T0189984

Lecture Notes in Computer Science   12238

Founding Editors

Gerhard Goos
Karlsruhe Institute of Technology, Karlsruhe, Germany
Juris Hartmanis
Cornell University, Ithaca, NY, USA

Editorial Board Members

Elisa Bertino
Purdue University, West Lafayette, IN, USA
Wen Gao
Peking University, Beijing, China
Bernhard Steffen ⓘ
TU Dortmund University, Dortmund, Germany
Gerhard Woeginger ⓘ
RWTH Aachen, Aachen, Germany
Moti Yung
Columbia University, New York, NY, USA

More information about this series at http://www.springer.com/series/7410

Clemente Galdi · Vladimir Kolesnikov (Eds.)

Security and Cryptography for Networks

12th International Conference, SCN 2020
Amalfi, Italy, September 14–16, 2020
Proceedings

 Springer

Editors
Clemente Galdi (iD)
Università degli Studi di Salerno
Fisciano, Italy

Vladimir Kolesnikov (iD)
Georgia Institute of Technology
Atlanta, GA, USA

ISSN 0302-9743   ISSN 1611-3349   (electronic)
Lecture Notes in Computer Science
ISBN 978-3-030-57989-0   ISBN 978-3-030-57990-6   (eBook)
https://doi.org/10.1007/978-3-030-57990-6

LNCS Sublibrary: SL4 – Security and Cryptology

© Springer Nature Switzerland AG 2020
This work is subject to copyright. All rights are reserved by the Publisher, whether the whole or part of the material is concerned, specifically the rights of translation, reprinting, reuse of illustrations, recitation, broadcasting, reproduction on microfilms or in any other physical way, and transmission or information storage and retrieval, electronic adaptation, computer software, or by similar or dissimilar methodology now known or hereafter developed.
The use of general descriptive names, registered names, trademarks, service marks, etc. in this publication does not imply, even in the absence of a specific statement, that such names are exempt from the relevant protective laws and regulations and therefore free for general use.
The publisher, the authors and the editors are safe to assume that the advice and information in this book are believed to be true and accurate at the date of publication. Neither the publisher nor the authors or the editors give a warranty, expressed or implied, with respect to the material contained herein or for any errors or omissions that may have been made. The publisher remains neutral with regard to jurisdictional claims in published maps and institutional affiliations.

This Springer imprint is published by the registered company Springer Nature Switzerland AG
The registered company address is: Gewerbestrasse 11, 6330 Cham, Switzerland

Preface

The 12th Conference on Security and Cryptography for Networks (SCN 2020) was held as a virtual event during September 14–16, 2020. The conference has traditionally been held in Amalfi, with the exception of the 5th edition, held in the nearby town of Maiori. After the editions of 1996, 1999, and 2002, it has been organized biennially thereafter.

The year 2020 will be remembered as the year of COVID-19 pandemic. During this hard period, humanity faced extraordinary difficulties. At the time of this writing, the number of infected people had nearly reached 23 million worldwide, while there had been more than half a million deaths. Our first thoughts go to people who suffered, fought, and, unfortunately, too often lost their battle. We also sincerely hope that many people view preventative isolation as an opportunity to spend more enjoyable time with family.

In this context, scientific research, basic and applied, has proven once more to be key for advancing and preserving the success of humanity. Biology, medicine, immunology, and statistics/modeling are clearly seen as crucial in our response to the virus. At the same time, it is crypto and security research, among other CS and engineering fields, that enabled the massive worldwide shift to online operations and social interactions. It is clear that security and privacy research must proceed at an even greater pace to both continue to support existing tools, as well as to enable other features, notably, privacy protection, e.g., via multiparty computation.

The SCN conference is an international meeting that focuses on the cryptographic and information security methodologies needed to address such challenges. SCN allows researchers, practitioners, developers, and users interested in the security of communication networks to meet and exchange ideas in the wonderful setting of the Amalfi Coast. SCN 2020 proceedings contain the 33 papers selected by the Program Committee (PC). The conference received 87 submissions of exceptional quality. Each submission was assigned to at least three reviewers. After an initial individual review phase, the submissions were discussed for a period of three additional weeks. During the discussion phase the PC used, rather intensively, a recently introduced feature of the review system, which allows PC members to anonymously ask questions directly to authors. Reviewing and selection among very high-quality submissions was a challenging and difficult task. We are grateful to the PC members and external reviewers for their hard and careful work. Special thanks to Vassilis Zikas for his extra work as shepherd of one of the papers.

The conference program also included an invited talk by Jesper Buus Nielsen. We would like to thank Jesper as well as all the other speakers for their contribution to the conference. SCN 2020 was organized in cooperation with the International Association for Cryptologic Research (IACR).

We thank all the authors who submitted papers to this conference, the Organizing Committee members, colleagues, and student helpers for their valuable time and effort, and all the conference attendees who made this event truly intellectually stimulating through their active participation.

August 2020   Clemente Galdi
                                                                              Vladimir Kolesnikov

Organization

Program Committee Chair

Vladimir Kolesnikov   Georgia Institute of Technology, USA

General Chair

Clemente Galdi   Università di Salerno, Italy

Steering Committee

Carlo Blundo	Università di Salerno, Italy
Alfredo De Santis	Università di Salerno, Italy
Ueli Maurer	ETH Zurich, Switzerland
Rafail Ostrovsky	University of California, Los Angeles, USA
Giuseppe Persiano	Università di Salerno, Italy
Jacques Stern	ENS Paris, France
Douglas Stinson	University of Waterloo, Canada
Gene Tsudik	University of California, Irvine, USA
Moti Yung	Google, USA

Program Committee

Divesh Aggarwal	National University of Singapore, Singapore
Elena Andreeva	Technical University of Denmark, Denmark
Gilad Asharov	Bar-Ilan University, Israel
Saikrishna Badrinarayanan	Visa Research, USA
Manuel Barbosa	INESC TEC, University of Porto, Portugal
Jeremiah Blocki	Purdue University, USA
David Cash	University of Chicago, USA
Dario Catalano	Università di Catania, Italy
Nishanth Chandran	Microsoft Research, India
Sebastian Faust	Technische Universität Darmstadt, Germany
Juan A. Garay	Texas A&M University, USA
Romain Gay	Cornell Tech, USA
Stanislaw Jarecki	University of California, Irvine, USA
Benoit Libert	CNRS, ENS Lyon, France
Vadim Lyubashevsky	IBM Zurich, Switzerland
Daniel Masny	VISA Research, USA
Payman Mohassel	Facebook, USA
Svetla Nikova	Katholieke Universiteit Leuven, Belgium
Ryo Nishimaki	NTT, Japan

Emmanuela Orsini	Katholieke Universiteit Leuven, Belgium
Giuseppe Persiano	Università di Salerno, Italy
Mike Rosulek	Oregon State University, USA
Elaine Shi	Cornell University, USA
Francois-Xavier Standaert	Université catholique de Louvain, Belgium
Marc Stevens	CWI, The Netherlands
Daniele Venturi	Sapienza Università di Roma, Italy
Damien Vergnaud	Sorbonne Université, IUF, France
Ivan Visconti	Università di Salerno, Italy
Xiao Wang	Northwestern University, USA
Daniel Wichs	Northeastern University, USA
Vassilis Zikas	The University of Edinburgh, UK

Local Organizing Committee

Luigi Catuogno	Università di Salerno, Italy
Giuseppe Fenza	Università di Salerno, Italy
Graziano Fuccio	Università di Salerno, Italy
Francesco Orciuoli	Università di Salerno, Italy
Rocco Zaccagnino	Università di Salerno, Italy

Additional Reviewers

Enrique Argones	Yash Kondi
Gennaro Avitabile	Lilia Kraleva
James Bartusek	Nikos Leonardos
Tim Beyne	Wei-Kai Lin
Sarani Bhattacharya	Julian Loss
Vincenzo Botta	Akash Madhusudan
Benedikt Bnz	Mohammad Mahmoody
Matteo Campanelli	Nathan Manohar
Wouter Castryck	Khoa Nguyen
Yilei Chen	Maciej Obremski
Poulami Das	Max Orlt
Julien Devigne	Hugo Pacheco
Andreas Erwig	Elena Pagnin
Xiong Fan	Thomas Peters
Rex Fernando	Bernardo Portela
Aarushi Goel	Willy Quach
Alonso Gonzlez	Srinivasan Raghuraman
Vincenzo Iovino	Adrin Ranea
Ruta Jawale	Siavash Riahi
Ilan Komargodski	Joao Ribeiro

Olivier Sanders
Pratik Sarkar
Mark Simkin

Luisa Siniscalchi
Azam Soleimanian
Fre Vercauteren

Contents

Blockchain

Account Management in Proof of Stake Ledgers

Dimitris Karakostas[1,3]($\boxtimes$), Aggelos Kiayias[1,3], and Mario Larangeira[2,3]

[1] University of Edinburgh, Edinburgh, UK
dimitris.karakostas@ed.ac.uk, akiayias@inf.ed.ac.uk
[2] Tokyo Institute of Technology, Tokyo, Japan
mario@c.titech.ac.jp
[3] IOHK, Wan Chai, Hong Kong

Abstract. Blockchain protocols based on Proof-of-Stake (PoS) depend—by nature—on the active participation of stakeholders. If users are offline and abstain from the PoS consensus mechanism, the system's security is at risk, so it is imperative to explore ways to both maximize the level of participation and minimize the effects of non-participation. One such option is stake representation, such that users can delegate their participation rights and, in the process, form "stake pools". The core idea is that stake pool operators always participate on behalf of regular users, while the users retain the ownership of their assets. Our work provides a formal PoS wallet construction that enables delegation and stake pool formation. While investigating the construction of addresses in this setting, we distil and explore *address malleability*, a security property that captures the ability of an attacker to manipulate the delegation information associated with an address. Our analysis consists of identifying multiple levels of malleability, which are taken into account in our paper's core result. We then introduce the first ideal functionality of a PoS wallet's core which captures the PoS wallet's capabilities and is realized as a secure protocol based on standard cryptographic primitives. Finally, consider the wallet core in conjunction with a PoS ledger and investigate how delegation and stake pools affect a PoS system's security.

1 Introduction

One of Bitcoin's [34] novelties was combining Proof-of-Work (PoW) with a hash-chain to solve the consensus problem. As shown in subsequent works [23,24,35], these elements enable Bitcoin to solve Byzantine Agreement (BA) under open participation. PoW is central in identifying the eligible party that acts at any given time. Specifically, the consensus participants, who generate blocks, are the *miners* which run the PoW mechanism. In turn, the users manage private keys

A. Kiayias—This work was supported in part by EU Project No. 780477, PRIV-ILEDGE.

M. Larangeira—This work was supported by the Input Output Cryptocurrency Collaborative Research Chair funded by Input Output HK.

© Springer Nature Switzerland AG 2020
C. Galdi and V. Kolesnikov (Eds.): SCN 2020, LNCS 12238, pp. 3–23, 2020.
https://doi.org/10.1007/978-3-030-57990-6_1

with which they control their assets by signing and publishing transactions on the ledger. PoW-based ledgers observe a decoupling between miners and users, as miners may not own digital assets and users may not participate in mining.

The costly nature of PoW though gave rise to alternative mechanisms, most notably Proof-of-Stake (PoS). In PoS, the eligible party, or "block minter", is also a "stakeholder" and is selected proportionally to its stake, i.e. its assets. Stakeholders can arbitrarily join and leave, while also remaining pseudonymous. Thus, the assets of a PoS ledger are dual in nature, acting as both transaction means and participation rights in the consensus protocol. This fundamental property of PoS systems raises two major considerations. First, using the same key for multiple operations increases its attack surface. For example, using the same key multiple times, e.g. to participate in consensus in a PoS setting, enables quantum attacks, given that most implementations employ non-post-quantum secure signature schemes. Furthermore, frequently using and keeping a key online counters security enhancements like hardware wallets. Second, users need to be online and perform complicated actions. In an environment where most users are offline and abstain from the protocol, the security guarantees are weakened.

The above issues are well known. For instance, the usage of multiple keys has been proposed to address the first consideration[1]. A possible countermeasure for reduced participation is to enable the delegation of participation in the PoS protocol. Users are then organized in "stake pools", i.e. consortiums managed by a single party, the pool's "leader", that runs the PoS protocol as a delegate of the pool's members. Stake pools also bring efficiency advantages, since the set of stake pool leaders is typically smaller than the entire stakeholders' set and thus overall the system can operate with better cost efficiency, since a smaller number of parties have to invest in running a transaction processing service.

PoS systems increasingly gain momentum. For instance, Cardano and EOS, both PoS-based systems, are among the top cryptocurrencies by market capitalization[2], while Ethereum [40], the second-biggest blockchain system, slowly transitions to a PoS protocol, Casper [7]. However, the literature lacks a comprehensive and formal treatment of a PoS system's account management. Due to the little systematization of PoS wallets, developers often resort to ad hoc solutions which, as our malleability attack showcases, may be vulnerable. Formalizing the PoS wallet is an important step, since wallets are the gateway through which users interact with a distributed ledger and a core element of consensus itself. Our work aims to act as a guideline for PoS designers, providing a composable scheme which can be used in a black-box manner. Finally, an important motivation is the low level of decentralization in PoS systems. Even in cases where stakeholders are arguably in control, they choose their representatives from a very narrow set of accounts; for instance, the EOS admits only 21 block producers at any given time. Our work helps alleviate centralization tendencies by allowing each user to either participate or delegate to *any* party of their choice.

---

[1] For one such discussion see https://reddit.com/r/ethereum/comments/6idf2c.
[2] https://coinmarketcap.com [April 2020].

1.1 Our Contributions and Roadmap

Our core contribution is a composable treatment of PoS wallets, which perform account management in distributed ledgers. Our work aims to be the basis of discussion and analysis of existing and future wallet designs and implementations. First, we distill the desiderata of a PoS wallet (Sect. 2). In turn, we describe the malleability attack (Sect. 3). Malleability enables an adversary to artificially inflate its delegated stake, by acquiring the delegation rights of assets without permission from their owner, potentially getting financial gains (e.g., in a PoS based financial system). However, as shown in Theorem 1, as long as malleability is mitigated and the utilized cryptographic primitives are sound, our wallet design is secure. We explore various protection levels against malleability, each offering security and performance guarantees suitable for a wide range of systems. Notably protection against malleability comes with relatively small cost in the size of addresses; specifically, a completely non malleable address scheme amounts to 129 bytes. The severity of malleability is shown via potential threat against Cardano's incentivized testnet, although no malleability attacks have been recorded yet. Interestingly, malleability may be of independent interest in any scheme which combines multiple attributes in a single identifier, for instance Decentralized Identifiers (DIDs) [37].

Our second contribution is a composable ideal functionality for the core of a Proof-of-Stake wallet (Sect. 4). Our analysis is based on the UC Framework [8] and is inspired by Canetti [9]. The ideal functionality $\mathcal{F}_{\text{CoreWallet}}$ epitomizes in a concise way a PoS wallet's properties. We realize $\mathcal{F}_{\text{CoreWallet}}$ in the form of the protocol $\pi_{\text{CoreWallet}}$. Both the functionality and the protocol are highly parametric, enabling different address and wallet recovery schemes to be employed. We also describe an address scheme which enables the recovery of the wallet's addresses and their balance given a master key and the ledger in $O(n \log(m))$ time complexity, n being the wallet's addresses and m all addresses in the ledger. Finally, we combine the core wallet with a PoS ledger to complete staking operations, like stake delegation and the formation of stake pools, as well as payments and block production (in the context of a PoS system). We also analyze the effects of delegation and stake pools on the security of a "vanilla" PoS system; our results confirm that, as long as the stake majority is managed by honest parties, be it pools or stakeholders, a PoS system is secure.

1.2 Related Work

Cryptographic literature has seen a multitude of PoS protocols in the past years. The first provably secure PoS protocol, Ouroboros [32], initiated a family of PoS protocols consisting of Ouroboros Praos [15], Genesis [3], Crypsinous [31], and Hydra [10]. These protocols are similar to Bitcoin, in the sense that they offer eventual guarantees of liveness and persistence, and cover issues including security, privacy, and availability. Another popular PoS protocol, Algorand [11,25], employs Byzantine Agreement to construct a secure PoS ledger with transaction finality in expected constant time. Similarly, Snow White [5,36] uses the notion of "robustly reconfigurable consensus", which is specially designed to cope with the lack of participation of users in the consensus protocol. Our work is complementary to these PoS protocols, offering the wallet interface that can be used in conjunction with them to construct a robust and secure PoS system.

However, formal wallet research has been sparse and limited on PoW. The widely implemented HD Wallet Standard BIP32 [41], based on deterministic wallets [33], was studied by Gutoski and Stebila [29] under partial key leakage, and by Das *et al.* [14], who provide a formal treatment of deterministic wallets. We also employ hierarchical key generation akin to BIP32 for address generation and recovery. Our work also builds on Courtois *et al.* [13], who investigated wallets and key management for Bitcoin [34]. Finally, Arapinis *et al.* [2] analyze specialized hardware wallets under UC, although focused only on PoW.

Various PoS systems employ delegation with varied results. "Delegated PoS", as deployed on Steem [38], EOS [12], and (with some amendments) Tezos [28], enables the voting of delegates. However, all use a single key for both payment and voting. Also Steem and EOS limit the number of potential delegates to 21 at any moment, while Tezos offers a more open setting, where users can vote for any delegate of their choice, but requires a delegate to own (and lock in a deposit) at least 8.25% of its delegated stake. On the other hand, Cardano[3] (at present) pins all stake to a closed set of block production nodes, i.e. does not offer open participation, while NEO[4] enables only 7 consensus nodes, 5 of which are controlled by a single entity. An alternative approach is taken by Decred [17], which uses a ticketing system, i.e. stakeholders buy a ticket for participation akin to using a separate key. However, like Tezos, it requires the locking of funds, i.e. it does not allow concurrent payments and staking. Our work provides a formal model that, combined with a PoS framework, can help avoid the security, centralization, and usability issues of these systems. Finally, the game theoretic analysis of reward allocation and stake pool formation is an interesting, though orthogonal, problem. Our work provides the cryptographic infrastructure, on top of which a reward scheme (e.g. [6,22]) can be deployed.

1.3   Preliminaries

Definitions and Notation. A ledger records and manages a set of fungible assets. For example, a "satoshi" is the asset maintained by the Bitcoin ledger. The users create **addresses** to interact with the ledger's assets. An **account**, i.e. a set of **addresses**, is denoted by $\Lambda \subseteq \{0,1\}^{p(\lambda)}$ for a given, fixed polynomially bounded function $p(\cdot)$ and the security parameter λ. An **attribute** δ is an object which identifies a property, so an address is associated with a number g of attributes of different types: i) **public** attributes are identifiable and used without any interaction with the account's owner; ii) **semi-public** attributes become public when a transaction that spends from the address is issued; iii) **private** attributes never become public. For instance, Bitcoin addresses comprise of the hash of a

---

[3] https://www.cardano.org/.
[4] https://neo.org.

verification key. Therefore, the verification key is *semi-public*, its hash is *public*, whereas the private key which signs transactions is *private*. Finally, $|\alpha|$ denotes the length (in bits) of the object α, $A||B$ denotes the concatenation of two objects A and B, and $head(C)$ denotes the last block in a chain C, i.e. $head(C||B) = B$.

Threat Model and Adversarial Motivation. We assume that the adversary *does not* control a majority of the stake, otherwise attacking the PoS protocol would be trivial. Instead, the adversary aims to inflate its stake by exploiting "staking operations" like delegation as described previously. We also assume that the adversary is "adaptive", i.e. it can corrupt parties on dynamically while the protocol is being executed, and "rushing", i.e. it retrieves and (possibly) delays the honest parties' messages before deciding its strategy.

2   General Desiderata

Before presenting our framework, we first identify the properties that the wallet in a PoS setting should offer. This investigation is an important step in understanding the restrictions in designing such systems, as well as evaluating the choices that a PoS protocol's designer should make, given that, as we show, a number of desirable properties may be conflicting. In a PoS system each account manages addresses, which own a non-negative amount of cryptocurrency assets. A PoS system should offer at minimum two basic operations for each user's account: i) *paying* and ii) *staking*. Addresses, simply put, are strings which have cryptocurrency balances associated with them. They may also contain metadata, in the form of arbitrary attributes, which are useful for particular system operations. We identify the following desiderata for addresses in a PoS setting:

Address Non-malleability: Given an address (and possibly also transactions associated with that address), it should be infeasible for an attacker to construct a different address that shares *only some* of its attributes, most importantly its payment key.

Address Uniqueness: The address generation process should not likely produce the same address for different attributes, i.e. addresses should be unique.

Short Addresses: The addresses should be relatively short, in order to be usable and storage efficient.

Multiple Types of Addresses: It should be possible to construct more than one type of addresses, with each type supporting a different subset of basic operations, e.g. to ban some addresses from staking or delegating to a stake pool.

Multiple Device Support: An account should be able to exist on multiple devices that share *no joint internal state*.

Address Recovery: An account should be able to identify its addresses, given the ledger and the payment keys which it controls.

Privacy and Unlinkability: Addresses should be indistinguishable and not publicly linkable to the account which manages them.

An additional and equally important concern in the PoS setting is the "nothing at stake" problem [21]. As opposed to PoW, in PoS a player can easily create blocks that extend multiple parallel chains, an adversarial behavior which diverges from every PoS protocol's rules. Thus, an adversary may profit by attacking the system in this manner, even as they own a large amount of the very assets which they attack. This problem becomes more apparent in the cases of custodian services, which manage assets on behalf of their clients, but assume no financial risk themselves. In this work, we sidestep this problem by introducing "exile" addresses, i.e. addresses excluded from the protocol's execution.

The two basic operations, i.e. *payment* and *staking*, are performed independently by two separate pieces of information, denoted $\mathcal{I}_p$ and $\mathcal{I}_s$ respectively. The main advantage here is that stake delegation does not require the use of $\mathcal{I}_p$, which is reserved only for transferring funds. Another desirable result is the ability to recover all addresses in a deterministic manner given a master key (cf. [29, 41]). This feature is particularly important in case the equipment which hosts the wallet is lost. We summarize the above, with some additions, as follows:

Account Master Key: There should exist a master key (or seed), that can be used to generate all of the account's management information.

Staking and Payment Separation: Compromising the staking operation should not affect the payment operation (and vice-versa).

Payment Key Information Safety: Apart from its hash, no other information about the payment key $\mathcal{I}_p$ should be public prior to issuing a payment.

Key Exposure Mitigation: Ownership of the account's assets and staking ability should be recoverable in case the staking information $\mathcal{I}_s$ is compromised.

Finally, the delegation mechanism boils down to the ability of a user to give the rights over her stake to another user. This action should be distinguishable from other actions, like payment, in order to protect the users and also facilitate automatic reward schemes to be implemented by the ledger. The desiderata for the delegation mechanism are as follows:

Cost Effective Delegation: Stake delegation, as well as changing an account's delegation profile, should be cost effective.

Chain Delegation Restriction: A limit to the number of permitted chain delegation assignments may be enforced.

Delegation Verification: Participants in the system should be able to verify the status of delegation assignments.

3   Address Malleability

Before designing our PoS wallet, a brief motivation behind researching malleability and its relation to our setting is needed. *Address malleability* is similar to the malleability notions that have been explored in existing literature (cf. [18]) and is intrinsically tied to address generation. Malleability here is observed in the relation between the payment and staking keys. Thus, this family of malleability attacks enables an adversary to construct addresses on behalf of honest users, which may correspond to the honest payment keys and adversarial staking keys. Such addresses are called *forgeries*. A forgery is successful if an honest wallet accepts a forgery as its own and can spend its assets, whereas it fails if it is impossible to send money to it or funds that it owns are unspendable.

We assume two types of adversaries, depending on the information to which they have access. The first is the *network adversary*, who can view the ledger's contents and the addresses produced by an honest party. The second is the *targeting adversary*, who accesses the same information as the network adversary, as well as the semi-public attributes of the addresses of the "victim", i.e. the honest user for which it attempts to produce a forgery. We showcase the different types of adversaries with the following example. Assume a company C that receives regular payments in cryptocurrencies. For security reasons, C stores the private keys of its addresses on an offline server, whereas the public keys are stored online, in order to easily compute and share new addresses with its clients. An adversary that pretends to be a client is a "network" adversary, i.e. may access some of C's addresses. Instead, an adversary that infiltrates the online server and accesses the public keys is "targeting". If the system does not protect against targeting adversaries, then malleability may be used to mount a covert attack, i.e. to obtain the staking rights of C's assets without raising flags.

Formal analysis of malleability takes the form of the malleability predicate M. M returns 1 or 0 to denote whether an address is valid or not. In this context, a valid address is either honestly-generated *or* is a successful forgery. The *fully non-malleable* construction is instantiated with the predicate $M_{\mathsf{NM}}^{\mathsf{L},\mathsf{T},P}$ of Algorithm 1. The predicate verifies that an recipient's address has been generated by some party following the correct process. Upon issuing a transaction (resp. upon verifying), the malleability predicate checks the address of the receiver (resp. sender) to ensure its legitimate and thus if the transaction is acceptable.

Algorithm 1. The *fully non-malleable* predicate.

---

    function $M_{\mathsf{NM}}^{\mathsf{L},\mathsf{T},P}(aux, \alpha)$
      switch "aux" **do**
        case "issue"
          if $\exists P'$ such that $\exists l_\alpha : (\alpha, l_\alpha) \in L_{P'}$ **then**
            return 1
          end if
        case "verify" OR "recover"
          if $\exists l_\alpha : (\alpha, l_\alpha) \in L_P$ **then**
            return 1
          end if
      return 0
    end function

Malleability attacks depend on who can mount them and to which extent. We identify these levels, ranging from *full*, with no inherent protection against malleability, to *non-malleable*. These levels are distinguished based on the following properties: i) the adversarial types, i.e. whether the adversary is on the network level or targeting, as described above; ii) "self-verification", i.e. whether a wallet can recognize a forgery for one of its own addresses; iii) "cross-verification", i.e. whether a wallet can recognize a forgery for *any* address.

Although high levels of protection are more desirable, there is a performance trade-off. Specifically, a fully malleable address scheme typically produces short addresses, thus is suitable for applications focused on performance rather than security. In contrast, a security-oriented project would rather aim for the higher levels of malleability protection. Following we briefly describe each level and offer indicative address implementations, assuming that SHA256 is the employed hash function and the signature scheme is ECDSA on secp256r1. We also assume that each address is associated with two keys, (vks, sks) for staking and (vkp, skp) payments. With the exception of ex post malleable addresses, the hash of the payment key also serves as the recovery tag. With foresight we note that all schemes are suitable for usage with the core-wallet protocol of Sect. 4.2. Also in all cases the user reveals the staking key, whereas in all levels except 4 they also reveal the payment key, in addition to publishing the address, thus the overall storage requirement is $|\alpha| + |\text{vkp}| + |\text{vks}|$.

Level 1, Full Malleability: Address schemes of this level enable forgeries from both network and targeting adversaries. To accept an address, a wallet only checks whether it controls its payment key. For instance, the address is constructed as the concatenation of the hashes of the payment and staking keys: $\alpha = \mathcal{H}(\text{vkp})||\mathcal{H}(\text{vks})$. Thus, given α, an adversary can replace $\mathcal{H}(\text{vks})$ with $\mathcal{H}(\text{vks}')$, for some adversarial key $\mathcal{H}(\text{vks}')$. The length of fully malleable addresses is 64 bytes, i.e. the sum of two hashes.

Level 2, Ex Post Malleability: This level prohibits network adversaries, though targeting adversaries can create successful forgeries. Ex post malleable addresses are constructed as follows: $\alpha = \mathcal{H}(\text{vkp}||\text{vks}||ht)||\mathcal{H}(\text{vks})||ht$. The first part of the address is the hashed root of its attribute tree. The attributes are the payment key vkp, the staking key vks, and the recovery tag ht. Now, given only α an attacker can no longer replace vks since, in doing so, the first part of the address would be invalidated. However, if the attacker also knows the payment key vkp, it can produce successful forgeries. The length of ex post malleable addresses is 96 bytes, i.e. the sum of three hashes.

Level 3, "Sink" Malleability: Sink malleable address schemes protect against both network and targeting adversaries. Now, a forgery is always rejected by the wallet and its funds are "burnt". Intuitively, imagine transactions as a graph, where the graph's nodes are addresses and its edges are transactions. Forgeries are "sinks", which trap all funds sent to them and no transaction can spend from them. Thus, a wallet can identify forgeries for one of its payment keys, but cannot identify whether an address with a key that it does not own is a forgery.

To construct a sink malleable address, the payment key certifies the staking key as follows: $\alpha = \mathcal{H}(\mathsf{vkp})||\mathsf{vks}||\mathsf{Sign}(\mathsf{skp}, \mathsf{vks})$. Clearly, even if an attacker knows the public payment key vkp, it cannot create a forgery, unless it forges a signature. The ECDSA signature is 512 bits, so the address is 128 bytes.

Level 4, Non-malleability: Non-malleable addresses offer the highest level of protection, as any party can identify whether *any* address is a forgery. Non-malleability is achieved by utilizing the signature of the sink malleable scheme and revealing the public payment key: $\alpha = \mathsf{vkp}||\mathcal{H}(\mathsf{vks})||\mathsf{Sign}(\mathsf{skp}, \mathsf{vks})$. Therefore, the address's length is about 129 bytes (33 bytes for the payment key, 32 bytes for the hash, and 64 for the signature).

Table 1 summarizes the above comparison. As expected, higher levels of malleability protection induce a higher performance cost, in terms of address length. Additionally, the fully non-malleable scheme reveals the public key by default, which opens the system to quantum attacks, assuming a non-post-quantum secure signature scheme like ECDSA is employed. Future work will explore the usage of non-interactive zero-knowledge proofs of knowledge, which enable the same level of security without revealing the public key.

Table 1. Comparison of malleability levels, from malleable to fully non-malleable, based on the types of adversaries that can successfully forge an address, the ability of a wallet to identify a forgery, and the address length. We note that the non-malleable scheme reveals the public payment key by default, whereas all other schemes reveal only its hash (and the public key is revealed only upon conducting a transaction).

Malleability level	Network protection	Targeting protection	Self-verification	Cross-verification	Address length (bytes)
1. Full	✗	✗	✗	✗	64
2. Ex post	✓	✗	✗	✗	96
3. Sink	✓	✓	✓	✗	128
4. Non-malleable	✓	✓	✓	✓	129

Address malleability is adjacent to (though more severe than) transaction malleability in Bitcoin [1, 16]. Using the latter, an attacker modifies a transaction and changes its identifier (i.e. its hash), such that the issuer is led to believe that the original transaction is unconfirmed. Although this attack may lead to loss of funds (e.g. as claimed in the Mt. Gox incident [16]), it does not compromise the ledger's consensus mechanism, due to the decoupling of the mining and the transaction processes. In contrast, address malleability directly affects a PoS ledger's security, since an attacker can use it to artificially inflate their delegated stake to the extent of (potentially) violating the honest majority assumption.

Finally, we present a real-world case of the address malleability hazard. On December 2019, Cardano released its Incentivized Testnet[5], a testnet aimed at

---

[5] https://staking.cardano.org/ [April 2020].

enabling Cardano stakeholders to create stake pools and delegate their stake on a preliminary level. In accordance to our setting, addresses are associated with two keys, for payments and staking operations, nevertheless addresses are fully malleable; specifically, they are constructed as the (Bech32-encoded) concatenation of the payment and staking keys[6], as in our malleable scheme. Although no real-world attacks have been recorded yet, our paper raises awareness about their possibility and the mitigation strategies that are available for practical systems.

4   The Core Proof-of-Stake Wallet

We now focus on defining the core of a PoS wallet. With malleability in mind, we first build the Core-Wallet ideal functionality, i.e. the security definition of the basic key-management operations that PoS wallet should complete. Following, we realize the functionality via a protocol which can be constructed using standard cryptographic primitives. The Core-Wallet protocol employs a number of sub-routines and, as we show in Theorem 1, securely realizes the ideal functionality, as long as a set of standard assumptions are ensured. By the end of the section we briefly discuss the construction of addresses and wallet recovery, i.e. the identification of the wallet's addresses and its balance given its private keys and the public ledger. First, we outline the core wallet's inner workings:

Initialization: During initialization, in the ideal functionality $\mathcal{F}_{\text{CoreWallet}}$, various global lists are initialized, while in the protocol $\pi_{\text{CoreWallet}}$, the master secret key is created, i.e. the wallet's *seed* which will be used to generate all keys and addresses; $\pi_{\text{CoreWallet}}$ also maintains lists for the wallet's keys.

Address Generation: During address generation, $\mathcal{F}_{\text{CoreWallet}}$ leaks to the adversary the new address; in fact the adversary chooses the address, which is then checked by $\mathcal{F}_{\text{CoreWallet}}$ for validity, e.g. to ensure that it is unique. This choice implies that the adversary knows the addresses of the wallet, i.e. there is no address privacy; future versions of the core wallet will aim to provide privacy guarantees. The address is then linked with a list of attributes, i.e. the payment and staking keys and helper attributes like the recovery tag, and are stored in the global arrays. In $\pi_{\text{CoreWallet}}$, address generation depends on the helper function GenAddr, given the child attributes generated using the master key.

Wallet Recovery: Wallet recovery is the process of retrieving the recovery tags of the wallet's addresses. In $\mathcal{F}_{\text{CoreWallet}}$ these are maintained in a list, while in $\pi_{\text{CoreWallet}}$ they are reconstructed from the master key and respective indices.

Address Recovery: This interface enables a wallet to verify whether an address α was among its first i constructed addresses; the verification process is as above. Interestingly, during address recovery the malleability predicate is also used; thus, depending on the level of malleability that we want to achieve, at this point the wallet may accept forgeries as valid.

---

[6] The Rust code of Cardano's testnet is on Github. Address construction and key concatenation can be found at https://git.io/Jvppa and https://git.io/Jvppr.

Issue Transaction: To issue a transaction, the wallet receives the sender and receiver addresses and the amount of assets to be transferred. Following the UC model of signatures [9], it retrieves from the adversary the signature object and, after a few checks (including for malleability), registers the signed transaction. Thus, although the adversary can partially affect the signature's structure, $\mathcal{F}_{\text{CoreWallet}}$ ensures that security is maintained. On the protocol's side, transaction issuing is achieved by simply signing the transaction with the payment key that corresponds to the sender's address.

Verify Transaction: Transaction verification is also similar to signature verification. Specifically, $\mathcal{F}_{\text{CoreWallet}}$ ensures that i) the malleability level is preserved (using the predicate), and ii) completeness, unforgeability, and consistency are ensured, i.e. a secure digital signature scheme's needed properties. On the other hand, $\pi_{\text{CoreWallet}}$ simply uses the Verify algorithm of the employed signature scheme to check the transaction's signature's validity.

Issue and Verify Staking: Issuing and verification of staking actions, e.g. the certificates which we explore in Sect. 5, is achieved similarly to payment transactions, with the usage of staking keys instead of payment keys.

4.1   The Core-Wallet Functionality

The goal of $\mathcal{F}_{\text{CoreWallet}}^{M}$ is to distill in a concise way the PoS wallet's properties and provide a formal basis of discussion. The ideal functionality $\mathcal{F}_{\text{CoreWallet}}$, inspired by Canetti [9], interacts with the ideal adversary $\mathcal{S}$ and a set of parties denoted by $\mathbb{P}$ and is parameterized by the malleability predicate $M(\cdot, \cdot, \cdot) \rightarrow \{0, 1\}$. It also keeps the, initially empty, lists S of staking actions and T of transactions. Without loss of generality, we assume that, given a list of attributes $l_{\alpha, Gen} = (\delta_1, \ldots, \delta_g)$, δ_1 is the staking key's information and δ_2 is the recovery tag. We note that the functionality distinguishes the addresses in three types, the "base", "pointer", and "exile" addresses, each with a specific utility. Briefly, base addresses bootstrap a wallet, pointer addresses are shorter, and exile addresses help bypass the nothing-at-stake problem described in Sect. 2.

Functionality $\mathcal{F}_{\text{CoreWallet}}^{M}$

Initialization: Upon receiving (INIT, sid) from $P \in \mathbb{P}$, forward it to $\mathcal{S}$ and wait for (INITOK, sid). Then initialize the empty lists L_P of addresses and attribute lists and K_P of staking keys, and send (INITOK, sid) to P.

Address Generation: Upon receiving (GENERATEADDRESS, sid, aux) from $P \in \mathbb{P}$, forward it to $\mathcal{S}$. Upon receiving (ADDRESS, sid, α, l_α) from $\mathcal{S}$, parse l_α as $(\delta_1, \ldots, \delta_g)$ and $\forall P' \in \mathbb{P}$ check if $\forall (\alpha', (\delta_1', \ldots, \delta_g')) \in L_{P'}$ it holds that $\alpha \neq \alpha'$, $\delta_2' \neq \delta_2$, and $\forall j \in [i, \ldots, g] : \delta_j' \neq \delta_j$, i.e. the address, recovery tag, and private attributes are unique. If so, then:

- if $aux = (\text{"base"})$, check that $\forall (\alpha', (\delta_1', \ldots, \delta_g')) \in L_P : \delta_1' \neq \delta_1$,
- else if $aux = (\text{"pointer"}, \text{vks})$, check that $\delta_1 = \text{vks}$,
- else if $aux = (\text{"exile"})$, check that $\delta_1 = \bot$.

If the checks hold or P is corrupted, then insert (α, l_α) to L_P and return (ADDRESS, sid, α) to P. If $aux = $ ("base") also insert δ_1 to K_P and return (STAKINGKEY, sid, δ_1) to P.

Wallet Recovery: Upon receiving (RECOVERWALLET, sid, i) from $P \in \mathbb{P}$, for the first i elements in L_P return (TAG, sid, δ_2).

Address Recovery: Upon receiving (RECOVERADDR, sid, α, i) from P, if (α, l) is one of the first i elements of L_P or $M(L_P, $"recover"$, \alpha) = 1$, return (RECOVEREDADDR, sid, α).

Issue Transaction: Upon receiving (PAY, $sid, \Theta, \alpha_s, \alpha_r, m$) from $P \in \mathbb{P}$, if $\exists l_\alpha : (\alpha_s, l_\alpha) \in L_P$ forward it to $\mathcal{S}$. Upon receiving (TRANSACTION, sid, tx, σ) from $\mathcal{S}$, such that $tx = (\Theta, \alpha_s, \alpha_r, m)$, check if $\forall (tx', \sigma', b') \in \mathcal{T} : \sigma' \neq \sigma$, $(tx, \sigma, 0) \notin \mathcal{T}$, and $M(L_P, $"issue"$, \alpha_r) = 1$. If all checks hold, then insert $(tx, \sigma, 1)$ to $\mathcal{T}$ and return (TRANSACTION, sid, tx, σ).

Verify Transaction: Upon receiving (VERIFYPAY, sid, tx, σ) from $P \in \mathbb{P}$, with $tx = (\Theta, \alpha_s, \alpha_r, m)$ for a metadata string m, forward it to $\mathcal{S}$ and wait for a reply message (VERIFIEDPAY, sid, tx, σ, ϕ). Then:

- if $M(L_P, $"verify"$, \alpha_s) = 0$, set $f = 0$
- else if $(tx, \sigma, 1) \in \mathcal{T}$, set $f = 1$
- else, if P is not corrupted and $(tx, \sigma, 1) \notin \mathcal{T}$, set $f = 0$ and insert $(tx, \sigma, 0)$ to $\mathcal{T}$
- else, if $(\Theta, \alpha_s, \alpha_r, m, \sigma, b) \in \mathcal{T}$, set $f = b$
- else, set $f = \phi$.

Finally, send (VERIFIEDPAY, sid, tx, σ, f) to P.

Issue Staking: Upon receiving (STAKE, sid, stx) from P, such that $stx = (\text{vks}, m)$ for a metadata string m, forward the message to $\mathcal{S}$. Upon receiving (STAKED, sid, stx, σ) from $\mathcal{S}$, if $\forall (stx', \sigma', b') \in S : \sigma' \neq \sigma$, $(stx, \sigma, 0) \notin S$, and $\text{vks} \in K_P$, add $(stx, \sigma, 1)$ to S and return (STAKED, sid, stx, σ) to P.

Verify Staking: Upon receiving (VERIFYSTAKE, sid, stx, σ) from $P \in \mathbb{P}$, forward it to $\mathcal{S}$ and wait for (VERIFIEDSTAKE, sid, stx, σ, ϕ), with $stx = (\text{vks}, m)$. Then find P_s, such that $\text{vks} \in K_{P_s}$, and:

- if $(stx, \sigma, 1) \in S$, set $f = 1$
- else if P_s is not corrupted and $(stx, \sigma, 1) \notin S$, set $f = 0$ and insert $(stx, \sigma, 0)$ to S
- else if exists an entry $(stx, \sigma, f') \in S$, set $f = f'$
- else set $f = \phi$ and insert (stx, σ, ϕ) to S.

Finally, return (VERIFIEDSTAKE, sid, stx, σ, f) to P.

We remark that $\mathcal{F}_{\text{CoreWallet}}$ does not consider *forward security* in the sense of Bellare and Miner [4]. Thus, it does not fit protocols which require stronger security guarantees, e.g. Ouroboros Praos [15] which relies on a forward secure digital signature scheme to provide security guarantees against fully-adaptive corruption in a semi-synchronous setting. Additionally, it does not allow arbitrary parties to generate addresses, unlike e.g. Cryptonote [39].

4.2   The Core-Wallet Protocol

We now introduce the core-wallet protocol $\pi_{\text{CoreWallet}}$ which realizes $\mathcal{F}_{\text{CoreWallet}}$. $\pi_{\text{CoreWallet}}$ abstracts address generation and is parameterized with various helper functions. parsePubAttrs returns an address's public attributes [vks, wrt, aux]. HKeyGen and RTagGen produce the child key pair and the recovery tag respectively. We also assume a signature scheme $\Sigma = \langle \text{KeyGen}, \text{Verify}, \text{Sign} \rangle$ (cf. [27]). $\pi_{\text{CoreWallet}}$ interacts with $\mathcal{P}_o$, the wallet's owner, and maintains the lists PK of payment keys and SK of staking keys. Theorem 1, a core result of this paper, proves $\pi_{\text{CoreWallet}}$'s security w.r.t. $\mathcal{F}_{\text{CoreWallet}}$. For readability purposes, we drop the generic notation δ and instead use names representative of each attribute; the staking and the payment keys are now (vks, sks) and (vkp, skp) respectively. The public attributes $d = [\text{vks}, wrt, aux]$ comprise of the public staking key, the recovery tag, and the address's auxiliary information, which identifies its type.

Protocol $\pi_{\text{CoreWallet}}$

Initialization: Upon receiving (INIT, sid) from $\mathcal{P}_o$, set $msk \xleftarrow{\$} \{0,1\}^\lambda$ and return (INITOK, sid) to $\mathcal{P}_o$.

Address Generation: Upon receiving (GENERATEADDRESS, sid, aux) from $\mathcal{P}_o$, compute the index and "child" attributes as follows: i) pick $i \leftarrow \mathcal{I}$; ii) compute $(\text{vkp}_c, \text{skp}_c) =$ HKeyGen($\langle msk, \text{"payment"}, i \rangle$); iii) compute $wrt = $ RTagGen(vkp_c). If $aux = (\text{"base"})$ compute $(\text{vks}_c, \text{sks}_c) = $ HKeyGen($\langle msk, \text{"staking"}, i \rangle$); else, if $aux = (\text{"pointer"}, \text{vks})$, find $(\text{vks}_c, \text{sks}_c) \in K : \text{vks} = \text{vks}_c$; else if $aux = (\text{"exile"})$ set $(\text{vks}_c, \text{sks}_c) = (\bot, \bot)$. Then insert $l_\alpha = \langle \text{vks}_c, wrt, aux, \text{vkp}_c, \text{skp}_c, \text{sks}_c \rangle$, generate the new address α as $\alpha = $ GenAddr($\langle aux, \text{vks}_c, \text{vkp}_c, wrt \rangle$), and insert the tuple $\langle \alpha, (\text{vkp}_c, \text{skp}_c) \rangle$ to PK. Then return (ADDRESS, sid, α) to $\mathcal{P}_o$. If $aux = \text{"base"}$ also insert $(\text{vks}_c, \text{sks}_c)$ to SK and send the message (STAKINGKEY, sid, vks_c) to $\mathcal{P}o$.

Wallet Recovery: Upon receiving (RECOVERWALLET, sid, i_{max}) from $\mathcal{P}_o$, $\forall i \in [0, i_{max}]$ set $(\text{vkp}_i, \text{skp}_i) = $ HKeyGen($\langle msk, \text{"payment"}, i \rangle$) and return (TAG, sid, RTagGen(vkp_i)).

Address Recovery: Upon receiving (RECOVERADDR, sid, α, i_{max}) from $\mathcal{P}_o$, parse the address's attributes $(\text{vks}, wrt, aux) = parsePubAttrs(\alpha)$. If exists $i \in \mathcal{I} : i < i_{max}$, where $(\text{vkp}_i, \text{skp}_i) = $ HKeyGen($\langle msk, \text{"payment"}, i \rangle$) and RTagGen($\text{vkp}_i$) $= wrt$, return (RECOVEREDADDR, sid, α).

Issue Transaction: Upon receiving (PAY, sid, Θ, α_s, α_r, m) from $\mathcal{P}_o$, find $\langle \alpha_s, (\text{vkp}, \text{skp}) \rangle \in PK$ and return (TRANSACTION, sid, tx, Sign(skp, tx)), such that $tx = (\Theta, \alpha_s, \alpha_r, m)$.

Verify Transaction: Upon receiving (VERIFYPAY, sid, tx, σ) from $\mathcal{P}_o$, with $tx = (\Theta, \alpha_s, \alpha_r, m)$ for some metadata string m, find an entry

$\langle \alpha_s, (\text{vkp}, \text{skp}) \rangle$ in PK and return ($\text{VERIFIEDPAY}, sid, tx, \sigma, \text{Verify}(tx, \sigma,$ vkp)) to $\mathcal{P}_o$.

Issue Staking: Upon receiving (STAKE, sid, stx) from $\mathcal{P}_o$ such that $stx = (\text{vks}, m)$, find $(\text{vks}, \text{sks}) \in SK$ and return ($\text{STAKED}, sid, stx, \text{Sign}(\text{sks}, stx)$).

Verify Staking: Upon receiving a message ($\text{VERIFYSTAKE}, sid, stx, \sigma$) from party $\mathcal{P}_o$, where $stx = (\text{vks}, m)$ for some metadata m, find $(\text{vks}, \text{sks}) \in SK$ and return ($\text{VERIFIEDSTAKE}, sid, stx, \sigma, \text{Verify}(stx, \sigma, \text{sks})$).

4.3 Security of the Core-Wallet Protocol

Like $\mathcal{F}_{\text{CoreWallet}}$, $\pi_{\text{CoreWallet}}$ accommodates multiple address schemes and levels of malleability. Next we present the definitions of the properties needed to prove its security, while Theorem 1 proves that $\pi_{\text{CoreWallet}}$ securely realizes $\mathcal{F}_{\text{CoreWallet}}$ assuming its sub-processes satisfy these definitions. The proof is heavily based on Canetti [9] for the signature's properties, while the address properties (cf. Definitions 1, 2, 3, 4) cover malleability and address generation.

Definition 1 (Collision resistance). *A function H is collision resistant if, given $h \leftarrow \{0,1\}^l$, it should be computationally infeasible for a probabilistic polynomial algorithm to find a value x such that $h = \mathcal{H}(x)$.*

Definition 2 (Address collision resistance). *Analogously to hash functions, GenAddr is collision resistant when it is infeasible to produce two different attribute lists $l_i = (\delta_1^i, \ldots, \delta_g^i)$ for $i \in \{1, 2\}$, i.e. they differ in at least one attribute like $\exists j \in [1, g]: \delta_j^1 \neq \delta_j^2$, such that $\text{GenAddr}(l_1) = \text{GenAddr}(l_2)$, after running $\text{GenAddr}(\cdot)$ a polynomial number of times.*

Definition 3 (Hierarchical Key Generation). *For a key generation function $\text{HKeyGen}(\cdot)$ and signature scheme $\Sigma = \langle \text{KeyGen}, \text{Verify}, \text{Sign} \rangle$, $\text{HKeyGen}(\cdot)$ is hierarchical for Σ if, for all i, the key distribution produced by $\text{HKeyGen}(i)$ is computationally indistinguishable from the key distribution produced by KeyGen.*

Definition 4 (Non-malleable attribute address generation). *Let $\mathcal{L}$ be a distribution of attribute lists and $l \leftarrow \text{DOM}(\mathcal{L})$ an attribute list, such that $\text{DOM}(\mathcal{L}) = \Delta_1 \times \ldots \times \Delta_g$. Let the first attributes of l $\delta_1, \ldots, \delta_i$ relate to a property over which we define non-malleability. Given an address α, it is infeasible for an adversary $\mathcal{A}$ to produce valid forgeries, i.e. acceptable addresses with the same payment key as α, without access to α's private attributes, even with access to the address's metadata, i.e. its semi-public attributes. Concretely, with Addrs the list of addresses queried by $\mathcal{A}$ to the oracle $\text{GenAddr}^d(\cdot)$, it holds that:*

$$\Pr \left[\begin{array}{c} l = (\delta_1, \ldots, \delta_g), \ \alpha \leftarrow \text{GenAddr}(l), \\ \mathcal{A}^{\text{GenAddr}^d(\cdot), \text{GenMeta}^d(\cdot)}(\delta_i, \ldots, \delta_g) \rightarrow (\alpha', \delta_i', \ldots, \delta_g') \end{array} : \right.$$
$$\left. (\text{GenAddr}^d(\delta_i', \ldots, \delta_g') = \alpha') \wedge (\alpha' \neq \alpha) \wedge (\alpha' \notin \text{Addrs}) \right] \leq negl(\lambda)$$

for probabilities over GenAddr's randomness, the PPT adversary $\mathcal{A}$, and l.

Theorem 1. *Let the generic protocol* $\pi_{\text{CoreWallet}}$ *be parameterized by a signature scheme* $\Sigma = \langle \text{KeyGen}, \text{Verify}, \text{Sign} \rangle$ *and the* RTagGen, HKeyGen, *and* GenAddr *functions. Then* $\pi_{\text{CoreWallet}}$ *securely realizes the ideal functionality* $\mathcal{F}^{M_{SM}}_{\text{CoreWallet}}$ *if and only if* Σ *is EUF-CMA,* GenAddr *is collision resistant and attribute nonmalleable (cf. Definitions 2 and 4),* RTagGen *is collision resistant (cf. Definition 1), and* HKeyGen *is hierarchical for* Σ *(cf. Definition 3).*

4.4 Address Construction and Wallet Recovery

Following the protocol's definition, we now provide a brief overview of the address generation and recovery. For the construction of a new, "child" address we utilize a hierarchical address generation scheme (cf. hierarchical deterministic wallets [33]). The child key, which is produced by the master key and an index i, is given to the address generation function GenAddr, which outputs the new address. The wallet produces three types of addresses with different staking information. The stake of a **base** address is controlled by a new staking key. A **pointer** address's staking key is associated with an existing key which is published in a past transaction in the ledger. Finally, an **exile** address is not associated with any staking key, thus cannot perform staking and its assets are automatically removed from the PoS protocol's execution.

Each address also contains the (public) recovery tag *wrt*. The tag is created by RTagGen and links the address to its attributes without revealing its semipublic attributes, e.g. the payment key. During recovery, a wallet retrieves from the ledger its addresses and their balance, using its master key. Specifically, we assume a well-defined list of domains, each having a finite cardinality. The wallet initially picks indexes from the first domain, constructs the recovery tag for each, and compares it to the ledger's addresses. After identifying all addresses from the indexes of the first domain, it proceeds with the second and so forth. If, for some domain, no index is associated with a ledger's address, recovery halts. The complexity of recovery is $O(n \log(m))$, n being the number of the wallet's addresses and m the number of the ledger's addresses.

5 Integration of the Core-Wallet with PoS Consensus

Combining the core wallet with a Proof-of-Stake ledger we can build a full PoS wallet. We abstract the PoS ledger in the following functions and properties:

  i) $F_\theta(\cdot)$: given an address α, F_θ returns the assets that α owns;
 ii) $F_{\Phi,tx}(\cdot)$: $F_{\Phi,tx}$ outputs the fees Φ of publishing a transaction on the ledger;
iii) $F_{otx}(\cdot)$: given an address, F_{otx} outputs its outgoing transactions;
 iv) Φ_{reg}: the cost of stake pool registration;
  v) α_{reg}: a special address that pertains to pool registration;
 vi) $F_{PoS,player}(\cdot)$: given a chain $\mathcal{C}$, $F_{PoS,player}$ outputs the next PoS participant.

The above take various forms in distributed ledgers, given the various PoS flavors. Following, we explore how payments and staking actions are conducted via the core wallet. Also we evaluate the impact of stake pools on the execution and security assumptions of a typical PoS protocol, various modes of operation for enhanced safety and privacy, as well as two noteworthy attack vectors.

5.1 The PoS Wallet's Actions

A PoS wallet performs two types of actions, *payment* and *staking*. Although payment, i.e. the transfer of assets between accounts, is straightforward, staking depends on the inner-workings of each PoS protocol, so here we cover only delegation and stake pool formation.

Payment: Payment is the transfer of Θ assets from a sender address α_s to a receiver address α_r. The wallet creates the transaction $tx = (\Theta, \alpha_s, \alpha_r, m)$, with metadata m like the amount of fees. Next it accesses the PAY interface of $\pi_{\mathrm{CoreWallet}}$, retrieves the signed transaction, and publishes it on the ledger.

Stake Pool Registration: A main staking operation that the wallet enables is the formation of stake pools, which participate in the PoS protocol on behalf of stakeholders. Every pool is identified by a registered staking key. Before registering the key, the wallet first uses the address generation interface of $\pi_{\mathrm{CoreWallet}}$ to produce a new staking key (vks, sks). It then creates a registration certificate $R = (\mathsf{vks}, m)$, where m is the pool's metadata, e.g. the name of the pool's leader. The certificate is passed to the STAKE interface of the core protocol, in order to sign it. Finally, the signed certificate is published on the ledger as part of the metadata of a payment, thus registering the key vks on behalf of the pool.

Delegation: Delegation enables a stakeholder to commission a stake pool to perform staking on its behalf. It is also based on certificates, like $\Sigma = (\mathsf{vks}_s, \langle \mathsf{vks}_d, m \rangle)$. vks_s is the staking key to which the certificate applies, i.e. the key which controls the stake of an address, vks_d is the delegate's key, i.e. the registered key of a stake pool, and m is the certificate's metadata. Again the wallet gives Σ to the STAKE interface of $\pi_{\mathrm{CoreWallet}}$ and then publishes the signed certificate via a payment transaction's metadata, similar to stake pool registration. When a staking key issues a delegation certificate, *all* addresses which are associated with it are re-delegated accordingly. For instance, if a pointer address points to a key vks_s, then the latest certificate issued by this key takes effect. Finally, a stake pool re-delegates via a lightweight certificate, i.e. a certificate not published via a transaction but included in the block's headers.

5.2 Participation in the PoS Protocol

PoS participation consists of regularly publishing blocks to extend a chain. A block $\mathcal{B}$ is a tuple (vks, m), where $(\mathsf{vks}, \mathsf{sks})$ is the key signing $\mathcal{B}$ and m are $\mathcal{B}$'s contents. As with the other staking actions, the wallet obtains a block's signature via the staking interface (and a verifier similarly checks it). However, a block's validity, i.e. whether it can extend a given chain, depends on the chain decision rules, which are affected by delegation as shown next.

Given its local chain $\mathcal{C}$, a player retrieves the address which is eligible to produce a block as $\alpha_{PoS} = F_{PoS,player}(\mathcal{C})$. α_{PoS} has staking key vks_{PoS}. A block $\mathcal{B}$ signed by a different staking key ($\mathsf{vks}, \mathsf{sks}$) is valid for $\mathcal{C}$ if i) $\mathcal{C}$ contains a certificate that delegates from vks_{PoS} to vks or ii) either vks_{PoS} has not delegated or a certificate that delegates from vks_{PoS} to vks_h is published in $\mathcal{C}$ and $\mathcal{B}$ contains a lightweight certificate delegating from vks_h to vks; otherwise $\mathcal{B}$ is invalid. Additionally, the empty chain $\mathcal{C} = \epsilon$ is valid and, given a chain $\mathcal{C} = \mathcal{C}'\|\mathcal{B}$, if $\mathcal{C}'$ is valid and B is valid for $\mathcal{C}'$, then $\mathcal{C}$ is valid. A chain is picked between the previously accepted chain $\mathcal{C}$ and the set of *valid* chains $\mathbb{C}$ available on the network: the longest chain from $\mathbb{C} \cup \{\mathcal{C}\}$ is chosen. In case of length tie between two chains $\mathcal{C}_1$ and $\mathcal{C}_2$, where $head(\mathcal{C}_1)$ and $head(\mathcal{C}_2)$ are signed by ($\mathsf{vks}_1, \mathsf{sks}_1$) and ($\mathsf{vks}_2, \mathsf{sks}_2$) respectively, the following rules apply:

- if vks_1 and vks_2 are delegated via two heavyweight certificates, then choose the certificate with the higher index
- else if vks_1 is delegated via the heavyweight certificate Σ_1 and vks_2 is delegated via the *lightweight* certificate Σ_2, then $\mathcal{C}_1$ is chosen
- else if vks_1 and vks_2 are delegated via the combination of heavyweight and lightweight certificates ($\Sigma_{1,1}, \Sigma_{1,2}$) and ($\Sigma_{2,1}, \Sigma_{2,2}$) respectively, then:
  - if they have different indexes, choose the one with the higher index
  - else if they have different counters, choose the one with the higher counter
  - else choose the first observed on the network.

5.3   Consensus Security Under Stake Pools

To argue about the security of a PoS stake-pooled variant we turn to the underlying protocol's honest stake threshold assumption τ. This parameter identifies the minimum percentage of stake that needs to be honest; typically, τ is set to $1/2 + \epsilon$ or $2/3 + \epsilon$ for some $\epsilon > 0$.

We assume that stake is delegated to P pools, of which P_h back the correct protocol execution and control ρ_h percentage of the total stake. In this setting we need to consider pools, rather than stake itself. Intuitively, when a player delegates, they relinquish their staking rights for block production (though they retain the right to choose their delegate). If an honest party delegates to the adversary, then its becomes adversarial in the stake-pooled setting. Thus, the adversary compromises the stake-pooled security by corrupting enough pools, such that the percentage of stake that honest pools control is less than τ. We stress that this does not necessarily imply that the adversary needs to corrupt a large number of pools. For instance, if a pool controls $\rho_a \geq 1 - \tau$ of the total stake, the adversary can compromise the stake-pooled variant's security by only corrupting this single large pool. Corollary 1 formalizes this argument; its proof following directly from the definition of the chain selection rules of Sect. 5.2.

Corollary 1. *Assume a PoS protocol π, the execution of which is secure if at least τ stake is honest. The execution of π and the core-wallet protocol $\pi_{\mathrm{CoreWallet}}$ under the chain selection rules of Sect. 5.2 is secure if $\rho_h \geq \tau$, where ρ_h is the percentage of stake controlled by pools that back the correct protocol execution.*

5.4 Attacks Against Stake Pooled PoS

Sybil Attacks. Using stake pools for the PoS protocol's execution, rather than the stakeholders themselves, introduces the possibility of *Sybil Attacks* [19]. Specifically, suppose that the adversary creates a large number of stake pools. Since it is hard for honest players to identify an adversarial pool, they could appear legitimate and users might be convinced to delegate to them, thus increasing the adversarial stake ratio. This is an inherent problem, since no form of external identification exists and an adversary can create a large number of staking keys and registration certificates. A potential countermeasure is to have pool leaders commit (some of) their own stake to their pool. In our setting, this method is facilitated by introducing an extra field in the delegation certificate's metadata, which identifies the leader's addresses and funds committed to the pool. As long as the funds are locked in these addresses, the leader cannot use them for multiple pool commitments. While this does not directly prevent a Sybil attack, it does bound the attacker's identity production capability.

Replay Attacks. An important consideration is *replay protection*. Replay attacks are prominent in account-based ledgers, where an adversary may republish an old transaction. For instance, suppose *Alice* sends x assets from her account A to *Bob*. After the payment is published, A controls $y = z - x$ assets, where z are the funds A held before the payment. In a replay scenario, the adversary re-publishes this payment, thus a further amount x of funds is sent from A to Bob. The same vulnerability exists against certificates, e.g. an attacker can re-publish a past certificate in order to forcefully change a user's delegation choice. Our solution is based on an *address whitelist*. The certificate defines the addresses which are allowed to publish it; naturally, this scheme assumes that, upon creating the certificate, the wallet knows the possible addresses that can publish it. In order to verify a certificate, a node checks whether it is published in a transaction issued by a whitelisted address. In order to replay the certificate, the adversary would need to infiltrate one of the whitelisted addresses. Notably, no state needs to be maintained by the verifiers. Indeed, the information which counters a replay attack, i.e. the address whitelist, is in the certificate, without the need to parse the entire ledger or maintain extra local state, as in the case of the counter-based mechanisms used in Ethereum, cf. [20]. Alternative, a deadline-based approach could be followed. Similar to a whitelist, a certificate also includes a block limit, i.e. the latest block in which the transaction can be published. The block limit should be carefully chosen, in order to allow the block producers enough time to include it in a block. On the one hand, if the limit is too low, then the block producers might not receive it on time or might not prioritize it, and thus not publish it at all after the limit has expired. On the other hand, if it is too high, the user needs to wait a large amount of time before being able to re-delegate their stake, which hurts the usability of the system.

References

1. Andrychowicz, M., Dziembowski, S., Malinowski, D., Mazurek, Ł.: On the malleability of bitcoin transactions. In: Brenner, M., Christin, N., Johnson, B., Rohloff, K. (eds.) FC 2015. LNCS, vol. 8976, pp. 1–18. Springer, Heidelberg (2015). https://doi.org/10.1007/978-3-662-48051-9_1
2. Arapinis, M., Gkaniatsou, A., Karakostas, D., Kiayias, A.: A formal treatment of hardware wallets. In: Goldberg and Moore [26], pp. 426–445. https://doi.org/10.1007/978-3-030-32101-7_26
3. Badertscher, C., Gaži, P., Kiayias, A., Russell, A., Zikas, V.: Ouroboros genesis: composable proof-of-stake blockchains with dynamic availability. In: Proceedings of the 2018 ACM SIGSAC Conference on Computer and Communications Security, CCS 2018, pp. 913–930. ACM, New York (2018). https://doi.org/10.1145/3243734.3243848. http://doi.acm.org/10.1145/3243734.3243848
4. Bellare, M., Miner, S.K.: A forward-secure digital signature scheme. In: Wiener, M. (ed.) CRYPTO 1999. LNCS, vol. 1666, pp. 431–448. Springer, Heidelberg (1999). https://doi.org/10.1007/3-540-48405-1_28
5. Bentov, I., Pass, R., Shi, E.: Snow white: provably secure proofs of stake. Cryptology ePrint Archive, Report 2016/919 (2016). http://eprint.iacr.org/2016/919
6. Bruenjes, L., Kiayias, A., Koutsoupias, E., Stouka, A.P.: Reward sharing schemes for stake pools. Computer Science and Game Theory (cs.GT) arXiv:1807.11218 (2018)
7. Buterin, V., Griffith, V.: Casper the friendly finality gadget. CoRR abs/1710.09437 (2017). http://arxiv.org/abs/1710.09437
8. Canetti, R.: Universally composable security: a new paradigm for cryptographic protocols. In: 42nd Annual Symposium on Foundations of Computer Science, Las Vegas, NV, USA, 14–17 October 2001, pp. 136–145. IEEE Computer Society Press (2001). https://doi.org/10.1109/SFCS.2001.959888
9. Canetti, R.: Universally composable signatures, certification and authentication. Cryptology ePrint Archive, Report 2003/239 (2003). http://eprint.iacr.org/2003/239
10. Chakravarty, M.M.T., et al.: Hydra: fast isomorphic state channels. Cryptology ePrint Archive, Report 2020/299 (2020). https://eprint.iacr.org/2020/299
11. Chen, J., Gorbunov, S., Micali, S., Vlachos, G.: ALGORAND AGREEMENT: super fast and partition resilient byzantine agreement. Cryptology ePrint Archive, Report 2018/377 (2018). https://eprint.iacr.org/2018/377
12. Community, E.: Eos.io technical white paper v2 (2018). https://github.com/EOSIO/Documentation/blob/master/TechnicalWhitePaper.md
13. Courtois, N.T., Emirdag, P., Valsorda, F.: Private key recovery combination attacks: on extreme fragility of popular bitcoin key management, wallet and cold storage solutions in presence of poor RNG events. Cryptology ePrint Archive, Report 2014/848 (2014). http://eprint.iacr.org/2014/848
14. Das, P., Faust, S., Loss, J.: A formal treatment of deterministic wallets. In: Cavallaro, L., Kinder, J., Wang, X., Katz, J. (eds.) ACM CCS 2019: 26th Conference on Computer and Communications Security, 11–15 November 2019, pp. 651–668. ACM Press (2019). https://doi.org/10.1145/3319535.3354236
15. David, B., Gaži, P., Kiayias, A., Russell, A.: Ouroboros Praos: an adaptively-secure, semi-synchronous proof-of-stake protocol. Cryptology ePrint Archive, Report 2017/573 (2017). http://eprint.iacr.org/2017/573

16. Decker, C., Wattenhofer, R.: Bitcoin transaction malleability and MtGox. In: Kutyłowski, M., Vaidya, J. (eds.) ESORICS 2014, Part II. LNCS, vol. 8713, pp. 313–326. Springer, Cham (2014). https://doi.org/10.1007/978-3-319-11212-1_18

17. decred.org: Decred–an autonomous digital currency (2019). https://decred.org

18. Dolev, D., Dwork, C., Naor, M.: Nonmalleable cryptography. SIAM Rev. **45**(4), 727–784 (2003)

19. Douceur, J.R.: The Sybil attack. In: Druschel, P., Kaashoek, F., Rowstron, A. (eds.) IPTPS 2002. LNCS, vol. 2429, pp. 251–260. Springer, Heidelberg (2002). https://doi.org/10.1007/3-540-45748-8_24

20. Ethereum: Glossary: Account nonce (2018). https://github.com/ethereum/wiki/wiki/Glossary

21. Ethereum: Proof of stake FAQs (2018). https://github.com/ethereum/wiki/wiki/Proof-of-Stake-FAQs

22. Fanti, G.C., Kogan, L., Oh, S., Ruan, K., Viswanath, P., Wang, G.: Compounding of wealth in proof-of-stake cryptocurrencies. In: Goldberg and Moore [26], pp. 42–61. https://doi.org/10.1007/978-3-030-32101-7_3

23. Garay, J., Kiayias, A., Leonardos, N.: The bitcoin backbone protocol: analysis and applications. In: Oswald, E., Fischlin, M. (eds.) EUROCRYPT 2015, Part II. LNCS, vol. 9057, pp. 281–310. Springer, Heidelberg (2015). https://doi.org/10.1007/978-3-662-46803-6_10

24. Garay, J.A., Kiayias, A., Leonardos, N.: The bitcoin backbone protocol with chains of variable difficulty. In: Katz and Shacham [30], pp. 291–323. https://doi.org/10.1007/978-3-319-63688-7_10

25. Gilad, Y., Hemo, R., Micali, S., Vlachos, G., Zeldovich, N.: Algorand: scaling byzantine agreements for cryptocurrencies. Cryptology ePrint Archive, Report 2017/454 (2017). http://eprint.iacr.org/2017/454

26. Goldberg, I., Moore, T. (eds.): FC 2019. LNCS, vol. 11598. Springer, Cham (2019). https://doi.org/10.1007/978-3-030-32101-7

27. Goldwasser, S., Micali, S., Rivest, R.L.: A "paradoxical" solution to the signature problem (abstract) (impromptu talk). In: Blakley, G.R., Chaum, D. (eds.) CRYPTO 1984. LNCS, vol. 196, p. 467. Springer, Heidelberg (1984)

28. Goodman, L.: Tezos—a self-amending crypto-ledger white paper (2014)

29. Gutoski, G., Stebila, D.: Hierarchical deterministic bitcoin wallets that tolerate key leakage. In: Böhme, R., Okamoto, T. (eds.) FC 2015. LNCS, vol. 8975, pp. 497–504. Springer, Heidelberg (2015). https://doi.org/10.1007/978-3-662-47854-7_31

30. Katz, J., Shacham, H. (eds.): CRYPTO 2017, Part I. LNCS, vol. 10401. Springer, Cham (2017). https://doi.org/10.1007/978-3-319-63688-7

31. Kerber, T., Kiayias, A., Kohlweiss, M., Zikas, V.: Ouroboros Crypsinous: privacy-preserving proof-of-stake. In: 2019 IEEE Symposium on Security and Privacy, San Francisco, CA, USA, 19–23 May 2019, pp. 157–174. IEEE Computer Society Press (2019). https://doi.org/10.1109/SP.2019.00063

32. Kiayias, A., Russell, A., David, B., Oliynykov, R.: Ouroboros: a provably secure proof-of-stake blockchain protocol. In: Katz and Shacham [30], pp. 357–388. https://doi.org/10.1007/978-3-319-63688-7_12

33. Maxwell, G., et al.: Deterministic wallets (2014)

34. Nakamoto, S.: Bitcoin: a peer-to-peer electronic cash system (2008)

35. Pass, R., Seeman, L., Shelat, A.: Analysis of the blockchain protocol in asynchronous networks. In: Coron, J.-S., Nielsen, J.B. (eds.) EUROCRYPT 2017, Part II. LNCS, vol. 10211, pp. 643–673. Springer, Cham (2017). https://doi.org/10.1007/978-3-319-56614-6_22

36. Pass, R., Shi, E.: The sleepy model of consensus. In: Takagi, T., Peyrin, T. (eds.) ASIACRYPT 2017, Part II. LNCS, vol. 10625, pp. 380–409. Springer, Cham (2017). https://doi.org/10.1007/978-3-319-70697-9_14
37. Reed, D., Sporny, M., Longley, D., Allen, C., Grant, R., Sabadello, M.: Decentralized identifiers (DIDs) v0. 11. W3C, Draft Community Group Report, vol. 9 (2018)
38. Steem: Steem whitepaper (2018). https://steem.com/steem-whitepaper.pdf
39. Van Saberhagen, N.: Cryptonote v 2.0 (2013)
40. Wood, G.: Ethereum: a secure decentralised generalised transaction ledger. Ethereum project yellow paper, vol. 151, pp. 1–32 (2014)
41. Wuille, P.: Hierarchical Deterministic Wallets (2017). Online January 2020. https://github.com/bitcoin/bips/blob/master/bip-0032.mediawiki

Afgjort: A Partially Synchronous Finality Layer for Blockchains

Thomas Dinsdale-Young[1], Bernardo Magri[3][iD], Christian Matt[2(✉)][iD],
Jesper Buus Nielsen[3][iD], and Daniel Tschudi[2,3][iD]

[1] Concordium, Aarhus, Denmark
{ty,cm,dt}@concordium.com
[2] Concordium, Zurich, Switzerland
[3] Concordium Blockchain Research Center, Aarhus University, Aarhus, Denmark
{magri,jbn}@cs.au.dk

Abstract. Most existing blockchains either rely on a Nakamoto-style of consensus, where the chain can fork and produce rollbacks, or on a committee-based Byzantine fault tolerant (CBFT) consensus, where no rollbacks are possible. While the latter ones offer better consistency, the former tolerate more corruptions. To achieve the best of both worlds, we initiate the formal study of finality layers. Such a finality layer can be combined with a Nakamoto-style blockchain (NSB) and periodically declare blocks as final, preventing rollbacks beyond final blocks.

As conceptual contributions, we formalize the concept of a finality layer and identify the following properties to be crucial for finality layers: finalized blocks form a chain (*chain-forming*), all parties agree on the finalized blocks (*agreement*), the last finalized block does not fall too far behind the last block in the underlying blockchain (*updated*), and all finalized blocks at some point have been on the chain adopted by honest parties holding at least k units of the resource on which consensus is based, e.g., stake or computing power (*k-support*).

As our main technical contribution we propose the finality layer protocol Afgjort. We prove that it satisfies all of the aforementioned requirements in the setting with less than 1/3 corruption among the finalizers and a partially synchronous network.

We further show that tolerating less than 1/3 corruption is optimal for partially synchronous finality layers. Finally, we provide data from experiments ran with an implementation of our protocol; the data confirms that finality is reached much faster than without our finality layer.

Keywords: Blockchain · Finality · Byzantine agreement

1 Introduction

In classical blockchains such as Bitcoin [22], parties that win a "lottery" are given the right to append blocks to a growing chain. Due to network delays, the chain can fork and become a tree since parties can append new blocks to the chain

© Springer Nature Switzerland AG 2020
C. Galdi and V. Kolesnikov (Eds.): SCN 2020, LNCS 12238, pp. 24–44, 2020.
https://doi.org/10.1007/978-3-030-57990-6_2

before even seeing other blocks already appended to the chain by other parties. Such forks can also be created intentionally due to adversarial behavior. Therefore, parties need a chain-selection rule, e.g., the longest-chain rule, determining which chain in the tree is considered valid and where to append new blocks. The chain selected by a given party can thus change over time, causing rollbacks and invalidating transactions on the previously selected chain. Since very long rollbacks are unlikely, the risk can be mitigated by waiting until "sufficiently many" blocks are below a certain block before considering it "final". This waiting time can, however, often be longer than what is desirable for applications: Even assuming perfect network conditions and $1/3$ corruption, the adversary can win k lotteries in a row with probability $1/3^k$ and thereby cause a rollback of length k. This means that to limit the rollback probability of a block to 2^{-80}, which is a desirable security level in a cryptographic setting, one needs to wait for at least 50 blocks appended to it. Taking Bitcoin as a general example, where a new block is generated roughly every 10 min, this results in waiting for more than 8 h for a block to be final. Considering more sophisticated attacks and unclear network conditions, an even longer waiting time would be necessary. The main reason for this slow finality is that the simplistic rule of looking far enough back in the chain needs to take a worst-case approach: it is extremely unlikely that the adversary wins 49 blocks in a row, but to obtain 2^{-80} security against $1/3$ corruption, you must assume all the time that it could just have happened.

NSB vs CBFT Blockhains. As an alternative to Nakamoto-style blockchains (NSBs), committee-based Byzantine fault tolerant (CBFT) consensus designs such as the ones employed by Tendermint [5,20] and Algorand [16,21] have been proposed. Such blockchains provide immediate finality, i.e., every block that makes it into such a blockchain can be considered final. They have, however, one big disadvantage when compared to NSBs: responsive CBFT protocols cannot tolerate more than $t < n/3$ corruptions (cf. [25]), while NSBs typically tolerate up to $t < n/2$ corruptions.

1.1 Our Contributions

Formalization of Finality Layers. To facilitate the formal study of finality layers, we identify the following properties to be crucial. (1) *Chain-forming* says that no forks should be in the final part of the tree, i.e., all finalized blocks should be on a chain. (2) *Agreement* further ensures that all honest parties agree on all finalized blocks. (3) The Δ-*updated* property guarantees that the chains held by honest parties are at most $\Delta \in \mathbb{N}$ blocks beyond the last finalized block; in other words, finalized blocks keep up with the chain growth. Finally, the (4) *k-support* property ensures that any finalized block must have been on the chain adopted by at least k honest parties[1]; a minimal requirement is 1-*support*, as otherwise,

---

[1] We note that whenever we mention number of parties in this work it should be interpreted as the number of parties weighted by the underlying resource of the blockchain, e.g., in a PoS system k parties should be read as the fraction k/n of the total stake n in the system.

finalized blocks are potentially not on the path of *any* honest party, forcing parties to "jump" to the finalized block and resulting in bad chain quality.

A New Partially Synchronous Finality Layer. We propose a partially synchronous[2] finality layer, called Afgjort, that can be composed with virtually any NSB (synchronous or partially synchronous) that has the standard properties of common prefix, chain growth, and chain quality (cf. [9,13,24]). Our finality layer allows a finalization committee to dynamically "checkpoint" the blockchain by using Byzantine agreement to identify and then mark common blocks in the honest users' chains as final. Our finality layer is responsive in the sense that blocks are declared as final as soon as they are in the common-prefix of honest parties, which is typically long before the worst-case common-prefix bound.

Experiments. We have implemented our finality layer on top of a proof-of-stake blockchain and ran experiments in different settings. In Sect. 7 our results show that our finality layer indeed provides finality much faster than the 50 blocks waiting time mentioned above. In all experiments, finality is typically reached after about 10 blocks, in favorable conditions even 3 to 4 blocks are mostly sufficient.

For a measure of comparison, consider the PoS blockchain Ouroboros Praos [9] with a 15 s block time, and say we want to limit the rollback probability to 2^{-80} under $1/3$ corruption. As discussed before, one needs to wait for at least 50 blocks in that setting, leading to more than 12 min for finality. In our experiments, finalization with Afgjort on top of Ouroboros Praos brings this time down to around 70–85 s on average, which is an improvement of around one order of magnitude.

1.2 The Two-Layer Approach

Using a two-layer approach with a finality layer on top of a NSB has several advantages over using a CBFT consensus design or using only a NSB. First of all, when the corruption is below $n/3$, the finality layer can declare blocks as final much faster than a pure NSB. Furthermore, when the corruption is between $n/3 < t < n/2$, a two-layer design can "turn off" the finality layer and rely on the NSB, whereas pure CBFT designs completely break in this setting. Additional features of a two-layer design include:

– A finality layer can be put on top of *any* NSB, yielding a modular design. This allows to optimize the two aspects separately. In particular, our finality layer can be put on top of existing blockchains to get responsive finality.
– A finality layer can prevent long-range attacks on proof-of-stake blockchains. In a long range attack, an attacker can in several plausible situations grow a deeper alternative chain from far back in time that overtakes the real one

---

[2] We consider the *partially synchronous* network model of [11], where there is an upper bound Δ_{net} on the network delay that is not known to the protocol designer or the honest parties. In particular, Δ_{net} cannot be used by a partially synchronous protocol.

[15]. To prevent this, many existing proof-of-stake protocols rely on a complex chain-selection rule including some form of checkpointing, which prevents honest parties from adopting such alternative chains [3,9]. A finality layer (such as Afgjort) can provide this checkpointing, which is then not needed anymore in the underlying blockchain. Therefore, one can use simpler chain-selection rules for these protocols, such as simply choosing the longest chain.

– In contrast to pure CBFT designs, a two-layer blockchain continuously keeps producing blocks in the NSB and can then finalize several of them at once. Therefore, a two-layer design can provide higher and more consistent through-put than pure CBFT designs in situations where the Byzantine agreement is slower than the NSB.

1.3   Our Techniques

We assume the existence of a *finalization committee* such that up to less than $1/3$ of the committee can be corrupted. We emphasize that techniques for selecting such a committee is an orthogonal problem, and we briefly discuss it in Sect. 5.

The finalization committee is responsible for finalizing the next block. The block they are to finalize is the one at depth d, where d is some depth in the tree that they all agree on and which is deeper than the currently last finalized block. To ensure all parties agree on the value of d, it can be deterministically computed from the blocks in the path of the last finalized block.

Why Not "off-the-shelf" Byzantine Agreement? At first, it may appear that there is an easy way to finalize a block at depth d: Simply let the committee run some existing "off-the-shelf" Byzantine agreement protocol to agree on a block at depth d, which is then declared final. Typical Byzantine agreement protocols, however, do not provide the guarantees we need: the usual validity property only guarantees that if all honest parties have the same input value, they agree on this value; if honest parties start with different values, the agreement can be on an arbitrary value. This means that if we use this approach and start finalization before depth d is in the common prefix of all honest parties, any block, even ones not on the chain of any honest party, can be declared as final. This is clearly undesirable and violates the support property we require from finality layers. Better guarantees could be achieved by using Byzantine agreement with strong validity introduced by Neiger [23]. This requires the agreed value to be the input of an honest party. Even this strong notion, however, only gives 1-support, while we aim for higher support. Furthermore, strong impossibility results are known [12,23] for this type of validity if the set of possible input values is large, which is the case in our setting since there could be many different blocks at depth d.

Protocol Description. The basic insight that allows us to overcome these limitations is that we can utilize the common-prefix property of the underlying blockchain: If we wait long enough, all honest parties will have the same block at depth d on their chain. In that case, they can decide on this block. If honest parties have different blocks at depth d, they can just agree to wait longer. More concretely, our protocol proceeds as follows.

When a committee member has a chain which reached depth $d + 1$, it votes on the block it sees at depth d on its chain using a committee-based Byzantine fault tolerance consensus protocol (CBFT). This protocol is designed such that it succeeds if all parties vote for the same block, otherwise it might fail. If the CBFT announces success, the block that it outputs is defined to be final. This is enforced by modifying the chain-selection rule to always prefer the chain with the most final blocks. If the CBFT reports failure, the committee members will iteratively retry until it succeeds. In the i'th retry they wait until they are at depth $d + 2^i$ and vote for the block they see at depth d on their chain. Eventually 2^i will be large enough that the block at depth d is in the common-prefix, and then the CBFT will succeed. The process then repeats with the next committee and the next depth $d' > d$.

This finality layer works under the assumption that there is some non-trivial common-prefix. It does not need to know how long it is, it only assumes that some unknown upper bound exists. Note that the length of the common prefix generally can, among other things, depend on the network delay, which is unknown in our partially synchronous model. This also gives responsive finality: when the number of blocks after the common-prefix value is low, we finalize quickly. Furthermore, it makes the finality layer work as a hedge against catastrophic events, during which there are more blocks than usual after the common prefix.

Common-Prefix and Uniquely Justified Votes. The procedure described above ensures that at some point, the block to be finalized at depth d is in the common-prefix. Then, the common-prefix property ensures that all *honest* parties vote for that block. However, it is still possible for dishonest parties to vote for another block.

Due to space limitations, in this extended abstract, we only present a simplified version of our protocol with the caveat that it requires an additional property of the underlying blockchain, which we call bounded *dishonest chain growth*. It implies that a chain only adopted by dishonest parties grows slower than the chains of honest parties. This holds for many blockchains (assuming honest majority of the relevant resource), but it may not hold, e.g., if the blockchain allows parties to adaptively adjust the hardness of newly added blocks. In that case, dishonest parties can grow long *valid* chains with low hardness quickly without violating the common-prefix property, since honest parties will not adopt chains with hardness lower than their own current chain. Given this additional property, we have that at some point, there will be only one block at depth d lying on a sufficiently long path. When a party votes for a block at depth d, we ask the party to *justify* the vote by sending along an extension of the path of length 2^i. So we can ask that our CBFT has success only when *all* parties vote the same, even the corrupted parties. In all other cases it is allowed to fail. Since any path can eventually grow to any length, the property that there is a unique justified vote is temporary. We therefore start our CBFT with a so-called **Freeze** protocol which in a constant number of rounds turns a temporarily uniquely justified vote into an eternally uniquely justified vote. After that, the CBFT can be finished by running a binary Byzantine agreement on whether Freeze succeeded.

In the full version [10] we present our full protocol that does not rely on bounded dishonest chain growth and consequently works on top of any blockchain with the typical properties. We still get from the common-prefix property that at some point, all *honest* parties will vote for the same block. We exploit this by adding an additional step at the beginning of the protocol which tries to filter out votes that come only from dishonest parties.

Keeping Up with Chain Growth. The updated property of the finality layer requires that the finalized blocks do not fall behind the underlying blockchain too much. To guarantee this, the depths for which finalization is attempted need to be chosen appropriately. Ideally, we would like the distance between two finalized blocks to correspond to the number of blocks the chain grows during the time needed for finalization. Since parties have to agree on the next depth to finalize beforehand, they can only use information that is in the chain up to the last finalized block to determine the next depth.

We use the following idea to ensure the chain eventually catches up with the chain growth: When parties add a new block, they include a pointer to the last block that has been finalized at that point. They also include a witness for that finalization, so that others can verify this. If the chain does not grow too fast, at the time a finalized block is added to the chain, the previously finalized block should already be known. If the chain grows too fast, however, we keep finalizing blocks that are too high in the tree. In the latter case, the pointer to the last finalized block in some block will be different from the actually last finalized block. If we detect this, we can adjust how far we need to jump ahead with the following finalization.

1.4 Related Work

A closely related work is Casper the Friendly Finality Gadget [6], which was (to the best of our knowledge) the first proposal of a modular finality layer that can be built on top of a Nakamoto-style blockchain. Casper presents a finality layer for PoW blockchains where a finalization committee is established by parties that are willing to "deposit" coins prior to joining the committee. The committee members can vote on blocks that they wish to make final and a CBFT protocol is used to achieve agreement; if more than 2/3 of the committee members (weighted by deposit value) vote on the same block, then the block becomes "final". However, since the authors do not present a precise network model and a detailed protocol description and analysis, it is not clear whether the Casper protocol guarantees liveness and/or safety in the partially synchronous model. In particular, the authors only consider what they call "plausible liveness", but there is no guarantee that liveness actually holds.

Another closely related, concurrent work is GRANDPA [27]. In contrast to our work and Casper FFG, parties in the initial phase of GRANDPA vote for their whole chain instead of a block on a predetermined depth. Parties then try to finalize the deepest block with more than 2/3 votes. This allows to finalize blocks as deep as possible. We note, however, that our mechanism of choosing the next finalization depth (see paragraph "keeping up with chain growth" above) also guarantees that we finalize sufficiently deep blocks. In contrast to our paper, GRANDPA only gives an informal treatment on several aspects. In particular, they do not consider the updated and support properties as we do, and they do not precisely specify which properties from the underlying NSB they need. From the properties they state, one can conclude that they achieve only 1-support, while our protocol has $n/3$-support. Furthermore, GRANDPA relies on a leader, what could be a problem for the liveness of the protocol if a DDoS attack is directed to the leader after his role is revealed. We remark that our protocol does not rely on a leader. Moreover, GRANDPA also uses a fixed timeout T; it inevitably prevents the protocol from being responsive in the sense that it will run slower than the network allows it when T is set too large. Our protocol does not rely on such fixed timeouts.

We stress that we are *not* presenting a blockchain protocol, yet it is instructive to compare our finality layer to existing consensus protocols. The consensus protocol closest to ours is Hybrid Consensus (HC) by Pass and Shi [25], and the closely related Thunderella [26]. They take an underlying synchronous blockchain and use it to elect a committee. To do so, they assume that the underlying blockchain has a known upper bound on how long rollbacks can be. Parties then look that far back in their currently adopted chain to elect the committee based on that blocks. Then the committee runs a CBFT protocol to get a responsive consensus protocol, i.e., the committee is producing the blocks. Note that this does not add finality to the underlying blockchain. We could cast our work in terms of theirs as follows: we can elect the next committee in the same way as HC. But our committee would not produce blocks, instead it introspectively tries to agree on a recent block in the underlying blockchain. We then do a binary search to look far enough back to reach agreement. When we agree, that block is defined as final. Now we could use that final block to elect the next committee in the same way as HC. That way, we can typically elect the next committee from a much more recent block. Thus, we do not need to assume that recent block winners stay online for as long as HC.

2   Preliminaries

2.1   Model and Network Assumptions

We assume that there is a physical time $\tau \in \mathbb{N}$ that is monotonously increasing and that parties have access to local clocks. These clocks do not have to be synchronized; we only require the clocks to run at roughly the same speed. We need that they drift from τ by at most some known bound Δ_{Time}. For the sake of simpler proofs we will pretend in proofs that $\Delta_{\text{Time}} = 0$. All proofs can easily be adapted to the case of a known $\Delta_{\text{Time}} > 0$. For simplicity, we assume that there is a fixed set of parties $\mathcal{P}$ with $n := |\mathcal{P}|$, where we denote the parties by

$P_i \in \mathcal{P}$. There is an adversary which can corrupt up to $t \in \mathbb{N}$ parties. We call P_i honest if it was not corrupted by the adversary. We use Honest to denote the set of all honest parties. For simplicity, we here assume static corruptions, i.e., the adversary needs to corrupt all parties at the beginning. The set of parties $\mathcal{P}$ constitutes what we call a committee. In Sect. 5 we discuss how the set $\mathcal{P}$ can be sampled from a blockchain.

We further assume parties have access to a gossip network which allows them to exchange messages. This models how the peer-to-peer layer distributes messages in typical blockchains. We work in a partially synchronous model, which means that there is a hidden bound Δ_{net} on message delays. In contrast to synchronous networks, Δ_{net} is not known, i.e., the protocols cannot use Δ_{net}; they can only assume the existence of some bound. One can think of Δ_{net} as an unknown parameter of the assumed network functionality, or alternatively as being chosen by the adversary at the beginning of the protocol execution (after the protocol has been fixed). More concretely, we make the following assumptions on the network:

- When an honest party sends a message at time τ, all honest parties receive this message at some time in $[\tau, \tau + \Delta_{net}]$.
- When an honest party receives a message at time τ (possibly sent by a dishonest party), all honest parties receive this message until time $\tau + \Delta_{net}$.

We finally assume that each party has a signing key for some cryptographic signature scheme where the verification key is publicly known (e.g., is on the blockchain). For our analysis, we assume signatures are perfect and cannot be forged. Formally, this can be understood as parties having access to some ideal signature functionality [2,8]. We do not model this in detail here because the involved technicalities are not relevant for our protocols.

We assume knowledge of basic concepts from graph theory (in particular rooted trees). We denote by $\text{PathTo}(T, v)$ the path from the root of tree T to node v. Let $\text{Depth}(T, v)$ be the length of $\text{PathTo}(T, v)$ and $\text{Height}(T, v)$ be the length of the longest path from v to a leaf. We refer to the full version [10], for more detailed definitions.

3   Abstract Model of Blockchains

We want to describe our finality layer independently of the underlying blockchain protocol. Therefore, we use an abstract model that captures only the relevant properties needed for our finalization layer. The properties are modeled via an ideal functionality $\mathcal{F}_{\text{TREE}}$, to which all parties have access. At a high level, $\mathcal{F}_{\text{TREE}}$ provides each party access to their view of all existing blocks arranged in a tree with the genesis block at its root. The adversary can grow these trees under certain constraints. Formally we give the adversary access to commands which grow the individual trees Tree_i of the parties P_i. We also give party P_i access to a GETTREE command which returns the current Tree_i. The functionality $\mathcal{F}_{\text{TREE}}$ maintains several variables that evolve over time. For a time τ and a variable X, we use X^τ to denote the value of the variable X at time τ. Inside $\mathcal{F}_{\text{TREE}}$ each P_i has an associated tree Tree_i. The nodes in these trees correspond to blocks and can contain several pieces of information, which we do not further specify since this is not relevant here. We only assume that blocks contain a field for some metadata data used by our finalization protocols. The party P_i can read Tree_i but is not allowed to modify it. All trees have a common root G, called genesis, and initially, all trees only consist of G. We let $\text{HonestTree} := \cup_{P_i \in \text{Honest}} \text{Tree}_i$ be the graph that consists of all blocks in the view of any honest party. The adversary can add nodes to any tree at will, under the constraint that HonestTree remains a tree at all times. All P_i also have a position $\text{Pos}_i \in \text{Tree}_i$. We require that Pos_i is a leaf of Tree_i and can be set at will by the adversary. If the adversary adds a node in Tree_i that is a child of Pos_i, Pos_i gets updated to be the new leaf. Recall that for a node B in Tree_i, $\text{PathTo}(\text{Tree}_i, B)$ denotes the (unique) path from the root to B. We define $\text{Path}_i := \text{PathTo}(\text{Tree}_i, \text{Pos}_i)$. In a typical blockchain protocol, Path_i corresponds to the chain currently adopted by P_i (e.g., the longest chain, or the chain with maximal total hardness).

Remark 1. New blocks are typically not added only by the adversary, but also by honest parties that are baking. Furthermore, the positions of honest parties are not set by the adversary, but by the parties themselves following some chain selection rule, e.g., by setting the position to the deepest leaf in the tree. We give the adversary full control over these two aspects for two reasons: First, it allows us to abstract away details about these mechanisms. Secondly, giving the adversary more power makes our results stronger.

Finalization Friendliness. To be able to finalize, we need the blockchain to be finalization friendly. This basically means that it needs to provide an interface for our finalization protocols. Concretely, parties need to additionally have access to the two commands SETFINAL and PROPDATA. A party calls (SETFINAL, R) once this party considers R to be final. More formally, each party has a variable $\text{lastFinal}_i \in \text{Tree}_i$, initially set to the genesis block G. The command (SETFINAL, R) for $R \in \text{Tree}_i$ sets lastFinal_i to R. Inputs (SETFINAL, R) by P_i where R is not a descendant of lastFinal_i are ignored. The intended effect on the blockchain is that parties will eventually set their position to be a descendant of R and maintain this indefinitely. In our formalization, this corresponds to a restriction on how the adversary sets the positions and is discussed in Sect. 3.1. In a real blockchain protocol, this can be achieved by modifying the chain selection rule to reject all chains not containing R. For honest P_i we use FinalTree_i to be the tree consisting of all paths in Tree_i going through lastFinal_i. Note that this consists of only a single path from G to lastFinal_i and then possibly a proper tree below lastFinal_i. We let $\text{FinalTree} = \cup_{P_i \in \text{Honest}} \text{FinalTree}_i$.

The command (PROPDATA, data) allows parties to propose some $\text{data} \in \{0, 1\}^*$ to be included in a future block. This is different from transactions being added to blocks in that we only have weak requirements on it: Roughly speaking, we want a constant fraction of all honest paths to contain data corresponding to the last proposal of some honest party at the time the block was first added.

This requirement is discussed in more detail in Sect. 3.1; here we only assume the adversary can add arbitrary data to blocks, which is implicit in the model since blocks are chosen by the adversary.

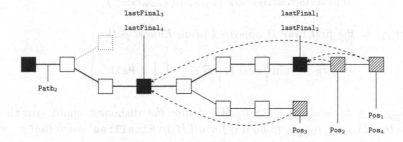

Fig. 1. Example of a possible `HonestTree` with honest parties P_1, P_2, P_3, and P_4. The block at the very left is the genesis block. Finalized blocks are drawn in solid black, blocks corresponding to positions of honest parties with a dashed pattern. The dashed arrows point to `lastFinal` of the parties having their positions at the origins of the arrows. In this example, P_3 and P_4 have not yet learned about the third finalized block. The dotted node does not belong to `FinalTree` because it is not on a path through `lastFinal` of any honest party. Everything else is part of `FinalTree`. The thick blue line corresponds to `Path`$_2$. (Color figure online)

Figure 1 shows an example of a tree with the relevant variables. The formal specification of the functionality $\mathcal{F}_{\text{TREE}}$ is given in the full version [10].

3.1 Desirable Properties and Bounds

We now state some important assumptions and properties of blockchain protocols in our model. All properties are essentially restrictions on how the adversary can grow the trees. The definitions below involve a number of so-called *hidden bounds*. These parameters are supposed to exist (possibly depending on the security parameter), but are *not* made public to the parties. In particular, they cannot be used in the protocols; one may only assume in proofs that these parameters exist. We require that the bounds are polynomial in the security parameter.

We assume some standard properties about the underlying blockchain such as common-prefix and chain growth. See the full version [10] for the formal definitions.

Dishonest Chain Growth. We here introduce a new property that is needed for the more efficient variant of our protocol. It is concerned with how fast dishonest parties can grow chains. The usual chain growth property bounds the growth of the positions of honest parties. We here consider a bound on the growth of chains no honest party is positioned on, i.e., we want to bound how fast dishonest parties can grow their chains.

Definition 1. *For $\tau \in \mathbb{N}$ and $B \in \texttt{FinalTree}^\tau$, let $\hat{B}$ be the deepest ancestor of B in $\texttt{FinalTree}^\tau$ that has at some point been on an honest path,*

$$\hat{B} := \underset{B' \in \text{PathTo}(\texttt{FinalTree}^\tau, B) \cap \left(\cup_{\tau' \le \tau} \cup_{P_i \in \texttt{Honest}} \texttt{Path}_i^{\tau'} \right)}{\text{argmax}} \{\text{Depth}(B')\},$$

and let $\hat{\tau}_B$ be the first time $\hat{B}$ appeared in an honest path:

$$\hat{\tau}_B := \min\left\{ \tau' \in \mathbb{N} \,\middle|\, \hat{B} \in \bigcup_{P_i \in \texttt{Honest}} \texttt{Path}_i^{\tau'} \right\}.$$

Let $\Delta_{\text{growth}} \in \mathbb{N}$, and $\rho_{\text{disgro}} \ge 0$. We define the dishonest chain growth *with parameters $\Delta_{\text{growth}}, \rho_{\text{disgro}}$ to hold if for all B in $\texttt{FinalTree}^\tau$ such that $\tau - \hat{\tau}_B \ge \Delta_{\text{growth}}$, the length of the path from $\hat{B}$ to B is bounded by $\rho_{\text{disgro}} \cdot (\tau - \hat{\tau}_B)$, and by $\rho_{\text{disgro}} \cdot \Delta_{\text{growth}}$ if $\tau - \hat{\tau}_B < \Delta_{\text{growth}}$:*

$$\text{DCGrowth}(\Delta_{\text{growth}}, \rho_{\text{disgro}}) :\equiv \forall \tau \in \mathbb{N} \;\forall B \in \texttt{FinalTree}^\tau$$
$$\text{Depth}(B) - \text{Depth}(\hat{B}) \le \rho_{\text{disgro}} \cdot \max\{\Delta_{\text{growth}}, \tau - \hat{\tau}_B\}.$$

Intuitively, the path from $\hat{B}$ to B is grown only by dishonest parties since no honest party was ever positioned on it, and $\tau - \hat{\tau}_B$ is the time it took to grow this path. Taking the maximum over Δ_{growth} and $\tau - \hat{\tau}_B$ allows that for periods shorter than Δ_{growth}, the growth can temporarily be faster. Note that it is possible that the adversary knows $\hat{B}$ before it appears on an honest path or even in $\texttt{FinalTree}$. In that case, there is actually more time to grow the chain. The definition thus implicitly excludes that dishonest parties know blocks honest parties will have on their path far in the future.

Remark 2. Note that Definition 1 only considers blocks in $\texttt{FinalTree}$, which by definition only contains blocks known to honest parties and considered valid by them. This in particular means that chains grown entirely "in the head" of an adversary and not presented to honest parties cannot be used to violate bounded dishonest chain growth; neither can blocks that honest parties currently consider invalid (e.g., blocks from "future" slots in proof-of-stake blockchains).

3.2   Discussion on Dishonest Chain Growth

Our more efficient protocol concretely needs that dishonest chain growth is strictly slower than honest chain growth. We next give some intuition why this is a natural assumption for many blockchains.

Typical Proof-of-Stake Blockchains. Consider a proof-of-stake blockchain such as Ouroboros [17] with the longest chain rule. If the honest parties hold more than 50% of the stake, they will be selected more often to produce blocks than corrupted parties. Hence, the corrupted parties are not able to produce a chain faster than the honest parties.

When a network model with bounded delays is assumed, such as in Ouroboros Praos [9], honest blocks can "collide" in the sense that a new block is created before the previous block is known to the new block producer. In that case, the honest chain will grow slower than if there were no collisions. Consequently, the gap between honest and dishonest stake needs to be larger to ensure the dishonest chain still grows slower for longer network delays. Note that the same analysis is required for proving the common-prefix property [9]: Intuitively, if dishonest parties can grow a chain faster than the honest parties, they can overtake the honest chain and create a fork. Bounded dishonest chain growth thus seems to fit nicely into existing analyses of different blockchain protocols.

Proof-of-Work Blockchains. In proof-of-work blockchains with fixed difficulty, the same intuition as above applies. Furthermore, the same reasoning about colliding honest blocks is required in that setting if network delays are considered [24]. In Bitcoin with variable difficulty [14], however, parties adopt not necessarily the longest chain, but the most difficult (or "heaviest") one. Therefore, an adversary could grow a very long chain with very small difficulty quickly, and thus violate bounded dishonest chain growth without violating the common-prefix property. Hence, dishonest chain growth holds for PoW blockchains with fixed difficulty but not necessarily when the difficulty can vary. Note however that one can still use our extended protocol [10] in the case of variable difficulty PoW, which in turn only requires the standard blockchain properties.

Long-Range Attacks. On a proof-of-stake blockchain, a long-range attack allows an attacker, given enough time, to grow a longer alternative chain from far back in time that overtakes the real one [15]. This is not a problem for us since we only need bounded dishonest chain growth while finalizing. That is, we need that the time required to finalize the next block is shorter than the time needed to mount a successful long-range attack. To put this into perspective, the analysis by Gaži et al. [15] of a hypothetical proof-of-stake blockchain suggests that, e.g., an attacker with 0.3 relative stake needs more than 5 years for the attack considered there. This is way longer than the typical time to finalize (see Sect. 7 for our experimental data).

4   The Finality Layer

4.1   Formalization

We now formalize the properties we want from a finality layer. The finality layer is a protocol that interacts with a blockchain as described above and uses the SETFINAL-command. The properties correspond to restrictions on how the SETFINAL-command is used.

Definition 2. *Let* $\Delta, k \in \mathbb{N}$. *We say a protocol achieves* (Δ, k)*-finality if it satisfies the following properties.*

Chain-forming: *If an honest party* $P_i \in \mathtt{Honest}$ *inputs* (SETFINAL, R) *at time* τ, *we have* $\mathtt{lastFinal}_i \in \mathrm{PathTo}(\mathtt{Tree}_i^\tau, R)$ *and* $R \neq \mathtt{lastFinal}_i$.

Agreement: *For all* $l \in \mathbb{N}$ *we have that if the l-th inputs* (SETFINAL, $\cdot$) *of honest* P_i *and* P_j *are* (SETFINAL, R_i) *and* (SETFINAL, R_j), *respectively, then* $R_i = R_j$.

Δ-Updated: *At any time* τ, *we have*

$$\max_{P_i \in \text{Honest}} \text{Depth}(\text{Pos}_i^\tau) - \min_{P_i \in \text{Honest}} \text{Depth}(\text{lastFinal}_i^\tau) \leq \Delta.$$

k-Support: *If honest* $P_i \in$ Honest *inputs* (SETFINAL, R) *at time* τ, *there are at least* k *honest parties* $P_j \in$ Honest *and times* $\tau_j \leq \tau$ *such that* $R \in \text{Path}_j^{\tau_j}$.

The chain-forming property guarantees that all finalized blocks are descendants of previously finalized blocks. That is, the finalized blocks form a chain and in particular, there are no forks. Agreement further guarantees that all honest parties agree on the same finalized blocks. This means that all ancestors of the last finalized block can be trusted to never disappear from the final chain of any honest party. The updated property ensures that the final chain grows roughly at the same speed as the underlying blockchain. This also implies liveness of the finalization protocol if the underlying blockchain keeps growing, in the sense that all honest parties will keep finalizing new blocks.

The property k-support finally ensures that whenever a block becomes finalized, at least k parties had this block on their path at some point. The smaller k is, the more honest parties need to "jump" to a new position under the next finalized block, which can cause rollbacks. We want to guarantee that *at least* $k \geq 1$ because otherwise we finalize blocks that are not supported by any honest party, what would inevitably lead to bad chain quality.

In the full version [10], we briefly show how to model security in the UC framework and how the proof that the finality layer has the desired properties translates into a UC proof. Moreover, in the full version [10], we show that our protocol is optimal in its corruption bound and that any hope of having a partially synchronous finality layer for $t \geq n/3$ is void.

5   Afgjort Protocol

In this section we describe our finality protocol. The protocol consists of a collection of algorithms that interacts with each other making finalization possible. In the main routine FinalizationLoop, parties regularly try to finalize new blocks by invoking the Finalization algorithm.

The goal of Finalization is to make all the honest parties agree on a common node R at depth d of their own local trees. This finalization happens with a "delay" of γ blocks, i.e., honest parties will only start the agreement process once their Path$_i$ has length at least $d + \gamma$. If the honest parties successfully agree on a block R, they will finalize it by re-rooting their own local tree for the new root R. If no agreement is achieved the parties increase the finalization delay γ and re-run the agreement protocol with the new delay; this process repeats until an agreement is met. The idea is that once γ is large enough, there will be only one candidate for a final block at depth d, which will then successfully be agreed on.

Justifications. We introduce the concept of *justifications*. A justification J is a predicate which takes as input a value v and the local state of a party (in particular its tree). We say that the value v is J-justified for party P_i if the predicate evaluates to true for v and P_i's state.

Definition 3. *For a value v that can be sent or received, a justification is a predicate J which can be applied to v and the local state of a party. Justifications are monotone with respect to time, i.e., if J is true for a value v at party P at time τ, then J is true (at that party) any time $\geq \tau$.*[3]

An example is the following justification $J_{\mathrm{INTREE}}^{d,\gamma}$ where the value v is a block.

Definition 4. *A block B is $J_{\mathrm{INTREE}}^{d,\gamma}$-justified for party P_i if B is at depth d of a path of length at least $d + \gamma$ in* FinalTree$_i$.

We call such justification *eventual*, in the sense that if a block is $J_{\mathrm{INTREE}}^{d,\gamma}$-justified for a honest party P_i, then it will be eventually $J_{\mathrm{INTREE}}^{d,\gamma}$-justified for any other honest party. This is a direct consequence of tree propagation.

Definition 5. *A justification J is an eventual justification if for any value v and parties P_i and P_j the following holds. If v becomes justified for party P_i at time τ and both P_i and P_j from that point in time are live and honest, then eventually v becomes justified for party P_j.*

Keeping Up with the Tree Growth. After a block at some depth d has successfully been finalized, one needs to choose the next depth d' for finalization. For the updated property, this new depth should ideally be chosen such that $d' - d$ corresponds to how long the chain grows during one finalization round. In case this value was set too small before, we need to temporarily increase it to catch up with the chain growth. In the finalization protocol, parties use the subroutine NextFinalizationGap, which returns an estimate ℓ, and set the next depth to $d' = d + \ell$. We discuss this procedure in the full version [10].

Finalization Witnesses. After a successful finalization, parties use PROPDATA to add a *finalization witness* W to the blockchain. A finalization witness has the property that whenever a valid witness for some R exists, then R indeed has been finalized. In our protocols, such a witness consists of $t + 1$ signatures on the outcome of the finalization. We put such witnesses on the blockchain for two reasons: First, it allows everyone (including parties not on the finalization

---

[3] Our finality layer repeatedly executes finalization in the FinalizationLoop. We require monotonicity only for each iteration separately, i.e., justified values can become unjustified in later iterations. We do not formalize this to simplify the presentation. This can in fact happen for the justification we use since they are with respect to FinalTree and nodes get removed from FinalTree after a successful finalization.

committee) to verify which blocks have been finalized. Secondly, we use the witnesses for computing the next finalization gap (see the full version [10]).

Finalization. The finalization loop algorithm FinalizationLoop is used to periodically invoke the finalization procedure to finalize blocks at increasing depths.

Protocol FinalizationLoop(sid)

Party P_i does the following:
1: Set $\gamma := 1$, $d := 5$, and $\ell := 5$
2: **for** ctr $= 1, 2, 3, \ldots$ **do**
3:     Set faid $:=$ (sid, ctr)
4:     Run $(R, \mathtt{W}, \gamma') :=$ Finalization(faid, $J_{\mathrm{INTREE}}^{d,\gamma}, d, \gamma$)
5:     Invoke (SETFINAL, R)
6:     Invoke (PROPDATA, $\mathtt{W}$)
7:     Set $\ell :=$ NextFinalizationGap(lastFinal$_i$, ℓ)
8:     Set $d := d + \ell$
9:     Set $\gamma := \lceil 0.8 \cdot \gamma' \rceil$
10: **end for**

The basic building block of our finality protocol is the algorithm Finalization which is used to agree on a final block for depth d. The algorithm takes as inputs a unique id faid, a depth d, and an integer $\gamma \geq 1$ corresponding to number of blocks that need to occur under the block that is attempted to be finalized. If there is no agreement on a final block, γ is doubled and the parties try again. Once the parties have agreed on a block R, the algorithm outputs R and the value γ. The finalization loop then again reduces γ by multiplying it with 0.8 so that over time, a good value for γ is found. The factor 0.8 is not significant and only used for simplicity here. In practice, one can use some heuristics to optimize efficiency.

Protocol Finalization(faid, $J_{\mathrm{INTREE}}^{d,\gamma}, d, \gamma$)

Party P_i does the following:
1: **repeat**
2:     Set baid $:=$ (faid, γ)
3:     Wait until lastFinal$_i$ is on Path$_i$ and Path$_i$ has length $\geq d + \gamma$
4:     Let B_d be the block at depth d on Path$_i$
5:     Run $(R, \mathtt{W}) :=$ WMVBA(baid, $J_{\mathrm{INTREE}}^{d,\gamma}$) with input B_d
6:     **if** $R = \bot$ **then** set $\gamma := 2\gamma$ **end if**
7: **until** $R \neq \bot$
8: **Output** $(R, \mathtt{W}, \gamma)$

The Finalization algorithm relies on a weak multi-valued Byzantine agreement protocol, that we call WMVBA. We discuss the general idea of the WMVBA protocol next, and we defer a more detailed treatment to Sect. 6.

WMVBA. The input to the WMVBA protocol are proposals in the form of blocks; we require all proposals in WMVBA to be $J_{\mathrm{INTREE}}^{d,\gamma}$ justified, i.e., the block proposal must be in the tree of honest parties at depth d and height γ. This prevents the corrupted parties from proposing arbitrary blocks. By the design of the Finalization protocol, where γ is doubled between the calls to WMVBA it will quickly happen that all honest parties agree on the block B at the depth where we try to finalize. Furthermore, by the assumed properties of the underlying blockchain, it will also happen that no other block is $J_{\mathrm{INTREE}}^{d,\gamma}$-justified. This moment where B is the only valid proposal is a sweet spot for agreement as we have pre-agreement. However, the sweet spot is temporary; if enough time passes, the corrupted parties could grow a long enough alternative chain which would make another proposal legitimate. We therefore want to quickly exploit the "sweet spot".

Existence of Unique Justified Proposals. For our more efficient finalization protocol to succeed, we need that there will be a unique justified proposal at some point such that all honest parties will agree on that. In the full version [10], we give a precise definition of this property and show that it follows from the dishonest chain growth property DCGrowth together with the standard chain properties.

Committee Selection. Properly selecting a committee is a challenging task that has been extensively studied [18, 19, 25]. The appropriate strategy to select a finalization committee is highly tied to the specific type of blockchain one considers. Therefore, it is out of the scope of this paper to propose a definitive answer on how to select a committee for each particular setting. In the full version [10], we discuss some possible approaches that can be used to select the finalization committee in a few settings.

Security Analysis. The theorem below summarizes the security guarantees of our finality layer. We provide a proof in the full version [10].

Theorem 1. *For $t < \frac{n}{3}$ and a blockchain satisfying common prefix, chain quality, bounded chain growth, and DCGrowth, there exists a Δ such that the Afgjort protocol described above satisfies $(\Delta, n/3)$-finality.*

6   Weak Multi-valued Byzantine Agreement

At the core of the Finalization algorithm from Sect. 5, parties use a Byzantine agreement protocol relative to a justification J (here $J = J_{\mathrm{INTREE}}^{d,\gamma}$). Each party P_i inputs a justified proposal p_i (a block) and gets a decision d_i (a block or $\bot$) as output. The Byzantine agreement must satisfy consistency and termination which are defined as follows.

Consistency: If some honest parties P_i and P_j output decisions d_i and d_j respectively, then $d_i = d_j$.

Termination: If all honest parties input some justified proposal, then eventually all honest parties output a decision.

For termination, Finalization requires that the agreement protocol satisfies a special form of validity. For blockchains satisfying DCGrowth, we propose the agreement protocol WMVBA. It is inspired by classic asynchronous BA protocol such as [7] and [4]. The WMVBA protocol satisfies weak validity and $n/3$-support:

Weak Validity: If during the protocol execution there exists a decision d such that no other decision d', where $d' \neq d$ is J-justified for any honest party, then no honest party P_i outputs a decision d' with $d' \neq d$.

$n/3$**-Support:** If some honest party P_i outputs decision d with $d \neq \perp$, then at least $n/3$ of the honest parties had J-justified input d.

Remark 3. The $n/3$-support property is a strengthening of *strong validity*, which has been introduced by Neiger [23]. Strong validity requires the output of honest parties to be the input of some honest party, i.e., it roughly corresponds to 1-support (ignoring $\perp$-outputs and justifications). As was shown by Neiger [23] in the information-theoretic setting, and later by Fitzi and Garay [12] in the computational setting, strong validity is impossible (even in a synchronous network) if $n \leq mt$, where m is the number of possible inputs. We circumvent these impossibilities by allowing parties to output $\perp$ when there are too many possible inputs (i.e., justified proposals).

Fitzi and Garay [12] further introduced another related notion, δ-*differential consensus*: If v is the output of honest parties and $\#v$ the number of honest parties with input v, then no other value $v' \neq v$ was the input of more than $\#v + \delta$ honest parties. Note that k-support implies that at most $n - k$ honest parties can have an input different from the agreed output (if all parties are honest). Thus, it implies $(n - 2k)$-differential consensus. On the other hand, δ-differential consensus does not imply k-support for any k since if no value is the input of more than δ honest parties, δ-differential consensus does not provide any guarantee.

Remark 4. Note that for termination WMVBA, it is required that at some point in time there exists a unique justified block in the tree; this is only guaranteed if the underlying blockchain satisfies bounds on both dishonest and honest chain growth. In the full version [10], we additionally describe an extended version of WMVBA that provides a stronger validity guarantee, and in particular it terminates if there is a point in time where all honest parties pre-agree on a block in the tree, which follows naturally from the standard blockchain properties. The extended version, however, only provides 1-support and requires one extra round of communication.

Protocol Intuition. At the beginning of the WMVBA protocol all parties first run the Freeze sub-protocol. In Freeze, parties send their proposals to all other parties and every party checks whether they received at least $n - t$ proposals for the same block. In that case, their output for Freeze is that block, otherwise it is $\bot$. Freeze thereby boils the decision for a finalized block down to the binary decision between $\bot$ and a unique block output by Freeze (if that exists). To this end, a binary Byzantine agreement protocol ABBA is run after Freeze. Details on the WMVBA protocol are found in the full version [10].

In contrast to many classical protocols, such as the one in [7], we implement a coin-flip using a VRF-based approach instead of a distributed coin-flip protocol. Also note that our protocols are not asynchronous; we explicitly make use of the partially synchronous network assumption. The idea of reducing a multivalued Byzantine agreement to a binary Byzantine agreement as used in WMVBA (via Freeze and ABBA) was first proposed by Turpin and Coan [28]. The idea of core-set selection as used in ABBA has been presented, e.g., in [1].

The most important difference of our protocol compared to classical ones is that classical protocols provide validity (i.e., if all honest parties have the same input v, then no honest party decides on $v' \neq v$), which is stronger than our weak validity. They do not, however, provide any support. In our setting, weak validity is sufficient and support is an important property for a finality layer. Hence, while we use mostly known techniques, we need different guarantees and cannot directly rely on existing protocols.

7   Experimental Results

In order to experimentally evaluate Afgjort, we ran a number of experiments using an industrially developed implementation of the protocol. As the underlying NSB, we use the PoS blockchain Ouroboros Praos [9]. Our test network consisted of 1000 baker nodes (i.e., nodes producing blocks) distributed in two datacenters with low-latency links (physical latency in the 1–2 ms range).

We ran six experiments varying the size of the finalization committee between 10, 100 and 1000 members, and varying the expected block production rate of the underlying blockchain between 1 and 15 seconds per block. In each configuration, there were 1000 baker nodes, and the finalizers where chosen randomly among them. To provide a load, 100 transactions were submitted to the system each second. The slot time of the underlying blockchain was fixed at 0.1 s; the block production rate was controlled by choosing the difficulty parameter. In each experiment, the network was started and allowed to stabilize for 1 h; the sample window was the blocks that were created in the second hour of operation (according to their slot times).

Table 1 shows the results of these experiments. The "target block time" is the expected time it takes to produce a new block based on the chosen slot time and difficulty. With 0.1 s slot time, this means, e.g., that a target block time of 1 s corresponds to a difficulty parameter such that in each slot, the probability that some party is eligible to create a block is 0.1. The "finalization gap" measures the "gap" in time and in number of blocks from when a block was first inserted in the tree to when it was considered final; the gap in time is taken to be the difference

Table 1. Experimental results.

Target block time (s)	# Finalizers	Finalization gap				# Blocks	Avg. block time (s)	# Tx
		Time (s)		# Blocks				
		Mean	SD	Mean	SD			
1	10	8.4	3.7	6.4	2.5	2776	1.3	359990
	100	7.3	3.1	5.6	2.1	2775	1.3	359968
	1000	19.3	6.1	10.3	3.1	1991	1.8	359232
15	10	69.9	41.8	3.6	1.2	189	19.0	355386
	100	66.2	35.4	3.6	1.2	190	18.9	359045
	1000	84.6	44.2	3.8	1.2	168	21.4	360955

in nominal (slot) time between a block and the first block that considers it to be finalized, and the gap in number of blocks is the difference in depth between a block and the first block that considers it to be finalized. For both measurements we give the mean and standard deviation (SD). "Blocks" is the total number of blocks on the finalized chain in the 1 h sample window, and "Average block time" is the average time between the creation of blocks on the finalized chain in that window. Finally, "Transactions" represents the total accumulated number of transactions in the blocks on the finalized chain inside the sample window.

Under ideal circumstances, the system should produce a chain with no branching, and we would expect the measured average block time to be equal to the target block time. The fact that this does not happen suggests that some branching does occur. It is also possible that a baker may fail to produce a block in a slot, despite having the right to do so, if the responsible thread fails to wake up in time. As one can see from the results, the average block time with 1000 finalizers is higher than with fewer finalizers. This can be explained by a much higher load on the network, which also affects the bakers. Overall, we picked the parameters rather aggressively to put some stress on our finality layer, since finalization in a perfect blockchain without any branching is a trivial task.

Curiously, the configurations with 100 finalizers consistently perform better than those with 10 and 1000 finalizers, in terms of time to finalize a block. Since a larger finalization committee equates to more messages being sent, we would tend to expect worse performance with a larger committee. One possible explanation for 100 finalizers outperforming 10 is that in the former, finalizers have fewer network hops between them on average. This may mean that a finalizer reaches the thresholds to progress with the finalization protocol more quickly.

We note that the constants used in NextFinalizationGap prevent the gap between finalized blocks going below 4. With 15 s expected block time, this gap was constantly 4 within the sample window. This suggests that more frequent finalization would be feasible by adjusting these constants.

Acknowledgements. We would like to thank Mateusz Tilewski for countless discussions during the design of the finality layer, his deep insights into practical distributed systems were valuable in designing a system which is at the same time efficient in practice and provably secure. We would like to thank Matias Frank Jensen and Emil Morre Christensen; their work on generalizing the Finality layer gave valuable insights which were adapted into the protocol presented in this paper. Finally, we thank the Concordium tech team that worked on the implementation and ran the experiments reported in this paper.

References

1. Attiya, H., Welch, J.: Distributed Computing: Fundamentals, Simulations, and Advanced Topics. Wiley Series on Parallel and Distributed Computing. Wiley, Hoboken (2004)
2. Backes, M., Hofheinz, D.: How to break and repair a universally composable signature functionality. In: Zhang, K., Zheng, Y. (eds.) ISC 2004. LNCS, vol. 3225, pp. 61–72. Springer, Heidelberg (2004). https://doi.org/10.1007/978-3-540-30144-8_6
3. Badertscher, C., Gazi, P., Kiayias, A., Russell, A., Zikas, V.: Ouroboros genesis: composable proof-of-stake blockchains with dynamic availability. In: ACM CCS 2018, pp. 913–930. ACM Press (2018)
4. Bracha, G.: An asynchronous [(n-1)/3]-resilient consensus protocol. In: Probert, R.L., Lynch, N.A., Santoro, N. (eds.) 3rd ACM PODC, pp. 154–162. ACM, August 1984
5. Buchman, E.: Tendermint: byzantine fault tolerance in the age of blockchains. Master's thesis, The University of Guelph, Guelph, Ontario, Canada, June 2016. http://hdl.handle.net/10214/9769
6. Buterin, V., Griffith, V.: Casper the friendly finality gadget. CoRR abs/1710.09437 (2017)
7. Cachin, C., Kursawe, K., Petzold, F., Shoup, V.: Secure and efficient asynchronous broadcast protocols. In: Kilian, J. (ed.) CRYPTO 2001. LNCS, vol. 2139, pp. 524–541. Springer, Heidelberg (2001). https://doi.org/10.1007/3-540-44647-8_31
8. Canetti, R.: Universally composable signature, certification, and authentication. In: Proceedings of the 17th IEEE Computer Security Foundations Workshop, June 2004
9. David, B., Gaži, P., Kiayias, A., Russell, A.: Ouroboros Praos: an adaptively-secure, semi-synchronous proof-of-stake blockchain. In: Nielsen, J.B., Rijmen, V. (eds.) EUROCRYPT 2018, Part II. LNCS, vol. 10821, pp. 66–98. Springer, Cham (2018). https://doi.org/10.1007/978-3-319-78375-8_3
10. Dinsdale-Young, T., Magri, B., Matt, C., Nielsen, J.B., Tschudi, D.: Afgjort: a partially synchronous finality layer for blockchains. Cryptology ePrint Archive, Report 2019/504 (2019). https://eprint.iacr.org/2019/504
11. Dwork, C., Lynch, N., Stockmeyer, L.: Consensus in the presence of partial synchrony. J. ACM 35(2), 288–323 (1988)
12. Fitzi, M., Garay, J.A.: Efficient player-optimal protocols for strong and differential consensus. In: Borowsky, E., Rajsbaum, S. (eds.) 22nd ACM PODC, pp. 211–220. ACM, July 2003
13. Garay, J., Kiayias, A., Leonardos, N.: The bitcoin backbone protocol: analysis and applications. In: Oswald, E., Fischlin, M. (eds.) EUROCRYPT 2015, Part II. LNCS, vol. 9057, pp. 281–310. Springer, Heidelberg (2015). https://doi.org/10.1007/978-3-662-46803-6_10

14. Garay, J., Kiayias, A., Leonardos, N.: The bitcoin backbone protocol with chains of variable difficulty. In: Katz, J., Shacham, H. (eds.) CRYPTO 2017, Part I. LNCS, vol. 10401, pp. 291–323. Springer, Cham (2017). https://doi.org/10.1007/978-3-319-63688-7_10

15. Gazi, P., Kiayias, A., Russell, A.: Stake-bleeding attacks on proof-of-stake blockchains. In: Crypto Valley Conference on Blockchain Technology, CVCBT (2018)

16. Gilad, Y., Hemo, R., Micali, S., Vlachos, G., Zeldovich, N.: Algorand: scaling byzantine agreements for cryptocurrencies. In: Proceedings of the 26th Symposium on Operating Systems Principles (2017)

17. Kiayias, A., Russell, A., David, B., Oliynykov, R.: Ouroboros: a provably secure proof-of-stake blockchain protocol. In: Katz, J., Shacham, H. (eds.) CRYPTO 2017, Part I. LNCS, vol. 10401, pp. 357–388. Springer, Cham (2017). https://doi.org/10.1007/978-3-319-63688-7_12

18. Kokoris-Kogias, E., Jovanovic, P., Gailly, N., Khoffi, I., Gasser, L., Ford, B.: Enhancing bitcoin security and performance with strong consistency via collective signing. In: 25th USENIX Security Symposium (2016)

19. Kokoris-Kogias, E., Jovanovic, P., Gasser, L., Gailly, N., Syta, E., Ford, B.: OmniLedger: a secure, scale-out, decentralized ledger via sharding. In: 2018 IEEE Symposium on Security and Privacy, pp. 583–598. IEEE Computer Society Press, May 2018

20. Kwon, J.: Tendermint: consensus without mining. Manuscript (2014). https://tendermint.com/static/docs/tendermint.pdf

21. Micali, S.: ALGORAND: the efficient and democratic ledger. CoRR (2016)

22. Nakamoto, S.: Bitcoin: a peer-to-peer electronic cash system. Manuscript (2009). http://www.bitcoin.org/bitcoin.pdf

23. Neiger, G.: Distributed consensus revisited. Inf. Process. Lett. **49**(4), 195–201 (1994)

24. Pass, R., Seeman, L., Shelat, A.: Analysis of the blockchain protocol in asynchronous networks. In: Coron, J.-S., Nielsen, J.B. (eds.) EUROCRYPT 2017, Part II. LNCS, vol. 10211, pp. 643–673. Springer, Cham (2017). https://doi.org/10.1007/978-3-319-56614-6_22

25. Pass, R., Shi, E.: Hybrid consensus: efficient consensus in the permissionless model. In: 31st International Symposium on Distributed Computing, DISC (2017)

26. Pass, R., Shi, E.: Thunderella: blockchains with optimistic instant confirmation. In: Nielsen, J.B., Rijmen, V. (eds.) EUROCRYPT 2018, Part II. LNCS, vol. 10821, pp. 3–33. Springer, Cham (2018). https://doi.org/10.1007/978-3-319-78375-8_1

27. Stewart, A.: Byzantine finality gadgets. Manuscript (2019). https://github.com/w3f/consensus/blob/master/pdf/grandpa.pdf

28. Turpin, R., Coan, B.A.: Extending binary byzantine agreement to multivalued byzantine agreement. Inf. Process. Lett. **18**(2), 73–76 (1984)

Aggregatable Subvector Commitments
for Stateless Cryptocurrencies

Alin Tomescu[1]([✉])[iD], Ittai Abraham[1], Vitalik Buterin[2], Justin Drake[2],
Dankrad Feist[2], and Dmitry Khovratovich[2]

[1] VMware Research, Palo Alto, CA, USA
{alint,iabraham}@vmware.com
[2] Ethereum Foundation, Singapore, Singapore
{vitalik,justin,dankrad,dmitry.khovratovich}@ethereum.org

Abstract. An *aggregatable subvector commitment (aSVC)* scheme is a
vector commitment (VC) scheme that can aggregate multiple proofs into
a single, small subvector proof. In this paper, we formalize aSVCs and
give a construction from constant-sized polynomial commitments. Our
construction is unique in that it has linear-sized public parameters, it can
compute all constant-sized proofs in quasilinear time, it updates proofs
in constant time and it can aggregate multiple proofs into a constant-
sized subvector proof. Furthermore, our concrete proof sizes are small
due to our use of pairing-friendly groups. We use our aSVC to obtain
a payments-only stateless cryptocurrency with very low communication
and computation overheads. Specifically, our constant-sized, aggregatable proofs reduce each block's proof overhead to a single group element,
which is optimal. Furthermore, our subvector proofs speed up block verification and our smaller public parameters further reduce block size.

1 Introduction

In a *stateless cryptocurrency*, neither *miners* nor cryptocurrency *users* need to
store the full *ledger state*. Instead, this state consisting of users' account balances
is split among all users using an *authenticated data structure*. This way, miners
only store a succinct *digest* of the ledger state and each user stores their account
balance. Nonetheless, miners can still validate transactions sent by users, who
now include *proofs* that they have sufficient balance. Furthermore, miners can
still propose new *blocks* of transactions and users can easily *synchronize* or *update*
their proofs as new blocks get published.

Stateless cryptocurrencies have received increased attention [Dry19, RMCI17,
CPZ18, BBF19, GRWZ20] due to several advantages. First, stateless cryptocurrencies eliminate hundreds of gigabytes of miner storage needed to validate
blocks. Second, statelessness makes scaling consensus via *sharding* much easier,
by allowing miners to efficiently switch from one shard to another [KJG+18].

An errata for this paper can be found at https://github.com/alinush/asvc-paper.

© Springer Nature Switzerland AG 2020
C. Galdi and V. Kolesnikov (Eds.): SCN 2020, LNCS 12238, pp. 45–64, 2020.
https://doi.org/10.1007/978-3-030-57990-6_3

Third, statelessness lowers the barrier to entry for full nodes, resulting in a much more resilient, distributed cryptocurrency.

Stateless Cryptocurrencies from VCs. At a high level, a VC scheme allows a *prover* to compute a succinct *commitment* c to a *vector* $\mathbf{v} = [v_0, v_1, \ldots, v_{n-1}]$ of *n elements* where $v_i \in \mathbb{Z}_p$. Importantly, the prover can generate a *proof* π_i that v_i is the element at position i in $\mathbf{v}$, and any *verifier* can check it against the commitment c. The prover needs a *proving key* prk to commit to vectors and to compute proofs, while the verifier needs a *verification key* vrk to verify proofs. (Usually $|\text{vrk}| \ll |\text{prk}|$.) Some VC schemes support *updates*: if one or more elements in the vector change, the commitment and proofs can be updated efficiently. For this, a static *update key* upk_j tied only to the updated position j is necessary. Alternatively, some schemes require dynamic *update hints* uph_j, typically consisting of the actual proof π_j. The proving, verification and update keys comprise the VC's *public parameters*. Lastly, *subvector commitment (SVC)* schemes [LM19] support computing succinct proofs for I-*subvectors* $(v_i)_{i \in I}$ where $I \subset [0, n)$. Furthermore, some schemes are *aggregatable*: multiple proofs π_i for $v_i, \forall i \in I$ can be aggregated into a single, succinct I-subvector proof.

Chepurnoy, Papamanthou and Zhang pioneered the idea of building *account-based* [Woo], stateless cryptocurrencies on top of any *vector commitment (VC)* scheme [CPZ18]. Ideally, such a VC would have (1) sublinear-sized, updatable proofs with sublinear-time verification, (2) updatable commitments and (3) sublinear-sized update keys. In particular, static update keys (rather than dynamic update hints) help reduce interaction and thus simplify the design (see Sect. 4.1). We say such a VC has *"scalable updates."* Unfortunately, most VCs do not have scalable updates (see Sect. 1.1) or, if they do [CPZ18, Tom20], they are not optimal in their proof and update key sizes. Lastly, while some schemes in hidden-order groups have scalable updates [CFG+20], they suffer from larger concrete proof sizes and are likely to require more computation in practice.

Our Contributions. In this paper, we formalize a new *aggregatable subvector commitment (aSVC)* notion that supports commitment updates, proof updates and aggregation of proofs into subvector proofs. Then, we construct an aSVC *with scalable updates* over pairing-friendly groups. Compared to other pairing-based VCs, our aSVC has constant-sized, aggregatable proofs that can be updated with constant-sized update keys (see Table 2). Furthermore, our aSVC supports computing all proofs in quasilinear time. We prove our aSVC secure under q-SBDH [Goy07] in the extended version of our paper [TAB+20].

A Highly-Efficient Stateless Cryptocurrency. We use our aSVC to construct a stateless cryptocurrency based on the elegant design of Edrax [CPZ18]. Our stateless cryptocurrency has very low storage, communication and computation overheads (see Table 1). First, our constant-sized update keys have a smaller impact on block size and help users update their proofs faster. Second, our proof aggregation drastically reduces block size and speeds up block validation. Third, our verifiable update keys removes the need for miners to either (1) store all $O(n)$ update keys or (2) interact during transaction validation to check update keys.

Table 1. Asymptotic comparison of our work with other stateless cryptocurrencies. n is the number of users, λ is the security parameter, and b is the number of transactions in a block. $\mathbb{G}$ is an *exponentiation* in a known-order group. $\mathbb{G}_?$ is a (slower) *exponentiation* (of size 2λ bits) in a hidden-order group. $\mathbb{P}$ is a pairing computation. $|\pi_i|$ is the size of a proof for a user's account balance. $|\mathsf{upk}_i|$ is the size of user i's update key. $|\pi_I|$ is the size of a proof aggregated from all π_i's in a block. We give each *Miner's storage* in terms of VC public parameters (e.g., update keys). A miner takes: (1) *Check digest time*, to check that, by "applying" the transactions from block $t+1$ to block t's digest, he obtains the correct digest for block $t+1$, (2) *Aggr. proofs time*, to aggregate b transaction proofs, and (3) *Vrfy.* $|\pi_I|$ *time*, to verify the aggregated proof. A user takes *Proof synchr. time* to "synchronize" or update her proof by "applying" all the transactions in a new block. We treat [GRWZ20] and [CFG+20] as a payments-only stateless cryptocurrency without smart contracts. Our aggregation and verification times have an extra $b\log^2 b\,\mathbb{F}$ term, consisting of very fast field operations.

Account-based stateless cryptocurrencies	Edrax [CPZ18]	Pointproofs [GRWZ20]	2nd VC of [CFG+20]	Our work
$|\pi_i|$	$\log n\ |\mathbb{G}|$	$1\ |\mathbb{G}|$	$1\ |\mathbb{G}_?|$	$1\ |\mathbb{G}|$
$|\mathsf{upk}_i|$	$\log n\ |\mathbb{G}|$	$n\ |\mathbb{G}|$	$1\ |\mathbb{G}_?|$	$1\ |\mathbb{G}|$
$|\pi_I|$	$b\log n\ |\mathbb{G}|$	$1\ |\mathbb{G}|$	$1\ |\mathbb{G}_?|$	$1\ |\mathbb{G}|$
Miner's storage	$n\ |\mathbb{G}|$	$n\ |\mathbb{G}|$	$1\ |\mathbb{G}_?|$	$b\ |\mathbb{G}|$
Vrfy. $|\pi_I|$ time	$b\log n\ \mathbb{P}$	$2\,\mathbb{P} + b\,\mathbb{G}$	$b\log b\ \mathbb{G}_?$	$2\,\mathbb{P} + b\,\mathbb{G} + b\lg^2 b\,\mathbb{F}$
Check digest time	$b\,\mathbb{G}$	$b\,\mathbb{G}$	$b\,\mathbb{G}_?$	$b\,\mathbb{G}$
Aggr. proofs time	$\times$	$b\,\mathbb{G}$	$b\log^2 b\ \mathbb{G}_?$	$b\,\mathbb{G} + b\lg^2 b\,\mathbb{F}$
Proof synchr. time	$b\log n\ \mathbb{G}$	$b\,\mathbb{G}$	$b\,\mathbb{G}_?$	$b\,\mathbb{G}$

1.1 Related Work

Vector Commitments (VCs). The notion of VCs appears early in [CFM08, LY10, KZG10] but Catalano and Fiore [CF13] are the first to formalize it. They introduce schemes based on the Computational Diffie-Hellman (CDH), with $O(n^2)$-sized public parameters, and on the RSA problem, with $O(1)$-sized public parameters, which can be *specialized* into $O(n)$-sized ones when needed. Lai and Malavolta [LM19] formalize *subvector commitments (SVCs)* and extend both constructions from [CF13] with constant-sized I-subvector proofs. Camenisch et al. [CDHK15] build VCs from KZG commitments [KZG10] to Lagrange polynomials that are not only *binding* but also *hiding*. However, their scheme intentionally prevents aggregation of proofs as a security feature. Feist and Khovratovich [FK20] introduce a technique for precomputing all *constant-sized* evaluation proofs in KZG commitments when the evaluation points are all roots of unity. We use their technique to compute VC proofs fast. Chepurnoy et al. [CPZ18] instantiate VCs using multivariate polynomial commitments [PST13] but with logarithmic rather than constant-sized proofs. Then, they build the first efficient, account-based, stateless cryptocurrency on top of their scheme. Later on, Tomescu [Tom20] presents a very similar scheme but from univariate polynomial commitments [KZG10] which supports subvector proofs.

Boneh et al. [BBF19] instantiate VCs using hidden-order groups. They are the first to support aggregating multiple proofs (under certain conditions). They are also the first to have constant-sized public parameters, without the need to specialize them into $O(n)$-sized ones. However, their VC uses update hints (rather than keys), which is less suitable for stateless cryptocurrencies. Campanelli et al. [CFG+20] also formalize SVCs with a more powerful notion of *infinite (dis)aggregation* of proofs. In contrast, our aSVC only supports "one hop" aggregation and does not support disaggregation. They also formalize a notion of updatable, distributed VCs as Verified Decentralized Storage (VDS). However, their use of hidden-order groups leads to larger concrete proof sizes.

Concurrent with our work, Gorbunov et al. [GRWZ20] also formalize aSVCs with a stronger notion of *cross-commitment aggregation*. However, their formalization lacks (verifiable) update keys, which hides many complexities that arise in stateless cryptocurrencies (see Sect. 4.2.2). Their VC scheme extends [LY10] with (1) aggregating proofs into I-subvector proofs and (2) aggregating multiple I-subvector proofs *with respect to different VCs* into a single, constant-sized proof. However, this versatility comes at the cost of (1) losing the ability to precompute all proofs fast, (2) $O(n)$-sized update keys for updating proofs, and (3) $O(n)$-sized verification key. This makes it difficult to apply their scheme in a stateless cryptocurrency for payments such as Edrax [CPZ18]. Furthermore, Gorbunov et al. also enhance KZG-based VCs with proof aggregation, but they do not consider proof updates. Lastly, they show it is possible to aggregate I-subvector proofs across different commitments for KZG-based VCs.

Kohlweiss and Rial [KR13] extend VCs with zero-knowledge protocols for proving correct computation of a new commitment, for opening elements at secret positions, and for proving secret updates of elements at secret positions.

Stateless Cryptocurrencies. The concept of stateless validation appeared early in the cryptocurrency community [Mil12, Tod16, But17] and later on in the academic community [RMCI17, Dry19, CPZ18, BBF19, GRWZ20]. Initial proposals for UTXO-based cryptocurrencies used Merkle hash trees [Mil12, Tod16, Dry19, CPZ18]. In particular, Dryja [Dry19] gives a beautiful Merkle forest construction that significantly reduces communication. Boneh et al. [BBF19] further reduce communication by using RSA accumulators.

Reyzin et al. [RMCI17] introduce a Merkle-based construction for account-based stateless cryptocurrencies. Unfortunately, their construction relies on *proof-serving nodes*: every user sending coins has to fetch the recipient's Merkle proof from a node and include it with her own proof in the transaction. Edrax [CPZ18] obviates the need for proof-serving nodes by using a vector commitment (VC) with update keys (rather than update hints like Merkle trees). Nonetheless, proof-serving nodes can still be used to assist users who do not want to manually update their proofs (which is otherwise very fast). Unfortunately, Edrax's (non-aggregatable) proofs are logarithmic-sized and thus sub-optimal.

Gorbunov et al. [GRWZ20] introduce *Pointproofs*, a versatile VC scheme which can aggregate proofs across *different* commitments. They use this power to solve a slightly different problem: stateless block validation for smart contract executions (rather than for payments as in Edrax). Unfortunately, their approach requires miners to store a different commitment for each smart contract, or around 4.5 GBs of (dynamic) state in a system with 10^8 smart contracts. This could be problematic in applications such as sharded cryptocurrencies, where miners would have to download part of this large state from one another when switching shards. Lastly, the verification key in Pointproofs is $O(n)$-sized, which imposes additional storage requirements on miners. Furthermore, Gorbunov et al. do not discuss how to update nor precompute proofs efficiently. Instead they assume that all contracts have $n \leq 10^3$ memory locations and users can compute all proofs in $O(n^2)$ time. In contrast, our aSVC can compute all proofs in $O(n \log n)$ time [FK20]. Nonetheless, their approach is a very promising direction for supporting smart contracts in stateless cryptocurrencies.

Bonneau et al. [BMRS20] use recursively-composable, succinct non-interactive arguments of knowledge (SNARKs) [BSCTV14] for stateless validation. However, while block validators do not have to store the full state in their system, miners who propose blocks still have to.

2 Preliminaries

Notation. λ is our security parameter. $\mathbb{G}_1, \mathbb{G}_2$ are groups of prime order p endowed with a *pairing* $e : \mathbb{G}_1 \times \mathbb{G}_2 \to \mathbb{G}_T$. (We assume symmetric pairings where $\mathbb{G}_1 = \mathbb{G}_2$ for simplicity of exposition.) $\mathbb{G}_?$ is a hidden-order group. We use multiplicative notation for all groups. ω is a primitive nth root of unity in $\mathbb{Z}_p$ [vzGG13a]. poly$(\cdot)$ is any function upper-bounded by some univariate polynomial. negl$(\cdot)$ is any negligible function. $\log x$ and $\lg x$ are shorthand for $\log_2 x$. $[i,j] = \{i, i+1, \ldots, j-1, j\}$, $[0, n) = [0, n-1]$ and $[n] = [1, n]$. $\mathbf{v} = (v_i)_{i \in [0,n)}$ is a vector of size n with elements $v_i \in \mathbb{Z}_p$.

Lagrange Interpolation. Given n pairs $(x_i, y_i)_{i \in [0,n)}$, we can find or *interpolate* the *unique* polynomial $\phi(X)$ of degree $< n$ such that $\phi(x_i) = y_i, \forall i \in [0, n)$ using *Lagrange interpolation* in $O(n \log^2 n)$ time [vzGG13b] as $\phi(X) = \sum_{i \in [0,n)} \mathcal{L}_i(X) y_i$, where $\mathcal{L}_i(X) = \prod_{j \in [0,n), j \neq i} \frac{X - x_j}{x_i - x_j}$. Recall that a *Lagrange polynomial* $\mathcal{L}_i(X)$ has the property that $\mathcal{L}_i(x_i) = 1$ and $\mathcal{L}_i(x_j) = 0, \forall i, j \in [0, n)$ with $j \neq i$. Note that $\mathcal{L}_i(X)$ is defined in terms of the x_i's which, throughout this paper, will be either $(\omega^i)_{i \in [0,n)}$ or $(\omega^i)_{i \in I}, I \subset [0, n)$.

2.1 KZG Polynomial Commitments

Kate, Zaverucha and Goldberg (KZG) proposed a *constant-sized* commitment scheme for degree n polynomials $\phi(X)$. Importantly, an *evaluation proof* for any $\phi(a)$ is constant-sized and constant-time to verify; it does not depend in any way on the degree of the committed polynomial. KZG requires public parameters $(g^{\tau^i})_{i \in [0,n]}$, which can be computed via a decentralized MPC protocol [BGM17] that hides the *trapdoor* τ. KZG is computationally-hiding under the discrete log assumption and computationally-binding under n-SDH [BB08].

Committing. Let $\phi(X)$ denote a polynomial of degree $d \leq n$ with coefficients $c_0, c_1, \ldots, c_d$ in $\mathbb{Z}_p$. A KZG commitment to $\phi(X)$ is a single group element $C = \prod_{i=0}^{d} \left(g^{\tau^i} \right)^{c_i} = g^{\sum_{i=0}^{d} c_i \tau^i} = g^{\phi(\tau)}$. Committing to $\phi(X)$ takes $\Theta(d)$ time.

Proving One Evaluation. To compute an *evaluation proof* that $\phi(a) = y$, KZG leverages the polynomial remainder theorem, which says $\phi(a) = y \Leftrightarrow \exists q(X)$ such that $\phi(X) - y = q(X)(X - a)$. The proof is just a KZG commitment to $q(X)$: a single group element $\pi = g^{q(\tau)}$. Computing the proof takes $\Theta(d)$ time. To verify π, one checks (in constant time) if $e(C/g^y, g) = e(\pi, g^\tau/g^a) \Leftrightarrow e(g^{\phi(\tau)-y}, g) = e(g^{q(\tau)}, g^{\tau-a}) \Leftrightarrow \phi(\tau) - y = q(\tau)(\tau - a)$.

Proving Multiple Evaluations. Given a set of points I and their evaluations $\{\phi(i)\}_{i \in I}$, KZG can prove all evaluations with a constant-sized *batch proof* rather than $|I|$ individual proofs. The prover computes an *accumulator polynomial* $a(X) = \prod_{i \in I}(X - i)$ in $\Theta(|I| \log^2 |I|)$ time and computes $\phi(X)/a(X)$ in $\Theta(d \log d)$ time, obtaining a quotient $q(X)$ and remainder $r(X)$. The batch proof is $\pi_I = g^{q(\tau)}$. To verify π_I and $\{\phi(i)\}_{i \in I}$ against C, the verifier first computes $a(X)$ from I and interpolates $r(X)$ such that $r(i) = \phi(i), \forall i \in I$ in $\Theta(|I| \log^2 |I|)$ time. Next, she computes $g^{a(\tau)}$ and $g^{r(\tau)}$. Finally, she checks if $e(C/g^{r(\tau)}, g) = e(g^{q(\tau)}, g^{a(\tau)})$. We stress that batch proofs are only useful when $|I| \leq d$. Otherwise, if $|I| > d$, the verifier can interpolate $\phi(X)$ directly from the evaluations, which makes verifying any $\phi(i)$ trivial.

2.2   Account-Based Stateless Cryptocurrencies

In a stateless cryptocurrency based on VCs [CPZ18], there are *miners* running a permissionless consensus algorithm [Nak08] and *users*, numbered from 0 to $n-1$ who have *accounts* with a *balance* of coins. (n can be ∞ if the VC is unbounded.) For simplicity of exposition, we do not give details on the consensus algorithm, on transaction signature verification nor on monetary policy.

The (Authenticated) State. The *state* is an *authenticated data structure (ADS)* mapping each user i's *public key* to their account balance bal_i. (In practice, the mapping is also to a *transaction counter* c_i, which is necessary to avoid transaction replay attacks. We address this in Sect. 4.3.1.) Importantly, miners and users are *stateless*: they do not store the state, just its *digest* d_t at the latest block t they are aware of. Additionally, each user i stores a proof $\pi_{i,t}$ for their account balance that verifies against d_t.

Miners. Despite miners being stateless, they can still validate transactions, assemble them into a new *block*, and propose that block. Specifically, a miner can verify every new transaction spends valid coins by checking the sending user's balance against the latest digest d_t. This requires each user i who sends coins to j to include her proof $\pi_{i,t}$ in her transaction. Importantly, user i should not have to include the recipient's proof $\pi_{j,t}$ in the transaction, since that would require interacting with *proof-serving nodes* (see Sect. 4.3.2)

Once the miner has a set V of valid transactions, he can use them to create the next block $t + 1$ and propose it. The miner obtains this new block's digest

d_{t+1} by "applying" all transactions in V to d_t. When other miners receive this new block $t + 1$, they can validate its transactions from V against d_t and check that the new digest d_{t+1} was produced correctly from d_t by "reapplying" all the transactions from V.

Users. When creating a transaction tx for block $t+1$, user i includes her proof $\pi_{i,t}$ for miners to verify she has sufficient balance. When she sees a new block $t + 1$, she can update her proof $\pi_{i,t}$ to a new proof $\pi_{i,t+1}$, which verifies against the new digest d_{t+1}. For this, she will look at all changes in balances $(j, \Delta\mathsf{bal}_j)_{j \in J}$, where J is the set of users with transactions in block $t + 1$, and "apply" those changes to her proof. Similarly, miners can also update proofs of pending transactions which did not make it in block t and now need a proof w.r.t. d_{t+1}.

Users assume that the consensus mechanism produces correct blocks. As a result, they do *not* need to verify transactions in the block; they only need to update their own proof. Nonetheless, since block verification is stateless and fast, users could easily participate as block validators, should they choose to.

3   Aggregatable Subvector Commitment (aSVC) Schemes

In this section, we introduce the notion of *aggregatable subvector commitments (aSVCs)* as a natural extension to *subvector commitments (SVCs)* [LM19] where anybody can aggregate b proofs for individual positions into a single constant-sized *subvector proof* for those positions. Our formalization differs from previous work [BBF19, GRWZ20] in that it accounts for (static) update keys as the *verifiable* auxiliary information needed to update commitments and proofs. This is useful in distributed settings where the public parameters of the scheme are split amongst many participants, such as in stateless cryptocurrencies.

3.1   aSVC API

Our API resembles the VC API by Chepurnoy et al. [CPZ18] and the SVC API by Lai and Malavolta [LM19], extended with an API for verifying update keys (see Section 4.2.2) and an API for aggregating proofs. Unlike [CPZ18], our VC.UpdateProof API receives both upk_i and upk_j as input. This is reasonable in the stateless setting, since each user has to store their upk_i anyway and they extract upk_j from the transactions (see Sect. 4).

VC.KeyGen($1^\lambda, n$) $\to$ prk, vrk, $(\mathsf{upk}_j)_{j \in [0,n)}$. Randomized algorithm that, given a security parameter λ and an upper-bound n on vector size, returns a *proving key* prk, a *verification key* vrk and *update keys* $(\mathsf{upk}_j)_{j \in [0,n)}$.

VC.Commit(prk, $\mathbf{v}$) $\to c$. Deterministic algorithm that returns a commitment c to any vector $\mathbf{v}$ of size $\leq n$.

VC.ProvePos(prk, I, $\mathbf{v}$) $\to \pi_I$. Deterministic algorithm that returns a proof π_I that $\mathbf{v}_I = (v_i)_{i \in I}$ is the I-subvector of $\mathbf{v}$. For notational convenience, I can be either an index set $I \subseteq [0, n)$ or an individual index $I = i \in [0, n)$.

VC.VerifyPos(vrk, c, $\mathbf{v}_I$, I, π_I) → T/F. Deterministic algorithm that verifies the
   proof π_I that $\mathbf{v}_I$ is the I-subvector of the vector committed in c. As before,
   I can be either an index set $I \subseteq [0, n)$ or an individual index $I = i \in [0, n)$.
VC.VerifyUPK(vrk, i, upk$_i$) → T/F. Deterministic algorithm that verifies that
   upk$_i$ is indeed the ith update key.
VC.UpdateComm(c, δ, j, upk$_j$) → c'. Deterministic algorithm that returns a new
   commitment c' to $\mathbf{v}'$ obtained by updating v_j to $v_j + \delta$ in the vector $\mathbf{v}$
   committed in c. Needs upk$_j$ associated with the updated position j.
VC.UpdateProof(π_i, δ, i, j, upk$_i$, upk$_j$) → π'_i. Deterministic algorithm that
   updates an old proof π_i for the ith element v_i, given that the jth element
   was updated to $v_j + \delta$. Note that i can be equal to j.
VC.AggregateProofs(I, $(\pi_i)_{i \in I}$) → π_I Deterministic algorithm that, given proofs
   π_i for v_i, $\forall i \in I$, aggregates them into a succinct I-subvector proof π_I.

3.2   aSVC Correctness and Security Definitions

Definition 1 (Aggregatable SVC Scheme). (VC.KeyGen, VC.Commit,
VC.ProvePos, VC.VerifyPos, VC.VerifyUPK, VC.UpdateComm, VC.UpdateProof,
VC.AggregateProofs) *is a secure aggregatable subvector commitment scheme if* $\forall$
upper-bounds $n = \mathsf{poly}(\lambda)$ *it satisfies the following properties:*

Definition 2 (Correctness). $\forall$ *honestly generated* prk, vrk, $(\mathsf{upk}_j)_{j \in [0,n)}$ *via*
VC.KeyGen, $\forall$ *vectors* $\mathbf{v} = (v_j)_{j \in [0,n)}$ *with commitment c obtained via* VC.Commit
and, optionally, VC.UpdateComm *calls,* $\forall I \subseteq [0, n)$, *if π_I is a (sub)vector
proof for* $\mathbf{v}_I = (v_i)_{i \in I}$ *obtained via any valid interleaving of* VC.ProvePos,
VC.AggregateProofs *and* VC.UpdateProof, *then* VC.VerifyPos(vrk, c, $\mathbf{v}_I$, I, π_I)
returns true. *Furthermore,* VC.VerifyUPK(vrk, i, upk_i) $= T$, $\forall i \in [0, n)$.

Definition 3 (Update Key Uniqueness). $\forall$ *adversaries* $\mathcal{A}$ *running in time*
$\mathsf{poly}(\lambda)$:

$$
\Pr \left[\begin{array}{c} \mathsf{prk}, \mathsf{vrk}, (\mathsf{upk}_j)_{j \in [0,n)} \leftarrow \mathsf{VC.KeyGen}(1^\lambda, n), \\ i, \mathsf{upk}, \mathsf{upk}' \leftarrow \mathcal{A}(1^\lambda, \mathsf{prk}, \mathsf{vrk}, (\mathsf{upk}_j)_{j \in [0,n)}) : \\ \mathsf{VC.VerifyUPK}(\mathsf{vrk}, i, \mathsf{upk}) = T \wedge \\ \mathsf{VC.VerifyUPK}(\mathsf{vrk}, i, \mathsf{upk}') = T \wedge \\ \mathsf{upk} \neq \mathsf{upk}' \end{array} \right] \leq \mathsf{negl}(\lambda)
$$

Observation: Definitions that allow for *dynamic* update hints rather than *unique*
update keys are possible too, but would be less simple to state and less useful
for stateless cryptocurrencies (see Sect. 4).

Definition 4 (Position Binding Security). $\forall$ *adversaries* $\mathcal{A}$ *running in time*
$\mathsf{poly}(\lambda)$, *if* $\mathbf{v}_I = (v_i)_{i \in I}$ *and* $\mathbf{v}'_J = (v'_j)_{j \in J}$, *then:*

$$
\Pr \left[\begin{array}{c} \mathsf{prk}, \mathsf{vrk}, (\mathsf{upk}_i)_{i \in [0,n)} \leftarrow \mathsf{VC.KeyGen}(1^\lambda, n), \\ (c, I, J, \mathbf{v}_I, \mathbf{v}'_J, \pi_I, \pi_J) \leftarrow \mathcal{A}(1^\lambda, \mathsf{prk}, \mathsf{vrk}, (\mathsf{upk}_i)_{i \in [0,n)}) : \\ \mathsf{VC.VerifyPos}(\mathsf{vrk}, c, \mathbf{v}_I, I, \pi_I) = T \wedge \\ \mathsf{VC.VerifyPos}(\mathsf{vrk}, c, \mathbf{v}'_J, J, \pi_J) = T \wedge \\ \exists k \in I \cap J, \text{ such that } v_k \neq v'_k \end{array} \right] \leq \mathsf{negl}(\lambda)
$$

Table 2. Asymptotic comparison of our aSVC with other (aS)VCs based on prime-order groups. n is the vector size and b is the subvector size. See our extended paper [TAB+20] for a more detailed analysis. All schemes have $O(n)$-sized parameters (except [LM19] has $O(n^2)$ and [CFG+20] has $O(1)$); can update commitments in $O(1)$ time (except for [KZG10]); have $O(1)$-sized proofs that verify in $O(1)$ time (except [CPZ18] and [Tom20] proofs are $O(\lg n)$). *Com.* is the time to commit to a size-n vector. *Proof upd.* is the time to update *one* individual proof π_i after a change to *one* vector element v_j. *Prove one*, *Prove subv.* and *Prove each* are the times to compute a proof π_i for one v_i, a size-b subvector proof π_I and proofs for all $(v_i)_{i \in [0,n)}$, respectively.

(aS)VC scheme	$|\text{vrk}|$	$|\text{upk}_i|$	Com.	Prove one	Proof upd.	Prove subv.	Verify subv.	Aggregate	Prove each
[LM19]	n	n	n	n	1	bn	b	$\times$	n^2
[KZG10]	b	$\times$	$n \lg^2 n$	n	$\times$	$b \lg^2 b + n \lg n$	$b \lg^2 b$	$\times$	n^2
[CDHK15]	n	n	$n \lg^2 n$	n	1	$n \lg^2 n$	$b \lg^2 b$	$\times$	n^2
[CPZ18]	$\lg n$	$\lg n$	n	n	$\lg n$	$\times$	$\times$	$\times$	n^2
[Tom20]	$\lg n + b$	$\lg n$	$n \lg n$	$n \lg n$	$\lg n$	$b \lg^2 b + n \lg n$	$b \lg^2 b$	$\times$	$n \lg n$
[GRWZ20]	n	n	n	n	1	bn	b	b	n^2
[CFG+20]	1	1	$n \lg n$	$n \lg n$	1	$(n - b) \lg (n - b)$	$b \lg b$	$b \lg^2 b$	$n \lg^2 n$
Our work	b	1	n	n	1	$b \lg^2 b + n \lg n$	$b \lg^2 b$	$b \lg^2 b$	$n \lg n$
Our work*	b	1	$n \lg n$	1	1	$b \lg^2 b$	$b \lg^2 b$	$b \lg^2 b$	$n \lg n$

3.3 aSVC from KZG Commitments to Lagrange Polynomials

In this subsection, we present our aSVC from KZG commitments to Lagrange polynomials. Similar to previous work, we represent a vector $\mathbf{v} = [v_0, v_1, \ldots, v_{n-1}]$ as a polynomial $\phi(X) = \sum_{i \in [0,n)} \mathcal{L}_i(X) v_i$ in Lagrange basis [KZG10, CDHK15, Tom20, GRWZ20]. However, unlike previous work, we add support for efficiently updating and aggregating proofs. For aggregation, we use known techniques for aggregating KZG proofs via *partial fraction decomposition* [But20]. For updating proofs, we introduce a new mechanism to reduce the update key size from linear to constant. We use *roots of unity* and "store" v_i as $\phi(\omega^i) = v_i$, which means our Lagrange polynomials are $\mathcal{L}_i(X) = \prod_{j \in [0,n), j \neq i} \frac{X - \omega^j}{\omega^i - \omega^j}$. For this to work *efficiently*, we assume without loss of generality that n is a power of two.

Committing. A commitment to $\mathbf{v}$ is just a KZG commitment $c = g^{\phi(\tau)}$ to $\phi(X)$, where τ is the trapdoor of the KZG scheme (see Sect. 2.1). Similar to previous work [CDHK15], the proving key includes commitments to all Lagrange polynomials $\ell_i = g^{\mathcal{L}_i(\tau)}$. Thus, we can compute $c = \prod_{i=1}^{n} (\ell_i)^{v_i}$ in $O(n)$ time without interpolating $\phi(X)$ and update it as $c' = c \cdot (\ell_i)^{\delta}$ after adding δ to v_i. Note that c' is just a commitment to an updated $\phi'(X) = \phi(X) + \delta \cdot \mathcal{L}_i(X)$.

Proving. A proof π_i for a single element v_i is just a KZG evaluation proof for $\phi(\omega^i)$. A subvector proof π_I for for $v_I, I \subseteq [0, n)$ is just a KZG batch proof for all $\phi(\omega^i)_{i \in I}$ evaluations. Importantly, we use the Feist-Khovratovich (FK) [FK20] technique to compute all proofs $(\pi_i)_{i\in[0,n)}$ in $O(n \log n)$ time. This allows us to aggregate I-subvector proofs faster in $O(|I| \log^2 |I|)$ time (see Table 2).

3.4   Partial Fraction Decomposition

A key ingredient in our aSVC scheme is *partial fraction decomposition*, which we re-explain from the perspective of Lagrange interpolation. First, let us rewrite the Lagrange polynomial for interpolating $\phi(X)$ given all $\big(\phi(\omega^i)\big)_{i\in I}$:

$$\mathcal{L}_i(X) = \prod_{j\in I, j\neq i} \frac{X - \omega^j}{\omega^i - \omega^j} = \frac{A_I(X)}{A_I'(\omega^i)(X - \omega^i)}, \text{ where } A_I(X) = \prod_{i\in I}(X - \omega^i) \quad (1)$$

Here, $A_I'(X) = \sum_{j\in[0,n)} A_I(X)/(X - \omega^j)$ is the derivative of $A_I(X)$ [vzGG13b]. Next, for any $\phi(X)$, we can rewrite the Lagrange interpolation formula as $\phi(X) = A_I(X) \sum_{i\in[0,n)} \frac{y_i}{A_I'(\omega^i)(X-\omega^i)}$. In particular, for $\phi(X) = 1$, this implies $\frac{1}{A_I(X)} = \sum_{i\in[0,n)} \frac{1}{A_I'(\omega^i)(X-\omega^i)}$. In other words, we can decompose $A_I(X)$ as:

$$\frac{1}{A_I(X)} = \frac{1}{\prod_{i\in I}(X - \omega^i)} = \sum_{i\in[0,n)} c_i \cdot \frac{1}{X - \omega^i}, \text{ where } c_i = \frac{1}{A_I'(\omega^i)} \quad (2)$$

$A_I(X)$ can be computed in $O(|I| \log^2 |I|)$ time [vzGG13b]. Its derivative, $A_I'(X)$, can be computed in $O(|I|)$ time and evaluated at all ω^i's in $O(|I| \log^2 |I|)$ time [vzGG13b]. Thus, all c_i's can be computed in $O(|I| \log^2 |I|)$ time. For the special case of $I = [0, n)$, we have $A_I(X) = A(X) = \prod_{i\in[0,n)}(X - \omega^i) = X^n - 1$ and $A'(\omega^i) = n\omega^{-i}$ [TAB+20, Appendix A]. In this case, any c_i can be computed in $O(1)$ time.

3.4.1   Aggregating Proofs

We build upon Drake and Buterin's observation [But20] that partial fraction decomposition (see Sect. 3.4) can be used to aggregate KZG evaluation proofs. Since our VC proofs are KZG proofs, we show how to aggregate a set of proofs $(\pi_i)_{i\in I}$ for elements v_i of $\mathbf{v}$ into a constant-sized I-subvector proof π_I for $(v_i)_{i\in I}$.

Recall that π_i is a commitment to $q_i(X) = \frac{\phi(X) - v_i}{X - \omega^i}$ and π_I is a commitment to $q(X) = \frac{\phi(X) - R(X)}{A_I(X)}$, where $A_I(X) = \prod_{i\in I}(X - \omega^i)$ and $R(X)$ is interpolated such that $R(\omega^i) = v_i, \forall i \in I$. Our goal is to find coefficients $c_i \in \mathbb{Z}_p$ such that $q(X) = \sum_{i\in I} c_i q_i(X)$ and thus aggregate $\pi_I = \prod_{i\in I} \pi_i^{c_i}$. We observe that:

$$q(X) = \phi(X)\frac{1}{A_I(X)} - R(X)\frac{1}{A_I(X)} \quad (3)$$

$$= \phi(X) \sum_{i\in I} \frac{1}{A_I'(\omega^i)(X - \omega^i)} - \left(A_I(X) \sum_{i\in I} \frac{v_i}{A_I'(\omega^i)(X - \omega^i)}\right) \cdot \frac{1}{A_I(X)} \quad (4)$$

$$= \sum_{i\in I} \frac{\phi(X)}{A_I'(\omega^i)(X - \omega^i)} - \sum_{i\in I} \frac{v_i}{A_I'(\omega^i)(X - \omega^i)} = \sum_{i\in I} \frac{1}{A_I'(\omega^i)} \cdot \frac{\phi(X) - v_i}{X - \omega^i} \quad (5)$$

$$= \sum_{i\in I} \frac{1}{A_I'(\omega^i)} \cdot q_i(X) \quad (6)$$

Thus, we can compute all $c_i = 1/A'_I(\omega^i)$ using $O(|I| \log^2 |I|)$ field operations (see Sect. 3.4) and compute $\pi_I = \prod_{i \in I} \pi_i^{c_i}$ with an $O(|I|)$-sized multi-exponentiation.

3.4.2   Updating Proofs

When updating π_i after a change to v_j, it could be that either $i = j$ or $i \neq j$. First, recall that π_i is a KZG commitment to $q_i(X) = \frac{\phi(X) - v_i}{X - \omega^i}$. Second, recall that, after a change δ to v_j, the polynomial $\phi(X)$ is updated to $\phi'(X) = \phi(X) + \delta \cdot \mathcal{L}_j(X)$. We refer to the party updating their proof π_i as the *proof updater*.

The $i = j$ Case. Consider the quotient polynomial $q'_i(X)$ in the updated proof π'_i after v_i changed to $v_i + \delta$:

$$q'_i(X) = \frac{\phi'(X) - (v_i + \delta)}{X - \omega^i} = \frac{(\phi(X) + \delta \mathcal{L}_i(X)) - v_i - \delta}{X - \omega^i} \tag{7}$$

$$= \frac{\phi(X) - v_i}{X - \omega^i} + \frac{\delta(\mathcal{L}_i(X) - 1)}{X - \omega^i} = q_i(X) + \delta \left(\frac{\mathcal{L}_i(X) - 1}{X - \omega^i} \right) \tag{8}$$

This means the proof updater needs a KZG commitment to $\frac{\mathcal{L}_i(X) - 1}{X - \omega^i}$, which is just a KZG evaluation proof that $\mathcal{L}_i(\omega^i) = 1$. This can be addressed very easily by making this commitment part of upk_i. To conclude, to update π_i, the proof updater obtains $u_i = g^{\frac{\mathcal{L}_i(\tau) - 1}{\tau - \omega^i}}$ from upk_i and computes $\pi'_i = \pi_i \cdot (u_i)^{\delta}$. (Remember that the proof updater, who calls $\mathsf{VC.UpdateProof}(\pi_i, \delta, i, i, \mathsf{upk}_i, \mathsf{upk}_i)$, has upk_i.)

The $i \neq j$ Case. Now, consider the quotient polynomial $q'_i(X)$ after v_j changed to $v_j + \delta$:

$$q'_i(X) = \frac{\phi'(X) - v_i}{X - \omega^i} = \frac{(\phi(X) + \delta \mathcal{L}_j(X)) - v_i}{X - \omega^i} \tag{9}$$

$$= \frac{\phi(X) - v_i}{X - \omega^i} + \frac{\delta \mathcal{L}_j(X)}{X - \omega^i} = q_i(X) + \delta \left(\frac{\mathcal{L}_j(X)}{X - \omega^i} \right) \tag{10}$$

In this case, the proof updater will need to construct a KZG commitment to $\frac{\mathcal{L}_j(X)}{X - \omega^i}$. For this, we put enough information in upk_i and upk_j, which the proof updater has (see Sect. 3.1), to help her do so.

Since $U_{i,j}(X) = \frac{A(X)}{A'(\omega^j)(X - \omega^j)(X - \omega^i)}$ and $A'(\omega^j) = n\omega^{-j}$, it is sufficient to reconstruct a KZG commitment to $W_{i,j}(X) = \frac{A(X)}{(X - \omega^j)(X - \omega^i)}$, which can be decomposed as $W_{i,j}(X) = A(X) \left(c_i \frac{1}{X - \omega^i} + c_j \frac{1}{X - \omega_j} \right) = c_i \frac{A(X)}{X - \omega^i} + c_j \frac{A(X)}{X - \omega^j}$, where $c_i = 1/(\omega^i - \omega^j)$ and $c_j = 1/(\omega^j - \omega^i)$ (see Sect. 3.4). Thus, if we include $a_j = g^{A(\tau)/(\tau - \omega^j)}$ in each upk_j, the proof updater can first compute $w_{i,j} = a_i^{c_i} a_j^{c_j}$, then compute $u_{i,j} = (w_{i,j})^{\frac{1}{A'(\omega^j)}}$ and finally update the proof as $\pi'_i = \pi_i \cdot (u_{i,j})^{\delta}$.

3.4.3   aSVC Algorithms

Having established the intuition for our aSVC, we can now describe it in detail using the aSVC API from Sect. 3.1.

VC.KeyGen$(1^\lambda, n) \to$ prk, vrk, $(\text{upk}_j)_{j\in[0,n)}$. Generates n-SDH public parameters $g, g^\tau, g^{\tau^2}, \ldots, g^{\tau^n}$. Computes $a = g^{A(\tau)}$, where $A(X) = X^n - 1$. Computes $a_i = g^{A(\tau)/(X-\omega^i)}$ and $\ell_i = g^{\mathcal{L}_i(\tau)}, \forall i \in [0, n)$. Computes KZG proofs $u_i = g^{\frac{\mathcal{L}_i(\tau)-1}{X-\omega^i}}$ for $\mathcal{L}_i(\omega^i) = 1$. Sets $\text{upk}_i = (a_i, u_i)$, prk $= \left((g^{\tau^i})_{i\in[0,n]}, (\ell_i)_{i\in[0,n)}, (\text{upk}_i)_{i\in[0,n)}\right)$ and vrk $= \left((g^{\tau^i})_{i\in[0,|I|]}, a\right)$.

VC.Commit$($prk, $\mathbf{v}) \to c$. Returns $c = \prod_{i\in[0,n)}(\ell_i)^{v_i}$.

VC.ProvePos$($prk, $I, \mathbf{v}) \to \pi_I$. Computes $A_I(X) = \prod_{i\in I}(X-\omega^i)$ in $O(|I| \log^2 |I|)$ time. Divides $\phi(X)$ by $A_I(X)$ in $O(n \log n)$ time, obtaining a quotient $q(X)$ and a remainder $r(X)$. Returns $\pi_I = g^{q(\tau)}$. (We give an $O(n)$ time algorithm in [TAB+20, Appendix D.7] for the $|I| = 1$ case.)

VC.VerifyPos$($vrk, $c, \mathbf{v}_I, I, \pi_I) \to T/F$. Computes $A_I(X) = \prod_{i\in I}(X-\omega^i)$ in $O(|I| \log^2 |I|)$ time and commits to it as $g^{A_I(\tau)}$ in $O(|I|)$ time. Interpolates $R_I(X)$ such that $R_I(i) = v_i, \forall i \in I$ in $O(|I| \log^2 |I|)$ time and commits to it as $g^{R_I(\tau)}$ in $O(|I|)$ time. Returns T iff. $e(c/g^{R_I(\tau)}, g) = e(\pi_I, g^{A_I(\tau)})$. (When $I = \{i\}$, we have $A_I(X) = X - \omega^i$ and $R_I(X) = v_i$.)

VC.VerifyUPK$($vrk, $i, \text{upk}_i) \to T/F$. Checks that ω^i is a root of $X^n - 1$ (which is committed in a) via $e(a_i, g^\tau/g^{(\omega^i)}) = e(a, g)$. Checks that $\mathcal{L}_i(\omega^i) = 1$ via $e(\ell_i/g^1, g) = e(u_i, g^\tau/g^{(\omega^i)})$, where $\ell_i = a_i^{1/A'(\omega^i)} = g^{\mathcal{L}_i(\tau)}$.

VC.UpdateComm$(c, \delta, j, \text{upk}_j) \to c'$. Returns $c' = c \cdot (\ell_j)^\delta$, where $\ell_j = a_j^{1/A'(\omega^j)}$.

VC.UpdateProof$(\pi_i, \delta, i, j, \text{upk}_i, \text{upk}_j) \to \pi_i'$. If $i = j$, returns $\pi_i' = \pi_i \cdot (u_i)^\delta$. If $i \neq j$, computes $w_{i,j} = a_i^{1/(\omega^i-\omega^j)} \cdot a_j^{1/(\omega^j-\omega^i)}$ and $u_{i,j} = w_{i,j}^{1/A'(\omega^j)}$ (see Sect. 3.4.2) and returns $\pi_i' = \pi_i \cdot (u_{i,j})^\delta$.

VC.AggregateProofs$(I, (\pi_i)_{i\in I}) \to \pi_I$. Computes $A_I(X) = \prod_{i\in I}(X-\omega^i)$, its derivative $A_I'(X)$ and all $c_i = (A_I'(\omega^i))_{i\in I}$ in $O(|I| \log^2 |I|)$ time. Returns $\pi_I = \prod_{i\in I} \pi_i^{c_i}$.

3.4.4   Distributing the Trusted Setup

Our aSVC requires a centralized, trusted setup phase that computes its public parameters. We can decentralize this phase using highly-efficient MPC protocols that generate (g^{τ^i})'s in a distributed fashion [BGM17]. Then, we can derive the remaining parameters from the (g^{τ^i})'s, which has the advantage of keeping our parameters *updatable*. First, the commitment $a = g^{A(\tau)}$ to $A(X) = X^n - 1$ can be computed in $O(1)$ time via an exponentiation. Second, the commitments $\ell_i = g^{\mathcal{L}_i(\tau)}$ to Lagrange polynomials can be computed via a single DFT on the (g^{τ^i})'s [Vir17, Sec 3.12.3, pg. 97]. Third, each $a_i = g^{A(\tau)/(\tau-\omega^i)}$ is a bilinear accumulator membership proof for ω^i w.r.t. $A(X)$ and can all be computed in $O(n \log n)$ time using FK [FK20]. But what about computing each $u_i = g^{\frac{\mathcal{L}_i(\tau)-1}{X-\omega^i}}$?

Computing All u_i's Fast. Inspired by the FK technique [FK20], we show how to compute all n u_i's in $O(n \log n)$ time using a single DFT on group elements. First, note that $u_i = g^{\frac{\mathcal{L}_i(\tau)-1}{X-\omega^i}}$ is a KZG evaluation proof for $\mathcal{L}_i(\omega^i) = 1$. Thus, $u_i = g^{Q_i(\tau)}$ where $Q_i(X) = \frac{\mathcal{L}_i(X)-1}{X-\omega^i}$. Second, let $\psi_i(X) = A'(\omega^i)\mathcal{L}_i(X) = $

$\frac{X^n-1}{X-\omega^i}$. Then, let $\pi_i = g^{q_i(\tau)}$ be an evaluation proof for $\psi_i(\omega^i) = A'(\omega^i)$ where $q_i(X) = \frac{\psi_i(X)-A'(\omega^i)}{X-\omega^i}$ and note that $Q_i(X) = \frac{1}{A'(\omega^i)}q_i(X)$. Thus, computing all u_i's reduces to computing all π_i's. However, since each proof π_i is for a *different* polynomial $\psi_i(X)$, directly applying FK does not work. Instead, we give a new algorithm that leverages the structure of $\psi_i(X)$ when divided by $X - \omega^i$. Specifically, in [TAB+20, Appendix B], we show that:

$$q_i(X) = \sum_{j\in[0,n-2]} H_j(X)\omega^{ij}, \forall i \in [0,n), \text{ where } H_j(X) = (j+1)X^{(n-2)-j} \quad (11)$$

If we let h_j be a KZG commitment to $H_j(X)$, then we have $\pi_i = \prod_{j\in[0,n-2]} h_j^{(\omega^{ij})}$, $\forall i \in [0,n)$. Next, recall that the Discrete Fourier Transform (DFT) *on a vector of group elements* $\mathbf{a} = [a_0, a_1, \ldots, a_{n-1}] \in \mathbb{G}^n$ is:

$$\mathsf{DFT}_n(\mathbf{a}) = \hat{\mathbf{a}} = [\hat{a}_0, \hat{a}_1, \ldots, \hat{a}_{n-1}] \in \mathbb{G}^n, \text{ where } \hat{a}_i = \prod_{j\in[0,n)} a_j^{(\omega^{ij})} \quad (12)$$

If we let $\pi = [\pi_0, \pi_1, \ldots, \pi_{n-1}]$ and $\mathbf{h} = [h_0, h_1, \ldots, h_{n-2}, 1_{\mathbb{G}}, 1_{\mathbb{G}}]$, then $\pi = \mathsf{DFT}_n(\mathbf{h})$. Thus, computing all n h_i's takes $O(n)$ time and computing all n π_i's takes an $O(n \log n)$ time DFT. As a result, computing all u_i's from the (g^{τ^i})'s takes $O(n \log n)$ time overall.

3.4.5 Correctness and Security

The correctness of our aSVC scheme follows naturally from Lagrange interpolation. Aggregation and proof updates are correct by the arguments laid out in Sects. 3.4.1 and 3.4.2, respectively. Subvector proofs are correct by the correctness of KZG batch proofs [KZG10]. We prove our aSVC is position binding and has update key uniqueness in the extended version [TAB+20, Appendix C].

4 A Highly-Efficient Stateless Cryptocurrency

In this section, we enhance Edrax's elegant design by replacing their VC with our secure *aggregatable* subvector commitment (aSVC) scheme from Sect. 3.3. As a result, our stateless cryptocurrency has smaller, aggregatable proofs and smaller update keys. This leads to smaller, faster-to-verify blocks for miners and faster proof synchronization for users (see Table 1). Furthermore, our verifiable update keys reduce the storage overhead of miners from $O(n)$ update keys to $O(1)$. We also address a denial of service (DoS) attack in Edrax's design.

4.1 From VCs to Stateless Cryptocurrencies

Edrax pioneered the idea of building account-based, stateless cryptocurrencies on top of any VC scheme [CPZ18]. In contrast, previous approaches were based on *authenticated dictionaries (ADs)* [RMCI17,But17], for which efficient constructions with static update keys are not known. In other words, these AD-based approaches used *dynamic update hints* uph_j consisting of the proof for position j. This complicated their design, requiring user i to ask a *proof-serving node* for user j's proof in order to create a transaction sending money to j.

Trusted Setup. To support up to n users, public parameters $(\mathrm{prk}, \mathrm{vrk}, (\mathrm{upk}_i)_{i \in [0,n)}) \leftarrow \mathrm{VC.KeyGen}(1^\lambda, n)$ are generated via a *trusted setup*, which can be decentralized using MPC protocols [BGM17]. Miners need to store all $O(n)$ update keys to propose blocks and to validate blocks (which we fix in Sect. 4.2.2). The prk is only needed for *proof-serving nodes* (see Sect. 4.3.2).

The (Authenticated) State. The state is a vector $\mathbf{v} = (v_i)_{i \in [0,n)}$ of size n that maps user i to $v_i = (\mathrm{addr}_i | \mathrm{bal}_i) \in \mathbb{Z}_p$, where bal_i is her balance and addr_i is her *address*, which we define later. (We discuss including transaction counters for preventing replay attacks in Sect. 4.3.1.) Importantly, since $p \approx 2^{256}$, the first 224 bits of v_i are used for addr_i and the last 32 bits for bal_i. The genesis block's state is the all zeros vector with digest d_0 (e.g., in our aSVC, $d_0 = g^0$). Initially, each user i is *unregistered* and starts with a proof $\pi_{i,0}$ that their $v_i = 0$.

"Full" vs. "Traditional" Public Keys. User i's address is computed as $\mathrm{addr}_i = H(\mathrm{FPK}_i)$, where $\mathrm{FPK}_i = (i, \mathrm{upk}_i, \mathrm{tpk}_i)$ is her *full public key*. Here, tpk_i denotes a *"traditional" public key* for a digital signature scheme, with corresponding secret key tsk_i used to authorize user i's transactions. To avoid confusion, we will clearly refer to public keys as either "full" or "traditional."

Registering via INIT Transactions. INIT transactions are used to *register* new users and assign them a unique, ever-increasing number from 1 to n. For this, each block t stores a *count of users registered so far* cnt_t. To register, a user generates a *traditional secret key* tsk with a corresponding *traditional public key* tpk. Then, she broadcasts an INIT transaction:

$$\mathrm{tx} = [\mathrm{INIT}, \mathrm{tpk}]$$

A miner working on block $t + 1$ who receives tx, proceeds as follows.

1. He sets $i = \mathrm{cnt}_{t+1}$ and increments the count cnt_{t+1} of registered users,
2. He updates the VC via $d_{t+1} = \mathrm{VC.UpdateComm}(d_{t+1}, (\mathrm{addr}_i | 0), i, \mathrm{upk}_i)$,
3. He incorporates tx in block $t + 1$ as $\mathrm{tx}' = [\mathrm{INIT}, (i, \mathrm{upk}_i, \mathrm{tpk}_i)] = [\mathrm{INIT}, \mathrm{FPK}_i]$.

The full public key with upk_i is included so other users can correctly update their VC when they process tx'. Note that to compute $\mathrm{addr}_i = H(\mathrm{FPK}_i)$, the miner needs to have the correct upk_i which requires $O(n)$ storage. We discuss how to avoid this in Sect. 4.2.2.

Transferring Coins via SPEND Transactions. When transferring v coins to user j, user i (who has $v' \geq v$ coins) must first obtain $\mathrm{FPK}_j = (j, \mathrm{upk}_j, \mathrm{tpk}_j)$. This is similar to existing cryptocurrencies, except the (full) public key is now slightly larger. Then, user i broadcasts a SPEND transaction, signed with her tsk_i:

$$\mathrm{tx} = [\mathrm{SPEND}, t, \mathrm{FPK}_i, j, \mathrm{upk}_j, v, \pi_{i,t}, v']$$

A miner working on block $t + 1$ processes this SPEND transaction as follows:

1. He checks that $v \leq v'$ and verifies the proof $\pi_{i,t}$ that user i has v' coins via VC.VerifyPos(vrk, d_t, (addr$_i|v'$), i, $\pi_{i,t}$). (If the miner receives another transaction from user i, it needs to carefully account for i's new $v' - v$ balance.)
2. He updates i's balance in block $t+1$ with $d_{t+1} = $ VC.UpdateComm($d_{t+1}, -v, i,$ upk$_i$), which only sets the lower order bits of v_i corresponding to bal$_i$, without touching the higher order bits for addr$_i$.
3. He does the same for j with $d_{t+1} = $ VC.UpdateComm($d_{t+1}, +v, j,$ upk$_j$).

Validating Blocks. Suppose a miner receives a new block $t+1$ with digest d_{t+1} that has b SPEND transactions:

$$\mathsf{tx} = [\mathsf{SPEND}, t, \mathsf{FPK}_i, j, \mathsf{upk}_j, v, \pi_{i,t}, v']$$

To validate this block, the miner (who has d_t) proceeds in three steps (INIT transactions can be handled analogously):

Step 1: Check Balances. First, for each tx, he checks that $v \leq v'$ and that user i has balance v' via VC.VerifyPos(vrk, d_t, (addr$_i|v'$), i, $\pi_{i,t}$) $= T$. Since the sending user i might have multiple transactions in the block, the miner has to carefully keep track of each sending user's balance to ensure it never goes below zero.

Step 2: Check Digest. Second, he checks d_{t+1} has been computed correctly from d_t and from the new transactions in block $t + 1$. Specifically, he sets $d' = d_t$ and for each tx, he computes $d' = $ VC.UpdateComm($d', -v, i,$ upk$_i$) and $d' = $ VC.UpdateComm($d', +v, j,$ upk$_j$). Then, he checks that $d' = d_{t+1}$.

Step 3: Update Proofs, If Any. If the miner lost the race to build block $t + 1$, he can start mining block $t + 2$ by "moving over" the SPEND transactions from his unmined block. For this, he updates all proofs in those SPEND transactions, so they are valid against the new digest d_{t+1}. Similarly, the miner must also "move over" all INIT transactions, since block $t + 1$ might have registered new users.

User Proof Synchronization. Consider a user i who has processed the ledger up to time t and has digest d_t and proof $\pi_{i,t}$. Eventually, she receives a new block $t + 1$ with digest d_{t+1} and needs to update her proof so it verifies against d_{t+1}. Initially, she sets $\pi_{i,t+1} = \pi_{i,t}$. For each [INIT, FPK$_j$] transaction, she updates her proof $\pi_{i,t+1} = $ VC.UpdateProof($\pi_{i,t+1}, (H(\mathsf{FPK}_j)|0), i, j,$ upk$_i$, upk$_j$). For each [SPEND, t, FPK$_j$, k, upk$_k$, v, $\pi_{j,t}$, v'], she updates her proof twice: $\pi_{i,t+1} = $ VC.UpdateProof($\pi_{i,t+1}, -v, i, j,$ upk$_i$, upk$_j$) and $\pi_{i,t+1} = $ VC.UpdateProof($\pi_{i,t+1},$ $+v, i, k,$ upk$_i$, upk$_k$). We stress that users can safely be offline and miss new blocks. Eventually, when a user comes back online, she downloads the missed blocks, updates her proof and is ready to transact.

4.2   Efficient Stateless Cryptocurrencies from aSVCs

In this subsection, we explain how replacing the Edrax VC with our aSVC from Sect. 3.3 results in a more efficient stateless cryptocurrency (see Table 1). Then, we address a denial of service attack on user registrations in Edrax.

4.2.1   Smaller, Faster, Aggregatable Proofs

Our aSVC enables miners to aggregate all b proofs in a block of b transactions into a single, constant-sized proof. This drastically reduces Edrax's per-block proof overhead from $O(b \log n)$ group elements to just one group element. Unfortunately, the b update keys cannot be aggregated, but we still reduce their overhead from $O(b \log n)$ to b group elements per block (see Sect. 4.2.3). Our smaller proofs are also faster to update, taking $O(1)$ time rather than $O(\log n)$. While verifying an aggregated proof in our aSVC is $O(b \log^2 b)$ time, which is asymptotically slower than the $O(b)$ time for verifying b individual ones, it is still *concretely* faster as it only requires two, rather than $O(b)$, cryptographic pairings. This makes validating new blocks much faster in practice.

4.2.2   Reducing Miner Storage Using Verifiable Update Keys

We stress that miners must validate update keys before using them to update a digest. Otherwise, they risk corrupting that digest, which results in a denial of service. Edrax miners sidestep this problem by simply storing all $O(n)$ update keys. Alternatively, Edrax proposes outsourcing update keys to an untrusted third party via a static Merkle tree. Unfortunately, this would either require interaction *during block proposal and block validation* or would double the update key size. Our implicitly-verifiable update keys avoid these pitfalls, since miners can directly verify the update keys in a SPEND transaction via VC.VerifyUPK. Furthermore, for INIT transactions, miners can fetch (in the background) a running window of the update keys needed for the next k registrations. By carefully upper-bounding the number of registrations expected in the near future, we can avoid interaction during the block proposal. This background fetching could be implemented in Edrax too, either with a small overhead via Merkle proofs or by making their update keys verifiable (which seems possible).

4.2.3   Smaller Update Keys

Although, in our aSVC, upk_i contains $a_i = g^{A(\tau)/(X-\omega^i)}$ and $u_i = g^{\frac{\mathcal{L}_i(\tau)-1}{X-\omega^i}}$, miners only need to include a_i in the block. This is because of two reasons. First, user i already has u_i to update her own proof after changes to her own balance. Second, no other user $j \neq i$ will need u_i to update her proof π_j. However, as hinted in Sect. 4.1, miners actually need u_i when only a subset of i's pending transactions get included in block t. In this case, the excluded transactions must have their proofs updated using u_i so they can be included in block $t + 1$. Fortunately, this is not a problem, since miners always receive u_i with user i's transactions. The key observation is that they do not have to include u_i in the mined block, since users do not need it.

4.2.4   Addressing DoS Attacks on User Registrations.

Unfortunately, the registration process based on INIT transactions is susceptible to Denial of Service (DoS) attacks: an attacker can simply send a large number of INIT transactions and quickly exhaust the free space in the vector **v**.

There are several ways to address this. First, one can use an aSVC from hidden-order groups, which supports an unbounded number of elements [CFG+20]. However, that would negatively impact performance. Second, as future work, one could develop and use unbounded, authenticated dictionaries *with scalable updates*. Third, one could simply use multiple bounded aSVCs together with cross-commitment proof aggregation, which our aSVC supports [GRWZ20]. Lastly, one can add a cost to user registrations via a new INITSPEND transaction that registers a user j by having user i send her some coins:

$$[\texttt{INITSPEND}, t, \mathsf{FPK}_i, \mathsf{tpk}, v, \pi_{i,t}, v'], \text{ where } 0 < v \le v'$$

Miners processing this transaction would first register a new user j with traditional public key tpk and then transfer her v coins. We stress that this is how existing cryptocurrencies operate anyway: in order to join, one has to be transferred some coins from existing users. Lastly, we can ensure that each tpk is only registered once by including in each INIT/INITSPEND transaction a non-membership proof for tpk in a Merkle prefix tree of all TPKs. We leave a careful exploration of this to future work.

Finally, miners (and only miners) will be allowed to create a *single* $[\texttt{INIT}, \mathsf{FPK}_i]$ transaction per block to register themselves. This has the advantage of letting new miners join, without "permission" from other miners or users, while severely limiting DoS attacks, since malicious miners can only register a new user per block. Furthermore, transaction fees and/or additional proof-of-work can also severely limit the frequency of INITSPEND transactions.

4.2.5 Minting Coins and Transaction Fees

Support for minting new coins can be added with a new MINT transaction type:

$$\mathsf{tx} = [\texttt{MINT}, i, \mathsf{upk}_i, v]$$

Here, i is the miner's user account and v is the amount of newly minted coins. (Note that miners must register as users using INIT transactions if they are to receive block rewards.) To support transaction fees, we can extend the SPEND transaction format to include a fee, which is then added to the miner's block reward specified in the MINT transaction.

4.3 Discussion

4.3.1 Making Room for Transaction Counters

As mentioned in Sect. 2.2, to prevent transaction replay attacks, account-based stateless cryptocurrencies such as Edrax should actually map a user i to $v_i = (\mathsf{addr}_i | c_i | \mathsf{bal}_i)$, where c_i is her *transaction counter*. This change is trivial, but does leave less space in v_i for addr_i, depending on how many bits are needed for c_i and bal_i. (Recall that $v_i \in \mathbb{Z}_p$ typically has ≈ 256 bits.) To address this, we propose using one aSVC for mapping i to addr_i and another aSVC for mapping i to $(c_i | \mathsf{bal}_i)$. Our key observation is that if the two aSVCs use different n-SDH parameters (e.g., (g^{τ^i})'s and (h^{τ^i})'s, such that $\log_g h$ is unknown), then we could aggregate commitments, proofs and update keys so as to introduce zero computational and communication overhead in our stateless cryptocurrency. Security of this scheme could be argued similar to security of perfectly hiding KZG commitments [KZG10], which commit to $\phi(X)$ as $g^{\phi(\tau)}h^{r(\tau)}$ in an analogous fashion. We leave investigating the details of this scheme to future work.

4.3.2 Overhead of Synchronizing Proofs

In a stateless cryptocurrency, users need to keep their proofs updated w.r.t. the latest block. For example, in our scheme, each user spends $O(b \cdot \Delta t)$ time updating her proof, if there are Δt new blocks of b transactions each. Fortunately, when the underlying VC scheme supports precomputing all n proofs fast [Tom20], this overhead can be shifted to untrusted third parties called *proof-serving nodes* [CPZ18]. Specifically, a proof-serving node would have access to the proving key prk and periodically compute all proofs for all n users. Then, any user with an out-of-sync proof could ask a node for their proof and then manually update it, should it be slightly out of date with the latest block. Proof-serving nodes save users a significant amount of proof update work, which is important for users running on constrained devices such as mobile phones.

5 Conclusion

In this paper, we formalized a new cryptographic primitive called an *aggregatable subvector commitment (aSVC)* that supports aggregating and updating proofs (and commitments) using only constant-sized, static auxiliary information referred to as an "update key." We constructed an efficient aSVC from KZG commitments to Lagrange polynomials which, compared to other pairing-based schemes, can precompute, aggregate and update proofs efficiently and, compared to schemes from hidden-order groups, has smaller proofs and should perform better in practice. Lastly, we continued the study of stateless validation initiated by Chepurnoy et al., improving block validation time and block size, while addressing attacks and limitations. We hope our work will ignite further research into stateless validation for payments and smart contracts and lead to improvements both at the theoretical and practical level.

Acknowledgements. The authors want to thank Madars Virza for pointing out the Lagrange-based approach to VCs and the DFT technique for computing all KZG commitments to Lagrange polynomials. We also thank Leonid Reyzin and Dimitris Kolonelos for corrections and productive conversations that helped improve this paper.

References

[BB08] Boneh, D., Boyen, X.: Short signatures without random oracles and the SDH assumption in bilinear groups. J. Cryptol. **21**(2), 149–177 (2007). https://doi.org/10.1007/s00145-007-9005-7

[BBF19]   Boneh, D., Bünz, B., Fisch, B.: Batching techniques for accumulators with applications to IOPs and stateless blockchains. In: Boldyreva, A., Micciancio, D. (eds.) CRYPTO 2019. LNCS, vol. 11692, pp. 561–586. Springer, Cham (2019). https://doi.org/10.1007/978-3-030-26948-7_20

[BGM17]   Bowe, S., Gabizon, A., Miers, I.: Scalable multi-party computation for zk-SNARK parameters in the random beacon model (2017). https://eprint.iacr.org/2017/1050

[BMRS20] Bonneau, J., Meckler, I., Rao, V., Shapiro, E.: Coda: Decentralized Cryptocurrency at Scale (2020). https://eprint.iacr.org/2020/352

[BSCTV14] Ben-Sasson, E., Chiesa, A., Tromer, E., Virza, M.: Scalable zero knowledge via cycles of elliptic curves. Algorithmica **79**(4), 1102–1160 (2016). https://doi.org/10.1007/s00453-016-0221-0

[But17]   Buterin, V.: The stateless client concept. ethresear.ch (2017). https://ethresear.ch/t/the-stateless-client-concept/172

[But20]   Buterin, V.: Using polynomial commitments to replace state roots (2020). https://ethresear.ch/t/using-polynomial-commitments-to-replace-state-roots/7095

[CDHK15] Camenisch, J., Dubovitskaya, M., Haralambiev, K., Kohlweiss, M.: Composable and modular anonymous credentials: definitions and practical constructions. In: Iwata, T., Cheon, J.H. (eds.) ASIACRYPT 2015. LNCS, vol. 9453, pp. 262–288. Springer, Heidelberg (2015). https://doi.org/10.1007/978-3-662-48800-3_11

[CF13]   Catalano, D., Fiore, D.: Vector commitments and their applications. In: Kurosawa, K., Hanaoka, G. (eds.) PKC 2013. LNCS, vol. 7778, pp. 55–72. Springer, Heidelberg (2013). https://doi.org/10.1007/978-3-642-36362-7_5

[CFG+20] Campanelli, M., Fiore, D., Greco, N., Kolonelos, D., Nizzardo, L.: Vector Commitment Techniques and Applications to Verifiable Decentralized Storage (2020). https://eprint.iacr.org/2020/149

[CFM08]   Catalano, D., Fiore, D., Messina, M.: Zero-knowledge sets with short proofs. In: Smart, N. (ed.) EUROCRYPT 2008. LNCS, vol. 4965, pp. 433–450. Springer, Heidelberg (2008). https://doi.org/10.1007/978-3-540-78967-3_25

[CPZ18]   Chepurnoy, A., Papamanthou, C., Zhang, Y.: Edrax: A Cryptocurrency with Stateless Transaction Validation (2018). https://eprint.iacr.org/2018/968

[Dry19]   Dryja, T.: Utreexo: A dynamic hash-based accumulator optimized for the Bitcoin UTXO set (2019). https://eprint.iacr.org/2019/611

[FK20]   Feist, D., Khovratovich, D.: Fast amortized Kate proofs (2020). https://github.com/khovratovich/Kate

[Goy07]   Goyal, V.: Reducing trust in the PKG in identity based cryptosystems. In: Menezes, A. (ed.) CRYPTO 2007. LNCS, vol. 4622, pp. 430–447. Springer, Heidelberg (2007). https://doi.org/10.1007/978-3-540-74143-5_24

[GRWZ20] Gorbunov, S., Reyzin, L., Wee, H., Zhang, Z.: Pointproofs: Aggregating Proofs for Multiple Vector Commitments (2020). https://eprint.iacr.org/2020/419

[KJG+18] Kokoris-Kogias, E., Jovanovic, P., Gasser, L., Gailly, N., Syta, E., Ford, B.: OmniLedger: a secure, scale-out, decentralized ledger via sharding. In: IEEE S&P 2018, May 2018

[KR13]   Kohlweiss, M., Rial, A.: Optimally private access control. In: ACM WPES 2013 (2013)

[KZG10]   Kate, A., Zaverucha, G.M., Goldberg, I.: Constant-size commitments to polynomials and their applications. In: Abe, M. (ed.) ASIACRYPT 2010. LNCS, vol. 6477, pp. 177–194. Springer, Heidelberg (2010). https://doi.org/10.1007/978-3-642-17373-8_11

[LM19]   Lai, R.W.F., Malavolta, G.: Subvector commitments with application to succinct arguments. In: Boldyreva, A., Micciancio, D. (eds.) CRYPTO 2019. LNCS, vol. 11692, pp. 530–560. Springer, Cham (2019). https://doi.org/10.1007/978-3-030-26948-7_19

[LY10]   Libert, B., Yung, M.: Concise mercurial vector commitments and independent zero-knowledge sets with short proofs. In: Micciancio, D. (ed.) TCC 2010. LNCS, vol. 5978, pp. 499–517. Springer, Heidelberg (2010). https://doi.org/10.1007/978-3-642-11799-2_30

[Mil12]   Miller, A.: Storing UTXOs in a balanced Merkle tree (zero-trust nodes with O(1)-storage) (2012). https://bitcointalk.org/index.php?topic=101734.msg1117428

[Nak08]   Nakamoto, S.: Bitcoin: A Peer-to-Peer Electronic Cash System (2008). https://bitcoin.org/bitcoin.pdf

[PST13]   Papamanthou, C., Shi, E., Tamassia, R.: Signatures of correct computation. In: Sahai, A. (ed.) TCC 2013. LNCS, vol. 7785, pp. 222–242. Springer, Heidelberg (2013). https://doi.org/10.1007/978-3-642-36594-2_13

[RMCI17]   Reyzin, L., Meshkov, D., Chepurnoy, A., Ivanov, S.: Improving authenticated dynamic dictionaries, with applications to cryptocurrencies. In: Kiayias, A. (ed.) FC 2017. LNCS, vol. 10322, pp. 376–392. Springer, Cham (2017). https://doi.org/10.1007/978-3-319-70972-7_21

[TAB+20]   Tomescu, A., Abraham, I., Buterin, V., Drake, J., Feist, D., Khovratovich, D.: Aggregatable Subvector Commitments for Stateless Cryptocurrencies (2020). https://eprint.iacr.org/2020/527

[Tod16]   Todd, P.: Making UTXO set growth irrelevant with low-latency delayed TXO commitments (2016). https://petertodd.org/2016/delayed-txo-commitments

[Tom20]   Tomescu, A.: How to Keep a Secret and Share a Public Key (Using Polynomial Commitments). PhD thesis, Massachusetts Institute of Technology, Cambridge, MA, USA (2020)

[Vir17]   Virza, M.: On Deploying Succinct Zero-Knowledge Proofs. PhD thesis, Massachusetts Institute of Technology, Cambridge, MA, USA (2017)

[vzGG13a]   von zur Gathen, J., Gerhard, J.: Fast multiplication. In: Modern Computer Algebra, 3rd edn, chapter 8, pp. 221–254. Cambridge University Press, Cambridge (2013)

[vzGG13b]   von zur Gathen, J., Gerhard, J.: Fast polynomial evaluation and interpolation. In: Modern Computer Algebra, 3rd edn, chapter 10, pp. 295–310. Cambridge University Press, Cambridge (2013)

[Woo]   Wood, G.: Ethereum: A Secure Decentralised Generalised Transaction Ledger (2014). http://gavwood.com/paper.pdf

Tight Verifiable Delay Functions

Nico Döttling[1], Sanjam Garg[2], Giulio Malavolta[2,3(✉)],
and Prashant Nalini Vasudevan[2]

[1] CISPA Helmholtz Center for Information Security, Saarbrücken, Germany
[2] University of California, Berkeley, USA
giulio.malavolta@hotmail.it
[3] Carnegie Mellon University, Pittsburgh, USA

Abstract. A Verifiable Delay Function (VDF) is a function that takes
at least T sequential steps to evaluate and produces a unique output
that can be verified efficiently, in time essentially independent of T. In
this work we study *tight* VDFs, where the function can be evaluated in
time not much more than the sequentiality bound T.

On the negative side, we show the impossibility of a black-box construction from random oracles of a VDF that can be evaluated in time
$T + O(T^\delta)$ for any constant $\delta < 1$. On the positive side, we show that
any VDF with an inefficient prover (running in time cT for some constant c) that has a natural self-composability property can be generically
transformed into a VDF with a tight prover efficiency of $T + O(1)$. Our
compiler introduces only a logarithmic factor overhead in the proof size
and in the number of parallel threads needed by the prover. As a corollary, we obtain a simple construction of a tight VDF from any succinct
non-interactive argument combined with repeated hashing. This is in
contrast with prior generic constructions (Boneh et al., CRYPTO 2018)
that required the existence of incremental verifiable computation, which
entails stronger assumptions and complex machinery.

1 Introduction

Verifiable Delay Functions (VDFs), introduced by Boneh et al. [5], is a recent
cryptographic primitive which allows one to put protocol parties on halt for a set
amount of time. VDFs are functions that are characterized by three properties.
For a time parameter T, (i) it should be possible to compute the function in
sequential time T. Furthermore, a VDF should be T-*sequential* in the sense that
(ii) it should not be possible to compute such a function in (possibly parallel)
time significantly less than T. Finally, (iii) the function should produce a proof π
which convinces a verifier that the function output has been correctly computed.
Such a proof π should be succinct, in the sense that the proof size and the verification complexity are (essentially) independent of T. These properties enable
a prover to prove to the verifier that a certain amount of time has elapsed, say,
by computing the function on an input provided by the verifier.

After the seminal work of Boneh et al. [5], VDFs have rapidly generated
interest in the community and several follow-up constructions have recently been

© Springer Nature Switzerland AG 2020
C. Galdi and V. Kolesnikov (Eds.): SCN 2020, LNCS 12238, pp. 65–84, 2020.
https://doi.org/10.1007/978-3-030-57990-6_4

proposed [18,22], and there is active work in implementing and optimizing them for near-term practical use [8]. This is partially motivated by the large range of applications of this primitive. As an example, VDFs can turn blockchains into randomness beacons – introducing a delay in the generation of the randomness prevents malicious miners from sampling blocks adaptively to bias the outcome of the beacon. VDFs are also useful as a computational time-stamp and have further applications in the context of proofs of replications [1] and resource-efficient blockchains [9].

One of the major efficiency metrics for a VDF is the prover's computational complexity, in relation to the time parameter T. This determines the time taken to evaluate a VDF by an honest prover, and therefore the gap with respect to the best possible successful malicious machine (which we bound to take time atleast T). In the ideal case this gap is non-existent, i.e., the prover can compute the VDF in time exactly T without resorting to massive parallelization. This work asks the following question:

When do VDFs with tight *prover complexity exist?*

Our Negative Result: Motivated by concerns about concrete efficiency, we first investigate the possibility of black-box constructions of VDFs from other cryptographic primitives. In particular, given the prevalence of strong and efficient candidates for simple cryptographic primitives like one-way functions and collision-resistant hash functions (SHA256, for instance), we would ideally like to use these as black-boxes to get similarly strong and efficient VDFs. As a negative result, we show that it is impossible to construct a T-sequential VDF where the prover runtime is close to T (with any number of processors) in a black-box manner from random oracles (and thus one-way functions or collision-resistant hash functions).

Theorem 1 (Informal). *There is no black-box construction of a T-sequential VDF from a random oracle where the prover makes at most $T + O(T^\delta)$ rounds of queries to the oracle for some constant $\delta < 1$.*

Our Positive Result: On the other hand, we find that the natural generic non-blackbox approach to constructing a VDF can actually be made tight. All known constructions of VDF proceed by iteratively applying some function f to the given input – that is, computing $f(x)$, $f(f(x))$, and so on. A proof that this was done correctly is computed either afterwards or during this computation. We show that, assuming a *modest* parallelism of the prover, we can bootstrap any such VDF where the prover complexity may not be tight into a VDF where the prover runtime matches the sequentiality bound T. More specifically, we construct VDFs that can be computed in parallel time $T + O(1)$ using $O(log(T))$ processors and space.

Our bootstrapping theorem consists of a compiler that transforms *any* VDF with a somewhat natural *self-composability* property into a VDF with a tight prover complexity. Roughly speaking, we require that the evaluation of a VDF on time parameter T can be decomposed into two (sequential) evaluations of the same VDF on parameters T_1 and T_2 such that $T_1 + T_2 = T$. This is satisfied by all known VDF candidates. The resulting scheme is as secure as the underlying VDF. Furthermore, the transformation is practically efficient and simple to implement.

Theorem 2 (Informal). *If there exists a self-composable VDF with a prover runtime bounded by $c \cdot T$ for some constant c, then there exists a VDF with prover runtime bounded by $T + O(1)$.*

As our transformation mentioned above is black-box, Theorems 1 and 2 together rule out black-box constructions from random oracles of a self-composable VDF where the prover makes at most cT rounds of queries for some constant c. We highlight a few other interesting corollaries of our theorem:

(1) Assuming the existence of an inherently sequential function and (not necessarily incremental) succinct non-interactive arguments [14,17], there exists a T-sequential VDF, for any T, where the prover runs in time T using a poly-logarithmic number of processors.

This improves over generic constructions from prior work [5], which required *incremental* verifiable computation [3,21], which is a stronger primitive.[1] Next, we turn our attention to specific number-theoretic constructions. In this context we improve the prover efficiency of the construction of Pietrzak [18], where the prover runs in time approximately $T + \sqrt{T}$.

(2) Assuming the security of Pietrzak's VDF, there exists a T-sequential VDF with prover parallel runtime exactly T using $log\,log(T)$ processors and space. The proof size is increased by a factor of $log\,log(T)$ and the verifier parallel complexity is unchanged.

Our result generalizes a prior work by Wesolowski [22] which obtains a specific construction of a tight VDF. We discuss the consequences of our bootstrapping theorem in greater detail in Appendix A. Regarding the additional parallelism used by our prover, we stress that a $log(T)$ parallelism by the prover is also (implicitly) assumed by prior work: In the circuit model, even computing a simple collision-resistant hash with security parameter λ already requires at least λ ($> log(T)$ in our setting) parallel processors. Our compiler adds an extra logarithmic factor, which is well in reach of modern GPUs.

1.1 Our Techniques

In this section we give a brief overview of the main ideas behind this work. To simplify the exposition, we first discuss our bootstrapping theorem and then we give some intuition behind our impossibility result.

---

[1] Known constructions of incremental verifiable computation require succinct arguments with knowledge extraction.

Self-composability and Weak Efficiency. In the standard syntax of VDFs, both the output value y and the proof π are computed by a single function Eval. For the purposes of this work, it is instructive to think of the algorithms which compute a VDF function values y and proofs π as separate algorithms Comp and Prove: Comp takes as input the time parameter T and an input x and outputs a function value y and auxiliary information α. On the other hand Prove takes as input α and outputs a proof π. The first property that we assume for the underlying VDF is *weak-efficiency*: On time parameter T, the Comp algorithm runs in time T whereas Prove runs in time at most cT, for some constant c. While our argument is generic, for the purpose of this outline we always assume that $c = 1$, i.e., it takes the same number of steps to compute the function via $(y, \alpha) \leftarrow \mathsf{Comp}(T, x)$ and to compute the proof $\pi \leftarrow \mathsf{Prove}(\alpha)$.

We also assume that the function Comp is *self-composable*. Namely, let that $T = T_1 + T_2$ for any $T_1, T_2 > 0$. For any input x, we require that if $(y_1, \cdot) \leftarrow \mathsf{Comp}(T_1, x)$, $(y_2, \cdot) \leftarrow \mathsf{Comp}(T_2, y_1)$ and $(y, \cdot) \leftarrow \mathsf{Comp}(T, x)$, then it holds that $y_2 = y$. In other words, we require that the function $(y, \cdot) \leftarrow \mathsf{Comp}(T, x)$ can be computed in two smaller steps, where we feed the result of the first step back into the function to obtain the actual output.

We argue that these are mild requirements for VDFs, in fact all of the recent constructions fit into this paradigm and therefore can be used as input for our compiler. This includes the more structured approach of repeated squaring over hidden order groups [18,22] and even the straightforward combination of repeated hashing and succinct arguments [5].

Bootstrapping VDFs. In favor of a simpler presentation, throughout the following informal discussion we assume that $T = 2^t$, for some integer t. The more general case is handled in the main body of the paper and follows with minor modifications. Recall that, by the self-composability property, we can split the computation $(y, \alpha) \leftarrow \mathsf{Comp}(2^t, x)$ into two separate blocks $(y_1, \alpha_1) \leftarrow \mathsf{Comp}(2^{t-1}, x)$ and $(y, \alpha_2) \leftarrow \mathsf{Comp}(2^{t-1}, y_1)$. Our main insight is that we do not need to compute a proof π for the full trace of the computation, instead we can compute two separate proofs for the corresponding subroutines. Then the final proof will consist of the concatenation of the two proofs. More specifically, we will set $\pi = (\pi_1, \pi_2)$, where $\pi_1 \leftarrow \mathsf{Prove}(\alpha_1)$ and $\pi_2 \leftarrow \mathsf{Prove}(\alpha_2)$.

This modification allows us to leverage parallelism. To evaluate the function on input x, one first computes $(y_1, \alpha_1) \leftarrow \mathsf{Comp}(2^{t-1}, x)$ in a single threaded computation. Once this step is reached, the computation forks into two parallel threads: A thread S_1 that computes $(y, \alpha_2) \leftarrow \mathsf{Comp}(2^{t-1}, y_1)$ and a thread S_2 which computes $\pi_1 \leftarrow \mathsf{Prove}(\alpha_1)$. Note that by the weak efficiency of the VDF, the runtime of the algorithm Prove is identical to that $\mathsf{Comp}(2^{t-1}, x)$, i.e., 2^{t-1} steps. It follows that S_1 and S_2 will terminate simultaneously. In other words, both y and π_1 will be available at the same time.

At this point only the computation of the proof π_2 is missing. If we were to do it naively, then we would need to add an extra 2^{t-1} steps to compute $\mathsf{Prove}(\alpha_2)$, after the computation of $(y, \alpha_2) \leftarrow \mathsf{Comp}(2^{t-1}, y_1)$ terminates. This would yield a total computation time of $T + T/2$, which is still far from optimal. However, observe that our trick has cut the original computation overhead by a factor of 2. This suggest a natural strategy to proceed: We recursively apply the same algorithm as above on $\mathsf{Comp}(2^{t-1}, y_1)$ and further split the proof π_2 into two sub-proofs for two equal-length chunks of computation. The recursion proceeds up to the point where the computation of the function consists of a single step, and therefore there is no proof needed. Note that this happens after $t = log(T)$ iterations. Since we spawn a new thread for each level of the recursion, this also bounds the total amount of parallelism of the prover.

Our actual proof π now consists of $((y_1, \pi_1), \ldots, (y_t, \pi_t))$, i.e. the proof π consists of t components. We verify π in the canonical way, that is, setting $y_0 = x$ we compute $\mathsf{Vf}(2^{t-i}, y_{i-1}, y_i, \pi_i)$ for all $1 \le i \le t$ and accept if all verify and $y_t = y$.

Black-Box Impossibility. We show that there cannot be a black-box construction of a VDF from a random oracle if the overhead in computing the proof in the VDF is small. That is, if the number of sequential rounds of queries that the algorithm Eval makes to the oracle is less than $T + O(T^\delta)$ for some constant $\delta < 1$. Note that our transformation sketched above is itself black-box, and thus our result also rules out black-box constructions of self-composable VDFs with a constant-factor overhead in generating the proof.

The central idea behind the impossibility is observation that since the verification algorithm Vf makes only a small number of queries, it cannot tell whether Eval actually made all the queries it was supposed to. For simplicity, suppose that Eval makes exactly T sequential rounds of queries, and that the sequentiality of the VDF guarantees that its output cannot be computed in less than T rounds of queries. On input x, suppose $\mathsf{Eval}(x) = (y, \pi)$. Efficiency and completeness of the VDF require that the verification algorithm Vf, making only $poly(log(T))$ queries to the oracle, accepts when given (x, y, π). Whereas, soundness requires that the same Vf rejects when given (x, y', π') for any $y' \ne y$ and any π'. We show that all of these cannot happen at the same time while making only black-box use of the random oracle, if this oracle is the only source of computational hardness.

Consider an alternative evaluation algorithm $\overline{\mathsf{Eval}}$ that behaves the same as Eval except that on one of the rounds of queries that Eval makes, instead of making the queries to the oracle, it sets their answers on its own to uniformly random strings of the appropriate length. Otherwise it proceeds as Eval does, and outputs whatever Eval would output. Now, unless the algorithm Vf makes one of the queries that $\overline{\mathsf{Eval}}$ skipped, it should not be able to distinguish between the outputs of Eval and $\overline{\mathsf{Eval}}$. As these skipped queries are only a $1/T$ fraction of the queries that $\overline{\mathsf{Eval}}$ made, Vf, which only makes $poly(log(T))$ queries, catches them with only this small probability. Thus, if Vf accepts the output (y, π) of $\mathsf{Eval}(x)$, then it should also mostly accept the output (y', π') of $\overline{\mathsf{Eval}}(x)$.

On the other hand, as $\overline{\mathsf{Eval}}$ made less than T rounds of queries to the oracle, sequentiality implies that y' should be different from y (except perhaps with negligible probability). Thus, with high probability, Vf accepts (y', π') where $y' \ne y$, contradicting soundness.

1.2 Related Work

A related concept is that of Proofs of Sequential Work (PoSW), originally introduced by Mahmoody, Moran, and Vadhan [15]. A PoSW can be seen as a relaxed version of a VDF where the output of the function is not necessarily unique: PoSW satisfy a loose notion of sequentiality where the prover is required to perform at least αT sequential steps, for some constant $\alpha \in [0, 1]$. In contrast with VDFs, PoSWs admit efficient instantiations that make only black-box calls to a random oracle [10,11].

Time-lock puzzles [20] allow one to hide some information for a certain (polynomial) amount of time. This primitive is intimately related to sequential computation as it needs to withstand attacks from massively parallel algorithms. Time lock-puzzles have been instantiated in RSA groups [20] or assuming the existence of succinct randomized encodings and of a worst case non-parallelizable language [4]. Time-lock puzzles can be seen as VDFs with an additional encryption functionality, except that there is no requirement for an efficient verification algorithm. In this sense the two primitives are incomparable.

Two constructions of tight VDFs were proposed in the seminal work of Boneh et al. [5], one assuming the existence of incremental verifiable computation and the other from permutation polynomials (shown secure against a new assumption). The latter scheme achieves only a weak form of prover efficiency since it requires T parallel processors to be evaluated tightly. Shortly after, two number theoretic constructions have been presented independently by Pietrzak [18] and Wesolowski [22], based on squaring in groups of unknown order. In their original presentation, neither of these schemes was tight as the prover required additional $\sqrt{T}$ and $T/logT$ extra steps, respectively [6].

However, Wesolowski [22] later updated his paper with a paragraph that sketches a method to improve the prover complexity of his construction from $T + O(T/logT)$ to $T + O(1)$, using techniques similar to the ones in our compiler. Our bootstrapping theorem can be seen as a generalization of these techniques and can be applied to a broader class of constructions. Finally we mention of a new VDF instance from supersingular isogenies [12] where the validity of the function output can be checked without the need to compute any extra proof, however the public parameters of such a scheme grow linearly with the time parameter T.

In a concurrent and independent work by Mahmoody et al. [16], an impossibility result is also shown. Compared to our result, their lower bound rules out the existence of blackbox VDFs for a looser set of parameters (i.e., it is a more general result). In contrast with our work, their paper does not contain any results on new instantiations of VDFs.

2   Verifiable Delay Functions

We denote by $\lambda \in \mathbb{N}$ the security parameter. We say that a function $negl$ is negligible if it vanishes faster than any polynomial. Given a set S, we denote by $s \leftarrow_\$ S$ the uniform sampling from S. We say that an algorithm runs in *parallel time* T with P-many processors if it can be implemented by a PRAM machine with P parallel processors running in time T. We say that an algorithm is PPT if it can be implemented by a probabilistic machine running in time polynomial in λ.

Here we recall the definition of verifiable delay functions (VDF) from [5].

Definition 1 (Verifiable Delay Function). *A VDF* $\mathfrak{V} =$ (Setup, Gen, Eval, Vf) *is defined as the following tuple of algorithms.*

Setup(1^λ) $\rightarrow pp$: *On input the security parameter* 1^λ, *the setup algorithm returns the public parameters* pp. *By convention, the public parameters encode an input domain* $\mathcal{X}$ *and an output domain* $\mathcal{Y}$.

Gen(pp) $\rightarrow x$: *On input the public parameters* pp, *the instance generation algorithm sample a random input* $x \leftarrow_s \mathcal{X}$.

Eval(pp, x, T) $\rightarrow (y, \pi)$: *On input the public parameters* pp, *an input* $x \in \mathcal{X}$, *and a time parameter* T, *the evaluation algorithm returns an output* $y \in \mathcal{Y}$ *together with a proof* π. *The evaluation algorithm may use random coins to compute* π *but not for computing* y.

Vf(pp, x, y, π, T) $\rightarrow \{0,1\}$: *On input the public parameters* pp, *an input* $x \in \mathcal{X}$, *an output* $y \in \mathcal{Y}$, *a proof* π, *and a time parameter* T, *the verification algorithm output a bit* $\{0,1\}$.

Efficiency. We require that the setup and the instance generation algorithms run in time $poly(\lambda)$, whereas the running time of the verification algorithm must be bounded by $poly(log(T), \lambda)$. For the evaluation algorithm, we require it to run in parallel time *exactly* T. We also consider less stringent notions of efficiency where its (parallel) running time is bounded by cT, for some constant c.

Completeness. The completeness property requires that correctly generated proofs always cause the verification algorithm to accept.

Definition 2 (Completeness). *A VDF* $\mathfrak{V} =$ (Setup, Gen, Eval, Vf) *is complete if for all* $\lambda \in \mathbb{N}$ *and all* $T \in \mathbb{N}$ *it holds that*

$$\Pr\left[\mathsf{Vf}(pp, x, y, \pi, T) = 1 \,\middle|\, \begin{array}{l} pp \leftarrow \mathsf{Setup}(1^\lambda) \\ x \leftarrow \mathsf{Gen}(pp) \\ (y, \pi) \leftarrow \mathsf{Eval}(pp, x, T) \end{array} \right] = 1.$$

Sequentiality. We require a VDF to be sequential in the sense that no machine should be able to gain a noticeable speed-up in terms of parallel running time, when compared with the honest evaluation algorithm.

Definition 3 (Sequentiality). *A VDF* $\mathfrak{V} =$ (Setup, Gen, Eval, Vf) *is sequential if for all* $\lambda \in \mathbb{N}$ *and for all pairs of PPT machines* $(\mathcal{A}_1, \mathcal{A}_2)$, *such that the parallel running time of* $\mathcal{A}_2$ *(with any polynomial amount of processors in* T*) is less than* T, *there exists a negligible function* negl *such that*

$$\Pr\left[(y, \cdot) = \mathsf{Eval}(pp, x, T) \,\middle|\, \begin{array}{l} pp \leftarrow \mathsf{Setup}(1^\lambda) \\ (T, \tau) \leftarrow \mathcal{A}_1(pp) \\ x \leftarrow \mathsf{Gen}(pp) \\ y \leftarrow \mathcal{A}_2(pp, x, T, \tau) \end{array} \right] = negl(\lambda).$$

Soundness. For soundness we require that it is computationally hard to find two valid outputs for a single instance of the VDF. Note that here we do not constrain the running time of the adversary, except for being polynomial in λ and T.

Definition 4 (Soundness). *A VDF* $\mathfrak{V} = (\mathsf{Setup}, \mathsf{Gen}, \mathsf{Eval}, \mathsf{Vf})$ *is sound if for all* $\lambda \in \mathbb{N}$ *and for all PPT machines* $\mathcal{A}$ *there exists a negligible function* negl *such that*

$$\Pr\left[\mathsf{Vf}(pp, x, y, \pi, T) = 1 \text{ and } (y, \cdot) \neq \mathsf{Eval}(pp, x, T) \,\middle|\, \begin{matrix} pp \leftarrow \mathsf{Setup}(1^\lambda) \\ (T, x, y, \pi) \leftarrow \mathcal{A}_1(pp) \end{matrix}\right] = negl(\lambda).$$

3 A Bootstrapping Theorem for VDFs

In this section we propose a compiler that takes as input any weakly efficient VDF (that satisfies some natural composability properties) and turns it into a fully-fledged efficient scheme. We first characterize the exact requirements of the underlying VDF, then we describe our construction and we show that it preserves all of the properties of the underlying scheme.

3.1 Building Block

We require that the underlying VDF can be composed with itself (possibly using different time parameters) arbitrarily many times, without altering the function output, i.e., $\mathsf{Eval}(pp, \cdot, T_1) \circ \mathsf{Eval}(pp, \cdot, T_2) = \mathsf{Eval}(pp, \cdot, T_1 + T_2)$. More concretely, we assume the existence of a VDF that satisfies the following.

Definition 5 (Self-Composability). *A VDF* $\mathfrak{V} = (\mathsf{Setup}, \mathsf{Gen}, \mathsf{Eval}, \mathsf{Vf})$ *is self-composable if, for all* pp *in the support of* $\mathsf{Setup}(1^\lambda)$, *for all* $x \in \mathcal{X}$, *all* (T_1, T_2) *bounded by a sub-exponential function in* λ, *we have that* $\mathsf{Eval}(pp, x, T_1 + T_2) = \mathsf{Eval}(pp, y, T_2)$, *where* $(y, \cdot) = \mathsf{Eval}(pp, x, T_2)$.

Note that this also implies that the domain and the range of the function are identical, i.e., $\mathcal{X} = \mathcal{Y}$. We stress that this property is satisfied by all known candidate VDF constructions [5,18,22]. To characterize the second requirement, it is going to be useful to refine the syntax of our primitive. We assume that the evaluation algorithm $\mathsf{Eval}(pp, x, T)$ is split in the following subroutines:

$\mathsf{Eval}(pp, x, T)$: On input the public parameters pp, and input $x \in \mathcal{X}$, and a time parameter T, execute the subroutine $(y, \alpha) \leftarrow \mathsf{Comp}(pp, x, T)$. Then compute $\pi \leftarrow \mathsf{Prove}(\alpha)$ and return (y, π).

This captures the compute-and-prove approach, where the prover evaluates some inherently sequential function and then computes a short proof of correctness, potentially using some information from the intermediate steps of the computation (α). Note that this refinement is done without loss of generality since one can recover the original syntax by encoding the proof π in the advice α and set the prove algorithm to be the identity function. We are now in the position of stating the efficiency requirements of the input VDF.

Definition 6 (Weak Efficiency). *A VDF* $\mathfrak{V}$ = (Setup, Gen, Eval, Vf) *is weakly efficient if there exists a function* $\Psi : \mathbb{N} \to \mathbb{N}$ *and a non-negative constant c such that for all* $T \in \mathbb{N}$ *it holds that* $0 \leq \Psi(T) \leq cT$ *and* Prove *runs in parallel time* $\Psi(T)$*, where T is the parallel running time of* Eval$(\cdot, \cdot, T)$.

Note that the total running time of the evaluation algorithm is bounded by $(c + 1)T$, for some constant c. This condition is again met by all known VDF instances [5,18,22], since they are all based on the compute-and-prove paradigm: Given a long sequential computation, the corresponding proof π can be computed in parallel time at most linear in T by using essentially any verifiable computation scheme.

3.2 Scheme Description

Let $\mathfrak{V}$ = (Setup, Gen, Eval, Vf) be a weakly efficient and self-composable VDF and let Ψ be the corresponding function such that, on input T, the running time of the subroutine Prove is bounded by $\Psi(T)$. Our construction $\overline{\mathfrak{V}}$ = ($\overline{\text{Setup}}, \overline{\text{Gen}}, \overline{\text{Eval}}, \overline{\text{Vf}}$) is shown below.

$\overline{\text{Setup}}(1^\lambda)$: Return Setup(1^λ).

$\overline{\text{Gen}}(pp)$: Return Gen(pp).

$\overline{\text{Eval}}(pp, x, T)$: Set S to be the smallest non-negative integer such that $S + \Psi(S) \geq T$.
  (1) If $S \leq 1$:
    (a) Compute $(y, \alpha) \leftarrow$ Comp(pp, x, T).
    (b) Return $(y, \emptyset)$.
  (2) Else:
    (a) Compute $(y, \alpha) \leftarrow$ Comp(pp, x, S).
    (b) Spawn a parallel thread to compute $\pi \leftarrow$ Prove(α).
    (c) Compute $(\tilde{y}, L) \leftarrow \overline{\text{Eval}}(pp, y, T - S)$ in the main thread.
    (d) Return $(\tilde{y}, (y, \pi) \cup L)$.

$\overline{\text{Vf}}(pp, x, y, \pi, T)$:
  (1) Parse π as $((y_1, \pi_1), \ldots, (y_n, \pi_n))$.
  (2) Set $S_0 = T$ and $y_0 = x$.
  (3) For all $1 \leq i \leq n$:
    (a) Define S_i to be the smallest integer such that $S_i + \Psi(S_i) \geq S_0 - \sum_{j=1}^{i-1} S_j$.
    (b) Compute in parallel $b_i = $ Vf(pp, y_{i-1}, y_i, S_i).
  (4) Return $(b_1 \wedge \cdots \wedge b_n \wedge (y, \cdot) = $ Eval$(pp, y_n, T - \sum_{j=1}^n S_j))$.

The setup and the instance generation algorithms are unchanged. The new evaluation algorithm is defined recursively: On input some time T, the algorithm defines S to be the smallest non-negative integer such that $S + \Psi(S) \geq T$. Recall that the correctness of the evaluation of the Comp algorithm on time parameter S can be proven in time $\Psi(S)$, by the weak efficiency condition of the VDF. Thus, S approximates from above the maximum amount of computation that can be performed and proven within time T. The algorithm then branches, depending on the value of S:

(1) $S \leq 1$: In this case the algorithm simply computes $\mathsf{Comp}(pp, x, T)$ and outputs the result of the computation, without computing a proof. Observe that since $S = 1$ it holds that $T \leq (1 + c)$, where c is the constant such that $\Psi(S) \leq cS$. Thus the algorithm runs for at most $c + 1$ steps. This corresponds to the last step of the recursion.

(2) $S > 1$: In this case the algorithm computes the underlying VDF on time parameter S and outputs the resulting $(y, \alpha) \leftarrow \mathsf{Comp}(pp, x, S)$. At this point the algorithm branches in two parallel threads:
   (a) The first thread computes the proof $\pi \leftarrow \mathsf{Prove}(\alpha)$.
   (b) The second thread calls the evaluation algorithm recursively on input $(pp, y, T - S)$, which returns an output $\tilde{y}$ and a list L.
   The algorithm returns the function output $\tilde{y}$ and the list L augmented (from the left) with the intermediate pair (y, π), i.e., $(y, \pi) \cup L$.

The output of the computation consists of n pairs $(y_1, \pi_1), \ldots, (y_n, \pi_n)$, where n is the depth of the recursion, and a function output $\tilde{y}$. Each output-proof pair can be verified independently and the correctness of the function output $\tilde{y}$ can be checked by recomputing at most c steps of the VDF on input y_n.

Note that the only parameter that affects the efficiency of the prover and the verifier and the size of the proof is the depth of the recursion n. Intuitively, each step of the recursion slices off a chunk of the computation without affecting the total runtime of the algorithm, until only a constant number of steps is left. If S and $\Psi(S)$ are not too far apart, then n can be shown to be bounded by a poly-logarithmic factor in T. We give a pictorial representation of the steps of the computation in Fig. 1.

3.3   Analysis

The completeness of our scheme follows from the self-composability of the underlying VDF. In the following we analyze the efficiency of our construction and we show that the properties of the underlying VDF are preserved under self-composition.

Efficiency. Recall that S is always a non-negative integers and therefore each step of the recursion is executed on input some integer $\leq T$. Thus we can bound the size of each proof π_i by the size of the proof of the underlying VDF on time parameter T. It follows that the proof size of our scheme is at most a factor n larger, where n is the depth of the recursion. In the following we bound the

depth of the recursion, thus establishing also a bound also on the proof size. We
begin by stating and proving the following instrumental lemma.

Lemma 1. *Let $\Psi : \mathbb{N} \rightarrow \mathbb{N}$ be a function such that there exists a constant c such
that for all $S \in \mathbb{N}$ it holds that $\Psi(S) \leq cS$. Fix an $S_0 \in \mathbb{N}$ and define S_i to be the
smallest non-negative integer such that $S_i + \Psi(S_i) \geq S_0 - \sum_{j=1}^{i-1} S_j$. Then for all
$S_0 \in \mathbb{N}$ and for all $i \geq 0$ it holds that $S_0 - \sum_{j=1}^{i} S_j \leq S_0 \left(\frac{c}{c+1} \right)^i$.*

Proof. We prove the claimed bound by induction over i. For the base case $i = 0$
we have $S_0 \leq S_0$, which is trivial. For the induction step, recall that S_i is defined
to be the smallest integer such that $S_i + \Psi(S_i) \geq S_0 - \sum_{j=1}^{i-1} S_j$. Since $\Psi(S_i) \leq cS_i$,
for some non-negative c, we have that

$$S_i + cS_i \geq S_0 - \sum_{j=1}^{i-1} S_j$$

$$S_i(c+1) \geq S_0 - \sum_{j=1}^{i-1} S_j$$

$$S_i \geq \frac{S_0 - \sum_{j=1}^{i-1} S_j}{c+1}.$$

By induction hypothesis, it follows that

$$S_0 - \sum_{j=1}^{i} S_j = S_0 - \sum_{j=1}^{i-1} S_j - S_i$$

$$\leq S_0 - \sum_{j=1}^{i-1} S_j - \frac{S_0 - \sum_{j=1}^{i-1} S_j}{c+1}$$

$$= \frac{(S_0 - \sum_{j=1}^{i-1} S_j)c}{c+1}$$

$$\leq S_0 \left(\frac{c}{c+1} \right)^{i-1} \left(\frac{c}{c+1} \right)$$

$$= S_0 \left(\frac{c}{c+1} \right)^i.$$

The bound on the depth of the recursion is obtained by observing that the i-th
copy of the evaluation algorithm is called on time parameter exactly $T - \sum_{j=1}^{i} S_j$,
where S_j is defined as above. Note that if $T - \sum_{j=1}^{i} S_j \leq 1$, then the recursion
always stops, since the condition $1 + \Psi(1) \geq 1$ is satisfied for all non-negative Ψ.
If we set $S_0 = T$ and apply Lemma 1 we obtain the following relation

$$T - \sum_{j=1}^{i} S_j \leq T \left(\frac{c}{c+1} \right)^i \leq 1.$$

Solving for i, we have that $log_{\left(\frac{c+1}{c}\right)}(T)$ iterations always suffice for the algorithm to terminate. This also implies a bound on the number of processors needed to evaluate the function. We now establish a bound on the parallel runtime of the evaluation algorithm.

Lemma 2. *Let $\mathfrak{V}$ be a weakly efficient VDF. Then, for all pp in the support of $\overline{\mathsf{Setup}}(1^\lambda)$, for all $x \in \mathcal{X}$, and for all $T \in \mathbb{N}$, the algorithm $\overline{\mathsf{Eval}}(pp, x, T)$ terminates in at most $T + c$ steps.*

Proof. We first consider the main thread of the execution. Set $S_0 = T$ and define S_i to be the smallest integer such that $S_i + \Psi(S_i) \geq S_0 - \sum_{j=1}^{i-1} S_j$. Observe that the main thread consists of n applications of the algorithm Comp on time parameter S_i, where n is the depth of the recursion, and one application on input $S_0 - \sum_{j=1}^{n} S_j$. Thus, by the weak efficiency of $\mathfrak{V}$, the total running time of the main thread is exactly

$$\sum_{j=1}^{n} S_j + S_0 - \sum_{j=1}^{n} S_j = S_0 = T.$$

To bound the runtime of the parallel threads we bound the difference with respect to the amount of steps needed for the main thread to terminate, starting from the moment the execution forks. We show a bound assuming $\Psi(S) = cS$, which implies a bound for the general case since the proving algorithm can only get faster. Consider the i-th recursive instance of the algorithm: After computing $(\alpha_i, y_i) \leftarrow \mathsf{Comp}(pp, x_i, S_i)$, the main thread proceeds by calling $\overline{\mathsf{Eval}}$ on input $T - S_i$ and spawns a new thread to compute a proof on input α_i. As discussed above, we know that the main thread will terminate within $T - S_i$ steps, thus all we need to do is bounding the amount of extra steps needed for the computation of the proof. Note that we have

$$(S_i - 1) + \Psi(S_i - 1) < T$$

since we assumed that S_i was the smallest integer that satisfies $S_i + \Psi(S_i) \geq T$. Substituting,

$$(S_i - 1) + \Psi(S_i - 1) < T$$
$$\Psi(S_i - 1) < T - S_i + 1$$
$$c(S_i - 1) < T - S_i + 1$$
$$cS_i - c < T - S_i + 1$$
$$\Psi(S_i) < T - S_i + c + 1$$

where $\Psi(S_i)$ is exactly the number of steps needed to compute π_i. This holds for all recursive instances of the algorithms and concludes our proof.

We remark that the extra c steps needed for our algorithm to terminate are due to the rounding that happens when S does not divide T. For the common case where T is a power of 2 and Ψ is the identity function, then $T = 2S$ in all of the recursive calls of the algorithm and the process terminates in exactly T steps. The verifier complexity is bounded by that of n parallel calls to the verifier of the underlying VDF on input some time parameter $\leq T$, where n is poly-logarithmic in T (see discussion above), plus an extra parallel instance that recomputes at most $c + 1$ steps of the Comp algorithm.

Sequentiality. In the following we show that our transformation preserves the sequentiality of the underlying VDF.

Theorem 3 (Sequentiality). *Let $\mathfrak{V}$ be a self-composable sequential VDF, then $\overline{\mathfrak{V}}$ is sequential.*

Proof. Let $\mathcal{A}$ be and adversary that, on input a random instance x, finds the corresponding image y in time less than T. By definition of our evaluation algorithm, y is computed as

$$(y, \cdot) \leftarrow \mathsf{Comp}\left(pp, y_n, T - \sum_{j=1}^{n} S_j\right),$$

where $(y_i, \cdot) \leftarrow \mathsf{Comp}(pp, y_{i-1}, S_i)$, for all $1 \leq i \leq n$, setting $y_0 = x$. Invoking the self-composability of the underlying VDF, we have that

$$(y, \cdot) = \mathsf{Comp}\left(pp, x, T\right) = \mathsf{Eval}\left(pp, x, T\right)$$

twhich implies that y is the correct image of the underlying VDF for the same time parameter T. Thus the existence of $\mathcal{A}$ contradicts the sequentiality of $\mathfrak{V}$.

Soundness. The following theorem establishes the soundness of our scheme. Note that the reduction is tight, which means that our construction is exactly as secure as the input VDF.

Theorem 4. *Let $\mathfrak{V}$ be a self-composable and sound VDF, then $\overline{\mathfrak{V}}$ is sound.*

Proof. Let $\mathcal{A}$ be an adversary that, on input the honestly generated public parameters pp, outputs some tuple (T, x, y, π) such that π is a valid proof, but $(y, \cdot) \neq \overline{\mathsf{Eval}}(pp, x, T)$. Let $\pi = ((y_1, \pi_1), \ldots, (y_n, \pi_n))$ and set $y_0 = x$. Then we claim that one of the following conditions must be satisfied:

(1) There exists some $i \in \{1, \ldots, n\}$ such that $(y_i, \cdot) \neq \mathsf{Comp}(pp, y_{i-1}, S_i)$, where S_i is defined as in the verification algorithm, or
(2) $(y, \cdot) \neq \mathsf{Comp}(pp, y_n, T - \sum_{j=1}^{n} S_j)$.

If none of the above conditions is met, then we have that

$$(y, \cdot) = \mathsf{Comp}\left(pp, x, T\right) = \overline{\mathsf{Eval}}\left(pp, x, T\right)$$

by the self-composability of $\mathfrak{V}$, which contradicts the initial hypothesis. It follows that a successful attack implies at least one of the above conditions. However, (1) implies that we can extract a tuple $(y_{i-1}, y_i, \pi_i, S_i)$, such that π_i is a valid proof but $(y_i, \cdot) \neq \mathsf{Eval}(pp, y_{i-1}, S_i)$, which contradicts the soundness of $\mathfrak{V}$. On the other hand, if (2) happens then the verifier always rejects. It follows that the existence of $\mathcal{A}$ implies that the underlying VDF is not sound.

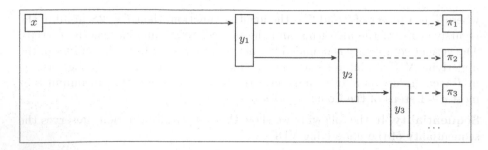

Fig. 1. Example of the execution trace of the evaluation algorithm for Ψ being the identity function. Solid lines denote the computation of the iterated function (Comp) and dashed lines denote the computation of the corresponding proof (Prove).

4   Black-Box Impossibility

In this section, we show that it is not possible to have a (tight) VDF whose only source of computational hardness is a random oracle. This implies that VDFs cannot be constructed by making just black-box use of several cryptographic primitives such as One-Way Functions and Collision-Resistant Hash Functions.

In this setting, we give all the algorithms in a VDF construction (that is, Setup, Gen, Eval, and Vf), as well as any adversaries, access to a random oracle that we denote by H. Our measure of the complexity of an algorithm will be the number of queries that it makes to H, and sequentiality is also measured by the number of rounds of queries made to H adaptively.

Theorem 5. *There is no black-box construction of a VDF* (Setup, Gen, Eval, Vf) *from a random oracle where* Eval$(\cdot, \cdot, T)$ *makes at most $T + O(T^\delta)$ rounds of queries for some $\delta < 1$, and is also T-sequential.*

Noting that our transformation from Sect. 3 (of any self-composable weakly efficient VDF into a VDF with constant proof overhead) is black-box, we can extend this impossibility as follows.

Corollary 1. *There is no black-box construction of a self-composable VDF* (Setup, Gen, Eval, Vf) *from a random oracle where* Eval$(\cdot, \cdot, T)$ *makes at most cT rounds of queries (for some constant c) and is also T-sequential.*

Our approach is as follows. Imagine replacing the answers to all but $(T - 1)$ rounds of queries that Eval makes to H with something completely random (independent of H). Since we only replaced a small fraction of the queries made, the output of Eval in this case should look the same to Vf, which makes very few queries to H. On the other hand, if this replacement did not change the value of y output by Eval, then it means that we could have computed Eval by answering these queries ourselves, and thus making only $(T-1)$ rounds of queries to H, contradicting sequentiality. Thus, if Eval is indeed T-sequential, then this replacement allows us to break soundness.

Proof (Theorem 5). Fix any alleged VDF (Setup, Gen, Eval, Vf) with access to a random oracle H. Suppose, for some $\delta < 1$, there is a function $p(\lambda, T)$ that is $O(poly(\lambda) \cdot T^\delta)$ such that, for any λ, T, and $pp \leftarrow \mathsf{Gen}^H(1^\lambda)$, the evaluation algorithm $\mathsf{Eval}(pp, \cdot, T)$ makes at most $T + p(\lambda, T)$ rounds of queries to H. Without loss of generality (since the algorithms are not bounded in the memory they use), we assume that an algorithm does not make the same query twice to H.

We construct an adversarial evaluator $\overline{\mathsf{Eval}}$ that works as follows on input (pp, x, T):

1. Pick a uniformly random set $I \subseteq [T + p(\lambda, T)]$ of size $(p(\lambda, T) + 1)$.
2. Run $\mathsf{Eval}(pp, x, T)$ as is whenever it is not making oracle queries.
3. When Eval makes the ith round of oracle queries $(q_1, \ldots, q_m)$,
   - if $i \notin I$, respond with $(H(q_1), \ldots, H(q_m))$.
   - if $i \in I$, respond with $(a_1, \ldots, a_m)$, where the a_i's are uniformly random strings of the appropriate length.
4. Output the (y, π) that Eval produces at the end.

The following claim states that if Vf makes only a small number of queries (which it has to for efficiency), it cannot distinguish between the outputs of Eval and $\overline{\mathsf{Eval}}$.

Claim (Indistinguishability). Suppose pp and x are generated from $\mathsf{Setup}^H(1^\lambda)$ and $\mathsf{Gen}^H(pp)$, respectively. Let $(y, \pi) \leftarrow \mathsf{Eval}^H(pp, x, T)$, and $(\overline{y}, \overline{\pi}) \leftarrow \overline{\mathsf{Eval}}^H(pp, x, T)$. If the algorithm $\mathsf{Vf}^H(pp, \cdot, \cdot, \cdot, T)$ makes at most $T/8p(\lambda, T)$ queries to H, then, for all $\lambda \in \mathbb{N}$ and all $T \in \mathbb{N}$, it holds that:

$$\left| \Pr\left[\mathsf{Vf}^H(pp, x, y, \pi, T) = 1 \right] - \Pr\left[\mathsf{Vf}^H(pp, x, \overline{y}, \overline{\pi}, T) = 1 \right] \right| \leq \frac{1}{4}$$

We defer the proof of the above to later in this section. The next claim states that, if the given VDF is sequential, then the output y as computed by $\overline{\mathsf{Eval}}$ has to differ with high probability from that computed by Eval. This follows immediately from the observation that $\overline{\mathsf{Eval}}$ makes at most $(T - 1)$ rounds of queries to H, and if so outputs that same y as Eval with non-negligible probability, this would immediately contradict T-sequentiality.

Claim (Sensitivity). Suppose the given VDF is T-sequential, and that pp and x are generated from $\mathsf{Setup}^H(1^\lambda)$ and $\mathsf{Gen}^H(pp)$, respectively. Let $(y, \pi) \leftarrow \mathsf{Eval}^H(pp, x, T)$, and $(\overline{y}, \overline{\pi}) \leftarrow \overline{\mathsf{Eval}}^H(pp, x, T)$. Then, there exists a negligible function *negl* such that for all $\lambda \in \mathbb{N}$ and all $T \in \mathbb{N}$ it holds that:

$$\Pr\left[y = \overline{y} \right] \leq negl(\lambda)$$

We now construct an adversary $\mathcal{A}$ that breaks the soundness of the supposed VDF. $\mathcal{A}$, on input the parameters pp, works as follows:

1. Generate $x \leftarrow \mathsf{Gen}^H(pp)$, and set $T = 2^\lambda$.
2. Compute $(\overline{y}, \overline{\pi}) \leftarrow \overline{\mathsf{Eval}}^H(pp, x, T)$.

3. Output $(T, x, \overline{y}, \overline{\pi})$.

Our argument now is based on the following three points:

- By the efficiency of the VDF, Vf makes much fewer than $T/8p(\lambda, T)$ $(= 2^{\Omega(\lambda)})$ queries.
- So, by the correctness of the VDF and Claim 4, the probability that $\mathsf{Vf}(pp, x, \overline{y}, \overline{\pi}, T)$ does not output 1 is at most $1/4$.
- By Claim 4, the probability that $\overline{y}$ agrees with the output of Eval is at most $negl(\lambda)$.

Together, by the union bound, we have:

$$\Pr\left[\mathsf{Vf}(pp, x, \overline{y}, \overline{\pi}, T) = 1 \text{ and } (y, \cdot) \neq \mathsf{Eval}(pp, x, T)\right] \geq 1 - \left(\frac{1}{4} + negl(\lambda)\right)$$

Noting that $\mathcal{A}$ runs in nearly the same time as Eval, this contradicts the claim that we started with a VDF that is both sequential and sound, proving the theorem.

Proof (Indistinguishability Claim). Recall that $\overline{\mathsf{Eval}}$ generates $(\overline{y}, \overline{\pi})$ just by altering the oracle that Eval has access to. Denoting this altered oracle by $\overline{H}$, note that $\overline{H}$ is also a random oracle, and that if Vf also had access to $\overline{H}$ instead of H, then the behavior of the whole system would not change. That is,

$$\Pr\left[\mathsf{Vf}^{\overline{H}}(pp, x, \overline{y}, \overline{\pi}, T) = 1\right] = \Pr\left[\mathsf{Vf}^{H}(pp, x, y, \pi, T) = 1\right] \tag{1}$$

Suppose, when given input (pp, x, y, π, T), the algorithm Vf^{H} makes N queries $q_1, \ldots, q_N$ to the oracle. Its behavior when given access to $\overline{H}$ instead of H is different only if the two oracles disagree on at least one of these queries. For any query q_i, the algorithm $\overline{\mathsf{Eval}}$ alters the oracle at this query if it happens to be made by Eval in a round contained in I. This happens with probability less than $(p(\lambda, T) + 1)/(T + p(\lambda, T))$. This implies that, for any $i \in [N]$,

$$\Pr\left[H(q_i) \neq \overline{H}(q_i)\right] \leq \frac{p(\lambda, T) + 1}{T + p(\lambda, T)} \leq \frac{2p(\lambda, T)}{T}$$

Thus, by the union bound, the probability that $\mathsf{Vf}^{\overline{H}}$ behaves differently from Vf^{H} on any input is at most $2Np(\lambda, T)/T$. If $N \leq T/8p(\lambda, T)$, together with (1), this implies that:

$$\left|\Pr\left[\mathsf{Vf}^{H}(pp, x, y, \pi, T) = 1\right] - \Pr\left[\mathsf{Vf}^{H}(pp, x, \overline{y}, \overline{\pi}, T) = 1\right]\right|$$
$$= \left|\Pr\left[\mathsf{Vf}^{\overline{H}}(pp, x, \overline{y}, \overline{\pi}, T) = 1\right] - \Pr\left[\mathsf{Vf}^{H}(pp, x, \overline{y}, \overline{\pi}, T) = 1\right]\right| \leq \frac{1}{4}.$$

Acknowledgments. S. Garg is supported in part from DARPA SIEVE Award, AFOSR Award FA9550-15-1-0274, AFOSR Award FA9550-19-1-0200, AFOSR YIP Award, NSF CNS Award 1936826, DARPA and SPAWAR under contract N66001-15-C-4065, a Hellman Award, a Sloan Research Fellowship and research grants by the Okawa Foundation, Visa Inc., and Center for Long-Term Cybersecurity (CLTC, UC Berkeley). The views expressed are those of the author and do not reflect the official policy or position of the funding agencies.

A   Instantiations

In the following we survey the existing candidate VDF schemes and we discuss the implications of our results.

A.1   Compute-and-Prove VDF

The original work of Boneh et al. [5] discusses an instantiation for VDF based on any (conjectured) inherently sequential function and a succinct non-interactive argument system (SNARG) [14,17]. The prover simply evaluates the function on a randomly chosen input and computes a short proof that the computation is done correctly. However, such an approach is dismissed since the time to compute a SNARG is typically much longer than that needed for the corresponding relation. Therefore, to achieve meaningful sequentiality guarantees, the prover needs to resort to massive parallelization which requires a number of processors linear in the time parameter T.

For this reason they turned their attention to incremental verifiable computation schemes [21]. Such a primitive derives from the recursive composition of SNARGs and allow one to compute the proof incrementally as the computation proceeds. However, this feature comes at a cost: The number of recursions introduces an exponential factor in the running time of the extractor and therefore the schemes can be shown sound only for a constant amount of iterations. Other constructions [3] circumvent this issue by constructing computation trees of constant depth, however the overhead given by the recursive application of a SNARG is typically the bottleneck of the computation.

Our approach can be seen as a lightweight composition theorem for VDFs and rehabilitates the compute-and-prove paradigm using standard SNARGs in conjunction with iterated sequential functions: Most of the existing SNARG schemes can be computed in time quasi-linear in T [2] and can be parallelized to meet our weak efficiency requirements using a poly-logarithmic amount of processors (in the time parameter T). Our compiler shows that the combination of SNARGs and iterated sequential functions already gives a tightly sequential VDF, for any value of T.

A.2   Wesolowski's VDF

A recent work by Wesolowski [22] builds an efficient VDF exploiting the conjectured sequentiality of repeated squaring in groups of unknown order, such as RSA groups [19] or class groups of imaginary quadratic order [7]. Loosely speaking, given a random instance $x \in \mathbb{G}$ and a time parameter T, the sequential function is defined as $f(x) = x^{2^T}$. Wesolowski proposes a succinct argument for the corresponding language

$$\mathcal{L} = \left\{ (\mathbb{G}, x, y, T) : y = x^{2^T} \right\}$$

where the verification is much faster than recomputing the function from scratch. The argument goes as follows:

(1) The verifier samples a random prime p from the set of the first 2^λ primes.
(2) The prover computes $q, r \in \mathbb{Z}$ such that $2^T = pq + r$ and outputs $\pi = x^q$ as the proof.
(3) The proof π can be verified by checking that $\pi^p x^r = y$, where r is computed as $2^T \bmod p$.

The argument can be made non-interactive using the Fiat-Shamir transformation [13]. Note that the value of q cannot be computed by the prover explicitly since the order of the group is unknown, however it can be computed in the exponent of x in time close to T.

Wesolowski's proof consists of a single group element and the verifier workload is essentially that of two exponentiations in $\mathbb{G}$. The main shortcoming of the scheme is that the time to compute a valid proof is proportional to the time to compute the function. However, Wesolowski briefly explains how to reduce this overhead to a constant factor using parallel processors. The modification sketched in his paper is essentially an ad-hoc version of our compiler.

A.3 Pietrzak's VDF

Recently, Pietrzak [18] also showed an efficient succinct argument for the same language $\mathcal{L}$, taking a slightly different route. In the following we briefly recall the backbone of the argument:

(1) If $T = 1$, the verifier simply checks that $x^2 = y$.
(2) Else the prover computes $z = x^{2^{T/2}}$ and sends it to the verifier.
(3) The verifier samples some $r \in \{1, \ldots, 2^\lambda\}$.
(4) The prover and the verifier recurse on input $(\mathbb{G}, x^r z, z^r y, T/2)$.

The resulting argument is less efficient than Wesolowski's approach in terms of proof size and verifier complexity by a factor of $log(T)$. However Pietrzak's argument can be computed in time approximately $\sqrt{T}$ using roughly $\sqrt{T}$ memory by storing some intermediate values of the function evaluation.

It is clear that such a VDF fulfills the conditions to apply our compiler and allows us to truncate the additional $\sqrt{T}$ factor from the proof computation. Due to the increased proof size, it might appear that the resulting scheme is strictly worse than that obtained by combining our compiler with Wesolowski's approach. However the significantly shorter proving time allows us to give a sharper bound on the number of recursion of our algorithm: In each iteration the new time parameter is computed as $1/2\sqrt{4T+1}-1$ and therefore approximately $log log(T)$ iterations suffice to hit the bottom of the recursion. As a consequence, Pietrzak's argument needs less parallelism to achieve optimal prover runtime. We also point out that Pietrzak's argument rests on a weaker assumption, as discussed in [6].

References

1. Armknecht, F., Barman, L., Bohli, J.-M., Karame, G.O.: Mirror: enabling proofs of data replication and retrievability in the cloud. In: 25th SENIX Security Symposium (USENIX Security 16), pp. 1051–1068 (2016)

2. Ben-Sasson, E., Chiesa, A., Tromer, E., Virza, M.: Scalable zero knowledge via cycles of elliptic curves. In: Garay, J.A., Gennaro, R. (eds.) CRYPTO 2014. LNCS, vol. 8617, pp. 276–294. Springer, Heidelberg (2014). https://doi.org/10.1007/978-3-662-44381-1_16

3. Bitansky, N., Canetti, R., Chiesa, A., Tromer, E.: Recursive composition and bootstrapping for SNARKS and proof-carrying data. In: Boneh, D., Roughgarden, T., Feigenbaum, J. (eds.) 45th Annual ACM Symposium on Theory of Computing, Palo Alto, CA, USA, 1–4 June, pp. 111–120. ACM Press (2013)

4. Bitansky, N., Goldwasser, S., Jain, A., Paneth, O., Vaikuntanathan, V., Waters, B.: Time-lock puzzles from randomized encodings. In: Sudan, M. (ed.) ITCS 2016: 7th Conference on Innovations in Theoretical Computer Science, Cambridge, MA, USA, 14–16 January, pp. 345–356. Association for Computing Machinery (2016)

5. Boneh, D., Bonneau, J., Bünz, B., Fisch, B.: Verifiable delay functions. In: Shacham, H., Boldyreva, A. (eds.) CRYPTO 2018. LNCS, vol. 10991, pp. 757–788. Springer, Cham (2018). https://doi.org/10.1007/978-3-319-96884-1_25

6. Boneh, D., Bünz, B., Fisch, B.: A survey of two verifiable delay functions. Cryptology ePrint Archive, Report 2018/712 (2018). https://eprint.iacr.org/2018/712

7. Buchmann, J., Williams, H.C.: A key-exchange system based on imaginary quadratic fields. J. Cryptol. 1(2), 107–118 (1988). https://doi.org/10.1007/BF02351719

8. Chia network second VDF competition. https://www.chia.net/2019/04/04/chia-network-announces-second-vdf-competition-with-in-total-prize-money.en.html. Accessed 22 Apr 2019

9. Cohen, B.: Proofs of space and time. Blockchain protocol analysis and security engineering (2017). https://cyber.stanford.edu/sites/default/files/bramcohen.pdf

10. Cohen, B., Pietrzak, K.: Simple proofs of sequential work. In: Nielsen, J.B., Rijmen, V. (eds.) EUROCRYPT 2018. LNCS, vol. 10821, pp. 451–467. Springer, Cham (2018). https://doi.org/10.1007/978-3-319-78375-8_15

11. Döttling, N., Lai, R.W.F., Malavolta, G.: Incremental proofs of sequential work. In: Ishai, Y., Rijmen, V. (eds.) EUROCRYPT 2019. LNCS, vol. 11477, pp. 292–323. Springer, Cham (2019). https://doi.org/10.1007/978-3-030-17656-3_11

12. De Feo, L., Masson, S., Petit, C., Sanso, A.: Verifiable delay functions from supersingular isogenies and pairings. Cryptology ePrint Archive, Report 2019/166 (2019). https://eprint.iacr.org/2019/166

13. Fiat, A., Shamir, A.: How to prove yourself: practical solutions to identification and signature problems. In: Odlyzko, A.M. (ed.) CRYPTO 1986. LNCS, vol. 263, pp. 186–194. Springer, Heidelberg (1987). https://doi.org/10.1007/3-540-47721-7_12

14. Kilian, J.: A note on efficient zero-knowledge proofs and arguments (extended abstract). In: 24th Annual ACM Symposium on Theory of Computing, Victoria, BC, Canada, 4–6 May, pp. 723–732. ACM Press (1992)

15. Mahmoody, M., Moran, T., Vadhan, S.P.: Publicly verifiable proofs of sequential work. In: Kleinberg, R.D. (ed.) ITCS 2013: 4th Innovations in Theoretical Computer Science, Berkeley, CA, USA, 9–12 January, pp. 373–388. Association for Computing Machinery (2013)

16. Mahmoody, M., Smith, C., Wu, D.J.: A note on the (im)possibility of verifiable delay functions in the random oracle model. Cryptology ePrint Archive, Report 2019/663 (2019). https://eprint.iacr.org/2019/663

17. Micali, S.: CS proofs (extended abstracts). In: 35th Annual Symposium on Foundations of Computer Science, Santa Fe, NM, USA, 20–22 November, pp. 436–453. IEEE Computer Society Press (1994)

18. Pietrzak, K.: Simple verifiable delay functions. In: Blum, A. (ed.) ITCS 2019: 10th Innovations in Theoretical Computer Science Conference, San Diego, CA, USA, 10–12 January, vol. 124, pp. 60:1–60:15. LIPIcs (2019)
19. Rivest, R.L., Shamir, A., Adleman, L.M.: A method for obtaining digital signature and public-key cryptosystems. Commun. Assoc. Comput. Mach. **21**(2), 120–126 (1978)
20. Rivest, R.L., Shamir, A., Wagner, D.A.: Time-lock puzzles and timed-release crypto. Technical Report MIT/LCS/TR-684 (1996)
21. Valiant, P.: Incrementally verifiable computation or proofs of knowledge imply time/space efficiency. In: Canetti, R. (ed.) TCC 2008. LNCS, vol. 4948, pp. 1–18. Springer, Heidelberg (2008). https://doi.org/10.1007/978-3-540-78524-8_1
22. Wesolowski, B.: Efficient verifiable delay functions. Cryptology ePrint Archive, Report 2018/623 (2018). https://eprint.iacr.org/2018/623

Multiparty Computation

Black-Box Constructions of
Bounded-Concurrent Secure Computation

Sanjam Garg[1], Xiao Liang[2]([✉])[iD], Omkant Pandey[2], and Ivan Visconti[3]

[1] University of California, Berkeley, USA
sanjamg@berkeley.edu
[2] Stony Brook University, Stony Brook, USA
{liang1,omkant}@cs.stonybrook.edu
[3] University of Salerno, Fisciano, Italy
visconti@unisa.it

Abstract. We construct a general purpose secure multiparty computation protocol which remains secure under (a-priori) bounded-concurrent composition and makes only black-box use of cryptographic primitives. Prior to our work, constructions of such protocols required non-black-box usage of cryptographic primitives; alternatively, black-box constructions could only be achieved for super-polynomial simulation based notions of security which offer incomparable security guarantees.

Our protocol has a constant number of rounds and relies on standard polynomial-hardness assumptions, namely, the existence of semi-honest oblivious transfers and collision-resistant hash functions. Previously, such protocols were not known even under sub-exponential assumptions.

Keywords: Multi-party computation · Bounded concurrent composition · Black-box construction · Straight-line extraction

S. Garg—Supported in part from DARPA SIEVE Award, AFOSR Award FA9550-15-1-0274, AFOSR Award FA9550-19-1-0200, AFOSR YIP Award, NSF CNS Award 1936826, DARPA and SPAWAR under contract N66001-15-C-4065, a Hellman Award, a Sloan Research Fellowship and research grants by the Okawa Foundation, Visa Inc., and Center for Long-Term Cybersecurity (CLTC, UC Berkeley). The views expressed are those of the author and do not reflect the official policy or position of the funding agencies.
X. Liang and O. Pandey—Supported in part by DARPA SIEVE Award HR00112 020026, NSF grant 1907908, and a Cisco Research Award. Any opinions, findings and conclusions or recommendations expressed in this material are those of the author(s) and do not necessarily reflect the views of the United States Government, DARPA, NSF, or Cisco.
I. Visconti—This research has been supported in part by the European Union's Horizon 2020 research and innovation programme under grant agreement No 780477 (project PRIViLEDGE.

© Springer Nature Switzerland AG 2020
C. Galdi and V. Kolesnikov (Eds.): SCN 2020, LNCS 12238, pp. 87–107, 2020.
https://doi.org/10.1007/978-3-030-57990-6_5

1 Introduction

Secure multiparty computation (MPC) allows n players to jointly compute a functionality, while no group of (malicious parties) learn anything beyond their inputs and prescribed outputs. Introduced in the seminal works of [25,58], this model has since been studied extensively. General constructions for computing any functionality even when a majority of players are adversarial have been long known. The focus of this work are MPC protocols that only make a black-box use of cryptographic primitives and maintain security in the concurrent setting where several instances of the protocol may execute simultaneously.

Black-Box Constructions. General purpose MPC protocols are often *non-black-box* in nature, i.e., they use the code of the underlying cryptographic primitives at some stage of the computation. For example, a common step in such protocols is to use general-purpose zero-knowledge proofs which perform NP reductions. Non-black use of primitives is usually undesirable since not only is it computationally expensive, it also renders the protocol useless in situations where such code is not available (e.g., primitives based on hardware-tokens). One therefore seeks *black-box* constructions of such protocols which use the underlying primitives only in black-box way (i.e., only through their input/output interfaces).

Black-box constructions of general MPC protocols have received considerable attention recently. In the standalone setting, Ishai et al. [35] (together with Haitner [32]) presented the first black-box construction of general purpose MPC under the minimal assumption of semi-honest oblivious Transfer (OT). Subsequently, Wee [57] reduced the round complexity of these constructions to $O(\log^* n)$, and Goyal [26] to only constant rounds. Very recently, Applebaum et al. [1] showed that 2-round MPC is unachievable by making only black-box use of 2-round OT. In the two-party setting, black-box construction were obtained by Pass and Wee [53] in constant-rounds and Ostrovsky et al. [47] in 5 rounds, which is optimal w.r.t. *black-box proof techniques* [37]. We discuss the concurrent setting next.

Concurrent Security. The standard notion of security for MPC, also called *stand-alone security* considers only a single execution of this protocol. While this is sufficient for many applications, other situations (such as protocol executions over the Internet) require stronger notions of security. This setting, where there may be many protocols executions at the same time, is called the *concurrent* setting. Unfortunately, it is known that stand-alone security does not necessarily imply security in the concurrent setting [19].

To address the above issue, Canetti [10] proposed the notion of *universally composable* (UC) security where protocols maintain their strong simulation based security guarantees even in the presence of other arbitrary protocols. Achieving such strong notion of UC-security turned out to be impossible in the plain model [10,11]. Moreover, Lindell [43,44] proved that even in the special case where only instantiations of the *same* protocol are allowed, standard notion of

polynomial-time simulation is impossible to achieve. (This is called "self composition" and also corresponds to the setting in this work.)

These strong negative results motivated the study of alternative notions of
security. Our focus is the *plain* model where no trusted setup is available. Two
directions that are relevant to us in this model are:

- **Bounded-Concurrent Composition:** in this model, a bound m is fixed
  a-priori, and the protocol design may depend on m. The adversary is allowed
  to participate in at most m simultaneous executions of the protocol. We consider security against *dishonest majority* with *interchangeable* roles, i.e., the
  adversary can choose an arbitrary subset of (all but one) parties to corrupt
  in each session. As in the original (unbounded) setting, the ideal-world simulator is required to run in (expected) polynomial time. Due to the a-priori
  bound, it is feasible to bypass the aforementioned negative results. Lindell
  presented a m-bounded concurrent two-party protocol in $O(m)$-rounds using
  black-box simulation [43]. Subsequently Pass and Rosen [52] presented a constant round two-party protocol and Pass [50] a constant round MPC protocol
  (under improved assumptions), using non-black-box simulation. All general-
  purpose secure-computation protocols in this setting make non-black-box use
  of the underlying cryptographic primitives.
- **Super-Polynomial Simulation:** while it is not directly relevant to this
  work, we build upon techniques developed in the context of super-polynomial
  simulation where the simulator is allowed to run in *super-polynomial time*.
  This relaxation provides somewhat weaker security guarantees (which are,
  nonetheless, meaningful for many functionalities), and allows (unbounded)
  concurrent composition. Three different ways to formulate this notion are
  super-polynomial simulation (SPS) [49], angel-based security [12,55], and
  security with shielded oracles [9].
  Prabhakaran and Sahai [55] provided the initial positive result for SPS security. Although, these early results [6,42,45,55] relied on non-standard/sub-
  exponential assumptions, Canetti, Lin and Pass achieved this notion under
  standard polynomial time assumptions [12] in polynomially many rounds,
  and soon after, Garg et al. [21] in *constant* rounds. The works in [12,45,55]
  actually achieve angel-based security, though only [12] relies on standard polynomial hardness. Subsequently, Goyal et al. [30] presented a $\tilde{O}(\log n)$ round
  construction under the same assumptions.
  Black-box constructions of angel-based secure computation were first presented by Lin and Pass [41] assuming the existence of semi-honest OT, in
  $O(\max(n^\epsilon, R_{OT}))$ rounds, where $\epsilon > 0$ is an arbitrary constant and R_{OT} is
  the round complexity of the underlying OT protocol. (Hence, if the under-
  lying OT protocol has only constant round, the round complexity is $O(n^\epsilon)$.)
  Subsequently, Kiyoshima [38] provided a $\tilde{O}(\log^2 n)$-round construction under
  the same assumption. To achieve constant round constructions, Broadnax
  et al. [9] proposed security with shielded oracles, a notion that lies strictly
  between SPS and angel-based security, along with a constant-round black-
  box construction under polynomial hardness assumptions. Recently, Garg,

Kiyoshima, and Pandey [22] presented a constant-round black-box MPC protocol which achieves SPS security under polynomial hardness assumptions (which are weaker than those in [9] at the cost of (weaker) SPS security).

State of the Art. The notion of bounded-concurrent composition requires standard polynomial-time simulation. It does not follow from security notions that rely on super-polynomial simulation (which are known to have black-box constructions). Consequently, all known constructions of bounded-concurrent secure MPC rely on non-black-box usage of underlying cryptographic primitives.

1.1 Our Contribution

In this work, we seek to construct general-purpose MPC protocols that make only black-box use of cryptographic primitives and remain secure under bounded-concurrent self composition. Furthermore, we seek constructions whose security can be proven under standard polynomial hardness assumptions (although, to the best of our knowledge, such protocols are not known even under, say, sub-exponential assumptions since the simulator must still run in polynomial time).

Towards this goal, we first aim to construct a black-box bounded-concurrent oblivious transfer (OT) protocol. At a high level, this construction relies on non-black-box simulation to handle simulation in the bounded-concurrent setting (along the lines of [3,50]); to ensure that this does not result in non-black-box use of cryptographic primitives, we implement this idea using the "black-box non-black-box" protocol of Goyal et al. [31]. Once we have control over bounded-concurrent simulation, we rely on the OT protocol of Garg et al. [22] to achieve the full oblivious transfer functionality. Unfortunately, implementing this idea is somewhat complex, perhaps in part because abstractions such as "straight-line simulation/extraction" are not straightforward to formalize despite their intuitive appeal. We mitigate this situation by defining a new abstraction which we call (bounded) *robust zero-knowledge*; this notion asks for simulators to work even in the presence of (bounded) external communication which cannot be "rewound" (and therefore, looks very close to UC zero-knowledge [10]). Similar notion has been defined by [40] in the context of non-malleable commitment w.r.t. an external party. Zero-knowledge ($\mathcal{ZK}$) with this robust property allows us to combine the non-black-box simulation techniques with the SPS based proof techniques of [22] to achieve black-box bounded-concurrent OT. An additional feature of our protocol is that it has *constant* rounds.

Along the way, we also present the first "straight-line"[1] extractable commitment scheme that only makes black-box use of semi-honest OTs. This primitive may be useful for other applications, especially for black-box constructions of MPC protocols from minimal assumption.

Having obtained bounded-concurrent security for OT, we proceed to construct bounded-concurrent MPC protocols for all functionalities. This step is executed almost identically to a similar step in [22] and does not require any

---

[1] It means the extraction strategy does not involve rewinding techniques.

additional assumptions. It also maintains the black-box and constant round properties of the original OT protocol. Consequently, we obtain the first general-purpose bounded-concurrent secure MPC protocol that makes only black-box use of cryptographic primitives; furthermore, the protocol has constant rounds and relies only on standard polynomial hardness assumptions.

Theorem 1 (Informal). *Assume the existence of constant-round semi-honest oblivious transfer protocols and collision-resistant hash functions. Then, there exists a constant-round black-box construction of general-purpose MPC that achieves bounded-concurrent security.*

The formal statement is given as Theorem 4 in Sect. 7. This result is essentially a black-box version of Pass's result [50].

1.2 Other Related Works

In addition to the works mentioned in the introduction, there are several works that study security in the concurrent setting. For SPS-security, Pass et al. [51] present a constant-round non-black-box construction of MPC from constant-round semi-honest OT. Dachman-Soled et al. and Venkitasubramaniam [17,56] present a non-black-box construction that satisfies adaptive security. And very recently, Badrinarayanan et al. [2] present a non-black-box 3-round construction assuming sub-exponential hardness assumptions. For angel-based security, Kiyoshima et al. [39] present a constant-round black-box construction albeit under a sub-exponential hardness assumption, and Hazay and Venkitasubramaniam [34] present a black-box construction that achieves adaptive security.

We have not discussed works that focus on other security notions, e.g., input-indistinguishable computation and multiple ideal-query model [28,46,50].

Black-box constructions have been extensively explored for several other primitives such as non-malleable or CCA-secure encryption, non-malleable commitments, zero-knowledge proofs and so on (e.g., [14,16,29,31,48,54]). For concurrent OT, Garay and MacKenzie [20] presented a protocol for independent inputs under the DDH assumption, and Garg et al. [23] proved the impossibility of this task for general input distributions.

2 Overview of Our Techniques

Before describing our approach, we first make some observations. We start by noting that in the context of concurrent secure computation, it is not possible to use rewinding-based simulation techniques since the simulator will have to provide additional outputs during rewinding but the ideal functionality does not deliver more than one output. This is in sharp contrast to concurrent zero-knowledge where the output is simply "yes" since the statement is in the language. While this can be salvaged for certain functionalities as shown by Goyal [27], it is essential to move to straight-line simulators for general functionalities.

In particular, in the bounded-concurrent setting we must move to non-black-box simulation techniques [4].

Let us also note that in some situations, particularly in the setting of resettable zero-knowledge, a long line of work shows that it is possible to perform non-black-box simulation under one-way functions [7,8,15]. Furthermore, a black-box version of these simulation techniques under one-way functions was obtained by Ostrovsky, Scafuro, and Venkitasubramaniam [48]. It therefore seems possible to construct bounded-concurrent MPC under the minimal assumption of semi-honest OT in a black-box manner.[2] Unfortunately, this approach is flawed since *all* known non-black-box simulation techniques are based on rewinding and therefore cannot be applied to the concurrent MPC setting. It is also not at all clear if "straight-line" simulatable zero-knowledge based only on one-way functions can be constructed from known approaches. Therefore, we stress that *even without the requirement of black-box usage of primitives, constructing bounded-concurrent MPC under semi-honest OT only remains as a fascinating open problem.*

We therefore attempt to obtain a construction that exploits collision-resistant hash functions, in addition to the minimal assumption of semi-honest OTs. Toward this goal, we build upon techniques developed in the following two works:

1. Garg, Kiyoshima, and Pandey [22] construct a constant-round black-box MPC protocol with SPS-security under polynomial hardness assumptions. The simulator works by extracting crucial information from adversary's messages via brute-force. The simulator is straight-line and such extraction steps are the only non-polynomial work in its execution.
2. Goyal et al. [31] present a black-box implementation of the non-black-box simulation techniques that rely on adversary's code [3]. Such techniques often (and certainly those of [3,31]) extend to situations where the adversary may receive arbitrary but *a-priori bounded* amount of external communication.

At a high level, our main idea is to use the simulation technique of [31] to replace the brute-force extraction steps in [22] with polynomial-time extraction using adversary's code. The corresponding commitment scheme will be interactive. Since this simulator is polynomial time, we can hope to get bounded-concurrent MPC (in contrast to SPS MPC). Implementing this idea turns out to be rather involved. The fact that the commitment protocol is interactive brings its own issues of non-malleability and also interferes with some key proof steps in [22] which rely on rewinding. It is also not enough that the underlying commitment protocol be extractable in a "bounded-concurrent" setting; instead we need a more flexible notion (that, roughly speaking, mirrors straight-line simulation).

Although we have non-black-box simulation techniques at our disposal, we do not rely on the multiple slots approach of Pass [50] to build simulation soundness directly into our protocols. Instead, by relying on the techniques in the

---

[2] In some works, when the construction is black-box but the proof of security uses non-black-box techniques (as in this paper), this is referred to as a semi-black-box protocol.

aforementioned two works, we obtain a more modular approach where non-malleability and simulation soundness are obtained with the help of an underlying non-malleable commitment. In this sense, the structure of our bounded-concurrent protocol is fundamentally different from that of [50] to achieve bounded-concurrent MPC. We now provide more details.

The high-level structure of our protocol is similar to that of [22] where the MPC protocol is obtained in two steps. First, we obtain a (constant-round) black-box construction of a bounded-concurrent OT protocol. Next, we compose this OT protocol with an existing constant-round OT-hybrid UC-secure MPC protocol. We elaborate on each step below. We remark that we consider concurrent security in the interchangeable-roles setting. So, in the case of OT, the adversary can participate in a session as the sender while concurrently participating in another session as the receiver.

2.1 Black-Box (Constant-Round) Bounded-Concurrent OT

Our OT protocol is very similar to the OT protocol of [22] (which in turn is based on the high-level cut-and-choose structure of [41] inspired from [13,33,57]) except that we will implement the basic commitment scheme using a "straight-line extractable" commitment (with some other properties that we will discussion soon). At a high level, the OT protocol of [22] proceeds as follows:

1. The protocol is based on cut-and-choose techniques. Therefore, as the first step of the protocol, the sender S and the receiver R commit to their challenges for future stages in advance. This step uses a two-round statistically binding commitment scheme Com. This step avoids selective opening attacks. The ideal-world simulator can extract these challenges by brute-force to perform the simulation. This is the only non-polynomial time step of this simulator (and the one we wish to replace).
2. Next, S and R execute many instances of a semi-honest OT protocol in parallel, where in each instance S and R use the inputs and the randomness that are generated by a coin-tossing protocol.
3. Next, S and R use a non-malleable commitment scheme NMCom to set up a "trapdoor statement" which, roughly speaking, commits a witness to the fact that the trapdoor statement is false. This step, following [21], makes it possible to commit to a false witness in the security proof while ensuring (due to non-malleability of NMCom) that the adversary still continues to commit to a correct witness (so that his statement is still false). The step is performed by modifying different stages of **one session at a time**. This ensures that changes in one interactive part of the protocol are not affected by what happens in later stages of that same session.
4. Finally, S and R use OT combiner which allows them to execute an OT with their real inputs securely when most of the OT instances in the previous steps are correctly executed. To check that most of the OT instances in the previous steps were indeed correctly executed, S and R do use cut-and-choose where S (resp., R) chooses a constant fraction of the OT instances randomly and

R (resp., S) reveals the input and randomness that it used in those instances so that S (resp., R) can verify whether R executed those instances correctly.

Replacing Com with Straight-Line Extractable Commitments. Our goal is to eliminate brute-force extraction using code of the adversary. In doing so, we have to ensure that (1) the interactive nature of the commitment protocol so obtained does not result into new malleability issues in the proof; and (2) the extraction step can be done in a modular fashion (especially in straight-line) so that we can keep the overall proof structure of [22] where one session is modified at a time.

As a starting point, let us consider the Barak-Lindell extractable commitment scheme [5]. In their construction, the committer C first sends an enhanced trapdoor permutation f.[3] Then the two parties involve in the following 3-step coin tossing: (1) R sends a commitment $\mathsf{Com}(r_1)$ to a random string r_1; (2) C replies with a random string r_2; (3) R then sends r_1 with a $\mathcal{ZK}$ argument on the fact that this r_1 is indeed the random string he committed in step (1). Both parties learn the value $r = r_1 \oplus r_2$ as the output of the coin tossing. To commit to a (single-bit) message σ, C sends σ masked by the hard-core bit of $f^{-1}(r)$. An extractor can use the $\mathcal{ZK}$ simulator to bias the coin-tossing result to some value r', for which it knows the preimage of $f^{-1}(r')$. Thus, it can extract the committed value.

Straight-Line Extraction. To adapt the above scheme for our purpose, we need to ensure that the construction is black-box *and* that the committed value can be extracted in a straight-line fashion. Toward this goal, we replace R's commitment and $\mathcal{ZK}$ argument with the protocol of Goyal et al. [31]. More specifically, [31] provides a "commit-and-prove" primitive Π_{ZK} where:

- they provide a (non-interactive statistically-binding) commitment scheme[4] called VSSCom using which one can send a commitment y to a string x;
- and later, prove to a verifier, that "y is a commitment to string x such that $\phi(x) = 1$" where ϕ is an arbitrary function.

In particular, ϕ is chosen to be the $\mathcal{NP}$-relation for an $\mathcal{NP}$-complete language in [31] to get a black-box version of Barak's result [3].

In our case, we will choose ϕ to be the identity function $I_x(\cdot)$.[5] Therefore, the Barak-Lindell commitment protocol mentioned above can be implemented in a black-box manner by ensuring that: (1) R uses VSSCom to prepare the

---

[3] In their original construction, C sends a trapdoor permutation (TDP) f and then proves in zero-knowledge that f is indeed a valid TDP. To make this step black-box, C can send an enhanced TDP instead (without the need of $\mathcal{ZK}$ proof).

[4] In [31], this commitment is actually required to be statistically-hiding. But it can be replaced with a statistically-binding scheme if certain modifications are made to the proof phase. See [24] for more details.

[5] Note $I_x(y) = 1$ if and only if $y = x$ is well defined and the "code" of I_x requires only the knowledge of x.

commitment to r_1, and (2) protocol Π_{ZK} is the aforementioned proof protocol with $\phi := I_{r_1}(\cdot)$.

At a high level, this approach meets our needs for a black-box construction that supports straight-line extraction. But more caution is needed to handle the actually simulation as we are in the (bounded) *concurrent* setting. We will address this concern soon (see the discussion in the **Robust-ZK for Bounded Concurrency** part below).

Removing TDPs. Since we aim to have a construction assuming only semi-honest OTs (and CRHFs), we also want to remove the reliance on the (enhanced) TDPs. As the first attempt, we ask C to secret-share the message σ to n random shares using exclusive-or. Then let the receiver learn through a special OT (e.g. an $n/2$-out-of-n OT) half of these shares. Next, we invoke the above (black-box) version of coin-tossing in Barak-Lindell protocol to determine another $n/2$ shares that C will decommit to. Due to the pseudo-randomness of the coin-tossing result, R will learn the the shares that "complement" what he learned through OT with only negligible probability. Thus, we can hope to achieve (computational) hiding. Meanwhile, an extractor could always bias the coin-tossing result to the complement shares, thus allowing it to extract the value σ.

However, there are several issues with this approach. First, the sender's (committer's) input to the OT must be the decommitment information to the secret shares. Otherwise, a malicious sender can use arbitrary values in the OT execution, which will disable our extraction strategy.[6] Also, this construction suffers from *selective opening attacks* (SOAs) as the values in the commitments are correlated. It is not clear how we can use standard techniques (e.g. asking R to commit to his challenges in advance, or using another coin-tossing to determine his challenges) to get rid of SOAs. This is because we need to keep R's challenges in this stage hidden from C (to ensure extractability).

To solve this problem, we let C commit to $2n$ secret shares of σ, denoted as $\{\mathsf{Com}(s_{i,b})\}_{i\in[n],b\in\{0,1\}}$. Then n 1-out-of-2 OT instances are executed in parallel, where R learns (the decommitment to) one share out of $(s_{i,0}, s_{i,1})$ in the i-th OT. Next, we can use the Barak-Lindell coin tossing to determine an n-bit string $r = r_1\|\ldots\|r_n$. Finally, C decommits to $\{\mathsf{Com}(s_{i,r_i})\}_{i\in[n]}$. In this construction, R's input to (a single) OT can be guessed correctly with probability $1/2$. By a careful design of hybrids, we show this is sufficient to get rid of SOAs, thus allowing us to prove hiding property (See Sect. 5). Moreover, the extractor can still learn all the shares by biasing r_i to the complement to its input in the i-th OT instance (for all $i \in [n]$).

Merging with [22]. Finally, to ensure that the interactive nature does not create non-malleability issues, we will ask each party to commit to a long-enough random string, using the above extractable commitment. This step is done as the foremost step in our OT protocol (called "Step 0"). Then each party will use

---

[6] Note that we cannot ask the committer to prove in zero-knowledge that he uses the committed shares as sender's input in the OT execution, because such proof will make non-black-box use of both the commitment and OT.

the long random string as one-time pad to "mask" the values that they want to commit to during the execution of our OT protocol. Now, we can rely on the structure of the hybrid proof of [22], which first deals with all stages of a given session and then moves on to the next session in a specific order (determined by the transcript). The key observation here is that since Step 0 is performed ahead of all other steps for a fixed session s, changes in later stages of s cannot affect what happens in Step 0 (for example, issues of malleability and simulation-soundness do not arise). Furthermore, since any rewinding-based proofs of [22] are only relevant to later stages, they do not rewind Step 0 of sessions s.

Remark 1. Ostrovsky et al. [48] showed how to achieve the same as [31] while relaxing the assumption from CRHFs to one-way functions (OWFs). But we cannot use their approach (or any of the prior approaches that perform non-black-box simulation under OWFs) since simulators in these approaches are not straight-line. It uses both the adversary's code **and** rewinding to get a OWF-based construction.

Robust-$\mathcal{ZK}$ for Bounded Concurrency. The final issue that we need to address is how the non-black-box simulation will actually be performed corresponding to protocol Π_{ZK} (in Step 0) mentioned above. The main issue is that there are concurrently many sessions of Π_{ZK} executing simultaneously. In particular, if there are m sessions of OT protocol, then there will be $\ell = 2m$ sessions of Π_{ZK}. Simply replacing the prover with the non-black-box simulator may not result in polynomial-time simulation.

An immediate idea is that if Π_{ZK} is *bounded-concurrent $\mathcal{ZK}$* for up to ℓ sessions, then we can use the *concurrent* non-black-box simulator to simulate Step 0 of all m sessions of the OT protocol at once. This allows us to bias coin-tossing for all m sessions and then we can design hybrids exactly as in [22].

Unfortunately, bounded-concurrent $\mathcal{ZK}$ only guarantees *self* composition; i.e., it can only deal with messages of protocol Π_{ZK}. In our case, Π_{ZK} is part of a larger protocol execution and the adversary receives messages from different stages of all sessions. We thus need a more robust notion of non-black-box simulation which, roughly speaking, (a) is straight-line, and (b) enables bounded-concurrent composition of $\mathcal{ZK}$ protocols *even in the presence of external messages* as long as the total communication outside the $\mathcal{ZK}$ protocol is a-priori bounded.

We formulate this notion explicitly in Sect. 4 and call it *robust zero-knowledge*. The notion requires that the view of a (standalone) verifier V^* who interacts with an external party B can be simulated by a simulator S only on input the code of V^*. The simulator is not allowed to rewind V^* or B. However, both B and S are allowed to see each others messages (which is essential to make sure that many concurrent instances of the simulators compose seamlessly). This yields a notion that is similar in spirit to UC zero-knowledge [10] and implies bounded-concurrent $\mathcal{ZK}$.

We remark that most $\mathcal{ZK}$ protocols based on non-black-box simulation, with suitable adjustment of parameters, can actually handle *arbitrary* external messages (and not just the messages of the same protocol) without any modification. This observation was first used in Barak's original work [3], and finds applications in other places [5,50,52]. In particular, it also holds for the protocol of Goyal et al. [31] and is implicit in their security proof. Thus, these protocols already achieve the (bounded) robust-$\mathcal{ZK}$ notion. Robust-$\mathcal{ZK}$ is just a convenient tool to help in the hybrid proofs.

By setting the parameters of Π_{ZK} so that it is ℓ-robust-$\mathcal{ZK}$ allows us to replace the provers of Π_{ZK} with simulator instances in Step 0 of any given session s while maintaining the overall structure and sequence of hybrids in [22] where stages of one session are handled at any given time. This gives us m-bounded concurrent OT.

2.2 Composition of OT with OT-hybrid MPC

The final step of our construction is the same as in [22]. Namely, we compose our bounded-concurrent OT protocol with a OT-hybrid UC-secure MPC protocol (i.e., replace each invocation of the ideal OT functionality in the latter with an execution of the former), thereby obtaining a MPC protocol in the plain model. While selecting the parameters, we have to ensure we adjust the parameters of Π_{ZK} to allow long enough messages so that simulation can be performed for the MPC protocol instead of the OT protocol. Since we only proved bounded-concurrent self composition for OT (not full UC-security), we do not get a proof for the MPC protocol right away. Hence, we prove the security by analyzing the MPC protocol directly. In essence, what we do is to observe that the security proof for our OT protocol (which consists of a hybrid argument from the real world to the ideal world) still works even after the OT protocol is composed with a OT-hybrid MPC protocol.

3 Preliminaries

We denote the security parameter by n. We use $\stackrel{c}{\approx}$ to denote computational indistinguishability between two probability ensembles. For a set S, we use $x \stackrel{\$}{\leftarrow} \mathsf{S}$ to mean that x is sampled uniformly at random from S. PPT denotes probabilistic polynomial time and $\mathsf{negl}(\cdot)$ denotes negligible functions. Other relevant concepts include verifiable secret sharing schemes, extractable commitments, (robust) non-malleable commitments, and bounded-concurrent MPC (with interchangeable roles). Due to space constraints, we provide formal descriptions for these definitions in the full version of this paper [24].

4 Robust Zero-Knowledge and Commit-and-Prove

Goyal et al. [31] present a new $\mathcal{ZK}$ argument for $\mathcal{NP}$, assuming only back-box access to CRHFs. Their protocol (with a slight modification) can be interpreted as a "commit-and-prove" ZK. The prove stage relies on Barak's non-black-box simulation [3], thus inheriting the following property: the protocol has a "preamble" phase where the verifier sends a random string r; the simulator is "straight-line" *even in the presence of arbitrary (external) incoming communication of a-priori bounded length $\ell(n)$ once $|r|$ is sufficiently bigger than $\ell(n)$*.

We capture this property by defining the notion of *robust zero-knowledge* in Definition 1. Roughly, it considers the interaction between a prover P and a (dishonest) verifier V^*, where V^* may also interact with an external PPT machine B. A protocol is ℓ-robust ZK if there is a straight-line simulator whose output (Sview) is indistinguishable from the view of V^* in the aforementioned real interaction (Rview), where the size of all the messages that V^* receives from B is bounded by ℓ.[7]

Definition 1 (Robust Zero-Knowledge (Informal)). *An interactive argument system Π for a language $L \in \mathcal{NP}$ is robust $\mathcal{ZK}$ w.r.t. a PPT ITM B if for all PPT ITM V^* there exists a PPT ITM S (called the robust simulator), such that:*

$$\left\{ \mathsf{Rview}_{\Pi,n,x}^{B(y)} \langle P(w), V^*(z) \rangle \right\}_{n,x,w,z,y} \overset{c}{\approx} \left\{ \mathsf{Sview}_{\Pi,n,x}^{B(y)} \langle S(\mathsf{code}[V^*], z), V^*(z) \rangle \right\}_{n,x,z,y}.$$

where $n \in \mathbb{N}, x \in L, w \in R_L(x), z \in \{0,1\}^*, y \in \{0,1\}^*$.

For a polynomial $\ell : \mathbb{N} \to \mathbb{N}$, Π is ℓ-robust zero-knowledge if it is robust w.r.t. every PPT ITM B that sends at most $\ell(n)$ bits. Π is robust zero-knowledge if it is ℓ-robust zero-knowledge for every polynomial ℓ.

It can be shown that the zero-knowledge protocol in [31, Section 4.2] is a black-box ℓ-robust commit-and-prove zero knowledge protocol. That protocol (with slight modifications) consists of two phase: (1) in **VSS Commit Phase**, the prover commits to a witness w; (2) in a **Proof Phase** that may happen alter, the prover proves that the value committed in previous phase is indeed the witness to the common theorem x. We denote this protocol as Π_{GOSV}. It will play an important role in next section (in Protocol 1). Due to page limits, we refer the reader to the full version [24], where we provide more details about Π_{GOSV}, a formal treatment of robust ZK and a lemma that robust ZK implies bounded-concurrent ZK.

5   Straight-Line Extractable Commitments

In this section, we construct an extractable commitment scheme, assuming black-box access to any semi-honest oblivious transfer. The construction (shown in Protocol 1) makes black-box use of a statistically-binding commitment Com and a maliciously-secure oblivious transfer OT. For the OT, we require (computational) indistinguishability-based security against malicious senders, and simulation-based security (ideal/real paradigm) against malicious receivers. Such OTs can be constructed in a black-box manner from any semi-honest OT [32]. To ease the presentation, we show in Protocol 1 a single-bit commitment. It can be easily extend to committing to multi-bit strings by standard techniques (see [24]).

---

[7] A related but very different notion of robustness appears explicitly in the context of non-malleability in [30,42].

Protocol 1. ℓ-Robust Extractable statistically-Binding Commitment

Common Input: Security parameter 1^n, robustness parameter ℓ
Auxiliary Input to C: A bit $\sigma \in \{0,1\}$ to be committed
Commit Phase:

1. C samples $2n$ random bits $\{s_{i,b}\}_{i\in[n],b\in\{0,1\}}$, whose exclusive-or equals σ.
2. C and R involves in $2n$ independent executions of Com in parallel, where C commits to each values in $\{s_{i,b}\}_{i\in[n],b\in\{0,1\}}$ separately. Let $c_{i,b}$ denote the commitment to $s_{i,b}$. Let $d_{i,b}$ denote the decommitment information w.r.t. $c_{i,b}$.
3. R samples independently $n-1$ random bits $\tau_1,\ldots,\tau_{n-1} \xleftarrow{\$} \{0,1\}^{n-1}$. C and R involves in n independent executions of OT in parallel. For the i-th OT execution ($i \in [n-1]$), C acts as the sender with the two private input set to $\mathsf{Inp}_0^{(i)} = d_{i,0}$ and $\mathsf{Inp}_1^{(i)} = d_{i,1}$. R acts as the receiver with input τ_i. Note that at the end of this stage R learns $\{d_{i,\tau_i}\}_{i\in[n-1]}$. R rejects if any of these decommitments are invalid.
4. R samples uniformly at random a bit $\tau_n \xleftarrow{\$} \{0,1\}$. C and R involves in an execution of OT where C acts as the sender with the two private input set to $\mathsf{Inp}_0^{(n)} = d_{n,0}$ and $\mathsf{Inp}_1^{(n)} = d_{n,1}$. R acts as the receiver with input τ_n. Note that at the end of this stage R learns d_{n,τ_n}. R rejects if d_{n,τ_n} is not a valid decommitment w.r.t. c_{n,τ_n}.[8]
5. C and R run a coin-tossing protocol:

    (a) R samples a random string $r_1 \xleftarrow{\$} \{0,1\}^n$ and runs the VSS **Commit Phase** of Protocol Π_{GOSV} to generate $c_{r_1} = \mathsf{VSSCom}(r_1)$. R sends c_{r_1}.
    (b) C chooses a random string $r_2 \xleftarrow{\$} \{0,1\}^n$ and sends r_2.
    (c) R sends r_1 (without decommitment information)
    (d) R and C run the **Proof Phase** of Protocol Π_{GOSV} with robustness parameter $\ell(n)$ to prove that the string r_1 sent by R in Step 5-(c) is indeed the value it committed to in Step 5-(a).

    The output of the coin-tossing phase is $\mathsf{ch} = r_1 \oplus r_2$. For $i \in [n]$, let ch_i denote the i-th bit of ch.
6. C sends to R the values $\{d_{i,\mathsf{ch}_i}\}_{i\in[n]}$. Note that these are the decommitments to $\{c_{i,\mathsf{ch}_i}\}_{i\in[n]}$ in Step 2. R rejects if any of these decommitments are invalid.

Reveal Phase:

1. C sends to R the values $\{d_{i,b}\}_{i\in[n],b\in\{0,1\}}$ (aka all the decommitments).
2. R rejects if any of the decommitments is invalid; otherwise, R computes the decommitted value as $\sigma = \oplus_{i,b}s_{i,b}$. (Note that $s_{i,b}$ is contained in $d_{i,b}$.)

Theorem 2. *Protocol 1 is a straight-line extractable statistically-binding commitment scheme, which accesses the underlying primitives in a black-box manner.*

---

[8] We remark that this step can actually happen in parallel with the OT instances in Step 3. It is put here (only) to ease the presentation of the security proof. In [24], we talk about how the proof can be modified to accommodate the case where the Step-4 OT happens in parallel with Step 3.

Proof. The construction is black-box as we use the black-box commit-and-prove of [31] in the coin-tossing step. Statistically-binding property follows directly from that of the Step-2 commitment scheme Com. But the proofs for hiding property and extractability are more involved. In the following, we describe the ideas behind them. The complete proof can be found in [24].

Computationally-Hiding Property. We want to build a sequence of hybrids, where we switch from the honest commitment to a bit σ to the commitments to $\overline{\sigma} := \sigma \oplus 1$, without being distinguished by any PPT malicious receiver R^*. To do that, we first substitute the OT instance in Step 4 with the ideal OT functionality $\mathcal{F}_{\mathsf{OT}}$ (thanks to its simulation-based security against malicious receivers). Now the hybrid will learn in Step 4 the (ideal-world) R^*'s input b to this OT instance, while R^* has (information-theoretically) no information about $s_{n,1-b}$. Recall that $\{s_{i,b}\}$ are random secret shares of σ. Thus, the hybrid can switch to a commitment to $\overline{\sigma}$ by simply changing $s_{n,1-b}$ to $\overline{s}_{n,1-b} := s_{n,1-b} \oplus 1$, in the Step-2 commitment. The computational indistinguishability can essentially be reduced to that of Com. Note that the hybrid will not learn b until Step 4, so it has to make a random guess when it prepares $\{s_{i,b}\}$ in Step 1 and 2. This will result in a loss of $1/2$ adversarial advantage in our reduction to the hiding of Com. Also, there is another $1/2$ factor due to the possibility that the last bit of Step-5 coin tossing hits $(1 - b)^9$ (recall that we cannot open $c_{n,1-b}$ as the hybrid lies about it). Therefore, the adversarial advantage will be reduced by a (multiplicative) factor of $1/4$ in total. But this is still enough for us to finish the reduction.

Extractability. First, note that there exists a simulator for Step-5 coin tossing which can bias the result to any target value. This can be done relying on the ZK simulator for Step 5d (same as in Barak-Lindell extractable commitment [5]) plus the sender's security of OT. Therefore, the extractor can work in the following way: it first uses a random τ as the honest receiver in the OT instances, which allows him to learn $\{s_{i,\tau_i}\}_{i\in[n]}$; then it biases the coin-tossing result to $\overline{\tau}$, which will let him learn $\{s_{i,\overline{\tau}_i}\}_{i\in[n]}$ from the committer's decommitments. With all shares $\{s_{i,b}\}$, the extractor can compute σ.

6 Our Bounded Concurrent OT Protocol

In this section, we prove the following theorem.

Theorem 3. *Assume the existence of constant-round semi-honest oblivious transfer protocols and collision-resistant hash functions. Then, for every polynomial m, there exists a constant-round protocol that securely computes the ideal OT functionality $\mathcal{F}_{\mathsf{OT}}$ under m-bounded concurrent composition, and it uses the underlying primitives in the black-box way.*

---

9 Note that the security of Step-5 coin tossing ensures that R^* can learn both (decommitments to) $s_{n,0}$ and $s_{n,1}$ with only negligible probability.

At a high-level, we obtain the OT claimed in Theorem 3 by replacing the statistically-binding commitment Com in the OT of [22] (denoted as GKP-OT) with a new commitment based on Protocol 1. Due to space constraints, we give only a high-level description of our construction, highlighting the modifications we made to the GKP-OT, and then talk about the security proof. The formal description of our protocol and security proof are given in the full version [24].

As mentioned in the technical overview (Sect. 2.1), we want to rely on the same simulation technique for GKP-OT, but with an (efficient) alternative way in which the simulator can "extract" the value committed in Com. Let us first recall the (only) two places where Com is used in GKP-OT:

1. In the very beginning (Stage 1), S (resp. R) uses Com to commit to a random set Γ_S (resp. Γ_R), which is used later for cut-and-chose.
2. Next, S (resp. R) uses Com to commit to a random string a^S (resp. a^R) in the (Stage-2) coin tossing, which will later be used as inputs to the parallel execution of several random OT instances (which are in turned used for an OT-combiner stage later).

Since we now have the straight-line extractable commitment (Protocol 1) at our disposal, we may replace Com with Protocol 1. We notice that the GKP simulator Sim_{OT} can be extended to our setting by substituting the brute-forcing with the Protocol-1 extractor. However, this method requires us to insert many intermediate hybrids in carefully-chosen places as we need to ensure that the extractions happen in time, while not disturbing the adjacent hybrids. We thus take the following alternative approach.

Our Approach. We add a new step (called **Stage 0**) in the beginning of GKP-OT, where S (resp. R) commits using Protocol 1 to two random strings ϕ^S and ψ^S (resp. ϕ^R and ψ^R) of proper length. We then continue identically as in GKP-OT with the following modifications:

- In Stage 1, when S (resp. R) needs to commit to Γ_S (resp. Γ_R), he simply sends $\phi^S \oplus \Gamma_S$ (resp. $\phi^R \oplus \Gamma_R$);
- In Stage 2, when S (resp. R) needs to commit to a^S (resp. a^R), he simply sends $\psi^S \oplus a^S$ (resp. $\psi^R \oplus a^R$).

Intuitively, we ask both parties commit to random strings which will later be used as one-time pads to "mask" the values they committed to by Com in the original GKP-OT. The hiding of Γ_S and a^S follows straightforwardly. To allow the simulator to extract them efficiently, it is sufficient to let Sim_{OT} use the extractor of Protocol 1 to extract ϕ^S and ψ^S. This can be done based on two important properties of the extractor for Protocol 1:

1. *Straight-line:* this guarantees that Sim_{OT} can finish the extraction efficiently, free of the exponential-time problem due to recursive rewinding (similar as that for concurrent zero-knowledges [18]).

2. *Robustness:* since Protocol 1 is based on the ℓ-robust ZK (Sect. 4), its extractor inherits the ℓ-robustness. By setting the parameter ℓ carefully, we make sure that the simulator can switch from honest receiver's strategy to the extractor's strategy session by session, even in the presence of (bounded-ly) many other sessions.

Since we put the commitments to those masks in the very beginning, all the extractions can be done before further hybrids are defined. Similar arguments also apply when the receiver is corrupted. Therefore, we can make use of the GKP technique in a modular way to finish the proof of Theorem 3. We refer the reader to [24] for more details.

7   Our Bounded-Concurrent MPC Protocol

In this section, we prove the following theorem.

Theorem 4. *Assume the existence of constant-round semi-honest oblivious transfer protocols and collision-resistant hash functions. Let $\mathcal{F}$ be any well-formed functionality. Then, for every polynomial m, there exists a constant-round protocol that securely computes $\mathcal{F}$ under m-bounded concurrent composition; furthermore, it uses the underlying primitives in the black-box way.*

The protocol and the proofs are identical to those in [22] except that we use the bounded-concurrent secure OT protocol described in previous section. We now provide more details. We focus on the two-party case below (the MPC case is analogous).

Protocol Description. Roughly speaking, we obtain our bounded-concurrent 2PC protocol by composing our bounded-concurrent OT protocol in Sect. 6 with a UC-secure OT-hybrid 2PC protocol. Concretely, let Π_{OT} be our ℓ-bounded-concurrent OT protocol in Sect. 6, and $\Pi_{2PC}^{\mathcal{F}_{OT}}$ be a UC-secure OT-hybrid 2PC protocol with the following property: The two parties use the OT functionality $\mathcal{F}_{OT}$ only at the beginning of the protocol, and they send only randomly chosen inputs to $\mathcal{F}_{OT}$. Then, we obtain our bounded-concurrent 2PC protocol Π_{2PC} by replacing each invocation of $\mathcal{F}_{OT}$ in $\Pi_{2PC}^{\mathcal{F}_{OT}}$ with an execution of Π_{OT} (i.e., the two parties execute Π_{OT} instead of calling to $\mathcal{F}_{OT}$), where all the executions of Π_{OT} are carried out in a synchronous manner, i.e., in a manner that the first message of all the executions are sent before the second message of any execution is sent etc.; furthermore, the bounded-concurrency parameter for Π_{OT} is set to be m' defined as follows: let ν_{2PC} denote the length of all messages of the hybrid 2PC protocol $\Pi_{2PC}^{\mathcal{F}_{OT}}$ protocol (which does not include the length of messages corresponding to OT calls since we are in the hybrid model). Then, we set m' so that the length ℓ of long messages of Π_{OT} would be n bits longer than $\nu_{OT} + \nu_{2PC}$. This can be ensured by setting $m' = a \cdot m$ where a is the smallest integer that is bigger than $\max(\nu_{OT}/\nu_{2PC}, \nu_{2PC}/\nu_{OT})$.

As the UC-secure OT-hybrid 2PC protocol, we use the constant-round 2PC (actually, MPC) protocol of Ishai et al. [36][10], which makes only black-box use of pseudorandom generators (which in turn can be obtained in the black-box way from any semi-honest OT protocol).

Since the OT-hybrid protocol of Ishai et al. [36] (as well as its modification in [22]) is a black-box construction and has only constant number of rounds, our protocol Π_{2PC} is also a black-box construction and has only constant number of rounds.

The security of this protocol can be proved in a similar way as our OT protocol. The formal proof is provided in the full version [24].

References

1. Applebaum, B., Brakerski, Z., Garg, S., Ishai, Y., Srinivasan, A.: Separating two-round secure computation from oblivious transfer. In: 11th Innovations in Theoretical Computer Science Conference (ITCS 2020). Schloss Dagstuhl-Leibniz-Zentrum für Informatik (2020)
2. Badrinarayanan, S., Goyal, V., Jain, A., Khurana, D., Sahai, A.: Round optimal concurrent MPC via strong simulation. In: Kalai, Y., Reyzin, L. (eds.) TCC 2017. LNCS, vol. 10677, pp. 743–775. Springer, Cham (2017). https://doi.org/10.1007/978-3-319-70500-2_25
3. Barak, B.: How to go beyond the black-box simulation barrier. In: 42nd FOCS, pp. 106–115. IEEE Computer Society Press (2001). https://doi.org/10.1109/SFCS.2001.959885
4. Barak, B.: Constant-round coin-tossing with a man in the middle or realizing the shared random string model. In: 43rd FOCS, pp. 345–355. IEEE Computer Society Press (2002). https://doi.org/10.1109/SFCS.2002.1181957
5. Barak, B., Lindell, Y.: Strict polynomial-time in simulation and extraction. In: 34th ACM STOC, pp. 484–493. ACM Press (2002). https://doi.org/10.1145/509907.509979
6. Barak, B., Sahai, A.: How to play almost any mental game over the net - concurrent composition via super-polynomial simulation. In: 46th FOCS, pp. 543–552. IEEE Computer Society Press (2005). https://doi.org/10.1109/SFCS.2005.43
7. Bitansky, N., Paneth, O.: From the impossibility of obfuscation to a new non-black-box simulation technique. In: 53rd FOCS, pp. 223–232. IEEE Computer Society Press (2012). https://doi.org/10.1109/FOCS.2012.40
8. Bitansky, N., Paneth, O.: On the impossibility of approximate obfuscation and applications to resettable cryptography. In: Boneh, D., Roughgarden, T., Feigenbaum, J. (eds.) 45th ACM STOC, pp. 241–250. ACM Press (2013). https://doi.org/10.1145/2488608.2488639
9. Broadnax, B., Döttling, N., Hartung, G., Müller-Quade, J., Nagel, M.: Concurrently composable security with shielded super-polynomial simulators. In: Coron, J.-S., Nielsen, J.B. (eds.) EUROCRYPT 2017. LNCS, vol. 10210, pp. 351–381. Springer, Cham (2017). https://doi.org/10.1007/978-3-319-56620-7_13

---

[10] The protocol of Ishai et al. [36] itself does not satisfy the above property, but as shown in [22], it can be easily modified to satisfy it.

10. Canetti, R.: Universally composable security: a new paradigm for cryptographic protocols. In: 42nd FOCS, pp. 136–145. IEEE Computer Society Press (2001). https://doi.org/10.1109/SFCS.2001.959888
11. Canetti, R., Kushilevitz, E., Lindell, Y.: On the limitations of universally composable two-party computation without set-up assumptions. In: Biham, E. (ed.) EUROCRYPT 2003. LNCS, vol. 2656, pp. 68–86. Springer, Heidelberg (2003). https://doi.org/10.1007/3-540-39200-9_5
12. Canetti, R., Lin, H., Pass, R.: Adaptive hardness and composable security in the plain model from standard assumptions. In: 51st FOCS, pp. 541–550. IEEE Computer Society Press (2010). https://doi.org/10.1109/FOCS.2010.86
13. Choi, S.G., Dachman-Soled, D., Malkin, T., Wee, H.: Simple, black-box constructions of adaptively secure protocols. In: Reingold, O. (ed.) TCC 2009. LNCS, vol. 5444, pp. 387–402. Springer, Heidelberg (2009). https://doi.org/10.1007/978-3-642-00457-5_23
14. Choi, S.G., Dachman-Soled, D., Malkin, T., Wee, H.: A black-box construction of non-malleable encryption from semantically secure encryption. J. Cryptol. 31(1), 172–201 (2017)
15. Chung, K.M., Pass, R., Seth, K.: Non-black-box simulation from one-way functions and applications to resettable security. In: Boneh, D., Roughgarden, T., Feigenbaum, J. (eds.) 45th ACM STOC, pp. 231–240. ACM Press (2013). https://doi.org/10.1145/2488608.2488638
16. Cramer, R., et al.: Bounded CCA2-secure encryption. In: Kurosawa, K. (ed.) ASIACRYPT 2007. LNCS, vol. 4833, pp. 502–518. Springer, Heidelberg (2007). https://doi.org/10.1007/978-3-540-76900-2_31
17. Dachman-Soled, D., Malkin, T., Raykova, M., Venkitasubramaniam, M.: Adaptive and concurrent secure computation from new adaptive, non-malleable commitments. In: Sako, K., Sarkar, P. (eds.) ASIACRYPT 2013. LNCS, vol. 8269, pp. 316–336. Springer, Heidelberg (2013). https://doi.org/10.1007/978-3-642-42033-7_17
18. Dwork, C., Naor, M., Sahai, A.: Concurrent zero-knowledge. In: 30th ACM STOC, pp. 409–418. ACM Press (1998). https://doi.org/10.1145/276698.276853
19. Feige, U., Shamir, A.: Witness indistinguishable and witness hiding protocols. In: 22nd ACM STOC, pp. 416–426. ACM Press (1990). https://doi.org/10.1145/100216.100272
20. Garay, J.A., MacKenzie, P.D.: Concurrent oblivious transfer. In: 41st FOCS, pp. 314–324. IEEE Computer Society Press (2000). https://doi.org/10.1109/SFCS.2000.892120
21. Garg, S., Goyal, V., Jain, A., Sahai, A.: Concurrently secure computation in constant rounds. In: Pointcheval, D., Johansson, T. (eds.) EUROCRYPT 2012. LNCS, vol. 7237, pp. 99–116. Springer, Heidelberg (2012). https://doi.org/10.1007/978-3-642-29011-4_8
22. Garg, S., Kiyoshima, S., Pandey, O.: A new approach to black-box concurrent secure computation. In: Nielsen, J.B., Rijmen, V. (eds.) EUROCRYPT 2018. LNCS, vol. 10821, pp. 566–599. Springer, Cham (2018). https://doi.org/10.1007/978-3-319-78375-8_19
23. Garg, S., Kumarasubramanian, A., Ostrovsky, R., Visconti, I.: Impossibility results for static input secure computation. In: Safavi-Naini, R., Canetti, R. (eds.) CRYPTO 2012. LNCS, vol. 7417, pp. 424–442. Springer, Heidelberg (2012). https://doi.org/10.1007/978-3-642-32009-5_25

24. Garg, S., Liang, X., Pandey, O., Visconti, I.: Black-box constructions of bounded-concurrent secure computation. Cryptology ePrint Archive, Report 2020/216 (2020). https://eprint.iacr.org/2020/216

25. Goldreich, O., Micali, S., Wigderson, A.: How to play any mental game or A completeness theorem for protocols with honest majority. In: Aho, A. (ed.) 19th ACM STOC, pp. 218–229. ACM Press (May 1987). https://doi.org/10.1145/28395.28420

26. Goyal, V.: Constant round non-malleable protocols using one way functions. In: Fortnow, L., Vadhan, S.P. (eds.) 43rd ACM STOC, pp. 695–704. ACM Press (2011). https://doi.org/10.1145/1993636.1993729

27. Goyal, V.: Positive results for concurrently secure computation in the plain model. In: 53rd FOCS, pp. 41–50. IEEE Computer Society Press (2012). https://doi.org/10.1109/FOCS.2012.13

28. Goyal, V., Jain, A.: On concurrently secure computation in the multiple ideal query model. In: Johansson, T., Nguyen, P.Q. (eds.) EUROCRYPT 2013. LNCS, vol. 7881, pp. 684–701. Springer, Heidelberg (2013). https://doi.org/10.1007/978-3-642-38348-9_40

29. Goyal, V., Lee, C.K., Ostrovsky, R., Visconti, I.: Constructing non-malleable commitments: a black-box approach. In: 53rd FOCS, pp. 51–60. IEEE Computer Society Press (2012). https://doi.org/10.1109/FOCS.2012.47

30. Goyal, V., Lin, H., Pandey, O., Pass, R., Sahai, A.: Round-efficient concurrently composable secure computation via a robust extraction lemma. In: Dodis, Y., Nielsen, J.B. (eds.) TCC 2015. LNCS, vol. 9014, pp. 260–289. Springer, Heidelberg (2015). https://doi.org/10.1007/978-3-662-46494-6_12

31. Goyal, V., Ostrovsky, R., Scafuro, A., Visconti, I.: Black-box non-black-box zero knowledge. In: Shmoys, D.B. (ed.) 46th ACM STOC, pp. 515–524. ACM Press (2014). https://doi.org/10.1145/2591796.2591879

32. Haitner, I.: Semi-honest to malicious oblivious transfer—the black-box way. In: Canetti, R. (ed.) TCC 2008. LNCS, vol. 4948, pp. 412–426. Springer, Heidelberg (2008). https://doi.org/10.1007/978-3-540-78524-8_23

33. Haitner, I., Ishai, Y., Kushilevitz, E., Lindell, Y., Petrank, E.: Black-box constructions of protocols for secure computation. SIAM J. Comput. 40(2), 225–266 (2011)

34. Hazay, C., Venkitasubramaniam, M.: Composable adaptive secure protocols without setup under polytime assumptions. In: Hirt, M., Smith, A. (eds.) TCC 2016. LNCS, vol. 9985, pp. 400–432. Springer, Heidelberg (2016). https://doi.org/10.1007/978-3-662-53641-4_16

35. Ishai, Y., Kushilevitz, E., Lindell, Y., Petrank, E.: Black-box constructions for secure computation. In: Kleinberg, J.M. (ed.) 38th ACM STOC, pp. 99–108. ACM Press (2006). https://doi.org/10.1145/1132516.1132531

36. Ishai, Y., Prabhakaran, M., Sahai, A.: Founding cryptography on oblivious transfer – efficiently. In: Wagner, D. (ed.) CRYPTO 2008. LNCS, vol. 5157, pp. 572–591. Springer, Heidelberg (2008). https://doi.org/10.1007/978-3-540-85174-5_32

37. Katz, J., Ostrovsky, R.: Round-optimal secure two-party computation. In: Franklin, M. (ed.) CRYPTO 2004. LNCS, vol. 3152, pp. 335–354. Springer, Heidelberg (2004). https://doi.org/10.1007/978-3-540-28628-8_21

38. Kiyoshima, S.: Round-efficient black-box construction of composable multi-party computation. In: Garay, J.A., Gennaro, R. (eds.) CRYPTO 2014. LNCS, vol. 8617, pp. 351–368. Springer, Heidelberg (2014). https://doi.org/10.1007/978-3-662-44381-1_20

39. Kiyoshima, S., Manabe, Y., Okamoto, T.: Constant-round black-box construction of composable multi-party computation protocol. In: Lindell, Y. (ed.) TCC 2014. LNCS, vol. 8349, pp. 343–367. Springer, Heidelberg (2014). https://doi.org/10.1007/978-3-642-54242-8_15

40. Lin, H., Pass, R.: Non-malleability amplification. In: Mitzenmacher, M. (ed.) 41st ACM STOC, pp. 189–198. ACM Press (2009). https://doi.org/10.1145/1536414.1536442

41. Lin, H., Pass, R.: Black-box constructions of composable protocols without set-up. In: Safavi-Naini, R., Canetti, R. (eds.) CRYPTO 2012. LNCS, vol. 7417, pp. 461–478. Springer, Heidelberg (2012). https://doi.org/10.1007/978-3-642-32009-5_27

42. Lin, H., Pass, R., Venkitasubramaniam, M.: A unified framework for concurrent security: universal composability from stand-alone non-malleability. In: Mitzenmacher, M. (ed.) 41st ACM STOC, pp. 179–188. ACM Press (2009). https://doi.org/10.1145/1536414.1536441

43. Lindell, Y.: Bounded-concurrent secure two-party computation without setup assumptions. In: 35th ACM STOC, pp. 683–692. ACM Press (2003). https://doi.org/10.1145/780542.780641

44. Lindell, Y.: Lower bounds for concurrent self composition. In: Naor, M. (ed.) TCC 2004. LNCS, vol. 2951, pp. 203–222. Springer, Heidelberg (2004). https://doi.org/10.1007/978-3-540-24638-1_12

45. Malkin, T., Moriarty, R., Yakovenko, N.: Generalized environmental security from number theoretic assumptions. In: Halevi, S., Rabin, T. (eds.) TCC 2006. LNCS, vol. 3876, pp. 343–359. Springer, Heidelberg (2006). https://doi.org/10.1007/11681878_18

46. Micali, S., Pass, R., Rosen, A.: Input-indistinguishable computation. In: 47th FOCS, pp. 367–378. IEEE Computer Society Press (2006). https://doi.org/10.1109/FOCS.2006.43

47. Ostrovsky, R., Richelson, S., Scafuro, A.: Round-optimal black-box two-party computation. In: Gennaro, R., Robshaw, M. (eds.) CRYPTO 2015. LNCS, vol. 9216, pp. 339–358. Springer, Heidelberg (2015). https://doi.org/10.1007/978-3-662-48000-7_17

48. Ostrovsky, R., Scafuro, A., Venkitasubramanian, M.: Resettably sound zero-knowledge arguments from OWFs - the (semi) black-box way. In: Dodis, Y., Nielsen, J.B. (eds.) TCC 2015. LNCS, vol. 9014, pp. 345–374. Springer, Heidelberg (2015). https://doi.org/10.1007/978-3-662-46494-6_15

49. Pass, R.: Simulation in quasi-polynomial time, and its application to protocol composition. In: Biham, E. (ed.) EUROCRYPT 2003. LNCS, vol. 2656, pp. 160–176. Springer, Heidelberg (2003). https://doi.org/10.1007/3-540-39200-9_10

50. Pass, R.: Bounded-concurrent secure multi-party computation with a dishonest majority. In: Babai, L. (ed.) 36th ACM STOC, pp. 232–241. ACM Press (2004). https://doi.org/10.1145/1007352.1007393

51. Pass, R., Lin, H., Venkitasubramaniam, M.: A unified framework for UC from only OT. In: Wang, X., Sako, K. (eds.) ASIACRYPT 2012. LNCS, vol. 7658, pp. 699–717. Springer, Heidelberg (2012). https://doi.org/10.1007/978-3-642-34961-4_42

52. Pass, R., Rosen, A.: Bounded-concurrent secure two-party computation in a constant number of rounds. In: 44th FOCS, pp. 404–415. IEEE Computer Society Press (2003). https://doi.org/10.1109/SFCS.2003.1238214

53. Pass, R., Wee, H.: Black-box constructions of two-party protocols from one-way Functions. In: Reingold, O. (ed.) TCC 2009. LNCS, vol. 5444, pp. 403–418. Springer, Heidelberg (2009). https://doi.org/10.1007/978-3-642-00457-5_24

54. Peikert, C., Waters, B.: Lossy trapdoor functions and their applications. SIAM J. Comput. **40**(6), 1803–1844 (2011)
55. Prabhakaran, M., Sahai, A.: New notions of security: achieving universal composability without trusted setup. In: Babai, L. (ed.) 36th ACM STOC, pp. 242–251. ACM Press (2004). https://doi.org/10.1145/1007352.1007394
56. Venkitasubramaniam, M.: On adaptively secure protocols. In: Abdalla, M., De Prisco, R. (eds.) SCN 2014. LNCS, vol. 8642, pp. 455–475. Springer, Cham (2014). https://doi.org/10.1007/978-3-319-10879-7_26
57. Wee, H.: Black-box, round-efficient secure computation via non-malleability amplification. In: 51st FOCS, pp. 531–540. IEEE Computer Society Press (2010). https://doi.org/10.1109/FOCS.2010.87
58. Yao, A.C.C.: How to generate and exchange secrets (extended abstract). In: 27th FOCS, pp. 162–167. IEEE Computer Society Press (1986). https://doi.org/10.1109/SFCS.1986.25

Communication-Efficient (Proactive) Secure Computation for Dynamic General Adversary Structures and Dynamic Groups

Karim Eldefrawy[1](✉) [iD], Seoyeon Hwang[2] [iD], Rafail Ostrovsky[3] [iD], and Moti Yung[4] [iD]

[1] SRI International, Menlo Park, CA, USA
karim.eldefrawy@sri.com
[2] University of California Irvine, Irvine, CA, USA
[3] University of California Los Angeles, Los Angeles, CA, USA
[4] Columbia University and Google, New York, NY, USA

Abstract. In modern distributed systems, an adversary's limitations when corrupting subsets of a system's components (e.g., servers) may not necessarily be based on threshold constraints, but rather based on other technical or organizational characteristics. This means that the corruption patterns (and thus protection guarantees) are based on the adversary being limited by what can be captured by a *General Adversary Structure (GAS)*. We consider efficient secure multiparty computation (MPC) under such dynamically-changing GAS settings. In such settings, one desires to protect against and during corruption profile changes; such adaptivity also renders some (secret sharing-based) encoding schemes underlying MPC protocols more efficient than others when operating with the (currently) considered GAS.

One of our contributions is a set of new protocols to efficiently and securely convert back and forth between different MPC schemes for GAS; this process is often called *share conversion*. We consider two MPC schemes, one based on additive secret sharing and the other based on Monotone Span Programs (MSP). The ability to convert between the secret sharing representations of these MPC schemes enables us to construct *the first communication-efficient structure-adaptive proactive MPC protocol for dynamic GAS settings*. By structure-adaptive, we mean that the choice of the MPC protocol to execute in future rounds after the GAS is changed (as specified by an administrative entity) is chosen to ensure communication-efficiency (the typical bottleneck in MPC). Furthermore, since such secure "collaborative" computing may be long-lived, we consider the *mobile adversary setting*, often called the *proactive security setting*. As our second contribution, we construct communication-efficient MPC protocols that can adapt to the proactive security setting. Proactive security assumes that at each (well defined) period of time the adversary corrupts different parties and may visit the entire system overtime and corrupt all parties, provided that in each period it controls groups obeying the GAS constraints. In our protocol, the shares

© Springer Nature Switzerland AG 2020
C. Galdi and V. Kolesnikov (Eds.): SCN 2020, LNCS 12238, pp. 108–129, 2020.
https://doi.org/10.1007/978-3-030-57990-6_6

can be refreshed, meaning that parties receive new shares reconstructing the same secret, and some parties who lost their shares because of the reboot/reset can recover their shares. As our third contribution, we consider another aspect of global long-term computations, namely, that of the dynamic groups. Settings with dynamic groups and GAS were not dealt with in existing literature on (proactive) MPC. In dynamic group settings, parties can be added and eliminated from the computation, under different GAS restrictions. We extend our protocols to this additional dynamic group settings defined by different GAS (see the full version of the paper [18] for formal details of protocols and proofs).

Keywords: Secure multiparty computation · Secret sharing · Share conversion · Dynamic general adversary structures · Monotone span programs · Proactive security

1 Introduction

Secure Multiparty Computation (MPC) is a general primitive consisting of several protocols executed among a set of parties, and has motivated the study of different adversary models and various new settings in cryptography [3,5,7,11,13,14,21,23,28,29]. For groups with more than two parties, i.e., the multiparty setting, secret sharing (SS) is often an underlying primitive used in constructing MPC; SS also has other applications in secure distributed systems and protocols used therein [2,9,10,15–17,20,22].

In typical arithmetic MPC, the underlying SS [8,30] is of the threshold type scheme, i.e., a dealer shares a secret s among n parties such that an adversary that corrupts no more than a threshold t of the parties (called corruption threshold) does not learn anything about s, while any $t + 1$ parties can efficiently recover it. MPC protocols built on top of SS allow a set of distrusting parties $P_1, \ldots, P_n$, with private inputs $x_1, \ldots, x_n$, to jointly compute (in a secure distributed manner) a function $f(x_1, x_2, \ldots, x_n)$ while guaranteeing correctness of its evaluation and privacy of inputs for honest parties. The study of secure computation was initiated by [31] for two parties and [21] for three or more parties. Constructing efficient MPC protocols withstanding stronger adversaries has been an important problem in cryptography and witnessed significant progress since its inception, e.g., [3,4,6,7,11,13,14,25,28,29].

Enforcing a bound on adversary's corruption limit is often criticized as being arbitrary for protocols with long execution times, especially when considering the so-called "reactive" functionalities that continuously run a control loop. Such reactive functionalities become increasingly important, as MPC is adopted to resiliently implement privacy-sensitive control functions in critical infrastructures such as power-grids or command-and-control in distributed network monitoring and defense infrastructure. In those two cases, one should expect resourceful adversaries to continuously attack parties/servers involved in such an MPC, and given enough time, vulnerabilities in underlying software will eventually be found.

An approach to deal with the ability of adversaries to eventually corrupt all parties is the *proactive security model* [28]. This model introduced the notion of a mobile adversary motivated by the persistent corruption of parties in an MPC protocol. A mobile adversary can corrupt all parties in a distributed protocol during the execution of said protocol, but with the following limitations: (i) only a constant fraction (in the threshold setting) of parties can be corrupted during any round of the protocol; (ii) parties periodically get rebooted to a clean initial state, guaranteeing small fraction of corrupted parties, assuming that the corruption rate is not more than the reboot rate[1]. The model also assumes that an adversary cannot predict or reconstruct the randomness used by parties in any uncorrupted period of time, as demarcated by rebooting.

In most (standard and proactive) MPC literature, the adversary's corruption capability is characterized by a threshold t (out of the n parties). More generally, however, the adversary's corruption capability could be specified by a so-called *general adversary structure (GAS)*, i.e., a set of potentially corruptible subsets of parties. Even more generally, it can be specified by a set of corruption scenarios, one of which the adversary can choose (secretly). For instance, each scenario can specify a set of parties that can be passively corrupted and a subset of them that can even be actively corrupted. Furthermore, such scenarios may change over time, thus effectively rendering the GAS describing them to itself be dynamically evolving. There are currently no proactive MPC protocols efficiently handling such dynamic general specifications of adversaries, especially when the group of parties performing MPC is dynamic. The need for secure computation for dynamic groups with changing specifications of the GAS is discussed in more detail in the full version of the paper [18].

Our main objective is to address a setting that is as close as possible to the complex dynamic reality of today's distributed systems. We accomplish this by answering the following question: *Can we design a communication-efficient proactively secure MPC (PMPC) protocol for dynamic groups with security against dynamic general adversary structures?*

Contributions: We answer the above question in the affirmative. One of our main contributions is to build a set of protocols to efficiently convert back and forth between two different MPC schemes for GAS; this process is often called *share conversion*. Specifically, we consider an MPC scheme based on additive secret sharing and another MPC scheme based on Monotone Span Programs (MSP). The ability to efficiently and securely convert between these MPCs enables us to construct *the first communication-efficient structure-adaptive proactive MPC (PMPC) protocol for dynamic GAS settings*. We note that *all* existing proactive secret sharing and PMPC protocols (details in Appendix A and Table 4 in the full version of this paper [18]) can only handle (threshold) adversary structures that describe sets of parties with cardinality less than a fraction of the total number of parties.

---

[1] In our model, rebooting to a clean state includes global information, e.g., circuits to be computed via MPC, identities of parties in the computation, and access to secure point-to-point channels and a broadcast channel.

Given the large number of "moving parts" and complexity of PMPC protocols and the additional complexity for specifying them for GAS, we start from a standard (i.e., non-proactive) MPC protocol with GAS and extend it to the proactive setting for static groups and then dynamic groups. Note that MPC protocols typically extend secret sharing and perform computations on secret shared inputs, we thus focus the discussion in this paper on MPC with the understanding that results also apply to secret sharing.

As part of the proactive protocols, we support the following three functionalities: refreshing shares that reconstructs the same secret, recovering shares of parties who lost them or were rebooted from clear state, and redistributing new shares of the same secret to another group of parties. This implies that we can also deal with dynamic sets of parties, where parties can be eliminated and where parties can be added (i.e., start with a recovery of their shares in a refresh phase). Also, we can deal with settings where the entire set of parties changes and existing secret shared data has to be moved to a new set of parties with a possibly new specification of the GAS they should protect against. This original set of parties then redistributes the shared secrets to the new set (which may, or may not, have some overlap with the original set).

Paper Outline: In Section 2, we overview the typical blueprint of PMPC and briefly discuss the related work and roadblocks/challenges facing constructing communication-efficient structure-adaptive PMPC protocols for dynamic groups and dynamic GAS settings. Section 3 contains necessary preliminaries and specifications of underlying network and communication models, the adversary model, and some other basic building blocks required in the rest of the paper. We then describe the details of the new protocols developed in this paper in Sect. 4. Due to the space limitations, we refer to the full version of the paper [18] for more details of security proofs, complexity comparison tables, and a deeper discussion of the considered settings and related work.

2   Overview of Proactive MPC and Design Roadblocks

This section reviews the typical blueprint of Proactive MPC (PMPC) protocols. Due to space constraints, we discuss details of related work in Appendix A of the full version of the paper [18]. We then discuss roadblocks facing designing communication-efficient structure-adaptive PMPC protocols for GAS.

2.1   Blueprint of Proactive Secret Sharing (PSS) and Proactive MPC (PMPC)

PMPC protocols [3,28] are usually constructed on top of (linear) secret sharing schemes, and involve alternating compute and refresh (and reboot/reset) phases. The refresh phases involve distributed re-randomization of the secret shares, and deleting old ones to ensure that a mobile adversary does not obtain enough shares (from the same phase) that can allow them to violate secrecy of the shared inputs and intermediate compute results. A PMPC protocol usually consist of the following six sub-protocols:

1. **Share**: allows a dealer (typically one of the parties) to share a secret s among the n parties.
2. **Reconstruct**: allows parties to reconstruct a shared secret s using the shares they collectively hold.
3. **Refresh**: is executed between two consecutive phases, w and $w + 1$, and generates new shares for phase $w + 1$ that encode the same secret as, but are independent of the shares in phase w, and erases the old shares.
4. **Recover**: allows parties that lost their shares (due to rebooting/resetting or other reasons) to obtain new shares encoding the same secret s, with the help of other online parties.
5. **Add**: allows parties holding shares of two secrets, s and t, to obtain shares encoding the sum, $s + t$.
6. **Multiply**: allows parties holding shares of two secrets, s and t, to obtain shares encoding the product, $s \cdot t$.

To deal with dynamic groups, where parties can leave, or new parties can join the group, the following additional sub-protocol **Redistribute** is required:

7. **Redistribute**: is executed between two consecutive protocol phases, w and $w + 1$, and allows parties in a new group (in phase $w + 1$) to obtain new shares that encode the same secret as the shares in phase w.

A communication-efficient protocol should thus be structure-adaptive when considering evolving GAS, this means that if the set of parties performing the MPC receives (from an administrator) a request to adapt to a new GAS, for which it is known that another (secret sharing) encoding scheme is more efficient, they need to convert. We stress that this is different than the **Redistribute** protocol, which re-shares a shared secret but *with the same secret sharing scheme*. We require a non-trivial additional protocol to perform such conversion:

8. **Convert**: is executed between two consecutive protocol phases, w and $w + 1$, and allows parties in a new group defined by a new GAS (in phase $w + 1$) to obtain new shares under a different secret sharing scheme but that encode the same secret as the shares in phase w (under the old secret sharing scheme and the old GAS).

2.2 Roadblocks Facing PMPC for Dynamic General Adversary Structures and Dynamic Groups

Starting with an appropriate SS scheme and an MPC protocol for GAS, the following is to be addressed to develop a communication-efficient PMPC protocol for dynamic groups and GAS: (1) design convert protocols to be structure-adaptive, (2) design refresh and recover protocols to proactivize the underlying SS scheme, (3) design a redistribute protocol for settings with dynamic groups, and (4) efficient communication in all protocols. These four issues are discussed in more detail in the full version [18].

3   Preliminaries

This section provides preliminaries required for the rest of the paper. We first provide terminology and other definitions used in this paper. We then discuss the underlying communication model, security guarantees, and the adversary model that we consider. The section concludes by reviewing the information checking and dispute control schemes used in the MPC protocols [24,26] on which we build our protocols.

3.1   Terminology of Proactive Security

Let $\mathcal{P} = \{P_1, ..., P_n\}$ be a set of n participating parties in PMPC protocols. The parties in $\mathcal{P}$ want to compute a function f over a finite field $\mathbb{F}$. Similar to the previous proactive security literature [1,3,19], a proactive protocol proceeds in *phases*. A phase consists of a number of consecutive rounds and every round belongs to exactly one phase. There are two types of phases, *refresh* and *operational*, which alternate. Intuitively, a refresh phase re-randomizes the secret shared data so that attacks in different phases cannot affect each other, while an operational phase performs whatever computations the protocol is designed for. Finally, a *stage* consists of an *opening* refresh phase, an operational phase, and a *closing* refresh phase, i.e., each refresh phase is not only the closing of one stage, but also the opening of another stage. If an adversary corrupts a party P_i during an operational phase, the adversary is given the view of P_i starting from its state at the beginning of the current operational phase. Else if the corruption is made during a refresh phase, the adversary gets the view of P_i in both stages, u and $u + 1$, that include the refresh phase as the closing and the opening and P_i is assumed to be corrupted for the stage $u + 1$. Detailed definitions can be found in Appendix A.4 in full version [18].

3.2   Definitions and Assumptions

In this work, we consider protocols with unconditional security for both passive and active adversaries. In terms of the communication model, we consider a synchronous network of n parties connected by an authenticated broadcast channel and point-to-point channels. Note that without this setting, we do not guarantee the information-theoretic security. The different security guarantees and communication models in the MPC literature are discussed in Appendix A.2 of the full version [18] in more detail. We consider the adversary's capabilities in terms of the *general adversary structure (GAS)*, which is a more general and flexible notion to reason about adversaries (compared to only the threshold limitation on corruptions) and applicable to various cases, e.g. when special combination of parties is needed, when some parties are authorized, etc.

Let $2^{\mathcal{P}}$ denote the set of all the subsets of $\mathcal{P}$. A subset of $2^{\mathcal{P}}$ is called *qualified* if parties in the subset can reconstruct/access the secret, while a subset of $2^{\mathcal{P}}$ that parties in the set obtain no information about the secret is called *ignorant*. Every subset of $\mathcal{P}$ is either qualified or ignorant. The secrecy condition is stronger: even if any ignorant set of parties holds any kind of partial information about the shared value, they must not obtain any additional information about the shared value.

The *access structure* Γ is the set of all qualified subsets of $\mathcal{P}$ and the *secrecy structure* Σ is the set of all ignorant subsets of $\mathcal{P}$. Naturally, Γ includes all supersets of each element in it (so often called *monotone access structure*), while Σ includes all subsets of each element in it. We call such minimum or maximum sets as *basis structure*, and denote it with $\tilde{\cdot}$. i.e., the basis access structure $\tilde{\Gamma}$ is the set of all minimal subsets in Γ, and the basis secrecy structure $\tilde{\Sigma}$ is the set of all maximal subsets in Σ. As a generalization of specifying the adversary's capabilities by a corruption type (passive or active) and a threshold t, an adversary can be described by a corruption type and an adversary structure $\Delta \subseteq \Sigma$. The *adversary structure* Δ is a set of subsets of parties that can be potentially corrupted. The adversary can choose a set in Δ and corrupt all the parties in the set. Note that the adversary structure in t-threshold SS is the set of all subsets of $\mathcal{P}$ of at most t parties and GAS extends this to non-threshold models. A GAS includes all of these structures, (Γ, Σ, Δ).

The types of adversaries can be classified as *passive adversary* and *active adversary*. A passive adversary can only perform passive corruptions on Σ, eavesdropping on all the inputs and outputs of corrupted parties in Σ. i.e., $\Delta = \Sigma$. On the other hand, an active adversary, which is also called (Σ, Δ)-adversary, can passively corrupt some parties in a set A and actively corrupt some parties in a set B, where $A \in \Delta$ and $(A \cup B) \in \Sigma$.

In real-world scenarios, it is natural to deal with *dynamic groups*, which means participating parties can leave and/or newly join in the group performing the computation. Then, the GAS (Γ, Σ, Δ) as well as the participating parties $\mathcal{P}$ may be changed. Therefore, we need one more protocol to deal with dynamic groups, which redistributes new shares to the new group that encodes the same secret as the ones in the previous group. It also needs to prevent leaving parties from using their shares to obtain any information about the secret.

3.3   Information Checking (IC) and Dispute Control

In some of the MPC protocols that we consider, an *information checking (IC)* technique is used to prevent active adversaries from announcing wrong values through corrupted parties. It is a three party protocol among a sender P_s, a receiver P_r, and a verifier P_v. When P_s sends a message m to P_r, P_s also encloses an authentication tag to P_r, while giving a verification tag to P_v through private channels. Whenever any disagreement about what P_s sent to P_r occurs, P_k acts as an objective third party and verifies the authenticity of m to P_r. The MPC protocols in this paper use different variants of IC, but the common idea is to check if all the points that P_r and P_v have lie on the polynomial of degree 1. Note that this can be naturally extended to the polynomial of degree l, where l is the number of secrets in a batch of sharing, as in [26]. An IC scheme consists of two protocols, called `Authenticate` and `Verify`, and because of the space limit, we present each IC protocols in our full version of the paper [18].

MPC protocols in this paper also use the *dispute control* to deal with detected cheaters. This means that each party P_i locally maintains a list $\mathcal{D}_i$ of parties that P_i distrusts, and the list $\mathcal{D}$ of pairs of parties who are in dispute with each other. These lists are empty when the MPC protocol begins, and whenever any dispute arises between two parties P_i and P_j (for example, P_i insists that P_j is lying), the pair $\{P_i, P_j\}$ is added to the dispute list $\mathcal{D}$. Since all disputes are broadcasted, each party P_i has the same list $\mathcal{D}$, while maintaining its own list $\mathcal{D}_i$. After P_j is added to $\mathcal{D}_i$, P_i behaves in all future invocations of the protocol for authentication and verification with P_j as if it fails whether this is the case or not. Some MPC schemes also maintain a list $\mathcal{C}$ of parties that everyone agrees are corrupted.

Table 1. Notations used in this paper. GAS denotes the general adversary structure.

Notation	Explanation
$\mathcal{P} = \{P_1, ..., P_n\}$	A set of participating parties in a protocol
(Γ, Σ, Δ)	The access/secrecy/adversary structures in a GAS
$\mathbb{S}$	A sharing specification describing how shares are distributed
$w, w+1$	A phase (number)
$[s]^w$	A sharing of a secret s in phase w, i.e., a set of shares of s
$\mathbb{F}$	A finite field
$\mathcal{D}$	The (public) list of pairs of parties who are in dispute with each other
$\mathcal{D}_i$	A (local) list of parties that P_i distrusts
$\mathcal{C}$	The (public) list of parties that everyone agrees to their corruptness
M	A matrix from a MSP $\widehat{M} = (\mathbb{F}, M, \rho, \mathbf{r})$[a]
$\mathbf{a}$	A vector (with bold texts)
M_i	A matrix of rows of M assigned to P_i according to an indexing function
M_A	A matrix of rows of M assigned to all $P_i \in A$ according to an indexing function
$\langle , \rangle$	The inner product
$A \setminus B$	The set difference of A and B, i.e., the set of elements in A but not in B
$a \xleftarrow{\$} \mathbb{F}$	Randomly chosen element a from the finite field $\mathbb{F}$

[a] Detailed definitions of components of MSP are provided in Sect. 4.2.

4 Proactive MPC Protocols for Dynamic GAS and Dynamic Groups

As mentioned in Sect. 2, our PMPC protocols build on two MPC protocols with different underlying secret sharing schemes. One is an MPC protocol [24] based on additive secret sharing and the other [26] is based on a monotone span program (MSP) with multiplication. For convenience, we call the former as *additive MPC* and the latter as *MSP-based MPC* in the rest of the paper. Both guarantee unconditional security against active $Q2$ adversaries. $Q2$ means no two sets in Δ cover the entire set of parties; i.e., for $\forall A, B \in \Delta$, $\mathcal{P} \not\subseteq A \cup B$. Table 1 summarizes the notations we use in this paper.

In Sect. 4.1 and Sect. 4.2, we present the *additive PMPC* and *MSP-based PMPC* schemes, respectively, with our new additional protocols to "proactivize" each MPC scheme. We formalize the base protocols of [24] and [26] in our full version [18] and focus on our new protocols in the main body of the paper. For proactivizing a MPC protocol, we develop two new main protocols, called Refresh and Recover, and add one more protocol, called Redistribute, for dynamic groups. The resulting PMPC is composed of 6 protocols, Share, Reconstruct, Add, Multiply, Refresh, and Recover, or 7 in the dynamic groups case when including Redistribute. For clarification, we denote each protocol with superscripts, A or M, for additive PMPC and MSP-based PMPC, respectively. Note that the complexity of additive PMPC protocols depends on $|\widetilde{\Sigma}|$ and n, while that of MSP-based PMPC protocols depends on d and n, where n is the number of participating parties, $|\widetilde{\Sigma}|$ is the size of the set of all maximal subsets in the secrecy structure, and d is the number of rows of the MSP matrix.

In Sect. 4.3, we develop *share conversion* protocols between the *additive PMPC* and *MSP-based PMPC* schemes to enable one to adapt/change the utilized protocols according to the dynamic GAS. This is necessary and important because one can become more communication-efficient than the other depending on the circumstances. For instance, considering the upper bound on d is about $|\widetilde{\Sigma}|^{2.7}$ [26], the MSP-based MPC is more expensive than the additive MPC, but d can be also low as $n = |\mathcal{P}|$ in some cases, which makes the MSP-based MPC more communication-efficient. Due to the space limit, we provide all the security proofs and formalized based protocols in our full version of the paper [18].

4.1 Additive PMPC

We build our additive PMPC protocol on top of Hirt and Tschudi's unconditional MPC [24] based on additive secret sharing. Assuming n participating parties $\mathcal{P} = \{P_1, ..., P_n\}$, parties want to share a sharing of a secret s according to the sharing specification $\mathbb{S}$. Any Δ-*private* sharing specification, which means for every $Z \in \Delta$, $\exists S \in \mathbb{S}$ such that $S \cup Z = \emptyset$, can be used to securely share a secret, and we adopt one from [27], $\mathbb{S} = (S_1, ..., S_k)$, where $S_i = \mathcal{P} \setminus T_i$ for $\widetilde{\Sigma} = \{T_1, ..., T_k\}$, the set of all maximal subsets in Σ. In [24], they use an IC scheme for dealing with active adversaries, which consists of $\text{Authenticate}^{\text{A}}$ and Verify^{A}. $\text{Authenticate}^{\text{A}}(P_s, P_r, P_v, m)$ is for P_s to distribute the authentication tag of m to P_r and the verification tag of m to P_v, and $\text{Verify}^{\text{A}}(P_s, P_r, P_v, m', tags)$ is for P_j to request P_v to verify the value m' with an authentication tag and a verification tag.

Definition 4.1. *A value s is **shared** with respect to a sharing specification $\mathbb{S} = (S_1, ..., S_k)$ by additive secret sharing, if the following holds:*

a) *There exists shares $s_1, ..., s_k$ such that $s = \sum_{i=1}^{k} s_i$.*
b) *Each s_i is known to every party in S_i, for all i.*
c) *$\forall P_s, P_r \in S_i$, $\forall P_v \in \mathcal{P}$, P_v can verify the value s_i using the IC, for each i.*

A secret value s is shared among $\mathcal{P}$ through the protocol $\texttt{Share}^\texttt{A}$ and any qualified subgroup B of $\mathcal{P}$ can reconstruct the secret value through $\texttt{Reconstruct}^\texttt{A}$. In $\texttt{Share}^\texttt{A}$ protocol, a dealing party randomly chooses $k-1$ values in $\mathbb{F}$, sets the k-th value as $s - \sum_{i=1}^{k-1} s_i$, and sends each i-th value to every player in S_i. Then multiple $\texttt{Authenticate}^\texttt{A}$ are invoked to generate the IC tags. In $\texttt{Reconstruct}^\texttt{A}$, parties in B verify the forwarded values of each share from the others using $\texttt{Verify}^\texttt{A}$ and reconstruct the secret value by locally adding all the verified share values. Note that the sharing of s is linear and does not leak any information about s without the whole set of sharing. Assuming the shares for the values s and t are already shared among $\mathcal{P}$, addition of s and t can be done naturally even without any interaction among n parties by the linearity. However, multiplication is quite tricky and requires a lot of communications to securely form the share of $(s \cdot t)$ among n parties, as $s \cdot t = \sum_{i=1}^{k} s_i \cdot \sum_{j=1}^{k} t_j = \sum_{i=1}^{k} \sum_{j=1}^{k} (s_i \cdot t_i)$. For more details of $\texttt{Add}^\texttt{A}$ and $\texttt{Multiply}^\texttt{A}$ are presented in the full version of the paper [18].

To make this additive MPC scheme to be a PMPC that can also handle dynamic groups, we build three protocols, called $\texttt{Refresh}^\texttt{A}$, $\texttt{Recover}^\texttt{A}$, and $\texttt{Redistribute}^\texttt{A}$. The protocol $\texttt{Refresh}^\texttt{A}$ periodically refreshes or rerandomizes the shares in a distributed manner. This can be done naturally by every party's sharing zero and locally adding all the received shares to the current holding share. The execution of this protocol does not reveal any additional information about the secret as only the shares of zeros are communicated.

Protocol $\texttt{Refresh}^\texttt{A}(w, [s]) \longrightarrow [s]^{w+1}$

Input: a phase w and a sharing of s
Output: new sharing of s in phase $w + 1$, $[s]^{w+1}$

1. Every party P_i in $\mathcal{P}$ invokes $\texttt{Share}^\texttt{A}(w, 0, \mathcal{P})$. (in parallel)
2. Each party adds all shares received in Step 1 to shares of s and sets result as the new share of s in phase $w + 1$.
3. parties in $\mathcal{P}$ collectively output $[s]^{w+1}$.

Theorem 4.1 *(Correctness and Secrecy of $\texttt{Refresh}^\texttt{A}$). When $\texttt{Refresh}^\texttt{A}$ terminates, all parties receive new shares encoding the same secret as old shares with error probability $n^4 |\mathbb{S}|/|\mathbb{F}|$, and cannot obtain any information about the secret by execution of the protocol. $\texttt{Refresh}^\texttt{A}$ requires $|\mathbb{S}|(7n^4 + n^2) \log |\mathbb{F}|$ bits of communication and broadcasts $|\mathbb{S}|((3n^4 + n) \log |\mathbb{F}| + n^3)$ bits.*

For the protocol $\texttt{Recover}^\texttt{A}$, we construct the following two sub-protocols, $\texttt{ShareRandom}^\texttt{A}$ and $\texttt{RobustReshare}^\texttt{A}$. $\texttt{ShareRandom}^\texttt{A}$ generates a sharing of a random element r in $\mathbb{F}$ and parties in the same S_i receive the i-th share of r for each i, but the value of r is not revealed to anyone. Since each iteration requires $O(|S_q|^2 \log |\mathbb{F}|)$ broadcast bits for each q and each $|S_q|$ is less than n, it broadcasts at most $O(|\mathbb{S}|n^2 \log |\mathbb{F}|)$ bits among parties and no communications is required.

Protocol $\mathtt{ShareRandom}^A(w, \mathcal{P}) \longrightarrow [r]^w$

Input: a phase w and a set of participating parties $\mathcal{P}$
Output: a sharing $[r]$ of a random number r, shared among $\mathcal{P}$

1.   For each $S_q \in \mathbb{S} = \{S_1, ..., S_k\}$:
2.   Each party $P_i \in S_q$ generates a random number r_{qi} and broadcast it among all parties in S_q.
3.   Each $P_i \in S_q$ locally adds up all values received in Step 2, and set it as r_q.
4.   The parties in $\mathcal{P}$ collectively output $[r]$, where $r = \sum_{q=1}^{k} r_q$.

The protocol $\mathtt{RobustReshare}^A$ allows parties in $\mathcal{P}_R \in \Gamma$ to receive a sharing of an input random number r (with the value of r) from the parties in $\mathcal{P}_S$, where everyone in $\mathcal{P}_S$ knows the value of r. Distributing one sharing of r is non-trivial in the active adversary model because we cannot trust one party who might be corrupted. Let $Honest := \{\mathcal{P} \setminus A \mid A \in \overline{\Delta}\}$, where $\overline{\Delta}$ is the set of all maximal subsets in Δ. Since the adversary can corrupt one set of parties in Δ in each phase, there exists at least one set of parties in $Honest$ that includes only honest parties in that phase. The main idea of the protocol $\mathtt{RobustReshare}^A$ below is to find such set by repeating to share and reconstruct for each party's holding value for r. At the end of the protocol, parties in $\mathcal{P}_R$ can set a sharing of r and also know the value of the random number r.

Protocol $\mathtt{RobustReshare}^A(w, r, \mathcal{P}_S, \mathcal{P}_R) \longrightarrow [r]^w$

Input: a phase w, a random number r, a set $\mathcal{P}_S$ of parties sending r, and a set $\mathcal{P}_R$ of receiving
            parties, where $\mathcal{P}_R \in \Gamma$
Output: a sharing of r in phase w, $[r]^w$

1.   Every party in $\mathcal{P}_S$ executes $\mathtt{Share}^A(w, r, \mathcal{P}_R)$ according to the sharing specification $\mathbb{S}_R$ on $\mathcal{P}_R$.
     Let $[r]^{(i)}$ be the sharing of r that $P_{k_i} \in \mathcal{P}_S$ shares.
2.   Parties in $\mathcal{P}_R$ invoke $\mathtt{Reconstruct}^A([r]^{(i)}, \mathcal{P}_R)$, for each $i = 1, 2, ..., |\mathcal{P}_S|$.
     Let $r^{(i)}$ be the output of each invocation.
3.   Each party chooses a set $H \in Honest$ such that $\exists v, v = r^{(i)}$ for all $P_{k_i} \in H$. If there are multiple such sets, choose the minimal set including P_i with lower id, i.
4.   Output the sharing of r from the party P_i in H with the minimum id, i.
     i.e. Output $[r] \leftarrow [r]^{(min)}$, where $min := \min_{P_i \in H}\{i\}$.

The security of $\mathtt{RobustReshare}^A$ relies on the security of $\mathtt{Share}^A$ and $\mathtt{Reconstruct}^A$, as the rest is executed locally. For complexities, as both protocols $\mathtt{Share}^A$ and $\mathtt{Reconstruct}^A$ are invoked for each party in $\mathcal{P}_S$ and $|Honest| = |\overline{\Delta}| \leq |\overline{\Sigma}| = |\mathbb{S}|$, the total communication and broadcast complexities of $\mathtt{RobustReshare}^A$ is $O(|\mathbb{S}|n^3 + |\mathcal{P}_S||\mathbb{S}|n^3 + |Honest|) = O(|\mathcal{P}_S||\mathbb{S}|n^3)$.

The protocol $\mathtt{Recover}^{\mathtt{A}}$ allows rebooted/reset parties to obtain new shares for the same secret s with the assistance of other parties. Let $R \subset \mathcal{P}$ be a set of parties who need to recover their shares. Note that $\mathcal{P} \backslash R$ must be still in Γ for the protocol $\mathtt{Recover}^{\mathtt{A}}$ to output a new sharing of s because otherwise, it contradicts to the definition of the access structure. It needs the condition $\mathcal{Q}^1(S_q, \mathcal{Z})$, which is already a necessary condition for the protocol $\mathtt{Reconstruct}^{\mathtt{A}}$. The main idea is as follows: a sharing of unknown random value r is generated among entire parties in $\mathcal{P}$ by $\mathtt{ShareRandom}^{\mathtt{A}}$ and the parties in $\mathcal{P} \backslash R$ holding the shares of s re-share the value $r' = r + s$ and a sharing of r' to entire parties. Then, all parties including R can compute the new shares of s by computing $[r'] - [r]$.

Protocol $\mathtt{Recover}^{\mathtt{A}}(w, [s], R) \longrightarrow [s]^{w+1}$ or $\perp$

Input: a phase w, a sharing of s, and a set of rebooted parties R
Output: new sharing of s in phase $w + 1$, $[s]^{w+1}$, or aborted

1. Parties in $\mathcal{P}$ invoke $\mathtt{ShareRandom}^{\mathtt{A}}(w, \mathcal{P})$ to generate a sharing $[r]$ of r, where r is a random in $\mathbb{F}$.
2. Each party in $\mathcal{P} \backslash R$ invokes $\mathtt{Add}^{\mathtt{A}}(w, [r], [s])$ to share the sharing of $r + s$.
3. $\mathtt{Reconstruct}^{\mathtt{A}}(w, [r + s], \mathcal{P} \backslash R)$ is invoked and every party in $\mathcal{P} \backslash R$ gets $r' := r + s$.
4. $\mathtt{RobustReshare}^{\mathtt{A}}(w, r', \mathcal{P} \backslash R, \mathcal{P})$ is invoked, and each party in $\mathcal{P}$ gets $[r']$.
5. Each party computes $[r'] - [r]$ by executing $\mathtt{Add}^{\mathtt{A}}(w, [r'], -[r])$, where $-[r]$ is the additive inverses of the shares in $\mathbb{F}$.

Theorem 4.2 *(Correctness and Secrecy of $\mathtt{Recover}^{\mathtt{A}}$). If $\mathbb{S}$ and $\mathcal{Z}$ satisfy $\mathcal{Q}^1(\mathbb{S}, \mathcal{Z})$, the protocol $\mathtt{Recover}^{\mathtt{A}}$ allows a set $\forall R \in \Delta$ of rebooted parties to recover their shares encoding the same secret with error probability $O((n - |R|)|\mathbb{S}|n^3/|\mathbb{F}| + (n - |R|)|\mathbb{S}|n^2/(|\mathbb{F}| - 2))$. $\mathtt{Recover}^{\mathtt{A}}$ does not reveal any additional information about the secret. $\mathtt{Recover}^{\mathtt{A}}$ requires $O((n - |R|)|\mathbb{S}|n^3 \log |\mathbb{F}|)$ bits of communication and broadcasts $O((n - |R|)|\mathbb{S}|n^3 \log |\mathbb{F}|)$ bits.*

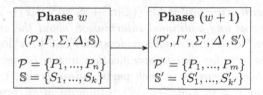

Fig. 1. Dynamic groups and GAS in two consecutive phases, w and $w + 1$

To handle dynamic groups and dynamic GASs, assume that the participating parties and structures are given as in Fig. 1. This phase information is specified by a trusted third party, such as Site Reliability Engineer in Google. Please refer to the full version [18] for the details of the real-life examples. The protocol

`Redistribute`[A] allows new participating parties to obtain a sharing of the same secret as the previous phase according to the new GAS. The idea is quite intuitive because of the repetitive sharing properties, which is to double-share the sharing of a secret from the previous participating group to the new group. Note that the protocol `Redistribute`[M] we will show in the next section has different, non-trivial idea, and reduced complexities.

Protocol $\mathtt{Redistribute}^A(w, s) \longrightarrow [s]^{w+1}$

Input: phase w and a secret s
Output: shares of s in phase $w + 1$
Precondition: parties in P share $[s]^w$ for a secret s
Postcondition: parties in P' share $[s]^{w+1}$ encoding the same secret s

1. For each $S_i \in \mathbb{S}$:
2.   Each party P_y in S_i forwards its holding value $[s_i]_y$ for s_i to every party in S_i who is supposed
    to hold the same share (over the secure channel).
3. $\mathtt{Verify}^A(P_S, P_R, P_V, w, [s_i]_y, A_{S,R,V}(s_i))$ is invoked for all $P_R, P_V \in S_i$, $\forall P_S \in S_i$. If P_V outputs
    $[s_i]_y$ in each invocation, P_V accepts it as value for s_i. Denote v_i as the accepted value for s_i,
    for each i.
4.   Each party $P_y \in S_i$ runs $\mathtt{Share}^A(w + 1, v_i, \mathcal{P}')$ according to $\mathbb{S}'$.
5. For each $S'_j \in \mathbb{S}'$:
6.   Each party in S'_j holds $\{v_{ij}\}_{i=1}^k$. For each v_{ij}, all $P_R, P_V \in S'_j$ invoke
    $\mathtt{Verify}^A(P_S, P_R, P_V, w, v_{ij}, A_{S,R,V(v_{ij})})$ for $\forall P_S \in S'_j$ and accept output value as v_{ij}.
7.   Each party in S'_j sums up all k values accpeted in step 6, and set it as new j-th share of s, i.e., $s'_j := \sum_{i=1}^k v_{ij}$.

Theorem 4.3 *(Correctness and Secrecy of* `Redistribute`[A]*). Executing* `Redistribute`[A]*, new participating parties receive a sharing of the same secret as the old shares with error probability* $(((|\mathbb{S}|n^3 + |\mathbb{S}'|m^3)/(|\mathbb{F}| - 2) + nm^3|\mathbb{S}'|/|\mathbb{F}|)$ *and it does not reveal any additional information about the secret. It communicates* $O(|\mathbb{S}||\mathbb{S}'|nm^3 \log |\mathbb{F}|)$ *bits and broadcasts* $O(|\mathbb{S}||\mathbb{S}'|nm^3 \log |\mathbb{F}|)$ *bits, where* $\mathbb{S}$ *and* $\mathbb{S}'$ *denote the sets for sharing specification in two consecutive phases and* n, m *are the number of parties in each participating group, i.e.,* $n = |\mathcal{P}|$ *and* $m = |\mathcal{P}'|$. *Assuming* $n = m$ *and* $|\mathbb{S}| = |\mathbb{S}'|$, *communication/broadcast complexities are* $O(|\mathbb{S}|^2 n^4 \log |\mathbb{F}|)$.

The function of `Recover`[A] can be naturally substituted with `Redistribute`[A] with the same participating groups and the same sharing specification, but using our `Recover`[A] protocol is more efficient as it has linear complexity in $|\mathbb{S}|$, while `Redistribute`[A] has quadratic complexities in $|\mathbb{S}|$. Due to the space limit, we provide the total analysis of communication and broadcast complexities with error probability for each protocol in our additive PMPC scheme in Table 2 in our full version of the paper.

4.2   MSP-Based PMPC

Lampkins and Ostrovsky [26] presented an unconditionally secure MPC protocol based on Monotone Span Program (MSP) secret sharing against any $Q2$-adversary, which has linear communication complexity in the size of multiplicative MSP. We build our MSP-based PMPC protocol on top of their MPC protocol, *without increasing the complexity in terms of the size of MSP, d*. We denote a vector with bold texts as in Table 1, and formalized protocols of [26] and all the security proofs of our protocols are given in the full version of our paper [18].

Definition 4.2. $(\mathbb{F}, M, \rho, \boldsymbol{a})$ *is called a monotone span program (MSP), if* $\mathbb{F}$ *is a finite field,* M *is a* $d \times e$ *matrix over* $\mathbb{F}$, $\rho : \{1, 2, ..., d\} \rightarrow \{1, 2, ..., n\}$ *is a surjective indexing function for each row of* M, *and* $\boldsymbol{a} \in \mathbb{F}^e \backslash \boldsymbol{0}$ *is a (fixed) target vector, where* $\boldsymbol{0} = (0, ..., 0) \in \mathbb{F}^e$. $(\mathbb{F}, M, \rho, \boldsymbol{a}, \boldsymbol{r})$ *is called a multiplicative MSP, if* $(\mathbb{F}, M, \rho, \boldsymbol{a})$ *is a MSP and* $\boldsymbol{r}$ *is a recombination vector, which means the vector* $\boldsymbol{r}$ *satisfies the property that* $\langle \boldsymbol{r}, M\boldsymbol{b} * M\boldsymbol{b}' \rangle = \langle \boldsymbol{a}, \boldsymbol{b} \rangle \cdot \langle \boldsymbol{a}, \boldsymbol{b}' \rangle$, *for all* $\boldsymbol{b}, \boldsymbol{b}'$, *where* $*$ *is the Hadamard product and* $\cdot$ *is the inner product.*

The target vector $\mathbf{a}$ can be any vector in $\mathbb{F}^e \backslash \boldsymbol{0}$; we use $\mathbf{a} = (1, 0, ..., 0)^t \in \mathbb{F}^e$ for convenience, as in [26]. Let $f : \{0, 1\}^n \rightarrow \{0, 1\}$ be a monotone function. A MSP $(\mathbb{F}, M, \rho, \mathbf{a})$ is said to compute f if for all nonempty set $A \subset \{1, ..., n\}$, $f(A) = 1 \Leftrightarrow \mathbf{a} \in \mathrm{Im}M_A^t$, i.e., $\exists \lambda_A$ such that $M_A^t \lambda_A = \mathbf{a}$. Also, a MSP $(\mathbb{F}, M, \rho, \mathbf{a})$ computing f is said to accept Γ if $B \in \Gamma \Leftrightarrow f(B) = 1$. Note that any given MSP computes a monotone Boolean function f, defined $f(x_1, ..., x_n) = 1 \Leftrightarrow \mathbf{a} \in \mathrm{Im}M_A^t$ where $A = \{1 \leq i \leq n | x_i = 1\}$, and it is well known that any monotone Boolean function can be computed by a MSP.

The SS scheme based on the MSP accepting Γ [12,26] also consists of **Share** and **Reconstruct** protocols. The protocol $\mathtt{BasicShare}^{\mathtt{M}}$ generates a sharing of s by sending each assigned row of $\mathbf{s} - M\mathbf{b}$ by the indexing function ρ, where $M \in \mathcal{M}(d \times e)$ is the matrix of the MSP corresponding to Δ and $\mathbf{b} := (s, r_2, ..., r_e) \in \mathbb{F}^e$ is a vector containing the secret value s and $(e - 1)$ random values r_i's. For reconstruction, since the MSP accepts Γ, $B \in \Gamma \Leftrightarrow f(B) = 1 \Leftrightarrow \mathbf{a} \in \mathrm{Im}M_B^t$, which means there is some vector λ_B such that $M_B^t \lambda_B = \mathbf{a}$. Therefore, parties can reconstruct the secret value with shares that parties in B hold by computing $\langle \lambda_B, [s]_B \rangle = \langle \lambda_B, M_B\mathbf{b} \rangle = \langle M_B^t \lambda_B, \mathbf{b} \rangle = \langle \mathbf{a}, \mathbf{b} \rangle = s$, because $\mathbf{a} = (1, 0, ..., 0)$ and $\mathbf{b} = (s, r_2, ..., r_e)$.

For dealing with active adversaries, they use a (different) IC scheme and dispute control. The IC scheme accepts the Shamir's secret sharing techniques [30] (See the full version [18] for details). For dispute control, one more list $\mathcal{C}$ is also used, where $\mathcal{C}$ is a set of parties known by all parties to be corrupted. That means, the list $\mathcal{D}$ maintains the parties in each dispute list $\mathcal{D}_i$, for all i, and some of them move to the list $\mathcal{C}$ when all parties agree that they are corrupted. Note that their SS scheme for active adversaries allows parties to share and reconstruct multiple secret values in one execution of the protocol, but we only consider the case with one secret value per execution to fairly compare the complexities with additive PMPC protocols. So we call the share and reconstruct protocols (with a batch of multiple secrets) in [26] as $\mathtt{ShareMultiple}^{\mathsf{M}}$ and $\mathtt{ReconstructMultiple}^{\mathsf{M}}$ and our considering special case protocols (with single secret) as $\mathtt{Share}^{\mathsf{M}}$ and $\mathtt{Reconstruct}^{\mathsf{M}}$. On the other hand, the protocol $\mathtt{LC\text{-}Reconstruct}^{\mathsf{M}}$ [26] allows parties to reconstruct linear combinations of multiple secrets that have been shared using $\mathtt{Share}^{\mathsf{M}}$ protocol and to detect corrupted parties while reconstructing. For computations, addition can be done with no communication thanks to the linearity of the shares, while multiplication needs a little trick. As we just adopt the protocols from [26] (with only small variants), we present the formal descriptions in [18].

To make this MPC scheme to PMPC handling dynamic groups, we build three new main protocols, called $\mathtt{Refresh}^{\mathsf{M}}$, $\mathtt{Recover}^{\mathsf{M}}$, and $\mathtt{Redistribute}^{\mathsf{M}}$. Recall that the protocol $\mathtt{Refresh}^{\mathsf{M}}$ re-randomizes the shares that each party has regularly so that the adversary cannot reconstruct the secret until he corrupts any set in the access structure in the period. By the linearity of the shares, the main idea is same as before.

Protocol $\mathtt{Refresh}^{\mathsf{M}}(w, [s]) \longrightarrow [s]^{w+1}$

Input: a phase w and a sharing of s
Output: new sharing of s in phase $w + 1$, $[s]^{w+1}$

1. Every party P_i in $\mathcal{P}$ invokes $\mathtt{Share}^{\mathsf{M}}(w, 0, P_i)$. (in parallel)
2. Each party locally does component-wise addition with all the shares received in Step 1 and the shares of s, and set it as the new share of s in phase $w + 1$.
3. parties in $\mathcal{P}$ collectively output $[s]^{w+1}$.

Theorem 4.4. *(Correctness and Secrecy of $\mathtt{Refresh}^{\mathsf{M}}$). When $\mathtt{Refresh}^{\mathsf{M}}$ terminates, all parties receive new shares encoding the same secret as old shares they had before, and they cannot get any information about the secret by the execution of the protocol. It communicates $O((n^2 d + n^3 \kappa) \log |\mathbb{F}| + n^3 \kappa \log d)$ bits and broadcasts $O(n^3 \log d + (n^3 + nd) \log |\mathbb{F}|)$ bits.*

For $\mathtt{Recover}^{\mathsf{M}}$ and $\mathtt{Redistribute}^{\mathsf{M}}$, we construct two protocols, $\mathtt{ShareRandom}^{\mathsf{M}}$ and $\mathtt{RobustReshare}^{\mathsf{M}}$. The goals of the protocols are similar to the ones in Sect. 4.1, but due to the fact that each party holds the unique share of a secret, $\mathtt{ShareRandom}^{\mathsf{M}}$ can be generalized for multiple groups of parties, which enables to build the efficient $\mathtt{Redistribute}^{\mathsf{M}}$ protocol. The protocol $\mathtt{ShareRandom}^{\mathsf{M}}$ allows participating parties to generate multiple sharings of a random value $r \in \mathbb{F}$ for each group without reconstructing the value r. Note that $W = \{w\}$ for $\mathtt{Recover}^{\mathsf{M}}$, while $W = \{w, w + 1\}$ for $\mathtt{Redistribute}^{\mathsf{M}}$. The protocol $\mathtt{ShareRandom}^{\mathsf{M}}$ outputs $|W|$ sharings of the same r, where r is the summation of all random elements from each party in each phase. For instance, when $W = \{w\}$, the output is one sharing of r, say $[r] = \{\mathbf{r}_1, ..., \mathbf{r}_n\}$, where $\mathtt{LC\text{-}Reconstruct}^{\mathsf{M}}(w, [r])$ reconstructs $r = \sum_{P_i \notin \mathcal{C}} r^{(i)}$. We denote $\mathtt{ShareRandom}^{\mathsf{M}}(w)$ in this case. On the other hand, when $W = \{w, w + 1\}$, it outputs two sharings of r, $[r]^w := \{\mathbf{r}_1^w, ..., \mathbf{r}_n^w\}$ and $[r]^{w+1} := \{\mathbf{r}_1^{w+1}, ..., \mathbf{r}_m^{w+1}\}$, where both sharings reconstruct the same r. i.e., $\mathsf{LC\text{-}Reconstruct}^{\mathsf{M}}(w, [r]^w) = \mathsf{LC\text{-}Reconstruct}^{\mathsf{M}}(w + 1, [r]^{w+1}) = r$, where $r = \sum_{P_i \notin \mathcal{C}^w} r^{(w,i)} + \sum_{P_j \notin \mathcal{C}^{w+1}} r^{(w+1,j)}$.

Protocol $\mathsf{ShareRandom}^{\mathsf{M}}(W) \longrightarrow \{[r]^w\}_{w \in W}$

Input: a list W of phases where participating parties generate sharing(s) of a random value

Output: $|W|$ sharing(s) of a random value r, for each $\mathcal{P}^w$ in $w \in W$

1. For each $w \in W$:
2.   Each party $P_i \notin \mathcal{C}^w$ chooses a random value $r^{(w,i)}$ and invokes $\mathsf{Share}^{\mathsf{M}}(w', r^{(w,i)}, \mathcal{P}^{w'})$ $|W|$ times
      in parallel with respect to $\mathbb{S}^w$, for each $w' \in W$.
3. For each $w \in W$:
4.   Each party $P_i \in \mathcal{P}^w$ locally computes $\mathbf{r}_i^w := \sum_{w' \in W} \sum_{P_j \notin \mathcal{C}^{w'}} [r^{(w',j)}]_i^w$, where $[r^{(w',j)}]_i^w$ is P_i's
      holding share of $r^{(w',j)}$ received in Step 2 from $P_j \notin \mathcal{C}^{w'}$.
5. $|W|$ sharings of r, $\{[r]^w\}_{w \in W}$, are collectively output, where $r := \sum_{P_j \notin \mathcal{C}^w, w \in W} r^{(w,j)}$ and
   $[r]^w := \{\mathbf{r}_1^w, ..., \mathbf{r}_{|\mathcal{P}^w|}^w\}$.

Note that all summand vectors $\{[r^{(w',j)}]_i^w\}$ have the same lengths for each party. For $N := \sum_{w \in W} |\mathcal{P}^w|$, the protocol communicates $O(N|W|((nd + n^2\kappa)\log|\mathbb{F}| + n^2\kappa \log d))$ bits and broadcasts $O(N|W|(n^2 \log d + (n^2 + d)\log|\mathbb{F}|))$ bits.

Recall that $Honest := \{\mathcal{P} \setminus A \mid A \in \overline{\Delta}\}$ is a set of potential honest parties sets. The protocol $\mathsf{RobustReshare}^{\mathsf{M}}$ similarly works as the one in Sect. 4.1. Every party in $\mathcal{P}_S \subseteq \mathcal{P}^{w_S}$ in phase w_S knows the value r and wants to send a right sharing of r to the parties in $\mathcal{P}_R \subseteq \mathcal{P}^{w_R}$ in phase w_R. As the adversary picks one subset of parties in Δ in each phase, there exists at least one set in $Honest$ consisting of only honest parties in that phase.

Protocol $\mathsf{RobustReshare}^{\mathsf{M}}(r, w_S, \mathcal{P}_S, w_R, \mathcal{P}_R) \longrightarrow [r]^{w_R}$

Input: a random element $r \in \mathbb{F}$, a phase w_S, a set of parties $\mathcal{P}_S$ in phase w_S, phase w_R, and
   a set of parties $\mathcal{P}_R \in \Gamma$ in phase w_R

Output: a sharing of r in phase w_R, $[r]^{w_R}$

Precondition: All parties in $\mathcal{P}_S$ know the value of r.

Postcondition: Each party in $\mathcal{P}_R$ receives the share of new sharing of r.

1. Every party in $\mathcal{P}_S$ executes $\texttt{Share}^{\texttt{M}}(w_R, r, \mathcal{P}_R)$ according to $\mathbb{S}_R$. Let $[r]^{(i)}$ be the sharing of r that $P_{k_i} \in \mathcal{P}_S$ shares.
2. For each $i = 1, 2, ..., |\mathcal{P}_S|$, $\texttt{Reconstruct}^{\texttt{M}}(w_R, [r]^{(i)}, \mathcal{P}_R)$ is invoked. Let $r^{(i)}$ be the result of each reconstruction.
3. Choose a value v such that $v = r^{(i)}$ for all $P_{k_i} \in H$, for some $H \in Honest$. Each party chooses such set $H \in Honest$. If there exists multiple such sets, the minimal set including P_i with lower id, i, is chosen.
4. Parties in $\mathcal{P}_R$ collectively outputs the sharing of r from the party P_i in H with the minimum id, i.
    i.e. Output $[r] \leftarrow [r]^{(min)}$, where $min := \min_{P_i \in H}\{i\}$.

Security of $\texttt{RobustReshare}^{\texttt{M}}$ relies on the security of $\texttt{Share}^{\texttt{M}}$ and $\texttt{Reconstruct}^{\texttt{M}}$ and communicates $O(|\mathcal{P}_S|(|\mathcal{P}_R|^2 \kappa \log d_R + (|\mathcal{P}_R|^3 + |\mathcal{P}_R|^2\kappa + |\mathcal{P}_R|d_R) \log |\mathbb{F}|))$ and broadcasts $O(|\mathcal{P}_S|(|\mathcal{P}_R|^2 \log d_R + (|\mathcal{P}_R|^2 + d_R) \log |\mathbb{F}|))$ bits.

Using these sub-protocols, $\texttt{Recover}^{\texttt{M}}$ allows the rebooted/reset parties to recover their shares, by generating new sharing of the same secret in $\mathcal{P}$ with the assistance of other parties. A sharing of a random element r is generated using $\texttt{ShareRandom}^{\texttt{M}}$, $\texttt{LC-Reconstruct}^{\texttt{M}}$ allows every party to reconstruct a publicly known random value $r' := r + s$, and $\texttt{RobustReshare}^{\texttt{M}}$ helps parties to set one same sharing of r'.

Protocol $\texttt{Recover}^{\texttt{M}}(w, [s], R) \longrightarrow [s]^{w+1}$ or $\perp$

Input: a phase w, a sharing of s, and a set of rebooted parties R
Output: new sharing of s in phase $w + 1$, $[s]^{w+1}$, or aborted

1. Invoke $\texttt{ShareRandom}^{\texttt{M}}(w)$ and generate a sharing $[r] := \{\mathbf{r}_1, ..., \mathbf{r}_n\}$ of a random r in $\mathbb{F}$.
2. Each party P_i in $\mathcal{P} \setminus R$ locally computes $\mathbf{r}_i + \mathbf{s}_i$, the share of $r' := r + s$.
3. $\texttt{LC-Reconstruct}^{\texttt{M}}(w, [r'])$ is invoked in $\mathcal{P} \setminus R$ and every party in $\mathcal{P} \setminus R$ gets r'.
4. $\texttt{RobustReshare}^{\texttt{M}}(r', w, \mathcal{P} \setminus R, w, \mathcal{P})$ is invoked, and each party in $\mathcal{P}$ gets $[r']^w := \{\mathbf{r}'_1, ..., \mathbf{r}'_n\}$.
5. Each party locally computes $\mathbf{r}'_i - \mathbf{r}_i$ and sets it as new share of s.

Theorem 4.5. *(Correctness and Secrecy of $\texttt{Recover}^{\texttt{M}}$). The protocol $\texttt{Recover}^{\texttt{M}}$ allows a set R of parties who were rebooted to recover their shares encoding the same secret, for any $R \in \Delta$, and does not reveal any additional information about the secret except the shares each party had before the execution of the protocol. It communicates $O(n^3 \kappa \log d + (n^4 + n^3\kappa + n^2d) \log |\mathbb{F}|)$ bits and broadcasts $O(n^3 \log d + (n^3 + nd) \log |\mathbb{F}|)$ bits.*

Considering the dynamic settings in Fig. 1, $\texttt{Redistribute}^{\texttt{M}}$ allows parties in the new group $\mathcal{P}'$ to receive the shares encoding the same secret. The main idea is similar to the one in $\texttt{Recover}^{\texttt{M}}$, but as parties might be different in two phases, it needs to be considered very carefully. To send a right sharing of s from $\mathcal{P}$ to

$\mathcal{P}'$ without revealing the secret value s to the parties, both parties in two phases generate a sharing of random value r without reconstructing the value r using ShareRandom$^\text{M}$. Then, parties holding the share of s locally compute the share of r to the share of s and reconstruct $s + r$ using them. Now, all parties in $\mathcal{P}$ knows the value $s + r$, but not s or r, so that they invoke RobustReshare$^\text{M}$ to send a right sharing of $s + r$ to the parties in $\mathcal{P}'$. As parties in $\mathcal{P}'$ are also holding the share of r, now each party can locally computes the share of s.

Protocol Redistribute$^\text{M}(w, [s]^w) \longrightarrow [s]^{w+1}$

Input: a phase w and the sharing of s in phase w, $[s]^w = \{\mathbf{s}_1^w, ..., \mathbf{s}_n^w\}$
Output: new sharing of s for phase $w + 1$, $[s]^{w+1} = \{\mathbf{s}_1^{w+1}, ..., \mathbf{s}_m^{w+1}\}$

1. Parties in $\mathcal{P}$ and $\mathcal{P}'$ invoke ShareRandom$^\text{M}(W)$, where $W = \{w, w+1\}$, to generate two sharings of a random value r, unknown to every party. That is, parties in $\mathcal{P}$ separately receive a sharing $[r]^w := \{\mathbf{r}_1^w, ..., \mathbf{r}_n^w\}$, while parties in $\mathcal{P}'$ receive a sharing $[r]^{w+1} := \{\mathbf{r}_1^{w+1}, ..., \mathbf{r}_m^{w+1}\}$, and no one knows the value of r.

2. Each party P_i in $\mathcal{P}$ locally computes $\mathbf{x}_i := \mathbf{r}_i^w + \mathbf{s}_i^w$, where $\mathbf{s}_i^w$ is the share of s.

3. Parties in $\mathcal{P}$ invoke LC-Reconstruct$^\text{M}(w, [x])$ with $[x] := \{\mathbf{x}_1, ..., \mathbf{x}_n\}$ and the result is denoted by x. Note that $x = s + r$, where r is random and unknown to everyone.

4. Parties invoke RobustReshare$^\text{M}(x, w, \mathcal{P}, w+1, \mathcal{P}')$ so that parties in $\mathcal{P}'$ receive a sharing of x, say $[x] := \{\mathbf{z}_1, ..., \mathbf{z}_m\}$, for $\mathbf{z}_i := M_i' \mathbf{X}$, where the vector $\mathbf{X} = (x, \$, ..., \$) \in \mathbb{F}^{e'}$ with random $\$$'s.

5. Each party P_i' in $\mathcal{P}'$ locally computes $\mathbf{s}_i^{w+1} := \mathbf{z}_i - \mathbf{r}_i^{w+1}$, for $i = 1, ..., m$.

6. Parties in $\mathcal{P}'$ collectively output $\{\mathbf{s}_1^{w+1}, ..., \mathbf{s}_m^{w+1}\}$ as a sharing of s in new phase.

Theorem 4.6. *(Correctness and Secrecy of* Redistribute$^\text{M}$*). When the protocol terminates, all parties in new participating group have the shares of the same secret as the old shares, and the protocol does not reveal any information about the secret. It communicates $O(n^2\kappa \log d + nm^2\kappa \log d' + ((n^2 + mn)d + (m^2 + mn)d' + (n^3 + m^3)\kappa + (m+n)mn\kappa + nm^3) \log |\mathbb{F}|)$ bits and broadcasts $O((n^3 + mn^2) \log d + nm^2 \log d' + (n^3 + (n+m)(mn+d) + nd') \log |\mathbb{F}|)$ bits, where $|\mathcal{P}| = n$, $|\mathcal{P}'| = m$, size$(M) = d$, and size$(M') = d'$.*

We provide the total analysis of MSP-based PMPC protocols based on the protocols in [26] in Table 3 in our full version of the paper [18].

4.3 Conversions Between Additive and MSP-Based MPC

Now, we present the way to convert the additive PMPC scheme into the MSP-based PMPC and the opposite direction. Recall that the complexity of an additive PMPC scheme depends on the size of the sharing specification $|\mathbb{S}|$ (we use the basic secrecy structure $|\widetilde{\Sigma}|$), while the one of a MSP-based PMPC scheme depends on the size of the MSP, d. Since d can be varied from n to $|\widetilde{\Sigma}|^{2.7}$ depending on the adversary structures [26], there are some cases worth to convert the schemes even though the conversion itself needs some resource. One PMPC scheme with better complexities can be chosen, only when participating groups or GAS are changed. That is, when dynamic groups and structures of two consecutive phases are given, participating parties can continue the current PMPC scheme by executing `Redistribute` protocol or they can convert the scheme from one to the other by calling the protocols, called `ConvertAdditiveIntoMSP` or `ConvertMSPIntoAdditive`. The security proofs for each conversion protocol are provided in the full version [18].

Let the groups and structures in consecutive phases be $\mathcal{S}^w := (\mathcal{P}, \Gamma, \Sigma, \Delta, \mathbb{S})$ and $\mathcal{S}^{w+1} := (\mathcal{P}', \Gamma', \Sigma', \Delta', \mathbb{S}')$ and assume the additive PMPC scheme has been used in phase w with sharing specification $\mathbb{S} = \{S_1, S_2, ..., S_k\}$. The protocol `ConvertAdditiveIntoMSP` converts additive sharing of s into a MSP-based sharing of s (the formal description of the protocol is in the full version [18]). By definition, if no qualified subset of parties in the access structure Γ remains in $\mathcal{P}$, then the secret value s cannot be reconstructed even though the protocol is executed. That is, there exists at least one honest party in each $S_i \in \mathbb{S}$. To deal with active adversaries, all parties in each S_i need to share their share s_i to parties in $\mathcal{P}'$ using `Share`^{M} protocol. Then parties in $\mathcal{P}'$ blind their shares with the shares of a random number and open (reconstruct) the blinded values to decide one sharing of s_i from the honest party in S_i. By linearity of shares, each party in $\mathcal{P}'$ can compute the MSP-based share of s by component-wise adding all its receiving shares.

Theorem 4.7. *(Correctness and Secrecy of* `ConvertAdditiveIntoMSP`*). When the protocol* `ConvertAdditiveIntoMSP` *terminates, all parties in new participating group have shares of the same secret encoded by the old shares, and the protocol does not reveal any information about the secret.* `ConvertAdditiveIntoMSP` *communicates* $O(k((m^2+mn)d+(m^3+m^2n)\kappa+nm^3)\log|\mathbb{F}|+k(m^3+m^2n)\kappa\log d)$ *bits and broadcasts* $O(k(mnd+m^3+m^2n)\log|\mathbb{F}|+k(m^3+m^2n)\log d)$ *bits, where* $|\mathcal{P}| = n$, $|\mathcal{P}'| = m$, $|\mathbb{S}| = k$, *and size(M)* $= d$.

When parties are using the MSP-based PMPC scheme and want to convert it to the additive PMPC in the next phase, they execute the protocol `ConvertMSPIntoAdditive` (the formal description of the protocol is in the full version [18]). It converts a MSP-based sharing of s in phase w into an additive sharing of s in phase $w + 1$. Note that each party P_i has different shares of s in MSP-based PMPC and P_i's share of s is the vector of length d_i. For these reasons, each party needs to invoke multiple `Share`^{A} protocols to share each component of the vector according to the sharing specification $\mathbb{S}'$ in phase $w + 1$. Each party in each $S_j \in \mathbb{S}$ collects all the shares received from the same party P_i and form a vector of length d_i. Then, all the parties in S_j hold the same n vectors of different lengths. When recomposing these n vectors according to the indexing function ρ of phase w, each party can compute its share of s by inner product with the vector λ such that $M^t\lambda = \mathbf{a}$.

Theorem 4.8. *(Correctness and Secrecy of* `ConvertMSPIntoAdditive`*). When the protocol terminates, all parties in new participating group have the shares* *of the same secret as the old shares, and the protocol does not reveal any information about the secret. It communicates $O(dkn^3 \log |\mathbb{F}|)$ bits and broadcasts $O(dkn^3 \log |\mathbb{F}|)$ bits, where $|\mathcal{P}| = n$, $|\mathcal{P}'| = m$, $|\mathbb{S}'| = k$, and size(M) = d.*

From the Theorem 4.7 and Theorem 4.8, we can derive the following corollary.

Corollary. *A proactive MPC scheme based on additive secret sharing and a proactive MPC scheme based on MSP-based secret sharing are convertible. That is, one can transform an additive sharing of a secret to a MSP-based sharing of the same secret and also transform a MSP-based sharing of a secret to an additive sharing of the same secret, without revealing any information about the secret among participating parties.*

Acknowledgements. Rafail Ostrovsky is supported in part by DARPA and NIWC Pacific under contract N66001-15-C-4065, DARPA under Cooperative Agreement No: HR0011-20-2-0025, the Office of the Director of National Intelligence (ODNI), Intelligence Advanced Research Projects Activity (IARPA), via 2019-1902070008, NSF-BSF Grant 1619348, US-Israel BSF grant 2012366, Google Faculty Award, JP Morgan Faculty Award, IBM Faculty Research Award, Xerox Faculty Research Award, OKAWA Foundation Research Award, B. John Garrick Foundation Award, Teradata Research Award, and Lockheed-Martin Corporation Research Award. The views and conclusions contained herein are those of the authors and should not be interpreted as necessarily representing the official policies, either expressed or implied, of ODNI, IARPA, the Department of Defense, or the U.S. Government. The U.S. Government is authorized to reproduce and distribute reprints for governmental purposes notwithstanding any copyright annotation therein.

References

1. Almansa, J.F., Damgård, I., Nielsen, J.B.: Simplified threshold RSA with adaptive and proactive security. In: Vaudenay, S. (ed.) EUROCRYPT 2006. LNCS, vol. 4004, pp. 593–611. Springer, Heidelberg (2006). https://doi.org/10.1007/11761679_35
2. Backes, M., Cachin, C., Strobl, R.: Proactive secure message transmission in asynchronous networks. In: Proceedings of the Twenty-Second ACM Symposium on Principles of Distributed Computing, PODC 2003, Boston, Massachusetts, USA, 13–16 July 2003, pp. 223–232 (2003)
3. Baron, J., Eldefrawy, K., Lampkins, J., Ostrovsky, R.: How to withstand mobile virus attacks, revisited. In: Proceedings of the 2014 ACM Symposium on Principles of Distributed Computing, PODC 2014, pp. 293–302 (2014)
4. Baron, J., Defrawy, K.E., Lampkins, J., Ostrovsky, R.: Communication-optimal proactive secret sharing for dynamic groups. In: Malkin, T., Kolesnikov, V., Lewko, A.B., Polychronakis, M. (eds.) ACNS 2015. LNCS, vol. 9092, pp. 23–41. Springer, Cham (2015). https://doi.org/10.1007/978-3-319-28166-7_2
5. Beerliová-Trubíniová, Z., Hirt, M.: Perfectly-secure MPC with linear communication complexity. In: Canetti, R. (ed.) TCC 2008. LNCS, vol. 4948, pp. 213–230. Springer, Heidelberg (2008). https://doi.org/10.1007/978-3-540-78524-8_13
6. Michael Ben-Or, S.G., Wigderson, A.: Completeness theorems for non-cryptographic fault-tolerant distributed computation (extended abstract). In: STOC, pp. 1–10 (1988)

7. Ben-Sasson, E., Fehr, S., Ostrovsky, R.: Near-linear unconditionally-secure multiparty computation with a dishonest minority. In: Safavi-Naini, R., Canetti, R. (eds.) CRYPTO 2012. LNCS, vol. 7417, pp. 663–680. Springer, Heidelberg (2012). https://doi.org/10.1007/978-3-642-32009-5_39

8. Blakley, G.R.: Safeguarding cryptographic keys. In: Proceedings of AFIPS National Computer Conference, vol. 48, pp. 313–317 (1979)

9. Canetti, R., Herzberg, A.: Maintaining security in the presence of transient faults. In: Desmedt, Y.G. (ed.) CRYPTO 1994. LNCS, vol. 839, pp. 425–438. Springer, Heidelberg (1994). https://doi.org/10.1007/3-540-48658-5_38

10. Castro, M., Liskov, B.: Practical byzantine fault tolerance and proactive recovery. ACM Trans. Comput. Syst. **20**(4), 398–461 (2002)

11. Chaum, D., Crépeau, C., Damgard, I.: Multiparty unconditionally secure protocols. In: Proceedings of the Twentieth Annual ACM Symposium on Theory of Computing, STOC 1988, pp. 11–19 (1988)

12. Cramer, R., Damgård, I., Maurer, U.: Span programs and general secure multiparty computation. BRICS Rep. Ser. **4**(28) (1997)

13. Damgård, I., Ishai, Y., Krøigaard, M.: Perfectly secure multiparty computation and the computational overhead of cryptography. In: Gilbert, H. (ed.) EUROCRYPT 2010. LNCS, vol. 6110, pp. 445–465. Springer, Heidelberg (2010). https://doi.org/10.1007/978-3-642-13190-5_23

14. Damgård, I., Ishai, Y., Krøigaard, M., Nielsen, J.B., Smith, A.: Scalable multiparty computation with nearly optimal work and resilience. In: Wagner, D. (ed.) CRYPTO 2008. LNCS, vol. 5157, pp. 241–261. Springer, Heidelberg (2008). https://doi.org/10.1007/978-3-540-85174-5_14

15. Dolev, S., Garay, J., Gilboa, N., Kolesnikov, V.: Swarming secrets. In: 47th Annual Allerton Conference on Communication, Control, and Computing, Allerton 2009, pp. 1438–1445, September 2009

16. Dolev, S., Garay, J.A., Gilboa, N., Kolesnikov, V.: Secret sharing Krohn-Rhodes: private and perennial distributed computation. In: Innovations in Computer Science - ICS 2010, Tsinghua University, Beijing, China, 7–9 January 2011. Proceedings, pp. 32–44 (2011)

17. Dolev, S., Garay, J.A., Gilboa, N., Kolesnikov, V., Yuditsky, Y.: Towards efficient private distributed computation on unbounded input streams. J. Mathe. Cryptol. **9**(2), 79–94 (2015)

18. Eldefrawy, K., Hwang, S., Ostrovsky, R., Yung, M.: Communication-efficient (proactive) secure computation for dynamic general adversary structures and dynamic groups. Cryptology ePrint Archive, Report 2020/747 (2020). https://eprint.iacr.org/2020/747.pdf

19. Eldefrawy, K., Ostrovsky, R., Park, S., Yung, M.: Proactive secure multiparty computation with a dishonest majority. In: Catalano, D., De Prisco, R. (eds.) SCN 2018. LNCS, vol. 11035, pp. 200–215. Springer, Cham (2018). https://doi.org/10.1007/978-3-319-98113-0_11

20. Frankel, Y., Gemmell, P., MacKenzie, P.D., Yung, M.: Proactive RSA. In: Kaliski, B.S. (ed.) CRYPTO 1997. LNCS, vol. 1294, pp. 440–454. Springer, Heidelberg (1997). https://doi.org/10.1007/BFb0052254

21. Goldreich, O., Micali, S., Wigderson, A.: How to play any mental game. In: Proceedings of the Nineteenth Annual ACM Symposium on Theory of Computing, STOC 1987, pp. 218–229 (1987)

22. Herzberg, A., Jarecki, S., Krawczyk, H., Yung, M.: Proactive secret sharing or: how to cope with perpetual leakage. In: Coppersmith, D. (ed.) CRYPTO 1995. LNCS, vol. 963, pp. 339–352. Springer, Heidelberg (1995). https://doi.org/10.1007/3-540-44750-4_27

23. Hirt, M., Maurer, U., Lucas, C.: A dynamic tradeoff between active and passive corruptions in secure multi-party computation. In: Canetti, R., Garay, J.A. (eds.) CRYPTO 2013. LNCS, vol. 8043, pp. 203–219. Springer, Heidelberg (2013). https://doi.org/10.1007/978-3-642-40084-1_12

24. Hirt, M., Tschudi, D.: Efficient general-adversary multi-party computation. In: Sako, K., Sarkar, P. (eds.) ASIACRYPT 2013. LNCS, vol. 8270, pp. 181–200. Springer, Heidelberg (2013). https://doi.org/10.1007/978-3-642-42045-0_10

25. Ishai, Y., Kushilevitz, E., Ostrovsky, R., Sahai, A.: Cryptography with constant computational overhead. In: STOC, pp. 433–442 (2008)

26. Lampkins, J., Ostrovsky, R.: Communication-efficient MPC for general adversary structures. In: Abdalla, M., De Prisco, R. (eds.) SCN 2014. LNCS, vol. 8642, pp. 155–174. Springer, Cham (2014). https://doi.org/10.1007/978-3-319-10879-7_10

27. Maurer, U.: Secure multi-party computation made simple. In: Cimato, S., Persiano, G., Galdi, C. (eds.) SCN 2002. LNCS, vol. 2576, pp. 14–28. Springer, Heidelberg (2003). https://doi.org/10.1007/3-540-36413-7_2

28. Ostrovsky, R., Yung, M.: How to withstand mobile virus attacks (extended abstract). In: PODC, pp. 51–59 (1991)

29. Rabin, T., Ben-Or, M.: Verifiable secret sharing and multiparty protocols with honest majority. In: Proceedings of the Twenty-First Annual ACM Symposium on Theory of Computing, STOC 1989, pp. 73–85 (1989)

30. Shamir, A.: How to share a secret. Commun. ACM 22(11), 612–613 (1979)

31. Yao, A.C.: Protocols for secure computations. In: Proceedings of the 23rd Annual Symposium on Foundations of Computer Science, FOCS 1982, pp. 160–164 (1982)

Efficient Protocols for Oblivious Linear Function Evaluation from Ring-LWE

Carsten Baum[1] [iD], Daniel Escudero[1] [iD], Alberto Pedrouzo-Ulloa[2] [iD],
Peter Scholl[1()] [iD], and Juan Ramón Troncoso-Pastoriza[3] [iD]

[1] Aarhus University, Aarhus, Denmark
{cbaum,escudero,peter.scholl}@cs.au.dk
[2] University of Vigo, Vigo, Galicia, Spain

[3] EPFL, Lausanne, Switzerland

Abstract. An oblivious linear function evaluation protocol, or OLE, is a two-party protocol for the function $f(x) = ax + b$, where a sender inputs the field elements a, b, and a receiver inputs x and learns $f(x)$. OLE can be used to build secret-shared multiplication, and is an essential component of many secure computation applications including general-purpose multi-party computation, private set intersection and more.

In this work, we present several efficient OLE protocols from the ring learning with errors (RLWE) assumption. Technically, we build two new passively secure protocols, which build upon recent advances in homomorphic secret sharing from (R)LWE (Boyle et al., Eurocrypt 2019), with optimizations tailored to the setting of OLE. We upgrade these to active security using efficient amortized zero-knowledge techniques for lattice relations (Baum et al., Crypto 2018), and design new variants of zero-knowledge arguments that are necessary for some of our constructions.

Our protocols offer several advantages over existing constructions. Firstly, they have the lowest communication complexity amongst previous, practical protocols from RLWE and other assumptions; secondly, they are conceptually very simple, and have just one round of interaction for the case of OLE where b is randomly chosen. We demonstrate this with an implementation of one of our passively secure protocols, which can perform more than 1 million OLEs per second over the ring $\mathbb{Z}_m$, for a 120-bit modulus m, on standard hardware.

1 Introduction

Oblivious linear function evaluation, or OLE, is a two-party protocol between a sender, with input $a, b \in \mathbb{F}$, and a receiver, who inputs $x \in \mathbb{F}$ and receives $y = ax + b$. OLE is an arithmetic generalization of oblivious transfer to a larger field $\mathbb{F}$, since OLE over $\mathbb{F}_2$ can be seen as equivalent to oblivious transfer on the messages z_0, z_1 by setting $a = z_0 + z_1$ and $b = z_0$, so the receiver learns $y = z_x$. Similarly to oblivious transfer, OLE can be used in constructions of secure two-party and multi-party computation, and is particularly useful for the setting of

© Springer Nature Switzerland AG 2020
C. Galdi and V. Kolesnikov (Eds.): SCN 2020, LNCS 12238, pp. 130–149, 2020.
https://doi.org/10.1007/978-3-030-57990-6_7

securely computing arithmetic circuits over $\mathbb{F}$ [3,19,20,23], where OT tends to be less efficient. As well as general secure computation protocols, OLE can be used to carry out specific tasks like private set intersection [22], secure matrix multiplication and oblivious polynomial evaluation [28,30].

OLE can be constructed from a range of "public-key" type assumptions. In the simplest, folklore construction, the receiver encrypts its input x using a linearly homomorphic encryption scheme and gives this to the sender. Using the homomorphic properties of the scheme, the sender computes an encryption of $y = ax + b$ and sends this back to the receiver to decrypt. This approach can be instantiated with Paillier encryption or lattice-based encryption based on the learning with errors (LWE) [29] or RLWE assumptions [26], and has been implicitly used in several secure multi-party computation protocols [8,24, 27]. There are also constructions of OLE from coding-theoretic assumptions [21, 23,28] which mostly rely on the hardness of decoding Reed-Solomon codes in certain parameter regimes with a high enough noise rate. These constructions are asymptotically efficient, but so far have not been implemented in practice, to the best of our knowledge. For the special (and easier) case of *vector-OLE*, which is a large batch of many OLEs with the same input x from the receiver, there are efficient constructions from more standard coding-theoretic assumptions over general codes, which also have good performance in practice [3,10,11,30].

Despite the fact there are many existing constructions of OLE, either implicit or explicit in the literature, very few of these works study the practical efficiency of OLE in its own right (except for the special case of vector-OLE). Instead, most of the aforementioned works either focus on the efficiency of higher-level primitives such as secure multi-party computation, or mainly discuss asymptotic efficiency rather than performance in practice. In this work, we advocate for the practical study of OLE as a *standalone primitive*. This has the benefits that it can be plugged into any higher-level application that needs it in a modular way, potentially simplifying analysis and security proofs compared with a more monolithic approach.

1.1 Our Contributions

We present and study new OLE protocols with security based on the ring learning with errors (RLWE) assumption, with passive and active security. Our passively secure protocols are very simple, consisting of just one message per party, and our most efficient variant achieves the lowest communication complexity of any practical (implemented) OLE protocol we are aware of, requiring around half the bandwidth of previous solutions. We add active security using zero-knowledge proofs, which have a low amortized complexity when performing a large number of OLEs, giving only a small communication overhead over the passive protocols. To adapt existing zero-knowledge proof techniques to our protocols, we have to make several modifications, and describe a new amortized proof of knowledge that can be used to show a batch of *secret-key* (R)LWE ciphertexts is well-formed (previous techniques only apply to *public-key* ciphertexts).

We have implemented and benchmarked our most efficient passively secure protocol, and show it can compute more than 1 million OLEs per second on a standard laptop, over a $\approx$ 120-bit ring $\mathbb{Z}_m$ where m is the product of two CPU word-sized primes. The communication cost per OLE is around 4 elements of $\mathbb{Z}_m$ per party, and the amortized complexity of our actively secure protocol is almost the same, when computing a large enough number of OLEs. This is almost half the communication cost of previous protocols based on RLWE, and less than 25% of the cost of an actively secure protocol based on oblivious transfer and noisy Reed-Solomon encodings [21].

1.2 Outline

In Sect. 1.3 below, we present an overview of the main techniques in our constructions. We then describe some preliminaries in Sect. 2. Section 3 contains our OLE protocols based on public-key RLWE encryption, which only require a standard public key infrastructure as a setup assumption. In Sect. 4, we present more efficient protocols which reduce communication using secret-key encryption, and a more specialized setup assumption. In the full version of this work, we give additional details on the zero-knowledge arguments which are used to make the previous protocols actively secure. Finally, in Sect. 5, we analyze the concrete efficiency of our solutions, compare this with previous OLE protocols, and present implementation results for our most efficient passively secure protocol.

1.3 Techniques

Our protocols construct a symmetric variant of OLE, where one party, Alice, inputs a field element $u \in \mathbb{F}$, the other party, Bob, inputs $v \in \mathbb{F}$, and the parties receive random values α and β (respectively) such that $\alpha + \beta = u \cdot v$. This can easily be used to construct an OLE by having the sender, say Alice, one-time-pad encrypt her additional input using α, allowing Bob to correct his output accordingly. In this formulation, OLE is also equivalent to producing an additive secret-sharing of the product of two private inputs; this type of secret-shared multiplication is an important building block in multi-party computation protocols, for instance in constructing Beaver multiplication triples [7]. In our protocols, we first create OLEs over a large polynomial ring $\mathcal{R}_m = \mathbb{Z}_m[X]/(X^N + 1)$, which comes from the RLWE assumption, and then convert each OLE over $\mathcal{R}_m$ to a batch of N OLEs over $\mathbb{Z}_m$, for some prime modulus m, using packing techniques from homomorphic encryption [31].

Our point of departure is the recent *homomorphic secret sharing* scheme by Boyle et al. [13], based on LWE or RLWE. Homomorphic secret sharing is a form of secret sharing in which shares can be computed upon non-interactively, such that the parties end up with an *additive* secret sharing of the result of the computation. HSS was first constructed under the DDH assumption [12] and variants of threshold and multi-key fully homomorphic encryption [18], followed by the more efficient lattice-based construction of [13], which supports homomorphic computation of branching programs (or, "restricted multiplication" circuits where every multiplication gate must involve at least one input wire). Note that any "public-key" type two-party HSS scheme that supports multiplication leads to a simple OLE protocol: each party sends a secret-sharing of its input, then both parties multiply the shares to obtain an additive share of the product.

Efficient OLE from a Public-Key Setup. Our first construction can be seen as taking the HSS scheme of Boyle et al. and optimizing it for the specific functionality of OLE. When plugging in their scheme to perform OLE, a single share from one party consists of two RLWE ciphertexts: one encrypting the message, and one encrypting a function of the secret key, which is needed to perform the multiplication. Our first observation is that, in the setting of OLE where we have two parties who each have one of the inputs to be multiplied, we can reduce this to just *one ciphertext per party*, where Alice sends an encryption of her input u multiplied by a secret key, and Bob sends an encryption of his input. Both of these ciphertexts, including the one dependent on the secret key, can be created from a standard public-key infrastructure-like setup where Alice and Bob have each others' RLWE public keys, thanks to a weak KDM security property of the scheme. This gives a communication complexity of two $\mathcal{R}_q$ elements per party, for a RLWE ciphertext modulus q, to create a single ring-OLE over $\mathcal{R}_m$. We can also obtain a further saving by sending one party's ciphertext at a smaller modulus $p < q$.

Reducing Communication with a Dedicated Setup. Our second protocol considers a different setup assumption, where the parties are assumed to have access to a single OLE over $\mathcal{R}_q$, which gives them secret shares of the product of two RLWE secret keys. With this, we are able to replace the public-key RLWE ciphertexts from the previous protocol with *secret-key* ciphertexts, which can be of size just one ring element instead of two. This cuts the overall communication in half, and also reduces computational costs.

Achieving Active Security. To obtain security against active corruptions, we need to ensure that both parties' RLWE ciphertexts are correctly generated, in particular, that the small "error" polynomials used as encryption randomness were generated correctly (and not too large). For a public key RLWE encryption, this boils down to proving knowledge of a short vector $s \in \mathbb{Z}_q^n$, such that $As = c$ where A, c are public values defined by the RLWE public key and ciphertext, respectively. In practice, we do not know efficient methods of proving the above statement. Instead, we can obtain good *amortized* efficiency when proving knowledge for *many* such relations of the form

$$A\overline{s}_i = c_i \tag{1}$$

for the same matrix A, where now the secret $\overline{s}_i$ may have slightly larger coefficients than the original secret s_i. This overhead is known as the *soundness slack* parameter, and comes from the fact that a dishonest prover can sometimes make the proof succeed even when s_i is slightly larger than the claimed bound. Efficient amortized proofs for (1) have been given in several works [5,15,16,25], most recently with a communication overhead that is *independent* of the number of relations being proven [4].

Proving correctness of a batch of public-key RLWE ciphertexts can be essentially done by proving a batch of relations of the form in (1), allowing use of these efficient amortized proofs. To achieve active security in our public-key OLE protocol, we use a slightly modified version of the proof from [4], by allowing different size bounds to be proven for different components of s_i. This gives us tighter parameters for the encryption scheme.

On the other hand, for our second protocol, things are not so straightforward. To see why, recall that a batch of secret-key RLWE ciphertexts have the form:

$$(a_i, a_i \cdot s + e_i + (q/p) \cdot x_i) \tag{2}$$

Here, a_i is a random element in the polynomial ring $\mathcal{R}_q = \mathbb{Z}_q[X]/(X^N + 1)$, e_i is a small error value in $\mathcal{R}_q$, and $s \in \mathcal{R}_q$ is the secret key. We want to prove that both s and e_i have small coefficients.

The problem is, since a_i is different for each ciphertext, these cannot be expressed in the form of (1), since they are not linear in a fixed public value. This was *not* the case for the public-key setting, where every ciphertext is linear in the fixed public key; here, by switching to a secret-key encryption scheme to improve efficiency, we can unfortunately no longer apply the amortization techniques of [4].

Furthermore, there is a second obstacle, since we now have a special preprocessing phase which gives out shares of $s_A \cdot s_B$, for the parties' RLWE secret keys s_A and s_B. These must be the *same* secret keys that are used to produce the encryptions, and to ensure this, we also have to tie these together into the ZK proof statement.

To work around these issues, we perform two steps. Firstly, we modify the preprocessing so that each party gets a *commitment* to its secret key, under a suitable homomorphic commitment scheme (which can also be based on lattices [6]). We then design a new proof of knowledge, which proves knowledge of short (s, e_i, x_i) satisfying (2) with similar amortized efficiency to the proof from [4] for (1). Our proof simultaneously guarantees the secret s is the same s that was committed to in the preprocessing, leveraging the homomorphic properties of the commitment scheme.

2   Preliminaries

In this section we introduce the basic notation we will need throughout our work. As basic notation, we write $\alpha \star \beta$ to denote the component-wise product of the vectors α, β.

Rings and Rounding. Let q be an odd integer and $N = 2^r$ be a power of two. We define the ring $\mathcal{R} := \mathbb{Z}[X]/\langle X^N + 1 \rangle$ as well as $\mathcal{R}_q = \mathcal{R}/\langle q \rangle$ as the reduction of the polynomials of $\mathcal{R}$ modulo q. Representing the coefficients of $f \in \mathcal{R}_q$ uniquely by its representatives from $[-(q-1)/2, (q-1)/2]$ we define $\|f\|_\infty$ as the largest norm of any coefficient of f when considered over the above interval. We define by $\mathcal{U}(R)$ the uniform distribution over the finite set R and furthermore let $S_\beta = \{x \in \mathcal{R} \mid \|x\|_\infty \leq \beta\}$.

Let $n, k \in \mathbb{N}^+$. In this work we consider the computational problems Ring-LWE, Module-LWE and Module-SIS. Their full description can be found in the full version of this manuscript.

We define by $\lfloor f \rceil_p$ the scaling of each coefficient of f by p/q over the reals and then rounding to the nearest element in $[-(p-1)/2, (p-1)/2]$ respectively. A simple but useful result we will use throughout our protocols is the following.

Lemma 1. *Let* $p|q$, $x \leftarrow \mathcal{R}_q^n$ *and* $y = x + e \bmod q$ *for some* $e \in \mathcal{R}_q^n$ *with* $\|e\|_\infty < B < q/p$. *Then* $\Pr[\lfloor y \rceil_p \neq \lfloor x \rceil_p \bmod p] \leq \frac{2npNB}{q}$.

Gaussian Distributions and Simulatability. We denote by $\rho_{v,\sigma}^m(x)$ the continuous normal distribution over $\mathbb{R}^m$ centered at $v \in \mathbb{R}^m$ with standard deviation $\sigma \in \mathbb{R}$. If $v = 0$ then we just write $\rho_\sigma^m(x)$. For a countable set $S \subset \mathbb{R}^m$ we furthermore define $\rho_\sigma^m(S) = \sum_{x \in S} \rho_\sigma^m(x)$. Finally, we define the discrete normal distribution over $\mathbb{Z}^m$ centered at $v \in \mathbb{Z}^m$ with standard deviation $\sigma \in \mathbb{R}^m$ as $\mathcal{D}_{v,\sigma}^m(x) = \rho_{v,\sigma}^m(x)/\rho_\sigma^m(\mathbb{Z}^m)$.

Throughout this work we apply $\mathcal{D}$ to vectors from $\mathcal{R}^k$ in which case we mean that $\mathcal{D}_\sigma(x)^k = \mathcal{D}_\sigma^{Nk}(\overline{x})$ with $\overline{x} \in \mathbb{Z}^{Nk}$ being the coefficient-wise embedding of $\mathcal{R}^k$ into $\mathbb{Z}^{Nk}$. We consider sampling $\mathcal{R}$-elements from $\mathcal{D}_\sigma$ as sampling each coefficient independently from this distribution.

Ring-LWE Based Encryption Scheme. In this work we use basic ideas from RLWE-based encryption, specially in our public key based construction from Sect. 3. We describe here a simplified version of the public-key encryption scheme from [26], which we refer to as LPR. We consider two distributions $\mathcal{D}_{\mathsf{sk}}$ and $\mathcal{D}$ over $\mathcal{R}_q$, bounded (with overwhelming probability) by B_{sk} and B_{err}, respectively. The key generation, encryption and decryption procedures are defined as follows:

Gen(a): On input a public random $a \in \mathcal{R}_q$, first sample $s \leftarrow \mathcal{D}_{\mathsf{sk}}$ and $e \leftarrow \mathcal{D}$. Output $\mathsf{sk} = (s)$ and $\mathsf{pk} = (a, b)$ where $b = a \cdot s + e$.

Enc$_{p,q}$(pk, x): On input $\mathsf{pk} \in \mathcal{R}_q^2$ and $x \in \mathcal{R}_p$, sample $w, e_0, e_1 \leftarrow \mathcal{D}$ and output (c_0, c_1), where $c_1 = -a \cdot w + e_1$ and $c_0 = b \cdot w + e_0 + (q/p) \cdot x$.

Dec($\mathsf{sk}, (c_0, c_1)$): Compute $x' = c_0 + s \cdot c_1 \bmod q$, and output $x = \lfloor x' \rceil_p \bmod p^1$. Notice that this works if the total noise $e = s \cdot e_1 + e \cdot w + e_0$ is bounded by $p/2q$.

---

[1] Our protocols do not directly use the decryption algorithm, but our simulator in the proof of Theorem 2 does.

On top of these standard procedures, we also use an algorithm KDMEnc which produces an encryption of $x \cdot s$, where s is the secret key. As observed in [13,14], this can be done using only the public key by adding the message to the second component of an encryption of zero.

KDMEnc$_{p,q}$(pk, x): Sample $w, e_0, e_1 \leftarrow \mathcal{D}$ and output (c_0, c_1), where $c_1 = (q/p) \cdot x - a \cdot w + e_1$ and $c_0 = b \cdot w + e_0$.

Commitments and Zero-Knowledge Arguments. In this work, in order to achieve active security, we make extensive use of commitments schemes and zero knowledge arguments of knowledge. We refer the reader to the full version of this manuscript for full definitions of these cryptographic notions. Here, we only introduce the basic notation.

Commitment Schemes. We consider an additively homomorphic statistically hiding commitment scheme, which we denote by a tuple $C = (\mathsf{KG}, \mathsf{Com}, \mathsf{Open})$. In this work we mainly use two different commitment schemes, namely the somewhat additively homomorphic commitment scheme of Baum et al. [6] (denoted as $C = (\mathsf{KG}, \mathsf{Com}, \mathsf{Open})$) as well as a compressing statistically secure commitment scheme $C_{\mathsf{aux}} = (\mathsf{KG}_{\mathsf{aux}}, \mathsf{KG}_{\mathsf{aux}}, \mathsf{Open}_{\mathsf{aux}})$.

One can easily instantiate C_{aux} either using the Random Oracle or [17]. The scheme of [6] is only somewhat homomorphic, meaning that it only supports a limited number of addition of commitments due to the growth of r. More details on the used commitment scheme can be found in the full version.

Zero-Knowledge Arguments of Knowledge (ZKA). Let $\mathcal{R}$ be an NP relation. For $(pp, x, w) \in \mathcal{R}$ we call pp the public parameter, x the statement and w the witness. A Zero-Knowledge Proof of Knowledge for $\mathcal{R}$ is an interactive protocol Π between a PPT prover $\mathcal{P}$ and a PPT verifier $\mathcal{V}$ satisfying completeness, soundness against bounded malicious provers and honest-verifier zero-knowledge. The actual zero-knowledge arguments that are used with respect to the commitment scheme C can be found in the full version.

Oblivious Linear Function Evaluation. The functionality we implement in this work is oblivious linear evaluation (OLE), which, in a nutshell, consists of producing an additive sharing of a multiplication. A bit more precisely, $\mathcal{P}_{\mathsf{Alice}}$ and $\mathcal{P}_{\mathsf{Bob}}$ have each one secret input $v \in \mathcal{R}_m$ and $u \in \mathcal{R}_m$, respectively, and their goal is to get additive random shares of the product $u \cdot v$. The formal description of the functionality appears in the full version of this manuscript.

SIMD for Lattice-Based Primitives. In this work we exploit plaintext packing techniques used in homomorphic encryption [31] based on the Chinese remainder theorem: We choose $m = 1 \bmod (2N)$ such that the polynomial $X^N + 1$ splits completely into a product of linear factors modulo m. This implies that $\mathcal{R}_m$ is isomorphic to N copies of $\mathbb{Z}_m$, so a single OLE over the ring $\mathcal{R}_m$ can be directly used to obtain a batch of N OLEs over $\mathbb{Z}_m$.

Protocol $\Pi_{\text{OLE-pk}}$

We use moduli $q > p > m$, where $m|p$ and $p|q$, and m is the final modulus of inputs and outputs.

1. *Setup.* The parties call $\mathcal{F}_{\text{PKI}}$, so that both parties obtain $\text{pk} = (a, b) \in \mathcal{R}_q^2$, while $\mathcal{P}_{\text{Alice}}$ gets $s_{\text{Alice}} \in \mathcal{R}_q$ and $\mathcal{P}_{\text{Bob}}$ gets $s_{\text{Bob}} \in \mathcal{R}_q$.
2. *First Message.* On input $u \in \mathcal{R}_m^n$ from $\mathcal{P}_{\text{Bob}}$:
   (a) $\mathcal{P}_{\text{Bob}}$ sends $(c_0, c_1) = \text{KDMEnc}_{p,q}(\text{pk}, u)$ to $\mathcal{P}_{\text{Alice}}$:

(b)	The parties engage in a zero-knowledge argument for the relation $\mathcal{R}_{\text{Bob}}^{\text{pk}}$ with $\mathcal{P}_{\text{Alice}}$ as the verifier and $\mathcal{P}_{\text{Bob}}$ as the prover. If this fails then the parties abort.

   (c) $\mathcal{P}_{\text{Alice}}$ computes $\rho_{\text{Alice}} = \lfloor s_{\text{Alice}} \cdot c_1 \rceil_p$ and $\mathcal{P}_{\text{Bob}}$ computes $\rho_{\text{Bob}} = \lfloor c_0 + s_{\text{Bob}} \cdot c_1 \rceil_p$ (it should hold that $\rho_{\text{Alice}} + \rho_{\text{Bob}} = s \cdot u \bmod p$)
3. *Second Message.* On input $v \in \mathcal{R}_m^n$ from $\mathcal{P}_{\text{Alice}}$:
   (a) $\mathcal{P}_{\text{Alice}}$ sends $(d_0, d_1) = \text{Enc}_{m,p}(\text{pk}, v)$ to $\mathcal{P}_{\text{Bob}}$

(b)	The parties engage in a zero-knowledge argument for the relation $\mathcal{R}_{\text{Alice}}^{\text{pk}}$ with $\mathcal{P}_{\text{Bob}}$ as the verifier and $\mathcal{P}_{\text{Alice}}$ as the prover. If this fails then the parties abort.

   (c) $\mathcal{P}_{\text{Alice}}$ outputs $\alpha = \lfloor d_1 \star \rho_{\text{Alice}} \rceil_m$.
   (d) $\mathcal{P}_{\text{Bob}}$ outputs $\beta = \lfloor d_0 \star u + d_1 \star \rho_{\text{Bob}} \rceil_m$.
   We should now have $\alpha + \beta = u \star v \bmod m$.

Fig. 1. Actively secure OLE protocol from a PKI setup. The passively secure version of the protocol is obtained by removing the framed steps.

3   OLE from PKI Setup

In this section we present our first OLE construction, which is particularly simple and efficient. Furthermore, the only setup required is a correlated form of public key infrastructure in which $\mathcal{P}_{\text{Alice}}$ and $\mathcal{P}_{\text{Bob}}$ have each a secret/public key pair for the LPR scheme, where the $a \in \mathcal{R}_q$ component of the public key is the same for both. This can be seen as a PKI setup in which the public keys are derived using some public randomness. The precise functionality $\mathcal{F}_{\text{PKI}}$ is given in the full version of this manuscript.

Our protocol, $\Pi_{\text{OLE-pk}}$, can be found in Fig. 1. The passively secure version $\Pi_{\text{OLE-pk}}^{\text{passive}}$ is obtained from the active one by removing the zero knowledge arguments, whose steps are framed in the description of the protocol. To provide a high level idea of our construction, we first recall the main techniques from the homomorphic secret-sharing scheme of Boyle et al. [13]. Suppose two parties have additive secret shares of a RLWE secret key $s \in \mathcal{R}_q$, and are also given secret shares modulo q of x, $x \cdot s$ and a public ciphertext $c_y = (c_0, c_1) = \text{Enc}(\text{pk}, y)$, for some messages x, y. Boyle et al. observed that if each party *locally* decrypts c_y using its shares, denoted $[x]$, $[x \cdot s]$, we have:

$$[x] \cdot c_0 + [x \cdot s] \cdot c_1 = [x \cdot (c_0 + c_1 \cdot s)] \approx [(q/p) \cdot x \cdot y].$$

Applying the rounding operation from decryption on the above shares then gives *exact* additive shares of $x \cdot y$, provided the error is much smaller than q/p.

To create the initial shares of x and $x \cdot s$, it is enough to start with shares of s and ciphertexts encrypting $x, x \cdot s$, since each ciphertext can then be locally decrypted to obtain shares of these values. Boyle et al. also described a variant which removes the need for encryptions of $x \cdot s$, but at the cost of an additional setup assumption involving shares of s^2.

Our OLE protocol from this section builds upon this blueprint, with some optimizations. First, we observe that in the two-party OLE setting, it is not necessary to give out $\mathsf{Enc}(\mathsf{pk}, x)$ to obtain shares of x, since one of the parties always knows x so they can simply choose these shares to be x and 0. (This is in contrast to the homomorphic secret-sharing setting, where the evaluating parties may be a set of servers who did not provide inputs.) Since we only do one multiplication, it's therefore enough to give out the two ciphertexts $c_x = \mathsf{Enc}(\mathsf{pk}, x \cdot s)$ and $c_y = \mathsf{Enc}(\mathsf{pk}, y)$, compared with four ciphertexts used in the HSS scheme from [13]. Since both ciphertexts can be easily generated from the public-key setup, this leads to a very simple protocol where each party (in parallel) sends a single message that is either an encryption of its input, or its input times s.

As an additional optimization, we show that the second ciphertext encrypting y can be defined at a smaller modulus p instead of q, since we only care about obtaining the result modulo $m < p$, which saves further on bandwidth[2].

The protocol described above is passively secure, but an active adversary can break the security of this construction by sending incorrectly-formed ciphertexts. Due to our simple communication pattern this turns out to be the only potential source of attack, which we rule out by having the parties prove, in zero knowledge, that their ciphertexts are correctly formed.

3.1 Passive Security

We now proceed to the security proof of our protocol $\Pi_{\mathsf{OLE\text{-}pk}}^{\mathsf{passive}}$, which consists of protocol $\Pi_{\mathsf{OLE\text{-}pk}}$ in Fig. 1 without the zero knowledge arguments framed in the protocol description.

Our proof requires that a random element of $\mathcal{R}_q$ is invertible with high probability. As we will see, this technicality allows the simulator to "solve equations", matching real and ideal views. For our choice of parameters this is always the case, and for this we make use of the following lemma whose proof appears in the full version.

Lemma 2. *Let* $q = \prod_{i=1}^{k} p_i$, *where each* p_i *is an* ℓ-*bit prime. If the polynomial* $f(x) \in \mathbb{Z}_q[x]$ *of degree* N *used to define* $\mathcal{R}_q$ *splits completely mod* p_i *as*

---

[2] This optimization is possible since we skip the "modulus lifting" step from [13], which is only needed when doing several repeated multiplications.

$f(x) = \prod_{j=1}^{N} f_{ij}(x) \bmod p_i$, where each $f_{ij}(x)$ is linear, then the probability that a uniformly random element from $\mathcal{R}_q$ is not invertible is upper bounded by $\frac{N \cdot k}{2^{\ell}}$.

Given the above, the probability that at least one component of a vector in $\mathcal{R}_q^n$ is not invertible is upper bounded by $n \cdot N \cdot k \cdot 2^{-\ell}$. For all our parameter sets in Sect. 5, this quantity is below $2^{-\lambda}$ for $\lambda \approx 36$, which is good enough for our purposes since we need it only as an artefact for the proof and it does not lead to any concrete attack or leakage[3]. We also use invertibility to argue correctness of the protocol, as it is required for being able to use Lemma 1 in our protocols. If this probability is not good enough for a certain application, the parties could use a PRF to rerandomize their shares so that this lemma can be applied without invertibility. However, in order to keep our exposition simple we do not discuss such extension.

Another simple but useful lemma for our construction is the following.

Lemma 3. *Assume that $p|q$. Given $y \in \mathcal{R}_p$, the set of $x \in \mathcal{R}_q$ such that $y = \lfloor x \rceil_p$ is given by $x = \left(\frac{q}{p}\right) \cdot y + e$ for $e \in \mathbb{Z} \cap (-q/2p, q/2p]$. In particular, the mapping $\mathcal{R}_q \to \mathcal{R}_p$ given by $x \mapsto \lfloor x \rceil_p$ is a surjective regular mapping, meaning that every element in the codomain has an equal number of preimages.*

Finally, we have the following proposition, concerning correctness of our construction. It follows as a corollary of Proposition 2 by setting the soundness slack parameter τ to be 1, so we defer the proof to that section.

Proposition 1. *Assume that $3 \cdot 2^{\kappa+1} \cdot n \cdot (mN)^2 \cdot B_{\text{err}} \cdot B_{\text{sk}} \leq p \leq \frac{q}{3 \cdot 2^{\kappa+1} \cdot n \cdot N^2 \cdot B_{\text{err}} \cdot B_{\text{sk}}}$. Let $\boldsymbol{u}, \boldsymbol{v} \in \mathcal{R}_m^n$ be the inputs to Protocol $\Pi_{\text{OLE-pk}}^{\text{passive}}$, and let $\boldsymbol{\alpha}, \boldsymbol{\beta} \in \mathcal{R}_m^n$ be the outputs. Then, with probability at least $1 - 2^{-\kappa}$, $\boldsymbol{u} \star \boldsymbol{v} = \boldsymbol{\alpha} + \boldsymbol{\beta}$.*

With these tools at hand we proceed with the main result from this section.

Theorem 1. *Assume that $3 \cdot 2^{\kappa+1} \cdot n \cdot (mN)^2 \cdot B_{\text{err}} \cdot B_{\text{sk}} \leq p \leq \frac{q}{3 \cdot 2^{\kappa+1} \cdot n \cdot N^2 \cdot B_{\text{err}} \cdot B_{\text{sk}}}$. Then protocol $\Pi_{\text{OLE-pk}}^{\text{passive}}$, which consists of protocol $\Pi_{\text{OLE-pk}}$ without the underlined steps, realizes functionality $\mathcal{F}_{\text{OLE}}$ in the $\mathcal{F}_{\text{PKI}}$-hybrid model under the RLWE assumption.*

The proof of this Theorem is presented in the full version.

3.2 Active Security

As we saw in the previous section, the correctness of our construction relies on the different terms involved having a certain bound: The input $\boldsymbol{u}$ must be smaller than m, the noise terms used for the encryption have to be upper bounded by B_{err}, and the randomness $\boldsymbol{w}$ and $\boldsymbol{w}'$ used for the encryption must be less than

---

[3] This restriction can be easily overcome by modifying the definition of security against passive adversaries, allowing the adversary to choose its output. However, we prefer to stick to more standard security definitions.

B_{sk}. An actively corrupted party who chooses randomness outside these bounds can easily distinguish between the real and ideal executions.

To achieve active security, each party proves in zero-knowledge that the ciphertexts they send are correctly formed. We begin by analyzing the case of a corrupt $\mathcal{P}_{\mathsf{Bob}}$. Consider the message from $\mathcal{P}_{\mathsf{Bob}}$, which consists of a batch of ciphertexts

$$(c_0, c_1) = (b \cdot w + e_0, (q/p) \cdot u - a \cdot w + e_1)$$

Rewriting this, $\mathcal{P}_{\mathsf{Bob}}$ has to prove knowledge of vectors (over $\mathcal{R}_q$) w, u, e_0, e_1 satisfying

$$\underbrace{\begin{pmatrix} b & 1 & 0 & 0 \\ -a & 0 & 1 & q/p \end{pmatrix}}_{A} \cdot \underbrace{(w \; e_0 \; e_1 \; u)^{\top}}_{S} = \underbrace{\begin{pmatrix} c_0 \\ c_1 \end{pmatrix}}_{T} \tag{3}$$

and $\|w\|_{\infty} \leq B_{\mathsf{sk}}$, $\|u\|_{\infty} \leq m$, $\|e_0\|_{\infty} \leq B_{\mathsf{err}}$ and $\|e_1\|_{\infty} \leq B_{\mathsf{err}}$. This can be written in matrix form as follows

$$\mathcal{R}_{\mathsf{Bob}}^{\mathsf{pk}} = \left\{ \begin{array}{c} (pp, u, w) = ((\mathcal{R}, q, n, \beta, A), T, S) \mid (A, S, T) \in \mathcal{R}_q^{2 \times 4} \times \mathcal{R}^{4 \times n} \times \mathcal{R}_q^{2 \times n} \\ \wedge \, AS = T \wedge \|s_i\|_{\infty} \leq \beta_i \end{array} \right\}$$

where s_i is the i-th row of S and the bound vector is $\beta = (B_{\mathsf{sk}}, B_{\mathsf{err}}, B_{\mathsf{err}}, B_{\mathsf{msg}})$. Such type of statements can be proven efficiently using the amortized proof from [4], as we discuss more thoroughly in the full version.

We can similarly define a relation for the message (d_0, d_1) that $\mathcal{P}_{\mathsf{Alice}}$ sends, and we call this relation $\mathcal{R}_{\mathsf{Alice}}^{\mathsf{pk}}$. We note however that in the proof of Theorem 1 we did not actually use any bound on the message v, so we may exclude the bound $\|v\|_{\infty} \leq m$ from this relation.

For the rest of this section we assume the existence of zero knowledge arguments of knowledge for the relations $\mathcal{R}_{\mathsf{Alice}}^{\mathsf{pk}}$ and $\mathcal{R}_{\mathsf{Bob}}^{\mathsf{pk}}$. Note that when proving knowledge of the relation $\mathcal{R}_{\mathsf{Bob}}^{\mathsf{pk}}$ or $\mathcal{R}_{\mathsf{Alice}}^{\mathsf{pk}}$ above, if the prover is malicious then our proof actually only guarantees that $\|s_i\|_2 \leq \tau \cdot \beta_i$, where τ is the soundness slack parameter of the zero knowledge argument. We therefore need to choose our parameters with respect to the larger bounds, to ensure correctness of the protocol.

We begin with the following proposition, which shows that, under an appropriate choice of parameters, our protocol guarantees correctness. Its proof appears in the full version.

Proposition 2. *Assume that* $3 \cdot 2^{\kappa+1} \cdot n \cdot \tau \cdot (mN)^2 \cdot B_{\mathsf{err}} \cdot B_{\mathsf{sk}} \leq p \leq \frac{q}{3 \cdot 2^{\kappa+1} \cdot n \cdot \tau \cdot N^2 \cdot B_{\mathsf{err}} \cdot B_{\mathsf{sk}}}$. *Let* $u, v \in \mathcal{R}_m^n$ *be the inputs to Protocol* $\Pi_{\mathsf{OLE\text{-}pk}}$, *and let* $\alpha, \beta \in \mathcal{R}_m^n$ *be the outputs. Assume that the relations* $\mathcal{R}_{\mathsf{Alice}}^{\mathsf{pk}}$ *and* $\mathcal{R}_{\mathsf{Bob}}^{\mathsf{pk}}$ *defined in Sect. 3.2 hold, but that at most one of them has slack parameter* τ^4. *Then, with probability at least* $1 - 2^{-\kappa}$, $u \star v = \alpha + \beta$.

---

[4] That is, the bounds in one of the two relations have an extra factor of τ. This corresponds to what can be guaranteed for a corrupt party via the zero knowledge argument.

With this tool at hand, the security of the actively secure version of our protocol can be proven. The proof appears in the full version.

Theorem 2. *Assume that* $3 \cdot 2^{\kappa+1} \cdot n \cdot \tau \cdot (mN)^2 \cdot B_{\mathrm{err}} \cdot B_{\mathrm{sk}} \leq p \leq \frac{q}{3 \cdot 2^{\kappa+1} \cdot n \cdot \tau \cdot N^2 \cdot B_{\mathrm{err}} \cdot B_{\mathrm{sk}}}$. *Protocol* $\Pi_{\mathrm{OLE\text{-}pk}}$ *realizes functionality* $\mathcal{F}_{\mathrm{OLE}}$ *under the RLWE assumption.*

4 OLE from Correlated Setup

Ciphertexts in the public key version of the LPR cryptosystem consist of two ring elements. However, in the secret key variant, we can reduce this to one element, since the first element is uniformly random so can be compressed using, for example, a PRG. Given this, a natural way of shaving off a factor of two in the communication complexity of our protocol from Sect. 3 would be to use secret key encryption instead of public key.

In this section we present an OLE protocol that instantiates precisely this idea. The communication pattern is very similar to the one from Protocol $\Pi_{\mathrm{OLE\text{-}pk}}$, in which there is a setup phase, then $\mathcal{P}_{\mathrm{Bob}}$ sends an encryption of his input u to $\mathcal{P}_{\mathrm{Alice}}$ (and proves in zero-knowledge its correctness for the actively secure version), and then $\mathcal{P}_{\mathrm{Alice}}$ does the same. The challenge, here, is that now, as we are using secret-key encryption to obtain his ciphertext in the first message, there is no way for Bob to encrypt u multiplied by the (combined) secret key.

To make this work, we replace the PKI setup functionality from the previous section with a more specialized setup, where $\mathcal{P}_{\mathrm{Bob}}$ gets $\sigma_{\mathrm{Bob}} \in \mathcal{R}_q$ and $\mathcal{P}_{\mathrm{Alice}}$ gets $\sigma_{\mathrm{Alice}} \in \mathcal{R}_q$ such that $s_{\mathrm{Alice}} \cdot s_{\mathrm{Bob}} = \sigma_{\mathrm{Alice}} + \sigma_{\mathrm{Bob}} \bmod q$. This can be seen as an OLE itself, where the values being multiplied are small RLWE secret keys; under this interpretation, our protocol can be seen as a form of "OLE extension" protocol. The intuition for why this setup is useful, is that Bob's secret-key ciphertext can now be distributively "decrypted" using the shares of $s_{\mathrm{Alice}} \cdot s_{\mathrm{Bob}}$, which (after rounding) leads to shares of $u \cdot s_{\mathrm{Alice}}$. In the second phase, these shares are then used to "decrypt" Alice's ciphertext, giving shares of the product $u \star v$.

The setup functionality is described in the full version of this manuscript, where we present both the passive and active versions of the functionality, with the main difference being that in the active setting we must ensure that the corrupt party uses the same secret key for encrypting its input as the secret key distributed in the setup phase. Thus, in this case, when the corrupted party proves in zero knowledge the correctness of its encryption, it also proves that the secret key is the same as in the setup phase. This requires the setup functionality in the active case to output some extra information that allows us to "bind" the key from the setup with the key from the encryption sent, for which we use commitments. We discuss this in more detail when we look at active security in Sect. 4.2.

Our protocol is described in full detail in Fig. 2. As in Sect. 3 , we present the full, actively secure version, but outline in a box those steps that are only necessary for active security.

Protocol $\Pi_{\text{OLE-sk}}$

We use moduli $q > p > m$, where m is the final modulus of inputs and outputs. We assume that m divides p and that p divides q.

1. *Setup phase.*
   (a) *Passive case.* $\mathcal{P}_{\text{Alice}}, \mathcal{P}_{\text{Bob}}$ each send (Sample, sid) to $\mathcal{F}_{\text{setup}}$. $\mathcal{P}_{\text{Alice}}$ obtains $s_{\text{Alice}}, \sigma_{\text{Alice}}$ while $\mathcal{P}_{\text{Bob}}$ obtains $s_{\text{Bob}}, \sigma_{\text{Bob}}$.

   > *Active case.* $\mathcal{P}_{\text{Alice}}, \mathcal{P}_{\text{Bob}}$ each send (Sample, sid) to $\mathcal{F}_{\text{setup}}$. $\mathcal{P}_{\text{Alice}}$ obtains $s_{\text{Alice}}, \sigma_{\text{Alice}}, r_{\text{Alice}}, c_{\text{Alice}}, c_{\text{Bob}}$ and $\mathcal{P}_{\text{Bob}}$ obtains $s_{\text{Bob}}, \sigma_{\text{Bob}}, r_{\text{Bob}}, c_{\text{Alice}}, c_{\text{Bob}}$.

   (b) The parties sample two public random values $a, a' \in \mathcal{R}_q^n$.[a]
2. *First Message.* On input $u \in \mathcal{R}_m^n$ from $\mathcal{P}_{\text{Bob}}$:
   (a) $\mathcal{P}_{\text{Bob}}$ samples a noise vector $e_{\text{Bob}} \leftarrow \mathcal{D}^n$ and sends $c = \left(\frac{q}{p}\right) \cdot u + (a \cdot s_{\text{Bob}} + e_{\text{Bob}})$ $\mod q$ to $\mathcal{P}_{\text{Alice}}$.

   > (b) The parties engage in a zero-knowledge argument for the relation $\mathcal{R}_{\text{Bob}}^{\text{sk}}$ with $\mathcal{P}_{\text{Alice}}$ as the verifier and $\mathcal{P}_{\text{Bob}}$ as the prover with witness $(u, e_{\text{Bob}}, s_{\text{Bob}}, r_{\text{Bob}})$. If this fails then the parties abort.

   (c) $\mathcal{P}_{\text{Alice}}$ computes $\rho_{\text{Alice}} = \lfloor s_{\text{Alice}} \cdot c - a \cdot \sigma_{\text{Alice}} \rceil_p$.
   (d) $\mathcal{P}_{\text{Bob}}$ computes $\rho_{\text{Bob}} = - \lfloor a \cdot \sigma_{\text{Bob}} \rceil_p$. It should now hold that $u \cdot s_{\text{Alice}} = \rho_{\text{Alice}} + \rho_{\text{Bob}} \mod p$.
3. *Second Message.* On input $v \in \mathcal{R}_m^n$ from $\mathcal{P}_{\text{Alice}}$.
   (a) $\mathcal{P}_{\text{Alice}}$ samples a noise vector $e_{\text{Alice}} \leftarrow \mathcal{D}^n$ and sends $d = \left(\frac{p}{m}\right) \cdot v + (a' \cdot s_{\text{Alice}} + e_{\text{Alice}}) \mod p$ to $\mathcal{P}_{\text{Bob}}$.

   > (b) The parties engage in a zero-knowledge argument for the relation $\mathcal{R}_{\text{Alice}}^{\text{sk}}$ with $\mathcal{P}_{\text{Bob}}$ as the verifier and $\mathcal{P}_{\text{Alice}}$ as the prover, with witness $(v, e_{\text{Alice}}, s_{\text{Alice}}, r_{\text{Alice}})$. If this fails then the parties abort.

   (c) $\mathcal{P}_{\text{Bob}}$ outputs, $\beta = \lfloor u \star d - a' \star \rho_{\text{Bob}} \rceil_m \mod m$.
   (d) $\mathcal{P}_{\text{Alice}}$ outputs, $\alpha = - \lfloor a' \star \rho_{\text{Alice}} \rceil_m \mod m$. It should hold that $u \star v = \alpha + \beta \mod m$

---

[a] In practice this can be done by using a PRF with some pre-shared key. In our proofs we use a random oracle that can be programmed by the simulator.

Fig. 2. Actively secure OLE protocol based on RLWE. The passively secure version of the protocol is obtained by removing the framed steps.

4.1 Passive Security

The following proposition states that our construction satisfies correctness when the parties are honest, and follows from Proposition 4 in Sect. 4.2, which analyzes the case where the bounds satisfied by the values from one of the parties may not be sharp.

Proposition 3. *Assume that $2^{\kappa+1} \cdot n \cdot (mN)^2 \cdot B_{\text{err}} \leq p \leq \frac{q}{2^{\kappa+1} \cdot n \cdot N^2 \cdot B_{\text{err}} \cdot B_{\text{sk}}}$. Let $u, v \in \mathcal{R}_m^n$ be the inputs to Protocol $\Pi_{\text{OLE-sk}}$, and let $\alpha, \beta \in \mathcal{R}_m^n$ be the outputs. Then, with probability at least $1 - 2^{-\kappa}$, $u \star v = \alpha + \beta$.*

With this proposition, we proceed to the proof of security of our passively secure protocol.

Theorem 3. *Assume that $m^2 \cdot B_{err} \cdot 2^{\kappa+1} \cdot n \cdot N^2 \leq p \leq \frac{q}{2^{\kappa+1} \cdot n \cdot N^2 \cdot B_{sk} \cdot B_{err}}$. Then protocol $\Pi_{OLE\text{-}sk}^{passive}$, which consists of protocol $\Pi_{OLE\text{-}sk}$ without the underlined steps, realizes functionality $\mathcal{F}_{OLE}$ in the $\mathcal{F}_{setup}$-hybrid model under the RLWE assumption.*

The proof bears similarity with the proof of Theorem 1, and we defer it to the full version.

4.2 Active Security

An active adversary in the protocol $\Pi_{OLE\text{-}sk}$ can cheat by sending incorrect messages. For example, a corrupt $\mathcal{P}_{Bob}$ may send an incorrectly formed c, and one can show that, in fact, by choosing c appropriately a corrupt $\mathcal{P}_{Bob}$ may learn some information about $\mathcal{P}_{Alice}$'s input v. A similar attack can be carried out by a corrupt $\mathcal{P}_{Alice}$. Hence, to achieve active security, we must ensure that the message c sent by $\mathcal{P}_{Bob}$ and the message d sent by $\mathcal{P}_{Alice}$ are computed honestly.

We implement zero knowledge arguments to show precisely these statements. $\mathcal{P}_{Bob}$ proves that he knows $\boldsymbol{u}, \boldsymbol{e}$ and s_{Bob} of the appropriate sizes such that $c = \left(\frac{q}{p}\right) \cdot \boldsymbol{u} + (\boldsymbol{a} \cdot s_{Bob} + \boldsymbol{e}_{Bob}) \bmod q$, and $\mathcal{P}_{Alice}$ proceeds similarly.

An additional technicality, however, is that s_{Bob} (and respectively s_{Alice}) has to be exactly the same value that was distributed during the setup phase. To enforce this, we consider a modified setup functionality for the actively secure setting that, on top of distributing $s_{Bob} \cdot s_{Alice} = \sigma_{Bob} + \sigma_{Alice}$, also distributes commitments to s_{Bob} and s_{Alice} that can be used in the relation of the zero knowledge argument.

Given that the protocol is essentially symmetric with respect to the roles of $\mathcal{P}_{Alice}$ and $\mathcal{P}_{Bob}$, from now on we focus on discussing the case of a corrupt $\mathcal{P}_{Bob}$. A similar argument applies for the case of corrupt $\mathcal{P}_{Alice}$. The message c that $\mathcal{P}_{Bob}$ sends is formed by adding n RLWE samples to $\left(\frac{q}{p}\right) \cdot \boldsymbol{u}$, which is a scaled version of its input $\boldsymbol{u}$. Furthermore, the RLWE samples must be generated using the secret s_{Bob} distributed in the setup phase. As a result, the relation that $\mathcal{P}_{Bob}$ will prove is

$$\mathcal{R}_{Bob}^{sk}(\tau) = \left\{ \begin{array}{c} (pp, u, w) = \\ \left((\mathcal{R}, q, p, m, \beta, \mathsf{pk}, \boldsymbol{a}, \mathsf{com}_{Bob}), \right. \\ \left. c, (\boldsymbol{u}, \boldsymbol{e}, s, r) \right) \end{array} \middle| \begin{array}{l} c = \left(\frac{q}{p}\right) \cdot \boldsymbol{u} + \boldsymbol{a} \cdot s + \boldsymbol{e} \bmod q \wedge \\ \|\boldsymbol{u}\|_{\infty} \leq \tau \cdot \beta_1 \wedge \|\boldsymbol{e}\|_{\infty} \leq \tau \cdot \beta_2 \wedge \\ \mathsf{Open}_{\mathsf{pk}}(\mathsf{com}_{Bob}, s, r) = 1 \end{array} \right\}$$

and $\mathcal{R}_{Alice}^{sk}$ can be defined similarly[5]. Here in the honest case $\mathcal{P}_{Bob}$ starts with $\mathcal{R}_{Bob}^{sk}$, but the guarantee given by the zero-knowledge argument will be for a substantially larger factor τ (see the full version). The relation essentially shows

---

[5] As in public-key protocol from Sect. 3.2, $\mathcal{P}_{Alice}$ does not need to prove the bound on her input v.

that the message that $\mathcal{P}_{\text{Bob}}$ sends is well formed, and furthermore, that the s_{Bob} used for constructing this message is exactly the same as the one provided in the setup phase.

For the purpose of this section we assume the existence of zero knowledge arguments for the relations $\mathcal{R}^{\text{sk}}_{\text{Alice}}$ and $\mathcal{R}^{\text{sk}}_{\text{Bob}}$. We develop such results in the full version.

Now, to proceed with the security proof of our protocol, we first present the following proposition, which states that our construction satisfies correctness even when the bound on the parameters may have some slack. This is similar to Proposition 2 and its proof is deferred to the full version.

Proposition 4. *Assume that* $2^{\kappa+1} \cdot n \cdot \tau \cdot (mN)^2 \cdot B_{\text{err}} \leq p \leq \frac{q}{2^{\kappa+1} \cdot n \cdot \tau \cdot N^2 \cdot B_{\text{err}} \cdot B_{\text{sk}}}$. *Let* $\boldsymbol{u}, \boldsymbol{v} \in \mathcal{R}^n_m$ *be the inputs to Protocol* $\Pi_{\text{OLE-sk}}$, *and let* $\boldsymbol{\alpha}, \boldsymbol{\beta} \in \mathcal{R}^n_m$ *be the outputs. Assume that the relations* $\mathcal{R}^{\text{sk}}_{\text{Alice}}$ *and* $\mathcal{R}^{\text{sk}}_{\text{Bob}}$ *hold, but that at most one of them has slack parameter* τ. *Then, with probability at least* $1 - 2^{-\kappa}$, $\boldsymbol{u} \star \boldsymbol{v} = \boldsymbol{\alpha} + \boldsymbol{\beta}$.

Given this, we can prove the security of our actively secure OLE protocol, as stated in the following theorem. The proof appears in the full version.

Theorem 4. *Assume that* $2^{\kappa+1} \cdot n \cdot \tau \cdot (mN)^2 \cdot B_{\text{err}} \leq p \leq \frac{q}{2^{\kappa+1} \cdot n \cdot \tau \cdot N^2 \cdot B_{\text{err}} \cdot B_{\text{sk}}}$. *Then protocol* $\Pi_{\text{OLE-sk}}$ *realizes functionality* $\mathcal{F}_{\text{OLE}}$ *in the* $\mathcal{F}_{\text{setup}}$-*hybrid model under the RLWE assumption.*

5   Evaluation

In this section, we evaluate the efficiency of our OLE protocols, and compare this with protocols based on previous techniques. Firstly, we look at the communication complexity and compare this with other protocols. Then, in Sect. 5.2, we present implementation results for our passively secure secret-key protocol to demonstrate its practicality.

Choosing Parameters. We estimate parameters for our OLE protocols according to the correctness requirement in Proposition 2. For RLWE we use a ternary secret distribution (so, $B_{\text{sk}} = 1$) a Gaussian error distribution with $\sigma = 3.19$ and $B_{\text{err}} = 6\sigma$; the soundness slack parameter is $\tau = 1$ for passive protocols and $\tau \approx 24\sqrt{8Nn\kappa}$ otherwise. The statistical security parameter is $\kappa = 40$.

5.1   Comparison to Previous Protocols

Table 1 presents the communication complexity, measured from the protocol specifications, of our two public-key and secret-key OLE protocols, and compares this with two other protocols based on RLWE-based homomorphic encryption, either additively homomorphic (AHE) or somewhat homomorphic (SHE), as well as a protocol based on noisy Reed-Solomon encodings (RS). As can be seen from the table, ours is the only protocol with just a single round of communication, where each party simultaneously sends just one message (as in a non-interactive

Table 1. Comparison of the complexity of our OLE protocols with previous works based on homomorphic encryption

Protocol	Security		Rounds*	Total comm. (bits)			
	Passive	Active		$\log m \approx 128$		$\log m \approx 64$	
				Passive	Active	Passive	Active
PK-OLE	RLWE	+ FS[†]	1	1516	1630	1004	1120
SK-OLE	RLWE	+ FS	1	758	815	502	560
AHE	RLWE	+ FS + LOE[‡]	2	1320	1476	800	956
SHE	RLWE	+ FS	2	3682	3682	2310	2310
RS	Noisy encodings	–	8	4096	4096	2048	2048

[†] FS is Fiat-Shamir
[‡] LOE is linear-only encryption [9]
* 1 round means that each party sends one message simultaneously. 2 rounds either means that each party sequentially sends one message (for AHE), or one simultaneous message, twice in succession (for SHE).

key exchange), whereas both other protocols require two rounds. Our secret-key protocol, which requires some special preprocessing, has the lowest communication cost of all the protocols, with both passive and active security. Furthermore, compared with the previously most efficient protocol based on AHE with active security, our active protocols avoid the need for assuming linear-only encryption, which is a relatively strong and un-studied assumption, compared with standard RLWE.

A full description of these protocols can be found in the full version.

5.2 Experimental Results

We have implemented the passive version of the secret-key protocol (see in Fig. 2) in Go language, making use of the ring package provided by the lattigo library [1]. Our implementation features a full-RNS (Residue Number System) realization of all the protocol operations, using a moduli of 60-bit limbs. For comparison purposes, we have also implemented an AHE-based OLE protocol (we refer the reader to the full version for more details).

The execution times of the protocol steps were tested on a laptop with an Intel Core i7-8550U processor with 16 GB RAM, running Arch Linux with kernel 5.6.4 and Go 1.14.2 The latency is not simulated, as it is highly dependent on the particular deployment; we include instead the communication complexity of the involved messages, from which the latency can be derived.

We have chosen two practical parameter sets for both protocols (see Tables 2a and 4a), both featuring more than 110 bits of security,[6] and achieving more than 2 million scalar OLEs per protocol run. Table 2b includes the run times

---

[6] We have used the LWE security estimator of Albrecht et al. [2] (available online in https://bitbucket.org/malb/lwe-estimator.) to give bit-security estimates.

Table 2. Parameter sets and run times in the passive case of Fig. 2

Parameter	Par. set 1	Par. set 2	Bob	Par. set 1	Par. set 2	Alice	Par. set 1	Par. set 2
q	360 bits (6 limbs)	480 bits (8 limbs)	Step 2.(a)	462 ms	601 ms	Step 2.(c)	564 ms	817 ms
p	240 bits (4 limbs)	360 bits (6 limbs)	Step 2.(d)	533 ms	772 ms	Step 3.(a)	350 ms	479 ms
m	60 bits (1 limb)	120 bits (2 limbs)	Step 3.(c)	263 ms	438 ms	Step 3.(d)	242 ms	412 ms
Bit security	≈ 159	≈ 116	1st msg	995 ms	1373 ms	1st msg	564 ms	817 ms
# OLEs	2097152	2097152	2nd msg	263 ms	438 ms	2nd msg	591 ms	890 ms

(a) Example parameter sets ($n = 128$ and $N = 16384$) and global run times for the passive case of Fig. 2 (uniformly random ternary secret keys $\{-1, 0, 1\}$ and Gaussian noise with $\sigma = 3.19$)

(b) Run times in the passive case of Fig. 2 for the example parameter sets of Table 2a ($n = 128$ and $N = 16384$, uniformly random ternary secret keys $\{-1, 0, 1\}$ and Gaussian noise with $\sigma = 3.19$)

Table 3. Total run times expressions and extrapolated run times in the passive case of Fig. 2

Run time expressions for Bob and Alice	Total time	600Mbit/s	1Gbit/s	10Gbit/s
$T_{\text{Bob}} = \max(T_{2.a} + T_{2.d}, T_{3.a} + T_d) + T_{3.c}$	Par. Set 1	2526 ms	2023 ms	1344 ms
$T_{\text{Alice}} = \max(T_{3.a}, T_{2.a} + T_c) + T_{2.c} + T_{3.d}$	Par. Set 2	3508 ms	2837 ms	1931 ms

(a) Total run time expressions for Bob (T_{Bob}) and Alice (T_{Alice})

(b) Extrapolated Run times $(\max(T_{\text{Bob}}, T_{\text{Alice}}))$ in the passive case of Fig. 2

Table 4. Parameter sets and communication costs for the passive case of Fig. 2 and AHE-based protocol (see full version)

Parameter	Par. set 1	Par. set 2
$\{n, N\}$	$\{256, 8192\}$	$\{128, 16384\}$
p	240 bits (4 limbs)	360 bits (6 limbs)
m	60 bits (1 limb)	120 bits (2 limbs)
bit security	≈ 115	≈ 159
# OLEs	2097152	2097152
Alice time	1441 ms	2129 ms
Bob time	1024 ms	1375 ms
Total time	2465 ms	3504 ms

Proposed protocol of Fig. 2		
$\{$Bob $|$ Alice$\}$	Par. set 1	Par. set 2
1st msg. $\{2.(a) \mid -\}$	$\{94.37 \mid -\}$ MB	$\{125.83 \mid -\}$ MB
2nd msg. $\{- \mid 3.(a)\}$	$\{- \mid 62.91\}$ MB	$\{- \mid 94.37\}$ MB
AHE-based protocol (see full version)		
1st round	$\{- \mid 62.91\}$ MB	$\{- \mid 94.37\}$ MB
2nd round	$\{125.83 \mid -\}$ MB	$\{188.74 \mid -\}$ MB

(a) Example parameter sets and global run times for the passively secure OLE based on AHE from the full version (uniformly random ternary secret keys $\{-1, 0, 1\}$ and Gaussian noise with $\sigma = 3.19$)

(b) Communication cost in the passive case of Fig. 2 and the passively secure OLE based on AHE from the full version corresponding to each party (Alice and Bob) and Table 4b (see full version) shows the communication costs.

It is worth noting that the public key version from Fig. 1 is not explicitly tested, but it incurs in a similar computational complexity as the one from Fig. 2; it presents, though, an increase on the communication complexity, as the interchanged messages are composed of two polynomials instead of one.

As the latency is not simulated, in order to compare with other protocols, we must consider that the total run time of ours would be $\max(T_{\mathsf{Bob}}, T_{\mathsf{Alice}})$, being T_{Bob} (resp. T_{Alice}) the corresponding run time for Bob (resp. Alice). Tables 3a and 3b include the corresponding expressions and also extrapolate total protocol run times for some specific values of network bandwidth $\{600\mathsf{Mbit/s}, 1\mathsf{Gbit/s}, 10\mathsf{Gbit/s}\}$. T_{step} corresponds to the time of each step included in Table 2b, and T_d (resp. T_c) is the time needed to transmit ciphertext d (resp. c)

Extrapolated runtimes are approximately equal or lower than those obtained with the protocol based on AHE (see full version); note that for the last one we are not taking into account transmission runtimes. Consequently, we can see that the proposed protocols in this paper achieve both a better efficiency and lower communication cost than the one based on AHE described in the full version.

Acknowledgements. We thank the anonymous reviewers for comments which helped to improve the paper. This work has been supported by the European Research Council (ERC) under the European Union's Horizon 2020 research and innovation programme under grant agreement No 669255 (MPCPRO), the Danish Independent Research Council under Grant-ID DFF–6108-00169 (FoCC), an Aarhus University Research Foundation starting grant, the Xunta de Galicia & ERDF under projects ED431G2019/08 and Grupo de Referencia ED431C2017/53, and by the grant #2017-201 (DPPH) of the Strategic Focal Area "Personalized Health and Related Technologies (PHRT)" of the ETH Domain.

References

1. Lattigo 1.3.1 (2020). http://github.com/ldsec/lattigo. EPFL-LDS
2. Albrecht, M.R., Player, R., Scott, S.: On the concrete hardness of learning with errors. J. Math. Cryptol. **9**(3), 169–203 (2015)
3. Applebaum, B., Damgård, I., Ishai, Y., Nielsen, M., Zichron, L.: Secure arithmetic computation with constant computational overhead. In: Katz, J., Shacham, H. (eds.) CRYPTO 2017. LNCS, vol. 10401, pp. 223–254. Springer, Cham (2017). https://doi.org/10.1007/978-3-319-63688-7_8
4. Baum, C., Bootle, J., Cerulli, A., del Pino, R., Groth, J., Lyubashevsky, V.: Sublinear lattice-based zero-knowledge arguments for arithmetic circuits. In: Shacham, H., Boldyreva, A. (eds.) CRYPTO 2018. LNCS, vol. 10992, pp. 669–699. Springer, Cham (2018). https://doi.org/10.1007/978-3-319-96881-0_23
5. Baum, C., Damgård, I., Larsen, K.G., Nielsen, M.: How to prove knowledge of small secrets. In: Robshaw, M., Katz, J. (eds.) CRYPTO 2016. LNCS, vol. 9816, pp. 478–498. Springer, Heidelberg (2016). https://doi.org/10.1007/978-3-662-53015-3_17

6. Baum, C., Damgård, I., Lyubashevsky, V., Oechsner, S., Peikert, C.: More efficient commitments from structured lattice assumptions. In: Catalano, D., De Prisco, R. (eds.) SCN 2018. LNCS, vol. 11035, pp. 368–385. Springer, Cham (2018). https://doi.org/10.1007/978-3-319-98113-0_20

7. Beaver, D.: Efficient multiparty protocols using circuit randomization. In: Feigenbaum, J. (ed.) CRYPTO 1991. LNCS, vol. 576, pp. 420–432. Springer, Heidelberg (1992). https://doi.org/10.1007/3-540-46766-1_34

8. Bendlin, R., Damgård, I., Orlandi, C., Zakarias, S.: Semi-homomorphic encryption and multiparty computation. In: Paterson, K.G. (ed.) EUROCRYPT 2011. LNCS, vol. 6632, pp. 169–188. Springer, Heidelberg (2011). https://doi.org/10.1007/978-3-642-20465-4_11

9. Boneh, D., Ishai, Y., Sahai, A., Wu, D.J.: Lattice-based SNARGs and their application to more efficient obfuscation. In: Coron, J.-S., Nielsen, J.B. (eds.) EUROCRYPT 2017. LNCS, vol. 10212, pp. 247–277. Springer, Cham (2017). https://doi.org/10.1007/978-3-319-56617-7_9

10. Boyle, E., Couteau, G., Gilboa, N., Ishai, Y.: Compressing vector OLE. In: Lie, D., Mannan, M., Backes, M., Wang, X. (eds.) ACM CCS 2018, pp. 896–912. ACM Press (2018)

11. Boyle, E., et al.: Efficient two-round OT extension and silent non-interactive secure computation. In: Cavallaro, L., Kinder, J., Wang, X., Katz, J. (eds.) ACM CCS 2019, pp. 291–308. ACM Press (2019)

12. Boyle, E., Gilboa, N., Ishai, Y.: Breaking the circuit size barrier for secure computation under DDH. In: Robshaw, M., Katz, J. (eds.) CRYPTO 2016. LNCS, vol. 9814, pp. 509–539. Springer, Heidelberg (2016). https://doi.org/10.1007/978-3-662-53018-4_19

13. Boyle, E., Kohl, L., Scholl, P.: Homomorphic secret sharing from lattices without FHE. In: Ishai, Y., Rijmen, V. (eds.) EUROCRYPT 2019. LNCS, vol. 11477, pp. 3–33. Springer, Cham (2019). https://doi.org/10.1007/978-3-030-17656-3_1

14. Brakerski, Z., Vaikuntanathan, V.: Fully homomorphic encryption from ring-LWE and security for key dependent messages. In: Rogaway, P. (ed.) CRYPTO 2011. LNCS, vol. 6841, pp. 505–524. Springer, Heidelberg (2011). https://doi.org/10.1007/978-3-642-22792-9_29

15. Cramer, R., Damgård, I., Xing, C., Yuan, C.: Amortized complexity of zero-knowledge proofs revisited: achieving linear soundness slack. In: Coron, J.-S., Nielsen, J.B. (eds.) EUROCRYPT 2017. LNCS, vol. 10210, pp. 479–500. Springer, Cham (2017). https://doi.org/10.1007/978-3-319-56620-7_17

16. Damgård, I., Pastro, V., Smart, N., Zakarias, S.: Multiparty computation from somewhat homomorphic encryption. In: Safavi-Naini, R., Canetti, R. (eds.) CRYPTO 2012. LNCS, vol. 7417, pp. 643–662. Springer, Heidelberg (2012). https://doi.org/10.1007/978-3-642-32009-5_38

17. Damgård, I.B., Pedersen, T.P., Pfitzmann, B.: On the existence of statistically hiding bit commitment schemes and fail-stop signatures. In: Stinson, D.R. (ed.) CRYPTO 1993. LNCS, vol. 773, pp. 250–265. Springer, Heidelberg (1994). https://doi.org/10.1007/3-540-48329-2_22

18. Dodis, Y., Halevi, S., Rothblum, R.D., Wichs, D.: Spooky encryption and its applications. In: Robshaw, M., Katz, J. (eds.) CRYPTO 2016. LNCS, vol. 9816, pp. 93–122. Springer, Heidelberg (2016). https://doi.org/10.1007/978-3-662-53015-3_4

19. Döttling, N., Ghosh, S., Nielsen, J.B., Nilges, T., Trifiletti, R.: TinyOLE: efficient actively secure two-party computation from oblivious linear function evaluation. In: Thuraisingham, B.M., Evans, D., Malkin, T., Xu, D. (eds.) ACM CCS 2017, pp. 2263–2276. ACM Press (2017)

20. Genkin, D., Ishai, Y., Prabhakaran, M., Sahai, A., Tromer, E.: Circuits resilient to additive attacks with applications to secure computation. In: Shmoys, D.B. (ed.) 46th ACM STOC, pp. 495–504. ACM Press (2014)
21. Ghosh, S., Nielsen, J.B., Nilges, T.: Maliciously secure oblivious linear function evaluation with constant overhead. In: Takagi, T., Peyrin, T. (eds.) ASIACRYPT 2017. LNCS, vol. 10624, pp. 629–659. Springer, Cham (2017). https://doi.org/10.1007/978-3-319-70694-8_22
22. Ghosh, S., Nilges, T.: An algebraic approach to maliciously secure private set intersection. In: Ishai, Y., Rijmen, V. (eds.) EUROCRYPT 2019. LNCS, vol. 11478, pp. 154–185. Springer, Cham (2019). https://doi.org/10.1007/978-3-030-17659-4_6
23. Ishai, Y., Prabhakaran, M., Sahai, A.: Secure arithmetic computation with no honest majority. In: Reingold, O. (ed.) TCC 2009. LNCS, vol. 5444, pp. 294–314. Springer, Heidelberg (2009). https://doi.org/10.1007/978-3-642-00457-5_18
24. Keller, M., Pastro, V., Rotaru, D.: Overdrive: making SPDZ great again. In: Nielsen, J.B., Rijmen, V. (eds.) EUROCRYPT 2018. LNCS, vol. 10822, pp. 158–189. Springer, Cham (2018). https://doi.org/10.1007/978-3-319-78372-7_6
25. Lyubashevsky, V.: Lattice signatures without trapdoors. In: Pointcheval, D., Johansson, T. (eds.) EUROCRYPT 2012. LNCS, vol. 7237, pp. 738–755. Springer, Heidelberg (2012). https://doi.org/10.1007/978-3-642-29011-4_43
26. Lyubashevsky, V., Peikert, C., Regev, O.: A toolkit for ring-LWE cryptography. In: Johansson, T., Nguyen, P.Q. (eds.) EUROCRYPT 2013. LNCS, vol. 7881, pp. 35–54. Springer, Heidelberg (2013). https://doi.org/10.1007/978-3-642-38348-9_3
27. Mohassel, P., Zhang, Y.: SecureML: a system for scalable privacy-preserving machine learning. In: 2017 IEEE Symposium on Security and Privacy, pp. 19–38. IEEE Computer Society Press (2017)
28. Naor, M., Pinkas, B.: Oblivious transfer and polynomial evaluation. In: 31st ACM STOC, pp. 245–254. ACM Press (1999)
29. Regev, O.: On lattices, learning with errors, random linear codes, and cryptography. In: Gabow, H.N., Fagin, R. (eds.) 37th ACM STOC, pp. 84–93. ACM Press (2005)
30. Schoppmann, P., Gascón, A., Reichert, L., Raykova, M.: Distributed vector-OLE: improved constructions and implementation. In: Cavallaro, L., Kinder, J., Wang, X., Katz, J. (eds.) ACM CCS 2019, pp. 1055–1072. ACM Press (2019)
31. Smart, N.P., Vercauteren, F.: Fully homomorphic SIMD operations. Des. Codes Cryptogr. 71(1), 57–81 (2012). https://doi.org/10.1007/s10623-012-9720-4

Multi-clients Verifiable Computation via Conditional Disclosure of Secrets

Rishabh Bhadauria$^{(\boxtimes)}$ and Carmit Hazay$^{(\boxtimes)}$ (iD)

Bar-Ilan University, Ramat-Gan, Israel
{rishabh.bhadauria,carmit.hazay}@biu.ac.il

Abstract. In this paper, we explore the connection between two-party conditional disclosure of secrets (CDS) and verifiable computation. Here, the integrity mechanism underlying CDS is leveraged to ensure two-clients verifiable computation, where the computation is outsourced to an external server by two clients that share the input to the function. Basing integrity on CDS enjoys several significant advantages such as non-interactivity, constant rate communication complexity, a simple verification procedure, easily batched, and more.

In this work, we extend the definition of plain CDS, considering two additional security properties of privacy and obliviousness that respectively capture input and output privacy. We then show that these extended notions of CDS are useful for designing secure two-party protocols in the presence of an untrusted third party.

We complement the above with a sequence of new CDS constructions for a class of predicates of interest, including private set-intersection (PSI) and set-union cardinality, comparison, range predicate, and more. Based on these constructions we design new non-interactive constant-rate protocols for comparing two strings based on symmetric-key cryptography, and without requiring bit-decomposition. We additionally design new protocols for PSI cardinality and PSI based on recent work by Le, Ranellucci, and Gordon (CCS 2019) with similar advantages.

1 Introduction

In this paper, we explore the connection between two-party conditional disclosure of secrets (CDS) [11] and verifiable computation. CDS is a generalization of secret-sharing, where two parties (denoted by Alice and Bob), that share a uniform string r, wish to disclose a secret s to a third party (denoted by Claire) if and only if their respective inputs x_1 and x_2 satisfy some predicate $f : \{0,1\}^n \times \{0,1\}^n \to \{0,1\}$ (we denote such inputs as 1-inputs). CDS is defined by two encoding algorithms $(\mathsf{Enc}_1, \mathsf{Enc}_2)$ for Alice and Bob to respectively compute their messages to Claire. Based on these encodings, and the knowledge of x_1 and x_2, Claire runs a decoding algorithm Dec to extract s. Note that CDS does

C. Hazay—This work is supported by the BIU Center for Research in Applied Cryptography and Cyber Security in conjunction with the Israel National Cyber Bureau in the Prime Minister's Office, and by ISF grant No. 1316/18.

© Springer Nature Switzerland AG 2020
C. Galdi and V. Kolesnikov (Eds.): SCN 2020, LNCS 12238, pp. 150–171, 2020.
https://doi.org/10.1007/978-3-030-57990-6_8

not maintain the privacy of Alice and Bob's inputs. In the past two decades, different aspects of CDS have been studied extensively exploring its communication complexity, the complexity of the decoder, and its expressibility; see some recent examples [1–3,17]. Concerning the latter aspect, note that garbled circuits [22] imply CDS for any polynomial function assuming only one-way functions and requiring communication complexity $O(\kappa \cdot |C|)$ where C is the computed circuit and κ is the security parameter.

Verifiable Computation from CDS. In this work, we explore the observation that for CDS with sufficiently long secrets, the secret can serve as proof for the fact that the output of f equals 1. Namely, at the heart of every CDS construction lies an integrity mechanism that prevents Claire from learning s for 0-inputs. This observation is not new and previously made in the context of attribute-based encryption [20], a public key object analogue to CDS. We exploit this mechanism to demonstrate the usefulness of CDS for designing non-interactive two-clients verifiable protocols in the presence of untrusted server, for a class of predicates that admit CDS. Informally, given two CDS schemes for f and $\bar{f}$, the clients forward the server the encoding of their inputs within these CDS. The server then replies with the decoded messages. From the secrecy property of the underlying CDS, the server should not extract both secrets.

In more detail, our basic two-client model includes three parties; two clients C_0 and C_1 that have an input and access to shared randomness, and a third untrusted server S. The clients wish to delegate the computation of some predicate f to an external unreliable server while performing less work than mutually evaluating the function. Note that this modeling differs from classic verifiable computation [9] by distributing the input between two clients. In this work, we prove that CDS gives rise to verifiable computation on distributed data. The security of our constructions holds in the presence of a malicious server (that follows an arbitrary attack strategy) and the semi-honest corruption of a single client (or any proper subset of the clients in the general setting). Some of our constructions also tolerate the malicious behaviour of the clients.

Prior work in the multi-client setting [6,13] showed generic solutions with a preprocessing phase whose running time depends on the complexity of f, which therefore must be amortized away. On the other hand, we only focus on a concrete set of predicates of interest where our solutions are not involved with a preprocessing phase. Moreover, the complexity of the input encoding algorithms of our underlying CDS schemes is strictly smaller than applying a multi-party protocol between the clients; we elaborate on this point more concretely below. We consider two flavours of privacy: input privacy where the server may only conclude the outcome of the predicate, and full privacy in the spirit of the simulation-based definition of secure computation, where only the clients learn the outcome of the predicate.

Applying the CDS abstraction for verifiable computation enjoys some qualitative advantages:

1. ROUND COMPLEXITY. First, CDS based constructions are non-interactive and require only a single message in each direction. Reducing the round

complexity of secure protocols is an important goal, where non-interactive protocols are particularly attractive. Here the clients can post the "encoding" of their inputs and go offline, allowing the server to evaluate the function on the inputs and sending a single message to the client.

2. HARDNESS ASSUMPTIONS. CDS is an information-theoretic object that can potentially be realized only based on one-way functions or even without any assumption. In this work, we additionally require using Σ-protocols.

3. CONSTANT RATE COMMUNICATION COMPLEXITY. The encoding messages sent from the clients imply constant upload rate communication complexity.[1] As demonstrated below, this complexity is much smaller than the complexity achieved in prior work for our particular class of predicates.

4. SIMPLICITY. The verification procedure of our schemes is as simple as checking equality between the untrusted party's response and the secret s.

5. BATCHING. The verification algorithm can be easily batched, taking the linear combination of many secrets and amortizing away the communication complexity of the server. This batching approach implies (amortized) download rate-1 which is much smaller than the solutions from [6,13] that incur download rate of κ.

6. POINT-TO-POINT CHANNELS. Our protocols do not employ any broadcast channels and only rely on point-to-point channels. This also means that Claire can launch a selective abort attack.

7. TRANSPARENT SETUP AND NO PREPROCESSING. Finally, recall that CDS schemes require common randomness between Alice and Bob. This can be viewed as mutual access to a common random string which is simpler to realize than employing a preprocessing phase that requires communication and has a secret trapdoor.

2PC with an Untrusted Helper from CDS. The second model where CDS is useful for is a two-party computation with an untrusted "helper". Namely, the classic notion of two-party computation is extended to the three-party setting, where the third party S performs the computation on the inputs of the other two parties. Security in this model holds as long as at most one of the parties is corrupted. This model has been recently considered in [16] with the aim of designing more practical set operations protocols. In order to use a simulation based definition for our protocols, we extend the security definition of plain CDS to support two additional features: privacy and obliviousness. Loosely speaking, privacy implies that only the output of the predicate may be leaked to Claire whereas obliviousness implies that nothing is leaked. This forms a hierarchy of definitions and captures additional scenarios that require both privacy and integrity.

New CDS Constructions. We design new (private/oblivious) CDS constructions for several important predicates. We then establish our verifiable schemes based on these CDS constructions.

---

[1] We measure the upload rate as the ratio between the size of the encoded messages and the inputs. We further define the download rate by the ratio between the size of $f(x_1, x_2)$ and s.

Equality/Inequality. We begin with CDS schemes for verifying equality and inequality of sufficiently long strings without requiring bit-decomposition. Protocols for securely comparing private values are fundamental building blocks of secure computation with numerous applications, initiated by the famous millionaires problem by Yao [22]. Nevertheless, designing concretely efficient protocols has remained a challenge. The state of the art concrete (amortized) analysis for semi-honest secure comparison [7] requires $O(\kappa \ell / \log \kappa)$ bits in the setup phase and $O(\ell)$ bits in the online phase, based on oblivious transfer. Another recent work [4] for equality based on function secret sharing requires $\lambda \ell$ bits in the setup phase and ℓ bits in the online phase. Currently, this work implies the best online communication in the semi-honest setting. Using somewhat homomorphic encryption scheme, the (amortized) bit complexity of [10] is $\tilde{O}(\ell + \kappa)$. Both [10] and [7] require non-constant round complexity.

In contrast, our non-interactive protocols achieve small upload rate (e.g., 10) for moderately long strings (e.g., polylogarithmic is κ), and rely on one-way functions and Σ-protocols.[2] Compared with [4], our scheme induces a higher upload rate in the online phase. Nevertheless, we require a simpler and more efficient setup, as our setup only requires a uniform random string while [4] requires correlated randomness (in the form of function secret sharing keys for computing a distributed point function), as well as more bits in the setup phase.

We introduce two CDS schemes for equality and inequality. One first scheme uses one-way functions (or pseudorandom functions (PRFs)) while the other scheme uses Σ-protocols as well. Specifically, we leverage the special soundness property of the Σ-protocol, which implies an algorithm that extracts the witness given two transcripts with the same first message and distinct challenges. In the semi-honest setting (where the clients are semi-honest and Claire may be malicious), we require one way functions and Σ-protocols. Specifically, we use one way functions to encode the input, and a Σ-protocol which is easily sampleable with respect to witness. This means that given a witness ω, we can generate a statement x. Moving to the malicious setting requires to replace the PRFs with PRPs as well as to utilize Σ-protocols that have an extractability algorithm for extracting the verifier's randomness given the transcript, witness, statement and prover's randomness. For instance, Schnorr's protocol [21] satisfies both of these properties. The verification algorithm provided by the Σ-protocol is also essential in allowing it to be maliciously secure. We note that this mechanism can also be extended to the multi-party case where we would use Σ-protocol with an extended special soundness property. We compare our construction to prior work in Table 1. Finally, we note that our protocols can be extended to a zero test with some tweaks.

---

[2] Loosely speaking, a Σ-protocol is a 3-round public-coin interactive proof for an NP relation, for which there exists an extractor that extracts the witness upon rewinding the prover. We require an additional transcript verifiability property that is leveraged for achieving correctness against malicious input encoding of Alice and Bob, going beyond semi-honest security.

PSI CARDINALITY. Private set-intersection (PSI) is an important functionality
that gained much attention from the cryptographic community due to its broad
applicability. It is defined by computing the intersection of two (or more) sets
X_1 and X_2. In this work, we show that a non-interactive variant of a recent
set-intersection protocol by Le et al. [16] implies CDS for the cardinality of
set-intersection based on one-way functions. More concretely, we show that (a
variant of one of) their protocols induces two CDS constructions for verifying upper and lower bounds on the intersection size, yielding the exact size of
the set-intersection with rate 3 communication complexity. We note that these
CDS techniques can be easily extended to address set-union cardinality, set-
membership and small domain range predicates. Using the CDS for verifying
upper bounds of PSI intersection as well as using our CDS for equality, we can
construct a two-party PSI with untrusted server and constant rate (4 in the
passive setting and 8 in the active setting). As above, we can extend the security
of our schemes to the malicious setting. Finally, we note that in order to use our
CDS schemes for verifiable computation, the soundness error probability $1/|\mathbb{F}|$
must be negligible. Therefore, $|\mathbb{F}|$ must be at least of size polylogarithmic in κ.

Table 1. A comparison of our equality protocol with prior work where λ is the security
parameter, the inputs are of size ℓ bits and OT is oblivious transfer.

Construction	Setup	Round complexity	Online comm.	Offline comm.	Hardness assump.	Security
[7]	Correlated[a]	≥ 3	$\mathcal{O}(\lambda\ell)$	$3\ell + o(\ell)$	OWF +OT	Passive
[18]	Uniform	3	$\mathcal{O}(\lambda\ell)$	$\mathcal{O}(\lambda\ell)$	OWF+OT	Active
[4]	Correlated[b]	2	ℓ	$\lambda\ell$	OWF	Passive
Fig. 7	Uniform	2	3ℓ	6ℓ	OWF	Passive
Fig. 7	Uniform	2	10ℓ	7ℓ	OWF+Σ-protocol[c]	Active

[a] This work uses two types of correlated randomness that are generated using OT
for XOR and AND shares.
[b] This correlation requires keys for computing distributed point functions.
[c] We concretely rely here on the hardness of discrete logarithm in groups.

Prior work on verifiable set operations for the single client setting [5,19]
relied on stronger hardness assumptions such as q-string Diffie-Hellman and
extractable collision-resistant hash functions, but also achieved stronger properties such as public verifiability and dynamically changing sets. [8] was the
first work which introduced the concept of server-aided two-party PSI where the
server is used as a helper party to resolve a dispute under stringer assumptions.
While the communication complexity is linear and the number of rounds is constant, the rate is higher (at least 16) and the number of rounds is at least 7

(excluding the extra rounds occurred due to zero-knowledge proofs). In a followup work [15], Kamara et al. constructed a 3-round server-aided two-party PSI with a malicious server where the communication complexity is inflated by some statistical parameter γ.

A recent work on threshold PSI [12] shows semi-honest protocols for comparing the union size of two sets when excluded with the intersection against some threshold parameter t. These protocols introduce communication complexity $\tilde{O}(t)$ (resp. $O(t^2)$ and $O(t^3)$) assuming fully homomorphic encryption (resp. additively homomorphic encryption and oblivious transfer). It is an interesting problem to extend these techniques to the non-interactive setting (where the second solution is not constant round).

2 Preliminaries

2.1 Σ-Protocols

A Σ-protocol is a 3-round primitive that implies zero-knowledge for honest verifiers with special soundness. In this work, we require the following additional properties:

- **Efficiently sampleable.** We require from the underlying Σ-protocol to be efficiently sampleable with respect to the witness. Formally, there exists an efficient algorithm $x \leftarrow \mathsf{Gen}(\omega, 1^\kappa)$ such that $(x, \omega) \in \mathcal{R}$.
- **Randomness extraction.** We require from the underlying Σ-protocol to have an extractability property where the extractor extracts the prover's randomness given the protocol's transcript, witness and statement of the Σ-protocol. More formally, there exist a PPT algorithm $\mathsf{RandExt}$ such that $p_r = \mathsf{RandExt}(x, \omega, T)$ which can extract the randomness r_p associated with the prover's algorithm in Σ-protocol, $(x, \omega) \in \mathcal{R}$ and T correspond to the transcript of Σ-protocol.

In this work, we employ Schnorr's Protocol [21] that satisfies these two properties. We also use the verification algorithm of the verifier to determine whether a transcript is accepting (or valid).

2.2 Conditional Disclosure of Secrets

We begin with the basic definition of CDS as given in [11]. We require computational privacy and thus implicitly assume that all our algorithms receive the security parameter κ as part of their input. Furthermore, some of our constructions will evaluate a predicate over a field $\mathbb{F}$ rather than on bit strings. We note that the input sizes will always be polynomially related to κ.

Definition 1 (CDS). *Let $f : \{0,1\}^n \times \{0,1\}^n \rightarrow \{0,1\}$ be a predicate. Let Enc_1 and Enc_2 be two PPT encoding algorithms and Dec be deterministic decoding algorithm. Let $s \in \{0,1\}^\kappa$ be a secret and r joint randomness drawn from the uniform distribution. Then the following conditions must hold:*

- **Correctness:** *For every input* (x_1, x_2) *which satisfies the condition* $f(x_1, x_2) = 1$ *and a secret* s, $\Pr[\mathsf{Dec}(x_1, x_2, \mathsf{Enc}_1(x_1, s, r), \mathsf{Enc}_2(x_2, s, r)) \neq s] \leq \mathsf{negl}(\kappa)$
- **Secrecy:** *There exists a* PPT *simulator* Sim *such that for every input* (x_1, x_2) *which satisfies the condition* $f(x_1, x_2) = 0$ *and a secret* $s \in \{0,1\}^\kappa$,

$$\big\{\mathsf{Sim}(x_1, x_2)\big\}_{x_1, x_2 \in \{0,1\}^n} \overset{c}{\approx} \big\{\mathsf{Enc}_1(x_1, s, r), \mathsf{Enc}_2(x_2, s, r)\big\}_{x_1, x_2 \in \{0,1\}^n}$$

2.3 Multi-clients Verifiable Computation

In this model, a set of clients outsource the computation of a function f over their distributed inputs to an untrusted server. We are interested in a non-interactive multi-client verifiable computation where the clients do not interact with each other after the setup phase (which is used to generate common randomness r and is independent of the function and the client's inputs). Note that this phase can be realized either via a one-time coin-tossing protocol or by accessing a public source of randomness, such as a random oracle applied on a fixed value. As in [13], we consider two security flavours for this setting, where the clients are either semi-honest or malicious whereas the servers are always malicious. We will continue with the syntax.

Syntax. An t-party multi-clients verifiable computation (MVC) scheme with semi-honest clients consists of the following algorithms:

- $r \leftarrow$ Setup: All clients receive a uniform string r.
- $(\tilde{x}_j, \tau_j) \leftarrow$ Input$(x_j, r, 1^\kappa)$. Each client C_j will run this *input encoding algorithm* on its input x_j and randomness r. The output of this algorithm is an encoded input $\tilde{x}_j$, which will be sent to the server, and the input decoding secret τ_j which will be kept private by the client.
- $(\alpha_1, \ldots, \alpha_t) \leftarrow$ Compute$(\tilde{x}_1, \ldots \tilde{x}_t, f)$. Given the encoded inputs $\{\tilde{x}_j\}_j$ and the function description, this *computation algorithm* computes an encoded output α_j.
- $y \cup \{\bot\} \leftarrow$ Verify(τ_j, α_j). Each client C_j runs this *verification algorithm* with the decoding secret τ_j, and the encoded output α_j. The algorithm outputs either a value y (that is supposed to be $f(x_1, \ldots, x_t)$), or $\bot$ indicating that the server attempted to cheat.

Note that the setup can also be made reusable using a pseudorandom function. In contrast, prior work requires a more complicated setup phase. Efficiency wise, we would like the time it takes for encoding the input and for verifying the output of the server to be less than computing f. Moreover, correctness can be defined naturally by requiring that the outcome of the computation algorithm passes the verification algorithm with overwhelming probability when correctly generated. We continue with a soundness definition.

Definition 2 (Soundness of MVC). *For a multi-client verifiable computation scheme MVC, consider the following experiment with respect to an adversarial server $\mathcal{A}$:*

$$
\Pr\left[y \neq f(x_1, \ldots, x_t) \,\middle|\, \begin{array}{l} \text{for all } j \in [t], \; r \leftarrow \mathsf{Setup}, (\tilde{x}_j, \tau_j) \leftarrow \mathsf{Input}(x_j, r, 1^\kappa), \\ (\alpha_1, \ldots, \alpha_t) \leftarrow \mathcal{A}(\tilde{x}_1, \ldots \tilde{x}_t, f) \; , \; y \leftarrow \mathsf{Verify}(\tau_j, \alpha_j) \end{array} \right]
$$
$$
\leq \mathsf{negl}(\kappa)
$$

Security Against Malicious Clients. The above definition holds for semi-honest clients (that follow the protocol faithfully) as long as they do not collude with the server. A stronger notion considers security in the presence of malicious clients (that follow an arbitrary attack strategy). In the two-client setting, our constructions are secure in the presence of a single malicious corruption of one of the clients.

Achieving Privacy. Our definition does not guarantee input or output privacy. These properties will be derived directly from the underlying CDS construction. Namely, if the CDS will be private or oblivious then the MVC will respectively maintain input or output privacy. For the constructions that achieve both privacy and correctness, we will use a simulation-based definition to prove security.

3 New Variants of CDS

In this section, we define two new variants of CDS: - private CDS and oblivious CDS. While private CDS hides the input of the clients achieving input privacy, oblivious CDS achieves input privacy as well as output privacy.

We extend Definition 1 by not giving the inputs x_1 and x_2 to both the decoder and the simulator Sim. This implies that Claire does not gain any information about x_1 and x_2 from the encoded messages of Alice and Bob, but may still conclude the outcome of the predicate. This definition will be useful for achieving input privacy in our multi-client verifiable computation constructions.

Definition 3 (Private CDS). *Let $f : \{0,1\}^n \times \{0,1\}^n \to \{0,1\}$ be a predicate. Let Enc_1 and Enc_2 be PPT encoding algorithms and Dec be deterministic decoding algorithm. Let $s \in \{0,1\}^\kappa$ be a secret and r joint randomness drawn from the uniform distribution. Then the following conditions must hold:*

- **Correctness:** *For every input (x_1, x_2) which satisfies the condition $f(x_1, x_2) = 1$ and a secret s, $\Pr[\mathsf{Dec}(\mathsf{Enc}_1(x_1, s, r), \mathsf{Enc}_2(x_2, s, r)) \neq s] \leq \mathsf{negl}(\kappa)$.*
- **Privacy:** *There exists a PPT simulator Sim such that for every input (x_1, x_2) and a secret s,*

$$
\left\{ \mathsf{Sim}(1^{|x_1|}, 1^{|x_2|}, y) \right\}_{x_1, x_2 \in \{0,1\}^n} \stackrel{c}{\approx} \left\{ \mathsf{Enc}_1(x_1, s, r), \mathsf{Enc}_2(x_2, s, r) \right\}_{x_1, x_2 \in \{0,1\}^n}
$$

$$
\left\{ \mathsf{Sim}(1^{|x_1|}, 1^{|x_2|}, y, s) \right\}_{x_1, x_2 \in \{0,1\}^n} \stackrel{c}{\approx} \left\{ \mathsf{Enc}_1(x_1, s, r), \mathsf{Enc}_2(x_2, s, r) \right\}_{x_1, x_2 \in \{0,1\}^n}
$$

where the first equation holds for $y = 0$ and the second equation holds for $y = 1$, and $y = f(x_1, x_2)$.

Finally, we consider a simulation-based definition, where we require that Claire cannot conclude any information about the secret. This definition is formalized by requiring that the encoded messages can be simulated without the knowledge of both the inputs nor the output (namely, the secret).

Definition 4 (Oblivious CDS). *Let* $f : \{0,1\}^n \times \{0,1\}^n \to \{0,1\}$ *be a predicate. Let* Enc_1 *and* Enc_2 *be two* PPT *encoding algorithms and* Dec *be deterministic decoding algorithm. Let* $s \in \{0,1\}^\kappa$ *be a secret and* r *a joint randomness drawn from the uniform distribution. Then the following conditions must hold:*

- **Correctness:** *For every input* (x_1, x_2) *which satisfies the condition* $f(x_1, x_2) = 1$ *and a secret* s, $\Pr[\mathsf{Dec}(\mathsf{Enc}_1(x_1, s, r), \mathsf{Enc}_2(x_2, s, r)) \neq s] \leq \mathsf{negl}(\kappa)$.
- **Indistinguishability:** *For every* PPT *active adversary* $\mathcal{A}$ *in real model corrupting Claire, there exists a* PPT *algorithm* Sim *in ideal world such that:*

$$\{\mathrm{REAL}_{f,A(z)}(x_1, x_2, s, n)\}_{x_1,x_2,s,n} \overset{c}{\approx} \{\mathrm{IDEAL}_{f,\mathsf{Sim}(z)}(x_1, x_2, s, n)\}_{x_1,x_2,s,n}$$

where f *is the computed predicate and* x_1 *and* x_2 *are the inputs of Alice and Bob, respectively.*

4   New CDS Constructions

In what follows, we discuss our CDS constructions for a class of predicates. In Sect. 4.1 we present private and oblivious CDS schemes for the equality predicate. In Sect. 4.2 we present two private CDS schemes for the inequality predicate. In Sect. 4.3 we present a CDS scheme for verifying lower and upper bounds of PSI cardinality. As a general note, we remark that our analysis relies on the fact that the secret is unpredictable (or uniformly random). This is sufficient for our applications, as the parties choose the secret by themselves. For applications where the parties have no control in choosing the secret, they can run our protocols with $F_k(s)$, where F is a PRF.

4.1   CDS for Equality

In this section, we present two CDS constructions for verifying the equality of two strings. Our first construction, presented in Fig. 1, shows a simple oblivious CDS scheme with information-theoretic security. Whereas our second CDS scheme, presented in Fig. 2, shows a private CDS scheme assuming one-way functions. The latter construction uses Σ-protocols as an underlying building block and can be extended to ensure the correctness of the encoding computations of Alice and Bob by relying on the verifiability property of the Σ-protocol, thus enhancing the security of the scheme.

The high level idea of our first construction is by generating two linearly independent equations such that extracting the secret is possible only if the inputs are equal. Due to the perfect secrecy nature of the two equations, the scheme preserves obliviousness, as Claire cannot detect whether she learned the correct secret or not. Specifically, our CDS achieves information-theoretic security and is computationally lightweight. This idea is similar to the multi-party CDS construction from [14].

$$\mathsf{CDS}_{\mathrm{EQ}_1}$$

- **Inputs.** The CDS protocol for equality is invoked by the interface $\mathsf{CDS}_{\mathrm{EQ}_1}(x_1, x_2, s, (r_1, r_2))$ where
    - x_1 and x_2 is input of Alice and Bob respectively over a field $\mathbb{F}$.
    - r_1 and r_2 are the shared randomness.
    - $s \in \mathbb{F}$ is a secret value which is shared between Alice and Bob.

  The computed function is $f(x_1, x_2) = \begin{cases} 1 & \text{if } x_1 = x_2 \\ 0 & \text{otherwise} \end{cases}$

- **Output.** Claire outputs s if $f(x_1, x_2) = 1$ and an independent string $s' \neq s$ otherwise.

- **Algorithms.**
    - $\mathsf{Enc}_1(x_1, s, (r_1, r_2)) = r_1 \cdot x_1 + r_2 + s$.
    - $\mathsf{Enc}_2(x_2, s, (r_1, r_2)) = r_1 \cdot x_2 + r_2$.
    - $\mathsf{Dec}(\tilde{x}_1, \tilde{x}_2) = \tilde{x}_1 - \tilde{x}_2$.

Fig. 1. Oblivious CDS for equality.

Theorem 4.1. *Protocol* $\mathsf{CDS}_{\mathrm{EQ}_1}$ *from Fig. 1 is an oblivious CDS (cf. Definition 4) for the equality predicate.*

Our second CDS construction for the equality predicate uses Σ-protocols as a platform to compare between two strings in a private manner. Namely, we leverage the (PRF evaluations of the) parties' inputs as the randomness sources to compute the prover's first message of the Σ-protocol and fix the secret as the witness for the corresponding relation. Then, only if equality holds we ensure that Claire can extract the secret due to the special soundness property of the protocol. Our detailed construction is given in Fig. 2. Note that this scheme achieves private CDS as Claire cannot conclude any information about the parties' inputs due to the privacy of the PRF. Nevertheless, it can conclude the outcome of the predicate.

Theorem 4.2. *Assume the existence of pseudorandom functions and a Σ-protocol for some predefined NP relation $\mathcal{R}$, then protocol $\mathsf{CDS}_{\mathrm{EQ}_2}$ from Fig. 2 is a private CDS (cf. Definition 3) for the equality predicate.*

$$\text{CDS}_{\text{EQ}_2}$$

- **Inputs.** The CDS protocol for equality is invoked by the interface $\text{CDS}_{\text{EQ}_2}(x_1, x_2, s, (r_1, r_2, r_{\text{PRF}}))$ where
    - x_1 and x_2 are the respective inputs of Alice and Bob from $\{0, 1\}^\kappa$.
    - r_1, r_2 and r_{PRF} are the shared randomness.
    - $s \in \{0, 1\}^\kappa$ is a secret value which is shared between Alice and Bob.

  The computed function is $f(x_1, x_2) = \begin{cases} 1 & \text{if } x_1 = x_2 \\ 0 & \text{otherwise} \end{cases}$

- **Notations.** We require that the fractions of r_1 and r_2 from the joint randomness should not be equal (namely, $r_1 \neq r_2$). This is necessary for the extractability of secret s. The protocol is parameterized by an NP relation $(x, \omega) \in \mathcal{R}$ and a Σ-protocol with an extractor $\mathcal{E}$, such that s serves as the witness and x is the corresponding public statement (we assume one can compute x from ω). The Σ-protocol transcript is generated by emulating $\mathcal{P}$ and $\mathcal{V}$ yielding $(a, e, z) = \langle \mathcal{P}(x, \omega; r), \mathcal{V}(x) \rangle$ where r is the prover's randomness.

- **Output.** Claire outputs s if $f(x_1, x_2) = 1$ and $\perp$ otherwise.

- **Algorithms.**
    - $\text{Enc}_1(x_1, s, (r_1, r_2, r_{\text{PRF}}))$:
        - A public statement x is generated as explained above using $\omega = s$ for the Σ-protocol.
        - A PRF key k is generated using r_{PRF}.
        - The input x_1 is encoded as $\mathbf{x}_1 = F_k(x_1)$.
        - The output is generated as

        $$\tilde{x}_1 = (x, (a_1, e_1, z_1)) = (x, \langle \mathcal{P}(x, \omega; \mathbf{x}_1), \mathcal{V}(x, r_1) \rangle).$$

    - $\text{Enc}_2(x_2, s, (r_1, r_2, r_{\text{PRF}}))$:
        - A public statement x is generated as explained above using $\omega = s$ for the Σ-protocol.
        - A PRF key k is generated using r_{PRF}.
        - The input x_2 is encoded as $\mathbf{x}_2 = F_k(x_2)$.
        - The output is generated as

        $$\tilde{x}_2 = (x, (a_2, e_2, z_2)) = (x, \langle \mathcal{P}(x, \omega; \mathbf{x}_2), \mathcal{V}(x, r_2) \rangle).$$

    - $\text{Dec}(\tilde{x}_1, \tilde{x}_2)$:
        - The message $\tilde{x}_1$ is broken down into $(x, (a_1, e_1, z_1))$ and the message $\tilde{x}_2$ is broken down into $(x, (a_2, e_2, z_2))$.
        - $s' = \begin{cases} \mathcal{E}(\tilde{x}_1, \tilde{x}_2) & \text{if } a_1 = a_2 \\ \perp & \text{otherwise} \end{cases}$

Fig. 2. Private CDS for equality.

The correctness property of Protocol CDS_{EQ_2} relies on the special soundness property. The messages sent by Alice and Bob to Claire consist of a statement of Σ-protocol along with the transcripts of Σ-protocol. In the case of the two input values of Alice and Bob are equal, this will result in the first message of the transcript being same. As we have two different transcripts with the same first message, the special soundness property of Σ-protocol always allows us to extract the secret s. The privacy property of the inputs in case of 0-output relies on the special honest verifier zero-knowledge which allows the Sim to generate valid transcripts of a given statement x based on inputting x and the random value e which acts as the second message in Σ protocol. We show that two transcripts generated through the above algorithm is indistinguishable to the message sent in the real protocol. The privacy property of the inputs in the case of 1-output is based on indistinguishability of pseudorandom functions from truly random functions.

Communication Complexity. Note that both our protocols achieve a constant upload rate. Specifically, the rate of our oblivious CDS (Fig. 1) is 1 whereas the rate of our private CDS (Fig. 2) is 5. These are the first protocols to achieve this rate for comparison based on symmetric-key assumptions and Σ-protocols.

Achieving Malicious Security. We further note that our private protocol can achieve stronger security for the clients by relying on the verifiability property of the Σ-protocol for NP statements with a single witness. In particular, before extracting the secret, Claire can check whether the transcripts are generated correctly and that $e_1 \neq e_2$. That would imply that the prover knows *some* secret, but not necessarily that it has used the correct secret. However, from the fact that the parties also send the statements as part of their messages, Claire can easily test whether the same secret was used by both parties and abort otherwise. This implies correctness with respect to the encoding algorithms. To prove malicious security, we would also need to extract the parties' inputs using the randomness extraction property specified in Definition 2.1.

4.2   CDS for Inequality

In this section, we present two CDS constructions for inequality for checking whether two strings are identical. Both constructions, presented in Figs. 3 and 4, achieve private CDS assuming one-way functions. The latter construction uses Σ-protocols as an underlying building block and can be extended to ensure the correctness of the encoding computations of the parties by relying on the verifiability property of the Σ-protocol, similar to the argument for the equality CDS scheme from the prior section.

Our first construction for the inequality predicate uses a 1-degree polynomial as the basis of the construction. The parties first apply a PRF on their inputs, and then utilize it to generate an evaluation of a polynomial that is embedded with the secret as the constant coefficient. Then if the inequality condition holds, algorithm Dec will be given two different evaluations of a 1-degree polynomial and can interpolate the polynomial, learning the secret. If inequality does not

---

$\mathrm{CDS}_{\mathrm{INEQ}_1}$

- **Inputs.** The CDS protocol for equality is invoked by the interface $\mathrm{CDS}_{\mathrm{INEQ}_1}(x_1, x_2, s, (r, r_{\mathrm{PRF}}))$ where:
  - x_1 and x_2 are the respective inputs of Alice and Bob over a field $\mathbb{F}$.
  - r and r_{PRF} are the shared randomness.
  - $s \in \mathbb{F}$ is a secret value which is shared between Alice and Bob.

  The computed functions if $f(x_1, x_2) = \begin{cases} 1 & \text{if } x_1 \neq x_2 \\ 0 & \text{otherwise} \end{cases}$

- **Output.** Claire outputs s if $f(x_1, x_2) = 1$ and $s' \neq s$ otherwise.

- **Algorithms.**
  - $\mathrm{Enc}_1(x_1, s, (r_1, r_2))$:
    - A PRF key k is generated using r_{PRF}.
    - The input x_1 is encoded as $\mathbf{x}_1 = F_k(x_1)$.
    - A polynomial is constructed as $p(x) = r \cdot x + s$.
    - The output is generated as $\tilde{x}_1 = (\mathbf{x}_1, p(\mathbf{x}_1))$.
  - $\mathrm{Enc}_2(x_2, s, (r_1, r_2))$:
    - A PRF key k is generated using r_{PRF}.
    - The input x_2 is encoded as $\mathbf{x}_2 = F_k(x_2)$.
    - A polynomial is constructed as $p(x) = r \cdot x + s$.
    - The output is generated as $\tilde{x}_2 = (\mathbf{x}_2, p(\mathbf{x}_2))$.
  - $\mathrm{Dec}(\tilde{x}_1, \tilde{x}_2)$:
    - The secret is generated by interpolating the points $\tilde{x}_1$ and $\tilde{x}_2$ to retrieve the polynomial $p'(\cdot)$ and output $s' = p'(0)$. If $\tilde{x}_1 = \tilde{x}_2$, then output $s' = \perp$

Fig. 3. First private CDS for inequality.

hold then there will be only one evaluation of the polynomial, resulting in Dec not being able to restore the polynomial and the secret.

Theorem 4.3. *Assume the existence of pseudorandom functions then protocol* $\mathrm{CDS}_{\mathrm{INEQ}_1}$ *from Fig. 3 is a private CDS (cf. Definition 3) for the inequality predicate.*

Our second private CDS construction from Fig. 4 for the inequality predicate uses Σ-protocols as a platform to compare between two strings in a private manner. Namely, we leverage the (PRF evaluations of the) parties' inputs as the public randomness of the verifier's algorithm to produce different challenges, while using the same randomness for the prover's algorithm to ensure that its first message is identical for both parties. The secret is fixed as the witness as before. Then, only if inequality holds Claire can extract the secret due to the special soundness of the protocol.

As before, note that this scheme achieves private CDS due to the privacy of the PRF.

$\mathsf{CDS}_{\mathrm{INEQ}_2}$

– **Input.** The CDS protocol for equality is invoked by the interface $\mathsf{CDS}_{\mathrm{INEQ}_2}(x_1, x_2, s, (r, r_{\mathrm{PRF}}))$ where:
  • x_1 and x_2 are the respective inputs of Alice and Bob from $\{0, 1\}^\kappa$.
  • r and r_{PRF} are the shared randomness.
  • $s \in \{0, 1\}^\kappa$ is a secret value which is shared between Alice and Bob.
  The computed function is $f(x_1, x_2) = \begin{cases} 1 & \text{if } x_1 \neq x_2 \\ 0 & \text{otherwise} \end{cases}$

– **Notations.** We require that the fractions of r_1 and r_2 from the joint randomness should not be equal (namely, $r_1 \neq r_2$). This is necessary for the extractability of secret s. The protocol is parameterized by an NP relation $(x, \omega) \in \mathcal{R}$ and a Σ-protocol with an extractor $\mathcal{E}$, such that s serves as the witness and x is the corresponding public statement (we assume one can compute x from ω). The Σ-protocol transcript is generated by emulating $\mathcal{P}$ and $\mathcal{V}$ yielding $(a, e, z) = \langle \mathcal{P}(x, \omega; r), \mathcal{V}(x) \rangle$ where r is the prover's randomness.

– **Output.** Claire outputs s if $f(x_1, x_2) = 1$ and $\perp$ otherwise.

– **Algorithms.**
  • $\mathsf{Enc}_1(x_1, s, (r, r_{\mathrm{PRF}}))$:
    – A public statement x is generated as explained above using $\omega = s$ for the Σ-protocol.
    – A PRF key k is generated using r_{PRF}.
    – The input x_1 is encoded as $\mathbf{x}_1 = F_k(x_1)$.
    – The output is generated as

$$\tilde{x}_1 = (x, (a_1, e_1, z_1)) = (x, \langle \mathcal{P}(x, \omega; r), \mathcal{V}(x; \mathbf{x}_1) \rangle).$$

  • $\mathsf{Enc}_2(x_2, s, (r_1, r_2, r_{\mathrm{PRF}}))$:
    – A public statement x is generated as explained above using $\omega = s$ for the Σ-protocol.
    – A PRF key k is generated using r_{PRF}.
    – The input x_2 is encoded as $\mathbf{x}_2 = F_k(x_2)$.
    – The output is generated as

$$\tilde{x}_2 = (x, (a_2, e_2, z_2)) = (x, \langle \mathcal{P}(x, \omega; r), \mathcal{V}(x; \mathbf{x}_2) \rangle).$$

  • $\mathsf{Dec}(\tilde{x}_1, \tilde{x}_2)$:
    – The message $\tilde{x}_1$ is broken down into $(x, (a_1, e_1, z_1))$ and the message $\tilde{x}_2$ is broken down into $(x, (a_2, e_2, z_2))$.
    – $s' = \begin{cases} \mathcal{E}(\tilde{x}_1, \tilde{x}_2) & \text{if } e_1 \neq e_2 \\ \perp & \text{otherwise} \end{cases}$

Fig. 4. Second private CDS for inequality.

Theorem 4.4. *Assume the existence of pseudorandom functions and a Σ-protocol for some predefined NP relation $\mathcal{R}$, then protocol $\mathsf{CDS}_{\mathrm{INEQ2}}$ from Fig. 4 is a private CDS (cf. Definition 3) for the inequality predicate.*

The proof idea of Protocol $\mathsf{CDS}_{\mathrm{INEQ2}}$ is almost similar to that of Protocol $\mathsf{CDS}_{\mathrm{EQ2}}$ with small modifications. In the equality protocol ($\mathsf{CDS}_{\mathrm{EQ2}}$), the input is encoded and utilized as the randomness of $\mathcal{P}$ algorithm in Σ-protocol. The latter protocol ($\mathsf{CDS}_{\mathrm{INEQ2}}$), the input is encoded and utilized as the randomness of $\mathcal{V}$ algorithm in Σ-protocol.

Note that the communication rate of our protocols is between 2 and 5 and that the security for Alice and Bob can be enhanced based on the verification procedure of the Σ-protocol (as discussed in the previous section) as well as extract the input of corrupt parties in malicious case by extracting the verifier's randomness (using Definition 2.1).

4.3   CDS for Bounds on PSI Cardinality

In this section, we present two CDS constructions for verifying the bound of PSI cardinality (namely, the intersection size). Figure 5 presents a CDS construction to verify a lower bound on the PSI cardinality while Fig. 6 presents a CDS construction to verify an upper bound on this cardinality. Our protocols leak the PSI cardinality to Claire. Technically, both constructions rely on polynomial evaluations as the base of the construction and utilize PRF for the privacy of parties' input. We remark that our protocols follow due simple modifications of one of the PSI protocols from [16]. Our main observation here shows that the techniques used in [16] induce CDS constructions on PSI (lower and upper bounds) cardinality.

Our first construction is a CDS scheme that verifies whether the PSI cardinality is lower bounded by some value t, that is hardcoded within the scheme. Namely, it utilizes the property that if t values are in common for both sets, then Claire should be able to extract the secret by recovering the polynomial $p(\cdot)$ of a degree $t-1$. In essence, the parties utilize an additive secret sharing on their polynomial evaluations to enable that. Claire can see which encoded elements are in common and retrieve their polynomial evaluations to extract the secret s. We next prove the following theorem.

Theorem 4.5. *Assume the existence of pseudorandom functions, then protocol $\mathsf{CDS}_{\geq t}$ from Fig. 5 is a private CDS (cf. Definition 3) for the greater than predicate.*

The second construction in Fig. 6 is a CDS scheme to verify if the PSI cardinality is of size at most t. It utilizes the property that if t values are in common for both sets, then the union $X_1 \cup X_2$ will include $n+m-t$ items. Therefore, Alice and Bob encode their inputs using a polynomial of degree $n+m-t-1$, embedding the secret s as the constant coefficient. As a result, given enough points, Claire should be able to extract the secret by recovering the polynomial $p(\cdot)$ of a degree $n+m-t-1$.

$$\mathsf{CDS}_{\geq t}$$

- **Inputs.** The CDS protocol for a lower bound of PSI cardinality is parameterized by t and invoked by the interface $\mathsf{CDS}_{\geq t}(X_1, X_2, s, (r_{\mathrm{poly}}, r_{\mathrm{PRF}_1}, r_{\mathrm{PRF}_2}))$ where:
  - X_1 and X_2 are the inputs of Alice and Bob over $\mathbb{F}$ of respective sizes n and m.
  - $r_{\mathrm{poly}}, r_{\mathrm{PRF}_1}$ and r_{PRF_2} are the shared randomness.
  - $s \in \mathbb{F}$ is a secret value which is shared between Alice and Bob.

  The computed function is $f(X_1, X_2) = \begin{cases} 1 & \text{if } |X_1 \cap X_2| \geq t \\ 0 & \text{otherwise} \end{cases}$

- **Output.** Claire outputs s if $f(X_1, X_2) = 1$ and $\bot$ or $s' \neq s$ otherwise.

- **Algorithms.**
  - $\mathsf{Enc}_1(X_1, s, (r_{\mathrm{poly}}, r_{\mathrm{PRF}_1}, r_{\mathrm{PRF}_2}))$:
    - Two PRF keys k_1 and k_2 are generated using r_{PRF_1} and r_{PRF_2}, respectively.
    - A polynomial $p(\cdot)$ of degree $t - 1$ is picked at random based on randomness r_{poly} and s as the constant coefficient of $p(\cdot)$ (namely, $p(0) = s$).
    - The input X_1 is encoded as $\mathcal{X}_1 = \{F_{k_1}(x_1) \mid \forall x_1 \in X_1\}$.
    - The output is generated as $\tilde{X}_1 = \{(\mathbf{x}_1, p(\mathbf{x}_1) - F_{k_2}(\mathbf{x}_1)) \mid \mathbf{x}_1 \in \mathcal{X}_1\}$.
  - $\mathsf{Enc}_2(X_2, s, (r_{\mathrm{poly}}, r_{\mathrm{PRF}_1}, r_{\mathrm{PRF}_2}))$:
    - Two PRF keys k_1 and k_2 are generated using r_{PRF_1} and r_{PRF_2}, respectively.
    - A polynomial $p(\cdot)$ of degree $t - 1$ is generated with randomness r_{poly} and s as the constant coefficient of s.
    - The input X_2 is encoded as $\mathcal{X}_2 = \{F_{k_1}(x_2) \mid \forall x_2 \in X_2\}$.
    - The output is generated as $\tilde{X}_2 = \{(\mathbf{x}_2, F_{k_2}(\mathbf{x}_2)) \mid \mathbf{x}_2 \in \mathcal{X}_2\}$.
  - $\mathsf{Dec}(\tilde{X}_1, \tilde{X}_2)$:
    - A set $\tilde{X} = \{(a, b + c) \mid (a, b) \in \tilde{X}_1 \text{ AND } (a, c) \in \tilde{X}_2\}$ is defined.
    - If $|\tilde{X}| \geq t$ then polynomial $p'(\cdot)$ is generated by interpolating the points in $\tilde{X}$.
    - $s' = \begin{cases} p'(0) & \text{if } |\tilde{X}| \geq t \\ \bot & \text{otherwise} \end{cases}$

Fig. 5. Private CDS for a lower bound on PSI cardinality.

Theorem 4.6. *Assume the existence of pseudorandom functions, then protocol* $\mathsf{CDS}_{\leq t}$ *from Fig. 6 is a private CDS (cf. Definition 3) for the less than predicate.*

5   Multi-clients Verifiable Computation via CDS

We next discuss how to use our CDS constructions from the previous section in order to construct verifiable computation schemes in the presence of two clients (Alice and Bob) and a server (Claire). We construct such schemes for the equality predicate (Sect. 5.1), for PSI cardinality (Sect. 5.2) and for PSI (Sect. 5.3). Our constructions follow the paradigm where we construct verifiable computation based on CDS schemes for predicate f and $\bar{f}$. Namely, security is proven in

---

$$\mathsf{CDS}_{\leq t}$$

- **Inputs.** The CDS protocol for an upper bound of PSI cardinality is parameterized by t and invoked by the interface $\mathsf{CDS}_{\leq t}(X_1, X_2, s, (r_{\mathrm{poly}}, r_{\mathrm{PRF}}))$ where:
    - X_1 and X_2 are the inputs of Alice and Bob over $\mathbb{F}$ of the respective sizes n and m.
    - r_{poly} and r_{PRF} are the shared randomness.
    - $s \in \mathbb{F}$ is a secret value which is shared between Alice and Bob.

    The computed function is $f(X_1, X_2) = \begin{cases} 1 & \text{if } |X_1 \cap X_2| \leq t \\ 0 & \text{otherwise} \end{cases}$

- **Output.** Claire outputs s if $f(X_1, X_2) = 1$ and $\perp$ or $s' \neq s$ otherwise.

- **Algorithms.**
    - $\mathsf{Enc}_1(X_1, s, (r_{\mathrm{poly}}, r_{\mathrm{PRF}}))$:
        - A PRF key k is generated using r_{PRF}.
        - A polynomial $p(\cdot)$ of degree $n + m - t - 1$ is picked at random based on randomness r_{poly} and s as the constant coefficient of $p(\cdot)$ (namely, $p(0) = s$).
        - The input X_1 is encoded as $\mathcal{X}_1 = \{F_k(x_1) \mid \forall x_1 \in X_1\}$.
        - The output is generated as $\tilde{X}_1 = \{(\mathbf{x}_1, p(\mathbf{x}_1)) \mid \mathbf{x}_1 \in \mathcal{X}_1\}$.
    - $\mathsf{Enc}_2(X_2, s, (r_{\mathrm{poly}}, r_{\mathrm{PRF}}))$:
        - A PRF key k is generated using r_{PRF}.
        - A polynomial $p(\cdot)$ of degree $n + m - t - 1$ is generated with randomness r_{poly} and s as the constant coefficient of s ($p(0) = s$).
        - The input X_2 is encoded as $\mathcal{X}_2 = \{F_k(x_2) \mid \forall x_2 \in X_2\}$.
        - The output is generated as $\tilde{X}_2 = \{(\mathbf{x}_2, p(\mathbf{x}_2)) \mid \mathbf{x}_2 \in \mathcal{X}_2\}$.
    - $\mathsf{Dec}(\tilde{X}_1, \tilde{X}_2)$:
        - A set is generated $\tilde{X} = \{(a, b) \mid (a, b) \in \tilde{X}_1 \text{ OR } (a, b) \in \tilde{X}_2\}$.
        - If $\left|\tilde{X}\right| \geq n + m - t$ then $p'(\cdot)$ is generated by interpolating the points in $\tilde{X}$.
        - $s' = \begin{cases} p'(0) & \text{if } \left|\tilde{X}\right| \geq n + m - t \\ \perp & \text{otherwise} \end{cases}$

Fig. 6. Private CDS construction for an upper bound on PSI cardinality.

the presence of a malicious server, and either semi-honest or malicious servers. We assume that the clients have access to a coin-tossing functionality $\mathcal{F}_{\mathrm{COIN}}$ that produces a sufficiently long string for the underlying CDS schemes, chosen uniformly at random.

5.1   MVC for Equality

We begin with a protocol for equality. Namely, Alice and Bob hold two strings they want to learn whether they are equal or not. Our protocol relies on the techniques used for the CDS constructions from Figs. 1 and 3, implying the following theorem.

Theorem 5.1. *Assume the existence of pseudorandom functions, then protocol* VC_{EQ} *from Fig. 7 is a two-clients verifiable computation for the equality predicate in the presence of semi-honest clients and malicious server.*

We prove that protocol VC_{EQ} is a verifiable computation in the presence of semi-honest Alice and Bob and malicious Claire. We actually prove that parties' views can be simulated. The only interesting case is when Claire is corrupted, since when either Alice or Bob are corrupted, the simulator can send then the corresponding secret (which is their only incoming message). When Claire is corrupted, the security follows from the privacy property of CDS for equality and inequality and so is straight forward.

$$VC_{EQ}$$

- **Inputs**. The VC protocol for equality is invoked by the interface $VC_{EQ_1}(x_1, x_2)$ where x_1 and x_2 are respective inputs of Alice and Bob over a field $\mathbb{F}$.
- **Setup**. $(s_0, s_1, r_1, r_2, r_3, r_4, r_{PRF}) \leftarrow G$

  An ideal functionality $\mathcal{F}_{COIN}$ is invoked to generate the shared randomness $(s_0, s_1, r_1, r_2, r_3, r_4, r_{PRF})$.
- **Protocol**.
    - Alice, Bob and Claire run $CDS_{INEQ_1}(x_1, x_2, s_0, (r_1, r_2, r_{PRF}))$ (cf. Figure 3). Claire sends s_0' to Alice and Bob as the output of the CDS protocol.
    - Alice and Bob run $CDS_{EQ_1}(x_1, x_2, s_1, (r_3, r_4))$ (cf. Figure 1). Claire sends s_1' to Alice and Bob as the output of the CDS protocol. In case $s_0' \neq \bot$, Claire sets $s_1' = \bot$ and sends it as the output of CDS_{EQ_1}. This step can run in parallel to the step above where Claire sends (s_0', s_1') together.
    - Upon receiving (s_0', s_1') from Claire, Alice/Bob outputs '0' if $s_0' = s_0$, '1' if $s_1' = s_1$ and outputs "ABORT" otherwise.

Fig. 7. 2-client VC for equality.

Recalling that we have two instantiations of both the equality and inequality CDS schemes. Then another construction can be defined based on CDS_{INEQ_2} and CDS_{EQ_2}. The difference between the two protocols is that in the former both underlying CDS schemes are based on Σ-protocols that we exploit to achieve malicious security. Specifically, Claire checks whether the transcripts are generated correctly and tries to extract one of the secrets.

5.2 MVC for PSI Cardinality

We continue with our construction for PSI cardinality. As a warmup, we describe a slight variant of [16], where the parties first learn from Claire (a possibly incorrect) size t of the intersection, and then invoke our CDS schemes $CDS_{\geq t}$ and

---

PSI – CA

- **Inputs.** The VC for PSI cardinality protocol is invoked by the interface PSI – $CA_1(X_1, X_2)$ where X_1 and X_2 are the inputs of Alice and Bob of the respective sizes n and m. Every element in the set is over a field $\mathbb{F}$.

- **Setup.** $(s_0, s_1, r_{\text{poly}_1}, r_{\text{poly}_2}, r_{\text{PRP}}, r_{\text{PRP}_2}) \leftarrow G$

  An ideal functionality $\mathcal{F}_{\text{COIN}}$ is invoked to generate the shared randomness $(s_0, s_1, r_{\text{poly}_1}, r_{\text{poly}_2}, r_{\text{PRP}}, r_{\text{PRP}_2})$.

- **Protocol.**
  - A PRP key k is generated using r_{PRP}.

  - Alice and Bob encode their inputs as $\mathcal{X}_1 = \{F_k(x_1) \mid x_1 \in X_1\}$ and $\mathcal{X}_2 = \{F_k(x_2) \mid x_2 \in X_2\}$ and send $\mathcal{X}_1$ and $\mathcal{X}_2$ to Claire respectively.

  - Claire sends $t = |\mathcal{X}_1 \cap \mathcal{X}_2|$ to Alice and Bob.

  - Alice, Bob and Claire run $\text{CDS}_{\geq t}(X_1, X_2, s_0, (r_{\text{poly}_1}, r_{\text{PRP}}, r_{\text{PRP}_2}))$. Claire sends s_0' to Alice and Bob as the output of the CDS protocol.

  - Alice, Bob and Claire run $\text{CDS}_{\leq t}(X_1, X_2, s_1, (r_{\text{poly}_2}, r_{\text{PRP@}Its}))$. Claire sends s_1' to Alice and Bob as the output of the CDS protocol. This step can run in parallel with the step above where Claire can send (s_0', s_1').

  - Upon receiving (s_0', s_1') from Claire, Alice/Bob outputs t if $(s_0', s_1') = (s_0, s_1)$ and outputs "ABORT" otherwise.

Fig. 8. 2-round PSI cardinality.

$\text{CDS}_{\leq t}$ for checking lower and upper bounds. Although we abstract the protocol differently, the end result is very similar to the protocol from [16], which can also be proven secure in the presence of malicious corruptions by replacing the PRF we use for the CDS with a pseudorandom permutation (PRP).

Theorem 5.2. *Assume the existence of pseudorandom permutations, then protocol* PSI – CA *from Fig. 8 is a 2-round two-clients verifiable computation for PSI cardinality in the presence of malicious parties.*

5.3 MVC for PSI

We conclude this section with a verifiable construction for PSI (given in Fig. 9) which extends the PSI cardinality from the previous section. In more detail, our scheme is built on the equality CDS scheme CDS_{EQ_2} from Fig. 2, taking a different approach than the PSI from [16] (which we build our PSI cardinality on). In the first phase, Claire provides the list of elements in the intersection together with an equality proof. This is required to ensure that the only attack Claire can carry out is excluding elements from the set. In particular, every

---

PSI_1

- **Inputs.** The MVC for PSI protocol is invoked by the interface $\mathsf{PSI}(X_1, X_2)$ where X_1 and X_2 are the respective inputs of Alice and Bob of sizes n and m.

- **Setup.** $(s, s_{\mathrm{poly}}, r_1, r_2, r_{\mathrm{poly}}, r_{\mathrm{PRP}}, r_{\mathrm{PRP}_2}) \leftarrow \mathsf{Setup}(1^\kappa)$.
  An ideal functionality $\mathcal{F}_{\mathrm{COIN}}$ is invoked to generate the shared randomness $(s, s_{\mathrm{poly}}, r_1, r_2, r_{\mathrm{poly}}, r_{\mathrm{PRP}}, r_{\mathrm{PRP}_2})$.

- **Protocol.**
  - A PRP key k and k_2 is generated using respective randomness r_{PRP} and r_{PRP_2}.

  - Alice and Bob encode their inputs as $\mathcal{X}_1 = \{F_k(x_1) \mid x_1 \in X_1\}$ and $\mathcal{X}_2 = \{F_k(x_2) \mid x_2 \in X_2\}$.

  - For each element $\mathbf{x}_1 \in \mathcal{X}_1$, Alice generates:
    * $s^{(\mathbf{x}_1)} = F_{k_2}(s\|\mathbf{x}_1)$.
    * $r_1^{(\mathbf{x}_1)} = F_{k_2}(r_1\|\mathbf{x}_1)$.
    * $r_2^{(\mathbf{x}_1)} = F_{k_2}(r_2\|\mathbf{x}_1)$.

  - For each element $\mathbf{x}_2 \in \mathcal{X}_2$, Bob generates:
    * $s^{(\mathbf{x}_2)} = F_{k_2}(s\|\mathbf{x}_2)$.
    * $r_1^{(\mathbf{x}_2)} = F_{k_2}(r_1\|\mathbf{x}_2)$.
    * $r_2^{(\mathbf{x}_2)} = F_{k_2}(r_2\|\mathbf{x}_2)$.

  - Alice generates
    $$\tilde{X}_1 = \{(\mathbf{x}_1, \mathsf{CDS}_{\mathrm{EQ}_2} : \mathsf{Enc}_1(\mathbf{x}_1, s^{(\mathbf{x}_1)}, (r_1^{(\mathbf{x}_1)}, r_2^{(\mathbf{x}_2)}, r_{\mathrm{PRP}}))) \mid \mathbf{x}_1 \in \mathcal{X}_1\}.$$

  - Bob generates
    $$\tilde{X}_2 = \{(\mathbf{x}_2, \mathsf{CDS}_{\mathrm{EQ}_2} : \mathsf{Enc}_2(\mathbf{x}_2, s^{(\mathbf{x}_2)}, (r_1^{(\mathbf{x}_2)}, r_2^{(\mathbf{x}_2)}, r_{\mathrm{PRP}}))) \mid \mathbf{x}_2 \in \mathcal{X}_2\}.$$

  - Alice and Bob send their respective messages $\tilde{X}_1$ and $\tilde{X}_2$ to Claire.

  - Claire generates $\tilde{X} = \{(\mathbf{x}, {}_{1,2}) \mid (\mathbf{x}, {}_1) \in \tilde{X}_1 \text{ and } (\mathbf{x}, {}_2) \in \tilde{X}_2\}$.

  - Claire generates a set $S = \{(\mathbf{x}, s) \mid \forall (\mathbf{x}, {}_{1,2}) \in \tilde{X} \text{ where each element } s = \mathsf{CDS}_{\mathrm{EQ}_2} : \mathsf{Dec}_{(1,2)} \neq \perp\}$ and sends S to Alice and Bob.

  - Alice and Bob calculate $t = |S|$ and check if all $(\mathbf{x}, s^{(\mathbf{x})}) \in S$ satisfy $F_{k_2}(s\|\mathbf{x}) = s^{(\mathbf{x})}$. If any check fails, they output "ABORT".

  - If Alice/Bob doesn't output "ABORT", $\mathsf{PSI} = \{v \mid (\mathbf{x}, s) \in S \text{ and } F_k(v) = \mathbf{x}\}$.

  - Alice, Bob and Claire run $\mathsf{CDS}_{\leq t}(X_1, X_2, s_{\mathrm{poly}}, (r_{\mathrm{poly}}, r_{\mathrm{PRP}}))$. Claire sends s'_{poly} to Alice and Bob as the output of the CDS protocol.

  - Upon receiving s'_{poly}, Alice/Bob output PSI if $s'_{\mathrm{poly}} = s_{\mathrm{poly}}$ otherwise they output "ABORT".

Fig. 9. 2-round PSI.

party can check whether the declared intersection is part of its input, and is also convinced that the same elements appear within the other party's input, as ensured by the security of the CDS for quality. In the second phase, the parties continue with a PSI cardinality based on the estimated outcome from the first phase.

Theorem 5.3. *Assume the existence of pseudorandom permutations, a Σ-protocol for some predefined NP relation $\mathcal{R}$, then protocol PSI from Fig. 9 is a 2-round two-clients verifiable computation for PSI in the presence of malicious parties.*

References

1. Applebaum, B., Arkis, B.: On the power of amortization in secret sharing: d-Uniform secret sharing and CDS with constant information rate. In: Beimel, A., Dziembowski, S. (eds.) TCC 2018. LNCS, vol. 11239, pp. 317–344. Springer, Cham (2018). https://doi.org/10.1007/978-3-030-03807-6_12
2. Applebaum, B., Arkis, B., Raykov, P., Vasudevan, P.N.: Conditional disclosure of secrets: amplification, closure, amortization, lower-bounds, and separations. In: Katz, J., Shacham, H. (eds.) CRYPTO 2017. LNCS, vol. 10401, pp. 727–757. Springer, Cham (2017). https://doi.org/10.1007/978-3-319-63688-7_24
3. Applebaum, B., Vasudevan, P.N.: Placing conditional disclosure of secrets in the communication complexity universe. In: ITCS, pp. 4:1–4:14 (2019)
4. Boyle, E., Gilboa, N., Ishai, Y.: Secure computation with preprocessing via function secret sharing. In: Hofheinz, D., Rosen, A. (eds.) TCC 2019. LNCS, vol. 11891, pp. 341–371. Springer, Cham (2019). https://doi.org/10.1007/978-3-030-36030-6_14
5. Canetti, R., Paneth, O., Papadopoulos, D., Triandopoulos, N.: Verifiable set operations over outsourced databases. In: Krawczyk, H. (ed.) PKC 2014. LNCS, vol. 8383, pp. 113–130. Springer, Heidelberg (2014). https://doi.org/10.1007/978-3-642-54631-0_7
6. Choi, S.G., Katz, J., Kumaresan, R., Cid, C.: Multi-client non-interactive verifiable computation. In: Sahai, A. (ed.) TCC 2013. LNCS, vol. 7785, pp. 499–518. Springer, Heidelberg (2013). https://doi.org/10.1007/978-3-642-36594-2_28
7. Couteau, G.: New protocols for secure equality test and comparison. In: Preneel, B., Vercauteren, F. (eds.) ACNS 2018. LNCS, vol. 10892, pp. 303–320. Springer, Cham (2018). https://doi.org/10.1007/978-3-319-93387-0_16
8. Dong, C., Chen, L., Camenisch, J., Russello, G.: Fair private set intersection with a semi-trusted arbiter. In: Wang, L., Shafiq, B. (eds.) DBSec 2013. LNCS, vol. 7964, pp. 128–144. Springer, Heidelberg (2013). https://doi.org/10.1007/978-3-642-39256-6_9
9. Gennaro, R., Gentry, C., Parno, B.: Non-interactive verifiable computing: outsourcing computation to untrusted workers. In: Rabin, T. (ed.) CRYPTO 2010. LNCS, vol. 6223, pp. 465–482. Springer, Heidelberg (2010). https://doi.org/10.1007/978-3-642-14623-7_25
10. Gentry, C., Halevi, S., Jutla, C., Raykova, M.: Private database access with HE-over-ORAM architecture. In: Malkin, T., Kolesnikov, V., Lewko, A.B., Polychronakis, M. (eds.) ACNS 2015. LNCS, vol. 9092, pp. 172–191. Springer, Cham (2015). https://doi.org/10.1007/978-3-319-28166-7_9

11. Gertner, Y., Ishai, Y., Kushilevitz, E., Malkin, T.: Protecting data privacy in private information retrieval schemes. J. Comput. Syst. Sci. **60**(3), 592–629 (2000)
12. Ghosh, S., Simkin, M.: The communication complexity of threshold private set intersection. In: Boldyreva, A., Micciancio, D. (eds.) CRYPTO 2019. LNCS, vol. 11693, pp. 3–29. Springer, Cham (2019). https://doi.org/10.1007/978-3-030-26951-7_1
13. Gordon, S.D., Katz, J., Liu, F.-H., Shi, E., Zhou, H.-S.: Multi-client verifiable computation with stronger security guarantees. In: Dodis, Y., Nielsen, J.B. (eds.) TCC 2015. LNCS, vol. 9015, pp. 144–168. Springer, Heidelberg (2015). https://doi.org/10.1007/978-3-662-46497-7_6
14. Ishai, Y., Kushilevitz, E., Paskin, A.: Secure multiparty computation with minimal interaction. In: Rabin, T. (ed.) CRYPTO 2010. LNCS, vol. 6223, pp. 577–594. Springer, Heidelberg (2010). https://doi.org/10.1007/978-3-642-14623-7_31
15. Kamara, S., Mohassel, P., Raykova, M., Sadeghian, S.: Scaling private set intersection to billion-element sets. In: Christin, N., Safavi-Naini, R. (eds.) FC 2014. LNCS, vol. 8437, pp. 195–215. Springer, Heidelberg (2014). https://doi.org/10.1007/978-3-662-45472-5_13
16. Le, P.H., Ranellucci, S., Gordon, S.D.: Two-party private set intersection with an untrusted third party. In: CCS (2019)
17. Liu, T., Vaikuntanathan, V., Wee, H.: Conditional disclosure of secrets via nonlinear reconstruction. In: Katz, J., Shacham, H. (eds.) CRYPTO 2017. LNCS, vol. 10401, pp. 758–790. Springer, Cham (2017). https://doi.org/10.1007/978-3-319-63688-7_25
18. Mohassel, P., Rindal, P.: ABY3: a mixed protocol framework for machine learning. IACR Cryptology ePrint Archive 2018, 403 (2018)
19. Papamanthou, C., Tamassia, R., Triandopoulos, N.: Optimal verification of operations on dynamic sets. In: Rogaway, P. (ed.) CRYPTO 2011. LNCS, vol. 6841, pp. 91–110. Springer, Heidelberg (2011). https://doi.org/10.1007/978-3-642-22792-9_6
20. Parno, B., Raykova, M., Vaikuntanathan, V.: How to delegate and verify in public: verifiable computation from attribute-based encryption. In: Cramer, R. (ed.) TCC 2012. LNCS, vol. 7194, pp. 422–439. Springer, Heidelberg (2012). https://doi.org/10.1007/978-3-642-28914-9_24
21. Schnorr, C.P.: Efficient signature generation by smart cards. J. Cryptology **4**(3), 161–174 (1991). https://doi.org/10.1007/BF00196725
22. Yao, A.C.: How to generate and exchange secrets (extended abstract). In: FOCS, pp. 162–167 (1986)

Private Identity Agreement for Private Set Functionalities

Ben Kreuter[1], Sarvar Patel[1], and Ben Terner[2(✉)]

[1] Google, New York, NY, USA
{benkreuter,sarvar}@google.com
[2] UC Santa Barbara, Santa Barbara, CA, USA
bterner@cs.ucsb.edu

Abstract. Private set intersection and related functionalities are among the most prominent real-world applications of secure multiparty computation. While such protocols have attracted significant attention from the research community, other functionalities are often required to support a PSI application in practice. For example, in order for two parties to run a PSI over the unique users contained in their databases, they might first invoke a support functionality to agree on the primary keys to represent their users.

This paper studies a secure approach to agreeing on primary keys. We introduce and realize a functionality that computes a common set of identifiers based on incomplete information held by two parties, which we refer to as *private identity agreement*, and we prove the security of our protocol in the honest-but-curious model. We explain the subtleties in designing such a functionality that arise from privacy requirements when intending to compose securely with PSI protocols. We also argue that the cost of invoking this functionality can be amortized over a large number of PSI sessions, and that for applications that require many repeated PSI executions, this represents an improvement over a PSI protocol that directly uses incomplete or fuzzy matches.

Keywords: Private set intersection · Private identity agreement · Garbled circuits

1 Introduction

In recent years *Private Set Intersection* (PSI) and related two-party protocols have been deployed in real-world applications [20]. In the simplest setting of PSI, each party has a set X_i as its input, and the output will be the intersection $\bigcap X_i$. More generally the parties may wish to compute some function f over the intersection and obtain output $f(\bigcap X_i)$ [8, 13, 20, 24, 25].

Owing to its importance in real-world applications, PSI has been the topic of a significant body of research. Common PSI paradigms include DDH-style protocols [1, 10, 18, 21, 28], approaches based on oblivious transfer [12, 23, 26, 27] or oblivious polynomial evaluation [9, 14], and approaches based on garbled circuits [17, 23, 24]. Performance improvements have been dramatic, especially the computational overhead of PSI.

© Springer Nature Switzerland AG 2020
C. Galdi and V. Kolesnikov (Eds.): SCN 2020, LNCS 12238, pp. 172–191, 2020.
https://doi.org/10.1007/978-3-030-57990-6_9

State-of-the-art PSI protocols require *exact* matches to compute the intersection; in other words, the intersection is based on bitwise equality. In real-world application scenarios the parties may not have inputs that match exactly. As an example, consider the case of two centralized electronic medical record (EMR) providers, which supply and aggregate medical records for medical practitioners, who wish to conduct a study about the number of patients who develop a particular disease after their recent medical histories indicate at-risk status. The EMR providers could use a PSI protocol to count the total number of unique diagnoses among their collective patients. Unfortunately, the EMR providers may not have the same set of information about each patient in their databases; for example, one might identify Alice by her street address and phone number, while the other might use her phone number and email address. Further complicating matters, Bob could use "bob@email.com" for one provider, but "BobDoe123@university.edu" for another.

It may appear that naively applying PSI to each column in two parties' databases would allow them to realize their desired functionality, but such an approach has many flaws. For example, in the case that individuals use different identifying information for the different services, this approach could incur false negatives. To remedy this issue, there has been previous research on the private record linkage problem, in which "fuzzy matches" between records are permitted [16,30]. In this problem, two rows from different parties' databases can be said to match if they satisfy some closeness relation, for example by matching approximately on t out of n columns. However, fuzzy matching PSI protocols are not as performant as exact-matching protocols.

As a design goal, we consider applications in which two parties would like to run PSI many times over respective databases. In our EMR example, the rows comprising users change slowly as new patients enter the system and some are expunged. However, auxiliary medical data could change frequently, at least daily. If the EMR providers wish to continuously update their medical models or run multiple analyses, they may run many PSI instances with auxiliary data [20].

In general, for many applications it is desirable for two parties to run PSI-style protocols many times over their respective data sets, and in this work we assume the parties will perform many joint queries. It is therefore advantageous for the parties to first to establish a new column for their databases, containing a single key for each row that can be used for the most performant exact-match PSI protocols.

As a second design goal, we relax an assumption that is standard for the private record linkage problem. We believe that it is not always realistic in practice to assume or to ensure that each participant's database uniquely maps its rows to identities. For example, one EMR provider may unknowingly have multiple records about the same person in its database, as a result of that person providing different identifying information to different medical providers. As part of a correct protocol, some preprocessing phase must identify records that belong to the same individual – using both parties' records – and group them accordingly. This is especially important for PSI applications that compute aggregate statistics.

This correctness requirement introduces an additional privacy concern. Consider the case in which party A has a single row in its database that matches more than one row in party B's database. Naively running a protocol to produce primary keys which link records would inevitably reveal some information to one of the parties. Either party A would learn that the party B is unaware that its rows could be merged, or party B would learn that it has several rows that correspond to a single person. Either way, one party will learn more about the other party's input than it should.

This work focuses on resolving the apparent trade-offs in privacy and performance between state-of-the-art exact-matching and fuzzy-matching PSI protocols. Our approach is to design a new two-party protocol that computes a new identifier for every row in both databases that will give exact matches. To avoid the additional leakage problem described above, our protocol outputs either (a) shares of the new identifiers, or (b) encryptions of the new identifiers for a generic CPA-secure encryption scheme with XOR homomorphism, which can be decrypted with a key held by the other party. (Our protocol can also output both share and encryptions, and we in fact prove security in the case that it outputs both.) The regime of PSI protocols that can be composed with our protocol is limited to those that can *combine shares or decrypt online* without revealing the plaintext to either party. However, the flexibility we provide in producing outputs offers flexibility to the design of PSI protocols which can be composed with ours. Additionally, although our identifier-agreement protocol is computationally intensive compared to the subsequent PSI protocol, we argue that this is a one-time cost that can be amortized over many PSI computations.

1.1 Our Contributions

This work addresses two problems: (1) The performance and accuracy tradeoffs between exact matching PSI and fuzzy matching PSI protocols. (2) The correctness and privacy problems introduced to PSI by the possibility of poorly defined rows. We address both of these problems in one shot by defining a functionality that computes shared primary keys for two parties' databases, such that the keys can be used multiple times as inputs to successive efficient PSI protocols, *without revealing the keys to the parties*. We refer to our stated problem as the *private identity agreement* functionality, and define it formally. We additionally discuss the security implications of composing our identity agreement functionality and subsequent PSI functionalities. We note that identity agreement is substantially more complex than private set intersection and private record linkage because of the concerns introduced by producing an intermediate output of a larger functionality.

After defining the identity agreement problem, we present a novel two-party protocol that solves the problem in the honest-but-curious model. We additionally describe a modification to our protocol that allows the outputs to naturally compose with DDH-style PSI protocols. Finally we present performance of a prototype implementation.

1.2 Related Work

Private set intersection with "fuzzy" matches has been considered in previous research. An early work by Freedman, Nissim, and Pinkas on PSI included a proposed fuzzy matching protocol based on oblivious polynomial evaluation [14]. Unfortunately that protocol had a subtle flaw identified by Chmielewski and Hoepman, who proposed solutions based on OPE, secret sharing, and private Hamming distance [7].

Concurrently with our work, Buddhavarapu et al. [6] presented *private matching for compute*, which addresses the problem of producing intermediate identifiers for repeated private set functionalities. They use different techniques and parallelize their implementation, which yields very good performance. However, they do not address the issues incurred by linking records between data sets, which is the most technically challenging and expensive aspect of the problem we consider.

Wen and Dong presented a protocol solving the *private record linkage* problem, which is similar to the common identifiers problem in this work [30]. In that setting the goal is to determine which records in several databases correspond to the same person, and to then reveal those records. Wen and Dong present two approaches, one for exact matches using the *garbled bloom filter* technique from previous work on PSI [12] and one for fuzzy matches that uses locality-sensitive hash functions [19] to build the bloom filter. One important difference between the PRL setting and ours is that our privacy goal requires the matches and non-matches to remain secret from both parties. We also assign a label to each record, with the property that when two records match they are assigned the same label.

Huang, Evans, and Katz compared the performance of custom PSI protocols to approaches based on garbled circuits [17]. One of their constructions, which they call *sort-compare-shuffle*, is familiar to our approach. Our protocol uses the sort-compare-shuffle technique as a repeated subroutine. Unlike their constructions, our output is not a set intersection.

2 Problem Definition

Our setting assumes two parties, each holding some database, that wish to engage in inner-join style queries on their two databases, which we refer to as the *private joint-database query* functionality $\mathcal{F}^{\text{Query}}$. The join will be over some subset of columns, and will be a disjunction i.e. two rows are matched if any of the columns in the join match. In Fig. 1 we present the ideal private joint-database query functionality.

We consider a scenario in which it is advantageous for the parties to first establish a new database column containing keys for each record, so that this key can be used for many exact-match PSI protocols. We refer to this as the *private identity agreement* functionality, denoted $\mathcal{F}^{\text{ID}}$ and described in Fig. 2. As we have explained, establishing these keys is a setup phase in a general protocol that realizes $\mathcal{F}^{\text{Query}}$. Importantly, the newly established identities should not be revealed to either party, as this could also reveal information about the other party's input. This makes it impossible to separate the protocol for $\mathcal{F}^{\text{ID}}$ from the subsequent PSI-style protocols that the parties will use for their joint queries. We must instead modify the PSI-style protocols as well to ensure a secure composition with $\mathcal{F}^{\text{ID}}$. Our security analysis must therefore consider the entire $\mathcal{F}^{\text{Query}}$ as a single system.

The Identity Agreement Functionality. We denote the set of possible identifiers that either party may hold by $I = \otimes I_i$, with each set I_i being one column and having $\perp \in I_i$. To define a "match" we define an equivalence relation $S_1 \overset{\text{user}}{\sim} S_2$ as follows: if there exists component of $s_{1,j} \neq \perp$ of S_1 and a component $s_{2,k} \neq \perp$ of S_2 such that

$s_{1,j} = s_{2,k}$ then $S_1 \overset{\text{user}}{\sim} S_2$. In other words, we consider two rows to be equivalent if any of their non-empty columns are equal.[1]

For each party p_i with database $\mathcal{D}_{p_i}$, we assume for simplicity of exposition that every pair of rows S_1 and S_2 satisfies $S_1 \overset{\text{user}}{\not\sim} S_2$. (This means that the party does not have sufficient information to conclude that the two rows represent the same element.) Note, however, that it is possible for p_1 to have rows $S_{1,1}, S_{1,2}$, and for p_2 to have a row S_2 such that $S_{1,1} \overset{\text{user}}{\sim} S_2 \overset{\text{user}}{\sim} S_{1,2}$. In such a situation, p_1 is not aware that its database contains two rows that represent the same element.

The goal of the identity agreement functionality $\mathcal{F}^{\text{ID}}$ is to compute a map $\Lambda \colon \mathcal{D}_{p_1} \cup \mathcal{D}_{p_2} \to \mathcal{U}$ such that for any $S_1 \overset{\text{user}}{\sim} S_2$, $\Lambda(S_1) = \Lambda(S_2)$, and for all $S_1 \overset{\text{user}}{\not\sim} S_2$, $\Lambda(S_1) \neq \Lambda(S_2)$. As we explain below, the parties will not learn $\Lambda(S_i)$ for their respective databases; they will only see encryptions of the map.

We define the privacy goals of $\mathcal{F}^{\text{ID}}$ in relation to the overall query functionality $\mathcal{F}^{\text{Query}}$: to compute some PSI functionality where the intersection is determined by the $\overset{\text{user}}{\sim}$ relation. Importantly, if $\mathcal{F}^{\text{ID}}$ is composed with other protocols to realize $\mathcal{F}^{\text{Query}}$, then $\mathcal{F}^{\text{ID}}$ may not reveal any information about $\overset{\text{user}}{\sim}$ to either party. Consider, for example, a situation where p_1 has in its input S_1 and S_2, and in p_2's input there is a S_* such that $S_1 \overset{\text{user}}{\sim} S_* \overset{\text{user}}{\sim} S_2$. It should not be the case that p_1 will learn $S_1 \overset{\text{user}}{\sim} S_2$, beyond what can be infered from the output of the PSI functionality. Likewise, p_2 should not learn that p_1 has such elements in its input. If $\mathcal{F}^{\text{ID}}$ revealed such information, then some party could learn more from the composition of $\mathcal{F}^{\text{ID}}$ with another functionality than it would learn from querying only $\mathcal{F}^{\text{Query}}$.

Private Query Functionality $\mathcal{F}^{\text{Query}}$

1. **Setup:** Upon receiving messages of the form $(\text{setup}, \text{sid}, \mathcal{D}_{p_i})$ from p_i, store $(\text{sid}, \mathcal{D}_{p_i}, i)$. After receiving setup from both parties with matching sid, ignore all future setup messages with sid.

2. **Queries:** Upon receiving messages of the form $(\text{query}, \text{sid}, f)$ from party p_i, where $f = (f_1, f_2)$ is the description of a two-party functionality over two databases:
   (a) If both parties have not sent setup messages for sid, ignore the message. Otherwise proceed as follows.
   (b) Record the message $(\text{query}, \text{sid}, (f_1, f_2), i)$. If have already recorded $(\text{query}, \text{sid}, (f_1, f_2), 3 - i)$, then send $(\text{response}, \text{sid}, f_1(\mathcal{D}_{p_1}, \mathcal{D}_{p_2}))$ to p_1 and $(\text{response}, \text{sid}, f_2(\mathcal{D}_{p_1}, \mathcal{D}_{p_2}))$ to p_2.

Fig. 1. Query functionality $\mathcal{F}^{\text{Query}}$, which receives two parties' databases and responds to queries over functions of the databases.

---

[1] It is possible to establish $\overset{\text{user}}{\sim}$ for S_1 and S_2 for any binary relation that $s_{1,j}$ and $s_{2,k}$ may satisfy; however, we feel that equality is the most natural, and consider only equality in this work. We remark later to indicate when one could substitute another relation for equality in the construction.

ID Agreement Functionality $\mathcal{F}^{ID}$

1. **Inputs:** Each party p_i has a tuple $\text{input}_{p_i} = (\mathcal{D}_{p_i}, k_{p_i}^{enc})$, where $\mathcal{D}_{p_i}$ is the party's database and $k_{p_i}^{enc}$ is an encryption key for a CPA-secure encryption scheme (referred to as CPA).
2. **Generate Identifiers:** Upon receiving $(\text{submit}, \text{sid}, \text{input}_{p_i})$ from each p_i for session sid, $\mathcal{F}^{ID}$ computes a map $\Lambda \colon \mathcal{D}_{p_1} \cup \mathcal{D}_{p_2} \to \mathcal{U}$, where $\mathcal{U} = \{0,1\}^\ell$ is a universe of user identities, such that for any two rows S_1 and S_2 for which $S_1 \overset{\text{user}}{\sim} S_2$, $\Lambda(S_1) = \Lambda(S_2)$, and for all two rows for which $S_1 \overset{\text{user}}{\not\sim} S_2$, $\Lambda(S_1) \neq \Lambda(S_2)$.
   Let $\Lambda(S)$ be the identifier assigned to a row S. For each row $S \in \mathcal{D}_{p_i}$, $\mathcal{F}^{ID}$ returns $(\text{sid}, S, \text{CPA.enc}(k_{p_{3-i}}^{enc}, \Lambda(S)))$ to p_i.

Fig. 2. ID agreement functionality $\mathcal{F}^{ID}$

Two-Party Component Labeling Functionality $\mathcal{F}^{lbl}$

1. **Inputs:** Each party p_i has a tuple $\text{input}_{p_i} = (G_{p_i}, k_{p_i}^{enc}, \rho_{p_i})$, where $G_{p_i} = (V_{p_i}, E_{p_i})$ is a graph, $k_{p_i}^{enc}$ is an encryption key for a CPA-secure encryption scheme (referred to as CPA), and $\rho_{p_i} = \{\rho_{p_i,j}\}_{j\in[N]}$ is a list of N ℓ-bit one-time pads.
2. **Generate Labels:** Upon receiving $(\text{submit}, \text{sid}, \text{input}_{p_i})$ from each p_i for session sid, $\mathcal{F}^{lbl}$ samples random elements from a universe $\mathcal{U} = \{0,1\}^\ell$ and computes a map $\Lambda \colon V_{p_1} \cup V_{p_2} \to \{0,1\}^\ell$ such that for any two vertices $v_1, v_2 \in V_{p_1} \cup V_{p_2}$, $\Lambda(v_1) = \Lambda(v_2)$ if and only if v_1 and v_2 are in the same connected component in $G_1 \cup G_2$.
   For $i \in \{1,2\}$ and $j \in [|V_{p_i}|]$, let $v_{p_i,j}$ be the jth vertex in V_{p_i}. $\mathcal{F}^{lbl}$ computes $f_{p_i}^{enc} = \{\text{CPA.enc}(k_{p_i}^{enc}, \Lambda(v_{p_i,j}))\}_{j\in[|V_{p_i}|]}$ and $f_{p_i}^{mask} = \{\rho_{p_i,j} \oplus \Lambda(v_{p_i,j})\}_{j\in[|V_{p_i}|]}$
   $\mathcal{F}^{lbl}$ sends $(\text{labeling}, \text{sid}, f_{p_1}^{enc}, f_{p_2}^{mask})$ to p_1 and $(\text{labeling}, \text{sid}, f_{p_2}^{enc}, f_{p_1}^{mask})$ to p_2.

Fig. 3. Two-party component labeling functionality $\mathcal{F}^{lbl}$

3 Security Primitives and Cryptographic Assumptions

Garbled Circuits. Garbled circuits were proposed by Andrew Yao [31] as a means to a generic two-party computation protocol. Yao's protocol consists of two subprotocols: a garbling scheme [5] and an oblivious transfer. Most of the CPU work of a garbled circuit protocol involves symmetric primitives, and as Bellare et al. show, garbling schemes can use a block cipher with a fixed key, further improving performance [5]. A drawback of garbled circuits is that they require as much communication as computation, but this can be mitigated by using garbled circuits to implement efficient subprotocols of a larger protocol.

ElGamal Encryption. The ElGamal encryption scheme is CPA-secure under the DDH assumption, and supports homomorphic group operations (denoted ElGl.*Mul* below). If the plaintext space is small, addition in the exponent can also be supported, but decryption in this case requires computing a discrete logarithm. Using the identity element of the group, EIGl.*Mul* can be used to re-randomize a ciphertext.

Definition 1 (ElGamal Encryption). *The ElGamal encryption scheme [15] is an additively homomorphic encryption scheme, consisting of the following probabilistic polynomial-time algorithms:*

EIGl.**Gen** *Given a security parameter λ, EIGl.Gen(λ) returns a public-private key pair (pk, sk), and specifies a message space $\mathcal{M}$.*

EIGl.**Enc** *Given the public key pk and a plaintext message $m \in \mathcal{M}$, one can compute a ciphertext EIGl.Enc(pk, m), an El Gamal encryption of m under pk.*

EIGl.**Dec** *Given the secret key sk and a ciphertext EIGl.Enc(pk, m), one can run EIGl.Dec to recover the plaintext m.*

EIGl.**Mul** *Given the public key pk and a set of ciphertexts $\{EIGl.Enc(pk, m_i)\}$ encrypting messages $\{m_i\}$, one can homomorphically compute a ciphertext encrypting the product of the underlying messages: EIGl.Enc($pk, \prod_i m_i$) = EIGl.Mul($\{EIGl.Enc(pk, m_i)\}_i$)*

As described in Sect. 4.4, we use EIGl.*Mul* to induce an XOR homomorphism by encrypting bit-by-bit. This allows us to avoid performing group operations in the garbled circuit subprotocol and reduces communication cost, at the cost of CPU effort.

4 Secure ID Agreement as Secure Two-Party Component Labeling

In this section, we define a graph problem that we call Two-Party Component Labeling, and provide a reduction between ID agreement and Two-Party Component Labeling. We then describe an algorithm to compute component labeling and a two-party protocol that securely implements it.

4.1 Two-Party Component Labeling

In the two-party component labeling problem, each party $p_i \in \{p_1, p_2\}$ has a graph $G_{p_i} = (V_{p_i}, E_{p_i})$, where there exists some universe of vertices V for which $V_{p_1} \subset V$ and $V_{p_2} \subset V$. Each party's graph contains at most N vertices, which are distributed among connected components of size at most m. Both N and m are parameters of the problem. As shorthand, we refer to a connected component as a component. As output, each party assigns a label to every component in its graph. If there are two components $C_1 \in G_{p_1}$ and $C_2 \in G_{p_2}$ for which C_1 and C_2 have a non-empty intersection, then p_1 and p_2 must assign the same label to C_1 and C_2. Just as we explained with ID Agreement, this property induces a transitive relation. If two vertices $v \in G_{p_1}$ and $u \in G_{p_2}$ are in the same component of $G = G_{p_1} \cup G_{p_2}$, then their components in G_{p_1} and G_{p_2}, respectively, must be assigned the same label.

More precisely, consider parties p_1 and p_2 with graphs G_{p_1} and G_{p_2}, respectively, and let C_{p_i} represent the set of components that constitute G_{p_i}. Moreover, assume the vertices in G_{p_1} and G_{p_2} are drawn from some universe of vertices V. The two-party component labeling problem is to construct a map $\Lambda \colon C_{p_1} \cup C_{p_2} \to \mathcal{U}$, where $\mathcal{U}$ is a universe of labels. For any two components $C_1, C_n \in C_{p_1} \cup C_{p_2}$, $\Lambda(C_1) = \Lambda(C_n)$ if and only if there is some series of components $C_2, \ldots, C_{n-1} \in C_{p_1} \cup C_{p_2}$ such that $C_i \cap C_{i+1} \neq \emptyset$ for $i \in \{1 \ldots n-1\}$.

4.2   Reducing ID Agreement to Two-Party Component Labeling

We reduce the two-party identity agreement problem to two-party component labeling. Each party p represents its database as a graph $G_p = (V_p, E_p)$ as follows. Each piece of identifying information in party p's database is represented by a vertex in p's graph. (Empty entries in a database are simply left out of the graph.) Edges in the graph connect vertices which represent identifying information of the same user. Therefore, each set in a party's database is represented as a component in the party's graph.

The component labeling of two graphs G_{p_1} and G_{p_2} can be trivially used to assign user identities. The identifier of a user represented by a component C in G_p is directly copied from the label assigned to C during component labeling.

Intuitively, the reduction works because the two parties compute ID agreement over their databases by computing a union of their graphs. If the two parties' graphs contain the same vertex v (meaning both databases contain the same piece of identifying information), then the components containing v in G_{p_1} and G_{p_2} are the same component in the union graph $G = G_{p_1} \cup G_{p_2}$.

4.3   An Algorithm for Two-Party Component Labeling

In this section, we present a component labeling algorithm without explicitly addressing privacy concerns. In Sect. 4.4, we present a protocol to implement the algorithm while preserving privacy. We illustrate an execution of our percolate-and-match algorithm in Fig. 4 and provide pseudo-code in Fig. 5.

Our component labeling algorithm is an iterative procedure in which the two parties assign labels to every vertex in their respective graphs and then progressively update their vertices' labels. To initialize the procedure, each party p constructs an initial labeling for its local graph by assigning a unique label to every vertex in its graph G_p. Specifically, every vertex v in G_p is assigned the label v, the encoding of the vertex itself.[2] Notice that in the initial labeling, no two vertices within a party's graph are assigned the same label. However, any vertex that is included in both graphs is assigned the same label by both parties.

By the end of the iterative procedure, two properties of the labelings must be met. First, within each component of a party's graph, all vertices must have the same label. Second, if any vertex is in both parties' graphs, then the vertex has the same label in both parties' labelings. Together, these two requirements enforce that every two vertices within a component of $C \subset G$ have the same label. This common label can then be taken as the component's label.

Each step in our iterative procedure is a two phase process. The first phase operates on each party's graph independently. It enforces the property that for each component in a party's graph, every vertex in the component has the same label. In this phase, the algorithm assigns to every vertex $v \in G_p$ the (lexicographic) minimum of all labels in its component in G_p. We call this a *percolation phase* because common labels are percolated to every vertex in a component.

---

[2] In an application, the label would be the data that the vertex represents. Additionally, if the parties agree on an encoding scheme beforehand, types (address, zip, phone) can be encoded as part of a label at the cost of only a few bits.

In the second phase, the algorithm operates on the vertices which are common to both parties' graphs. It ensures that every vertex v which is common to both parties' graphs has been assigned the same label in the two parties' labelings. If one party's label for v differs from the other party's label for v, then both labels are updated to the minimum of two labels that have been assigned to v. We call this a *matching phase* because vertices which are common to both graphs are assigned matching labels in the two labelings.

If some vertex's label is updated in a matching phase, then its label may differ from the labels of the other vertices in its component. Therefore, the iterative procedure repeats until labelings stabilize. During percolation, each vertex's label is set to the minimum label of all vertices in its component. If some vertex's label changes during a matching phase, its new label must be "smaller" than its previous label. During the next percolation phase, the change is propagated by again updating the label of each vertex in the component is to the minimum label in the component. In the full version, we prove that if m denotes the maximum size of a component in $G_{p_1} \cup G_{p_2}$, then at most $m - 1$ iterations are necessary for vertex labels to stabilize.

4.4 Private Component Labeling

We now provide a protocol which implements the component labeling algorithm described in Sect. 4.3 while preserving privacy. The ideal functionality $\mathcal{F}^{|b|}$ for private two-party component labeling is given in Fig. 3.

Approach. The challenge of securely implementing the percolate-and-match algorithm arises from the fact that percolate-and-match performs two operations: (1) comparisons on vertices, and (2) updates on vertex labels. However, if either party knew the output of any such operation on its vertices, then it would learn information about the other party's graph. Consider that if a participant learns that its vertex's label changed during the any matching phase or during a percolation phase, it learns that one of the vertices in its graph has a matching vertex in the other party's graph. Similarly, it a party learns that its vertex's label *isn't* updated during the first matching or percolation phase, it learns its vertex isn't in the other party's graph.

Our approach is to perform both vertex comparisons and label updates without revealing the output of any comparison or update, and to encrypt all intermediate and output labels so that no information is leaked about the computation. Naively adapting state-of-the-art PSI protocols in order to perform our matching phase does not work for this approach, because in addition to finding the common vertices in the two parties' graphs, we must also perform updates on matching labels; state of the art PSI protocols do not provide easy ways to modify auxiliary data without revealing information.

To implement comparisons and updates, we use garbled circuits. Importantly, garbled circuits must implement oblivious algorithms, whose operation is independent of the input data. Notably, for any branch in the execution tree of an oblivious algorithm, we must perform operations for both possible paths, replacing the untaken path with dummy operations. Additionally, random accesses to an array (i.e. those for which the index being read is input-dependent) must either scan over the entire array, incurring

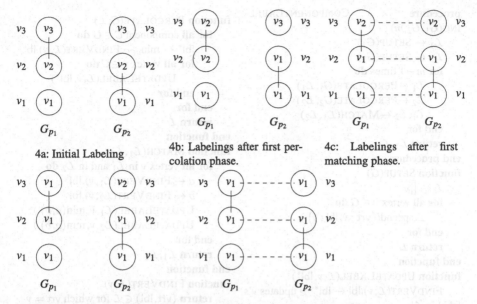

4a: Initial Labeling

4b: Labelings after first percolation phase.

4c: Labelings after first matching phase.

4d: Labelings after second percolation phase.

4e: Labelings after second matching phase.

Fig. 4. Depiction of the percolate-and-match algorithm for component labeling. v_1, v_2, and v_3 are common to both G_{p_1} an G_{p_2}. Each vertex's label is drawn inside the vertex, and its identity is on the side. p_1's graph has an edge between v_2 and v_3, while p_2's graph has an edge between v_1 and v_2. Solid lines depict edges in each party's graph. Dotted lines depict matches that occur during matching phases. The figures show the evolution of the algorithm over 2 iterations.

a $O(N)$ cost, or use *Oblivious RAM* techniques, which incurs $\log(N)$ communication overhead per access [2,22].

Matching via Garbled Circuits. To perform our matching phase obliviously, we adapt a technique described by Huang, Evans, and Katz for PSI [17]. In their scheme, called Sort-Compare-Shuffle, each party sorts its elements, then provides its sorted list to a garbled circuit which merges the two lists. If two parties submit the same element, then the two copies of the element land in adjacent indices in the merged list. The circuit iterates through the list, comparing elements at adjacent indices in order to identify common elements. After comparing, their circuit shuffles the sorted list before revealing elements in the intersection.

Our construction adapts the sort-compare-shuffle technique to efficiently perform our matching phase with label updates as follows. Each party submits a sorted list of vertices to a garbled circuit, including auxiliary information for each vertex that represents the vertex's currently assigned label. To perform matching, we merge the two parties' lists of vertices into one sorted list L and iterate through L. At each pair of adjacent indices in L, we conditionally assign both elements' current labels to the minimum of the two labels only if the vertices match. Matching in this way via garbled

procedure   COMPONENTLABEL-
ING(G_1, G_2, m)
 $L_1 \leftarrow$ SETUP(G_1)
 $L_2 \leftarrow$ SETUP(G_2)
 for $m - 1$ **times do**
  $L_1 \leftarrow$ PERCOLATE(G_1, L_1)
  $L_2 \leftarrow$ PERCOLATE(G_2, L_2)
  $L_1, L_2 \leftarrow$ MATCH(L_1, L_2)
 end for
 return L_1, L_2
end procedure
function SETUP(G)
 $L \leftarrow []_N$
 for all vertex $v \in G$ **do**
  L.append$((\text{vrt} : v, \text{lbl} : v))$
 end for
 return L
end function
function UPDATELABEL(L, v, lbl^*)
 FINDVERT(L, v).lbl $\leftarrow$ lbl* ▷ updates v's
label in L
end function

function PERCOLATE(G, L)
 for all component $C \in G$ **do**
  lbl$^* \leftarrow \min_{u \in C}$ FINDVERT(L, u).lbl
  for all vertex $v \in C$ **do**
   UPDATELABEL(L, v, lbl^*)
  end for
 end for
 return L
end function
function MATCH(L_1, L_2)
 for all vertex v in L_1 and in L_2 **do**
  $a \leftarrow$ FINDVERT(L_1, v).lbl
  $b \leftarrow$ FINDVERT(L_2, v).lbl
  UPDATELABEL$(L_1, v, \min(a, b))$
  UPDATELABEL$(L_2, v, \min(a, b))$
 end for
 return L_1, L_2
end function
function FINDVERT(L, v)
 return $(\text{vrt}, \text{lbl}) \in L$ for which vrt $= v$
end function

Fig. 5. Pseudocode for component labeling algorithm.

circuit hides from both parties all of the matches that are made between the two parties' graphs and their respective label updates.

Percolation via Garbled Circuits. To percolate labels within a component, a party can submit all of the vertices in one of its components to a garbled circuit along with each vertex's current label. The circuit computes the minimum of the labels and assigns the minimum label to each vertex in the component.

Stitching Percolation and Matching Together. The remaining question is how to efficiently stitch together percolation phases and matching phases without revealing intermediate labels of any vertices. We perform percolation and matching in the same circuit. To transition between percolation and matching phases, we permute the list of vertices. We define a permutation π which is hidden from both parties, and apply π and π^{-1} to L to transition from matching phase to percolation phase and back.

Our garbled circuit begins by merging the two parties' sorted lists into one large list L. We then apply π to the list to shuffle the list, hiding all information about the sorted order of L. Next, we reveal indices of each party's components in $\pi(L)$. For the graph G_{p_i} of each party i, and for each component $C \subset G_{p_i}$, both parties learn the indices of C's vertices in $\pi(L)$. We use these indices to hard-wire the min-circuit that percolates labels within C. After percolating, we apply the inverse permutation π^{-1} to $\pi(L)$ and can again iterate through L to merge. The circuit repeatedly applies π and π^{-1} to L to

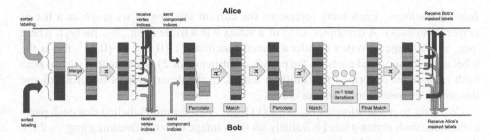

Fig. 6. Illustration of the percolate-and-match garbled circuit approach.

transition from matching phase to percolation phase and back. After $m-1$ iterations, the circuit outputs encrypted labels to the two parties.

We remark that permuting L and revealing indices of each party's components avoids in-circuit random access to look up current vertex labels for each percolation circuit, and hence the overhead of ORAM. Revealing indices allows our circuit to hard-wire the indices of the min-circuits that perform percolation, achieving $O(1)$ cost per label lookup at the expense of an $O(n \log n)$ shuffle between phases. We can consider that this technique allows us to amortize the expense of two permutations with cost $n \log n$ over the n memory accesses we do for each iteration, which yields the same asymptotic complexity as ORAM [2,22].

Graph Structure. There is one additional caveat. Revealing the indices of the vertices of each component in L reveals the structure of the parties' graphs. To prevent this, we require that both parties pad their graphs to some predetermined structure. To simplify the presentation, we set a number of components C and a maximum size of each component m, and then have each party pad its graphs using randomly selected vertices until each graph contains $N = Cm$ vertices.

Outputs. Each party receives as output XOR-shares of both parties' labels and their own labels encrypted under a key held by the other party.

Protocol in Depth. We now describe how to privately implement our percolate-and-match algorithm. Figure 6 illustrates our approach, Fig. 7 contains the full protocol, and Fig. 8 describes our garbled circuits.

Protocol Inputs. As input, each party p has a graph $G_p = (V_p, E_p)$. If some party has fewer than m vertices in some component(s) of its graph, it pads its graph by randomly sampling vertices to add to its component(s). The two parties must agree on a number of components C and the maximum size of a component m, and each must pad its graph until it has $N = Cm$ vertices.

In addition, each party p_i has a key $k_{p_i}^{enc}$ for a CPA-Secure encryption scheme with XOR homomorphism. Third, it has a list of N ℓ-bit random strings ρ_p. The key and random strings are used for the output; the key will encrypt the other party's output labels, and random strings will hide p's own labels from the other party.

Initial Labelings. Each party represents the current labeling of its graph as a list of *vertex descriptors.* A descriptor $\mathcal{L}(v)$ of a vertex v is a triple $(\text{img}_v, \text{lbl}_v, \text{party}_v)$, where img_v is the image of vertex v under a shared function $H \colon \{0,1\}^* \rightarrow \{0,1\}^\ell$, lbl_v is the label assigned to v, and party_v is the party's identifier (1 or 2). We note that we use H to hash each vertex descriptor to a uniform length. In the description of the protocol and the proof, we treat H as a random oracle.

We refer to p's labeling as $\mathcal{L}_p = \{\mathcal{L}(v)\}_{v \in G_p}$. In the initial labeling that each party constructs, each vertex's label is initially set to its image under H (meaning $\text{img}_v = \text{lbl}_v$). After constructing its labeling $\mathcal{L}_{p_i}$, each party sorts its labeling $\mathcal{L}_{p_i}$ on the images of its vertices under H.

Garbled Circuit Part 1: Merge, Permute, and Reveal Order. After the parties set up their inputs, they invoke a garbled circuit that merges their descriptors into a combined labeling $\mathcal{L}$ and reveals the indices of their descriptors under a random permutation. First, each party p_i submits its sorted labeling $\mathcal{L}_{p_i}$ to a garbled circuit. The garbled circuit merges $\mathcal{L}_{p_1}$ and $\mathcal{L}_p$ into one list $\mathcal{L}$ using a Batcher Merge [3]. Second, the circuit shuffles $\mathcal{L}$ using a permutation π unknown to either party using Waksman networks [4,29]. Each party p_i randomly samples a permutation π_{p_i} on $2N$ elements and inputs its selection bits s_{p_i} to the circuit. We define $\pi = \pi_{p_1} \circ \pi_{p_2}$; the circuit permutes $\mathcal{L}$ as $\pi(\mathcal{L})$.

Next, the circuit reveals to each party the indices of its own vertices in $\pi(\mathcal{L})$. First, each party samples $2N$ one-time pads σ_{p_i} and submits them to the circuit. The garbled circuit then iterates through $\pi(\mathcal{L})$, and at each index, the descriptor's third element (which is the party identity) determines what to output to each party. If the vertex at index j was submitted by p_i, then p_i receives from the garbled circuit $\pi(\mathcal{L})[j].\text{img}$, the image of the vertex at index j in the permuted list, and p_{3-i} receives $\pi(\mathcal{L})[j].\text{img} \oplus \sigma_{p_i,j}$, which is the same image but masked by p_1's jth one-time pad.

Given the indices of each of its vertices in $\pi(\mathcal{L})$, each party computes the indices composing each of its components. Let $\text{idx}(v)$ denote the index of vertex v in $\pi(\mathcal{L})$. For each component $C \subset G_{p_i}$, p_i computes $\text{idx}(C) = \{\text{idx}(v)\}_{v \in C}$. For each component C in G_{p_i}, p_i shares $\text{idx}(C)$ with p_{3-i}. Note that each party p_i learns the indices of its own vertices in $\pi(\mathcal{L})$ *and* it learns the indices corresponding to each of p_{3-i}'s components in $\pi(\mathcal{L})$. However, neither party learns the original positions of either party's vertices in $\mathcal{L}$. In the proof, we show that revealing these indices in $\pi(\mathcal{L})$ reveals no information about the other party's inputs.

Garbled Circuit Part 2: Percolate and Match. In the second subcircuit, the parties perform percolation and matching. The parties use the information revealed about their components' indices in $\pi(\mathcal{L})$ to hard-wire the indices of each component in order to perform percolation. Percolation happens via independent subcircuit for each component in both parties' graphs. For each component C, let $\text{idx}(C)$ be the indices of the component's vertices in $\pi(\mathcal{L})$. The circuit computes $\text{lbl}^* \leftarrow \min_{j \in \text{idx}(C)} \pi(\mathcal{L})[j].\text{lbl}$, and then assigns $\pi(\mathcal{L})[j].\text{lbl} \leftarrow \text{lbl}^*$ for each $j \in \text{idx}(C)$.

Given a circuit with the parties' descriptors arranged as $\pi(\mathcal{L})$, the circuit applies $\pi^{-1} = \pi_{p_2}^{-1} \circ \pi_{p_1}^{-1}$ to $\pi(\mathcal{L})$ to retrieve $\mathcal{L}$. It then performs matching by iterating through

$\mathcal{L}$ and obliviously comparing the descriptors at each pair of adjacent indices in $\mathcal{L}$.[3] Let $\mathcal{L}[i] = (\mathsf{img}_i, \mathsf{lbl}_i, \mathsf{party}_i)$ be the descriptor at index i in $\mathcal{L}$, and let $\mathcal{L}[i+1] = (\mathsf{img}_{i+1}, \mathsf{lbl}_{i+1}, \mathsf{party}_{i+1})$ be the descriptor at index $i+1$. If $\mathsf{img}_i = \mathsf{img}_{i+1}$, then both lbl_i and lbl_{i+1} are set to be the minimum among lbl_i and lbl_{i+1}.

The circuit iterates between percolation and matching $m-1$ times, applying π to transition from matching to percolation, and π^{-1} to transition from percolation to matching. After the final matching, the circuit applies π to transition to the output phase.

Encrypting Vertex Labels. At the end of the protocol, each party must receive its vertex labels encrypted under a key known only to the other party. We show how to move encryption outside of the garbled circuit in order to save the cost of online encryption at the expense of a few extra rounds of communication.

For a generic CPA-secure encryption scheme, we use the following technique. Consider a message m, computed within a circuit, that needs to be encrypted under a key k known only to p_1 without either party learning m. At the end, p_2 should learn $c = \mathsf{enc}(k, m)$. We can encrypt m under k as follows. p_2 samples a one-time pad υ and submits it to the circuit. The circuit outputs $m \oplus \upsilon$ to p_1. p_1 computes $c' = \mathsf{enc}(\mathsf{key}, m \oplus \upsilon)$. Then, p_1 sends c' to p_2, and p_2 computes $c = c' \oplus \upsilon = \mathsf{enc}(k, m)$.

The garbled circuit produces outputs to the parties as follows. Let out_i be the set of indices of p_i's vertices in $\pi(\mathcal{L})$. For the jth index in out_i, p_{3-i} receives $\pi(\mathcal{L})[\mathsf{out}_i[j]].\mathsf{lbl} \oplus \rho_{p_i}[j]$, which is p_i's jth label masked by p_i's jth random pad. The parties use the technique above to recover their encrypted labels.

Interfacing with DDH-Style PSI Protocols. We present our technique for ElGamal encrypting vertex labels. As we show below, DDH-style PSI protocols can be modified to accept ElGamal-encrypted inputs.

First, the parties agree on ℓ group elements $\{h_{j,0}\}_{j \in [\ell]}$. They then compute $h_{j,1} = h_{i,0}^{-1}$ as the inverse of each element. Neither party should know the discrete logarithm of these group elements; this can be accomplished, for example, by using the Diffie-Hellman key exchange to agree on $h_{j,0}$ for each j.

We represent a label m using these group elements by letting each pair of group elements $(h_{j,0}, h_{j,1})$ corresponds to the possible values of the bit at position j of the label (the same group elements are used for all labels). Let m_j be the jth bit of m. m can be represented as $\{h_{j,m_j}\}_{j \in [|m|]}$. Notice that each bit can be inverted by computing $h_{i,b}^{q-2}$ where q is the order of the group. Therefore, to compute $m \oplus p$, it is sufficient to invert the elements representing m where the bits of p are 1.

Suppose m is the label of one of p_i's vertices. As we described above, p_i submits a mask υ to the circuit, and the circuit outputs $m' = m \oplus \upsilon$ to p_{3-i}. For each bit m'_j in m', p_{3-i} will encrypt h_{j,m'_j} under its public key, and will send the ℓ ciphertexts for m' to p_i. When p_i receives its ciphertexts, it removes υ as follows. For each bit υ_j of υ where $\upsilon_j = 1$, p_i uses $\mathsf{ElGl}.Mul$ to invert the plaintext of the corresponding bit ciphertext. Finally, p_i uses $\mathsf{ElGl}.Mul$ to combine the bit-ciphertexts into a single label.

---

[3] If not using equality to compare the descriptors, then one could substitute any other comparison circuit to evaluate matching between two elements.

Recall that DDH-style PSI protocols proceed as follows:

1. p_1 chooses a random exponent R_1 and, for each element $S_{1,i}$ in its set, sends $S_{1,i}^{R_1}$ to p_2.
2. p_2 chooses a random exponent R_2 and, for each element $S_{2,j}$ in its set, computes $S_{2,j}^{R_2}$. It then computes $(S_{1,i}^{R_1})^{R_2}$, and sends $\{S_{1,i}^{R_1 R_2}\}$ and $\{S_{2,j}^{R_2}\}$ to p_1.
3. p_1 computes $(S_{2,j}^{R_2})^{R_1}$ and the intersection.

We note that the exponentiations of each party's input elements can actually be performed using EIGl.*Mul*. Since the other party has the key to decrypt these ciphertexts, the protocol proceeds as follows:

1. p_1 samples a random exponent R_1 and, for each element $\text{enc}_{pk_2}(S_{1,i})$ in its set, sends $\text{enc}_{pk_2}(S_{1,i}^{R_1})$ to p_2.
2. p_2 samples a random exponent R_2 and, for each element $\text{enc}_{pk_1}(S_{2,j})$ in its set, computes $\text{enc}_{pk_1}(S_{2,j}^{R_2})$. p_2 computes $S_{1,i}^{R_1} \leftarrow \text{dec}_{sk_2}(\text{enc}_{pk_2}(S_{1,i}^{R_1}))$ and then $(S_{1,i}^{R_1})^{R_2}$, and sends $\{S_{1,i}^{R_1 R_2}\}$ and $\{\text{enc}_{pk_1}(S_{2,j}^{R_2})\}$ to p_1.
3. p_1 decrypts, computes $(S_{2,j}^{R_2})^{R_1}$, and computes the intersection.

Protocol Outputs. Each party outputs two sets of encrypted labels. First, each party outputs the other party's masked labels, which it receives from the garbled circuit. Second it output its own vertices' encrypted labels.

Parties associate their encrypted labels with their vertices based on the order in which they receive their encrypted labels. In the earlier reveal phase, the parties learn the indices of their own vertices in the permuted list. They sort their vertices based on their indices in that list, and then associate the sorted vertices in order with the encrypted labels they receive. To choose a component label, a party arbitrarily selects any label assigned to a vertex in the component.

5   Evaluation

Asymptotic Analysis. The offline cost of the protocol is dominated by setup and encryption phases. In the setup, sorting a list of N of vertices offline requires $O(N \log N)$ offline comparisons. During the encryption phase, each party encrypts the other party's N labels and performs N XOR operations to retrieve its own encrypted labels.

The garbled circuit performs the following computations for the percolate-and-match algorithm. Merging two sorted lists of size N requires $O(N \log N)$ oblivious comparisons using a Batcher merge. Each percolation phase requires computing C (the number of components) min-circuits over m-sized lists. We can find the minimum of a list with m elements using m comparisons; therefore, in total the min circuits require $N = Cm$ comparisons per percolation phase. To perform each matching phase, we require $O(N)$ pairwise comparisons and updates. In addition, each Waksman network requires $O(N \log N)$ oblivious swaps, and two permutation networks are computed per iteration. Therefore, each iteration of the loop requires $O(N \log N)$ operations, and the

Secure Two-Party Component Labeling Protocol

- **Shared Inputs** The two parties share a security parameter λ and a random oracle $H: \{0,1\}^* \to \{0,1\}^{\ell}$
- **Local Input** Each party $p_i \in \{p_1, p_2\}$ has the following inputs:
  - $G_{p_i} = (V_{p_i}, E_{p_i})$ is a party's graph. For each party, V_{p_i} is a subset of a universal set V. Moreover, $|V_{p_i}| = N$. Each graph G_{p_i} is composed of components containing at most m vertices.
  - $k_{p_i}^{enc}$ is an encryption key for a CPA-secure encryption scheme with XOR homomorphism
  - $\rho_{p_i} = \{\rho_{p_i,j}\}_{j \in N}$ is a set of N ℓ-bit strings.
- **Setup**: Each party p_i
  - Randomly selects a permutation on $2N$ elements π_{p_i} and generates its Waksman select bits s_{p_i}.
  - Samples $2N$ ℓ-bit masks $\sigma_{p_i} = \{\sigma_{p_i,j}\}_{j \in [2N]}$ uniformly at random.
  - Computes $V_{p_i}^H \leftarrow \text{sort}(\text{map}(V_{p_i}, \lambda(x): H(x)), \lambda(x,y): x < y)$, which applies H to each of p_i's vertices and then sorts the images lexicographically.
  - Computes $\mathcal{L}_{p_i} = \{(\text{img}: V_{p_i,j}^H, \text{lbl}: V_{p_i,j}^H, \text{party}: i)\}_{j \in [N]}$
- **Revealing order under permutation**. Each party p_i:
  - Submits $\mathcal{L}_{p_i}$, σ_{p_i}, and s_i to the garbled circuit $\text{GC}^{\text{RevealOrder}}$, which merges $\mathcal{L}_{p_1}$ and $\mathcal{L}_{p_2}$ as $\mathcal{L}$, and permutes $\mathcal{L}$ as $\pi(\mathcal{L})$. Each party receives $2N$ ℓ-bit outputs from $\text{GC}^{\text{RevealOrder}}$. Let $o_{p_i}^{\text{order}} = \{o_{p_i,j}^{\text{order}}\}_{j \in [2N]}$ be the set of outputs received by party p_i.
  - Computes the indices of both parties' labels in the list $\pi(\mathcal{L})$ computed by $\text{GC}^{\text{RevealOrder}}$. p_i sets $\text{out}_{p_i} \leftarrow \{j: o_{p_i,j}^{\text{order}} \in V_{p_i}^H\}$, and sets $\text{out}_{p_{3-i}} \leftarrow \{j: o_{p_i,j}^{\text{order}} \notin V_{p_i}^H\}$, where out_{p_i} is the set of indices of p_i's vertices in $\pi(\mathcal{L})$.
  - Records the index of each of its vertices in $\pi(\mathcal{L})$. For all $v \in V_{p_i}$, assigns $\text{idx}(v) \leftarrow j: o_{p_i,j}^{\text{order}} = H(v)$.
  - Groups the indices in $o_{p_i}^{\text{order}}$ by component. For each component $C \in G_{p_i}$, assign $\text{idx}(C) \leftarrow \{\text{idx}(v)\}_{v \in C}$.
  - Sends $I_{p_i} = \{\text{idx}(C)\}_{C \in G_{p_i}}$ to p_{3-i}.
- **Percolate and Match**
  - The parties use and I_{p_1}, I_{p_2}, out_{p_1}, and out_{p_2} to hard-wire $\text{GC}_{I_{p_1}, I_{p_2}, \text{out}_{p_1}, \text{out}_{p_2}}^{\text{Perc\&Match}}$. Each party p_i submits ρ_{p_i} to the circuit and receives the other party's masked labels. Let $\{o_{p_i,j}^{\text{pm}}\}_{j \in [N]}$ be p_i's final output from the garbled circuit.
- **Encrypting Labels**. Each party p_i:
  - Encrypts the other party's masked labels using $k_{p_i}^{enc}$ and sends them to p_{3-i}. For all $j \in [N]$, p_i computes $\phi_{p_{3-i},j} = \text{CPA.enc}(k_{p_i,\text{l}}^{enc}, o_{p_i,j}^{\text{pm}})$ and sends $\{\phi_{p_{3-i},j}\}_{j \in [N]}$ to p_{3-i}.
- **PostProcessing**. Each party p_i:
  - Removes the masks from the encrypted labels it receives. p_i receives $\{\phi_{p_i,j}\}_{j \in [N]}$ from p_{3-i}, and computes $\gamma_{p_i,j} \leftarrow \phi_{p_i,j} \oplus \rho_{p_i,j}$.
  - Maps its vertices to its encrypted output labels. p_i computes $Y \leftarrow \text{sort}(V_{p_i}, \lambda(x,y): \text{idx}(x) < \text{idx}(y))$. Then p_i constructs $\Lambda_{p_i} = \{(Y_j, \gamma_{p_i,j})\}_{j \in [N]}$.
- **Outputs** Each party p_i outputs $\{o_{p_i,j}^{\text{pm}}\}_{j \in [N]}$ and Λ_{p_i}.

Fig. 7. Full protocol for secure component labeling.

procedure
REVEALORDER($\mathcal{L}_{p_1}, \mathcal{L}_{p_2}, \sigma_{p_1}, \sigma_{p_2}, s_{p_1}, s_{p_2}$)
// Merge, Permute, and Reveal the permuted index of each vertex to the vertex's owner
  $\mathcal{L} \leftarrow$ BATCHER-MERGE($\mathcal{L}_{p_1}, \mathcal{L}_{p_2}$, CmpImg)
  $\mathcal{L} \leftarrow$ PERMUTE($\mathcal{L}, s_{p_1}, s_{p_2}$)
  $o_{p_1} \leftarrow []_{2N}, o_{p_2} \leftarrow []_{2N}$
  for all $j \in [2N]$ **do**
    if $\mathcal{L}[j].\text{party} = p_1$ **then**
      $o_{p_1}[j] \leftarrow \mathcal{L}[j].\text{img}$
      $o_{p_2}[j] \leftarrow \mathcal{L}[j].\text{img} \oplus \sigma_{p_1,j}$
    else
      $o_{p_1}[j] \leftarrow \mathcal{L}[j].\text{img} \oplus \sigma_{p_2,j}$
      $o_{p_2}[j] \leftarrow \mathcal{L}[j].\text{img}$
    end if
  end for
  Output o_{p_1} to p_1 and o_{p_2} to p_2
end procedure

procedure PERC&MATCH($\mathcal{L}, \rho_{p_1}, \rho_{p_2}, s_{p_1}, s_{p_2}$)
// $I_{p_1}, I_{p_2}, \text{out}_{p_1}, \text{out}_{p_2}$ must be hard-coded
// $\mathcal{L}$ is passed to this subcircuit already permuted
  for all $i \in [m-1]$ **do**
    $\mathcal{L} \leftarrow$ PERCOLATE($\mathcal{L}, I_{p_1}$)
    $\mathcal{L} \leftarrow$ PERCOLATE($\mathcal{L}, I_{p_2}$)
    $\mathcal{L} \leftarrow$ INVERTPERMUTE($\mathcal{L}, s_{p_1}, s_{p_2}$)
    $\mathcal{L} \leftarrow$ MATCH($\mathcal{L}$)
    $\mathcal{L} \leftarrow$ PERMUTE($\mathcal{L}, s_{p_1}, s_{p_2}$)
  end for
  $o_{p_1} \leftarrow$ MASKFIXEDOUTPUTS($\mathcal{L}, \rho_{p_2}, \text{out}_{p_2}$)
  $o_{p_2} \leftarrow$ MASKFIXEDOUTPUTS($\mathcal{L}, \rho_{p_1}, \text{out}_{p_1}$)
  Output o_{p_1} to p_1 and o_{p_2} to p_2
end procedure

function PERMUTE(L, s_1, s_2)
  return Waksman(Waksman(L, s_1), s_2)
end function

function INVERTPERMUTE(L, s_1, s_2)
  return Waksman^{-1}(Waksman$^{-1}(L, s_2), s_1$)
end function

function PERCOLATE($\mathcal{L}, I$)
// I provides the indices in $\mathcal{L}$ that compose each component C in some party's graph.
  for all $\text{idx}(C) \in I$ **do**
    $\psi \leftarrow []_m$
    for all $j \in [m]$ **do**
      $\psi[j] \leftarrow \mathcal{L}[\text{idx}(C)[j]].\text{lbl}$
    end for
    $\text{minlbl} \leftarrow \min_{j \in [m]} \psi[j]$
    for all $j \in [m]$ **do**
      $\mathcal{L}[\text{idx}(C)[j]].\text{lbl} \leftarrow \text{minlbl}$
    end for
  end for
  return $\mathcal{L}$
end function

function MATCH($\mathcal{L}$)
  for all $i \in [2N-1]$ **do**
    $\text{lbl}^* \leftarrow \min(\mathcal{L}[i].\text{lbl}, \mathcal{L}[i+1].\text{lbl})$
    if $\mathcal{L}[i].\text{img} = \mathcal{L}[i+1].\text{img}$ **then**
      $\mathcal{L}[i].\text{lbl} \leftarrow \text{lbl}^*$
      $\mathcal{L}[i+1].\text{lbl} \leftarrow \text{lbl}^*$
    end if
  end for
  return $\mathcal{L}$
end function

function MASKFIXEDOUTPUTS($\mathcal{L}, \rho, \text{out}$)
  $j \leftarrow 0$
  $o \leftarrow []_N$
  for all $i \in \text{out}$ **do**
    $o[j] \leftarrow \mathcal{L}[i] \oplus \rho[j]$
    $j \leftarrow j+1$
  end for
  return o
end function

function CMPIMG(l_1, l_2)
  return $l_1.\text{img} \leq l_2.\text{img}$
end function

Fig. 8. Garbled circuit for secure component labeling. The subcircuits GC^{RevealOrder} and GC$^{\text{Perc&Match}}$ are defined by the procedures RevealOrder and PercAndMatch. In GC$^{\text{Perc&Match}}$, variables out$_{p_i}$ and I_{p_i} are public and must be hard-coded.

iterative procedure loops $m-1$ times. In total, the garbled circuit performs $O(Nm\log N)$ comparisons and swaps. The circuit must also compute $2N$ conditional XOR operations for the first output to the two parties, and an addition N XORs for the final output.

The total cost of the protocol is dominated by the garbled circuit. The circuit size depends on the output length ℓ of the hash function H because each comparison is performed over ℓ-bit values. The total cost of the circuit is therefore $O(Nm\ell\log N)$ gates. In the full version, we set ℓ as a function of the input size N and the tolerable correctness error ε. Specifically, we set $\ell \geq \lceil 2\log(2N) - \log(\varepsilon) - 1 \rceil$, making the total size of the circuit $O(Nm\log(N)(\log(N) + \log(\frac{1}{\varepsilon})))$ gates.

Experiments. We implemented our protocol using Obliv-C [32] and Absentminded Crypto Kit [11], adding our own optimizations to Obliv-C. Our tests were performed in parallel on Google Compute Platform (GCP) on n1-highmem-32 (32 vCPUs with 208GB memory) machines between pairs of machines in the same datacenter. El-Gamal operations were performed over elliptic curve secp256r1. We present our experimental results in the full version.

Security Analysis. We prove our protocol secure in the honest-but-curious model. The proof is presented in the full version. Adaptation to malicious security is future work.

6 Conclusion and Future Work

We have presented a two-party protocol that can be used as a setup for subsequent PSI-style computations. Our ID-agreement protocol was designed for use with DDH-style PSI protocols. In particular, we rely on the fact that in DDH-style protocols it is straightforward to work with ElGamal encryptions by taking advantage of the homomorphism over the group operation. We believe similar techniques can be applied to other PSI paradigms, which we leave for future work.

In a real-world application it is possible that the parties will update their respective databases and require new encrypted labels for their modified rows. One approach to computing the updated labels would be to run the entire protocol again, but this would be expensive if the updates occur frequently. More efficiently updating labels without scanning over bother parties' entire inputs is an interesting future direction.

Acknowledgement. We would like thank Samee Zahur for his assistance with the Obliv-C compiler and Jack Doerner for his assistance with Absentminded Crypto Kit.

References

1. Agrawal, R., Evfimievski, A., Srikant, R.: Information sharing across private databases. In: Proceedings of the 2003 ACM SIGMOD International Conference on Management of Data, SIGMOD 2003, pp. 86–97. ACM, New York (2003). https://doi.org/10.1145/872757.872771
2. Asharov, G., Komargodski, I., Lin, W.K., Nayak, K., Peserico, E., Shi, E.: Optorama: optimal oblivious ram. Cryptology ePrint Archive, Report 2018/892 (2018). https://eprint.iacr.org/2018/892

3. Batcher, K.E.: Sorting networks and their applications. In: Proceedings of the April 30-May 2, 1968, Spring Joint Computer Conference, pp. 307–314. ACM (1968)
4. Beauquier, B., Darrot, É.: On arbitrary size waksman networks and their vulnerability. Parallel Process. Lett. **12**(03n04), 287–296 (2002)
5. Bellare, M., Hoang, V.T., Rogaway, P.: Foundations of garbled circuits. Cryptology ePrint Archive, Report 2012/265 (2012). https://eprint.iacr.org/2012/265
6. Buddhavarapu, P., Knox, A., Mohassel, P., Sengupta, S., Taubeneck, E., Vlaskin, V.: Private matching for compute. Cryptology ePrint Archive, Report 2020/599 (2020). https://eprint.iacr.org/2020/599
7. Chmielewski, L., Hoepman, J.H.: Fuzzy private matching. In: Third International Conference on Availability, Reliability and Security, ARES 2008, pp. 327–334. IEEE (2008)
8. Ciampi, M., Orlandi, C.: Combining private set-intersection with secure two-party computation. In: Catalano, D., De Prisco, R. (eds.) SCN 2018. LNCS, vol. 11035, pp. 464–482. Springer, Cham (2018). https://doi.org/10.1007/978-3-319-98113-0_25
9. Dachman-Soled, D., Malkin, T., Raykova, M., Yung, M.: Efficient robust private set intersection. In: Abdalla, M., Pointcheval, D., Fouque, P.-A., Vergnaud, D. (eds.) ACNS 2009. LNCS, vol. 5536, pp. 125–142. Springer, Heidelberg (2009). https://doi.org/10.1007/978-3-642-01957-9_8
10. De Cristofaro, E., Kim, J., Tsudik, G.: Linear-complexity private set intersection protocols secure in malicious model. In: Abe, M. (ed.) ASIACRYPT 2010. LNCS, vol. 6477, pp. 213–231. Springer, Heidelberg (2010). https://doi.org/10.1007/978-3-642-17373-8_13
11. Doerner, J.: Absentminded crypto kit (2017)
12. Dong, C., Chen, L., Wen, Z.: When private set intersection meets big data: an efficient and scalable protocol. In: Proceedings of the 2013 ACM SIGSAC Conference on Computer & Communications Security, CCS 2013, pp. 789–800. ACM, New York (2013). https://doi.org/10.1145/2508859.2516701
13. Falk, B.H., Noble, D., Ostrovsky, R.: Private set intersection with linear communication from general assumptions. Cryptology ePrint Archive, Report 2018/238 (2018). https://eprint.iacr.org/2018/238
14. Freedman, M.J., Nissim, K., Pinkas, B.: Efficient private matching and set intersection. In: Cachin, C., Camenisch, J.L. (eds.) EUROCRYPT 2004. LNCS, vol. 3027, pp. 1–19. Springer, Heidelberg (2004). https://doi.org/10.1007/978-3-540-24676-3_1
15. Gamal, T.E.: A public key cryptosystem and a signature scheme based on discrete logarithms. IEEE Trans. Inf. Theory **31**(4), 469–472 (1985)
16. He, X., Machanavajjhala, A., Flynn, C., Srivastava, D.: Composing differential privacy and secure computation: a case study on scaling private record linkage. In: Proceedings of the 2017 ACM SIGSAC Conference on Computer and Communications Security, CCS 2017, pp. 1389–1406. ACM, New York (2017). https://doi.org/10.1145/3133956.3134030
17. Huang, Y., Evans, D., Katz, J.: Private set intersection: are garbled circuits better than custom protocols? In: 19th Annual Network and Distributed System Security Symposium, NDSS 2012, San Diego, California, USA, 5–8 February 2012 (2012). http://www.internetsociety.org/private-set-intersection-are-garbled-circuits-better-custom-protocols
18. Huberman, B.A., Franklin, M., Hogg, T.: Enhancing privacy and trust in electronic communities. In: Proceedings of the 1st ACM Conference on Electronic Commerce, pp. 78–86. ACM (1999)
19. Indyk, P., Motwani, R.: Approximate nearest neighbors: towards removing the curse of dimensionality. In: Proceedings of the Thirtieth Annual ACM Symposium on Theory of Computing, pp. 604–613. ACM (1998)
20. Ion, M., Kreuter, B., Nergiz, E., Patel, S., Saxena, S., Seth, K., Shanahan, D., Yung, M.: Private intersection-sum protocol with applications to attributing aggregate ad conversions. Technical report, Cryptology ePrint Archive, Report 2017/738 (2017)

21. Lambæk, M.: Breaking and fixing private set intersection protocols. Technical report, Cryptology ePrint Archive, Report 2016/665 (2016). http://eprint.iacr.org/2016/665
22. Larsen, K.G., Nielsen, J.B.: Yes, there is an oblivious RAM lower bound!. In: Shacham, H., Boldyreva, A. (eds.) CRYPTO 2018. LNCS, vol. 10992, pp. 523–542. Springer, Cham (2018). https://doi.org/10.1007/978-3-319-96881-0_18
23. Pinkas, B., Schneider, T., Segev, G., Zohner, M.: Phasing: private set intersection using permutation-based hashing. In: 24th USENIX Security Symposium (USENIX Security 2015), pp. 515–530. USENIX Association, Washington, D.C. (2015). https://www.usenix.org/conference/usenixsecurity15/technical-sessions/presentation/pinkas
24. Pinkas, B., Schneider, T., Tkachenko, O., Yanai, A.: Efficient circuit-based psi with linear communication. Cryptology ePrint Archive, Report 2019/241 (2019), https://eprint.iacr.org/2019/241
25. Pinkas, B., Schneider, T., Weinert, C., Wieder, U.: Efficient circuit-based psi via cuckoo hashing. Cryptology ePrint Archive, Report 2018/120 (2018). https://eprint.iacr.org/2018/120
26. Pinkas, B., Schneider, T., Zohner, M.: Faster private set intersection based on ot extension. Usenix Secur. 14, 797–812 (2014)
27. Rindal, P., Rosulek, M.: Improved private set intersection against malicious adversaries. In: Coron, J.-S., Nielsen, J.B. (eds.) EUROCRYPT 2017. LNCS, vol. 10210, pp. 235–259. Springer, Cham (2017). https://doi.org/10.1007/978-3-319-56620-7_9
28. Segal, A., Ford, B., Feigenbaum, J.: Catching bandits and only bandits: privacy-preserving intersection warrants for lawful surveillance. In: FOCI (2014)
29. Waksman, A.: A permutation network. J. ACM (JACM) 15(1), 159–163 (1968)
30. Wen, Z., Dong, C.: Efficient protocols for private record linkage. In: Proceedings of the 29th Annual ACM Symposium on Applied Computing, pp. 1688–1694. ACM (2014)
31. Yao, A.C.: Protocols for secure computations. In: Proceedings of the 23rd Annual Symposium on Foundations of Computer Science, SFCS 1982, pp. 160–164. IEEE Computer Society, Washington, DC (1982). https://doi.org/10.1109/SFCS.1982.88
32. Zahur, S., Evans, D.: Obliv-C: a language for extensible data-oblivious computation. IACR Cryptology ePrint Archive 2015, 1153 (2015)

UC-Secure OT from LWE, Revisited

Willy Quach[✉][iD]

Northeastern University, Boston, USA
quach.w@husky.neu.edu

Abstract. We build a two-round, UC-secure oblivious transfer protocol
(OT) in the common reference string (CRS) model under the Learning
with Errors assumption (LWE) with super-polynomial modulus-to-noise
ratio. We do so by instantiating the dual-mode encryption framework of
Peikert, Vaikuntanathan and Waters (CRYPTO'08). The resulting OT
can be instantiated in either one of two modes: one providing statistical
sender security, and the other statistical receiver security. Furthermore,
our scheme allows the sender and the receiver to reuse the CRS across
arbitrarily many executions of the protocol. To our knowledge, this is the
first construction of an UC-secure OT from LWE that achieves either
statistical receiver security or unbounded reusability of the CRS. For
comparison, the construction of UC-secure OT from LWE of Peikert,
Vaikuntanathan and Waters only provides computational receiver security and bounded reusability of the CRS.

Our main technical contribution is a public-key encryption scheme
from LWE where messy public keys (under which encryptions hide the
underlying message statistically) can be tested in time essentially independent of the LWE modulus q.

1 Introduction

Oblivious Transfer (OT), introduced by Rabin [Rab81], is now one of the most
fundamental cryptographic primitives, especially in the context of secure multi-
party computation [Yao86, GMW87]. Using OT, a sender with two messages
m_0, m_1 can send, to a receiver with choice bit b, the message m_b. Intuitively,
security ensures that the sender does not learn anything about the receiver's
choice bit, and that the receiver does not learn anything about the other message
m_{1-b}.

We would like OTs to provide security against *malicious* adversaries, who
might deviate arbitrarily from the specifications of the protocol, and ideally
achieve the strong guarantees of simulation-based security, where any malicious
adversary induces an ideal adversary against an ideal OT functionality. Among
the different flavors of simulation-based security is the powerful notion of Universal Composability (UC) [Can01], which additionally ensures that security is
preserved whenever the OT is executed within larger protocols.

Independently, one would ideally guarantee security against *computationally unbounded* adversaries. While OTs cannot simultaneously ensure statistical

© Springer Nature Switzerland AG 2020
C. Galdi and V. Kolesnikov (Eds.): SCN 2020, LNCS 12238, pp. 192–211, 2020.
https://doi.org/10.1007/978-3-030-57990-6_10

security for both receivers and senders, we can hope to provide statistical security for one specific party at a time.

Another desirable property is to require minimal interaction between the sender and the receiver. Two-round OT, which consists of a message from the receiver to the sender and a response from the sender to the receiver, is the best we can hope for. Unfortunately two-round, simulation-secure OT is impossible to achieve in the plain model. We therefore need to rely on some trusted setup assumption, the most standard one (at least in theory) being the availability of a *common reference string* (CRS) to both parties. In this context, we would like to generate a CRS once for all and be able to *reuse* it across many executions of the OT, as opposed to using a fresh CRS every time.

Two-round UC-secure OTs in the CRS model exist under several widely believed assumptions such as the Decisional Diffie-Hellman assumption (DDH), the Quadratic Residuosity assumption (QR), or the Learning with Errors assumption (LWE) [PVW08]. However, to our knowledge, current constructions of UC-secure OT from LWE only achieve weaker security guarantees compared to their group-based or number-theoretic counterparts. More precisely, current UC-secure OTs from LWE [PVW08] only achieve computational receiver security and each CRS can only be securely used a bounded number of times. This is all the more surprising as LWE seems in general much stronger at enabling powerful cryptographic primitives than DDH or QR.

Our Results. Our main result is the construction of a UC-secure OT scheme from the LWE assumption, with *statistical receiver security* and where the CRS can be reused an *unbounded* number of times (between a fixed sender and a fixed receiver). To our knowledge, this gives the first UC-secure OT from LWE achieving either of these two properties. We more precisely obtain the following:

Theorem 1.1 (informal). *Assuming LWE with super-polynomial modulus-to-noise ratio, there exists a two-round UC-secure OT in the common reference string (CRS) model, where the common reference string can be instantiated in two modes:*

- *One provides statistical receiver security and computational sender security;*
- *The other provides statistical sender security and computational receiver security. Furthermore, the CRS in this mode is a common random string.*

In either case, one single CRS can be reused for arbitrarily many executions between the sender and the receiver. Moreover, the two modes for the CRS are computationally indistinguishable.

For comparison, [PVW08] constructs OTs with the same properties as Theorem 1.1 from either DDH or QR. However, their construction from LWE (with polynomial modulus-to-noise ratio) only achieves weaker security guarantees. Namely, the CRS of the resulting OT can only be reused a bounded number of times, and receiver security is always computational (regardless of the mode). We stress that, in order to reuse the construction of [PVW08] from LWE an unbounded number of times, one would need the trusted setup to generate as many CRSs.

We point out that the original OT construction of [PVW08] from LWE (with weaker security guarantees) uses a *polynomial* LWE modulus, whereas our construction requires a super-polynomial one. As such, our construction is technically incomparable to the one of [PVW08]. We leave the construction of an OT with security properties similar to Theorem 1.1 from LWE with polynomial modulus as a natural open question.

We also note that the reusability property of the CRS only holds between a *fixed* (ordered) pair of sender and receiver (which is the same reusability property achieved by the constructions from DDH or QR of [PVW08]). While it is possible to generate a fresh CRS for every pair of parties executing the OT, one would ideally have one single "short" CRS of length independent from the number of parties. We leave such a possibility as another interesting open problem.

Related Work. The work of [PVW08] provides a construction of a UC-secure OT from LWE. Even though the latter construction only requires a *polynomial* LWE modulus (while ours requires a super-polynomial one), it only achieves weaker security guarantees, namely a non-reusable CRS and receiver security against computationally bounded senders. We provide a more detailed overview of their construction in Sect. 1.1. In terms of efficiency, our scheme essentially computes λ instances of [PVW08] (where λ is the security parameter), while using a larger modulus q.

There has been recent works building maliciously-secure OT from LWE. The work of [BD18] builds a *statistically sender-private* OT from LWE in the *plain model* (from LWE with polynomial modulus-to-noise ratio). For comparison, our construction achieves the stronger simulation-based security of UC (as opposed to indistinguishability-based security), at the cost of relying on a trusted common reference string,[1] and can further be instantiated to provide statistical receiver security, and is therefore less practically efficient.

The recent work of [DGH+20] gives a generic construction of UC-secure OT, which can be instantiated from CDH or LPN. As far as we understand, their construction provides unbounded reusability of the CRS, and is instantiable from LWE by relying further on either [PVW08] or [BD18]. In comparison, our construction can provide statistical security for either one of the parties (depending on the mode of Theorem 1.1), while [DGH+20] only provides computational security for both sides. Furthermore, our construction is significantly simpler and arguably more efficient.[2] Notably, we do not require the use of any non black-box techniques.

Non-interactive Zero-Knowledge Proofs. Recently, [CCH+19, PS19] obtained the first construction of non-interactive zero-knowledge proofs (NIZK) (for all NP)

---

[1] One such setup is necessary to achieve simulation-based security.

[2] Our construction essentially computes λ Regev ciphertexts. In comparison, [DGH+20] uses (among others) a generic zero-knowledge proof (for all NP) to ensure honest evaluation of a garbled circuit encoding an encryption procedure.

from LWE. This NIZK is *dual-mode*, meaning that according to the distribution of the CRS, the resulting NIZK is either statistically sound or statistical zero-knowledge; and those distributions are computationally indistinguishable. Therefore, starting with any *semi-maliciously* secure *dual-mode* OT (where the mode of the CRS gives either statistical receiver privacy or statistical sender privacy), one could potentially obtain a maliciously-secure dual-mode OT using the NIZK of [CCH+19, PS19].

There are, however, several caveats to this approach. First, in order to build dual-mode OT, we would have to start with a dual-mode (semi-malicious) OT. As is, [PVW08], even seen as a semi-malicious protocol, only achieves computational receiver security from LWE. Similarly to our approach, this can be fixed using noise flooding, and would therefore result on also relying on LWE with super-polynomial modulus-to-noise ratio. Second, the NIZKs of [CCH+19, PS19] are *not* adaptively sound when instantiated in statistical zero-knowledge mode. This seems inherent as the reductions for the soundness of [CCH+19, PS19] are black-box [Pas13]. This can be generically fixed using complexity leveraging, but would result in further relying on the *sub-exponential hardness* of LWE. Third, because [CCH+19, PS19] are generic NIZKs for all NP, compiling the OT of [PVW08] would most likely result in practially quite inefficient proofs. As a result, our approach results in an arguably simpler and more efficient protocol, and is provably secure under weaker assumptions (namely, under the *polynomial* hardness of LWE with super-polynomial modulus-to-noise ratio). Even though the need for sub-exponential hardness seems hard to avoid in the approach above, building a semi-malicious dual-mode OT from LWE with polynomial modulus-to-noise ratio does not seem out of reach, and we leave it as a natural open question.

Hash proof systems [CS98, CS02] are well-known to enable constructions of OTs. Notably, [Kal05] builds maliciously secure OTs starting from hash proof systems over languages with special properties. However, the resulting constructions only achieve the weaker guarantees of game-based security. Interestingly, one can interpret our construction as following a blueprint similar to [Kal05], using the (weak) hash proof system of Benhamouda et al. [BBDQ18]. However, our strong simulation-security guarantees seem to mainly stem from algebraic properties of LWE, as opposed to the hash proof system blueprint itself. In some sense, we use the hash proof system of [BBDQ18] to relax the task of our simulator (used to argue sender security) to a regime where lattice trapdoor techniques directly apply.

Curiously, while hash proof systems are usually defined over languages of *ciphertexts*, we implicitly consider in this work the language of valid *public keys* (and indeed the hash proof system of [BBDQ18] is originally defined over a *dual* Regev scheme, in which ciphertexts correspond to public keys in our construction).

1.1 Technical Overview

Our construction instantiates the dual-mode encryption framework introduced in [PVW08], which results in an OT with the properties of Theorem 1.1. In the same paper, [PVW08] only builds a weaker variant of dual-mode encryption from LWE, which results in a weaker form of OT, namely with neither a reusable CRS nor statistical receiver security. In this work, we build on this original construction of [PVW08] to obtain the original (stronger) version of dual-mode encryption from LWE.

We first upgrade reusability and receiver security by using a standard noise flooding technique, which requires the LWE modulus q to be super-polynomial. Unfortunately, the proof of *sender security* breaks down if we do so. This is because the simulator of [PVW08, GPV08] used to argue sender security runs in time linear in q, and therefore does not run in polynomial time if combined with noise flooding.

We therefore modify the scheme further by incorporating an appropriate *randomized rounding function* to the encryption scheme, which enables an alternative, polynomial time simulator for sender security. Such a rounding function was introduced by Benhamouda et al. [BBDQ18] in the seemingly unrelated context of hash proof systems over lattice languages. In a nutshell, while the simulator of [PVW08, GPV08] needs to test that q different points are far from a certain lattice, ours only tests a single point. More details follow.

Dual-Mode Encryption. The *dual-mode encryption* framework, introduced in [PVW08], serves as a modular way to build UC-secure OTs. A dual-mode encryption scheme uses a common reference string (CRS). Given this CRS, a receiver can, given some *branch* $b \in \{0,1\}$, create a pair of public/secret keys. Using the receiver's public key and the CRS, a sender can encrypt messages with respect to a branch $b' \in \{0,1\}$. The receiver can then use his secret key to decrypt the message corresponding to the branch $b' = b$ he initially used to create his pair of keys. Looking ahead, in an OT, the branch b corresponds to the receiver's choice bit, and the sender encrypts each his messages $m_{b'}$ to branch b'.

A dual-mode encryption scheme is set up in either one of two modes - messy or decryption - which determines the distribution of the CRS.

In *messy* mode, for all potentially maliciously generated public keys, (at least) one of the encryption branches hides its underlying message *statistically*. Combined with an efficient procedure to identify such so-called messy branches (given an appropriate trapdoor to the CRS), this ensures simulation-based statistical sender security.

In *decryption* mode, one can sample (given an appropriate trapdoor to the CRS) one public key along with two secret keys, one for each of the two branches, such that each of the two potential public/secret key pairs are individually *statistically indistinguishable* from honestly generated keys. This in particular implies that public keys statistically hide their branch b, and more generally, enables a simulator to extract messages encrypted to both branches, thus ensuring simulation-based receiver security.

Finally, a dual-mode encryption requires the two setup modes to be *computationally indistinguishable*. This allows us to argue both computational receiver security in messy mode, and computational sender security in decryption mode, by first switching to the other mode and then relying on the security of the latter.

Overall, [PVW08] showed that dual-mode encryption directly implies a UC-secure OT, where the mode used to pick the CRS - messy or decryption - induces which side is provided statistical security - sender or receiver, respectively. They furthermore show that the CRS can be reused between a fixed pair of sender and receiver, using the Joint-state UC framework of [CR03].

Weak Dual-Mode Encryption from LWE ([PVW08]). Our starting point is the construction of a weak form of dual-mode encryption from LWE of [PVW08]. The construction is a tweak on the (primal) Regev encryption scheme [Reg05], and works as follows. The CRS is set to be a uniformly random matrix $\mathbf{A} \xleftarrow{\$} \mathbb{Z}_q^{m \times n}$, along with an offset vector $\mathbf{v} \in \mathbb{Z}_q^m$. Key generation for a branch $b \in \{0, 1\}$ works as the Regev scheme, that is, by picking a uniform secret vector $\mathbf{s} \xleftarrow{\$} \mathbb{Z}_q^n$, a "short" error term $\mathbf{e}$, and setting $\mathsf{pk}_b = \mathbf{As} + \mathbf{e} \in \mathbb{Z}_q^m$, and $\mathsf{sk}_b = \mathbf{s}$. In particular $(\mathbf{A}, \mathsf{pk}_b)$ is a properly generated Regev public key with secret key sk_b. A crucial feature of the construction is that the two public keys (one for each branch) differ by the public offset $\mathbf{v} \in \mathbb{Z}_q^m$, that is: $\mathsf{pk}_1 - \mathsf{pk}_0 = \mathbf{v}$. This in particular defines pk_{1-b}. The public key of the dual-mode encryption scheme is then set to be, say, pk_0 (which given $\mathbf{v}$ determines pk_1), and the secret key sk_b.

To encrypt a message μ with respect to a branch b', one computes a Regev encryption using $(\mathbf{A}, \mathsf{pk}_{b'})$ as the Regev public key. That is, if $\mathsf{pk}_b = \mathbf{As} + \mathbf{e}$, one samples a "short" vector $\mathbf{r} \in \mathbb{Z}_q^m$, and outputs $\mathbf{r}^t \mathbf{A}, \mathbf{r}^t (\mathbf{As} + \mathbf{e}) + \mathsf{Encode}(\mu)$, where Encode is a fixed encoding procedure. In particular, using sk_b, one can decrypt ciphertexts for branch $b' = b$.

In messy mode, the offset term $\mathbf{v}$ is chosen uniformly at random in $\mathbb{Z}_q^m$. To argue security, the works of [GPV08, PVW08] introduce the notion of *messy* public keys, under which (Regev) encryptions statistically hide their message (and in our context the index of a messy public key corresponds to a messy branch). A core observation, made in [GPV08], is that for $\mathsf{pk} = \mathbf{c}$, if a certain quantity called the *smoothing parameter* of a certain lattice $\Lambda^{\perp}(\mathbf{A}\|\mathbf{c})$ is sufficiently small, then the public key pk is messy. Using a counting argument, [PVW08] shows that with overwhelming probability over the choice of $\mathbf{A}$ and $\mathbf{v}$, we have that *for all* public key $\mathsf{pk}_0 \in \mathbb{Z}_q^m$, (at least) one of pk_0 or $\mathsf{pk}_1 = \mathsf{pk}_0 + \mathbf{v}$ is messy. Finally, one builds an *extractor* that efficiently identifies one such messy public key. This is done, given an appropriate trapdoor for $\mathbf{A}$, by testing whether all (non-zero) multiples of $\mathsf{pk} = \mathbf{c}$ modulo q are sufficiently far from the lattice $\Lambda(\mathbf{A})$. If so, $\Lambda(\mathbf{A}\|\mathbf{c})$ essentially has a large minimum distance, which in turn implies that $\Lambda^{\perp}(\mathbf{A}\|\mathbf{c})$ indeed has a small smoothing parameter [MR04, Pei08, GPV08].[3]

---

[3] More precisely, the counting argument of [PVW08] actually shows that for all pair of public keys, such a test exhibits (at least) one messy public key.

In decryption mode, the offset term $\mathbf{v}$ is set to be the difference of two LWE samples: $\mathbf{v} = (\mathbf{A}\mathbf{s}_1 + \mathbf{e}_1) - (\mathbf{A}\mathbf{s}_0 + \mathbf{e}_0)$, which is pseudorandom by the LWE assumption; and therefore the two modes are computationally indistinguishable. In particular, one can now set $\widetilde{\mathsf{pk}}_0 = \mathbf{A}\mathbf{s}_0 + \mathbf{e}_0$ (and implicitly $\widetilde{\mathsf{pk}}_1 = \mathbf{A}\mathbf{s}_1 + \mathbf{e}_1$), so that the secret keys of *both* branches are known (namely $\mathbf{s}_0$ and $\mathbf{s}_1$, respectively), while all the keys follow the proper distribution. Doing so, however, presents several drawbacks. First, the "trapdoored" public key pk_0 is *fixed* by the CRS. This is ultimately why the CRS can only be reused a bounded number of times fixed in advance. Second, an unbounded adversary can potentially learn non-trivial information about $\mathbf{e}_0$ (and $\mathbf{e}_1$) from $\mathbf{v}$, in which case the trapdoored key $\widetilde{\mathsf{pk}}_0$ does *not* look like a freshly sampled public key. While one can actually argue security against a computationally bounded sender (using LWE), this prevents the scheme from achieving statistically receiver security.

Upgrading Security in Decryption Mode via Noise Flooding. Our first observation is that all the issues in decryption mode pointed above can be swiftly solved using *noise flooding*. Namely, we define the new public key as $\mathsf{pk}_b = \mathbf{A}\mathbf{s} + \mathbf{e} + \mathbf{f}$, where we flood the LWE error $\mathbf{e}$ using a much larger error term $\mathbf{f} \in \mathbb{Z}_q^m$ (which should still not be too large so as to allow decryption). Doing so hides the initial error term $\mathbf{e}$ *statistically*.

We now set the offset term to be a regular LWE sample $\mathbf{v} = \mathbf{A}\mathbf{s}^* + \mathbf{e}^*$, and sample our trapdoored public key as $\widetilde{\mathsf{pk}}_0 = \mathbf{A}\mathbf{s} + \mathbf{e} + \mathbf{f}$ using a fresh secret $\mathbf{s}$, error $\mathbf{e}$, and flooding term $\mathbf{f}$, along with $\mathsf{sk}_0 = \mathbf{s}$ and $\mathsf{sk}_1 = \mathbf{s} + \mathbf{s}^*$. Now the flooding term $\mathbf{f}$ statistically hides the error $\mathbf{e}^*$ in $\widetilde{\mathsf{pk}}_1 = \mathbf{A}(\mathbf{s} + \mathbf{s}^*) + (\mathbf{e} + \mathbf{e}^*) + \mathbf{f}$, and we therefore obtain both statistical receiver security and reusability of the CRS.

Fixing the Extractor in Messy Mode. One drawback of noise flooding is that it requires a *super-polynomial* modulus q. This is because the flooding term $\mathbf{f}$ should be super-polynomially larger than the LWE error $\mathbf{e}$. Therefore, we now have to rely on the hardness of LWE with super-polynomial modulus-to-noise ratio.

But the most dire issue is that the extractor used to argue security in messy mode is now inefficient. Recall that the extractor of [PVW08] tests that all of the $q - 1$ multiples of $\mathsf{pk} = \mathbf{c}$ are far from the lattice $\Lambda(\mathbf{A})$: its runtime is inherently (at least) *linear in q*, and in particular now runs in super-polynomial time if combined with noise flooding. This, in turn, makes the simulator used to argue sender security of the OT run in super-polynomial time. Fixing this issue is the main technical insight of this work.

Instead, we focus on designing an encryption scheme such that messy public keys can be recognized more efficiently. In other words, we would like an efficiently checkable condition on $\mathbf{c} \in \mathbb{Z}_q^m$ under which $\mathbf{r}^t \cdot \mathbf{c}$ (which is the masking term computed during an encryption) is uniform given $\mathbf{r}^t \mathbf{A}$, where $\mathbf{r}$ is drawn from a "small" distribution. To do so, we use the techniques developed in [BBDQ18], which introduces an explicit *randomized rounding function R* (with output $\{0,1\}$) with the following (informal) properties:

1. If $\mathbf{c} \in \mathbb{Z}_q^m$ is *"sufficiently far"* from the lattice $\Lambda(\mathbf{A})$, then $R(\mathbf{r}^t \cdot \mathbf{c})$ is *statistically close* to uniform, even given $\mathbf{r}^t \cdot \mathbf{A}$;
2. If $\mathbf{c} = \mathbf{As} + \mathbf{e} \in \mathbb{Z}_q^m$ is *"sufficiently close"* to the lattice $\Lambda(\mathbf{A})$, then $R(\mathbf{r}^t \cdot \mathbf{As}) = R(\mathbf{r}^t \cdot \mathbf{c})$ with good probability (say $\geq 2/3$).

In a nutshell, the rounding function R is defined in such a way so that the other multiples $k \cdot \mathbf{c}$, $k \neq 1$ are in some sense filtered out by (the absence of) corresponding harmonics of its density function. We refer the reader to Lemma 2.7 or [BBDQ18] for more details on the construction of this rounding function.

This induces a variant of the Regev encryption scheme, where the Regev public key is $(\mathbf{A}, \mathbf{c})$, and the message is now masked using $R(\mathbf{r}^t \cdot \mathbf{c})$, where approximate correctness is ensured by providing $\mathbf{r}^t \cdot \mathbf{A}$ in the ciphertext, and relying on Property 2. Correctness can then be amplified by giving many independent such ciphertexts.

By Property 1, public keys $(\mathbf{A}, \mathbf{c})$ are messy as soon as $\mathbf{c}$ is "sufficiently far" from $\Lambda(\mathbf{A})$ - and crucially, independently of the other multiples of $\mathbf{c}$ - which can be tested efficiently using an appropriate trapdoor for $\mathbf{A}$ [AR03, Pei08, GPV08, MP12]. In our construction, we use the LWE decoder of [MP12], which (arguably) results in a substantially simpler extractor than the original versions [GPV08, PVW08].

To finish the proof, it suffices to note that the random offset $\mathbf{v}$ is, with high probability, "sufficiently far" from the lattice $\Lambda(\mathbf{A})$, in which case *for all* public key $\mathsf{pk}_0 = \mathbf{c}$, either $\mathbf{c}$ or $\mathbf{c} + \mathbf{v}$ is "sufficiently far" from $\Lambda(\mathbf{A})$. Otherwise their difference $\mathbf{v}$ would not be "sufficiently far" from the lattice. Therefore at least one of them is messy and recognized as such by the extractor.

2 Preliminaries

Notations. Throughout the paper, λ will denote a security parameter, and $n = n(\lambda)$ the dimension of the LWE problem. We will often abuse notation and use n as the security parameter.

We denote by $\mathsf{poly}(n)$ any function f such that $f(n) = O(n^c)$ for some constant c; and $\mathsf{negl}(n)$ denotes any function such that $f(n) = n^{-\omega(1)}$. We will denote (column) vectors by bold lower cases (e.g., $\mathbf{c}$) and matrices by bold upper cases (e.g, $\mathbf{A}$). We denote the transposition operation by $\cdot^t$ (e.g., $\mathbf{c}^t$). For $\mathbf{A} \in \mathbb{Z}_q^{m \times n}$ and $\mathbf{B} \in \mathbb{Z}_q^{m \times k}$, we denote by $(\mathbf{A} \| \mathbf{B}) \in \mathbb{Z}_q^{m \times (n+k)}$ their horizontal concatenation. Unless specifically stated otherwise, all the distances $d(\cdot, \cdot)$ and norms $\| \cdot \|$ we use are in the ℓ_2 norm. $\| \cdot \|_\infty$ denotes the infinity norm. We use the notation $[k]$ for the set of integers $[1, \ldots, k]$. For a set E, we will sometimes denote by $\mathcal{U}(E)$ the uniform distribution over E, and we will use $x \xleftarrow{\$} E$ to denote the uniform sampling $x \leftarrow \mathcal{U}(E)$.

We define the statistical distance between two random variables X and Y over some domain Ω as $\mathsf{SD}(X, Y) = \frac{1}{2} \sum_{w \in \Omega} |X(w) - Y(w)|$. We say that two ensembles of random variables $X = \{X_\lambda\}_\lambda, Y = \{Y_\lambda\}_\lambda$ are *statistically indistinguishable* if $\mathsf{SD}(X_\lambda, Y_\lambda) \leq \mathsf{negl}(\lambda)$; and we denote it with $X \approx_s Y$.

We say that two ensembles of random variables $X = \{X_\lambda\}_\lambda, Y = \{Y_\lambda\}_\lambda$ are *computationally indistinguishable* if for all probabilistic, polynomial time (PPT) distinguisher $\mathcal{A} \to \{0,1\}$, we have: $|\Pr[\mathcal{A}(X_\lambda) = 1] - \Pr[\mathcal{A}(Y_\lambda) = 1]| \leq \mathsf{negl}(\lambda)$; and we denote it with $X \approx_c Y$.

For $B \in \mathbb{R}$, we say that a distribution ψ is *B-bounded* if $\Pr_{x \leftarrow \psi}[|x| \geq B] \leq \mathsf{negl}(\lambda)$.

2.1   Dual Mode Encryption

We recall the definition of dual-mode encryption [PVW08].

Definition 2.1 (Dual Mode Encryption). *A Dual-Mode Encryption scheme with message space $\{0,1\}^k$ is a tuple of PPT algorithms* (SetupMessy, SetupDec, KeyGen, Enc, Dec, FindMessy, TrapKeyGen) *with the following syntax:*

- SetupMessy(1^λ) $\to$ (crs, td$_M$)*: Given the security parameter λ, the setup algorithm outputs a common reference string* crs *along with a trapdoor* td$_M$.
- SetupDec(1^λ) $\to$ (crs, td$_D$)*: Given the security parameter λ, the setup algorithm outputs a common reference string* crs *along with a trapdoor* td$_D$.
- KeyGen(crs, b) $\to$ (pk, sk$_b$)*: Given a reference string* crs *and a branch $b \in \{0,1\}$, the key-generation algorithm outputs a public key* pk *and a secret key* sk$_b$ *for branch b.*
- Enc(crs, pk, b', μ) $\to$ ct*: Given a reference string* crs*, a public key* pk*, a branch $b' \in \{0,1\}$ and a message $\mu \in \{0,1\}^k$, the encryption algorithm outputs a ciphertext* ct.
- Dec(crs, sk, ct) $\to$ μ*: Given a reference string* crs*, a secret key* sk *and a ciphertext* ct*, the decryption algorithm outputs a message μ.*
- FindMessy(crs, td$_M$, pk) $\to$ $\bar{b}$*: Given a reference string* crs*, a trapdoor in messy mode* td$_M$ *and a (possibly malformed) public key* pk*, the algorithm outputs a branch $\bar{b} \in \{0,1\}$.*
- TrapKeyGen(crs, td$_D$)*: Given a reference string* crs*, a trapdoor in decryption mode* td$_D$*, the algorithm outputs keys* (pk, sk$_0$, sk$_1$) *where* pk *is a public-key, and* sk$_0$ *and* sk$_1$ *are secret keys for branches 0 and 1, respectively.*

We require the following properties to hold:

- **Completeness on decryptable branch:** *For all $\mu \in \{0,1\}^k$ and $b \in \{0,1\}$:*

$$\Pr[\mathsf{Dec}(\mathsf{crs}, \mathsf{sk}_b, \mathsf{Enc}(\mathsf{crs}, \mathsf{pk}, b, \mu)) = \mu] \geq 1 - \mathsf{negl}(\lambda),$$

whether (crs, td) $\leftarrow$ SetupMessy(1^λ) *or* (crs, td) $\leftarrow$ SetupDec(1^λ)*, and where* (pk, sk$_b$) $\leftarrow$ KeyGen(crs, b).
- **Indistinguishability of modes:** *We have:*

$$\mathsf{crs}_M \approx_c \mathsf{crs}_D,$$

where (crs$_M$, td$_M$) $\leftarrow$ SetupMessy(1^λ) *and* (crs$_D$, td$_D$) $\leftarrow$ SetupDec(1^λ).

- **Security in messy mode** *(a.k.a. trapdoor identification of a messy branch):* With overwhelming probability over $(\mathsf{crs}, \mathsf{td}_M) \leftarrow \mathsf{SetupMessy}(1^\lambda)$, *it holds that for all (possibly malformed)* pk *and all messages* $\mu_0, \mu_1 \in \{0, 1\}^k$:

$$\mathsf{Enc}(\mathsf{crs}, \mathsf{pk}, \bar{b}, \mu_0) \approx_s \mathsf{Enc}(\mathsf{crs}, \mathsf{pk}, \bar{b}, \mu_1),$$

where $\bar{b} \leftarrow \mathsf{FindMessy}(\mathsf{crs}, \mathsf{td}_M, \mathsf{pk})$.
- **Security in decryption mode** *(a.k.a. trapdoor generation of keys decryptable on both branches):* With overwhelming probability over $(\mathsf{crs}, \mathsf{td}_D) \leftarrow \mathsf{SetupDec}(1^\lambda)$, *we have that for every* $b \in \{0, 1\}$:

$$(\mathsf{crs}, \mathsf{pk}, \mathsf{sk}_b) \approx_s (\mathsf{crs}, \mathsf{KeyGen}(1^\lambda)),$$

where $(\mathsf{pk}, \mathsf{sk}_0, \mathsf{sk}_1) \leftarrow \mathsf{TrapKeyGen}(\mathsf{td}_D)$.

[PVW08] showed that any dual-mode encryption scheme implies a "dual-mode" UC-secure OT. We refer to [PVW08] for more precise definitions of UC security.

Theorem 2.1 (Dual-Mode Encryption implies UC-Secure OT [PVW08]). *Assume* $(\mathsf{SetupMessy}, \mathsf{SetupDec}, \mathsf{KeyGen}, \mathsf{Enc}, \mathsf{Dec}, \mathsf{FindMessy}, \mathsf{TrapKeyGen})$ *is a dual-mode encryption scheme. Then, there exists a protocol realizing the multi-session functionality* $\widehat{\mathcal{F}}_{OT}$ *in the* $\mathcal{F}_{CRS}$*-hybrid model, under static corruptions.*

Furthermore the protocol can be instantiated in two modes (each over a distinct functionality $\mathcal{F}_{CRS}$*): one providing statistical sender security and computational receiver security; and the other statistical receiver security and computational sender security.*

2.2   Lattices and Learning with Errors

We will use the following lemma:

Lemma 2.2 (Noise flooding (e.g [AJL+12])). *Let* $B = B(\lambda)$, $B' = B'(\lambda) \in \mathbb{Z}$ *be two integers, and let* $e_1 \in [-B, B]$. *Suppose that* $B/B' = \mathsf{negl}(\lambda)$. *Then:*

$$\mathcal{U}([-B', B']) \approx_s \mathcal{U}([-B', B']) + e_1.$$

The following lemma states that for appropriate parameters, random q-ary lattices have a large minimum distance and are full-rank:

Lemma 2.3 *[GPV08, Lemmas 5.1 and 5.3] Suppose* $m \geq 2n \log q$. *Then:*

$$\Pr_{\mathbf{A} \xleftarrow{\$} \mathbb{Z}_q^{m \times n}} [\lambda_1^\infty(\Lambda(\mathbf{A})) \geq q/4 \quad \wedge \quad \mathbf{A} \text{ is full-rank}] \geq 1 - 2q^{-n}.$$

We define the *Gaussian weight function* on $\mathbb{R}^m$ with parameter $\tau > 0$ as:

$$\rho_\tau : x \mapsto \exp(-\pi\|x\|^2/\tau^2).$$

The *discrete Gaussian distribution* over $\mathbb{Z}$ with parameter $\tau > 0$ is defined as:

$$\forall x \in \mathbb{Z}, D_{\mathbb{Z},\tau}(x) = \frac{\rho_\tau(x)}{\sum_{y\in\mathbb{Z}} \rho_\tau(y)}.$$

The following lemma states that random q-ary lattices have a small smoothing parameter:

Lemma 2.4 ([MR04, Pei08, GPV08]). *For any m-dimensional lattice Λ and real $\epsilon > 0$, we have:*

$$\eta_\epsilon(\Lambda) \leq \frac{\sqrt{\log(2m/(1+1/\epsilon))/\pi}}{\Lambda_1^\infty(\Lambda^*)}.$$

In particular, with overwhelming probability over the choice of $\mathbf{A} \xleftarrow{\$} \mathbb{Z}_q^{m\times n}$, we have that for any function $\omega(\sqrt{\log m})$, there exists a negligible function $\epsilon(m)$ such that

$$\eta_\epsilon(\Lambda^\perp(\mathbf{A})) \leq \omega(\sqrt{\log m}).$$

Lattices and Gaussians. We recall basic definitions related to lattices.

For an integer m, an m-dimensional lattice Λ is a discrete subgroup of $\mathbb{R}^m$. For a lattice Λ, its dual Λ^* is defined as $\Lambda^* = \{\mathbf{r} \in \mathrm{Span}_{\mathbb{R}}(\Lambda) \,|\, \forall \mathbf{x} \in \Lambda, \langle \mathbf{x}, \mathbf{r} \rangle \in \mathbb{Z}\}$.

The *minimum distance* (in infinity norm) of a lattice is defined as $\lambda_1^\infty(\Lambda) = \min_{x\in\Lambda\setminus\{0\}} \|x\|_\infty$.

For $\mathbf{A} \in \mathbb{Z}_q^{m\times n}$, we will use the following q-ary lattices defined by $\mathbf{A}$:

$$\Lambda(\mathbf{A}) = \{\mathbf{As}\,|\,\mathbf{s} \in \mathbb{Z}_q^n\} + q\mathbb{Z}^m, \quad \Lambda^\perp(\mathbf{A}) = \{\mathbf{r} \in \mathbb{Z}^m \,|\, \mathbf{r}^t\mathbf{A} = \mathbf{0}^t \bmod q\}.$$

The lattices $\Lambda(\mathbf{A})$ and $\Lambda^\perp(\mathbf{A})$ are dual to each other up to a scaling factor: $\Lambda(\mathbf{A}) = q \cdot \Lambda^\perp(\mathbf{A})^*$.

We say, for $\mathbf{A} \in \mathbb{Z}_q^{m\times n}$, that $\mathbf{A}$ is *full-rank* the columns of $\mathbf{A}$ are linearly independent.

For $\epsilon > 0$, the *smoothing parameter* of a lattice Λ, introduced in [MR04] and denoted $\eta_\epsilon(\Lambda)$, is the smallest $\tau > 0$ such that $\rho_{1/\tau}(\Lambda^* \setminus \{\mathbf{0}\}) \leq \epsilon$. Intuitively, for $\tau \geq \eta_\epsilon(\Lambda)$ for some small ϵ, we have that for $\mathbf{r} \leftarrow D_{\mathbb{Z},\tau}^m$, $\mathbf{r} \bmod \Lambda$ is roughly uniform. In particular, if $\mathbf{A} \in \mathbb{Z}_q^{m\times n}$ is full-rank and $\tau \geq \eta_\epsilon(\Lambda^\perp(\mathbf{A}))$, then for $\mathbf{r} \leftarrow D_{\mathbb{Z},\tau}^m$, $\mathbf{r}^t\mathbf{A} \bmod q$ is roughly uniform in $\mathbb{Z}_q^{1\times n}$.

Learning with Errors. We recall the definition of the Learning with Errors assumption.

Definition 2.5 (Decisional Learning with Errors assumption [Reg05]). *Let n and $q = q(n) \geq 2$ be integers, and χ a distribution over $\mathbb{Z}$. The* Learning with Errors *assumption* $\mathsf{LWE}_{q,\chi,n}$ *states that for all* $m = \mathsf{poly}(n)$ *the following distributions are computationally indistinguishable:*

$$(\mathbf{A}, \mathbf{A}\mathbf{s} + \mathbf{e}) \approx_c (\mathbf{A}, \mathbf{b}),$$

where $\mathbf{A} \xleftarrow{\$} \mathbb{Z}_q^{m \times n}$, $\mathbf{e} \leftarrow \chi^m$, $\mathbf{s} \xleftarrow{\$} \mathbb{Z}_q^n$ *and* $\mathbf{b} \xleftarrow{\$} \mathbb{Z}_q^m$.

[Reg05] showed that for all $B \geq \widetilde{\Omega}(\sqrt{n})$, there exists a B-bounded distribution $\chi = \chi(n)$ such for all $q = q(n) \geq 2$, breaking $\mathsf{LWE}_{q,\chi,n}$ is as hard as (quantumly) solving GapSVP_γ and SIVP_γ within approximation factor $\gamma = \widetilde{O}(\sqrt{n}q/B)$. For comparison, the best known (provable) algorithm for GapSVP_γ runs in time $2^{\widetilde{\Omega}(n/\log\gamma)}$ [Sch87].

Lattice Trapdoors

Lemma 2.6 (Lattice trapdoors [MP12]). *There exists a PPT algorithm* $\mathsf{TrapGen}(1^n, 1^m, q) \rightarrow (\mathbf{A}, \mathbf{T})$, *which on input some integers* n, $q \geq 2$ *and* $m \geq \Omega(n \log q)$, *satisfies the following properties:*

- *The distribution of* $\mathbf{A}$ *is within negligible statistical distance from* $\mathcal{U}(\mathbb{Z}_q^{m \times n})$;
- *There exists a polynomial-time, deterministic algorithm* $\mathsf{Invert}(\mathbf{T}, \mathbf{A}, \mathbf{c})$, *which on input* $\mathbf{c} = \mathbf{A}\mathbf{s} + \mathbf{e}$ *where* $\mathbf{s} \in \mathbb{Z}_q^m$ *and* $\mathbf{e} \in \mathbb{Z}_q^m$ *such that* $\|\mathbf{e}\| < q/6\sqrt{m}$, *outputs* $(\mathbf{s}, \mathbf{e})$.

Without loss of generality, the algorithm Invert only outputs some $(\mathbf{s}, \mathbf{e})$ whenever $\mathbf{c} = \mathbf{A}\mathbf{s} + \mathbf{e}$ and $\|\mathbf{e}\| < q/6(\sqrt{m})$, as these conditions can be checked efficiently.

2.3 Smooth Rounding over Lattices

We recall the properties of the rounding function defined in [BBDQ18].

Lemma 2.7 (Statistically smooth rounding [BBDQ18]). *Suppose* $m = \Theta(n \log q)$. *Let* $R : \mathbb{Z}_q \mapsto \{0, 1\}$ *be a randomized rounding function defined as:*

$$R(x) = \begin{cases} 1 \text{ with probability } \frac{1}{2} + \frac{\cos(2\pi x/q)}{2} \\ 0 \text{ with probability } \frac{1}{2} - \frac{\cos(2\pi x/q)}{2} \end{cases}.$$

Let $\mathbf{A} \in \mathbb{Z}_q^{m \times n}$, $\mathbf{p} \in \mathbb{Z}_q^n$, *and* $\tau \geq \eta_\epsilon(\Lambda^\perp(\mathbf{A}))$ *for some* $\epsilon = \mathsf{negl}(n)$. *Then the following properties hold:*

- **Statistical Smoothness:** *Suppose* $\mathbf{A}$ *is full rank. Then, for all* $\mathbf{c} \in \mathbb{Z}_q^m$ *such that* $d(\mathbf{c}, \Lambda(\mathbf{A})) \geq q\sqrt{m}/\tau$, *we have:*

$$\left| \Pr_{R, \mathbf{r} \leftarrow D_{\mathbb{Z},\tau}^m} \left[R(\langle \mathbf{r}, \mathbf{c} \rangle) = 1 \mid \mathbf{r}^t \mathbf{A} = \mathbf{p}^t \right] - 1/2 \right| \leq \mathsf{negl}(n),$$

where the probability is taken over $\mathbf{r} \leftarrow D_{\mathbb{Z},\tau}^m$ *and the internal randomness of* R.

- *Approximate Correctness:* For all $\mathbf{c} = \mathbf{A}\mathbf{s} + \mathbf{e}$ where $\mathbf{s} \in \mathbb{Z}_q^n$ and $\mathbf{e} \in \mathbb{Z}_q^m$ satisfies $\|\mathbf{e}\| \leq B$ (i.e., $d(\mathbf{c}, \Lambda(\mathbf{A})) \leq B$) where $B \cdot \tau \cdot \sqrt{m} = o(q)$, then for all large enough n:

$$\Pr_{R,\, \mathbf{r} \leftarrow D_{\mathbb{Z},\tau}^m} [R(\mathbf{r}^t \mathbf{A}\mathbf{s}) = R(\mathbf{r}^t \mathbf{c}))] \geq 2/3.$$

Remark 2.8 (Statistically correct rounding). In addition to the rounding function presented above, [BBDQ18] also defines a rounding function with *statistically correctness* and *approximate smoothness* (meaning that its bias is bounded). For our ultimate purpose of building a dual-mode encryption scheme from LWE, such a rounding scheme would also suffice (modulo direct modifications in the encryption scheme). However the parameters imposed by such a rounding function are slightly more constraining, and in particular require a super-polynomial modulus q in the first place. This for instance disallows the use of the scheme described in Sect. 3.1 with a polynomial modulus q (even though our final construction requires a super-polynomial modulus anyway).

3 Dual-Mode Encryption from LWE

We now focus on building a dual-mode encryption scheme from LWE. In Sect. 3.1, we introduce a public-key encryption scheme where most messy public keys can be tested efficiently. This serves as a basis for our actual construction of a dual-mode encryption scheme in Sect. 3.2.

3.1 A Messy Public-Key Encryption Scheme

We use the rounding function defined in Lemma 2.7 to define a variant of the (primal) Regev encryption scheme, where the message is now masked by a *rounded* bit (instead of a value in $\mathbb{Z}_q$). Looking ahead, this scheme has the crucial property that public key messiness is efficiently testable (given an appropriate trapdoor) in time essentially independent of the LWE modulus q.

Parameters. Let $n = n(\lambda) = \lambda$, $q = q(\lambda) \geq 2$ be integers. Let $m \geq 2(n+1)\log q$.
   Let $\tau \geq 4\sqrt{m}$ (and $\tau \geq 6(m)$ if one wants to test messy public keys).
   Let $\chi = \chi(n)$ given by Definition 2.5 be a $B = B(n)$ bounded distribution where $B = \widetilde{\Omega}(\sqrt{n})$.
   Let $B' \in \mathbb{Z}$ be such that $(B + B') \cdot \tau\sqrt{m} = o(q)$ (which implies $q \geq \omega(B' + \sqrt{n})m)$).
   Let R be the rounding function defined in Lemma 2.7.

Construction. We define our public key encryption scheme (SmoothKeyGen, SmoothEnc, SmoothDec) over message space $\mathcal{M} = \{0,1\}$ as follows:

- Smooth.KeyGen(1^λ): Sample $\mathbf{A} \xleftarrow{\$} \mathbb{Z}_q^{m \times n}$, $\mathbf{s} \xleftarrow{\$} \mathbb{Z}_q^n$, $\mathbf{e} \leftarrow \chi^m$, $\mathbf{f} \xleftarrow{\$} [-B', B']$ and set $\mathbf{c} = \mathbf{A}\mathbf{s} + \mathbf{e} + \mathbf{f}$. Output:

$$\mathsf{pk} = (\mathbf{A}, \mathbf{c}), \quad \mathsf{sk} = \mathbf{s}.$$

- Smooth.Enc(pk, $\mu \in \{0,1\}$): For $i \in [\lambda]$, sample $\mathbf{r}_i \leftarrow D_{\mathbb{Z},\tau}^m$. Compute $\mathbf{p}_i^t = \mathbf{r}_i^t \cdot \mathbf{A} \in \mathbb{Z}_q^{1 \times n}$, and:

$$\beta_i \leftarrow R(\mathbf{r}_i^t \cdot \mathbf{c}) \oplus \mu,$$

and output:

$$\mathsf{ct} = (\{\mathbf{p}_i, \beta_i\}_{i \leq \lambda}).$$

- Smooth.Dec(sk, ct): Compute, for all $i \in [\lambda]$:

$$b_i \leftarrow R(\mathbf{p}_i^t \cdot \mathbf{s}) \oplus \beta_i,$$

and output the majority bit of the b_i's.

Looking ahead, the additional term $\mathbf{f}$ added to $\mathbf{c}$ will be used in the dual-mode encryption scheme to help arguing security in decryption mode. We note that removing this term from $\mathbf{c}$ does not affect any of the properties listed below.

Properties. We first argue correctness the scheme.

Lemma 3.1 (Correctness). *Suppose* $(B + B') \cdot \tau \cdot \sqrt{m} = o(q)$ *and* $\tau \geq \omega(\sqrt{\log m})$. *Then the scheme above is correct.*

Proof. By Lemma 2.4, there exists some $\epsilon = \mathsf{negl}(n)$[4], such that with overwhelming probability over the choice of $\mathbf{A}$, we have $\tau \geq \eta_\epsilon(\Lambda^\perp(\mathbf{A}))$.

By approximate correctness of the rounding function R (Lemma 2.7), for all $i \in [\lambda]$, we have:

$$\Pr_{R, \mathbf{r}_i \leftarrow D_{\mathbb{Z},\tau}^m} [b_i = \beta_i] \geq 2/3,$$

over the internal randomness of R and $\mathbf{r}_i \leftarrow D_{\mathbb{Z},\tau}^m$ alone. Using a Chernoff bound, we obtain that decryption is correct with overwhelming probability. $\square$

Next, we give a sufficient condition over public-keys so that the associated encryption hides the message information-theoretically. Looking ahead, this will be used to argue both security of the scheme above, and messy mode security of the derived dual-mode encryption scheme.

Following the terminology of [PVW08, GPV08], we say that a public key pk is *messy* (which stands short for *message-lossy*) if SmoothEnc(pk, m) *statistically hides* the message m for all m, that is:

$$\mathsf{SmoothEnc}(\mathsf{pk}, 0) \approx_s \mathsf{SmoothEnc}(\mathsf{pk}, 1).$$

Lemma 3.2 (Sufficient condition for public key messiness). *Let* $\mathbf{A} \xleftarrow{\$} \mathbb{Z}_q^{m \times n}$, *and* $\mathbf{c} \in \mathbb{Z}_q^m$. *Fix* $\epsilon = \mathsf{negl}(n)$, *and suppose* $\tau \geq \eta_\epsilon(\Lambda(\mathbf{A}))$.

If $d(\mathbf{c}, \Lambda(\mathbf{A})) \geq q\sqrt{m}/\tau$ *and* $\mathbf{A}$ *is full rank, then the public key* $(\mathbf{A}, \mathbf{c})$ *is messy, that is:*

$$\mathsf{SmoothEnc}(\mathsf{pk}, 0) \approx_s \mathsf{SmoothEnc}(\mathsf{pk}, 1).$$

---

[4] Looking more closely at Lemma 2.4, ϵ can be exponentially small if $\tau \geq m$.

Proof. By statistical smoothness of the rounding function (Lemma 2.7), every bit $R(\mathbf{r}_i^t \cdot \mathbf{c})$ is *statistically close to uniform* given $\mathbf{A}, \mathbf{c}, \mathbf{p}_i$ over the internal randomness of R and $\mathbf{r}_i \leftarrow D_{\mathbb{Z},\tau}^m$ alone. In particular, $\{\beta_i\}_{i \in [\lambda]}$ are statistically close to uniform bits.

Lemma 3.3 (Most public keys are messy). *Suppose $m \geq 2(n+1)\log q$ and $\tau \geq 4\sqrt{m}$.*

Let $(\mathbf{A}, \mathbf{c}) \xleftarrow{\$} \mathbb{Z}_q^{m \times n} \times \mathbb{Z}_q^m$. Then with overwhelming probability, $d(\mathbf{c}, \Lambda(\mathbf{A})) \geq q/4$ and in particular $(\mathbf{A}, \mathbf{c})$ is messy.

Proof. By Lemma 2.3, $(\mathbf{A} \| \mathbf{c})$ is full-rank except with negligible probability $q^{-(n+1)}$.

Furthermore, we have that for any fixed $\mathbf{A} \in \mathbb{Z}_q^{m \times n}$, $d_\infty(\mathbf{c}, \Lambda(\mathbf{A})) \geq q/4$ with overwhelming probability over the choice of $\mathbf{c}$. This is because the set of points within distance $q/4$ (in ℓ_∞ norm) from $\Lambda(\mathbf{A})$ has size at most $q^n \cdot (q/2)^m$. As $m \geq 2n \log q$, the probability that $\mathbf{c} \xleftarrow{\$} \mathbb{Z}_q^m$ belongs to those points is at most q^{-n}, which is negligible.

This implies that for any fixed $\mathbf{A}$, $d(\mathbf{c}, \Lambda(\mathbf{A})) \geq d_\infty(\mathbf{c}, \Lambda(\mathbf{A})) \geq q\sqrt{m}/\tau$ with overwhelming probability over the randomness of $\mathbf{c} \xleftarrow{\$} \mathbb{Z}_q^m$ alone. The result then follows by Lemma 3.2. $\quad\square$

The observation above allows us to argue security of the scheme:

Lemma 3.4 (Security). *Suppose $m \geq 2(n+1)\log q$ and $\tau \geq 4\sqrt{m}$. Then the encryption scheme is secure under the $\mathsf{LWE}_{q,\chi,n}$ assumption.*

Proof. By the $\mathsf{LWE}_{q,\chi,n}$ assumption, given $\mathbf{A}$, the vector $\mathbf{c}$ in the public key is computationally indistinguishable from uniform in $\mathbb{Z}_q^m$. Now, if $(\mathbf{A}, \mathbf{c}) \xleftarrow{\$} \mathbb{Z}_q^{m \times n} \times \mathbb{Z}_q^m$, we have that $(\mathbf{A}, \mathbf{c})$ is messy with overwhelming probability by Lemma 3.3, and security follows. $\quad\square$

Next, we describe how to identify messy public keys given an appropriate trapdoor.

Lemma 3.5 (Weak identification of messy public keys). *Suppose $\tau \geq 6m$. Let $(\mathbf{A}, \mathbf{T}) \leftarrow \mathsf{TrapGen}(1^n, 1^m, q)$. Suppose $\mathbf{A}$ is full-rank and $\tau \geq 6m$. Then there exists a polynomial-time algorithm $\mathsf{IsMessy}$ which on input a vector $\mathbf{c}$ decides whether $d(\mathbf{c}, \Lambda(\mathbf{A})) \geq q\sqrt{m}/\tau)$. In particular, if this is the case, the public key $(\mathbf{A}, \mathbf{c})$ is identified as messy.*

Proof. We define the algorithm $\mathsf{IsMessy}$ as follows:

$\mathsf{IsMessy}(\mathbf{T}, \mathbf{A}, \mathbf{c})$:

1. Run $\mathsf{Invert}(\mathbf{T}, \mathbf{A}, \mathbf{c})$ from Lemma 2.6.
2. If the output is $(\mathbf{s}, \mathbf{e})$ with $\|\mathbf{e}\| \leq q/6\sqrt{m}$, then output not sure, Otherwise output messy.

By Lemma 2.6, if $d(\mathbf{c}, \Lambda(\mathbf{A})) \geq q/6\sqrt{m} \geq q\sqrt{m}/\tau$, then IsMessy outputs messy.

As in [PVW08], IsMessy might output not sure even though the public key is actually messy. This is because we only test for a sufficient condition for messiness in Lemma 3.3. However if IsMessy$(\mathbf{T}, \mathbf{A}, \mathbf{c})$ outputs messy, then the public key $(\mathbf{A}, \mathbf{c})$ is indeed messy. Looking ahead, in our construction of a dual-mode encryption scheme, we will ensure that at least one of the two branches is recognized as messy.

3.2 Dual-Mode Encryption

We now describe our dual-mode encryption scheme.

Parameters. The constraints over the parameters mostly inherits from Sect. 3.1:

Let $n = n(\lambda)$, $q = q(\lambda) \geq 2$ be integers. Let $m \geq 2(n+1)\log q$.

Let $\tau \geq 6m$ (from Lemma 3.5);

Let $\chi = \chi(n)$ given by Definition 2.5 be a $B = B(n)$ bounded distribution where $B = \widetilde{\Omega}(\sqrt{n})$.

Let $B' \in \mathbb{Z}$ be such that $(B + B') \cdot \tau\sqrt{m} = o(q)$ (which implies $q \geq \omega(B' + \sqrt{n})m))$.

Let R be the randomized rounding function defined in Lemma 2.7.

Suppose furthermore that:

- $B/B' = \mathsf{negl}(n)$.

For instance, one can set (without trying to optimize the parameters): $n = \lambda$, $q = n^{\omega(1)}$ (with $q \leq 2^n$), $m = 2\log q$, $B = n$, $B' = q/n^3$, $\tau = 6m$.

Construction. In the following, the input and output public keys pk of the dual-mode scheme are implicitly public keys for the branch $b = 0$.

- SetupMessy$(1^\lambda) \rightarrow (\mathsf{crs}, \mathsf{td}_M)$: Sample $(\mathbf{A}, \mathbf{T}) \leftarrow \mathsf{TrapGen}(1^n, 1^m, q)$. Pick $\mathbf{v} \xleftarrow{\$} \mathbb{Z}_q^m$. Output:

$$\mathsf{crs} = (\mathbf{A}, \mathbf{v}), \quad \mathsf{td}_M = \mathbf{T}.$$

- SetupDec$(1^\lambda) \rightarrow (\mathsf{crs}, \mathsf{td}_D)$: Sample $\mathbf{A} \xleftarrow{\$} \mathbb{Z}_q^{m \times n}$. Pick $\mathbf{s}^* \xleftarrow{\$} \mathbb{Z}_q^n$ and $\mathbf{e}^* \leftarrow \chi^m$. Set $\mathbf{v} = \mathbf{A}\mathbf{s}^* + \mathbf{e}^*$, and output:

$$\mathsf{crs} = (\mathbf{A}, \mathbf{v}), \quad \mathsf{td}_D = \mathbf{s}^*.$$

- KeyGen$(\mathsf{crs}, b) \rightarrow (\mathsf{pk}_0, \mathsf{sk}_b)$: Pick $\mathbf{s} \xleftarrow{\$} \mathbb{Z}_q^n$, $\mathbf{e} \leftarrow \chi^m$, and $\mathbf{f} \xleftarrow{\$} [-B', B']$. Output:

$$\mathsf{pk}_0 = \mathbf{A}\mathbf{s} + \mathbf{e} + \mathbf{f} - b \cdot \mathbf{v}, \quad \mathsf{sk}_b = \mathbf{s}.$$

In particular, we have $\mathsf{pk}_b = \mathbf{A}\mathbf{s} + \mathbf{e} + \mathbf{f}$ and $\mathsf{pk}_1 - \mathsf{pk}_0 = \mathbf{v}$.

- $\mathsf{Enc}(\mathsf{crs}, \mathsf{pk}_0, b', \mu) \to \mathsf{ct}$: Compute $\mathsf{pk}_{b'} = \mathbf{c} := \mathsf{pk}_0 + b' \cdot \mathbf{v}$.
  For $i \in [\lambda]$, sample $\mathbf{r}_i \leftarrow D_{\mathbb{Z},\tau}^m$. Compute $\mathbf{p}_i^t = \mathbf{r}_i^t \cdot \mathbf{A} \in \mathbb{Z}_q^{1 \times n}$, and:

$$\beta_i \leftarrow R(\mathbf{r}_i^t \cdot \mathbf{c}) \oplus \mu,$$

and output:
$$\mathsf{ct} = (\{\mathbf{p}_i, \beta_i\}_{i \leq \lambda}).$$

- $\mathsf{Dec}(\mathsf{crs}, \mathsf{sk}_b, \mathsf{ct}) \to \mu$: Parse the ciphertext as $\mathsf{ct} = (\{\mathbf{p}_i, \beta_i\}_{i \leq \lambda})$. Compute, for all $i \in [\lambda]$:

$$b_i \leftarrow R(\mathbf{p}_i^t \cdot \mathbf{s}) \oplus \beta_i,$$

and output the majority bit of the b_i's as μ.
- $\mathsf{FindMessy}(\mathsf{td}_M, \mathsf{pk}_0) \to \bar{b}$: Run $\mathsf{IsMessy}(\mathsf{pk}_0)$ (defined in Lemma 3.5). If it outputs messy, output 0.
  Otherwise, output 1.
- $\mathsf{TrapKeyGen}(\mathsf{td}_D)$: Pick $\mathbf{s} \overset{\$}{\leftarrow} \mathbb{Z}_q^n$, $\mathbf{e} \leftarrow \chi^m$, $\mathbf{f} \overset{\$}{\leftarrow} [-B', B']$. Output:

$$\mathsf{pk}_0 = \mathbf{As} + \mathbf{e} + \mathbf{f}, \quad \mathsf{sk}_0 = \mathbf{s}, \quad \mathsf{sk}_1 = \mathbf{s} + \mathbf{s}^*.$$

Remark 3.6 (Common random string in messy mode). The CRS in messy mode is *statistically* close to uniform. As the trapdoor is only used in the proof of security, we can replace the CRS in messy mode with a common *random* string instead, and adding an appropriate hybrid in the proof of security. The original construction of [PVW08] also satisfies this property.

3.3   Dual-Mode Properties

Lemma 3.7 (Completeness on decryptable branch). *Suppose* $(B + B') \cdot \tau \cdot \sqrt{m} = o(q)$ *and* $\tau \geq \omega(\sqrt{\log m})$. *Then the scheme above is correct.*

Proof. This follows directly by correctness of $(\mathsf{SmoothKeyGen}, \mathsf{SmoothEnc}, \mathsf{SmoothDec})$, as $(\mathbf{A}, \mathsf{pk}_b)$ (where $\mathsf{pk}_0 \leftarrow \mathsf{KeyGen}(\mathsf{crs}, b)$ and $\mathsf{pk}_b = \mathsf{pk}_0 + b \cdot \mathbf{v}$) is distributed identically as $\mathsf{SmoothKeyGen}(1^\lambda)$, and Enc and Dec procede as $\mathsf{SmoothEnc}$ and $\mathsf{SmoothDec}$, respectively.

Lemma 3.8 (Indistinguishability of modes). *Assuming* $\mathsf{LWE}_{q,\chi,n}$, *the scheme satisfies indistinguishability of modes.*

Proof. By Lemma 2.6, the CRS in messy mode $\mathsf{crs}_M = (\mathbf{A}, \mathbf{v}) \leftarrow \mathsf{SetupMessy}(1^\lambda)$ is statistically close to uniform over $\mathbb{Z}_q^{m \times n} \times \mathbb{Z}_q^m$.

Now, by the $\mathsf{LWE}_{q,\chi,n}$ assumption, $(\mathbf{A}, \mathbf{v}) \overset{\$}{\leftarrow} (\mathbb{Z}_q^{m \times n} \times \mathbb{Z}_q^m)$ is computationally indistinguishable from $(\mathbf{A}, \mathbf{v} = \mathbf{As}^* + \mathbf{e}^*)$, where $\mathbf{A} \overset{\$}{\leftarrow} \mathbb{Z}_q^{m \times n}$, $\mathbf{s}^* \overset{\$}{\leftarrow} \mathbb{Z}_q^n$ and $\mathbf{e}^* \leftarrow \chi^m$, which is identically distributed as $\mathsf{crs}_D \leftarrow \mathsf{SetupDec}(1^\lambda)$.

Lemma 3.9 (Security in messy mode). *Suppose that* $\tau \geq 6m$, *and* $m \geq 2(n+1)\log q$. *Then the scheme satisfies security in messy mode.*

Proof. We first argue that with overwhelming probability over the probability of $(\mathbf{A}, \mathbf{v}) \leftarrow \mathsf{SetupMessy}(1^\lambda)$ alone, we have that *for all* public key pk_0, at least one of the public keys $\mathsf{pk}_0 = \mathbf{c}_0$ or $\mathsf{pk}_1 = \mathbf{c}_1$ satisfies $d(\mathbf{c}_b, \Lambda(\mathbf{A})) \geq q/6\sqrt{m}$, and is in particular messy by Lemma 3.3 (conditioned on $\mathbf{A}$ being full-rank and $\tau \geq \eta_\epsilon(\Lambda^\perp(\mathbf{A}))$, which happen with overwhelming probability over the choice of $\mathbf{A}$ by Lemma 2.3 and Lemma 2.4).

This is simply because if both $\mathbf{c}_0$ and $\mathbf{c}_1$ are close to $\Lambda(\mathbf{A})$, then by triangular inequality $\mathbf{v} = \mathbf{c}_1 - \mathbf{c}_0$ must be as well, which only happens with negligible probability over the randomness of $\mathsf{SetupMessy}$. More precisely, if $d(\mathbf{c}_b, \Lambda(\mathbf{A})) \leq q/6\sqrt{m}$ for both $b \in \{0,1\}$, then $d(\mathbf{v}, \Lambda(\mathbf{A})) \leq q/3\sqrt{m}$, which only happens with negligible probability over the randomness of $(\mathbf{A}, \mathbf{v}) \leftarrow \mathbb{Z}_q^{m \times n} \times \mathbb{Z}_q^m$, by Lemma 3.3.

Now conditioned on the above, by Lemma 3.5, we have that if $\mathsf{FindMessy}$ $(\mathbf{T}, \mathbf{A}, \mathsf{pk}_0)$ does not output 0, then it outputs 1, which is therefore a messy branch. In particular, for all pk_0, the output branch of $\bar{b} = \mathsf{FindMessy}(\mathsf{td}_M, \mathsf{pk}_0)$ is messy and therefore:

$$\mathsf{Enc}(\mathsf{crs}, \mathsf{pk}, \bar{b}, \mu_0) \approx_s \mathsf{Enc}(\mathsf{crs}, \mathsf{pk}, \bar{b}, \mu_1).$$

Lemma 3.10 (Security in decryption mode). *Assuming $B'/B = \mathsf{negl}(n)$, the scheme satisfies security in decryption mode.*

Proof. Because $\mathsf{pk}_1 - \mathsf{pk}_0 = \mathbf{v}$ is in the CRS, it suffices to argue that the distributions $(\mathsf{pk}_b, \mathsf{sk}_b)$ generated using either $\mathsf{KeyGen}(\mathsf{crs}_D, b)$ or $\mathsf{TrapKeyGen}(\mathsf{td}_D)$ are statistically close.

Fix $(\mathsf{crs}_D, \mathsf{td}_D) \leftarrow \mathsf{SetupDec}(1^\lambda)$, where $\mathsf{crs}_D = (\mathbf{A}, \mathbf{v} = \mathbf{A}\mathbf{s}^* + \mathbf{e}^*)$ and $\mathsf{td}_D = \mathbf{s}^*$.

Let $(\mathsf{pk}_0, \mathsf{sk}_0, \mathsf{sk}_1) \leftarrow \mathsf{TrapKeyGen}(\mathsf{td}_D)$. We have:

$$\mathsf{pk}_0 = \mathbf{A}\mathbf{s} + \mathbf{e} + \mathbf{f}, \quad \mathsf{sk}_0 = \mathbf{s};$$

$$\mathsf{pk}_1 = \mathbf{A}(\mathbf{s} + \mathbf{s}^*) + (\mathbf{e} + \mathbf{e}^*) + \mathbf{f}, \quad \mathsf{sk}_1 = (\mathbf{s} + \mathbf{s}^*),$$

which is, by Lemma 2.2, distributed statistically close to:

$$\mathsf{pk}_1 = \mathbf{A}(\mathbf{s} + \mathbf{s}^*) + \mathbf{e} + \mathbf{f}, \quad \mathsf{sk}_1 = (\mathbf{s} + \mathbf{s}^*).$$

Regular keys for branch b (output by $\mathsf{KeyGen}(\mathsf{crs}, b)$) are generated as:

$$\widetilde{\mathsf{pk}}_b = \mathbf{A}\mathbf{s} + \mathbf{e} + \mathbf{f} \quad, \quad \widetilde{\mathsf{sk}}_b = \mathbf{s},$$

where $\mathbf{s} \xleftarrow{\$} \mathbb{Z}_q^n$, $\mathbf{e} \leftarrow \chi^m$, $\mathbf{f} \xleftarrow{\$} [-B', B']$, and $\widetilde{\mathsf{pk}}_1 - \widetilde{\mathsf{pk}}_0 = \mathbf{v}$.

Therefore, for all $b \in \{0,1\}$ the joint distributions $(\mathsf{crs}_D, \mathsf{pk}_b, \mathsf{sk}_b)$ and $(\mathsf{crs}_D, \widetilde{\mathsf{pk}}_b, \widetilde{\mathsf{sk}}_b)$ are statistically close to each other.

Finally, using Theorem 2.1, we obtain the following:

Corollary 3.11. *Assuming $\mathsf{LWE}_{q,\chi,n}$ with the parameters defined in the construction, there exists an UC-secure OT with the specifications of Theorem 2.1.*

Acknowledgements. We thank Vinod Vaikuntanathan and Daniel Wichs for helpful discussions and comments about this work. Part of this work was done while the author was visiting the Simons Institute for the Theory of Computing for the Spring 2020 program "Lattices: Algorithms, Complexity, and Cryptography".

References

[AJL+12] Asharov, G., Jain, A., López-Alt, A., Tromer, E., Vaikuntanathan, V., Wichs, D.: Multiparty computation with low communication, computation and interaction via threshold FHE. In: Pointcheval and Johansson [PJ12], pp. 483–501

[AR03] Aharonov, D., Regev, O.: A lattice problem in quantum NP. In: 44th FOCS, pp. 210–219. IEEE Computer Society Press, October 2003

[BBDQ18] Benhamouda, F., Blazy, O., Ducas, L., Quach, W.: Hash proof systems over lattices revisited. In: Abdalla, M., Dahab, R. (eds.) PKC 2018. LNCS, vol. 10770, pp. 644–674. Springer, Cham (2018). https://doi.org/10.1007/978-3-319-76581-5_22

[BD18] Brakerski, Z., Döttling, N.: Two-message statistically sender-private OT from LWE. In: Beimel, A., Dziembowski, S. (eds.) TCC 2018. LNCS, vol. 11240, pp. 370–390. Springer, Cham (2018). https://doi.org/10.1007/978-3-030-03810-6_14

[Can01] Canetti, R.: Universally composable security: a new paradigm for cryptographic protocols. In: 42nd FOCS, pp. 136–145. IEEE Computer Society Press, October 2001

[CCH+19] Canetti, R., et al.: Fiat-Shamir: from practice to theory. In: 51st ACM STOC, pp. 1082–1090. ACM Press (2019)

[CR03] Canetti, R., Rabin, T.: Universal composition with joint state. In: Boneh, D. (ed.) CRYPTO 2003. LNCS, vol. 2729, pp. 265–281. Springer, Heidelberg (2003). https://doi.org/10.1007/978-3-540-45146-4_16

[CS98] Cramer, R., Shoup, V.: A practical public key cryptosystem provably secure against adaptive chosen ciphertext attack. In: Krawczyk, H. (ed.) CRYPTO 1998. LNCS, vol. 1462, pp. 13–25. Springer, Heidelberg (1998). https://doi.org/10.1007/BFb0055717

[CS02] Cramer, R., Shoup, V.: Universal hash proofs and a paradigm for adaptive chosen ciphertext secure public-key encryption. In: Knudsen, L.R. (ed.) EUROCRYPT 2002. LNCS, vol. 2332, pp. 45–64. Springer, Heidelberg (2002). https://doi.org/10.1007/3-540-46035-7_4

[DGH+20] Döttling, N., Garg, S., Hajiabadi, M., Masny, D., Wichs, D.: Two-round oblivious transfer from CDH or LPN. In: Canteaut, A., Ishai, Y. (eds.) EUROCRYPT 2020. LNCS, vol. 12106, pp. 768–797. Springer, Cham (2020). https://doi.org/10.1007/978-3-030-45724-2_26

[GMW87] Goldreich, O., Micali, S., Wigderson, A.: How to play any mental game or a completeness theorem for protocols with honest majority. In: Aho, A. (ed.) 19th ACM STOC, pp. 218–229. ACM Press, May 1987

[GPV08] Gentry, C., Peikert, C., Vaikuntanathan, V.: Trapdoors for hard lattices and new cryptographic constructions. In: Ladner, R.E., Dwork, C. (eds.) 40th ACM STOC, pp. 197–206. ACM Press, May 2008

[Kal05] Kalai, Y.T.: Smooth projective hashing and two-message oblivious transfer. In: Cramer, R. (ed.) EUROCRYPT 2005. LNCS, vol. 3494, pp. 78–95. Springer, Heidelberg (2005). https://doi.org/10.1007/11426639_5

[MP12] Micciancio, D., Peikert, C.: Trapdoors for lattices: simpler, tighter, faster, smaller. In: Pointcheval and Johansson [PJ12], pp. 700–718

[MR04] Micciancio, D., Regev, O.: Worst-case to average-case reductions based on Gaussian measures. In: 45th FOCS, pp. 372–381. IEEE Computer Society Press, October 2004

[Pas13] Pass, R.: Unprovable security of perfect NIZK and non-interactive non-malleable commitments. In: Sahai, A. (ed.) TCC 2013. LNCS, vol. 7785, pp. 334–354. Springer, Heidelberg (2013). https://doi.org/10.1007/978-3-642-36594-2_19

[Pei08] Peikert, C.: Limits on the hardness of lattice problems in LP norms. Comput. Complex. **17**(2), 300–351 (2008)

[PJ12] Pointcheval, D., Johansson, T. (eds.): EUROCRYPT 2012. LNCS, vol. 7237. Springer, Heidelberg (2012)

[PS19] Peikert, C., Shiehian, S.: Noninteractive zero knowledge for NP from (Plain) learning with errors. In: Boldyreva, A., Micciancio, D. (eds.) CRYPTO 2019. LNCS, vol. 11692, pp. 89–114. Springer, Cham (2019). https://doi.org/10.1007/978-3-030-26948-7_4

[PVW08] Peikert, C., Vaikuntanathan, V., Waters, B.: A framework for efficient and composable oblivious transfer. In: Wagner, D. (ed.) CRYPTO 2008. LNCS, vol. 5157, pp. 554–571. Springer, Heidelberg (2008). https://doi.org/10.1007/978-3-540-85174-5_31

[Rab81] Rabin, M.O.: How to Exchange Secrets with Oblivious Transfer, 1981. Harvard Aiken Computational Laboratory TR-81

[Reg05] Regev, O.: On lattices, learning with errors, random linear codes, and cryptography. In: Gabow, H.N., Fagin, R. (eds.) 37th ACM STOC, pp. 84–93. ACM Press, May 2005

[Sch87] Schnorr, C.P.: A hierarchy of polynomial time lattice basis reduction algorithms. Theor. Comput. Sci. **53**(2), 201–224 (1987)

[Yao86] Yao, A.C.-C.: How to generate and exchange secrets (extended abstract). In: 27th FOCS, pp. 162–167. IEEE Computer Society Press, October 1986

Oblivious RAM

Efficient 3-Party Distributed ORAM

Paul Bunn[1(✉)], Jonathan Katz[2], Eyal Kushilevitz[3], and Rafail Ostrovsky[4]

[1] Stealth Software Technologies, Inc., Los Angeles, USA
paul@stealthsoftwareinc.com
[2] Department of Computer Science, George Mason University, Fairfax, USA
jkatz2@gmail.com
[3] Computer Science Department, Technion, Haifa, Israel
eyalk@cs.technion.ac.il
[4] Department of Computer Science and Department of Mathematics,
University of California, Los Angeles, USA
rafail@cs.ucla.edu

Abstract. *Distributed Oblivious RAM (DORAM)* protocols—in which parties obliviously access a shared location in a shared array—are a fundamental component of secure-computation protocols in the RAM model. We show here an efficient, 3-party DORAM protocol with semi-honest security for a single corrupted party. To the best of our knowledge, ours is the first protocol for this setting that runs in constant rounds, requires sublinear communication and linear work, and makes only black-box use of cryptographic primitives. Our protocol also appears to be concretely more efficient than existing solutions.

As a building block of independent interest, we construct a 3-server distributed point function (DPF) with security against *two* colluding servers that is arguably simpler and has better concrete efficiency than prior work. We also show how to distribute the key-generation protocol of this DPF (in a black-box manner).

Keywords: Oblivious RAM (ORAM) · Distributed computation · Function Secret Sharing (FSS) · Secure Multiparty Computation (MPC)

1 Introduction

A fundamental problem in the context of privacy-preserving protocols for large data is ensuring efficient oblivious read/write access to memory. Research in this area originated with the classical work on oblivious RAM (ORAM) [12], which can be viewed as allowing a stateful client to store an (encrypted) array on a server, and then obliviously read/write data from/to specific addresses of that array with sublinear client-server communication. Roughly, *obliviousness* here means that for each memory access the server learns nothing about which address is being accessed, the specific data being read or written, and even whether a read or a write is being performed. A long line of work [1,3,10,13,18,

© Springer Nature Switzerland AG 2020
C. Galdi and V. Kolesnikov (Eds.): SCN 2020, LNCS 12238, pp. 215–232, 2020.
https://doi.org/10.1007/978-3-030-57990-6_11

23, 26–29, 32, 34, 35] has shown both asymptotic and concrete improvements to ORAM protocols. More recently [1, 7, 19, 22, 25, 31] ORAM has been extended to a *multi-server* setting in which a client stores data on two or more servers and obliviousness must hold with respect to each of them.

In all the aforementioned work, there is a fundamental distinction between the client and the server(s): the client knows the address being accessed and, in the case of writes, the data being written; following a read, the client learns the data that was read. That is, there are no privacy/obliviousness requirements with respect to the client.

One of the primary applications of ORAM protocols is in the realm of secure computation in the random-access machine (RAM) model of computation [2, 7–10, 14, 15, 17, 21, 24, 25, 32, 33, 35]. In this setting, parties may store an array in a distributed fashion (such that none of them know its contents), and may need to read from or write to the array during the course of executing some algorithm. Memory accesses must now be oblivious to *all* parties; that is, there is no one party who can act as a "client" and is allowed to learn information about, e.g., the positions in memory being accessed. There is thus a need for a new primitive, referred to as *distributed ORAM* (DORAM), that allows the parties to collectively share an array and perform oblivious reads/writes on that array at addresses that are themselves distributed among the parties.

An n-party DORAM protocol can be constructed from any n'-party ORAM scheme (with $n' \leq n$) using generic secure computation. The main idea is for n' of the parties to act as the servers in the underlying ORAM scheme; a memory access for an address that is shared among the n parties is carried out by having those parties run a secure-computation protocol to evaluate the client algorithm of the underlying ORAM scheme. This approach (with various optimizations) was followed in some prior work on RAM-model secure computation, and motivated efforts to design ORAM schemes in which the client algorithm can be implemented by a low-complexity circuit [30, 32]. In addition to the constructions of DORAM that are implied by prior work on ORAM, or that are implicit in previous work on RAM-based secure computation, dedicated DORAM schemes have been given in the 2-party [7, 14] and 3-party [8, 16] settings.

1.1   Our Contribution

We present a 3-party DORAM protocol, secure against semi-honest corruption of one of the parties. To the best of our knowledge, it is the first such protocol that simultaneously runs in constant rounds, requires sublinear communication and linear work, and makes only black-box use of cryptographic primitives. (The last property rules out constructions that apply generic secure computation to known ORAM schemes.) We believe our protocol is concretely more efficient than existing solutions (we leave a thorough experimental validation of this for future (ongoing) work).

Our protocol is inspired by the work of Doerner and Shelat [7], who use function secret sharing [4, 5, 11] (specifically, a distributed point function) to construct what can be viewed as a DORAM protocol in the two-party setting.

Our work shows that this approach can be applied in the three-party setting as well. As a building block of independent interest, we show a new construction of a 3-party distributed point function (see Sect. 2) that is secure against any *two* colluding servers. Our construction has communication complexity $O(\sqrt{N})$, where N is the size of the domain. This matches the asymptotic communication complexity of the only previous construction [4], but we believe that our scheme is both simpler and has better concrete efficiency. More importantly, our construction supports distributed key generation in a black-box manner, which we exploit in our DORAM protocol.

Outline of the Paper. We describe a construction of a 3-server distributed point function (DPF), with privacy against two semi-honest corruptions, in Sect. 2. In Sect. 3 we review known DPF-based multi-server constructions for oblivious reading (PIR) [6,20] or writing (PIW) [25]. We show in Sect. 4 how to combine our 3-server DPF with 2-server PIR/PIW to obtain a 3-server ORAM scheme, secure against semi-honest corruption of one server. Finally, in Sect. 5 we discuss how to extend our ORAM scheme to obtain a 3-party *distributed* ORAM protocol, secure against one semi-honest corruption. Relevant definitions are given in each of the corresponding sections, although due to space constraints we omit standard definitions of PIR [6], PIW [25], and ORAM [12].

2   A 2-Private, 3-Server Distributed Point Function

2.1   Definitions

Distributed point functions were introduced by Gilboa and Ishai [11], and further generalized and improved by Boyle et al. [4,5].

Fix some parameters N and B. For $y \in [N] = \{1, \ldots, N\}$ and $v \in \{0,1\}^B$, define the *point function* $F_{y,v} : \{1, \ldots, N\} \rightarrow \{0,1\}^B$ to be the function that outputs v on input y, and otherwise outputs 0^B for any other input. A distributed point function provides a way for a client to "secret share" a point function among a set of servers. We define it for the case of three servers with privacy against any set of two colluding servers (the definitions can be extended in the natural way for other cases).

Definition 1. *A 3-server distributed point function consists of a pair of algorithms* (Gen, Eval) *with the following functionality:*

- Gen *takes as input the security parameter* 1^κ, *an index* $y \in \{1, \ldots, N\}$, *and a value* $v \in \{0,1\}^B$. *It outputs keys* K^1, K^2, K^3.
- Eval *is a deterministic algorithm that takes as input a key* K *and an index* $x \in \{1, \ldots, N\}$, *and outputs a string* $\tilde{v} \in \{0,1\}^B$.

Correctness requires that for any κ, *any* $(y,v) \in \{1, \ldots, N\} \times \{0,1\}^B$, *any* K^1, K^2, K^3 *output by* Gen$(1^\kappa, y, v)$, *and any* $x \in \{1, \ldots, N\}$, *we have:*

$$\mathsf{Eval}(K^1, x) \oplus \mathsf{Eval}(K^2, x) \oplus \mathsf{Eval}(K^3, x) = F_{y,v}(x).$$

Definition 2. *A 3-server DPF is* 2-private *if for any* $i_1, i_2 \in \{1, 2, 3\}$ *and any* PPT *adversary A, the following is negligible in κ:*

$$\left| \Pr \left[\begin{array}{l} (y_0, v_0, y_1, v_1) \leftarrow A(1^\kappa); b \leftarrow \{0, 1\}; \\ (K^1, K^2, K^3) \leftarrow \mathsf{Gen}(1^\kappa, y_b, v_b) \end{array} : A(K^{i_1}, K^{i_2}) = b \right] - \frac{1}{2} \right|.$$

2.2 Our Construction

Let $N = \ell^2$, for some ℓ. Let $G : \{0, 1\}^\kappa \to (\{0, 1\}^B)^{\sqrt{N}}$ be a pseudorandom generator. We describe a construction of a 2-private, 3-server DPF:

$\underline{\mathsf{Gen}(1^\kappa, y, v)}$: View $y \in \{1, \dots, N\}$ as a pair (i, j) with $i, j \in [\sqrt{N}]$. Then:

1. Choose uniform $I^1, I^2, I^3 \in \{0, 1\}^{\sqrt{N}}$ subject to constraint: $I^1 \oplus I^2 \oplus I^3 = (0, \dots, 0, 1, 0, \dots, 0)$, where the '1' appears in coordinate i.
2. For $k = 1, \dots, \sqrt{N}$ do:

   If $k \neq i$, then choose random seeds $a_k, b_k, c_k \leftarrow \{0, 1\}^\kappa$ and define:

   $$S_k^1 = \{a_k, b_k\}, \quad S_k^2 = \{b_k, c_k\}, \quad S_k^3 = \{c_k, a_k\}. \tag{1}$$

   Note that each seed is in exactly two of the above sets.
   If $k = i$, then choose random seeds $a_k, b_k, c_k, d_k \leftarrow \{0, 1\}^\kappa$ and define:

   $$S_k^1 = \{a_k, d_k\}, \quad S_k^2 = \{b_k, d_k\}, \quad S_k^3 = \{c_k, d_k\}. \tag{2}$$

   Note that in this case, each seed is in an odd number of sets (d_k is in S_k^1, S_k^2, and S_k^3, and the other seeds are each in exactly one set).
   We stress that the S_i^j are all *unordered* pairs, e.g., each set is specified by writing its elements in lexicographic order.
3. Let $\mathbf{e}_{j,v} \in (\{0, 1\}^B)^{\sqrt{N}} = (0^B, \dots, 0^B, v, 0^B, \dots, 0^B)$ denote a "characteristic vector" that is zero everywhere except position j, where it has value v. Compute the *correction word*:

   $$C = G(a_i) \oplus G(b_i) \oplus G(c_i) \oplus G(d_i) \oplus \mathbf{e}_{j,v}. \tag{3}$$

   (The inputs to G are from the iteration of Step 2 when $k = i$.)
4. Gen outputs keys: $K^1 = (S_1^1, \dots, S_{\sqrt{N}}^1, I^1, C)$, $K^2 = (S_1^2, \dots, S_{\sqrt{N}}^2, I^2, C)$, $K^3 = (S_1^3, \dots, S_{\sqrt{N}}^3, I^3, C)$, each of length $O((\kappa + B) \cdot \sqrt{N})$.

$\underline{\mathsf{Eval}(K, x)}$. View $x \in \{1, \dots, N\}$ as a pair (i', j') with $i', j' \in [\sqrt{N}]$. Let $K = (S_1, \dots, S_{\sqrt{N}}, I, C)$, where $S_k = \{\alpha_k, \beta_k\}$ for $k = 1, \dots, \sqrt{N}$.
Compute the vector: $\tilde{V} = G(\alpha_{i'}) \oplus G(\beta_{i'}) \oplus (I_{i'} \cdot C) \in (\{0, 1\}^B)^{\sqrt{N}}$, where $I_{i'}$ is the i'-th bit of I. Output the B-bit string in position j' of $\tilde{V}$.

Correctness. Let $y = (i, j)$ and say K^1, K^2, K^3 are output by $\mathsf{Gen}(1^\kappa, y, v)$. Let $x = (i', j')$ and consider the outputs $\tilde{v}^1 = \mathsf{Eval}(K^1, x)$, $\tilde{v}^2 = \mathsf{Eval}(K^2, x)$, and $\tilde{v}^3 = \mathsf{Eval}(K^3, x)$. Let $\tilde{V}^1, \tilde{V}^2, \tilde{V}^3$ denote the intermediate vectors computed by these three executions of Eval, respectively. Consider two cases:

1. Say $i' \neq i$. Then: $\tilde{V}^1 \oplus \tilde{V}^2 \oplus \tilde{V}^3 = 0^{B \cdot \sqrt{N}}$, where we have used that each PRG seed appears exactly twice as per (1) and that $I_{i'}^1 \oplus I_{i'}^2 \oplus I_{i'}^3 = 0$ when $i' \neq i$. Hence $\tilde{v}^1 \oplus \tilde{v}^2 \oplus \tilde{v}^3 = 0^B$ for any j'.

2. Say $i' = i$. Then: $\tilde{V}^1 \oplus \tilde{V}^2 \oplus \tilde{V}^3 = \mathbf{e}_{j,v}$, where we have used that each PRG seed $\{a_i, b_i, c_i, d_i\}$ appears an odd number of times as per (2) and that $I_{i'}^1 \oplus I_{i'}^2 \oplus I_{i'}^3 = 1$ when $i' = i$, and thus the correction word C cancels the PRG outputs as per (3). Hence $\tilde{v}^1 \oplus \tilde{v}^2 \oplus \tilde{v}^3$ is equal to 0^B if $j' \neq j$, and is equal to v if $j' = j$.

Theorem 1. *The above scheme is 2-private.*

Proof. By symmetry we may assume, without loss of generality, that servers 1 and 2 are corrupted. Fix a PPT algorithm A and let Expt_0 denote the experiment as in Definition 2. Let ϵ_0 denote the probability with which A correctly outputs b in that experiment, i.e.,

$$\epsilon_0 = \Pr\left[\begin{array}{l} (y_0, v_0, y_1, v_1) \leftarrow A(1^\kappa); b \leftarrow \{0,1\}; \\ (K^1, K^2, K^3) \leftarrow \mathsf{Gen}(1^\kappa, y_b, v_b) \end{array} : A(K^1, K^2) = b \right].$$

Now consider an experiment Expt_1 in which Gen is modified as follows, where we let $y_b = (i, j)$.

1. For $k = 1, \ldots, \sqrt{N}$, compute S_k^1 and S_k^2 as before. (Note that S_k^3 need not be defined, since we only care about the keys K^1, K^2 provided to A. In particular, we never need to define the value of seed c_i.
2. Set C to a uniform value in $(\{0,1\}^B)^{\sqrt{N}}$.
3. Set I^1, I^2 to uniform values in $\{0,1\}^{\sqrt{N}}$.
4. Keys K^1, K^2 are then defined as before.

It follows from pseudorandomness of G that the view of A in Expt_1 is computationally indistinguishable from its view in Expt_0; hence if we let ϵ_1 denote the probability that A correctly outputs b in Expt_1 we must have $|\epsilon_1 - \epsilon_0| \leq \mathsf{negl}(\kappa)$.

It may be observed that the view of A in Expt_1 is independent of i and j. In particular, the joint distributions of S_i^1, S_i^2 and S_k^1, S_k^2 (for $k \neq i$) are identical (namely, the distribution defined by choosing three uniform seeds $a, b, c \in \{0,1\}^\kappa$ and letting the first set be $\{a, b\}$ and the second set be $\{b, c\}$). Thus, $\epsilon_1 = 1/2$, concluding the proof. $\square$

3   Oblivious Reading and Writing

We describe here known n-server protocols [11] for private information retrieval (PIR) for oblivious reading, and private information writing (PIW) for oblivious writing, based on any n-server DPF. In the context, as in the case of ORAM, we have a client interacting with these servers, and there is no obliviousness requirement with respect to the client. If the DPF is t-private, these protocols are t-private as well. (Formal definitions are given by Gilboa and Ishai [11].)

PIR. Let $D \in (\{0,1\}^B)^N$ be an encrypted data array. Let (Gen, Eval) be an n-server DPF with domain $[N]$ and range $\{0,1\}$. Each of the n servers is given a copy of D. To retrieve the data $D[y]$ stored at address y, the client computes $\mathsf{Gen}(1^\kappa, y, 1)$ to obtain keys $K^1, \ldots, K^n$, and sends K^i to the ith server. The ith server computes $c_x^i = \mathsf{Eval}(K^i, x)$ for $x \in \{1, \ldots, N\}$, and sends $r^i = \bigoplus_{x \in \{1, \ldots, N\}} c_x^i \cdot D[x]$ to the client. Finally, the client computes $\bigoplus_{i=1}^n r^i$. Correctness holds since:

$$\bigoplus_{i=1}^n r^i = \bigoplus_{x \in \{1, \ldots, N\}} \bigoplus_{i=1}^n c_x^i \cdot D[x] = \bigoplus_{x \in \{1, \ldots, N\}} F_{y,1}(x) \cdot D[x] = D[y].$$

Privacy follows immediately from privacy of the DPF.

PIW. Let $D \in (\{0,1\}^B)^N$ be a data array. Let (Gen, Eval) be an n-server DPF for point functions with domain $[N]$ and range $\{0,1\}^B$. Now, each of the servers is given an *additive share* D^i of D, where $\bigoplus D^i = D$. When the client wants to write the value v to address y, we require the client to know the current value v_{old} stored at that address. (Here, we simply assume the client knows this value; in applications of PIW we will need to provide a way for the client to learn it.) The client computes $\mathsf{Gen}(1^\kappa, y, v \oplus v_{\mathsf{old}})$ to obtain keys $K^1, \ldots, K^n$, and sends K^i to the ith server. The ith server computes $\mathsf{Eval}(K^i, x)$ for $x = 1, \ldots, N$ to obtain a sequence of B-bit values $\tilde{V}^i = (\tilde{v}_1^i, \ldots, \tilde{v}_N^i)$, and then updates its share D^i to $\tilde{D}^i = D^i \oplus \tilde{V}^i$. Note that if we define $\tilde{D} = \bigoplus \tilde{D}^i$, then $\tilde{D}$ is equal to D everywhere except at address y, where the value at that address has been "shifted" by $v \oplus v_{\mathsf{old}}$ so that the new value stored there is v.

4   3-Server ORAM

In this section we describe a 3-server ORAM scheme secure against a *single* semi-honest server. The scheme can be built from any 2-private, 3-server DPF together with any 2-server PIR protocol. (As discussed previously, a 2-server PIR protocol can be constructed from any 1-private, 2-server DPF; efficient constructions of the latter are known [5,11].)

A 4-Server ORAM Scheme. As a warm-up, we sketch a 4-server ORAM protocol (secure against a single semi-honest server), inspired by ideas of [25], based on 2-server PIR and PIW schemes constructed as in the previous section. Let $D \in (\{0,1\}^B)^N$ be the client's (encrypted) data, and let D^1, D^2 be shares so that $D^1 \oplus D^2 = D$. Servers 1 and 2 store D^1, and servers 3 and 4 store D^2. The client can then obliviously read from and write to D as follows: to read the value at address y, the client runs a 2-server PIR protocol with servers 1 and 2 to obtain $D^1[y]$ and with servers 3 and 4 to obtain $D^2[y]$. It then computes $D[y] = D^1[y] \oplus D^2[y]$.

To write the value v to address y, the client first performs an oblivious read (as above) to learn the value v_{old} currently stored at that address. It then runs a 2-server PIW protocol with servers 1 and 3 to store v at address y in the array shared by those servers. Next, it sends the *same* PIW messages to servers 2 and 4, respectively. (The client does *not* run a fresh invocation of the PIW scheme; rather, it sends server 2 the same message it sent to server 1 and sends server 4 the same message it sent to server 3.) This ensures that (1) servers 1 and 2 hold the same updated data $\tilde{D}^1$; (2) servers 3 and 4 hold the same updated data $\tilde{D}^2$; and (3) the updated array $\tilde{D} = \tilde{D}^1 \oplus \tilde{D}^2$ is identical to the previously stored array except at position y (where the value stored is now v).

A 3-Server ORAM Scheme. We now show how to adapt the above ideas to the 3-server case, using a 2-server PIR scheme and a 2-private, 3-server DPF. The data D of the client is again viewed as an N-element array of B-bit entries. The invariant of the ORAM scheme is that at all times there exist shares D^1, D^2, D^3 with $D^1 \oplus D^2 \oplus D^3 = D$; server 1 will hold $\{D^1, D^2\}$, server 2 will hold $\{D^2, D^3\}$, and server 3 will hold $\{D^3, D^1\}$.

Before describing how reads and writes are performed, we define two subroutines GetValue and ShiftValue.

GetValue. To learn the entry at address y, the client uses three independent executions of a 2-server PIR scheme. Specifically, it uses an execution of the PIR protocol with servers 1 and 2 to learn $D^2[y]$; an execution of the PIR protocol with servers 2 and 3 to learn $D^3[y]$; and an execution of the PIR protocol with servers 1 and 3 to learn $D^1[y]$. Finally, it XORs the three values just obtained to obtain $D[y] = D^1[y] \oplus D^2[y] \oplus D^3[y]$.

ShiftValue. This subroutine allows the client to shift the value at position y by $\Delta \in \{0,1\}^B$, i.e., to change D to $\tilde{D}$ where $\tilde{D}[x] = D[x]$ for $x \neq y$ and $\tilde{D}[y] = D[y] \oplus \Delta$. Let (Gen, Eval) be a 2-private, 3-server DPF scheme with domain $[N]$ and range $\{0,1\}^B$. The client computes $K^1, K^2, K^3 \leftarrow \text{Gen}(y, \Delta)$ and sends K^1 to server 1, K^2 to server 2, and K^3 to server 3. Each server s respectively computes $\text{Eval}(K^s, x)$ for $x = 1, \dots, N$ to obtain a sequence of B-bit values $\tilde{V}^s = (\tilde{v}_1^s, \dots, \tilde{v}_N^s)$, and then updates its share D^s to $\tilde{D}^s = D^s \oplus \tilde{V}^s$. Note that if $\tilde{D}$ denotes the updated version of the array, then $\tilde{D}^1 \oplus \tilde{D}^2 \oplus \tilde{D}^3 = \tilde{D}$.

After the above, server 1 holds $\{\tilde{D}^1, D^2\}$, server 2 holds $\{\tilde{D}^2, D^3\}$, and server 3 holds $\{\tilde{D}^3, D^1\}$, and so the desired invariant does not hold. To fix this, the client also sends K^1 to server 3, K^2 to server 1, and K^3 to server 2. (We stress that the *same* keys used before are being used here, i.e., the client does not run a fresh execution of the DPF.) This allows each server to update its "other" share to the same value held by the corresponding other server, and hence restore the invariant.

With these in place, we may now define our read and write protocols.

Read. To read the entry at index y, the client runs GetValue(y) followed by ShiftValue($y, 0^B$).

Write. To write value v to index y, the client runs GetValue(y) to learn the current value v_{old} stored at index y, and then runs ShiftValue($y, v \oplus v_{\text{old}}$).

Correctness of the construction is immediate. Security against a single semi-honest server follows from security of the GetValue and ShiftValue subroutines, which in turn follow from security of the primitives used: GetValue is secure because the PIR scheme hides y from any single corrupted server; ShiftValue is secure against any single corrupted server—even though that server sees *two* keys from the DPF—by virtue of the fact that the DPF is 2-private.

5   3-Party Distributed ORAM

5.1   Definition

In the previous section we considered the client-server setting where a single client outsources its data to three servers, and can perform reads and writes on that data. In that setting, the client knows the index y when reading and knows the index y and value v when writing. Here, in contrast, we consider a setting where three parties P_1, P_2, P_3 distributively implement the client (as well as the servers), and none of them should learn the input(s) or output of read/write requests—in fact, they should not even learn whether a read or a write was performed. Instead, all inputs/outputs are additively shared among the three parties, and should remain hidden from any single (semi-honest) party.

More formally, we define in Fig. 1 an ideal, reactive functionality $\mathcal{F}_{\text{mem}}$ corresponding to distributed storage of an array with support for memory accesses. (For simplicity we leave initialization implicit, and so assume the functionality always stores an array $D \in (\{0,1\}^B)^N$.) We then define a *1-private, 3-party distributed ORAM* (DORAM) protocol to be a 3-party protocol that realizes this ideal functionality in the presence of a single (semi-honest) corrupted party.

Our DORAM protocol will utilize a 3-Server DPF protocol as a subroutine. Our use of DPF requires a *dealerless* variant, where instead of utilizing a single party for the Gen protocol to distribute keys corresponding to the secret location y and secret value v, instead y and v are secret-shared amongst three ORAM parties.[1] While a standard DPF protocol can be converted into a "dealerless" protocol using generic MPC, this introduces inefficiencies that may outweight the benefit of using a DPF-based approach in the first place. Instead, we will directly construct a 3-party dealerless DPF protocol.

5.2   Our Construction

We give a construction of a 3-party DORAM protocol inspired by the 3-server ORAM scheme described in the previous section. Here, however, we rely on the specific 3-server DPF constructed in Sect. 2.

Our construction follows closely the strategy of the previous section: start with a three way sharing of the database as $D = D^1 \oplus D^2 \oplus D^3$ where each

---

[1] Some of the subprotocols will require that secret location y is (XOR) secret shared amongst the three parties, while others require i and j (where $y = (i,j)$) to be secret shared. For simplicity, we assume that both variants are provided as inputs to each of the three parties, and note that generic MPC can be applied to convert from one variant to the other, if necessary.

Functionality $\mathcal{F}_{\mathsf{mem}}$

The functionality is assumed to be initialized with an array $D \in (\{0,1\}^B)^N$.

1. On input additive shares of (op, y, v) from the three parties, do:
   (a) If $\mathsf{op} = \mathsf{read}$ then set $o = D[y]$.
   (b) If $\mathsf{op} = \mathsf{write}$ then set[a] $o = D[y]$ and $D[y] = v$.
2. Let o^1, o^2, o^3 be random, additive shares of o. Return o^s to party s.

---

[a] For the purposes of the functionality, o can be an arbitrary value when $\mathsf{op} = \mathsf{write}$. For concreteness, we set $o = D[y]$ in this case so as to slightly optimize our protocol.

Fig. 1. Functionality $\mathcal{F}_{\mathsf{mem}}$ for distributed memory access.

of the three parties knows two of these three shares, and then define subroutines GetValue and ShiftValue that maintain the invariant that at all times the database continues to be three-way shared with each party knowing two of the three shares. The primary challenge for the present distributed setting will be to modify the GetValue and ShiftValue subroutines to be "dealerless," whereby the input location y and write value v are secret-shared amongst the three parties.

At a high-level, the subroutine GetValue will be modified by running a shifted-index 2-PIR scheme, whereby one party acts as the PIR client with shifted index $i + \omega$ (this party does not know the shift ω), and the other two parties act as the PIR servers on a shifted (by ω) database. Then this shifted-database 2-PIR protocol is run three times, once with party 1 acting as the client on PIR database D^2, once with party 2 acting as the client on PIR database D^3, and once with party 3 acting as the PIR client on PIR database D^1.

Meanwhile, the challenge for making the ShiftValue subroutine "dealerless" lies in making the Gen subprotocol of the 2-out-of-3 DPF from Sect. 2 dealerless. Recall that our DPF protocol had three main steps: (i) Generating shares of a characteristic vector $I = I^1 \oplus I^2 \oplus I^3$ with the unique '1' in position i (where $y = (i, j)$ is the secret location); (ii) Dealing two PRG seeds for each of the $\sqrt{N}$ segments that satisfy (1) and (2); and (iii) Generating shares of the "characteristic vector" $\mathbf{e}_{j,v}$ that is zero everywhere except in coordinate j where it has value v. We show below how each of these steps can be done in a dealerless setting (where inputs $y = (i, j)$ and v are secret-shared amongst the three parties).

GetValue. Here the parties hold y^1, y^2, y^3, respectively, with $y = y^1 \oplus y^2 \oplus y^3$; after running this protocol the parties should hold additive shares v^1, v^2, v^3 of the value $D[y]$. This is accomplished as follows:

1. P_2 chooses uniform $r^2 \in [N]$ and sends r^2 to P_1 and $y^2 \oplus r^2$ to P_3. Party P_3 chooses uniform $r^3 \in [N]$ and sends r^3 to P_1 and $y^3 \oplus r^3$ to P_2. Then P_2 and P_3 each compute $\omega = y^2 \oplus r^2 \oplus y^3 \oplus r^3$, and P_1 computes $y^1 \oplus r^2 \oplus r^3 = y \oplus \omega$.
2. P_1 runs the client algorithm in the 2-server PIR protocol using the "shifted index" $y \oplus \omega$. Parties P_2 and P_3 will play the roles of the servers using the

"shifted database" that results by shifting the position of every entry in D^3 by ω. Rather than sending their responses to P_1, however, P_2 and P_3 simply record those values locally. Note that this results in P_2 and P_3 holding additive shares of $D^3[y]$.

Repeating the above with P_2 as client (reading from D^1) and again with P_3 as client (reading from D^2)—and then having the parties locally XOR their shares together—results in the three parties holding additive shares $\hat{o}^1, \hat{o}^2, \hat{o}^3$ of $D[y]$. Finally, the parties re-randomize their shares. Namely, each party P_s chooses uniform Δ_s and sends it to P_{s+1}; it then sets its output share equal to $o^s = \hat{o}^s \oplus \Delta_s \oplus \Delta_{s-1}$.

ShiftValue. Here we assume the parties have shares i^1, i^2, i^3 and j^1, j^2, j^3 such that, if $i = i^1 \oplus i^2 \oplus i^3$ and $j = j^1 \oplus j^2 \oplus j^3$, the shared index is $y = (i, j)$. The parties also have shares v^1, v^2, v^3 with $v^1 \oplus v^2 \oplus v^3 = v$. At the end of this protocol, the parties should hold shares of the updated data $\tilde{D}$ where all entries are the same as in the original data D except that $\tilde{D}[y] = D[y] \oplus v$.

We show how to implement a *distributed* version of the Gen algorithm in our 3-server DPF, whereby the Gen algorithm is modified so that no single party knows the secret location y nor secret value v (instead, these are secret-shared amongst the three parties). Namely, the parties will run a protocol that results in party 1 holding K^1, party 2 holding K^2, and party 3 holding K^3, where K^1, K^2, K^3 are distributed as in an execution of $\mathsf{Gen}(1^\kappa, y, v)$. Given this primitive, a distributed version of ShiftValue can then be implemented following the ideas from the previous section.

We now describe the distributed version of the DPF. For clarity, we describe sub-protocols for each of the steps of the Gen algorithm from Sect. 2; these sub-protocols can be parallelized in the obvious way.

1. The sub-protocol for step 1 proceeds as follows:
   (a) P_2 chooses uniform $r^2 \in [\sqrt{N}]$ and sends r^2 to P_1 and $i^2 \oplus r^2$ to P_3. Party P_3 chooses uniform $r^3 \in [\sqrt{N}]$ and sends r^3 to P_1 and $i^3 \oplus r^3$ to P_2. Then P_2 and P_3 each compute $\omega = i^2 \oplus r^2 \oplus i^3 \oplus r^3$, and P_1 computes $i^1 \oplus r^2 \oplus r^3 = i \oplus \omega$.
   (b) P_1 runs $\mathsf{Gen}(1^\kappa, i \oplus \omega, 1)$, where Gen denotes the key-generation algorithm for a 2-server DPF with domain $[\sqrt{N}]$ and range $\{0, 1\}$. This results in keys K^2, K^3 that are sent to P_2 and P_3, respectively.
   (c) For $k = 1, \ldots, \sqrt{N}$, party P_2 sets $\hat{I}^2[k] = \mathsf{Eval}(K^2, k \oplus \omega)$ to obtain a string $\hat{I}^2 \in \{0, 1\}^{\sqrt{N}}$. Similarly, P_3 computes $\hat{I}^3 \in \{0, 1\}^{\sqrt{N}}$. Finally, P_1 sets $\hat{I}^1 = 0^{\sqrt{N}}$. Note that $(\hat{I}^2[k] \oplus \hat{I}^3[k])$ equals one if $k = i$ and otherwise equals zero everywhere else, and so $\hat{I}^1 \oplus \hat{I}^2 \oplus \hat{I}^3 = (0, \ldots, 0, 1, 0, \ldots, 0)$ with the '1' in coordinate i.
   (d) The parties re-randomize their shares: Each party P_s chooses uniform Δ_s and sends it to P_{s+1}; it then sets its output share equal to $I_s = \hat{I}_s \oplus \Delta_s \oplus \Delta_{s-1}$.
2. Here we describe the sub-protocol corresponding to step 2. Let I^1, I^2, I^3 be the respective outputs of the parties after step 1, above, and let $I^s[k]$ denote the kth bit of I^s. For $k = 1, \ldots, \sqrt{N}$ do:

(a) Party P_s chooses $\alpha_k^s, \beta_k^s, \gamma_k^s, \delta_k^s \leftarrow \{0,1\}^\kappa$. Each party P_s then sends $I^s[k]$ to P_{s-1} together with three of these four quantities chosen: P_1 sends $I^1[k], \alpha_k^1, \beta_k^1, \delta_k^1$ to P_3; P_2 sends $I^2[k], \beta_k^2, \gamma_k^2, \delta_k^2$ to P_1; and P_3 sends $I^3[k], \alpha_k^3, \gamma_k^3, \delta_k^3$ to P_2.

(b) The parties run the following steps:

   i. P_2 chooses $\alpha_k', \beta_k', \delta_k' \leftarrow \{0,1\}^\kappa$ and $z \leftarrow \{0,1\}$, and sends those values to P_3. Parties P_2 and P_3 then compute:

$$
\begin{array}{ll}
\quad\quad P_2 & \quad\quad P_3 \\
x_0 := \alpha_k^2 \oplus \alpha_k' & y_0 := \alpha_k^{\bar{1}} \oplus \alpha_k^3 \oplus \alpha_k' \\
x_1 := \beta_k^2 \oplus \beta_k' & y_1 := \beta_k^{\bar{1}} \oplus \beta_k^3 \oplus \beta_k' \\
x_2 := \delta_k^2 \oplus \delta_k' & y_2 := \delta_k^{\bar{1}} \oplus \delta_k^3 \oplus \delta_k'
\end{array}
$$

   ii. P_2 computes two ordered pairs S_0, S_1 as follows:

$$
S_{I^2[k] \oplus I^3[k]} = \begin{cases} (x_0, x_1) & \text{if } z = 0 \\ (x_1, x_0) & \text{if } z = 1 \end{cases}
$$

$$
S_{1 \oplus I^2[k] \oplus I^3[k]} = \begin{cases} (x_0, x_2) & \text{if } z = 0 \\ (x_2, x_0) & \text{if } z = 1. \end{cases}
$$

P_3 computes two ordered pairs T_0, T_1 as follows:

$$
T_{I^3[k]} = \begin{cases} (y_0, y_1) & \text{if } z = 0 \\ (y_1, y_0) & \text{if } z = 1 \end{cases}
$$

$$
T_{1 \oplus I^3[k]} = \begin{cases} (y_0, y_2) & \text{if } z = 0 \\ (y_2, y_0) & \text{if } z = 1. \end{cases}
$$

   iii. P_1 runs a 1-out-of-2 oblivious-transfer protocol[2] with P_2, where P_1 uses selection bit $I^1[k]$ and P_2 uses inputs S_0, S_1; let (x, x') be the output of P_1. Similarly, P_1 runs a 1-out-of-2 oblivious-transfer protocol with P_3, where P_1 uses selection bit $I^1[k] \oplus I^2[k]$ and P_3 uses inputs T_0, T_1; let (y, y') be the output of P_1. Finally, P_1 defines $S_k^1 = \{x \oplus y, \ x' \oplus y'\}$.

Note that if $k \neq i$ then $I^1[k] \oplus I^2[k] \oplus I^3[k] = 0$; in that case, we have $\{x, x'\} = \{x_0, x_1\}$ and $\{y, y'\} = \{y_0, y_1\}$, and so

$$
S_k^1 = \{\alpha_k^1 \oplus \alpha_k^2 \oplus \alpha_k^3, \ \beta_k^1 \oplus \beta_k^2 \oplus \beta_k^3\}.
$$

On the other hand, if $k = i$ then $I^1[k] \oplus I^2[k] \oplus I^3[k] = 1$; in that case, $\{x, x'\} = \{x_0, x_2\}$ and $\{y, y'\} = \{y_0, y_2\}$, and so

$$
S_k^1 = \{\alpha_k^1 \oplus \alpha_k^2 \oplus \alpha_k^3, \ \delta_k^1 \oplus \delta_k^2 \oplus \delta_k^3\}.
$$

---

[2] In our setting, with three parties and one semi-honest corruption, a simple oblivious-transfer protocol with information-theoretic security can be constructed using standard techniques, e.g. having one player act as a dealer of correlated randomness.

(c) The parties run (b) two more times, changing the roles of the parties (and modifying the values used) in the analogous way so that each party P_s ends up learning the appropriate S_k^s.

3. The sub-protocol corresponding to step 3 proceeds as follows:

(a) The parties run a protocol analogous to step 1 to generate uniform $\hat{C}^1, \hat{C}^2, \hat{C}^3 \in (\{0,1\}^B)^{\sqrt{N}}$, held by the respective parties, such that

$$\hat{C}^1 \oplus \hat{C}^2 \oplus \hat{C}^3 = e_{j,v} = (\overbrace{0^B, \ldots, 0^B, v, 0^B, \ldots, 0^B}^{j}). \tag{4}$$
$$\underbrace{}_{\sqrt{N}}$$

In detail:

i. P_2 chooses uniform $r^2 \in [\sqrt{N}]$ and sends r^2 to P_1 and $j^2 \oplus r^2$ to P_3. Party P_3 chooses uniform $r^3 \in [\sqrt{N}]$ and sends r^3 to P_1 and $j^3 \oplus r^3$ to P_2. Then P_2 and P_3 each compute $\omega = j^2 \oplus r^2 \oplus j^3 \oplus r^3$, and P_1 computes $j^1 \oplus r^2 \oplus r^3 = j \oplus \omega$.

ii. P_1 runs the $\mathsf{Gen}(1^\kappa, j \oplus \omega, v^1)$, where Gen is the key-generation algorithm for a 2-server DPF with range $\{0,1\}^B$ and domain $[\sqrt{N}]$. (Note the differences from the corresponding part of step 1.) This results in keys K^2, K^3 that are sent to P_2 and P_3, respectively.

iii. For $k = 1, \ldots, \sqrt{N}$, party P_2 sets $\hat{C}_1^2[k] = \mathsf{Eval}(K^2, k \oplus \omega)$. Similarly, P_3 computes $\hat{C}_1^3 \in \{0,1\}^{\sqrt{N}}$. Note that

$$\hat{C}_1^2[k] \oplus \hat{C}_1^3[k] = \begin{cases} v^1 & \text{if } k = j \\ 0 & \text{otherwise.} \end{cases} \tag{5}$$

The above steps are carried out twice more in a symmetric fashion, with each of P_2 and P_3 acting as client in a 2-server DPF. This results in P_1 and P_3 holding $\hat{C}_2^1$ and $\hat{C}_2^3$, respectively, satisfying a relation as in (5) but with v^2 in place of v^1, and P_1 and P_2 holding $\hat{C}_3^1$ and $\hat{C}_3^2$, respectively, also satisfying a relation as in (5) but with v^3 in place of v^1. Next, P_1 sets $\hat{C}^1 = \hat{C}_2^1 \oplus \hat{C}_3^1$, with P_2, P_3 acting analogously. Finally, the parties re-randomize their shares (in the same way as in earlier steps). The end result is that the parties hold uniform $\hat{C}^1, \hat{C}^2, \hat{C}^3$ satisfying (4).

(b) Recall that from step 2, each party P_s holds sets $S_1^s, \ldots, S_{\sqrt{N}}^s$. Each party P_s now computes: $C^s = \hat{C}^s \oplus (\bigoplus_k G(S_k^s))$, where $G(\{s_1, s_2\}) = G(s_1) \oplus G(s_2)$. It can be verified that:

$$C^1 \oplus C^2 \oplus C^3 = \hat{C}^1 \oplus \hat{C}^2 \oplus \hat{C}^3 \oplus G(a_i) \oplus G(b_i) \oplus G(c_i) \oplus G(d_i),$$

where we define:

$$a_i = \alpha_i^1 \oplus \alpha_i^2 \oplus \alpha_i^3$$
$$b_i = \beta_i^1 \oplus \beta_i^2 \oplus \beta_i^3$$
$$c_i = \gamma_i^1 \oplus \gamma_i^2 \oplus \gamma_i^3$$
$$d_i = \delta_i^1 \oplus \delta_i^2 \oplus \delta_i^3.$$

(c) Each party P_s sends C^s to the other two parties, so they can all compute $C = C^1 \oplus C^2 \oplus C^3$.

Note that after the above, each party P_s has a key K^s corresponding to the output of the Gen algorithm for our 3-server DPF from Sect. 2.

Memory Access. We can handle a memory access by suitably modifying the approach from the previous section. The parties begin holding additive shares of a memory-access instruction (op, y, v) and data D, and do:

1. The parties run the GetValue protocol using their shares of y, and end up holding shares o^1, o^2, o^3 with $o = o^1 \oplus o^2 \oplus o^3 = D[y]$.
2. The parties run a secure multi-party computation implementing the following functionality:

   If $\mathsf{op} = \mathsf{read}$ then set $w = 0^B$; otherwise, set $w = v \oplus o$. Output random additive shares w^1, w^2, w^3 of w.

   This functionality can be realized in our setting using a simple protocol with information-theoretic security. Specifically, let $\mathsf{op} \in \{0, 1\}$ with 0 indicating read. The parties hold additive shares of op, v, and o, and need only to compute a (random) additive sharing of $w = \mathsf{op} \cdot (v \oplus o)$. This can be computed via a standard protocol for distributed multiplication.
3. The parties run the ShiftValue protocol using their shares of y and their shares of w. The parties locally output their shares of o.

Theorem 2. *The above is a 1-private, 3-party DORAM protocol where each memory access requires $O(1)$ rounds and $O(\sqrt{N})$ communication.*

Proof. We prove security by showing that our GetValue protocol securely realizes an appropriately defined functionality for reading a value from the parties' shared data, and that our ShiftValue protocol securely computes the Gen algorithm of our 3-server DPF. (Our notion of securely realizing a functionality is the standard one from the secure-computation literature, for one semi-honest corruption. In particular, we consider indistinguishability of the joint distribution consisting of the corrupted party's view and the outputs of the other parties.) Security of the overall DORAM protocol then follows in a straightforward manner.

Security of GetValue. For security of GetValue, we consider the functionality $\mathcal{F}_{\mathsf{read}}$ in Fig. 2. This functionality is non-reactive, and takes the current array (shared as in our protocol) as input from the parties.

Claim. Our GetValue protocol securely realizes $\mathcal{F}_{\mathsf{read}}$ for a single, semi-honest corruption.

Proof. Since the protocol is symmetric, we may without loss of generality assume P_1 is corrupted. We show a simulator that takes as input values D^1, D^2, and y^1 used as input by P_1 along with an output value o^1, and simulates a view of P_1 in an execution of the protocol. The simulator works as follows:

Functionality $\mathcal{F}_{\text{read}}$

On input D^1, D^2, y^1 from P_1, along with D^2, D^3, y^2 from P_2 and D^1, D^3, y^3 from P_3, do:

1. Let $D = D^1 \oplus D^2 \oplus D^3$ and $y = y^1 \oplus y^2 \oplus y^3$.
2. Set $o = D[y]$.
3. Let o^1, o^2, o^3 be random, additive shares of o. Return o^s to party s.

Fig. 2. Functionality $\mathcal{F}_{\text{read}}$ for a distributed read access.

First iteration: Choose uniform r_1^2 and r_1^3, and send these to P_1 on behalf of P_2 and P_3, respectively.

Second iteration, step 1: Choose uniform r_2^1 on behalf of P_1 (i.e., as part of P_1's random tape). Choose uniform r_2^3 and send it to P_1 on behalf of P_3.

Second iteration, step 2: Run the 2-server PIR scheme using address 1 to obtain keys K_2^1, K_2^3. Send K_2^1 to P_1 on behalf of P_2. Let o_2^1 be the local value that P_1 would compute in this step.

Third iteration: This is simulated analogously to the second iteration. Let o_3^1 be the local value that P_1 would compute in this step.

Re-randomization: Choose uniform Δ_1 on behalf of P_1, and let Δ_3 be such that $o_2^1 \oplus o_3^1 \oplus \Delta_1 \oplus \Delta_3 = o^1$. Send Δ_3 to P_1 on behalf of P_3.

Security of the PIR scheme readily implies that the distribution of the simulated view of P_1 in the ideal world is computationally indistinguishable from the distribution of its view in a real execution of the protocol. Moreover, even conditioned on P_1's view, the outputs of P_2 and P_3 are uniform (subject to XORing to the correct output) in both the ideal- and real-world executions.

Next, we show that the ShiftValue protocol securely computes the Gen algorithm of our 3-server DPF, i.e., that it securely realizes the functionality that takes additive shares of y and v from the three parties, computes $K^1, K^2, K^3 \leftarrow \text{Gen}(1^\kappa, y, v)$, and returns K^s to P_s. For ease of exposition, we show that each step of the ShiftValue protocol securely computes the corresponding step of Gen.

Security of ShiftValue (step 1). The desired functionality here is simple: the parties's inputs are additive shares i^1, i^2, i^3 of a value $i = i^1 \oplus i^2 \oplus i^3$, and the parties' outputs are I^1, I^2, I^3, respectively, that are uniformly distributed subject to: $I^1 \oplus I^2 \oplus I^3 = (0, \dots, 0, 1, 0, \dots, 0)$ with the '1' in coordinate i.

Claim. The first step of the GetValue protocol securely realizes the functionality just described for a single, semi-honest corruption.

Proof. We consider separately the case where P_1 is corrupted, and the case where either P_2 or P_3 is corrupted. For corrupted P_1, we define a simulator that takes as input a value i^1 used as input by P_1 along with an output value I^1, and simulates a view of P_1 in an execution of the protocol. The simulator works as follows:

1. Choose uniform r^2 and r^3, and send these to P_1 on behalf of P_2 and P_3, respectively.
2. Choose uniform Δ_1 on behalf of P_1. Set $\Delta_3 = I^1 \oplus \Delta_1$ and send that value to P_1 on behalf of P_3.

It is immediate that the distribution of the simulated view of P_1 in the ideal world is identical to the distribution of its view in a real execution of the protocol. Moreover, even conditioned on P_1's view, the outputs of P_2 and P_3 are uniform (subject to XORing to the correct output) in both the ideal- and real-world executions.

For the other case, assume P_2 is corrupted without loss of generality, and let i^2, I^2 be the corresponding input and output values given to the simulator. Here, the simulator works as follows:

1. Choose uniform r^2 on behalf of P_2. Choose uniform $\hat{r}^3$ and send it to P_2 on behalf of P_3.
2. Run $K^2, K^3 \leftarrow \mathsf{Gen}(1^\kappa, 1, 1)$, where Gen denotes the key-generation algorithm for a 2-server DPF with the appropriate domain and range. Send K^2 to P_2 on behalf of P_1. Let $\hat{I}^2$ be the local value that P_1 would compute in this step.
3. Choose uniform Δ_2 on behalf of P_2. Set $\Delta_1 = I^2 \oplus \hat{I}^2 \oplus \Delta_2$ and send that value to P_2 on behalf of P_2.

Security of the DPF implies that the distribution of the simulated view of P_2 in the ideal world is computationally indistinguishable from the distribution of its view in a real execution. Moreover, even conditioned on P_2's view, the outputs of P_1 and P_3 are uniform (subject to XORing to the correct output) in both the ideal- and real-world executions.

Security of ShiftValue (step 2). The desired ideal functionality in this case takes additive shares I^1, I^2, I^3 of $I = I^1 \oplus I^2 \oplus I^3$ (which is a unary representation of i) as input from the parties, and then does the following for $k = 1, \ldots, \sqrt{N}$: choose $a_k, b_k, c_k, d_k \leftarrow \{0,1\}^\kappa$. Then if $k \neq i$, output to the parties: $S_k^1 = \{a_k, b_k\}$, $S_k^2 = \{b_k, c_k\}$, $S_k^3 = \{c_k, a_k\}$, respectively, while if $k = i$, output to the parties: $S_k^1 = \{a_k, d_k\}$, $S_k^2 = \{b_k, d_k\}$, $S_k^3 = \{c_k, d_k\}$, respectively. (In all cases, the elements in the set are randomly permuted so their order does not reveal information.)

In analyzing step 2 of ShiftValue, we assume the parties re-randomize their shares of I before running the protocol. This is justified by the fact that the parties re-randomize their shares at the end of step 1.

Claim. The second step of the GetValue protocol (with re-randomization of shares done first) securely realizes the functionality just described for a single, semi-honest corruption.

Proof. We analyze the protocol in a hybrid model where the parties have access to an oblivious-transfer (OT) functionality. By symmetry, we may assume without loss of generality that P_1 is corrupted. We describe a simulator that takes as input a value I^1 used as input by P_1 along with output values $S_1^1, \ldots, S_{\sqrt{N}}^1$, where $S_k^1 = \{a_k, b_k\}$, and simulates a view of P_1 in an execution of the protocol. The simulator works as follows:

1. Choose uniform Δ_1 on behalf of P_1. Choose uniform Δ_3 and send it to P_1 on behalf of P_3. (This simulates the re-randomization step.)
2. For $k = 1, \ldots, \sqrt{N}$, do:
   (a) Choose uniform $\alpha_k^1, \beta_k^1, \gamma_k^1, \delta_k^1$ on behalf of P_1. Choose uniform $I^2[k]$, β_k^2, γ_k^2, δ_k^2 and send them to P_1 on behalf of P_2.
   (b) Choose uniform x, y such that $x \oplus y = a_k$, and uniform x', y' such that $x' \oplus y' = b_k$. Simulate the OTs (with P_1 as receiver and P_2 as sender in one execution and P_3 as sender in the other execution) by giving P_1 outputs (x, x') and (y, y') from the two executions with probability $1/2$, and outputs (x', x) and (y', y) with probability $1/2$.
   (c) Choose uniform $\beta_k'', \gamma_k'', \delta_k''$, z'' on behalf of P_1.
   (d) Choose uniform $\alpha_k''', \gamma_k''', \delta_k'''$, z''' and send them to P_1 on behalf of P_2.

It is immediate that the distribution of the simulated view of P_1 in the ideal world is identical to the distribution of its view in a real execution of the protocol. Moreover, the distribution of the outputs of P_2 and P_3, conditioned on the inputs of all the parties and the output of P_1, is identically distributed in the ideal- and real-world executions.

Security of ShiftValue (step 3). The proof of security here follows closely along the lines of the proof for step 1, and is therefore omitted. $\square$

Acknowledgments. This work was supported by DARPA and NIWC Pacific under contract N66001-15-C-4065, as well as the Office of the Director of National Intelligence (ODNI), Intelligence Advanced Research Projects Activity (IARPA), via 2019-1902070008. The views and conclusions contained herein are those of the authors and should not be interpreted as necessarily representing the official policies, either expressed or implied, of ODNI, IARPA, the Department of Defense, or the U.S. Government. The U.S. Government is authorized to reproduce and distribute reprints for governmental purposes notwithstanding any copyright annotation therein. Work of Jonathan Katz was supported in part by NSF award #1563722. Research of Eyal Kushilevitz is supported by ISF grant 1709/14, BSF grant 2012378, NSF-BSF grant 2015782, and a grant from the Ministry of Science and Technology, Israel, and the Department of Science and Technology, Government of India. Rafail Ostrovsky is supported in part by NSF-BSF Grant 1619348, US-Israel BSF grant 2012366, Google Faculty Award, JP Morgan Faculty Award, IBM Faculty Research Award, Xerox Faculty Research Award, OKAWA Foundation Research Award, B. John Garrick Foundation Award, Teradata Research Award, and Lockheed-Martin Corporation Research Award.

Thanks also to Steve Lu and the anonymous reviewers for helpful comments and suggestions.

References

1. Abraham, I., Fletcher, C.W., Nayak, K., Pinkas, B., Ren, L.: Asymptotically tight bounds for composing ORAM with PIR. In: Fehr, S. (ed.) PKC 2017. LNCS, vol. 10174, pp. 91–120. Springer, Heidelberg (2017). https://doi.org/10.1007/978-3-662-54365-8_5

2. Afshar, A., Hu, Z., Mohassel, P., Rosulek, M.: How to efficiently evaluate RAM programs with malicious security. In: Oswald, E., Fischlin, M. (eds.) EUROCRYPT 2015. LNCS, vol. 9056, pp. 702–729. Springer, Heidelberg (2015). https://doi.org/10.1007/978-3-662-46800-5_27

3. Apon, D., Katz, J., Shi, E., Thiruvengadam, A.: Verifiable oblivious storage. In: Krawczyk, H. (ed.) PKC 2014. LNCS, vol. 8383, pp. 131–148. Springer, Heidelberg (2014). https://doi.org/10.1007/978-3-642-54631-0_8

4. Boyle, E., Gilboa, N., Ishai, Y.: Function secret sharing. In: Oswald, E., Fischlin, M. (eds.) EUROCRYPT 2015. LNCS, vol. 9057, pp. 337–367. Springer, Heidelberg (2015). https://doi.org/10.1007/978-3-662-46803-6_12

5. Boyle, E., Gilboa, N., Ishai, Y.: Function secret sharing: improvements and extensions. In: CCS, pp. 1292–1303. ACM Press (2016)

6. Chor, B., Goldreich, O., Kushilevitz, E., Sudan, M.: Private information retrieval. In: FOCS, pp. 41–50 (1995)

7. Doerner, J., Shelat, A.: Scaling ORAM for secure computation. In: CCS, pp. 523–535. ACM Press (2017)

8. Faber, S., Jarecki, S., Kentros, S., Wei, B.: Three-party ORAM for secure computation. In: Iwata, T., Cheon, J.H. (eds.) ASIACRYPT 2015. LNCS, vol. 9452, pp. 360–385. Springer, Heidelberg (2015). https://doi.org/10.1007/978-3-662-48797-6_16

9. Garg, S., Gupta, D., Miao, P., Pandey, O.: Secure multiparty RAM computation in constant rounds. In: Hirt, M., Smith, A. (eds.) TCC 2016. LNCS, vol. 9985, pp. 491–520. Springer, Heidelberg (2016). https://doi.org/10.1007/978-3-662-53641-4_19

10. Gentry, C., Goldman, K.A., Halevi, S., Julta, C., Raykova, M., Wichs, D.: Optimizing ORAM and using it efficiently for secure computation. In: De Cristofaro, E., Wright, M. (eds.) PETS 2013. LNCS, vol. 7981, pp. 1–18. Springer, Heidelberg (2013). https://doi.org/10.1007/978-3-642-39077-7_1

11. Gilboa, N., Ishai, Y.: Distributed point functions and their applications. In: Nguyen, P.Q., Oswald, E. (eds.) EUROCRYPT 2014. LNCS, vol. 8441, pp. 640–658. Springer, Heidelberg (2014). https://doi.org/10.1007/978-3-642-55220-5_35

12. Goldreich, O., Ostrovsky, R.: Software protection and simulation on oblivious RAMs. J. ACM 43(3), 431–473 (1996)

13. Goodrich, M.T., Mitzenmacher, M.: Privacy-preserving access of outsourced data via oblivious RAM simulation. In: Aceto, L., Henzinger, M., Sgall, J. (eds.) ICALP 2011. LNCS, vol. 6756, pp. 576–587. Springer, Heidelberg (2011). https://doi.org/10.1007/978-3-642-22012-8_46

14. Gordon, S.D.: Secure two-party computation in sublinear (amortized) time. In: CCS, pp. 512–524. ACM Press (2012)

15. Hazay, C., Yanai, A.: Constant-round maliciously secure two-party computation in the RAM model. In: Hirt, M., Smith, A. (eds.) TCC 2016. LNCS, vol. 9985, pp. 521–553. Springer, Heidelberg (2016). https://doi.org/10.1007/978-3-662-53641-4_20

16. Jarecki, S., Wei, B.: 3PC ORAM with low latency, low bandwidth, and fast batch retrieval (2018). https://eprint.iacr.org/2018/347.pdf

17. Keller, M., Yanai, A.: Efficient maliciously secure multiparty computation for RAM. In: Nielsen, J.B., Rijmen, V. (eds.) EUROCRYPT 2018. LNCS, vol. 10822, pp. 91–124. Springer, Cham (2018). https://doi.org/10.1007/978-3-319-78372-7_4

18. Kushilevitz, E., Lu, S., Ostrovsky, R.: On the (in)security of hash-based oblivious ram and a new balancing scheme. In: SODA, pp. 143–156. ACM-SIAM (2012)

19. Kushilevitz, E., Mour, T.: Sub-logarithmic distributed oblivious RAM with small block size (2018). https://arxiv.org/pdf/1802.05145.pdf

20. Kushilevitz, E., Ostrovsky, R.: Replication is not needed: single database, computationally-private information retrieval. In: FOCS, pp. 364–373 (1997)

21. Liu, C., Huang, Y., Shi, E., Katz, J., Hicks, M.W.: Automating efficient RAM-model secure computation. In: IEEE Symposium on Security and Privacy, pp. 218–234. IEEE (2016)

22. Lu, S., Ostrovsky, R.: Distributed oblivious RAM for secure two-party computation. In: Sahai, A. (ed.) TCC 2013. LNCS, vol. 7785, pp. 377–396. Springer, Heidelberg (2013). https://doi.org/10.1007/978-3-642-36594-2_22

23. Mayberry, T., Blass, E.-O., Chan, A.H.: Efficient private file retrieval by combining ORAM and PIR. In: 21st Annual Network and Distributed System Security Symposium, NDSS 2014, San Diego, California, USA, 23–26 February 2014. The Internet Society (2014)

24. Nayak, K., Wang, X.S., Ioannidis, S., Weinsberg, U., Taft, N., Shi, E.: GraphSC: parallel secure computation made easy. In: IEEE Symposium on Security and Privacy, pp. 377–394. IEEE (2015)

25. Ostrovsky, R., Shoup, V.: Private information storage. In: STOC, pp. 294–303. Springer (1997)

26. Pinkas, B., Reinman, T.: Oblivious RAM revisited. In: Rabin, T. (ed.) CRYPTO 2010. LNCS, vol. 6223, pp. 502–519. Springer, Heidelberg (2010). https://doi.org/10.1007/978-3-642-14623-7_27

27. Ren, L., et al.: Constants count: practical improvements to oblivious RAM. In: Jung, J., Holz, T., (eds.) 24th USENIX Security Symposium, USENIX Security 15, Washington, D.C., USA, 12–14 August 2015, pp. 415–430. USENIX Association (2015)

28. Shi, E., Chan, T.-H.H., Stefanov, E., Li, M.: Oblivious RAM with $O((\log N)^3)$ Worst-Case Cost. In: Lee, D.H., Wang, X. (eds.) ASIACRYPT 2011. LNCS, vol. 7073, pp. 197–214. Springer, Heidelberg (2011). https://doi.org/10.1007/978-3-642-25385-0_11

29. Stefanov, E., et al.: Path ORAM: an extremely simple oblivious RAM protocol. In: CCS, pp. 299–310. ACM Press (2013)

30. Wang, X., Chan, H., Shi, E.: Circuit ORAM: on tightness of the Goldreich-Ostrovsky lower bound. In: CCS, pp. 850–861. ACM Press (2015)

31. Wang, X., Gordon, D., Katz, J.: Simple and efficient two-server ORAM (2018). https://eprint.iacr.org/2018/005.pdf

32. Wang, X., Huang, Y., Chan, H., Shelat, A., Shi, E.: SCORAM: oblivious ram for secure computation. In: CCS, pp. 191–202. ACM Press (2014)

33. Wang, X., Gordon, S.D., McIntosh, A., Katz, J.: Secure computation of MIPS machine code. In: Askoxylakis, I., Ioannidis, S., Katsikas, S., Meadows, C. (eds.) ESORICS 2016. LNCS, vol. 9879, pp. 99–117. Springer, Cham (2016). https://doi.org/10.1007/978-3-319-45741-3_6

34. Williams, P., Sion, R.: Single round access privacy on outsourced storage. In: CCS, pp. 293–304. ACM Press (2012)

35. Zahur, S., et al.: Revisiting square-root ORAM: efficient random access in multiparty computation. In: IEEE Symposium on Security and Privacy, pp. 218–234. IEEE (2016)

Gradual GRAM and Secure Computation
for RAM Programs

Carmit Hazay[✉] and Mor Lilintal

Bar-Ilan University, Ramat-Gan, Israel
carmit.hazay@biu.ac.il, mor.tzoomi@gmail.com

Abstract. Despite the fact that the majority of applications encountered in practice today are captured more efficiently by RAM programs, the area of secure two-party computation (2PC) has seen tremendous improvement mostly when the function is represented by Boolean circuits. One of the most studied objects in this domain is garbled circuits. Analogously, garbled RAM (GRAM) provide similar security guarantees for RAM programs with applications to constant round 2PC. In this work we consider the notion of *gradual GRAM* which requires no memory garbling algorithm. Our approach provides several qualitative advantages over prior works due to the conceptual similarity to the analogue garbling mechanism for Boolean circuits. We next revisit the GRAM construction from [11] and improve it in two orthogonal aspects: match it directly with tree-based ORAMs and explore its consistency with gradual ORAM.

1 Introduction

Background. Secure multi-party computation (MPC) protocols allow a group of parties to compute some function f on the parties' private inputs, while preserving a number of security properties such as *privacy* and *correctness*. This area has witnessed a tremendous progress in the past two decades both in the two-party setting [18,19,25,26,33,34,37,40,41,46], and with a larger number of parties [5,7,20,27,42]. Nevertheless, most of this research has been conducted for Boolean circuits and falls short when the computation involves accesses to a large memory, which are translated into a linear scan of the memory inside the circuit. This translation is required for every memory access and causes a huge blowup in the description of the circuit. Moreover, the majority of applications encountered in practice today are more efficiently captured using *random-access memory (RAM)* programs that allow constant-time memory lookup and contain branches, recursions and loops. This covers graph algorithms such as the known Dijkstra's shortest path algorithm, binary search on sorted data, finding the kth-ranked element, the Gale-Shapely stable matching algorithm and many more.

C. Hazay—Supported by the BIU Center for Research in Applied Cryptography and Cyber Security in conjunction with the Israel National Cyber Bureau in the Prime Minister's Office, and by ISF grant No. 1316/18.

© Springer Nature Switzerland AG 2020
C. Galdi and V. Kolesnikov (Eds.): SCN 2020, LNCS 12238, pp. 233–252, 2020.
https://doi.org/10.1007/978-3-030-57990-6_12

Generic transformations from RAM programs that run in time T imply circuits of size $O(T^3 \log T)$ which are non-scalable even for relatively small memory sizes [4,36].

To address these limitations secure protocols have been designed directly in the RAM model, either with round complexity that grows with the running-time of the RAM program [6,8,17,23,24] or with constant round complexity [1,8–13,21,28–30,43]. A fundamental tool in designing protocols in the RAM model is Oblivious RAM (ORAM) [14,16,35], which supports dynamic memory access with polylogarithmic cost while preventing any leakage from the memory. Namely, ORAM is a technique for hiding all the information about the memory of a RAM program, including both the content of the memory and the access pattern to it. The efficiency of ORAM constructions is evaluated by their bandwidth and storage blowups where the former refers to the number of data blocks that are sent between the parties per memory access and the later refers to the multiplicative overhead of the oblivious memory size. Recent constructions incur practical polylogarithmic overheads in the size of memory [3,38,39].

1.1   Constant Round 2PC for RAM Programs

Similarly to two-party protocols for Boolean circuits, achieving constant round for RAM programs is carried out by adapting the garbled circuits technique [45] to support RAM computations [10,11,13,29]. Nevertheless, as opposed to classic garbled circuits where the computation is large and the inputs are relatively small, in RAM programs the accessed memory can be huge whereas the running time of the program is typically much smaller (e.g., polylogarithmic in the memory size). Informally, garbled RAM (GRAM) is a non-interactive object that garbles the memory D into $\widetilde{D}$, the program P into $\widetilde{P}$ and the input x into $\widetilde{x}$ such that only $P^D(x)$ (the execution of such a program) is revealed from $\widetilde{D}, \widetilde{P}, \widetilde{x}$. Moreover, the size of $\widetilde{D}$ (reps. $\widetilde{x}$) is proportional to D (resp. x), and the size and evaluation-time of $\widetilde{P}$ grows with the running-time of $P^D(x)$. At the heart of every GRAM construction lies a mechanism that prevents the evaluator from rolling back and evaluates the CPU circuits on an older version of the data elements (namely, before the most recent update took place). Consequently, memory garbling algorithms must be embedded with authenticating tools (even in the semi-honest setting). As for Boolean circuits, combined with semi-honest oblivious transfer, GRAM immediately implies semi-honest 2PC for RAM programs.

In order to hide the access pattern to the memory, all these schemes are built on top of ORAMs. Recall that the original motivation of ORAM was to protect memory accesses to the physical RAM (or to a server with a large storage capacity), by some remote CPU (or by a client with a small storage). Nevertheless, in the distributed setting, the memory is initially empty and is occupied on the fly (see [1]). Therefore, it makes no sense to initially run the garbled memory algorithm. Another drawback is regarding the amplification from semi-honest to malicious security, which either involves using zero-knowledge proofs for highly complicated statements or running a distributed protocol for the memory initialization. For instance, proving correctness within [11] requires proving the correctness of κ^2 PRF evaluation per tree node. Moreover, current GRAM constructions do not support the useful offline/online paradigm, where most of the work can be offloaded to an offline phase which is independent of the parties' inputs.[1]

Finally, the security analysis of these constructions have been proven relative to the weaker Unprotected Memory Access (UMA) notion, where the attacker may learn the initial contents of the memory D as well as the complete memory-access pattern throughout the computation. A transformation from any GRAM scheme with UMA security into one with full security has shown in [13].[2] With the exception of the GRAM from [29],[3] all prior constructions garble the memory using a tree that is built on top of the data. Namely, in [10,11] the leaves are associated with the memory contents, whereas in [13] a binary tree is added on top of the original data in order to construct Oblivious RAM with Predictably Timed Writes. Finally, the revocable PRF is based on the GGM tree-based PRF construction of [15]. This adds another layer of complication to the garbled memory when combining the GRAM tree with one of the recent ORAM constructions.

These drawbacks demonstrate that there is much room for improving the current state of affairs of GRAM schemes both theoretically and practically.

1.2   Our Results

Gradual ORAM for Tree-Based ORAMs. Motivated by the discussion above and the fact that all GRAM constructions are based on binary trees, we start by examining tree-based ORAM constructions and explore the flexible notion of *gradual ORAM*. This notion is an extension of the classic notion of ORAM that does not require an initialization phase to compile the data. Instead, a new algorithm is considered, that handles the memory insertions separately and can be skipped directly to the RAM program set of instructions. An immediate advantage that is derived by the flexibility of gradual ORAM is *resizability* [31]. Namely, the inherent dependence on a fixed-size tree is removed, allowing flexible storage. We note that this concept is not new and has been considered before.

Gradual GRAM. Next we extend the notion of GRAM and consider an analogue *gradual GRAM* notion with no memory garbling algorithm. Namely, this object is defined by only two algorithms for garbling the program and the input, where all the memory operations are incorporated within the program. This modification implies that the garbling mechanism is now only involved with a

---

[1] While some of the computation of these garbled memory algorithms can be carried out offline, it requires storing a large state that grows with the memory size.

[2] Informally, the transformation encrypts the memory elements and apply an ORAM construction to hide the access pattern.

[3] Note that this construction suffers from a circularity issue in its security analysis; see [13] for a detailed discussion.

sequence of small CPU-steps that are garbled using the classic garbled circuits approach. Therefore, it is conceptually closer to the analogue garbling mechanism for Boolean circuits. This new concept also introduces several advantages:

1. The scheme enjoys all the advancements of garbled circuits such as half gates, Free-XOR, Pipelining, and OT extension, that lead to highly optimizes semihonest protocols. We note that garbling a large set of circuits can benefit from recent techniques for batch garbling [32] (due to garbling a large sequence of small CPU-steps).
2. The bulk of work (e.g., generating the garbled circuits) can be shifted to an offline phase, performed independently of the data and the parties' inputs.
3. Amplifying security to the malicious setting is immediate by applying standard techniques such as cut-and-choose [26] or authenticated garbling [22,41], or any futuristic alternative approaches.
4. The parties can directly proceed with the program execution whenever the initial memory is empty and build the tree on the fly.
5. The space complexity of the garbler algorithm can be made minimal by processing each garbled circuit at the time rather than storing the entire tree of memory.

In addition, gradual GRAM can serve as a step towards supporting a broader class of data processing algorithms such as data streams or online algorithms, where the data is processed serially (compatible with memory on the fly access). We also stress that our notion maintains persistent data, where the memory updates are persistent for future executions, as similarly considered in prior work.

We next revisit the GRAM scheme from [11] and improve it in two dimensions:

1. We first prove that it can be combined directly with tree-based ORAMs, where the best matches are with the Simple ORAM [3] and the Circuit ORAM [39] due to their root-to-leaf eviction algorithms. We observe that for some ORAM constructions it is beneficial to build a combined tree that contains the ORAM buckets and the GRAM information, and is proven directly secure rather than via UMA. This allows to reduce the number of visited nodes in the GRAM and simplifies the CPU-steps circuits; see more discussion below and a comparison in Table 1. We remark that combining a tree-based ORAM with other data structures also appeared in [44].
2. In addition, we observe that [11] can be made consistent with our notion of gradual GRAM, where the combined tree is built on the fly based on gradual ORAM. This requires adjusting the GRAM algorithms to support an incomplete tree while maintaining authentication. Furthermore, it allows to avoid the expensive initialization phase and saves on space resources, as the size of the tree is minimized rather then growing with the maximum size of the data. To handle the case where an internal node may not have any children, we store two additional bits that notify whether the current node has a left (resp. right) child. We remark that our insights also apply to [10],

which introduces a more complex scheme where each internal tree node of $\widetilde{D}$ corresponds to a garbled circuit but the OWF is black-box accessed.

Efficiency Gains. To understand the quantitative differences between our gradual GRAM constructions and [11], we compare in Table 1 the number of nodes visited in the garbled memory in both cases, and the sizes of the garbled circuits involved a single ORAM access. Note first that all tree-based ORAMs require reading $O(1)$ root-to-leaf paths which implies reading $O(\log n)$ nodes per original memory access. Moreover, the GLOS construction implies a tree with $O(n \log n)$ leaves (each containing a bucket of size B). Therefore, accessing an ORAM node requires reading $\log n$ nodes, where the size of the $\log n - 1$ navigation circuits grows with κ^2 PRF evaluations whereas the leaf circuits involve $O(\kappa \cdot B)$ PRF evaluations.[4] Thus, the total number of steps in GLOS is $O((n + T) \cdot \log^2 n)$ and the overall circuits sizes of accessing a single ORAM element involve $O((\log n - 1) \cdot \kappa^2 + \kappa \cdot B)$ PRF evaluations.

In contrast, our construction combines the ORAM tree with the GRAM tree which eliminates a factor of $\log n$ in the overhead, implying running time of $O((n + T) \cdot \log n)$ (where the $n \cdot \log n$ overhead is due to the insertion program which may be eliminated in some cases such as when the initial memory is empty). Furthermore, each circuit involves $O(\kappa^2 + \kappa \cdot B)$ PRF evaluations as each node is also associated with a bucket (which implies that the node's size is larger). When instantiating the underlying ORAM with Simple ORAM each node contains a bucket of $O(\log n)$ values of size U, then we achieve circuit size proportional to $O(\kappa^2 + \kappa \cdot U \cdot \log n)$ PRF evaluations. In the Circuit ORAM each node contains a bucket with $O(1)$ values where only the stash is of size $O(\log n)$. Therefore in this case only the stash circuit is of size $O(\kappa^2 + \kappa \cdot U \cdot \log n)$, while the other circuits are of size $O(\kappa^2 + \kappa \cdot U)$. See Sect. 3.2 for more discussion.

Table 1. Communication and computation costs for the different GRAMs schemes. We use n to denote the number of memory entries, κ the security parameter and U the size of a bucket value.

Approach	Overall number of steps	Overall CPU-steps circuits sizes per a single ORAM access
[11]	$O((n + T) \cdot \log^2 n)$	$O((\log n - 1) \cdot \kappa^2 + \kappa \cdot B)$
Gradual [11] + Simple ORAM	$O((n + T) \cdot \log n)$	$O(\kappa^2 + \kappa \cdot U \cdot \log n)$
Gradual [11] + Circuit ORAM	$O((n + T) \cdot \log n)$	$O(\kappa^2 + \kappa \cdot U)$

---

[4] This is because the translation mapping in [11] involves a PRF evaluation per stored bit.

Extending to the Multi-party Setting. Due to the conceptual similarity to the garbled circuits approach for Boolean circuits, our approach is also easily extendable to the multi-party setting as well by applying different distributed garbling approaches [2,20,42]. These protocols scale much better than when running a distributed protocol for computing the garbled memory algorithm as done in all prior work, due to all recent optimizations.

2 Preliminaries

2.1 The RAM Model of Computation

We start with the notation of computation in the RAM model. Given a program P, with access to memory D of size n, that obtains a "short" input x which we alternatively think of as the initial state of the program. We use the notation $P^D(x)$ to denote the execution of program P with initial memory contents D and input x. The program can read/write to various locations in memory D throughout its execution. We also consider the case where several different programs are executed sequentially and the memory persists between executions. Specifically, this process is denoted by $(y_1, ..., y_c) = (P_1(x_1), .., P_c(x_c))^D$ to indicate that $P_1^D(x_1)$ is executed first, resulting in some memory contents D_1 and an output y_1, following that $P_2^{D_1}(x_2)$ is executed resulting in some memory contents D_2 and an output y_2 and so on.

CPU-Step Circuit. We consider a RAM program as a sequence of at most T small CPU-steps, where each of them is represented by a circuit that computes the following functionality:

$$C_{\mathrm{CPU}}^P\left(\mathsf{state}_t, v_t^{\mathsf{read}}\right) = \left(\mathsf{state}_{t+1}, i_{t+1}^{\mathsf{read}}, v_{t+1}^{\mathsf{write}}\right), \quad 1 \leq t \leq T$$

2.2 Garbled RAM

Analogously to garbled circuits for Boolean circuits [45], garbled RAM (GRAM) provide similar guarantees in the RAM model of computation. Namely, it is a non-interactive object that ensures privacy and correctness, and implies semi-honest two-round secure two-party computation when combined with OT. The standard definition of GRAM [13] is composed out of four algorithms defined as follows.

Syntax. A garbled RAM scheme consists of four PPT algorithms (GData, GProg, GInput, GEval) defined as follows:

- $\widetilde{D} \leftarrow$ GData(D, k): Takes as input a memory $D \in \{0, 1\}^n$ and a key k, and outputs the garbled memory $\widetilde{D}$.

- $(\widetilde{P}, k^{\mathsf{Inp}}) \leftarrow \mathsf{GProg}(P, k, n, t)$: takes a key k and a description of a RAM program P with memory-size n and run-time consisting of t CPU steps, and outputs a garbled program $\widetilde{P}$ and input garbling key labels k^{Inp}.
- $\tilde{x} \leftarrow \mathsf{GInput}(x, k^{\mathsf{Inp}})$: Takes as input a small input x and input garbling key labels k^{Inp}, and outputs a garbled input $\tilde{x}$.
- $y \leftarrow \mathsf{GEval}^{\widetilde{D}}(\widetilde{P}, \widetilde{D}, \tilde{x})$: Takes as input a garbled program $\widetilde{P}$, garbled memory data $\widetilde{D}$ and garbled input $\tilde{x}$ and computes the output $y = P^D(x)$. We model GEval as a RAM program that can read and write to arbitrary locations of its memory initially containing $\widetilde{D}$.

Correctness. We require that for any program P, initial memory D and input x it holds that: $\Pr[\mathsf{GEval}^{\widetilde{D}}(\widetilde{P}, \widetilde{D}, \tilde{x}) = P^D(x)] = 1$ where $\widetilde{D} \leftarrow \mathsf{GData}(D, k)$, $(\widetilde{P}, k^{\mathsf{Inp}}) \leftarrow \mathsf{GProg}(P, k, n, t)$ and $\tilde{x} \leftarrow \mathsf{GInput}(x, k^{\mathsf{Inp}})$.

Security. We require that there exists a simulator SIM such that: $(\widetilde{D}, \widetilde{P}, \tilde{x}) \overset{c}{\approx} \mathsf{SIM}(n, T, P, y)$ where $\widetilde{D} \leftarrow \mathsf{GData}(D, k), (\widetilde{P}, k^{\mathsf{Inp}}) \leftarrow \mathsf{GProg}(P, k, n, t)$ and $\tilde{x} \leftarrow \mathsf{GInput}(x, k^{\mathsf{Inp}})$.

2.3 The Details of the GLOS GRAM

In this construction each internal node node is associated with a PRF key r that is encrypted under a PRF key associated with node's parent, and each memory access is translated into a sequence of $d' - 1$ navigation circuits (where d' is the depth of the [11] tree) and a step circuit. During the evaluation, each navigation circuit outputs a translation mapping that allows the evaluator to learn the input label for the next node (either the left or the right child of node) based on the path to the read position in the memory. In addition, the circuit refreshes the PRF key associated with node and computes a new set of PRF values based on this new key to be stored on node. The step circuit finally performs the read or write operation. When proving security via the UMA setting first, this technique incurs a multiplicative overhead of d' on top of the running time of the program since for each memory access the evaluator has to traverse a tree of depth d' and only then perform the actual operation.

Data Garbling: $\widetilde{D} \leftarrow \mathsf{GData}(D, k)$. Let the memory data D be of size n where each block is of size κ, then the garbled memory $\widetilde{D}$ is a binary tree of depth d where the real data is associated with the leaves of the tree. Furthermore, the content of the internal nodes is determined based on computations made using the PRF keys $r^{i,j} \in \{0,1\}^{\kappa}$ where i is the level (or the depth) of the tree and j is the index of that node within the ith level (where the ith level includes 2^i keys). Namely, these keys are used to encrypt the data or the input labels keys for the next CPU-step circuit. In particular at the leaves level, the 2κ bits $D_{j\kappa} \ldots D_{j\kappa+2\kappa-1}$ are encrypted using the key $r^{d-1, \lfloor j/2 \rfloor}$ for every j, where the first κ bits are encrypted with a tag left and the remaining κ bits are encrypted with the tag right. In addition, each value within an internal node is encrypted by the key that is associated with its parent node. The concrete realization requires that each bit of the key $r^{i,j}$ is encrypted under the key $r^{i-1, \lfloor j/2 \rfloor}$.

Program Garbling: $(\widetilde{P}, k^{\mathsf{Inp}}) \leftarrow \mathsf{GProg}(P, k, n, t)$. Each CPU-step in the original program P is performed using d steps in this scheme, where the first $d-1$ steps navigate the tree to the required data block whereas the last step performs the CPU-step of the program on this block and continues with the next CPU-step cycle. In the following, we provide the details of these two sub-circuits navigation and step:

Navigation Circuit. The navigation circuits enable to traverse the tree. Each circuit $nav_{i,j}$ for $i \in [T]$ and $j \in [d]$, denotes the jth circuit within the ith group of circuits that navigates the jth level of the tree while computing the ith CPU-step. This circuit takes as input two PRF keys x, y and a location L. In addition, it is hardwired with the PRF keys s, r' and the labels $\mathsf{lbl}_0^{\mathsf{left}}, \mathsf{lbl}_1^{\mathsf{left}}, \mathsf{lbl}_0^{\mathsf{right}}, \mathsf{lbl}_1^{\mathsf{right}}$ where s is a fresh key that will replace the key associated with the parent of the two nodes associated with keys x and y, and r' is a fresh key that will replace either x or y (depends on the location L). Moreover, the set of labels $\overline{\mathsf{lbl}}_b^z$ corresponds to the input labels for the next navigation circuit with respect to the keys x and y (for $z \in \{\mathsf{left}, \mathsf{right}\}, b \in \{0, 1\}$). The output of $nav_{i,j}$ is the result of the PRF F applied on the pair of keys using the parent key s and a translation table that initiates the evaluation of the next circuit in the ith group of circuits, which is either circuit $nav_{i,j+1}$ or $step_i$. In more details, the $nav_{i,j}$ circuit is defined as follows:

– If $L_j = 0$ (namely, the jth bit of L equals 0), then replace x with r', otherwise replace y with r'. Call the new key pair $\widehat{x}, \widehat{y}$. Encrypt this pair using their parent's key s (hardwired) and output

$$\mathsf{write} = (\mathsf{F}_s(\mathsf{left}, \widehat{x}), \mathsf{F}_s(\mathsf{right}, \widehat{y}), L, \mathsf{state})$$

which implies that these PRF values stored on the nodes associated with keys x and y will replace the PRF values currently written there (obviously we only replace one key amongst (x, y) and thus only replace its associated PRF values).[5] Furthermore, the circuit outputs a translation table that enables the evaluator to obtain the input keys labels for the next level when following the path via the left node. Specifically, the circuit outputs

$$\mathsf{translate} = \{\underbrace{\mathsf{F}_x(\mathsf{left}, 0)}_{\mathsf{padding}} \oplus \underbrace{\mathsf{lbl}_0^{\mathsf{left}}}_{\mathsf{key\ label}}, \mathsf{F}_x(\mathsf{left}, 1) \oplus \mathsf{lbl}^{\mathsf{left}},$$

$$\mathsf{F}_x(\mathsf{right}, 0) \oplus \mathsf{lbl}_0^{\mathsf{right}}, \mathsf{F}_x(\mathsf{right}, 1) \oplus \mathsf{lbl}^{\mathsf{right}}\}$$

Similarly, if $L_j = 1$ then the circuit outputs a translation table using the key y and replaces y with a fresh PRF key.

---

[5] We note that our description is informal. Specifically, the keys are encrypted bit-by-bit implying 2κ ciphertexts, as each key is of size κ.

Step Circuit. The circuit $step_i$ takes as input two data items D_x, D_y along with the location L and the current state of the program. As before, the values r and s, as well as a set of labels $\overline{\mathsf{lbl}}_b^z$ (for $z \in \{\mathsf{left}, \mathsf{right}\}$, $b \in \{0, 1\}$) are hardcoded into this circuit, where r is a fresh key that replaces the key that is associated with the parent of D_x, D_y and s is the PRF key of the root of the tree. Moreover, $\overline{\mathsf{lbl}}_b^z$ are the key labels for the input wires used by the next navigation circuit $nav_{i+1,0}$, which is the first navigation circuit of the next CPU-step. In more details, circuit $step_i$ is defined as follows:

- If $L_{d-1} = 0$ then set $D_{\mathsf{read}} = D_x$ to be the data item that is required for the ith CPU-step. Upon reading D_{read}, the evaluator computes $(\mathsf{state}', L', D_{\mathsf{write}})$ $= \mathsf{C}_{\mathrm{CPU}}^P(\mathsf{state}, D_{\mathsf{read}})$ where state' is the new state of the program, L' is the next location to be read from and D_{write} is the value to overwrite location D_{read} with. Encrypt the updated data items $(D_{\mathsf{write}}, D_y)$ (where D_{write} replaces D_x) with their fresh parent's key r and output $\mathsf{write} = (L, \mathsf{F}_r(\mathsf{left}, D_{\mathsf{write}}), \mathsf{F}_r(\mathsf{right}, D_y))$. Similarly, if $L_{d-1} = 1$ then follows this step with $D_{\mathsf{read}} = D_y$.
- Note that the following circuit $nav_{i+1,0}$ restarts the navigation from layer 1 toward location L' (skipping layer 0). Thus, it expects to be given as input the two PRF keys $r_{1,0}, r_{1,1}$. These keys are encrypted by the root key s which, as mentioned earlier, is hardwired into the current $step_i$ circuit. Thus $step_i$ also outputs a translation table in order to map these keys into the corresponding input labels for the circuit $nav_{i+1,0}$.
- The circuit also outputs (state', L') where state' is the updated state for the next CPU-step and L' is the next location to read from.

3   Gradual GRAM

In this section we define the notion of gradual GRAM where the memory is not garbled separately, but rather occupied via a sequence of insert operations.

Syntax. The new garbled GRAM notion consists of four PPT algorithms $(\mathsf{GProg}, \mathsf{GInputInsertion}, \mathsf{GInput}, \mathsf{GEval})$ defined as follows:

- $(\widetilde{P}, \bar{k}_{\mathrm{INS}}^{\mathsf{Inp}}, \bar{k}_D^{\mathsf{Inp}}, \bar{k}_{\mathrm{RAM}}^{\mathsf{Inp}}, s) \leftarrow \mathsf{GProg}(P, k, n, t)$: Takes as input a program P that is represented as a sequence of T CPU-steps with memory size n and outputs a garbled program $\widetilde{P}$ and input garbling key labels $k_{\mathrm{INS}}^{\mathsf{Inp}}, \bar{k}_D^{\mathsf{Inp}}, \bar{k}_{\mathrm{RAM}}^{\mathsf{Inp}}, s$. The garbled program $\widetilde{P}$ consists of a garbled insertion program $\widetilde{P}_{\mathrm{INS}}$ and a garbled RAM program $\widetilde{P}_{\mathrm{RAM}}$ corresponding to P. The input garbling keys $k_{\mathrm{INS}}^{\mathsf{Inp}}$ correspond to the inputs labels of the first circuit in $\widetilde{P}_{\mathrm{INS}}$ excluding the input labels for the first element from the memory D_1. The key s is the root PRF key generated upon running the garbling insertion program.
- $\{\widetilde{D}_e\}_{e \in [n]} \leftarrow \mathsf{GInputInsertion}(D, \bar{k}_D^{\mathsf{Inp}})$: Takes as input a memory D of size n and insertion garbling keys $\bar{k}_D^{\mathsf{Inp}}$ and outputs a garbled data element $\widetilde{D}_e$ for each $e \in [n]$ (where $\widetilde{D}_e$ is the garbled memory for the eth address).

- $\tilde{k} \leftarrow \mathsf{GInput}(x, \bar{k}_{\mathrm{RAM}}^{\mathsf{Inp}}, s)$: Takes as input an input x, input garbling keys $\bar{k}_{\mathrm{RAM}}^{\mathsf{Inp}}$ and root key s and outputs a garbled input $\tilde{k}$ which is the set of input key labels for the first circuit in garbled RAM program $\widetilde{P}_{\mathrm{RAM}}$.
- $y \leftarrow \mathsf{GEval}(\widetilde{P}, k_{\mathrm{INS}}^{\mathsf{Inp}}, \{\widetilde{D}_e\}_{e \in [n]}, \tilde{k})$: Takes as input a garbled program $\widetilde{P}$, the insertion garbling inputs keys $k_{\mathrm{INS}}^{\mathsf{Inp}}$, garbled data elements $\{\widetilde{D}_e\}_{e \in [n]}$ and a garbled input $\tilde{k}$ and computes the output $y = P^D(x)$.

Correctness. We require that for any program P, memory D and input x it holds that: $\Pr[\mathsf{GEval}(\widetilde{P}, k_{\mathrm{INS}}^{\mathsf{Inp}}, \{\widetilde{D}_e\}_{e \in [n]}, \tilde{k}) = P^D(x)] = 1$ where $(\widetilde{P}, \bar{k}_{\mathrm{INS}}^{\mathsf{Inp}}, \bar{k}_D^{\mathsf{Inp}}, \bar{k}_{\mathrm{RAM}}^{\mathsf{Inp}}, s) \leftarrow \mathsf{GProg}(P, k, n, t)$, $\{\widetilde{D}_e\}_{e \in [n]} \leftarrow \mathsf{GInputInsertion}(D, \bar{k}_D^{\mathsf{Inp}})$ and $\tilde{k} \leftarrow \mathsf{GInput}(x, \bar{k}_{\mathrm{RAM}}^{\mathsf{Inp}}, s)$.

Security. We require that there exists a simulator SIM such that: $(\widetilde{P}, k_{\mathrm{INS}}^{\mathsf{Inp}}, \{\widetilde{D}_e\}_{e \in [n]}, \tilde{k}) \overset{c}{\approx} \mathsf{SIM}(n, T, P, y)$ where $(\widetilde{P}, \bar{k}_{\mathrm{INS}}^{\mathsf{Inp}}, \bar{k}_D^{\mathsf{Inp}}, \bar{k}_{\mathrm{RAM}}^{\mathsf{Inp}}, s) \leftarrow \mathsf{GProg}(P, k, n, t)$, $\{\widetilde{D}_e\}_{e \in [n]} \leftarrow \mathsf{GInputInsertion}(D, \bar{k}_D^{\mathsf{Inp}})$, $\tilde{k} \leftarrow \mathsf{GInput}(x, \bar{k}_{\mathrm{RAM}}^{\mathsf{Inp}}, s)$ and $y = P^D(x)$.

3.1   The Modified GLOS GRAM

We next discuss how to combine the GLOS with Simple/Circuit ORAMs while building the tree gradually, starting with the "Program Garbling" algorithm.

Program Garbling: $(\widetilde{P}, \bar{k}_{\mathrm{INS}}^{\mathsf{Inp}}, \bar{k}_D^{\mathsf{Inp}}, \bar{k}_{\mathrm{RAM}}^{\mathsf{Inp}}, s) \leftarrow \mathsf{GProg}(P, k, n, t)$. In order to combine the GLOS construction with Simple ORAM, we extend GLOS by storing additional information on each non-leaf node. More formally, the root, denoted by $n_{0,0}$, is associated with a PRF key $r^{0,0}$. Moreover, each internal node $n_{i,j}$ is associated with a PRF key $r^{i,j}$ where $i \in \{1, .., d-1\}$ refers to the node's depth whereas $j \in \{0, .., 2^i - 1\}$ refers to its position on its row. Recall that the garbled memory is created gradually during the execution of the garbled program. Consequently, the garbled memory may correspond to an incomplete data structure, implying that upon reading some node it does not have any children. In this case, we should not output a translate table for the missing children or try to rewrite their values. To identify this case, each node will store two additional bits $\mathsf{cdn} = \{\mathsf{cdn}[0], \mathsf{cdn}[1]\}$ which respectively indicate the existence of the left or right children. Namely, $\mathsf{cdn}[0] = 1$ if and only if the specified node has a left child, and similarly for $\mathsf{cdn}[1]$. To conclude, each non-leaf node $n_{i,j}$ stores three types of PRF evaluations computed under its parent's PRF key $r^{i-1, \lfloor j/2 \rfloor}$ (or under the key r^{ROOT} for the case of the root):

1. Navigation information that includes the PRF evaluations over the key $r^{i,j}$ (as in GLOS).
2. ORAM information that includes the PRF evaluations over the bucket $B^{i,j}$ associated with this node. Each such bucket contains d tuples of size U of the form (i, pos, v) where v is the memory content for the address i and pos is the leaf index associated with that address.

3. Information about the children, that includes the PRF evaluations over cdn.

The leaf nodes, denoted by $n_{d,j}$ for $j \in [0, n-1]$, only contain the PRF evaluations over the bucket $B^{d,j}$.

Our garbling procedure has four subroutines: (1) reading from the root, (2) reading from the internal nodes, (3) reading from a leaf and (4) the final circuit. Each subroutine outputs a translation mapping for the children of the node it is reading from (where at the leaf level the mapping is for the root), which allows to extract the input labels for the next circuit on the navigation path (where in case a child does not exist, then the translation mapping outputs labels corresponding to 0). We denote the set of input labels corresponding to a circuit in our construction, $\mathsf{type} \in \{\mathsf{left}, \mathsf{right}, \mathsf{root}\}$

$$\{\overline{\mathsf{lbl}_b^{\mathsf{type}}}\}_{b \in \{0,1\}} = \Big(\underbrace{\{\mathsf{lbl}_b^{\mathsf{type},0,k}\}_{b \in \{0,1\}, k \in [\kappa]}}_{\text{navigation labels (GLOS)}},$$

$$\underbrace{\{\mathsf{lbl}_b^{\mathsf{type},h,u}\}_{b \in \{0,1\}, h \in [d], u \in [U]}}_{\text{bucket labels}}, \underbrace{\{\mathsf{lbl}_b^{\mathsf{type},c}\}_{b \in \{0,1\}, c \in [0,1]}}_{\text{children's labels}} \Big)$$

Procedure trans

Procedure trans outputs the translation mapping for some node node.
Input.

- A PRF key r of node's parent.
- A parameter type $\in \{\mathsf{left}, \mathsf{right}, \mathsf{root}\}$.
- A set of input labels $\{\mathsf{lbl}_0^{\mathsf{type},0,k}, \mathsf{lbl}^{\mathsf{type},0,k}\}_{k \in [\kappa]}$ for a PRF key.
- A set of input labels $\{\mathsf{lbl}_0^{\mathsf{type},h,u}, \mathsf{lbl}^{\mathsf{type},h,u}\}_{h \in [d], u \in [U]}$ for a bucket.
- A pair of input labels $\{\mathsf{lbl}_0^{\mathsf{type},c}, \mathsf{lbl}^{\mathsf{type},c}\}_{c \in [0,1]}$ for cdn.

Output.

- Return

translate =

$$\Big\{ \mathsf{F}_r(\mathsf{type}, 0, k, 0) \oplus \underbrace{\mathsf{lbl}_0^{\mathsf{type},0,k}}_{\substack{\text{padding that is stored} \\ \text{on the GRAM node node}}}, \mathsf{F}_r(\mathsf{type}, 0, k, 1) \oplus \underbrace{\mathsf{lbl}^{\mathsf{type},0,k}}_{\substack{\text{input labels for the} \\ \text{circuit visiting node}}} \Big\}_{k \in [\kappa]}$$

$$\big\{ \mathsf{F}_r(\mathsf{type}, h, u, 0) \oplus \mathsf{lbl}_0^{\mathsf{type},h,u}, \mathsf{F}_r(\mathsf{type}, h, u, 1) \oplus \mathsf{lbl}^{\mathsf{type},h,u} \big\}_{h \in [d], u \in [U]}$$

$$\big\{ \mathsf{F}_r(\mathsf{type}, c, 0) \oplus \mathsf{lbl}_0^{\mathsf{type},c} \big\}_{c \in [0,1]}$$

$$\big\{ \mathsf{F}_r(\mathsf{type}, c, 1) \oplus \mathsf{lbl}^{\mathsf{type},c} \big\}_{c \in [0,1]}$$

Fig. 1. The translation mapping procedure.

An important building block of these subroutines is the procedure trans that outputs a translation mapping of a node. This procedure obtains the input labels of the next circuit and outputs a translate table for the PRF values associated with this node. We present its details in Fig. 1.

An Overview of the Circuits. The program garbling procedure contains four different types of circuits: C_{ROOT} that enables to read from the root, C_{INTER} that enables to read from an internal (non-leaf and non-root) node, C_{LEAF} that enables to read from a leaf node and a concluding circuit C_{FINAL}.

As in the GLOS construction each internal circuit C_{INTER} takes two PRF keys r^{left}, r^{right} associated with two adjacent nodes $(n_{i,j}, n_{i,j+1})$ in some level i and an auxiliary input aux which includes additional information such as the state state and the index level. The circuit is also given the buckets B^{left} and B^{right} stored on these nodes, and the values cdn^{left} and cdn^{right} corresponding to the children's information of each node. Finally, the circuit is hardwired with fresh PRF keys r', r and the input labels to the next circuit $\{\overline{lbl_b^{left}, lbl_b^{right}}\}_{b \in \{0,1\}}$.

Upon given these inputs, each circuit runs a CPU-step of the Simple ORAM which uses one of the buckets $\{B^{left}, B^{right}\}$ according to the reading location stored at aux and outputs an updated bucket B^{write}. It further outputs a tuple (aux', write, translate) where aux' denote an updated auxiliary information, write consists of the values to be written into nodes $n_{i,j}, n_{i,j+1}$ and translate consists of the translation mapping for the two children in the next level on the navigation path using the labels $\{\overline{lbl_b^{left}, lbl_b^{right}}\}_{b \in \{0,1\}}$. Moreover, the write output contains PRF evaluation under the fresh key r' which replaces the key associated with the parent of the nodes $n_{i,j}, n_{i,j+1}$. The second fresh key r will replace one of the keys r^{left}, r^{right} which will be determined according to the reading location. Namely, the PRF evaluations will be computed now over the new key r and the other old key associated with the node in the other direction. Next, the updated bucket B^{write} is written to the appropriate node together with the updated values cdn^{left} and cdn^{right}.

The three other circuits are described similarly to the internal circuit with the following modifications. First, the input to the root circuit includes a single PRF key $r^{0,0}$, a bucket $B^{0,0}$ and $cdn^{0,0}$. Furthermore, the leaf circuit is hardwired with the input labels of the next root circuit their output translate refers to the root, whereas the final circuit is not hardwired with any input labels. In addition, the later two circuits do not take any PRF keys. For the following formal description, we use the notation $B_u^{h,write}$ denoting the bit u within the tuple h in the bucket B^{write} and the notation pos[i] denotes the bit i in the leaf pos (which contains d bits enumerated from 1 to d). We continue with the detailed descriptions of the garbling program subroutines and circuits functionalities.

– **Reading from the root (circuit C_{ROOT}).** This circuit takes as input a key associated with the root $r^{0,0}$, a bucket $B^{0,0}$, an auxiliary input aux = {state, t, $i, i^{read}, v^{read}, v^{write}$} and a pair of bits cdn. For the first $t < n \cdot \log n$ steps, the circuit also obtains i^{insert}, v^{insert} (per entry from the real memory data

D). In addition, the circuit is hardwired with the PRF keys s, r' and labels $\{\mathsf{lbl}_b^{\mathsf{left}}, \mathsf{lbl}_b^{\mathsf{right}}\}_{b \in \{0,1\}}$ where s and r' are fresh PRF keys that will respectively replace the keys r^{ROOT} and $r^{0,0}$. In more details,

1. Initialize pos, $B^{\mathsf{temp}} = \mathsf{NULL}$ and set $B^{\mathsf{read}} = B^{0,0}, r^{\mathsf{trans}} = r^{0,0}$.
2. If $t = 0$ set mode = Read/Write. Else set mode $= 1 - \mathsf{mode}$.[6]
3. If $t < n \cdot \log n$ run

$$(\mathsf{pos}, B^{\mathsf{write}}, B^{\mathsf{temp}}) \leftarrow \underbrace{C_{\mathrm{CPU}}^{P_{\mathrm{INS}}'}(i^{\mathsf{insert}}, v^{\mathsf{insert}}, i, \mathsf{pos}, B^{\mathsf{read}}, B^{\mathsf{temp}})}_{\text{Simple ORAM insertion}}$$

else, run

$$(\mathsf{state}', \mathsf{pos}, B^{\mathsf{write}}, B^{\mathsf{temp}}, i^{\mathsf{read}}, v^{\mathsf{read}}, v^{\mathsf{write}})$$
$$\leftarrow \underbrace{C_{\mathrm{CPU}}^{P'}(\mathsf{state}, i, \mathsf{mode}, \mathsf{pos}, B^{\mathsf{read}}, B^{\mathsf{temp}}, i^{\mathsf{read}}, v^{\mathsf{read}}, v^{\mathsf{write}})}_{\text{Simple ORAM read/write instruction for the compiled P'}}$$

4. Set $\mathsf{transLeft} = \mathsf{trans}(r^{\mathsf{trans}}, \mathsf{left}, \{\mathsf{lbl}_b^{\mathsf{left}}\}_{b \in \{0,1\}})$.
5. Set $\mathsf{transRight} = \mathsf{trans}(r^{\mathsf{trans}}, \mathsf{right}, \{\mathsf{lbl}_b^{\mathsf{right}}\}_{b \in \{0,1\}})$.
6. Set

$$\left\{ \begin{array}{ll} \mathsf{translate} = \overline{\mathsf{lbl}_0^{\mathsf{left}}} \parallel \overline{\mathsf{lbl}_0^{\mathsf{right}}}, & \text{if cdn} = 00; \\ \mathsf{translate} = \overline{\mathsf{lbl}_0^{\mathsf{left}}} \parallel \mathsf{transRight}, & \text{if cdn} = 01; \\ \mathsf{translate} = \mathsf{transLeft} \parallel \overline{\mathsf{lbl}_0^{\mathsf{right}}}, & \text{if cdn} = 10; \\ \mathsf{translate} = \mathsf{transLeft} \parallel \mathsf{transRight}, & \text{if cdn} = 11; \end{array} \right\}.$$

7. Below, IsOtherNode contains a one-bit flag to indicate the existence of a node that does not reside on the reading path. The next circuit uses IsOtherNode in order to tell whether to rewrite the other node that is not on the path. Specifically, if $\mathsf{pos}[i+1] = 0$ then set $\mathsf{cdn}[0] = 1$ and IsOtherNode $= \mathsf{cdn}[1]$, else set $\mathsf{cdn}[1] = 1$ and IsOtherNode $= \mathsf{cdn}[0]$.
8. Set

$$\mathsf{write} = \Big(\mathsf{root}, \{F_s(\mathsf{root}, 0, k, r_k')\}_{k \in [\kappa]} \parallel \{F_s(\mathsf{root}, h, u, B_u^{h, \mathsf{write}})\}_{h \in [d], u \in [U]}$$
$$\parallel F_s(\mathsf{root}, 0, \mathsf{cdn}[0]) \parallel F_{r'}(\mathsf{root}, 1, \mathsf{cdn}[1]) \Big)$$

9. Output:

$$\mathsf{aux}' = (\{\mathsf{state}', \mathsf{IsOtherNode}, \mathsf{pos}, t+1, 1, \mathsf{mode}, B^{\mathsf{temp}}, i^{\mathsf{read}}, v^{\mathsf{read}}, v^{\mathsf{write}}\},$$
$$\mathsf{translate}, \mathsf{write}).$$

- **Reading from an internal node (circuit C_{INTER}).** This circuit takes as input two PRF keys r^{left} and r^{right} that are associated with the two nodes $(n_{i,j}, n_{i,j+1})$, their corresponding buckets B^{left} and B^{right}, an auxiliary input

---

[6] We use the variable mode to interchange between Read/Write and Eviction. We abuse notation and denote by $1 - \mathsf{mode}$ the "opposite" (namely, the other) value of mode.

$\mathsf{aux} = \{t, i, \mathsf{state}, \mathsf{IsOtherNode}, \mathsf{pos}, \mathsf{mode}, B^{\mathsf{temp}}, i^{\mathsf{read}}, v^{\mathsf{read}}, v^{\mathsf{write}}\}$ and the two values $\mathsf{cdn}^{\mathsf{left}}$ and $\mathsf{cdn}^{\mathsf{right}}$. In addition, the circuit is hardwired with the PRF keys r', r, and labels $\{\mathsf{lbl}_b^{\mathsf{left}}, \mathsf{lbl}_b^{\mathsf{right}}\}_{b \in \{0,1\}}$ where r' is the key associated with the parent's node of $(n_{i,j}, n_{i,j+1})$ and r is a fresh key that will replace either r^{left} or r^{right} (depends on the value pos). In more details,

1. Deciding whether the next move is left or right based on the next position bit. Namely, if $\mathsf{pos}[i] = 0$ then set $\mathsf{type} = \mathsf{left}$, else $\mathsf{type} = \mathsf{right}$. Also set $B^{\mathsf{read}} = B^{\mathsf{type}}, r^{\mathsf{trans}} = r^{\mathsf{type}}, \mathsf{cdn} = \mathsf{cdn}^{\mathsf{type}}$.

2. Initializing $i^{\mathsf{insert}}, v^{\mathsf{insert}} = \mathsf{NULL}$ (since these inputs are only used at the root level).

3. Run Steps 3–6 from the procedure for $\mathrm{C}_{\mathrm{ROOT}}$.

4. If $\mathsf{pos}[i + 1] = 0$ then set $\mathsf{cdn}^{\mathsf{type}}[0] = 1$ and $\mathsf{IsOtherNode} = \mathsf{cdn}^{\mathsf{type}}[1]$, else $\mathsf{cdn}^{\mathsf{type}}[1] = 1$ and $\mathsf{IsOtherNode} = \mathsf{cdn}^{\mathsf{type}}[0]$.

5. Set

$$\mathsf{write} = \Big(\mathsf{type}, \{\mathsf{F}_{r'}(\mathsf{type}, 0, k, r_k)\}_{k \in [\kappa]} \,\|\, \{\mathsf{F}_{r'}(\mathsf{type}, h, u, B_u^{h,\mathsf{write}})\}_{h \in [d], u \in [U]}$$
$$\|\,\mathsf{F}_{r'}(\mathsf{type}, 0, \mathsf{cdn}^{\mathsf{type}}[0]) \,\|\, \mathsf{F}_{r'}(\mathsf{type}, 1, \mathsf{cdn}^{\mathsf{type}}[1])\Big)$$

6. Set also the output writing values for the opposite direction, which is not on the reading path.[7]

$$\mathsf{writeOpp} = \Big(\overline{\mathsf{type}}, \{\mathsf{F}_{r'}(\overline{\mathsf{type}}, 0, k, r_k^{\overline{\mathsf{type}}})\}_{k \in [\kappa]}$$
$$\|\, \{\mathsf{F}_{r'}(\overline{\mathsf{type}}, h, u, B_u^{h,\overline{\mathsf{type}}})\}_{h \in [d], u \in [U]}$$
$$\|\, \mathsf{F}_{r'}(\overline{\mathsf{type}}, 0, \mathsf{cdn}^{\overline{\mathsf{type}}}[0]) \,\|\, \mathsf{F}_{r'}(\overline{\mathsf{type}}, 1, \mathsf{cdn}^{\overline{\mathsf{type}}}[1])\Big)$$

7. If $\mathsf{IsOtherNode} = 1$ then set $\mathsf{write} = \mathsf{write} \,\|\, \mathsf{writeOpp}$.

8. Output:

$$\mathsf{aux}' = (\mathsf{state}, \mathsf{IsOtherNode}, \mathsf{pos}, t + 1, i + 1, \mathsf{mode}, B^{\mathsf{temp}}, i^{\mathsf{read}}, v^{\mathsf{read}},$$
$$v^{\mathsf{write}}, \mathsf{translate}, \mathsf{write}).$$

– **Reading from a leaf (circuit $\mathrm{C}_{\mathrm{LEAF}}$).** This circuit takes as input two buckets B^{left} and B^{right} that are associated with the two nodes $(n_{i,j}, n_{i,j+1})$ and an auxiliary input

$$\mathsf{aux} = \{t, i, \mathsf{state}, \mathsf{mode}, \mathsf{IsOtherNode}, \mathsf{pos}, B^{\mathsf{temp}}, i^{\mathsf{read}}, v^{\mathsf{read}}, v^{\mathsf{write}}\}.$$

In addition, the circuit is hardwired with the PRF keys r', s and the labels $\{\mathsf{lbl}_b^{\mathsf{root}}\}_{b \in \{0,1\}}$, where r' is the key associated with the parent's node of $(n_{i,j}, n_{i,j+1})$ and s is the key of the parent of $r^{0,0}$. In more details,

1. If $\mathsf{pos}[i - 1] = 0$ then set $\mathsf{type} = \mathsf{left}$, else $\mathsf{type} = \mathsf{right}$. Also set $B^{\mathsf{read}} = B^{\mathsf{type}}$.

---

[7] The syntax $\overline{\mathsf{type}}$ refers to the opposite of the variable type. For example, if $\mathsf{type} = \mathsf{left}$ then $\overline{\mathsf{type}} = \mathsf{right}$.

2. Set $i^{\mathsf{insert}}, v^{\mathsf{insert}} = \mathrm{NULL}$.
3. Run Step 3 from the procedure for C_{ROOT}.
4. Set $\mathsf{translate} = \mathsf{trans}\Big(s, \mathsf{root}, \{\overline{\mathsf{lbl}_b^{\mathsf{root}}}\}_{b \in \{0,1\}}\Big)$
5. Set $\mathsf{write} = \Big(\mathsf{type}, \{F_{r'}(\mathsf{type}, h, u, B_u^{h,\mathsf{write}})\}_{h \in [d], u \in [U]}\Big)$
6. Set
$$\mathsf{writeOpp} = \Big(\overline{\mathsf{type}}, \{F_{r'}(\mathsf{type}, h, u, B_u^{h,\overline{\mathsf{type}}})\}_{h \in [d], k \in [U]}\Big)$$

7. If $\mathsf{IsOtherNode} = 1$ then set $\mathsf{write} = \mathsf{write} \,\|\, \mathsf{writeOpp}$.
8. Output:

$$\mathsf{aux'} = (\{\mathsf{state}, \mathsf{pos}, t + 1, 0, \mathsf{mode}, i^{\mathsf{read}}, v^{\mathsf{read}}, v^{\mathsf{write}}\},$$

$$\mathsf{translate}, \mathsf{write})$$

- **The final step (circuit C_{FINAL}).** The circuit takes as input two buckets B^{left} and B^{right} that are associated with the two nodes $(n_{i,j}, n_{i,j+1})$ and an auxiliary input $\mathsf{aux} = \{t, \mathsf{state}, \mathsf{IsOtherNode}, \mathsf{pos}, B^{\mathsf{temp}}, i^{\mathsf{read}}, v^{\mathsf{read}}, v^{\mathsf{write}}\}$. In addition, the circuit is hardwired with a PRF key r' where r' is the key associated with the parent's node of $(n_{i,j}, n_{i,j+1})$. In more details,
  1. Run Steps 1–3 and 5–7 from the procedure for C_{LEAF}.
  2. Output: $(\mathsf{state'}, \mathsf{write})$.

3.2   The Complete GRAM Construction

Summarizing the descriptions of the above four subroutines, the final garbling procedure consists of multiple instances of these circuits. More specifically, our complete garbling program procedure consists of two sub-procedures: the insertion program garbling denoted by $\mathsf{GProg}_{\mathrm{INS}}$ and the garbling RAM program P denoted by $\mathsf{GProg}_{\mathrm{RAM}}$. Each of them call algorithm GCircuit in order to garble each circuit. Note that each circuit is hardwired with the input labels for the next circuit and we therefore need to garble the circuits in the opposite order.

In the insertion garbled program $\mathsf{GProg}_{\mathrm{INS}}$, the program only follows the Eviction procedure as defined in the Simple ORAM. Therefore, for each memory entry D_e for $e \in [n]$, the garbled RAM traverses the tree from the root to some leaf implying that it will consist of one instance of C_{ROOT}, $(d-1)$ instances of C_{INTER} and one instance of C_{LEAF}, where in the last step one instance of C_{LEAF} is replaced with an instance of C_{FINAL}. This program garbling outputs a set of garbled circuits denoted by $\{\widetilde{C}_{\tau,i}\}$ where $\tau \in [n]$ is the time step and $i \in [0, d]$ is the level in the tree. As in the GLOS construction, we parse the inputs labels of each garbled circuit $\widetilde{C}_{\tau,i}$ as $\overline{\mathsf{lbl}}^{\tau,i} = (\overline{\mathsf{lbl}}^{\tau,i,\mathsf{read}}, \overline{\mathsf{lbl}}^{\tau,i,\mathsf{aux}})$, where the former set of labels correspond to the inputs $r^{\mathsf{left}}, r^{\mathsf{right}}, B^{\mathsf{left}}, B^{\mathsf{right}}, \mathsf{cdn}^{\mathsf{left}}$ and $\mathsf{cdn}^{\mathsf{right}}$ (that should be read from the memory) and are embedded in the previous circuit. Whereas the later set of labels correspond to the data elements from D and other information that depends on the input such as the state.

On the other hand, for each memory access in the garbled RAM program $\mathsf{GProg}_{\mathrm{RAM}}$, the program traverses the tree twice, reading two root-to-leaf paths (one in Read/Write mode and another in Eviction mode) implying that the garbled program will consist of two instances of C_{ROOT}, $2 \cdot (d-1)$ instances of C_{INTER} and two instances of C_{LEAF}, where in the last step one instance of C_{LEAF} is replaced with an instance of C_{FINAL}. The garbling RAM program GProg_{RAM} outputs a set of garbled circuits denoted by $\{\widetilde{C}_{\tau,p,i}\}$ where $\tau \in [n+1, n+T]$ is a RAM step, $p \in \{0,1\}$ indicates whether this is the first or the second root-to-leaf pass and $i \in [0,d]$ is the tree level. Note that the same circuits are garbled for both paths where the functionality differs as a function of the mode.

Program Garbling GProg. Informally, the garbling procedure $\mathsf{GProg}(P, k, n, t)$ proceeds as follows:

1. Run $(\widetilde{P}_{INS}, k_{INS}^{Inp}, \bar{k}_{D}^{Inp}, s) \leftarrow \mathsf{GProg}_{INS}(k, n)$.
2. Run $(\widetilde{P}_{RAM}, \bar{k}_{RAM}^{Inp}) \leftarrow \mathsf{GProg}_{RAM}(P, k, n, t)$.
3. Output $(\widetilde{P} = \{\widetilde{P}_{INS}, \widetilde{P}_{RAM}\}, k_{INS}^{Inp}, \bar{k}_{D}^{Inp}, \bar{k}_{RAM}^{Inp}, s)$.

Data Elements Garbling $\{\widetilde{D}_e\}_{e \in [n]} \leftarrow \mathsf{GInputInsertion}(D, \bar{k}_{D}^{Inp})$. This algorithm outputs input labels for the elements in D, namely for each $\{D_e\}_{e \in [n]}$. These labels will constitute the inputs labels to the first instance of $\widetilde{C}_{ROOT}$ in the sequence of insertion circuits. Specifically, upon given the inputs $\left(D, \bar{k}_{D}^{Inp} = \{\overline{\mathsf{lbl}}^{e,0,i^{insert},v^{insert}}\}_{e \in [n]}\right)$, the algorithm $\mathsf{GInputInsertion}$ outputs

$$\{\widetilde{D}_e\} = \left(\{\mathsf{lbl}_{e_\gamma}^{e,0,i_\gamma^{insert}}\}_{\gamma \in [\log n]}, \{\mathsf{lbl}_{D_{e_\beta}}^{e,0,v_\beta^{insert}}\}_{\beta \in [U']}\right), \quad 1 \le e \le n$$

where e_γ is the γth bit of the index e, D_{e_β} is the βth bit in the element D_e and U' is the size of an element in D.

Input Garbling $\tilde{k} \leftarrow \mathsf{GInput}(x, \bar{k}_{RAM}^{Inp}, s)$. This algorithm outputs the input labels for the garbled program $\widetilde{P}_{RAM}$. Upon given the inputs $(x, \bar{k}_{RAM}^{Inp} = \{\overline{\mathsf{lbl}}^{root}, \overline{\mathsf{lbl}}^{aux}\}, s)$, the algorithm proceed as follows:

– Set
$$\mathsf{translate} = \begin{bmatrix} \{F_s(\mathsf{root}, 0, k, 0) \oplus \mathsf{lbl}_0^{root,0,k}, \\ F_s(\mathsf{root}, 0, k, 1) \oplus \mathsf{lbl}^{root,h,k}\}_{k \in [\kappa]} \\ \{F_s(\mathsf{root}, h, u, 0) \oplus \mathsf{lbl}_0^{root,h,u}, \\ F_s(\mathsf{root}, h, u, 1) \oplus \mathsf{lbl}^{root,h,u}\}_{h \in [d], u \in [U]} \\ \{F_s(\mathsf{root}, c, 0) \oplus \mathsf{lbl}_0^{root,c}\}_{c \in [0,1]} \\ \{F_s(\mathsf{root}, c, 1) \oplus \mathsf{lbl}_0^{root,c}\}_{c \in [0,1]} \end{bmatrix}$$

– Set $\tilde{x} = \{\mathsf{lbl}_{x_\sigma}^{aux,state_\sigma}\}_{\sigma \in [|x|]}$ where x_σ is the σth bit of x.
– Set $\overline{\mathsf{lbl}}^{aux'} = \overline{\mathsf{lbl}}^{aux} / \overline{\mathsf{lbl}}^{aux,state}$ (the auxiliary labels apart from state).
– Output $\tilde{k} = \{\mathsf{translate}, \tilde{x}, \overline{\mathsf{lbl}}_0^{aux'}\}$.

Garbled Evaluation $y \leftarrow \mathsf{GEval}(\widetilde{P}, k_{INS}^{Inp}, \{\widetilde{D}_e\}_{e \in [n]}, \tilde{k})$. This algorithm sequentially evaluates the garbled circuits created by GProg and calls procedure Eval in order to evaluate the underlying garbled circuits.

We conclude with the following theorem which we prove in the full version.

Theorem 31. *Assuming one-way functions, then our construction is secure garbled RAM scheme (cf. Sect. 2.2).*

An Overview of the Proof of Theorem 31. In this proof we construct a simulator that outputs a sequence of simulated garbled circuits generated from the end to start. Since the simulator does not know the real input values (D, x) it writes random values to the memory (rather than PRF evaluations). Moreover, by definition, the simulator knows only one label per input wire and hence cannot compute the complete translate table as required by the garbling program. It therefore uses random values for the missing labels in the translation mapping. Note that, as in the real execution, the values written to the memory must be consistent with the translate table of some future circuit. Namely, if the value $\alpha \oplus \mathsf{lbl}$ is output as part of the translate table of circuit $\tilde{C}^\tau$, then the value α should be written to the same location by the last circuit $\tilde{C}^{\tau'}, \tau' < \tau$ that writes to that location. To address these limitations, the simulator maintains an updated table that contains all the values output as part of the translate table. The simulator also keeps a flag table in order to avoid accessing nodes that do not exist yet. Intuitively, in order to argue that the simulated output is indistinguishable from the real distribution, we first define a hybrid experiment **Hyb** for which the simulator access the real memory access locations. We then prove that the simulation and the hybrid experiment are indistinguishable, relying on the security of the Simple ORAM. Next, we follow the proof outline of GLOS and reduce security to the PRF security and privacy of garbled circuits.

Efficiency. In our construction, the size of the garbled program, as well as the time it takes to create and evaluate it is $O((n+T) \cdot \mathsf{poly}(\kappa, U \cdot \tilde{B}))$ where an ORAM bucket contains $\tilde{B}$ tuples of size U (where in the Simple ORAM $\tilde{B} = O(\log n)$ whereas in the Circuit ORAM $\tilde{B} = O(1)$ for internal nodes and $O(\log n)$ stash size). Moreover, the overall running time of GProg and GInputInsertion, as well as the running time of GEval is $O((n + T) \cdot \log n)$. Note that there is a tradeoff between the unit size that is read per access and the overall number of accesses per original access. The analyze of most tree-based ORAMs is based on reading a single memory unit per access which implies that the running time is $O(\log^2 n)$ per one original access. On the other hand, when reading the whole bucket in a single access as we analyze above, the overhead per one original access is $O(\log n)$ but requires garbling larger CPU-steps circuits. A similar analysis holds for the [11] GRAM as well.

References

1. Afshar, A., Hu, Z., Mohassel, P., Rosulek, M.: How to efficiently evaluate RAM programs with malicious security. In: Oswald, E., Fischlin, M. (eds.) EUROCRYPT 2015. LNCS, vol. 9056, pp. 702–729. Springer, Heidelberg (2015). https://doi.org/10.1007/978-3-662-46800-5_27
2. Beaver, D., Micali, S., Rogaway, P.: The round complexity of secure protocols (extended abstract). In: STOC, pp. 503–513 (1990)

3. Chung, K.-M., Pass, R.: A simple ORAM. IACR Cryptology ePrint Archive 2013/243 (2013)
4. Cook, S.A., Reckhow, R.A.: Time-bounded random access machines. In: STOC, pp. 73–80 (1972)
5. Damgård, I., Keller, M., Larraia, E., Pastro, V., Scholl, P., Smart, N.P.: Practical covertly secure MPC for dishonest majority – or: breaking the SPDZ limits. In: Crampton, J., Jajodia, S., Mayes, K. (eds.) ESORICS 2013. LNCS, vol. 8134, pp. 1–18. Springer, Heidelberg (2013). https://doi.org/10.1007/978-3-642-40203-6_1
6. Damgård, I., Meldgaard, S., Nielsen, J.B.: Perfectly secure oblivious RAM without random oracles. In: Ishai, Y. (ed.) TCC 2011. LNCS, vol. 6597, pp. 144–163. Springer, Heidelberg (2011). https://doi.org/10.1007/978-3-642-19571-6_10
7. Damgård, I., Pastro, V., Smart, N., Zakarias, S.: Multiparty computation from somewhat homomorphic encryption. In: Safavi-Naini, R., Canetti, R. (eds.) CRYPTO 2012. LNCS, vol. 7417, pp. 643–662. Springer, Heidelberg (2012). https://doi.org/10.1007/978-3-642-32009-5_38
8. Doerner, J., Shelat, A.: Scaling ORAM for secure computation. In: CCS, pp. 523–535 (2017)
9. Garg, S., Gupta, D., Miao, P., Pandey, O.: Secure multiparty RAM computation in constant rounds. In: Hirt, M., Smith, A. (eds.) TCC 2016. LNCS, vol. 9985, pp. 491–520. Springer, Heidelberg (2016). https://doi.org/10.1007/978-3-662-53641-4_19
10. Garg, S., Lu, S., Ostrovsky, R.: Black-box garbled RAM. In: FOCS, pp. 210–229 (2015)
11. Garg, S., Lu, S., Ostrovsky, R., Scafuro, A.: Garbled RAM from one-way functions. In: STOC, pp. 449–458 (2015)
12. Gentry, C., Goldman, K.A., Halevi, S., Julta, C., Raykova, M., Wichs, D.: Optimizing ORAM and using it efficiently for secure computation. In: De Cristofaro, E., Wright, M. (eds.) PETS 2013. LNCS, vol. 7981, pp. 1–18. Springer, Heidelberg (2013). https://doi.org/10.1007/978-3-642-39077-7_1
13. Gentry, C., Halevi, S., Lu, S., Ostrovsky, R., Raykova, M., Wichs, D.: Garbled RAM revisited. In: Nguyen, P.Q., Oswald, E. (eds.) EUROCRYPT 2014. LNCS, vol. 8441, pp. 405–422. Springer, Heidelberg (2014). https://doi.org/10.1007/978-3-642-55220-5_23
14. Goldreich, O.: Towards a theory of software protection and simulation by oblivious rams. In: STOC, pp. 182–194 (1987)
15. Goldreich, O., Goldwasser, S., Micali, S.: How to construct random functions. J. ACM 33(4), 792–807 (1986)
16. Goldreich, O., Ostrovsky, R.: Software protection and simulation on oblivious rams. J. ACM 43(3), 431–473 (1996)
17. Gordon, S.D., et al.: Secure two-party computation in sublinear (amortized) time. In: CCS, pp. 513–524 (2012)
18. Gueron, S., Lindell, Y., Nof, A., Pinkas, B.: Fast garbling of circuits under standard assumptions. In: CCS, pp. 567–578 (2015)
19. Hazay, C., Ishai, Y., Venkitasubramaniam, M.: Actively secure garbled circuits with constant communication overhead in the plain model. In: Kalai, Y., Reyzin, L. (eds.) TCC 2017. LNCS, vol. 10678, pp. 3–39. Springer, Cham (2017). https://doi.org/10.1007/978-3-319-70503-3_1
20. Hazay, C., Scholl, P., Soria-Vazquez, E.: Low cost constant round MPC combining BMR and oblivious transfer. In: Takagi, T., Peyrin, T. (eds.) ASIACRYPT 2017. LNCS, vol. 10624, pp. 598–628. Springer, Cham (2017). https://doi.org/10.1007/978-3-319-70694-8_21

21. Hazay, C., Yanai, A.: Constant-round maliciously secure two-party computation in the RAM model. In: Hirt, M., Smith, A. (eds.) TCC 2016. LNCS, vol. 9985, pp. 521–553. Springer, Heidelberg (2016). https://doi.org/10.1007/978-3-662-53641-4_20
22. Ishai, Y., Kushilevitz, E., Ostrovsky, R., Prabhakaran, M., Sahai, A.: Efficient non-interactive secure computation. In: Paterson, K.G. (ed.) EUROCRYPT 2011. LNCS, vol. 6632, pp. 406–425. Springer, Heidelberg (2011). https://doi.org/10.1007/978-3-642-20465-4_23
23. Keller, M., Scholl, P.: Efficient, oblivious data structures for MPC. In: Sarkar, P., Iwata, T. (eds.) ASIACRYPT 2014. LNCS, vol. 8874, pp. 506–525. Springer, Heidelberg (2014). https://doi.org/10.1007/978-3-662-45608-8_27
24. Keller, M., Yanai, A.: Efficient maliciously secure multiparty computation for RAM. In: Nielsen, J.B., Rijmen, V. (eds.) EUROCRYPT 2018. LNCS, vol. 10822, pp. 91–124. Springer, Cham (2018). https://doi.org/10.1007/978-3-319-78372-7_4
25. Kolesnikov, V., Schneider, T.: Improved garbled circuit: free XOR gates and applications. In: Aceto, L., Damgård, I., Goldberg, L.A., Halldórsson, M.M., Ingólfsdóttir, A., Walukiewicz, I. (eds.) ICALP 2008. LNCS, vol. 5126, pp. 486–498. Springer, Heidelberg (2008). https://doi.org/10.1007/978-3-540-70583-3_40
26. Lindell, Y., Pinkas, B.: An efficient protocol for secure two-party computation in the presence of malicious adversaries. In: Naor, M. (ed.) EUROCRYPT 2007. LNCS, vol. 4515, pp. 52–78. Springer, Heidelberg (2007). https://doi.org/10.1007/978-3-540-72540-4_4
27. Lindell, Y., Pinkas, B., Smart, N.P., Yanai, A.: Efficient constant round multi-party computation combining BMR and SPDZ. In: Gennaro, R., Robshaw, M. (eds.) CRYPTO 2015. LNCS, vol. 9216, pp. 319–338. Springer, Heidelberg (2015). https://doi.org/10.1007/978-3-662-48000-7_16
28. Liu, C., Huang, Y., Shi, E., Katz, J., Hicks, M.W.: Automating efficient RAM-model secure computation. In: IEEE Symposium on Security and Privacy, pp. 623–638 (2014)
29. Lu, S., Ostrovsky, R.: How to garble RAM programs? In: Johansson, T., Nguyen, P.Q. (eds.) EUROCRYPT 2013. LNCS, vol. 7881, pp. 719–734. Springer, Heidelberg (2013). https://doi.org/10.1007/978-3-642-38348-9_42
30. Miao, P.: Cut-and-choose for garbled RAM. IACR Cryptology ePrint Archive 2016/907 (2016)
31. Moataz, T., Mayberry, T., Blass, E.-O., Chan, A.H.: Resizable tree-based oblivious RAM. In: Böhme, R., Okamoto, T. (eds.) FC 2015. LNCS, vol. 8975, pp. 147–167. Springer, Heidelberg (2015). https://doi.org/10.1007/978-3-662-47854-7_9
32. Mohassel, P., Rosulek, M.: Non-interactive secure 2PC in the offline/online and batch settings. In: Coron, J.-S., Nielsen, J.B. (eds.) EUROCRYPT 2017. LNCS, vol. 10212, pp. 425–455. Springer, Cham (2017). https://doi.org/10.1007/978-3-319-56617-7_15
33. Nielsen, J.B., Nordholt, P.S., Orlandi, C., Burra, S.S.: A new approach to practical active-secure two-party computation. In: Safavi-Naini, R., Canetti, R. (eds.) CRYPTO 2012. LNCS, vol. 7417, pp. 681–700. Springer, Heidelberg (2012). https://doi.org/10.1007/978-3-642-32009-5_40
34. Nielsen, J.B., Orlandi, C.: LEGO for two-party secure computation. In: Reingold, O. (ed.) TCC 2009. LNCS, vol. 5444, pp. 368–386. Springer, Heidelberg (2009). https://doi.org/10.1007/978-3-642-00457-5_22
35. Ostrovsky, R.: Efficient computation on oblivious RAMs. In: STOC, pp. 514–523 (1990)

36. Pippenger, N., Fischer, M.J.: Relations among complexity measures. J. ACM **26**(2), 361–381 (1979)
37. Rindal, P., Rosulek, M.: Faster malicious 2-party secure computation with online/offline dual execution. In: USENIX, pp. 297–314 (2016)
38. Stefanov, E., et al.: Path ORAM: an extremely simple oblivious RAM protocol. J. ACM **65**(4), 18:1–18:26 (2018)
39. Wang, X., Chan, T.-H.H., Shi, E.: Circuit ORAM: on tightness of the Goldreich-Ostrovsky lower bound. In: CCS, pp. 850–861 (2015)
40. Wang, X., Malozemoff, A.J., Katz, J.: Faster secure two-party computation in the single-execution setting. In: Coron, J.-S., Nielsen, J.B. (eds.) EUROCRYPT 2017. LNCS, vol. 10212, pp. 399–424. Springer, Cham (2017). https://doi.org/10.1007/978-3-319-56617-7_14
41. Wang, X., Ranellucci, S., Katz, J.: Authenticated garbling and efficient maliciously secure two-party computation. In: CCS, pp. 21–37 (2017)
42. Wang, X., Ranellucci, S., Katz, J.: Global-scale secure multiparty computation. In: CCS, pp. 39–56 (2017)
43. Wang, X.S., Huang, Y., Chan, T.-H.H., Shelat, A., Shi, E.: SCORAM: oblivious RAM for secure computation. In: CCS, pp. 191–202 (2014)
44. Wang, X.S., et al.: Oblivious data structures. In: CCS, pp. 215–226 (2014)
45. Yao, A.C.-C.: How to generate and exchange secrets (extended abstract). In: FOCS, pp. 162–167 (1986)
46. Zahur, S., Rosulek, M., Evans, D.: Two halves make a whole. In: Oswald, E., Fischlin, M. (eds.) EUROCRYPT 2015. LNCS, vol. 9057, pp. 220–250. Springer, Heidelberg (2015). https://doi.org/10.1007/978-3-662-46803-6_8

Oblivious Tight Compaction In $O(n)$ Time with Smaller Constant

Sam Dittmer[1($\boxtimes$)] and Rafail Ostrovsky[2]

[1] Stealth Software Technologies, Inc., Los Angeles, CA, USA
samdittmer@stealthsoftwareinc.com
[2] Department of Computer Science and Mathematics,
University of California, Los Angeles, Los Angeles, CA, USA
rafail@cs.ucla.edu

Abstract. Oblivious compaction is a crucial building block for hash-based oblivious RAM. Asharov et al. recently gave a $O(n)$ algorithm for oblivious tight compaction [2]. Their algorithm is deterministic and asymptotically optimal, but the implied constant is $\gg 2^{111}$. We give a new algorithm for oblivious tight compaction that runs in time $< 23913.17n + o(n)$. As part of our construction, we give a new result in the bootstrap percolation of random regular graphs.

1 Introduction

1.1 Oblivious RAM

Oblivious RAM has been a critical object of study in cryptography since its introduction by Goldreich and Ostrovksy [15]. ORAM now arises in a number of contexts such as improving security on SGX chips [10], garbled RAM programs [21] and cloud computing [34]. Many implementations and variations of ORAM exist, including distributed ORAM, where multiple clients jointly access a shared array (see e.g. [7,20]) and parallel ORAM (see e.g. [25]). Many variations have explored optimizations with larger block sizes or client memory, such as the well-known Path ORAM [31], which has blocks of size $\Omega(\log^2 n)$ and $O(\log n) \cdot \omega(1)$ blocks of client storage.

In this paper, we consider the classic ORAM model, with a single server, a single client, blocks of size $O(\log n)$, and $O(1)$ blocks of client storage. Recently Asharov et al. [1] gave the first ever asymptotically optimal ORAM construction under these conditions, with $O(\log n)$ amortized overhead, which they called OptORAMa. A key building block in their construction is an oblivious tight compaction algorithm with $O(n)$ runtime, which was improved on in [2].

OptORAMa is noteworthy for being asymptotically optimal and deterministic, but it is not intended for practical applications. The implied constant in the big-O notation for the oblivious tight compaction algorithm is enormous, $\gg 2^{111}$.

We construct a new oblivious tight compaction algorithm that matches the asymptotics of OptORAMa and makes a substantial improvement to the constant. We do this in part by removing the requirement that the algorithm be

© Springer Nature Switzerland AG 2020
C. Galdi and V. Kolesnikov (Eds.): SCN 2020, LNCS 12238, pp. 253–274, 2020.
https://doi.org/10.1007/978-3-030-57990-6_13

deterministic, and by analyzing the behavior of expander graphs under majority bootstrap percolation. Our algorithm requires $23913.17n$ steps to compact an array of length n with negligible failure probability. This is still far too large of a constant for the algorithm to be used in practical applications, but we hope the techniques presented here take us a step closer to practicality.

1.2 Main Results

Our main theorem is our oblivious tight compaction algorithm:

Theorem 1. *There is an algorithm to obliviously tightly compact an array in* $23913.17n + o(n)$ *time.*

To demonstrate the correctness of our algorithm, we need the following new result on bootstrap percolation, which we prove in Appendix C. The proof builds on the expander graph mixing lemma and generalizes the proof of Lemma 10 in [9].

Theorem 2. *Let G be a d-regular Ramanujan graph. For $d \geq 13$ odd and $d \geq 16$ even there is some constant $c < 1$ such that every subset $S \subseteq G$ with $|S|/|G| \geq c$ is a percolating set for majority bootstrap percolation.*

1.3 Bootstrap Percolation

Bootstrap percolation of a graph is type of cellular automaton where, at each time step, a vertex's behavior is determined by the behavior of its neighbors. It is an area of extensive research in computer science and combinatorics, and also arises in areas from physics studies of the Bethe lattice [8] and Ising model [30] to the study of social networks [11,19]. One prominent area of research is on the size of percolating sets, which are sets that, if activated initially, will cause the entire graph to be activated.

One common way to phrase this question is to ask when choosing vertices from a graph with probability p gives a percolating set with high probability (see e.g. [3,6,33]). In the case of random regular graphs, Balogh and Pittel compute the p^* at which a transition from probability almost zero to probability almost one occurs [5]. We use their result to determine the density of bins needed for majority bootstrap percolation to occur with high probability However, we also desire bounds on initial sets above which percolation to the entire graph is guaranteed, rather than occurring with high probability. We give such bounds in Theorem 2 and prove them in Appendix C.

There has been broad interest in the question of the smallest possible percolating set for many different families of graphs, including expander graphs [9], regular graphs [16], d-dimensional hypercubes [23,24], and powers of complete graphs [4]. Coja-Oghlan, Feige, Krivelevich and Reichman studied the size of the *largest* minimal percolating set for expander graphs [9] in the case of a constant size activation threshold. This question has also been studied for the grid [23], hypercubes [27] and trees [28].

We are interested in majority bootstrap percolation, where a vertex becomes active if a majority of its neighbors are active. Gärtner and Zehmakan gave a result equivalent to establishing an upper bound on the size of the largest minimal percolating set for expander graphs of sufficiently large degree in [14], (see also [35]) but their result is for two-way majority bootstrap percolation, a different cellular automaton.

1.4 Comparison to OptORAMa

To clearly present both the similarities to and the improvements over the OptORAMa compaction algorithm [1] and its follow-up [2], we describe below several of the key features of OptORAMa that facilitate its asymptotic optimality and drive its large runtime. We also describe the approach our algorithm takes to address the same problems.

1. In the OptORAMa compaction algorithms, large arrays are divided into smaller bins, where all but a constant fraction of bins have their density of marked elements bounded above by some constant. In [1], for large enough arrays (compared to W, the word size) this subdivision step happens twice. In [2], this subdivision step only needs to happen once.
   In our algorithm, we likewise divide large arrays into much smaller bins, using a single subdivision step, and use bins of size $O(W/\log W)$.
   Our algorithm relies on bin distribution schemes that only produces overly dense bins with non-negligible probability $n^{-\frac{a}{\log\log n}}$ or n^{-c}. We then collect the elements from the dense bins into another large runoff array, which we must also compact.
2. In OptORAMa, private data about small bins are packed into $O(1)$ memory words, so that this data can be accessed obliviously in $O(1)$ time. We use the same bitpacking schemes in a similar way.
3. In OptORAMa, expander graphs are used to simulate random access. This is used in particular for their LooseSwapMisplaced algorithm, which controls density of marked elements. Our LOOSESWAP algorithm is essentially the "re-randomised" version of OptORAMa's "de-randomised" LooseSwapMisplaced algorithm.
4. In OptORAMa, expander graphs are also used as a building block for linear superconcentrators on small bins. OptoRAMa adapts the non-oblivious Pippenger construction [26] that builds from a bipartite expander graph.
   We replace linear superconcentrators with bootstrap percolation on expander graphs. This allows to distribute balls evenly between buckets without forcing us to designate a certain set of vertices as "input" or "output" vertices.
5. Estimate of OptORAMa runtime: In the fastest variation presented in [2], the authors use the Jimbo-Maruoka expander graph, [18] a bipartite expander graph with degree at least d^k, where $d = 8$, and k is an integer such that $(8/(5\sqrt{2}))^k > L = 64$. This forces $k \geq 37$, so the degree is at least 2^{111}, and the runtime at least $2^{111}n$.

2   Structure of Paper

Our algorithm is made up of three rounds of compaction, and three levels of compaction. We give an overview of the construction, including a summary of the accounting of the overall cost of the algorithm, in Sect. 3. We describe the top level of the construction in Sect. 4 and the next two levels of construction in Sect. 5. The descriptions of some sub-algorithms are moved to the appendices.

In the first round, we extract most marked elements, leaving behind a shortened array of size $O(n/\log^3 n)$, which can be Batcher sorted, and a sparse array of density $n^{-a/\log\log n}$, for some absolute constant $a > 0$. In the second round, we reduce the density from $n^{-a/\log\log n}$ to n^{-c}, for some constant $c > 0$. In the third round, we complete the compaction.

At the top level, we control density through LooseSwap. At the middle level we shuffle elements into bins via LooseCompact or SparseLooseCompact. At the bottom level, we perform loose compaction on bins of size $W/\log W$ using majority bootstrap percolation via BinCompact or BinCompactMargulis.

We follow [1] in using *tight compaction* to refer to moving all marked elements to the left of all unmarked elements, and *loose compaction* to refer to moving all marked elements into an array whose size is decreased by some constant fraction. As in [1], we note that tight compaction can be reduced to loose compaction.

Our loose compaction algorithm uses an involved construction to control the density of marked elements on part of the array. It then shuffles elements from that part of the array into bins of size $\Theta(\log n)$, i.e. proportional to $W/\log W$. We then run BinCompact to loosely compact each bin. This produces a sparse runoff array and a discard array populated with unmarked and dummy elements. The sparse runoff array we compact with a modified bin compaction algorithm BinCompactMargulis. The discard array we compact by running TightCompact again, since the discard array produced in this iteration is made up entirely of dummy elements. We give a more detailed description of how these algorithms interact in Sect. 4.

In the algorithm BinCompact, we shuffle each bin into buckets of constant size, and identify each bucket with the vertex of an expander graph G. Via bitpacking, we can store the private data of G in a single memory word.

By treating empty buckets as active in the sense of majority bootstrap percolation, and applying Theorem 2, we assign weights to edges of G, so that every non-empty vertex has a majority of edges pointing away from it. This algorithm is essentially nonoblivious, since we can analyze the private data of G locally. Once the edge weights are set, we perform oblivious swaps in the directions indicated by the edge weights. We give a more detailed description of BinCompact in Sect. 5.

For sparse arrays with density bounded above by $\exp\left(-O(\log n(\log\log n)^t)\right)$, for $t \in \{-1, 0\}$, we use a variant of BinCompact built on Margulis graphs that we call BinCompactMargulis. We use here a tree traversal algorithm that is similar to bootstrap percolation in its effects. We give the details in Appendix A.

We defer proofs of a number of lemmas to Appendix B. The proof of Theorem 2 is given in Appendix C. A careful accounting of runtime cost is given in the full version of this paper [12].

3   Main Algorithm

3.1   Description of Algorithm

In the first round of compaction, we use TIGHTCOMPACTBYTWO to produce arrays with density $\gamma < 0.005307$. Then we shuffle into bins of size $O(\log n / \log \log n)$ in LOOSECOMPACT. By Lemma 6, we find that the probability of density greater than γ is

$$e^{-O(\log n / \log \log n)}.$$

For each bin, we run BINCOMPACT, using a random expander graph of degree $d = 13$. By Corollary C1, all elements will be reached by majority bootstrap percolation unless the density is greater than γ. When the density is greater than γ, we transfer the entire bin to the runoff array.

When we complete this process, we have a sorted array with $ne^{-O(\log n / \log \log n)}$ dummy elements, and a runoff array of size $14n$ and density $e^{-O(\log n / \log \log n)}$. Running SPARSELOOSECOMPACT repeatedly gives a new runoff array of size $21n$ and density n^{-c}, for some constant $c < 1$. Running SPARSELOOSECOMPACT repeatedly again gives no runoff, since by Lemma 7 we now have negligible failure probability in BINCOMPACTMARGULIS. We account for the sparse runoff of the discard arrays similarly in § 3.2 and § 4.2.

We run the LOOSECOMPACT array in all three rounds to extract most of the marked elements, leaving behind three sub-arrays of size $O(n / \log^3 n)$, which can be compacted in $o(n)$ time by Batcher sort.

3.2   Runtime of Main Algorithm

Here we give the cost of our main algorithm by analyzing the previous section, summarizing the argument in the full version of this paper [12]. The first round of the algorithm, achieving $O(e^{-O(\log n / \log \log n)})$ compaction, has a cost of

$$\left[\left(7 + 3\lg(d) + \frac{(1 - (1 - \gamma)^{d+1} + \varepsilon)(5d + 1) + 4 - 6\lg(d)}{2d + 2} \right) \cdot \left((d + 1) + (d + 1)^2 \right) + \frac{\alpha}{\beta}(d + 1) \right] n$$
$$+ \left[\left(1 - \frac{\beta}{1 - \alpha} \right)^{-1} (\log(1 + 1/d)d + (1 - \alpha) \log(\beta/\gamma)) + 2(d^2 - 1) \log(1 + 1/d) \right] n$$
$$+ \left(\frac{1}{\beta} - 2 \right) n + (d - 1)(1 - \frac{2}{d}) \log(d/\gamma) n + \frac{2}{d + 1} U(n).$$

Taking $d = 13, \alpha = 0.01, \beta = 0.2801, \gamma = 0.005307$, gives a run time of

$$4644.59n.$$

We then have to run the remainder of our algorithm on the array of size $14n$ with density $e^{-O(\log n/\log\log n)}$. However, the guarantee of low density eliminates the costs from α and β. The cost for the second round is:

$$(14 + 21 + 196)(3/2)8n,$$

since $|R| = 14n$ initially, $|C| = 196n$ initially, and $\cup C' = 21n$, taking the union over all sets C' that occur in the loop. The term $(3/2)$ is the contribution from summing the geometric series $\sum(1/3)^k$ to account for the repeated calls to SPARSELOOSECOMPACT on the gemetrically decreasing R and C. Similarly, the cost for the third round is

$$(21 + 63/2 + 63/2 + 294)(3/2)8n,$$

summing over $S = S' \cup S''$, T, and T'. This gives a cost of

$$7308n$$

for the second and third rounds together. Adding back in the cost of the original algorithm gives a cost of

$$U(n) = 11952.58n + o(n),$$

for TIGHTCOMPACTBYTWO and a cost of

$$T(n) = 23913.17n + o(n)$$

for general tight compaction.

4   Compaction Algorithms

4.1   General Tight Compaction from Compaction by Two

In Algorithm 1, we reduce tight compaction to the case where exactly half of the elements are marked. First, we observe that compressing marked elements to the left side of an array is equivalent to compressing unmarked elements to the right half. The formal implementation of this observation is given in lines 1–5 and lines 10–15.

Next, assume less than or equal to half of the elements are marked. If we can loosely compact those elements into the left half of the array, then, by induction we can tightly compact the left half of the array. Equivalently, we mark additional elements until exactly half of the elements are marked, and then compact those elements tightly into the left half. The formal implementation is given in lines 6–9.

The correctness of this algorithm is an immediate consequence of induction and the correctness of Algorithm 2, TIGHTCOMPACTBYTWO, as shown in § 4.2.

Algorithm 1. Oblivious tight compaction

Require: Array A of size n with some subset of elements marked
Ensure: Obliviously shuffle A so that all marked elements are at the front of the array
1: **procedure** TIGHTCOMPACT(A)
2:     $s \leftarrow 0$
3:     **if** More than half of A is marked **then**
4:         $s \leftarrow 1$
5:         Switch all markings
6:     **end if**
7:     Temporarily mark additional elements until exactly half of A is marked
8:     TIGHTCOMPACTBYTWO(A)
9:     Unmark the temporarily marked elements
10:     TIGHTCOMPACT($A[1 : \frac{n}{2}]$)
11:     **if** $s = 1$ **then**
12:         Swap element in position i with position $n + 1 - i$
13:         Unswitch all markings
14:     **else**
15:         Perform dummy access to positions i and $n + 1 - i$
16:     **end if**
17: **end procedure**

Algorithm 2. Tight compaction by two

Require: Array I of size n with exactly half of I marked, constants α, β, γ,γ', W, and d
Ensure: Obliviously shuffle I so that all marked elements are at the front of the array
1: **procedure** TIGHTCOMPACTBYTWO($A, \alpha, \beta, \gamma, W, d$)
2:     $(A, B, R, \tilde{A}, \tilde{B}, \tilde{R}) \leftarrow$ MIRRORCOMPACT($A, \alpha, \beta, \gamma, W, d$)
3:     For every statement in lines 4–17, execute the statement again replacing all sets U with $\tilde{U}$
4:     $(A', V, R') \leftarrow$ DUMMYCOMPACT($B, \alpha, \beta, \gamma, W, d$)
5:     $C \leftarrow R'$
6:     **while** $|R| + |C| > n/(\log^3 n)$ **do**
7:         $(R, C', S') \leftarrow$ SPARSELOOSECOMPACT(R)
8:         Append C' to C
9:         $(C, \text{DUMMY}, S'') \leftarrow$ SPARSELOOSECOMPACT(C)
10:         Append S' and S'' to S
11:     **end while**
12:     $T \leftarrow \{\}$
13:     **while** $|S| + |T| > n/(8\log^3 n)$ **do**
14:         $(S, T', \text{DUMMY}) \leftarrow$ SPARSELOOSECOMPACT(S)
15:         $T \leftarrow T \cup T'$
16:         $(T, \text{DUMMY}, \text{DUMMY}) \leftarrow$ SPARSELOOSECOMPACT(T)
17:     **end while**
18:     $I \leftarrow$ Batcher sort of $(A \cup A' \cup R \cup C \cup S \cup T) \cup (\tilde{A} \cup \tilde{A}' \tilde{R} \cup \check{C} \cup \tilde{S} \cup \tilde{T})$, sorted with marked elements first, then unmarked elements, then dummy elements
19:     $I \leftarrow$ leading $|A| + |\tilde{A}|$ elements of I
20:     $I \leftarrow \tilde{V} \cup I \cup V$
21: **end procedure**

4.2   Tight Compaction by Two

In TIGHTCOMPACTBYTWO, Algorithm 2, we describe all three *rounds* of our compaction algorithm, at the top *level*. The first round is the most complicated, and relies on the two sub-protocols MIRRORCOMPACT and DUMMYCOMPACT (Algorithms 3 and 4).

We introduce a number of constants, to be optimized later. The constant α represents the fraction of the array on which we will perform LOOSECOMPACT, while β, γ, and γ' are bounds on density of marked elements in subarrays. The degree of the expander graph is given by d, and the word size is $W = \Theta(\log n)$.

The purpose of MIRRORCOMPACT is to isolate a subarray $A_1 \subseteq I$ whose density of marked elements is very low. We then call LOOSECOMPACT on A_1, which in turn calls BINCOMPACT. We require A_1 to have density $\leq \gamma'$, which ensures that all but an $n^{-c/\log\log n}$ fraction of the bins created in LOOSECOMPACT will have density $\leq \gamma$, for some constant $c > 0$ (where c is a function of γ, γ' and W; see Lemma 6).

The algorithm relies on *exactly* half of the elements being marked. This allows us to divide the array in half and control the density in both halves. We write $I = A \cup \tilde{A}$, and treat $\tilde{A}$ as the mirror of A, reversing the role of marked and unmarked balls. To begin, we use LOOSESWAP to force the density of A to be less than β, which pushes the density of $\tilde{A}$ above $1 - \beta$.

We divide A into $A = A_1 \cup A_2$, with $|A_1| = \alpha|A|$, and likewise divide $\tilde{A} = \tilde{A}_1 \cup \tilde{A}_2$. We push the density of A_2 below γ' by running LOOSESWAP on A_1 and A_2, and likewise push the density of $\tilde{A}_2$ above γ'. We have now increased the density of A_1 and decreased the density of $\tilde{A}_1$, so we use LOOSESWAP to push their densities back to β and $1 - \beta$. Note that, by Lemma 5, the densities at every stage of the algorithm can, in principle, be computed exactly up to a term of order $1 + O(n^{-1/4})$.

We can now run LOOSECOMPACT on A_1 and $\tilde{A}_1$. This compacts A_1 by a factor of $\frac{d}{d+1}$, and so increases the density of A_1 by a factor of $(1 + \frac{1}{d})$. It compacts A by a factor of $(1 - \frac{\alpha}{d+1})$. We adjust the borders of A_1 and A_2 so that A_1 again covers α of A. We now need to run LOOSESWAP twice, both to push down the density of the former A_1 array from $(1 + \frac{1}{d})\gamma'$ to γ', and to push down the density of what used to be A_2 from β to γ'. We can then run LOOSECOMPACT again on the new A_1.

After executing MIRRORCOMPACT, we have to deal with the discard array B, which has size $(d + 1)A$, and the runoff array R, of the same size. The claimed sizes of the discard and runoff arrays are a result of summing a geometric series, and are proven in [12].

To deal with the discard array, which is a mix of unmarked and dummy elements, we apply DUMMYCOMPACT. We show in § 4.3 that the density of unmarked elements is exactly $\frac{1}{d+1}$. We no longer can exchange with the mirror $\tilde{B}$, since $\tilde{B}$ also has mostly dummy elements. However, using a slightly modified version of our loop in lines 4–8, we can compact the non-dummy elements of B until B is roughly half dummy and half unmarked elements. When we run LOOSECOMPACT on B, the discard array is a mix of dummy elements and more dummy elements, so we can discard it entirely.

Once we have an array that is half dummy and half unmarked, we apply DUM-MYCOMPACTBYTWO to extract the unmarked elements only. This algorithm is similar to TIGHTCOMPACTBYTWO, but requires additionally a REROUTE algorithm which re-directs marked elements to any fixed private locations in the array. REROUTE is constructed recursively from a call to TIGHTCOMPACT on an array of size n/d, and allows calls to LOOSECOMPACT on arrays with γn dummy elements to be implemented with a call of LOOSECOMPACT on an array with $(1 - \gamma)$ dummy elements. We give a detailed description in the full version of this paper [12].

Algorithm 3. Mirror compaction

Require: Array I of size n with exactly half of I marked, constants α, β, γ, γ', W, and d

Ensure: Return $(A, B, R, \tilde{A}, \tilde{B}, \tilde{R})$ with A and $\tilde{A}$ of size $O(n/\log^3 n)$, $|B| = |\tilde{B}| = |R| = |\tilde{R}| = (d+1)n/2$, with B and $\tilde{B}$ the DISCARD arrays with only dummy and unmarked elements and dummy and marked elements, respectively, and R and $\tilde{R}$ the RUNOFF arrays with non-dummy elements of density $\exp(-a \log n / \log \log n)$.

1: **procedure** MIRRORCOMPACT($A, \alpha, \beta, \gamma, W, d$)
2:     Divide I into its left and right half, $I = A \cup \tilde{A}$
3:     LOOSESWAP($A, \tilde{A}, \frac{1}{2}, \frac{1}{2}, \beta$)
4:     For every statement in lines 5–21 other than line 12, execute the statement again on $\tilde{A}$, reversing the role of marked and unmarked elements
5:     Divide $A = A_1 \cup A_2$ with $|A_1| = \alpha n/2$ and $|A_2| = (1 - \alpha)n/2$
6:     LOOSESWAP($A_1, A_2, \beta, \beta, \gamma'$)
7:     $B, R, S \leftarrow \{\}$
8:     LOOSECOMPACT($A_1, \gamma', \gamma, W, d$)
9:     Append RUNOFF(A_1) to R
10:    Append DISCARD(A_1) to B
11:    **while** $|A_1| + |A_2| > n/(6\log^3 n)$ **do**
12:        Divide $A_2 = A_1' \cup A_2'$ so that $(1 - \alpha)(|A_1| + |A_1'|) = \alpha|A_2'|$
13:        LOOSESWAP($A_2, \tilde{A}_2, \frac{\beta}{1-\alpha}, 1 - \frac{\beta}{1-\alpha}, \beta$)
14:        LOOSESWAP($A_1, A_2', \gamma'(1 + \frac{1}{d}), \beta, \gamma'$)
15:        LOOSESWAP($A_1', A_2', \beta, \beta, \gamma'$)
16:        $A_1 \leftarrow A_1 \cup A_1'$
17:        $A_2 \leftarrow A_2'$
18:        $(A_1, \text{DISCARD}(A_1), \text{RUNOFF}(A_1)) \leftarrow$ LOOSECOMPACT($A_1, \gamma', \gamma, W, d$).
19:        Append RUNOFF(A_1) to R
20:        Append DISCARD(A_1) to B
21:    **end while**
22:    Return $(A_1 \cup A_2, B, R, \tilde{A}_1 \cup \tilde{A}_2, \tilde{B}, \tilde{R})$
23: **end procedure**

The second and third rounds of TIGHTCOMPACTBYTWO are given in lines 5–11 and 12–17, respectively. In lines 5–11, we deal with arrays with density of non-dummy elements $\exp(-a \log n / \log \log n)$. In lines 12–17, we deal with arrays with density $\exp(-a \log n) = n^{-a}$. In both cases, we distinguish between arrays with marked, unmarked and dummy elements (B, S), and arrays with only unmarked and dummy elements (C, T).

Algorithm 4. Dummy compaction

Require: Array A of size $(d+1)n$ with $(1 - \exp(-a \log n / \log \log n))n$ elements unmarked, and the rest dummies, constants γ, γ', W, and d

Ensure: Return an ordered pair $(U, V, \text{RUNOFF}(A))$, where $|U| = n/log^3 n$, $|U| + |V| = n$, and $|\text{RUNOFF}(A)| = (d+1)^2 n$. U, V and A each hold a mix of dummy and unmarked elements. All but $\exp(-a \log n / \log \log n)$ of the elements of V are unmarked, and all but $\exp(-a \log n / \log \log n)$ of the elements of A are dummy.

1: **procedure** DUMMYCOMPACT$(A, \alpha, \beta, \gamma, W, d)$
2:      Divide $A = A_1 \cup A_2$ with $|A_1| = \frac{d-1}{d+1}|A|$ and $|A_2| = \frac{2}{d+1}|A|$
3:      LOOSESWAP$(A_1, A_2, \frac{1}{d}, \frac{1}{d}, \gamma')$
4:      **while** $|A_1| > \frac{n}{\log^3 n}$ **do**
5:          LOOSESWAP$(R_1, R_2, \gamma'(1 + \frac{1}{d}), \frac{1}{2}, \gamma')$
6:          $(A_1, \text{DUMMY}, B) \leftarrow$ LOOSECOMPACT$(A_1, \gamma', \gamma, W, d)$
7:          Append B to RUNOFF(R)
8:      **end while**
9:      $(U, \text{DUMMY}, B, \text{DUMMY}, V, \tilde{B}) \leftarrow$ DUMMYCOMPACTBYTWO$(R_1 \cup R_2, \alpha, \beta, \gamma, W, d)$
10:      Return $(U, V, B \cup \tilde{B})$
11: **end procedure**

We show in §4.3 and §4.4 that the probability of failure for LOOSECOMPACT and SPARSELOOSECOMPACT, respectively, is negligible in n for $|A| = \Omega(n/\log^3 n)$. By a similar argument, we show that LOOSESWAP is negligible in n in the full version of this paper [12]. The loops in this subsection will run at most $O(\log \log n)$ times, so by a union bound the probability of failure of this algorithm is also negligible.

4.3 Analysis of Algorithm 6

This algorithm shuffles elements into bins where we can then apply BINCOMPACT. By Lemma 6, the probability that a bin D_i has more than $\gamma|D_i|$ marked balls is $n^{-c/\log \log n}$, for some constant $c < 1$.

The proof of correctness is an immediate consequence of the proof of correctness of BINCOMPACT given in §5.1.

4.4 Analysis of Algorithm 7

This is the sparse analogue of LOOSECOMPACT given in the previous section.

Algorithm 5. Loose swap misplaced

Require: Arrays A_1 and A_2 with densities of marked elements bounded above by ρ_1 and ρ_2 respectively and $|A_i| = \Omega(n/\log^3 n)$.

Ensure: Density of A_1 bounded above by $\rho_1' < \rho_1$ with all but negligible probability

1: **procedure** LOOSESWAP($A_1,A_2,\rho_1,\rho_2,\rho_1'$)
2:     $t \leftarrow 0$
3:     $T \leftarrow \epsilon n + |A_1| \int_{\rho_1'}^{\rho_1} \left(1 - \frac{|A_1|(\rho_1-\rho)+|A_2|\rho_2}{|A_2|}\right)^{-1} \frac{d\rho}{\rho}$
4:     **for** $t < T$ **do**
5:         $t \leftarrow t+1$
6:         Choose random indices i_1 and i_2 from A_1 and A_2
7:         **if** $A_1[i_1]$ is marked and $A_2[i_2]$ is unmarked **then**
8:             Obliviously swap the contents of i_1 and i_2
9:         **else**
10:           Perform fake accesses
11:         **end if**
12:     **end for**
13: **end procedure**

Algorithm 6. Loose compaction

Require: Array A with $|A| = \Omega(n/\log^3 n)$ and at most $\gamma'|A|$ marked elements, for some constant $\gamma' < \gamma$.

Ensure: Triple $(B, \text{DISCARD}(A), \text{RUNOFF}(A))$ such that $|B| = (1 - \frac{1}{d+1})|A|$ and $|\text{DISCARD}(A)| = |\text{RUNOFF}(A)| = |A|$. These three sets together contain the elements of A and additional dummy elements. All marked elements of A are in B or $\text{RUNOFF}(A)$ and, with all but negligible probability, the density of non-dummy elements in $\text{RUNOFF}(A)$ is $\exp((c-1)\log n/\log\log n)$.

1: **procedure** LOOSECOMPACT(A,γ,W,d)
2:     Shuffle A in the clear with Fischer-Yates.
3:     Divide A into bins $\{D_i\}$ of size $(d+1)W/(d\log W + 1 + \lg(d) + \frac{d}{2})$.
4:     $A \leftarrow \{\}$
5:     $\text{RUNOFF}(A) \leftarrow \{\}$
6:     $\text{DISCARD}(A) \leftarrow \{\}$
7:     **for** bin D_i **do**
8:         $(D_i, \text{DISCARD}(D_i), \text{RUNOFF}(D_i)) \leftarrow \text{BINCOMPACT}(D_i, W, d)$
9:         Append $\text{RUNOFF}(D_i)$ to $\text{RUNOFF}(A)$
10:         Append $\text{DISCARD}(D_i)$ to $\text{DISCARD}(A)$
11:         Append D_i to A
12:     **end for**
13: **end procedure**

By Lemma 7, the probability that a fixed bin has more than $\log\log n$ elements is negligible in n. By taking a union bound over the bins, the probability that at least one bin has more than $\log\log n$ marked elements is also negligible in n.

The proof of correctness relies on the proof of correctness of BINCOMPACTMARGULIS given in § A.1.

Algorithm 7. Sparse loose compaction

Require: Array A with $|A| = \Omega(n/\log^3 n)$ and at most $|A| \exp((c-1)\log n(\log \log n)^t)$ marked elements, for $c < 1$ and $t \in \{-1, 0\}$.

Ensure: Triple $(B, \text{DISCARD}(A), \text{RUNOFF}(A))$ such that $|B| = |A|/3$ and $|\text{DISCARD}(A)| = |\text{RUNOFF}(A)| = |A|$. These three sets together contain the elements of A and additional dummy elements. All marked elements of A are in B or $\text{RUNOFF}(A)$ and, with all but negligible probability, the density of non-dummy elements in $\text{RUNOFF}(A)$ is $\exp((c-1)\log n(\log \log n)^{t+1})$.

1: **procedure** SPARSELOOSECOMPACT(A, c, W)
2:     Shuffle A in the clear with Fischer-Yates
3:     Divide A into bins $\{D_i\}$ of size $3W/2$.
4:     $B \leftarrow \{\}$
5:     $\text{DISCARD}(A) \leftarrow \{\}$
6:     $\text{RUNOFF}(A) \leftarrow \{\}$
7:     **for** bin D_i **do**
8:         $(D_i, \text{DISCARD}(D_i), \text{RUNOFF}(D_i)) \leftarrow$ BINCOMPACTMARGULIS(D_i, W)
9:         Append D_i to A
10:        Append $\text{DISCARD}(D_i)$ to $\text{DISCARD}(A)$
11:        Append $\text{RUNOFF}(D_i)$ to $\text{RUNOFF}(A)$
12:    **end for**
13: **end procedure**

---

5   Bin Compaction with Bootstrap Percolation

In this section, we give the algorithm BINCOMPACT, and related algorithms needed to implement it. The algorithm BINCOMPACTMARGULIS used for SPARSECOMPACT is similar, and we describe it in Appendix A. In both algorithms, the idea is the same: we assign elements to buckets of constant size, place each bucket at the vertex of an expander graph, and use some graph algorithm to assign directions to the edges of the graph.

5.1   Analysis of Algorithm 8

The algorithm BINCOMPACT(A, W, d) replaces A with a new array that is $(1 - \frac{1}{d+1})$ times smaller, with all marked elements from the old A moved into the new A. In this process, some unmarked elements will be removed from A. They are placed into a new array $\text{DISCARD}(A)$, which also contains a number of dummy elements.

The first time we call BINCOMPACT, we generate a d-regular expander graph G of size $|G| = W/(\log W + 1 + \lg d + \frac{d}{2})$. This takes polylogarithmic time, as shown in Lemmas 2, 3 and 4.

Each time we call BINCOMPACT, we also assign to G a set of private data so that the edge set of G and its private data fit into a single memory word. The edge set and private data of G can therefore be accessed and altered without revealing the access pattern.

Algorithm 8. Loose bin compaction with degree d Rucinski-Wormald graphs

---

Require: Array A with $|A| = (d+1)W/(d \log W + 1 + \lg d + \frac{d}{2})$, and some constant γ
Ensure: Triple $(B, \text{DISCARD}(A), \text{RUNOFF}(A))$ such that Compact $|B| = (1 - \frac{1}{d+1})|A|$ and $|\text{RUNOFF}(A)| = |\text{DISCARD}(A)| = |A|$. With probability $1 - \exp(-c \log n / \log \log n)$, all marked elements from A are in B and $\text{RUNOFF}(A) = \text{DUMMY}$. Otherwise B and $\text{DISCARD}(A)$ are DUMMY and $\text{RUNOFF}(A) = A$.

1: **procedure** $\text{BINCOMPACT}(A, W, d)$
2:     **if** more than $\gamma|A|$ marked elements **then**
3:         $\text{RETURN } (\text{DUMMY}, \text{DUMMY}, A)$
4:     **end if**
5:     $k \leftarrow |A|/(d+1)$
6:     $G \leftarrow$ a d-regular expander graph with k vertices $\{v_1, \dots, v_k\}$
7:     Divide A into k bins $D_1, \dots, D_k$ of size $(d+1)$
8:     Let w be a single memory word of W bits
9:     $w \leftarrow wt(v_i) \in \{\text{EMPTY}, \text{NONEMPTY}\} \cup wt(e(v_i, v_j)) \in \{\text{INCOMING}, \text{OUTGOING}\} \cup$
        $\text{COUNT}(v_i) \in \{0, \dots, d\}$
10:     **for** $i \in \{1, \dots, k\}$ **do**
11:         $\text{COUNT}(v_i) = 0$
12:         **if** D_i contains no marked elements **then**
13:             $wt(v_i) \leftarrow \text{EMPTY}$
14:         **else**
15:             $wt(v_i) \leftarrow \text{NONEMPTY}$
16:         **end if**
17:     **end for**
18:     **if** proportion of vertices marked EMPTY is less than $(1 - \gamma)^{d+1} - \varepsilon$ **then**
19:         $\text{RETURN } (\text{DUMMY}, \text{DUMMY}, A)$
20:     **end if**
21:     **for** $v \in V$ **do**
22:         $\text{EXPLORE}(v)$
23:     **end for**
24:     **for** $i \in \{1, \dots, k\}$ **do**
25:         Add d dummy elements to D_i
26:     **end for**
27:     **for** $v_i \in V$ **do**
28:         **for** neighbors $\{v_{i_1}, \dots, v_{i_j}, \dots, v_{i_d}\}$ of v_i **do**
29:             **if** $wt(e(v_i, v_{i_j})) = \text{OUTGOING}$ **then**
30:                 $j' \leftarrow$ index of v_i in list of neighbors of v_{i_j}
31:                 Swap element j in D_i with element $d + 1 + j'$ in D_{i_j}
32:             **else**
33:                 Perform dummy memory accesses
34:             **end if**
35:         **end for**
36:     **end for**
37:     $A, \text{DISCARD}(A) \leftarrow \{\}$
38:     **for** $i \in \{1, \dots, k\}$ **do**
39:         $\text{SLOWCOMPACT}(D_i)$
40:         Append leading d elements of D_i to A
41:         Append the remainder of D_i to $\text{DISCARD}(A)$
42:     **end for**
43: **end procedure**

The array A is required to have size $|A| = (d+1)|G|$ so that we can assign $d+1$ elements of A to each vertex of G. We consider a vertex to be EMPTY if it contains no marked elements, and NONEMPTY otherwise. As part of the private data of G, for each vertex we store a single bit representing EMPTY or NONEMPTY, and another $\lg(d)$ bits to store a variable COUNT that counts the number of EMPTY neighbors. COUNT is used only in the EXPLORE subroutine.

The rest of the private data of G is made up of edge weights. We use $kd/2$ bits to assign a direction to each edge of the graph. Formally, we replace each edge e between vertices v_i and v_j with a pair of directed edges $e(v_i, v_j)$ and $e(v_j, v_i)$. To indicate an edge pointing from v_i to v_j, we assign OUTGOING to $wt(e(v_i, v_j))$ and INCOMING to $wt(e(v_j, v_i))$. To indicate an edge pointing in the opposite direction, we reverse the labels. Of course, since the weights of $e(v_i, v_j)$ and $e(v_j, v_i)$ are always opposite, it only requires one bit to store both weights. The total storage cost for the private data of G is thus

$$|G|(1 + \lg d + \tfrac{d}{2})$$

bits, which explains our choice of the size of $|G|$.

We can now describe the algorithm BINCOMPACT in terms of the private data of G. In lines 2–25, we mark vertices as EMPTY or NONEMPTY and check against certain failure conditions. In lines 26–28, we mark every edge as INCOMING or OUTGOING. Then in lines 29–47 we swap elements between vertices in the directions indicated by the edge weights, and compact each vertex's elements.

The edge weights are assigned by the subroutine EXPLORE, which guarantees that every vertex with marked elements has more OUTGOING edges than INCOMING edges. We show this in § 5.2.

The loop in lines 32–41 ensures that every bucket D_i holds at most d marked elements, and at least $d + 1$ dummy elements. Indeed, vertices marked initially as EMPTY will receive at most d marked elements from their d neighbors. Vertices marked initially as NONEMPTY will have more edges marked OUTGOING than INCOMING. Note that the swap in line 37 does not necessarily transfer a marked element, but it does guarantee that position j in D_i holds an unmarked element. Let the number of OUTGOING edges be o and the number of INCOMING edges be i. After lines 33–42 the number of marked elements will be at most $d + 1 - o + i = d$. Likewise the number of dummy elements for an initially NONEMPTY vertex will be exactly $d + 1 - o + i = d$.

Now D_i has $2d + 1$ elements, with at most d elements marked, so we can run the algorithm SLOWCOMPACT(D_i) described in § 5.3. We obtain an output array A of size dk holding all the marked elements from the original A along with an array DISCARD(A) of size $(d + 1)k$, as desired.

BINCOMPACT fails when A begins with more than $\gamma|A|$ elements marked, or when fewer than $(1 - \gamma)^{d+1} - \varepsilon$ bins contain no marked elements. Since $|A| = \Omega(W/\log W) = \Omega(\log n)$, the two events occurs with probability $\exp(-c \log n(\log \log n)^t)$, by Lemma 6 and Lemma 8, respectively. In case of failure, the contents of A are emptied into RUNOFF(A), and BINCOMPACT(A) returns an array of dummy elements.

Algorithm 9. Explore subroutine for Rucinski-Wormald graphs

```
1: procedure EXPLORE(vertex v)
2:     if wt(v) = NONEMPTY then
3:         if COUNT = 0 then
4:             for neighbors w of v do
5:                 if wt(w) = EMPTY then
6:                     COUNT ← COUNT + 1
7:                 end if
8:             end for
9:         else
10:            COUNT = COUNT + 1
11:        end if
12:        if COUNT > d/2 then
13:            wt(v) ← EMPTY
14:            for neighbors w of v do
15:                if wt(w) = EMPTY then
16:                    wt(e(v, w)) ← OUTGOING
17:                else
18:                    wt(e(v, w)) ← INCOMING
19:                    EXPLORE(w)
20:                end if
21:            end for
22:        end if
23:    end if
24: end procedure
```

5.2 Analysis Of Explore

We desire to implement majority bootstrap percolation, where EMPTY vertices are treated as active, and NONEMPTY vertices are inactive. Then vertices that are initially NONEMPTY will be activated when a majority of their neighbors are active, so that a majority of its edges will be marked as OUTGOING.

Let S be the collection of vertices marked EMPTY. We show in Corollary C1 that, for $\frac{|S|}{|G|} \geq (1 - \gamma)^{d+1}$, $|S|$ is a percolating set, i.e. majority bootstrap percolation activates every vertex.

However, running majority bootstrap percolation would take time superlinear in $|A|$. The EXPLORE subroutine is similar to majority bootstrap percolation, but activates neighbors of active vertices as they become available, rather than looping through the entire array at each time step.

Claim 51. *The set of vertices activated after the* EXPLORE *subroutine has been run on every vertex is the same as when we run majority bootstrap percolation on G.*

We give the proof in the full version of this paper [12].

Algorithm 10. Slow loose compaction

Require: Array A of size t with at most $t/2$ marked elements
Ensure: compact A so that all marked elements are in the first $\lfloor t/2 \rfloor$ positions
 1: **procedure** SLOWCOMPACT(A)
 2:     $u \leftarrow \lfloor t/2 \rfloor$, LCOUNT $\leftarrow 0$ and RCOUNT $\leftarrow t - 2u$
 3:     **for** $i \in \{1, \ldots, u\}$ **do**
 4:         **if** $A[i]$ is marked **then**
 5:             LCOUNT $\leftarrow$ LCOUNT $+ 1$
 6:         **end if**
 7:         **if** $A[u + i]$ is marked **then**
 8:             RCOUNT $\leftarrow$ RCOUNT $+ 1$
 9:         **end if**
10:         **if** $|\text{LCOUNT} - \text{RCOUNT}| = 2$ **then**
11:             Swap $A[i]$ and $A[u + i]$
12:             LCOUNT $\leftarrow$ LCOUNT ± 1
13:             RCOUNT $\leftarrow$ RCOUNT ∓ 1
14:         **end if**
15:     **end for**
16:     SLOWCOMPACT($A[1 \ldots u]$) and SLOWCOMPACT($A[u + 1 \ldots t]$)
17:     **for** $i \in 1, \ldots, \lfloor u/2 \rfloor$ **do**
18:         Swap $A[u + i]$ and $A[u + 1 - i]$
19:     **end for**
20: **end procedure**

5.3   Analysis of Algorithm 10

The loop in lines 3–15 ensures that both the left and right half of A have at most half of their elements marked. The correctness of this algorithm follows by induction. The runtime analysis showing $O(n \log n)$ cost is given in the full version of this paper, [12].

Funding acknowledgements. This work was supported in part by DARPA and NIWC Pacific under contract N66001-15-C-4065, as well as the Office of the Director of National Intelligence (ODNI), Intelligence Advanced Research Projects Activity (IARPA), via 2019-1902070008. The views and conclusions contained herein are those of the authors and should not be interpreted as necessarily representing the official policies, either expressed or implied, of ODNI, IARPA, the Department of Defense, or the U.S. Government. The U.S. Government is authorized to reproduce and distribute reprints for governmental purposes notwithstanding any copyright annotation therein.

Rafail Ostrovsky was supported in part by NSF-BSF Grant 1619348, US-Israel BSF grant 2012366, DARPA under Cooperative Agreement No: HR0011-20-2-0025, Google Faculty Award, JP Morgan Faculty Award, IBM Faculty Research Award, Xerox Faculty Research Award, OKAWA Foundation Research Award, B. John Garrick Foundation Award, Teradata Research Award, and Lockheed-Martin Corporation Research Award.

A   Margulis Graph Compaction

A.1   Analysis of Algorithm 11

The argument here is similar to the argument in § 5.1, and is given in full in the full version of this paper [12].

B   Combinatorial Lemmas

We state here a number of combinatorial lemmas we need throughout the paper, and give a citation if the result is well-known. For proofs and discussion, we refer to the full version of this paper [12].

Lemma 1. *[Margulis [22]] There is a family of 4-regular expander graphs $\{G_k\}_{k\geq 0}$ with girth satisfying $|G_k| \geq 0.756 \log G_k$, with $G_k = (p_k^3 - p_k)$, for p_k the kth prime.*

The following result is due to Friedman [13] proving a conjecture of Alon.

Lemma 2 (Friedman). *The probability that a random d-regular graph G on n vertices, with dn even and $n > d$, has second eigenvalue $\leq 2\sqrt{d-1} + \epsilon$, is $1 - O(n^{-c})$.*

The following is due to Steger and Wormald [32], though the algorithm was first studied by Rucinski and Wormald [29].

Lemma 3 (Steger, Wormald). *There is an algorithm for generating a random d-regular graph, uniformly, in time $O(nd^2)$.*

Lemma 4. *It is possible to test whether a d-regular graph G on n vertices is Ramanujan in time poly(n).*

Combining these three results gives us an algorithm for generating a d-regular expander graph on n vertices in time $poly(n)$. Since our expander graphs will have $O(\log n)$ vertices, and we only need to generate $O(\log n)$ such graphs, this is sufficient for our needs.

Lemma 5. *Consider a random walk along the integers $\mathbb{Z}$ where the probability of moving from i to $i+1$ is $f(\frac{i}{n})$ for some increasing function f. Let X be a random variable denoting the time it takes to walk from ρn to $\rho' n$. Then*

$$\Pr\left(|X - n \int_\rho^{\rho'} \frac{dx}{f(x)}| > \epsilon n^{3/4} \right) = e^{-8(\rho'-\rho)\epsilon^2 \sqrt{n}}.$$

Lemma 6. *Fix constants $\gamma' < \gamma$, and let A be an array of length n with $\gamma'n$ marked balls. Then if $k \log n / \log\log n$ balls are chosen at random from A, the probability there are more than $\gamma k \log n$ marked balls chosen is $n^{-\frac{(\gamma-\gamma')^2 k}{(\gamma+\gamma')\log\log n}}$.*

Algorithm 11. Loose compaction for bins of Margulis graphs

Require: Array A with $|A| \leq 3W/(4 \log W + 5)$ and $\exp\left((c-1)\log n (\log\log n)^t\right) |A|$ elements marked, for $t \in \{-1, 0\}$.

Ensure: Triple $(B, \text{DISCARD}(A), \text{RUNOFF}(A))$ such that $|B| = |A|/3$, $|\text{DISCARD}(A)| = |\text{RUNOFF}(A)| = |A|$, all of the marked elements of A are in B with probability $1 - \exp\left((c-1)\log n(\log\log n)^{t+1}\right)$, and otherwise all of the marked elements of A are in $\text{RUNOFF}(A)$.

```
 1: procedure BINCOMPACTMARGULIS(A, W, b = 3, ℓ = 3, d = 4)
 2:     p ← min{prime i|i³ − i ≥ |A|/3}
 3:     k ← p³ − p
 4:     G ← a 4-regular Margulis expander graph with k vertices, i.e. a Cayley graph
           for SL₂(𝔽ₚ)
 5:     Label the vertices V of G as V = {v₁, ..., vₖ}
 6:     Divide A into k bins D₁, ..., Dₖ of size 3, adding dummy elements if necessary
 7:     Let w be a single memory word of W bits
 8:     w ← wt(vᵢ) ∈ {EMPTY, NONEMPTY, TERMINAL} ∪ wt(e(vᵢ, vⱼ)) ∈
           {INCOMING, OUTGOING, OFF}
 9:     for i ∈ {1, ..., k} do
10:        if Dᵢ contains no marked elements then
11:            wt(vᵢ) ← EMPTY
12:        else
13:            wt(vᵢ) ← NONEMPTY
14:        end if
15:     end for
16:     if more than ℓ log |G| NONEMPTY vertices then
17:        RUNOFF(A) ← A
18:        RETURN (DUMMY, DUMMY, RUNOFF(A))
19:     end if
20:     for v ∈ V do
21:        EXPLOREMARGULIS(v)
22:     end for
23:     for i ∈ {1, ..., k} do
24:        Add 1 dummy element to Dᵢ
25:     end for
26:     for vᵢ ∈ V do
27:        for First three neighbors {vᵢ₁, vᵢ₂, vᵢ₃} of vᵢ do
28:            if wt(e(vᵢ, vᵢⱼ)) = OUTGOING then
29:                Swap element j in Dᵢ with element 4 in Dᵢⱼ
30:            else
31:                Perform dummy memory accesses
32:            end if
33:        end for
34:        for j ∈ {1, 2, 3} do
35:            if Dᵢ[j] is marked and wt(e(vᵢ, vᵢ₄)) = OUTGOING then
36:                t ← Dᵢ[j] and Dᵢ[j] ← DUMMY
37:            else
38:                Perform dummy memory accesses
39:            end if
40:        end for
41:        Dᵢ₄[4] ← t
42:     end for
43:     RETURN ((Dᵢ[4]), (Dᵢ[1 : 3]), RUNOFF(A))
44: end procedure
```

Algorithm 12. Explore subroutine for Margulis graphs

```
1: procedure EXPLOREMARGULIS(vertex v)
2:    if wt(v) = NONEMPTY then
3:        SUBEXPLOREMARGULIS(v)
4:    end if
5: end procedure
6: procedure SUBEXPLOREMARGULIS(v)
7:    if wt(v) = NONEMPTY then
8:        wt(v) ← EMPTY
9:        for neighbors w of v do
10:            if wt(e(v, w)) = OFF then
11:                wt(e(v, w)) ← OUTGOING
12:                SUBEXPLOREMARGULIS(w)
13:            end if
14:        end for
15:    else
16:        for neighbors w of v do
17:            if wt(e(v, w)) = OFF then
18:                if wt(w) = NONEMPTY then
19:                    wt(e(v, w)) ← OUTGOING
20:                    SUBEXPLOREMARGULIS(w)
21:                end if
22:            end if
23:        end for
24:    end if
25: end procedure
```

Lemma 7. *Fix a constant $c < 1$, and let A be an array of $\Omega(n/\log^3 n)$ balls with at most $|A|\exp\left((c-1)\log n(\log\log n)^t\right)$ marked balls, for $t > -2$. Then if $k\log n/\log\log n$ balls are chosen at random from A, the probability there are more than $\ell\log\log n$ marked balls chosen is $\exp\left(-O(\log n(\log\log n)^{t+1})\right)$, for every choice of $k, \ell > 0$. In particular, for $t = 0$, it is negligible in n.*

Lemma 8. *Fix constants ε, γ and k. Let A be an array of kn balls, with γkn balls marked. Shuffle A and divide it into bins of size k. The probability that there are fewer than $\left((1-\gamma)^k - \varepsilon\right)n$ empty bins is e^{-cn}, for some constant c.*

C   Proof of Theorem 2

Proof. Choose $c > \frac{1}{2}$ and suppose by way of contradiction there is some set U with $\frac{|U|}{|G|} > c$ that does not activate all of G under percolation. Let S be the set that is activated by U. Then we also have $\frac{|S|}{|G|} > c$, and all vertices in $T = G\backslash S$ have fewer than $\lceil\frac{d+1}{2}\rceil$ edges to S. By the expander mixing lemma (see e.g. [17])

we have

$$e(T,T) \leq \frac{d|T|^2}{|G|} + \lambda|T|$$

$$\leq \left(\frac{d|T|}{|G|} + 2\sqrt{d-1}\right)|T|,$$

when G is an expander graph. Taking $T = G\backslash S$ gives

$$e(T,T) \leq \left(d - \frac{dS}{G} + 2\sqrt{d-1}\right)|T|$$

$$\leq \left(d(1-c) + 2\sqrt{d-1}\right)|T|.$$

First consider the case when d is odd. We have

$$2\sqrt{d-1} < \frac{d+1}{2}$$

for $d \geq 13$, so that, for c sufficiently close to 1, we have

$$e(T,T) < \frac{d+1}{2}|T|$$

and

$$e(S,T) > \frac{d-1}{2}|T|.$$

Thus at least one vertex of T has at least $\frac{d+1}{2}$ edges to S, and can be activated, a contradiction.

The proof for d even is similar, and relies on the fact that $d = 16$ is the smallest value with

$$2\sqrt{d-1} < \frac{d}{2}.$$

Corollary C1. *For* $d = 13$, *there is some constant* γ *such that every set* S *with* $|S|/|G| \geq (1-\gamma)^{d+1}$ *is a percolating set for majority bootstrap percolation.*

Proof. This is an immediate consequence of Theorem 2 but we derive γ explicitly. We desire

$$\left(d - d(1-\gamma)^{d+1} + 2\sqrt{d-1}\right) < \frac{d+1}{2},$$

and so choose $\gamma < 0.005307$.

References

1. Asharov, G., Komargodski, I., Lin, W.-K., Nayak, K., Peserico, E., Shi, E.: Optorama: optimal oblivious RAM. Cryptology ePrint Archive, Report 2018/892 (2018). https://eprint.iacr.org/2018/892
2. Asharov, G., Komargodski, I., Lin, W.-K., Peserico, E., Shi, E.: Oblivious parallel tight compaction. Cryptology ePrint Archive, Report 2020/125 (2020). https://eprint.iacr.org/2020/125
3. Balogh, J., Bollobás, B., Morris, R.: Graph bootstrap percolation. Random Struct. Algorithms 41(4), 413–440 (2012)
4. Balogh, J., Bollobás, B., Morris, R., Riordan, O.: Linear algebra and bootstrap percolation. J. Comb. Theor. Ser. A 119(6), 1328–1335 (2012)
5. Balogh, J., Pittel, B.G.: Bootstrap percolation on the random regular graph. Random Struct. Algorithms 30(1–2), 257–286 (2007)
6. Bradonjić, M., Saniee, I.: Bootstrap percolation on random geometric graphs. Probab. Eng. Informational Sci. 28(2), 169–181 (2014)
7. Bunn, P., Katz, J., Kushilevitz, E., Ostrovsky, R.: Efficient 3-party distributed ORAM. IACR Cryptology ePrint Arch. 2018, 706 (2018)
8. Chalupa, J., Leath, P.L., Reich, G.R.: Bootstrap percolation on a bethe lattice. J. Phys. C Solid State Phys. 12(1), L31 (1979)
9. Coja-Oghlan, A., Feige, U., Krivelevich, M., Reichman, D.: Contagious sets in expanders. In: Proceedings of the Twenty-Sixth Annual ACM-SIAM Symposium on Discrete Algorithms, SIAM, pp. 1953–1987 (2014)
10. Cui, S., Belguith, S., Zhang, M., Asghar, M.R., Russello, G.: Preserving access pattern privacy in SGX-assisted encrypted search. In: 2018 27th International Conference on Computer Communication and Networks (ICCCN), pp. 1–9. IEEE (2018)
11. Di Muro, M.A., Buldyrev, S.V., Braunstein, L.A.: Reversible bootstrap percolation: fake news and fact-checking. arXiv preprint arXiv:1910.09516 (2019)
12. Dittmer, S., Ostrovsky, R.: Oblivious tight compaction in o(n) time with smaller constant. Cryptology ePrint Archive, Report 2020/377 (2020). https://eprint.iacr.org/2020/377
13. Friedman, J., et al.: Relative expanders or weakly relatively ramanujan graphs. Duke Math. J. 118(1), 19–35 (2003)
14. Gärtner, B., Zehmakan, A.N.: Majority model on random regular graphs. In: Bender, M.A., Farach-Colton, M., Mosteiro, M.A. (eds.) LATIN 2018. LNCS, vol. 10807, pp. 572–583. Springer, Cham (2018). https://doi.org/10.1007/978-3-319-77404-6_42
15. Goldreich, O., Ostrovsky, R.: Software protection and simulation on oblivious RAMs. J. ACM (JACM) 43(3), 431–473 (1996)
16. Guggiola, A., Semerjian, G.: Minimal contagious sets in random regular graphs. J. Stat. Phys. 158(2), 300–358 (2015)
17. Haemers, W.H.: Interlacing eigenvalues and graphs. Linear Algebra Appl. 226(228), 593–616 (1995)
18. Jimbo, S., Maruoka, A.: Expanders obtained from affine transformations. In: Proceedings of the Seventeenth Annual ACM Symposium on Theory of Computing, pp. 88–97 (1985)
19. Lelarge, M.: Diffusion and cascading behavior in random networks. ACM SIGMETRICS Performance Eval. Rev. 39(3), 34–36 (2011)
20. Lu, S., Ostrovsky, R.: Distributed oblivious RAM for secure two-party computation. In: Sahai, A. (ed.) TCC 2013. LNCS, vol. 7785, pp. 377–396. Springer, Heidelberg (2013). https://doi.org/10.1007/978-3-642-36594-2_22

21. Lu, S., Ostrovsky, R.: How to garble RAM programs? In: Johansson, T., Nguyen, P.Q. (eds.) EUROCRYPT 2013. LNCS, vol. 7881, pp. 719–734. Springer, Heidelberg (2013). https://doi.org/10.1007/978-3-642-38348-9_42
22. Margulis, G.A.: Explicit constructions of graphs without short cycles and low density codes. Combinatorica 2(1), 71–78 (1982)
23. Morris, R.: Minimal percolating sets in bootstrap percolation. Electron. J. Comb. 16(1), R2 (2009)
24. Morrison, N., Noel, J.A.: Extremal bounds for bootstrap percolation in the hypercube. J. Comb. Theo. Ser. A 156, 61–84 (2018)
25. Nayak, K., Katz, J.: An oblivious parallel ram with o (log2 n) parallel runtime blowup. IACR Cryptology ePrint Arch. 2016, 1141 (2016)
26. Pippenger, N.: Self-routing superconcentrators. J. Comput. Syst. Sci. 52(1), 53–60 (1996)
27. Riedl, E.: Largest minimal percolating sets in hypercubes under 2-bootstrap percolation. Electron. J. Comb. 17(R80), 1 (2010)
28. Riedl, E.: Largest and smallest minimal percolating sets in trees. Electron. J. Comb. 19, P64 (2012)
29. Ruciński, A., Wormald, N.C.: Random graph processes with degree restrictions. Comb. Probab. Comput. 1(2), 169–180 (1992)
30. Sabhapandit, S., Dhar, D., Shukla, P.: Hysteresis in the random-field ising model and bootstrap percolation. Phys. Rev. Lett. 88(19), 197202 (2002)
31. Stefanov, E., et al.: Path ORAM: an extremely simple oblivious RAM protocol. In: Proceedings of the 2013 ACM SIGSAC Conference on Computer & Communications Security, pp. 299–310 (2013)
32. Steger, A., Wormald, N.C.: Generating random regular graphs quickly. Comb. Probab. Comput. 8(4), 377–396 (1999)
33. Turova, T.S., Vallier, T.: Bootstrap percolation on a graph with random and local connections. J. Stat. Phys. 160(5), 1249–1276 (2015)
34. Williams, P., Sion, R.: Single round access privacy on outsourced storage. In: Proceedings of the 2012 ACM Conference on Computer and Communications Security, pp. 293–304 (2012)
35. Zehmakan, A.N.: Opinion forming in erdős-rényi random graph and expanders. Discrete Appl. Math. (2019)

Primitives and Constructions

Anonymity and Rewards in Peer Rating Systems

Lydia Garms[1]([✉]), Siaw–Lynn Ng[1], Elizabeth A. Quaglia[1], and Giulia Traverso[2]

[1] Royal Holloway, University of London, Egham, UK
{Lydia.Garms,S.Ng,Elizabeth.Quaglia}@rhul.ac.uk
[2] Cysec, Lausanne, Switzerland
giulia.traverso@cysec.systems

Abstract. When peers rate each other, they may rate inaccurately to boost their own reputation or unfairly lower another's. This could be mitigated by having a reputation server incentivise accurate ratings with a reward. However, assigning rewards becomes challenging when ratings are anonymous, since the reputation server cannot tell which peers to reward for rating accurately. To address this, we propose an anonymous peer rating system in which users can be rewarded for accurate ratings, and we formally define its model and security requirements. In our system ratings are rewarded in batches, so that users claiming their rewards only reveal they authored one in this batch of ratings. To ensure the anonymity set of rewarded users is not reduced, we also split the reputation server into two entities, the Rewarder, who knows which ratings are rewarded, and the Reputation Holder, who knows which users were rewarded. We give a provably secure construction satisfying all the security properties required. For our construction we use a modification of a Direct Anonymous Attestation scheme to ensure that peers can prove their own reputation when rating others, and that multiple feedback on the same subject can be detected. We then use Linkable Ring Signatures to enable peers to be rewarded for their accurate ratings, while still ensuring that ratings are anonymous. Our work results in a system which allows accurate ratings to be rewarded, whilst still providing anonymity of ratings with respect to the central entities managing the system.

1 Introduction

Anonymity has long been a sought-after property in many cryptographic primitives, such as public-key encryption [5], identity-based encryption [2,15], and a defining one in others, such as group signatures [16] and ring signatures [46]. A plethora of more complex protocols, from broadcast encryption [35] to cryptocurrencies [32], have been enhanced by user anonymity.

L. Garms—The author was supported by the EPSRC and the UK government as part of the Centre for Doctoral Training in Cyber Security at Royal Holloway, University of London (EP/K035584/1) and by the InnovateUK funded project AQuaSec.

© Springer Nature Switzerland AG 2020
C. Galdi and V. Kolesnikov (Eds.): SCN 2020, LNCS 12238, pp. 277–297, 2020.
https://doi.org/10.1007/978-3-030-57990-6_14

An example of such protocols are *rating systems*, also referred to as reputation systems, in which users can be rated by providing feedback on goods or services, with the support of a reputation server. Each user has a reputation value based on these ratings, which can be used to evaluate their trustworthiness. In this context, the value of anonymity lies in the fact that users are able to give honest feedback without fear of repercussions. This may occur when there is a lack of trust for the reputation server, or when users are concerned about retaliation.

Anonymity has received a great amount of attention in this area and abundant existing literature covers a range of anonymous rating systems in both the centralised and distributed settings. Distributed systems, e.g., [38], have no reputation server and use local reputation values, i.e., reputation values created by users on other users. For example, a user may generate a reputation value based on feedback from querying other users. This means a user does not have a unique reputation value, but many other users hold their own reputation value for them. In this setting, privacy preserving decentralised reputation systems [43] are designed to maintain anonymity when answering queries from other users.

We focus on centralised systems, since the reputation systems used by most service providers such as Airbnb, Uber and Amazon are of this type. In the centralised setting, a central reputation server enrols users and forms reputation values on these users. In [10,11,17,18,23] anonymity of a rating is provided to all except the reputation server, and multiple ratings cannot be given on the same subject. In [51], multiple reputation servers are used so that anonymity of ratings holds, unless all reputation servers collude. Other works provide anonymity of ratings in the presence of a corrupted reputation server [25,27,44,47]. In [3,8] anonymity is achieved with a different approach. The reputation server still enrols users, but no longer forms reputations. Instead users collect tokens based on anonymous ratings from other users and prove their own reputation.

Whilst the benefits of anonymity are clear, it is also understood that this same property can provide an opportunity for malicious users to misbehave. They may "bad mouth" other users, for instance competitors, giving dishonest negative feedback to these users to decrease their reputation. Or they may collude and give each other positive feedback in order to inflate their own reputation. To avoid this, the system can provide either a mechanism to revoke the malicious user's anonymity (typically achieved through a traceability property), or incentivize good behaviour by rewarding users. The rating systems proposed so far approach this issue via user tracing. Indeed, in schemes where the reputation server can de–anonymise ratings [11,17,18,23], inaccurate ratings can be punished.

We take a different approach by rewarding honest ratings in *anonymous peer rating systems*, where users are peers and anonymously rate each other. Examples include peer-to-peer file sharing [1], collaborative knowledge production [14,28,40], and shared knowledge of internet and software vulnerabilities [30,48]. In such systems the rewarding approach works well since raters are also participating within the system and so have an interest in rating accurately to increase their reputation through rewards. The use of incentives to encourage accurate feedback has already been discussed in [42,50], but ratings are not anonymous.

Privacy-preserving incentive schemes [9,12,29,33,39], where users can be incentivised anonymously without their transactions being linked, have also been proposed. In [39] it is described how such incentives could contribute towards a reputation value. However, these schemes do not capture the ability to reward accurate ratings. Firstly, ratings must be incentivised as they are submitted, at which point it is not known whether a rating is accurate. When accurate ratings are determined it is then difficult to return the incentive to the relevant user. Secondly, in [9,12,29,33], a user's balance is updated each time a user receives an incentive. However, a user may have submitted k accurate rating on other users, which are unlinkable. Then their balance of n should increase by k, but instead they receive k updated tokens for a balance of $n + 1$. Finally, in [9,12,29,39] a user would have to participate in an interactive protocol to rate others.

Therefore the challenge remains to rewards users that rate accurately, whilst preserving the anonymity of their ratings even with respect to the reputation server. This is what we address in this paper.

1.1 Our Work

We consider an anonymous peer rating system in which, at each round of inter-action, users rate each other by providing feedback to the reputation server.

Our contribution is to allow accurate ratings to be incentivised and weighted by reputation, whilst still ensuring anonymity of ratings. Achieving this is chal-lenging for two reasons. First, the reputation used to weight feedback could be used to de-anonymise a user. We can partially mitigate this by ensuring reputa-tion is coarse-grained as in [8] (by rounding the reputation value, for instance), which ensures that a user who has a unique reputation score does not reveal their identity. The trade off between precision of reputation and size of anonymity sets is further discussed in [45]. Second, and crucially, accurate ratings must be incen-tivised without being de-anonymised. We achieve this by incentivising a large set of ratings simultaneously, and rewarding the users responsible for such ratings. With this approach, however, the anonymity set can be reduced substantially. Indeed, a malicious reputation server could decide to only reward a small number of ratings it seeks to de-anonymise, and then check which users are rewarded with an increase in reputation. These users then must have authored these ratings.

A way to lessen the impact in both cases is to restrict access to reputation. A specific trusted entity, the Reputation Holder, holds the reputations of users, and the latter should only be revealed sparingly. We do not specify exactly when and how reputations should be revealed in order to allow for a flexible scheme, and because this has been discussed in the existing literature. For example, in [27,47], users can prove their reputation and so can decide which users to reveal it to. A simpler example is that a user would have to demonstrate a good reason to learn another's reputation from the Reputation Holder.

We go further and introduce a new entity, the Rewarder, who chooses which ratings to reward, and who cannot see which users have their reputation increase. As the Reputation Holder no longer knows which ratings were rewarded, they cannot compare these ratings with the users that claim rewards and so reduce the anonymity set. We formalise this in the Anonymity of Ratings under a Corrupt Reputation Holder requirement. For completeness, we also consider the case that the Reputation Holder and the Rewarder collude or are the same entity. Clearly they learn that each user that was rewarded n times, authored n of the ratings rewarded, however they should learn no more than this. We formalise this in our Anonymity of Ratings under Full Corruption requirement.

Although we are aware that using reputation values and incentivising accurate ratings both inescapably reduce the anonymity sets of ratings, in this work we aim to provide the best anonymity achievable given the functionality. Furthermore, we also must ensure that users do not attempt to subvert the system by claiming rewards that they are not entitled to, by providing multiple ratings on the same user per round, by lying about their reputation, or by framing other users so that they seem to be cheating. We formalise this in our Fair Rewards, Traceability[1], Unforgeability of Reputation and Non–Frameability requirements.

In this work we first provide a model and security requirements for an anonymous peer rating system APR, which formalises the necessary privacy and security properties discussed above. We use property-based definitions, which are intuitive and useful when proving security. We then give a construction that is provably secure given these security requirements. Our construction makes use of Direct Anonymous Attestation (DAA) [13], which we use to sign feedback. This ensures that, whilst signed feedback are unlinkable, multiple feedback on the same user can be detected, due to the user controlled linkability feature of DAA. We modify the DAA scheme so that when giving feedback a user can prove they have a particular reputation for that round, so that feedback can be weighted. We then make use of Linkable Ring Signatures [36] to allow to incentivise users who rate accurately. For every rating a freshly generated verification key is attached, encrypted under the Rewarder's public key. When the Rewarder rewards a rating, they publish the corresponding decrypted verification keys. The user can then sign a linkable ring signature with the corresponding secret key and claim their incentive from the Reputation Holder. The linkability of the signature scheme can be used to detect if a user tries to claim for the same incentive twice, whilst its anonymity ensures that ratings remain anonymous.

Although DAA and Linkable Ring Signature schemes are similar primitives, we note that they have subtly different properties that make them exactly suited to their particular role in building an APR scheme. As ring signature key pairs can be generated without involving any central entity, this allows a new verification key to be generated for every rating. The fact that a central entity, in our case the Reputation Holder, must authorise the creation of a new DAA key pair, prevents sybil attacks. Otherwise, users could easily create multiple identities and rate other users as many times as they wish per round. Unlike group signatures [16], DAA schemes do not allow a trusted opener to de–anonymise signatures, ensuring that anonymity of ratings holds with respect to the Rewarder.

---

[1] Traceability here refers to the requirement that multiple ratings cannot be given on the same subject per round.

While the main aim of our anonymous peer rating system is to ensure anonymous and honest feedback, it is also important to consider how it is affected by many other conventional attacks on rating systems. The unfair ratings attack [21] is mitigated by the detection of multiple ratings per subject per round. The incentives also encourage users to give more accurate feedback. The self–rating or self–promoting attack [31] is mitigated by encouraging all users to give feedback on their own performance. Sybil attacks [22], where a user creates multiple identities to join the system to give unfair feedback, can be mitigated by making joining the system expensive, and by a robust registration process. This also mitigates against whitewashing attacks [19], where a user leaves and rejoins to shed a bad reputation. The on-off attack [49], where a user behaves honestly to increase their reputation before behaving dishonestly, can be somewhat mitigated by adjusting the weighting of the final reputation formation in our system, so that bad behaviour will cause the reputation to deteriorate quickly. Reputation lag exploitation [34], where a user exploits the interval before the latest round of ratings takes effect, cannot be prevented but, as before, we can mitigate it by making the reputation deteriorate faster on bad behaviour.

2 Anonymous Peer Rating Systems: Definitions and Security Models

In this section, we introduce and formally define an anonymous peer rating (APR) system, and the security and privacy properties it should satisfy. We consider a set of users $\mathcal{U} = \{uid_i\}$ interacting with each other in rounds. At the end of each round they rate each other's performance, by anonymously sending a numerical feedback alongside their reputation to the Rewarder. The Rewarder collects ratings, discards multiple ratings on the same subject, and rewards accurate feedback by outputting a set of incentives. A user claims to the Reputation Holder that they were responsible for a number of these incentives. The final reputation held by the Reputation Holder on a user is based on three components: weighted feedback from other users, the number of incentives they have successfully claimed, and their previous reputation. We present an illustration of our model in Fig. 1 and formally capture this as follows.

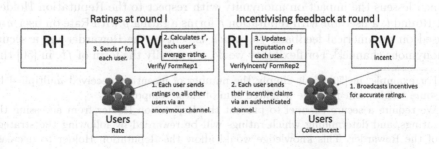

Fig. 1. Diagram illustrating our model.

Setup and Key Generation. The Reputation Holder and Rewarder generate their own key pairs. The group public key $gpk = (\text{param}, rwpk, rhpk)$ consists of the public keys of both entities.

Setup$(1^\tau, f_1, f_2) \to$ **param:** input a security parameter 1^τ, and two generic functions f_1 and f_2 which calculate the reputations of users. The function f_1 is input the number of ratings a user is being rewarded for, and outputs the second component, $\mathbf{r}''$, of their reputation for this round. The function f_2 is input the two components of a user's reputation for this round, and their reputation from the previous round, and outputs their final reputation for this round[2]. Setup outputs the public parameters param which include f_1, f_2.

RHKeyGen(**param**) $\to (rhsk, rhpk)$: performed by the Reputation Holder, outputs the Reputation Holder's secret key $rhsk$ and public key $rhpk$.

RWKeyGen(**param**) $\to (rwsk, rwpk)$: performed by the Rewarder, outputs the Rewarder's secret key $rwsk$ and public key $rwpk$.

Join. When a user joins the system they engage in an interactive protocol with the Reputation Holder after which they are issued with secret keys used to provide anonymous ratings and to collect rewards for giving honest feedback. We assume users must join the system before a round of ratings begins.

⟨**Join**$(gpk),$ **Issue**$(rhsk, gpk)$⟩: a user uid joins the system by engaging in an interactive protocol with the Reputation Holder. The user uid and Reputation Holder perform algorithms Join and Issue respectively. These are input a state and an incoming message M_{in}, and output an updated state, an outgoing message M_{out}, and a decision, either cont, accept, or reject, which denote whether the protocol is still ongoing, has ended in acceptance or has ended in rejection respectively. (States are values necessary for the next stage of the protocol.) The initial input to Join is the group public key, gpk, whereas the initial input to Issue is the Reputation Holder's secret key, $rhsk$, and the group public key gpk. If the user uid accepts, Join privately outputs the user's secret key $\mathbf{gsk}[uid]$, and Issue outputs $\mathbf{reg}[uid]$, which stores the user's registration and will be used to later allocate that user a reputation.

Ratings at Round l. Each user uid has a reputation $\mathbf{r}[uid, l]$ at round l, also held by the Reputation Holder. We assume that reputation is coarse-grained, which lessens the impact on anonymity with respect to the Reputation Holder. At Round l, a user uid with reputation r forms a rating ρ with Rate on user uid' based on a numerical feedback fb, which is sent to the Rewarder via a secure anonymous channel[3]. For flexibility we do not specify the form of fb, in [50] this

---

[2] For example, in [50], f_1 is simply the number of incentives received multiplied by some weight, and f_2 is the weighted sum of these components.

[3] We require a secure channel to prevent the Reputation Holder from accessing the ratings, and determining which ratings will be rewarded by following the strategy of the Rewarder. This knowledge would allow the Reputation Holder to decrease the anonymity set of the users claiming incentives, as in the case when both the Rewarder and Reputation Holder are corrupted.

a real number between 0 and 1. The user stores a trapdoor td for each rating for later use when claiming incentives. The Rewarder can verify ratings with Verify.

After collecting the valid ratings weighted by reputation, the Rewarder calculates an intermediate value $\mathbf{r}'[uid, l]$ for each uid with FormRep1, through which it also detect multiple ratings on the same subject. This value captures the average feedback given on uid weighted by the reputation of the rater, and is sent to the Reputation Holder via a secure authenticated channel.

Rate($\mathbf{gsk}[uid], gpk, fb, uid', l, r, \omega$) $\rightarrow$ (ρ, td) : performed by the user with identifier uid, with input the user's secret key $\mathbf{gsk}[uid]$, the group public key gpk, a feedback fb, the user who they are rating uid', the current round l, their reputation r, and a reputation token ω output in the previous round by AllocateRep. Outputs a rating ρ and a trapdoor td.

Verify($fb, uid', l, r, \rho, gpk$) $\rightarrow$ $\{0, 1\}$: a public function that is performed by the Rewarder when receiving a rating tuple (fb, uid', r, ρ). Outputs 1 if ρ is valid on the feedback fb for user uid' at round l for reputation r under the group public key gpk, and 0 otherwise.

FormRep1($uid, l, (fb_1, r_1, \rho_1), \cdots (fb_k, r_k, \rho_k), gpk$) $\rightarrow$ $\mathbf{r}'[uid, l]$: performed by the Rewarder with input k valid rating tuples $\{(fb_i, uid, r_i, \rho_i) : i \in [1, k]\}$ on user uid at round l, and the group public key gpk. Outputs $\mathbf{r}'[uid, l] = \frac{\sum_{i=1}^{k} r_i fb_i}{\sum_{i=1}^{k} r_i}$ if all ratings originate from different users' secret keys. Otherwise outputs $\perp$ (in practice also outputs ratings that should be discarded).

Incentivising Accurate Feedback. The Rewarder compares each feedback on uid'. If this is close to $\mathbf{r}'[uid', l]$ then this rating will be considered to be accurate and will be given an incentive. We define accurate as close to $\mathbf{r}'$. However, our model could simply be adapted to incorporate different metrics of accuracy.

The Rewarder inputs the k accurate ratings in this round to Incent, which outputs k incentives which are broadcast publicly to all users. Incent must be deterministic, to allow users to identify which incentives match their ratings.

A user collects all its incentives and can then use CollectIncent, along with the trapdoors stored earlier, to output an incentive claim σ for each of their incentives. They send these incentive claims to the Reputation Holder over a secure authenticated channel. Incentive claims are verified by the Reputation Holder with VerifyIncent. After gathering all the valid incentive claims, the Reputation Holder calculates the second component $\mathbf{r}''[uid, l+1]$ of a user's reputation at round l with FormRep2, which also checks that no user has claimed the same incentive twice. This value reflects how in line the feedback of uid is with respect to other users' feedback, incentivising users to give honest feedback.

Incent($(fb_1, uid_1, r_1, \rho_1), \cdots, (fb_k, uid_k, r_k, \rho_k), l, rwsk, gpk$) $\rightarrow$ $t_1, \cdots, t_k$: a deterministic function performed by the Rewarder on input k rating tuples $\{(fb_i, uid_i, r_i, \rho_i) : i \in [1, k]\}$ from round l and its secret key $rwsk$. Outputs k incentives $t_1, \cdots, t_k$.

CollectIncent($uid, (fb, uid', l, r, \rho, td), t_1, \cdots, t_k, gpk$) $\rightarrow$ σ: performed by the user uid who gave the rating tuple (fb, uid', r, ρ) for round l corresponding to trapdoor td, with input the incentives output by the Rewarder $t_1, \cdots, t_k$. Outputs an incentive claim σ if the rating tuple (fb, uid', r, ρ) corresponds to an incentive in list $t_1, \cdots, t_k$ and $\perp$ otherwise.

VerifyIncent$(uid, \sigma, t_1, \cdots, t_k, gpk) \rightarrow \{0, 1\}$: performed by the Reputation Holder when receiving an incentive claim σ from user uid on incentives $t_1, \cdots, t_k$. Outputs 1 if the incentive claim is valid on $uid, t_1, \cdots t_k$ and 0 otherwise.

FormRep2$(uid, \sigma_1, \cdots \sigma_{k_1}, t_1, \cdots, t_{k_2}, gpk) \rightarrow \mathbf{r}''[uid, l]$: performed by the Reputation Holder with input a user uid, k_1 valid incentive claims $\sigma_1, \cdots \sigma_{k_1}$ and k_2 incentives $t_1, \cdots, t_{k_2}$. Outputs $\mathbf{r}''[uid, l] = f_1(k_1)$ if no incentive has been claimed twice, and otherwise $\perp$.

Allocate Reputation For Next Round. For the first round, all users' reputations are set to an initial value. The reputation of user uid for round $l + 1$, $\mathbf{r}[uid, l + 1]$, is set by the Reputation Holder as $f_2(\mathbf{r}'[uid, l], \mathbf{r}''[uid, l], \mathbf{r}[uid, l])$ combining the user's previous reputation and the two intermediate values $\mathbf{r}'[uid, l], \mathbf{r}''[uid, l]$. This reputation value $\mathbf{r}[uid, l + 1]$, which we refer to as r, and a reputation token ω obtained from AllocateRep are given to the user via a secure authenticated channel to allow them to prove they have this reputation in the next round.

AllocateRep$(uid, r, l, rhsk, \mathbf{reg}) \rightarrow \omega$: performed by the Reputation Holder with input a user uid with reputation r during round l, the Reputation Holder's secret key $rhsk$ and the registration table $\mathbf{reg}$. Outputs reputation token ω.

2.1 Security Requirements

An APR system must satisfy Correctness, as well as the following security requirements: *Anonymity of Ratings under Full Corruption*, which formalises the strongest anonymity that can be achieved when the Rewarder and Reputation Holder are corrupted; *Anonymity of Ratings under a Corrupt Reputation Holder*, which ensures that ratings cannot be de-anonymised or linked by the Reputation Holder[4]; *Traceability*, which ensures that multiple ratings cannot be given on the same user per round; *Non–Frameability*, which ensures that users cannot be impersonated when giving ratings or claiming incentives; *Unforgeability of Reputation*, which ensures that a user cannot lie about their reputation, and *Fair Rewards*, which ensures that users can only successfully claim for the number of incentives they were awarded. We focus here on the Anonymity of Ratings and Fair Rewards requirements as these are the most novel, directly relating to the problem of incentivising anonymous ratings. However, the Traceability, Non–Frameability and Unforgeability of Reputation requirements are given in the full version of this paper [26].

We provide definitions in the computational model of cryptography. These are typically formulated as experiments in which an adversary, having access

---

[4] The case of a corrupt Rewarder is captured in the Anonymity of Ratings under Full Corruption requirement.

to a certain number of *oracles*, is challenged to produce an output. Such output captures an instance of the system in which the security requirement does not hold. In Fig. 2, we provide the oracles used in our security requirements: AddU, SndToU, SndToRH, AllocateRep, USK, Rate, TD, Incent, Collect, based on notation from [6]. We give a high level description below:

- AddU (Add User): creates an honest user *uid*.
- SndToU (Send to User): creates honest users when the adversary has corrupted the Reputation Holder. The adversary impersonates the RH, and engages in a <Join, Issue> protocol with an honest user.
- SndToRH (Send to RH): creates corrupted users, when the adversary has not corrupted the Reputation Holder. The adversary impersonates a user and engages in a < Join, Issue > protocol with an honest RH.
- AllocateRep: allows an adversary to obtain outputs of AllocateRep.
- USK: allows an adversary to obtain the secret key of an honest user.
- Rate: allows an adversary to perform Rate on behalf of an honest user.
- TD: allows an adversary to obtain a trapdoor associated to a rating that has been obtained through the Rate oracle.
- Incent: allows an adversary to obtain outputs of Incent.
- Collect: allows an adversary to obtain outputs of CollectIncent for a rating that has been output by the Rate oracle and then input to the Incent oracle.

All oracles have access to the following records maintained as global state which are initially set to ∅:

HL List of *uids* of honest users. New honest users can be added by queries to the AddU oracle (for an honest RH) or SndToU oracle (for a corrupt RH).

CL List of corrupt users that have requested to join the group. New corrupt users can be added through the SndToRH oracle if the RH is honest. If the RH is corrupt, we do not keep track of corrupt users.

AL List of all queries to the AllocateRep oracle for corrupt users.

SL List of queries and outputs from the Rate oracle.

TDL List of queries to the TD oracle.

IL List of queries, and outputs of the Incent oracle.

CLL List of queries, and outputs of the Collect oracle.

Correctness. An APR system is correct, if when Rate is input an honestly generated secret key and a reputation token, it will output a valid rating. Provided all ratings input to FormRep1 originate from different users it will output the correct function. Also, if Incent and CollectIncent are performed honestly on k valid ratings, the resulting incentive claims will be valid. Provided each incentive is only claimed once, FormRep2 will output $f_1(k)$. We give the full requirement in the full version of this paper [26].

Fig. 2. Oracles used in our security requirements

Anonymity of Ratings. We now give the requirements for both corruption settings that ensure ratings cannot be de-anonymised or linked by user, provided multiple ratings on the same user per round are not given. We also must ensure that ratings cannot be linked to the corresponding incentive claim. This is crucial to ensuring ratings are anonymous, as incentive claims are sent fully authenticated and so, if linkable to the corresponding rating, they could be used to de-anonymise such ratings.

Anonymity of Ratings under Full Corruption. We first formally define anonymity of ratings in the case both the Rewarder and the Reputation Holder have been corrupted. In this setting, the following attack can always be mounted: The adversary, having corrupted the Rewarder and Reputation Holder, wishes to de-anonymise a specific rating and so simply only rewards this rating. The author of the rating then claims their reward from the Reputation Holder, revealing their identity. Such an attack is unavoidable when incentivising accurate feedback.

However, we can still provide some guarantee of anonymity, namely that the adversary should learn no more than the following: a user that has been rewarded n times per round is responsible for n of the rewarded ratings for that round. When $n = 1$ the above attack still holds, but this dishonest behaviour of the Rewarder can be detected as only one incentive would be publicly broadcast. Our security requirement achieves this by allowing the challenge rating to be input to the Collect oracle, on the condition that an additional rating authored by the other challenged user is added to the inputs. By including ratings originating from both challenged users, the incentives claimed by both of these users will increase by 1, and so the adversary cannot use this to trivially win. We note that this notion implies the anonymity requirement when just the Rewarder is corrupted, i.e., it is the strongest of the two requirements.

In the security game the Reputation Holder and Rewarder are corrupted, and so the adversary can create corrupted users. The adversary chooses two honest users, as well as a feedback, a user who is the subject of the feedback, and a reputation. The adversary must give reputation tokens for each user for this reputation. The adversary is returned with a challenge rating authored by one of these users, with this reputation, on this feedback and user (subject), and they must guess which user authored the rating. The challenge rating as well as another rating authored by the other challenged user is saved in RL, for later use in the Collect oracle. The adversary can create honest users with the SndToU oracle and obtain their ratings with the Rate oracle. However they cannot query to the Rate oracle either of the users that were challenged as well as the challenge subject/round. Otherwise the FormRep1 algorithm could be used to trivially win, due to the detection of multiple ratings on the same user/round. We also must check that both ratings computed from the challenged users are valid, to ensure that both ω_0 or ω_1 output by the adversary were correctly formed. The adversary can also reveal the trapdoor from each Rate oracle query with the TD oracle, but not for the challenge ratings as this would lead to a trivial win by detecting double claims with FormRep2. They also have access to an Incent oracle. The adversary can query incentives from the Incent oracle, that originate from the Rate oracle, to the Collect oracle. If they include the challenge rating, an additional rating from the other challenged user is added to the inputs. The adversary is returned with the incentive claims for these ratings along with the user who claims them. This captures the fact that claiming incentives should not violate the anonymity of ratings. We give the full game below:

Experiment: $\mathsf{Exp}_{\mathcal{A},\mathsf{APR}}^{anon\text{-}fullcorr}(\tau, f_1, f_2)$

$b \leftarrow_\$ \{0,1\}, \mathsf{RL}, \mathsf{RL}^\dagger \leftarrow \emptyset, param \leftarrow_\$ \mathsf{Setup}(1^\tau, f_1, f_2), (rhsk, rhpk) \leftarrow_\$ \mathsf{RHKeyGen}(param)$

$(rwsk, rwpk) \leftarrow_\$ \mathsf{RWKeyGen}(param), gpk \leftarrow (param, rwpk, rhpk)$

$(st, uid_0^*, uid_1^*, l^*, fb^*, uid'^*, r^*, \omega_0, \omega_1) \leftarrow_\$ \mathcal{A}^{\mathsf{SndToU,Rate,TD,Incent,Collect}}(\text{choose}, gpk, rhsk, rwsk)$

if $uid_0^*, uid_1^* \notin \mathsf{HL}$ or $\mathbf{gsk}[uid_0^*], \mathbf{gsk}[uid_1^*] = \perp$ return $\perp$

$\forall b' \in \{0,1\}$ $(td_{b'}^*, \rho_{b'}^*) \leftarrow_\$ \mathsf{Rate}(\mathbf{gsk}[uid_{b'}^*], gpk, fb^*, uid'^*, l^*, r^*, \omega_{b'})$

// Compute both ratings for use in Collect oracle and to check ω_0, ω_1

$\mathsf{RL} \leftarrow \{(uid_{b'}^*, uid'^*, fb^*, r^*, \rho_{b'}^*, td_{b'}^*, l^*) : b' \in \{0,1\}\}$ // Save both ratings for use in Collect

$d \leftarrow_\$ \mathcal{A}^{\mathsf{SndToU,Rate,TD,Incent,Collect}}(\text{guess}, st, \rho_b^*)$

if ρ_0^* or $\rho_1^* = \perp$ or $\exists b' \in \{0,1\}$ s.t $(uid_{b'}^*, uid'^*, \cdot, \cdot, \cdot, \cdot, l^*) \in \mathsf{SL}$

// Check ω_0, ω_1 are both valid and FormRep1 can't be used to trivially win by detecting multiple ratings

   return $d \leftarrow_\$ \{0,1\}$

if $d = b$ return 1   else return 0

An APR system satisfies Anonymity of Ratings under Full Corruption if for all functions f_1, f_2, for all polynomial time adversaries $\mathcal{A}$, the following advantage is negligible in τ:

$$|\Pr[\mathsf{Exp}_{\mathcal{A},\mathsf{APR}}^{anon-fullcorr}(\tau, f_1, f_2) = 1] - 1/2|.$$

Anonymity of Ratings under a Corrupt Reputation Holder. We next define anonymity in the setting where the Reputation Holder has been corrupted, but not the Rewarder. This means that the adversary now does not know which ratings have been rewarded. The challenge rating and a rating authored by the other challenged user are now stored in list $\mathsf{RL}^\dagger$. The adversary has full access to the Collect oracle, modelling the role of the Reputation Holder. However, if the challenge rating is input to the Incent oracle, the rating authored by the other challenged user stored in $\mathsf{RL}^\dagger$ is also added to the inputs. The Incent oracle shuffles the outputs. This represents that the Reputation Holder no longer knows which rating is linked to each incentive.

Experiment: $\mathsf{Exp}_{\mathcal{A},\mathsf{APR}}^{anon\text{-}rh}(\tau, f_1, f_2)$

$b \leftarrow_\$ \{0,1\}, \mathsf{RL}, \mathsf{RL}^\dagger \leftarrow \emptyset, param \leftarrow_\$ \mathsf{Setup}(1^\tau, f_1, f_2), (rhsk, rhpk) \leftarrow_\$ \mathsf{RHKeyGen}(param)$

$(rwsk, rwpk) \leftarrow_\$ \mathsf{RWKeyGen}(param), gpk \leftarrow (param, rwpk, rhpk)$

$(st, uid_0^*, uid_1^*, l^*, fb^*, uid'^*, r^*, \omega_0, \omega_1) \leftarrow_\$ \mathcal{A}^{\mathsf{SndToU,Rate,TD,Incent,Collect}}(\text{choose}, gpk, rhsk)$

if $uid_0^*, uid_1^* \notin \mathsf{HL}$ or $\mathbf{gsk}[uid_0^*], \mathbf{gsk}[uid_1^*] = \perp$ return $\perp$

$\forall b' \in \{0,1\}$ $(td_{b'}^*, \rho_{b'}^*) \leftarrow_\$ \mathsf{Rate}(\mathbf{gsk}[uid_{b'}^*], gpk, fb^*, uid'^*, l^*, r^*, \omega_{b'})$

// Compute both ratings for use in Incent oracle and to check ω_0, ω_1

$\mathsf{RL}^\dagger \leftarrow \{(uid_{b'}^*, uid'^*, fb^*, r^*, \rho_{b'}^*, td_{b'}^*, l^*) : b' \in \{0,1\}\}$ // Save both ratings for use in Incent

$d \leftarrow_\$ \mathcal{A}^{\mathsf{SndToU,Rate,TD,Incent,Collect}}(\text{guess}, st, \rho_b^*)$

if ρ_0^* or $\rho_1^* = \perp$ or $\exists b' \in \{0,1\}$ s.t $(uid_{b'}^*, uid'^*, \cdot, \cdot, \cdot, \cdot, l^*) \in \mathsf{SL}$

// Check ω_0, ω_1 are both valid and FormRep1 can't be used to trivially win by detecting multiple ratings

   return $d \leftarrow_\$ \{0,1\}$

if $d = b$ return 1   else return 0

An APR system satisfies Anonymity of Ratings under a Corrupt Reputation Holder if for all f_1, f_2, for all polynomial time adversaries $\mathcal{A}$, the following advantage is negligible in τ:

$$|\Pr[\mathsf{Exp}_{\mathcal{A},\mathsf{APR}}^{anon-rh}(\tau, f_1, f_2) = 1] - 1/2|.$$

Fair Rewards. This requirement ensures that an adversary cannot increase the number of incentives they were allocated, or steal incentives allocated to other users. In the security game the Rewarder and the Reputation Holder are corrupted, so the adversary can create corrupted users. The adversary is given the SndToU and Rate oracles to create honest users, and obtain their ratings. They have access to the Collect oracles to obtain incentive claims on incentives obtained from the Rate oracle followed by the Incent oracle. They have access to the trapdoor oracle, to obtain trapdoors associated to ratings output by Rate. The adversary must choose k_1 incentives obtained from the Incent oracle, and k_2 valid incentive claims, not output by the Collect oracle, corresponding to a single user identifier. If FormRep2 doesn't detect cheating, and more incentive claims are output than incentives corresponding to ratings not obtained through the Rate oracle or queried to the trapdoor oracle, then the adversary wins. We give the full game below:

Experiment: $\mathsf{Exp}_{\mathcal{A},\mathsf{APR}}^{fair-rew}(\tau, f_1, f_2)$

$\mathsf{RL}, \mathsf{RL}^\dagger \leftarrow \emptyset, \mathsf{param} \leftarrow_\$ \mathsf{Setup}(1^\tau, f_1, f_2), (rhsk, rhpk) \leftarrow_\$ \mathsf{RHKeyGen}(\mathsf{param})$

$(rwsk, rwpk) \leftarrow_\$ \mathsf{RWKeyGen}(\mathsf{param}), gpk \leftarrow (\mathsf{param}, rwpk, rhpk)$

$(uid, (\sigma_1, \cdots \sigma_{k_2}), (t_1, \cdots t_{k_1}), l) \leftarrow_\$ \mathcal{A}^{\mathsf{SndToU},\mathsf{Rate},\mathsf{TD},\mathsf{Incent},\mathsf{Collect}}(gpk, rwsk, rhsk)$

if $\exists i \in [k_1]$ s.t $(t_i, (fb_i, uid_i', r_i, \rho_i)) \notin \mathsf{IL}$ **return** 0

return 1   **if**   the following conditions hold

    $\forall i \in [k_2]$ σ_i not returned by Collect oracle and $\mathsf{VerifyIncent}(uid, \sigma_i, (t_1, \cdots, t_{k_1})) = 1$ and

    $\mathsf{FormRep2}(uid, \sigma_1, \cdots \sigma_{k_2}, t_1, \cdots t_{k_1}, gpk) \neq \perp$ and

    $k_2 > |\{i \in [k_1] : (\cdot, uid_i', fb_i, r_i, \rho_i, \cdot, l) \notin \mathsf{SL}$ or $(fb_i, uid_i', l, r_i, \rho_i) \in \mathsf{TDL}\}|$

An APR system satisfies Fair Rewards if for all functions f_1, f_2, for all polynomial time adversaries $\mathcal{A}$, the advantage $\Pr[\mathsf{Exp}_{\mathcal{A},\mathsf{APR}}^{fair-rew}(\tau, f_1, f_2) = 1]$ is negligible in τ.

3   Construction

We propose a construction for an APR system which makes use of three building blocks: Linkable Ring Signatures (LRS), a modified Direct Anonymous Attestation (DAA*) scheme and a public–key encryption scheme.

Ring signatures [46] allow users to sign on behalf of a ring of users, without revealing their identity within the ring. There is no central entity involved, and users generate their own signing and verification keys. Linkable ring signatures [36] allow for the public linking of signatures by signer. We exploit these features to allow for incentivising accurate ratings as follows. Each rating includes a freshly generated verification key encrypted under the public key of the Rewarder, and the user who has generated the rating stores the corresponding signing key as a trapdoor. The Rewarder publishes these decrypted verification keys as incentives. Then to claim an incentive the user uses the signing key to sign a ring signature on their user identifier with respect to the ring of verification keys given as incentives. The anonymity of Linkable Ring Signatures ensures that claiming incentives will not de-anonymise ratings. The unforgeability property ensures that only users that have been rewarded can claim an incentive, and the linking function ensures that only one reward can be claimed per rating.

Direct Anonymous Attestation (DAA) [13] allows users to sign on behalf of a group, whilst remaining anonymous within the group. The user-controlled linkability feature, where two signatures on the same basename by the same user are linked, whilst all other signatures are unlinkable, can be used to detect multiple feedback on the same subject. In our setting, the basename can be set to be the user who is the subject of the feedback and the round. In our system we also wish to ensure feedback is weighted by reputation. However, this must also be balanced with anonymity of feedback. For this to be possible the reputation of users must be coarse-grained enough that they cannot be identified by their reputation. To ensure this, we bind reputation into a Direct Anonymous Attestation scheme, which we will call a DAA* scheme. Now a user proves their reputation when signing, allowing for the weighting of feedback.

3.1   Public-Key Encryption Schemes

Our scheme makes use of a public–key encryption scheme, which consists of the following: $\mathsf{EncSetup}(1^\tau)$, which is input the security parameter 1^τ and outputs parameters $\mathsf{param}_{\mathsf{Enc}}$; $\mathsf{EncKeyGen}(\mathsf{param}_{\mathsf{Enc}})$, which is input the parameters and outputs secret key sk and the public key pk; $\mathsf{Enc}(pk, m)$, which is input the public key pk and a message m from the message space, and outputs a ciphertext c; and $\mathsf{Dec}(sk, c)$, which is input the secret key sk and a ciphertext c, and outputs a message m or a decryption failure $\perp$. We require the encryption scheme to be correct and satisfy indistinguishability under adaptive chosen ciphertext attacks.

3.2   Linkable Ring Signatures

We use the model in [4] for one-time linkable ring signatures, which gives the strongest security yet. The scheme from [4] has the shortest signatures to date. We give the security requirements: Correctness Linkability, Linkable Anonymity, Non–Frameability and Unforgeability in the full version [26].

Definition 1 (Linkable Ring Signatures). A linkable ring signature scheme LRS is given by polynomial time algorithms (LRKeyGen, LRSign, LRVerify, LRLink):

LRKeyGen(1^τ): takes as input the security parameter 1^τ and outputs a pair (vk, sk) of verification and signing keys.

LRSign(sk, m, R): takes as input a signing key sk, a message m, and a list of verification keys $R = (vk_1, ..., vk_q)$, and outputs a signature Σ.

LRVerify(R, m, Σ): takes as input a ring $R = (vk_1, ..., vk_q)$, a message m, and a signature Σ, and outputs either 0 or 1.

LRLink($\Sigma_1, \Sigma_2, m_1, m_2$) : is input two signatures/ messages, outputs 0 or 1.

3.3   DAA* Signatures

The security model of DAA* closely follows that of pre–DAA signatures [7]. We give the security requirements for DAA* signatures in the full version [26].

Definition 2 (DAA*). A DAA* scheme consists of the following algorithms:

DAA*Setup(1^τ): input the security parameter τ, outputs parameters param.

DAA*KeyGen(param): input the parameters param, outputs the group public key gpk, and the issuing secret key isk.

⟨DAA*Join(gpk), DAA*Issue(isk, gpk)⟩: a user i joins the group by engaging in an interactive protocol with the Issuer. The user i and Issuer perform algorithms DAA*Join and DAA*Issue respectively. These are input a state and an incoming message respectively, and output an updated state, an outgoing message, and a decision, either cont, accept, or reject. The initial input to DAA*Join is the group public key, whereas the initial input to DAA*Issue is the issuer secret key, isk, and the group public key. If the issuer accepts, DAA*Join has a private output of **gsk**[i], DAA*Issue has a private output of **reg**[i].

DAA*Update($r, t, isk, i, $**reg**$, gpk$): input a reputation r, a time t, the issuing secret key isk, a user i, the registration list **reg**, gpk. Outputs a token ω.

DAA*Sign($bsn, m, $**gsk**$[i], \omega, gpk, r, t$): input a basename bsn, a message m, a user secret key **gsk**[i], a token ω output by DAA*Update, a group public key gpk, a reputation r and time t. It checks that ω is valid for user i, reputation r and time t and outputs a signature Ω. Otherwise it outputs $\perp$.

DAA*Verify($bsn, m, r, t, \Omega, gpk$): input a basename bsn, a message m, a reputation r, time t, a signature Ω, and a group public key gpk. It outputs 1 if Ω is valid for the item I, reputation r and time t, and 0 otherwise.

DAA*Link($(bsn_0, m_0, r_0, t_0, \Omega_0), (bsn_1, m_1, r_1, t_1, \Omega_1), gpk$): input two signatures Ω_0, Ω_1 each on a basename, a message, a reputation, a time, and a group public key gpk. It outputs 1 if both signatures are valid, $bsn_0 = bsn_1$ and the two signatures have the same author, and 0 otherwise.

DAA*Identify$_T(\mathcal{T}, gsk$): outputs 1 if $\mathcal{T}$ corresponds to a valid transcript of <DAA*Join, DAA*Issue>, with output gsk to DAA*Join, and otherwise 0.

DAA*Identify$_S(bsn, m, r, t, \Omega, gsk$): outputs 1 if the signature Ω could have been produced with user secret key gsk, and 0 otherwise.

3.4   Our Construction

We now present our construction that securely realizes an APR system, using a PKE scheme, an LRS scheme and a DAA* scheme. We give our construction in Fig. 3, except for the <Join, Issue> protocol which is identical to the

$\underline{\text{Setup}(1^r, f_1, f_2)}$

return $(\text{DAA*Setup}(1^r), \text{EncSetup}(1^r), f_1, f_2)$

$\underline{\text{RHKeyGen}(\text{param}_{\text{DAA*}}, \text{param}_{\text{Enc}}, f_1, f_2)}$

$(rhsk, rhpk) \leftarrow_s \text{DAA*KeyGen}(\text{param}_{\text{DAA*}})$ return $(rhsk, rhpk)$

$\underline{\text{RWKeyGen}(\text{param}_{\text{DAA*}}, \text{param}_{\text{Enc}}, f_1, f_2)}$

$(rwsk, rwpk) \leftarrow_s \text{EncKeyGen}(\text{param}_{\text{Enc}})$ return $(rwsk, rwpk)$

$\underline{\text{Rate}(\text{gsk}[uid], gpk, fb, uid', l, r, \omega)}$

$(vk, td) \leftarrow_s \text{LRKeyGen}(1^r), \bar{vk} \leftarrow_s \text{Enc}(rwpk, vk)$

$\Omega \leftarrow_s \text{DAA*Sign}((uid', l), (fb, \bar{vk}), \text{gsk}[uid], \omega, gpk, r, l), \rho \leftarrow (\Omega, \bar{vk})$

$\underline{\text{Verify}(fb, uid', l, r, \rho = (\Omega, \bar{vk}), gpk)}$

$\text{DAA*Verify}((uid', l), (fb, \bar{vk}), r, l, \Omega, gpk)$

$\underline{\text{FormRep1}(uid, l, (fb_1, r_1, (\Omega_1, \bar{vk}_1)), \cdots, (fb_k, r_k, (\Omega_k, \bar{vk}_k)), gpk)}$

$\forall (i, j) \in [k]$ s.t $i \neq j$ **if** $\text{DAA*Link}(((uid, l), (fb_i, \bar{vk}_i), r_i, l, \Omega_i), ((uid, l), (fb_j, \bar{vk}_j), r_j, l, \Omega_j), gpk) = 1$ **return** $\perp$

else return $\frac{\sum_{i=1}^k r_i fb_i}{\sum_{i=1}^k r_i}$

$\underline{\text{Incent}(\{(fb_i, uid_i, r_i, (\Omega_i, \bar{vk}_i)) : i \in [k]\}, l, rwsk, gpk)}$

$\forall i \in [k]$ $t_i \leftarrow \text{Dec}(rwsk, \bar{vk}_i)$ **return** $(t_1, \cdots, t_k)$

$\underline{\text{CollectIncent}(uid, (fb, uid', l, r, \rho, td), t_1, \cdots, t_k, gpk)}$

return $\sigma \leftarrow_s \text{LRSign}(td, uid, (t_1, \cdots t_k))$

$\underline{\text{VerifyIncent}(uid, \sigma, t_1, \cdots, t_k, gpk)}$

return $\text{LRVerify}((t_1, \cdots t_k), uid, \sigma)$

$\underline{\text{FormRep2}(uid, \sigma_1, \cdots \sigma_{k_1}, t_1, \cdots, t_{k_2}, gpk)}$

$\forall i, j \in [k_1]$ s.t $i \neq j$ **if** $\text{LRLink}(\sigma_i, \sigma_j, uid, uid) = 1$ **return** $\perp$ **else return** $f_1(k_1)$

$\underline{\text{AllocateRep}(uid, r[uid, l], l, isk, reg)}$

return $\text{DAA*Update}(r[uid, l], l, isk, uid, reg, gpk)$

Fig. 3. Our APR construction

<DAA*Join, DAA*Issue> protocol for DAA* signatures such that DAA*Join is input $rhpk$, and DAA*Issue is input $(rhsk, rhpk)$.

3.5   Security of Our Construction

We show that our construction satisfies the security requirements for an APR system defined in Sect. 2. We need one further property than the security of the LRS and DAA* building blocks. In the <Join, Issue> protocol, the RH must be sent an SPK of the user's secret key. SPK denotes a signature proof of knowledge, that is a non-interactive transformation of a proof PK. These proofs can be extended to be online-extractable [24], by verifiably encrypting the witness to a public key defined in the common reference string. We require the proof system to be simulation-sound, online–extractable and zero-knowledge. We give further details on the proof protocols used in the full version [26].

Theorem 1. *The construction presented in Fig. 3 is a secure APR, as defined in Sect. 2, if the LRS scheme, DAA* scheme and PKE scheme used are secure, and the SPK is online extractable, simulation sound, and zero-knowledge.*

The detailed proofs of Lemmata 1–6 are given in the full version [26].

Lemma 1. *The construction satisfies Anonymity of Ratings under Full–Corruption if the LRS and DAA* schemes satisfy Anonymity, and the SPK is zero-knowledge.*

Proof intuition. A distinguisher between the original game and one where the challenged user identifiers are swapped in the `Collect` oracle when the challenge rating is input, can break the anonymity of linkable ring signatures. A reduction can now be made to the anonymity of our DAA* scheme. □

Lemma 2. *The construction satisfies Anonymity of Ratings under a Corrupt Reputation Holder if the DAA* scheme satisfies Anonymity and the PKE scheme satisfies indistinguishability under adaptive chosen ciphertext attacks, and the SPK is zero-knowledge.*

Proof intuition. A distinguisher between the original game and a game where the `Collect` oracle, on input an incentive from the ratings in $RL^\dagger$, swaps the user identifiers, can break the IND–CCA2 security of the encryption scheme. A reduction can now be made to the anonymity of our DAA* scheme. □

Lemma 3. *The construction satisfies Traceability if the DAA* scheme satisfies both Traceability and Non–Frameability, and the SPK is online extractable and simulation sound.*

Lemma 4. *The construction satisfies Non–Frameability if the LRS and DAA* schemes both satisfy Non–Frameability, and the SPK is zero-knowledge.*

Lemma 5. *The construction satisfies Unforgeability of Reputation if the DAA* scheme satisfies Unforgeability of Reputation, and the SPK is online extractable and simulation sound.*

Lemma 6. *The construction satisfies Fair Rewards if the LRS scheme satisfies Linkability and Non–Frameability.*

Proof intuition. An adversary breaks fair rewards either by "stealing" an incentive from an honest user, in which case we could break the non–frameability of LRS, or by expanding the incentives that were fairly allocated to corrupted users, in which case we could break the Linkability of LRS. □

3.6   Concrete Instantiation and Efficiency

We give a DAA* construction, and prove that it securely realizes a DAA* scheme in the full version [26], assuming the LRSW [37], DCR [41], and DDH assumptions and the random oracle model. The <DAA*Join, DAA*Issue> protocol already contains a suitable SPK of the user secret key. A linkable ring signature scheme that securely realises the model in Sect. 3.2 is given in [4]. An incentive claim would have size $\log(l)\mathsf{poly}(\tau)$, where l is the number of incentives. This is the current state of the art for linkable ring signatures, and is reasonable, albeit large. Ratings are reasonably small, and consist of 7 τ-bit elements, and an encryption of 3 commitments.

4   Conclusion and Future Work

We give a security model for an anonymous peer rating system APR that allows accurate ratings to be incentivised, feedback to be weighted by reputation, and multiple feedback on the same subject to be detected, whilst still ensuring ratings remain anonymous. We use Linkable Ring Signatures and a modification of DAA to build a construction that is secure under these requirements.

The DAA and Linkable Ring Signature primitives are not inherent in realising our anonymous peer ratings system. Different primitives could be used to build constructions that are more efficient or rely on different assumptions.

In a peer rating system, a high reputation score leads to a real payoff for users, corresponding to an increase in utility. When increasing one's utility is the ultimate goal, game theory helps to gain new insights. A peer rating system formalised through game theory, which also follows the strategies of weighting feedback and incentivising accurate ratings, is proposed in [50] and experimentally simulated when used in collaborative intrusion detection systems in [20]. It is shown in [50] to what extent it pays off for users to rate accurately given the size of incentives and the size of the coalition(s) of dishonest users. However, anonymity of ratings is not taken into account and a fully trusted central authority receives the ratings and issues the incentives. As future work, we want to determine game theoretically whether our scheme incentivises accurate ratings.

References

1. Gnutella. https://en.wikipedia.org/wiki/Gnutella. Accessed 30 Aug 2019
2. Abdalla, M., et al.: Searchable encryption revisited: consistency properties, relation to anonymous IBE, and extensions. In: Shoup, V. (ed.) CRYPTO 2005. LNCS, vol. 3621, pp. 205–222. Springer, Heidelberg (Aug (2005)
3. Androulaki, E., Choi, S.G., Bellovin, S.M., Malkin, T.: Reputation systems for anonymous networks. In: Borisov, N., Goldberg, I. (eds.) PETS 2008. LNCS, vol. 5134, pp. 202–218. Springer, Heidelberg (2008). https://doi.org/10.1007/978-3-540-70630-4_13
4. Backes, M., Döttling, N., Hanzlik, L., Kluczniak, K., Schneider, J.: Ring signatures: logarithmic-size, no setup—from standard assumptions. In: Ishai, Y., Rijmen, V. (eds.) EUROCRYPT 2019. LNCS, vol. 11478, pp. 281–311. Springer, Cham (2019). https://doi.org/10.1007/978-3-030-17659-4_10
5. Bellare, M., Boldyreva, A., Desai, A., Pointcheval, D.: Key-privacy in public-key encryption. In: Boyd, C. (ed.) ASIACRYPT 2001. LNCS, vol. 2248, pp. 566–582. Springer, Heidelberg (2001). https://doi.org/10.1007/3-540-45682-1_33
6. Bellare, M., Shi, H., Zhang, C.: Foundations of group signatures: the case of dynamic groups. In: Menezes, A. (ed.) CT-RSA 2005. LNCS, vol. 3376, pp. 136–153. Springer, Heidelberg (2005). https://doi.org/10.1007/978-3-540-30574-3_11
7. Bernhard, D., Fuchsbauer, G., Ghadafi, E.M., Smart, N.P., Warinschi, B.: Anonymous attestation with user-controlled linkability. Int. J. Inf. Secur. 12(3), 219–249 (2013)

8. Bethencourt, J., Shi, E., Song, D.: Signatures of reputation. In: Sion, R. (ed.) FC 2010. LNCS, vol. 6052, pp. 400–407. Springer, Heidelberg (2010). https://doi.org/10.1007/978-3-642-14577-3_35

9. Blömer, J., Bobolz, J., Diemert, D., Eidens, F.: Updatable anonymous credentials and applications to incentive systems. In: Cavallaro, L., Kinder, J., Wang, X., Katz, J. (eds.) ACM CCS 2019, pp. 1671–1685. ACM Press, November 2019

10. Blömer, J., Eidens, F., Juhnke, J.: Practical, anonymous, and publicly linkable universally-composable reputation systems. In: Smart, N.P. (ed.) CT-RSA 2018. LNCS, vol. 10808, pp. 470–490. Springer, Cham (2018). https://doi.org/10.1007/978-3-319-76953-0_25

11. Blömer, J., Juhnke, J., Kolb, C.: Anonymous and publicly linkable reputation systems. In: Böhme, R., Okamoto, T. (eds.) FC 2015. LNCS, vol. 8975, pp. 478–488. Springer, Heidelberg (2015). https://doi.org/10.1007/978-3-662-47854-7_29

12. Bobolz, J., Eidens, F., Krenn, S., Slamanig, D., Striecks, C.: Privacy-preserving incentive systems with highly efficient point-collection. In: To Apppear at Proceedings of the 2020 ACM Asia Conference on Computer and Communications Security (2020)

13. Brickell, E.F., Camenisch, J., Chen, L.: Direct anonymous attestation. In: Atluri, V., Pfitzmann, B., McDaniel, P. (eds.) ACM CCS 2004, pp. 132–145. ACM Press, October 2004

14. Brinckman, A., et al.: Collaborative circuit designs using the CRAFT repository. Future Gener. Comput. Syst. **94**, 841–853 (2019)

15. Camenisch, J., Kohlweiss, M., Rial, A., Sheedy, C.: Blind and anonymous identity-based encryption and authorised private searches on public key encrypted data. In: Jarecki, S., Tsudik, G. (eds.) PKC 2009. LNCS, vol. 5443, pp. 196–214. Springer, Heidelberg (2009). https://doi.org/10.1007/978-3-642-00468-1_12

16. Chaum, D., van Heyst, E.: Group signatures. In: Davies, D.W. (ed.) EUROCRYPT 1991. LNCS, vol. 547, pp. 257–265. Springer, Heidelberg (1991). https://doi.org/10.1007/3-540-46416-6_22

17. Chen, L., Li, Q., Martin, K.M., Ng, S.L.: A privacy-aware reputation-based announcement scheme for VANETs. In: 2013 IEEE 5th International Symposium on Wireless Vehicular Communications (WiVeC), pp. 1–5. IEEE (2013)

18. Chen, L., Li, Q., Martin, K.M., Ng, S.L.: Private reputation retrieval in public - a privacy-aware announcement scheme for vanets. IET Inf. Secur. **11**(4), 204–210 (2017)

19. Chuang, J.: Designing incentive mechanisms for peer-to-peer systems. In: 1st IEEE International Workshop on Grid Economics and Business Models, 2004, GECON 2004, pp. 67–81. IEEE (2004)

20. Cordero, C.G., et al.: Sphinx: a colluder-resistant trust mechanism for collaborative intrusion detection. IEEE Access **6**, 72427–72438 (2018)

21. Dellarocas, C.: Immunizing online reputation reporting systems against unfair ratings and discriminatory behavior. In: Proceedings of the 2nd ACM Conference on Electronic Commerce, March 2001

22. Douceur, J.R.: The sybil attack. In: Druschel, P., Kaashoek, F., Rowstron, A. (eds.) IPTPS 2002. LNCS, vol. 2429, pp. 251–260. Springer, Heidelberg (2002). https://doi.org/10.1007/3-540-45748-8_24

23. El Kaafarani, A., Katsumata, S., Solomon, R.: Anonymous reputation systems achieving full dynamicity from lattices. In: Proceedings of the 22nd International Conference on Financial Cryptography and Data Security (FC) (2018)

24. Fischlin, M.: Communication-efficient non-interactive proofs of knowledge with online extractors. In: Shoup, V. (ed.) CRYPTO 2005. LNCS, vol. 3621, pp. 152–168. Springer, Heidelberg (2005). https://doi.org/10.1007/11535218_10
25. Garms, L., Martin, K.M., Ng, S.L.: Reputation schemes for pervasive social networks with anonymity. In: Proceedings of the Fifteenth International Conference on Privacy, Security and Trust (PST 2017), pp. 1–6. IEEE, August 2017
26. Garms, L., Quaglia, E., Ng, S.L., Traverso, G.: Anonymity and rewards in peer rating systems. Cryptology ePrint Archive, Report 2020/790 (2020). https://eprint.iacr.org/2020/790
27. Garms, L., Quaglia, E.A.: A new approach to modelling centralised reputation systems. In: Buchmann, J., Nitaj, A., Rachidi, T. (eds.) AFRICACRYPT 2019. LNCS, vol. 11627, pp. 429–447. Springer, Cham (2019). https://doi.org/10.1007/978-3-030-23696-0_22
28. Giannoulis, M., Kondylakis, H., Marakakis, E.: Designing and implementing a collaborative health knowledge system. Expert Syst. Appl. **126**, 277–294 (2019)
29. Hartung, G., Hoffmann, M., Nagel, M., Rupp, A.: BBA+: improving the security and applicability of privacy-preserving point collection. In: Thuraisingham, B.M., Evans, D., Malkin, T., Xu, D. (eds.) ACM CCS 2017, pp. 1925–1942. ACM Press (October/November 2017)
30. Hawley, M., Howard, P., Koelle, R., Saxton, P.: Collaborative security management: developing ideas in security management for air traffic control. In: 2013 International Conference on Availability, Reliability and Security, pp. 802–806 (September 2013)
31. Hoffman, K., Zage, D., Nita-Rotaru, C.: A survey of attack and defense techniques for reputation systems. ACM Comput. Surv. **42**(1), 1–31 (2009)
32. Hopwood, D., Bowe, S., Hornby, T., Wilcox, N.: Zcash protocol specification. Tech. rep. Zerocoin Electric Coin Company (2016)
33. Jager, T., Rupp, A.: Black-box accumulation: collecting incentives in a privacy-preserving way. PoPETs **2016**(3), 62–82 (2016)
34. Jøsang, A., Golbeck, J.: Challenges for robust trust and reputation systems. In: 5th International Workshop on Security and Trust Management (STM 2009) (2009)
35. Libert, B., Paterson, K.G., Quaglia, E.A.: Anonymous broadcast encryption: adaptive security and efficient constructions in the standard model. In: Fischlin, M., Buchmann, J., Manulis, M. (eds.) PKC 2012. LNCS, vol. 7293, pp. 206–224. Springer, Heidelberg (2012). https://doi.org/10.1007/978-3-642-30057-8_13
36. Liu, J.K., Wei, V.K., Wong, D.S.: Linkable spontaneous anonymous group signature for ad hoc groups. In: Wang, H., Pieprzyk, J., Varadharajan, V. (eds.) ACISP 2004. LNCS, vol. 3108, pp. 325–335. Springer, Heidelberg (2004). https://doi.org/10.1007/978-3-540-27800-9_28
37. Lysyanskaya, A., Rivest, R.L., Sahai, A., Wolf, S.: Pseudonym systems. In: Heys, H., Adams, C. (eds.) SAC 1999. LNCS, vol. 1758, pp. 184–199. Springer, Heidelberg (2000). https://doi.org/10.1007/3-540-46513-8_14
38. Mármol, F.G., Pérez, G.M.: Security threats scenarios in trust and reputation models for distributed systems. Comput. Secur. **28**(7), 545–556 (2009)
39. Milutinovic, M., Dacosta, I., Put, A., Decker, B.D.: uCentive: an efficient, anonymous and unlinkable incentives scheme. In: 2015 IEEE Trustcom/BigDataSE/ISPA, vol. 1, pp. 588–595 (2015)
40. Nabuco, O., Bonacin, R., Fugini, M., Martoglia, R.: Web2touch 2016: evolution and security of collaborative web knowledge. In: 2016 IEEE 25th International Conference on Enabling Technologies: Infrastructure for Collaborative Enterprises (WETICE), pp. 214–216, June 2016

41. Paillier, P.: Public-key cryptosystems based on composite degree residuosity classes. In: Stern, J. (ed.) EUROCRYPT 1999. LNCS, vol. 1592, pp. 223–238. Springer, Heidelberg (1999). https://doi.org/10.1007/3-540-48910-X_16
42. Papaioannou, T.G., Stamoulis, G.D.: An incentives' mechanism promoting truthful feedback in peer-to-peer systems. In: CCGrid 2005. IEEE International Symposium on Cluster Computing and the Grid, 2005, vol. 1, pp. 275–283, May 2005
43. Pavlov, E., Rosenschein, J.S., Topol, Z.: Supporting privacy in decentralized additive reputation systems. In: Jensen, C., Poslad, S., Dimitrakos, T. (eds.) iTrust 2004. LNCS, vol. 2995, pp. 108–119. Springer, Heidelberg (2004). https://doi.org/10.1007/978-3-540-24747-0_9
44. Petrlic, R., Lutters, S., Sorge, C.: Privacy-preserving reputation management. In: Proceedings of the 29th Annual ACM Symposium on Applied Computing, SAC 2014, pp. 1712–1718. ACM, New York (2014)
45. Pingel, F., Steinbrecher, S.: Multilateral secure cross-community reputation systems for internet communities. In: Furnell, S., Katsikas, S.K., Lioy, A. (eds.) TrustBus 2008. LNCS, vol. 5185, pp. 69–78. Springer, Heidelberg (2008). https://doi.org/10.1007/978-3-540-85735-8_8
46. Rivest, R.L., Shamir, A., Tauman, Y.: How to leak a secret. In: Boyd, C. (ed.) ASIACRYPT 2001. LNCS, vol. 2248, pp. 552–565. Springer, Heidelberg (2001). https://doi.org/10.1007/3-540-45682-1_32
47. Schiffner, S., Clauß, S., Steinbrecher, S.: Privacy and liveliness for reputation systems. In: Martinelli, F., Preneel, B. (eds.) EuroPKI 2009. LNCS, vol. 6391, pp. 209–224. Springer, Heidelberg (2010). https://doi.org/10.1007/978-3-642-16441-5_14
48. Sillaber, C., Sauerwein, C., Mussmann, A., Breu, R.: Data quality challenges and future research directions in threat intelligence sharing practice. In: Proceedings of the 2016 ACM on Workshop on Information Sharing and Collaborative Security, WISCS 2016, pp. 65–70. ACM, New York (2016)
49. Sun, Y.L., Han, Z., Yu, W., Ray Liu, K.J.: Attacks on trust evaluation in distributed networks. In: 2006 40th Annual Conference on Information Sciences and Systems, pp. 1461–1466 (2006)
50. Traverso, G., Butin, D., Buchmann, J.A., Palesandro, A.: Coalition-resistant peer rating for long-term confidentiality. In: 2018 16th Annual Conference on Privacy, Security and Trust (PST), pp. 1–10, August 2018
51. Zhai, E., Wolinsky, D.I., Chen, R., Syta, E., Teng, C., Ford, B.: AnonRep: towards tracking-resistant anonymous reputation. In: 13th USENIX Symposium on Networked Systems Design and Implementation (NSDI 16), pp. 583–596. USENIX Association (2016)

Secure Generalized Deduplication via Multi-Key Revealing Encryption

Daniel E. Lucani[1] [iD], Lars Nielsen[1] [iD], Claudio Orlandi[1] [iD], Elena Pagnin[2] [iD], and Rasmus Vestergaard[1] [iD]

[1] Aarhus University, Aarhus, Denmark
{daniel.lucani,lani,rv}@eng.au.dk, orlandi@cs.au.dk
[2] Lund University, Lund, Sweden
elena.pagnin@eit.lth.se

Abstract. Cloud Storage Providers (CSPs) offer solutions to relieve users from locally storing vast amounts of data, including personal and sensitive ones. While users may desire to retain some privacy on the data they outsource, CSPs are interested in reducing the total storage space by employing compression techniques such as deduplication. We propose a new cryptographic primitive that simultaneously realizes both requirements: Multi-Key Revealing Encryption (MKRE). The goal of MKRE is to disclose the result of a pre-defined function over multiple ciphertexts, even if the ciphertexts were generated using different keys, while revealing *nothing else* about the data. We present a formal model and a security definition for MKRE and provide a construction of MKRE for generalized deduplication that only uses symmetric key primitives in a black-box way. Our construction allows *(a)* cloud providers to reduce the storage space by using generalized deduplication to compress encrypted data across users, and *(b)* each user to maintain a certain privacy level for the outsourced information. Our scheme can be proven secure in the random oracle model (and we argue that this is a necessary evil). We develop a proof-of-concept implementation of our solution. For a test data set, our MKRE construction achieves secure generalized deduplication with a compression ratio of 87% for 1 KB file chunks and 82.2% for 8 KB chunks. Finally, our experiments show that, compared to generalized deduplication setup with un-encrypted files, adding privacy via MKRE introduces a compression overhead of less than 3% and reduces the storage throughput by at most 6.9%.

Keywords: Private cloud storage · Secure deduplication · Revealing encryption

1 Introduction

Cloud Storage Providers (CSPs) are offering vast amounts of storage at a low cost to users who desire to outsource their data storage. In order to provide this service at a low cost, CSPs employ compression techniques to reduce their

© Springer Nature Switzerland AG 2020
C. Galdi and V. Kolesnikov (Eds.): SCN 2020, LNCS 12238, pp. 298–318, 2020.
https://doi.org/10.1007/978-3-030-57990-6_15

storage cost. In particular, *data deduplication* has become a popular technique for compression of data across files generated by users of the system. For example, if two users upload the same file to the server, only one copy is stored, which both users are allowed to retrieve. Deduplication is often carried out across file chunks (parts), which increases the potential to reduce the storage footprint of the system, as two files that are different as a whole may have significant portions that are equal, *e.g.*, when different versions of the same file are stored.

Generalized deduplication [32] is a recent generalization of this principle. By enabling deduplication of data chunks that are similar, rather than identical, this method can achieve a better compression than classic deduplication techniques. As a conceptual and oversimplified example of generalized deduplication, consider two users that hold identical pictures of the Eiffel tower, except for a different person in the foreground. If the CSP could see the two plaintext files, it could easily identify the two pictures as "almost identical", and store the background only once, reducing the overall storage space required. As a great number of people take pictures of the Eiffel tower, we could imagine that many users might upload similar images to the CSP, which would allow the data to be compressed more than is possible when only exact copies of files are deduplicated.

In order to compress the data it stores, the CSP will need to access it to identify where (generalized) deduplication can be used. A naïve implementation would allow CSPs to directly access all uploaded files in cleartext to determine how the data can be compressed. Such a solution will unfortunately undermine the privacy of the data, reducing the types of files that the CSP should be trusted with. A privacy-conscious user could patch this weakness by encrypting their data under a private key before uploading it, but using semantically secure encryption schemes would prevent the CSP from performing any meaningful deduplication. Therefore, previous work has established encryption schemes with relaxed security guarantees that can enable the server to identify when two files are identical and thus enable secure deduplication over encrypted data (see, *e.g.*, convergent [13] or message-locked [6] encryption).

In this paper, we propose an encryption scheme that allows the server to identify when encrypted data corresponds to similar, rather than identical, data. In particular, using such an encryption scheme, CSPs can apply generalized deduplication directly on the encrypted data. Albeit the server learns whether two ciphertexts correspond to similar plaintexts or not, nothing else is revealed about the original plaintext data. This provides another opportunity for protecting sensitive information while enabling storage compression techniques.

Overview of Contributions. Our first contribution is a definitional model that generalizes the notion of Revealing Encryption[1] (RE) [15,24] to the multi-user setting, thus the name Multi-Key Revealing Encryption (MKRE). In a nutshell, a RE scheme is parametrized by some function f, and, given two ciphertexts c_1, c_2 obtained by encrypting x_1, x_2 respectively (under the same key), there

---

[1] The term "Revealing Encryption" was first introduced in an oral presentation by Adam O'Neill.

exist some public evaluation function g such that $g(c_1, c_2) = f(x_1, x_2)$.[2] MKRE extends this to the case where the data is encrypted with different, potentially independent keys.[3]

In this paper, we are mostly interested with the case where the function f computes whether x_1, x_2 are "similar" or not, as this is the function required for secure generalized deduplication. Note that MKRE for this f can also be seen as a natural generalization of message-locked encryption (and indeed message-locked encryption is a crucial component of our solution) and therefore we share the same issues in providing a meaningful and intelligible security definition. In a nutshell, in message-locked encryption a message is encrypted using the message itself as the key. Thus, any user encrypting the same message will produce the same ciphertext, allowing to check equality (and therefore perform deduplication) across encryptions performed by different users. Defining security for message-locked encryption is however quite tricky: The problem is that we cannot prevent the adversary from encrypting messages locally and compare them with the output of the challenge oracle, and we encountered similar challenges when attempting to define security for MKRE. Previous work in message-locked encryption solved this issue by parameterizing the security definition via a message distribution. We find those definitions to be quite complex to parse and therefore quite unfriendly to the practitioners who should decide whether such a primitive provides the right level of security for their applications. As our work is motivated by real-world interest in secure deduplication, we decided to provide what we see as a simpler alternative, which instead relies on idealized primitives: In our definition the adversary can only perform encryptions interacting with the challenger or the random oracle. Looking ahead, this will allow the reduction to "know everything that the adversary knows" and therefore we do not need to worry about trivial attacks. Intuitively, our definition guarantees that the adversary learns nothing about the content of a ciphertext, unless it ever requests an encryption of a "close" message, in which case it is allowed to learn this fact and nothing else. As a downside, our definition implies that our construction must use idealized primitives (e.g., random oracles).

We provide a generic construction of MKRE for our use case from a black-box combination of message-locked, deterministic, and randomized encryption schemes. Furthermore, we show a concrete instantiation based solely on hash functions and prove its security in the random oracle model, which we have argued is a necessary evil given our security definition. In a nutshell, our technique splits files into two parts: one that we consider less sensitive and deduplication-friendly (*e.g.*, the background with the Eiffel tower) and one more sensitive, on which no public clustering is desired (*e.g.*, the person in the foreground). Then a form of deterministic encryption is applied to the former part of the data (*e.g.*, the image backgrounds) while semantically secure

---

[2] Revealing encryption can be seen as a special case of functional encryption where a single decryption key is published together with the public parameters when the system is initialized.

[3] Similarly, MKRE can be seen as a special case of multi-input functional encryption.

encryption is applied to "fully" protect the other, more sensitive part (*e.g.*, the image foregrounds), which thus cannot be deduplicated. While, in retrospect, our construction is really simple, we find it very fascinating that it is at all possible to perform any kind of meaningful computation across ciphertexts encrypted independently by different users using independent keys, and we leave as a major open problem whether there exist "simple" MKRE schemes for other natural, useful functions.

Our findings are supported by a software implementation that allows us to characterize the trade-off among added security, processing speed of the system, and overall compression performance. Our experiments show that our construction is only negligibly less efficient than generalized deduplication applied to the plaintexts directly, while achieving a greater privacy level: Adding MKRE to generalized deduplication reduces the overall system storage throughput by no more than 6.9%, and the compression capabilities by at most 3%.[4]

Limitations. As any revealing encryption scheme, MKRE for generalized deduplication reveals some specific information about the uploaded data to the CSP. This leakage is unavoidable: if one wishes to deduplicate *similar* data, then deduplicated chunks must come from similar files. This means that a malicious CSP can see how many ciphertexts of the same user are deduplicated and learn the statistical distribution of the deduplications. Frequency analysis on deduplication reveals the distribution of messages which obviously impacts the security of the system. This cannot be mitigated while targeting high-compression deduplication and thus falls outside the scope of this work.

2 Related Work

The conflicting interests of CSPs employing deduplication and privacy-concerned users have been studied from many angles. A generic framework that explains the various constraints and allows for comparison of secure deduplication strategies is presented in [8].

To enable privacy-aware server-side deduplication, the most common approach is to force users with the same plaintext to arrive at the same ciphertext. The first work of this nature was convergent encryption [13], followed by the more general Message-Locked Encryption (MLE) scheme in [6], where a hash of the plaintext is used as the encryption key. Some recent developments seek to optimize MLE, *e.g.*, for deduplication of file chunks rather than the entire files and enable efficient updates to the stored data [35]. Other proposals use an oblivious PRF against a key-server to determine the file-derived keys [5], or have clients determine the keys in a distributed manner using a PAKE-based protocol [21,22]. All of these schemes reveal that deduplicated ciphertexts correspond

---

[4] In this work, we perform generalized deduplication based on Hamming codes, however, the principles we develop are general and can be easily transferred to any transformation function.

to *identical* data. In contrast, our scheme only reveals that deduplicated cipher-texts correspond to *similar* data. Deduplication of similar data is also dealt with in [19], albeit quite differently. They have a highly specific use case in mind and remove perceptually similar images by comparing a 'perceptual hash' calculated over the plaintext images, which can lead to duplicate detection under modifications such as resizing, compression, or flipping. Thus, their compression is lossy, not every image can be retrieved as it was uploaded, but something "similar" might be returned. On the contrary, our method is lossless and everything can be retrieved exactly as it was uploaded. Further, what is considered similar in our method is more general, as the notion of similarity is tied to the chosen transformation function for generalized deduplication.

We view our privacy-aware server-side deduplication scheme as a generalization to the multi-user setting of the notion of Revealing Encryption (RE) [15]. Our approach also shares similarities with Predicate Encryption (PE) [17], Searchable Encryption (SE) [12], Multi-Input Functional Encryption (MIFE) [14], ad-hoc MIFE [1] and Multi-Client FE (MCFE) [11,20]. At a very abstract level, all these primitives share a common goal, *i.e.*, to allow to encrypt data in such a way that it is possible to perform *computation on a set of cipher-texts*. However, they do so by exploiting different mechanisms and assumptions, and allow for different degrees of freedom in choosing which function f should be computed and which users should be able to compute the function. In PE, SE, and (MK)RE the function f is determined a priori; the different flavors of functional encryption allow f to be chosen adaptively. In contrast to other primitives, the function computed by (MK)RE is *public* and can be evaluated on set of ciphertexts *without* the need of a secret key (or secret state). Notably, in functional encryption f is linked to the decryption algorithm, and thus it is intrinsically a secret-key operation. This is a core difference to the RE setting. Moreover, in (MK)RE data are encrypted using a secret key, which is different from what happens in all other settings.[5]

As the names suggest MIFE, MCFE and MKRE are the only primitives that consider multi-user settings. Unfortunately, it is known that MIFE and MCFE for generic functionalities can only be realized using "heavy tools", such as obfuscation and multi linear maps [14], and is therefore not currently of practical interest. Recent work has thus favored concrete and efficient realizations for more restricted functionalities that rely on less demanding assumptions, *e.g.*, MCFE for inner product in the random oracle model from DDH [11] and MCFE for linear functions in the standard model from LWE [20]. Following this philosophy, our aim is to build MKRE from "minimalist tools", *i.e.*, hash functions, and instantiate a scheme with immediate practical applications.

3   Preliminaries

Notation. For $n, n_1, n_2 \in \mathbb{N}$, let $[n_1 : n_2]$ be the set $\{n_1, n_1 + 1, \ldots, n_2\}$ and $[n]$ be the set $[1 : n]$. For $x \in \mathbb{Z}$, let $|x|$ denote the absolute value of x. Let $x \xleftarrow{\$} S$

---

[5] With the exception of SE for which there exist realization both in the asymmetric [3] and in the symmetric settings [29].

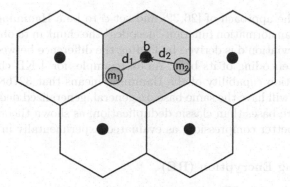

Fig. 1. Visualizing generalized deduplication. Similar chunks map to the same base, but different deviations

denote that x is sampled uniform random from the set S. We denote the security parameter of cryptographic primitives as λ.

3.1 Generalized Deduplication

A typical deduplication strategy is to segment files into chunks and look for chunks that appear more than once in the file or that match a chunk from previously stored files [34]. We will use the terms "file" and "chunk" interchangeably, since they both denote the object to be deduplicated, albeit at different granularities. In many settings, this works well. However, deduplication is traditionally limited by the fact that it requires chunks to be identical. Thus, even if just one bit differs between two chunks, they are stored independently.

Generalized deduplication can alleviate this issue [26,32] by allowing a systematic deduplication of near-identical chunks. The idea is to employ a transformation function ϕ which takes as input an n-bit chunk m and decomposes it into a k-bit *base*, b, and an l-bit *deviation*, d. Concretely, $\phi : \{0,1\}^n \to \{0,1\}^k \times \{0,1\}^l$ with $\phi(\mathsf{m}) = (\mathsf{b},\mathsf{d})$, and there exists a function $\phi^{-1} : \{0,1\}^k \times \{0,1\}^l \to \{0,1\}^n$ that reconstructs a data chunk from a given base and a deviation, *i.e.*, for any chunk $\mathsf{m} \in \{0,1\}^n$ it holds that $\phi^{-1}(\phi(\mathsf{m})) = \mathsf{m}$. Figure 1 visualizes the partition induced by ϕ on the chunk space: two similar chunks, m_1 and m_2, are mapped to the same base b, with different deviations ($\mathsf{d}_1 \neq \mathsf{d}_2$). For usability, we require $k > l$, meaning that the base contains most of the chunk's information and the deviation is small. In our example of portrait pictures with the Eiffel tower, the background image corresponds to the (common) base, while the person's figure is the (file-dependent) deviation. The bases can then be deduplicated, so that each base is stored only once. Finally, the deviation is stored alongside a reference to the base, which ensures that each file can be reconstructed without any loss of information. Classic deduplication can be obtained by letting the transformation function be the identity function, so bases are the original chunks and the deviation is empty.

We follow the approach of [26,32] and set ϕ to be a Hamming code [16]. In this case, the transformation function "decodes" the chunk m to obtain its base b, and then the deviation d is derived by finding the difference between the original chunk and the encoding of its base. As an example, for 4 KB chunks the one-bit error-correction capability of the Hamming means that 32768 different, but similar, chunks will have the same base. In general, generalized deduplication can thus match more bases than classic deduplication, as shown theoretically in [32] and achieve a better compression, as evaluated experimentally in [26,31,33].

3.2 Revealing Encryption (RE)

The first ingredient in RE schemes is an *authorized function* f from a set of inputs $\mathcal{M}^n$ to a set of output values $\mathcal{V}$. Formally, $f : \mathcal{M}^n \to \mathcal{V}$. Examples of authorized functions are $f = \max\{\cdots\}$ and $f = \mathtt{deduplicate}(\cdot,\cdot)$ (see Definition 7). Revealing encryption schemes are built around the chosen *authorized function* and are defined as follows.[6]

Definition 1 (Revealing encryption (RE) [15]). *Let* $f : \mathcal{M}^n \to \mathcal{V}$ *be an n-ary authorized function. An RE scheme for the function f is a tuple of algorithms* $\mathsf{RE}_f = (\mathsf{Setup}, \mathsf{Enc}, \mathsf{Reveal})$ *defined as follows:*

$\mathsf{Setup}(1^\lambda)$: *on input security parameter* λ *(in unary), this randomized algorithm outputs a secret key* sk *and some public parameters* pp. pp *are input to all the following algorithms even when not explicitly written.*

$\mathsf{Enc}(\mathsf{sk}, \mathsf{m})$: *on input the secret key* sk *and a message* $\mathsf{m} \in \mathcal{M}$, *this randomized algorithm outputs a ciphertext* c.

$\mathsf{Reveal}(\mathsf{c}_1, \ldots, \mathsf{c}_n)$: *on input the public parameters* pp *and n ciphertexts this deterministic algorithm outputs a value* $v \in \mathcal{V}$.

Revealing correctness essentially states that the output of Reveal evaluated on a set of ciphertexts should equal the output of the authorized function f evaluated on the corresponding set of plaintexts. Security is defined using a *leakage function* that sizes what the adversary learns from evaluating Reveal on any collection of n ciphertexts.

Definition 2 (Leakage function and optimal RE_f). *A function* $L : \mathcal{M}^* \to \{0,1\}^*$ *is a leakage function for a revealing encryption scheme* RE_f *if, given any tuple of input values, L outputs the information leaked by* RE_f *when running* Reveal *on any possible size-n subset of the corresponding ciphertexts. A* RE_f *is said to be optimal if it leaks precisely what is required by the functionality, that is:*

$$L(\mathsf{m}_1, \ldots, \mathsf{m}_q) = \{f(\mathsf{m}_i \,;\, i \in S), \, S \subseteq [q], |S| = n\}.$$

Further details on RE and its security notion can be found in [10,15].

---

[6] To improve readability and have an homogeneous language when extending RE to multiple users (MKRE), we use Reveal instead of Eval in [15]. Also, in Sect. 4 we will split the algorithm Setup from [15] into a global set up procedure, called Setup, and a user-dependent KeyGen.

4   Multi-Key Revealing Encryption

We now introduce Multi-Key Revealing Encryption (MKRE), a cryptographic primitive that extends revealing encryption to handle functions evaluated on data encrypted using distinct secret keys. In addition to the standard algorithms of RE, MKRE includes KeyGen, needed to extract user specific key material from the common parameters, and Dec, that allows users to efficiently retrieve their data. After presenting the MKRE framework, we provide detailed discussions of our security notions in Sect. 4.1 and of the need for random oracles to tolerate user corruption in Sect. 4.2.

Definition 3 (Multi-key revealing encryption (MKRE)). *Let* f : $\mathcal{M}^n \to \mathcal{V}$ *be an n-ary authorized function. A multi-key revealing encryption scheme for the function* f *is a tuple of algorithms* MKRE_f = $(\mathsf{Setup}, \mathsf{KeyGen}, \mathsf{Enc}, \mathsf{Reveal}, \mathsf{Dec})$ *defined as follows:*

$\mathsf{Setup}(1^\lambda)$: *this randomized algorithm outputs a master public key* mpk *containing at least a description of the function* f *The* mpk *serves as public parameters and is implicitly input to all subsequent algorithms.*

$\mathsf{KeyGen}()$: *this randomized algorithm outputs a user secret key* sk *.*

$\mathsf{Enc}(\mathsf{sk}, \mathsf{m})$: *on input a secret key* sk *and a message* $\mathsf{m} \in \mathcal{M}$, *this randomized algorithm outputs a ciphertext* c.

$\mathsf{Reveal}(c_1, \ldots, c_n)$: *on input the master public key* mpk *and* n *ciphertexts this deterministic algorithm outputs* $v \in \mathcal{V}$.

$\mathsf{Dec}(\mathsf{sk}, c)$: *on input a secret key* sk *and a ciphertext* c, *this deterministic algorithm returns a plaintext* m.

We depart from the convention of omitting the decryption algorithm in RE schemes. This is motivated by the fact that in many practical cases, *e.g.*, cloud storage, it is essential for users to be able to recover the plaintext data at a later point in time. We define two notions of correctness: one for the public revealing method and one for the secret decryption.

Definition 4 (MKRE_f revealing correctness). *A MKRE scheme* MKRE_f *satisfies revealing correctness if, for any n-tuple of messages* $\mathsf{m}_1, \ldots, \mathsf{m}_n \in \mathcal{M}^n$, *for any n-tuple of keys* $\mathsf{sk}_1, \ldots, \mathsf{sk}_n$ *generated by* KeyGen, *and for any* $c_i \leftarrow$ $\mathsf{Enc}(\mathsf{sk}_i, \mathsf{m}_i)$ *with* $i \in [n]$, *it holds that*

$$\mathsf{Reveal}\,(c_1, \ldots, c_n) = f\,(\mathsf{m}_1, \ldots, \mathsf{m}_n)$$

with all but negligible probability. Note that the n *ciphertexts may be encrypted under up to* n *different secret keys.*

Definition 5 (MKRE_f decryption correctness). *A MKRE scheme* MKRE_f *satisfies decryption correctness if for any message* $\mathsf{m} \in \mathcal{M}$ *and for any secret key* sk *generated by* KeyGen *it holds that*

$$\mathsf{Dec}(\mathsf{sk}, \mathsf{Enc}(\mathsf{sk}, \mathsf{m})) = \mathsf{m}.$$

Next, we define security using the real versus ideal world paradigm.

Definition 6 (MKRE$_f$ security). *Let λ be a security parameter, f a revealing function, MKRE$_f$ a multi-key revealing encryption scheme for f with associated leakage function L. Consider the experiments $\mathsf{REAL}_{\mathcal{A}}^{\mathsf{MKRE}_f}(\lambda)$ and $\mathsf{IDEAL}_{\mathcal{A},\mathcal{S},L}^{\mathsf{MKRE}_f}(\lambda)$ depicted below, where $\mathcal{C}$ denotes the corruption oracle, $\mathcal{RO}$ the random oracle, $\mathcal{E}$ the encryption oracle, and prepending an $\mathcal{S}$ denotes a simulated oracle.*

$\mathsf{REAL}_{\mathcal{A}}^{\mathsf{MKRE}_f}(\lambda)$	$\mathsf{IDEAL}_{\mathcal{A},\mathcal{S},L}^{\mathsf{MKRE}_f}(\lambda)$
$\mathsf{mpk} \leftarrow \mathsf{Setup}(1^{\lambda})$	$\mathsf{mpk} \leftarrow \mathsf{Setup}(1^{\lambda})$
$b \leftarrow \mathcal{A}^{\mathcal{C}(\cdot),\mathcal{RO}(\cdot),\mathcal{E}(\cdot)}(\mathsf{mpk})$	$b \leftarrow \mathcal{A}^{\mathcal{SC}(\cdot),\mathcal{SRO}(\cdot),\mathcal{SE}(\cdot)}(\mathsf{mpk})$

We say that MKRE$_f$ is a secure MKRE scheme with respect to L if, for all adversaries $\mathcal{A}$ that make at most $q = \mathsf{poly}(\lambda)$ queries, there exists a simulator $\mathcal{S}$ such that the output distributions of the two experiments described above are computationally indistinguishable, i.e.:

$$\mathsf{REAL}_{\mathcal{A}}^{\mathsf{MKRE}_f}(\lambda) \sim_c \mathsf{IDEAL}_{\mathcal{A},\mathcal{S},L}^{\mathsf{MKRE}_f}(\lambda)$$

We assume that oracles and simulators are stateful. Thus, whenever we query a new message, its leakage can be assumed to be the output of the reveal function evaluated against every previously queried message. To keep track of relevant information contained in the state, we use the following dictionaries:

$\mathcal{D}_{\mathsf{id}}$: Set of pairs (identity-identifier, user secret key),
$\mathcal{D}_{\mathsf{corr}}$: Set of identity-identifiers corresponding to corrupted users,
$\mathcal{D}_{\mathsf{ro}}$: Set of (input, output) pairs generated by queries to the random oracle,
$\mathcal{D}_{\mathsf{enc}}$: Set of tuples (identity-identifier, message, ciphertext) generated by encryption queries.

They are all empty at the beginning of the MKRE$_f$ security game and are populated as shown in Fig. 2.

4.1   Discussion of Our Definitions

We now compare our security definitions for MKRE with the corresponding notions in RE. We first highlight the similarities, then motivate our changes.

Similarities. In the ideal world, the MKRE$_f$ simulated encryption oracle has to produce ciphertexts having access only to the natural leakage inherent in the revealing encryption scheme and without seeing the actual query. The structure of our simulator for MKRE is similar to the RE simulator [15]: In order to generate a ciphertext for a queried message m, $\mathcal{S}$ is *not* given m; instead it has access

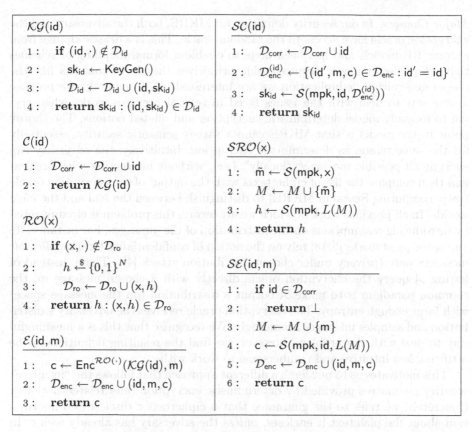

Fig. 2. Real vs ideal world: $\mathcal{KG}$ (key generation subroutine, $\mathcal{A}$ cannot query directly), $\mathcal{C}$ (corruption oracle), $\mathcal{SC}$ (simulated corruption oracle), $\mathcal{RO}$ (random oracle), $\mathcal{SRO}$ (simulated random oracle), $\mathcal{E}$ (encryption oracle), $\mathcal{SE}$ (simulated encryption oracle). In line 3 of $\mathcal{SRO}$ and in line 4 of $\mathcal{SE}$, $L(M) = L(m_1, m_2, \ldots, m_n)$ denotes the leakage produced from all messages encrypted so far, including the new message ($\tilde{m}$ or m).

to the *leakage* produced by m against all the previously encrypted messages ($L(M)$ in Fig. 2). This exploits the *revealing* feature natural to RE schemes and does not disclose more than what the simulator can learn by applying the public Reveal procedure to the ciphertexts. We remark that giving $\mathcal{S}$ access to $L(M)$ is crucial to ensure that real world ciphertexts only reveal the desired information about the plaintexts and nothing else.

Minor Additions. Our system involves multiple users, and we let the adversary $\mathcal{A}$ corrupt some and learn their secret keys. Our $\mathcal{SE}$ rejects encryption queries for corrupted users. This limitation is done solely to simplify the model and does not restrict the adversary, who can encrypt messages for corrupted parties without interacting with the encryption oracle. (Yet, $\mathcal{A}$ needs to query the random oracle, as we discuss in the next paragraph.)

Major Changes. In our security definition for MKRE, both the adversary and the encryption oracle have access to the random oracle. This is a drastic change from current RE models and has been done to enable a formal handling of schemes that adopt deterministic cryptographic primitives (handy in contexts like the one of generalized deduplication we are interested in). Concretely, we propose a new way to deal with the issues faced in several previous works when trying to formally model deterministic encryption and related notions. The thorny point in the model is that MKRE cannot satisfy semantic security, essentially for the same reason as deterministic encryption. Intuitively, the adversary can encrypt all possible messages "locally" (*i.e.*, without interacting with oracles) and then compare the list of ciphertexts with the output of the encryption oracle (resp. computing Reveal in MKRE) to distinguish between the real and the ideal worlds. In all previous work of which we are aware, this problem is circumvented by introducing assumptions on the distribution of the messages. For instance, [6] and subsequent works [5,18] rely on the notion of confidentiality for *unpredictable* messages only (privacy under chosen-distribution attack [4]). There, instead of letting $\mathcal{A}$ query the encryption oracle directly with a chosen message m, the common paradigm is to make $\mathcal{A}$ output a distribution (on the message space) with large enough entropy. The encryption oracle receives the adversary's distribution and samples messages accordingly. We recognize that this is a meaningful way to deal with the problem, however, we find the resulting definitions to be artificial, less intuitive and cumbersome to work with.

This motivates us to put forth a different approach that follows the "intuitive" security guarantees provided by deterministic encryption (and related notions). Concretely, we refer to the guarantee that a ciphertext c discloses no information about the plaintext it encloses, *unless* the adversary has already seen c. In the standard model, since the adversary can perform encryptions locally, without informing any oracle, it is not possible to meaningfully reason about which messages $\mathcal{A}$ has encrypted or not. In contrast, in the random oracle model, the adversary must interact with some oracle (and thus, the simulator) to perform encryptions. Intuitively, the random oracle model makes it possible to "extract" from the adversary the set of messages that $\mathcal{A}$ is encrypting "locally". In MKRE, at every random oracle query we allow the simulator to guess what $\mathcal{A}$ is doing and extract information from it. Concretely, at every random oracle query, $\mathcal{S}$ can use x, the input to $\mathcal{RO}$, to guess a message $\tilde{m}$, which it adds to the set of simulated messages M and can get the leakage for. We believe that this approach gives the simulator a "more fair" task than what is required by previous models, e.g., [6]. In particular, our model lets the simulator learn the same information the adversary can derive locally by computing f (the authorized function) on messages encrypted both locally and via the encryption oracle.

We stress that without the extra leakage during random oracle queries (line 3 in $\mathcal{SRO}$), the definition could not be instantiated due to the following trivial attack. First, the adversary makes one query, m_1, to the encryption oracle and receives c_1. Then, $\mathcal{A}$ computes "local" encryptions of other message m_i for $i \in [2, n]$ such that $f(m_1, \ldots, m_n) = v$ for a random value $v \in \mathcal{V}$ in the range of

f. In the real world, the ciphertexts satisfy $\mathsf{Reveal}(c_1, \ldots, c_n) = v$. In the ideal world (without $\mathcal{SRO}$ leakage), instead, the simulator gets no leakage, since the encryption oracle is queried only once. When simulating the random oracle, $\mathcal{S}$ has no access to the global leakage $L(m_1, \ldots, m_n) = v$. As a result, no simulator can guarantee that the "locally encrypted" ciphertexts will match the random value v, so the adversary distinguishes the two worlds with non-negligible probability $1 - 1/|\mathcal{V}|$.

4.2 On the Need for Random Oracles to Tolerate Corruptions

Any secure MKRE construction that tolerates corruption of users must rely on *adaptive primitives* such as non-committing encryption [9]. To give an intuition of why this is the case, consider the following trivial attack. First, the adversary asks for encryptions of many random messages m_i for the same identity id^*. Then $\mathcal{A}$ corrupts id^*. In the real world, the secret key for id^* is chosen at the beginning of the game, thus each ciphertext c_i received by $\mathcal{A}$ is indeed an encryption of m_i under the same sk_{id^*}. On the other hand, in the ideal world the simulator does not have access to the random messages during the encryption queries, and therefore returns ciphertexts that are independent of the m_i. Only upon corruption the simulator learns what message m_i each ciphertext should decrypt to (line 3 in $\mathcal{SC}$). At this moment, $\mathcal{S}$ has to come up with *one* secret key that "explains" all of the previously generated ciphertexts (*i.e.*, such that $\mathsf{Dec}(\mathsf{sk}_{id^*}, c_i) = m_i$). Due to the incompressibility of random data, such a secret key must be at least as long as the number of encrypted messages. This means that in the standard model there exists no secure construction of an MKRE scheme that tolerates user corruption *and* has fixed sized key. Thus, efficient MKRE schemes exist only in the random oracle model. This incompressibility issue is known for encryption schemes with adaptive properties, *e.g.*, [2, 7, 25].

5   MKRE for Generalized Deduplication of Private Data

In this section, we show how to instantiate MKRE for generalized deduplication of private data. In Sect. 5.1 we propose a high-level compiler that combines well-established cryptographic primitives in a black-box way into an MKRE scheme for generalized deduplication. In Sect. 5.2 we describe how to instantiate our compiler and its building blocks using solely random oracles. This concrete construction is simulatable secure in the model introduced in Sect. 4. Due to space limitations, we defer to the full version [23] a discussion on how to generically turn our compiler (and thus our explicit construction) from the ad-hoc setting, where each user generates keys independently, to a centralized setting. The latter setting provides an additional layer of security against nosy servers and may be useful in systems that employ a key distribution center.

Setup Assumptions. Throughout this section we assume that the function for generalized deduplication ϕ is given and known to all parties involved in the scheme (in our experiments ϕ is a Hamming code, see Sect. 6 for further details). In detail, we require ϕ to be a function that maps a chunk $m \in \{0,1\}^n$ into a base and a deviation:

$$\phi(m) = (\phi_1(m), \phi_2(m)) = (b, d) \in \{0,1\}^k \times \{0,1\}^l.$$

For recovery purposes, ϕ needs to be invertible, i.e., there exists a function $\phi^{-1} : \{0,1\}^k \times \{0,1\}^l \to \{0,1\}^n$ such that $\phi^{-1}(\phi(m)) = m$ for any chunk $m \in \{0,1\}^n$. Finally, in our use case the size of bases is larger than the security parameter, i.e., $k > \lambda$. We are interested in the following authorized function.

Definition 7 (Authorized function for generalized deduplication). *We define the authorized (revealing) function for generalized deduplication as $f = $ deduplicate : $\{0,1\}^n \times \{0,1\}^n \to \{0,1\}$ where*

$$f(m_1, m_2) = \mathtt{deduplicate}(m_1, m_2) = \begin{cases} 1 \text{ if } \phi_1(m_1) = \phi_1(m_2) \\ 0 \text{ otherwise} \end{cases}.$$

We note that f returns 1 (deduplication is possible) only on similar chunks, i.e., chunks with the same base b, independently of the deviations.

5.1   Our MKRE Compiler

Our MKRE compiler for generalized deduplication of private data uses three building blocks: a message-locked encryption scheme, a deterministic secret key encryption scheme, and a randomized secret key encryption scheme. The authorized function is $f = \mathtt{deduplicate}$ (see Definition 7).

Definition 8 (An MKRE compiler for generalized deduplication). *Let $f : \{0,1\}^n \times \{0,1\}^n \to \{0,1\}$ be the authorized function for generalized deduplication from Definition 7. Our MKRE scheme for generalized deduplication is defined by the following algorithms:*

Setup(1^λ): *Set up a message-locked encryption scheme $ML = (\mathtt{mlSetup}, \mathtt{mlKD}, \mathtt{mlE}, \mathtt{mlD})$, a secret-key deterministic encryption scheme $DetE = (\mathtt{detKG}, \mathtt{detE}, \mathtt{detD})$, and a randomized (secret key) encryption scheme $RandE = (\mathtt{randKG}, \mathtt{randE}, \mathtt{randD})$. Publish as mpk all public parameters of the schemes.*
KeyGen(): *Run $\mathsf{detk_{id}} \leftarrow \mathtt{detKG}()$ and $\mathsf{randkey_{id}} \leftarrow \mathtt{randKG}()$. Let $\mathsf{sk_{id}} \leftarrow (\mathsf{detk_{id}}, \mathsf{randkey_{id}})$ and return $\mathsf{sk_{id}}$.*
Enc($\mathsf{sk_{id}}, m$): *Parse the secret key as $(\mathsf{detk_{id}}, \mathsf{randkey_{id}})$ and apply the generalized deduplication transformation to the data record m to obtain its base and deviation: $\phi(m) = (b, d)$. Perform the following steps:*

    1. $\mathsf{mk} \leftarrow \mathtt{mlKD}(b)$, (generate a base-derived key using ML),
    2. $\beta \leftarrow \mathtt{mlE}(\mathsf{mk}, b)$, (ML encrypt the base using the base-derived key),
    3. $\gamma \leftarrow \mathtt{detE}_{\mathsf{detk_{id}}}(\mathsf{mk})$, (encrypt the base-derived key using DetE),
    4. $\delta \leftarrow \mathtt{randE}_{\mathsf{randkey_{id}}}(d)$, (encrypt deviation using RandE).

Return the ciphertext $c = (\beta, \gamma, \delta)$.

Reveal(c_1, c_2): *Parse* $c_i = (\beta_i, \gamma_i, \delta_i)$ *for* $i \in \{1, 2\}$. *If the first ciphertext components are equal, i.e.,* $\beta_1 = \beta_2$, *output 1, otherwise, output 0.*

Dec(sk_{id}, c): *Parse the secret key* sk_{id} *as* $(\mathtt{detk}_{id}, \mathtt{randkey}_{id})$ *and the ciphertext* c *as* (β, γ, δ). *Perform the following steps:*

  1. $mk \leftarrow \mathtt{detD}_{\mathtt{detk}_{id}}(\gamma)$, *(DetE decrypt the base-derived key);*
  2. $b \leftarrow \mathtt{mlD}(mk; \beta)$, *(Recover the base using ML);*
  3. $d \leftarrow \mathtt{randD}_{\mathtt{randkey}_{id}}(\delta)$, *(RandE decrypt the deviation)*
Return the plaintext record $m = \phi^{-1}(b, d)$.

Figure 3 visualizes the workflow of the algorithms in our high-level MKRE scheme of Definition 8. Next, we show the correctness of the Reveal and the Dec procedures. Security is proven after we describe a concrete instantiation of the building blocks using a random oracle in Sect. 5.2.

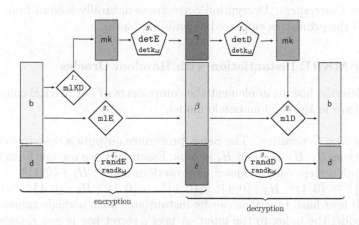

Fig. 3. Visual representation of the workflow of our MKRE construction for generalized deduplication (notation according to Definition 8).

Revealing Correctness. Following Definition 4 for the revealing function f of Definition 7, we now prove that, for any pair of messages $m_1, m_2 \in \{0, 1\}^n$ and for any pair of keys sk_1, sk_2 (potentially belonging to different users), the output of Reveal evaluated on the ciphertexts $c_i \leftarrow \mathsf{Enc}(sk_i, m_i)$, $i \in [2]$ equals the output of the authorized function from Definition 7. In detail, we show that $\Pr[\mathsf{Reveal}(c_1, c_2) = f(m_1, m_2)] \geq 1 - \mathsf{negl}(\lambda)$, where the probability is taken over the choice of keys and the random coins of the algorithms. The functions are defined as:

$$\mathsf{Reveal}(c_1, c_2) = \begin{cases} 1 \text{ if } \beta_1 = \beta_2, \text{ where } c_i = (\beta_i, \gamma_i, \delta_i) \\ 0 \text{ otherwise} \end{cases}$$

$$f(m_1, m_2) = \begin{cases} 1 \text{ if } \phi_1(m_1) = \phi_1(m_2), \text{ i.e. } b_1 = b_2 \\ 0 \text{ otherwise} \end{cases}$$

We distinguish two cases according to the output of f.

$f(m_1, m_2) = 0$. By definition of f, the event $f(m_1, m_2) = 0$ corresponds to the event $b_1 \neq b_2$ (recall that $\phi_1(m_i) = b_i$). We prove that Reveal outputs 0 as well (with all but negligible probability). This holds since the β component of a ciphertext is generated deterministically from b_i, and by assumption $b_1 \neq b_2$. In detail, $\beta_i = \mathtt{mlE}(mk_i, b_i)$. Now since $b_1 \neq b_2$, it holds that $\mathtt{mlKD}(b_1) \to mk_1 \neq mk_2 \leftarrow \mathtt{mlKD}(b_2)$ with all but negligible probability. Likewise, $\mathtt{mlE}(mk_1; b_1) \to \beta_1 \neq \beta_2 \leftarrow \mathtt{mlE}(mk_2; b_2)$ also holds with overwhelming probability.

$f(m_1, m_2) = 1$. By definition of f, the event $f(m_1, m_2) = 1$ corresponds to the event $b_1 = b_2$. We prove that in this case Reveal always outputs 1 as well. From the assumption that $b_1 = b_2$, it follows that $\mathtt{mlKD}(b_1) = \mathtt{mlKD}(b_2) =: mk$, i.e., the two chunks lead to the same message-locked key. In addition, given that message-locked encryption is deterministic, it holds that $\mathtt{mlE}(mk; b_1) = \beta_1 = \mathtt{mlE}(mk; b_2) = \beta_2 =: \beta$.

Decryption Correctness. Decryption correctness naturally follows from the correctness of the primitives employed as building blocks.

5.2   Our MKRE Instantiation with Random Oracles

We now describe how to implement the components of our MKRE construction of Definition 8 in the random oracle model.

Setup and Key Generation. The Setup procedure outputs a description of four hash functions H_1, H_2, H_3, and H_4 in mpk. Essentially, we use one hash function per encryption step, each modeled as a random oracle: $H_1 : \{0,1\}^k \to \{0,1\}^\lambda$; $H_2 : \{0,1\}^\lambda \to \{0,1\}^k$; $H_3 : \{0,1\}^\lambda \times \{0,1\}^k \to \{0,1\}^k$; $H_4 : \{0,1\}^\lambda \times \{0,1\}^\lambda \to \{0,1\}^l$. All four hash functions can be instantiated with a single random oracle by prepending the index to the input. A user's secret key is *one* random string $sk_{id} = detk_{id} = randkey_{id} \xleftarrow{\$} \{0,1\}^\lambda$.

Message-Locked Encryption. This primitive is instantiated using the two hash functions H_1 and H_2. The base-derived key is generated as

$$mk \leftarrow \mathtt{mlKD}(b) := H_1(b).$$

The message-locked encryption of b is then computed as

$$\beta \leftarrow \mathtt{mlE}(mk, b) := H_2(mk) \oplus b.$$

Finally, the ciphertext β can be decrypted with mk as

$$b \leftarrow \mathtt{mlD}(mk; \beta) := H_2(mk) \oplus \beta.$$

Deterministic Encryption. This primitive is instantiated using H_3. Recall that in the random oracle $\mathsf{detk_{id}} = \mathsf{sk_{id}} \in \{0,1\}^\lambda$. To implement deterministic encryption of the message-locked key mk in the random oracle model (which cannot be inverted), we must depart slightly from the abstract construction in the previous section and use the encryption of the base β "as IV":

$$\gamma \leftarrow \mathsf{detE_{detk_{id}}}(\mathsf{mk}) := H_3(\mathsf{sk_{id}}, \beta) \oplus \mathsf{mk}.$$

The decryption of a deterministic ciphertext γ (using the "random IV" β) is performed as

$$\mathsf{mk} \leftarrow \mathsf{detD_{detk_{id}}}(\mathsf{mk}) := H_3(\mathsf{sk_{id}}, \beta) \oplus \gamma.$$

Randomized Encryption. This primitive is instantiated using H_4. Recall that in the random oracle $\mathsf{randkey_{id}} = \mathsf{sk_{id}} \in \{0,1\}^\lambda$. The randomized encryption is performed as:

$$\delta \leftarrow \mathsf{randE_{randkey_{id}}}(\mathsf{d}) := (\delta_1, \delta_2),$$

where $\delta_1 \xleftarrow{\$} \{0,1\}^\lambda$ and $\delta_2 := (H_4(\mathsf{sk_{id}}, \delta_1) \oplus \mathsf{d})$. The randomized decryption is performed as:

$$\mathsf{d} \leftarrow \mathsf{randD_{randkey_{id}}}(\delta) := H_4(\mathsf{sk_{id}}, \delta_1) \oplus \delta_2.$$

Analysis of Construction. Correctness of the above algorithms can be easily verified by inspection. We can now prove the security of our scheme.

Theorem 1. *The MKRE construction of Sect. 5.2 is simulation secure in our framework (Definition 6) in the random oracle model.*

Due to space constraints, we only provide a brief overview of the core parts of the proof, which is how to deal with random oracle and corruption queries. The full proof is given in the full version of the paper [23]. In the case of queries to H_1, our model lets the simulator $\mathcal{S}$ learn the adversary's queries to the oracle. If $H_1(\mathsf{x})$ has not yet been initialized, the simulator has the chance to make a guess, $\tilde{\mathsf{m}}$, for the chunk corresponding to the query (step 1 in $\mathcal{SRO}$, see Fig. 2). Concretely, $\mathcal{S}$ asks for $\tilde{\mathsf{m}} = \phi^{-1}(\mathsf{x}, 0)$, and therefore $\mathcal{S}$ learns whether any file with the same base has been queried to $\mathcal{SE}$ previously (thanks to leakage received in step 3, see Fig. 2). The simulator uses the leakage to identify the list of ciphertexts "matching" the queried base x and can set its answer consistently. In case of corruption queries, $\mathcal{S}$ needs to produce a secret key which explains all of the previously produced encryptions for the corrupted identity. To do so, $\mathcal{S}$ receives the list of such ciphertexts and the corresponding plaintexts (line 2 of $\mathcal{SC}$ in Fig. 2). Then $\mathcal{S}$ can pick a random key $\mathsf{sk_{id}} \xleftarrow{\$} \{0,1\}^\lambda$, and for all $(\mathsf{m}, \mathsf{c}) \in \mathcal{D}_{\mathsf{enc}}^{(\mathsf{id})}$, it can program the random oracles to match the expected output. In case H_3 or H_4 were initialized before the corruption query was made the simulator fails in this task and aborts, but this happens with negligible probability.

6   Proof-of-Concept Implementation and Evaluation

Having obtained an understanding of the security of our MKRE scheme in the random oracle model, it is interesting to evaluate its practical merits. To do this, we developed a proof-of-concept implementation of the instantiation presented in Sect. 5.2. Our implementation follows the software architecture of Nielsen et al. [26] and adopts the Hamming code also used in [32] as an example of a generalized deduplication transformation. We run our experiments with parameter $l \in \{13, 14, 15, 16\}$ for the Hamming code. A Hamming code has a codeword length of $n = 2^l - 1$ bits and a message length of $k = 2^l - l - 1$ bits. To ensure that the data chunks always align with the data's byte boundaries, we use data chunks of $2^l = n+1$ bits. The transformation function ϕ then operates as follows. The first n bits are decoded using the Hamming code, providing the k bit base. Then, the last bit and the l-bit syndrome of the Hamming code (representing the location of a single bit difference between the reencoded base and the original chunk) are concatenated to form a deviation of $l+1$ bits. As a result, our experiments with generalized deduplication transformation based on the Hamming code will ingest chunks with a size between 1 KB and 8 KB.

To instantiate the cryptographic primitives, we use the OpenSSL library [30]. In particular, we chose AES-128-CTR and HMAC-SHA-1 for encryption and hashing, respectively. This choice is somewhat arbitrary, and another choice may be made as desired. We use HMAC-SHA-1 to derive the message-locked keys from bases. Deterministic encryption (and thus the message-locked encryption) is implemented by using an all-zero IV in AES. Randomized encryption utilizes a randomly chosen IV for AES, which is concatenated with the ciphertext. While this choice of algorithms is not equivalent to the random oracle model, we assume that this provides a "good enough" approximation to the random oracle behavior. This choice of algorithms allows us to implement an efficient practical solution. Our evaluation is run on a publicly available dataset of images provided by Plant Labs Inc. [28] consisting of 69 high-resolution .tiff images of approximately 50 MB each. As a result, our experiments deal with 3.5 GB of data. We compare the overall performance of applying MKRE for privacy-aware deduplication across users with the unsecured case of storing the unencrypted files directly on the server. The experiments are run on a Backblaze Storage Pod 6.0 with a 3.7 GHz Intel Xeon E5-1620 v2 Quad-Core CPU.

The first point of comparison is compression ratio $= \frac{\text{compressed size}}{\text{original size}}$. A compression ratio of 1 indicates that no compression is achieved, i.e., that the compressed version takes up 100% of the original size. A low compression ratio is clearly desired. Figure 4 compares the compression ratios achieved with encrypted and unencrypted generalized deduplication, using chunks of 1 KB and 8 KB. We remark that in [26], it was shown that, for the same data set, ZFS, a state-of-the-art file system utilizing classic deduplication [27], achieved negligible compression. Our experiments show that, as expected, the compression ratio of the encrypted version follows the unencrypted ratio closely. The only difference is that some overhead must be stored for the encrypted version, e.g., from padding and IVs. In particular, we see that for 1 KB chunks the overhead is more

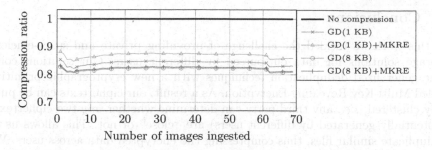

Fig. 4. Compression ratio, as images are stored on the server using generalized deduplication. Each image has a size of approximately 50 MB.

significant, increasing the average compression ratio from 84% to 87%. On the other hand, the overhead has smaller impact on the ratio when the chunks are longer, as seen for 8 KB chunks, where the average increase is just from 81.8% to 82.2%. This validates that it indeed is possible to achieve similar compression levels when operating on encrypted data, as desired.

A second, equally important, point is the impact on system throughput. This is shown on Fig. 5. Obviously, adding an encryption step can only decrease the system throughput. In our experiments, the drop in throughput is larger for larger chunks. Indeed, there is actually no significant difference in throughput when chunks are 1 KB. The worst case is seen for 8 KB chunks, where the throughput drops 6.9%. We note that although our system is not thoroughly optimized, throughputs on the order of $2-16$ MB/s is observed. This is promising, as with some optimization a throughput on the order of 100s of MB/s should be achievable. Such a throughput will allow our method to be deployed in real-time cloud systems, where the bottleneck then is the read/write speeds of the hard drives or SSDs.

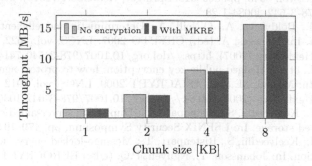

Fig. 5. System-level throughput of our proof-of-concept implementation storing files with generalized deduplication and MKRE.

7 Conclusions

In this work we tackled the challenge of providing private and space-efficient storage solutions for data outsourced by different users. Our solutions combine generalized deduplication techniques with a new cryptographic primitive called Multi-Key Revealing Encryption. As a result, our ciphertexts can be publicly clustered, *i.e.*, any third party can determine whether *any* two ciphertexts (potentially generated by different users) are "close" or not. This allows us to deduplicate similar files, thus compressing the encrypted data across users. We tested a practical implementation of our proposal on a real world dataset. These experiments show that, for a range of common deduplication chunk sizes, our privacy-aware solution achieves a compression ratio that is only 3% worse (in the worst case) than the one provided by generalized deduplication on unencrypted data, and the maximum loss in throughput is 6.9%.

We leave the investigation of other applications which benefit from MKRE as an interesting direction for future research.

Acknowledgements. This work was partially financed by: the SCALE-IoT project (Grant No. DFF-7026-00042B) and FoCC (Grant No. DFF-6108-00169) granted by the Danish Council for Independent Research; the AUFF Starting Grant AUFF-2017-FLS-7-1; Aarhus University's DIGIT Centre; the strategic research area ELLIIT; the Concordium Blockhain Research Center, Aarhus University, Denmark; the European Research Council (ERC) under the European Unions's Horizon 2020 research and innovation programme under grant agreement No 803096 (SPEC).

References

1. Agrawal, S., Clear, M., Frieder, O., Garg, S., O'Neill, A., Thaler, J.: Ad hoc multi-input functional encryption (2019). https://eprint.iacr.org/2019/356
2. Agrawal, S., Gorbunov, S., Vaikuntanathan, V., Wee, H.: Functional encryption: new perspectives and lower bounds. In: Canetti, R., Garay, J.A. (eds.) CRYPTO 2013. LNCS, vol. 8043, pp. 500–518. Springer, Heidelberg (2013). https://doi.org/10.1007/978-3-642-40084-1_28
3. Bellare, M., Boldyreva, A., O'Neill, A.: Deterministic and efficiently searchable encryption. In: Menezes, A. (ed.) CRYPTO 2007. LNCS, vol. 4622, pp. 535–552. Springer, Heidelberg (2007). https://doi.org/10.1007/978-3-540-74143-5_30
4. Bellare, M., et al.: Hedged public-key encryption: how to protect against bad randomness. In: Matsui, M. (ed.) ASIACRYPT 2009. LNCS, vol. 5912, pp. 232–249. Springer, Heidelberg (2009). https://doi.org/10.1007/978-3-642-10366-7_14
5. Bellare, M., Keelveedhi, S., Ristenpart, T.: DupLESS: server-aided encryption for deduplicated storage. In: USENIX Security Symposium, pp. 179–194 (2013)
6. Bellare, M., Keelveedhi, S., Ristenpart, T.: Message-locked encryption and secure deduplication. In: Johansson, T., Nguyen, P.Q. (eds.) EUROCRYPT 2013. LNCS, vol. 7881, pp. 296–312. Springer, Heidelberg (2013). https://doi.org/10.1007/978-3-642-38348-9_18
7. Bendlin, R., Nielsen, J.B., Nordholt, P.S., Orlandi, C.: Lower and upper bounds for deniable public-key encryption. In: Lee, D.H., Wang, X. (eds.) ASIACRYPT 2011. LNCS, vol. 7073, pp. 125–142. Springer, Heidelberg (2011). https://doi.org/10.1007/978-3-642-25385-0_7

8. Boyd, C., Davies, G.T., Gjøsteen, K., Raddum, H., Toorani, M.: Security notions for cloud storage and deduplication. In: Baek, J., Susilo, W., Kim, J. (eds.) ProvSec 2018. LNCS, vol. 11192, pp. 347–365. Springer, Cham (2018). https://doi.org/10.1007/978-3-030-01446-9_20
9. Canetti, R., Feige, U., Goldreich, O., Naor, M.: Adaptively secure multi-party computation. In: ACM STOC, pp. 639–648 (1996)
10. Chenette, N., Lewi, K., Weis, S.A., Wu, D.J.: Practical order-revealing encryption with limited leakage. Fast Softw. Encryption 2016, 474–493 (2016)
11. Chotard, J., Dufour Sans, E., Gay, R., Phan, D.H., Pointcheval, D.: Decentralized multi-client functional encryption for inner product. In: Peyrin, T., Galbraith, S. (eds.) ASIACRYPT 2018. LNCS, vol. 11273, pp. 703–732. Springer, Cham (2018). https://doi.org/10.1007/978-3-030-03329-3_24
12. Curtmola, R., Garay, J.A., Kamara, S., Ostrovsky, R.: Searchable symmetric encryption: improved definitions and efficient constructions. J. Comput. Secur. 19(5), 895–934 (2011)
13. Douceur, J.R., Adya, A., Bolosky, W.J., Simon, D., Theimer, M., Simon, P.: Reclaiming space from duplicate files in a serverless distributed file system. ICDCS 2002, 617–624 (2002)
14. Goldwasser, S., et al.: Multi-input functional encryption. In: Nguyen, P.Q., Oswald, E. (eds.) EUROCRYPT 2014. LNCS, vol. 8441, pp. 578–602. Springer, Heidelberg (2014). https://doi.org/10.1007/978-3-642-55220-5_32
15. Haagh, H., Ji, Y., Li, C., Orlandi, C., Song, Y.: Revealing encryption for partial ordering. In: O'Neill, M. (ed.) IMACC 2017. LNCS, vol. 10655, pp. 3–22. Springer, Cham (2017). https://doi.org/10.1007/978-3-319-71045-7_1
16. Hamming, R.W.: Error detecting and error correcting codes. Bell Syst. Tech. J. 29(2), 147–160 (1950)
17. Katz, J., Sahai, A., Waters, B.: Predicate encryption supporting disjunctions, polynomial equations, and inner products. J. Cryptol. 26, 191–224 (2013)
18. Li, J., Chen, X., Li, M., Li, J., Lee, P.P., Lou, W.: Secure deduplication with efficient and reliable convergent key management. IEEE Trans. Parallel Distrib. Syst. 25(6), 1615–1625 (2013)
19. Li, X., Li, J., Huang, F.: A secure cloud storage system supporting privacy-preserving fuzzy deduplication. Soft Comput. 20(4), 1437–1448 (2015). https://doi.org/10.1007/s00500-015-1596-6
20. Libert, B., Ţiţiu, R.: Multi-client functional encryption for linear functions in the standard model from LWE. In: Galbraith, S.D., Moriai, S. (eds.) ASIACRYPT 2019. LNCS, vol. 11923, pp. 520–551. Springer, Cham (2019). https://doi.org/10.1007/978-3-030-34618-8_18
21. Liu, J., Asokan, N., Pinkas, B.: secure deduplication of encrypted data without additional independent servers. In: ACM CCS, pp. 874–885 (2015)
22. Liu, J., Duan, L., Li, Y., Asokan, N.: Secure deduplication of encrypted data: refined model and new constructions. In: Smart, N.P. (ed.) CT-RSA 2018. LNCS, vol. 10808, pp. 374–393. Springer, Cham (2018). https://doi.org/10.1007/978-3-319-76953-0_20
23. Lucani, D.E., Nielsen, L., Orlandi, C., Pagnin, E., Vestergaard, R.: Secure generalized deduplication via multi-key revealing encryption. Cryptology ePrint Archive, Report 2020/799 (2020). https://eprint.iacr.org/2020/799 (full version of this work)
24. Michalevsky, Y., Joye, M.: Decentralized policy-hiding ABE with receiver privacy. In: Lopez, J., Zhou, J., Soriano, M. (eds.) ESORICS 2018. LNCS, vol. 11099, pp. 548–567. Springer, Cham (2018). https://doi.org/10.1007/978-3-319-98989-1_27

25. Nielsen, J.B.: Separating random oracle proofs from complexity theoretic proofs: the non-committing encryption case. In: Yung, M. (ed.) CRYPTO 2002. LNCS, vol. 2442, pp. 111–126. Springer, Heidelberg (2002). https://doi.org/10.1007/3-540-45708-9_8
26. Nielsen, L., Vestergaard, R., Yazdani, N., Talasila, P., Lucani, D.E., Sipos, M.: Alexandria: a proof-of-concept implementation and evaluation of generalised data deduplication. In: IEEE GLOBECOM Workshop on Advances in Edge Computing (2019)
27. Oracle: What Is ZFS? (2019). https://docs.oracle.com/cd/E23823_01/html/819-5461/zfsover-2.html. Accessed 12 Oct 2019
28. Planet Labs Inc: download samples of our, high resolution imagery, for monitoring, tasking and large area mapping (2019). https://info.planet.com/download-free-high-resolution-skysat-image-samples/. Accessed 17 Jun 2019
29. Stefanov, E., Papamanthou, C., Shi, E.: Practical dynamic searchable encryption with small leakage. NDSS **71**, 72–75 (2014)
30. The OpenSSL Project: OpenSSL: the open source toolkit for SSL/TLS. www.openssl.org. Accessed 23 Sep 2019
31. Vestergaard, R., Lucani, D.E., Zhang, Q.: A randomly accessible lossless compression scheme for time-series data. In: IEEE INFOCOM (2020)
32. Vestergaard, R., Zhang, Q., Lucani, D.E.: Generalized deduplication: bounds, convergence, and asymptotic properties. In: IEEE GLOBECOM (2019)
33. Vestergaard, R., Zhang, Q., Lucani, D.E.: Lossless compression of time series data with generalized deduplication. In: IEEE GLOBECOM (2019)
34. Xia, W., et al.: A comprehensive study of the past, present, and future of data deduplication. Proc. IEEE **104**(9), 1681–1710 (2016)
35. Zhao, Y., Chow, S.S.M.: Updatable block-level message-locked encryption. IEEE Trans. Dependable Secure Comput. (2019)

Signatures, Encryption, and Algebraic Constructions

A Simple and Efficient CCA-Secure Lattice KEM in the Standard Model

Xavier Boyen[1], Malika Izabachène[2], and Qinyi Li[3(✉)]

[1] QUT, Brisbane, Australia
xb@boyen.org
[2] CEA LIST, Point Courrier 172, 91191 Gif-sur-Yvette Cedex, France
malika.izabachene@cea.fr
[3] Griffith University, Brisbane, Australia
qinyi.li@griffith.edu.au

Abstract. We present, to date, the most efficient public-key encapsulation mechanism from integer lattices in the standard model. Our construction achieves adaptive CCA security through a "direct" chosen-ciphertext security technique without relying on any generic transformation. The security of our construction is based on the standard learning-with-errors assumption. The efficiency of our construction is almost the same as the best known non-adaptive CCA-secure construction.

1 Introduction

Public-key encryption (PKE) is one of the most essential cryptographic primitives that provide data confidentiality. It is the *de facto* requirement that a PKE scheme should be CCA-secure, i.e., secure against adaptive chosen-ciphertext attack for internet applications. In general, the security definitions for PKE involve a game in which the adversary receives a challenge ciphertext ct^* and tries to extract non-trivial information about the underlying message $m*$. With the power of adaptive chosen-ciphertext attack, after receiving ct^*, the adversary can make decryption queries, i.e., adaptively formulating arbitrary ciphertexts that are different from but possibly related to the challenge ciphertext ct^*, and obtain the corresponding plaintexts. Such decryption queries could be helpful to the adversary. For instance, if the adversary can modify the challenge ciphertext ct^* to get a valid (i.e., properly decipherable) ciphertext $ct \neq ct^*$ such that m, the message that ct encrypts, is related to m^* in some known way, the adversary can learn something about m^*. This can be done by sending through ct as a decryption query and receiving back the m^*-related message m.

For efficiency reasons, the main use of public-key encryption is as a key encapsulation mechanism (KEM) for exchanging or delivering random session keys. For example, in the paradigm of "hybrid encryption" [13], a KEM scheme is used in conjunction with a data encapsulation mechanism (DEM) scheme which is a basically a symmetric-key cipher: the KEM encrypts a random session key and the DEM uses the random session key to encrypt the actual message. It is

© Springer Nature Switzerland AG 2020
C. Galdi and V. Kolesnikov (Eds.): SCN 2020, LNCS 12238, pp. 321–337, 2020.
https://doi.org/10.1007/978-3-030-57990-6_16

known that if both KEM and DEM are CCA-secure, then the hybrid encryption is CCA-secure [13]. While any PKE scheme is also a KEM scheme (by sampling then encrypting a random symmetric keys), KEM schemes may be constructed in more efficient ways.

One of the most common ways of constructing a CCA-secure KEM is to apply the Fujisaki-Okamoto transformation [16] to a weakly secure PKE/KEM scheme (e.g., one with chosen-plaintext or CPA security). This approach has produced many practical KEMs that are CCA-secure in the random oracle model. Alas, the security argument from this approach is merely heuristic since random oracles are fictions that cannot be instantiated in the real world. There have been plentiful works on building efficient PKE/KEM schemes from various of number-theoretic assumptions, e.g., [9,13,17,19], without using random oracles. Since these schemes are insecure against quantum adversaries, it is desirable to find "quantum-safe" alternatives, e.g., lattice-based constructions.

There are three current approaches for constructing CCA-secure PKE/KEM from lattices in the standard model, i.e., without using random oracles. The first one is to apply the BCHK transformation [9] to tag-based encryption (TBE) or identity-based encryption (IBE). This approach introduces noticeable extra overheads in computation and ciphertext size to the underlying TBE/IBE scheme. The second one is to resort to lossy trapdoor functions (LTFs) [31], as in the construction from [10]. One of the main issue with this approach is that the known lattice-based lossy trapdoor functions (e.g., [5,8,31]) require relatively large parameters and rely on strong lattice assumptions (e.g., LWE with large (but still polynomial) modulus-to-noise ratio). For example, the recent simple construction of CCA-secure KEM scheme from [10] uses a stronger LWE assumption than the CCA-secure PKE/KEM obtained by applying BCHK transform to the identity/tag-based encryption schemes in [1,24]. The third approach is to instantiate the Naor-Yung paradigm [14,26,33] using a non-interactive zero-knowledge (NIZK) proof system from lattices, such as [30], but at the moment this approach is not even remotely practical.

In this paper, we propose a fourth approach, for constructing an efficient KEM in the standard model from standard lattice assumptions, without appealing to generic transformation, LTFs or NIZKs.

1.1 Our Approach

At a high level, we adopt the "direct chosen-ciphertext" approach from [11], previously used in pairing-based CCA-secure PKE constructions ([11,20]), and adapt it for use with an TBE/IBE from the learning-with-errors (LWE) problem, e.g., [1,24]. However, contrarily to pairing-based constructions, the ciphertexts in lattice-based constructions often contain noise terms. Varying the noise terms within a small interval results in slightly different ciphertexts which are still valid and properly decrypt to the same message. This is because those noise terms are removed by the error-correction mechanism of the decryption algorithms as long as they are "small" enough. While those noise terms are crucial for security, they also impede the making of the ciphertexts non-malleable for CCA security.

Let's take the tag-based PKE scheme from [24] as an example. The ciphertext of the scheme is

$$\mathbf{c}_0^t = \mathbf{s}^t \mathbf{A} + \mathbf{e}_0^t \quad ; \quad \mathbf{c}_1^t = \mathbf{s}^t(\mathbf{A}_1 + H(\mathsf{id})\mathbf{G}) + \mathbf{e}_1^t$$

where matrices $\mathbf{A}$, $\mathbf{A}_1 \in \mathbb{Z}_q^{n \times m}$ are public keys, H is a full-rank difference encoding (FRD) which is either injective or with second pre-image resistance, and $\mathbf{G} \in \mathbb{Z}_q^{n \times m}$ is a "gadget" matrix. (We refer to [1] for the details of FRD and to [24] for the detail of $\mathbf{G}$.) Here we ignore how the actual message is hidden for simplicity. Notice that this ciphertext essentially contains many LWE samples and $\mathbf{e}_0$, $\mathbf{e}_1$ are the LWE noise terms. To prove security [1], the simulator embeds the challenge tag $H(\mathsf{id}^*)$ in $\mathbf{A}_1$ such that all ciphertexts with $H(\mathsf{id}) \neq H(\mathsf{id}^*)$ can be decrypted, except for the challenge ciphertext whose tag is $H(\mathsf{id}^*)$.

Drawing inspiration from [11,20,35], we would replace the identity id by $\mathbf{c}_0$ and obtain

$$\mathbf{c}_0^t = \mathbf{s}^t \mathbf{A} + \mathbf{e}_0^t \quad ; \quad \mathbf{c}_1^t = \mathbf{s}^t(\mathbf{A}_1 + H(\mathbf{c}_0)\mathbf{G}) + \mathbf{e}_1^t$$

The tag $H(\mathbf{c}_0)$ binds $\mathbf{s}$ and $\mathbf{e}_0$. Given a challenge ciphertext $(\mathbf{c}_0^*, \mathbf{c}_1^*)$, if the attacker modifies $\mathbf{c}_0^*$ or $\mathbf{c}_1^*$ by changing $\mathbf{s}$, the tag $H(\mathbf{c}_0^*)$ changes, and, by the same argument as in [1], decryption queries on such a modified ciphertext can be answered. However, this does not make the ciphertext non-malleable because adding a small error $\mathbf{e}$ to $\mathbf{e}_1$ results in a ciphertext that decrypts to the same message with high probability. In fact, a recent lattice-based public-key encryption scheme [15] does not appear to live up to its claim of CCA security, precisely for this reason.

Therefore, an additional mechanism is needed in order to prevent the adversary from modifying $\mathbf{e}_1$ while keeping the ciphertext valid. Our idea is simple. We add a hash of $\mathbf{e}_1$ to the ciphertext, where hashing is from the short integer solution (SIS) problem, i.e., $\mathbf{c}_2 = \mathbf{U}\mathbf{e}_1$ where $\mathbf{U} \in \mathbb{Z}_q^{n \times m}$ is a random matrix. We also input $\mathbf{c}_2$ to the FRD function. This gives a ciphertext

$$\mathbf{c}_0^t = \mathbf{s}^t \mathbf{A} + \mathbf{e}_0^t \quad ; \quad \mathbf{c}_1^t = \mathbf{s}^t(\mathbf{A}_1 + H(\mathbf{c}_0, \mathbf{c}_2)\mathbf{G}) + \mathbf{e}_1^t \quad ; \quad \mathbf{c}_2 = \mathbf{U}\mathbf{e}_1$$

This provides non-malleability, since modifying $\mathbf{e}_1$ into a "small" $\mathbf{e}_2'$ without changing $\mathbf{c}_2$ is infeasible, without also producing a solution to the SIS problem for the random matrix $\mathbf{U}$, given by $\mathbf{U}(\mathbf{e}_1 - \mathbf{e}_1') = \mathbf{0}$.

Lastly, we observe that it is enough to use $H(\mathbf{c}_0, \mathbf{c}_2)$, a hash value which can be as short as the security parameter, to make the ciphertext non-malleable, instead of $\mathbf{c}_2$. Therefore, the final ciphertext of our construction consists of three elements:

$$\mathbf{c}_0^t = \mathbf{s}^t \mathbf{A} + \mathbf{e}_0^t \quad ; \quad \mathbf{c}_1^t = \mathbf{s}^t(\mathbf{A}_1 + H(\mathbf{c}_0, \mathbf{U}\mathbf{e}_1)\mathbf{G}) + \mathbf{e}_1^t \quad ; \quad H(\mathbf{c}_0, \mathbf{U}\mathbf{e}_1)$$

which can be of the same size as the *non-adaptive* CCA1-secure PKE scheme proposed in [24].

The security rationale behind this simple idea is the duality between the lattice problems LWE and SIS [21,22]. LWE and SIS are "syntactically equivalent" in the sense that adding an SIS hash of the noise term of the given LWE samples is essentially equivalent to providing a redundant description of the LWE problem, and therefore would not make the LWE problem any significantly easier.

1.2 Comparison and Related Work

Our construction achieves *adaptive* CCA security (a.k.a. CCA2 security) while being almost as concise as the best-known *non-adaptive* CCA1-secure scheme without random oracles from [24] (dubbed "MP12" henceforward). Public key size is essentially the same except for one extra public matrix U^1. Our ciphertexts are as short as those of CCA1-secure MP12 under the same message encoding, hence shorter than any CCA2-secure ciphertext that could be obtained by upgrading MP12 through the BCHK transform (yielding "MP12-BCHK").

In terms of encapsulation (encryption) and decapsulation (decryption) speed, even though our construction incurs one extra matrix-vector multiplication Ue_1, performance is very comparable to MP12-BCHK with commitments and message authentication codes, and better than the MP12-BCHK with one-time signatures (recall that the generic BCHK transform works in either of those ways). In terms of computational assumptions, we rely on almost the same LWE assumption as the one used in MP12. Crucially, the LWE noise-to-modulus ratio in both schemes is the same. The only difference is that to prove security, our construction requires a slightly larger number of LWE samples than needed by MP12, as these extra LWE samples are used to simulate Ue_1. This, however, is a mostly academic distinction with limited bearing on security, as the hardness of the LWE problem is not sensitive to the number of samples.

Duong et al. [15] recently proposed a lattice-based PKE scheme with equality test. However, the scheme is not CCA-secure as the ciphertext is malleable, as we noted before. It would be interesting to work out if our technique is applicable to leverage their scheme to achieve CCA security without losing efficiency.

Zhang et al. [35] recently proposed another lattice-based PKE scheme with claimed CCA security. One similarity with ours is that they require the random session key to be encoded in the LWE secret; we elected to do the same to make our construction more compact. It should be noted, however, that the security proof of [35] seems incomplete, although no attack seems to have been found.

Table 1 below gives a comparison amongst efficient public-key encryption and encapsulation schemes from lattices in the standard model. To be generous, we assume that all schemes use the same efficient way of encoding the message into the normal-form LWE secret vectors, with the caveat that the resulting secrets post-encoding must retain sufficiently high entropy. (The original MP12 encodes messages into the LWE noise vectors, making its ciphertexts larger.) In Table 1, the pub, com and tag overheads affecting MP12-MAC, refer to public parameters, weak commitment and MAC tag borne by the "MAC" version of

---

[1] A common practical implementation heuristic would be to expand U from a public seed using a secure pseudorandom number generator; for the security reduction U needs to be truly random.

the BCHK transform. Likewise, vk and sig in MP12-SIG are the public key and signature in a strongly unforgeable one-time signature scheme incurred by the "SIG" version of the BCHK transform. Their size will generally be much larger than the security parameter, which we conventionally write λ. Both MP12 and our work have a ciphertext overhead component of size λ: in MP12 it is a random tag; in our case it is a second-preimage-resistant hash function. Given a modulus q and dimension n (suitably determined from the security parameter λ), the hardness of the LWE problem is mostly determined by the noise-to-modulus ratio parameter α. The smaller $\alpha > 0$ is, the easier the LWE problem becomes. As noted above, α is essentially the same across the relevant constructions.

Table 1. Comparison for PKE schemes

	Param. α	$|\mathsf{pk}|$	$|\mathsf{ct}|$	Security	Type
MP12 [24]	$\tilde{O}(1/n)$	$2(n \log q)^2$	$3n \log q + \lambda$	CCA1	PKE
MP12-MAC [9,24]	$\tilde{O}(1/n)$	$2(n \log q)^2 + |\mathsf{pub}|$	$3n \log q + |\mathsf{tag}| + |\mathsf{com}|$	CCA	PKE
MP12-SIG [9,24]	$\tilde{O}(1/n)$	$2(n \log q)^2$	$3n \log q + |\mathsf{sig}| + |\mathsf{vk}|$	CCA	PKE
This work	$\tilde{O}(1/n)$	$3(n \log q)^2$	$3n \log q + \lambda$	CCA	KEM

2 Preliminaries

We denote the security parameter by λ. We use bold lowercase letters (e.g. $\mathbf{a}$) to denote vectors and bold capital letters (e.g. $\mathbf{A}$) to denote matrices. For a positive integer $q \geq 2$, let $\mathbb{Z}_q$ be the ring of integers modulo q. We denote the group of $n \times m$ matrices in $\mathbb{Z}_q$ by $\mathbb{Z}_q^{n \times m}$. Vectors are treated as column vectors. The transpose of a vector $\mathbf{a}$ is denoted by $\mathbf{a}^\top$. For $\mathbf{A} \in \mathbb{Z}_q^{n \times m}$ and $\mathbf{B} \in \mathbb{Z}_q^{n \times m'}$, let $[\mathbf{A}|\mathbf{B}] \in \mathbb{Z}_q^{n \times (m+m')}$ be the concatenation of $\mathbf{A}$ and $\mathbf{B}$. We denote by $\|\mathbf{x}\|$ the ℓ_2 norm of a vector $\mathbf{x}$. $\|\mathbf{X}\|$ denotes the ℓ_2 length of the longest column of $\mathbf{R}$. Let $\mathbf{x} = (x_1, x_2, ..., x_n)$ be s vector over $\mathbb{Z}_q^n$, $\|\mathbf{x}\| = \max(|x_1|, |x_2|, ..., |x_n|)$. Let X and Y be two random variables taking values in some finite set Ω. Their statistical distance, denoted $\Delta(X, Y)$, is $\Delta(X, Y) = \frac{1}{2} \sum_{s \in \Omega} |\Pr[X = s] - \Pr[Y = s]|$.

The following lemma will be useful in our security proofs.

Lemma 1 (Lemma 1 of [34]). *Let X_1, X_2, B be events defined in some probability distribution, and suppose that $X_1 \wedge \neg B \Leftrightarrow X_2 \wedge \neg B$. Then $|\Pr[X_1] - \Pr[X_2]| \leq \Pr[B]$.*

2.1 Lattices, Discrete Gaussians, and Trapdoors

Definition 1 (Random Integer Lattice). *For a positive integer q (later to be prime), a matrix $\mathbf{A} \in \mathbb{Z}_q^{n \times m}$ and a vector $\mathbf{u} \in \mathbb{Z}_q^n$, define the m-dimensional full-rank integer lattices*

$$\Lambda(\mathbf{A}) = \{\mathbf{y} \in \mathbb{Z}^m \; s.t. \; \exists \mathbf{x} \in \mathbb{Z}_q^n \; where \; \mathbf{x}^t \mathbf{A} = \mathbf{y} \pmod{q}\}$$

$$\Lambda^{\perp}(\mathbf{A}) := \{\mathbf{y} \in \mathbb{Z}^m \ s.t. \ \mathbf{A}\mathbf{y} = \mathbf{0} \pmod{q}\}$$

In fact, up to a scaling factor of q, $\Lambda(\mathbf{A})$ and $\Lambda^{\perp}(\mathbf{A})$ are dual to each other.

Definition 2. *Let $m \in \mathbb{Z}_{>0}$ be a positive integer and $\Lambda \subset \mathbb{Z}^m$. For any real vector $\mathbf{c} \in \mathbb{R}^m$ and positive parameter $\sigma \in \mathbb{R}_{>0}$, $\forall \mathbf{y} \in \Lambda$, the discrete Gaussian distribution over Λ with center $\mathbf{c}$ and parameter σ is denoted by $D_{\Lambda,\sigma,\mathbf{c}} = \rho_{\sigma,\mathbf{c}}(\mathbf{y})/\rho_{\sigma,\mathbf{c}}(\Lambda)$ where $\rho_{\sigma,\mathbf{c}}(\mathbf{x}) = \exp\left(-\pi\|\mathbf{x}-\mathbf{c}\|^2/\sigma^2\right)$ is the Gaussian function and $\rho_{\sigma,\mathbf{c}}(\Lambda) = \sum_{\mathbf{x} \in \Lambda} \rho_{\sigma,\mathbf{c}}(\mathbf{x})$. For notational convenience, $\rho_{\sigma,\mathbf{0}}$ and $D_{\Lambda,\sigma,\mathbf{0}}$ are abbreviated as ρ_σ and $D_{\Lambda,\sigma}$.*

Lemma 2 (special case of Lemma 4.4 of [25]). *For $\mathbf{x} \leftarrow D_{\mathbb{Z}^m,s}$, $\Pr[\|\mathbf{x}\| > s\sqrt{m}] < 1 - 2^{-\Omega(m)}$.*

Lemma 3 (Proposition 5.1 of [18]). *Let $q \geq 2$. For all but a $2q^{-n}$ fraction of all $\mathbf{A} \in \mathbb{Z}_q^{n \times m}$ and for any $s \geq \omega(\sqrt{\log n})$, the distribution of $\mathbf{A}\mathbf{e} \bmod q$ is statistically close to uniform over $\mathbb{Z}_q^n$, where $\mathbf{e} \sim D_{\mathbb{Z}^m,s}$.*

We will use the super-increasing vector $\mathbf{g}^t = (1, 2, 4, \ldots, 2^{k-1})$, for $k = \lceil \log_2 q \rceil$ and extend it to form a "gadget" matrix $\mathbf{G} = diag(\mathbf{g}^t, \ldots, \mathbf{g}^t) \in \mathbb{Z}_q^{n \times nk}$ as in [24]. Here we use a base 2 but other choices of base can be used. We formulate the following lemma which is directly derived from the Theorem 4.1 and Theorem 5.4 and of [24].

Lemma 4. *Let $w = n\lceil \log q \rceil$. Let $\mathbf{F} = [\mathbf{A}|\mathbf{A}\mathbf{R} + \mathbf{H}\mathbf{G}]$ where $\mathbf{R} \in \mathbb{Z}^{m \times w}$, $\mathbf{H} \in \mathbb{Z}_q^{n \times n}$ is invertible in $\mathbb{Z}_q$, and $\mathbf{G} \in \mathbb{Z}_q^{n \times w}$ is the gadget matrix. Given $\mathbf{b}^t = \mathbf{s}^t\mathbf{F} + \mathbf{e}^t$ where $\mathbf{e}^t = [\mathbf{e}_0^t | \mathbf{e}_1^t]$, there exists a p.p.t algorithm $\mathsf{Invert}(\mathbf{R}, \mathbf{F}, \mathbf{b})$ that outputs $\mathbf{s}$ and $\mathbf{e}$ when $\|\mathbf{e}_1^t - \mathbf{e}_0^t\mathbf{R}\|_\infty < q/4$.*

2.2 Hardness Assumptions

Definition 3 (Short-Integer-Solution Problem). *Let λ be the security parameter, $n = n(\lambda)$, $m = m(\lambda)$, $q = q(\lambda)$ and $\beta = \beta(\lambda)$. The advantage of an algorithm $\mathcal{A}$ that solves the problem $\mathsf{SIS}_{n,m,q,\beta}$, denoted by $\mathsf{Adv}_{\mathcal{A}}^{\mathsf{SIS}_{n,m,q,\beta}}(\lambda)$, is defined as $\Pr[\mathcal{A}(\mathbf{A}, \beta) \to \mathbf{e} \neq \mathbf{0} : \mathbf{A}\mathbf{e} = \mathbf{0} \bmod q \wedge \|\mathbf{e}\| \leq \beta]$ where $\mathbf{A} \leftarrow \mathbb{Z}_q^{n \times m}$. We say $\mathsf{SIS}_{n,m,q,\beta}$ is hard if for all p.p.t algorithms $\mathcal{A}$, $\mathsf{Adv}_{\mathcal{A}}^{\mathsf{SIS}_{n,m,q,\beta}}(\lambda) \leq \mathsf{negl}(\lambda)$.*

A series of works show that solving the $\mathsf{SIS}_{n,m,q,\beta}$ problem is as hard as approximating classic lattice problems, e.g., GapSVP and SIVP, for some approximation factor $\gamma = \beta \cdot \mathsf{poly}(n)$. We refer to [29] and the references therein for further details.

Definition 4 (Learning-With-Errors Problem). *Let λ be the security parameter, $n = n(\lambda)$, $m = m(\lambda)$, $q = q(\lambda)$ and an error distribution $\chi = \chi(n)$ over $\mathbb{Z}_q$. The advantage of a p.p.t adversary $\mathcal{A}$ for the learning with errors problem $\mathsf{LWE}_{n,m,q,\chi}$, denoted by $\mathsf{Adv}_{\mathcal{A}}^{\mathsf{LWE}_{n,m,q,\chi}}(\lambda)$, is defined as*

$$\left|\Pr[\mathcal{A}(\mathbf{A}, \mathbf{s}^t\mathbf{A} + \mathbf{e}^t) = 1] - \Pr[\mathcal{A}(\mathbf{A}, \mathbf{b}^t) = 1]\right|$$

where $\mathbf{A} \leftarrow \mathbb{Z}_q^{n \times m}$, $\mathbf{s} \leftarrow \mathbb{Z}_q^n$, $\mathbf{e} \leftarrow \chi^m$. The $\mathsf{LWE}_{n,m,q,\chi}$ problem is hard if $\mathsf{Adv}_{\mathcal{A}}^{\mathsf{LWE}_{n,m,q,\chi}}(\lambda) \leq \mathsf{negl}(\lambda)$ for all p.p.t adversary $\mathcal{A}$.

Regev [32] shows that, for $\alpha q > \sqrt{n}$, LWE is as hard as approximating some traditional worst-case lattice problems, e.g., SIVP. We refer to [29, 32] for details.

We prove the CCA security of our KEM scheme based on a variant of the LWE problem with a uniformly distributed SIS "hint", that we call the SISnLWE problem ("n" stands for "normal form"). It can also be seen as another variant of the Extended LWE problem [3,4,6,12,27] which has been studied in several different contexts. In Sect. 4.1, we prove that SISnLWE problem is hard as the LWE problem.

Definition 5 (Normal-form LWE with SIS hint). *Let λ be the security parameter, $n = n(\lambda)$, $m = m(\lambda)$, $q = q(\lambda)$ and an error distribution $\chi = \chi(n)$ over $\mathbb{Z}_q$. The advantage of a p.p.t. adversary $\mathcal{A}$ for the learning with errors problem $\mathsf{SISnLWE}_{n,m,q,\chi}$, denoted by $\mathsf{Adv}_{\mathcal{A}}^{\mathsf{SISnLWE}_{n,m,q,\chi}}(\lambda)$, is defined as*

$$\left| \Pr[\mathcal{A}(\mathbf{A}, \mathbf{s}^t \mathbf{A} + \mathbf{e}^t, \mathbf{Z}\mathbf{e}, \mathbf{Z}) = 1] - \Pr[\mathcal{A}(\mathbf{A}, \mathbf{b}^t, \mathbf{Z}\mathbf{e}, \mathbf{Z}) = 1] \right|$$

where $\mathbf{A}, \mathbf{Z} \leftarrow \mathbb{Z}_q^{n \times m}$, $\mathbf{s} \leftarrow \chi^n$, $\mathbf{e} \leftarrow \chi^m$. The $\mathsf{SISnLWE}_{n,m,q,\chi}$ problem is hard if $\mathsf{Adv}_{\mathcal{A}}^{\mathsf{SISnLWE}_{n,m,q,\chi}}(\lambda) \leq \mathsf{negl}(\lambda)$ for all p.p.t adversary $\mathcal{A}$.

We note that unlike the Extended LWE problems studied in [3,4,6] where $\mathbf{Z}$ is of low-norm, here $\mathbf{Z}$ is chosen uniformly at random which makes arguing the hardness of this new SISnLWE problem a lot easier.

Definition 6 (Second Pre-Image Collision Resistance). *Let λ be the security parameter. Let $H : \{0,1\}^* \rightarrow \{0,1\}^\ell$ be a hash function. We say that H is second-pre-image resistant if for all p.p.t algorithms $\mathcal{A}$, the advantage,*

$$\mathsf{Adv}_{\mathcal{A}}^{\mathsf{coll}}(\lambda) = \Pr[\mathcal{A}(H, x) \rightarrow x' \neq x \; : \; H(x) = H(x')]$$

where $x \leftarrow \{0,1\}^*$ and $x' \in \{0,1\}^*$ is negligible in λ.

We note that the notion of second pre-image collision resistance (or just second pre-image resistance) is weaker than the notion of collision resistance.

2.3 Public-Key Encapsulation

A public-key encapsulation (KEM) scheme $\Pi = (\mathsf{KeyGen}, \mathsf{Enc}, \mathsf{Dec})$ with key space $\mathcal{K}_\lambda$ consists of three polynomial-time algorithms. The key generation algorithm $\mathsf{KeyGen}(1^\lambda)$ generates a public key pk and a private key sk. The randomised key encapsulation algorithm $\mathsf{Enc}(\mathsf{pk})$ generates a session key $K \in \mathcal{K}_\lambda$ and a ciphertext ct. The decapsulation algorithm $\mathsf{Dec}(\mathsf{pk}, \mathsf{sk}, \mathsf{ct})$ returns the session key K or the error symbol $\perp$. The correctness of a KEM scheme requires that for all $\lambda \in \mathbb{N}$, and all $(K, \mathsf{ct}) \leftarrow \mathsf{Enc}(\mathsf{pk})$,

$$\Pr[\mathsf{Dec}(\mathsf{pk}, \mathsf{sk}, \mathsf{ct}) = K] \geq 1 - \mathsf{negl}(\lambda)$$

where the probability is taken over the random coins of KeyGen and Enc.

We recall the adaptive chosen-ciphertext security of KEM. The IND-CCA security of a KEM scheme Π with session key space $\mathcal{K}_\lambda$ is defined by the following security game. The challenger $\mathcal{C}$ runs $(\mathsf{pk}, \mathsf{sk}) \leftarrow \mathsf{KeyGen}(1^\lambda)$, chooses a random coin $\mu \leftarrow_\$ \{0,1\}$, samples $K_0^* \leftarrow_\$ \mathcal{K}_\lambda$, and computes $(K_1^*, \mathsf{ct}^*) \leftarrow \mathsf{Enc}(\mathsf{pk})$. Then $\mathcal{C}$ passes $(\mathsf{pk}, K_\mu^*, \mathsf{ct}^*)$ through to the adversary. The adversary launches adaptive chosen-ciphertext attacks: It repeatedly chooses any ciphertext $\mathsf{ct} \neq \mathsf{ct}^*$ and sends it over to $\mathcal{C}$ and $\mathcal{C}$ returns $\mathsf{Dec}(\mathsf{pk}, \mathsf{sk}, \mathsf{ct})$. Finally, $\mathcal{A}$ outputs μ' and wins if $\mu' = \mu$. We define $\mathcal{A}$'s advantage in the above security game as

$$\mathsf{Adv}^{\mathsf{ind-cca}}_{\mathcal{A},\Pi}(\lambda) = |\Pr[\mu' = \mu] - 1/2|.$$

We say Π is IND-CCA-secure if $\mathsf{Adv}^{\mathsf{ind-cca}}_{\mathcal{A},\Pi}(\lambda)$ is negligible in λ.

3   CCA-Secure KEM

We use the $\mathsf{SISnLWE}_{n,m,q,D_{\mathbb{Z},\alpha q}}$ problem for security where q is prime, $D_{\mathbb{Z},\alpha q}$ denotes the discrete Gaussian distribution with parameter αq, and $m \geq 2n\lceil \log q\rceil$. The following specifications are shared across instances of our scheme.

1. A full-rank difference encoding [1] $\mathsf{FRD} : \mathbb{Z}_q^n \to \mathsf{GL}(n,q)$ where $\mathsf{GL}(n,q)$ denotes the set of modulo-q invertible matrices in $\mathbb{Z}_q^{n \times n}$.
2. $\mathbf{G} \in \mathbb{Z}_q^{n \times w}$ for $w = n\lceil \log q\rceil$ is the gadget matrix originally defined in [24].
3. The LWE error rate α such that $1/\alpha = 8 \cdot O(w) \cdot \omega(\sqrt{\log n})$.
4. A second-pre-image resistant hash function $H : \{0,1\}^* \to \{0,1\}^\lambda \setminus \{0^\lambda\}$ where 0^λ is the length-λ string with all 0's. W.l.o.g, we assume there is an efficient injective encoding that encodes the outputs of H to elements in $\mathbb{Z}_q^n$.

- $\mathsf{KeyGen}(1^\lambda)$ The key generation algorithm does:
    1. Sample $\mathbf{A} \leftarrow \mathbb{Z}_q^{n \times m}$, $\mathbf{R} \leftarrow D^{m \times w}_{\mathbb{Z},\omega(\sqrt{\log n})}$ and set $\mathbf{A}_1 \leftarrow \mathbf{AR}$.
    2. Sample $\mathbf{U} \leftarrow \mathbb{Z}_q^{n \times w}$.
    3. Return the public key $\mathsf{pk} = (\mathbf{A}, \mathbf{A}_1, \mathbf{U})$
- $\mathsf{Enc}(\mathsf{pk})$ The key encapsulation algorithm does:
    1. Sample a session key $\mathbf{k} \leftarrow \{0,1\}^n$, $\bar{\mathbf{s}} \leftarrow \mathbb{Z}_q^n$; Set $\mathbf{s} \leftarrow \mathbf{k}\lfloor q/2\rfloor + \bar{\mathbf{s}}$.
    2. Sample $\mathbf{e}_0 \leftarrow D^m_{\mathbb{Z},\alpha q}$, $\mathbf{e}_1 \leftarrow D^w_{\mathbb{Z},s}$ where $s^2 = (\|\mathbf{e}_0\|^2 + m(\alpha q)^2) \cdot \omega(\sqrt{\log n})^2$.
    3. Compute $\mathbf{c}_0^t \leftarrow \mathbf{s}^t \mathbf{A} + \mathbf{e}_0^t$, and $\mathbf{c}_2 \leftarrow \mathbf{U}\mathbf{e}_1$.
    4. Compute $\mathbf{c}_1^t \leftarrow \mathbf{s}^t(\mathbf{A}_1 + \mathsf{FRD}(\mathbf{t})\mathbf{G}) + \mathbf{e}_1^t$ where $\mathbf{t} = H(\mathbf{c}_0, \mathbf{c}_2)$ is encoded as an element in $\mathbb{Z}_q^n$ before being sent to $\mathsf{FRD}(\cdot)$.
    5. Return the ciphertext $\mathsf{ct} = (\mathbf{c}_0, \mathbf{c}_1, \mathbf{t})$ and session key $\mathbf{k}$.
- $\mathsf{Dec}(\mathsf{pk}, \mathsf{sk}, \mathsf{ct})$ The decapsulation algorithm does:
    1. Parse $\mathsf{ct} = (\mathbf{c}_0, \mathbf{c}_1, \mathbf{t})$; Output $\perp$ if ct doesn't parse.
    2. Call $\mathsf{Invert}(\mathbf{R}, \mathbf{F}, [\mathbf{c}_0^t | \mathbf{c}_1^t])$ where $\mathbf{F} = [\mathbf{A} | \mathbf{A}_1 + \mathsf{FRD}(\mathbf{t})\mathbf{G}]$ to get $\mathbf{e}_0$ and $\mathbf{e}_1$.
    3. If $\|\mathbf{e}_0\| > \alpha q\sqrt{m}$ or $\|\mathbf{e}_1\| > \alpha q\sqrt{2mw} \cdot \omega(\sqrt{\log n})$, output $\perp$.
    4. If $H(\mathbf{c}_0, \mathbf{U}\mathbf{e}_1) \neq \mathbf{t}$, output $\perp$.
    5. Let $\mathbf{s}[i]$ be the i-th coordinate of $\mathbf{s}$; Set $\mathbf{k}[i] \leftarrow 0$ if $\mathbf{s}[i]$ is closer to 0 or $\mathbf{k}[i] \leftarrow 1$ if $\mathbf{s}[i]$ is closer to $q/2$.
    6. Output $\mathbf{k}$ if $\|\mathbf{s} - \mathbf{k}\| \leq \alpha q\sqrt{n}$; Otherwise output $\perp$.

The ciphertext consists of three elements, i.e., $\mathbf{c}_0 \in \mathbb{Z}_q^m$, $\mathbf{c}_1 \in \mathbb{Z}_q^w$, and $\mathbf{t} \in \{0,1\}^\lambda$.

Decapsulation Correctness. It is sufficient to show that for a correctly generated ciphertext, the algorithm $\mathsf{Invert}(\mathbf{R}, \mathbf{F}, [\mathbf{c}_0^t | \mathbf{c}_1^t])$ will output $\mathbf{s}$ with overwhelming probability. Let $\mathbf{e}^t = [\mathbf{e}_0^t | \mathbf{e}_1^t]$. By Lemma 2, we have $\|\mathbf{e}_1\| \le s\sqrt{w}$, $\|\mathbf{e}_0\| \le \alpha q \sqrt{m}$, and $\|\mathbf{R}\| \le \sqrt{m} \cdot \omega(\sqrt{\log n})$ except with negligible probability. By Lemma 4,

$$
\begin{aligned}
\left\| \mathbf{e}_1^t - \mathbf{e}_0^t \mathbf{R} \right\|_\infty &\le \left\| \mathbf{e}_1^t - \mathbf{e}_0^t \mathbf{R} \right\| \le \left\| \mathbf{e}_1^t \right\| + \left\| \mathbf{e}_0^t \mathbf{R} \right\| \\
&\le 2\alpha q \cdot O(\sqrt{w}) \cdot \omega(\sqrt{\log n}) \cdot \sqrt{3w} \\
&\le 2\alpha q \cdot O(w) \cdot \omega(\sqrt{\log n}) \\
&\le q/4
\end{aligned}
$$

holds with overwhelming probability. So $\mathsf{Invert}(\mathbf{R}, \mathbf{F}, [\mathbf{c}_0^t | \mathbf{c}_1^t])$ correctly recovers $\mathbf{e}$ and $\mathbf{s}$ with overwhelming probability. Finally, since $\bar{\mathbf{s}} \sim D_{\mathbb{Z},\alpha q}^n$, we have $\|\bar{\mathbf{s}}\|_\infty \le q/4$ (i.e., $|\bar{\mathbf{s}}[i]| < q/4$ for all i) with overwhelming probability. So, $\mathbf{k}$ can be recovered from $\mathbf{s} = \mathbf{k}\lfloor q/2 \rfloor + \bar{\mathbf{s}}$ with overwhelming probability.

4 Security Analysis

The security of our KEM scheme is based on a variant of LWE problem we call SISnLWE (normal-form LWE with a SIS hint). In this section, we first show that SISnLWE is as hard as the standard LWE problem. Then we give the security proof of the KEM scheme.

4.1 The SISnLWE Problem

Let q, n, m, $m' \ge 2$ be integers where $m = O(n \log q)$ and $m' = m + n$. Let χ be a noise distribution on $\mathbb{Z}_q$. The $\mathsf{SISnLWE}_{n,m,q,\chi}$ problem gives as challenge

$$
(\mathbf{A}, \mathbf{b}^t, \mathbf{z} = \mathbf{Z}\mathbf{e} \bmod q, \mathbf{Z})
$$

where $\mathbf{A} \leftarrow \mathbb{Z}_q^{n \times m}$, $\mathbf{b} \in \mathbb{Z}_q^m$, $\mathbf{Z} \leftarrow \mathbb{Z}_q^{n \times m}$ and $\mathbf{e} \leftarrow \chi^m$. It asks to tell if there exists a vector $\mathbf{s} \sim \chi^n$ such that $\mathbf{b}^t = \mathbf{s}^t \mathbf{A} + \mathbf{e}^t \pmod q$ or if $\mathbf{b} \in \mathbb{Z}_q^n$ is random.

Instead of reducing the problem to standard LWE problem directly, we reduce the SISnLWE problem to the equivalent "knapsack" form of LWE, defined by Micciancio and Mol [23]. The Knapsack LWE problem, $\mathsf{KLWE}_{m'-n,m',q,\chi}$, gives $(\mathbf{B}, \mathbf{c})$ where $\mathbf{B} \leftarrow \mathbb{Z}_q^{(m'-n) \times m'}$, $\mathbf{c} \in \mathbb{Z}_q^{m'-n}$ and asks to determine if $\mathbf{c} = \mathbf{B}\mathbf{x}$ $\pmod q$ for some $\mathbf{x} \leftarrow \chi^{m'}$ or if $\mathbf{c}$ is uniformly random. The hardness of the knapsack-form LWE problem is in turn implied by the hardness of the standard LWE problem. This is shown by Micciancio and Mol (Lemma 10, [23]). We also note that the knapsack-form LWE problem has been used to prove the hardness of a version of the Extended LWE problem in [4].

We first define an intermediate problem $\mathsf{SISLWE}_{n,m,q,\chi}$ (LWE with a SIS hint): Given $(\mathbf{A}, \mathbf{b}^t, \mathbf{Z}\mathbf{e}, \mathbf{Z})$ where $\mathbf{A} \in \mathbb{Z}_q^{n \times m}$, $\mathbf{b} \in \mathbb{Z}_q^m$, $\mathbf{Z} \in \mathbb{Z}_q^{n \times m}$ and $\mathbf{e} \leftarrow \chi^m$, decide if $\mathbf{b}^t = \mathbf{s}^t \mathbf{A} + \mathbf{e}^t$ for some $\mathbf{s} \leftarrow \mathbb{Z}_q^n$ or if $\mathbf{b}$ is random. Note the only difference between the $\mathsf{SISnLWE}_{n,m,q,\chi}$ problem and the $\mathsf{SISLWE}_{n,m,q,\chi}$ problem is that in the former one $\mathbf{s}$ are sampled from the noise distribution χ^n and the in the latter one $\mathbf{s} \leftarrow \mathbb{Z}_q^n$.

Lemma 5. $\text{SISLWE}_{n,q,m',\chi}$ *is no easier than* $\text{KLWE}_{m'-n,q,m',\chi}$.

Proof. We show how to turn a $\text{KLWE}_{m'-n,q,m',\chi}$ problem instance $(\mathbf{B}, \mathbf{c}) \in \mathbb{Z}_q^{(m'-n) \times m'} \times \mathbb{Z}_q^{m'-n}$ to an $\text{SISLWE}_{n,m',q,\chi}$ problem instance. Let $\mathbf{B} = \begin{bmatrix} \mathbf{H} \\ \mathbf{Z} \end{bmatrix}$ and $\mathbf{c} = \begin{bmatrix} \mathbf{h} \\ \mathbf{z} \end{bmatrix}$ where $\mathbf{H} \in \mathbb{Z}_q^{(m'-2n) \times m'}$, $\mathbf{Z} \in \mathbb{Z}_q^{n \times m'}$, $\mathbf{h} \in \mathbb{Z}_q^{m'-2n}$, and $\mathbf{z} \in \mathbb{Z}_q^n$. The transformation directly follows from the proof of Lemma 4.9, [23]. Since $\mathbf{H}$ is random, the columns of $\mathbf{H}$ generates the set $\mathbb{Z}_q^{m'-2n}$ except with all but negligible probability. Using linear algebra, we first find a matrix $\mathbf{A}' \in \mathbb{Z}_q^{n \times m'}$ such that the rows of $\mathbf{A}'$ generates the set $S = \{\mathbf{x} \in \mathbb{Z}_q^{m'} : \mathbf{Hx} = \mathbf{0} \pmod q\}$. We randomise $\mathbf{A}'$ by left-multiplying it by a unimodular matrix $\mathbf{U} \in \mathbb{Z}_q^{n \times n}$ to get $\mathbf{A} \in \mathbb{Z}_q^{n \times m'}$. We set $\mathbf{b}^t = \tilde{\mathbf{s}}^t \mathbf{A} + \mathbf{r}^t$ where $\tilde{\mathbf{s}} \leftarrow \mathbb{Z}_q^n$ and $\mathbf{r} \in \mathbb{Z}_q^{m'}$ be an arbitrary solution to $\mathbf{Hr} = \mathbf{h} \pmod q$. Finally, $(\mathbf{A}, \mathbf{b}, \mathbf{z}, \mathbf{Z})$ is returned as an $\text{SISLWE}_{n,m',q,\chi}$ challenge.

We analyse the transformation. If $\mathbf{Hx} = \mathbf{h}$ and $\mathbf{Zx} = \mathbf{z}$, we can write $\mathbf{r} = \mathbf{r}' + \mathbf{x}$ where $\mathbf{Hr}' = \mathbf{0} \pmod q$. As the row of $\mathbf{A}$ generates S, we have $\mathbf{r}' = \mathbf{A}^t \mathbf{v}$ for some $\mathbf{v} \in \mathbb{Z}_q^n$. This shows that $\mathbf{b}^t = \mathbf{s}^t \mathbf{A} + \mathbf{x}^t$ for some random $\mathbf{s}$ $(= \tilde{\mathbf{s}} + \mathbf{v})$ and therefore $(\mathbf{A}, \mathbf{b}^t, \mathbf{z} = \mathbf{Zx}, \mathbf{Z})$ is distributed as SISLWE samples. On the other hand, if $\mathbf{c}$ is random, $\mathbf{b}^t = \tilde{\mathbf{s}}^t \mathbf{A} + \mathbf{r}^t$ is uniformly random on $\mathbb{Z}_q^n$. So, in the tuple $(\mathbf{A}, \mathbf{b}^t, \mathbf{z}, \mathbf{Z})$, $\mathbf{b}$ is uniformly random and there exists an (unknown) $\mathbf{e} \sim \chi^{m'}$ such that $\mathbf{z} = \mathbf{Ze}$. $\quad\square$

Lemma 6. $\text{SISnLWE}_{n,q,m,\chi}$ *is no easier than* $\text{SISLWE}_{n,m',q,\chi}$.

Proof. We essentially apply the proof of [7], Lemma 2. Let $(\bar{\mathbf{A}}, \bar{\mathbf{b}}, \bar{\mathbf{z}}, \bar{\mathbf{Z}})$ be an instance of $\text{SISLWE}_{n,m',q,\chi}$ where $m' = n + m$. Without loss of generality, let $\bar{\mathbf{A}} = [\bar{\mathbf{A}}_1 | \bar{\mathbf{A}}_2]$, $\bar{\mathbf{b}}^t = [\bar{\mathbf{b}}_1^t | \bar{\mathbf{b}}_2^t]$ where $\bar{\mathbf{A}}_1 \in \mathbb{Z}_q^{n \times n}$ is invertible over $\mathbb{Z}_q$ (recall the random matrices $\bar{\mathbf{A}}$ and $\bar{\mathbf{Z}}$ have $m' = O(n \log q)$ columns so with overwhelming probability they have n linearly independent columns), $\bar{\mathbf{b}}_1 \in \mathbb{Z}_q^n$. We first set

$$\mathbf{A} \leftarrow -\bar{\mathbf{A}}_1^{-1} \bar{\mathbf{A}}_2 \quad \text{and} \quad \mathbf{b}^t \leftarrow \bar{\mathbf{b}}_2^t + \bar{\mathbf{b}}_1^t \mathbf{A}$$

Let $\bar{\mathbf{Z}} = [\bar{\mathbf{Z}}_1 | \bar{\mathbf{Z}}_2]$ where $\bar{\mathbf{Z}}_1 \in \mathbb{Z}_q^{n \times n}$ is invertible modulus q. We set

$$\mathbf{z} = \mathbf{S}\bar{\mathbf{z}} \quad \text{and} \quad \mathbf{Z} = \mathbf{S}\bar{\mathbf{Z}}_2$$

where $\mathbf{S} \in \mathbb{Z}_q^{n \times n}$ such that $\mathbf{S}\bar{\mathbf{Z}}_1 = \mathbf{0} \pmod q$ ($\mathbf{S}$ can be constructed by left-multiplying a random $\mathbb{Z}_q^{n \times n}$-matrix to the solution of $\mathbf{X}\bar{\mathbf{Z}}_1 = \mathbf{0} \bmod q$). Then $(\mathbf{A}, \mathbf{b}, \mathbf{z}, \mathbf{Z})$ is returned as an $\text{SISnLWE}_{n,m,q,\chi}$ problem instance. We analyse the transformation. If there exists $\mathbf{s} \leftarrow \mathbb{Z}_q^n$, $\mathbf{x} \leftarrow \chi^{m'}$ where $\mathbf{x}^t = [\mathbf{x}_1^t | \mathbf{x}_2^t]$ and $\mathbf{x}_1 \leftarrow \chi^n$ such that

$$\bar{\mathbf{b}}^t = \mathbf{s}^t [\bar{\mathbf{A}}_1 | \bar{\mathbf{A}}_2] + [\mathbf{x}_1^t | \mathbf{x}_2^t] \quad \text{and} \quad \bar{\mathbf{z}} = \bar{\mathbf{Z}}_1 \mathbf{x}_1 + \bar{\mathbf{Z}}_2 \mathbf{x}_2.$$

The transformation gives us

$$\mathbf{b}^t = \mathbf{x}_1^t \mathbf{A} + \mathbf{x}_2^t \quad \text{and} \quad \mathbf{z} = \mathbf{Zx}_2$$

where $\mathbf{Z}$ is uniformly random (because $\bar{\mathbf{Z}}$ is uniformly random). So $(\mathbf{A}, \mathbf{b}^t, \mathbf{z}, \mathbf{Z})$ has pseudorandom distribution. If $\bar{\mathbf{b}}$ and $\bar{\mathbf{z}}$ are uniformly random, then $\mathbf{b}$ and $\mathbf{z}$ are uniformly random. So $(\mathbf{A}, \mathbf{b}^t, \mathbf{z}, \mathbf{Z})$ has random distribution.   □

4.2   Security Games

In order to prove security, we proceed by games. For $i = 0, 1, 2, 3$, we denote by G_i the i-th security game and S_i the event that the adversary $\mathcal{A}$ wins the security game G_i, e.g., by outputting $\mu' = \mu$.

G_0: The first game is the real IND-CCA security game. Let $\mathbf{k}_0, \mathbf{k}_1 \leftarrow \{0,1\}^n$ and let $\mathbf{s} = \mathbf{k}_1 \cdot \lfloor q/2 \rfloor + \bar{\mathbf{s}}$. The adversary $\mathcal{A}$ gets $\mathsf{pk} = (\mathbf{A}, \mathbf{A}_1, \mathbf{U})$, the hash function H, and a challenge ciphertext $\mathsf{ct}^* = (\mathbf{c}_0^*, \mathbf{c}_1^*, \mathbf{t}^*)$, where

$$\mathbf{c}_0^* = \mathbf{s}^t \mathbf{A} + \mathbf{e}_0^t, \quad \mathbf{c}_1^* = \mathbf{s}^t (\mathbf{A}_1 + \mathsf{FRD}(\mathbf{t}^*)\mathbf{G}) + \mathbf{e}_1^t, \quad \mathbf{t}^* = H(\mathbf{c}_0^*, \mathbf{U}\mathbf{e}_1)$$

and a session key $\mathbf{k}_\mu$ where $\mu \leftarrow \{0,1\}$. The simulator $\mathcal{B}$ implements the decapsulation oracle by following the real decapsulation algorithm. $\mathcal{A}$ eventually outputs a bit μ' and it wins if $\mu' = \mu$.

G_1: Game G_1 is identical to G_0 except that the decapsulation oracle rejects any ciphertext $\mathsf{ct} = (\mathbf{c}_0, \mathbf{c}_1, \mathbf{t})$ where $\mathbf{c}_0 \neq \mathbf{c}_0^*$ but $\mathbf{t} = \mathbf{t}^*$.

G_2: Game G_2 is identical to G_1 except that the decapsulation oracle rejects any ciphertext $\mathsf{ct} = (\mathbf{c}_0, \mathbf{c}_1, \mathbf{t})$ where $\mathbf{c}_0 = \mathbf{c}_0^*$ and $\mathbf{c}_1 \neq \mathbf{c}_1^*$.

G_3: Game G_3 is identical to G_2 except that the public key and the challenge ciphertext are simulated as follows.

1. Choose a hash function $H : \{0,1\}^* \rightarrow \{0,1\}^\lambda \setminus \{0^\lambda\}$.
2. Sample $\mathbf{A} \leftarrow \mathbb{Z}_q^{n \times m}$;
3. Sample $\mathbf{Z} \leftarrow \mathbb{Z}_q^{n \times w}$, $\mathbf{R}^t \leftarrow D_{\mathbb{Z}, \omega(\sqrt{\log n})}^{w \times m}$. If $\mathbf{R}$ has rank $< w$, the simulator aborts the simulation and exits without proceeding to the next step.
4. Using linear algebra to find $(\mathbf{R}^t)^{-1} \in \mathbb{Z}^{m \times w}$ such that $\mathbf{R}^t \cdot (\mathbf{R}^t)^{-1} = \mathbf{I}_w$; Set $\mathbf{U} \leftarrow \mathbf{Z}(\mathbf{R}^t)^{-1}$.
5. Sample $\mathbf{e}_0 \leftarrow D_{\mathbb{Z}, \alpha q}^m$, $\mathbf{v} \leftarrow D_{\mathbb{Z}, \alpha q \sqrt{m} \cdot \omega(\sqrt{\log n})}^w$; Set $\mathbf{e}_1^t \leftarrow \mathbf{e}_0^t \mathbf{R} + \mathbf{v}^t$.
6. Sample the session key $\mathbf{k}_1 \leftarrow \{0,1\}^n$, $\bar{\mathbf{s}} \leftarrow D_{\mathbb{Z}, \alpha q}^n$; Set $\mathbf{s} \leftarrow \mathbf{k}_1 \cdot \lfloor q/2 \rfloor + \bar{\mathbf{s}}$.
7. Compute $\mathbf{c}_0^{*t} \leftarrow \mathbf{s}^t \mathbf{A} + \mathbf{e}_0^t$ and $\mathbf{c}_2^* \leftarrow \mathbf{Z}\mathbf{e}_0 + \mathbf{U}\mathbf{v}$ (which equals to $\mathbf{U}\mathbf{e}_1$).
8. Set $\mathbf{A}_1 \leftarrow \mathbf{A}\mathbf{R} - \mathsf{FRD}(\mathbf{t}^*)\mathbf{G}$ and $\mathbf{c}_1^{*t} \leftarrow \mathbf{c}_0^{*t} \mathbf{R} + \mathbf{v}^t$ where $\mathbf{t}^* \leftarrow H(\mathbf{c}_0^*, \mathbf{c}_2^*)$.
9. Return $\mathsf{pk} = (\mathbf{A}, \mathbf{A}_1, \mathbf{U})$, public parameter H, $\mathsf{sk} = \mathbf{R}$, and $\mathsf{ct}^* = (\mathbf{c}_0^*, \mathbf{c}_1^*, \mathbf{t}^*)$

G_4: Game G_4 is the identical to G_3 except that both session keys $\mathbf{k}_0^*$ and $\mathbf{k}_1^*$ are sampled uniformly at random and, in particular, independently of the challenge ciphertext. We note that in this game, the adversary has no advantage in winning the game.

4.3   Security Proofs

Theorem 1. *Under the assumptions that H be second-pre-image resistant, the problem $\mathsf{SIS}_{n,q,\beta}$ be hard, and the problem $\mathsf{SISnLWE}_{n,m,q,D_{\mathbb{Z}, \alpha q}}$ be hard, the KEM* *scheme presented in Sect. 3 is IND-CCA secure. In particular, we have*

$$\mathsf{Adv}_{\mathcal{A},\Pi}^{\mathsf{ind-cca}}(\lambda) \leq \mathsf{Adv}_{\mathcal{B}_1,\mathcal{H}}^{\mathsf{coll}}(\lambda) + \mathsf{Adv}_{\mathcal{B}_2}^{\mathsf{SIS}_{n,q,\beta}}(\lambda) + \mathsf{Adv}_{\mathcal{B}_3}^{\mathsf{SISnLWE}_{n,m,q,D_{\mathbb{Z},\alpha q}}}(\lambda) + \mathsf{negl}(\lambda)$$

for some algorithms $\mathcal{B}_1$ $\mathcal{B}_2$ and $\mathcal{B}_3$, and $\mathsf{negl}(\lambda)$ is negligible in λ.

Proof. We establish the theorem by showing that the neighbour games are indistinguishable (either computationally or statistically) based on our assumptions.

Lemma 7. *G_0 and G_1 are computationally indistinguishable if $H : \{0,1\} \to \{0,1\}^{\lambda} \setminus \{0^{\lambda}\}$ is second-pre-image collision resistant. In particular,*

$$|\Pr[S_0] - \Pr[S_1]| \leq \mathsf{Adv}_{\mathcal{B}_1,\mathcal{H}}^{\mathsf{coll}}(\lambda) \tag{1}$$

for some algorithm $\mathcal{B}_1$.

Proof. First of all, we have, by definition,

$$\Pr[S_0] = \Pr[\mu = \mu'] = 1/2 \cdot \mathsf{Adv}_{\mathcal{A},\Pi}^{\mathsf{ind-cca}}(\lambda) + 1/2 \tag{2}$$

Let E_1 be the event that the adversary $\mathcal{A}$ issues a valid ciphertext (i.e., which can be decrypted properly) $\mathsf{ct} = (\mathbf{c}_0, \mathbf{c}_1, \mathbf{t})$ where $\mathbf{c}_0 \neq \mathbf{c}_0^*$ but $\mathbf{t} = \mathbf{t}^*$. We note that G_0 is identical to G_1 unless E_1 happens. So by Lemma 1 we have $|\Pr[S_0] - \Pr[S_1]| \leq \Pr[E_1]$. One the other hand, it is readily seen that E_1 implies a collision of H under a given pre-image $\mathbf{c}_0^*$. Therefore, $|\Pr[S_0] - \Pr[S_1]| \leq \mathsf{Adv}_{\mathcal{B},\mathcal{H}}^{\mathsf{coll}}(\lambda)$.

Lemma 8. *G_1 and G_2 are computationally indistinguishable if $\mathsf{SIS}_{n,q,\beta}$ problem is hard. In particular, for some algorithm $\mathcal{B}_2$*

$$|\Pr[S_1] - \Pr[S_2]| \leq \mathsf{Adv}_{\mathcal{B}_2}^{\mathsf{SIS}_{n,q,\beta}}(\lambda) \tag{3}$$

where $\beta = 2s\sqrt{w}$ for $s \leq \sqrt{6w} \cdot \alpha q \cdot \omega(\sqrt{\log n})$.

Proof. Recall that in G_2, the simulator $\mathcal{B}$ runs the real $\mathsf{KeyGen}(1^{\lambda})$ to generate $\mathsf{pk} = (\mathbf{A}, \mathbf{A}_1, \mathbf{U})$ and private key $\mathbf{R}$ as well as the public hash function H. It also computes a real challenge ciphertext $\mathsf{ct}^* = (\mathbf{c}_0^*, \mathbf{c}_1^*, \mathbf{t}^*)$ where

$$\mathbf{c}_0^{*t} = \mathbf{s}_1^t \mathbf{A} + \mathbf{e}_0^t, \quad \mathbf{c}_1^{*t} = \mathbf{s}_1^t(\mathbf{A}_1 + \mathsf{FRD}(\mathbf{t}^*)\mathbf{G}) + \mathbf{e}_1^t, \quad \mathbf{t}^* = H(\mathbf{c}_0^*, \mathbf{U}\mathbf{e}_1)$$

Let E_2 be the event that the adversary issues a *valid* ciphertext (i.e., which can be decrypted properly to a valid session key) $\mathsf{ct} = (\mathbf{c}_0, \mathbf{c}_1, \mathbf{t})$ where $\mathbf{c}_0 = \mathbf{c}_0^*$ (thus $\mathbf{t} = \mathbf{t}^*$) and $\mathbf{c}_1 \neq \mathbf{c}_1^*$. Since G_1 and G_2 are identical unless E_2 happens, by Lemma 1 we have $|\Pr[S_1] - \Pr[S_2]| \leq \Pr[E_2]$.

Next we show $\Pr[E_2]$ is bounded by the probability of successfully solving the SIS problem. A SIS adversary $\mathcal{B}_2$ receives its challenge, a random matrix $\mathbf{U} \in \mathbb{Z}_q^{n \times w}$. It generates $\mathbf{A}$, $\mathbf{A}_1$, H exactly as in the algorithm KeyGen, and publishes $\mathsf{pk} = (\mathbf{A}, \mathbf{A}_1, \mathbf{U}, H)$. It is easy to see that pk has the correct distribution. $\mathcal{B}_2$ simulates the security game G_1, interrupting the simulation whenever E_2 happens and using the corresponding query to solve its SIS instance.

Assume the decapsulation query is $\mathsf{ct} = (\mathbf{c}_0^*, \mathbf{c}_1, \mathbf{t}^*)$ where $\mathbf{c}_1^t = \tilde{\mathbf{s}}^t(\mathbf{A}_1 + \mathsf{FRD}(\mathbf{t}^*)\mathbf{G}) + \tilde{\mathbf{e}}_1^t$. We must have $\mathbf{U}\tilde{\mathbf{e}} = \mathbf{U}\mathbf{e}_1$. $\mathcal{B}$ uses its trapdoor $\mathbf{R}$ to recover $\tilde{\mathbf{e}}_1$, and outputs $\mathbf{e} \leftarrow \tilde{\mathbf{e}}_1 - \mathbf{e}_1$. Now we argue that $\mathbf{e}$ is indeed a correct solution to the SIS problem instance. First, we must have $\tilde{\mathbf{e}}_1 \neq \mathbf{e}_1$ with overwhelming probability. Otherwise, since $\mathbf{c}_0 = \mathbf{c}_0^*$ and $\mathbf{t} = \mathbf{t}^*$, we have to have $\mathbf{c}_1 = \mathbf{c}_1^*$, and thus the decapsulation query is the challenge ciphertext. This shows that $\mathbf{e} \neq \mathbf{0}$. Second, since ct is a valid ciphertext, $\|\tilde{\mathbf{e}}_1\| \leq s\sqrt{w}$ by construction. To bound the norm of $\mathbf{e}$, we have

$$\|\mathbf{e}\| \leq 2s\sqrt{w} = 2\sqrt{(\|\mathbf{e}_0\|^2 + m(\alpha q)^2) \cdot \omega(\sqrt{\log n})^2} \cdot \sqrt{w}$$
$$\leq \sqrt{6w} \cdot \alpha q \cdot \omega(\sqrt{\log n})$$

as required. This shows that $\Pr[E_2] \leq \mathsf{Adv}_{\mathcal{B}_2}^{\mathsf{SIS}_{n,q,\beta}}(\lambda)$.

Lemma 9. *There exist a negligible function* $\mathsf{negl}(\lambda)$ *such that*

$$|\Pr[S_2] - \Pr[S_3]| \leq \mathsf{negl}(\lambda) \tag{4}$$

Proof. First of all, let Abort be the event that the simulation aborts due to the fact that the matrix $\mathbf{R}$'s rows (i.e. $\mathbf{R}^t$'s columns) are not all linearly independent. Recall that $m \geq 2w = 2n\log q$ which means $\mathbf{R}$ has (at least) $m = 2w$ independent samples from $D_{\mathbb{Z}^w, \omega(\sqrt{\log n})}$. As shown in [2], the matrix $\mathbf{R}$ has rank w, i.e., the event Abort happens with a negligible probability.

In the following, we show that the public key and the challenge ciphertext simulated in G_3 is indistinguishable from those output in G_2 from the adversary's view, conditioned on that Abort did not happen.

For pk in G_3, we can see that $\mathbf{A}$ and H are correctly distributed. Since $\mathbf{R}^t \leftarrow D_{\mathbb{Z},\omega(\sqrt{\log n})}^{w \times m}$ (i.e., the coordinates of $\mathbf{R}$ are independent and each of them has distribution $D_{\mathbb{Z},\omega(\sqrt{\log n})}$), by Lemma 3, $\mathbf{A}_1$ generated in G_3 (i.e., $\mathbf{A}\mathbf{R} - \mathsf{FRD}(\mathbf{t}^*)\mathbf{G}$) and G_2 (i.e., $\mathbf{A}\mathbf{R}$) are statistically close (both are statistically close to the uniform distribution over $\mathbb{Z}_q^{n \times m}$). Moreover, by the fact that $\mathbf{Z} \in \mathbb{Z}_q^{n \times m}$ is uniformly random, we have $\mathbf{U} = \mathbf{Z}(\mathbf{R}^t)^{-1}$ is also uniformly random as in G_2.

Now we look at the challenge ciphertext. First of all, $\mathbf{c}_0^t$ is correctly distributed. Second, recall $\mathbf{e}_1^t \leftarrow \mathbf{e}_0^t\mathbf{R} + \mathbf{v}^t$. By adapting Theorem 3.1 of [28] and Corollary 3.10 of [32], conditioned on $\mathbf{A}_1$ and $\mathbf{U}$, $\mathbf{e}_1$ has a distribution that is statistically close to $D_{\mathbb{Z},s}^w$, where $s^2 = (\|\mathbf{e}_0\|^2 + m(\alpha q)^2) \cdot \omega(\sqrt{\log n})^2$. So, $\mathbf{e}_1$ has the required distribution except with negligible probability. Moreover,

$$\mathbf{c}_1^{*t} = \mathbf{c}_0^{*t}\mathbf{R} + \mathbf{v}^t = (\mathbf{s}^t\mathbf{A} + \mathbf{e}_0^t)\mathbf{R} + \mathbf{v}^t$$
$$= \mathbf{s}^t(\mathbf{A}_1 + \mathsf{FRD}(\mathbf{t}^*)\mathbf{G}) + (\mathbf{e}_0^t\mathbf{R} + \mathbf{v}^t)$$
$$= \mathbf{s}^t(\mathbf{A}_1 + \mathsf{FRD}(\mathbf{t}^*)\mathbf{G}) + \mathbf{e}_1^t$$

and

$$\mathbf{t}^* = H(\mathbf{c}_0^*, \mathbf{Z}\mathbf{e}_0 + \mathbf{U}\mathbf{v}) = H(\mathbf{c}_0^*, \mathbf{U}\mathbf{R}^t\mathbf{e}_0 + \mathbf{U}\mathbf{v}) = H(\mathbf{c}_0^*, \mathbf{U}\mathbf{e}_1)$$

which shows that $\mathbf{c}_1^*$ and $\mathbf{t}^*$ are also correctly distributed.mp

Finally, notice that the simulator in G_3 cannot decapsulate any ciphertext $\mathsf{ct} = (\mathbf{c}_0, \mathbf{c}_1, \mathbf{t})$ where $\mathbf{c}_0 = \mathbf{c}_0^*$ and $\mathbf{t} = \mathbf{t}^*$. However, such a decapsulation query has already been excluded in G_2. Summing up, G_3 is distributed the same as G_2 except with negligible statistical error $\mathsf{negl}(\lambda)$. So, we have Eq. (4).

Lemma 10. G_3 and G_4 are computationally indistinguishable if $\mathsf{SISnLWE}_{n,m,q}$, $D_{\mathbb{Z},\alpha q}$ is hard. In particular,

$$|\Pr[S_3] - \Pr[S_4]| \leq \mathsf{Adv}_{\mathcal{B}_3}^{\mathsf{SISnLWE}_{n,m,q,D_{\mathbb{Z},\alpha q}}}(\lambda) \qquad (5)$$

where $\chi = D_{\mathbb{Z},\alpha q}$ for some algorithm $\mathcal{B}_3$. Moreover the adversary has no advantage in G_4, i.e.,

$$\Pr[S_4] = 1/2 \qquad (6)$$

Proof. We show a simulator that simulates $\mathcal{S}$ either G_3 or G_4 from an instance of $\mathsf{SISnLWE}_{n,m,q,D_{\mathbb{Z},\alpha q}}$ problem. $\mathcal{S}$ receives its challenge $(\mathbf{A}, \mathbf{b}^t, \mathbf{z} = \mathbf{Z}\mathbf{e}_0, \mathbf{Z})$ for some $\mathbf{e}_0 \sim \chi^m$ and needs to decide if there are vectors $\bar{\mathbf{s}} \leftarrow D_{\mathbb{Z},\alpha q}^n$ such that $\mathbf{b}^t = \bar{\mathbf{s}}^t \mathbf{A} + \mathbf{e}_0^t$. $\mathcal{S}$ does the following to prepare pk, H and ct^*.

1. Set a hash function $H : \{0,1\}^* \to \{0,1\}^\lambda \setminus \{0^\lambda\}$.
2. Set $\mathbf{A}$ from the challenge.
3. Sample $\mathbf{R}^t \leftarrow D_{\mathbb{Z},\omega(\sqrt{\log n})}^{w \times m}$. If the columns of $\mathbf{R}$ are not linearly independent, the simulator aborts the simulation and exits without going to the next step.
4. Use linear algebra to find $(\mathbf{R}^t)^{-1} \in \mathbb{Z}^{m \times w}$ such that $\mathbf{R}^t \cdot (\mathbf{R}^t)^{-1} = \mathbf{I}_w$; Set $\mathbf{U} \leftarrow \mathbf{Z}(\mathbf{R}^t)^{-1} \in \mathbb{Z}_q^{n \times w}$.
5. Sample $\mathbf{k}_0, \mathbf{k}_1 \leftarrow \{0,1\}^n$; Set $\mathbf{c}_0^{*t} \leftarrow (\mathbf{k}_1 \lfloor q/2 \rfloor)^t \mathbf{A} + \mathbf{b}^t$.
6. Sample $\mathbf{v} \leftarrow D_{\mathbb{Z},\alpha q \sqrt{m} \cdot \omega(\sqrt{\log n})}^w$; Set $\mathbf{c}_1^{*t} \leftarrow \mathbf{c}_0^{*t} \mathbf{R} + \mathbf{v}^t$.
7. Set $\mathbf{t}^* = H(\mathbf{c}_0^*, \mathbf{z} + \mathbf{U}\mathbf{v})$ and $\mathbf{A}_1 \leftarrow \mathbf{A}\mathbf{R} - \mathsf{FRD}(\mathbf{t}^*)\mathbf{G}$ where $\mathbf{z} \in \mathbb{Z}_q^n$ is from the challenge.
8. Return $\mathsf{pk} = (\mathbf{A}, \mathbf{A}_1, \mathbf{U}, H)$, $\mathsf{ct}^* = (\mathbf{c}_0^*, \mathbf{c}_1^*, \mathbf{t}^*)$, and $\mathbf{k}_\mu$ for $\mu \leftarrow \{0,1\}$
9. Keep $\mathbf{R}$ for further use (i.e., implementing the decapsulation oracle).

Firstly, we can see that both games abort with the same probability. Conditioned on that both games do not abort, it is easy to see that pk has the correct distribution. Secondly, the trapdoor $\mathbf{R}$ enables answering all kinds of decapsulation queries except the ones that have already been excluded in G_1 and G_2.

We argue that depending on the $\mathsf{SISnLWE}_{n,m,q,D_{\mathbb{Z},\alpha q}}$ challenge, the simulator $\mathcal{S}$ either simulates G_4 or G_5. In the first case where $\mathbf{b}$ and $\mathbf{z}$ from the $\mathsf{SISnLWE}_{n,m,q,D_{\mathbb{Z},\alpha q}}$ challenge is random, $\mathbf{c}_0^*$ statistically hides $\mathbf{k}_1$ meaning that the challenge session $\mathbf{k}_\mu^*$ is anyway independent from ct^*. Therefore, $\mathcal{S}$ is simulating G_4. In the other case where $\mathbf{b}^t = \bar{\mathbf{s}}^t \mathbf{A} + \mathbf{e}_0^t$, the challenge ciphertext follows the correct distribution of G_3. To see this, we have

$$\mathbf{c}_0^* = (\mathbf{k}_1 \lfloor q/2 \rfloor)^t \mathbf{A} + \mathbf{b}^t = (\mathbf{k}_1 \lfloor q/2 \rfloor + \bar{\mathbf{s}})^t \mathbf{A} + \mathbf{e}_0^t = \mathbf{s}^t \mathbf{A} + \mathbf{e}_0^t$$

and

$$\mathbf{t}^* = H(\mathbf{c}_0^*, \mathbf{z} + \mathbf{Uv}) = H(\mathbf{c}_0^*, \mathbf{Ze}_0 + \mathbf{Uv}) = H(\mathbf{c}_0^*, \mathbf{Ue}_1)$$

and

$$\begin{aligned}
\mathbf{c}_1^{*t} &= \mathbf{c}_0^{*t}\mathbf{R} + \mathbf{v}^t = (\mathbf{s}^t\mathbf{A} + \mathbf{e}_0^t)\mathbf{R} + \mathbf{v}^t \\
&= \mathbf{s}^t(\mathbf{A}_1 + \mathsf{FRD}(\mathbf{t}^*)\mathbf{G}) + (\mathbf{e}_0^t\mathbf{R} + \mathbf{v}^t) \\
&= \mathbf{s}^t(\mathbf{A}_1 + \mathsf{FRD}(\mathbf{t}^*)\mathbf{G}) + \mathbf{e}_1^t
\end{aligned}$$

This shows that $\mathcal{S}$ is simulating G_3. So we have an efficient distinguisher of G_3 and G_4 which in turn leads to an efficient algorithm that solves the problem $\mathsf{SISLWE}_{n,m,q,\chi,D_{\mathbb{Z},\alpha q}}$. Equation (5) follows.

Finally, we note that in G_4, both $\mathbf{k}_0$ and $\mathbf{k}_1$ are independent of the challenge ciphertext ct* and the adversary has no advantage in winning the security game. So, we have Eq. (6)

We conclude the proof by combing inequalities (1), (2), (3), (4), (5), and (6). □

Acknowledgements. Second author acknowledges the support of the french Programme d'Investissement d'Avenir under the national project RISQ.

References

1. Agrawal, S., Boneh, D., Boyen, X.: Efficient lattice (H)IBE in the standard model. In: Gilbert, H. (ed.) EUROCRYPT 2010. LNCS, vol. 6110, pp. 553–572. Springer, Heidelberg (2010). https://doi.org/10.1007/978-3-642-13190-5_28

2. Agrawal, S., Boneh, D., Boyen, X.: Lattice basis delegation in fixed dimension and shorter-ciphertext hierarchical IBE. In: Rabin, T. (ed.) CRYPTO 2010. LNCS, vol. 6223, pp. 98–115. Springer, Heidelberg (2010). https://doi.org/10.1007/978-3-642-14623-7_6

3. Agrawal, S., Libert, B., Stehlé, D.: Fully secure functional encryption for inner products, from standard assumptions. In: Robshaw, M., Katz, J. (eds.) CRYPTO 2016. LNCS, vol. 9816, pp. 333–362. Springer, Heidelberg (2016). https://doi.org/10.1007/978-3-662-53015-3_12

4. Alperin-Sheriff, J., Peikert, C.: Circular and KDM security for identity-based encryption. In: Fischlin, M., Buchmann, J., Manulis, M. (eds.) PKC 2012. LNCS, vol. 7293, pp. 334–352. Springer, Heidelberg (2012). https://doi.org/10.1007/978-3-642-30057-8_20

5. Alwen, J., Krenn, S., Pietrzak, K., Wichs, D.: Learning with rounding, revisited. In: Canetti, R., Garay, J.A. (eds.) CRYPTO 2013. LNCS, vol. 8042, pp. 57–74. Springer, Heidelberg (2013). https://doi.org/10.1007/978-3-642-40041-4_4

6. Apon, D., Fan, X., Liu, F.-H.: Deniable attribute based encryption for branching programs from LWE. In: Hirt, M., Smith, A. (eds.) TCC 2016. LNCS, vol. 9986, pp. 299–329. Springer, Heidelberg (2016). https://doi.org/10.1007/978-3-662-53644-5_12

7. Applebaum, B., Cash, D., Peikert, C., Sahai, A.: Fast cryptographic primitives and circular-secure encryption based on hard learning problems. In: Halevi, S. (ed.) CRYPTO 2009. LNCS, vol. 5677, pp. 595–618. Springer, Heidelberg (2009). https://doi.org/10.1007/978-3-642-03356-8_35

8. Bellare, M., Kiltz, E., Peikert, C., Waters, B.: Identity-based (lossy) trapdoor functions and applications. In: Pointcheval, D., Johansson, T. (eds.) EUROCRYPT 2012. LNCS, vol. 7237, pp. 228–245. Springer, Heidelberg (2012). https://doi.org/10.1007/978-3-642-29011-4_15

9. Boneh, D., Canetti, R., Halevi, S., Katz, J.: Chosen-ciphertext security from identity-based encryption. SIAM J. Comput. **36**(5), 1301–1328 (2006)

10. Boyen, X., Li, Q.: Direct CCA-secure KEM and deterministic PKE from plain LWE. In: Ding, J., Steinwandt, R. (eds.) PQCrypto 2019. LNCS, vol. 11505, pp. 116–130. Springer, Cham (2019). https://doi.org/10.1007/978-3-030-25510-7_7

11. Boyen, X., Mei, Q., Waters, B.: Direct chosen ciphertext security from identity-based techniques. In: Proceedings of the 12th ACM Conference on Computer and Communications Security, pp. 320–329. ACM (2005)

12. Brakerski, Z., Langlois, A., Peikert, C., Regev, O., Stehlé, D.: Classical hardness of learning with errors. In Proceedings of the Forty-fifth Annual ACM Symposium on Theory of Computing (STOC 2013), pp. 575–584, New York, NY, USA. ACM (2013)

13. Cramer, R., Shoup, V.: Design and analysis of practical public-key encryption schemes secure against adaptive chosen ciphertext attack. SIAM J. Comput. **33**(1), 167–226 (2003)

14. Dolev, D., Dwork, C., Naor, M.: Nonmalleable cryptography. SIAM Rev. **45**(4), 727–784 (2003)

15. Duong, D.H., Fukushima, K., Kiyomoto, S., Roy, P.S., Susilo, W.: A lattice-based public key encryption with equality test in standard model. In: Jang-Jaccard, J., Guo, F. (eds.) ACISP 2019. LNCS, vol. 11547, pp. 138–155. Springer, Cham (2019). https://doi.org/10.1007/978-3-030-21548-4_8

16. Fujisaki, E., Okamoto, T.: Secure integration of asymmetric and symmetric encryption schemes. J. Cryptol. **26**(1), 80–101 (2013)

17. Gay, R., Hofheinz, D., Kiltz, E., Wee, H.: Tightly CCA-secure encryption without pairings. In: Fischlin, M., Coron, J.-S. (eds.) EUROCRYPT 2016. LNCS, vol. 9665, pp. 1–27. Springer, Heidelberg (2016). https://doi.org/10.1007/978-3-662-49890-3_1

18. Gentry, C., Peikert, C., Vaikuntanathan, V.: Trapdoors for hard lattices and new cryptographic constructions. In: Proceedings of the 40th Annual ACM Symposium on Theory of Computing (STOC 2008), pp. 197–206, New York, NY, USA. ACM (2008)

19. Hofheinz, D., Kiltz, E.: Practical chosen ciphertext secure encryption from factoring. In: Joux, A. (ed.) EUROCRYPT 2009. LNCS, vol. 5479, pp. 313–332. Springer, Heidelberg (2009). https://doi.org/10.1007/978-3-642-01001-9_18

20. Lai, J., Deng, R.H., Liu, S., Kou, W.: Efficient CCA-secure PKE from identity-based techniques. In: Pieprzyk, J. (ed.) CT-RSA 2010. LNCS, vol. 5985, pp. 132–147. Springer, Heidelberg (2010). https://doi.org/10.1007/978-3-642-11925-5_10

21. Lindner, R., Peikert, C.: Better key sizes (and attacks) for LWE-based encryption. In: Kiayias, A. (ed.) CT-RSA 2011. LNCS, vol. 6558, pp. 319–339. Springer, Heidelberg (2011). https://doi.org/10.1007/978-3-642-19074-2_21

22. Daniele, M.: Duality in lattice cryptography. In: Public-Key Cryptography, Invited Talk (2010)

23. Micciancio, D., Mol, P.: Pseudorandom knapsacks and the sample complexity of LWE search-to-decision reductions. In: Rogaway, P. (ed.) CRYPTO 2011. LNCS, vol. 6841, pp. 465–484. Springer, Heidelberg (2011). https://doi.org/10.1007/978-3-642-22792-9_26

24. Micciancio, D., Peikert, C.: Trapdoors for lattices: simpler, tighter, faster, smaller. In: Pointcheval, D., Johansson, T. (eds.) EUROCRYPT 2012. LNCS, vol. 7237, pp. 700–718. Springer, Heidelberg (2012). https://doi.org/10.1007/978-3-642-29011-4_41

25. Micciancio, D., Regev, O.: Worst-case to average-case reductions based on gaussian measures. SIAM J. Comput. **37**(1), 267–302 (2007)

26. Naor, M., Yung, M.: Public-key cryptosystems provably secure against chosen ciphertext attacks. In: Proceedings of the Twenty-Second Annual ACM Symposium on Theory of Computing, pp. 427–437 (1990)

27. O'Neill, A., Peikert, C., Waters, B.: Bi-deniable public-key encryption. In: Rogaway, P. (ed.) CRYPTO 2011. LNCS, vol. 6841, pp. 525–542. Springer, Heidelberg (2011). https://doi.org/10.1007/978-3-642-22792-9_30

28. Peikert, C.: An efficient and parallel gaussian sampler for lattices. In: Rabin, T. (ed.) CRYPTO 2010. LNCS, vol. 6223, pp. 80–97. Springer, Heidelberg (2010). https://doi.org/10.1007/978-3-642-14623-7_5

29. Peikert, C., et al.: A decade of lattice cryptography. Found. Trends® Theor. Comput. Sci. **10**(4), 283–424 (2016)

30. Peikert, C., Shiehian, S.: Noninteractive zero knowledge for NP from (plain) learning with errors. In: Boldyreva, A., Micciancio, D. (eds.) CRYPTO 2019. LNCS, vol. 11692, pp. 89–114. Springer, Cham (2019). https://doi.org/10.1007/978-3-030-26948-7_4

31. Peikert, C., Vaikuntanathan, V., Waters, B.: A framework for efficient and composable oblivious transfer. In: Wagner, D. (ed.) CRYPTO 2008. LNCS, vol. 5157, pp. 554–571. Springer, Heidelberg (2008). https://doi.org/10.1007/978-3-540-85174-5_31

32. Regev, O.: On lattices, learning with errors, random linear codes, and cryptography. In: Proceedings of the Thirty-seventh Annual ACM Symposium on Theory of Computing (STOC 2005), pp. 84–93, New York, NY, USA. ACM (2005)

33. Sahai, A.: Non-malleable non-interactive zero knowledge and adaptive chosen-ciphertext security. In: 40th Annual Symposium on Foundations of Computer Science (Cat. No. 99CB37039), pp. 543–553. IEEE (1999)

34. Shoup, V.: Sequences of games: a tool for taming complexity in security proofs. Cryptology ePrint Archive, Report 2004/332 (2004). https://eprint.iacr.org/2004/332

35. Zhang, J., Yu, Y., Fan, S., Zhang, Z.: Improved lattice-based CCA2-secure PKE in the standard model. Cryptology ePrint Archive, Report 2019/149 (2019). https://eprint.iacr.org/2019/149

Double-Authentication-Preventing Signatures in the Standard Model

Dario Catalano[1], Georg Fuchsbauer[2], and Azam Soleimanian[3,4]([✉])

[1] Dipartimento di Matematica e Informatica – Universitàă di Catania,
Catania, Italy
catalano@dmi.unict.it
[2] TU Wien, Vienna, Austria
[3] Inria de Paris, Paris, France
[4] École normale supérieure, CNRS, PSL University, Paris, France
{georg.fuchsbauer,azam.soleimanian}@ens.fr

Abstract. A double-authentication preventing signature (DAPS) scheme is a digital signature scheme equipped with a self-enforcement mechanism. Messages consist of an address and a payload component, and a signer is penalized if she signs two messages with the same addresses but different payloads. The penalty is the disclosure of the signer's signing key. Most of the existing DAPS schemes are proved secure in the random oracle model (ROM), while the efficient ones in the standard model only support address spaces of polynomial size.

We present DAPS schemes that are efficient, secure in the standard model under standard assumptions and support large address spaces. Our main construction builds on vector commitments (VC) and double-trapdoor chameleon hash functions (DCH). We also provide a DAPS realization from Groth-Sahai (GS) proofs that builds on a generic construction by Derler et al., which they instantiate in the ROM. The GS-based construction, while less efficient than our main one, shows that a general yet efficient instantiation of DAPS in the standard model is possible.

An interesting feature of our main construction is that it can be easily modified to guarantee security even in the most challenging setting where no trusted setup is provided. It seems to be the first construction achieving this in the standard model.

Keywords: Double-spending · Digital signature · Cryptocurrencies · Certificate subversion

1 Introduction

Digital signatures (DS) are a cryptographic primitive that guarantees authenticity and integrity. Its security is defined via the notion of unforgeability, which protects the signer, and there is no notion of a signer behaving badly. There are however applications in which the signer should be restricted; for example,

© Springer Nature Switzerland AG 2020
C. Galdi and V. Kolesnikov (Eds.): SCN 2020, LNCS 12238, pp. 338–358, 2020.
https://doi.org/10.1007/978-3-030-57990-6_17

a certificate authority should not certify two different public keys for the same domain.

Double-authentication-prevention signatures (DAPS) are a natural extension of digital signatures that prevent malicious behavior of the signer by a self-enforcement strategy. A message for DAPS consists of two parts, called address and payload i.e., $m = (a, p)$. A signer behaves maliciously if it signs two messages with the same addresses but different payloads, that is, $m_1 = (a_1, p_1)$ and $m_2 = (a_2, p_2)$ with $a_1 = a_2$ and $p_1 \neq p_2$. Such a pair (m_1, m_2) is called *compromising* and the signer is penalized for signing a compromising pair by having its signing key revealed. We next discuss typical applications of DAPS.

Certificate Subversion. Consider a certificate authority (CA) issuing certificates to different severs. A certificate is of the form $(server.com, \mathsf{pk}_s, \sigma_s)$, where *server.com* is the domain, pk_s is the server's public key and σ_s is a signature on $(server.com, \mathsf{pk}_s)$ by the CA. Entities that trust the CA's public key can now securely communicate with *server.com* by using pk_s. Consider a national state court that has jurisdiction over the CA and compels it to issue a rogue certificate for *server.com* for a public key under the control of an intelligence agency. The latter can then impersonate *server.com* without its clients detecting the attack. Using DAPS for certification gives the CA a strong argument to deny the order, as otherwise its key is leaked. It leads to an all-or-nothing situation where if one certificate has been subverted then all have (as once the key is revealed, everything can be signed).

Cryptocurrencies and Non-equivocation Contracts. In cryptographic e-cash systems (a.k.a. "Chaumian" e-cash), double-spending is prevented by revealing the identity of the misbehaving party [9]. This works well in systems where some central authority (e.g. a bank) can take concrete actions to penalize dishonest behaviors (such as blocking their accounts). In the setting of "cryptocurrencies", disclosing the identity of users is much harder to implement because of the decentralized nature of these systems, and indeed double-spending is typically prevented by consensus. Transactions are considered effective only after a certain amount of time. This naturally prevents double-spending but induces delays to reach agreement. Using DAPS to sign transactions could provide a strong deterrent to malicious behaviors. Double-spenders would disclose their secret signing keys, which, for the case of Bitcoin, could translate to a financial loss.

Translating to the DAPS setting, the address would be the coin and the payload the receiver when spending it. This is reminiscent to accountable assertions [20] (who give a ROM instantiation). For cryptocurrencies it is natural to implement this mechanism via DAPS, as digital signatures are already needed to authenticate transactions.

Practically, one can make non-equivocation contracts (i.e. contracts that allow to penalize parties that make conflicting statements to others, by the loss of money) by combining a DAPS scheme and a deposit. To ensure that an extracted DAPS secret key is a worthy secret, it can be associated to a deposit. Each party is required to put aside a certain amount of currency in a deposit which can be securely retrieved by the owner at the end of a time-locked session if the owner has not made conflicting statements during the session. Otherwise, anyone obtaining the extracted secret key also has access to the funds.

1.1 Challenges in Constructing DAPS

We next discuss some general challenges in constructing DAPS regarding their security, efficiency and functionality. Our aim is to construct a scheme that achieves a good balance among them.

Exponentially Large Address Space. The address part of a message for DAPS typically refers to a user/coin identity. Only allowing a polynomial number of predefined identities [12,18] severely limits the possible applications, while an exponential number of addresses practically amounts to no restrictions, as one can use a collision-resistant hash function to map into the address space.

Security When no Trusted Setup is Provided. DAPS schemes should satisfy two security notions. *Unforgeability* ensures that signatures from an honest signer (who does not sign compromising message pairs) are secure against an outside attacker. *Key extractability* requires that issuing signatures on compromising message pairs leaks the signer's signing key; the notion can be defined with respect to a trusted or untrusted setup. In the latter case, each signer generates its own key pair, while assuming a trusted setup, which generates and distributes key pairs to the signers, is arguably unrealistic.

The majority of existing DAPS constructions assumes a *trusted setup* [2,12,18,19]. Those that do not, are in the random oracle model [20] or have polynomial-size signatures (w.r.t. the length of the address) [4] or only support small address spaces [12,18].

Standard Assumptions. While giving reductionist security proofs is the preferred method of gaining trust in a cryptosystem, these guarantees are only meaningful if the underlying hardness assumptions have been well-studied. Moreover, such analyses often rely on idealizations like assuming hash functions are random functions (in the ROM). Our schemes are proven secure from very well-studied assumptions (e.g. RSA, CDH) and we do not make idealizing assumptions in our proofs, i.e., they are in the standard model.

Efficient/Concrete Instantiations. Some prior DAPS schemes [11] that claim short signatures or achieve others of the above properties are black-box constructions from building blocks whose instantiation is often left open. This can be a non-trivial task and leaves the concrete efficiency of such schemes unclear.

1.2 Our Contribution

In this paper we present new DAPS constructions that address all of the above challenges. Our main contributions are as follows.

Exponentially Large Address Spaces Without Random Oracles. Most of the existing DAPS schemes supporting an exponentially large address space need to rely on the RO heuristic (e.g. [2,4,19,20]). For some of these constructions such as the one based on ID-protocols, the need for the RO assumption is a result of the transformation of an interactive protocol to an non-interactive version like Poettering's scheme [18]. In the other schemes it is due to the fact that the simulator cannot simulate the signatures in the security reduction. The RO assumption then lets the simulator program its responses without having access to the signing key [20]. We circumvent many of the difficulties arising in previous works by combining vector commitments [7] and double-trapdoor chameleon hash functions [5,6]. Our methodology follows the authentication tree approach also adopted in a previous work [20]: a signature is an authenticated path from a leaf (whose position is the address part of the message) to a given root (the public key).

In previous work, the signer either had to create the whole tree in advance (thus forcing the address space to be polynomial-size) or use the random oracle to be able to deal with exponentially large address spaces. In our construction the signer creates the tree incrementally using the equivocation properties of the chameleon hash. Moreover, we prove our schemes secure by relying on the double-trapdoor property: the simulator will be able to issue signatures by knowing *only one* of the two trapdoors. If an adversary manages to create a forgery (or if it signs a compromising pair), our reduction uses this information to extract the *other* trapdoor with non-negligible probability. We moreover use vector commitments [7] to realize a "flat" authentication tree (i.e. a tree with branching degree $q > 2$). Since both vector commitments [7] and double-trapdoor chameleon hash [5,6] (see also our DCH scheme in the full version) can be realized under standard assumptions, the security of our schemes relies on the same assumptions (w.r.t. the trusted setup for the VC scheme).

Security Without Trusted Setup. Interestingly, our construction can be easily adapted to the setting where no trusted setup is available. This comes at the cost of slightly longer signatures and is in contrast to previous proposals that all rely on trusted setup (or random oracles). The basic intuition here is that double-trapdoor chameleon hash functions can be realized in an untrusted setup (we present one in the full version), and substituting the vector commitments with a *standard* collision-resistant hash function, the construction highlighted above still works. The downside is that the produced signatures are now longer, as more values have to be stored in the authentication chain. Very informally this is because, replacing Vector Commitments with collision resistant hash functions, leads to a *binary* (rather than "flat") authentication tree.

We remark that the DCH schemes originally suggested in [5,6] implicitly assume trusted setup. Here we present a DCH scheme that *does not need* a trusted setup. While our proposed DCH scheme was informally suggested in [6] (Sect. 3.1 of the full version), here we present a concrete construction and prove its security for the general setting where no trusted setup is available.

A More General Definition. We also propose a slightly more general (with respect to previous work) definition of key-extractability that, we believe, could be useful in other contexts as well. Our definition introduces a predicate $\mathsf{Comp}_{vk}(\cdot)$ that indicates evidence that the signer misbehaved. Slightly more in detail, the predicate aims at formalizing the fact that, from a compromising pair of signed messages, it may be possible to extract some sensitive information sk' (not necessarily the full signing key sk) that is compatible with the verification key, i.e. $\mathsf{Comp}_{vk}(\mathsf{sk}') = 1$. In order for this formalization to be any useful we also require that producing an sk' such that $\mathsf{Comp}_{vk}(\mathsf{sk}') = 1$ is hard (without a compromising pair of signed messages).

A Groth-Sahai-Based Construction. As additional contribution of this paper we propose a DAPS construction from Groth Sahai proofs [14] (DAPS-GS), which builds upon a construction proposed by Derler et al. [11]. The scheme, which we will refer to as DAPS-DRS, supports an exponentially large address space and is based on NIZK proofs, which the authors instantiated in the random oracle model (ROM). We modify their construction so that the NIZK proof system can be instantiated with the Groth-Sahai proof system [14]. This system provides efficient NIZK proofs in the standard model and under standard assumptions for a restricted class of languages.

An interesting difference between our DAPS-GS scheme and DAPS-DRS is that the latter uses a *fixed-value key-binding* PRF. We assign this task to a commitment scheme and can therefore relax the requirements on the PRF to standard PRF security. The authors of DAPS-DRS instantiate their key-value binding PRF F with the block cipher *LowMC* [1]. They thus need to make the (arguably non-standard) assumption that this block cipher is a fixed-value key-binding PRF. The commonality of our DAPS schemes (DAPS-VC-DCH and DAPS-GS) is that they are both in the standard model and support large address spaces. In fact, we instantiate the generic construction of [11] by Groth-Sahai NIZK proof system (as DAPS-GS) to provide a standard-model scheme and compare it against our main, more efficient, DAPS-VC-DCH (DAPS-DCH).

As a final note, we remark that our solutions compare favorably to previous work not only in terms of security guarantees, but also in terms of efficiency. Our most efficient construction based on vector commitments also provides nice trade-offs between the size of its signatures and the size of its verification keys: verification keys grow with the branching degree q of the underlying authentication tree, while signatures grow with the depth h of the tree. A more precise comparison with previous works is given in Table 1.

1.3   Related Work

Ruffing, Kate, and Schröder [20] present a DAPS scheme based on Merkle trees and chameleon hash functions in the random oracle model. Their scheme supports an exponentially large address space by using a flat-tree construction. They associate each leaf with a unique address and some values are assigned on the

Table 1. Comparison to prior work. Here n is the bit length of the address, written as $n = h \cdot \log q$ for integers h and q; values n_0 and $q_0 = \text{poly}(n_0)$ are LWE parameters, and $\ell_\pi(n)$ denotes the proof size in the underlying NIZK system for statements of length n. Finally, $|\mathbb{G}|$ stands for the size of group elements, λ_H is the bit length of the random oracle output, and N is an RSA modulus.

Scheme	Signature size	vk size	Address space	Assumption	ROM	No trusted setup
[18]	$|\mathbb{G}|$	$O(2^n)$	poly.	DLog	yes	no
[20]	$q \cdot h \cdot |\mathbb{G}|$	$O(1)$	exp.	DLog	yes	yes
[19]	$(\lambda_H + 1) \cdot \log N$	$O(1)$	exp.	Fact	yes	no
[2]	$\log N$	$O(1)$	exp.	Fact	yes	no
[4]	$O(n_0^2 \log q_0)$	$O(n_0^4 \log^3 q_0)$	exp.	LWE/SIS	yes	yes
[12]	$\ell_\pi(n)$	$O(2^n)$	poly.	DLog	yes	yes
[16]	$\log N$ or $2 \cdot |\mathbb{G}|$	$O(1)$	exp.	Fact or CDH	yes	yes
[11]	$\ell_\pi(n)$	$O(1)$	exp.	PRF & OWF	yes	yes
DAPS-GS	$36n \cdot |\mathbb{G}|$	$O(1)$	exp.	SXDH	no	no
DAPS-VC-DCH	$3h \cdot |\mathbb{G}|$	q	exp.	CDH	no	no
DAPS-DCH	$q \cdot h \cdot |\mathbb{G}|$	$O(1)$	exp.	DLog	no	yes

fly to nodes from a leaf to the root. A signature is an authentication chain. This flat-tree construction and the idea of assigning values on the fly has also been used in other constructions [8,10].

Poettering [18] gives a DAPS scheme based on a three-move identification scheme in the ROM. The scheme only supports small address spaces, essentially because each address is associated with a verification key.

Bellare, Poettering and Stebila [2] propose a similar solution but managed to avoid the restriction to small address spaces by introducing a trapdoor-ID scheme. Their solution still relies on random oracles and requires a trusted setup.

Poettering and Stebila [19] present a DAPS based on extractable 2-to-1 trapdoor functions (2:1-TF) in the ROM. A 2:1-TF is a trapdoor one-way function for which every element of the range has precisely two preimages and holding the trapdoor allows to efficiently invert the function. Again, the scheme requires a trusted setup and the ROM.

Other schemes in the random oracle model are those of Boneh, Kim, and Nikolaenko [4] and Gao et al. [16].

Derler, Ramacher, and Slamanig [11] present a generic DAPS construction from non-interactive zero-knowledge (NIZK) proof systems that supports an exponentially large address space. They instantiate the construction in the ROM using the Fiat-Shamir transformation [13]. NIZK proofs in the *common reference string* (CRS) model rely on a trusted setup, and so does any DAPS construction based on NIZK.

2   Preliminaries

Notations. We denote the security parameter by $\kappa \in \mathbb{N}$ and $x \leftarrow X$ means that element x is chosen uniformly at random from set X. If A is a probabilistic algorithm, $y \leftarrow A(x_1, x_2, \dots)$ denotes running A on input $x_1, x_2, \dots$, and assigning its output to y. All algorithms run in probabilistic polynomial-time (p.p.t.) unless stated otherwise. We denote concatenation by $\|$ and the set $\{1, \dots, n\}$ by $[n]$. We say $f(\kappa)$ is negligible, and write $f(\kappa) = \mathrm{negl}(\kappa)$, if for every positive polynomial $p(\kappa)$ there exists $\kappa_0 \in \mathbb{N}$ such that for all $\kappa > \kappa_0$: $f(\kappa) < 1/p(\kappa)$.

2.1   Digital Signatures

A digital signature (DS) scheme is defined as follows.

Definition 1 (Digital signature scheme). *A digital signature scheme Σ consists of the* p.p.t. *algorithms* (KeyGen, Sign, Verif) *where*

- KeyGen(1^κ), *on input the security parameter κ in unary, outputs a signing key* sk *and a verification key* vk *(which implicitly defines the message space $\mathcal{M}$).*
- Sign(sk, m), *on input signing key* sk *and message $m \in \mathcal{M}$, outputs a signature σ.*
- Verif(vk, m, σ), *on input verification key* vk, *message $m \in \mathcal{M}$ and signature σ, outputs either 0 or 1.*

Correctness. Signature scheme Σ is correct if for all $\kappa \in \mathbb{N}$, for all (sk, vk) $\leftarrow$ KeyGen(1^κ), for all $m \in \mathcal{M}$, and $\sigma \leftarrow$ Sign(sk, m), we have Verif(vk, m, σ) = 1.

2.2   Double-Authentication-Preventing Signatures

Double-authentication-preventing signature (DAPS) schemes are a subclass of digital signatures where the message to be signed is split into two parts; an address and a payload,[1] i.e., in Definition 1 we have $m = (a, p) \in \mathcal{U} \times \mathcal{P}$.

Informally, compromising messages are (signed) pairs of messages with the same addresses but different payloads.

Definition 2 (Compromising pair of signatures [19]). *For a verification key* vk, *a pair (S_1, S_2) where $S_1 = (a_1, p_1; \sigma_1)$ and $S_2 = (a_2, p_2; \sigma_2)$, is compromising if*

$$\text{Verif}(\text{vk}, (a_1, p_1), \sigma_1) = 1, \quad \text{Verif}(\text{vk}, (a_2, p_2), \sigma_2) = 1, \quad a_1 = a_2 \text{ and } p_1 \neq p_2.$$

---

[1] In [19] these two parts are referred as subject and message, and in [20] as context and statement. Here we are following the terminologies from [18].

$\mathsf{KExt}^{\mathsf{Tr}}_{\mathsf{DAPS},\mathcal{A}}(\kappa)$:	$\mathsf{KExt}^{\mathsf{nTr}}_{\mathsf{DAPS},\mathcal{A}}(\kappa)$:
$(\mathsf{sk},\mathsf{vk}) \leftarrow \mathsf{KeyGen}(1^\kappa)$	$(\mathsf{vk}; S_1, S_2) \leftarrow \mathcal{A}(1^\kappa)$
$(S_1, S_2) \leftarrow \mathcal{A}(\mathsf{sk},\mathsf{vk})$	$\mathsf{sk}' \leftarrow \mathsf{Ext}(\mathsf{vk}, S_1, S_2)$
$\mathsf{sk}' \leftarrow \mathsf{Ext}(\mathsf{vk}, S_1, S_2)$	Return 1 iff
Return 1 iff	$\;-\;(S_1, S_2)$ is compromising
$\;-\;(S_1, S_2)$ is compromising	$\;-\;0 \leftarrow \mathsf{Comp}_{\mathsf{vk}}(\mathsf{sk}')$
$\;-\;0 \leftarrow \mathsf{Comp}_{\mathsf{vk}}(\mathsf{sk}')$	

Fig. 1. Game for key-extractability of DAPS.

A key property of DAPS schemes is key-extractability (KE). It requires that no malicious signer can produce a compromising pair of signatures which does not lead to the revelation of a signing key that is compatible with its verification key. To make the definition more general, we allow the adversary to succeed even when it manages to produce compromising messages that do not reveal sensitive information about the secret key (and not necessarily the whole secret key).

This is captured via the Comp predicate that, informally, outputs 1 if the input is compatible with the public verification key. The exact meaning of this "compatible" depends on the specific application, but clearly for any $(\mathsf{sk},\mathsf{vk}) \leftarrow \mathsf{KeyGen}(1^\kappa)$ it should be the case that $1 \leftarrow \mathsf{Comp}_{\mathsf{vk}}(\mathsf{sk})$. If $\mathsf{Comp}_{\mathsf{vk}}(\cdot) = 1$ is constant, we have nothing more than an ordinary signature without any prevention. The main requirement here is that producing sk' such that $\mathsf{Comp}_{\mathsf{vk}}(\mathsf{sk}') = 1$ must be hard without a compromising pair of signed messages.

Definition 3 (Key-extractability [19]). *A DAPS scheme is key-extractable if there exists a* p.p.t. *algorithm* Ext *as follows:*

– Ext(vk, S_1, S_2), *on input a verification key* vk *and a compromising pair* (S_1, S_2), *outputs a signing key* sk',

such that $\Pr[\mathsf{KExt}^{\mathsf{Tr/nTr}}_{\mathsf{DAPS},\mathcal{A}}(\kappa) = 1] = \mathsf{negl}(\kappa)$ *for all* p.p.t. *adversaries* $\mathcal{A}$, *where experiment* $\mathsf{KExt}^{\mathsf{Tr/nTr}}_{\mathsf{DAPS},\mathcal{A}}(\kappa)$ *is as described in Fig. 1.*

We say that a DAPS scheme is KE for trusted setups if this holds for experiment $\mathsf{KExt}^{\mathsf{Tr}}_{\mathsf{DAPS},\mathcal{A}}$, *and it is KE without trusted setup if it holds for* $\mathsf{KExt}^{\mathsf{nTr}}_{\mathsf{DAPS},\mathcal{A}}$.

Since DAPS schemes are a subclass of digital signatures, the standard existential unforgeability should also be satisfied for a DAPS scheme. This requires a restriction though, as the adversary could obtain the signing key if it was allowed to query compromising pairs to its signing oracle.

Definition 4 (Unforgeability of DAPS). *A DAPS scheme Σ is existentially unforgeable under adaptive chosen-message attacks (EUF-CMA) if for all* p.p.t. *adversaries* $\mathcal{A}$, *we have* $\Pr[\mathsf{Forg}^{\mathcal{A}}_{\mathsf{DAPS}}(\kappa) = 1] = \mathsf{negl}(\kappa)$, *where* $\mathsf{Forg}^{\mathcal{A}}_{\mathsf{DAPS}}(\kappa)$ *is as described in Fig. 2.*

$$
\begin{array}{|ll|}
\hline
\underline{\mathsf{Forg}^{\mathcal{A}}_{\mathsf{DAPS}}(\kappa)\colon} & \underline{\text{Oracle } \mathsf{Sign}(\mathsf{sk},(a,p))\colon} \\
(\mathsf{sk},\mathsf{vk}) \leftarrow \mathsf{KeyGen}(1^{\kappa}) & \text{If } \exists p' \neq p : (a,p') \in Q \text{ then} \\
Q \leftarrow \emptyset & \quad \text{return } \bot \\
(a^*,p^*,\sigma^*) \leftarrow \mathcal{A}^{\mathsf{Sign}(\mathsf{sk},\cdot)}(\mathsf{vk}) & \sigma \leftarrow \mathsf{Sign}(\mathsf{sk},a,p) \\
\text{Return } 1 \text{ iff:} & Q \leftarrow Q \cup \{(a,p)\} \\
\quad - \text{ } \mathsf{Verif}(\mathsf{vk},a^*,p^*,\sigma^*)=1 & \text{Return } \sigma \\
\quad - \text{ } (a^*,p^*) \notin Q & \\
\hline
\end{array}
$$

Fig. 2. Game for EUF-CMA security of DAPS

$$
\begin{array}{|l|}
\hline
\underline{\mathsf{PBind}^{\mathcal{A}}_{\mathsf{VC}}(\kappa)\colon} \\
\mathsf{pp} \leftarrow \mathsf{Setup}(1^{\kappa}) \\
(C,m,m',i,\Lambda,\Lambda') \leftarrow \mathcal{A}(\mathsf{pp}) \\
\text{Return } 1 \text{ iff } m \neq m' \text{ and } \mathsf{Verif}_{\mathsf{pp}}(C,m,i,\Lambda)=1 \\
\qquad\qquad\qquad\quad \text{and } \mathsf{Verif}_{\mathsf{pp}}(C,m',i,\Lambda')=1 \\
\hline
\end{array}
$$

Fig. 3. Game for position-binding of a VC scheme

2.3 Vector Commitments

A vector commitment (VC) is a primitive allowing to commit to an ordered sequence of q values, rather than to single messages [7]. One can later open the commitment at a specific position.

Definition 5 (Vector commitments [7]). *A VC scheme is a tuple of* p.p.t. *algorithms* $\mathsf{VC} = (\mathsf{Setup}, \mathsf{Cmt}, \mathsf{Open}, \mathsf{Verif})$ *where*

- $\mathsf{Setup}(1^{\kappa}, q)$, *on input the security parameter* κ *and the length* q *of committed vectors (with* $q = poly(k)$*), outputs public parameters* pp *(which defines the message space* $\mathcal{M}$*).*
- $\mathsf{Cmt}_{\mathsf{pp}}(m_0, \dots, m_{q-1})$, *on input a sequence of* q *messages* $m_0, \dots, m_{q-1} \in \mathcal{M}$, *outputs a commitment string* C.
- $\mathsf{Open}_{\mathsf{pp}}(m_0, \dots, m_{q-1}, m, i)$ *produces a proof* Λ_i *that* m *is the* i-*th committed message in the sequence* $m_0, \dots, m_{q-1}$.
- $\mathsf{Verif}_{\mathsf{pp}}(C, m, i, \Lambda_i)$ *outputs 1 if* Λ_i *is a valid proof that* C *commits to a sequence* $m_0, \dots, m_{q-1}$ *with* $m = m_i$, *and 0 otherwise*

Definition 6 (Correctness of VC). *A VC is correct if for all* $\kappa \in \mathbb{N}$ *and* $q = \mathrm{poly}(\kappa)$, *all* $\mathsf{pp} \leftarrow \mathsf{Setup}(1^{\kappa}, q)$ *and all vectors* $(m_0, \dots, m_{q-1}) \in \mathcal{M}^q$, *we have*

$$
\Pr\left[
\begin{array}{l}
C \leftarrow \mathsf{Cmt}_{\mathsf{pp}}(m_0, \dots, m_{q-1}) \\
\Lambda_i \leftarrow \mathsf{Open}_{\mathsf{pp}}(m_i, i)
\end{array}
: \mathsf{Verif}_{\mathsf{pp}}(C, m_i, i, \Lambda_i) = 1
\right] = 1.
$$

The security notion for a VC scheme is called *position-binding* and requires that for any p.p.t. adversary, given pp, it should be infeasible to produce a commitment C and openings to two different messages for the same position.

Definition 7 (Position binding). *A VC scheme* VC *is position-binding if for all* $i \in \{0, \ldots, q-1\}$ *and* p.p.t. *adversary* $\mathcal{A}$ *we have* $\Pr[\mathsf{PBind}^{\mathcal{A}}_{\mathsf{VC}}(\kappa) = 1] = \mathsf{negl}(\kappa)$, *where game* $\mathsf{PBind}^{\mathcal{A}}_{\mathsf{VC}}(\kappa)$ *is as defined in Fig. 3.*

Finally, a VC scheme is *concise* if the size of the commitment string C and the output of algorithm Open are both independent of q.

2.4 Double-Trapdoor Chameleon Hash Functions

A chameleon hash function is a (collision-resistant) hash function, where given a trapdoor one can find collisions efficiently. A double-trapdoor chameleon hash (DCH) function scheme has two independent such trapdoors.

$\mathsf{DTCR}^{\mathcal{A}}_{\mathsf{DCH}}(\kappa)$:

$(\mathsf{pk}, \mathsf{tk}_0, \mathsf{tk}_1) \leftarrow \mathsf{KeyGen}(1^\kappa); \ b \xleftarrow{R} \{0, 1\}$

$\mathsf{tk}' \leftarrow \mathcal{A}(\mathsf{pk}, \mathsf{tk}_b)$

Output 1 iff $\mathsf{tk}' = \mathsf{tk}_{1-b}$.

Fig. 4. Collision-resistance game for a DCH scheme

Definition 8 (DC hash function [6]). *A DCH scheme* $\mathcal{H}$ *is a tuple of* p.p.t. *algorithms* $\mathcal{H} = (\mathsf{KeyGen}, \mathsf{TrChos}, \mathsf{CHash}, \mathsf{Coll})$ *where*

- $\mathsf{KeyGen}(1^\kappa)$, *on input the security parameter* κ, *outputs a public key* pk *(which implicitly defines the message space* $\mathcal{M}$*) and private keys* tk_0 *and* tk_1.
- $\mathsf{TrChos}(1^\kappa, i)$, *on input the security parameter* κ *and a bit* i, *outputs a pair of public/private keys* $(\mathsf{pk}, \mathsf{tk}_i)$.
- $\mathsf{CHash}_{\mathsf{pk}}(m, r)$, *on input the public key* pk, *a message* $m \in \mathcal{M}$ *and one (or more) random nonce* $r \in \mathcal{R}$, *outputs a hash value.*
- $\mathsf{Coll}(\mathsf{pk}, \mathsf{tk}_i, m', m, r)$, *on input one of the two trapdoor keys* tk_i, *two messages* m, m' *and a nonce* r, *outputs a nonce* r' *such that* $\mathsf{CHash}_{\mathsf{pk}}(m, r) = \mathsf{CHash}_{\mathsf{pk}}(m', r')$.

In the definition of algorithm Coll, the pair (m, r) and (m', r') is called a collision pair where $\mathsf{CHash}_{\mathsf{pk}}(m, r) = \mathsf{CHash}_{\mathsf{pk}}(m', r')$. For a DCH scheme, the following security requirements were given [6].

Definition 9 (Security of DCH). *We require double-trapdoor chameleon hash functions to satisfy the following properties:*

Distribution of keys. *The output of* $\mathsf{TrChos}(1^\kappa, i)$ *is distributed like a public key* pk *and the* i-*th private key* tk_i *output by* $\mathsf{KeyGen}(1^\kappa)$.

Double-trapdoor collision-resistance (DTCR). *Let* $(\mathsf{pk}, \mathsf{tk}_0, \mathsf{tk}_1)$ *be output by* $\mathsf{KeyGen}(1^\kappa)$. *For all* $i = 0, 1$, *given* pk *and* tk_i *it is infeasible to find* tk_{1-i}. *Formally, for all* p.p.t. *adversary* $\mathcal{A}$, *we have* $\Pr[\mathsf{DTCR}^{\mathcal{A}}_{\mathsf{DCH}}(\kappa) = 1] = \mathsf{negl}(\kappa)$, *where game* $\mathsf{DTCR}^{\mathcal{A}}_{\mathsf{DCH}}$ *is defined in Fig. 4.*

Key-extractability (KE) *(w.r.t. predicate* $\mathsf{Comp}(\cdot)$*). There exists a* p.p.t. *algorithm* Ext *as follows:*

- $\mathsf{Ext}(\mathsf{pk}, S_1, S_2)$, *on input the public key* pk *and a collision pair* (S_1, S_2), *outputs a (single) secret key* tk',

such that $\Pr[\mathsf{KExt}^{\mathsf{Tr/nTr}}_{\mathsf{DCH}, \mathcal{A}}(\kappa) = 1] = \mathsf{negl}(\kappa)$ *for all* p.p.t. *adversaries* $\mathcal{A}$, *with game* $\mathsf{KExt}^{\mathsf{Tr/nTr}}_{\mathsf{DCH}, \mathcal{A}}(\kappa)$ *as defined in Fig. 5.*

Uniformity. *For* r *chosen uniformly at random in* $\mathcal{R}$, *all messages* m *induce the same probability distribution on* $\mathsf{CHash}_{\mathsf{pk}}(m, r)$. *This implies that* $\mathsf{CHash}_{\mathsf{pk}}(m, r)$ *for randomly chosen* r *information-theoretically hides* m. *As for standard chameleon hash functions [15] this can be relaxed to computational indistinguishability of the above distributions for any two messages.*

Distribution of collisions. *For every* m, m', *and a uniformly random* r, *the distributions of* $r' = \mathsf{Coll}(\mathsf{tk}_i, m, m', r)$ *are identical (uniform) for* $i = 0, 1$, *even when given* $\mathsf{CHash}_{\mathsf{pk}}(m, r)$, m *and* m'.

$\mathsf{KExt}^{\mathsf{Tr}}_{\mathsf{DCH}, \mathcal{A}}(\kappa)$:	$\mathsf{KExt}^{\mathsf{nTr}}_{\mathsf{DCH}, \mathcal{A}}(\kappa)$:
$(\mathsf{pk}; \mathsf{tk}_0, \mathsf{tk}_1) \leftarrow \mathsf{KeyGen}(1^{\kappa})$	$(\mathsf{pk}; S_1, S_2) \leftarrow \mathcal{A}(1^{\kappa})$
$(S_1, S_2) \leftarrow \mathcal{A}(\mathsf{pk}, \mathsf{tk}_0, \mathsf{tk}_1)$	$\mathsf{tk}' \leftarrow \mathsf{Ext}(\mathsf{pk}, S_1, S_2)$
$\mathsf{tk}' \leftarrow \mathsf{Ext}(\mathsf{pk}, S_1, S_2)$	Output 1 iff
Output 1 iff	- (S_1, S_2) is a collision pair
- (S_1, S_2) is a collision pair	- $0 \leftarrow \mathsf{Comp}_{\mathsf{pk}}(\mathsf{tk}')$
- $\mathsf{tk}' \neq \mathsf{tk}_0$ and $\mathsf{tk}' \neq \mathsf{tk}_1$.	

Fig. 5. KE game for a DCH scheme. The left game is in the trusted setup and the right game is in the untrusted setup.

Remark 1 (On defining Key Extractability). Our definitions above of Key Extractability implicitly assume that some appropriate predicate Comp is *always* associated with a DCH. This might seem surprising at first as, for DCH, Comp is formally required only for the untrusted setup setting. However, even if one only cares about the trusted setup setting, we require the underlying DCH to have an associated predicate Comp, which lets us define Key Extractability for DAPS.

We thus assume, unless otherwise stated, that every DCH has an efficiently computable predicate Comp, so that for any $\kappa \in \mathbb{N}$ and any $(\mathsf{pk}, \mathsf{tk}_0, \mathsf{tk}_1)$ output by $\mathsf{KeyGen}(1^{\kappa})$ we have $\mathsf{Comp}_{\mathsf{pk}}(\mathsf{tk}_0) = \mathsf{Comp}_{\mathsf{pk}}(\mathsf{tk}_1) = 1$ and $\mathsf{Comp}_{\mathsf{pk}}(\mathsf{tk}') = 0$ for any $\mathsf{tk}' \notin \{\mathsf{tk}_0, \mathsf{tk}_1\}$.

2.5 Non-interactive Zero-Knowledge Proofs

Let $L = \{x \mid \exists w : R(x, w) = 1\}$ be a language in NP. A non-interactive zero knowledge (NIZK) proof system for L is formally defined as follows.

Definition 10 (NIZK proof system). *A NIZK proof system* Π *for the language* L *consists of three* p.p.t. *algorithms* (Setup, Prove, Verif) *where*

- Setup(1^κ) *takes the security parameter* κ *as input and outputs a common reference string* crs.
- Prove(crs, x, w), *takes the* crs, *a statement* x *and a witness* w *as input and outputs a proof* π.
- Verif(crs, x, π) *takes the* crs, *the statement* x, *and a proof* π *as input and outputs either 0 or 1.*

For a proof system $\Pi = $ (Setup, Prove, Verif), in addition to completeness and zero-knowledge we require *simulation-sound extractability*, which is a strengthening of knowledge soundness: even after the adversary has seen simulated proofs, from any valid (fresh) proof output by the adversary, a witness can be extracted.

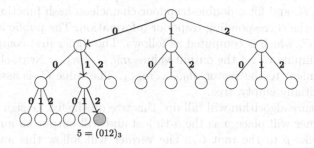

$$5 = (012)_3$$

Fig. 6. Assigning addresses to leafs.

3   A DAPS Scheme from VC and DCH (DAPS-VC-DCH)

3.1   Construction

In this section we present our DAPS scheme based on vector commitments and double-trapdoor chameleon hash function. Our scheme will make use of a "flat" q-ary tree (i.e. a tree with branching degree q) of height h, which we call the signing tree. The root of the tree will be a public value C_ϵ that will be part of the public key. Recall that in DAPS, messages are tuples of the form (a, p). The first component is interpreted as an integer in the range $\{0, \ldots, q^h - 1\}$. We can univocally associate each a to a path connecting the root with one leaf of the tree. In particular, a can be viewed as a number representing the labeling of the leaf in q-ary encoding (see the toy example in Fig. 6 for $q = 3$). In what follows, $\text{path}_{u \to w}$ denotes the ordered sequence of nodes connecting node u to node w. The root will be denoted by ϵ. Note that each node u has a unique position in the tree which we denote by pos_u; when u is the i-th node, from left-to-right, in the j-th level of the tree, we define $\text{pos}_u = j \| i$.

Overview of the Scheme. We start with an informal description of the stateful version of our scheme where the signer needs to keep track of the produced

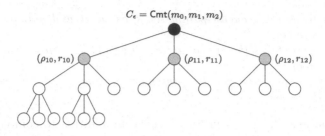

Fig. 7. Key generation: verification key.

signatures. The public key contains the public parameters for a vector commitment scheme VC and for a double-trapdoor chameleon hash function DCH. The private key is the corresponding trapdoor information. The public key also contains a value C_ϵ which is computed as follows. The signer first computes CHash on q random inputs to get the output values $m_0, \ldots, m_{q-1}$. Next, she sets C_ϵ as a VC commitment to the vector $m_0, \ldots, m_{q-1}$. The value C_ϵ is assigned to the root of an, initially empty, tree.

The signature algorithm will "fill up" this tree on the fly. To sign the message (a, p), the signer will place p as the a-th leaf and will output an authentication chain that links p to the root C_ϵ. The verifier will follow this authentication chain and if the end of the chain matches the value in the public key, accepts the signature.

We describe more in detail how the signer creates the authentication chain. Starting from the a-th leaf the signer produces the signature by augmenting the existing tree with the new authentication path. This is done using the following create-and-connect approach. First, the signer generates the possibly missing portion of the subtree containing the a-th leaf. Next, it connects this portion to the signing tree. Creating the missing portion of the tree essentially amounts to creating all the missing nodes. Specifically, and letting $a = (a_0, \ldots, a_h)$ be the q-ary encoding of a, the signer computes $m_{a_h} = \mathsf{CHash}(p_h, r)$ where $p_h = p$ (for some randomness r) and, for $i \in \{0, \ldots, q-1\} \setminus \{a_h\}$, $m_i = \mathsf{CHash}(\rho_i, r_i)$ for random ρ_i, r_i. Next the signer computes $p_{h-1} = \mathsf{Cmt}(\boldsymbol{m})$ with $\boldsymbol{m} = (m_0, \ldots, m_{q-1})$. The process is then repeated node by node moving up the path until no more nodes need to be created. This happens when the newly created p_j needs to be inserted in a position already occupied by some other value $\rho_j \neq p_j$ (i.e. for which a value $\mathsf{CHash}(\rho_j, r_j)$ was previously computed). This is when the connect phase begins. The signer uses knowledge of the trapdoor key to find a "colliding" r such that $\mathsf{CHash}(\rho_j, r_j) = \mathsf{CHash}(p_j, r)$.

In Fig. 7 we provide a pictorial representation of the key generation phase (for the toy case with branching degree 3). Black nodes indicate values that are obtained as outputs of the (vector) commitment and will not be altered any further in the future. Gray nodes indicate the frontier of the tree, i.e., nodes that are either leaves or roots of subtrees not yet explored.

Similarly, Fig. 8 pictorially describes (a toy example of) the signing procedure. To sign the message $(a = 000, p)$, one first creates the missing part of the tree, as sketched above. This also requires the signer to store all the commitments associated to each node. Once the procedure reaches a frontier node, the signer uses knowledge of the trapdoor to find a collision for CHash. In Fig. 8 this is what happens to node 1 that, once connected with the newly created subtree, becomes black. Notice that the collision finding procedure typically alters the associated randomness $\hat{r}_{10}$. This change will be done once and for all at this stage, as once the node is blackened no further modifications are allowed. To complete the procedure, the signer also produces valid openings Λ for all the commitments encountered in the path from the leaf p to the root and updates the lists of data associated to each node.

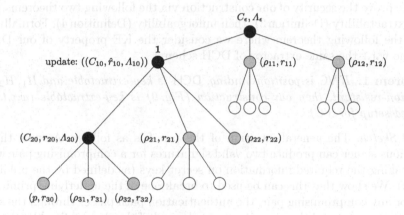

Fig. 8. Signature procedure.

Formal Description of the Scheme. We are now ready to present a formal description of our scheme. Let $VC = (VC.Setup, Cmt, Open, VC.Verif)$ be a vector commitment (VC) scheme and $DCH = (DCH.KeyGen, Trapdr, CHash, Coll)$ be a double-trapdoor chameleon hash (DCH) function with $Cmt: \mathcal{M}^q \to \mathcal{O}_{vc}$ and $CHash: (\mathcal{P}, \mathcal{R}) \to \mathcal{O}_{DCH}$. Let $H_1: \mathcal{O}_{vc} \to \mathcal{P}$ and $H_2: \mathcal{O}_{DCH} \to \mathcal{M}$ be two collision-resistant hash functions, used to map between different data types. The underlying data structure will be a tree T of branching degree q and height h. Messages are tuples of the form (a, p) with payload component $p \in \mathcal{P}$ and address $a \in \mathcal{U} := \{0, \ldots, q^h - 1\}$. We use the label ϵ for the root. Also, we say that v is a child of u in position i, when v is the i-th child of u (counting from left).

We use a pseudo-random function F to generate the random values (ρ_{ji}, r_{ji}) as $\rho_{ji} = F_k(j||i, 0)$ and $r_{ji} = F_k(j||i, 1)$, where k is part of the signing key. This makes signing deterministic (but still stateful, see below) and minimizes the information that has to be stored by the signer. Recall that $pos_u = j||i$ denotes the unique position of node u in the tree. A complete description of the scheme is given in Fig. 9 and Fig. 10

Remark 2. For DAPS schemes, signing is inherently stateful as the signer needs to remember the signed addresses in order not to sign a compromising pair. This is important for unforgeability rather than for correctness. Keeping track of the signed addresses can be efficiently done using a bloom filter [20]. In our scheme, the signer must in addition remember the payloads that it has signed in the past (but no further information, such as past signatures). This suffices to regenerate the tree during the signing of a new message.

3.2   Security Analysis

We prove the security of our construction via the following two theorems, first key-extractability (Definition 3), then unforgeability (Definition 4). Formally, we have the following theorem where we consider the KE property of our DAPS scheme w.r.t the same extractor of DCH scheme.

Theorem 1. *If* VC *is position-binding,* DCH *is key-extractable and* H_1, H_2 *are collision-resistant, then our construction (Fig. 9) is key-extractable (w.r.t. the trusted setup for* VC*).*

Proof Sketch. The general intuition of the proof is as follows. Assume that a malicious signer can produce two valid signatures for a compromising pair without leaking the required information on secret keys (as defined by the predicate Comp). We show that this can be used to break one of the underlying primitives.

For any compromising pair, the authentication path passes through the same nodes to the root and the commitment at the end of the chain is fixed by the verification key. This means the two valid signatures for a compromising pair have a "collision node" on the path, where at and above that node, the commitments of the authentication chains for these two signatures must be equal. Due to the security of hash functions H_1 and H_2 and the position-binding property of the VC scheme (which only rely on public parameters over which the signer has no control), and the fact that the two payloads are different, the signer must create a DCH collision. As this DCH collision can be obtained from the signatures, and extraction did not work, this breaks key-extractability of DCH. We make this intuition formal in the full version.

Theorem 2. *If* VC *is position-binding,* DCH *is a secure DCH scheme (Definition 9),* F *is pseudo-random, and* H_1 *and* H_2 *are collision-resistant, then our DAPS scheme is EUF-CMA secure.*

Proof Sketch. The first step in the proof is to replace all PRF outputs by uniformly random values, which is indistinguishable by pseudo-randomness. The rest of the proof crucially relies on various properties of the DCH scheme. First note that instead of using tk_0 as specified by the signing protocol, the game can choose $b \xleftarrow{R} \{0, 1\}$ and use tk_b when answering the adversary's signing queries.

KeyGen($1^\kappa, q, h,$):

- choose $k \xleftarrow{R} \mathcal{K}_F$ and hash functions H_1 and H_2
- run $\mathsf{pp}_{\mathsf{VC}} \leftarrow \mathsf{VC.Setup}(1^\kappa)$ and $(\mathsf{pk}_{\mathsf{DCH}}, \mathsf{tk}_0, \mathsf{tk}_1) \leftarrow \mathsf{DCH.KeyGen}(1^\kappa)$
- set $\rho_{1i} = F_k(1||i, 0)$ and $r_{1i} = F_k(1||i, 1)$, for $i = 0, \ldots, q-1$
- compute the DCH value $m_i = H_2(\mathsf{CHash}(\rho_{1i}, r_{1i}))$, $i = 0, \ldots, q-1$
- compute the VC value $C_\epsilon = \mathsf{Cmt}_{\mathsf{pp}_{\mathsf{VC}}}(m_0, \ldots, m_{q-1})$
- return $\mathsf{vk} = (H_1, H_2, \mathsf{pp}_{\mathsf{VC}}, \mathsf{pk}_{\mathsf{DCH}}, C_\epsilon)$ and $\mathsf{sk} = (\mathsf{tk}_0, \mathsf{tk}_1, k)$

Sign($\mathsf{vk}, \mathsf{sk}, (a, p)$):

- set $\sigma = \emptyset$
- **Frontier node.** let $u^* \in \mathsf{path}_{a \to \epsilon}$ be the frontier-node of the existing part of the tree (the first node on $\mathsf{path}_{a \to \epsilon}$ such that a DCH value was assigned)
- **Creation phase** (of the subtree rooted in u^*). for $u \in \mathsf{path}_{a \to u^*}$ (except u^*):
  1. if u is a leaf: set $r_u = F_k(\mathsf{pos}_u, 1)$, $p_u = p$, $m_u = H_2(\mathsf{CHash}(p_u, r_u))$ and $\sigma := \sigma || r_u$
     if u is not a leaf: set $C_u = \mathsf{Cmt}(m_0, \ldots, m_{q-1})$ where m_i is assigned to the ith child of u; set $p_u = H_1(C_u)$, $r_u = F_k(\mathsf{pos}_u, 1)$, $m_u = H_2(\mathsf{CHash}(p_u, r_u))$ and $\sigma = \sigma || (r_u, C_u, \Lambda_u)$ where $\Lambda_u = \mathsf{Open}(m_v, i)$ such that $v \in \mathsf{path}_{a \to \epsilon}$ is the i-th child of u
  2. for each sibling v of u, set $\rho_v = F_k(\mathsf{pos}_v, 0)$ and $r_v = F_k(\mathsf{pos}_v, 1)$, then compute $m_v = H_2(\mathsf{CHash}(\rho_v, r_v))$
- **Connection phase** (at node u^*).
  1. if u^* is a leaf: set $p_{u^*} = p$, run $\hat{r}_{u^*} \leftarrow \mathsf{Coll}(\mathsf{tk}_0, (\rho_{u^*}, r_{u^*}), p_{u^*})$ and set $\sigma || \hat{r}_{u^*}$
     if u^* is not a leaf: compute $C_{u^*} = \mathsf{Cmt}(m_0, \ldots, m_{q-1})$ and set $p_{u^*} = H_1(C_{u^*})$; run $\hat{r}_{u^*} \leftarrow \mathsf{Coll}(\mathsf{tk}_0, (\rho_{u^*}, r_{u^*}), p_{u^*})$ and set $\sigma || (\hat{r}_{u^*}, C_{u^*}, \Lambda_{u^*})$ where $\Lambda_{u^*} = \mathsf{Open}(m_v, i)$ such that $v \in \mathsf{path}_{a \to \epsilon}$ is the i-th child of u^*
  2. let w be the parent of u^*, update Λ_w as $\Lambda_w \leftarrow \mathsf{Open}(m_{u^*}, i)$ such that u^* is the i-th child of w; if $w \neq \epsilon$, set $\sigma := \sigma || \sigma_{w \to \epsilon}$ where $\sigma_{w \to \epsilon}$ is the authentication-chain from w to the root (with updated Λ_w); else, set $\sigma := \sigma || \Lambda_w$
- return σ

Verif($\mathsf{vk}, (a, p), \sigma$):

- parse vk as $(H_1, H_2, \mathsf{pp}_{\mathsf{VC}}, \mathsf{pk}_{\mathsf{DCH}}, C_\epsilon)$ and σ as $(r_h, (r_{h-1}, C_{h-1}, \Lambda_{h-1}), \ldots, (r_1, C_1, \Lambda_1), \Lambda_\epsilon)$; then consider $\mathsf{path}_{a \to \epsilon}$ identified by the representation $a = a_0, \ldots, a_h$.
- set $m_h = H_2(\mathsf{CHash}(p, r_h))$ and $m_j = H_2(\mathsf{CHash}(H_1(C_j), r_j))$ for $j = h-1, \ldots, 1$
- for $j = h-1, \ldots, 0$: check that $\mathsf{VC.Verif}(C_j, m_{j+1}, a_{j+1}, \Lambda_j) = 1$
- if all the verifications pass, return 1, otherwise return 0

Fig. 9. Our DAPS-VC-DCH scheme.

By *distribution of collisions* (Definition 9), the game is distributed as the original game (with PRF values replaced by random).

Consider a forgery $\sigma^* = (r_h^*, (r_{h-1}^*, C_{h-1}^*, \Lambda_{h-1}^*), \ldots, (r_1^*, C_1^*, \Lambda_1^*), \Lambda_\epsilon^*)$ for a message (a^*, p^*) that was not signed by the game. Let i be the signing query whose address a_i shares the longest prefix with a^* and let ℓ be the length of this prefix. Let $(r_{\ell+1}, (r_\ell, C_\ell, \Lambda_\ell), \ldots, (r_1, C_1, \Lambda_1), \Lambda_\epsilon)$ be the part of the signature resulting from this i-th signing query (note that all signatures on addresses with the same prefix end with the same elements). We consider two cases:

- $(C_\ell^*, \ldots, C_1^*) \neq (C_\ell, \ldots, C_1)$: Let j be the smallest index so that $C_j^* \neq C_j$. If $p_j^* := H_1(C_j^*) = H_1(C_j) =: p_j$ then we have found an H_1 collision

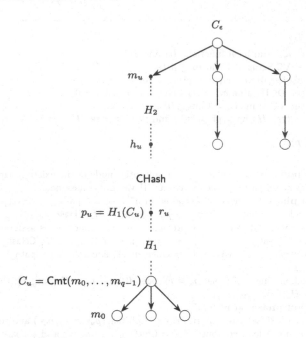

Fig. 10. Detailed figure for the construction and the security proof. Here dotted edges denote operations in a single node.

(see Fig. 10 for the required computations/operations in this node). Else if $h_j^* := \mathsf{CHash}(p_j^*, r_j^*) = \mathsf{CHash}(p_j, r_j) =: h_j$ then (since $p_j^* \neq p_j$), by key-extractability of DCH we can extract a trapdoor tk^*. Else if $m_j^* := H_2(h_j^*) = H_2(h_j) =: m_j$, then (since $h_j^* \neq h_j$) we have found an H_2 collision. Else we have $m_j^* \neq m_j$ and since $C_{j-1}^* = C_{j-1}$, this breaks position-binding of VC.

- $(C_\ell^*, \ldots, C_1^*) = (C_\ell, \ldots, C_1)$: Let $(\rho_{\ell+1}, r_{\ell+1}')$ be the values chosen for the $a_{\ell+1}^*$-th child of the node corresponding to C_ℓ when C_ℓ was first computed. Let $\rho^* := p^*$ if $\ell = h - 1$; else let $\rho* := H_1(C_{\ell+1}^*)$. If $\rho^* = \rho_{\ell+1}$ then we abort. (*)

  If $h_j^* := \mathsf{CHash}(\rho^*, r_{\ell+1}^*) = \mathsf{CHash}(\rho_{\ell+1}, r_{\ell+1}') =: h_j^*$ then (since $\rho^* \neq \rho_{\ell+1}$) by key-extractability, we extract a trapdoor tk^*. Otherwise, since $C_\ell^* = C_\ell$, but $h_j^* \neq h_j$, we either found a collision for H_2 or we broke position-binding of VC.

By *uniformity* of hashes (Definition 9) of the chameleon hash function DCH, the adversary has no information on $\rho_{\ell+1}$, so the probability of aborting in line (*) is negligible. Moreover, if we did not break CR of H_1 or H_2, or position-binding of VC or key-extractability of DCH, then we have extracted a valid trapdoor tk^*. Since the adversary obtains no information on the bit b (determining which trapdoor was used by the game), the probability that $\mathsf{tk}^* = \mathsf{tk}_{1-b}$ is $\frac{1}{2}$. The reduction can thus return tk^* and break *double-trapdoor collision-resistance* (Definition 9).

Finally, note that the restriction on the signing queries in the unforgeability game (Fig. 2) is crucial: if the adversary could obtain signatures on compromising pairs, then these would reveal tk_b. The formal proof is given in the full version.

3.3 Extension to Untrusted Setup (DAPS-DCH)

We discuss a simple modification of DAPS-VC-DCH that makes it secure when there is no trusted setup. What we mean by this is that, while we might trust standardized hash functions (such as SHA3) to be collision-resistant (CR), we might not trust a malicious signer to honestly generate its public key vk.

Under a maliciously generated key, the signer might be able to produce signatures on a compromising pair from which no secret key can be extracted, unless the DAPS scheme satisfies key extractability for untrusted setups (defined via the game on the right in Fig. 2). For this to hold for our DAPS, the underlying primitives need to be secure in untrusted setups. For DCH, a candidate satisfying this was informally discussed in [6] and is explicitly formalized in the full version of this paper. Unfortunately, for VC no instantiations without a trusted setup are known.

We therefore remove the VC scheme (and H_1) from the construction and replace it with a CR hash function $H \colon \mathcal{M}^q \to \mathcal{P}$. For each node u we include all chameleon-hash values associated with its children (except the child on the current path to the root) in the authentication chain. This modification, which we call DAPS-DCH, has q times longer signatures. Security of the scheme is immediate, since we could view H as a VC with an opening of $(m_0, \ldots, m_{q-1}, m, i)$ defined as $(m_0, \ldots, m_{i-1}, m_{i+1}, \ldots, m_{q-1})$ (Definition 5), which is position-binding by CR of H.

4   A DAPS Scheme Based on NIZK Proofs

We start with recalling the generic DAPS construction proposed by Derler et al. [11]. Their scheme, which we will refer to as DAPS-DRS, supports an exponentially large address space and is based on (simulation-sound) NIZK proofs of knowledge, which they instantiated using the Fiat-Shamir transformation [13] in the random oracle model. We will give an instantiation without random oracles and from standard assumptions by relying on the Groth-Sahai proof system [14]. This allows us to compare a standard-model version of an existing work to our DAPS-VC-DCH.

In DAPS-DRS scheme a signature contains a value $z := \gamma \cdot p + \mathsf{sk}_\Sigma$ where p is the payload of the message, sk_Σ is a signing key for a digital signature scheme Σ, and γ is derived from the address part a of the message via a pseudo-random function (PRF) F as $\gamma := F(\mathsf{sk}_{\mathsf{PRF}}, a)$. If the values z, z' for a compromising pair $(a, p), (a, p')$ have been correctly computed then they reveal $\mathsf{sk}_\Sigma = (zp' - z'p)/(p' - p)$.

To "commit" the signer to the values sk_Σ and $\mathsf{sk}_{\mathsf{PRF}}$, a one-way function is used: the public key contains $\mathsf{vk}_\Sigma := f(\mathsf{sk}_\Sigma)$ and moreover values β and

$c := F(\mathsf{sk}_{\mathsf{PRF}}, \beta)$. For (β, c) to fix $\mathsf{sk}_{\mathsf{PRF}}$, the PRF needs to assumed to be *fixed-value key-binding*, that is, it should be hard to find another key $\mathsf{sk}'_{\mathsf{PRF}}$ with $F(\mathsf{sk}_{\mathsf{PRF}}, \beta) = F(\mathsf{sk}'_{\mathsf{PRF}}, \beta)$.

A DAPS signature on a message $m = (a, p)$ under a public key $\mathsf{pk} = (\mathsf{crs}, \mathsf{vk}_\Sigma, (\beta, c))$ then consists of the value z together with a NIZK proof under crs that $(\mathsf{vk}_\Sigma, \beta, c, a, p, z)$ belongs to the following language:

$$L = \left\{ (\mathsf{vk}_\Sigma, \beta, c, a, p, z) \;\middle|\; \begin{array}{l} \exists (\mathsf{sk}_\Sigma, \mathsf{sk}_{\mathsf{PRF}}) : c = F(\mathsf{sk}_{\mathsf{PRF}}, \beta) \\ \wedge\, \mathsf{vk}_\Sigma = f(\mathsf{sk}_\Sigma) \wedge z = F(\mathsf{sk}_{\mathsf{PRF}}, a) \cdot p + \mathsf{sk}_\Sigma \end{array} \right\}.$$

We instantiate the NIZK proofs using the Groth-Sahai system over asymmetric bilinear groups. While the security of this proof system relies on a standard assumption (SXDH, that is, decisional Diffie-Hellman (DDH) holds in $\mathbb{G}_1$ and $\mathbb{G}_2$), it only supports a restricted class of languages, so the signature scheme and the PRF need to be compatible.

This is the case for the variant [3] of Waters' signature scheme [21] over asymmetric bilinear groups, which is secure under a variant of the *computational Diffie-Hellman assumption*, and the Naor-Reingold PRF [17], which is pseudorandom under DDH. Waters secret keys and Naor-Reingold PRF outputs are in $\mathbb{G}_1$.

In order to avoid additional assumptions on the PRF, we slightly modify the DAPS-DRS construction [11] (and call it DAPS-GS): to bind the signer to the value $\mathsf{sk}_{\mathsf{PRF}}$, we simply commitment to it in the public key using a commitment scheme $\mathcal{C}$. This lets us only rely on standard assumptions, while DRS had to assume that LowMC [1] is a fixed-value key-binding PRF.

In our variant DAPS-GS the language for the proof system is as follows:

$$L = \left\{ (\mathsf{vk}_\Sigma, \mathsf{pp}_\mathcal{C}, C, a, p, z) \;\middle|\; \begin{array}{l} \exists (\mathsf{sk}_\Sigma, \mathsf{sk}_{\mathsf{PRF}}) : C = \mathsf{Cmt}(\mathsf{pp}_\mathcal{C}, \mathsf{sk}_{\mathsf{PRF}}) \\ \wedge\, \mathsf{vk}_\Sigma = f(\mathsf{sk}_\Sigma) \wedge z = F(\mathsf{sk}_{\mathsf{PRF}}, a)^p \cdot \mathsf{sk}_\Sigma \end{array} \right\}$$

(recall that secret keys and PRF outputs are group elements, hence the multiplicative notation). Despite our efforts in optimizing the scheme, DAPS-GS is less efficient than our scheme DAPS-VC-DCH from Sect. 3, as shown in Table 1.

Acknowledgments. The first author is supported by the Programma ricerca di ateneo UNICT 2020-22 linea 2. The second author is supported by the Vienna Science and Technology Fund (WWTF) through project VRG18-002. The third author is supported by the European Union's Horizon 2020 Project FENTEC (Grant Agreement no. 780108).

References

1. Albrecht, M.R., Rechberger, C., Schneider, T., Tiessen, T., Zohner, M.: Ciphers for MPC and FHE. In: Oswald, E., Fischlin, M. (eds.) EUROCRYPT 2015. LNCS, vol. 9056, pp. 430–454. Springer, Heidelberg (2015). https://doi.org/10.1007/978-3-662-46800-5_17

2. Bellare, M., Poettering, B., Stebila, D.: Deterring certificate subversion: efficient double-authentication-preventing signatures. In: Fehr, S. (ed.) PKC 2017. LNCS, vol. 10175, pp. 121–151. Springer, Heidelberg (2017). https://doi.org/10.1007/978-3-662-54388-7_5

3. Blazy, O., Fuchsbauer, G., Pointcheval, D., Vergnaud, D.: Signatures on randomizable ciphertexts. In: Catalano, D., Fazio, N., Gennaro, R., Nicolosi, A. (eds.) PKC 2011. LNCS, vol. 6571, pp. 403–422. Springer, Heidelberg (2011). https://doi.org/10.1007/978-3-642-19379-8_25

4. Boneh, D., Kim, S., Nikolaenko, V.: Lattice-based DAPS and generalizations: self-enforcement in signature schemes. In: Gollmann, D., Miyaji, A., Kikuchi, H. (eds.) ACNS 2017. LNCS, vol. 10355, pp. 457–477. Springer, Cham (2017). https://doi.org/10.1007/978-3-319-61204-1_23

5. Bresson, E., Catalano, D., Gennaro, R.: Improved on-line/off-line threshold signatures. In: Okamoto, T., Wang, X. (eds.) PKC 2007. LNCS, vol. 4450, pp. 217–232. Springer, Heidelberg (2007). https://doi.org/10.1007/978-3-540-71677-8_15

6. Catalano, D., Di Raimondo, M., Fiore, D., Gennaro, R.: Off-line/on-line signatures: theoretical aspects and experimental results. In: Cramer, R. (ed.) PKC 2008. LNCS, vol. 4939, pp. 101–120. Springer, Heidelberg (2008). https://doi.org/10.1007/978-3-540-78440-1_7

7. Catalano, D., Fiore, D.: Vector commitments and their applications. In: Kurosawa, K., Hanaoka, G. (eds.) PKC 2013. LNCS, vol. 7778, pp. 55–72. Springer, Heidelberg (2013). https://doi.org/10.1007/978-3-642-36362-7_5

8. Catalano, D., Gennaro, R.: Cramer-Damgård signatures revisited: efficient flat-tree signatures based on factoring. In: Vaudenay, S. (ed.) PKC 2005. LNCS, vol. 3386, pp. 313–327. Springer, Heidelberg (2005). https://doi.org/10.1007/978-3-540-30580-4_22

9. Chaum, D., Fiat, A., Naor, M.: Untraceable electronic cash. In: Goldwasser, S. (ed.) CRYPTO 1988. LNCS, vol. 403, pp. 319–327. Springer, New York (1990). https://doi.org/10.1007/0-387-34799-2_25

10. Cramer, R., Damgård, I.: New generation of secure and practical RSA-based signatures. In: Koblitz, N. (ed.) CRYPTO 1996. LNCS, vol. 1109, pp. 173–185. Springer, Heidelberg (1996). https://doi.org/10.1007/3-540-68697-5_14

11. Derler, D., Ramacher, S., Slamanig, D.: Generic double-authentication preventing signatures and a post-quantum instantiation. In: Baek, J., Susilo, W., Kim, J. (eds.) ProvSec 2018. LNCS, vol. 11192, pp. 258–276. Springer, Cham (2018). https://doi.org/10.1007/978-3-030-01446-9_15

12. Derler, D., Ramacher, S., Slamanig, D.: Short double- and n-times-authentication-preventing signatures from ECDSA and more. In: 2018 IEEE European Symposium on Security and Privacy (EuroS&P 2018), London, United Kingdom, 24–26 April 2018, pp. 273–287 (2018)

13. Fiat, A., Shamir, A.: How to prove yourself: practical solutions to identification and signature problems. In: Odlyzko, A.M. (ed.) CRYPTO 1986. LNCS, vol. 263, pp. 186–194. Springer, Heidelberg (1987). https://doi.org/10.1007/3-540-47721-7_12

14. Groth, J., Sahai, A.: Efficient non-interactive proof systems for bilinear groups. In: Smart, N. (ed.) EUROCRYPT 2008. LNCS, vol. 4965, pp. 415–432. Springer, Heidelberg (2008). https://doi.org/10.1007/978-3-540-78967-3_24

15. Krawczyk, H., Rabin, T.: Chameleon signatures. In: NDSS 2000. The Internet Society, February 2000

16. Li, F., Gao, W., Wang, G., Chen, K., Tang, C.: Double-authentication-preventingsignatures revisited: new definition and construction from chameleon hash. Front. IT EE **20**(2), 176–186 (2019). https://doi.org/10.1631/FITEE. 1700005

17. Naor, M., Reingold, O.: Number-theoretic constructions of efficient pseudo-random functions. In: 38th FOCS, pp. 458–467. IEEE Computer Society Press, October 1997. https://doi.org/10.1109/SFCS.1997.646134

18. Poettering, B.: Shorter double-authentication preventing signatures for small address spaces. In: Joux, A., Nitaj, A., Rachidi, T. (eds.) AFRICACRYPT 2018. LNCS, vol. 10831, pp. 344–361. Springer, Cham (2018). https://doi.org/10.1007/978-3-319-89339-6_19

19. Poettering, B., Stebila, D.: Double-authentication-preventing signatures. In: Kutyłowski, M., Vaidya, J. (eds.) ESORICS 2014. LNCS, vol. 8712, pp. 436–453. Springer, Cham (2014). https://doi.org/10.1007/978-3-319-11203-9_25

20. Ruffing, T., Kate, A., Schröder, D.: Liar, liar, coins on fire! Penalizing equivocation by loss of bitcoins. In: Ray, I., Li, N., Kruegel, C. (eds.) ACM CCS 2015. pp. 219–230. ACM Press, October 2015. https://doi.org/10.1145/2810103.2813686

21. Waters, B.: Efficient identity-based encryption without random oracles. In: Cramer, R. (ed.) EUROCRYPT 2005. LNCS, vol. 3494, pp. 114–127. Springer, Heidelberg (2005). https://doi.org/10.1007/11426639_7

Efficient Signatures on Randomizable Ciphertexts

Balthazar Bauer[1,2(✉)] and Georg Fuchsbauer[3]

[1] Inria, Paris, France
[2] ENS, CNRS, PSL University, Paris, France
balthazar.bauer@ens.fr
[3] TU Wien, Vienna, Austria
georg.fuchsbauer@tuwien.ac.at

Abstract. Randomizable encryption lets anyone randomize a cipher-text so it is distributed like a fresh encryption of the same plaintext. *Signatures on randomizable ciphertexts* (SoRC), introduced by Blazy et al. (PKC'11), let one adapt a signature on a ciphertext to a randomization of the latter. Since signatures can only be adapted to ciphertexts that encrypt the same message as the signed ciphertext, signatures obliv-iously authenticate plaintexts. SoRC have been used as a building block in e-voting, blind signatures and (delegatable) anonymous credentials.

We observe that SoRC can be seen as *signatures on equivalence classes* (JoC'19), another primitive with many applications to anony-mous authentication, and that SoRC provide better anonymity guaran-tees. We first strengthen the unforgeability notion for SoRC and then give a scheme that provably achieves it in the generic group model. Signatures in our scheme consist of 4 bilinear-group elements, which is considerably more efficient than prior schemes.

1 Introduction

A standard approach for anonymous authentication is to combine signatures, which yield authentication, with zero-knowledge proofs, which allow to prove possession of a signature without revealing information about the latter and thus provide anonymity. This approach has been followed for (multi-show) anonymous credentials schemes, for which several showings of the same credential cannot be linked (in contrast to one-show credentials, e.g. [Bra00,BL13]).

The zero-knowledge proofs for these schemes are either instantiated using Σ-protocols [CL03,CL04] (and are thus interactive or in the random oracle model) or in the standard model [BCKL08] using Groth-Sahai proofs [GS08]. As this proof system only supports very specific types of statements in bilinear ("pairing-friendly") groups, signature schemes whose verification is of this type have been introduced: *structure-preserving signatures* [AFG10] sign messages from a group $\mathbb{G}$ and are verified by checking equivalences of products of pairings of group elements from the verification key, the message and the signature.

© Springer Nature Switzerland AG 2020
C. Galdi and V. Kolesnikov (Eds.): SCN 2020, LNCS 12238, pp. 359–381, 2020.
https://doi.org/10.1007/978-3-030-57990-6_18

Equivalence-Class Signatures. Hanser and Slamanig [HS14] extended this concept to *structure-preserving signatures on equivalence classes* (later improved in [FHS19]) for messages from $\mathbb{G}^2$, by adding a functionality called *signature adaptation*: given a signature on a message $\mathbf{m} \in \mathbb{G}^2$ and a scalar r, anyone can "adapt" the signature so it verifies for the message $r \cdot \mathbf{m}$. A signature thus authenticates the equivalence class of all multiples of the signed message.

Equivalence-class signatures (ECS) enable anonymous authentication that completely forgoes the layer of zero-knowledge proofs and thus yields considerable efficiency gains. Consider anonymous credentials. A credential is a signature on a message $\mathbf{m}$ (which typically contains a commitment to the user's attributes). In previous schemes, when authenticating, the user proves in zero knowledge that she knows a message $\mathbf{m}$ (and an opening of the contained commitment to the attributes she wants to show) as well as a signature on $\mathbf{m}$; several authentications with the same credential are thus unlinkable. Using ECS, this is possible *without* using any proof system [FHS19]: the user simply shows $r \cdot \mathbf{m}$ for a fresh random r together with an adapted signature. Anonymity is implied by the following property of ECS: to someone that is given $\mathbf{m}$ and a signature on $\mathbf{m}$, the pair consisting of $\mathbf{m}' := r \cdot \mathbf{m}$ for a random r and the signature adapted to $\mathbf{m}'$ is indistinguishable from a random element $\mathbf{m}''$ from $\mathbb{G}^2$ together with a *fresh* signature on $\mathbf{m}''$.

Besides the first attribute-based anonymous credential scheme whose showing efficiency is independent of the number of attributes [FHS19], ECS have been used to build very efficient blind signatures with minimal interaction between the signer and the user that asks for the signature [FHS15,FHKS16], revocable anonymous credentials [DHS15], as well as very efficient constructions [FGKO17, DS18] of both access-control encryption [DHO16] and dynamic group signatures [BSZ05].

The most efficient construction of ECS is the one from [FHS19], which was proven secure in the generic group model [Sho97]. A signature consist of 3 elements from a bilinear group, which the authors show to be optimal by relying on a result by Abe et al. [AGHO11]. Moreover, there is strong evidence that structure-preserving signatures of this size cannot be proved secure by a reduction to non-interactive assumptions [AGO11], meaning a proof in the generic group model is the best we can hope for. Less efficient constructions of EQS from standard assumptions have since then been given in the standard model by weakening the security guarantees [FG18] and in the common-reference string model [KSD19] (with signatures 6 times longer than [FHS19]).

Signatures with flexible public key [BHKS18] and *mercurials signatures* [CL19] are extensions of ECS that allow signatures to be adapted not only to multiples of the signed message, but also to multiples of the verification key. This has been used to build delegatable anonymous credentials [BCC09] in [CL19]. Delegatable credentials allow for hierarchical structures, in which users can delegate obtained credentials to users at lower levels.

Shortcomings of ECS. While schemes based on ECS offer (near-)optimal efficiency, a drawback is their weak form of anonymity. Consider a user who asks for a signature on $\mathbf{m} = (m_0 G, m_1 G)$ (where G is the generator of the group $(\mathbb{G}, +)$). If the user later sees a randomization (M_0', M_1') of this message, she can easily identify it as hers by checking whether $m_1 M_0' = m_0 M_1'$. The notion of anonymity (which is called *class-hiding* in ECS) that can be achieved for these equivalence classes is thus akin to what has been called *selfless* anonymity [CG05] in the context of group signatures: in contrast to *full* anonymity [BMW03], signatures are only anonymous to those that do not know the secret values used to construct them (the signing key for group signatures; the values m_0 and m_1 in our example above).

This weakness can have concrete repercussions on the anonymity guarantees provided by schemes built from ECS, for example delegatable credentials. In previous instantiations [BCC09, Fuc11] of the latter, the showing of a credential is anonymous to anyone, in particular to a user that has delegated said credential to the one showing it. However, in the construction from the ECS variant *mercurial signatures* [CL19], if Alice delegates a credential to Bob, she can identify Bob whenever he uses the credential to authenticate, which represents a serious infringement to Bob's privacy. In fact, anonymity towards the authority issuing (or delegating) credentials has been considered a fundamental property of anonymous credential schemes.

In [CL19], when Alice delegates a credential to Bob, she uses her secret key $(x_0, x_1) \in (\mathbb{Z}_{|\mathbb{G}|}^*)^2$ to sign Bob's pseudonym under her own pseudonym $(P_0, P_1) = (rx_0 G, rx_1 G)$ for a random r, which becomes part of Bobs credential. When Bob shows it, he randomizes Alice's pseudonym to $(P_0', P_1') := (r'P_0, r'P_1)$ for a random r', which Alice can recognize by checking whether $x_1 P_0' = x_0 P_1'$.

Signatures on Randomizable Ciphertexts. To overcome this weakness in anonymity in ECS, we use a different type of equivalence class. Consider an ElGamal [ElG85] encryption $(C_0, C_1) = (rG, M + rP)$ of a message M under an encryption key P. Such ciphertexts can be *randomized* by anyone, that is, without knowing the underlying message, a fresh encryption of the same message can be computed by choosing r' and setting $(C_0', C_1') := (C_0 + r'G, C_1 + r'P) = ((r + r')G, M + (r + r')P)$. All possible encryptions of a message form an equivalence class, which, in contrast to multiples of pairs of group elements, satisfy a "full" anonymity notion: after randomization, the resulting ciphertext looks random *even to the one that created the original ciphertext* (see Proposition 1).

If such equivalence classes yield better anonymity guarantees, the question is whether we can have adaptable signatures on them, that is, signatures on ciphertexts that can be adapted to randomizations of the signed ciphertext. It turns out that this concept exists and even predates that of ECS and is called *signatures on randomizable ciphertexts* (SoRC) [BFPV11]. Since their introduction, SoRC have been extensively used in e-voting [CCFG16, CFL19, CGG19, HPP20] and other primitives, such as blind signatures and extensions thereof [BFPV13]. Blazy et al. [BFPV11] prove their instantiation of SoRC unforgeable under standard assumptions in bilinear groups. Its biggest drawback is that it only allows for efficiently signing messages that consist of a few bits.

Our Contribution. Our aim was to construct a scheme of signatures on randomizable ciphertexts with a large message space and short signatures. But first we strengthen the notion of signature unforgeability. In SoRC, signatures are produced (and verified) on pairs of encryption keys and ciphertexts (ek, c). In the original unforgeability notion [BFPV11] the adversary is given a signature verification key and a set of encryption keys $ek_1, \ldots, ek_n$ and can then make queries (i, c) to get a signature for (ek_i, c). Its goal is to return (i^*, c^*) and a signature for (ek_{i^*}, c^*), so that c^* encrypts a message of which no encryption has been submitted to the signing oracle. Signatures thus authenticate plaintexts irrespective of the encryption key.

In more detail, once a query $(1, \mathsf{Enc}(ek_1, m))$ was made, a signature for $(ek_2, \mathsf{Enc}(ek_2, m))$ is *not* considered a forgery. In contrast, in our new definition (Definition 6), this is considered a forgery, since we view a signature as (obliviously) authenticating a message *for a particular encryption key*. That is, if from a signature on an encryption of a message for one key one can forge a signature on the same message for another key, this is considered a break of the scheme. A further difference is that, while in [BFPV11] encryption keys are generated by the challenger, we let the adversary choose (in any, possibly malicious, way) the encryption keys (in addition to the ciphertexts) on which it wishes to see a signature, as well as the key for its forgery.

We then construct a scheme which signs ElGamal ciphertexts and whose signatures consist of 4 elements of an (asymmetric) bilinear group (3 elements from $\mathbb{G}_1$ and 1 from $\mathbb{G}_2$). Our scheme (given in Fig. 3) is inspired by the original equivalence-class signature scheme [FHS19], whose equivalence classes only provide "selfless" anonymity. We show that signatures adapted to a randomization of a ciphertext are equivalently distributed to fresh signatures on the new ciphertext (Proposition 2). We then prove that our scheme satisfies our strengthened unforgeability notion in the generic group model (Theorem 1).

Comparison with Blazy et al. Apart from the stronger unforgeability notion we achieve, the main improvement of our scheme over [BFPV11] concerns its efficiency. The Blazy et al. scheme builds on (a new variant of) Waters signatures [Wat05] and Groth-Sahai proofs [GS08], which allows them to prove unforgeability from standard assumptions. However, encrypting and signing a k-bit message yields a ciphertext/signature pair consisting of $12 + 12k$ group elements of an asymmetric bilinear group. In our scheme, a message is a group element (as for ElGamal encryption), which lets us encode 128-bit messages (or messages of unbounded length by hashing into the group). A ciphertext/signature pair consists of 6 group elements. We also propose a generalization to messages of n group elements for which a ciphertext/signature pair consists of $n + 5$ group elements.

The price we pay for this length reduction by a factor of over 250 (for 128-bit messages or longer) is an unforgeability proof in the generic group model. But, as we argue next, this is to be expected. Since we sign group elements and verification consists in checking pairing-product equations, our scheme is *structure-preserving* [AFG10]. Signatures for such schemes must at least contain 3 group elements [AGHO11] and schemes with such short signatures cannot be proved from non-interactive (let alone standard) assumptions [AGO11]. Our 4-element signatures, which provide additional functionalities, and its unforgeability proof are therefore close to being optimal. We also note that a security reduction to computational hardness assumptions for schemes satisfying our unforgeability notion seems challenging, as the challenger cannot efficiently decide whether the adversary has won (in contrast to the weaker notion [BFPV11]).

2 Premilinaries

A function $\epsilon\colon \mathbb{N} \to \mathbb{R}$ is called negligible if for all $c > 0$ there is a k_0 such that $\epsilon(k) < \frac{1}{k^c}$ for all $k > k_0$. By $a \xleftarrow{\$} S$, we denote that a is picked uniformly at random from a set S. By $y \xleftarrow{\$} A(x)$ we denote running a probabilistic algorithm A on input x and assigning the output to y. We write $A(x; r)$ to make the randomness r explicit.

Bilinear Groups. We assume the existence of a probabilistic polynomial-time (p.p.t.) algorithm BGGen that takes as input an integer λ in unary and outputs a description of an (asymmetric) bilinear group $(p, \mathbb{G}, G, \hat{\mathbb{G}}, \hat{G}, \mathbb{G}_T, e)$ consisting of groups $(\mathbb{G}, +)$ and $(\hat{\mathbb{G}}, +)$, generated by G and $\hat{G}$, resp., and $(\mathbb{G}_T, \cdot)$, all of cardinality a prime number $p \in \{2^\lambda, \ldots, 2^{\lambda+1}\}$, and a bilinear map $e\colon \mathbb{G} \times \hat{\mathbb{G}} \to \mathbb{G}_T$, such that $e(G, \hat{G})$ generates $\mathbb{G}_T$, called *pairing*.

The *decisional Diffie-Hellman assumption* for BGGen states that no p.p.t. adversary $\mathcal{A}$ can distinguish a triple (dG, rG, drG) for $d, r \xleftarrow{\$} \mathbb{Z}_p$ from a random triple from $\mathbb{G}^3$ with better than negligible advantage (see also Fig. 4).

Rational Fractions. We define the *total degree* of a polynomial $P(X_1, \ldots, X_m) = \sum_{i \in \mathbb{N}^m} a_{i_1, \ldots, i_m} \prod_{j=1}^m X_j^{i_j} \in \mathbb{Z}_p[X_1, \ldots, X_m]$ as $\max_{i \in \mathbb{N}^m \,:\, a_{i_1, \ldots, i_m} \not\equiv_p 0} \{\sum_{j=1}^m i_j\}$.

In our main proof (Theorem 1), we make extensive use of multivariate rational fractions from $\mathbb{Z}_p(X_1, \ldots, X_m)$ and argue using their degrees, for which we will use the "French" Definition [AW98]: For $(P, Q) \in \mathbb{Z}_p[X_1, \ldots, X_m] \times (\mathbb{Z}_p[X_1, \ldots, X_m] \setminus \{0\})$, we define $\deg(P/Q) := \deg P - \deg Q$.

We recall some properties of this definition:

- It generalizes the one for polynomials.
- The degree does not depend on the choice of the representative.
- As for polynomials, we have $\deg(F_1 \cdot F_2) = \deg F_1 + \deg F_2$ and $\deg(F_1 + F_2) \leq \max\{\deg F_1, \deg F_2\}$.

We use subscripts for degrees in a specific indeterminate, e.g., $\deg_{x_i}$ denotes the degree in variable x_i.

3 Signatures on Randomizable Ciphertexts

We start with the definition of a *signatures on randomizable ciphertexts* scheme, which consists of a randomizable public-key encryption scheme and a signature

364   B. Bauer and G. Fuchsbauer

scheme, whose signatures are computed and verified on pairs (encryption key, ciphertext). In addition, there is an algorithm Adapt, which lets one adapt a signature on a ciphertext to any randomization of the latter.

3.1 Syntax

Definition 1. *We denote by $\mathcal{PP}$ the set of public parameters, and for $pp \in \mathcal{PP}$ we let $\mathcal{M}_{pp}$ be the set of messages, $\mathcal{DK}_{pp}$ the set of decryption keys, $\mathcal{EK}_{pp}$, the set of encryption keys, $\mathcal{C}_{pp}$ the set of ciphertexts, $\mathcal{R}_{pp}$ the set of ciphertext randomness, $\mathcal{SK}_{pp}$ the set of signature keys, $\mathcal{VK}_{pp}$ the set of verification keys and $\mathcal{S}_{pp}$ the set of signatures.*

A scheme of signatures on randomizable ciphertexts $\mathcal{SRC}$ consists of the following probabilistic algorithms, of which all except Setup *are implicitly parameterized by an element $pp \in \mathcal{PP}$.*

$$\mathsf{Setup} : \mathbb{N} \to \mathcal{PP}$$

$$\mathsf{KeyGen} : \emptyset \to \mathcal{DK}_{pp} \times \mathcal{EK}_{pp} \qquad \mathsf{SKeyGen} : \emptyset \to \mathcal{SK}_{pp} \times \mathcal{VK}_{pp}$$

$$\mathsf{Enc} : \mathcal{EK}_{pp} \times \mathcal{M}_{pp} \times \mathcal{R}_{pp} \to \mathcal{C}_{pp} \qquad \mathsf{Sign} : \mathcal{SK}_{pp} \times \mathcal{EK}_{pp} \times \mathcal{C}_{pp} \to \mathcal{S}_{pp}$$

$$\mathsf{Rndmz} : \mathcal{EK}_{pp} \times \mathcal{C}_{pp} \times \mathcal{R}_{pp} \to \mathcal{C}_{pp} \qquad \mathsf{Verify} : \mathcal{VK}_{pp} \times \mathcal{EK}_{pp} \times \mathcal{C}_{pp} \times \mathcal{S}_{pp} \to \{0,1\}$$

$$\mathsf{Dec} : \mathcal{DK}_{pp} \times \mathcal{C}_{pp} \to \mathcal{M}_{pp} \qquad \mathsf{Adapt} : \mathcal{S}_{pp} \times \mathcal{R}_{pp} \to \mathcal{S}_{pp}$$

We define the equivalence class $[c]_{ek}$ of a ciphertext c under encryption key ek as all randomizations of c, that is, $[c]_{ek} := \{c' \mid \exists\, r \in \mathcal{R}_{pp} : c' = \mathsf{Rndmz}(ek, c, r)\}$.

3.2 Correctness and Security Definitions

Correctness of SoRC requires that the encryption scheme and the signature scheme are correct.

Definition 2. *A SoRC scheme is* correct *if for all $pp \in \mathcal{PP}$, for all pairs (ek, dk) and (sk, vk) in the range of* KeyGen(pp) *and* SKeyGen(pp), *respectively, and all $m \in \mathcal{M}_{pp}$, $r \in \mathcal{R}_{pp}$ and $c \in \mathcal{C}_{pp}$:*

$$\mathsf{Dec}\big(dk, \mathsf{Enc}(ek, m, r)\big) = m \quad and \quad \Pr\left[\mathsf{Verify}\big(vk, ek, c, \mathsf{Sign}(sk, ek, c)\big) = 1\right] = 1.$$

Note that together with signature-adaptation (Definition 5 below), this implies that adapted signatures verify as well. We also require that the encryption scheme satisfies the standard security notion.

Definition 3. *Let game* **IND-CPA** *be as defined in Fig. 1. A SoRC scheme is* IND-CPA *secure if for all p.p.t. adversary $\mathcal{A}$ the following function is negligible in λ:*

$$\left| \Pr\left[\mathbf{IND\text{-}CPA}_{\mathcal{SRC}}^{\mathcal{A}}(\lambda, 1) = 1\right] - \Pr\left[\mathbf{IND\text{-}CPA}_{\mathcal{SRC}}^{\mathcal{A}}(\lambda, 0) = 1\right] \right|.$$

IND-CPA$_{SRC}^{A}(\lambda, b)$:	CL-HID$_{SRC}^{A}(\lambda, b)$:
01 $pp \xleftarrow{\$} \text{Setup}(1^{\lambda})$	01 $pp \xleftarrow{\$} \text{Setup}(\lambda)$
02 $(dk, ek) \xleftarrow{\$} \text{KeyGen}(pp)$	02 $(dk, ek) \xleftarrow{\$} \text{KeyGen}(pp)$
03 $(m_0, m_1, st) \xleftarrow{\$} A(ek)$	03 $(c, st) \xleftarrow{\$} A(ek)$
04 $r \xleftarrow{\$} \mathcal{R}_{pp}$	04 $c_0 \xleftarrow{\$} \mathcal{C}_{pp}$
05 $c := \text{Enc}(ek, m_b, r)$	05 $r \xleftarrow{\$} \mathcal{R}_{pp}$; $c_1 := \text{Rndmz}(ek, c, r)$
06 $b' \xleftarrow{\$} A(st, c)$	06 $b' \xleftarrow{\$} A(st, c_b)$
07 Return b'	07 Return b'

Fig. 1. Games for ciphertext-indistinguishability and class-hiding

Class-hiding is a property of equivalence-class signatures that states that given a representative of an equivalence class, then a random member of that class is indistinguishable from a random element of the whole space. We give a stronger definition, which we call *fully class-hiding* (analogously to full anonymity). Whereas in the original notion [FHS19, Def. 18], the representative is uniformly picked by the experiment, in our notion it is chosen by the adversary.

Definition 4. *Let game* **CL-HID** *be as defined in Fig. 1. A SoRC scheme is fully class-hiding if for all p.p.t. adversary A, the following function is negligible in λ:*

$$\left| \Pr\left[\text{CL-HID}_{SRC}^{A}(\lambda, 1) = 1\right] - \Pr\left[\text{CL-HID}_{SRC}^{A}(\lambda, 0) = 1\right] \right| .$$

Signature-adaptation requires that signatures that have been adapted to a randomization of the signed ciphertext are distributed like fresh signatures on the randomized ciphertext. A strengthening is the following variant, which also holds for maliciously generated verification keys [FHS19, Def. 20].

Definition 5. *A SoRC scheme is* signature-adaptable (under malicious keys) *if for all $pp \in \mathcal{PP}$, all $(vk, ek, c, sig) \in \mathcal{VK}_{pp} \times \mathcal{EK}_{pp} \times \mathcal{C}_{pp} \times \mathcal{S}_{pp}$ that satisfy* $\text{Verify}(vk, ek, c, sig) = 1$ *and all $r \in \mathcal{R}_{pp}$, the output of $\text{Adapt}(sig, r)$ is uniformly distributed over the set*

$$\{ sig' \in \mathcal{S}_{pp} \mid \text{Verify}(vk, ek, \text{Rndmz}(ek, c, r), sig') = 1 \} .$$

Note that if Sign outputs a uniform element in the set of valid signatures (which is the case in the ECS scheme from [FHS19] and our scheme) then Definition 5 implies that for all honestly generated (sk, vk) and all ek, c and r the outputs of the following two procedures are distributed equivalently:

$$\text{Adapt}(\text{Sign}(sk, ek, c), r') \quad \text{and} \quad \text{Sign}(sk, ek, \text{Rndmz}(ek, c, r')) .$$

Together, full class-hiding and signature-adaptability under malicious keys imply that for an adversary that creates a signature verification key as well as a ciphertext and a signature on it, a randomization of this ciphertext together with

---

$\mathbf{EUF}^{\mathcal{A}}_{\mathcal{SRC}}(\lambda):$

01 $Q := \emptyset$; $pp \xleftarrow{\$} \mathsf{Setup}(1^\lambda)$

02 $(sk, vk) \xleftarrow{\$} \mathsf{SKeyGen}(pp)$

03 $((ek^*, c^*), sig^*) \xleftarrow{\$} \mathcal{A}^{\mathsf{Sign}(sk, \cdot, \cdot)}_2(vk)$

04 Return $\big(\mathsf{Verify}(vk, ek^*, c^*, sig^*) = 1 \wedge (ek^*, c^*) \notin Q\big)$

$\mathsf{Sign}(sk, ek, c)$

01 $Q := Q \cup \{ek\} \times [c]_{ek}$

02 Return $\mathsf{Sign}(sk, ek, c)$

Fig. 2. Unforgeability game

an adapted signature looks like a random ciphertext with a fresh signature on it. (In contrast, for equivalence-class signatures, this was only true if the signed message was not chosen by the adversary [FHS19].)

Unforgeability. Finally, we present our strengthened notion of unforgeability, which is defined w.r.t. keys and equivalence classes. That is, after the adversary queries a signature for (ek, c), all tuples (ek, c') with $c' \in [c]_{ek}$ (that is, c' encrypts the same message as c under ek) are added to a set Q of signed objects. The adversary's goal is to produce a signature on a pair (ek^*, c^*) that is not contained in Q. (In the original definition [BFPV11], Q would contain the equivalence classes of c under *all* encryption keys, i.e., all encryptions of the plaintext of c under all keys.)

Definition 6. *Let* **EUF** *be the game defined in Fig. 2. A SoRC scheme is unforgeable is for all p.p.t. adversary $\mathcal{A}$ the following function is negligible in λ:*

$$\Pr\left[\mathbf{EUF}^{\mathcal{A}}_{\mathcal{SRC}}(\lambda) = 1\right].$$

4 Instantiation

Our instantiation of SoRC is given in Fig. 3. Its signatures sign ElGamal ciphertexts (C_0, C_1), and the signature elements $(Z, S, \hat{S})$ constitute a structure-preserving signature on (C_0, C_1) similar to the optimal scheme from [AGHO11]. (And removing G from the definition of Z would yield the equivalence-class scheme from [FHS19]: note that, without G, multiplying Z by r yields a signature on the message $r \cdot (C_0, C_1)$.) The new element T in our scheme allows for adaptation of signatures to randomizations of the signed ciphertext. Randomization implicitly defines the following equivalence classes: for $P \in \mathcal{EK}_{pp}$ and $(C_0, C_1), (C'_0, C'_1) \in \mathcal{C}_{pp}$:

$$(C'_0, C'_1) \in \big[(C_0, C_1)\big]_P \iff \exists r \in \mathbb{Z}_p : (C'_0, C'_1) = (C_0 + rG, C_1 + rP).$$

5 Security of Our Scheme

Correctness of our scheme follows by inspection. Moreover, ElGamal encryption [ElG85] satisfies IND-CPA if the decisional Diffie-Hellman (DDH) assumption holds for BGGen.

Setup(1^λ): Return $pp = (p, \mathbb{G}, G, \hat{\mathbb{G}}, \hat{G}, \mathbb{G}_T, e) \xleftarrow{\$} \mathsf{BGGen}(1^\lambda)$, which define
$\quad \mathcal{M}_{pp} := \mathbb{G}$, $\mathcal{C}_{pp} := \mathbb{G}^2$, $\mathcal{R}_{pp} := \mathbb{Z}_p$, $\mathcal{SK}_{pp} := (\mathbb{Z}_p^*)^2$, $\mathcal{VK}_{pp} := (\hat{\mathbb{G}}^*)^2$,
$\quad \mathcal{EK}_{pp} := \mathbb{G}^*$, $\mathcal{DK}_{pp} := \mathbb{Z}_p^*$ and $\mathcal{S}_{pp} := \mathbb{G} \times \mathbb{G}^* \times \hat{\mathbb{G}}^* \times \mathbb{G}$.

KeyGen(pp): Parse pp as $(p, \mathbb{G}, G, \hat{\mathbb{G}}, \hat{G}, \mathbb{G}_T, e)$
$\qquad dk := d \xleftarrow{\$} \mathbb{Z}_p^*$; $ek = P = dG$; return (dk, ek)

Enc(P, M, r): Return $(rG, M + rP)$

Dec($d, (C_0, C_1)$): Return $M := C_1 - dC_0$

Rndmz($P, (C_0, C_1), r'$): Return $(C_0 + r'G, C_1 + r'P)$

SKeyGen(pp): Parse pp as $(p, \mathbb{G}, G, \hat{\mathbb{G}}, \hat{G}, \mathbb{G}_T, e)$
$\qquad sk := (x_0, x_1) \xleftarrow{\$} (\mathbb{Z}_p^*)^2$; $vk := (\hat{X}_0 = x_0\hat{G}, \hat{X}_1 = x_1\hat{G})$; return (sk, vk)

Sign($(x_0, x_1), P, (C_0, C_1)$): $s \xleftarrow{\$} \mathbb{Z}_p^*$; return $(Z, S, \hat{S}, T)$ with

$$Z := \frac{1}{s}\big(G + x_0C_0 + x_1C_1\big) \qquad S := sG \qquad \hat{S} := s\hat{G} \qquad T := \frac{1}{s}\big(x_0G + x_1P\big)$$

Adapt($(Z, S, \hat{S}, T), r'$): $s' \xleftarrow{\$} \mathbb{Z}_p^*$; return $(Z', S', \hat{S}', T')$ with

$$Z' := \frac{1}{s'}\big(Z + r'T\big) \qquad\qquad S' := s'S \qquad \hat{S}' := s'\hat{S} \qquad T' := \frac{1}{s'}T$$

Verify($(\hat{X}_0, \hat{X}_1), P, (C_0, C_1), (Z, S, \hat{S}, T)$): Return 0 if $P = 0$ or $S = 0$. Return 1 if the following equations hold and 0 otherwise:

$$e(Z, \hat{S}) = e(G, \hat{G})e(C_0, \hat{X}_0)e(C_1, \hat{X}_1) \qquad e(G, \hat{S}) = e(S, \hat{G})$$
$$e(T, \hat{S}) = e(G, \hat{X}_0)e(P, \hat{X}_1)$$

Fig. 3. Our instantiation $\mathcal{SRC}$ of SoRC

Proposition 1. *If DDH holds for BGGen then the scheme in Fig. 3 is fully class-hiding (Definition 4).*

Proof. We first recall the game **DDH**, which formalizes the DDH assumption in Fig. 4 (left). Next, we instantiate **CL-HID** with our scheme from Fig. 3 and rewrite it in Fig. 4 (right). In particular, instead of choosing $c_0 \xleftarrow{\$} \mathbb{G}^2$, we compute it as $c + c_0'$ for a uniform $c_0' \xleftarrow{\$} \mathbb{G}^2$.

Let $\mathcal{A}$ be an adversary against $\mathbf{CL - HID}$. We define an adversary $\mathcal{B}$ against **DDH**, which upon receiving a challenge (P, R, S), sends P to $\mathcal{A}$ to get c and then sends $c + (R, S)$ to $\mathcal{A}$. Finally, $\mathcal{B}$ returns $\mathcal{A}$'s output b'.

Since for all λ and b we have that $\mathbf{DDH}^{\mathcal{B}^\mathcal{A}}_{\mathcal{SRC}}(\lambda, b)$ and $\mathbf{CL\text{-}HID}^{\mathcal{A}}_{\mathcal{SRC}}(\lambda, b)$ follow the same distribution, $\mathcal{B}$'s advantage in breaking DDH is the same as $\mathcal{A}$'s advantage in breaking full class-hiding.

Proposition 2. *The SoRC scheme in Fig. 3 is signature-adaptable under malicious keys (Definition 5).*

Proof. Let $pp = (p, \mathbb{G}, G, \hat{\mathbb{G}}, \hat{G}, \mathbb{G}_T, e) \in \mathcal{PP}$, let $vk = (x_0\hat{G}, x_1\hat{G})$, $ek = dG$, $C_0 = c_0G$, $C_1 = c_1G$ and $sig = (Z = zG, S = sG, \hat{S} = \hat{s}\hat{G}, T = tG)$ be such that

$\mathbf{DDH}^{\mathcal{B}}_{\mathsf{BGGen}}(\lambda, b):$	$\mathbf{CL\text{-}HID}^{\mathcal{A}}_{\mathcal{SRC}}(\lambda, b):$
01 $(p, \mathbb{G}, G, \hat{\mathbb{G}}, \hat{G}, \mathbb{G}_T, e) \xleftarrow{\$} \mathsf{BGGen}(\lambda)$	01 $pp \xleftarrow{\$} \mathsf{Setup}(\lambda)$
02 $P \xleftarrow{\$} \mathbb{G}$	02 $(d, P) \xleftarrow{\$} \mathsf{KeyGen}(pp)$
03 $r \xleftarrow{\$} \mathbb{Z}_p$	03 $(c, st) \xleftarrow{\$} \mathcal{A}(P)$
04 $S_1 := rP$	04 $c'_0 \xleftarrow{\$} \mathbb{G} \times \mathbb{G}$
05 $S_0 \xleftarrow{\$} \mathbb{G}$	05 $r \xleftarrow{\$} \mathcal{R}_{pp}$; $c'_1 := (rG, rP)$
06 $b' \xleftarrow{\$} \mathcal{B}(pp, (P, rG, S_b))$; Return b'	06 $b' \xleftarrow{\$} \mathcal{A}(st, c + c'_b)$; Return b'

Fig. 4. Games for decisional Diffie-Hellman and class-hiding instantiated with $\mathcal{SRC}$ from Fig. 3

$\mathsf{Verify}(vk, ek, (C_0, C_1), sig) = 1$. Taking the logarithms in basis $e(G, \hat{G})$ of the verification equations yields $\hat{s} = s$ and, using this,

$$zs = z\hat{s} = 1 + c_0 x_0 + c_1 x_1 \tag{1}$$
$$ts = t\hat{s} = x_0 + dx_1 \tag{2}$$

Let us now consider a uniform random element $sig' = (Z' = z'G, S' = s'G, \hat{S}' = \hat{s}'\hat{G}, T' = t'G)$ from the set $\{sig' \in \mathcal{S}_{pp} \mid \mathsf{Verify}(vk, ek, \mathsf{Rndmz}(ek, c, r), sig') = 1\}$. Again considering logarithms of the verification equation yields $\hat{s}' = s'$ and

$$z's' = 1 + (c_0+r)x_0 + (c_1+rd)x_1 = 1 + c_0 x_0 + c_1 x_1 + r(x_0+dx_1) \overset{(1),(2)}{=} zs + rts$$

$$t's' = x_0 + dx_1 \overset{(2)}{=} ts$$

Moreover, by signature validity, we have $s \neq 0$ and $s' \neq 0$. We thus have $Z' = \frac{s}{s'}(Z + rT)$ and $T' = \frac{s}{s'}T$, as well as $S' = \frac{s'}{s}S$ and $\hat{S}' = \frac{s'}{s}\hat{S}$ (since $\hat{s} = s$ and $\hat{s}' = s'$). In other words, sig' is a uniform element from the set $\{(\frac{1}{s^*}(Z + rT), s^*S, s^*\hat{S}, T' = \frac{1}{s^*}T) \mid s^* \in \mathbb{Z}_p^*\}$. Since $\mathsf{Adapt}(sig, r)$ outputs a uniform random element from that set, this concludes the proof.

Proof of Unforgeability

Our main technical result is to prove that our scheme satisfies unforgeability (Definition 6) in the generic group model [Sho97] for asymmetric ("Type-3") bilinear groups (for which there are no efficiently computable homomorphisms between $\mathbb{G}$ and $\hat{\mathbb{G}}$). In this model, the adversary is only given *handles* of group elements, which are just uniform random strings. To perform group operations, it uses an oracle to which it can submit handles and is given back the handle of the sum, inversion, etc of the group elements for which it submitted handles.

Theorem 1. *A generic adversary $\mathcal{A}$ that computes at most q group operations and makes up to k queries to its signature oracle cannot win the game $\mathbf{EUF}^{\mathcal{A}}_{\mathcal{SRC}}(\lambda)$ from Fig. 2 for $\mathcal{SRC}$ defined in Fig. 3 with probability greater than $2^{-\lambda+1} k (q + 3k + 3)^2$.*

Proof. We consider an adversary that only uses generic group operations on the group elements it receives. After getting a verification key $(\hat{X}_0 = x_0\hat{G}, \hat{X}_1 = x_1\hat{G})$ and signatures $(Z_i, S_i, \hat{S}_i, T_i)_{i=1}^{k}$ computed with randomness s_i on queries $((P^{(i)}, (C_0^{(i)}, C_1^{(i)})))_{i=1}^{k}$, the adversary outputs an encryption key $P^{(k+1)}$, a ciphertext $((C_0^{(k+1)}, C_1^{(k+1)}))$ and a signature $(Z^*, S^*, \hat{S}^*, T^*)$ for them. As it must compute any new group element by combining received group elements, it must choose coefficients $\psi^{(i)}, \psi_{z,1}^{(i)}, \ldots, \psi_{z,i-1}^{(i)}, \psi_{s,1}^{(i)}, \ldots, \psi_{s,i-1}^{(i)}, \psi_{t,1}^{(i)}, \ldots, \psi_{t,i-1}^{(i)}, \gamma^{(i)}, \gamma_{z,1}^{(i)}, \ldots, \gamma_{z,i-1}^{(i)}, \gamma_{s,1}^{(i)}, \ldots, \gamma_{s,i-1}^{(i)}, \gamma_{t,1}^{(i)}, \ldots, \gamma_{t,i-1}^{(i)}, \kappa^{(i)}, \kappa_{z,1}^{(i)}, \ldots, \kappa_{z,i-1}^{(i)}, \kappa_{s,1}^{(i)}, \ldots, \kappa_{s,i-1}^{(i)}, \kappa_{t,1}^{(i)}, \ldots, \kappa_{t,i-1}^{(i)}$ for all $i \in \{1, \ldots, k+1\}$, as well as $\sigma, \sigma_{z,1}, \ldots, \sigma_{z,k}, \sigma_{s,1}, \ldots, \sigma_{s,k}, \sigma_{t,1}, \ldots, \sigma_{t,k}, \tau, \tau_{z,1}, \ldots, \tau_{z,k}, \tau_{s,1}, \ldots, \tau_{s,k}, \tau_{t,1}, \ldots, \tau_{t,k}, \zeta, \zeta_{z,1}, \ldots, \zeta_{z,k}, \zeta_{s,1}, \ldots, \zeta_{s,k}, \zeta_{t,1}, \ldots, \zeta_{t,k}, \phi, \phi_0, \phi_1, \phi_{s,1}, \ldots, \phi_{s,k}$, which define

$$P^{(i)} = \psi^{(i)}G + \sum_{j=1}^{i-1} \left(\psi_{z,j}^{(i)}Z_j + \psi_{s,j}^{(i)}S_j + \psi_{t,j}^{(i)}T_j\right)$$

$$C_0^{(i)} = \gamma^{(i)}G + \sum_{j=1}^{i-1} \left(\gamma_{z,j}^{(i)}Z_j + \gamma_{s,j}^{(i)}S_j + \gamma_{t,j}^{(i)}T_j\right)$$

$$C_1^{(i)} = \kappa^{(i)}G + \sum_{j=1}^{i-1} \left(\kappa_{z,j}^{(i)}Z_j + \kappa_{s,j}^{(i)}S_j + \kappa_{t,j}^{(i)}T_j\right)$$

$$Z^* = \zeta G + \sum_{j=1}^{k} \left(\zeta_{z,j}Z_j + \zeta_{s,j}S_j + \zeta_{t,j}T_j\right)$$

$$S^* = \sigma G + \sum_{j=1}^{k} \left(\sigma_{z,j}Z_j + \sigma_{s,j}S_j + \sigma_{t,j}T_j\right)$$

$$T^* = \tau G + \sum_{j=1}^{k} \left(\tau_{z,j}Z_j + \tau_{s,j}S_j + \tau_{t,j}T_j\right)$$

$$\hat{S}^* = \phi\hat{G} + \phi_0\hat{X}_0 + \phi_1\hat{X}_1 + \sum_{j=1}^{k} \phi_{s,j}\hat{S}_j$$

Using this, we can write, for all $1 \le i \le k$, the discrete logarithms z_i and t_i in basis G of the elements $Z_i = \frac{1}{s_i}\left(G + x_0C_0^{(i)} + x_1C_1^{(i)}\right)$ and $T_i = \frac{1}{s_i}\left(x_0G + x_1P^{(i)}\right)$ from the oracle answers.

$$z_i = \frac{1}{s_i}\left(1 + x_0\left(\gamma^{(i)} + \sum_{j=1}^{i-1}\left(\gamma_{z,j}^{(i)}z_j + \gamma_{s,j}^{(i)}s_j + \gamma_{t,j}^{(i)}t_j\right)\right)\right.$$

$$\left. + x_1\left(\kappa^{(i)} + \sum_{j=1}^{i-1}\left(\kappa_{z,j}^{(i)}z_j + \kappa_{s,j}^{(i)}s_j + \kappa_{t,j}^{(i)}t_j\right)\right)\right) \qquad (3)$$

$$t_i = \frac{1}{s_i}\left(x_0 + x_1\left(\psi^{(i)} + \sum_{j=1}^{i-1}\left(\psi_{z,j}^{(i)}z_j + \psi_{s,j}^{(i)}s_j + \psi_{t,j}^{(i)}t_j\right)\right)\right) \qquad (4)$$

We interpret these values as multivariate rational functions in variables $x_0, x_1, s_1, \ldots, s_k$. A successful forgery $(Z^*, S^*, \hat{S}^*, T^*)$ on $\big(P^{(k+1)}, (C_0^{(k+1)}, C_1^{(k+1)})\big)$ satisfies the verification equations

$$e(Z^*, \hat{S}^*) = e(G, \hat{G})e(C_0^{(k+1)}, \hat{X}_0)e(C_1^{(k+1)}, \hat{X}_1) \qquad e(G, \hat{S}^*) = e(S^*, \hat{G})$$

$$e(T^*, \hat{S}^*) = e(G, \hat{X}_0)e(P^{(k+1)}, \hat{X}_1)$$

Using the coefficients defined above and considering the logarithms in base $e(G, \hat{G})$ we obtain

$$\left(\zeta + \sum_{j=1}^{k}\left(\zeta_{z,j}z_j + \zeta_{s,j}s_j + \zeta_{t,j}t_j\right)\right)\left(\phi + \phi_0 x_0 + \phi_1 x_1 + \sum_{i=1}^{k}\phi_{s,i}s_i\right)$$

$$= 1 + x_0 c_0^{(k+1)} + x_1 c_1^{(k+1)} \tag{5}$$

$$\phi + \phi_0 x_0 + \phi_1 x_1 + \sum_{i=1}^{k}\phi_{s,i}s_i = \sigma + \sum_{j=1}^{k}\left(\sigma_{z,j}z_j + \sigma_{s,j}s_j + \sigma_{t,j}t_j\right) \tag{6}$$

$$\left(\tau + \sum_{j=1}^{k}\left(\tau_{z,j}z_j + \tau_{s,j}s_j + \tau_{t,j}t_j\right)\right)\left(\phi + \phi_0 x_0 + \phi_1 x_1 + \sum_{i=1}^{k}\phi_{s,i}s_i\right)$$

$$= x_0 + x_1 d^{(k+1)} \tag{7}$$

where for all $i \in \{1, \ldots, k+1\}$:

$$c_0^{(i)} = \log C_0^{(i)} = \gamma^{(i)} + \sum_{j=1}^{i-1}\left(\gamma_{z,j}^{(i)}z_j + \gamma_{s,j}^{(i)}s_j + \gamma_{t,j}^{(i)}t_j\right)$$

$$c_1^{(i)} = \log C_1^{(i)} = \kappa^{(i)} + \sum_{j=1}^{i-1}\left(\kappa_{z,j}^{(i)}z_j + \kappa_{s,j}^{(i)}s_j + \kappa_{t,j}^{(i)}t_j\right)$$

$$\text{and } d^{(i)} = \log P^{(i)} = \psi^{(i)} + \sum_{j=1}^{i-1}\left(\psi_{z,j}^{(i)}z_j + \psi_{s,j}^{(i)}s_j + \psi_{t,j}^{(i)}t_j\right) \tag{8}$$

We follow the standard proof technique for results in the generic group model and now consider an "ideal" game in which the challenger treats all the (handles of) group elements as elements of $\mathbb{Z}_p(s_1, \ldots, s_k, x_0, x_1)$, that is, rational functions whose variables represent the secret values chosen by the challenger.

We first show that in the ideal game if the adversary's output satisfies the verification equations, then the second winning condition, $\big(P^{(k+1)}, (C_0^{(k+1)}, C_1^{(k+1)})\big) \notin Q$, is not satisfied, which demonstrates that the ideal game cannot be won. We then compute the statistical distance from the adversary's point of view between the real and the ideal game at the end of the proof.

In the ideal game we thus interpret the three equalities (5), (6) and (7) as polynomial equalities over the field $\mathbb{Z}_p(s_1, \ldots, s_k, x_0, x_1)$. More precisely, we consider the equalities in the ring $\mathbb{Z}_p(s_1, \ldots, s_k)[x_0, x_1]$, that is, the polynomial ring with x_0 and x_1 as indeterminates over the field $\mathbb{Z}_p(s_1, \ldots, s_k)$. (Note that this interpretation is possible because x_0 and x_1 never appear in the denominators of any expressions.) As one of our proof techniques, we will also consider the equalities over the ring factored by (x_0, x_1), the ideal generated by x_0 and x_1:[1]

$$\mathbb{Z}_p(s_1, \ldots, s_k)[x_0, x_1]/(x_0, x_1) \cong \mathbb{Z}_p(s_1, \ldots, s_k).$$

From (3) and (4), over this quotient we have $z_i = \frac{1}{s_i}$ and $t_i = 0$ and thus (5)–(7) become

$$\left(\zeta + \sum_{j=1}^{k} \left(\zeta_{z,j} \frac{1}{s_j} + \zeta_{s,j} s_j \right) \right) \left(\phi + \sum_{i=1}^{k} \phi_{s,i} s_i \right) = 1 \tag{9}$$

$$\phi + \sum_{i=1}^{k} \phi_{s,i} s_i = \sigma + \sum_{i=1}^{k} \left(\sigma_{z,i} \frac{1}{s_i} + \sigma_{s,i} s_i \right) \tag{10}$$

$$\left(\tau + \sum_{i=1}^{k} \left(\tau_{z,i} \frac{1}{s_i} + \tau_{s,i} s_i \right) \right) \left(\phi + \sum_{i=1}^{k} \phi_{s,i} s_i \right) = 0 \tag{11}$$

We first consider (10). By equating coefficients, we deduce:

$$\phi = \sigma \qquad \forall i \in \{1, \ldots, k\} : \ \phi_{s,i} = \sigma_{s,i} \quad \text{and} \quad \sigma_{z,i} = 0 \tag{12}$$

We now turn to (9) and first notice that

$$\left(\phi + \sum_{i=1}^{k} \phi_{s,i} s_i \right) \neq 0, \tag{13}$$

because it is a factor of a non-zero product in (9). We next consider the degrees of the factors in (9), using the fact that the degree of a product is the sum of the degrees of the factors. Let $i \in \{1, \ldots, k\}$. Since $\deg_{s_i}(1) = 0$ and $\deg_{s_i} \left(\phi + \sum_{i=1}^{k} \phi_{s,i} s_i \right) \geq 0$, we have $\deg_{s_i} \left(\zeta + \sum_{j=1}^{k} (\zeta_{z,j} \frac{1}{s_j} + \zeta_{s,j} s_j) \right) \leq 0$, from which we get

$$\forall i \in \{1, \ldots, k\} : \zeta_{s,i} = 0. \tag{14}$$

(Note that $\deg_{s_i} \left(\frac{1}{s_i} + s_i \right) = \deg_{s_i} \left(\frac{1+s_i^2}{s_i} \right) = 1$.) We next show that there is at most one $\phi_{s,i}$ that is non-zero. Suppose there exist $i_1 \neq i_2 \in \{1, \ldots, k\}$

---

[1] Considering an equation of rational functions over this quotient can also be seen as simply setting $x_0 = x_1 = 0$. Everything we infer about the coefficients from these modified equations is also valid for the original equation, since these must hold for all values $(x_0, x_1, s_1, \ldots, s_k)$ and so in particular for $(0, 0, s_1, \ldots, s_k)$.

    Yet another interpretation when equating coefficients in equations modulo (x_0, x_1) is that one equates coefficients only of monomials that do not contain x_0 or x_1.

such that $\phi_{s,i_1} \neq 0$ and $\phi_{s,i_2} \neq 0$. This implies that $\deg_{s_{i_1}} \left(\phi + \sum_{i=1}^{k} \phi_{s,i} s_i \right) = \deg_{s_{i_2}} \left(\phi + \sum_{i=1}^{k} \phi_{s,i} s_i \right) = 1$. By considering these degrees in (9), the left factor must be of degree -1, that is (recall that $\zeta_{s,i} = 0$ for all i by (14)):

$$\deg_{s_{i_1}} \left(\zeta + \sum_{j=1}^{k} \zeta_{z,j} \frac{1}{s_j} \right) = -1 \quad \text{and} \quad \deg_{s_{i_2}} \left(\zeta + \sum_{j=1}^{k} \zeta_{z,j} \frac{1}{s_j} \right) = -1 . \tag{15}$$

This is a contradiction since the former implies that $\zeta_{z,i_1} \neq 0$, while the latter implies that $\zeta_{z,i_1} = 0$, as we show next. Consider the expression $\deg_{s_{i_2}} \left((\zeta + \sum_{j=1, j \neq i_2}^{k} \zeta_{z,j} \frac{1}{s_j}) s_{i_2} + \zeta_{z,i_2} \right) = \deg_{s_{i_2}} \left((\zeta + \sum_{j=1}^{k} \zeta_{z,j} \frac{1}{s_j}) s_{i_2} \right) = -1 + \deg_{s_{i_2}} (s_{i_2}) = 0$, by using (15). This implies $(\zeta + \sum_{j=1, j \neq i_2}^{k} \zeta_{z,j} \frac{1}{s_j}) = 0$ and thus $\zeta_{z,i_1} = 0$, which was our goal.

Therefore, there exists i_0 such that, for all $i \neq i_0$, $\phi_{s,i} = 0$ and by (12):

$$\forall i \in \{1, \ldots, k\} \backslash \{i_0\} : \sigma_{s,i} = \phi_{s,i} = 0. \tag{16}$$

Together with (14), this means that we can rewrite (9) as $(\zeta + \sum_{j=1}^{k} \zeta_{z,j} \frac{1}{s_j})(\phi + \phi_{s,i_0} s_{i_0}) = 1$. Since for all $i \neq i_0$, s_i does not appear in 1, we have

$$\forall i \in \{1, \ldots, k\} \backslash \{i_0\} : \zeta_{z,i} = 0. \tag{17}$$

We now consider Eq. (6) modulo (x_1). Since, by (12), $\phi = \sigma$ and $\phi_{s,i} = \sigma_{s,i}$ for all i, two terms cancel on both sides. Moreover, by (12), $\sigma_{z,i} = 0$ for all i and thus, using $t_i \bmod (x_1) = \frac{x_0}{s_i}$ for all i, yields

$$\phi_0 x_0 = \sum_{i=1}^{k} \sigma_{t,i} \frac{x_0}{s_i}. \tag{18}$$

By identifying coefficients, we deduce that

$$\forall i \in \{1, \ldots, k\} : \sigma_{t,i} = \phi_0 = 0. \tag{19}$$

Using all of this in the original Eq. (6) (that is, "putting back" x_1 in (18) and applying (19)) yields $\phi_1 x_1 = 0$ and thus

$$\phi_1 = 0. \tag{20}$$

We now turn to (11), in which by (13) we have $(\tau + \sum_{i=1}^{k} (\tau_{z,i} \frac{1}{s_i} + \tau_{s,i} s_i)) = 0$. From this we get by equating coefficients:

$$\forall i \in \{1, \ldots, k\} : \tau_{z,i} = \tau_{s,i} = \tau = 0 .$$

Going back to Eq. (7) and applying the latter, as well as (19), (20) and (16) yields

$$\left(\sum_{i=1}^{k} \tau_{t,i} t_i\right)(\phi + \phi_{s,i_0} s_{i_0}) = x_0 + x_1\left(\psi^{(k+1)} + \sum_{j=1}^{k}\left(\psi_{z,j}^{(k+1)} z_j + \psi_{s,j}^{(k+1)} s_j + \psi_{t,j}^{(k+1)} t_j\right)\right).$$
(21)

Computing this modulo (x_1) and recalling $t_i \bmod (x_1) = \frac{x_0}{s_i}$ yields

$$\left(\sum_{i=1}^{k} \tau_{t,i} \frac{x_0}{s_i}\right)(\phi + \phi_{s,i_0} s_{i_0}) = x_0, \text{ and thus}$$

$$\sum_{i=1}^{k} \phi \tau_{t,i} \frac{x_0}{s_i} + \sum_{i=1, i \neq i_0}^{k} \phi_{s,i_0} \tau_{t,i} s_{i_0} \frac{x_0}{s_i} + \phi_{s,i_0} \tau_{t,i_0} x_0 = x_0.$$

By equating the coefficients for x_0, we deduce that

$$\phi_{s,i_0} \tau_{t,i_0} = 1 \quad (\text{and thus } \phi_{s,i_0} \neq 0 \text{ and } \tau_{t,i_0} \neq 0). \tag{22}$$

Moreover, for all $i \in \{1, \ldots, k\}\setminus\{i_0\}$, we deduce $\phi_{s,i_0} \tau_{t,i} = 0$ and $\phi \tau_{t,i_0} = 0$, which by applying (22) to both yields

$$\forall i \in \{1, \ldots, k\}\setminus\{i_0\} : \tau_{t,i} = 0 \quad \text{and} \quad \phi = 0. \tag{23}$$

Using this, the left-hand side of (21) becomes $\phi_{s,i_0} \tau_{t,i_0} t_{i_0} s_{i_0}$, which, applying (22) and (4), becomes $\frac{1}{s_{i_0}}(x_0 + x_1 d^{(i_0)}) s_{i_0}$. This means that (21) becomes $x_0 + x_1 d^{(i_0)} = x_0 + x_1 d^{(k+1)}$, which implies $x_1(d^{(i_0)} - d^{(k+1)}) = 0$. Since a polynomial ring over a integral domain such as $\mathbb{Z}_p(s_1, \ldots, s_k)$ is an integral domain, and $x_1 \neq 0$, the last equality implies $d^{(i_0)} = d^{(k+1)}$. This means

$$P^{(i_0)} = P^{(k+1)}, \tag{24}$$

that is, the encryption key of the forgery is the same as used in the i_0-th query. We next show that the ciphertext $(C_0^{(k+1)}, C_1^{(k+1)})$ of the forgery is a randomization of the one from the i_0-th query.

Consider Eq. (9). Since $\zeta_{z,i} = 0$ for $i \neq i_0$ (by (17)), all $\zeta_{s,i} = 0$ (by (14)), $\phi = 0$ (by (23)) and $\phi_{s,i} = 0$ for $i \neq i_0$ (by (16)), it simplifies to

$$\left(\zeta + \zeta_{z,i_0} \frac{1}{s_{i_0}}\right)\phi_{s,i_0} s_{i_0} = \zeta \phi_{s,i_0} s_{i_0} + \zeta_{z,i_0} \phi_{s,i_0} = 1, \tag{25}$$

from which we deduce

$$\zeta_{z,i_0} \phi_{s,i_0} = 1 \quad \text{and} \quad \zeta = 0. \tag{26}$$

We now consider (5) modulo (x_1) and apply what we have deduced so far, that is $\zeta = 0$ by (26), the coefficients previously mentioned above (25) and

$\phi_0 = 0$ by (19). The left-hand side of (5) modulo (x_1) becomes thus $\left(\zeta_{z,i_0} z_{i_0} + \sum_{j=1}^{k} \zeta_{t,j} t_j\right) \phi_{s,i_0} s_{i_0} \mod (x_1)$. Using moreover (26), we get that (5) modulo (x_1) becomes

$$z_{i_0} s_{i_0} + \left(\sum_{j=1}^{k} \zeta_{t,j} t_j\right) \phi_{s,i_0} s_{i_0} \mod (x_1)$$

$$= 1 + x_0\left(\gamma^{(k+1)} + \sum_{j=1}^{k}\left(\gamma_{z,j}^{(k+1)} z_j + \gamma_{s,j}^{(k+1)} s_j + \gamma_{t,j}^{(k+1)} t_j\right)\right) \mod (x_1), \quad (27)$$

and using $z_i \mod (x_1) = \frac{1+c_0^{(i)} x_0}{s_i} \mod (x_1)$ and $t_i \mod (x_1) = \frac{x_0}{s_i}$ for all i (cf. (3) and (4)) we get

$$\left(1 + c_0^{(i_0)}\right)x_0 + \left(\sum_{j=1}^{k} \zeta_{t,j} \frac{x_0}{s_j}\right) \phi_{s,i_0} s_{i_0} \mod (x_1)$$

$$= 1 + x_0\left(\gamma^{(k+1)} + \sum_{j=1}^{k}\left(\gamma_{z,j}^{(k+1)} \frac{1+c_0^{(j)} x_0}{s_j} + \gamma_{s,j}^{(k+1)} s_j + \gamma_{t,j}^{(k+1)} \frac{x_0}{s_j}\right)\right) \mod (x_1).$$

$$(28)$$

Let $i > i_0$ and let us consider the monomials of degree -1 in s_i and degree 0 in s_j, for all $j > i$. Note that all monomials of $c_0^{(j)} = \gamma^{(j)} + \sum_{\ell=1}^{j-1}\left(\gamma_{z,\ell}^{(j)} z_\ell + \gamma_{s,\ell}^{(j)} s_\ell + \gamma_{t,\ell}^{(j)} t_\ell\right)$ are of degree 0 in s_ℓ, for $\ell \geq j$. Therefore, we do not consider any $\frac{c_0^{(j)}}{s_j}$ for $j < i$ (because they do not contain the term s_i) nor $\frac{c_0^{(j)}}{s_j}$ for $j > i$ (since the contained monomials are of degree -1 in s_j for $j > i$). For the monomials of degree -1 in s_i and degree 0 in s_j for $j > i$ in (28) we thus have

$$\forall i > i_0 : \frac{\zeta_{t,i} x_0 \phi_{s,i_0} s_{i_0}}{s_i} = x_0\left(\gamma_{z,i}^{(k+1)} \frac{1+c_0^{(i)} x_0}{s_i} + \gamma_{t,i}^{(k+1)} \frac{x_0}{s_i}\right) \mod (x_1) = 0.$$

Multiplying by s_i yields

$$\zeta_{t,i} x_0 \phi_{s,i_0} s_{i_0} - x_0\left(\gamma_{z,i}^{(k+1)}(1 + x_0 c_0^{(i)}) + \gamma_{t,i}^{(k+1)} x_0\right) \mod (x_1) = 0$$

and after reordering the monomials according to their degree in x_0 we get

$$\forall i > i_0 : -x_0^2\left(\gamma_{z,i}^{(k+1)} c_0^{(i)} + \gamma_{t,i}^{(k+1)}\right) + x_0\left(\zeta_{t,i} \phi_{s,i_0} s_{i_0} - \gamma_{z,i}^{(k+1)}\right) \mod (x_1) = 0. \quad (29)$$

Considering the linear coefficient in x_0, and recalling that $\phi_{s,i_0} \neq 0$ by (22), we deduce

$$\forall i > i_0 : \gamma_{z,i}^{(k+1)} = \zeta_{t,i} = 0. \quad (30)$$

Applying this to Eq. (29) yields $x_0^2 \gamma_{t,i}^{(k+1)} \bmod (x_1) = 0$ for all $i > i_0$, and therefore

$$\forall i > i_0 : \gamma_{t,i}^{(k+1)} = 0. \tag{31}$$

Since by (30) and (31) for all $i > i_0 : \zeta_{t,i} = \gamma_{z,i}^{(k+1)} = \gamma_{t,i}^{(k+1)} = 0$, we can rewrite (27) as

$$z_{i_0} s_{i_0} + \Big(\sum_{i=1}^{i_0} \zeta_{t,i} t_i \Big) \phi_{s,i_0} s_{i_0} \bmod (x_1)$$

$$= 1 + x_0 \Big(\gamma^{(k+1)} + \sum_{i=1}^{i_0} \big(\gamma_{z,i}^{(k+1)} z_i + \gamma_{t,i}^{(k+1)} t_i \big) + \sum_{i=1}^{k} \gamma_{s,i}^{(k+1)} s_i \Big) \bmod (x_1). \tag{32}$$

For $i > i_0$, from the coefficients of $x_0 s_i$ we get $\gamma_{s,i}^{(k+1)} = 0$. Applying this, (30) and (31) to (8) yields

$$c_0^{(k+1)} = \gamma^{(k+1)} + \sum_{i=1}^{i_0} \big(\gamma_{z,i}^{(k+1)} z_i + \gamma_{s,i}^{(k+1)} s_i + \gamma_{t,i}^{(k+1)} t_i \big); \tag{33}$$

and the right-hand side of (32) becomes

$$1 + x_0 \Big(\gamma^{(k+1)} + \sum_{i=1}^{i_0} \big(\gamma_{z,i}^{(k+1)} z_i + \gamma_{s,i}^{(k+1)} s_i + \gamma_{t,i}^{(k+1)} \frac{x_0}{s_i} \big) \Big) \bmod (x_1).$$

Since $z_i \bmod (x_1) = \frac{1 + x_0 c_0^{(i)}}{s_i} \bmod (x_1)$ and $t_i \bmod (x_1) = \frac{x_0}{s_i}$, for all i, (32) becomes

$$1 + x_0 c_0^{(i_0)} + \Big(\sum_{i=1}^{i_0} \zeta_{t,i} \frac{x_0}{s_i} \Big) \phi_{s,i_0} s_{i_0} \bmod (x_1)$$

$$= 1 + x_0 \Big(\gamma^{(k+1)} + \sum_{i=1}^{i_0} \big(\gamma_{z,i}^{(k+1)} \frac{1 + x_0 c_0^{(i)}}{s_i} + \gamma_{s,i}^{(k+1)} s_i + \gamma_{t,i}^{(k+1)} \frac{x_0}{s_i} \big) \Big) \bmod (x_1).$$

We will now look at the coefficients of s_{i_0} and of $\frac{1}{s_{i_0}}$. For this, we first note that for $j \geq i$ no s_j appears in $c_0^{(i)}$ (cf. (8)) and therefore for all $i \leq i_0 : c_0^{(i)}$ is constant in s_{i_0}. From the coefficients of s_{i_0} and of $\frac{1}{s_{i_0}}$ we thus get, respectively:

$$\phi_{s,i_0} \sum_{i=1}^{i_0-1} \zeta_{t,i} \frac{x_0}{s_i} = x_0 \gamma_{s,i_0}^{(k+1)} \tag{34}$$

$$0 = x_0 \big(\gamma_{z,i_0}^{(k+1)} (1 + x_0 c_0^{(i_0)}) + \gamma_{t,i_0}^{(k+1)} x_0 \big) \bmod (x_1) \tag{35}$$

From (34) we get $\gamma_{s,i_0}^{(k+1)} = 0$ and, since $\phi_{s,i_0} \neq 0$ by (22),

$$\forall i < i_0 : \zeta_{t,i} = 0, \tag{36}$$

and from (35) we get $\gamma_{z,i_0}^{(k+1)} = 0$ (from the coefficient of x_0) and therefore $\gamma_{t,i_0}^{(k+1)} = 0$. Together, this lets us rewrite (33) as

$$c_0^{(k+1)} = \gamma^{(k+1)} + \sum_{i=1}^{i_0-1} \left(\gamma_{z,i}^{(k+1)} z_i + \gamma_{s,i}^{(k+1)} s_i + \gamma_{t,i}^{(k+1)} t_i \right). \qquad (37)$$

Recall that $\hat{S}^* = \phi\hat{G} + \phi_0\hat{X}_0 + \phi_1\hat{X}_1 + \sum_{j=1}^{k} \phi_{s,j}\hat{S}_j$ and $Z^* = \zeta G + \sum_{j=1}^{k} (\zeta_{z,j}Z_j + \zeta_{s,j}S_j + \zeta_{t,j}T_j)$. By (23), (19), (20) and (16) we have $\hat{S}^* = \phi_{s,i_0}\hat{S}_{i_0}$ Moreover, by (26), (17), (14), (30) and (36) we have $Z^* = \zeta_{z,i_0}Z_{i_0} + \zeta_{t,i_0}T_{i_0}$. We can now rewrite (5) as:

$$(\zeta_{z,i_0}z_{i_0} + \zeta_{t,i_0}t_{i_0})(\phi_{s,i_0}s_{i_0}) = 1 + x_0 c_0^{(k+1)} + x_1 c_1^{(k+1)}.$$

Since, by (26), $\zeta_{z,i_0}\phi_{s,i_0} = 1$ and plugging in the definitions of z_{i_0} and t_{i_0}, this yields

$$1 + x_0 c_0^{(i_0)} + x_1 c_1^{(i_0)} + \zeta_{t,i_0}\phi_{s,i_0}(x_0 + x_1 d^{(i_0)}) = 1 + x_0 c_0^{(k+1)} + x_1 c_1^{(k+1)},$$

and thus

$$x_0 \left(c_0^{(i_0)} + \zeta_{t,i_0}\phi_{s,i_0} - c_0^{(k+1)} \right) = -x_1 \left(c_1^{(i_0)} + \zeta_{t,i_0}\phi_{s,i_0}d^{(i_0)} - c_1^{(k+1)} \right). \qquad (38)$$

By considering the above modulo (x_1), plugging in the definition of $c_0^{(i)}$ from (8) and using (37), we get

$$0 = \zeta_{t,i_0}\phi_{s,i_0} + c_0^{(i_0)} - c_0^{(k+1)} \mod (x_1)$$

$$= \zeta_{t,i_0}\phi_{s,i_0} + \gamma^{(i_0)} - \gamma^{(k+1)}$$

$$+ \sum_{j=1}^{i_0-1} \left((\gamma_{z,j}^{(i_0)} - \gamma_{z,j}^{(k+1)})z_j + (\gamma_{s,j}^{(i_0)} - \gamma_{s,j}^{(k+1)})s_j + (\gamma_{t,j}^{(i_0)} - \gamma_{t,j}^{(k+1)})t_j \right) \mod (x_1)$$

$$= \zeta_{t,i_0}\phi_{s,i_0} + \gamma^{(i_0)} - \gamma^{(k+1)} + \sum_{j=1}^{i_0-1} \left((\gamma_{z,j}^{(i_0)} - \gamma_{z,j}^{(k+1)})\frac{(1 + x_0 c_0^{(j)})}{s_j} \right.$$

$$\left. + (\gamma_{s,j}^{(i_0)} - \gamma_{s,j}^{(k+1)})s_j + (\gamma_{t,j}^{(i_0)} - \gamma_{t,j}^{(k+1)})\frac{x_0}{s_j} \right) \mod (x_1). \qquad (39)$$

Taking the above modulo (x_0) we get

$$\zeta_{t,i_0}\phi_{s,i_0} + \gamma^{(i_0)} - \gamma^{(k+1)}$$

$$+ \sum_{j=1}^{i_0-1} \left((\gamma_{z,j}^{(i_0)} - \gamma_{z,j}^{(k+1)})\frac{1}{s_j} + (\gamma_{s,j}^{(i_0)} - \gamma_{s,j}^{(k+1)})s_j \right) \mod (x_0, x_1) = 0.$$

By looking at the coefficients of the constant monomial and of $\frac{1}{s_i}$ and s_i for all $i < i_0$, we deduce the following:

$$\zeta_{t,i_0}\phi_{s,i_0} + \gamma^{(i_0)} - \gamma^{(k+1)} = 0 \tag{40}$$

$$\forall i < i_0 : \gamma_{z,i}^{(i_0)} - \gamma_{z,i}^{(k+1)} = 0 \quad \text{and} \quad \gamma_{s,i}^{(i_0)} - \gamma_{s,i}^{(k+1)} = 0 \tag{41}$$

This lets us rewrite (39) as $\sum_{j=1}^{i_0-1} (\gamma_{t,j}^{(i_0)} - \gamma_{t,j}^{(k+1)})\frac{x_0}{s_j} \bmod (x_1) = 0$, and equating the coefficients of $\frac{x_0}{s_j}$ for all $j < i_0$ yields

$$\forall i < i_0 : \gamma_{t,i}^{(i_0)} = \gamma_{t,i}^{(k+1)}. \tag{42}$$

Applying (40), (41) and (42) to (37) yields

$$c_0^{(k+1)} = \zeta_{t,i_0}\phi_{s,i_0} + \gamma^{(i_0)} + \sum_{i=1}^{i_0-1} (\gamma_{z,i}^{(i_0)} z_i + \gamma_{s,i}^{(i_0)} s_i + \gamma_{t,i}^{(i_0)} t_i)).$$

Recalling the definition of $c_0^{(i_0)}$ form (8), we can conclude that:

$$c_0^{(k+1)} = \zeta_{t,i_0}\phi_{s,i_0} + c_0^{(i_0)}.$$

Therefore (38) becomes $0 = -x_1(c_1^{(i_0)} + \zeta_{t,i_0}\phi_{s,i_0}d^{(i_0)} - c_1^{(k+1)})$, in other words

$$c_1^{(k+1)} = \zeta_{t,i_0}\phi_{s,i_0}d^{(i_0)} + c_1^{(i_0)}.$$

The last two equations mean that $(C_0^{(k+1)}, C_1^{(k+1)}) = (C_0^{(i_0)} + rG, \ C_1^{(i_0)} + rP^{(i_0)})$, for $r = \zeta_{t,i_0}\phi_{s,i_0}$, which together with (24) means that

$$(P^{(k+1)}, (C_0^{(k+1)}, C_1^{(k+1)})) \in \{P^{(i_0)}\} \times [(C_0^{(i_0)}, C_1^{(i_0)})]_{P^{(i_0)}} \subset Q.$$

We have thus shown that in the "ideal" model, the attacker cannot win the game. It remains to upper-bound the statistical distance from the adversary point of view between these two models.

Difference Between Ideal and Real Game. We start with upper-bounding the degree of the denominators and numerators of the rational functions that can be generated by the adversary.

We first show that by induction on the number of queries k, that all the elements returned by the challenger in the ideal game are divisors of $\prod_{i=1}^{k} s_i$. In the base case, when no queries are made, no s_i appears and the elements returned by the adversary are polynomials. For the induction step, assume the statement holds for ℓ queries. Consider the reply to the $(\ell + 1)$-th query: $S_{\ell+1}$ and $\hat{S}_{\ell+1}$ are monomials; $Z_{\ell+1}$ and $T_{\ell+1}$ are sums of polynomials and elements output by the adversary divided by $s_{\ell+1}$. Using the induction hypothesis on the adversary's outputs, we deduce that the denominators divide $\prod_{i=1}^{\ell+1} s_i$.   □

Similarly, we can show that the numerators of each element output by the challenger can be written as a sum of divisors of $x_0^k x_1^k \prod_{i=1}^k s_i$.

The "ideal" model and the generic group model differ if and only if two elements are distinct as rational functions but identical as (handle of a) group element. That is, if we evaluate two different rational functions at scalar values $x_0, x_1, s_1, \ldots, s_k$ and obtain the same result.

Any such equality of rational functions generated during the game can be rewritten as a polynomial equation of degree $3k + k$ ($3k$ upper-bounding the degree of the numerator and k that of the denominator). Because the values $x_0, x_1, s_1, \ldots, s_k$ are uniformly random (and hidden from the adversary), the Schwartz-Zippel lemma [Sch80] yields that the probability of this equality holding is at most $\frac{4k}{p-1}$.

If the adversary computes at most q group operations, then there are at most $q + 3 + 3k$ group elements, where 3 comes from the generator and the verification key, and $3k$ corresponds to the answers to the signing queries (note that $\hat{S}$ and S correspond to the same monomial). There are therefore

$$\tfrac{1}{2}(q + 3k + 3)(q + 3k + 2)$$

pairs of rational functions. Using the union bound, we conclude that the adversary can distinguish the two models with probability at most $\frac{4k}{2(p-1)}(q + 3k + 3)(q + 3k + 2) < \frac{2k}{2^\lambda}(q + 3k + 3)^2$, since $p - 1 > 2^\lambda$, which is the bound claimed by the theorem.

Generalization of Our Scheme. We conclude by mentioning that our scheme easily generalizes to ElGamal encryptions of vectors of group elements without increasing the size of signatures: for an encryption key $(P_1, \ldots, P_n)$ and a signing key $(x_0, \ldots, x_n)$, a ciphertext consisting of $C_0 = rG$ and $C_i = M_i + rP_i$ for $1 \leq i \leq n$, a signature on randomizable ciphertexts is defined as:

$$Z := \frac{1}{s}\left(G + \sum_{i=0}^n x_i C_i\right) \quad S := sG \quad \hat{S} := s\hat{G} \quad T := \frac{1}{s}\left(x_0 G + \sum_{i=1}^n x_i P_i\right)$$

Acknowledgement. This is work is funded in part by the MSR–Inria Joint Centre. Fuchsbauer is supported by the Vienna Science and Technology Fund (WWTF) through project VRG18-002.

References

[AFG10] Abe, M., Fuchsbauer, G., Groth, J., Haralambiev, K., Ohkubo, M.: Structure-preserving signatures and commitments to group elements. In: Rabin, T. (ed.) CRYPTO 2010. LNCS, vol. 6223, pp. 209–236. Springer, Heidelberg (2010). https://doi.org/10.1007/978-3-642-14623-7_12

[AGHO11] Abe, M., Groth, J., Haralambiev, K., Ohkubo, M.: Optimal structure-preserving signatures in asymmetric bilinear groups. In: Rogaway, P. (ed.) CRYPTO 2011. LNCS, vol. 6841, pp. 649–666. Springer, Heidelberg (2011). https://doi.org/10.1007/978-3-642-22792-9_37

[AGO11] Abe, M., Groth, J., Ohkubo, M.: Separating short structure-preserving signatures from non-interactive assumptions. In: Lee, D.H., Wang, X. (eds.) ASIACRYPT 2011. LNCS, vol. 7073, pp. 628–646. Springer, Heidelberg (2011). https://doi.org/10.1007/978-3-642-25385-0_34

[AW98] Deschamps, C., Warusfel, A., Moulin, F.: Mathématiques 1ère année: Cours et exercices corrigés. Editions Dunod (1998)

[BCC09] Belenkiy, M., Camenisch, J., Chase, M., Kohlweiss, M., Lysyanskaya, A., Shacham, H.: Randomizable proofs and delegatable anonymous credentials. In: Halevi, S. (ed.) CRYPTO 2009. LNCS, vol. 5677, pp. 108–125. Springer, Heidelberg (2009). https://doi.org/10.1007/978-3-642-03356-8_7

[BCKL08] Belenkiy, M., Chase, M., Kohlweiss, M., Lysyanskaya, A.: P-signatures and noninteractive anonymous credentials. In: Canetti, R. (ed.) TCC 2008. LNCS, vol. 4948, pp. 356–374. Springer, Heidelberg (2008). https://doi.org/10.1007/978-3-540-78524-8_20

[BFPV11] Blazy, O., Fuchsbauer, G., Pointcheval, D., Vergnaud, D.: Signatures on randomizable ciphertexts. In: Catalano, D., Fazio, N., Gennaro, R., Nicolosi, A. (eds.) PKC 2011. LNCS, vol. 6571, pp. 403–422. Springer, Heidelberg (2011). https://doi.org/10.1007/978-3-642-19379-8_25

[BFPV13] Blazy, O., Fuchsbauer, G., Pointcheval, D., Vergnaud, D.: Short blind signatures. J. Comput. Secur. **21**(5), 627–661 (2013)

[BHKS18] Backes, M., Hanzlik, L., Kluczniak, K., Schneider, J.: Signatures with flexible public key: introducing equivalence classes for public keys. In: Peyrin, T., Galbraith, S. (eds.) ASIACRYPT 2018. LNCS, vol. 11273, pp. 405–434. Springer, Cham (2018). https://doi.org/10.1007/978-3-030-03329-3_14

[BL13] Baldimtsi, F., Lysyanskaya, A.: Anonymous credentials light. In: Sadeghi, A.-R., Gligor, V.D., Yung, M. (eds.) ACM CCS 2013, pp. 1087–1098. ACM Press, November 2013

[BMW03] Bellare, M., Micciancio, D., Warinschi, B.: Foundations of group signatures: formal definitions, simplified requirements, and a construction based on general assumptions. In: Biham, E. (ed.) EUROCRYPT 2003. LNCS, vol. 2656, pp. 614–629. Springer, Heidelberg (2003). https://doi.org/10.1007/3-540-39200-9_38

[Bra00] Brands, S.: Rethinking Public-Key Infrastructures and Digital Certificates: Building in Privacy. MIT Press, Cambridge (2000)

[BSZ05] Bellare, M., Shi, H., Zhang, C.: Foundations of group signatures: the case of dynamic groups. In: Menezes, A. (ed.) CT-RSA 2005. LNCS, vol. 3376, pp. 136–153. Springer, Heidelberg (2005). https://doi.org/10.1007/978-3-540-30574-3_11

[CCFG16] Chaidos, P., Cortier, V., Fuchsbauer, G., Galindo, D.: BeleniosRF: a noninteractive receipt-free electronic voting scheme. In: Weippl, E.R., Katzenbeisser, S., Kruegel, C., Myers, A.C., Halevi, S. (eds.) ACM CCS 2016, pp. 1614–1625. ACM Press, October 2016

[CFL19] Cortier, V., Filipiak, A., Lallemand, J.: BeleniosVS: secrecy and verifiability against a corrupted voting device. In: 2019 IEEE 32nd Computer Security Foundations Symposium (CSF), pp. 367–36714. IEEE (2019)

[CG05] Camenisch, J., Groth, J.: Group signatures: better efficiency and new theoretical aspects. In: Blundo, C., Cimato, S. (eds.) SCN 2004. LNCS, vol. 3352, pp. 120–133. Springer, Heidelberg (2005). https://doi.org/10.1007/978-3-540-30598-9_9

[CGG19] Cortier, V., Gaudry, P., Glondu, S.: Belenios: a simple private and verifiable electronic voting system. In: Guttman, J.D., Landwehr, C.E., Meseguer, J., Pavlovic, D. (eds.) Foundations of Security, Protocols, and Equational Reasoning. LNCS, vol. 11565, pp. 214–238. Springer, Cham (2019). https://doi.org/10.1007/978-3-030-19052-1_14

[CL03] Camenisch, J., Lysyanskaya, A.: A signature scheme with efficient protocols. In: Cimato, S., Persiano, G., Galdi, C. (eds.) SCN 2002. LNCS, vol. 2576, pp. 268–289. Springer, Heidelberg (2003). https://doi.org/10.1007/3-540-36413-7_20

[CL04] Camenisch, J., Lysyanskaya, A.: Signature schemes and anonymous credentials from bilinear maps. In: Franklin, M. (ed.) CRYPTO 2004. LNCS, vol. 3152, pp. 56–72. Springer, Heidelberg (2004). https://doi.org/10.1007/978-3-540-28628-8_4

[CL19] Crites, E.C., Lysyanskaya, A.: Delegatable anonymous credentials from mercurial signatures. In: Matsui, M. (ed.) CT-RSA 2019. LNCS, vol. 11405, pp. 535–555. Springer, Cham (2019). https://doi.org/10.1007/978-3-030-12612-4_27

[DHO16] Damgård, I., Haagh, H., Orlandi, C.: Access control encryption: enforcing information flow with cryptography. In: Hirt, M., Smith, A. (eds.) TCC 2016. LNCS, vol. 9986, pp. 547–576. Springer, Heidelberg (2016). https://doi.org/10.1007/978-3-662-53644-5_21

[DHS15] Derler, D., Hanser, C., Slamanig, D.: A new approach to efficient revocable attribute-based anonymous credentials. In: Groth, J. (ed.) IMACC 2015. LNCS, vol. 9496, pp. 57–74. Springer, Cham (2015). https://doi.org/10.1007/978-3-319-27239-9_4

[DS18] Derler, D., Slamanig, D.: Highly-efficient fully-anonymous dynamic group signatures. In: Kim, J., Ahn, G.-J., Kim, S., Kim, Y., López, J., Kim, T. (eds.) ASIACCS 18, pp. 551–565. ACM Press, April 2018

[ElG85] ElGamal, T.: A public key cryptosystem and a signature scheme based on discrete logarithms. IEEE Trans. Inf. Theor. $31(4)$, 469–472 (1985)

[FG18] Fuchsbauer, G., Gay, R.: Weakly secure equivalence-class signatures from standard assumptions. In: Abdalla, M., Dahab, R. (eds.) PKC 2018. LNCS, vol. 10770, pp. 153–183. Springer, Cham (2018). https://doi.org/10.1007/978-3-319-76581-5_6

[FGKO17] Fuchsbauer, G., Gay, R., Kowalczyk, L., Orlandi, C.: Access control encryption for equality, comparison, and more. In: Fehr, S. (ed.) PKC 2017. LNCS, vol. 10175, pp. 88–118. Springer, Heidelberg (2017). https://doi.org/10.1007/978-3-662-54388-7_4

[FHKS16] Fuchsbauer, G., Hanser, C., Kamath, C., Slamanig, D.: Practical round-optimal blind signatures in the standard model from weaker assumptions. In: Zikas, V., De Prisco, R. (eds.) SCN 2016. LNCS, vol. 9841, pp. 391–408. Springer, Cham (2016). https://doi.org/10.1007/978-3-319-44618-9_21

[FHS15] Fuchsbauer, G., Hanser, C., Slamanig, D.: Practical round-optimal blind signatures in the standard model. In: Gennaro, R., Robshaw, M. (eds.) CRYPTO 2015. LNCS, vol. 9216, pp. 233–253. Springer, Heidelberg (2015). https://doi.org/10.1007/978-3-662-48000-7_12

[FHS19] Fuchsbauer, G., Hanser, C., Slamanig, D.: Structure-preserving signatures on equivalence classes and constant-size anonymous credentials. J. Cryptology $32(2)$, 498–546 (2019)

[Fuc11]   Fuchsbauer, G.: Commuting signatures and verifiable encryption. In: Pater-
          son, K.G. (ed.) EUROCRYPT 2011. LNCS, vol. 6632, pp. 224–245.
          Springer, Heidelberg (2011). https://doi.org/10.1007/978-3-642-20465-
          4_14
[GS08]   Groth, J., Sahai, A.: Efficient non-interactive proof systems for bilinear
          groups. In: Smart, N. (ed.) EUROCRYPT 2008. LNCS, vol. 4965, pp.
          415–432. Springer, Heidelberg (2008). https://doi.org/10.1007/978-3-540-
          78967-3_24
[HPP20]   Hébant, C., Phan, D.H., Pointcheval, D.: Linearly-homomorphic signatures
          and scalable mix-nets. In: Kiayias, A., Kohlweiss, M., Wallden, P., Zikas, V.
          (eds.) PKC 2020. LNCS, vol. 12111, pp. 597–627. Springer, Cham (2020).
          https://doi.org/10.1007/978-3-030-45388-6_21
[HS14]   Hanser, C., Slamanig, D.: Structure-preserving signatures on equiva-
          lence classes and their application to anonymous credentials. In: Sarkar,
          P., Iwata, T. (eds.) ASIACRYPT 2014. LNCS, vol. 8873, pp. 491–511.
          Springer, Heidelberg (2014). https://doi.org/10.1007/978-3-662-45611-
          8_26
[KSD19]   Hanser, C., Slamanig, D.: Structure-preserving signatures on equiva-
          lence classes and their application to anonymous credentials. In: Sarkar,
          P., Iwata, T. (eds.) ASIACRYPT 2014. LNCS, vol. 8873, pp. 491–511.
          Springer, Heidelberg (2014). https://doi.org/10.1007/978-3-662-45611-
          8_26
[Sch80]   Schwartz, J.T.: Fast probabilistic algorithms for verification of polynomial
          identities. J. ACM (JACM) **27**(4), 701–717 (1980)
[Sho97]   Shoup, V.: Lower bounds for discrete logarithms and related problems.
          In: Fumy, W. (ed.) EUROCRYPT 1997. LNCS, vol. 1233, pp. 256–266.
          Springer, Heidelberg (1997). https://doi.org/10.1007/3-540-69053-0_18
[Wat05]   Waters, B.: Efficient identity-based encryption without random oracles.
          In: Cramer, R. (ed.) EUROCRYPT 2005. LNCS, vol. 3494, pp. 114–127.
          Springer, Heidelberg (2005). https://doi.org/10.1007/11426639_7

Fast Threshold ECDSA with Honest Majority

Ivan Damgård[1], Thomas Pelle Jakobsen[2](✉) (iD), Jesper Buus Nielsen[1], Jakob Illeborg Pagter[2], and Michael Bæksvang Østergaard[2]

[1] Aarhus University, Aarhus, Denmark
{ivan,jb}@cs.au.dk
[2] Sepior, Aarhus, Denmark
{tpj,jip,mbo}@sepior.com

Abstract. ECDSA is a widely adopted digital signature standard. A number of threshold protocols for ECDSA have been developed that let a set of parties jointly generate the secret signing key and compute signatures, without ever revealing the signing key. Threshold protocols for ECDSA have seen recent interest, in particular due to the need for additional security in cryptocurrency wallets where leakage of the signing key is equivalent to an immediate loss of money.

We propose a threshold ECDSA protocol secure against an active adversary in the honest majority model with abort. Our protocol is efficient in terms of both computation and bandwidth usage, and it allows the parties to pre-process parts of the signature, such that once the message to sign becomes known, the they can compute a secret sharing of the signature very efficiently, using only local operations. We also show how to obtain fairness in the online phase at the cost of some additional work in the pre-processing, i.e., such that it either aborts during pre-processing phase, in which case nothing is revealed, or the signature is guaranteed to be delivered to all honest parties.

1 Introduction

A hot topic of the 80s was *threshold cryptography* [11,12]. This notion covers encryption and signature schemes where the key is secret shared among a number of parties in a way that lets the parties sign or decrypt messages despite the fact that the key remains secret shared. The key remains protected as long as at most a certain threshold t of the parties are corrupted.

Threshold cryptography, being a special kind of *secure multiparty computation*, is stronger than simply secret sharing the key, since it allows to sign or encrypt without any one party reconstructing the key. Threshold cryptography therefore increases security by ensuring that an attacker must compromise $t+1$ points instead of a single point. It is also well-suited in cases with multiple owners of the key and where it should be enforced that signing or decryption only occur when a certain threshold of the owners agree.

© Springer Nature Switzerland AG 2020
C. Galdi and V. Kolesnikov (Eds.): SCN 2020, LNCS 12238, pp. 382–400, 2020.
https://doi.org/10.1007/978-3-030-57990-6_19

The elliptic curve digital signature standard ECDSA [21,23] has recently become very popular. It has for example been adopted by TLS and popular cryptocurrencies such as Bitcoin and Ethereum. This has caused a growing need for a threshold version of ECDSA. In particular, its use in cryptocurrencies implies that loss of the secret signing key immediately translates to a loss of money.[1]

However, while efficient threshold versions of e.g. RSA and ElGamal encryption and Schnorr signatures have been proposed early [31,33], efficient threshold variants of DSA/ECDSA have proved hard to achieve.

1.1 Related Work and Our Contribution

Gennaro et al. proposed one of the first threshold protocols for DSA signatures [18–20]. The authors give a simulation-based proof that the protocol is secure and robust against a static, malicious adversary corrupting at most t out of n parties for $n \geq 4t + 1$. (A solution for $n \geq 3t + 1$ is also sketched with no proof.) The protocol assumes a consistent and reliable broadcast channel and uses Pedersen's verifiable secret sharing [28].

Another line of work has focused on DSA/ECDSA threshold signatures in the case of a dishonest majority, i.e., with full threshold $t = n - 1$. This was initiated by MacKenzie and Reiter [27] who proposed a two-party protocol. Gennaro et al. later followed up with ECDSA schemes for more than two parties [3,17]. Common to these protocols were that they were not really practical, especially due to the work required by the distributed key generation.

Lindell and others [6,13,24] later improved on this in the two-party setting. Finally, recent results [14,16,26] provide full threshold ECDSA for any number of parties.

Recent results [9,32] show how to do threshold ECDSA based on schemes for general MPC. As shown by Dalskov et al. [9] this can lead to very practical protocols when instantiating the MPC with protocols for honest majority with abort.

Our Protocol Compared to Existing Dishonest Majority Protocols. The ECDSA protocols for dishonest majority [3,6,13,14,16,17,24,26,27] all rely on computationally heavy primitives such as Paillier encryption and zero-knowledge proofs, or they are based on oblivious transfer [13,14] which incurs high bandwidth. In comparison, our protocol is considerably simpler and efficient in terms of *both* computation and bandwidth usage.

In addition, except from Doerner et al. [14], these protocols somehow relax security, either by relying on assumptions not implied by ECDSA itself, such as decisional Diffie-Hellman [26] or the quadratic residuosity assumption [16,24], or they implement relaxed versions of the ECDSA functionality [13]. In contrast,

---

[1] For this reason Bitcoin uses *multisignatures* [1]. But as discussed in length in e.g. Gennaro et al. [17] threshold signatures are in several ways more suited.

we provide a proof in the UC model that our protocol (perfectly) implements the standard ECDSA functionality without additional assumptions.

Finally, most of these protocols are restricted to the two-party setting and/or require one or more rounds of *interaction* between the parties in the online phase, i.e., after the message to be signed is known. Contrary to this, our protocol allows the parties to locally compute a sharing of the final signature without interaction, given suitable preprocessing prior to knowing the message. The only other protocol comparable to ours in this regard is Doerner *et al.* [14] which, as mentioned, has a higher bandwidth consumption than our protocol.

That said, all of these protocols of course achieve stronger security in the sense that they can tolerate up to $n - 1$ corruptions.

Our Protocol Compared to the GJKR Protocol [18–20]. The protocol of Gennaro *et al.* [18–20] was designed for the honest majority setting and, like ours, avoids additional cryptographic assumptions and has a non-interactive online phase. Assuming a reliable broadcast channel, Gennaro *et al.* provides full security (including both termination guarantee and fairness) as long as $n \geq 4t + 1$.

From a practical perspective the $n \geq 4t + 1$ constraint can be problematic. It means that one has to find at least five parties that are willing to run the protocol, and even if found, only one corrupt party can be handled.

Another practical problem is the network model used by Gennaro *et al.* The fairness and termination guarantees they provide rely on the existence of a broadcast channel with guaranteed consistency and message delivery. As the internet lacks both of these properties, one has to implement them. This can be done, but it leads to additional rounds of communication, something that negatively affects the performance, especially when running the protocol in a WAN setting.

Moreover, to simulate guaranteed message delivery on the internet where message delivery is inherently unreliable, one has to resort to using timeouts: If an expected message is not received within a given timeout, the receiver continues, treating the sender as corrupt. A practical problem with this is that if the timeouts are too small, then otherwise honest parties will soon be deemed corrupt due to the message delays that naturally occur on the internet, and soon enough parties are corrupt to exceed the security threshold. To avoid this, large timeouts must be used. But using large timeouts lets a single malicious party cause the protocol to run exceptionally slow.

In many practical cases, the termination and fairness guarantees as provided by Gennaro *et al.* [18] may not be required.[2] We instead follow a recent trend also seen in the construction of general honest majority MPC protocols [7,15,25] of giving up on these guarantees to achieve faster, more practical protocols. Doing so, the above issues are avoided. If for example a message is lost, the parties can simply abort after a short timeout and retry later.

---

[2] In fact, in the case of a dishonest majority these guarantees are generally impossible to achieve, and therefore usually not addressed. This is the case for all the dishonest majority ECDSA protocols above [3,13,14,16,17,24,26,27].

As a result of this, where Gennaro *et al.* [18] require $12t + 8n + 1$ long curve multiplications per party, primarily due to the use of computationally heavy Pedersen commitments, we manage to reduce this to only 5. Consequently, with parties connected on a local network, under the reasonable assumption that long curve multiplications in this setting are the performance bottleneck, our protocol will have a signature throughput 7.4 times than of Gennaro *et al.* [18–20] for $n = 3$, and 13 times Gennaro *et al.* for $n = 5$, etc.

Sometimes, however, fairness is important. To address this, we show how to achieve fairness in our online phase, at the cost of some additional work which can be pre-processed. This means that the protocol may abort during pre-processing, in which case nothing leaks, but if it does not, then it is guaranteed to deliver the signature to all honest parties in the online phase.

Importantly, both versions of our protocol achieve a better security threshold of $n \geq 2t + 1$, which means that it can run with only three parties and only requires pairwise authentic and private channels.

Our Contribution

- We provide a practical and efficient threshold protocol for DSA and ECDSA signatures in the honest majority model with abort. It is secure against an active adversary and works for any number of parties n and security thresholds t as long as $n \geq 2t + 1$.
- The protocol is accompanied by a full proof in the UC model [5]. The proof shows that our protocol (perfectly) realizes the standard ECDSA functionality, and it relies on no additional assumptions.
- The protocol is well-suited for pre-processing: Most of the work can be done before the message to be signed is known, and if doing so, the protocol achieves excellent online performance. In the basic variant, when the parties receive the message to be signed, they can compute a sharing of the signature using only local operations, without interacting with each other.
- We show how to extend our basic protocol to ensure fairness and termination in the online phase.
- We demonstrate practicality by benchmarking in the LAN as well as the WAN setting. Using a *close-to-real-world* deployment with load balancers and authenticated channels we show that our protocol achieves both low latency and high throughput.

2   Our Threshold ECDSA Protocol

In this section we describe our basic protocol and the overall strategy for its simulation. To keep the description simple, we focus on the basic protocol and consider pre-processing and fairness later.

We assume familiarity with the DSA/ECDSA signature scheme and Shamir sharing. We will use $F(R)$ to denote the mapping of a point R to Z_q, i.e., for ECDSA $F(R)$ will output the x-coordinate of R, for DSA $F(R) = R \mod q$. We will use $[x] \leftarrow \text{RSS}(t)$ to denote joint random secret sharing where the parties obtain a sharing of a random value $x \in Z_q$ over a random polynomial of degree t. It is done simply by having each party create a random sharing, and then adding up the shares. Similarly, we use $[x] \leftarrow \mathtt{ZSS}(t)$ for a random sharing of zero. Given shares x_i over a polynomial f, corresponding points $y_i = g^{x_i}$ for a generator g, and $x_0 \in Z_q$ we use $\mathtt{ExpInt}(y_i; x_0) = g^{f(x_0)}$ to denote Lagrange interpolation "in the exponent". A more detailed recap of ECDSA and interpolation in the exponent can be found in Appendix A.

2.1 Technical Overview

At a high level, we follow the scheme of Gennaro et al. [20]. The parties first generate the private key $[x]$ using joint random secret sharing. Then they run a protocol to reveal the public key $y = g^x$. To avoid certain subtleties related to joint random secret sharing with guaranteed termination [19], and to avoid additional assumptions, Gennaro et al. use a rather complicated protocol based on Pedersen verifiable secret sharing. Since we allow abort, we can use plain Shamir secret sharing along with a simpler protocol for revealing g^x. Our protocol for revealing g^x works despite malicious parties and is designed to abort also if $[x]$ is not a consistent sharing.

When signing a message M, the parties generate a sharing of the nonce $[k]$ using joint random secret sharing and reveal g^k using the same protocol as for revealing the public key g^x. They then use Beaver's inversion trick to compute $[k^{-1}]$: They first generate a random sharing $[a]$, then multiply and open $w = [a][k]$. This is done using a simple passively secure protocol where the parties just reveal the product of their shares. Since this is a degree $2t$ sharing of ak they can recover ak as long as all parties participate honestly. With malicious parties the result is not necessarily correct. Gennaro et al. used error correcting codes to handle this. We tolerate abort and can instead use the same protocol as before to correctly open an authenticator $W = g^{ak}$ that lets the parties verify the correctness by checking that $g^w = W$.

If ok, the parties compute $[a] \cdot w^{-1} = [k^{-1}]$ and $m = H(M)$, and they can now compute and open $[s] = [k^{-1}](m + r[x])$ as they opened $[a][k]$ before. This time, however, since we tolerate abort, it suffices to check correctness of s by validating the resulting signature (r, s) on M using the public key y.

2.2 Computing Powers of a Point

A central building block in our protocol is a subprotocol that given a sharing $[x]$ and a generator $g \in G$ (on which all honest parties agree) reveals the value $y = g^x$. We let $y \leftarrow \mathtt{POWOPEN}(g, [x])$ denote this protocol.

The protocol works as follows:

1. Each party P_i sends $y_i = g^{x_i}$ to all the other parties. Let f be the unique degree t polynomial defined by the $t + 1$ (or more) honest parties' shares, i.e. $f(0) = x$.

2. When P_i receives all g^{x_j} for each $y_j \in \{y_{t+2}, y_{t+3}, \ldots, y_n\}$ it verifies that y_j is consistent with the degree t polynomial defined by the first $t + 1$ values $y_1, y_2, \ldots, y_{t+1}$. It does so by doing Lagrange interpolation "in the exponent".
3. If so, P_i knows that $y_1, \ldots, y_{t+1}$ are valid points on f, and P_i then uses again Lagrange interpolation "in the exponent" on $y_1, y_2, \ldots, y_{t+1}$ to compute $y = g^x = g^{f(0)}$.

Since $n \geq 2t + 1$ there are at least $t + 1$ honest parties. This means that each honest party will receive at least $t + 1$ correct shares "in the exponent", enough to uniquely define f. Hence, if any of the t corrupted parties cheat, all honest parties will abort in Step 2.

Intuitively, seeing the values g^{x_i} reveals nothing on the shares x_i since computing discrete logarithms in G is assumed to be hard. As we will later see, our simulation does in fact not rely on this property. The simulation works even for computationally unbounded adversaries.

A notable feature of POWOPEN is that for $n \geq 2t+1$ all honest parties will abort if the input sharing defined by the honest parties is inconsistent, i.e., if these shares are not points on a degree t polynomial, no matter what the corrupted parties do.

Simulation. Consider how to simulate POWOPEN. The simulator does not know the value x and so must use random shares x_j for the corrupted parties. During simulation each party P_i reveals g^{x_i} to all other parties. The challenge is that the simulator only knows t points on the polynomial f, namely $f(j)$ for the corrupted parties P_j. (This follows from the context in which POWOPEN is used, see e.g. next section on key generation.) But the simulated adversary sees all $y_i = g^{x_i}$. So in order to succeed, the simulator must make these values consistent with the environment's view (which includes $y = g^x$). In other words, the simulator must use values y_i' such that $\text{ExpInt}(y_i'; 0) = y = g^x$, but without knowing x.

Simulation is possible since the simulator knows an additional point on f "in the exponent", namely $y = g^x = g^{f(0)}$ (this requires that y is leaked to the adversary/simulator at the beginning of the protocol). So "in the exponent" the simulator knows $t + 1$ points on f, enough to fully determine f. Thus, using Lagrange interpolation "in the exponent" with y and the t random shares of the corrupted parties, the simulator can compute points to use for the honest parties in the simulation that are consistent with the adversary's view that includes $y = g^x$.

2.3 Key Generation

The aim of key generation is to have the parties generate a sharing $[x]$ of a uniformly random value $x \in Z_q$ and reveal to each party $y = g^x$. To generate $[x]$ the parties run $[x] \leftarrow \text{RSS}(t)$ to obtain a sharing of a random value $x \in Z_q$ over a random polynomial. To obtain $y = g^x$ we let the parties run the protocol $y \leftarrow \text{POWOPEN}(g, [x])$.

Regarding correctness: We use plain Shamir sharing and not verifiable secret sharing (VSS). This means that a single malicious party P_i may cause $[x]$ to be an inconsistent sharing, by dealing inconsistently for $x^{(i)}$. As discussed above, this will cause POWOPEN to abort, which is enough in our case, as we allow abort. Also, at least one party P_j will correctly choose uniform shares $x_j^{(i)}$, which is enough to ensure that $[x]$ is random and that all honest parties' shares of x are random.

An important part of the protocol is that no honest party P_i reveals his value g^{x_i} until he has received shares x_j from all other parties P_j. This forces the corrupt parties P_j to "commit" to their values $x^{(j)}$ before they see y. Without this, a corrupt party P_j could let $x^{(j)}$ depend on y.

The protocol guarantees that if two parties output a public key, they output the same public key y. In addition, all subsets of $t+1$ honest parties that receive output, will receive shares of the same private key x satisfying $g^x = y$. The protocol also ensures that each share x_i and the private key x (and hence also the public key) is uniformly distributed.

By having all parties send an ACK message to the others once they have succeeded, and require that parties only continue once an ACK have been received from all other parties, we get the property that the adversary can decide to abort or not, but if an honest party delivers output then so do all honest parties.

Regarding simulation, RSS is information-theoretically secure so the simulator can just simulate the protocol using random values x_i', and we already described how to simulate POWOPEN.

2.4   Signature Generation

Assume that key generation has been done without abort, such that the parties hold a consistent sharing of a random key $[x]$ and each party holds the corresponding public key $y = g^x$. Assume also that the parties agree on the (hashed) message $m \in Z_q$ to be signed. Then the signature protocol proceeds as follows.

First a random sharing $[k]$ is generated and $R = g^k$ is revealed, using the RSS and POWOPEN protocols. We then compute $[k^{-1}]$ using Beaver's inversion protocol. The idea is to compute a random $[a]$ and open $[a][k]$ (a is used to blind k). Then $[k^{-1}]$ can be computed locally as $[a] \cdot w^{-1}$.

So we let the parties generate $[a]$ using RSS and then compute $[w] = [a][k]$ and open $[w]$. The multiplication is done as follows: The parties simply compute their shares $w_i = a_i k_i$. This results in shares on a polynomial f_w of degree $2t$ with $f_w(0) = w$. But since $n \geq 2t + 1$ there are enough parties $(2t + 1)$ to interpolate w if they all reveal their shares. To avoid that their shares leak unintended information, they first compute a random degree $2t$ zero sharing $[b] \leftarrow \text{ZSS}(2t)$ and then reveal instead shares $a_i k_i + b_i$. We denote this protocol $w \leftarrow \text{WMULOPEN}([a], [k]; [b])$. The "w" is for "weak", since a single malicious party can cause the protocol to output anything. The only guarantee provided by the protocol is that it reveals no information about a and k, except of course the product ak.

Recall that $[a]$ and $[b]$, being generated using RSS and ZSS, are not known to be consistent sharings at this point. But at least each share b_i is known to be a random value that blinds the share $a_i k_i$, which is not necessarily random.

Note that there is not enough shares for any error detection on w: A single corrupt party could reveal a bad share w_i resulting in the parties ending up with a wrong value of w. To deal with this we use a trick in order to compute an authenticator $W = g^{ak}$. This allows each party to check that $g^w = W$ and abort if not. W is computed as follows: Recall that g^k was correctly computed by POWOPEN. The parties then invoke POWOPEN again, this time using g^k as the base, i.e. they compute $g^{ak} \leftarrow$ POWOPEN$(g^k, [a])$. Since correctness of POWOPEN is ensured as explained above, even if $[a]$ is not a consistent sharing, all honest parties will abort at this point unless $w = ak$.

Finally, given $[x]$, $[k^{-1}]$, $r = F(g^k)$ and the message m to sign, the parties compute the value

$$[s] = [k^{-1}](m + r[x]) \,.$$

Note that this boils down to another multiplication of two degree t sharings, which can be done locally since $n \geq 2t+1$, resulting in a degree $2t$ sharing, Again, to avoid that the shares leak information, a random degree $2t$ zero sharing $[c]$ is created using ZSS and each party reveals $s_i = h_i(m + rx_i) + ci$ where h_i is party P_i's share of k^{-1}.

As before when opening ak, the resulting value s can be recovered from $2t+1$ shares, but when $n = 2t+1$ there is not enough shares to do any error detection. So a single party can introduce any error on s. Before, we detected this by computing correctly the authenticator g^{ak}. This time we instead just lets the parties verify the resulting signature (r, s) on the message m using the public key y. Our analysis below shows that the only way the adversary can make the protocol succeed is by not introducing any fault on s.

Coping with Message Disagreement. To obtain a practical protocol we must make sure that the protocol aborts and no information leaks even if the *honest* parties do not agree on the message m to sign. Suppose that honest party P_1 got message $m + \Delta$ while the other honest parties used m. Then P_1 would reveal $s_1 = h_1(m + \Delta + rx_1) + c_1$. Anyone receiving all shares could then compute $s' = \sum \lambda_i s_i = s + \lambda_1 h_1 \Delta$ (where λ_i are the Lagrange coefficients). This shows that if an adversary could introduce an error on the message used by an honest party and somehow obtain the correct signature s then that party's share of k would have leaked.

To avoid this, the parties could of course send the message to each other and abort if there is any mismatch, and then proceed by opening s. But for efficiency, we would like a protocol that only requires one round once the message is known. To achieve this, we do as follows: During the initial rounds, we generate not just one zero-sharing $[c]$, but two degree $2t$ sharings of zero, $[d]$, $[e]$, using ZSS$(2t)$. When signing we then compute

$$[s] = [k^{-1}](m + r[x]) + [d] + m[e] \,.$$

If all parties are honest and agree on m then $[d]+m[e] = [0]$. If not, then $[d]+m[e]$ turns into a random pad that completely hides the honest parties shares s_i and ensures that the verification will fail. Note that $[d]$ and $[e]$ may not be zero, or may even be inconsistent, but it is guaranteed that each share of d and e are at least random, which is all that we need here.

Simulation. The simulator uses the same simulation strategy when simulating $R \leftarrow \texttt{POWOPEN}(g, [k])$ as when simulating $y \leftarrow \texttt{POWOPEN}(g, [x])$, i.e., where Lagrange interpolation "in the coefficient" allows to patch the honest parties' values g^{k_i}. The use of a uniformly random $[a]$ to blind $[k]$ means that the simulator can run $W \leftarrow \texttt{POWOPEN}(R, [a])$ and $w \leftarrow \texttt{WMULOPEN}([a], [k]; [b])$ without patching. Finally, $s \leftarrow \texttt{WMULOPEN}([k^{-1}], [m + rx]; [c])$ can be simulated because the simulator knows the correct value s as well as the corrupted parties' shares s_j of s (these are defined by the simulators choice of the corrupted parties's shares of k, a, b, d, e). This fixes $t + 1$ points on the a degree $2t$ polynomial f_s over which s is shared, and because $[s]$ includes the random zero sharing $[c]$ which effectively randomizes the polynomial, the simulator can simulate by picking a random degree $2t$ polynomial as long as it is consistent with these $t + 1$ points.

We emphasize that the simulation is in fact perfect as it relies on no computational assumptions and works even when Z_q and G are small.

Security. This completes our informal description of the protocol. We informally state security of the protocol in the following theorem. A full UC-proof (including a proof that re-running the protocol a reasonable number of times if it aborts) can be found in the full version of this paper [10].

Theorem 1 *(informal). The described protocol for ECDSA signatures achieves perfect UC-security with abort against a static, malicious adversary corrupting at most t parties if the total number of parties n satisfies $n \geq 2t + 1$.*

3   Fairness in the Online Phase

Unlike Gennaro et al. [18] (but like the ECDSA protocols for dishonest majority [13,16,24,26,27]) our basic protocol described above has no fairness or termination guarantee. So the adversary gets to see the signature r, s and may then abort the protocol before any honest party receives the signature. In practice, parties will retry on abort and the adversary may therefore end up with several valid signatures $(r_1, s_1), \ldots (r_L, s_L)$ on message M without any of the honest parties knowing any of these signatures.

This is of course not a forgery, since it can only happen with messages that the honest parties actually intended to sign. But it may nevertheless be unacceptable in some applications. For example if presenting a fresh signature allows to transfer a certain additional amount of money from someone's bank account.

Since we assume an honest majority it is indeed possible to achieve fairness. In fact, our basic protocol can be extended with just two additional pre-processing rounds in order to achieve fairness. The main idea is that in addition to R and

$[k^{-1}]$ the parties also prepare a sharing of $[x \cdot k^{-1}]$ in the pre-processing. Doing so, $[s]$ can be computed as $[s] = m[k^{-1}] + r[xk^{-1}]$, using only *linear* operations. Taking this one step further, by reducing the degree of $[x \cdot k^{-1}]$ to t and turning both $[k^{-1}]$ and $[xk^{-1}]$ into suitable *verifiable* secret sharings [28], we achieve the property that online, when M is known, the signature can be computed given only $t + 1$ correct shares and the correctness of each share can be validated.

The extended protocol works as follows. Let $[[a]]_t$ denote a verifiable secret sharing (VSS) of a, that is, every party is committed to his share of a via a Pedersen commitment, and shares are guaranteed to be consistent with a polynomial of degree at most t. Such sharings are additive, we have $[[a]] + [[x]] = [[a+x]]$, where addition denotes local addition of shares and commitment opening data [28].

To create a verifiable secret sharing $[[s]]_t$, a party P commits to the coefficients of a polynomial f of degree at most t, including a commitment to s that plays the role of the degree 0 coefficient. Now anyone can compute a commitment to $f(i)$ for $i = 1 \dots n$ using the homomorphic property of commitments. P sends privately opening information for this commitment to P_i. In the next round, P_i will complain if what he gets does not match his commitment. In the same way, we can get a pair $[[s]]_t, [[s]]_{2t}$ if P uses the same commitment to s in both VSSs. If each party P_j creates $[[s_j]]_t, [[s_j]]_{2t}$ in this way, we can add them all and get $[[s]]_t, [[s]]_{2t}$ where s is random and unknown to the adversary.

Using this in the context of our threshold signature protocol, we can assume that we have $[[x]]_t$ once and for all from the key generation phase. Using our protocol as described before, we can create r and $[k^{-1}]$. Now, the goal of the following subprotocol is to start from $[[x]]_t$ and $[k^{-1}]$ and obtain $[[k^{-1}x]]_t$.

So we do the following:

1. At the start of the entire protocol, each party will send his contribution to creating a pair $[[s]]_t, [[s]]_{2t}$ and one VSS $[[b]]_t$ as described above, to all other parties. In the following round, the objects $[[s]]_t, [[s]]_{2t}, [[b]]_t$ can be computed (or we abort). Therefore we can assume that when $[k^{-1}]$ is ready, the VSSs are also ready. We can also assume that each party P_i has committed to his share k_i in k^{-1}, as he can do this as soon as he knows this share.
2. Now, each P_i opens the difference between k_i and his share of b to all parties.
3. If the set of opened differences are consistent with a degree t polynomial, we continue, else we abort. Adjust the commitments to shares in $[[b]]_t$ using the opened differences to get $[[k^{-1}]]_t$ (only local computation). Now each party commits to the product of his share in k^{-1} and in x and does a standard ZK proof that this was done correctly. This implicitly forms $[[k^{-1}x]]_{2t}$. He also opens the difference between his share in $k^{-1}x$ and in $[[s]]_{2t}$.
4. Using the differences just opened, all parties reconstruct $k^{-1}x - s$ and add this $[[s]]_t$ so we now have $[[k^{-1}x]]_t$.
5. Finally, each party broadcasts a hash of his public view of the protocol so far (i.e., all the messages that he received and which were supposed to be sent to all parties) together with "OK" if he thinks the protocol went well so far.

Each party aborts unless he gets an "OK" from all other parties and the hash of his own public view matches the hashes he receives from all other parties.

Given this, once the message M is known, the parties can compute $m = H(M)$ and $[[s]]_t = m \cdot [[k^{-1}]]_t + r \cdot [[k^{-1}x]]_t$ using only local operations. To output the signature (r, s) each party sends r along with its share of s and the corresponding commitment opening to the receiver. Since the degree of $[[s]]_t$ is t the receiver only needs $t + 1$ correct shares, and by verifying the commitment of each share, the receiver knows which shares are correct. Since we assume $n \geq 2t + 1$ we know that at least $t + 1$ parties are honest, and thus the receiver is guaranteed to get the signature.

In other words, we get the desired property that either the protocol aborts during pre-processing and neither the adversary nor any other party gets the signature, or intended receiver(s) are guaranteed to get the signature.[3]

4   Performance

In this section we elaborate the performance of our basic protocol (with abort).

The protocol requires four rounds of interaction between the servers to generate a signature. But the first three rounds can be processed before the message to be signed is known.

We let a *presignature* denote the value R and the sharings $[k^{-1}], [e], [d]$ produced during the first three rounds. Each party can save R and its shares of k^{-1}, e, d under a unique presignature id (such as R). When the message M is known, the parties need only then agree on a presignature id in order to complete the signature protocol in one round.

The protocol is designed to run with any number of $n \geq 2t + 1$ parties. Recall that a random element $r \in Z_q$ can be represented using $\log_2 q$ bits and an element in $G \subset Z_p \times Z_p$ using $\log_2 p$ bits (roughly) using point compression. The protocol is constant-round and the communication complexity is $O(\kappa n^2)$ assuming that both $\log p$ and $\log q$ are proportional to a security parameter κ.

For a small number of parties, unless special hardware acceleration is available, the computational bottleneck is likely to be the "long" curve exponentiations, i.e., computing g^r for random values $r \in Z_q$. However, each party only needs to do a constant number of these operations. The constants are quite small as shown in Table 1.[4]

For large n, since the protocol is constant round, the $O(n^2)$ amount of arithmetics in Z_q that each does, will eventually become the bottleneck. In this case,

---

[3] It still holds that no interaction is required among the parties in the online phase. But the trick used in our basic protocol of blinding $[s]$ with $m[d] + [e]$ only works for degree $2t$ sharings. So unlike our basic protocol, we here require that the honest parties agree on M.

[4] Interpolating in the exponent requires $t + 1$ exponentiations, but the exponents in this case are Lagrange coefficients, which for realistic parameters are quite small. For example, for $n = 3$ and $t = 1$ the exponents are $(\lambda_1, \lambda_2) = (-1, 2)$, and so these are not considered "long" curve multiplications.

Table 1. Concrete performance

Protocol	Bits sent per party	Long curve multiplications per party
KEYGEN	$n \log q + n \log p$	1
PRESIG	$6n \log q + 2n \log p$	3
SIGN	$n \log q$	2

a more efficient protocol can be obtained by using hyperinvertible matrices [2] to improve performance of RSS and the (passively secure) multiplication of w and s. Note however, that $O(n^2)$ communication is still required for POWOPEN.

For small n we can save bandwidth and one round by computing the sharings $[k], [a], [b], [e], [d]$ using *pseudo-random* secret sharing [8].

4.1 Benchmarks

In order to determine the actual performance of our protocol we have implemented it and run a number of benchmarks. We have done several things to ensure that our benchmarks best reflect a real deployment scenario.

First, we benchmark the *client-server* setting where we include the time it takes for an external client to initiate the protocol by sending a request to the parties and receive a response when the operation is done. Also, we ensure that the parties are connected with secure channels. Note that this requires an additional round trip and computation for key agreement using mechanisms from the Noise Protocol framework [29]. We also let each party store its key shares in encrypted form in a PostgreSQL database. For elliptic curve operations we use OpenSSL v1.1.1b which provides the required timing attack resistant implementation for long curve multiplications. However when no secret values are involved we use the faster version also provided by OpenSSL. In the latter case we use precomputation to speed up the curve multiplication when using the default generator for the given elliptic curve.

Finally, as mentioned above, we split the protocol up in pre-processing and online processing. Hence we benchmark the individual operations (1) keygen, (2) presig, and (3) sign.

Latency. For a threshold signature scheme to be useful in practice it is important that a user should not be forced to wait for minutes before his key is generated or before he receives the signature that he requested.

To measure the latency we deploy each party on a separate m5.xlarge Amazon EC2 instance. Each instance runs CoreOS with two Docker containers: One with the actual implementation of the threshold protocol party, implemented in Java, and another container with a PostgreSQL instance for storing key and presignature shares.

We then let a single client issue a single requests to the servers, causing the servers to generate a single key, presignature or signature. In this benchmark, the servers are configured to use a single worker thread, i.e., each server uses only one CPU core for executing the protocol (including computing the long curve multiplications).

We run this benchmark for various combinations of parties and security thresholds, in both the LAN setting and the WAN setting. In the LAN setting all servers are located in the same Amazon region, where the network latency is usually less than 1 ms, whereas in the WAN setting the servers are located in different regions (Frankfurt, California, Tokyo) where package latency is often in the order of 50–200 ms.[5]

Table 2 shows the average time it takes for the keygen, presig and sign requests to finish in these settings after a number of warm-up requests. In the keygen operation, a client sends a keygen request to the servers, which run the keygen protocol and return a key id to the client. In the presig operation, a client sends a presig request to the servers which then generate the presignature and return a presignature id to the client. In the sign operation, the client sends a key id and a presignature id to the servers (for a key and a presignature that have previously been generated), and the servers then compute and return their signature shares to the client who recombines and verifies the signature.

It can be seen that in the LAN setting the latency increases with the number of parties and the security threshold. This is because the amount of work, especially the number of long curve multiplications that each party must compute, increases (quadratically) with the number of parties, and with low network latency, this is significant for the overall latency. In the WAN setting, however, the network latency is high enough that it almost completely dominates the overall latency. (At least for up to 9 parties. Adding parties, the latency caused by local computation will eventually dominate also in the WAN setting.)

Table 2. Latency per operation

n, t	LAN			WAN		
	keygen	presig	sign	keygen	presig	sign
3, 1	28.2 ms	34.2 ms	19.9 ms	1.22 s	1.47 s	0.73 s
5, 2	39.9 ms	44.8 ms	25.0 ms	1.47 s	1.71 s	0.98 s
7, 3	54.6 ms	60.0 ms	30.8 ms	1.48 s	1.72 s	0.98 s
9, 4	66.4 ms	74.0 ms	34.8 ms	1.48 s	1.72 s	1.00 s

Throughput. In realistic deployments, as mentioned above, a threshold signature scheme like ours will often run in the *client-server* setting with many concurrent

---

[5] In the WAN setting, since we use only three different regions, with $n > 3$ this means that some of the parties run in the same region. However, since the overall latency of the protocol is determined by the pair-wise connection with the *largest* latency, this makes no difference.

key generation and signature protocol instances on behalf of clients. We therefore measure the throughput, that is, the number of operations that the servers can handle per second in this setting.

It is likely that signing will happen more often than key generation. If for example BIP-32 key derivation [34] is used, key generation is only run once to obtain a sharing of the master key whereas subsequent keys are derived in an efficient non-interactive manner.

Also, given already computed presignatures, generating the final signature is a lightweight operation for the servers, since signing for the servers then only imply a few local operations in Z_q and sending a share of s to the client who verifies it. For these reasons, in a real deployment, we expect that presignature generation will be the overall bottleneck with respect to throughput. We therefore focus on presignature generation in this benchmark.

We run this benchmark with tree servers ($n = 3$) and security threshold $t = 1$. To best reflect an actual real-world deployment, each server consists of a load balancer (haproxy), a database server (PostgreSQL), and a number of worker hosts. Clients contact the load balancer using a secure channel. The load balancer ensures that the workload is distributed evenly among the workers based on the key id. All workers connect to the database server where the key shares are stored in encrypted form. Load balancer, database server and workers as well as all clients run on separate m5.xlarge Amazon EC2 instances (4 vCPUs, 16 GiB memory) in the same Amazon region.

Figure 1 illustrates this deployment: A client requests a presignature by contacting the three servers. Based on the given key id, one worker at each server is assigned the task (marked with bold lines). These workers then execute the presignature generation protocol and returns the presignature id to the client.

To benchmark, once the servers are ready, we spin up enough clients, each client sending a lot of presig requests to the server, such that the servers are completely busy and no increase in throughput is achieved by adding more clients. Table 3 shows the resulting throughput in the case where each client requests a single presignature per request as well as in the case where each client requests 100 presignatures in per request.

As expected, throughput scales almost linearly with the number of workers used by each server.

On m5.xlarge we have benchmarked that each (timing attack resistant) long curve multiplication occupies a core (i.e., 2 vCPU) for roughly 0.5 ms. Since each presig requires three multiplication, if these were the only thing to compute, we would expect 2 multiplications per ms or 666 presig/s.

In the batched setting where 100 presignatures are computed per client request, we are close to this limit and the bottleneck clearly is the CPU required to do the long curve multiplications, getting a throughput of roughly 600 presig/s. Thus, for each additional m5.xlarge worker, the system can handle roughly 600 extra presignatures per second.

In the case where only a single presignature is computed per request, the throughput is lower, since the servers must spend a larger fraction of their

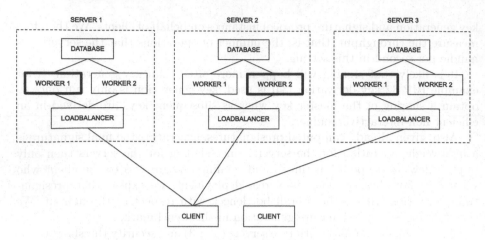

Fig. 1. A deployment in the client-server setting with three servers and two workers per server.

resources by handling the many active sessions. In this case each worker can handle roughly 150 additional presigs per second.

Table 3. Throughput for presignature generation

Workers per server	1 presig per request	100 presigs per request
2	347 presig/s	1,249 presig/s
4	649 presig/s	2,464 presig/s
6	919 presig/s	3,606 presig/s

A   Basic Tools and Definitions

A.1   Signature Schemes

Recall that a signature scheme is defined by three efficient algorithms: $pk, sk \leftarrow \mathtt{Gen}(1^\kappa)$; $\sigma \leftarrow \mathtt{Sign}_{sk}(M)$; $b \leftarrow \mathtt{Verify}_{pk}(M, \sigma)$ [22]. A signature scheme satisfies two properties:

- *Correctness.* With overwhelmingly high probability (in the security parameter κ) it must hold that all valid signatures must verify.
- *Existential unforgeability.* This is modeled with the following game $\mathsf{G_{FORGE}}$:
  - Run $pk, sk \leftarrow \mathtt{Gen}(1^\kappa)$; input pk to the adversary A.
  - On $(\mathtt{SIGN}, M)$ from A:
    Return $\sigma \leftarrow \mathtt{Sign}_{sk}(M)$ to A and add M to a set Q.

- On $(\texttt{FORGE}, M', \sigma')$ from A:

  If $M' \notin Q$ and $\texttt{Verify}_{pk}(M', \sigma') = \top$, output $\top$ and halt; else output $\bot$ and halt.

The signature scheme is existentially unforgeable if for any PPT A the probability $\Pr[\mathsf{G}_{\texttt{FORGE}} = \top]$ is negligible in κ. That is, even with access to a signing oracle, no adversary can produce a valid signature.

A correct and existentially unforgeable signature scheme is simply called secure.

A.2   The DSA/ECDSA Standard

An instance of the DSA signature scheme [21,23] has the parameters

$$(G, q, g, H, F) \leftarrow \texttt{Gen}(1^\kappa)$$

where G is a cyclic group of order q with generator $g \in G$, H a hash function $H : \{0,1\}^* \mapsto Z_q$ and F a function $F : G \mapsto Z_q$.

For $a, b \in G$ we will let ab denote the group operation (multiplicative notation). For $c \in Z_q$ and $g \in G$ we let g^c denote $gg \cdots g$, i.e., the group operation applied c times on g.

A key pair is generated by sampling uniformly the private key $x \in Z_q$ and computing the public key as $y = g^x$. Given a message $M \in \{0,1\}^*$ a signature is computed as follows: Let $m = H(M)$. Pick a random $k \in Z_q$, set $R = g^k$, $r = F(R)$, $s = k^{-1}(m + rx)$. The resulting signature is r, s. Given a public key y, a message M and signature r, s, one can verify the signature by computing $m = H(M)$ and checking that $r = F(g^{ms^{-1}} y^{rs^{-1}})$.

In DSA G is Z_p for some prime $p > q$. In ECDSA G is generated by a point g on an elliptic curve over Z_p for some $p > q$. In this case $F : G \mapsto Z_q$ is the function that given $R = (R_x, R_y) \in G \subset Z_p \times Z_p$ outputs $R_x \mod q$.

ECDSA has been proved secure in the Generic Group Model assuming that computing the discrete log in G is hard, and assuming that H is collision resistant and uniform [4].

Our protocol works for both DSA and ECDSA. In particular, it is suitable for ECDSA with the "Bitcoin" curve secp256k1 that is believed to have a 128-bit security level.

A.3   Shamir's Secret Sharing

Recall that in Shamir's secret sharing scheme [30] a dealer can secret share a value $m \in Z_q$ (for a prime number q) among n parties by choosing a random degree t polynomial $f(x)$ over Z_q subject to $f(0) = m$. The dealer then sends a share $m_i = f(i)$ to each party P_i. This reveals no information about m as long as at most t parties are corrupted. We will use $[m]$ to denote such a sharing where each party P_i holds a share m_i.

If the dealer is honest, any subset of $t + 1$ parties can reconstruct the secret using Lagrange interpolation. More generally, one can compute the value $f(j)$ for any value $j \in Z_q$ on a degree t polynomial $f()$ using Lagrange interpolation given values $y_i = f(x_i)$ for any $t + 1$ distinct values x_i. For the specific values $f(1), f(2), \ldots, f(t + 1)$ we can efficiently compute $f(j)$ for any $j \in Z_q$ as

$$f(j) = \lambda_1 f(1) + \lambda_2 f(2) + \cdots + \lambda_{t+1} f(t + 1)$$

where the Lagrange coefficients are defined as

$$\lambda_i := \prod_{1 < m < t+1, m \neq i} \frac{j - m}{i - m} .$$

For example, for $n = 3$, $t = 1$ and $j = 3$ we have $\lambda_1 = (3 - 2)/(1 - 2) = -1$ and $\lambda_2 = (3 - 1)/(2 - 1) = 2$ so for any degree-1 polynomial $f(x) = ax + b$ we can compute $f(3) = -1 \cdot f(1) + 2 \cdot f(2)$.

For $g \in G$ we will sometimes do Lagrange interpolation in "the exponent" as follows: For $Y_1 = g^{f(1)}, Y_2 = g^{f(2)}, \ldots, Y_{t+1} = g^{f(t+1)}$ define

$$\texttt{ExpInt}(Y_1, Y_2, \ldots Y_{t+1}; j) := \prod_{i=1}^{t+1} Y_i^{\lambda_i} = g^{\sum_{i=1}^{t+1} \lambda_i y_i} = g^{f(j)} .$$

We will also need to interpolate the value $p(0)$ on a degree $2t$ polynomial $p(x)$ from the $2t + 1$ values $p(1), p(2), \ldots, p(2t + 1)$. We denote this function

$$\texttt{Int2t}(p(1), p(2), \ldots, p(2t + 1)) .$$

Recall that Shamir's secret sharing scheme is linear. This means that once sharings $[m_1]$ and $[m_2]$ are established, and if the parties agree on a public constant $a \in Z_q$ then they can compute $[a \cdot m_1]$ and $[m_1 + m_2]$ efficiently, without communicating. We use $a \cdot [m_1]$ and $[m_1] + [m_2]$ to denote these operations.

References

1. Andresen, G.: BIP-11: M-of-n standard transactions. https://github.com/bitcoin/bips/blob/master/bip-0011.mediawiki. Accessed 15 Apr 2020
2. Beerliová-Trubíniová, Z., Hirt, M.: Perfectly-secure MPC with linear communication complexity. In: Canetti, R. (ed.) TCC 2008. LNCS, vol. 4948, pp. 213–230. Springer, Heidelberg (2008). https://doi.org/10.1007/978-3-540-78524-8_13
3. Boneh, D., Gennaro, R., Goldfeder, S.: Using level-1 homomorphic encryption to improve threshold DSA signatures for bitcoin wallet security. In: Lange, T., Dunkelman, O. (eds.) LATINCRYPT 2017. LNCS, vol. 11368, pp. 352–377. Springer, Cham (2019). https://doi.org/10.1007/978-3-030-25283-0_19
4. Brown, D.R.L.: Generic groups, collision resistance, and ECDSA. Des. Codes Cryptography **35**(1), 119–152 (2005). https://doi.org/10.1007/s10623-003-6154-z
5. Canetti, R., Fischlin, M.: Universally composable commitments. In: Kilian, J. (ed.) CRYPTO 2001. LNCS, vol. 2139, pp. 19–40. Springer, Heidelberg (2001). https://doi.org/10.1007/3-540-44647-8_2

6. Castagnos, G., Catalano, D., Laguillaumie, F., Savasta, F., Tucker, I.: Two-party ECDSA from hash proof systems and efficient instantiations. In: Boldyreva, A., Micciancio, D. (eds.) CRYPTO 2019, Part III. LNCS, vol. 11694, pp. 191–221. Springer, Cham (2019). https://doi.org/10.1007/978-3-030-26954-8_7

7. Chida, K., et al.: Fast large-scale honest-majority MPC for malicious adversaries. In: Shacham, H., Boldyreva, A. (eds.) CRYPTO 2018, Part III. LNCS, vol. 10993, pp. 34–64. Springer, Cham (2018). https://doi.org/10.1007/978-3-319-96878-0_2

8. Cramer, R., Damgård, I., Ishai, Y.: Share conversion, pseudorandom secret-sharing and applications to secure computation. In: Kilian, J. (ed.) TCC 2005. LNCS, vol. 3378, pp. 342–362. Springer, Heidelberg (2005). https://doi.org/10.1007/978-3-540-30576-7_19

9. Dalskov, A.P.K., Keller, M., Orlandi, C., Shrishak, K., Shulman, H.: Securing DNSSEC keys via threshold ECDSA from generic MPC. IACR Cryptology ePrint Archive, vol. 2019, p. 889 (2019). https://eprint.iacr.org/2019/889

10. Damgård, I., Jakobsen, T.P., Nielsen, J.B., Pagter, J.I., Østergård, M.B.: Fast threshold ECDSA with honest majority. IACR Cryptology ePrint Archive, vol. 2020, p. 501 (2020). https://eprint.iacr.org/2020/501

11. Desmedt, Y.: Society and group oriented cryptography: a new concept. In: Pomerance, C. (ed.) CRYPTO 1987. LNCS, vol. 293, pp. 120–127. Springer, Heidelberg (1988). https://doi.org/10.1007/3-540-48184-2_8

12. Desmedt, Y., Frankel, Y.: Threshold cryptosystems. In: Brassard, G. (ed.) CRYPTO 1989. LNCS, vol. 435, pp. 307–315. Springer, New York (1990). https://doi.org/10.1007/0-387-34805-0_28

13. Doerner, J., Kondi, Y., Lee, E., Shelat, A.: Secure two-party threshold ECDSA from ECDSA assumptions. In: 2018 IEEE Symposium on Security and Privacy, SP 2018, Proceedings, San Francisco, California, USA, 21–23 May 2018, pp. 980–997. IEEE Computer Society (2018). https://doi.org/10.1109/SP.2018.00036

14. Doerner, J., Kondi, Y., Lee, E., Shelat, A.: Threshold ECDSA from ECDSA assumptions: the multiparty case. In: 2019 IEEE Symposium on Security and Privacy, SP 2019, San Francisco, CA, USA, 19–23 May 2019, pp. 1051–1066. IEEE (2019). https://doi.org/10.1109/SP.2019.00024

15. Furukawa, J., Lindell, Y., Nof, A., Weinstein, O.: High-throughput secure three-party computation for malicious adversaries and an honest majority. In: Coron, J.-S., Nielsen, J.B. (eds.) EUROCRYPT 2017, Part II. LNCS, vol. 10211, pp. 225–255. Springer, Cham (2017). https://doi.org/10.1007/978-3-319-56614-6_8

16. Gennaro, R., Goldfeder, S.: Fast multiparty threshold ECDSA with fast trustless setup. In: Lie, D., Mannan, M., Backes, M., Wang, X. (eds.) Proceedings of the 2018 ACM SIGSAC Conference on Computer and Communications Security, CCS 2018, Toronto, ON, Canada, 15–19 October 2018, pp. 1179–1194. ACM (2018). https://doi.org/10.1145/3243734.3243859

17. Gennaro, R., Goldfeder, S., Narayanan, A.: Threshold-optimal DSA/ECDSA signatures and an application to bitcoin wallet security. In: Manulis, M., Sadeghi, A.-R., Schneider, S. (eds.) ACNS 2016. LNCS, vol. 9696, pp. 156–174. Springer, Cham (2016). https://doi.org/10.1007/978-3-319-39555-5_9

18. Gennaro, R., Jarecki, S., Krawczyk, H., Rabin, T.: Robust threshold DSS signatures. In: Maurer, U. (ed.) EUROCRYPT 1996. LNCS, vol. 1070, pp. 354–371. Springer, Heidelberg (1996). https://doi.org/10.1007/3-540-68339-9_31

19. Gennaro, R., Jarecki, S., Krawczyk, H., Rabin, T.: Secure distributed key generation for discrete-log based cryptosystems. In: Stern, J. (ed.) EUROCRYPT 1999. LNCS, vol. 1592, pp. 295–310. Springer, Heidelberg (1999). https://doi.org/10.1007/3-540-48910-X_21

20. Gennaro, R., Jarecki, S., Krawczyk, H., Rabin, T.: Robust threshold DSS signatures. Inf. Comput. **164**(1), 54–84 (2001). https://doi.org/10.1006/inco.2000.2881
21. Johnson, D., Menezes, A., Vanstone, S.A.: The elliptic curve digital signature algorithm (ECDSA). Int. J. Inf. Sec. **1**(1), 36–63 (2001). https://doi.org/10.1007/s102070100002
22. Katz, J., Lindell, Y.: Introduction to Modern Cryptography, 2nd edn. CRC Press, Boca Raton (2014)
23. Kerry, C.F., Secretary, A., Director, C.R.: FIPS PUB 186-4: Digital Signature Standard (DSS), July 2013. http://nvlpubs.nist.gov/nistpubs/FIPS/NIST.FIPS.186-4.pdf
24. Lindell, Y.: Fast secure two-party ECDSA signing. In: Katz, J., Shacham, H. (eds.) CRYPTO 2017, Part II. LNCS, vol. 10402, pp. 613–644. Springer, Cham (2017). https://doi.org/10.1007/978-3-319-63715-0_21
25. Lindell, Y., Nof, A.: A framework for constructing fast MPC over arithmetic circuits with malicious adversaries and an honest-majority. In: Thuraisingham, B.M., Evans, D., Malkin, T., Xu, D. (eds.) Proceedings of the 2017 ACM SIGSAC Conference on Computer and Communications Security, CCS 2017, Dallas, TX, USA, 30 October–03 November 2017, pp. 259–276. ACM (2017). https://doi.org/10.1145/3133956.3133999
26. Lindell, Y., Nof, A.: Fast secure multiparty ECDSA with practical distributed key generation and applications to cryptocurrency custody. In: Lie, D., Mannan, M., Backes, M., Wang, X. (eds.) Proceedings of the 2018 ACM SIGSAC Conference on Computer and Communications Security, CCS 2018, Toronto, ON, Canada, 15–19 October 2018, pp. 1837–1854. ACM (2018). https://doi.org/10.1145/3243734.3243788
27. MacKenzie, P., Reiter, M.K.: Two-party generation of DSA signatures. Int. J. Inf. Secur. **2**(3), 218–239 (2004). https://doi.org/10.1007/s10207-004-0041-0
28. Pedersen, T.P.: Non-interactive and information-theoretic secure verifiable secret sharing. In: Feigenbaum, J. (ed.) CRYPTO 1991. LNCS, vol. 576, pp. 129–140. Springer, Heidelberg (1992). https://doi.org/10.1007/3-540-46766-1_9
29. Perrin, T.: The noise protocol framework (2015). http://www.noiseprotocol.org
30. Shamir, A.: How to share a secret. Commun. ACM **22**(11), 612–613 (1979). https://doi.org/10.1145/359168.359176. http://doi.acm.org/10.1145/359168.359176
31. Shoup, V.: Practical threshold signatures. In: Preneel, B. (ed.) EUROCRYPT 2000. LNCS, vol. 1807, pp. 207–220. Springer, Heidelberg (2000). https://doi.org/10.1007/3-540-45539-6_15
32. Smart, N.P., Talibi Alaoui, Y.: Distributing any elliptic curve based protocol. In: Albrecht, M. (ed.) IMACC 2019. LNCS, vol. 11929, pp. 342–366. Springer, Cham (2019). https://doi.org/10.1007/978-3-030-35199-1_17
33. Stinson, D.R., Strobl, R.: Provably secure distributed Schnorr signatures and a (t, n) threshold scheme for implicit certificates. In: Varadharajan, V., Mu, Y. (eds.) ACISP 2001. LNCS, vol. 2119, pp. 417–434. Springer, Heidelberg (2001). https://doi.org/10.1007/3-540-47719-5_33
34. Wuille, P.: BIP-32: hierarchical deterministic wallets. https://github.com/bitcoin/bips/blob/master/bip-0032.mediawiki. Accessed 15 Apr 2020

Short Threshold Dynamic Group Signatures

Jan Camenisch[1], Manu Drijvers[1], Anja Lehmann[2], Gregory Neven[1],
and Patrick Towa[3,4(✉)]

[1] DFINITY, Zurich, Switzerland
{jan,manu,gregory}@dfinity.org
[2] Hasso-Plattner-Institute, University of Potsdam, Potsdam, Germany
anja.lehmann@hpi.de
[3] IBM Research, Zurich, Switzerland
tow@zurich.ibm.com
[4] DIENS, École Normale Supérieure, CNRS, PSL University, Paris, France

Abstract. Traditional group signatures feature a single issuer who can add users to the group of signers and a single opening authority who can reveal the identity of the group member who computed a signature. Interestingly, despite being designed for privacy-preserving applications, they require strong trust in these central authorities who constitute single points of failure for critical security properties. To reduce the trust placed on authorities, we introduce dynamic group signatures which distribute the role of issuer and opener over several entities, and support t_I-out-of-n_I issuance and t_O-out-of-n_O opening. We first define threshold dynamic group signatures and formalize their security. We then give an efficient construction relying on the pairing-based Pointcheval–Sanders (PS) signature scheme (CT-RSA 2018), which yields very short group signatures of two first-group elements and three field elements. We also give a simpler variant of our scheme in which issuance requires the participation of all n_I issuers, but still supports t_O-out-of-n_O opening. It is based on a new multi-signature variant of the PS scheme which allows for efficient proofs of knowledge and is a result of independent interest. We prove our schemes secure in the random-oracle model under a non-interactive q-type of assumption.

Keywords: Group signatures · Threshold cryptography

1 Introduction

Group signatures [19] are a fundamental cryptographic primitive which allows members of a user group to anonymously sign on behalf of the group after interacting with an issuer. That is, anyone can verify that a signature was computed by a group member, but only a designated authority called opener can reveal the identity of the signer. Variants of group signatures are for instance used for privacy-preserving authentication of Trusted Platform Modules (TPMs) in

© Springer Nature Switzerland AG 2020
C. Galdi and V. Kolesnikov (Eds.): SCN 2020, LNCS 12238, pp. 401–423, 2020.
https://doi.org/10.1007/978-3-030-57990-6_20

user devices [13,14,25,29,45] and of vehicles in Vehicle-to-Vehicle (V2V) and Vehicle-to-Infrastructure (V2I) communication [39,40,46].

The standard definition of group signatures places trust on a single issuer and a single opener. It means that a corrupt issuer can create credentials of which the signatures would open to no group member, and that there is no anonymity against a corrupt opener. For many applications, and in particular for V2V communication, it is simply prohibitive to have a single authority able to issue untraceable credentials or to have a single opener able to trace all users. The standard solution in such cases is to use threshold cryptography [21,43] to distribute the capabilities of the issuer and opener over multiple entities, of whom a threshold number must collaborate to add a user or open a signature.

Many group signature schemes follow a modular "sign-and-encrypt-and-prove" approach [1,3,8], where a user's signing key is a certificate on her identity, and a group signature contains an encryption of her identity and a zero-knowledge proof (bound to the signed message) that the user knows a valid certificate for the encrypted identity. The modular use of encryption to enable opening readily allows for threshold opening: it suffices to replace the underlying encryption scheme with another that supports threshold decryption [21], as Blömer et al. [6] pointed out. Nevertheless, lifting a group-signature scheme to a threshold-issuance setting is not as straightforward.

Short Group Signatures. The most efficient ("GetShorty") group signatures [5, 41] depart from the sign-and-encrypt paradigm though, yielding the shortest signature sizes to date [36]. Instead of adding an encryption of the user's identity to every signature, they rely on the issuer for opening. To reveal the identity of the user that generated a signature, the issuer maintains a list of the membership credentials he has generated and tests the signature against each entry. It makes opening expensive for the benefit of having short signatures, which perfectly fits for all applications where signatures must be short and opening an uncommon practice, such as in V2X communication. A disadvantage of this GetShorty approach is that it merges the roles of issuer and opener into a single party that has to be trusted for anonymity and unforgeability.

Unfortunately, these schemes are difficult to map to a threshold setting. A first problem is that to trace the signatures of a user, her identifier generated during the issuance protocol is necessary. A second issue is that their underlying base signature schemes, namely Camenisch–Lysyanskaya [18] and Pointcheval–Sanders [41,42] signatures, are not a priori suitable to a multi-signer setting as needed to distribute issuance. Indeed, with those signature schemes, all signers would have to agree on a common randomness.

Contributions. In this paper, we propose the first provably-secure group signatures that no longer require trust in single authorities for issuance and opening, but instead distribute their roles over several parties.

Security Model for Threshold Group Signatures. We start by formalizing threshold dynamic group signatures and define their security in the presence of multiple issuers and openers. Our model features a number n_I of issuers and a number n_O of openers separate from the issuers. Any quorum of $t_I + 1$ issuers can add users to the group, whereas no collusion of t_I issuers can generate a valid credential. Besides, any $t_O + 1$ openers can recover the identity of a signer, but anonymity is guaranteed against up to t_O corrupt openers.

Short Threshold Group Signatures. We then present an efficient, provably secure instantiation based on Pointcheval–Sanders (PS) signatures [42]. It shares ideas with the "GetShorty" approach and adapts them to a threshold setting. We show that the roles of issuer and opener can be separate even with this approach, as long as the openers can still access the opening information generated during issuance. Nevertheless, the openers do not partake in the issuance protocol and are the only parties who should be able to retrieve it. The challenge thus consists in making sure, during issuance, that the opening information is correct, and that the openers (and only them) can later retrieve it.

The signatures of our scheme are short as they comprise only 2 first-group elements and 3 exponents. The computation and verification of our group signatures only costs a few exponentiations in the first group and pairing computations (see Sect. 4.2). They respectively consist in proving and verifying knowledge of a PS signature obtained from a threshold number of issuers. The size and computational efficiency of our threshold group signatures therefore make them suitable for practical privacy-preserving applications. We prove our construction secure in the random-oracle model under a non-interactive q-type of assumption.

Simpler Distributed Group Signatures and Multi-signatures. In the full version of this paper [15], we also present a variant of our scheme that requires the participation of all n_I issuers to add users to the group, but still caters for threshold opening. It has the benefit of permitting the corruption of all issuers but one. It is based on a multi-signature variant of the PS scheme that we build therein and prove secure in the plain public-key model (i.e., the signers do not have to prove knowledge of their secret keys) under the same q-assumption. This PS multi-signature scheme constitutes a contribution of independent interest. Multi-signatures compress the signatures of multiple signers on the same message into a single compact signature and are for instance used to optimize consensus protocols in distributed ledgers and blockchains. Unlike existing multi-signature schemes [7,9,37,38], PS multi-signatures allow for efficient zero-knowledge proofs of signatures, making them an interesting tool for the design of privacy-enhancing cryptographic protocols.

Related Work. Soon after their introduction by Chaum and Van Heyst [19], several group-signature schemes were presented, but Bellare, Micciancio and Warinschi [3] were the first to formalize the security properties of static group signatures. Later on, Bellare, Shi and Zhang [4] gave formal security definitions for dynamic group signatures in which users can join the group at any time. Early schemes were based on the strong RSA assumption [1,17], but the focus later shifted to bilinear maps [5,8,11,18,20,32,41] for their better efficiency. Recently, with the possible advent of quantum computers, several group-signature schemes [10,12,31,33,34] have been proposed, but they remain inefficient compared to their pairing-based counterparts in terms of key or signature sizes, and signing cost. Even the scheme of Ling et al. [34] is far from being as efficient as pairing-based schemes, although it is the first scheme with signature size independent of the group size. Moreover, none of the post-quantum schemes so far supports threshold issuance, and building a fully distributed post-quantum group signature scheme is still an open problem.

Ghadafi [28] and Blömer et al. [6] considered group signatures with threshold opening, but did not address the more challenging task of threshold issuance. Manulis [35] introduced democratic group signatures in which there is no group manager. All members must participate to add a user to the group, and any member can open all group signatures, i.e., there is no anonymity within the group. Zheng et al. [47] extended democratic group signatures to enforce that at least a threshold number of members must collaborate to open signatures. In a sense, the extension of democratic group signatures due to Zheng et al. can be viewed as group signature schemes with distributed issuance and threshold opening. However, in addition to the poor anonymity guarantees that they provide, democratic group signature schemes are not applicable to a dynamic setting in which members join the group at a high frequency since public keys must then be refreshed. Furthermore, the public keys and signatures of the constructions of Manulis and of Zheng et al. are linear in the group size, making them impractical.

In their "Coconut" paper [44], Sonnino et al. proposed an anonymous credential system with threshold issuance and selective disclosure of user attributes. Though their techniques to achieve threshold issuance are similar to ours, their solution does not consider the issue of threshold opening, and therefore leaves aside the difficulty of realizing both threshold issuance and threshold opening while having short signatures. Besides, the authors do not provide a security model to analyze the security of their scheme. They only informally state properties that a scheme with threshold issuance and selective disclosure should satisfy, and then argue that their scheme does.

Gennaro, Goldfeder and Ithurburn recently proposed [26] extensions of the BBS [8] and CL [18] group-signature schemes that support threshold issuance. To achieve threshold opening, since those schemes follow the sign-and-encrypt paradigm, the authors point out that it suffices to replace the underlying encryption scheme with a threshold one as did Ghadafi [28] and Blömer et al. [6]. Nonetheless, this paradigm results in large signatures as explained above. Furthermore, Gennaro et al. do not provide a security model for threshold group-signature schemes. For the BBS scheme, they give a simulation argument for their threshold issuance protocol. For the CL scheme, they give a game-based proof that an adversary controlling less than a threshold number of parties cannot issue new credentials. Without a model that takes into account all the other aspects of group signatures scheme, especially threshold opening, it is difficult to grasp the exact security guarantees of their schemes.

2   Preliminaries

This section introduces the notations used throughout the paper, as well as the hardness assumptions and building blocks on which our constructions rely.

2.1   Notation

Vectors are denoted in bold font. For an integer $n \geq 1$, $[n]$ denotes the set $\{1, \ldots, n\}$. For an integer k, $\binom{[n]}{k}$ represents the set of subsets of $[n]$ of cardinality k. If $k \leq 0$ or $k > n$, then $\binom{[n]}{k} := \emptyset$. The notation $\binom{[n]}{\leq k}$ stands for the set of subsets of $[n]$ of cardinality no greater than k. Given a group $\mathbb{G}$ with neutral element $1_{\mathbb{G}}$, $\mathbb{G}^*$ denotes $\mathbb{G} \backslash \{1_{\mathbb{G}}\}$.

2.2   Pairing Groups

An asymmetric pairing group consists of a tuple $(p, \mathbb{G}, \tilde{\mathbb{G}}, \mathbb{G}_T, e)$ such that p is a prime number, $\mathbb{G}$, $\tilde{\mathbb{G}}$ and $\mathbb{G}_T$ are p-order groups, and such that $e: \mathbb{G} \times \tilde{\mathbb{G}} \to \mathbb{G}_T$ is a pairing, i.e., an efficiently computable non-degenerate ($e \neq 1_{\mathbb{G}_T}$, i.e., the constant map to $1_{\mathbb{G}_T}$) bilinear map. Type-3 pairing groups are pairing groups for which there is no efficiently computable homomorphism from $\tilde{\mathbb{G}}$ to $\mathbb{G}$.

2.3   Hardness Assumptions

Strong Diffie–Hellman Assumption. Pointcheval and Sanders introduced [42] a new non-interactive q-type of assumption that they called the Modified q-Strong Diffie–Hellman (q-MSDH-1) assumption. They proved that it holds in the generic bilinear group model.

Definition 1 (q-MSDH-1 Assumption). *Let* G *be a type-3 pairing-group generator. The q-MSDH-1 assumption over* G *is that for all PPT adversary* $\mathcal{A}$, *for all* $\lambda \in \mathbb{N}$, *for all* $\Gamma = \left(p, \mathbb{G}, \tilde{\mathbb{G}}, \mathbb{G}_T, e\right) \leftarrow \mathsf{G}\left(1^{\lambda}\right)$, *given* Γ, $g \in_R \mathbb{G}^*$, $\tilde{g} \in_R \tilde{\mathbb{G}}^*$, *and two tuples* $\left(g^{x^{\ell}}, \tilde{g}^{x^{\ell}}\right)_{\ell=0}^{q} \in (\mathbb{G} \times \tilde{\mathbb{G}})^{q+1}$ *and* $(g^a, \tilde{g}^a, \tilde{g}^{ax}) \in \mathbb{G} \times \tilde{\mathbb{G}}^2$ *for* $x, a \in_R \mathbb{Z}_p^*$, *the probability that* $\mathcal{A}$ *computes a tuple* $\left(w, P, h^{1/x+w}, h^{a/P(x)}\right)$, *with* $h \in \mathbb{G}^*$, P *a polynomial in* $\mathbb{Z}_p[X]$ *of degree at most* q *and* $w \in \mathbb{Z}_p$ *such that the polynomials* $X + w$ *and* P *are coprime, is negligible.*

Symmetric Discrete-Logarithm Assumption. The following assumption a generalization of the standard discrete-logarithm assumption to bilinear-group structures.

Definition 2 (Symmetric Discrete-Logarithm Assumption). *Let* G *be a type-3 pairing-group group generator. The Symmetric Discrete-Logarithm (SDL) assumption [5] over* G *is that for all PPT adversary* $\mathcal{A}$, *for all* $\lambda \in \mathbb{N}$ $\Gamma = \left(p, \mathbb{G}, \tilde{\mathbb{G}}, \mathbb{G}_T, e\right) \leftarrow \mathsf{G}\left(1^{\lambda}\right)$, $g \in_R G^*$, $\tilde{g} \in_R \tilde{\mathbb{G}}^*$, $x \in_R \mathbb{Z}_p^*$, *given* $(\Gamma, g, \tilde{g}, g^x, \tilde{g}^x)$ *as an input, the probability that* $\mathcal{A}$ *returns* x *is negligible.*

Note that given $(\Gamma, g, \tilde{g}, h, \tilde{h})$, one can always verify that it is a valid SDL tuple by testing the equality $e(g, \tilde{h}) = e(\tilde{g}, h)$. Notice also that the SDL assumption is implied by the q-MSDH-1 assumption (Definition 1).

Knowledge-of-Exponent Assumption. Fuchsbauer and Orru introduced an analog of the Diffie–Hellman Knowledge-of-Exponent assumption [2] in an asymmetric setting called the Asymmetric Diffie–Hellman Knowledge-of-Exponent assumption [24]. It is primarily used in the context of subversion-resistant non-interactive witness-indistinguishable proofs.

Definition 3 (Asymmetric Diffie–Hellman Knowledge-of-Exponent Assumption). *The (first-group) Asymmetric Diffie–Hellman Knowledge-of-Exponent (ADH-KE) game, parametrized by $\lambda \in \mathbb{N}$, for a type-3 pairing-group generator* G, *an adversary* $\mathcal{A}$ *and an extractor* Ext *is defined as follows:*

- $\Gamma := (p, \mathbb{G}, \tilde{\mathbb{G}}, \mathbb{G}_T, e) \leftarrow \mathsf{G}(1^\lambda); \ g \in_R \mathbb{G}^*$
- $(X, Y, Z) \leftarrow \mathcal{A}(\Gamma, g)$
- $s \leftarrow \mathsf{Ext}(\Gamma, g, X, Y, Z)$
- *return* $b \leftarrow \left(g^s \neq X \wedge g^s \neq Y \wedge Z = Y^{\mathrm{dlog}_g(X)}\right).$

In other words, $\mathcal{A}$ *wins the game if* (g, X, Y, Z) *is a Diffie–Hellman tuple, but algorithm* Ext *can extract neither* $\mathrm{dlog}_g(X)$ *nor* $\mathrm{dlog}_g(Y)$.

The ADH-KE assumption over a type-3 pairing-group generator G *is that there exists an efficient algorithm* Ext *such that for all efficient adversary* $\mathcal{A}$ *for the ADH-KE game,* $\Pr[b = 1]$ *is negligible in* λ.

2.4   Signatures

A signature scheme consists of 4 algorithms: a setup algorithm $\mathsf{Setup}(1^\lambda) \to pp$, a key-generation algorithm $\mathsf{KG}(pp) \to (vk, sk)$, a signing algorithm $\mathsf{Sign}(sk, m) \to \sigma$ and a verification algorithm $\mathsf{Verf}(vk, m, \sigma) \to \{0, 1\}$.

2.5   Pointcheval–Sanders Signature Scheme

Pointcheval and Sanders [42] proposed an efficient signature scheme that allows to sign message blocks $(m_1, \ldots, m_k)$ at once, and also to efficiently prove knowledge of signatures in zero-knowledge. They proved this scheme to be existential unforgeable under the q-MDSH-1 assumption [42] stated in Definition 1.

Given a type-3 pairing-group generator G and security parameter $\lambda \in \mathbb{N}$, the PS-signature scheme in a pairing-group $\Gamma = \left(p, \mathbb{G}, \tilde{\mathbb{G}}, \mathbb{G}_T, e\right) \leftarrow \mathsf{G}(1^\lambda)$ consists of the following algorithms.

$\mathsf{PS.Setup}(1^\lambda, \Gamma, k) \to pp$: generate $\tilde{g} \in \tilde{\mathbb{G}}^*$. Return $pp \leftarrow (\Gamma, \tilde{g}, k)$.
$\mathsf{PS.KG}(pp) \to (vk, sk)$: generate $x, y_1, \ldots, y_{k+1} \in_R \mathbb{Z}_p$, compute $\tilde{X} \leftarrow \tilde{g}^x$, $\tilde{Y}_j \leftarrow \tilde{g}^{y_j}$ for $j \in [k+1]$, and set and return $vk \leftarrow (\tilde{X}, \tilde{Y}_1, \ldots, \tilde{Y}_{k+1})$ and $sk \leftarrow (x, y_1, \ldots, y_{k+1})$.

PS.Sign $(sk, (m_1, \ldots, m_k)) \to \sigma$: choose $h \in_R \mathbb{G}^*$, $m' \in_R \mathbb{Z}_p$ and return the tuple $\left(m', h, h^{x + \sum_{j=1}^{k} y_j m_j + y_{k+1} m'}\right)$.

PS.Verf $(vk, (m_1, \ldots, m_k), \sigma) \to b$: parse σ as (m', σ_1, σ_2), verify that $\sigma_1 \neq 1_{\mathbb{G}}$ and that $e\left(\sigma_1, \tilde{X} \prod_{j=1}^{k} \tilde{Y}_j^{m_j} \tilde{Y}_{k+1}^{m'}\right) = e(\sigma_2, \tilde{g})$. If so, return 1, otherwise return 0.

In the random oracle model, the scheme remains secure under the same assumption if m' is computed as $\mathcal{H}(m_1, \ldots, m_k)$ [42, Corollary 12]. Noticing that the verification algorithm does *not* verify any property on m', and in particular that $m' = \mathcal{H}(m_1, \ldots, m_k)$, the scheme still allows for efficient zero-knowledge proofs of knowledge if m' is computed as such.

3 Threshold Dynamic Group Signatures

This section formally defines threshold dynamic group signatures. Classical dynamic group signatures [4] allow users to join a group of signers at any time by interacting with an issuer, and then sign anonymously on behalf of the group. A verifier is then assured that a valid signature stems from a group member but cannot infer any information about her identity. Only a dedicated authority, the opener, can recover the identity of a member who computed a valid signature.

In terms of security, group signatures should guarantee anonymity even in the presence of a corrupt issuer and unforgeability (also known as traceability) even when the opener is corrupt. Still, trust in each entity is necessary for the respective properties. It is even worse for schemes in which the roles of issuer and opener are assumed by the same party [11, 16] who then has to be trusted for both anonymity and unforgeability. This holds in particular for the GetShorty-type of signatures [5, 41] which yield the most efficient instantiations to date.

The capabilities of the issuer and the opener are here distributed over several entities to prevent them from becoming single points of failure. To reflect the difference between issuer and opener, two thresholds are introduced: schemes are defined with $n_I > 1$ issuers of whom $t_I + 1 \leq n_I$ are required to add users to the group. Similarly, there are $n_O > 1$ openers and at least $t_O + 1$ openers must collaborate to open a signature and reveal the signer's identity. This distinction of the thresholds is also to account for the fact that in practice, the issuance threshold would typically be lower than the opening threshold. Indeed, the issuance threshold would not be too high to ensure service availability, whereas the opening threshold would be high to protect users' privacy.

First comes the syntax of dynamic group signatures with threshold issuance and threshold opening. The security requirements that can be expected from such schemes are then formalized.

3.1 Syntax

Formally, a (t_I, t_O)-out-of-(n_I, n_O) DGS scheme, or $\binom{n_I, n_O}{t_I, t_O}$-DGS scheme, with identity space *ID* (assumed not to contain $\perp$) consists of the following algorithms:

$\mathsf{GSetup}(1^\lambda, n_I, n_O, t_I, t_O) \to pp$: on the input of a security parameter, a number n_I of issuers, a number n_O of openers and two integer threshold values, generates public parameters which are assumed to be an implicit input to all the other algorithms. Those parameters are also assumed to contain n_I, n_O, t_I and t_O. Moreover, each issuer is assigned a public, fixed index $i \in [n_I]$. Similarly, each opener is assigned a public index $i \in [n_O]$.

$\langle\{\mathsf{IKG}(pp, i)\}_{i=1}^{n_I}\rangle \to \langle\{(ipk, isk_i, st_i)\}_{i=1}^{n_I}\rangle$: a key-generation protocol between all n_I issuers. At the end of the protocol, the issuers agree on a public key, and each of them holds a secret key and a state (initially empty). The state later contains the identities of the users that are added to the group. The issuer public key is used to add users to the group, and to compute and verify group signatures.

$\langle\{\mathsf{OKG}(pp, i)\}_{i=1}^{n_O}\rangle \to \langle\{(opk, osk_i, \mathbf{reg}_i)\}_{i=1}^{n_O}\rangle$: a key-generation protocol run by the openers. At the end of the protocol, the issuers agree on a public opening key opk, an each of them holds a secret key osk_i (assumed to contain i and opk) and a register $\mathbf{reg}_i$ initially empty. The public opening key is needed to add users to the group, and to compute and verify signatures. The secret keys and the registers are needed to open signatures.

The group public key gpk consists of ipk and opk, i.e., $gpk \leftarrow (ipk, opk)$.

$\langle\mathsf{GJoin.U}(id, I, gpk) \rightleftharpoons \{\mathsf{GJoin.I}(st_i, isk_i, id, I, gpk)\}_{i \in I}\rangle \to \langle\mathbf{gsk}[id]/\bot, st_i'\rangle$: is a protocol between a user with identity id and $t_I + 1 =: |I|$ issuers. If $id \in st_i$ for any $i \in [n_I]$, then the ith issuer aborts the protocol. At the end of the protocol, the user algorithm returns a user group secret key $\mathbf{gsk}[id]$ (or $\bot$ if the protocol fails) and the state st_i of each issuer is updated.

$\mathsf{GSign}(gpk, \mathbf{gsk}[id], m) \to \sigma$: a probabilistic algorithm that computes a signature σ on a message m on behalf of the group.

$\mathsf{GVerf}(gpk, m, \sigma) \to b \in \{0, 1\}$: a deterministic algorithm that verifies a group signature σ on a message m w.r.t. to a group public key gpk.

$\langle\{\mathsf{GOpen}(\mathbf{reg}_i, osk_i, O, gpk, m, \sigma)\}_{i \in I}\rangle \to \langle\{id_i/\bot\}_{i \in O}\rangle$: is a protocol between $t_O + 1 =: |O|$ openers, at the end of which each algorithm returns the identity of the user who computed σ on m, or $\bot$ in case of failure. It is here assumed that the openers are given access to public and authentic information from all the successful issuance protocol executions, and that they use it to update their registers. Although this information is public, it is clear that for anonymity to later hold, no information about a signer can be inferred from it without the opener secret keys.

Note that contrarily to the model of Bellare et al. [4], in the model above, each opener maintains a register separate from the state of the issuers. These registers are necessary to open signatures, in addition to the opener secret keys. Those registers should rather be thought as the registers in the model of Bichsel et al. [5].

Correctness. Correctness captures the property that all honest issuers must agree on the same group public key. A signature σ computed on a message m with the secret key of a group-member id should also be accepted by the verification algorithm. Lastly, by executing the opening protocol, any set of $t_O + 1$ openers should all return id. These properties should hold with overwhelming probability regardless of the order in which users are added to the group.

3.2   Security Model

The security requirements for threshold DGS schemes are similar to the conventional ones for dynamic group signatures with a single issuer and a single opener [4], but adapted to a threshold setting. Those requirements are *anonymity*, which guarantees that a group signature reveals no information about the member who computed it, and *traceability*, which expresses the unforgeability property of group signatures.

Essentially, no collusion of t_I issuers should be able to add users and no collusion of t_O openers should be able to open signatures. The definitions are flexible in the sense that they can require an additional fraction of openers to be honest for traceability, and of issuers to be honest for anonymity. This allows for more efficient schemes that may need slightly stronger assumptions to prove their security.

Corruption. The corruption of the authorities is static, i.e., the authorities are corrupted at the beginning of the security experiments. As for the users, they are dynamically corrupted during the experiments.

Global Variables. In the security experiments for $\binom{n_I,n_O}{t_I,t_O}$-DGS schemes, the challenger maintains global variables which are accessible to the experiment oracles (defined hereunder). These variables are a group public gpk, a table of honest-user group secret keys **gsk** of size $|ID|$, and

- Q_{GJoin} a set of user identities id that have joined the group, whether honestly via a GJoin.U query or dishonestly via a GJoin.I_i query
- Q_{Corrupt} a set of user identities id either corrupt from the beginning via a GJoin.I_i query or of which the group secret key has been revealed
- Q_{GSign} a set of signing queries (id, m, σ) made by the adversary and the responses to those
- Q_{GOpen} a set of message–signature pairs (m, σ) for which the adversary has made an opening query.

The sets Q_{GJoin}, Q_{Corrupt}, Q_{GSign} and Q_{GOpen} are initially empty, and the entries of gpk and **gsk** are initially set to $\bot$.

Oracles. This sections describes the oracles in the security experiments for $\binom{n_I,n_O}{t_I,t_O}$-DGS schemes. The oracles have access to global variables priorly defined and maintained by the challenger in each security experiment. Whenever the adversary queries a protocol-algorithm (for joining or opening) oracle, a protocol execution is triggered with all the other honest parties on the same inputs, and the adversary plays the role of the dishonest parties (dishonest users, or dishonest issuers or openers). During these executions, the adversary controls the network, i.e., it can forward, delay, drop or modify the messages sent by the various parties. However, as in prior models [5], protocols can only be executed in sequential order, i.e., the adversary cannot start a protocol execution if all the prior ones have not terminated. In particular, the adversary cannot interleave messages between protocol executions or execute multiple sessions of the same protocol in parallel.

In the following description of the oracles, if a verification fails, the oracle returns $\bot$. It is implicitly assumed that id is always in ID. Given a set Q, the statement "adds x to Q" means that $Q \leftarrow Q \cup \{x\}$. The oracles in the security experiments are then

$\mathcal{O}.\mathsf{GJoin.U}(id, I)$: checks that $I \in \binom{[n_I]}{t_I+1}$. It adds id to Q_{GJoin}. It runs the user joining algorithm on (id, I, gpk). An execution of protocol GJoin is triggered and during it, the challenger plays the role of the (honest) user and of the honest issuers, and the adversary plays the role of the corrupt issuers. At the end of the protocol, if algorithm GJoin.U returns a key $\mathbf{gsk}[id]$, the challenger updates $\mathbf{gsk}$ accordingly.

$\mathcal{O}.\mathsf{GJoin.I}_i(id, I)$: (for each honest issuer i) checks that $i \in I \in \binom{[n_I]}{t_I+1}$. It adds id to Q_{GJoin} and Q_{Corrupt}. It runs the issuer joining algorithm on $(st_i, isk_i, id, I, gpk)$. An execution of protocol GJoin is triggered and during it, the adversary plays the role of the (corrupt) user and of the corrupt issuers. The challenger plays the role of the honest issuers.

$\mathcal{O}.\mathsf{GSign}(id, m)$: checks that $id \in Q_{\mathsf{GJoin}} \setminus Q_{\mathsf{Corrupt}}$. It computes $\sigma \leftarrow \mathsf{GSign}(gpk, \mathbf{gsk}[id], m)$. It adds (id, m, σ) to Q_{GSign} and returns σ.

$\mathcal{O}.\mathsf{GOpen}_i(O, m, \sigma)$: (for each honest opener i) checks that $i \in O \in \binom{[n_O]}{t_O+1}$. It adds (m, σ) to Q_{GOpen}. It runs the opening algorithm on $(\mathbf{reg}_i, osk_i, O, gpk, m, \sigma)$. A GOpen protocol execution is triggered and the adversary plays the role of the corrupt openers, while the challenger plays that of the honest ones.

$\mathcal{O}.\mathsf{RevealU}(id)$: adds id to Q_{Corrupt} and returns $\mathbf{gsk}[id]$.

$\mathcal{O}.\mathsf{ReadReg}(i, id)$: returns $\mathbf{reg}_i[id]$.

$\mathcal{O}.\mathsf{WriteReg}(i, id, v)$: (for each honest opener i) sets $\mathbf{reg}_i[id] \leftarrow v$, i.e., it write value v on the register of the ith opener for user id.

Anonymity. Anonymity ensures that a group signature reveals no information about the identity of the member who computed it as long as at most t_O openers are corrupt and the signature has not been opened. User identities are not hidden during the joining protocol, and it is in fact necessary to open signatures. In other words, anonymity is only guaranteed w.r.t. to group signatures, but it is not a restriction per se as in most practical scenarios, group signatures are computed at a much higher frequency than members are added. Signatures are therefore much more critical from a privacy perspective.

The definition is indistinguishability-based as the adversary chooses two honest users and a message. It receives a group signature computed with the key of either of them, and it must determine the signer's identity better than by guessing. The adversary is given access to an opening oracle which it can query

---

Experiment $\mathbf{Exp}^{\mathrm{ano}-b}_{\mathrm{DGS},\lambda,n_I,n_O,t_I,t_O}(\mathcal{A})$:

$pp \leftarrow \mathsf{GSetup}(1^\lambda, n_I, n_O, t_I, t_O)$

$\langle st_{\mathcal{A}}, \{(ipk_i, isk_i, st_i)\}_{i>t^*_I}\rangle \leftarrow \langle \mathcal{A}(\mathsf{keygen}, pp), \{\mathsf{IKG}(pp, i)\}_{i>t^*_I}\rangle$

$\langle st'_{\mathcal{A}}, \{(opk_i, osk_i, st_i)\}_{i>t_O}\rangle \leftarrow \langle \mathcal{A}(st_{\mathcal{A}}), \{\mathsf{OKG}(pp, i)\}_{i>t_O}\rangle$

$gpk \leftarrow (ipk, opk)$

$\mathcal{O} \leftarrow \Big\{ \mathsf{GJoin.U}, (\mathsf{GJoin.I}_i)_{i>t^*_I}, \mathsf{GSign}, (\mathsf{GOpen}_i)_{i>t_O}, \mathsf{RevealU}, \mathsf{WriteReg}\Big\}$

$(st''_{\mathcal{A}}, id^*_0, id^*_1, m^*) \leftarrow \mathcal{A}^{\mathcal{O}(gpk, (\mathbf{reg}_i), \mathbf{gsk}, \cdot)}(\mathsf{choose}, st'_{\mathcal{A}})$

$\sigma^* \leftarrow \mathsf{GSign}(gpk, \mathbf{gsk}[id^*_b], m^*)$

$b' \leftarrow \mathcal{A}^{\mathcal{O}(gpk, \mathbf{reg}, \mathbf{gsk}, \cdot)}(st''_{\mathcal{A}}, \sigma^*)$

if $id^*_0, id^*_1 \in Q_{\mathsf{GJoin}} \setminus Q_{\mathsf{Corrupt}}$ and $\mathbf{gsk}[id^*_0], \mathbf{gsk}[id^*_1] \neq \bot$ and $(m^*, \sigma^*) \notin Q_{\mathsf{GOpen}}$

   return b'

else

   return 0

Experiment $\mathbf{Exp}^{\mathrm{trace}}_{\mathrm{DGS},\lambda,n_I,n_O,t_I,t_O}(\mathcal{A})$:

$pp \leftarrow \mathsf{GSetup}(1^\lambda, n_I, n_O, t_I, t_O)$

$\langle st_{\mathcal{A}}, \{(ipk_i, isk_i, st_i)\}_{i>t_I}\rangle \leftarrow \langle \mathcal{A}(\mathsf{keygen}, pp), \{\mathsf{IKG}(pp, i)\}_{i>t_I}\rangle$

$\langle st'_{\mathcal{A}}, \{(opk_i, osk_i, st_i)\}_{i>t^*_O}\rangle \leftarrow \langle \mathcal{A}(st_{\mathcal{A}}), \{\mathsf{OKG}(pp, i)\}_{i>t^*_O}\rangle$

$gpk \leftarrow (ipk, opk)$

$\mathcal{O} \leftarrow \Big\{ \mathsf{GJoin.U}, (\mathsf{GJoin.I}_i)_{i>t_I}, \mathsf{GSign}, (\mathsf{GOpen}_i)_{i>t^*_O}, \mathsf{RevealU}, \mathsf{ReadReg}\Big\}$

$(O^*, m^*, \sigma^*) \leftarrow \mathcal{A}^{\mathcal{O}(gpk, (\mathbf{reg}_i), \mathbf{gsk}, \cdot)}(\mathsf{forge}, st'_{\mathcal{A}})$

if $O^* \not\subseteq \binom{\{t^*_O+1,\ldots,n_O\}}{t_O+1}$ then return 0

$(\{id^*_i\}_{i\in O^*}) \leftarrow (\{\mathsf{GOpen}(\mathbf{reg}_i, osk_i, O^*, gpk, m^*, \sigma^*)\}_{i\in O^*})$

if $\mathsf{GVerf}(gpk, m^*, \sigma^*) = 1$ and (case 1 or case 2)

with

   case 1) opening failed i.e.,

      $\exists i \in O^* : id^*_i = \bot$ or $\exists i, j \in O^* : id^*_i \neq id^*_j$

   case 2) opening was "incorrect", i.e., setting $id^* \leftarrow id^*_{\max O^*}$,

      $id^* \notin Q_{\mathsf{GJoin}}$ or $(id^* \in Q_{\mathsf{GJoin}} \setminus Q_{\mathsf{Corrupt}}$ and $(id^*, m^*, \sigma^*) \notin Q_{\mathsf{GSign}})$

   return 1

else

   return 0

Fig. 1. Security experiments for $\binom{n_I, n_O}{t_I, t_O}$-DGS schemes.

on all but the challenge signature, capturing a CCA-2 type of anonymity [8]. Dynamic corruption of group members is allowed, i.e., a signer may initially be honest but later corrupt. However, anonymity is guaranteed only for fully honest users, i.e., there is no forward anonymity. See Fig. 1 for the detailed experiment.

The classical notion of anonymity relies on the honesty of the opener, which is adjusted to a threshold setting and allows the adversary to corrupt up to t_O out of n_O openers. Without loss of generality, corrupt entities are always assumed to be the first ones, i.e., openers $1, \ldots, t_O$ are controlled by the adversary and $t_O + 1, \ldots, n_O$ are run by the challenger.

Concerning the issuers, the definition is flexible. Ideally, in schemes where the issuer and the opener are distinct entities, the issuer can be fully malicious in the anonymity game. In a distributed setting, it would translate in corrupting all n_I issuers. However, enforcing the corruption of all issuers may exclude some efficient schemes. The anonymity definition is thus parametrized to additionally limit the number of issuers that may be corrupt. In the experiment, the adversary corrupts t_I^* issuers, with t_I^* being a function of t_I. The strongest anonymity guarantees are achieved when $t_I^* = n_I$, in which case the adversary would output the issuer public key itself. The scheme presented in Sect. 4 realizes anonymity for $t_I^* = t_I < n_I/2$, i.e., the largest possible value for an interactive key-generation process to guarantee termination (robustness).

Lastly, it is worth noting that w.r.t. key generation, this model is stronger than that of Bellare et al. [4] in the sense that the keys of corrupt authorities are not assumed to be honestly generated.

Definition 4 (Anonymity). *A $\binom{n_I, n_O}{t_I, t_O}$-DGS scheme DGS is anonymous if for every efficient adversary $\mathcal{A}$, the advantage $\mathbf{Adv}^{\mathrm{ano}}_{\mathsf{DGS}, n_I, n_O, t_I, t_O, \mathcal{A}}(\lambda)$ of $\mathcal{A}$ defined as*

$$\left| \Pr[\mathbf{Exp}^{\mathrm{ano}-0}_{\mathsf{DGS}, \lambda, n_I, n_O, t_I, t_O}(\mathcal{A}) = 1] - \Pr[\mathbf{Exp}^{\mathrm{ano}-1}_{\mathsf{DGS}, \lambda, n_I, n_O, t_I, t_O}(\mathcal{A}) = 1] \right|$$

is negligible in λ.

Traceability. This notion captures the unforgeability property expected from dynamic group signatures and guarantees that only users who have joined the group can compute valid group signatures. With single authorities, the opener can be corrupt but the issuer must be honest. Therefore, adapted to a threshold setting, up to t_I out of n_I issuers can be corrupt.

Traceability is then formalized through the opening capabilities of group signatures as described in Fig. 1. It guarantees that for any valid signature σ on a message m, opening can neither fail (Case 1) nor reveal an "incorrect" identity (Case 2). The first case means that an opener cannot identify any signer or that the openers do not agree on the identity of the signer. The second case means that the revealed identity has either never joined the group of signers, or has joined and is honest, but never signed m. The latter is sometimes formalized through a dedicated *non-frameability* requirement, and the choice of combining both notions is discussed below.

Similarly to the case of anonymity, the number of openers that the adversary can additionally corrupt is parametrized via a bound t_O^*. The strongest traceability notion is achieved when $t_O^* = n_O$, i.e., when all openers can be corrupted. This is however not achievable when openers maintain state critical for opening, since the winning condition depends on a correct execution of protocol GOpen. In case of stateful opening, this requires the non-corrupt registers of at least $t_O + 1$ openers. Therefore, in such settings, at most $t_O^* = n_O - t_O - 1$ openers can be corrupt.

In comparison, in the traceability definition of Bellare et al. [4] for single-authority dynamic group signatures, the opener can be fully corrupt since the register needed to open signatures is rather maintained by the issuer (and the opener must have read access to it). However, this has the effect that in their anonymity definition, even if the honestly generated issuer key is given to the adversary, the challenger must maintain a register on its own to answer opening queries, and the adversary cannot read the register (though it can write on it) otherwise it would trivially win the anonymity game. It means that their model only captures a situation in which the issuer's key is compromised, but its state is not entirely. In this sense, even if their traceability definition captures a full corruption of the opener, the consequence is that their anonymity definition does not capture full corruption of the issuer.

Definition 5 (Traceability). *A* $\binom{n_I, n_O}{t_I, t_O}$*-DGS scheme* DGS *is traceable if for all efficient adversary* $\mathcal{A}$, $\Pr\left[\mathbf{Exp}_{\mathsf{DGS}, \lambda, n_I, n_O, t_I, t_O}^{\mathrm{trace}}(\mathcal{A}) = 1\right]$ *is negligible in* λ.

On Non-frameability. Classical definitions of group signatures with single authorities also include the notion of non-frameability. It reflects the idea that even if the issuer and opener are corrupt, they cannot falsely claim that an honest user computed a given valid signature. Since the opening algorithm in those definitions returns a long-term user public key, *in practice*, a public-key infrastructure would have to bind those keys to real-world identities; and such an infrastructure would be built with one or several certification authorities. However, if these certification authorities collude with the issuer and the opener, they would be able to frame an honest user. In other words, in real-world applications, users still need to trust some certification authority to protect them from malicious group-signature authorities even though the goal of non-frameability is precisely to avoid trust assumptions.

On the other hand, the rationale of threshold cryptography is that if there are many parties, some of them might in practice be corrupt but not all. Since group-signature schemes with several issuers and openers are now considered, the requirement is that if less than respective threshold numbers of them are corrupt, no efficient adversary can forge a signature and falsely claim that an honest user computed it. It is precisely this requirement that is captured by the last winning condition of the above definition of traceability. The scheme in Sect. 4 satisfies this property, but would not satisfy a definition in which all group-signature authorities are corrupt.

4   Our Threshold Dynamic Group Signatures

In this section, we build a threshold DGS scheme from (a variant of) PS signatures. We adopt the GetShorty approach of Bichsel et al. [5] instead of the traditional sign-and-encrypt paradigm. This approach avoids the extra encryption of user identities and enables schemes with highly compact signatures despite supporting signature opening. Our resulting signatures are short, and computing and verifying them only require a few exponentiations in the first group and some pairing computations (see Sect. 4.2).

The efficiency of the GetShorty scheme of Bichsel et al. [5] comes at the price of fully trusted authority responsible for both issuance and opening. A threshold setting allows to preserve the efficiency of the GetShorty approach, yet avoid the need for a single trusted entity. Our scheme shows that even with the GetShorty approach, the role of issuer and opener can be separated and distributed, and it enables t_I-out-of-n_I issuance and t_O-out-of-n_O opening. We still pay a small price for the efficiency, as not all issuers can be corrupt for anonymity and, likewise, not all openers can be malicious for traceability (contrarily to what might be expected). Still, moving to a threshold setting already avoids the most critical assumption, namely a fully trusted party, and instead tolerates corruption of some of them.

One challenge in designing our scheme is to separate the role of issuers and openers. It is necessary in the scheme of Bichsel et al. as the information needed for opening is created during issuance. Our scheme avoids that by assuming a public ledger to which users can upload their opening information during isssuance. This information is encrypted under the opener keys during issuance, and a user must prove to the issuers that she uploaded a valid ciphertext. In the full version [15], we also present a scheme that does not assume a ledger but instead combines the roles of issuer and opener anew, and supports threshold issuance and opening.

We first define the variant of the PS signature scheme on which our scheme is based and then describe our threshold group signatures.

4.1 Variant of the PS Signature Scheme

Consider the PS signature scheme (Sect. 2.5) in which the extra scalar m' is computed as $\mathcal{H}(m)$. In the same vein, the group element h could also be returned by the hash function, i.e., $(m', h) \leftarrow \mathcal{H}(m)$. This would allow several signers of the same message to agree on a common base h. The scheme remains unforgeable and the main difference from the unforgeability proof of Pointcheval and Sanders [42, Section 4.3] is that when $\mathcal{H}$ is queried on a message m different from the challenge message, the reduction algorithm already prepares (σ_1, σ_2) to be later returned in case the adversary makes a signing query on m.

This technique is similar to that of Sonnino et al. [44] for their credential system. They hash a commitment to the signed message to obtain a base h, even though they apply it to the CT-RSA'16 version of the PS scheme (so without m') and do not formally prove that the scheme remains secure.

Moreover, assume that the messages to be signed are publicly indexed, i.e., that for every message m there exists a unique value idx_m known to any signer. To sign a message m, instead of hashing to determine a scalar m' and a base h, a signer could instead compute m' as $\mathcal{H}(idx_m)$. If the number of messages to be signed is known in advance to be polynomial, the scheme remains unforgeable under the same assumption since indexing messages to determine (m', h) is equivalent to specifying in the public parameters a pair (m', h) for each message m. It is this variant of the scheme that is considered in our construction of threshold group signatures in Sect. 4.2. Therein, the messages signed are user secret keys sk_{id} indexed by the user identities id.

4.2 Construction with Separate Issuers and Openers

We first explain the main ideas of our construction, and then detail the protocols and algorithms.

Key Generation. During set-up, the issuers run the distributed key-generation protocol of Gennaro et al. [27] with t_I as a threshold to generate a public key for the PS signature scheme so that each of them holds a share of the secret key. The protocol guarantees that if $t_I < n_I/2$, then the protocol terminates (which cannot be enforced with a dishonest majority) and no colluding t_I issuers can infer any information about the secret key, whereas any $t_I + 1$ issuers can reconstruct it.

As for the openers, each of them simply generates a pair of ElGamal keys.

Join. For $t_I + 1$ issuers to add a user to the group, they all blindly sign with their PS secret-key share a random secret key sk_{id} chosen by the user. To do so, they need to agree on a common PS base h, so we used the variant from Sect. 4.1 of the PS signature scheme. The user group secret key consists of sk_{id} and the PS signature on it.

For each opener, the user encrypts a t_O-out-of-n_O Shamir share of sk_{id} and proves that the ciphertexts are correctly computed. With the ElGamal public keys of the openers, the issuers can verify the proofs and thus be convinced that the any $t_O + 1$ openers will later be able to retrieve correct shares of the user secret key if they can access the ciphertexts.

To make sure that these shares can later be retrieved by the openers, we assume the existence of an append-only ledger L accessible to all users, issuers and openers. Once the user has encrypted the shares of her secret key and has proved that she did so, she writes the encrypted shares and the proofs on the ledger. The issuers then send their PS signature-shares only after verifying the proofs. Therefore, each opener can later retrieve his shares of all group-member secret keys from the ledger.

Note that since honest issuers add a given user identity id to the group only once and when the proofs are correct, there is only one entry with valid proofs per user that can open her signatures. This entry is the one denoted $L[id]$ in the description of the opening algorithm.

Sign & Verify. To compute a group signature on a message m, the user computes a signature of knowledge on m of a valid PS signature on a user secret key sk_{id}. Verifying a signature on a message simply consists in verifying the signature of knowledge on it.

Open. To open a signature, any $t_O + 1$ openers first retrieve from the ledger their shares of user secret keys and store them in their registers. Once the openers' registers are updated, they test the signature to be opened against each entry in their registers until they find a user for which the shares match. It makes opening expensive for the benefit of having short signatures, which perfectly fits most practical scenarios, in which signatures should be short and opening an uncommon practice performed by resourceful authorities.

Scheme Description. To formally define the construction, let $\mathcal{H}_0 \colon \{0,1\}^* \to \mathbb{Z}_p \times \mathbb{G}^*$, and $\mathcal{H}_1 \colon \{0,1\}^* \to \mathbb{Z}_p$ be two random oracles (the latter is to compute non-interactive proofs of knowledge via the Fiat–Shamir heuristic [23]). Let also $ID \subseteq \mathbb{Z}_p$ denote a user identity space. The construction requires as building blocks

- the Sect. 4.1 variant of the PS signature scheme, further denoted PS, to sign user secret keys.
- an append-only ledger L with user identities as keys that is available to all users, issuers and openers
- secure (i.e., authenticated and confidential) channels
- a broadcast channel, i.e., a protocol between several parties that allows a sender to distribute a value to all the other parties so that the following three properties are satisfied:
  1. (termination) the protocol terminates
  2. (consistency) all honest parties receive the same value and
  3. (validity) if the sender is honest, then the value received by all honest parties is that of the sender.

Given a type-3 pairing group generator G and a security parameter $\lambda \in \mathbb{N}$, Our $\binom{n_I, n_O}{t_I, t_O}$-DGS scheme PS-DGS in a pairing group $\Gamma = \left(p, \mathbb{G}, \tilde{\mathbb{G}}, \mathbb{G}_T, e\right) \leftarrow G(1^\lambda)$ is the following:

$\mathsf{GSetup}(1^\lambda, n_I, n_O, t_I, t_O) \to pp$: generate $(g, \tilde{g}) \in_R \mathbb{G}^* \times \tilde{\mathbb{G}}^*$. Set $pp_{\mathsf{PS}} \leftarrow (\Gamma, \tilde{g}, 1)$ and return $pp \leftarrow (pp_{\mathsf{PS}}, g, n_I, n_O, t_I, t_O)$.

$\langle \{\mathsf{IKG}(pp, i)\}_{i=1}^{n_I} \rangle \to \langle \{(ipk, isk_i, st_i)\}_{i=1}^{n_I} \rangle$: is a protocol between all the issuers who proceed as follows

- the issuers run three times the distributed key-generation protocol of Gennaro et al. [27] with t_I as a threshold in group $\tilde{\mathbb{G}}$ to obtain three uniformly distributed public values $\tilde{X}$, $\tilde{Y}_0$ and $\tilde{Y}_1$. At the end of the protocol, each issuer $i \in [n_I]$ holds shares x_i, $y_{0,i}$ and $y_{1,i}$ such that for any $I \in \binom{[n_I]}{t_I+1}$, if w_i denotes the Lagrange coefficient of issuer i, then $x := \mathrm{dlog}_{\tilde{g}} \tilde{X} = \sum_{i \in I} x_i w_i$, and similarly for $y_0 := \mathrm{dlog}_{\tilde{g}} \tilde{Y}_0$ and $y_1 := \mathrm{dlog}_{\tilde{g}} \tilde{Y}_1$.

- issuer $i \in [n_I]$ returns $\left(ipk \leftarrow \left(\tilde{X}, \tilde{Y}_0, \tilde{Y}_1\right), isk_i \leftarrow (i, x_i, y_{0,i}, y_{1,i}), st_I \leftarrow \bot\right)$. The issuers send ipk to a certification authority which is assumed to make it publicly available so that anyone can get an authentic copy of it.

$\langle \{\mathsf{OKG}(pp, i)\}_{i=1}^{n_O} \rangle \to \langle \{(opk, osk_i, \mathbf{reg}_i)\}_{i=1}^{n_O} \rangle$: for each opener, generate an ElGamal pair of keys $(\tilde{f}_i \leftarrow \tilde{g}^{z_i}, z_i) \in \tilde{\mathbb{G}}^* \times \mathbb{Z}_p^*$ and initialize an empty register $\mathbf{reg}_i$. Set $opk_i \leftarrow \tilde{f}_i$ and $osk_i \leftarrow (i, \tilde{f}_i, z_i)$, and $opk \leftarrow ((i, opk_i))_{i=1}^{n_O}$. For each opener, return $(opk, osk_i, \mathbf{reg}_i)$. The opener send opk to a certification authority.

The group public key gpk is set to (ipk, opk).

GJoin : Assume that there is a broadcast channel between a user $\mathcal{U}$ and the $t_I + 1$ issuers $\mathcal{I}_i$ in $I \in \binom{[n_I]}{t_I+1}$. Assume also that there is a secure channel between $\mathcal{U}$ and every issuer $\mathcal{I}_i$. In particular, this implies that an adversary cannot modify the messages sent by the user to the issuers: it can only forward, delay or drop them. Throughout the following description of the protocol, whenever an algorithm receives an abort or an ill-formed message, or when a verification fails, it interrupts the protocol execution by broadcasting an abort message to all participants and returning $\perp$. The joining protocol between the user and the issuers is as follows:

1. GJoin.U, on input $\left(id, I, gpk = \left(ipk = (\tilde{X}, \tilde{Y}_0, \tilde{Y}_1), opk \right) \right)$,
   - choose $sk_{id} \in_R \mathbb{Z}_p^*$
   - $(a', h) \leftarrow \mathcal{H}_0(id)$
   - $h_{sk} \leftarrow h^{sk_{id}}$; $g_{sk} \leftarrow g^{sk_{id}}$. Therefore, (g, h, g_{sk}, h_{sk}) is a DDH tuple. It helps the reduction algorithm of the traceability proof to efficiently extract the secret keys of adversarial users (under the ADH-KE assumption).
   - $\pi \leftarrow$ NIZK.Prove$\{sk_{id}: h_{sk} = h^{sk_{id}} \wedge g_{sk} = g^{sk_{id}}\}$
   - generate $p_1, \ldots, p_{t_O} \in_R \mathbb{Z}_p$ and set $P \leftarrow sk_{id} + \sum_{\ell=1}^{t_O} p_\ell X^\ell \in \mathbb{Z}_p[X]$
   - for $i \in [n_O]$, compute $s_i \leftarrow P(i)$, i.e., Shamir shares of sk_{id} for each opener
   - for $\ell \in [t_O]$, compute $h_\ell \leftarrow h^{p_\ell}$, i.e., verification values as in the Feldman verifiable secret sharing scheme [22]
   - for all $i \in [n_O]$:
     * $r_i \leftarrow_\$ \mathbb{Z}_p$
     * $\tilde{C}_i := (\tilde{C}_{i,0}, \tilde{C}_{i,1}) \leftarrow \left(\tilde{g}^{r_i}, \tilde{f}_i^{r_i} \tilde{Y}_0^{s_i} \right)$
     * $\pi_i \leftarrow$ NIZK.Prove $\left\{ r_i: \tilde{C}_{i,0} = \tilde{g}^{r_i}, e\left(h, \tilde{C}_{i,1}/\tilde{f}_i^{r_i} \right) = e\left(h_{sk} \prod_{\ell=1}^{t_O} h_\ell^{i^\ell}, \tilde{Y}_0 \right) \right\}$ i.e., compute a proof that $\tilde{C}_i$ encrypts the ith share of sk_{id}
   - set $L[id] \leftarrow \left(g_{sk}, h_{sk}, h_1, \ldots, h_{t_O}, \pi, \left(\tilde{C}_i, \pi_i \right)_{i \in [n_O]} \right)$
   - broadcast written to all $\mathcal{I}_i$

2. GJoin.I, for $i \in I$, on input $(st_i, isk_i = (i, x_i, y_{0,i}, y_{1,i}), id, I, gpk)$
   - abort if $id \in st_i$
   - upon receiving written from $\mathcal{U}$:
     * $(a', h) \leftarrow \mathcal{H}_0(id)$
     * parse $L[id]$ as $\left(g_{sk}, h_{sk}, h_1, \ldots, h_{t_O}, \pi, \left(\tilde{C}_i, \pi_i \right)_{i \in [n_O]} \right)$
     * NIZK.Verf$(g, h, g_{sk}, h_{sk}, \pi) \stackrel{?}{=} 1$, i.e., verify that it is a DDH tuple
     * for $j \in [n_O]$, NIZK.Verf $\left(h, (h_\ell)_{\ell=1}^{t_O}, \tilde{Y}_0, \tilde{f}_j, \tilde{C}_j, \pi_j \right) \stackrel{?}{=} 1$, i.e., verify that the ciphertexts encrypt correct shares for each opener
     * $\Sigma_{i,2} \leftarrow h^{x_i + y_{i,1} a'} h_{sk}^{y_{i,0}}$ (i.e., blindly sign sk_{id} via h_{sk})
     * $st_i \leftarrow st_i \cup \{id\}$

         * send $\Sigma_{i,2}$ to $\mathcal{U}$ over a secure channel

3. GJoin.U, upon receiving $\Sigma_{i,2}$ from all $\mathcal{I}_i$ for $i \in I$,

    – $\Sigma \leftarrow \left(a', h, \prod_{i \in I} \Sigma_{i,2}^{w_i} = h^{x + y_0 sk_{id} + y_1 a'} \right)$, i.e., reconstruct the PS signature w.r.t. to ipk

    – PS.Verf$(ipk, sk_{id}, \Sigma) \stackrel{?}{=} 1$

    – return $\mathbf{gsk}[id] \leftarrow (sk_{id}, \Sigma)$

GSign$(ipk, \mathbf{gsk}[id], m) \rightarrow \sigma$: parse $\mathbf{gsk}[id] = (sk_{id}, \Sigma = (a', \Sigma_1, \Sigma_2))$. Generate $r \in_R \mathbb{Z}_p^*$. Compute $(\Sigma_1', \Sigma_2') \leftarrow (\Sigma_1^r, \Sigma_2^r)$ and

$$\pi \leftarrow \text{NIZK.Prove}\{(sk_{id}, a') \colon \text{PS.Verf}(ipk, sk_{id}, (a', \Sigma_1', \Sigma_2')) = 1\}(m).$$

That is, compute, with $\mathcal{H}_1$ as random oracle, a Schnorr signature of knowledge $\pi = (c, v_{sk}, v_{a'}) \in \mathbb{Z}_p^3$ on m of a pair (sk_{id}, a') such that $e\left({\Sigma_1'}^{sk_{id}}, \tilde{Y}_0 \right)$ $e\left({\Sigma_1'}^{a'}, \tilde{Y}_1 \right) = e(\Sigma_2', \tilde{g})e(\Sigma_1', \tilde{X})^{-1}$. Return $\sigma \leftarrow (\Sigma_1', \Sigma_2', \pi)$.

GVerf$(ipk, m, \sigma) \rightarrow b \in \{0,1\}$: parse σ as $(\Sigma_1, \Sigma_2, \pi)$. Return NIZK.Verf$(gpk, \Sigma_1, \Sigma_2, m, \pi)$. That is, return 1 if

$$c = \mathcal{H}_1 \left(ipk, \Sigma_1, \Sigma_2, e\left(\Sigma_1^{v_{sk}}, \tilde{Y}_0 \right) e\left(\Sigma_1^{v_{a'}}, \tilde{Y}_1 \right) e\left(\Sigma_2^{c}, \tilde{g} \right) e\left(\Sigma_1^{-c}, \tilde{X} \right), m \right)$$

and 0 otherwise.

GOpen : is run by $t_O + 1$ openers $\mathcal{O}_i$ (for $i \in O$) to recover the identity of the user who computed a valid group signature $\sigma = (\Sigma_1, \Sigma_2, \pi)$ on a message m. To do so, the openers first update their registers by checking the public ledger L. Then, the opening algorithms loop over the entries of their registers $\mathbf{reg}_i$ containing encryptions of shares $\tilde{Y}_0^{s_i}$ recorded during executions of protocol GJoin. For each identity id for which they have a share, the opening algorithms use their shares to determine whether (a', Σ_1, Σ_2) (with $(a', h) = \mathcal{H}_0(id)$) is a valid PS signature on the unique value determined by their $t_O + 1$ shares of the secret key of user id. If it is the case, the algorithms return id. If no such identity is found, the opening algorithm returns $\perp$. The protocol assumes a broadcast channel between the participating openers, and also that the protocol is aborted as soon as an algorithm receives an abort or an ill-formed message.

Formally, GOpen $(\mathbf{reg}_i, osk_i = (i, z_i), I, gpk, m, \sigma = (\Sigma_1, \Sigma_2, \pi))$ proceeds as follows:

1. if GVerf$(ipk, m, \sigma) = 0$ then return $\perp$
2. for all id such that $L[id] \neq \perp$, if $\mathbf{reg}_i[id] = \perp$ then parse $L[id]$ as $\left(g_{sk}, h_{sk}, h_1, \ldots, h_{t_O}, \pi, (\tilde{C}_i, \pi_i)_{i \in [n_O]} \right)$ and set $\mathbf{reg}_i[id] \leftarrow \tilde{C}_{i,1}/\tilde{C}_{i,0}^{z_i}$
3. for all id such that $\mathbf{reg}_i[id] \neq \perp$, compute $T_{id,i} \leftarrow e\left(\Sigma_1, \tilde{C}_{i,1}/\tilde{C}_{i,0}^{z_i} \right)$
4. broadcast $S_i \leftarrow \{(id, T_{id,i})\}_{id \,:\, \mathbf{reg}_i[id] \neq \perp}$ to all the openers in I

5. upon receiving S_j from all the other openers $\mathcal{O}_j$ (for $j \in I \setminus \{i\}$),
   - for $j \in I$, compute $w_j \leftarrow \prod_{\ell \in I \setminus \{j\}} \ell/(\ell - j)$, i.e., the jth Lagrange coefficient
   - for all $(id, T_{id,i}) \in S_i$ (in lexicographic order of user identities)
     * if $\exists j \in I \colon (id, *) \notin S_j$ then continue
     * $(a', h) \leftarrow \mathcal{H}_0(id)$
     * for all $j \in I \setminus \{i\}$, retrieve $(id, T_{id,j})$ from S_j
     * if $e\left(\Sigma_1, \tilde{X} \tilde{Y}_1^{a'}\right) \prod_{j \in I} T_{id,j}^{w_j} = e(\Sigma_2, \tilde{g})$ then return id
6. return $\perp$ (i.e., in case the previous equality holds for no tuple in $\mathbf{reg}_i$).

Remark 1. The signing and verification algorithms only need the short issuer public key, not the entire group public key.

Correctness & Security. PS-DGS is correct. In the random-oracle model, it is also anonymous under the first-group DDH and the SDL assumptions over the pairing-group generator G for any $t_O < n_O/2$ and $t_I = t_I^* < n_I/2$. Moreover, denoting by $q_{\mathcal{H}_0}$ the number of $\mathcal{H}_0$ queries, scheme PS-DGS satisfies traceability in the random-oracle model under the $q_{\mathcal{H}_0}$-MSDH-1, the ADH-KE and the SDL assumptions over the pairing-group generator G for any $t_I < n_I/2$, $t_O < n_O$ and $t_O^* = \min(t_O, n_O - t_O - 1)$. Proofs of these statements are given in the full version [15].

Discussion. The anonymity of the scheme is only guaranteed if less than half of the issuers are corrupt, and not all as one would hope. One reason is that the generation of the issuer keys is interactive, so for the protocol to terminate, there cannot be a dishonest majority. Another reason is that the reduction to the DDH requires to know all issuer secret keys which are shares of the PS secret key obtained during the key-generation protocol. To be able to reconstruct the shares of the corrupt issuers, the number $n - t_I^*$ of honest issuers must be greater than t_I^*.

Concerning traceability, it requires the number of corrupt openers not only to be smaller than $n_O - t_O - 1$ as explained in Sect. 3, but also smaller than t_O. It is due to the fact that even though the openers are separate from the issuers, they must still obtain user secret key shares from the joining protocol to be able to open signatures. In this sense, opening is not completely independent of issuance, and it is precisely what allows the signatures of the scheme to be so short. This constraint on the number of corrupt openers appears in the security proof in which the forked algorithm must simulate shares of user secret keys, and it can only do so if at most t_O openers are corrupt since the opening threshold is $t_O + 1$.

Efficiency. On a Cocks–Pinch pairing curve [30] defined over a field of order 2^{544} and with embedding degree 8, group elements in G take 68 Bytes for a group of 256-bit order. Note that this curve provides 131 bits of security [30].

A group signature from our scheme consists of two $\mathbb{G}$ elements and three $\mathbb{Z}_p$ elements, totalling 232 Bytes. The hash value in the proof of knowledge of a multi-signature can actually be shortened to second-preimage resistant length, further shortening a group signature to 216 Bytes.

Considering only group operations, computing a signature costs 4 exponentiations in $\mathbb{G}$ and the product of 2 pairing values. Verifying a signature costs 4 exponentiations in $\mathbb{G}$ and the multiplication of 4 pairing values.

In the full version [15], we also compare our scheme with previous ones in terms of size and efficiency.

Acknowledgements. Most of the work of the first four authors was done while being at IBM Research – Zurich. The authors thank David Pointcheval for helpful discussions. This work was supported by the CHIST-ERA USEIT project and the EU H2020 Research and Innovation Program under Grant Agreement No. 786725 (OLYMPUS).

References

1. Ateniese, G., Camenisch, J., Joye, M., Tsudik, G.: A practical and provably secure coalition-resistant group signature scheme. In: Bellare, M. (ed.) CRYPTO 2000. LNCS, vol. 1880, pp. 255–270. Springer, Heidelberg (2000). https://doi.org/10.1007/3-540-44598-6_16
2. Bellare, M., Fuchsbauer, G., Scafuro, A.: NIZKs with an untrusted CRS: security in the face of parameter subversion. In: Cheon, J.H., Takagi, T. (eds.) ASIACRYPT 2016, Part II. LNCS, vol. 10032, pp. 777–804. Springer, Heidelberg (2016). https://doi.org/10.1007/978-3-662-53890-6_26
3. Bellare, M., Micciancio, D., Warinschi, B.: Foundations of group signatures: formal definitions, simplified requirements, and a construction based on general assumptions. In: Biham, E. (ed.) EUROCRYPT 2003. LNCS, vol. 2656, pp. 614–629. Springer, Heidelberg (2003). https://doi.org/10.1007/3-540-39200-9_38
4. Bellare, M., Shi, H., Zhang, C.: Foundations of group signatures: the case of dynamic groups. In: Menezes, A. (ed.) CT-RSA 2005. LNCS, vol. 3376, pp. 136–153. Springer, Heidelberg (2005). https://doi.org/10.1007/978-3-540-30574-3_11
5. Bichsel, P., Camenisch, J., Neven, G., Smart, N.P., Warinschi, B.: Get shorty via group signatures without encryption. In: Garay, J.A., De Prisco, R. (eds.) SCN 2010. LNCS, vol. 6280, pp. 381–398. Springer, Heidelberg (2010). https://doi.org/10.1007/978-3-642-15317-4_24
6. Blömer, J., Juhnke, J., Löken, N.: Short group signatures with distributed traceability. In: Kotsireas, I.S., Rump, S.M., Yap, C.K. (eds.) MACIS 2015. LNCS, vol. 9582, pp. 166–180. Springer, Cham (2016). https://doi.org/10.1007/978-3-319-32859-1_14
7. Boldyreva, A.: Threshold signatures, multisignatures and blind signatures based on the gap-Diffie-Hellman-group signature scheme. In: Desmedt, Y.G. (ed.) PKC 2003. LNCS, vol. 2567, pp. 31–46. Springer, Heidelberg (2003). https://doi.org/10.1007/3-540-36288-6_3
8. Boneh, D., Boyen, X., Shacham, H.: Short group signatures. In: Franklin, M. (ed.) CRYPTO 2004. LNCS, vol. 3152, pp. 41–55. Springer, Heidelberg (2004). https://doi.org/10.1007/978-3-540-28628-8_3

9. Boneh, D., Drijvers, M., Neven, G.: Compact multi-signatures for smaller blockchains. In: Peyrin, T., Galbraith, S. (eds.) ASIACRYPT 2018, Part II. LNCS, vol. 11273, pp. 435–464. Springer, Cham (2018). https://doi.org/10.1007/978-3-030-03329-3_15

10. Boneh, D., Eskandarian, S., Fisch, B.: Post-quantum EPID group signatures from symmetric primitives. Cryptology ePrint Archive, Report 2018/261 (2018). https://eprint.iacr.org/2018/261

11. Boneh, D., Shacham, H.: Group signatures with verifier-local revocation. In: Atluri, V., Pfitzmann, B., McDaniel, P. (eds.) ACM CCS 2004, pp. 168–177. ACM Press, New York (2004)

12. Boschini, C., Camenisch, J., Neven, G.: Floppy-sized group signatures from lattices. In: Preneel, B., Vercauteren, F. (eds.) ACNS 2018. LNCS, vol. 10892, pp. 163–182. Springer, Cham (2018). https://doi.org/10.1007/978-3-319-93387-0_9

13. Brickell, E.F., Camenisch, J., Chen, L.: Direct anonymous attestation. In: Atluri, V., Pfitzmann, B., McDaniel, P. (eds.) ACM CCS 2004, pp. 132–145. ACM Press, New York (2004)

14. Camenisch, J., Chen, L., Drijvers, M., Lehmann, A., Novick, D., Urian, R.: One TPM to bind them all: fixing TPM 2.0 for provably secure anonymous attestation. In: 2017 IEEE Symposium on Security and Privacy, pp. 901–920. IEEE Computer Society Press, May 2017

15. Camenisch, J., Drijvers, M., Lehmann, A., Neven, G., Towa, P.: Short threshold dynamic group signatures. Cryptology ePrint Archive, Report 2020/016 (2020). https://eprint.iacr.org/2020/016

16. Camenisch, J., Groth, J.: Group signatures: better efficiency and new theoretical aspects. In: Blundo, C., Cimato, S. (eds.) SCN 2004. LNCS, vol. 3352, pp. 120–133. Springer, Heidelberg (2005). https://doi.org/10.1007/978-3-540-30598-9_9

17. Camenisch, J., Lysyanskaya, A.: Dynamic accumulators and application to efficient revocation of anonymous credentials. In: Yung, M. (ed.) CRYPTO 2002. LNCS, vol. 2442, pp. 61–76. Springer, Heidelberg (2002). https://doi.org/10.1007/3-540-45708-9_5

18. Camenisch, J., Lysyanskaya, A.: Signature schemes and anonymous credentials from bilinear maps. In: Franklin, M. (ed.) CRYPTO 2004. LNCS, vol. 3152, pp. 56–72. Springer, Heidelberg (2004). https://doi.org/10.1007/978-3-540-28628-8_4

19. Chaum, D., van Heyst, E.: Group signatures. In: Davies, D.W. (ed.) EUROCRYPT 1991. LNCS, vol. 547, pp. 257–265. Springer, Heidelberg (1991). https://doi.org/10.1007/3-540-46416-6_22

20. Derler, D., Slamanig, D.: Highly-efficient fully-anonymous dynamic group signatures. In: Kim, J., Ahn, G.J., Kim, S., Kim, Y., López, J., Kim, T. (eds.) ASIACCS 2018, pp. 551–565. ACM Press, New York (2018)

21. Desmedt, Y., Frankel, Y.: Threshold cryptosystems. In: Brassard, G. (ed.) CRYPTO 1989. LNCS, vol. 435, pp. 307–315. Springer, New York (1990). https://doi.org/10.1007/0-387-34805-0_28

22. Feldman, P.: A practical scheme for non-interactive verifiable secret sharing. In: 28th FOCS, pp. 427–437. IEEE Computer Society Press, October 1987

23. Fiat, A., Shamir, A.: How to prove yourself: practical solutions to identification and signature problems. In: Odlyzko, A.M. (ed.) CRYPTO 1986. LNCS, vol. 263, pp. 186–194. Springer, Heidelberg (1987). https://doi.org/10.1007/3-540-47721-7_12

24. Fuchsbauer, G., Orrù, M.: Non-interactive zaps of knowledge. In: Preneel, B., Vercauteren, F. (eds.) ACNS 2018. LNCS, vol. 10892, pp. 44–62. Springer, Cham (2018). https://doi.org/10.1007/978-3-319-93387-0_3

25. Garfinkel, T., Pfaff, B., Chow, J., Rosenblum, M., Boneh, D.: Terra: a virtual machine-based platform for trusted computing. In: Proceedings of the Nineteenth ACM Symposium on Operating Systems Principles, SOSP 2003. ACM (2003)
26. Gennaro, R., Goldfeder, S., Ithurburn, B.: Fully distributed group signatures (2019). https://www.orbs.com/wp-content/uploads/2019/04/Crypto_Group_signatures-2.pdf
27. Gennaro, R., Jarecki, S., Krawczyk, H., Rabin, T.: Secure distributed key generation for discrete-log based cryptosystems. In: Stern, J. (ed.) EUROCRYPT 1999. LNCS, vol. 1592, pp. 295–310. Springer, Heidelberg (1999). https://doi.org/10.1007/3-540-48910-X_21
28. Ghadafi, E.: Efficient distributed tag-based encryption and its application to group signatures with efficient distributed traceability. In: Aranha, D.F., Menezes, A. (eds.) LATINCRYPT 2014. LNCS, vol. 8895, pp. 327–347. Springer, Cham (2015). https://doi.org/10.1007/978-3-319-16295-9_18
29. Trusted Computing Group: Trusted platform module library specification, family "2.0" (2014). https://trustedcomputinggroup.org/resource/tpm-library-specification/
30. Guillevic, A., Masson, S., Thomé, E.: Cocks-pinch curves of embedding degrees five to eight and optimal ate pairing computation (2019). https://eprint.iacr.org/2019/431.pdf
31. Libert, B., Ling, S., Mouhartem, F., Nguyen, K., Wang, H.: Adaptive oblivious transfer with access control from lattice assumptions. In: Takagi, T., Peyrin, T. (eds.) ASIACRYPT 2017, Part I. LNCS, vol. 10624, pp. 533–563. Springer, Cham (2017). https://doi.org/10.1007/978-3-319-70694-8_19
32. Libert, B., Yung, M.: Dynamic fully forward-secure group signatures. In: Feng, D., Basin, D.A., Liu, P. (eds.) ASIACCS 2010, pp. 70–81. ACM Press, New York (2010)
33. Ling, S., Nguyen, K., Wang, H., Xu, Y.: Lattice-based group signatures: achieving full dynamicity with ease. In: Gollmann, D., Miyaji, A., Kikuchi, H. (eds.) ACNS 2017. LNCS, vol. 10355, pp. 293–312. Springer, Cham (2017). https://doi.org/10.1007/978-3-319-61204-1_15
34. Ling, S., Nguyen, K., Wang, H., Xu, Y.: Constant-size group signatures from lattices. In: Abdalla, M., Dahab, R. (eds.) PKC 2018, Part II. LNCS, vol. 10770, pp. 58–88. Springer, Cham (2018). https://doi.org/10.1007/978-3-319-76581-5_3
35. Manulis, M.: Democratic group signatures on example of joint ventures. Cryptology ePrint Archive, Report 2005/446 (2005). http://eprint.iacr.org/2005/446
36. Manulis, M., Fleischhacker, N., Günther, F., Kiefer, F., Poettering, B.: Group signatures: authentication with privacy (2012). https://www.bsi.bund.de/SharedDocs/Downloads/EN/BSI/Publications/Studies/GruPA/GruPA.pdf
37. Maxwell, G., Poelstra, A., Seurin, Y., Wuille, P.: Simple Schnorr multi-signatures with applications to bitcoin. Designs, Codes and Cryptography (2019). https://doi.org/10.1007/s10623-019-00608-x
38. Micali, S., Ohta, K., Reyzin, L.: Accountable-subgroup multisignatures: extended abstract. In: ACM CCS 2001, pp. 245–254. ACM Press, November 2001
39. Neven, G., Baldini, G., Camenisch, J., Neisse, R.: Privacy-preserving attribute-based credentials in cooperative intelligent transport systems. In: 2017 IEEE Vehicular Networking Conference, VNC 2017, pp. 131–138. IEEE (2017)
40. Petit, J., Schaub, F., Feiri, M., Kargl, F.: Pseudonym schemes in vehicular networks: a survey. IEEE Commun. Surv. Tut. 17(1), 228–255 (2015)

41. Pointcheval, D., Sanders, O.: Short randomizable signatures. In: Sako, K. (ed.) CT-RSA 2016. LNCS, vol. 9610, pp. 111–126. Springer, Cham (2016). https://doi.org/10.1007/978-3-319-29485-8_7
42. Pointcheval, D., Sanders, O.: Reassessing security of randomizable signatures. In: Smart, N.P. (ed.) CT-RSA 2018. LNCS, vol. 10808, pp. 319–338. Springer, Cham (2018). https://doi.org/10.1007/978-3-319-76953-0_17
43. Shamir, A.: How to share a secret. Commun. Assoc. Comput. Mach. **22**(11), 612–613 (1979)
44. Sonnino, A., Al-Bassam, M., Bano, S., Danezis, G.: Coconut: threshold issuance selective disclosure credentials with applications to distributed ledgers. CoRR abs/1802.07344 (2018). http://arxiv.org/abs/1802.07344
45. International Organization for Standardization: ISO/IEC 11889: Information technology - Trusted platform module library (2015). https://www.iso.org/standard/66510.html
46. Whyte, W., Weimerskirch, A., Kumar, V., Hehn, T.: A security credential management system for V2V communications. In: 2013 IEEE Vehicular Networking Conference, pp. 1–8. IEEE (2013)
47. Zheng, D., Li, X., Ma, C., Chen, K., Li, J.: Democratic group signatures with threshold traceability. Cryptology ePrint Archive, Report 2008/112 (2008). http://eprint.iacr.org/2008/112

Symmetric Crypto

Fully Collision-Resistant Chameleon-Hashes from Simpler and Post-quantum Assumptions

David Derler[1], Stephan Krenn[2], Kai Samelin[3], and Daniel Slamanig[2(✉)]

[1] DFINITY, Zurich, Switzerland
david@dfinity.org
[2] AIT Austrian Institute of Technology, Vienna, Austria
{stephan.krenn,daniel.slamanig}@ait.ac.at
[3] Independent, Landshut, Germany
kaispapers@gmail.com

Abstract. Chameleon-hashes are collision-resistant hash-functions parametrized by a public key. If the corresponding secret key is known, arbitrary collisions for the hash can be found. Recently, Derler et al. (PKC '20) introduced the notion of *fully* collision-resistant chameleon-hashes. Full collision-resistance requires the intractability of finding collisions, even with full-adaptive access to a collision-finding oracle. Their construction combines simulation-sound extractable (SSE) NIZKs with perfectly correct IND-CPA secure public-key encryption (PKE) schemes. We show that, instead of perfectly correct PKE, non-interactive commitment schemes are sufficient. For the first time, this gives rise to efficient instantiations from plausible post-quantum assumptions and thus candidates of chameleon-hashes with strong collision-resistance guarantees and long-term security guarantees. On the more theoretical side, our results relax the requirement to not being dependent on public-key encryption.

1 Introduction

Chameleon-hashes (CHs) are collision-resistant hash-functions parametrized by a public key. Knowledge of the corresponding secret key allows finding arbitrary collisions. Chameleon-hashes were initially introduced by Krawczyk and Rabin [35]. Similar underlying ideas even date back to the introduction of "trapdoor commitments" by Brassard et al. [14]. They are an integral part of many cryptographic constructions, both in theory and practice. For instance, CHs find usage in on/offline signatures [18,27,43], to generically lift non-adaptively secure signature schemes to adaptively secure ones [32,43], or as a building block for tightly-secure signatures [11]. Likewise, they find applications in strong one-time signatures [38], the construction of IND-CCA secure public-key encryption [46] or to extend Schnorr and RSA signatures to the universal designated-verifier setting [44]. CHs are also widely used in sanitizable signatures [2,7,15,16], i.e., signatures where a designated entity can alter certain parts of a signed message while also deriving a valid new signature for the altered message. Bellare

© Springer Nature Switzerland AG 2020
C. Galdi and V. Kolesnikov (Eds.): SCN 2020, LNCS 12238, pp. 427–447, 2020.
https://doi.org/10.1007/978-3-030-57990-6_21

and Ristov have shown that chameleon-hashes and Σ-protocols (meaning three-round public-coin honest-verifier zero-knowledge proofs of knowledge), are equivalent [8,9]. Likewise, several extensions such as (hierarchical) identity-based [4–6], policy-based chameleon-hash functions [21,42], or multi-trapdoor CHs [16,36] have been studied.

Derler et al. [20] recently studied existing collision-resistance notions of CHs and introduced the notion of full collision-resistance, which is the strongest known such notion and arguably the most natural one. Compared to prior notions, their definition requires that an adversary which has full adaptive access to a collision-finding oracle cannot find any collisions that it did not receive from the oracle. For comparison, the weakest meaningful notion (those satisfied by trapdoor commitments) does not allow the adversary to see *any* collision.

Contribution. Given the wide variety of application scenarios relying on CHs as building blocks, striving to find efficient instantiations and construction paradigms, based on minimal assumptions, yet with strong security guarantees, is an important task. Our contributions are along those lines, and, in particular, include:

- A black-box construction of fully collision-resistant chameleon-hashes based on SSE NIZKs and non-interactive commitment schemes. Most importantly, this construction manages to remove the requirement to rely on public-key encryption. While this is interesting from a practical point of view as it gives more freedom for possible instantiations, it is also interesting from a theoretical perspective, as we can instantiate our constructions from primitives which require weaker assumptions. Besides that, our construction offers strong indistinguishability, a strong privacy notion recently introduced by Derler et al. [21].
- An efficient instantiation from post-quantum assumptions. In particular, we present a concrete construction from the learning parity with noise (LPN) problem. This yields the first chameleon-hash from post-quantum assumptions that provides a collision-resistance notion stronger than that provided by trapdoor commitments (e.g., the lattice-based chameleon-hash by Cash et al. [17]). We note that although the security of the used SSE NIZKs obtained from the Fiat-Shamir transform are just argued in the random oracle model (ROM), there is a recent line of works [25,26,37] that prove security of (SSE) NIZKs obtained via Fiat-Shamir in the quantum accessible ROM (QROM) [13]. Latter gives evidence that security in the ROM based on post-quantum assumptions is a meaningful security guarantee in practice. We leave it as an interesting open question to study the security of instantiations from other post-quantum assumptions in the QROM.
- An efficient instantiation from the discrete logarithm (DL) assumption, in contrast to the DDH assumption used by Derler et al. [20].
- The new notion of randomness unforgeability of chameleon-hashes. Intuitively, it requires that the adversary cannot find new randomness for an honestly generated hash. This notion is weaker than the uniqueness notion

by Camenisch et al. [16], but may find its usage in cases where neither the holder of the secret key nor the hashing party is adversarial, protecting against outsiders tempering with the generated values.

2 Preliminaries

Notation. With $\lambda \in \mathbb{N}$ we denote our security parameter. All algorithms implicitly take 1^λ as an additional input. We write $a \leftarrow_r A(x)$ if a is assigned to the output of an algorithm A with input x (and use $a \leftarrow A(x)$ if A is deterministic). An algorithm is efficient, if it runs in probabilistic polynomial time (PPT) in the length of its input. All algorithms are PPT, if not explicitly mentioned otherwise. Most algorithms may return a special error symbol $\bot \notin \{0,1\}^*$, denoting an exception. Returning output ends execution of an algorithm or an oracle. In order to make the presentation in the security proofs more compact, we occasionally use $(a, \bot) \leftarrow_r A(x)$ to indicate that the second output is either ignored or not returned by A. If S is a finite set, we write $a \leftarrow_r S$ to denote that a is chosen uniformly at random from S. $\mathcal{M}$ denotes a message space of a scheme, and we generally assume that $\mathcal{M}$ is derivable from the scheme's public parameters or its public key. For a list we require that there is an injective, and efficiently reversible, encoding, that maps the list to $\{0,1\}^*$. A function $\nu : \mathbb{N} \to \mathbb{R}_{\geq 0}$ is negligible, if it vanishes faster than every inverse polynomial, i.e., $\forall k \in \mathbb{N}$, $\exists n_0 \in \mathbb{N}$ such that $\nu(n) \leq n^{-k}$, $\forall n > n_0$.

2.1 One-Way Functions

A one-way function f is a function, where computing the function is easy, but reversing the function is hard.

Definition 1 (One-Way Functions). *A function* $f : \{0,1\}^* \to \{0,1\}^*$ *is one-way, if (1) there exists a PPT algorithm* $\mathcal{A}_1$ *so that for all* $\forall\, x \in \{0,1\}^* : \mathcal{A}_1(x) = f(x)$, *and (2) for every PPT adversary* $\mathcal{A}_2$ *there exists a negligible function* ν *such that:*

$$\Pr[x \leftarrow_r \{0,1\}^\lambda, x' \leftarrow_r \mathcal{A}_2(f(x)) : f(x) = f(x')] \leq \nu(\lambda).$$

2.2 Non-interactive Commitment Schemes

Non-interactive commitment schemes allow one party to commit itself to a value without revealing it [12]. Later, the committing party can give some opening information to the receiver to "open" the commitment.

Definition 2 (Non-interactive Commitments). *A non-interactive commitment scheme* Γ *is a tuple of PPT algorithms defined as follows:*

ParGen$_\Gamma$. *This algorithm takes as input a security parameter* λ *and outputs the public parameters* pp$_\Gamma$:

$$\mathsf{pp}_\Gamma \leftarrow_r \mathsf{ParGen}_\Gamma(1^\lambda)$$

Commit$_\Gamma$. *This algorithm takes as input a message m, and outputs a commitment C together with corresponding opening information O:*

$$(C, O) \leftarrow_r \mathsf{Commit}_\Gamma(\mathsf{pp}_\Gamma, m)$$

Open$_\Gamma$. *This deterministic algorithm takes as input a commitment C, a message m, and some opening information O. It outputs a decision $d \in \{0, 1\}$:*

$$d \leftarrow \mathsf{Open}_\Gamma(\mathsf{pp}_\Gamma, C, O, m)$$

Definition 3 (Correctness). *A non-interactive commitment scheme Γ is said to be (perfectly) correct, if for all $\lambda \in \mathbb{N}$, all $\mathsf{pp}_\Gamma \leftarrow_r \mathsf{ParGen}_\Gamma(1^\lambda)$, for all messages $m \in \mathcal{M}$, for all $(C, O) \leftarrow_r \mathsf{Commit}_\Gamma(\mathsf{pp}_\Gamma, m)$, it holds that $\mathsf{Open}_\Gamma(\mathsf{pp}_\Gamma, C, O, m) = 1$.*

Definition 4 (Binding). *A non-interactive commitment scheme is binding, if for all PPT adversaries $\mathcal{A}$ there exists a negligible function ν such that:*

$$\Pr[\mathbf{Exp}_{\mathcal{A},\Gamma}^{\mathsf{Binding}}(\lambda) = 1] \leq \nu(\lambda),$$

where the corresponding experiment is depicted in Fig. 1.

Definition 5 (Hiding). *A non-interactive commitment scheme Γ is hiding, if for any PPT adversary $\mathcal{A}$, there exists a negligible functions ν such that:*

$$\left| \Pr[\mathbf{Exp}_{\mathcal{A},\Gamma}^{\mathsf{Hiding}}(\lambda) = 1] - 1/2 \right| \leq \nu(\lambda),$$

where the corresponding experiment is depicted in Fig. 1.

$\mathbf{Exp}_{\mathcal{A},\Gamma}^{\mathsf{Binding}}(\lambda)$
$\mathsf{pp}_\Gamma \leftarrow_r \mathsf{ParGen}_\Gamma(1^\lambda)$
$(C^*, O^*, O'^*, m^*, m'^*) \leftarrow_r \mathcal{A}(\mathsf{pp}_\Gamma)$
return 1, if $\mathsf{Open}_\Gamma(\mathsf{pp}_\Gamma, C^*, O^*, m^*) = 1 \wedge$
$\qquad \mathsf{Open}_\Gamma(\mathsf{pp}_\Gamma, C^*, O'^*, m'^*) = 1 \wedge$
$\qquad m^* \neq m'^*$
return 0

(a) Binding

$\mathbf{Exp}_{\mathcal{A},\Gamma}^{\mathsf{Hiding}}(\lambda)$
$\mathsf{pp}_\Gamma \leftarrow_r \mathsf{ParGen}_\Gamma(1^\lambda)$
$b \leftarrow_r \{0, 1\}$
$b^* \leftarrow_r \mathcal{A}^{\mathsf{Commit}'_\Gamma(\mathsf{pp}_\Gamma, \cdot, \cdot, b)}(\mathsf{pp}_\Gamma)$
$\quad$ where Commit'_Γ on input pp_Γ, m_0, m_1, and b:
$\qquad$ return $\bot$, if $m_0 \notin \mathcal{M} \vee m_1 \notin \mathcal{M}$
$\qquad (C, O) \leftarrow_r \mathsf{Commit}_\Gamma(\mathsf{pp}_\Gamma, m_b)$
$\qquad$ return C
return 1, if $b^* = b$
return 0

(b) Hiding

Fig. 1. Security games for non-interactive commitments

2.3   Non-interactive Proof Systems

Let L be an NP-language with associated witness relation R, i.e., such that $L = \{x \mid \exists w : R(x, w) = 1\}$. A non-interactive proof system allows to prove membership of some statement x in the language L. More formally, such a system is defined as follows.

Definition 6 (Non-interactive Proof System). *A non-interactive proof system Π for language L consists of three algorithms $\{\mathsf{PG}_\Pi, \mathsf{Prf}_\Pi, \mathsf{Vfy}_\Pi\}$, such that:*

PG_Π. *The algorithm PG_Π outputs public parameters of the scheme, where λ is the security parameter:*

$$\mathsf{crs}_\Pi \leftarrow_r \mathsf{PG}_\Pi(1^\lambda)$$

Prf_Π. *The algorithm Prf_Π outputs the proof π, on input of the CRS crs_Π, statement x to be proven, and the corresponding witness w:*

$$\pi \leftarrow_r \mathsf{Prf}_\Pi(\mathsf{crs}_\Pi, x, w)$$

Vfy_Π. *The deterministic algorithm Vfy_Π verifies the proof π by outputting a bit $d \in \{0, 1\}$, w.r.t. to some CRS crs_Π and some statement statement x:*

$$d \leftarrow \mathsf{Vfy}_\Pi(\mathsf{crs}_\Pi, x, \pi)$$

Definition 7 (Correctness). *A non-interactive proof system is called correct, if for all $\lambda \in \mathbb{N}$, for all $\mathsf{crs}_\Pi \leftarrow_r \mathsf{PG}_\Pi(1^\lambda)$, for all $x \in L$, for all w such that $R(x, w) = 1$, for all $\pi \leftarrow_r \mathsf{Prf}_\Pi(\mathsf{crs}_\Pi, x, w)$, it holds that $\mathsf{Vfy}_\Pi(\mathsf{crs}_\Pi, x, \pi) = 1$.*

In the context of (zero-knowledge) proof-systems, correctness is sometimes also referred to as completeness. In addition, we require two standard security notions for zero-knowledge proofs of knowledge: zero-knowledge and simulation-sound extractability (also known as simulation-extractability). We define them analogously to the definitions given in [22].

Informally speaking, zero-knowledge says that the receiver of the proof π does not learn anything except the validity of the statement. It is required that the distribution of crs_Π output by SIM_1 is distributed identically to PG_Π.

Definition 8 (Zero-Knowledge). *A non-interactive proof system Π for language L is zero-knowledge, if for any PPT adversary $\mathcal{A}$, there exists an PPT simulator $\mathsf{SIM} = (\mathsf{SIM}_1, \mathsf{SIM}_2)$ such that there exist negligible functions ν_1 and ν_2 such that*

$$\Big| \Pr\left[\mathsf{crs}_\Pi \leftarrow_r \mathsf{PG}_\Pi(1^\lambda) : \mathcal{A}(\mathsf{crs}_\Pi) = 1 \right] -$$

$$\Pr\left[(\mathsf{crs}_\Pi, \tau) \leftarrow_r \mathsf{SIM}_1(1^\lambda) : \mathcal{A}(\mathsf{crs}_\Pi) = 1 \right] \Big| \leq \nu_1(\lambda),$$

and that

$$\Big| \Pr\left[\mathbf{Exp}_{\mathcal{A},\Pi,\mathsf{SIM}}^{\text{Zero-Knowledge}}(\lambda) = 1 \right] - 1/2 \Big| \leq \nu_2(\lambda),$$

where the corresponding experiment is depicted in Fig. 2a.

$$\mathbf{Exp}_{\mathcal{A},\Pi,\mathsf{SIM}}^{\mathsf{Zero\text{-}Knowledge}}(\lambda)$$
$(\mathsf{crs}_\Pi, \tau) \leftarrow_r \mathsf{SIM}_1(1^\lambda)$
$b \leftarrow_r \{0,1\}$
$b^* \leftarrow_r \mathcal{A}^{P_b(\cdot,\cdot)}(\mathsf{crs}_\Pi)$
  where P_0 on input x, w:
    return $\pi \leftarrow_r \mathsf{Prf}_\Pi(\mathsf{crs}_\Pi, x, w)$, if $R(x,w) = 1$
    return $\bot$
  and P_1 on input x, w:
    return $\pi \leftarrow_r \mathsf{SIM}_2(\mathsf{crs}_\Pi, \tau, x)$, if $R(x,w) = 1$
    return $\bot$
return 1, if $b^* = b$
return 0

$$\mathbf{Exp}_{\mathcal{A},\Pi,\mathcal{E}}^{\mathsf{SimSoundExt}}(\lambda)$$
$(\mathsf{crs}_\Pi, \tau, \zeta) \leftarrow_r \mathcal{E}_1(1^\lambda)$
$\mathcal{Q} \leftarrow \emptyset$
$(x^*, \pi^*) \leftarrow_r \mathcal{A}^{\mathsf{SIM}(\cdot)}(\mathsf{crs}_\Pi)$
  where SIM on input x:
    obtain $\pi \leftarrow_r \mathsf{SIM}_2(\mathsf{crs}_\Pi, \tau, x)$
    $\mathcal{Q} \leftarrow \mathcal{Q} \cup \{(x, \pi)\}$
    return π
$w^* \leftarrow_r \mathcal{E}_2(\mathsf{crs}_\Pi, \zeta, x^*, \pi^*)$
return 1, if $\mathsf{Vfy}_\Pi(\mathsf{crs}_\Pi, x^*, \pi^*) = 1 \wedge$
  $R(x^*, w^*) = 0 \wedge (x^*, \pi^*) \notin \mathcal{Q}$
return 0

(a) Zero-Knowledge   (b) Simulation-Sound Extractability

Fig. 2. Security games for non-interactive proof systems

Simulation-sound extractability says that every adversary which is able to come up with a proof π^* for a statement must know the witness, even when seeing proofs for statements potentially not in L [41]. Clearly, this implies that the proofs output by a simulation-sound extractable proof-systems are non-malleable. Note that the definition of simulation-sound extractability of [30] is stronger than ours in the sense that the adversary also gets the trapdoor ζ as input. However, in our context this weaker notion (previously also used e.g. in [1,24]) suffices.

Definition 9 (Simulation-Sound Extractability). *A zero-knowledge non-interactive proof system Π for language L is said to be simulation-sound extractable, if for any PPT adversary $\mathcal{A}$, there exists a PPT extractor $\mathcal{E} = (\mathcal{E}_1, \mathcal{E}_2)$, such that*

$$\Big| \Pr\big[(\mathsf{crs}_\Pi, \tau) \leftarrow_r \mathsf{SIM}_1(1^\lambda) : \mathcal{A}(\mathsf{crs}_\Pi, \tau) = 1\big] -$$
$$\Pr\big[(\mathsf{crs}_\Pi, \tau, \zeta) \leftarrow_r \mathcal{E}_1(1^\lambda) : \mathcal{A}(\mathsf{crs}_\Pi, \tau) = 1\big] \Big| = 0,$$

and that there exist a negligible function ν so that

$$\Pr\Big[\mathbf{Exp}_{\mathcal{A},\Pi,\mathcal{E}}^{\mathsf{SimSoundExt}}(\lambda) = 1\Big] \le \nu(\lambda),$$

where the corresponding experiment is depicted in Fig. 2b.

3   Syntax and Security of Chameleon-Hashes

We next present the formal framework for CHs used by Derler et al. [20], which itself is based on prior work [3,15,16].

Definition 10. *A chameleon-hash CH is a tuple of five PPT algorithms (CHPG, CHKG, CHash, CHCheck, CHAdapt), such that:*

CHPG. *The algorithm* CHPG, *on input a security parameter* λ *outputs public parameters of the scheme:*

$$pp_{ch} \leftarrow_r CHPG(1^\lambda)$$

We assume that pp_{ch} *contains* 1^λ *and is implicit input to all other algorithms.* CHKG. *The algorithm* CHKG, *on input the public parameters* pp_{ch} *outputs the private and public keys of the scheme:*

$$(sk_{ch}, pk_{ch}) \leftarrow_r CHKG(pp_{ch})$$

CHash. *The algorithm* CHash *gets as input the public key* pk_{ch}, *and a message* m *to hash. It outputs a hash* h, *and some randomness* r:[1]

$$(h, r) \leftarrow_r CHash(pk_{ch}, m)$$

CHCheck. *The deterministic algorithm* CHCheck *gets as input the public key* pk_{ch}, *a message* m, *randomness* r, *and a hash* h. *It outputs a bit* $d \in \{0, 1\}$, *indicating whether the hash* h *is valid:*

$$d \leftarrow CHCheck(pk_{ch}, m, r, h)$$

CHAdapt. *The algorithm* CHAdapt *on input of a secret key* sk_{ch}, *the message* m, *the randomness* r, *hash* h, *and a new message* m' *outputs new randomness* r':

$$r' \leftarrow_r CHAdapt(sk_{ch}, m, m', r, h)$$

Definition 11 (Correctness). *A chameleon-hash is called correct, if for all security parameters* $\lambda \in \mathbb{N}$, *for all* $pp_{ch} \leftarrow_r CHPG(1^\lambda)$, *for all* $(sk_{ch}, pk_{ch}) \leftarrow_r CHKG(pp_{ch})$, *for all* $m \in \mathcal{M}$, *for all* $(h, r) \leftarrow_r CHash(pk_{ch}, m)$, *for all* $m' \in \mathcal{M}$, *we have for all* $r' \leftarrow_r CHAdapt(sk_{ch}, m, m', r, h)$, *that* $1 = CHCheck(pk_{ch}, m, r, h) = CHCheck(pk_{ch}, m', r', h)$.

Full Collision-Resistance. Derler et al. [20] recently defined the notion of full collision-resistance. Here, the adversary gets access to a collision-finding oracle CHAdapt', which outputs a collision for the adversarially chosen hash, but also keeps track of each of the queried and returned hash/message *pairs* (h, m) and (h, m'), using the list $\mathcal{Q}$. The adversary wins, if it comes up with a hash/message pair (h^*, m^*) colliding with (m'^*, r'^*), for the given public key, where (m'^*, r'^*) was never queried to or output from the collision-finding oracle.

Definition 12 (Full Collision-Resistance). *A chameleon-hash* CH *provides full collision-resistance, if for any PPT adversary* $\mathcal{A}$ *there exists a negligible function* ν *such that*

$$\Pr[\mathbf{Exp}_{\mathcal{A},CH}^{F\text{-CollRes}}(\lambda) = 1] \le \nu(\lambda)$$

The corresponding experiment is depicted in Fig. 3a.

---

[1] We note that the randomness r is also sometimes called "check value" [3].

$\mathbf{Exp}_{\mathcal{A},\mathsf{CH}}^{\mathsf{F\text{-}CollRes}}(\lambda)$

  $\mathsf{pp_{ch}} \leftarrow_r \mathsf{CHPG}(1^\lambda)$
  $(\mathsf{sk_{ch}}, \mathsf{pk_{ch}}) \leftarrow_r \mathsf{CHKG}(\mathsf{pp_{ch}})$
  $\mathcal{Q} \leftarrow \emptyset$
  $(m^*, r^*, m'^*, r'^*, h^*) \leftarrow_r \mathcal{A}^{\mathsf{CHAdapt}'(\mathsf{sk_{ch}}, \cdots, \cdot)}(\mathsf{pk_{ch}})$
    oracle $\mathsf{CHAdapt}'$ on input $\mathsf{sk_{ch}}, m, m', r, h$:
      return $\bot$, if $\mathsf{CHCheck}(\mathsf{pk_{ch}}, m, r, h) \neq 1$
      $r' \leftarrow_r \mathsf{CHAdapt}(\mathsf{sk_{ch}}, m, m', r, h)$
      Return $\bot$, if $r' = \bot$
      $\mathcal{Q} \leftarrow \mathcal{Q} \cup \{(h, m), (h, m')\}$
      return r'
  return 1, if $\mathsf{CHCheck}(\mathsf{pk_{ch}}, m^*, r^*, h^*) = 1 \wedge$
    $\mathsf{CHCheck}(\mathsf{pk_{ch}}, m'^*, r'^*, h^*) = 1 \wedge$
    $m^* \neq m'^* \wedge (h^*, m^*) \notin \mathcal{Q}$
  return 0

(a) Full Collision-Resistance

$\mathbf{Exp}_{\mathcal{A},\mathsf{CH}}^{\mathsf{S\text{-}Ind}}(\lambda)$

  $\mathsf{pp_{ch}} \leftarrow_r \mathsf{CHPG}(1^\lambda)$
  $(\mathsf{sk_{ch}}, \mathsf{pk_{ch}}) \leftarrow_r \mathsf{CHKG}(\mathsf{pp_{ch}})$
  $b \leftarrow_r \{0, 1\}$
  $b^* \leftarrow_r \mathcal{A}^{\mathsf{HashOrAdapt}(\mathsf{sk_{ch}}, \mathsf{pk_{ch}}, \cdot, \cdot, b)}(\mathsf{sk_{ch}}, \mathsf{pk_{ch}})$
    where $\mathsf{HashOrAdapt}$ on input $\mathsf{sk_{ch}}, \mathsf{pk_{ch}}, m, m', b$:
      $(h, r) \leftarrow_r \mathsf{CHash}(\mathsf{pk_{ch}}, m')$
      $(h', r') \leftarrow_r \mathsf{CHash}(\mathsf{pk_{ch}}, m)$
      $r'' \leftarrow_r \mathsf{CHAdapt}(\mathsf{sk_{ch}}, m, m', r', h')$
      return $\bot$, if $r'' = \bot \vee r' = \bot \vee r = \bot$
      if $b = 0$, return (h, r)
      if $b = 1$, return (h', r'')
  return 1, if $b^* = b$
  return 0

(b) Strong Indistinguishability

Fig. 3. Security games for Chameleon-Hashes

Strong Indistinguishability. Strong indistinguishability is a strong privacy notion [21]. It requires that a randomness r does not reveal whether it was generated using CHash or CHAdapt, even if the adversary $\mathcal{A}$ knows all secret keys.

Definition 13 (Strong Indistinguishability). *A chameleon-hash* CH *provides strong indistinguishability, if for any PPT adversary $\mathcal{A}$ there exists a negligible function ν such that*

$$\left| \Pr[\mathbf{Exp}_{\mathcal{A},\mathsf{CH}}^{\mathsf{S\text{-}Ind}}(\lambda) = 1] - 1/2 \right| \leq \nu(\lambda)$$

The corresponding experiment is depicted in Fig. 3b.

Randomness Unforgeability. Uniqueness, introduced by Camenisch et al. [16], requires that an adversary controlling *all* values (but the public parameters) cannot find two distinct randomness values $r^* \neq r'^*$ for the same hash/message pair (h, m). Uniqueness is a very strong notion that is hard to achieve, and, in this strong form, only seems to be required in one particular use case [7,16,33,42]. To this end, we introduce a slightly weaker variant that is easier to achieve while still being useful in other applications. It requires that an adversary cannot find new randomness for hashes it did not create by itself. We call this notion randomness unforgeability.

In our formalization, the challenger generates the key pair and parameters honestly, and uses $\mathsf{pk_{ch}}$ to initialize the adversary. The adversary gains access to two oracles. The oracle CHash' allows the adversary to adaptively receive hashes on messages of its choice. The generated hash/randomness pairs (h, r) are stored in a set $\mathcal{Q}$. The oracle $\mathsf{CHAdapt}'$ allows the adversary to adaptively find collisions for hashes. If the adversary queries a hash/randomness pair which is an element of $\mathcal{Q}$, the resulting (h, r') is also added to $\mathcal{Q}$. The adversary wins, if it can come up with a new randomness r^* (i.e., not stored in $\mathcal{Q}$) for whatever message m^*, verifying for a hash h^* which was output by CHash'.

$$\mathbf{Exp}_{\mathcal{A},\mathsf{CH}}^{\mathsf{Rand\text{-}Uf}}(\lambda)$$

$\mathsf{pp}_{\mathsf{ch}} \leftarrow_r \mathsf{CHPG}(1^\lambda)$
$(\mathsf{sk}_{\mathsf{ch}}, \mathsf{pk}_{\mathsf{ch}}) \leftarrow_r \mathsf{CHKG}(\mathsf{pp}_{\mathsf{ch}})$
$\mathcal{Q} \leftarrow \emptyset$
$(m^*, h^*, r^*) \leftarrow_r \mathcal{A}^{\mathsf{CHash}'(\mathsf{pk}_{\mathsf{ch}}, \cdot), \mathsf{CHAdapt}'(\mathsf{sk}_{\mathsf{ch}}, \cdot, \cdot, \cdot, \cdot)}(\mathsf{pk}_{\mathsf{ch}})$
    oracle CHash' on input $\mathsf{pk}_{\mathsf{ch}}, m$:
        $(h, r) \leftarrow_r \mathsf{CHash}(\mathsf{pk}_{\mathsf{ch}}, m)$
        $\mathcal{Q} \leftarrow \mathcal{Q} \cup \{(h, r)\}$
        return (h, r)
    oracle $\mathsf{CHAdapt}'$ on input $\mathsf{sk}_{\mathsf{ch}}, m, m', r, h$:
        $r' \leftarrow_r \mathsf{CHAdapt}(\mathsf{sk}_{\mathsf{ch}}, m, m', r, h)$
        return $\perp$, if $\mathsf{CHCheck}(\mathsf{pk}_{\mathsf{ch}}, m', r', h) \neq 1$
        If $\exists (h, \cdot) \in \mathcal{Q}$:
            $\mathcal{Q} \leftarrow \mathcal{Q} \cup \{(h, r')\}$
        return r'
return 1, if $\mathsf{CHCheck}(\mathsf{pk}_{\mathsf{ch}}, m^*, r^*, h^*) = 1 \wedge$
    $(h^*, \cdot) \in \mathcal{Q} \wedge (h^*, r^*) \notin \mathcal{Q}$
return 0

Fig. 4. Randomness unforgeability

Definition 14 (Randomness Unforgeability). *A chameleon-hash* CH *offers randomness unforgeability, if for any PPT adversary* $\mathcal{A}$ *there exists a negligible function* ν *such that*

$$\Pr[\mathbf{Exp}_{\mathcal{A},\mathsf{CH}}^{\mathsf{Rand\text{-}Uf}}(\lambda) = 1] \leq \nu(\lambda)$$

The corresponding experiment is depicted in Fig. 4.

4   Generic Construction

The main idea of our generic construction follows the original idea by Derler et al. [20], but slightly altered to meet our requirements. Namely, hashing a message m means committing to it. The randomness r is a SSE NIZK proving membership of a tuple containing the opening O for the commitment, and the pre-image x of a one-way function f, fulfilling the following NP-relation:

$$L := \{(\mathsf{pp}_\Gamma, h, m, y) \mid \exists (O, x) : \mathsf{Open}_\Gamma(\mathsf{pp}_\Gamma, h, O, m) = 1 \vee y = f(x)\} \quad (1)$$

Informally, this language requires the prover to demonstrate that it either knows an opening O such that h is a well-formed commitment of m under pp_Γ, or the pre-image x corresponding to $f(x)$ of a one-way function f is known. Our construction of a fully collision-resistant, strongly indistinguishable, and weakly unique, CH is presented as Construction 1.

4.1   Security

Subsequently, we prove the security of our CH in Construction 1.

Theorem 1. *If* Γ *is correct, and* Π *is complete, then* CH *in Construction 1 is correct.*

CHPG′(1^λ) : Fix a commitment scheme Γ, a one-way function f, and a compatible NIZK proof system for language L in (1). Return $pp_{ch} = (f, pp_\Gamma, crs_\Pi)$, where

$$pp_\Gamma \leftarrow_r \mathsf{ParGen}_\Gamma(1^\lambda), \text{ and } crs_\Pi \leftarrow_r \mathsf{PG}_\Pi(1^\lambda).$$

CHKG(pp_{ch}) : Return $(sk_{ch}, pk_{ch}) = (x, y)$, where

$$x \leftarrow_r \{0,1\}^\lambda, y \leftarrow f(x).$$

CHash(pk_{ch}, m) : Parse pk_{ch} as $((f, pp_\Gamma, crs_\Pi), y)$ and return $(h, r) = (C, \pi)$, where

$$(C, O) \leftarrow_r \mathsf{Commit}_\Gamma(pp_\Gamma, m), \text{ and } \pi \leftarrow_r \mathsf{Prf}_\Pi(crs_\Pi, (pp_\Gamma, h, m, y), (O, \bot)).$$

CHCheck(pk_{ch}, m, r, h) : Parse pk_{ch} as $((f, pp_\Gamma, crs_\Pi), y)$ and r as π, and return 1, if the following holds, and 0 otherwise:

$$m \in \mathcal{M} \wedge \mathsf{Vfy}_\Pi(crs_\Pi, (pp_\Gamma, h, m, y), \pi) = 1.$$

CHAdapt(sk_{ch}, m, m', r, h) : Parse sk_{ch} as x, and set $y \leftarrow f(x)$. Check that $m' \in \mathcal{M}$ and $\mathsf{CHCheck}(y, m, r, h) = 1$. Return $\bot$, if not. Otherwise, return $r' = \pi'$, where

$$\pi' \leftarrow_r \mathsf{Prf}_\Pi(crs_\Pi, (pp_\Gamma, h, m', y), (\bot, x)).$$

Construction 1: Our Construction of a Fully Collision-Resistant CH

Correctness follows from inspection and the (perfect) correctness of the used primitives.

Theorem 2. *If Γ is binding, f is a one-way function, and Π is simulation-sound extractable, then CH in Construction 1 is fully collision-resistant.*

The proof of this theorem is along the same lines as that in Derler et al. [20].

Proof. We prove full collision-resistance using a sequence of games.

Game 0: The original full collision-resistance game.
Game 1: As Game 0, but we replace the CHPG algorithm with an algorithm CHPG′ and modify the CHAdapt′ oracle as follows:

CHPG′(1^λ) :

$$crs_\Pi \leftarrow_r \mathsf{PG}_\Pi(1^\lambda) \rightsquigarrow \boxed{(crs_\Pi, \tau) \leftarrow_r \mathsf{SIM}_1(1^\lambda)}.$$

CHAdapt′(sk_{ch}, m, m', r, h) : In CHAdapt:

$$\pi \leftarrow_r \mathsf{Prf}_\Pi(crs_\Pi, (pp_\Gamma, h, m, y), (x, \bot)) \rightsquigarrow \boxed{\pi \leftarrow_r \mathsf{SIM}_2(crs_\Pi, \tau, (pp_\Gamma, h, m, y))}.$$

Transition - Game 0 → Game 1: We bound the probability for an adversary to detect this game change by presenting a hybrid game, which, depending on a zero-knowledge challenger $\mathcal{C}^{zk}$, either produces the distribution in Game 0 or Game 1, respectively. In particular, assume that we use the following algorithm CHPG″ instead of CHPG and CHPG′:

$\underline{\mathsf{CHPG}''(1^\lambda)}$:

$$(\mathsf{crs}_\Pi, \tau) \leftarrow_r \mathsf{SIM}_1(1^\lambda) \rightsquigarrow \boxed{\mathsf{crs}_\Pi \leftarrow_r \mathcal{C}^{\mathsf{zk}}}.$$

$\underline{\mathsf{CHAdapt}'(\mathsf{sk}_{\mathsf{ch}}, m, m', r, h)}$: In CHAdapt:

$$\pi' \leftarrow_r \mathsf{SIM}_2(\mathsf{crs}_\Pi, \tau, (\mathsf{pp}_\Gamma, h, m', y)) \rightsquigarrow \boxed{\pi' \leftarrow_r \mathcal{C}^{\mathsf{zk}}.P_b((\mathsf{pp}_\Gamma, h, m', y), (\bot, x))}.$$

Clearly, if the challenger's internal bit is 0 we simulate the distribution in Game 0, whereas we simulate the distribution in Game 1 otherwise. We have that $|\Pr[S_0] - \Pr[S_1]| \leq \nu_{\mathsf{zk}}(\lambda)$.

Game 2: As Game 1, but we replace the CHPG' algorithm with an algorithm CHPG''' which works as follows:

$\underline{\mathsf{CHPG}'''(1^\lambda)}$:

$$(\mathsf{crs}_\Pi, \tau) \leftarrow_r \mathsf{SIM}_1(1^\lambda) \rightsquigarrow \boxed{(\mathsf{crs}_\Pi, \tau, \zeta) \leftarrow_r \mathcal{E}_1(1^\lambda)}.$$

Transition - Game 1 → Game 2: Under simulation-sound extractability, Game 1 and Game 2 are indistinguishable. That is, $|\Pr[S_1] - \Pr[S_2]| = 0$.

Game 3: As Game 2, but we keep a list $\mathcal{Q}$ of all tuples (h, r, m) previously submitted to the collision-finding oracle which are accepted by the CHCheck algorithm, where h was never submitted to the collision-finding oracle before.

Transition - Game 2 → Game 3: This change is conceptual, i.e., $|\Pr[S_2] - \Pr[S_3]| = 0$.

Game 4: As Game 3, but for every valid collision $(m^*, r^*, m'^*, r'^*, h^*)$ output by the adversary we observe that either (m^*, r^*) or (m'^*, r'^*) must be a "fresh" collision, i.e., one that was never output by the collision-finding oracle. We assume, without loss of generality, that (m'^*, r'^*) is the "fresh" collision. We run $(x', O') \leftarrow_r \mathcal{E}_2(\mathsf{crs}_\Pi, \zeta, (\mathsf{pp}_\Gamma, h^*, m'^*, y), r'^*)$ and abort if the extraction fails. We call this event E_1.

Transition - Game 3 → Game 4: Game 3 and Game 4 proceed identically, unless E_1 occurs. Assume, towards contradiction, that event E_1 occurs with non-negligible probability. We now construct an adversary $\mathcal{B}$ which breaks the simulation-sound extractability property of the NIZK proof-system with non-negligible probability. We engage with a simulation-sound extractability challenger $\mathcal{C}^{\mathsf{sse}}$ and modify the algorithms as follows:

$\underline{\mathsf{CHPG}''''(1^\lambda)}$:

$$(\mathsf{crs}_\Pi, \tau, \zeta) \leftarrow_r \mathcal{E}_1(1^\lambda) \rightsquigarrow \boxed{(\mathsf{crs}_\Pi, \bot, \bot) \leftarrow_r \mathcal{C}^{\mathsf{sse}}}.$$

$\underline{\mathsf{CHAdapt}''(\mathsf{sk}_{\mathsf{ch}}, m, m', r, h)}$:

$$\pi' \leftarrow_r \mathsf{SIM}_2(\mathsf{crs}_\Pi, \tau, (\mathsf{pp}_\Gamma, h, m', y)) \rightsquigarrow \boxed{\pi' \leftarrow_r \mathcal{C}^{\mathsf{sse}}.\mathsf{SIM}(\mathsf{pp}_\Gamma, h, m', y)}.$$

In the end we output $((\mathsf{pp}_\Gamma, h^*, m'^*, y), r'^*)$ to the challenger. This shows that we have $|\Pr[S_3] - \Pr[S_4]| \leq \nu_{\mathsf{sse}}(\lambda)$.

Game 5: As Game 4, but we observe that if (m^*, r^*) does not correspond to a fresh collision for h^* in the above sense, then we will have an entry $(h^*, r, m) \in$

$\mathcal{Q}$ where (m, r) is a "fresh" collision, i.e., one computed by the adversary. We run the extractor for the fresh collision, i.e., either obtain $(x'', O'') \leftarrow_r \mathcal{E}_2(\mathsf{crs}_\Pi, \zeta, (\mathsf{pp}_\Gamma, h^*, m^*, y), r^*)$ or $(x'', O'') \leftarrow_r \mathcal{E}_2(\mathsf{crs}_\Pi, \zeta, (\mathsf{pp}_\Gamma, h^*, m, y), r)$, respectively. In case the extraction fails, we abort. We call the abort event E_2.

Transition - Game 4 → Game 5: Analogously to the transition between Game 3 and Game 4, we argue that Game 4 and Game 5 proceed identically unless E_2 occurs which is why we do not restate the reduction to simulation-sound extractability here. We have that $|\Pr[S_4] - \Pr[S_5]| \leq \nu_{\mathsf{sse}}(\lambda)$.

Reduction to Binding and One-Wayness: We are now ready to construct an adversary $\mathcal{B}$ which breaks either the binding property of the used one-way function or the binding property of the underlying Γ. Our adversary $\mathcal{B}$ proceeds as follows. It receives pp_Γ from its binding challenger, as well as, f and y from a one-way challenger. It embeds them straightforwardly as $\mathsf{pp}_{\mathsf{ch}}$ and $\mathsf{pk}_{\mathsf{ch}}$ to initialize $\mathcal{A}$. Now we know that we have extracted two witnesses (x, O) as well as (x'', O'') where one attests membership of $(\mathsf{pk}_\Omega, h^*, m'^*, y)$ in L and one attests membership of $(\mathsf{pk}_\Omega, h^*, m'', y)$ for some $m'' \neq m'^*$ in L. In either case, $\mathcal{B}$ can check whether $f(x) = y$ or $f(x'') = y$ holds. In this case, it can return x, or x'' resp., to its one-way challenger. In all other cases, O and O'' open the commitment h^* to different messages. Thus, $\mathcal{B}$ can directly return (h^*, O, O'', m^*, m'^*) as its own forgery. A union bound gives us $\Pr[S_5] \leq \nu_{\mathsf{owf}}(\lambda) + \nu_{\mathsf{binding}}(\lambda)$. This concludes the proof. $\square$

Remark 1. Note that, like Derler et al. [20], we conduct a full collision-resistance proof that only requires extracting twice. While the formal notion of simulation-sound extractability would allow us to simply extract in every oracle query, and, thus, obtain a more general result, this is to ensure that one can plug in proof systems that rely on a rewinding extractor without putting a restriction on the allowed adversarial queries. We note, however, that this way of proving the theorem implies some limitations and if one can not afford these limitations one would need to prove it via extracting in every oracle query, thus excluding some of the proof systems we can plausibly plug in when only extracting twice. The limitations are as follows: Observe that the extractor is formally only guaranteed to work as long as either the proof we want to extract from, or the corresponding statement does not correspond to an output of a query to the simulator. For the proof above to go through, this means that the concrete proof system plugged into our generic construction needs to have the property that for any given valid proof for some statement the probability that the proof output by an honest run of the simulator for the same statement will only collide with this proof with negligible probability. This is a pretty common property for proof systems, and all proof systems we can think of provide the required guarantees (e.g., Groth-Sahai proofs [31], or Fiat-Shamir transformed Σ protocols).

Theorem 3. *If Γ is hiding, and Π is zero-knowledge, then CH in Construction 1 is strongly indistinguishable.*

In the proof, we use $\boxed{\text{frameboxes}}$ and $\rightsquigarrow$ to highlight the changes we make in the algorithms throughout a sequence of games (and we only show the changes).

Proof. To prove strong indistinguishability, we use a sequence of games:

Game 0: The original strong indistinguishability game.

Game 1: As Game 0, but we modify the algorithms CHPG and the HashOrAdapt oracle as follows:

$\underline{\mathsf{CHPG}'(1^\lambda)}$:

$$\mathsf{crs}_\Pi \leftarrow_r \mathsf{PG}_\Pi(1^\lambda) \rightsquigarrow \boxed{(\mathsf{crs}_\Pi, \tau) \leftarrow_r \mathsf{SIM}_1(1^\lambda)}.$$

$\underline{\mathsf{HashOrAdapt}'(\mathsf{pk}_{ch}, \mathsf{sk}_{ch}, m, m', b)}$: In CHash:

$$\pi \leftarrow_r \mathsf{Prf}_\Pi(...) \rightsquigarrow \boxed{\pi \leftarrow_r \mathsf{SIM}_2(\mathsf{crs}_\Pi, \tau, (\mathsf{pp}_\Gamma, h, m, \mathsf{pk}_{ch}))}$$

and CHAdapt:

$$\pi' \leftarrow_r \mathsf{Prf}_\Pi(...) \rightsquigarrow \boxed{\pi' \leftarrow_r \mathsf{SIM}_2(\mathsf{crs}_\Pi, \tau, (\mathsf{pk}_\Omega, h, m', f(\mathsf{sk}_{ch})))}.$$

Transition - Game 0 → Game 1: We bound the probability for an adversary to detect this game change by presenting a hybrid game, which, depending on a zero-knowledge challenger $\mathcal{C}^{zk}$, either produces the distribution in Game 0 or Game 1, respectively. In particular, assume that we use the following changes:

$\underline{\mathsf{CHPG}''(1^\lambda)}$:

$$(\mathsf{crs}_\Pi, \tau) \leftarrow_r \mathsf{SIM}_1(1^\lambda) \rightsquigarrow \boxed{\mathsf{crs}_\Pi \leftarrow_r \mathcal{C}^{zk}}$$

$\underline{\mathsf{HashOrAdapt}''(\mathsf{pk}_{ch}, \mathsf{sk}_{ch}, m, m', b)}$: In CHash:

$$\pi \leftarrow_r \mathsf{SIM}_2(...) \rightsquigarrow \boxed{\pi \leftarrow_r \mathcal{C}^{zk}.P_b((\mathsf{pp}_\Gamma, h, m, \mathsf{pk}_{ch}), (O, \perp))}.$$

and CHAdapt:

$$\pi' \leftarrow_r \mathsf{SIM}_2(...) \rightsquigarrow \boxed{\pi' \leftarrow_r \mathcal{C}^{zk}.P_b((\mathsf{pp}_\Gamma, h, m', f(\mathsf{sk}_{ch})), (\perp, x))}.$$

Clearly, if the challenger's internal bit is 0 we simulate the distribution in Game 0, whereas we simulate the distribution in Game 1 otherwise. We have that $|\Pr[S_0] - \Pr[S_1]| \le \nu_{zk}(\lambda)$.

Game 2: As Game 1, but we modify the HashOrAdapt oracle as follows:

$\underline{\mathsf{HashOrAdapt}'''(\cdot, \cdot, \cdot, b)}$: In CHash:

$$(C, O) \leftarrow_r \mathsf{Commit}_\Gamma(\mathsf{pp}_\Gamma, m) \rightsquigarrow \boxed{(C, O) \leftarrow_r \mathsf{Commit}_\Gamma(\mathsf{pp}_\Gamma, 0)}.$$

Transition - Game 1 → Game 2: We bound the probability for an adversary to distinguish between two consecutive games by introducing a hybrid game which uses a hiding challenger to interpolate between two consecutive games.

$\underline{\mathsf{CHPG'''(\lambda)}}$:

$$\mathsf{pp}_\Gamma \leftarrow_r \mathsf{ParGen}_\Gamma(1^\lambda) \rightsquigarrow \boxed{\mathsf{pp}_\Gamma \leftarrow_r C^{\mathsf{hiding}}}.$$

$\underline{\mathsf{HashOrAdapt''''}(\mathsf{pk}_{\mathsf{ch}}, \mathsf{sk}_{\mathsf{ch}}, \mathsf{m}, \mathsf{m}', \mathsf{b})}$: In CHash:

$$(C, O) \leftarrow_r \mathsf{Commit}_\Gamma(\mathsf{pp}_\Gamma, 0) \rightsquigarrow \boxed{(C, \bot) \leftarrow_r C^{\mathsf{hiding}}.\mathsf{Commit}'_\Gamma(m, 0)}.$$

Now, depending on the challenger's bit, we either simulate Game 1 or Game 2. Thus we have that $|\Pr[S_1] - \Pr[S_2]| \le \nu_{\mathsf{hiding}}(\lambda)$.

Now, the strong indistinguishability game is independent of the bit b, proving strong indistinguishability.   □

Theorem 4. *If Γ is binding and hiding, f is a one-way function, Π is simulation-sound extractable, and CH fully collision-resistant, then CH in Construction 1 is randomness unforgeable.*

The proof of this theorem is presented in the full versions and omitted here due to the lack of space.

5   Concrete Instantiations

5.1   Concrete Instantiation from Pre-quantum Primitives

Our pre-quantum instantiation follows our generic compiler. As instantiation for Γ we use Pedersen commitments [39] in discrete-logarithm (DL) hard groups. For f we use is the exponentiation in the aforementioned group, which is a one-way function under the DL assumption. For the non-interactive proof system, we use Fiat-Shamir (FS) transformed Σ-protocols for DLOG relations in the random-oracle model [29] and additionally apply the compiler by Faust et al. [28] to make it simulation-sound extractable. This compiler requires additionally including the statement x upon hashing in the challenge computation. In addition the Σ-protocol needs to provide a property called quasi-unique responses for this compiler to apply, which is straight forward for our statements. See, e.g., [23], for a detailed discussion of this transformation. Although when using FS we have to rely on a rewinding extractor, this choice is suitable as in our security proofs we only need to extract a bounded number of times (i.e., twice).

   We provide this concrete instantiation as Construction 2, where we let $(\mathbb{G}, g_1, q) \leftarrow_r \mathsf{GGen}(1^\lambda)$ be an instance generator which returns a prime-order, and multiplicatively written, group $\mathbb{G}$, where the DL problem is hard, along with two generators g_1, g_2 as the Pedersen parameters (we compute $g_2 = H'(g_1)$ where H' is a random oracle to avoid a trusted setup). Note that an SSE NIZK for the required L in (2) is obtained using an *or* composition of a proof of a discrete logarithm [19] of Fiat-Shamir transformed Σ-protocols.

$$L := \{(y, h, m) \mid \exists\, (x, \xi)\ :\ h = (g_1^m g_2^\xi) \ \lor\ y = g_1^x\}. \tag{2}$$

$\mathsf{CHPG}(1^\lambda)$: Outputs the public parameters $(\mathbb{G}, g_1, g_2, q, H)$, where $\mathsf{pp_{ch}} = (\mathbb{G}, g_1, q) \leftarrow_r \mathsf{GGen}(1^\lambda)$, $g_2 \leftarrow H'(g_1)$, and a hash-functions $H : \{0,1\}^* \to \mathbb{Z}_q$ and $H' : \{0,1\}^* \to \mathbb{G}$ (which we assume to behave like a random oracle and to be implicitly available to all algorithms below).

$\mathsf{CHKG}(\mathsf{pp_{ch}})$: Return $(\mathsf{sk_{ch}}, \mathsf{pk_{ch}}) = (x, y)$, where $x \leftarrow_r \mathbb{Z}_q$ and $y \leftarrow g_1^x$.

$\mathsf{CHash}(\mathsf{pk_{ch}}, m)$: Parse $\mathsf{pk_{ch}}$ as y and $m \in \mathbb{Z}_q$, choose $(\xi, k_{1,1}, k_{1,2}, k_2, e_2, s_2) \leftarrow_r \mathbb{Z}_q^6$, set $u_1 \leftarrow g_1^{k_{1,1}} g_2^{k_{1,2}}$, $u_2 \leftarrow g_1^{s_2} \cdot y^{-e_2}$, $e \leftarrow H((y, h, m), (u_1, u_2))$ and $e_1 \leftarrow e - e_2 \bmod q$. Then compute $s_{1,1} \leftarrow k_{1,1} + e_1 m \bmod q$, $s_{1,2} = k_{1,2} + e_1 \xi$ and finally, return $(h, r) = (O, \pi)$, where

$$O \leftarrow g_1^m g_2^\xi \text{ , and } \pi \leftarrow (e_1, e_2, s_{1,1}, s_{1,2}, s_2).$$

$\mathsf{CHCheck}(\mathsf{pk_{ch}}, m, r, h)$: Parse $\mathsf{pk_{ch}}$ as y and r as $(e_1, e_2, s_{1,1}, s_{1,2}, s_2)$, and h as O. Return 1 if the following holds, and 0 otherwise:

$$m \in \mathbb{Z}_q \ \wedge \ e_1 + e_2 = H((y, h, m), (g_1^{s_{1,1}} g_2^{s_{1,2}} \cdot O^{-e_1}, g^{s_2} \cdot y^{-e_2})).$$

$\mathsf{CHAdapt}(\mathsf{sk_{ch}}, m, m', r, h)$: Parse $\mathsf{sk_{ch}}$ as x, and h as O. Set $y \leftarrow g_1^x$. Verify whether $m' \in \mathbb{Z}_q$, and $\mathsf{CHCheck}(y, m, r, h) = 1$. Return $\bot$ if not. Otherwise, choose $(k_{1,1}, k_{1,2}, e_1, s_{1,1}, s_{1,2}) \leftarrow_r \mathbb{Z}_q^5$, set $u_1 \leftarrow g_1^{s_{1,1}} \cdot g_2^{s_{1,2}} \cdot O^{-e_1}$, $u_2 \leftarrow g_1^{k_2}$, $e \leftarrow H((y, h, m'), (u_1, u_2))$, and $e_2 \leftarrow e - e_1 \bmod q$. Finally compute $s_2 \leftarrow k_2 + e_2 x \bmod q$, and return $r' = \pi'$, where

$$\pi' \leftarrow (e_1, e_2, s_{1,1}, s_{1,2}, s_2).$$

Construction 2: Concrete instantiation from DLOG

5.2   Concrete Instantiation from Post-quantum Primitives

Our post-quantum instantiation follows the paradigm of the previous instantiation, however leveraging the hardness of the Learning Parity with Noise (LPN) problem instead of that of DLOG, cf., e.g., Pietrzak [40] for an overview. The computational LPN assumption says that it is computationally infeasible (and actually NP hard) to distinguish samples of the form $(A, As \oplus e)$ from such of the (A, r), where $A \leftarrow_r \{0,1\}^{k \times \lambda}$, $s \leftarrow_r \{0,1\}^\lambda$, $x \leftarrow_r \{0,1\}^k$, and $e \leftarrow_r \chi$; the computational problem is defined analogously. In the standard LPN problem, χ is an k-dimensional Bernoulli distribution with parameter τ, i.e., each entry of e equals 1 with probability τ and 0 otherwise. Following Jain et al. [34], we will rely on the *exact* LPN (xLPN) problem in the following, where χ is an k-dimensional Bernoulli distribution conditioned on $\|e\|_1 = \lceil k\tau \rfloor$ and $\lceil . \rfloor$ denotes rounding to the nearest integer. It is easy to see that xLPN is computationally related to the standard LPN problem.

Let the message length be denoted by v, let $\tau \in [0, 0.25)$ and $k \in \mathcal{O}(v+\lambda)$ such that the linear code generated by $A \leftarrow_r \{0,1\}^{k \times (v+\lambda)}$ has a distance of more than $2\lceil k\tau \rfloor$ with overwhelming probability. The commitment scheme in [34] now works as follows. The public parameters consist of a matrix $A \leftarrow_r \{0,1\}^{k \times (v+\lambda)}$ and the value τ. A commitment to $m \in \{0,1\}^v$ is now given by choosing $\xi_1 \leftarrow_r \{0,1\}^\lambda$

$\mathsf{CHPG}(1^\lambda)$: Outputs the public parameters (A, τ, H, H'), where $\mathsf{pp}_{\mathsf{ch}} = (A, \tau)$ for $A \leftarrow_r \{0, 1\}^{(v+\lambda) \times k}$ and $\tau \in [0, 0.25)$ as above, $H : \{0, 1\}^* \to \{0, 1, 2\}^\ell$ is a hash-function (which we assume to behave like a random oracle and to be implicitly available to all algorithms below), and $H' : \{0, 1\}^* \to \{0, 1\}^{2\lambda}$ is a cryptographic hash function (which will be used as a computationally binding and statistically hiding auxiliary commitment scheme).

$\mathsf{CHKG}(\mathsf{pp}_{\mathsf{ch}})$: Return $(\mathsf{sk}_{\mathsf{ch}}, \mathsf{pk}_{\mathsf{ch}}) = ((x_1, x_2), y)$, where $x_1 \leftarrow_r \{0, 1\}^{v+\lambda}$, $x_2 \leftarrow_r \chi$, and $y \leftarrow Ax_1 \oplus x_2$, where as before χ indicates a Bernoulli distribution with parameter τ conditioned on $\|x_2\|_1 = \lceil \tau k \rfloor$.

$\mathsf{CHash}(\mathsf{pk}_{\mathsf{ch}}, m)$: Parse $\mathsf{pk}_{\mathsf{ch}}$ as y, then proceed as follows:

- *Compute h:* Draw $\xi_1 \leftarrow_r \{0, 1\}^\lambda$ and $\xi_2 \leftarrow_r \chi$. Set $h \leftarrow A(m\|\xi_1) \oplus \xi_2$.
- *Simulate proof for y:* Choose $e_2 \leftarrow_r \{0, 1, 2\}$ and $r_{2,0}, r_{2,1}, r_{2,2} \leftarrow_r \{0, 1\}^{2\lambda}$.
  - If $e_2{=}0$, let $\pi_2 \leftarrow_r S_k$, $v_2 \leftarrow_r \{0, 1\}^{v+\lambda}$, $f_2 \leftarrow_r \{0, 1\}^k$, $c_{2,0} \leftarrow_r H'((\pi_2, Av_2 \oplus f_2), r_{2,0})$, $c_{2,1} \leftarrow_r H'(\pi_2(f_2), r_{2,1})$ and $c_{2,2} \leftarrow_r H'(0, r_{2,3})$. Set $s_0 \leftarrow_r (\pi_2, Av_2 \oplus f_2, r_{2,0})$, $s_1 \leftarrow_r (\pi_2(f_2), r_{2,1})$, $s_2 \leftarrow_r \perp$.
  - If $e_2{=}1$, let $\pi_2 \leftarrow_r S_k$, $b \leftarrow_r \{0, 1\}^{v+\lambda}$, $a \leftarrow_r \{0, 1\}^k$, $c_{2,0} \leftarrow_r H'((\pi_2, Ab \oplus y \oplus a), r_{2,0})$, $c_{2,1} \leftarrow_r H'(0, r_{2,1})$ and $c_{2,2} \leftarrow_r H'(\pi_2(a), r_{2,3})$. Set $s_0 \leftarrow_r (\pi_2, Ab \oplus y \oplus a, r_{2,0})$, $s_1 \leftarrow_r \perp$, $s_2 \leftarrow_r (\pi_2(a), r_{2,2})$.
  - If $e_2{=}2$, let $b \leftarrow_r \chi$, $a \leftarrow_r \{0, 1\}^k$, $c_{2,0} \leftarrow_r H'(0, r_{2,0})$, $c_{2,1} \leftarrow_r H'(a, r_{2,1})$ and $c_{2,2} \leftarrow_r H'(a \oplus b, r_{2,3})$. Set $s_0 \leftarrow_r \perp$, $s_1 \leftarrow_r (a, r_{2,1})$, $s_2 \leftarrow_r (a \oplus b, r_{2,2})$.
- *Compute first message for h:* Choose $r_{1,0}, r_{1,1}, r_{1,2} \leftarrow_r \{0, 1\}^{2\lambda}$. Draw $\pi_1 \leftarrow_r S_k$, $v_1 \leftarrow_r \{0, 1\}^{v+\lambda}$, $f_1 \leftarrow_r \{0, 1\}^k$, $c_{1,0} \leftarrow_r H'((\pi_1, Av_1 \oplus f_1), r_{1,0})$, $c_{1,1} \leftarrow_r H'(\pi_1(f_1), r_{1,1})$ and $c_{1,2} \leftarrow_r H'(\pi(f_1 \oplus \xi_2), r_{1,2})$
- *Compute   challenge   for h:*   Compute $e \leftarrow H((y, h, m), (c_{1,0}, c_{1,1}, c_{1,2}, c_{2,0}, c_{2,1}, c_{2,2}))$. Set $e_1 \leftarrow e - e_2 \bmod 3$.
- *Compute proof for h:*
  - If $e_1{=}0$, set $s_0 \leftarrow_r (\pi_1, Av_1 \oplus f_1, r_{1,0})$, $s_1 \leftarrow_r (\pi_1(f_1), r_{1,1})$, $s_2 \leftarrow_r \perp$.
  - If $e_1{=}1$, set $s_0 \leftarrow_r (\pi_1, Av_1 \oplus f_1, r_{1,0})$, $s_1 \leftarrow_r \perp$, $s_2 \leftarrow_r (\pi_1(f_1 \oplus \xi_2), r_{1,2})$.
  - If $e_1{=}2$, set $s_0 \leftarrow_r \perp$, $s_1 \leftarrow_r (\pi_1(f_1), r_{1,1})$, $s_2 \leftarrow_r (\pi_1(f_1 \oplus \xi_2), r_{1,2})$.
- *Generate output:* Return (h, r), where $r \leftarrow ((c_{1,0}, c_{1,1}, c_{1,2}, c_{2,0}, c_{2,1}, c_{2,2}), (e_1, e_2), (s_{1,0}, s_{1,1}, s_{1,2}, s_{2,0}, s_{2,1}, s_{2,2}))$.

Construction 3: Instantiation from LPN: Key Generation and Hashing

and $\xi_2 \leftarrow_r \chi$, and setting $h = A(m\|\xi_1) \oplus \xi_2$; upon receiving the opening (ξ_1, ξ_2) of a commitment h, one checks that h has the correct form and that $\|\xi_2\|_1 = \lceil \tau k \rfloor$.

As before, we use plain xLPN as a one-way function using the same generator matrix A, leading to the following language underlying our construction:

$$L := \{(y, h, m) \mid \exists(x_1, x_2, \xi_1, \xi_2) : h = A(m\|\xi_1) \oplus \xi_2 \lor y = Ax_1 \oplus x_2\}. \quad (3)$$

The zero-knowledge proofs for xLPN presented in [34] are based on those by Stern [45] and come with a soundness error of $2/3$, therefore requiring about $\ell = 1.7\lambda$ parallel repetitions to achieve a soundness error or $2^{-\lambda}$. We note that the compiler to obtain simulation-sound extractability due to Faust et al. [28] also applies here: violating quasi-unique responses would imply finding a collision

---

$\underline{\mathsf{CHCheck}(\mathsf{pk}_{ch}, m, r, h)}$: Parse pk_{ch} as y and r as $((c_{1,0}, c_{1,1}, c_{1,2}, c_{2,0}, c_{2,1}, c_{2,2}),$
$(e_1, e_2), (s_{1,0}, s_{1,1}, s_{1,2}, s_{2,0}, s_{2,1}, s_{2,2}))$, then proceed as follows:

- *Check message and challenges*: Return 0 if $m \notin \{0,1\}^v$ or $e_1 + e_2 \neq$
  $H((y, h, m), (c_{1,0}, c_{1,1}, c_{1,2}, c_{2,0}, c_{2,1}, c_{2,2}))$.
- *Verify proofs*: Return 1 if all following tests succeed for $j = 1, 2$, where
  $z \leftarrow h$ for $j = 1$ and $z \leftarrow y$ for $j = 2$, and return 0 otherwise:
  - If $e_j = 0$, parse $s_{j,0}$ as $((\pi_j, t_{j,0}), r_{j,0})$ and $s_{j,1}$ as $(t_{j,1}, r_{j,1})$. Check if
    $c_{j,0} = H'((\pi_j, t_{j,0}), r_{j,0})$ and $c_{j,1} = H'(t_{j,1}, r_{j,1})$. Check if $\pi_j \in \mathcal{S}_k$ and
    $t_{j,0} \oplus \pi_j^{-1}(t_{j,1}) \in \operatorname{img} A$.
  - If $e_j = 1$, parse $s_{j,0}$ as $((\pi_j, t_{j,0}), r_{j,0})$ and $s_{j,2}$ as $(t_{j,2}, r_{j,2})$. Check if
    $c_{j,0} = H'((\pi_j, t_{j,0}), r_{j,0})$ and $c_{j,2} = H'(t_{j,2}, r_{j,2})$. Check if $\pi_j \in \mathcal{S}_k$ and
    $t_{j,0} \oplus \pi_j^{-1}(t_{j,2}) \oplus z \in \operatorname{img} A$.
  - If $e_j = 2$, parse $s_{j,1}$ as $(t_{j,1}, r_{j,1})$ and $s_{j,2}$ as $(t_{j,2}, r_{j,2})$. Check if $c_{j,1} =$
    $H'(t_{j,1}, r_{j,1})$ and $c_{j,2} = H'(t_{j,2}, r_{j,2})$. Check if $\|t_{j,1} \oplus t_{j,2}\|_1 = \lceil \tau k \rceil$.

$\underline{\mathsf{CHAdapt}(\mathsf{sk}_{ch}, m, m', r, h)}$: Parse sk_{ch} as (x_1, x_2), and with $y = Ax_1 \oplus x_2$:

- *Check inputs*: Return $\perp$ if $\mathsf{CHCheck}(y, m, r, h) = 0$ or $m' \notin \{0,1\}^v$.
- *Simulate proof for h*: Choose $e_1 \leftarrow_r \{0,1,2\}$ and $r_{1,0}, r_{1,1}, r_{1,2} \leftarrow_r \{0,1\}^{2\lambda}$.
  - If $e_1 = 0$, let $\pi_1 \leftarrow_r \mathcal{S}_k$, $v_1 \leftarrow_r \{0,1\}^{v+\lambda}$, $f_1 \leftarrow_r \{0,1\}^k$, $c_{1,0} \leftarrow_r$
    $H'((\pi_1, Av_1 \oplus f_1), r_{1,0})$, $c_{1,1} \leftarrow_r H'(\pi_1(f_1), r_{1,1})$ and $c_{1,2} \leftarrow_r H'(0, r_{1,3})$.
    Set $s_0 \leftarrow_r (\pi_1, Av_1 \oplus f_1, r_{1,0})$, $s_1 \leftarrow_r (\pi_1(f_1), r_{1,1})$, $s_2 \leftarrow_r \perp$.
  - If $e_1 = 1$, let $\pi_1 \leftarrow_r \mathcal{S}_k$, $b \leftarrow_r \{0,1\}^{v+\lambda}$, $a \leftarrow_r \{0,1\}^k$, $c_{1,0} \leftarrow_r$
    $H'((\pi_1, Ab \oplus y \oplus a), r_{1,0})$, $c_{1,1} \leftarrow_r H'(0, r_{1,1})$ and $c_{1,2} \leftarrow_r H'(\pi_1(a), r_{1,3})$.
    Set $s_0 \leftarrow_r (\pi_1, Ab \oplus y \oplus a, r_{1,0})$, $s_1 \leftarrow_r \perp$, $s_2 \leftarrow_r (\pi_1(a), r_{1,2})$.
  - If $e_1 = 2$, let $b \leftarrow_r \chi$, $a \leftarrow_r \{0,1\}^k$, $c_{1,0} \leftarrow_r H'(0, r_{1,0})$, $c_{1,1} \leftarrow_r$
    $H'(a, r_{1,1})$ and $c_{1,2} \leftarrow_r H'(a \oplus b, r_{1,3})$. Set $s_0 \leftarrow_r \perp$, $s_1 \leftarrow_r (a, r_{1,1})$,
    $s_1 \leftarrow_r (a \oplus b, r_{1,2})$.
- *Compute first message for y*: Choose $r_{2,0}, r_{2,1}, r_{2,2} \leftarrow_r \{0,1\}^{2\lambda}$. Draw $\pi_2 \leftarrow_r$
  $\mathcal{S}_k$, $v_2 \leftarrow_r \{0,1\}^{v+\lambda}$, $f_2 \leftarrow_r \{0,1\}^k$, $c_{2,0} \leftarrow_r H'((\pi_2, Av_2 \oplus f_2), r_{2,0})$, $c_{2,1} \leftarrow_r$
  $H'(\pi_2(f_2), r_{2,1})$ and $c_{2,2} \leftarrow_r H'(\pi(f_2 \oplus \xi_2), r_{2,2})$.
- *Compute challenge for h*: Compute $e \leftarrow$
  $H((y, h, m), (c_{1,0}, c_{1,1}, c_{1,2}, c_{2,0}, c_{2,1}, c_{2,2}))$. Set $e_2 \leftarrow e - e_1 \bmod 3$.
- *Compute proof for y*:
  - If $e_2 = 0$, set $s_0 \leftarrow_r (\pi_2, Av_2 \oplus f_2, r_{2,0})$, $s_2 \leftarrow_r (\pi_2(f_2), r_{2,1})$, $s_2 \leftarrow_r \perp$.
  - If $e_2 = 1$, set $s_0 \leftarrow_r (\pi_2, Av_2 \oplus f_2, r_{2,0})$, $s_2 \leftarrow_r \perp$, $s_2 \leftarrow_r (\pi_2(f_1 \oplus x_2), r_{2,2})$.
  - If $e_2 = 2$, set $s_0 \leftarrow_r \perp$, $s_2 \leftarrow_r (\pi_2(f_2), r_{2,1})$, $s_2 \leftarrow_r (\pi_2(f_2 \oplus x_2), r_{x,2})$.
- *Generate output*: Return $r' \leftarrow_r ((c_{1,0}, c_{1,1}, c_{1,2}, c_{2,0}, c_{2,1}, c_{2,2}), (e_1, e_2), (s_{1,0},$
  $s_{1,1}, s_{1,2}, s_{2,0}, s_{2,1}, s_{2,2})$.

Construction 4: Instantiation from LPN: Verify and Adapt

for the hash function used to instantiate the random oracle and the statement is included when hashing the challenge.[2]

We present the instantiation as Construction 3–4 and note that for notational convenience and readability, we only consider $\ell = 1$. For practical parameters, all

---

[2] We note that replacing LPN by learning with errors (LWE) and using the commitment scheme and zero-knowledge proofs of Benhamouda et al. [10] gives an immediate post-quantum instantiation that does not require parallel repetitions, yet requiring assumptions that give rise to public-key encryption.

proofs need to be simulated or computed ℓ times in parallel, with the challenges being computed via a single invocation of H. In the following we denote the symmetric group on k elements (i.e., the set of all permutations on k elements) by $\mathcal{S}_k$. Furthermore, for $A \in \{0,1\}^{m \times n}$, $\text{img}(A)$ we denote the image of the linear function characterized by A, i.e., $\text{img}(A) = \{Ax \mid x \in \{0,1\}^n\}$. Checking whether or not $y \in \text{img}(A)$ can efficiently be done by seeking a solution to the linear system $y = Ax$, e.g., using Gaussian elimination.

Acknowledgements. This work was supported by the European Union H2020 Programme under grant agreement n°830929 (CyberSec4Europe), the H2020 ECSEL Joint Undertaking under grant agreement n°783119 (SECREDAS), and by the Austrian Science Fund (FWF) and netidee SCIENCE under grant agreement P31621-N38 (PROFET).

References

1. Abe, M., David, B., Kohlweiss, M., Nishimaki, R., Ohkubo, M.: Tagged one-time signatures: tight security and optimal tag size. In: Kurosawa, K., Hanaoka, G. (eds.) PKC 2013. LNCS, vol. 7778, pp. 312–331. Springer, Heidelberg (2013). https://doi.org/10.1007/978-3-642-36362-7_20

2. Ateniese, G., Chou, D.H., de Medeiros, B., Tsudik, G.: Sanitizable signatures. In: di Vimercati, S.C., Syverson, P., Gollmann, D. (eds.) ESORICS 2005. LNCS, vol. 3679, pp. 159–177. Springer, Heidelberg (2005). https://doi.org/10.1007/11555827_10

3. Ateniese, G., Magri, B., Venturi, D., Andrade, E.R.: Redactable blockchain - or - rewriting history in bitcoin and friends. In: EuroS&P, pp. 111–126 (2017)

4. Ateniese, G., de Medeiros, B.: Identity-based Chameleon Hash and applications. In: Juels, A. (ed.) FC 2004. LNCS, vol. 3110, pp. 164–180. Springer, Heidelberg (2004). https://doi.org/10.1007/978-3-540-27809-2_19

5. Ateniese, G., de Medeiros, B.: On the key exposure problem in Chameleon Hashes. In: Blundo, C., Cimato, S. (eds.) SCN 2004. LNCS, vol. 3352, pp. 165–179. Springer, Heidelberg (2005). https://doi.org/10.1007/978-3-540-30598-9_12

6. Bao, F., Deng, R.H., Ding, X., Lai, J., Zhao, Y.: Hierarchical identity-based Chameleon Hash and its applications. In: Lopez, J., Tsudik, G. (eds.) ACNS 2011. LNCS, vol. 6715, pp. 201–219. Springer, Heidelberg (2011). https://doi.org/10.1007/978-3-642-21554-4_12

7. Beck, M.T., et al.: Practical strongly invisible and strongly accountable sanitizable signatures. In: Pieprzyk, J., Suriadi, S. (eds.) ACISP 2017. LNCS, vol. 10342, pp. 437–452. Springer, Cham (2017). https://doi.org/10.1007/978-3-319-60055-0_23

8. Bellare, M., Ristov, T.: Hash functions from sigma protocols and improvements to VSH. In: Pieprzyk, J. (ed.) ASIACRYPT 2008. LNCS, vol. 5350, pp. 125–142. Springer, Heidelberg (2008). https://doi.org/10.1007/978-3-540-89255-7_9

9. Bellare, M., Ristov, T.: A characterization of Chameleon Hash functions and new, efficient designs. J. Cryptol. **27**(4), 799–823 (2014)

10. Benhamouda, F., Krenn, S., Lyubashevsky, V., Pietrzak, K.: Efficient zero-knowledge proofs for commitments from learning with errors over rings. In: Pernul, G., Ryan, P.Y.A., Weippl, E. (eds.) ESORICS 2015. LNCS, vol. 9326, pp. 305–325. Springer, Cham (2015). https://doi.org/10.1007/978-3-319-24174-6_16

11. Blazy, O., Kakvi, S.A., Kiltz, E., Pan, J.: Tightly-secure signatures from Chameleon Hash functions. In: Katz, J. (ed.) PKC 2015. LNCS, vol. 9020, pp. 256–279. Springer, Heidelberg (2015). https://doi.org/10.1007/978-3-662-46447-2_12
12. Blum, M.: Coin flipping by telephone. In: Crypto, pp. 11–15 (1981)
13. Boneh, D., Dagdelen, Ö., Fischlin, M., Lehmann, A., Schaffner, C., Zhandry, M.: Random Oracles in a quantum world. In: Lee, D.H., Wang, X. (eds.) ASIACRYPT 2011. LNCS, vol. 7073, pp. 41–69. Springer, Heidelberg (2011). https://doi.org/10.1007/978-3-642-25385-0_3
14. Brassard, G., Chaum, D., Crépeau, C.: Minimum disclosure proofs of knowledge. J. Comput. Syst. Sci. **37**(2), 156–189 (1988)
15. Brzuska, C., et al.: Security of sanitizable signatures revisited. In: Jarecki, S., Tsudik, G. (eds.) PKC 2009. LNCS, vol. 5443, pp. 317–336. Springer, Heidelberg (2009). https://doi.org/10.1007/978-3-642-00468-1_18
16. Beck, M.T., et al.: Practical strongly invisible and strongly accountable sanitizable signatures. In: Pieprzyk, J., Suriadi, S. (eds.) ACISP 2017. LNCS, vol. 10342, pp. 437–452. Springer, Cham (2017). https://doi.org/10.1007/978-3-319-60055-0_23
17. Cash, D., Hofheinz, D., Kiltz, E., Peikert, C.: Bonsai trees, or how to delegate a lattice basis. In: Gilbert, H. (ed.) EUROCRYPT 2010. LNCS, vol. 6110, pp. 523–552. Springer, Heidelberg (2010). https://doi.org/10.1007/978-3-642-13190-5_27
18. Chen, X., Zhang, F., Susilo, W., Mu, Y.: Efficient generic on-line/off-line signatures without key exposure. In: Katz, J., Yung, M. (eds.) ACNS 2007. LNCS, vol. 4521, pp. 18–30. Springer, Heidelberg (2007). https://doi.org/10.1007/978-3-540-72738-5_2
19. Cramer, R., Damgård, I., Schoenmakers, B.: Proofs of partial knowledge and simplified design of witness hiding protocols. In: Desmedt, Y.G. (ed.) CRYPTO 1994. LNCS, vol. 839, pp. 174–187. Springer, Heidelberg (1994). https://doi.org/10.1007/3-540-48658-5_19
20. Derler, D., Samelin, K., Slamanig, D.: Bringing order to chaos: the case of collision-resistant Chameleon-Hashes. In: Kiayias, A., Kohlweiss, M., Wallden, P., Zikas, V. (eds.) PKC 2020. LNCS, vol. 12110, pp. 462–492. Springer, Cham (2020). https://doi.org/10.1007/978-3-030-45374-9_16
21. Derler, D., Samelin, K., Slamanig, D., Striecks, C.: Fine-grained and controlled rewriting in blockchains: Chameleon-hashing gone attribute-based. In: NDSS (2019)
22. Derler, D., Slamanig, D.: Key-homomorphic signatures: definitions and applications to multiparty signatures and non-interactive zero-knowledge. Des. Codes Crypt. **87**(6), 1373–1413 (2018). https://doi.org/10.1007/s10623-018-0535-9
23. Derler, D., Slamanig, D.: Highly-efficient fully-anonymous dynamic group signatures. In: AsiaCCS, pp. 551–565 (2018)
24. Dodis, Y., Haralambiev, K., López-Alt, A., Wichs, D.: Efficient public-key cryptography in the presence of key leakage. In: Abe, M. (ed.) ASIACRYPT 2010. LNCS, vol. 6477, pp. 613–631. Springer, Heidelberg (2010). https://doi.org/10.1007/978-3-642-17373-8_35
25. Don, J., Fehr, S., Majenz, C.: The measure-and-reprogram technique 2.0: Multi-round Fiat-Shamir and more. Cryptology ePrint Archive, Report 2020/282 (2020). https://eprint.iacr.org/2020/282
26. Don, J., Fehr, S., Majenz, C., Schaffner, C.: Security of the Fiat-Shamir transformation in the quantum random-oracle model. In: Boldyreva, A., Micciancio, D. (eds.) CRYPTO 2019. LNCS, vol. 11693, pp. 356–383. Springer, Cham (2019). https://doi.org/10.1007/978-3-030-26951-7_13

27. Even, S., Goldreich, O., Micali, S.: On-line/off-line digital signatures. J. Cryptol. **9**(1), 35–67 (1996). https://doi.org/10.1007/BF02254791
28. Faust, S., Kohlweiss, M., Marson, G.A., Venturi, D.: On the non-malleability of the Fiat-Shamir transform. In: Galbraith, S., Nandi, M. (eds.) INDOCRYPT 2012. LNCS, vol. 7668, pp. 60–79. Springer, Heidelberg (2012). https://doi.org/10.1007/978-3-642-34931-7_5
29. Fiat, A., Shamir, A.: How to prove yourself: practical solutions to identification and signature problems. In: Odlyzko, A.M. (ed.) CRYPTO 1986. LNCS, vol. 263, pp. 186–194. Springer, Heidelberg (1987). https://doi.org/10.1007/3-540-47721-7_12
30. Groth, J.: Simulation-sound NIZK proofs for a practical language and constant size group signatures. In: Lai, X., Chen, K. (eds.) ASIACRYPT 2006. LNCS, vol. 4284, pp. 444–459. Springer, Heidelberg (2006). https://doi.org/10.1007/11935230_29
31. Groth, J., Sahai, A.: Efficient non-interactive proof systems for bilinear groups. In: Smart, N. (ed.) EUROCRYPT 2008. LNCS, vol. 4965, pp. 415–432. Springer, Heidelberg (2008). https://doi.org/10.1007/978-3-540-78967-3_24
32. Hohenberger, S., Waters, B.: Short and stateless signatures from the RSA assumption. In: Halevi, S. (ed.) CRYPTO 2009. LNCS, vol. 5677, pp. 654–670. Springer, Heidelberg (2009). https://doi.org/10.1007/978-3-642-03356-8_38
33. Huang, K., Zhang, X., Mu, Y., Rezaeibagha, F., Wang, X., Li, J., Xia, Q., Qin, J.: EVA: efficient versatile auditing scheme for iot-based datamarket in jointcloud. IEEE Internet Things J. **7**(2), 882–892 (2020)
34. Jain, A., Krenn, S., Pietrzak, K., Tentes, A.: Commitments and efficient zero-knowledge proofs from learning parity with noise. In: Wang, X., Sako, K. (eds.) ASIACRYPT 2012. LNCS, vol. 7658, pp. 663–680. Springer, Heidelberg (2012). https://doi.org/10.1007/978-3-642-34961-4_40
35. Krawczyk, H., Rabin, T.: Chameleon signatures. In: NDSS, pp. 143–154 (2000)
36. Krenn, S., Pöhls, H.C., Samelin, K., Slamanig, D.: Chameleon-Hashes with dual long-term trapdoors and their applications. In: Joux, A., Nitaj, A., Rachidi, T. (eds.) AFRICACRYPT 2018. LNCS, vol. 10831, pp. 11–32. Springer, Cham (2018). https://doi.org/10.1007/978-3-319-89339-6_2
37. Liu, Q., Zhandry, M.: Revisiting post-quantum Fiat-Shamir. In: Boldyreva, A., Micciancio, D. (eds.) CRYPTO 2019. LNCS, vol. 11693, pp. 326–355. Springer, Cham (2019). https://doi.org/10.1007/978-3-030-26951-7_12
38. Mohassel, P.: One-time signatures and Chameleon Hash functions. In: Biryukov, A., Gong, G., Stinson, D.R. (eds.) SAC 2010. LNCS, vol. 6544, pp. 302–319. Springer, Heidelberg (2011). https://doi.org/10.1007/978-3-642-19574-7_21
39. Pedersen, T.P.: Non-interactive and information-theoretic secure verifiable secret sharing. In: Feigenbaum, J. (ed.) CRYPTO 1991. LNCS, vol. 576, pp. 129–140. Springer, Heidelberg (1992). https://doi.org/10.1007/3-540-46766-1_9
40. Pietrzak, K.: Cryptography from learning parity with noise. In: Bieliková, M., Friedrich, G., Gottlob, G., Katzenbeisser, S., Turán, G. (eds.) SOFSEM 2012. LNCS, vol. 7147, pp. 99–114. Springer, Heidelberg (2012). https://doi.org/10.1007/978-3-642-27660-6_9
41. Sahai, A.: Non-malleable non-interactive zero knowledge and adaptive chosen-ciphertext security. In: FOCS, pp. 543–553 (1999)
42. Samelin, K., Slamanig, D.: Policy-based sanitizable signatures. In: Jarecki, S. (ed.) CT-RSA 2020. LNCS, vol. 12006, pp. 538–563. Springer, Cham (2020). https://doi.org/10.1007/978-3-030-40186-3_23
43. Shamir, A., Tauman, Y.: Improved online/offline signature schemes. In: Kilian, J. (ed.) CRYPTO 2001. LNCS, vol. 2139, pp. 355–367. Springer, Heidelberg (2001). https://doi.org/10.1007/3-540-44647-8_21

44. Steinfeld, R., Bull, L., Wang, H., Pieprzyk, J.: Universal designated-verifier signatures. In: Laih, C.-S. (ed.) ASIACRYPT 2003. LNCS, vol. 2894, pp. 523–542. Springer, Heidelberg (2003). https://doi.org/10.1007/978-3-540-40061-5_33
45. Stern, J.: A new identification scheme based on syndrome decoding. In: Stinson, D.R. (ed.) CRYPTO 1993. LNCS, vol. 773, pp. 13–21. Springer, Heidelberg (1994). https://doi.org/10.1007/3-540-48329-2_2
46. Zhang, R.: Tweaking TBE/IBE to PKE transforms with Chameleon Hash functions. In: Katz, J., Yung, M. (eds.) ACNS 2007. LNCS, vol. 4521, pp. 323–339. Springer, Heidelberg (2007). https://doi.org/10.1007/978-3-540-72738-5_21

Generalized Matsui Algorithm 1 with Application for the Full DES

Tomer Ashur[1,2], Raluca Posteuca[1(✉)], Danilo Šijačić[1], and Stef D'haeseleer[1]

[1] Imec-COSIC, KU Leuven, Leuven, Belgium
{tomer.ashur,raluca.posteuca}@esat.kuleuven.be
[2] TU Eindhoven, Eindhoven, The Netherlands

Abstract. In this paper we introduce the strictly zero-correlation attack. We extend the work of Ashur and Posteuca in BalkanCryptSec 2018 and build a 0-correlation key-dependent linear trails covering the full DES. We show how this approximation can be used for a key recovery attack and empirically verify our claims through a series of experiments. To the best of our knowledge, this paper is the first to use this kind of property to leverage a meaningful attack against a symmetric-key algorithm.

Keywords: Linear cryptanalysis · DES · Poisonous hull

1 Introduction

Linear cryptanalysis is one of the most important tools used in the security evaluation of block ciphers. It was introduced in 1993, by Mitsuru Matsui, and used to attack the DES cipher. The technique became intensively studied, the formalism of linear cryptanalysis being extended in e.g., [Bih94, Nyb94]. This approach is widely applicable and produced many variants and generalizations such as multiple linear cryptanalysis [JR94, BCQ04], differential-linear cryptanalysis [CV94], zero-correlation linear cryptanalysis [BR11], etc.

Usually, linear cryptanalysis is used to launch a known-plaintext attack. The setting of a known-plaintext attack is that the attacker has a set of plaintexts and their corresponding ciphertexts, enciphered using a fixed key. The goal of the attack is to recover information regarding the secret key that was used.

Matsui's initial idea was to analyze probabilistic linear relations between a set of plaintexts, their ciphertexts, and the secret key. In order to distinguish a particular linear relation (called linear approximation), its probability should be observably different from 0.5. Estimating the quality of a linear approximation, usually measured by its correlation or bias, is one of the open problems in linear cryptanalysis and it is directly related to the success probability and the data complexity of the attack.

In order to construct a linear approximation of an iterated cipher, Matsui proposed to sequentially linearize each round. The resulting set of linear approximations is called a linear trail. The correlation of a linear trail is computed by multiplying the correlations of each 1-round linear approximation.

© Springer Nature Switzerland AG 2020
C. Galdi and V. Kolesnikov (Eds.): SCN 2020, LNCS 12238, pp. 448–467, 2020.
https://doi.org/10.1007/978-3-030-57990-6_22

1.1   Related Work

In [Nyb94] it was first observed that in some cases, there could be more than a single linear trail involving the same plaintext and ciphertext bits. This phenomenon is called *the linear hull effect*, a linear hull being defined as the set of all linear trails with the same input and output bits. The correlation of a linear hull is computed by summing up all underlying linear trails' correlations. Thus, the correlation of the linear hull may be significantly different from that of any of the underlying trails. When a linear attack is used, both the success rate and the data complexity of the attack are closely related to the hull's correlation and not to that of the trail.

In [AR16], Ashur and Rijmen showed that the linear hull effect can appear already within a single round of a cipher. All their experiments and key-recovery attacks were applied to the lightweight block cipher SIMON. Following up on this work, Ashur and Posteuca analyzed in [AP18] this phenomenon for the Data Encryption Standard (DES). They showed that under certain constraints, the f-function of DES exhibits 0-correlation key-dependent one-round linear hulls.

1.2   Our Contribution

In this paper we present a new type of zero-correlation attack, which we call "strictly zero-correlation" and apply it to the full DES. The attack uses a 1-round 0-correlation linear hull and embeds it into Matsui's 8-round linear trail. This results in a 16-round 0-correlation linear trail for DES under certain conditions for particular key bits. We then show how this linear trails can be used for key recovery by exploiting the key-dependent behavior of the correlation.

The contribution of the paper is therefore threefold:

1. We introduce a new type of attack based on linear cryptanalysis, called "strictly zero-correlation" attack;
2. We present a new attack covering the full DES;
3. We show how the key-dependent behavior of a linear trail can be used for key recovery.

1.3   Structure of This Paper

In Sect. 2, we introduce our notation, revisit some terminology regarding linear cryptanalysis, including the notion of poisonous round, and briefly describe the block cipher DES. In Sect. 3 we introduce strictly zero-correlation linear approximation covering the full DES and show how it can be used for key recovery. In Sect. 4 we present a series of experiments validating our analysis. Section 5 offers future research directions and concludes the paper.

2   Preliminaries

In this section we introduce the notation used in the rest of this paper and recall some terminology regarding linear cryptanalysis. We also present the DES cipher.

2.1   The Data Encryption Standard

The Data Encryption Standard (DES) [DES] is a block cipher developed by IBM during the early 1970's and published as an NBS (now NIST) standard in 1977.

DES has a Feistel structure with a round function which employs a non-linear function f. The overall structure of DES consists of an initial permutation, 16 enciphering rounds and a final permutation. The plaintext and the key are 64-bit each, even though only 56 out of 64 key-bits are actually used by the algorithm.

The input to the round function is a 48-bit round key (denoted by k) and two 32-bit intermediate cipherwords (denoted by x and y).

The round function is then given by:

$$R_k(x,y) = (y \oplus f(x,k), x)$$

The f-function consists of four layers:

1. *Expansion*: the 32-bit input x is expanded into a 48-bit output in the form presented in Fig. 1a. The reader may notice that after applying the expansion function, 16 out of 32 input bits are used twice. We will use this observation for our attack. In the sequel, we denote the expansion function by E.

32	1	2	3	4	5
4	5	6	7	8	9
8	9	10	11	12	13
12	13	14	15	16	17
16	17	18	19	20	21
20	21	22	23	24	25
24	25	26	27	28	29
28	29	30	31	32	1

16	7	20	21
29	12	28	17
1	15	23	26
5	18	31	10
2	8	24	14
32	27	3	9
19	13	30	6
22	11	4	25

(a) The expansion function E   (b) The permutation P

Fig. 1. DES round operations - Expansion (E) and Permutation (P)

2. *Key addition*: the output of the expansion function is XORed with the 48-bit round key. We denote the most significant bit of the subkey in round i by k_0^i and the least significant bit by k_{47}^i; when the round number is clear from context we may omit the superscript;

3. *Substitution*: the output of the key addition is divided into eight 6-bit chunks. Each of these blocks is given as an input to a different 6×4-bit S-box, resulting in eight 4-bit outputs. The specification of the S-boxes can be found in [DES]. We denote the substitution layer by S.

   Note that due to the expansion function a single input bit may influence two adjacent S-boxes. In this paper, we consider the first and the last S-boxes as being adjacent (i.e., we view the property of being adjacent as circular).

4. *Permutation*: a fixed 32-bit permutation is applied to the output of the substitution layer. This permutation, denoted by P, is described in Fig. 1b.

The Key Schedule. The key schedule of DES is a linear function where the round keys are basically obtained by selecting 48 out of the 56 bits of the master key. For a description of the key schedule we refer the interested reader to [DES].

Decryption. Since DES has a Feistel structure, the decryption function, DES^{-1}, uses the same structure as the encryption, but with the keys used in reverse order.

2.2 Masks and Approximations

Let a be a binary value of length n and let $a^t x = \bigoplus_{i=0}^{n-1} a_i x_i$, where a_i and x_i are the ith bit of a and x, respectively. We then say that a is the mask of x. Given that applying a mask to a bit-string represents, in essence, a selection of bits of x, we will also use the description of a mask as a set of positions:

$$ X = \{i_1, i_2, \ldots, i_v\} \Leftrightarrow \begin{cases} x_j = 1, \forall j \in X \\ x_j = 0, \forall j \notin X \end{cases} $$

The bits in positions $\{i_1, i_2, \ldots, i_v\}$ are called *active bits*, while the remaining bits of x are said to be inactive.

Let $R_k(x) = y$ denote the round function of a block cipher, where x, y and k are the plaintext, the ciphertext and the key, respectively. A linear approximation for R_k is a tuple (α, β, κ), where α, β and κ are the input mask, the output mask and the key mask, respectively. Let p be the probability that the equation $\alpha^t x \oplus \beta^t y \oplus \kappa^t k = 0$ holds for a uniformly selected x. Then the correlation of the linear approximation (α, β, κ) is defined as $corr(\alpha, \beta, \kappa) = 2p - 1$. In general, both p and $corr(\alpha, \beta, \kappa)$ are key-dependent (see, e.g., [AÅBL12])

A pair of masks (α, β) is said to be connectable if and only if β can be obtained from α using the rules of propagation introduced in [Bih94, Mat93]. Otherwise, the pair (α, β) is said to be non-connectable.

2.3 Linear Hulls and Trails

An iterated block cipher with r rounds can be described as the composition of $r - 1$ round functions, i.e. $Enc_k = R_{k_{r-i}} \circ \ldots \circ R_{k_0}$, where k_i denotes the round key and k denotes the encryption key. A linear trail covering r rounds of a block cipher is a sequence of $r + 1$ linear approximations such that the mask corresponding to the output of round i is the same as the one corresponding to the input of round $i+1$. Hence, a linear trail can be viewed as an $(r+1)$-dimension vector $(\lambda_1, \lambda_2, \ldots, \lambda_{r+1})$, where the pair $(\lambda_i, \lambda_{i+1})$ denotes the input and output masks at round i, respectively. The correlation of the linear trail is computed by multiplying the correlation of all single-round linear approximations:

$$corr(\lambda_1, \ldots, \lambda_{r+1}) = \prod_{i=1}^{r} corr(\lambda_i, \lambda_{i+1})$$

A linear hull covering r rounds is a pair (α, β) which represents the set of all linear trails with input mask α and output mask β (i.e., the input and output masks are fixed, but intermediate round masks may vary). The correlation of a linear hull is computed by summing the correlations of all linear trails in the set:

$$corr(\alpha, \beta) = \sum_{\lambda_1 = \alpha, \lambda_{r+1} = \beta} corr(\lambda_1, \ldots, \lambda_{r+1})$$

The round function of a block cipher can also be viewed as a composition of its atomic operations. Thus, the methods described above for computing the correlation of a linear trail can also be applied on a smaller scale to these atomic operations. In [AR16], the authors observed that, in some cases, it is possible to construct more than a single linear trail covering the round function. Likewise, in [AP18], the authors showed that this is specifically true for DES' f-function, and hence that the linear hull effect may appear already inside one round of DES. Our paper uses the latter observation to construct an attack on the full cipher.

2.4   One-Round Key-Dependent Linear Hulls in des

Following the notations of [AP18] we describe a linear approximation of the f-function as a tuple $(\alpha, \beta, \kappa, \tau, \lambda, \gamma)$, where α, β, κ are the input mask, the output mask and the key mask, respectively. The remaining components represent the intermediate masks of the trail: τ is the output mask of the expansion layer, and λ, γ are the input and the output masks of the substitution layer, respectively. Given the parallel nature of the S-boxes, we consider λ and γ as a concatenation of eight components of equal size. For example, the input mask $\lambda = (\lambda_1, \ldots, \lambda_8)$ is viewed as a concatenation of 6-bit masks and the output mask $\gamma = (\gamma_1, \ldots, \gamma_8)$ is viewed as a concatenation of 4-bit masks. Figure 2 depicts the propagation of linear masks through the f-function.

The rules of propagation for linear masks impose some constraints on these masks:

1. τ, κ and λ must all be the same;
2. each pair (λ_i, γ_i) must be connectable respective to the ith S-box, more precisely, the linear approximation table (LAT) of S_i must contain a non-zero entry at the intersection of λ_i and γ_i;
3. $\beta = P(\gamma)$.

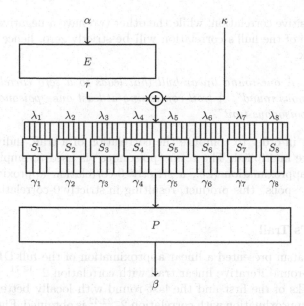

Fig. 2. A linear trail through the f-function of DES

Definition 1. S_i *is an active S-box if and only if the input and the output masks are nonzero, more precisely* $\lambda_i, \gamma_i \neq 0$.

Per [AP18], in the case of DES the linear hull effect may appear already within one round if at least one pair of adjacent S-boxes is active. This leads to the following observation:

Observation 1. *Given the constraints imposed by the rules of propagation for linear masks, two trails that are contained in the same 1-round hull (α, β) share the form $(\alpha, \beta, \tau_i, \tau_i, \tau_i, P^{-1}(\beta))$, where P^{-1} is the inverse of P. Thus, the only difference between two trails in the same 1-round linear hull is given by the intermediate mask τ.*

Corollary 2. *Given that each trail has a different mask after applying the expansion layer, the key masks will also be different, leading to the hull's correlation being key-dependent.*

2.5 Zero-Correlation Linear Approximations

Due to the presence of the linear hull effect, linear trails may interfere with each other, influencing the correlation of the hull in a constructive or destructive manner or, in some cases, even canceling out.

An example of a one-round linear hull containing four linear trails was described in [AP18] with the correlation of each of these trails having the same absolute value. One may notice that for certain values of the key, two linear trails will have a positive correlation, while the other two have a negative one. In this case, the value of the hull's correlation will be strictly zero, hence the name of our new attack.

Definition 2. *A one-round linear hull that leads to a zero correlation is said to be a "poisonous round". A trail containing at least one "poisonous" round is said to be a "poisonous trail".*

Recall that in order to compute the correlation of a trail, individual round correlations are multiplied. The term "poisonous" is used to emphasize that a single "bad" approximation (i.e., a strictly 0-correlation approximation) in a certain round "spoils" this product, resulting in strictly 0-correlation trail.

2.6   Matsui's Trail

In [Mat93], Matsui presented a linear approximation of the full DES, obtained by using an 8-round iterative linear trail with correlation $2^{-12.71}$. By replacing the linear masks of the first and the last round with locally better ones, a 16-rounds linear approximation with correlation $2^{-22.42}$ is obtained. Figure 3 depicts Matsui's 8-round iterative linear trail when circularly moved down by two rounds such that the last round of the original trail is now the second round. Since Matsui's 8-round trail is iterative, it can start in any of the trail rounds and extend naturally over the next seven rounds.

3   Constructing Poisonous Trails for DES

In this section we introduce a new linear trail for DES, containing a key-dependent poisonous round. This linear trail is obtained by replacing the last two rounds in Matsui's iterative trail, where the new last round is a poisonous round. This new linear approximation allows to take advantage of the key constraints that are imposed by the poisonous round, thus leading directly to a key-recovery attack.

The structure of this section is as follows: In Subsect. 3.1 we introduce a 1-round poisonous trail for DES. We extend this into a 2-round linear trail in Subsect. 3.2 and connect it to Matsui's trail in Subsect. 3.3. In Subsect. 3.4 we present some particular properties of our 16-round trail and discuss how different correlations can be distinguished. Finally, in Subsect. 3.5 we describe a key recovery attack based on our approach. Empirical validation of this analysis is provided in Sect. 4.

3.1   A Strictly Zero-Correlation 1-Round Linear Hull for des

In [AP18] the authors introduced the first strictly zero-correlation 1-round linear hull for the f-function of DES. In their example, the hull is defined by the input-output masks pair $(0x65000000, P(0x5A000000))$.

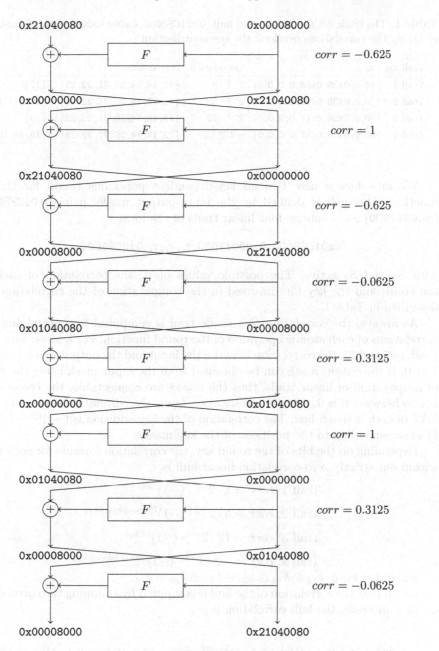

Fig. 3. Matsui's 8-round iterative linear approximation circularly moved down by 2 rounds

Table 1. The trails within the 1-round hull (0x01CF8000, 0x00440000) of the f-function of DES. The correlations overlook the key contribution.

Trail no.	τ_i	Correlation	Key masks
Trail 1	$(0, 0, 0\text{x}39, 0\text{x}0F, 0, 0, 0, 0)$	$2^{-8} \cdot 5$	$\{12, 13, 14, 20, 21, 22, 23\} \cup \{17\}$
Trail 2	$(0, 0, 0\text{x}3B, 0\text{x}2F, 0, 0, 0, 0)$	$2^{-8} \cdot 5$	$\{12, 13, 14, 20, 21, 22, 23\} \cup \{16, 17, 18\}$
Trail 3	$(0, 0, 0\text{x}38, 0\text{x}1F, 0, 0, 0, 0)$	$2^{-8} \cdot 12$	$\{12, 13, 14, 20, 21, 22, 23\} \cup \{19\}$
Trail 4	$(0, 0, 0\text{x}3A, 0\text{x}3F, 0, 0, 0, 0)$	$-2^{-8} \cdot 2$	$\{12, 13, 14, 20, 21, 22, 23\} \cup \{16, 18, 19\}$

We introduce a new 1-round key-dependent poisonous round for the f-function. This hull is defined by the input-output masks pair (0x01CF8000, 0x00011000) and contains four linear trails of the form

$$(0\text{x}01\text{CF}8000, 0\text{x}00011000, \tau_i, \tau_i, \tau_i, 0\text{x}0044000),$$

with S_3 and S_4 active. The possible values of τ_i, the correlation of each of the trails, and the key bits involved in the computation of the correlation are described in Table 1.

As always, the correlation of a single trail is computed by multiplying the correlations of each atomic operation of the round function. For a linear function (such as E and P), the correlation between the input and the output mask is either 1 or 0. If the output mask can be obtained from the input mask using the rules of propagation of linear trails, thus the masks are connectable, the correlation is 1; otherwise, it is 0. For the substitution layer, the correlation is given by the LAT of each active S-box. The correlation of the key addition is $(-1)^{\oplus_{i \in \kappa} k_i}$, for k_i's corresponding to the positions of the key mask.

Depending on the bits of the round key, the correlation formula for each trail within our strictly zero-correlation linear hull is

$$\text{Trail 1: } corr = 5 \cdot 2^{-8} \cdot (-1)^{l \oplus k_{17}}$$

$$\text{Trail 2: } corr = 5 \cdot 2^{-8} \cdot (-1)^{l \oplus k_{16} \oplus k_{17} \oplus k_{18}}$$

$$\text{Trail 3: } corr = 12 \cdot 2^{-8} \cdot (-1)^{l \oplus k_{19}}$$

$$\text{Trail 4: } corr = -2 \cdot 2^{-8} \cdot (-1)^{l \oplus k_{16} \oplus k_{18} \oplus k_{19}}$$

where $l = k_{12} \oplus k_{13} \oplus k_{14} \oplus k_{20} \oplus k_{21} \oplus k_{22} \oplus k_{23}$.

Given that the correlation of the hull is computed by summing the correlation of the four trails, the hull correlation is

$$corr = 2^{-8} \cdot (-1)^l \cdot [5 \cdot (-1)^{k_{17}} + 5 \cdot (-1)^{k_{16} \oplus k_{17} \oplus k_{18}} + 12 \cdot (-1)^{k_{19}} - 2 \cdot (-1)^{k_{16} \oplus k_{18} \oplus k_{19}}]$$

Note that the key bits in positions $k_{12}, k_{13}, k_{14}, k_{20}, k_{21}, k_{22}$, and k_{23} (i.e., the key bits shared among all 1-round trails) influence the sign of the correlation, while the key bits in positions k_{16}, k_{17}, k_{18}, and k_{19} (i.e., the key bits defining the individual 1-round trails) influence its magnitude.

The correlation of the 1-round linear hull, depending on the values of the round key, is

$$corr = \begin{cases} \pm 2^{-8} \cdot 14 & k_{16} \neq k_{18} \\ \pm 2^{-8} \cdot 20 & k_{16} = k_{18} \text{ and } k_{17} = k_{19} \\ 0 & \text{otherwise} \end{cases} \tag{1}$$

3.2 A 2-Round Poisonous Trail for DES

In order to connect it to Matsui's trail we extend the above 1-round linear hull into a 2-rounds linear trail, where the input mask is one of the masks used in Matsui's trail. This 2-round linear trail is described in Fig. 4.

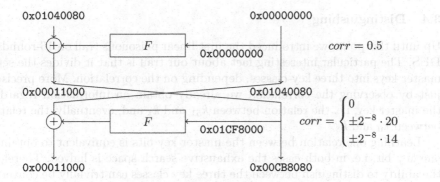

Fig. 4. A 2-round poisonous trail of DES. The last round is the poisonous one.

The correlation for the trail described above, depending on the values of the second round key, is:

$$corr = \begin{cases} \pm 2^{-9} \cdot 14 & k_{16} \neq k_{18} \\ \pm 2^{-9} \cdot 20 & k_{16} = k_{18} \text{ and } k_{17} = k_{19} \\ 0 & \text{otherwise} \end{cases} \tag{2}$$

3.3 A Poisonous 16-Round Trail for DES

We now adapt Matsui's trail into a poisonous 16-round trail by replacing the last two rounds with the trail described in Sect. 3.2. Since the last round of the new trail is poisonous, the entire trail becomes poisonous. The last 8 rounds of our new trail are presented in Fig. 5.

Given that the last round of the new trail is the poisonous one, the correlation of the 16-round trail depends on the bits in positions 16, 17, 18 and 19 of the last round key. Taking into account the key schedule, the correlation depends in the bits on positions 51, 0, 1 and 8 of the master key, and we get

$$corr = \begin{cases} \pm 2^{-24.95} & k_{51} \neq k_1 \\ \pm 2^{-24.42} & k_{51} = k_1 \text{ and } k_0 = k_8 \\ 0 & \text{otherwise} \end{cases} \quad (3)$$

We note that now the last two rounds of the trail presented in Fig. 3 have the smallest correlation, and that our 2-round trail from Sect. 3.2 has the same input mask. Thus, by replacing the last two rounds with our 2-round poisonous trail we improve the correlation. Whereas the correlation of the two rounds that we just replaced was $2^{-5.67}$, the new 2-round trail has a correlation that is 1.38 times better (for some keys).

3.4   Distinguishing

Up until this point, we introduced the first linear poisonous trail on 16-rounds of DES. The particular interesting fact about our trail is that it divides the set of master keys into three key-classes, depending on the correlation. More precisely, just by observing the correlation we already obtain an information regarding the master key, i.e. the relation between k_{51} and k_1 and, eventually, the relation between k_0 and k_8.

Learning one relation between the master key bits is equivalent to obtaining one key bit, i.e. in both cases the exhaustive search space is halved. Therefore, the ability to distinguish between the three key classes can trivially be converted into a key-recovery attack.

While in theory the computation of the correlation is straightforward, in practice there are some issues that we need to take into account. One of them is the data complexity required to compute the correlation.

Generally speaking, to detect a correlation c, an adversary needs to encrypt roughly $2 \cdot c^{-2}$ plaintexts. As per [Mat93], the larger the size of data sample, the more accurate the results are.

In order to gain the ability to distinguish between the three key-classes, i.e. between the three correlations, we choose the data size in accordance to the smallest non-zero correlation, that is, $2^{-24.95}$, and encrypt $2^{50.9}$ random plaintexts.

After computing the empirical correlation, we compare it to each of the three expected values. In the case of the non-zero correlations, we compare the empirical value to the theoretical one. For the zero-correlation case, we compare the empirical correlation to the inverse of the squared root of the data complexity; this is a good approximation for the expected empirical correlation for a sample with correlation 0.

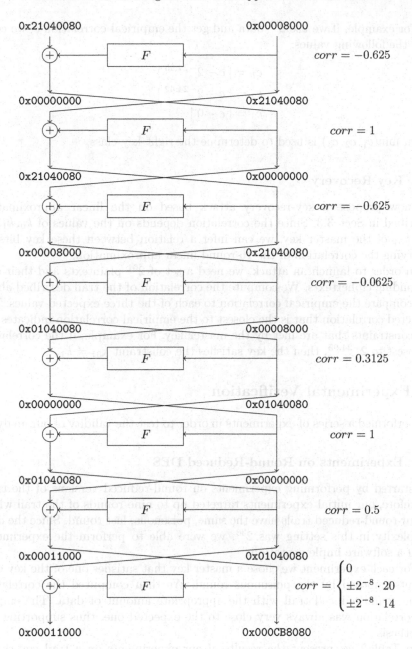

Fig. 5. The last eight rounds of our new linear approximation

For example, if we use 2^{51} data and get the empirical correlation c, we compute the following values:

$$c_1 = \mid c - 2^{-24.95} \mid$$
$$c_2 = \mid c - 2^{-24.42} \mid$$
$$c_3 = \mid c - 0 \mid .$$

Then, $\min(c_1, c_2, c_3)$ is used to determine the right key class.

3.5 Key Recovery

We now propose a key-recovery attack based on the linear approximation described in Sect. 3.3. Since the correlation depends on the values of k_0, k_1, k_8, and k_{51} of the master key, we can infer a relation between these key bits by observing the correlation of the 16-round linear approximation.

In order to launch an attack, we need a set of 2^{51} plaintexts and their corresponding ciphertexts. We compute the correlation of the trail described above and compare the empirical correlation to each of the three expected values. The expected correlation that is the closest to the empirical correlation indicates the key constraints that are met by the master key. For example, if the correlation is closest to $2^{-24.95}$, then the key satisfies the constraint $k_{51} \neq k_1$.

4 Experimental Verification

We performed a series of experiments in order to test the validity of our analysis.

4.1 Experiments on Round-Reduced DES

We started by performing experiments on round-reduced versions of the trail. Therefore, our initial experiments targeted up to nine rounds of the trail where all our round-reduced trails have the same, poisonous, last round. Since the data complexity in this setting was 2^{38}, we were able to perform the experiments using a software implementation.

For each experiment we chose a master key that satisfies one of the key constraints imposed by the poisonous round. We then computed the correlation of the round-reduced trail with the appropriate amount of data. The empirical correlation was always very close to the expected one, thus supporting our hypothesis.

In Table 2 we present the results of our experiments on a trail covering 9 rounds using 2^{38} data. The expected correlation of the trail, depending on the bits of the 9th round key is:

$$corr = \begin{cases} \pm 2^{-16.245} & k_{16} \neq k_{18} \\ \pm 2^{-15.714} & k_{16} = k_{18} \text{ and } k_{17} = k_{19} \\ 0 & \text{otherwise} \end{cases} \tag{4}$$

The smallest non-zero correlation of the trail is $2^{-16.245}$, thus the minimum amount of data needed is 2^{35}. We chose to use 2^{38} to improve the significance of the results. The weights of the expected and empirical correlations are given in Table 2.

Table 2. Experimental results of the last 9 rounds from the trail presented in Subsect. 3.3

Expected weight	Empirical correlation	Key constraint on RK_9
$-\infty$	-18.608	$k_{16} = k_{18}$ and $k_{17} \neq k_{19}$
-16.245	-16.055	$k_{16} \neq k_{18}$
-15.714	-15.631	$k_{16} = k_{18}$ and $k_{17} = k_{19}$

4.2 Experiments on Full DES

In order to empirically verify the validity of our analysis on the full DES, we used a custom hardware design. A brief description of the experimental setup can be found in Subsect. 4.3 with a detailed description in [D'h19].

Taking into consideration that the smallest correlation of the trail on the full DES is $2^{-24.95}$, the minimum amount of data needed for our experiments is $2^{50.9}$. We approximated this to 2^{51} data. For a better understanding of our results, we have empirically computed the correlation for the full DES using 144 different keys, as follows:

- 48 keys satisfy the constraint $k_{51} \neq k_1$; thus, their expected correlation is $\pm 2^{-24.95}$;
- 48 keys satisfy the constraint $k_{51} = k_1$ and $k_0 = k_8$; hence their expected correlation is $\pm 2^{-24.42}$;
- 48 keys satisfy the constraint leading to strictly zero-correlation.

In order to interpret our results, for each key-class we computed the log_2 of the absolute value of the mean of the empirical correlations, the results of this experiment are presented in Table 3. In Fig. 6 we depict in green the full distribution together with the respective expected distribution in blue. Note that Fig. 6b and Fig. 6c use the absolute value of the correlations while this is not necessary for Fig. 6a due to the convergence of ± 0 into a single case.

All our experiments, both on round-reduced and on full DES, support the hypothesis that different key-classes can be distinguished, therefore the correlation discloses the constraints that the key fulfils.

Table 3. Experimental results of the full DES using the trail described in Sect. 3.3

Expected weight	Average weight (empirical)	Key constraint (respective to the master key)	Success probability
-24.95	-24.90	$k_{51} \neq k_1$	62.5%
-24.42	-24.41	$k_{51} = k_1$ and $k_0 = k_8$	66.6 %
$-\infty$	-26.39	$k_{51} = k_1$ and $k_0 \neq k_8$	39.5 %

Average success probability: 51.9%

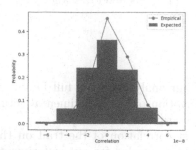

(a) Expected correlation $= 0$. Each of the 7 bins is of size $2^{-25.57}$ starting from $-2^{-23.76}$.

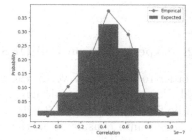

(b) Expected correlation $= \pm 2^{-24.42}$. Each of the 7 bins is of size $2^{-25.73}$ starting from $2^{-25.72}$.

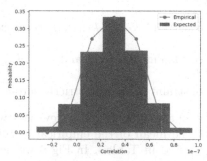

(c) Expected correlation $= \pm 2^{-24.95}$. Each of the 7 bins is of size $2^{-25.69}$ starting from $2^{-24.83}$.

Fig. 6. The distribution of the empirical correlations from 3×48 experiments (green) compared against histograms of the respective expected values (blue). Absolute values of the correlations are used in the top-right and bottom plots. (Color figure online)

4.3 Experimental Setup

We design and implement a custom DES accelerator to speed up the experiments. Figure 7 depicts the architecture of our computing system. It fits on a single instance of Zynq UltraScale+ MPSoC ZCU102. We boot PetaLinux on its hardwired quad-core Arm Cortex-A53 to make it an easily controllable standalone computing system, controllable through a flexible Python interface. We use the AXI interface provided by Xilinx to map 128 cryptanalitic cores as peripherals. This design is easily portable and expandable. Running at a clock speed of 250 MHz the throughput of each core is $2^{27.89}$ encryptions per second, requiring 19.17 h to run a single experiment consisting of 2^{51} encryptions using 128 cores.

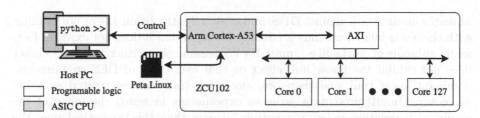

Fig. 7. Architecture of the accelerator for cryptanalysis of DES.

Figure 8 depicts architecture of each core. A core contains a round-pipelined implementation of DES with the supporting logic for cryptanalysis. Said logic includes: pseudo-random plaintext generation, masking the plaintext and the ciphertext values, evaluating the linear approximation and keeping the correlation. We increase flexibility and usability of the platform by allowing runtime reconfiguration of: masks, keys, pseudo-random number generation and the number of experiments. Therefore, experiments are performed fully in hardware. To the best of our knowledge, this is the first application of hardware for cryptanalysis of this sort.

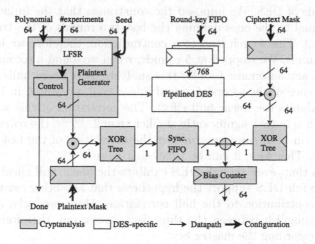

Fig. 8. Architecture of a cryptanalytic core.

We generate plaintexts using 64-bit Linear Feedback Shift Registers (LFSRs). LFSR hardware allows us to configure each with a different polynomial and starting value (seed). We ensure that pseudo-random sequences do not repeat by using primitive 64-bit polynomials—leading to sequence length of 2^{64}—for each LFSR. For more implementation details and source code we refer the interested reader to [D'h19].

5   Discussion

Matsui's linear attack against DES, and especially Algorithm 1, was not familiar with the linear hull effect, thus it trivially assumed that it does not exist. In fact, many subsequent works like [Jun01, BV17] assume that either the DES cipher does not exhibit the linear hull effect or that every hull of DES contains one dominant linear trail, and therefore, any other trails can be treated as noise. Moreover, [Jun01] presents a series of experiments in which the mean of the empirical correlation is not perceptibly greater than the theoretical one, the author concluding that the linear hull effect is not visible for DES.

In Sect. 4 we presented experimental verification for our distinguisher. As can be seen in Tables 2–3, while the empirical results are indeed "close enough" to their expected values, they are not quite the same. These small differences may be ignored as sample error (see also [BT13]) but they may also mean that another trail exists within Matsui's hull. As per Ashur and Rijmen in [AR16] ignoring some of the linear trails inside the hull leads to an over- or under-estimation of the expected correlation, leading in turn to a different success probability than what the adversary expects.

In our research we questioned the presence of the linear hull effect for the DES cipher. Since it can be challenging to identify another trail for the full DES, we restricted our search to round-reduced versions of the cipher. We performed our search by trial and error, starting by analyzing the existence of a second trail for two rounds of DES. We imposed the constraints that the input and output masks are equal to the ones defining the last two rounds of the trail presented in Subsect. 3.3. This search lead to a contradiction, therefore we increased the number of rounds. We stopped at 5 rounds, when we found a second trail. Since we didn't use any automatic tool for this analysis, more linear hulls might exist.

The existence of the second 5-round linear trail, presented in Fig. 9, proves that DES exhibits the linear hull effect. The correlation of this second trail is $2^{-21.19}$, which is indeed significantly smaller than $2^{-10.89}$, the correlation of the original trail (in both cases we consider the correlation of the last round equal to $\pm 2^{-8} \cdot 14$). Therefore, it can be treated as noise.

We stress that, even though DES exhibits the linear hull effect, our experiments on the full DES support the hypothesis that any other existing trail has a negligible contribution to the hull correlation. More precisely, an adversary is able to distinguish between the three key-classes and, therefore, gaining an information regarding the master key.

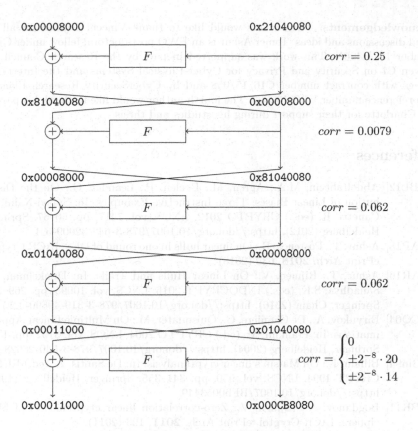

Fig. 9. The second 5-round linear trail

5.1 Conclusion

In this paper we extended the work in [AP18] by constructing a 0-correlation key-dependent linear trails that cover more than a single round of DES. First, we presented a 2-round linear approximation where the last round may have correlation 0, depending on the key. We showed how to connect these two rounds to Matsui's trail, resulting in 0-correlation key-dependent trails covering the full DES.

The work described can be extended in different directions. For example, it will be interesting to identify other block ciphers that exhibit "poisonous" linear trails and revisit, if exist, the linear attacks published against them. It also remains to be investigated if and how the attacks presented in this paper can be improved in term of both data and time complexity and how they affect the security of 3DES. Future research should also consider the extension of these attacks to the case of multiple linear cryptanalysis.

Acknowledgements. The authors would like to thank Vincent Rijmen for all the useful discussions and ideas. Tomer Ashur is an FWO post-doctoral fellow under Grant Number 12ZH420N. This work was supported in part by the Research Council KU Leuven C1 on Security and Privacy for Cyber-Physical Systems and the Internet of Things with contract number C16/15/058 and by CyberSecurity Research Flanders with reference number VR20192203. The fourth author would like to thank his parents and Charlotte for their support during his studies and thesis.

References

[AÅBL12]   Abdelraheem, M.A., Ågren, M., Beelen, P., Leander, G.: On the Distri-
           bution of Linear Biases: Three Instructive Examples. In: Safavi-Naini, R.,
           Canetti, R. (eds.) CRYPTO 2012. LNCS, vol. 7417, pp. 50–67. Springer,
           Heidelberg (2012). https://doi.org/10.1007/978-3-642-32009-5_4
[AP18]   Ashur, T., Posteuca, R.: On linear hulls in one round of DES. IACR Cryptol.
           ePrint Arch. **2018**, 635 (2018)
[AR16]   Ashur, T., Rijmen, V.: On Linear Hulls and Trails. In: Dunkelman, O.,
           Sanadhya, S.K. (eds.) INDOCRYPT 2016. LNCS, vol. 10095, pp. 269–286.
           Springer, Cham (2016). https://doi.org/10.1007/978-3-319-49890-4_15
[BCQ04]   Biryukov, A., De Cannière, C., Quisquater, M.: On Multiple Linear Approx-
           imations. In: Franklin, M. (ed.) CRYPTO 2004. LNCS, vol. 3152, pp. 1–22.
           Springer, Heidelberg (2004). https://doi.org/10.1007/978-3-540-28628-8_1
[Bih94]   Biham, E.: On Matsui's linear cryptanalysis. In: De Santis, A. (ed.) EURO-
           CRYPT 1994. LNCS, vol. 950, pp. 341–355. Springer, Heidelberg (1995).
           https://doi.org/10.1007/BFb0053449
[BR11]   Bogdanov, A., Rijmen, V.: Zero-correlation linear cryptanalysis of block
           ciphers. IACR Cryptol. ePrint Arch. **2011**, 123 (2011)
[BT13]   Bogdanov, A., Tischhauser, E.: On the Wrong Key Randomisation and Key
           Equivalence Hypotheses in Matsuis Algorithm 2. In: Moriai, S. (ed.) FSE
           2013. LNCS, vol. 8424, pp. 19–38. Springer, Heidelberg (2014). https://doi.
           org/10.1007/978-3-662-43933-3_2
[BV17]   Bogdanov, A., Vejre, P.S.: Linear Cryptanalysis of DES with Asymmetries.
           In: Takagi, T., Peyrin, T. (eds.) ASIACRYPT 2017. LNCS, vol. 10624,
           pp. 187–216. Springer, Cham (2017). https://doi.org/10.1007/978-3-319-
           70694-8_7
[CV94]   Chabaud, F., Vaudenay, S.: Links between differential and linear crypt-
           analysis. In: De Santis, A. (ed.) EUROCRYPT 1994. LNCS, vol. 950, pp.
           356–365. Springer, Heidelberg (1995). https://doi.org/10.1007/BFb0053450
[DES]   FIPS publication 46-3: Data Encryption Standard (DES)
[D'h19]   D'haeseleer, S.: Hardware design for cryptanalysis. Master's thesis, KU Leu-
           ven (2019). Ashur, T., Sijacic, D., Verbauwhede, I. (promotors)
[JR94]   Kaliski, B.S., Robshaw, M.J.B.: Linear Cryptanalysis Using Multiple
           Approximations. In: Desmedt, Y.G. (ed.) CRYPTO 1994. LNCS, vol.
           839, pp. 26–39. Springer, Heidelberg (1994). https://doi.org/10.1007/3-540-
           48658-5_4
[Jun01]   Junod, P.: On the Complexity of Matsuis Attack. In: Vaudenay, S., Youssef,
           A.M. (eds.) SAC 2001. LNCS, vol. 2259, pp. 199–211. Springer, Heidelberg
           (2001). https://doi.org/10.1007/3-540-45537-X_16

[Mat93] Matsui, M.: Linear Cryptanalysis Method for DES Cipher. In: Helleseth, T. (ed.) EUROCRYPT 1993. LNCS, vol. 765, pp. 386–397. Springer, Heidelberg (1994). https://doi.org/10.1007/3-540-48285-7_33

[Nyb94] Nyberg, K.: Linear approximation of block ciphers. In: De Santis, A. (ed.) EUROCRYPT 1994. LNCS, vol. 950, pp. 439–444. Springer, Heidelberg (1995). https://doi.org/10.1007/BFb0053460

[San95] Santis, A. (ed.): EUROCRYPT 1994. LNCS, vol. 950. Springer, Heidelberg (1995). https://doi.org/10.1007/BFb0053418

Theory and Lower Bounds

Anonymous Symmetric-Key Communication

Fabio Banfi(✉) ⓘ and Ueli Maurer

Department of Computer Science, ETH Zurich, 8092 Zurich, Switzerland
{fabio.banfi,maurer}@inf.ethz.ch

Abstract. We study anonymity of *probabilistic encryption* (pE) and *probabilistic authenticated encryption* (pAE). We start by providing concise game-based security definitions capturing anonymity for both pE and pAE, and then show that the commonly used notion of *indistinguishability from random ciphertexts* (IND$) indeed implies the anonymity notions for both pE and pAE. This is in contrast to a recent work of Chan and Rogaway (Asiacrypt 2019), where it is shown that IND$-secure nonce-based authenticated encryption can only achieve anonymity if a sophisticated transformation is applied. Moreover, we also show that the *Encrypt-then-MAC* paradigm is anonymity-preserving, in the sense that if both the underlying probabilistic MAC (pMAC) and pE schemes are anonymous, then also the resulting pAE scheme is. Finally, we provide a composable treatment of anonymity using the constructive cryptography framework of Maurer and Renner (ICS 2011). We introduce adequate abstractions modeling various kinds of anonymous communication channels for many senders and one receiver in the presence of an active man-in-the-middle adversary. Then we show that the game-based notions indeed are anonymity-preserving, in the sense that they imply constructions between such anonymous channels, thus generating authenticity and/or confidentiality as expected, but crucially retaining anonymity if present.

1 Introduction

When transmitting messages in the symmetric-key setting, where communicating parties share secret keys a priori, traditionally *confidentiality* and *authenticity* are the security properties that are mostly considered. Confidentiality guarantees exclusivity of the receiving party (no one but the receiver should be able to gain any partial information about the transmitted message, possibly other than its length), while authenticity guarantees exclusivity of the sending party (no one except the sender should be able to convince the receiver that it indeed originated the message). But in a scenario where there are more than just two communicating parties using the same protocol, e.g., many senders and one receiver (as considered in this work), another important security property must be taken into account, namely *anonymity*.

For the mentioned setting, we are more specifically interested in *external sender anonymity*, that is, the property that guarantees that no one but the

© Springer Nature Switzerland AG 2020
C. Galdi and V. Kolesnikov (Eds.): SCN 2020, LNCS 12238, pp. 471–491, 2020.
https://doi.org/10.1007/978-3-030-57990-6_23

receiver can learn from which sender a message originated. The main focus of our work is on security definitions which capture exactly this guarantee.

1.1   Background

Anonymity, as opposed to confidentiality and authenticity, in most settings (as is the case for the one considered here) cannot be "created out of the blue"; rather, an intrinsic property of anonymity is that it can be *preserved*. In the game-based spirit of security definitions, this is reflected by the fact that conventional anonymity notions are captured by the concept of *key-indistinguishability* of a scheme originally intended to provide other forms of security, as confidentiality or authenticity. More specifically, in the symmetric-key setting this means that anonymity is a property that needs to be provided in conjunction with confidentiality for encryption schemes and with authenticity for MAC schemes.

But when considered from a composable standpoint, the fact that anonymity can merely be preserved becomes even more evident: consider for example a protocol employing a MAC scheme and shared secret keys between the senders and the receiver, which is executed on top of an insecure channel to obtain an authenticated channel; if one wishes for the constructed channel to additionally be also anonymous, it must be the case that the insecure channel is anonymous as well, and this construction is still possible precisely if the employed MAC scheme not only is unforgeable, but is also key-indistinguishable.

The latter considerations were made explicit by Alwen, Hirt, Maurer, Patra, and Raykov in [4], and our work can be seen as a continuation and refinement of this line of research: Here we consider the construction of an anonymous *secure* (confidential *and* authenticated) channel from an anonymous authenticated one, and show that this is possible precisely if the employed encryption scheme not only has indistinguishable ciphertexts, but also indistinguishable keys. Moreover, we show that only if a secure authenticated encryption scheme which is key-indistinguishable is employed, one can construct the anonymous secure channel directly from the anonymous insecure one.

1.2   Contributions

We consider the following setting: n parties, the senders, wish to securely and anonymously transmit messages to the same party, the receiver, and we assume that the receiver a priori shares a (different) secret key with each of the n senders. Since all of our treatment is in the *symmetric-key* setting, and the considered protocols employ *probabilistic* (as opposed to nonce-based) schemes, we often tacitly assume these two facts throughout the paper. Moreover, since the meaning of security usually depends on the context, we adopt the convention that for a cryptographic scheme by *anonymous security* we mean anonymity (in form of key-indistinguishability) in conjunction with its conventionally associated security notion, that is, confidentiality for encryption, authenticity for MAC, and confidentiality plus authenticity (usually simply referred to as just security) for authenticated encryption.

Game-Based Security Definitions. We start by providing game-based security definitions capturing anonymity for both *probabilistic encryption* (pE) and *probabilistic authenticated encryption* (pAE). For the former, we revisit the notion of *key-indistinguishability*, originally put forth by Fischlin [13], and subsequently treated in [12] by Desai and in [1] by Abadi and Rogaway. In all three works this notion has been expressed for $n = 2$ senders; here we generalize it to an arbitrary number of senders. For *nonce-based* authenticated encryption (nAE), the analogous notion of key-indistinguishability has been recently put forth by Chan and Rogaway [11]. Here we propose a concise definition for the case of pAE instead.

For both pE and pAE, we show the relevant implications among the introduced security definitions, exposing the concrete security losses surfacing from the reductions (in the full version [5]). Furthermore, we formally show that indeed the strong security notion of *indistinguishability from random ciphertexts* (dubbed IND\$, and valid for both schemes) implies key-indistinguishability. Finally, we prove that the Encrypt-then-MAC (EtM) paradigm, applied on secure and anonymous pE and probabilistic MAC (pMAC), yields pAE which is not only secure, but crucially also anonymous, thus confirming that EtM is *anonymity-preserving.*

Composable Security Definitions. We next move to the focal point of our work, the composable treatment of anonymity. Here we introduce alternative security definitions within the *constructive cryptography* (CC) framework of Maurer and Renner [17, 19], which enjoy composability and allow to make explicit security goals from an application point of view.

First we phrase the desired security properties of (symmetric-key) protocols as specific constructions of cryptographic communication channels. More concretely, we start by defining the following resources which expose n interfaces to send messages and one to receive them: the *insecure anonymous channel* (A-INS), the *authenticated anonymous channel* (A-AUT), and the *secure anonymous channel* (A-SEC). Then we state that a protocol (executed by the senders and the receiver, which share secret keys a priori) provides *authenticity in conjunction with anonymity* if it constructs A-AUT from A-INS, provides *confidentiality in conjunction with anonymity* if it constructs A-SEC from A-AUT, and provides *security (i.e., confidentiality and authenticity) in conjunction with anonymity* if it constructs A-SEC directly from A-INS.

Secondly, we establish relations between the previously introduced game-based security definitions and their composable counterparts, that is, we show sufficiency conditions in terms of game-based definitions for the above mentioned constructions. As already mentioned earlier, in [4] it was shown that key-indistinguishable pMAC schemes enable the construction of A-AUT from A-INS. Here we show that anonymous secure pE enables the next logical step, namely the construction of A-SEC from A-AUT. In terms of time-complexity, this significantly improves upon the MAC-based solution proposed in [4] for the same construction. Furthermore, we show that these two steps can be performed in one shot using authenticated encryption instead, that is, we show that anonymous secure pAE constructs a A-SEC directly from A-INS. Again, this significantly improves upon the MAC-based solution proposed in [4] for the same construction. Moreover, this provides further evidence of the anonymity preservation of EtM.

Preferring Probabilistic Schemes for Anonymity. We observe that our constructive treatment strengthens the role of probabilistic authenticated encryption in contrast to its nonce-based counterpart when it comes to anonymity. According to Rogaway [20], a main advantage provided by nonces is that

> *"encryption schemes constructed to be secure under nonce-based security notions may be less prone to misuse".*

Nevertheless, this raises concerns about attacks in the multi-user (mu) setting, where crucially anonymity lives. For this reason in TLS 1.3 a *randomized nonces* mechanism has been proposed for the employed nAE scheme, AES with GCM (Galois/Counter Mode). This recently spawned work by Bellare and Tackmann [9] and Hoang, Tessaro, and Thiruvengadam [14], which initiated and refined the study of mu security of nAE in order to rigorously formalize security under such randomized nonces mechanism (but they did not address anonymity, in the form of key-indistinguishability).

But quoting again Rogaway [21, I.8 (page 22)],

> *"[if] an IV-based encryption scheme [...] is good in the nonce-based framework [...] then it is also good in the probabilistic setting",*

which implies that an IND\$-secure nAE scheme is an IND\$-secure pAE scheme, when the nonce is randomized (if one ignores the concept of *associated data*). Therefore, in view of our previously mentioned result attesting that IND\$-secure pAE implies anonymity, our work can be considered as a confirmation that the random nonce mechanism, if used with an IND\$-secure nAE scheme and under the assumption that the nonces are indeed truly uniformly random, also provides anonymity. Note that our consideration here is rather informal, and a more thorough study should be carried out to also incorporate the issue of nonce repetition and related birthday paradox security bounds (in our discussion, we are assuming a setting where not too many messages are exchanged).

This is to be compared to a recent work by Chan and Rogaway [11], which studies the anonymity of nAE: the authors observe that because of the session-related nature of the nonces, nAE actually fails to generally provide anonymity. For this reason, they introduce a transformation (dubbed NonceWrap) which converts an nAE scheme into a (syntactically different) new scheme, *anonymous* nAE (anAE), which they show does achieve anonymity (i.e., key-indistinguishability).

A Framework for Security Definitions and Proofs. We formulate all of the above mentioned security definitions in a systematic and concise language. We see the framework we put forth as an independent contribution, since it allows for compact formulations of security definitions, and enables easy and short (*reduction*-based) proofs of security, which in principle could be formally verified in a rather direct way (we leave this task open). Our proposed framework is based on the earlier work on *cryptographic systems* of Maurer, Pietrzak, and Renner [16,18], can be seen as a specialization of the recent work of Brzuska, Delignat-Lavaud, Fournet, Kohbrok, and Kohlweiss [10], and is inspired by the approach taken by Rosulek in [24].

1.3 Outline

We begin by providing the necessary background in Sect. 2, where we introduce our notation and the framework we use to state and prove security notions. As motivating examples, we revisit the classical security definitions for pE and pAE by capturing them within our framework. We proceed in Sect. 3 by providing game-based security definitions of anonymity, in terms of key-indistinguishability, for both pE and pAE. We introduce different notions, some capturing single security goals while others capturing more together, and then we show the relevant relations among them. Moreover, we show that for both pE and pAE, their respective stronger IND\$ security notions imply anonymity. As a last result within the realm of game-based security notions, we show that the Encrypt-then-MAC paradigm, used to build secure pAE from secure pE and secure pMAC, not only preserves security, but anonymity as well. Finally, in Sect. 4 we provide composable security definitions capturing anonymity for both pE and pAE, and show that these notions are implied by the previously introduced game-based definitions. This is our main contribution, and it should be seen as shedding light into what anonymity (in the sense of key-indistinguishability) of symmetric cryptographic primitives really achieves from an application point of view. Our analysis makes it explicit that in this setting, key-indistinguishability must be understood as a tool that *preserves* anonymity, rather than creating it. The proofs of all of our results are deferred to the full version [5].

2 Preliminaries

2.1 Notation

We write $x, \ldots \leftarrow y$ to assign the value y to variables $x, \ldots$, and $w, \ldots \overset{iid}{\leftarrow} \mathcal{D}$ to assign independently and identically distributed values to variables $w, \ldots$ according to distribution $\mathcal{D}$. $\varnothing$ denotes the empty set, $\mathbb{N} \doteq \{0, 1, 2, \ldots\}$ denotes the set of natural numbers, and for $n \in \mathbb{N}$, we use the convention $[n] \doteq \{1, \ldots, n\}$. For $n \in \mathbb{N}$, $\{0, 1\}^n$ denotes the set of bitstrings of length n, $\{0, 1\}^* \doteq \bigcup_{i \geq 0} \{0, 1\}^i$ denotes the set of all finite length bitstrings, for $s \in \{0, 1\}^*$, $|s|$ denotes the length of s (in bits), and $\$^n$ represent a uniformly sampled random bitstring of length n. Finally, for a random variable X over a set $\mathcal{X}$, $\operatorname{supp} X \doteq \{x \in \mathcal{X} \mid \Pr[X = x] > 0\}$.

2.2   Cryptographic Systems

We model cryptographic objects as *discrete reactive systems with interfaces*, that is, systems that can be queried with labeled inputs in a sequential fashion, where each distinct label corresponds to a distinct interface, and for each such input generate (possibly probabilistically) an equally labeled output depending on the input and the current state (formally defined by the sequence of all previous inputs and the associated outputs). Such systems can be formally described by conditional distributions of output values given input values, that is, by their *input-output behavior* (often described with *pseudocode*), as they formally correspond to *random systems* originally introduced in [16], and later refined in [18]. For two such systems $\mathbf{S}$ and $\mathbf{T}$ having the same input-output behavior (but possibly different implementation), we write $\mathbf{S} \equiv \mathbf{T}$.

In cryptography we are also interested in other objects (which can be formally modeled as special kinds of random systems). The first type we consider are *distinguishers*, which are just like the systems mentioned above, but enhanced with a special initial output which does not require an input, and a special final binary output. Formally, we usually consider a random experiment involving a distinguisher $\mathbf{D}$ and a system $\mathbf{S}$ which interact as follows: first $\mathbf{D}$ starts by (possibly probabilistically) generating the first output X_1 with some label (corresponding to a specific interface of $\mathbf{S}$), which will be used as the first input for $\mathbf{S}$ at that interface, which in turn will generate its first output Y_1 at the same interface, to be used as first input for $\mathbf{D}$. From Y_1 and the current state (X_1), $\mathbf{D}$ will then generate its second output X_2, with some (possibly different) label, and $\mathbf{S}$ will respond with Y_2 (depending on X_1, Y_1, and X_2), and so on, until $\mathbf{D}$ stops and outputs a bit Z. We call the operation of connecting $\mathbf{D}$ and $\mathbf{S}$ in the described way *sequential composition* and we syntactically represent it by the expression $\mathbf{DS}$, which is only valid if the number and types of labels (interfaces) match. We use the expression $\mathbf{DS}$ to also denote the random variable Z representing $\mathbf{D}$'s final binary output.

The second type of special objects are *converters*, which are similar to systems but defining two disjoint sets of labels, and which can be used to extend either distinguishers (with labels matching the one in the first set) or systems (with labels matching the ones in the second set). We refrain from defining this concept on a formal level, and limit ourselves to give an intuitive description: a converter $\mathbf{C}$ is an object such that $\mathbf{DC}$ (the sequential composition restricted to the first set of labels of distinguisher $\mathbf{D}$ with $\mathbf{C}$) is again a distinguisher, and $\mathbf{CS}$ (the sequential composition restricted to the second set of labels of $\mathbf{C}$ with system $\mathbf{S}$) is again a system.

As for example also done in [10] and [24], it is then possible to formalize an (associative) algebra of systems. Let $\mathbf{D}$ be a distinguisher, $\mathbf{C}$ a converter, and $\mathbf{S}$ a (regular) system. Then the experiment where $\mathbf{DC}$ interacts with $\mathbf{S}$ is the same experiment where $\mathbf{D}$ interacts with $\mathbf{CS}$, and we just denote this by $\mathbf{DCS}$ (again with the understanding that this expression also represents the final binary output of $\mathbf{D}$). Syntactically, this could be expressed as $(\mathbf{DC})\mathbf{S} = \mathbf{D}(\mathbf{CS}) = \mathbf{DCS}$.

We next define another way to compose systems, *parallel composition*: given two (or more) systems $\mathbf{S}$ and $\mathbf{T}$, a new system $\mathbf{V}$ is the (independent) parallel composition of $\mathbf{S}$ and $\mathbf{T}$, denoted $\mathbf{V} = [\mathbf{S}, \mathbf{T}]$, if a system $\mathbf{D}$ interacting with $\mathbf{V}$ can (independently) access system $\mathbf{S}$ and system $\mathbf{T}$. We remark that $\mathbf{V}$ is merely a "wrapper" for two independent instances of systems $\mathbf{S}$ and $\mathbf{T}$. On the other hand, it is often also the case that two systems composed in parallel need some correlation, that is, need to lose their independence (usually trough a shared random variable or, more in general, some shared state); two such systems $\mathbf{S}$ and $\mathbf{T}$ might be used to create what is called a *correlated* parallel composition, which we formalize as a new system $\mathbf{V}$ such that $\mathbf{V} = \mathbf{C}[\mathbf{S}, \mathbf{T}]$, for some system $\mathbf{C}$ accessing the independent systems $\mathbf{S}$ and $\mathbf{T}$, and emulating two (correlated) systems towards a system $\mathbf{D}$ interacting with $\mathbf{V}$. We introduce the notation $\mathbf{V} = \langle \mathbf{S}, \mathbf{T} \rangle$, which makes the correlating system $\mathbf{C}$ implicit in the following sense: a system $\mathbf{D}$ interacting with $\mathbf{V}$ can access the system $\mathbf{S}$ and system $\mathbf{T}$, but only through $\mathbf{C}$, and $\mathbf{S}$ and $\mathbf{T}$ become "labels" for the correlated systems emulated by $\mathbf{C}$. Figure 1 illustrates the two different concepts. Note that we can naturally extend both definitions to the case of n systems.

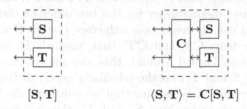

$$[\mathbf{S}, \mathbf{T}] \qquad\qquad \langle \mathbf{S}, \mathbf{T} \rangle = \mathbf{C}[\mathbf{S}, \mathbf{T}]$$

Fig. 1. Representation of the difference between *(independent) parallel composition* $[\mathbf{S}, \mathbf{T}]$ and *correlated parallel composition* $\langle \mathbf{S}, \mathbf{T} \rangle$.

Definition 1 (Systems Parallel Composition). *Given the sequence of systems* $\mathbf{S}_1, \ldots, \mathbf{S}_n$, *for* $n \in \mathbb{N}$, *define:*

- *Their (independent) parallel composition, denoted* $[\mathbf{S}_1, \ldots, \mathbf{S}_n]$, *as the system that exports n interfaces labeled* $\mathbf{S}_1, \ldots, \mathbf{S}_n$, *where label* $\mathbf{S}_i$ *is directly connected to system* $\mathbf{S}_i$, *for* $i \in [n]$.
- *Their correlated parallel composition, denoted* $\langle \mathbf{S}_1, \ldots, \mathbf{S}_n \rangle$, *as the system* $\mathbf{C}[\mathbf{S}_1, \ldots, \mathbf{S}_n]$, *where* $\mathbf{C}$ *is some (implicit) system which exports n interfaces labeled* $\mathbf{S}_1, \ldots, \mathbf{S}_n$.[1]

2.3 Indistinguishability of Cryptographic Systems

In cryptography, we are usually interested in how similarly two systems $\mathbf{S}$ and $\mathbf{T}$ (with matching interfaces) behave. Intuitively, the more indistinguishable their

---

[1] Note that correlated parallel composition is merely syntactic construct, and we only use this notation throughout our paper for easier (and nicer) statements.

behavior is, the closer $\mathbf{S}$ and $\mathbf{T}$ are. We can measure such closeness by means of the indistinguishability between systems $\mathbf{S}$ and $\mathbf{T}$ from the perspective of a distinguisher $\mathbf{D}$ which interacts with either of them, and outputs the bit denoted by $\mathbf{DV}$, for $\mathbf{V} \in \{\mathbf{S}, \mathbf{T}\}$, indicating its guess as to which system it is interacting with, where the understanding is that 0 indicates $\mathbf{S}$ and 1 indicates $\mathbf{T}$.

Definition 2. *For distinguisher $\mathbf{D}$ and systems $\mathbf{S}$ and $\mathbf{T}$, $\mathbf{D}$'s advantage in distinguishing between $\mathbf{S}$ and $\mathbf{T}$ is*

$$\Delta^{\mathbf{D}}(\mathbf{S}, \mathbf{T}) \doteq \Pr\left[\mathbf{DS} = 0\right] - \Pr\left[\mathbf{DT} = 0\right]$$

Moreover, in cryptography security statements are often conditional, as is the case for the present work. This means that, given two systems $\mathbf{S}$ and $\mathbf{T}$, we do not give a concrete value for the distinguishing advantage depending on a distinguisher $\mathbf{D}$, but rather relate this quantity to the distinguishing advantage of *another* distinguisher $\mathbf{D}'$ for two different systems $\mathbf{S}'$ and $\mathbf{T}'$. Such a relation should entail that if $\mathbf{S}'$ and $\mathbf{T}'$ are close (which usually can be either in turn related to the distinction between two further systems, or just crystallized as an *hardness assumption*), then so are $\mathbf{S}$ and $\mathbf{T}$. Such a relation can be carried out by using the same distinguisher for the two different distinction problems, but more in general usually requires a *reduction* system $\mathbf{C}$ which translates $\mathbf{S}'$ and $\mathbf{T}'$ into two systems $\mathbf{CS}'$ and $\mathbf{CT}'$ that, towards $\mathbf{D}$, behave similarly to $\mathbf{S}$ and $\mathbf{T}$, respectively. Turned around, this also means that $\mathbf{C}$ translates the distinguisher $\mathbf{D}$ for $\mathbf{S}$ and $\mathbf{T}$ into the (similarly good) distinguisher $\mathbf{D}' = \mathbf{DC}$ for $\mathbf{S}'$ and $\mathbf{T}'$.[2] Therefore, if we assume that no (efficient) distinguisher can have a good advantage in distinguishing $\mathbf{S}'$ and $\mathbf{T}'$, then so does $\mathbf{D}'$, and in turn also $\mathbf{D}$ in distinguishing $\mathbf{S}$ and $\mathbf{T}$. By Definition 2 and associativity of sequential systems composition this in particular implies $\Delta^{\mathbf{D}}(\mathbf{S}, \mathbf{T}) = \Delta^{\mathbf{D}}(\mathbf{CS}', \mathbf{CT}') = \Delta^{\mathbf{DC}}(\mathbf{S}', \mathbf{T}') = \Delta^{\mathbf{D}'}(\mathbf{S}', \mathbf{T}')$.

2.4   Probabilistic (Authenticated) Encryption (pE/pAE)

Syntactically, *probabilistic encryption* (pE) and *probabilistic authenticated encryption* (pAE) are the same object, which we generally call an *encryption scheme*. The distinction is merely on the level of security: if an encryption scheme provides *confidentiality* (or is IND-CPA-secure), we consider it *secure* pE, whereas if it provides *both confidentiality and authenticity* (or is IND-CCA3-secure), we consider it *secure* pAE.

Definition 3 (Encryption Scheme). *A (probabilistic) encryption scheme $\Pi \doteq (\mathsf{Gen}, \mathsf{Enc}, \mathsf{Dec})$ over key-space $\mathcal{K}$, message-space $\mathcal{M}$, and ciphertext-space $\mathcal{C}$ (with $\bot \notin \mathcal{K} \cup \mathcal{M} \cup \mathcal{C}$), is such that*

- Gen *is an (efficiently samplable) distribution over $\mathcal{K}$;*

---

[2] In this work, we assume that such translations (reductions) are *black-box*, that is, $\mathbf{C}$ only has access to the outputs of $\mathbf{D}$, not to its internal behavior.

- $\texttt{Enc}: \mathcal{K} \times \mathcal{M} \to \mathcal{C}$ *is a (efficiently computable) probabilistic function;*
- $\texttt{Dec}: \mathcal{K} \times \mathcal{C} \to \mathcal{M} \cup \{\bot\}$ *is an (efficiently computable) deterministic function.*

As customary, for $k \in \mathcal{K}$ we use the short-hand notation $\texttt{Enc}_k(\cdot)$ for $\texttt{Enc}(k, \cdot)$ and $\texttt{Dec}_k(\cdot)$ for $\texttt{Dec}(k, \cdot)$, and we also assume that $\mathcal{M} \subseteq \{0,1\}^*$ and for any $m \in \mathcal{M}$, $\{0,1\}^{|m|} \subseteq \mathcal{M}$, whereas $\mathcal{C} = \{0,1\}^*$, but for any $m \in \mathcal{M}$ and $k \in \mathcal{K}$, $|\texttt{Enc}_k(m)| = |m| + \tau$ for some fixed expansion factor $\tau \in \mathbb{N}$. Moreover, we assume correctness of Π, that is, for all keys k distributed according to $\texttt{Gen}$, and all ciphertexts $c \in \mathcal{C}$, $\texttt{Dec}_k(c) = m$ if $c \in \mathrm{supp}\,(\texttt{Enc}_k(m))$ and $\texttt{Dec}_k(c) = \bot$ otherwise.

In order to define the security (and later also anonymity) of a fixed scheme Π, we define the following single and double interface systems (where the dependency on Π is implicit), parameterized by a fixed key $k \in \mathcal{K}$:

- $\mathbf{E}_k$: On input a message $m \in \mathcal{M}$, return $\texttt{Enc}_k(m) \in \mathcal{C}$.
- $\mathbf{E}_k^\$$: On input a message $m \in \mathcal{M}$, return $\texttt{Enc}_k(\tilde{m}) \in \mathcal{C}$ for freshly and uniformly sampled $\tilde{m} \in \mathcal{M}$ with $|\tilde{m}| = |m|$.
- $\langle \mathbf{E}_k, \mathbf{D}_k \rangle$:
  - On input a message $m \in \mathcal{M}$, return $\texttt{Enc}_k(m) \in \mathcal{C}$.
  - On input a ciphertext $c \in \mathcal{C}$, return $\texttt{Dec}_k(c) \in \mathcal{M} \cup \{\bot\}$.
- $\langle \mathbf{E}_k, \mathbf{D}^\bot \rangle$: Initially set $\mathcal{Q} \subseteq \mathcal{M} \times \mathcal{C}$ to $\varnothing$ and then:
  - On input a message $m \in \mathcal{M}$, return $c \doteq \texttt{Enc}_k(m) \in \mathcal{C}$ and set $\mathcal{Q}$ to $\mathcal{Q} \cup \{(m, c)\}$.
  - On input a ciphertext $c \in \mathcal{C}$, if there is an $m \in \mathcal{M}$ such that $(m, c) \in \mathcal{Q}$, then return m, otherwise return $\bot$.
- $\langle \mathbf{E}_k^\$, \mathbf{D}^\bot \rangle$: Initially set $\mathcal{Q} \subseteq \mathcal{M} \times \mathcal{C}$ to $\varnothing$ and then:
  - On input a message $m \in \mathcal{M}$, return $c \doteq \texttt{Enc}_k(\tilde{m}) \in \mathcal{C}$ for freshly and uniformly sampled $\tilde{m} \in \mathcal{M}$ with $|\tilde{m}| = |m|$, and set $\mathcal{Q}$ to $\mathcal{Q} \cup \{(m, c)\}$.
  - On input a ciphertext $c \in \mathcal{C}$, if there is an $m \in \mathcal{M}$ such that $(m, c) \in \mathcal{Q}$, then return m, otherwise return $\bot$.

In our definitions, the key k will *always* be replaced by a random variable (usually denoted K or K_i, for some $i \in \mathbb{N}$) distributed according to Π's $\texttt{Gen}$.

We remark that in our security definitions below we will slightly abuse notation and informally refer to *efficient* distinguishers and *negligible* advantages; both concepts should be properly defined asymptotically, which we do not explicitly do, since we do not define any *security parameter*. Nevertheless, correct asymptotic security statements may be easily recovered by considering sequences of our security statements, and taking the limit. Still, when relating such definitions, we will not (need to) use such asymptotic concepts, since we will employ a *concrete approach*, as done for example by Bellare, Desai, Jokipii, and Rogaway [6].

2.5   Game-Based Security of pE/pAE

Following [6], we first define the game-based security of pE in the *real-or-random* fashion, where the adversary must distinguish between a true encryption oracle and one which ignores inputs and encrypts random messages of the same length instead. For this reason we interchangeably talk about adversary and distinguisher. The following definition captures well-known IND-CPA security notions commonly found in the literature.

Definition 4 (Game-Based Security of pE). *An encryption scheme Π is secure* pE *(or* IND-CPA-*secure) if*

$$\Delta^{\mathbf{D}}(\mathbf{E}_K, \mathbf{E}_K^{\$})$$

is negligible for any efficient distinguisher $\mathbf{D}$.

For pAE we closely follow the *all-in-one* security definition style originally introduced by Shrimpton in [25] and dubbed IND-CCA3, where an adversary must distinguish between two sets of oracles: the first set consists of true encryption and decryption oracles, whereas the second set consists of a fake encryption oracle which ignores inputs and encrypts random messages of the same length instead, and a fake decryption oracle which always return $\perp$, except if the provided ciphertext was previously output upon (fake) encryption, in which case the original message is returned. Note that this is actually a slightly different version than Shrimpton's original definition, and was put forth in [2] by Alagic, Gagliardoni, and Majenz, where the equivalence with the former is shown.

Definition 5 (Game-Based Security of pAE). *An encryption scheme Π is secure* pAE *(or* IND-CCA3-*secure) if*

$$\Delta^{\mathbf{D}}(\langle \mathbf{E}_K, \mathbf{D}_K \rangle, \langle \mathbf{E}_K^{\$}, \mathbf{D}^{\perp} \rangle)$$

is negligible for any efficient distinguisher $\mathbf{D}$.

3   Game-Based Anonymous Security of pE/pAE

We define game-based anonymity of pE and pAE in terms of what in the literature is usually termed *key-indistinguishability*. For this, recall from our discussion above (see Fig. 1) that the system $[\mathbf{S}_{K_1}, \ldots, \mathbf{S}_{K_n}]$ provides the distinguisher with n interfaces to n *distinct* and *independent* copies of system $\mathbf{S}_k$, each of which is parameterized by a *different*, freshly and independently sampled key K_i. On the other hand, the system $\langle \mathbf{S}_K, \ldots, \mathbf{S}_K \rangle$ provides the distinguisher with n interfaces to essentially the *same* copy of system $\mathbf{S}_k$, each of which is parameterized by the *same* key K (previously freshly sampled).

While here we only provide definitions, in the full version [5] we also show the relevant relations among them. We begin by providing a game-based security definition capturing exclusively the notion of anonymity (in terms of key-indistinguishability) of pE and pAE. In the following, when dropping the term $[n\text{-}]$ we mean *"for any integer $n \geq 2$"*.

Definition 6 (Game-Based Anonymity of pE). *An encryption scheme* Π *is* [n-]anonymous pE *(or* [n-]IK-CPA-secure*) if*

$$\Delta^{\mathbf{D}}([\mathbf{E}_{K_1}, \ldots, \mathbf{E}_{K_n}], \langle \mathbf{E}_K, \ldots, \mathbf{E}_K \rangle)$$

is negligible for any efficient distinguisher $\mathbf{D}$.

Definition 7 Game-Based Anonymity of pAE). *An encryption scheme* Π *is* [n-]anonymous pAE *(or* [n-]IK-CCA3-secure*) if*

$$\Delta^{\mathbf{D}}([\langle \mathbf{E}_{K_1}, \mathbf{D}_{K_1} \rangle, \ldots, \langle \mathbf{E}_{K_n}, \mathbf{D}_{K_n} \rangle], \langle \langle \mathbf{E}_K, \mathbf{D}^\perp \rangle, \ldots, \langle \mathbf{E}_K, \mathbf{D}^\perp \rangle \rangle)$$

is negligible for any efficient distinguisher $\mathbf{D}$.

Next, we define the coupling of the traditional security goal of pE/pAE with anonymity. For both notions, we use the term *anonymous security*; specifically, by anonymous and secure pE we mean key-indistinguishable and confidential encryption, whereas by anonymous and secure pAE we mean key-indistinguishable, confidential, and authenticated encryption.

Definition 8 (Game-Based Anonymous Security of pE). *An encryption scheme* Π *is* [n-]anonymous secure pE *(or* [n-]IND-IK-CPA-secure*) if*

$$\Delta^{\mathbf{D}}([\mathbf{E}_{K_1}, \ldots, \mathbf{E}_{K_n}], \langle \mathbf{E}_K^\$, \ldots, \mathbf{E}_K^\$ \rangle)$$

is negligible for any efficient distinguisher $\mathbf{D}$.

Definition 9 (Game-Based Anonymous Security of pAE). *An encryption scheme* Π *is* [n-]anonymous secure pAE (or [n-]IND-IK-CCA3-secure*) if*

$$\Delta^{\mathbf{D}}([\langle \mathbf{E}_{K_1}, \mathbf{D}_{K_1} \rangle, \ldots, \langle \mathbf{E}_{K_n}, \mathbf{D}_{K_n} \rangle], \langle \langle \mathbf{E}_K^\$, \mathbf{D}^\perp \rangle, \ldots, \langle \mathbf{E}_K^\$, \mathbf{D}^\perp \rangle \rangle)$$

is negligible for any efficient distinguisher $\mathbf{D}$.

Remark. The concept of key-indistinguishability has been first introduced under the name of *"key-hiding private-key encryption"* by Fischlin in [13] as 2- IK-CPA according to Definition 6. Subsequently, in [12], Desai also studied the problem introducing the concept of *"non-separability of keys"*, but specifically for encryption schemes based on block ciphers. Later, in [1], Abadi and Rogaway presented a security notion called *"which-key concealing"*, that is basically identical to Fischlin's, but they defined security as a combination of key-indistinguishability and ciphertext-indistinguishability, that is, as 2- IND-IK-CPA according to Definition 8. They also claimed that popular modes of operation for symmetric encryption yield key-private encryption schemes. We will prove this formally in Sect. 3.1. Interestingly, the concept of key-indistinguishability was successfully translated to the public-key setting by Bellare, Boldyreva, Desai, and Pointcheval in [7], where the terms *key-privacy* and *indistinguishability of keys* were originally suggested.

As previously mentioned, regarding key-indistinguishability of AE, in a very recent work Chan and Rogaway [11] introduce the nonce-based counterpart of our notion for pAE, Definition 9, which is crucially *not* directly applicable to nAE, but rather to anAE, a syntactically different scheme which can be obtained from nAE through the transformation NonceWrap that they introduce.

3.1 Computationally Uniform Ciphertexts Imply Anonymity

In this section we revisit a stronger security notion for symmetric encryption, which we call *indistinguishability from uniform ciphertexts, strong security*, or IND\$-{CPA,CCD3}-*security*, and show a simple folklore result that was stated in [1] (of which, to the best of our knowledge, there is no formal proof yet). This definition intuitively should capture indistinguishability of ciphertexts, but it actually overshoots this goal, and it is stronger in the sense that it also implies indistinguishability of keys. Recall that IND-{CPA,CCD3}-security *does not* imply indistinguishability of keys, but it turns out to be easier to prove that schemes meet the stronger notion, which is also conceptually simpler. Essentially, instead of choosing a random message to be encrypted in the ideal world, a random ciphertext is output (thus neglecting encryption altogether).

In order to formalize this notion, we need to introduce the system \$ (with implicit dependency on a fixed encryption scheme Π) which on input any message $m \in \mathcal{M}$ simply outputs a uniformly sampled ciphertext of appropriate length, that is, according to our Definition 3, a uniform random bitstring of length $|m| + \tau$, where $\tau \in \mathbb{N}$ is the expansion factor defined by Π (thus, in particular, \$ does not make use of the underlying encryption function defined by Π). Then for the case of pE we can increase the security requirement as follows.

Definition 10 (Game-Based Strong Security of pE). *An encryption scheme Π is* strongly secure pE *(or* IND\$-CPA-secure*) if*

$$\Delta^{\mathbf{D}}(\mathbf{E}_K, \$)$$

is negligible for any efficient distinguisher $\mathbf{D}$.

The analogous notion for pAE was introduced by Rogaway and Shrimpton in [23], and is adapted within our framework as follows.

Definition 11 (Game-Based Strong Security of pAE). *An encryption scheme Π is secure* pE *(or* IND\$-CCA3-secure*) if*

$$\Delta^{\mathbf{D}}(\langle \mathbf{E}_K, \mathbf{D}_K \rangle, \langle \$, \mathbf{D}^{\perp} \rangle)$$

is negligible for any efficient distinguisher $\mathbf{D}$.

Next, starting with the case of pE, we show that the stronger notion of IND\$-CPA indeed implies IND-IK-CPA (and thus also both IK-CPA and IND-CPA), as originally pointed out in [1]. This is captured formally by the following statement, shown for 2 users for cleaner presentation, but easily generalized to n users.

Theorem 1. *For every distinguisher* $\mathbf{D}$, *there exists a reduction* $\mathbf{C}$ *such that*

$$\Delta^{\mathbf{D}}([\mathbf{E}_{K_1}, \mathbf{E}_{K_2}], \langle \mathbf{E}_K^{\$}, \mathbf{E}_K^{\$} \rangle) = 3 \cdot \Delta^{\mathbf{DC}}(\mathbf{E}_K, \$).$$

In particular, this implies that if an encryption scheme is IND\$-CPA-*secure, then it is also* IND-IK-CPA-*secure*.

Finally, the analogous statement for the case of pAE just follows as a natural lifting of Theorem 1, but since we consider this result rather important, instead of only providing a corollary we actually state it as a theorem, that is, we show that the stronger notion of IND\$-CCA3 indeed implies IND-IK-CCA3 (and thus also both IK-CCA3 and IND-CCA3). We remark that this fact was informally pointed out by Rogaway [22].

Theorem 2. *For every distinguisher* $\mathbf{D}$, *there exists a reduction* $\mathbf{C}$ *such that*

$$\Delta^{\mathbf{D}}([\langle \mathbf{E}_{K_1}, \mathbf{D}_{K_1} \rangle, \langle \mathbf{E}_{K_2}, \mathbf{D}_{K_2} \rangle], \langle \langle \mathbf{E}_K^{\$}, \mathbf{D}^{\perp} \rangle, \langle \mathbf{E}_K^{\$}, \mathbf{D}^{\perp} \rangle \rangle)$$
$$= 3 \cdot \Delta^{\mathbf{DC}}(\langle \mathbf{E}_K, \mathbf{D}_K \rangle, \langle \$, \mathbf{D}^{\perp} \rangle).$$

In particular, this implies that if an encryption scheme is IND\$-CCA3-*secure, then it is also* IND-IK-CCA3-*secure.*

3.2   Anonymity Preservation of Encrypt-then-MAC

After having related the various game-based notions for pE and for pAE separately, we finally show how the anonymity enhanced security definitions for pE relate with those of pAE. For this, we need to introduce the concept of *message authentication code (MAC)* and its security and anonymity notions, which we only introduce in an intuitive and informal way here (see the full version [5] for more details). Recall that Bellare and Namprempre [8] and Krawczyk [15] have shown that the combination of an unforgeable (UF-CMA) MAC and a secure (IND-CPA) encryption scheme, performed according to the *Encrypt-then-MAC* (EtM) paradigm, yields an encryption scheme which is both secure (IND-CPA) and unforgeable (INT-CTXT, the equivalent notion of UF-CMA for encryption). Later, Shrimpton [25] showed that a nice *all-in-one* security definition for secure authenticated encryption, IND-CCA3, is equivalent to the combination IND-CPA and INT-CTXT, thus attesting that EtM performed on a UF-CMA-secure MAC scheme and an IND-CPA-secure encryption scheme, yields a IND-CCA3-secure authenticated encryption scheme. The encryption scheme $\mathtt{EtM}(\Pi, \Sigma) \doteq (\widehat{\mathtt{Gen}}, \widehat{\mathtt{Tag}}, \widehat{\mathtt{Vrf}})$, resulting from this specific composition of an encryption scheme $\Pi \doteq (\mathtt{Gen}_{\Pi}, \mathtt{Enc}, \mathtt{Dec})$ (with key-space $\mathcal{K}_{\Pi}$) and a MAC scheme $\Sigma \doteq (\mathtt{Gen}_{\Sigma}, \mathtt{Tag}, \mathtt{Vrf})$ (with key-space $\mathcal{K}_{\Sigma}$, $\mathtt{Tag} : \mathcal{K} \times \mathcal{C} \to \mathcal{C} \times \mathcal{T}$, and $\mathtt{Vrf} : \mathcal{K} \times \mathcal{C} \times \mathcal{T} \to \mathcal{C} \cup \{\perp\}$) is defined as follows:

- $\widehat{\mathtt{Gen}}$ is the product distribution of $\mathtt{Gen}_{\Pi}$ and $\mathtt{Gen}_{\Sigma}$ over $\mathcal{K}_{\Pi} \times \mathcal{K}_{\Sigma}$;
- $\widehat{\mathtt{Enc}}_{(k_e, k_a)} \doteq \mathtt{Tag}_{k_a} \circ \mathtt{Enc}_{k_e}$;
- $\widehat{\mathtt{Vrf}}_{(k_e, k_a)} \doteq \mathtt{Dec}_{k_e} \circ \mathtt{Vrf}_{k_a}$.

If we now want to define security of the composed scheme $\widehat{\Pi} \doteq \mathtt{EtM}(\Pi, \Sigma)$, we need to introduce a simple operator between (single-interface) systems, namely *cascading*: Informally, given systems $\mathbf{S}$ and $\mathbf{T}$, we define the new system $\mathbf{S} \triangleright \mathbf{T}$ as the system that on input x computes $y \doteq \mathbf{S}(x)$, and returns $z \doteq \mathbf{T}(y)$ (where we are assuming matching domains). As we did for Π, we can define systems

484   F. Banfi and U. Maurer

$\mathbf{T}_k$, $\mathbf{V}_k$, $\langle \mathbf{T}_k, \mathbf{V}_k \rangle$ and $\langle \mathbf{T}_k, \mathbf{V}^{\perp} \rangle$ relative to Σ. Then $\widehat{\mathsf{Enc}}_{(k_e, k_a)}$ is modeled by $\widehat{\mathbf{E}}_{(k_e, k_a)} \doteq \mathbf{E}_{k_e} \triangleright \mathbf{T}_{k_a}$, and $\widehat{\mathsf{Dec}}_{(k_e, k_a)}$ by $\widehat{\mathbf{D}}_{(k_e, k_a)} \doteq \mathbf{V}_{k_a} \triangleright \mathbf{D}_{k_e}$.

We can now show that EtM is *anonymity-preserving*, in the sense that if an encryption scheme Π is both IND-CPA-secure and IK-CPA-secure (that is, IND-IK-CPA-secure) and a MAC scheme Σ is both UF-CMA-secure and IK-CMA-secure (the analogous anonymity property of pMAC introduced in [3], which combined with that UF-CMA results in UF-IK-CMA-security, as we show in the full version [5]), then EtM(Π, Σ) not only is IND-CCA3-secure, but also IK-CCA3-secure (that is, IND-IK-CCA3-secure). This is captured formally by the following statement, shown for 2 users for cleaner presentation, but easily generalized to n users.

Theorem 3. *For every distinguisher* $\mathbf{D}$, *there exist reductions* $\mathbf{C}$ *and* $\mathbf{C}'$ *such that*

$$\Delta^{\mathbf{D}}([\langle \widehat{\mathbf{E}}_{K_1}, \widehat{\mathbf{D}}_{K_1} \rangle, \langle \widehat{\mathbf{E}}_{K_2}, \widehat{\mathbf{D}}_{K_2} \rangle], \langle \langle \widehat{\mathbf{E}}_K^{\$}, \widehat{\mathbf{D}}^{\perp} \rangle, \langle \widehat{\mathbf{E}}_K^{\$}, \widehat{\mathbf{D}}^{\perp} \rangle \rangle)$$

$$= \Delta^{\mathbf{DC}}([\mathbf{E}_{K_1}, \mathbf{E}_{K_2}], \langle \mathbf{E}_K^{\$}, \mathbf{E}_K^{\$} \rangle)$$

$$+ \Delta^{\mathbf{DC}'}([\langle \mathbf{T}_{K_1}, \mathbf{V}_{K_1} \rangle, \langle \mathbf{T}_{K_2}, \mathbf{V}_{K_2} \rangle], \langle \langle \mathbf{T}_K, \mathbf{V}^{\perp} \rangle, \langle \mathbf{T}_K, \mathbf{V}^{\perp} \rangle \rangle).$$

In particular, this implies that if Π *is* IND-IK-CPA-*secure and* Σ *is* UF-IK-CMA-*secure,*[3] *then* EtM(Π, Σ) *is* IND-IK-CCA3-*secure.*

4   Composable Security of Anonymous Communication

In this section we turn our attention to *composable security*, as opposed to game-based security. For this, we make use of the *constructive cryptography* (CC) framework by Maurer [17], which is a specialization of the *abstract cryptography* theory by Maurer and Renner [19].

4.1   Constructive Cryptography

In essence, CC allows to define security of cryptographic protocols as statements about constructions of resources from other resources, which we model as cryptographic systems from Sect. 2.2. For such systems, we might at times use suggestive words typed in sans-serif rather than bold-faced letters. The various interfaces of a resource should be thought of as being assigned to parties. In this work, all resources are parameterized by an integer $n \geq 2$ (the case $n = 1$ would be pointless for anonymity), and each defines $n + 2$ interfaces: n for the *senders*, denoted S_i, for $i \in [n]$, one for the *adversary*, denoted E, and one for the *receiver*, denoted R. Therefore, in the following we use the expression n-resource to make explicit such parameter. Another crucial ingredient of CC are *converters*, also formally modeled as systems (labeled by lower-case sans-serif suggestive words), which when applied to interfaces of n-resources, give raise to a new n-resource.

---

[3] In the full version [5] we show that indeed the last term captures UF-IK-CMA-security.

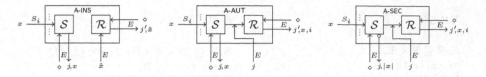

Fig. 2. Sketches of the channels (blue: interfaces; green: inputs; red: outputs). (Color figure online)

Within our formalization of cryptographic systems, CC converters thus correspond to converters of systems as defined in Sect. 2.2, but where we extend the sequential composition notion by allowing a (single-interface) converter system to be attached to just one of the interfaces of another n-resource system. Given a converter cnv and an n-resource $\mathbf{R}$, for $i \in [n]$ we denote the new n-resource system resulting from *attaching converter* cnv *to interface* S_i *of* n-resource $\mathbf{R}$ as $\mathsf{cnv}^{S_i} \mathbf{R}$. Note that this automatically implies commutativity of converters attached to different interfaces, that is, considering a second converter $\widehat{\mathsf{cnv}}$ and letting $j \in [n]$ such that $j \neq i$, then $\mathsf{cnv}^{S_i} \widehat{\mathsf{cnv}}^{S_j} \mathbf{R} \equiv \widehat{\mathsf{cnv}}^{S_j} \mathsf{cnv}^{S_i} \mathbf{R}$.

To make security statements within CC, we model protocols as lists of converters. For n-resources, this means that a protocol π executed by n senders and one receiver (an n-protocol) is a list of $n+1$ converters $(\mathsf{cnv}_1, \ldots, \mathsf{cnv}_{n+1})$, where the adopted convention is that cnv_i is attached to sender interface S_i, for $i \in [n]$, while cnv_{n+1} is attached to the receiver interface R. In the following, we use the short-hand notation $\pi\mathbf{R}$ for the n-resource $\mathsf{cnv}_1^{S_1} \cdots \mathsf{cnv}_n^{S_n} \mathsf{cnv}_{n+1}^{R} \mathbf{R}$. Moreover, for a second n-protocol $\hat{\pi} \doteq (\widehat{\mathsf{cnv}}_1, \ldots, \widehat{\mathsf{cnv}}_{n+1})$, we define the *composition* of $\hat{\pi}$ and π as $\hat{\pi}\pi \doteq (\widehat{\mathsf{cnv}}_1\mathsf{cnv}_1, \ldots, \widehat{\mathsf{cnv}}_{n+1}\mathsf{cnv}_{n+1})$, and therefore $\hat{\pi}\pi\mathbf{R}$ is the n-resource $(\widehat{\mathsf{cnv}}_1\mathsf{cnv}_1)^{S_1} \cdots (\widehat{\mathsf{cnv}}_n\mathsf{cnv}_n)^{S_n} (\widehat{\mathsf{cnv}}_{n+1}\mathsf{cnv}_{n+1})^{R} \mathbf{R}$. The last ingredient we need is that of a simulator, which can be simply understood as a converter to be attached to the adversarial interface E. With this, we can now express composable security of an n-protocol π in terms of indistinguishability as follows.

Definition 12 (Construction). *For n-resources $\mathbf{R}$ and $\mathbf{S}$, and function ε mapping distinguishers to real values, we say that an n-protocol π constructs $\mathbf{S}$ from $\mathbf{R}$ within ε, denoted $\mathbf{R} \xrightarrow{\pi, \varepsilon} \mathbf{S}$, if there exists a simulator sim such that for all distinguishers $\mathbf{D}$, $\Delta^{\mathbf{D}}(\pi\mathbf{R}, \mathsf{sim}^E \mathbf{S}) \leq \varepsilon(\mathbf{D})$.*

The intuition is that, if lifted to the asymptotic setting, Definition 12 implies that if $\varepsilon(\mathbf{D})$ is negligible for every efficient distinguisher $\mathbf{D}$, then the real n-resource $\mathbf{R}$ looks indistinguishable from the ideal n-resource $\mathbf{S}$. This naturally hints to the intuition that in any context where $\mathbf{S}$ is needed, $\pi\mathbf{R}$ can be safely used instead. This is the central point of composable security definitions, and is formalized by the following theorem, following directly from [19].

Theorem 4 (Composition). *Let $\mathbf{R}, \mathbf{S}, \mathbf{T}$ be n-resources, and π_1, π_2 n-protocols. If $\mathbf{R} \xrightarrow{\pi_1, \varepsilon_1} \mathbf{S}$ and $\mathbf{S} \xrightarrow{\pi_2, \varepsilon_2} \mathbf{T}$, then $\mathbf{R} \xrightarrow{\pi_2\pi_1, \hat{\varepsilon}_1 \oplus \hat{\varepsilon}_2} \mathbf{T}$, where $\hat{\varepsilon}_1(\mathbf{D}) \doteq \varepsilon_1(\mathbf{D}\pi_2)$, $\hat{\varepsilon}_2(\mathbf{D}) \doteq \varepsilon_2(\mathbf{D}\,\mathsf{sim}_2^E)$, sim_2 is any simulator whose existence justifies $\mathbf{S} \xrightarrow{\pi_2, \varepsilon_2} \mathbf{T}$, and $(\hat{\varepsilon}_1 \oplus \hat{\varepsilon}_2)(\mathbf{D}) \doteq \hat{\varepsilon}_1(\mathbf{D}) + \hat{\varepsilon}_2(\mathbf{D})$.*

A-INS$_\mathcal{X}^n$

$\mathcal{S}, \mathcal{R} \subseteq \mathbb{N} \times \mathcal{X},$
$c_S, c_R, t_S, t_R \in \mathbb{N}$
Initialize:
  $\mathcal{S}, \mathcal{R} \leftarrow \varnothing$
  $c_S, c_R \leftarrow 1$
  $t_S, t_R \leftarrow 0$
Interface $S_i(x \in \mathcal{X})$:
  $t_S \leftarrow t_S + 1$
  $\mathcal{S} \leftarrow \mathcal{S} \cup \{(t_S, x)\}$
Interface $E(\diamond)$:
  $\mathcal{O} \leftarrow \{(j, x) \in \mathcal{S} \mid c_S \leq j \leq t_S\}$
  $c_S \leftarrow t_S + 1$
  return $\mathcal{O}$
Interface $E(x \in \mathcal{X})$:
  $t_R \leftarrow t_R + 1$
  $\mathcal{R} \leftarrow \mathcal{R} \cup \{(t_R, x)\}$
Interface $R(\diamond)$:
  $\mathcal{O} \leftarrow \{(j, x) \in \mathcal{R} \mid c_R \leq j \leq t_R\}$
  $c_R \leftarrow t_R + 1$
  return $\mathcal{O}$

A-AUT$_\mathcal{X}^n$

$\mathcal{S}, \mathcal{R} \subseteq (\mathbb{N} \times \mathcal{X} \times \mathbb{N}) \cup (\mathbb{N} \times \{\bot\}^2),$
$c_S, c_R, t_S, t_R \in \mathbb{N}$
Initialize:
  $\mathcal{S}, \mathcal{R} \leftarrow \varnothing, c_S, c_R \leftarrow 1,\ t_S, t_R \leftarrow 0$
Interface $S_i(x \in \mathcal{X})$:
  $t_S \leftarrow t_S + 1,\ \mathcal{S} \leftarrow \mathcal{S} \cup \{(t_S, x, i)\}$
Interface $E(\diamond)$:
  $\mathcal{O} \leftarrow \{(j, x) \in \mathbb{N} \times \mathcal{X} \mid$
      $\exists i \in [n] : (j, x, i) \in \mathcal{S},$
      $c_S \leq j \leq t_S\}$
  $c_S \leftarrow t_S + 1$
  return $\mathcal{O}$
Interface $E(j \in \mathbb{N} \cup \{-1\})$:
  if $\exists x \in \mathcal{X}, i \in [n] : (j, x, i) \in \mathcal{S}$ **then**
    $t_R \leftarrow t_R + 1$
    $\mathcal{R} \leftarrow \mathcal{R} \cup \{(t_R, x, i)\}$
  else if $j = -1$ **then**
    $t_R \leftarrow t_R + 1$
    $\mathcal{R} \leftarrow \mathcal{R} \cup \{(t_R, \bot, \bot)\}$
Interface $R(\diamond)$:
  $\mathcal{O} \leftarrow \{(j, x, i) \in \mathcal{R} \mid c_R \leq j \leq t_R\}$
  $c_R \leftarrow t_R + 1$
  return $\mathcal{O}$

A-SEC$_\mathcal{X}^n$

$\mathcal{S}, \mathcal{R} \subseteq (\mathbb{N} \times \mathcal{X} \times \mathbb{N}) \cup (\mathbb{N} \times \{\bot\}^2),\ c_S, c_R, t_S, t_R \in \mathbb{N}$
Initialize:
  $\mathcal{S}, \mathcal{R} \leftarrow \varnothing,\ c_S, c_R \leftarrow 1,\ t_S, t_R \leftarrow 0$
Interface $S_i(x \in \mathcal{X})$:
  $t_S \leftarrow t_S + 1,\ \mathcal{S} \leftarrow \mathcal{S} \cup \{(t_S, x, i)\}$
Interface $E(\diamond)$:
  $\mathcal{O} \leftarrow \{(j, |x|) \in \mathbb{N} \times \mathbb{N} \mid \exists i \in [n] : (j, x, i) \in \mathcal{S}, c_S \leq j \leq t_S\},\ c_S \leftarrow t_S + 1$
  return $\mathcal{O}$
Interface $E(j \in \mathbb{N} \cup \{-1\})$:
  if $\exists x \in \mathcal{X}, i \in [n] : (j, x, i) \in \mathcal{S}$ **then**
    $t_R \leftarrow t_R + 1,\ \mathcal{R} \leftarrow \mathcal{R} \cup \{(t_R, x, i)\}$
  else if $j = -1$ **then**
    $t_R \leftarrow t_R + 1,\ \mathcal{R} \leftarrow \mathcal{R} \cup \{(t_R, \bot, \bot)\}$
Interface $R(\diamond)$:
  $\mathcal{O} \leftarrow \{(j, x, i) \in \mathcal{R} \mid c_R \leq j \leq t_R\},\ c_R \leftarrow t_R + 1$
  return $\mathcal{O}$

Fig. 3. Formal description of the *insecure* (A-INS$_\mathcal{X}^n$), *authenticated* (A-AUT$_\mathcal{X}^n$), and *secure* (A-SEC$_\mathcal{X}^n$) *anonymous channels.*

Anonymous Channels. There are four n-resources that we consider in this work. The first, $\mathsf{KEY}_{\mathcal{K}}^n$, models the initial symmetric-key setup: it generates n independent keys $K_1, \ldots, K_n \in \mathcal{K}$ according to an implicitly defined distribution Gen over $\mathcal{K}$, and for $i \in [n]$ it outputs K_i at interface S_i; at interface R it outputs the list $(K_1, \ldots, K_n)$ of all generated keys, while it outputs nothing at interface E. The remaining three n-resources model the anonymous channels for n senders and one receiver mentioned above (for messages over some set $\mathcal{X}$), where we assume a central adversary that is in full control of the physical communication between the senders and the receiver, that is, an adversary that can *delete*, *repeat*, and *reorder* messages.[4] $\mathsf{A\text{-}INS}_{\mathcal{X}}^n$ models the channel which leaks every message input by any sender (but not their identities) directly to the adversary. Note that in particular this means that the receiver does not directly receive the messages sent by the senders. Moreover, $\mathsf{A\text{-}INS}_{\mathcal{X}}^n$ allows the adversary to inject any message to the receiver (thus, in particular, also the ones originally sent by the senders). Note that this channel, while providing anonymity, is per se pretty useless, since the receiver has also no information about the identity of the sender of any message. Instead, $\mathsf{A\text{-}AUT}_{\mathcal{X}}^n$, while still leaking all the messages sent by the senders directly to the adversary, does not allow the latter to inject any message; instead, the adversary can now *select* messages that it wants to be forwarded to the receiver. Moreover, the forwarded messages also carry the identity of the original sender, still hidden to the adversary. Finally, $\mathsf{A\text{-}SEC}_{\mathcal{X}}^n$ essentially works as $\mathsf{A\text{-}AUT}_{\mathcal{X}}^n$, except that now only the *lengths* of the messages sent by the senders are leaked directly to the adversary. We sketch the three anonymous channels in Fig. 2 and provide a formal description of the behavior of the systems implementing such n-resources in Fig. 3.

4.2 Composable Anonymous Security of pE

In this section we first introduce a composable definition of anonymous security for pE, and then we show that the previously introduced game-based notion of IND-IK-CPA-security implies the former. The composable definition can be interpreted as providing *composable semantics* to IND-IK-CPA-security for pE, in the sense that the result we show here attests that if an encryption scheme is IND-IK-CPA-secure, then it can be safely used to construct a secure channel from an authenticated one, *while preserving anonymity*.

In the following, for a fixed encryption scheme Π let the converter enc behave as follows when connected to interface S_i of $\mathsf{KEY}_{\mathcal{K}}$ and interface S_i of $\mathsf{A\text{-}AUT}_{\mathcal{C}}$, for $i \in [n]$: on input a message $m \in \mathcal{M}$ from the outside, if not already done so before, output $\diamond$ to $\mathsf{KEY}_{\mathcal{K}}$ in order to fetch key K_i, then compute $c \leftarrow \mathsf{Enc}_{K_i}(m) \in \mathcal{C}$ and output c to $\mathsf{A\text{-}AUT}_{\mathcal{C}}$. Also let the converter dec (where again the dependency on Π is implicit) behave as follows when connected to interface R of $\mathsf{KEY}_{\mathcal{K}}$ and interface R of $\mathsf{A\text{-}AUT}_{\mathcal{C}}$: on input $\diamond$ from the

---

[4] Note that while deletion is a physical phenomenon, and can thus not be prevented using cryptography, it is in principle possible to prevent repetition and reordering, concretely by means of *sequence numbers*. But we do not cover this aspect of security in this work.

outside, if not already done so before, output $\diamond$ to $\mathsf{KEY}_\mathcal{K}$ in order to fetch keys $K_1, \ldots, K_n$, and then output $\diamond$ to $\mathsf{A\text{-}AUT}_\mathcal{C}$; for each obtained tuple (j, c, i), compute $m \leftarrow \mathsf{Dec}_{K_i}(c)$, and output the collection of all such resulting tuples (j, m, i) to the outside. Finally, we define the n-protocol $\pi_{\mathsf{enc}} \doteq (\mathsf{enc}, \ldots, \mathsf{enc}, \mathsf{dec})$.

Definition 13 (Composable Anonymous Security of pE). *An encryption scheme Π achieves* composable anonymous confidentiality *if*

$$[\mathsf{KEY}^n_\mathcal{K}, \mathsf{A\text{-}AUT}^n_\mathcal{C}] \xrightarrow{\pi_{\mathsf{enc}}, \varepsilon} \mathsf{A\text{-}SEC}^n_\mathcal{M},$$

that is, if there exists a simulator sim *such that for all distinguishers* **D**,

$$\Delta^\mathbf{D}(\pi_{\mathsf{enc}}[\mathsf{KEY}^n_\mathcal{K}, \mathsf{A\text{-}AUT}^n_\mathcal{C}], \mathsf{sim}^E\, \mathsf{A\text{-}SEC}^n_\mathcal{M}) \le \varepsilon(\mathbf{D}).$$

We next relate our game-based notion from Definition 8 to the above, and defer an in-depth discussion of the result to the full version [5].

Theorem 5. *If an encryption scheme Π is* IND-IK-CPA-*secure, then it achieves composable anonymous confidentiality, that is,*

$$[\mathsf{KEY}^n_\mathcal{K}, \mathsf{A\text{-}AUT}^n_\mathcal{C}] \xrightarrow{\pi_{\mathsf{enc}}, \varepsilon} \mathsf{A\text{-}SEC}^n_\mathcal{M},$$

with $\varepsilon(\mathbf{D}) \doteq \Delta^{\mathbf{DC}}([\mathbf{E}_{K_1}, \ldots, \mathbf{E}_{K_n}], \langle \mathbf{E}^\$_K, \ldots, \mathbf{E}^\$_K \rangle)$ and appropriate reduction system **C**.

4.3   Composable Anonymous Security of pAE

In this section we first introduce a composable definition of anonymous security for pAE, and then we show that the previously introduced game-based notion of IND-IK-CCA3-security implies the former. The composable definition can be interpreted as providing *composable semantics* to IND-IK-CCA3-security for pAE, in the sense that the result we show here attests that if an (authenticated) encryption scheme is IND-IK-CCA3-secure, then it can be safely used to construct a secure channel from an insecure one, *while preserving anonymity*.

In the following, for a fixed (authenticated) encryption scheme Π let the converter ae (where the dependency on Π is implicit) behave as follows when connected to interface S_i of $\mathsf{KEY}_\mathcal{K}$ and interface S_i of $\mathsf{A\text{-}INS}_\mathcal{C}$, for $i \in [n]$: on input a message $m \in \mathcal{M}$ from the outside, if not already done so before, output $\diamond$ to $\mathsf{KEY}_\mathcal{K}$ in order to fetch key K_i, then compute $c \leftarrow \mathsf{Enc}_{K_i}(m) \in \mathcal{C}$ and output c to $\mathsf{A\text{-}INS}_\mathcal{C}$. Also let the converter ad (where again the dependency on Π is implicit) behave as follows when connected to interface R of $\mathsf{KEY}_\mathcal{K}$ and interface R of $\mathsf{A\text{-}INS}_\mathcal{C}$: on input $\diamond$ from the outside, if not already done so before, output $\diamond$ to $\mathsf{KEY}_\mathcal{K}$ in order to fetch keys $K_1, \ldots, K_n$, and then output $\diamond$ to $\mathsf{A\text{-}INS}_\mathcal{C}$; for each obtained tuple (j, c), find the index $i \in [n]$ such that $m \ne \bot$, for $m \leftarrow \mathsf{Dec}_{K_i}(c)$, and output the collection of all such resulting tuples (j, m, i) to the outside. Finally, we define the n-protocol $\pi_{\mathsf{ae}} \doteq (\mathsf{ae}, \ldots, \mathsf{ae}, \mathsf{ad})$.

Definition 14 (Composable Anonymous Security of pAE). *An (authenticated) encryption scheme* Π *achieves composable anonymous security if*

$$[\mathsf{KEY}_{\mathcal{K}}^n, \mathsf{A\text{-}INS}_{\mathcal{C}}^n] \xrightarrow{\pi_{\mathsf{ae}}, \varepsilon} \mathsf{A\text{-}SEC}_{\mathcal{M}}^n,$$

that is, if there exists a simulator sim *such that for all distinguishers* $\mathbf{D}$,

$$\Delta^{\mathbf{D}}(\pi_{\mathsf{ae}}[\mathsf{KEY}_{\mathcal{K}}^n, \mathsf{A\text{-}INS}_{\mathcal{C}}^n], \mathsf{sim}^E \, \mathsf{A\text{-}SEC}_{\mathcal{M}}^n) \leq \varepsilon(\mathbf{D}).$$

We next relate our game-based notion from Definition 9 to the above, and defer an in-depth discussion of the result to the full version [5].

Theorem 6. *If an (authenticated) encryption scheme* Π *is* IND-IK-CCA3-*secure, then it achieves composable anonymous security, that is,*

$$[\mathsf{KEY}_{\mathcal{K}}^n, \mathsf{A\text{-}INS}_{\mathcal{C}}^n] \xrightarrow{\pi_{\mathsf{ae}}, \varepsilon} \mathsf{A\text{-}SEC}_{\mathcal{M}}^n,$$

with $\varepsilon(\mathbf{D}) \doteq \Delta^{\mathbf{DC}}([\langle \mathbf{E}_{K_1}, \mathbf{D}_{K_1} \rangle, \dots, \langle \mathbf{E}_{K_n}, \mathbf{D}_{K_n} \rangle], \langle\langle \mathbf{E}_K^{\$}, \mathbf{D}^{\perp} \rangle, \dots, \langle \mathbf{E}_K^{\$}, \mathbf{D}^{\perp} \rangle\rangle)$ *and appropriate reduction system* $\mathbf{C}$.

References

1. Abadi, M., Rogaway, P.: Reconciling two views of cryptography. In: van Leeuwen, J., Watanabe, O., Hagiya, M., Mosses, P.D., Ito, T. (eds.) TCS 2000. LNCS, vol. 1872, pp. 3–22. Springer, Heidelberg (2000). https://doi.org/10.1007/3-540-44929-9_1

2. Alagic, G., Gagliardoni, T., Majenz, C.: Unforgeable quantum encryption. In: Nielsen, J.B., Rijmen, V. (eds.) EUROCRYPT 2018. LNCS, vol. 10822, pp. 489–519. Springer, Cham (2018). https://doi.org/10.1007/978-3-319-78372-7_16

3. Alwen, J., Hirt, M., Maurer, U., Patra, A., Raykov, P.: Key-indistinguishable message authentication codes. In: Abdalla, M., De Prisco, R. (eds.) SCN 2014. LNCS, vol. 8642, pp. 476–493. Springer, Cham (2014). https://doi.org/10.1007/978-3-319-10879-7_27

4. Alwen, J., Hirt, M., Maurer, U., Patra, A., Raykov, P.: Anonymous authentication with shared secrets. In: Aranha, D.F., Menezes, A. (eds.) LATINCRYPT 2014. LNCS, vol. 8895, pp. 219–236. Springer, Cham (2015). https://doi.org/10.1007/978-3-319-16295-9_12

5. Banfi, F., Maurer, U.: Anonymous symmetric-key communication. Cryptology ePrint Archive, Report 2020/073 (2020). https://eprint.iacr.org/2020/073

6. Bellare, M., Desai, A., Jokipii, E., Rogaway, P.: A concrete security treatment of symmetric encryption. In: Proceedings 38th Annual Symposium on Foundations of Computer Science – FOCS 1997, pp. 394–403, October 1997

7. Bellare, M., Boldyreva, A., Desai, A., Pointcheval, D.: Key-privacy in public-key encryption. In: Boyd, C. (ed.) ASIACRYPT 2001. LNCS, vol. 2248, pp. 566–582. Springer, Heidelberg (2001). https://doi.org/10.1007/3-540-45682-1_33

8. Bellare, M., Namprempre, C.: Authenticated encryption: relations among notions and analysis of the generic composition paradigm. In: Okamoto, T. (ed.) ASIACRYPT 2000. LNCS, vol. 1976, pp. 531–545. Springer, Heidelberg (2000). https://doi.org/10.1007/3-540-44448-3_41

9. Bellare, M., Tackmann, B.: The multi-user security of authenticated encryption: AES-GCM in TLS 1.3. In: Robshaw, M., Katz, J. (eds.) CRYPTO 2016. LNCS, vol. 9814, pp. 247–276. Springer, Heidelberg (2016). https://doi.org/10.1007/978-3-662-53018-4_10

10. Brzuska, C., Delignat-Lavaud, A., Fournet, C., Kohbrok, K., Kohlweiss, M.: State separation for code-based game-playing proofs. In: Peyrin, T., Galbraith, S. (eds.) ASIACRYPT 2018. LNCS, vol. 11274, pp. 222–249. Springer, Cham (2018). https://doi.org/10.1007/978-3-030-03332-3_9

11. Chan, J., Rogaway, P.: Anonymous AE. In: Galbraith, S.D., Moriai, S. (eds.) ASIACRYPT 2019. LNCS, vol. 11922, pp. 183–208. Springer, Cham (2019). https://doi.org/10.1007/978-3-030-34621-8_7

12. Desai, A.: The security of all-or-nothing encryption: protecting against exhaustive key search. In: Bellare, M. (ed.) CRYPTO 2000. LNCS, vol. 1880, pp. 359–375. Springer, Heidelberg (2000). https://doi.org/10.1007/3-540-44598-6_23

13. Fischlin, M.: Pseudorandom function tribe ensembles based on one-way permutations: improvements and applications. In: Stern, J. (ed.) EUROCRYPT 1999. LNCS, vol. 1592, pp. 432–445. Springer, Heidelberg (1999). https://doi.org/10.1007/3-540-48910-X_30

14. Hoang, V.T., Tessaro, S., Thiruvengadam, A.: The multi-user security of GCM, revisited: tight bounds for nonce randomization. In: Proceedings of the 2018 ACM SIGSAC Conference on Computer and Communications Security – CCS 2018, pp. 1429–1440. Association for Computing Machinery, New York (2018)

15. Krawczyk, H.: The order of encryption and authentication for protecting communications (or: How secure is SSL?). In: Kilian, J. (ed.) CRYPTO 2001. LNCS, vol. 2139, pp. 310–331. Springer, Heidelberg (2001). https://doi.org/10.1007/3-540-44647-8_19

16. Maurer, U.: Indistinguishability of random systems. In: Knudsen, L.R. (ed.) EUROCRYPT 2002. LNCS, vol. 2332, pp. 110–132. Springer, Heidelberg (2002). https://doi.org/10.1007/3-540-46035-7_8

17. Maurer, U.: Constructive cryptography – a new paradigm for security definitions and proofs. In: Mödersheim, S., Palamidessi, C. (eds.) TOSCA 2011. LNCS, vol. 6993, pp. 33–56. Springer, Heidelberg (2012). https://doi.org/10.1007/978-3-642-27375-9_3

18. Maurer, U., Pietrzak, K., Renner, R.: Indistinguishability amplification. In: Menezes, A. (ed.) CRYPTO 2007. LNCS, vol. 4622, pp. 130–149. Springer, Heidelberg (2007). https://doi.org/10.1007/978-3-540-74143-5_8

19. Maurer, U., Renner, R.: Abstract cryptography. In: Innovations in Theoretical Computer Science – ICS 2011, pp. 1–21. Tsinghua University Press (2011)

20. Rogaway, P.: Nonce-based symmetric encryption. In: Roy, B., Meier, W. (eds.) FSE 2004. LNCS, vol. 3017, pp. 348–358. Springer, Heidelberg (2004). https://doi.org/10.1007/978-3-540-25937-4_22

21. Rogaway, P.: Evaluation of some blockcipher modes of operation. Cryptography Research and Evaluation Committees (CRYPTREC) for the Government of Japan (2011). https://web.cs.ucdavis.edu/~rogaway/papers/modes.pdf

22. Rogaway, P.: The evolution of authenticated encryption. In: Workshop on Real-World Cryptography (2013). https://crypto.stanford.edu/RealWorldCrypto/slides/phil.pdf

23. Rogaway, P., Shrimpton, T.: A provable-security treatment of the key-wrap problem. In: Vaudenay, S. (ed.) EUROCRYPT 2006. LNCS, vol. 4004, pp. 373–390. Springer, Heidelberg (2006). https://doi.org/10.1007/11761679_23

24. Rosulek, M.: The joy of cryptography. Oregon State University EOR (2018). http://web.engr.oregonstate.edu/~rosulekm/crypto/
25. Shrimpton, T.: A characterization of authenticated-encryption as a form of chosen-ciphertext security. Cryptology ePrint Archive, Report 2004/272 (2004). https://eprint.iacr.org/2004/272

Cryptographic Divergences:
New Techniques and New Applications

Marc Abboud[1]([✉])(iD) and Thomas Prest[2]([✉])(iD)

[1] École Normale Supérieure, Paris, France
marc.abboud@ens.fr
[2] PQShield, Oxford, UK
thomas.prest@pqshield.com

Abstract. In the recent years, some security proofs in cryptography have known significant improvements by replacing the statistical distance with alternative divergences. We continue this line of research, both at a theoretical and practical level. On the theory side, we propose a new cryptographic divergence with quirky properties. On the practical side, we propose new applications of alternative divergences: circuit-private FHE and prime number generators. More precisely, we provide the first formal security proof of the prime number generator PRIMEINC [8], and improve by an order of magnitude the efficiency of a prime number generator by Fouque and Tibouchi [16,17] and the *washing machine* technique by Ducas and Stehlé [15] for circuit-private FHE.

1 Introduction

Cryptographic divergences play an essential role in cryptography. Most of the time, they provide rigorous theoretical tools to prove that the concrete instantiation of a cryptosystem is as secure as an idealized description. Typically, the idealized scheme will rely on an ideal distribution $\mathcal{Q}$, whereas its instantiation will rely on a distribution $\mathcal{P}$. If $\mathrm{Div}(\mathcal{P}; \mathcal{Q})$ is small for some divergence Div, then one can predict the security of the concrete cryptosystem based on the security of the ideal one. Similarly, cryptographic divergences can help to connect a cryptosystem to a hard problem.

The statistical distance is by far the most prevalent cryptographic divergence. It is simple and versatile, making it the swiss army knife of cryptography. However, these last years have seen a number of works using alternative divergences. A compelling example is the Rényi divergence, which use has been spearheaded by lattice-based cryptography to improve security reductions [3,4,6,26,29,39]. When the number of queries is limited and in the presence of a search problem, it can provide significant gains. Another example is the Kullback-Leibler divergence, which has been used at a more foundational level.

M. Abboud—Most of this work was done while Marc Abboud was an intern at PQShield.

© Springer Nature Switzerland AG 2020
C. Galdi and V. Kolesnikov (Eds.): SCN 2020, LNCS 12238, pp. 492–511, 2020.
https://doi.org/10.1007/978-3-030-57990-6_24

1.1   Our Contributions

In this work, we continue the exploration of alternative divergences to improve security proofs. This is done at two levels: by providing new theoretical tools, and by finding new applications to specialized divergences.

A New Cryptographic Divergence. Our first contribution is to propose a parametric divergence called RE_α divergence (RE_α stands for *relative error of order* α). We believe it is interesting for theoretic and practical reasons. On the theory side, it connects several divergences: it is a continuous trade-off between the statistical distance and the relative error, and enjoys desirable properties of both divergences. It is also (non-tightly) equivalent to the Rényi divergence. On the practical side, it satisfies an unusual amplification property with cryptographic applications. Relations between divergences is given in Fig. 1.

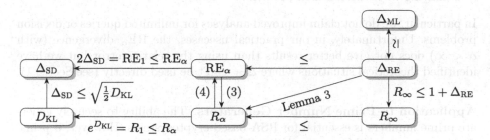

Fig. 1. Relations between cryptographic divergences: max-log distance Δ_{ML}, statistical distance Δ_{SD}, RE_α divergence, relative error Δ_{RE}, Kullback-Leibler divergence D_{KL}, Rényi divergence R_α.

New Applications: Proof Outline. As new applications of our new techniques and of existing ones, we provide improved analyses for circuit-private FHE and prime number generators. Our proofs follow this blueprint – already implicit in [39]:

(a) Bound the relative error $\Delta_{RE}(\mathcal{R}\|\mathcal{I})$ between a real distribution $\mathcal{R}$ and ideal distribution $\mathcal{I}$;
(b) Deduce the Rényi divergence $R_\alpha(\mathcal{R}\|\mathcal{I})$ between $\mathcal{R}$ and $\mathcal{I}$;
(c) Conclude that an adversary making Q queries to $\mathcal{I}$ and trying to solve a search problem does not increase his advantage by more than $O(1)$ when replacing $\mathcal{I}$ by $\mathcal{R}$.

Our proofs follow either the logical structure $(a) \Rightarrow (b) \Rightarrow (c)$, or $(b) \Rightarrow (c)$. The justification for $(a) \Rightarrow (b)$ is given by Lemma 3, and the one for $(b) \Rightarrow (c)$ by Lemma 4. We emphasize that using the Rényi divergence instead of the statistical distance does not mean we prove something weaker or different; both divergences are merely tools in proofs strategies, and we compare our improved analyses with existing ones in the exact same setting (search problem, Q queries).

Applications. We provide two applications of our techniques: circuit privacy for FHE and prime number generators. As is now customary when using the Rényi divergence (and this is also true for the RE_α divergence), two conditions are required to fully exploit the Rényi divergence:

- The number of queries Q should be much lower than 2^λ, where λ denotes the security level. In practice $128 \leq \lambda \leq 256$. On the other hand NIST's call for post-quantum cryptography standards suppose $Q \leq 2^{64}$, and we may assume even lower bounds for computation- and bandwidth-heavy primitives such as FHE. Finally, when generating a single public key, the number of queries to the key generation algorithm is as small as 1 (in the single-target setting).
- The underlying problem should be a search problem. One of our applications targets RSA-based signatures, where this is obviously the case. We also believe that most practical usecases of circuit-private FHEs can be described in a satisfying way with a search problem.

In particular, we do not claim improved analyses for unlimited queries or decision problems. Unfortunately, in our practical usecases, the RE_α divergence (with $\alpha < \infty$) does not give better results than using the relative error but we have identified theoretical situations where Δ_{RE} can't be used directly (see Sect. 5.1).

Application to Prime Number Generators. The ability to securely generate prime numbers is essential for RSA-based cryptosystems. However, if prime numbers are sampled from a weak distribution, it can lead to a variety of attacks. The most common ones are *GCD attacks*, where an attacker collects RSA public keys $N_i = p_i \cdot q_i$ with low collision entropy and extracts private keys (p_i, q_i) by computing GCDs. This multi-target attack has plagued the last decade, with several papers [5,24,27] compromising a total of more than 1 million keypairs. Primes sampled from highly structured distributions may also be vulnerable, as demonstrated by Coppersmith's attack [9,10] and its follow-up ROCA [37].

To mitigate attacks, several algorithms have been proposed to securely generate prime numbers. One obviously desirable property is to sample from a distribution with high collision entropy, lest the generated primes be vulnerable to GCD attacks. However, we note that having a high collision entropy does not preclude Coppersmith's attack, so it is not a necessary and sufficient condition for security. To offer stronger security guarantees, some prime numbers generators sample statistically close to the uniform distribution over primes in $[2^d; 2^{d+1}]$.[1] Some schemes based on the strong RSA assumption explicitly require this. In this work, we focus on two prime number generators and provide substantially improved security proofs for them.

The PRIMEINC *Generator.* A prominent generator is PRIMEINC, proposed by Brandt and Damgård [8]. Due to its simplicity and entropy efficiency, it is

---

[1] Typically, additional requirements are mandated, such as $(p+1)$ and $(p-1)$ having a large prime factor; but these can be added on top of the sampling procedure.

commonly used; see the PyCrypto[2] and OpenSSL[3] libraries. Despite its longevity and prevalence, PRIMEINC's concrete security had remained an open question. Circumstantial arguments were presented, leaning either towards weak security guarantees [8,34] or suggesting potential weaknesses [16,17], but no definite answer had been presented.

We clarify the situation by providing formal arguments which guarantee PRIMEINC's security in clearly defined scenarii or against common attacks. Our work for PRIMEINC uses only the Rényi divergence. More precisely, we show that:

- In the single-target setting, any scheme that is secure with the uniform distribution $\mathcal{U}$ (over primes in $[2^d; 2^{d+1}]$) remains secure when replacing $\mathcal{U}$ by the output distribution $\mathcal{P}$ of PRIMEINC, as long as there are $O(1)$ calls to $\mathcal{P}$; this covers for example RSA key generation. This argument is tight (only $O(1)$ bits of security are lost) and fully generic.
- In the multi-target setting, PRIMEINC has enough collision entropy to be secure against GCD attacks.

The Fouque-Tibouchi Generator. Fouque and Tibouchi [16,17] proposed prime number generators with an appealing feature; the statistical distance between their output distribution $\mathcal{P}$ and the uniform distribution $\mathcal{U}$ (over primes in an $[2; x]$) is upper bounded by $\log(x) \cdot x^{-\epsilon/4}$, where ϵ is an input parameter, and it can therefore be proven arbitrarily close to 0 by increasing ϵ. These generators are provably secure. However, the entropy consumption is linear in ϵ: thus there is a trade-off between statistical closeness to $\mathcal{U}$ and the entropy consumption. A standard statistical distance argument would mandate $\epsilon \geq \frac{4\lambda \log \log x}{\log x}$, where λ is the security level.

We provide a Rényi divergence-based security argument that only mandates $\epsilon \geq \frac{2\log(\lambda Q) \log \log x}{\log x}$, where Q is the number of queries to the generator. The entropy gain is significant when Q is much smaller than 2^λ, which is always the case in real applications. For practical usecases, we gain an order of magnitude in entropy consumption. Our proof uses the RE_α divergence for the computations.

Application to Circuit-Private FHE. (Fully) homomorphic encryption – or (F)HE – allows to securely evaluate circuits on encrypted data. Following Gentry's breakthrough [20], it has known an exponential growth in the last decade, and is now being advertised as a product by companies (Duality, Inpher, Zama) and standardized.

Circuit privacy is an increasingly relevant security notion for FHE. The setting is the following: a client $\mathcal{C}$ sends a (fully homomorphic) ciphertext $c = \mathsf{Enc}(m)$ to a server $\mathcal{S}$, which then homomorphically computes $c' = \mathsf{Enc}(f(m))$ for some function f, and sends it back to $\mathcal{C}$. A standard security requirement is that $\mathcal{S}$ doesn't learn anything about m or $f(m)$. Conversely, circuit privacy

---

[2] https://github.com/dlitz/pycrypto/blob/master/lib/Crypto/Util/number.py.
[3] https://github.com/openssl/openssl/blob/master/crypto/bn/bn_prime.c.

requires that $\mathcal{C}$ doesn't learn anything about the circuit f in the process. Circuit privacy is useful when f is a secret intellectual property of $\mathcal{S}$; without circuit privacy, a user might learn f and set up his own server. The lack of circuit privacy can be a strong deterrent for a company wishing to provide its services on encrypted data.

Today's most efficient method to realize circuit privacy in a generic way is the *washing machine* technique by Ducas and Stehlé [15].[4] In a nutshell, it first bootstraps the ciphertext, then injects entropy. One iteration of this *bootstrap-then-inject-entropy* process is called a *cycle*. [15] prove that their technique ensure circuit privacy if $\Theta(\lambda)$ cycles are sequentially applied to the ciphertext, where λ is the security level. However, despite recent improvements, bootstrapping remains an expensive operation. Thus circuit privacy can be a computational bottleneck.

We provide an improved analysis of Ducas and Stehlé's washing machine technique. We reduce the number of cycles by a factor essentially $\frac{2\lambda}{\log Q}$, where Q is the total number of (evaluation of f) queries made to the server. For realistic parameters, our new analysis improves the one of [15] by an order of magnitude. At a technical level, our proof leverages our proxy amplification property.

1.2 Related Works

These last years have seen a surge of papers using other divergences than the statistical distance in the cryptographic literature. For example, the Hellinger distance has been used to study key-alternating ciphers [43], the χ^2 divergence to study a few symmetric-key constructions [13], and the max-log distance [32] in the context of lattice-based cryptography.

The Kullback-Leibler divergence has been used to improve parameters in lattice-based cryptography [14,38], to redefine the advantage [33], to unify computational entropy notions [1], and indirectly (via the mutual information) in side-channel analysis [22].

The Rényi divergence has several applications in lattice-based cryptography [3,4,6,26,29,39,44]. Differential privacy [30,35] and leakage-resilient cryptography [40] have also benefitted from its use.

2 Preliminaries

Asymptotic Notations. For asymptotics, we use Laudau's notation. For two real functions $f, g : \mathbb{R}^+ \to \mathbb{R}$, we note $f = O(g)$ if there exists a constant C such that $|f| \leq C \cdot |g|$. Similarly, we note $f = o(g)$ if $f = \epsilon \cdot g$ for some function ϵ such that $\epsilon(x) \xrightarrow[x \to \infty]{} 0$. We note $f = \Theta(g)$ if $f = O(g)$ and $g = O(f)$. If f and g have several variables, we note $f = O_x(g)$ to specify that the assertion holds for the variable x (and similarly for the other notations). We will also use the notation $f \ll_x g$ for $f = O_x(g)$ when the articles we cite use it.

---

[4] The work of [7] requires no bootstrapping, but only applies to GSW-based schemes and is restricted to NC^1.

Integers (modulo n). $\mathbb{Z}$ denotes the set of integers. Let n be an integer, $\mathbb{Z}_n$ will denote the set of integers $\bmod n$ and $\mathbb{Z}_n^{\times}$ will denote the group of invertible elements of $\mathbb{Z}_n$. Euler's totient function is $\varphi(n) = |\mathbb{Z}_n^{\times}|$.

2.1 *f*-Divergences

f-divergences were first introduced by Csiszar [12], Morimoto [36] and Ali-Sirvey [2]. They provide a wide class of divergences between distributions, and encompass several divergences used in cryptography.

Definition 1 (*f*-Divergences). *Let* $f : \mathbb{R} \to \mathbb{R}$ *be a convex function such that* $f(1) = 0$. *Let* $\mathcal{P}, \mathcal{Q}$ *be two distributions over a countable space* X *such that* $\operatorname{Supp} \mathcal{P} \subset \operatorname{Supp} \mathcal{Q}$. *The f-divergence between* $\mathcal{P}$ *and* $\mathcal{Q}$ *is:*

$$\operatorname{Div}_f(\mathcal{P}; \mathcal{Q}) := \mathbb{E}_{\mathcal{Q}}\left[f\left(\frac{\mathcal{P}}{\mathcal{Q}}\right)\right] = \sum_{x \in \operatorname{Supp} \mathcal{Q}} \mathcal{Q}(x) f\left(\frac{\mathcal{P}(x)}{\mathcal{Q}(x)}\right)$$

Special cases of f-divergences are the following:

- *Statistical distance:* $\Delta_{\mathrm{SD}}(\mathcal{P}; \mathcal{Q}) = \operatorname{Div}_f(\mathcal{P}; \mathcal{Q})$ *for* $f : x \mapsto \frac{1}{2}|x - 1|$;
- *Kullback-Leibler divergence:* $D_{\mathrm{KL}}(\mathcal{P}; \mathcal{Q}) = \operatorname{Div}_f(\mathcal{P}; \mathcal{Q})$ *for* $f : x \mapsto x \ln(x)$;
- χ^2 *divergence:* $\chi^2(\mathcal{P}; \mathcal{Q}) = \operatorname{Div}_f(\mathcal{P}; \mathcal{Q})$ *for* $f : x \mapsto (x - 1)^2$;

We note that *all* *f*-divergences satisfy a few cryptographically useful properties such as the data processing inequality, probability preservation properties and joint convexity (see resp. Lemma 1, Corollary 2 and Corollary 3 of [21]). We state them here.

Lemma 1 (Data-processing inequality, Lemma 1 [21]). *Let* $\mathcal{P}, \mathcal{Q}$ *be two distributions over a space* X *and let* T *be a random function over* X. *Denote by* $\mathcal{P}^T, \mathcal{Q}^T$ *the composition of respectively* $\mathcal{P}$ *and* $\mathcal{Q}$ *with* T, *then*

$$\operatorname{Div}_f(\mathcal{P}^T; \mathcal{Q}^T) \leq \operatorname{Div}_f(\mathcal{P}; \mathcal{Q}).$$

Corollary 1 (Joint convexity of Div_f, **Corollary 2 [21]).** *All f-divergences are jointly convex, i.e, for all distributions* $\mathcal{P}_1, \mathcal{P}_2, \mathcal{Q}_1, \mathcal{Q}_2$ *over a space* X *and for all* $\lambda \in [0, 1]$, *one has*

$$\operatorname{Div}_f((1-\lambda)\mathcal{P}_1 + \lambda\mathcal{P}_2; (1-\lambda)\mathcal{Q}_1 + \lambda\mathcal{Q}_2) \leq (1-\lambda)\operatorname{Div}_f(\mathcal{P}_1, \mathcal{Q}_1) + \lambda\operatorname{Div}_f(\mathcal{P}_2, \mathcal{Q}_2).$$

Two divergences that are not *f*-divergences are also used in cryptography. If $\operatorname{Supp} \mathcal{P} = \operatorname{Supp} \mathcal{Q} = \Omega$, we define the following divergences:

- **Relative error:** $\Delta_{\mathrm{RE}}(\mathcal{P}; \mathcal{Q}) = \max_{\Omega} |\frac{\mathcal{P}}{\mathcal{Q}} - 1|$;
- **Max-log distance:** $\Delta_{\mathrm{ML}}(\mathcal{P}; \mathcal{Q}) \max_{\Omega} |\ln \mathcal{P} - \ln \mathcal{Q}|$;

Around 0, both divergences are equivalent [32]: $\Delta_{\mathrm{RE}}(\mathcal{P}; \mathcal{Q}) \sim \Delta_{\mathrm{ML}}(\mathcal{P}; \mathcal{Q})$.

2.2   Rényi Divergences and Rényi Entropies

In this section, we recall the definitions of Rényi divergences and entropies.

Definition 2 (Rényi divergence). *Let $\mathcal{P}, \mathcal{Q}$ be two discrete distributions over a space X such that* $\operatorname{Supp} \mathcal{P} \subset \operatorname{Supp} \mathcal{Q}$. *The Rényi divergence of order α is:*

$$
R_\alpha(\mathcal{P}; \mathcal{Q}) := \begin{cases} \left(\sum_{x \in \operatorname{Supp} \mathcal{Q}} \frac{\mathcal{P}(x)^\alpha}{\mathcal{Q}(x)^{\alpha-1}} \right)^{\frac{1}{\alpha-1}} & \text{if } 1 < \alpha < \infty \\ \max_{x \in \operatorname{Supp} \mathcal{Q}} \frac{\mathcal{P}(x)}{\mathcal{Q}(x)} & \text{if } \alpha = \infty \\ e^{D_{\mathrm{KL}}(\mathcal{P}; \mathcal{Q})} & \text{if } \alpha = 1 \end{cases}
$$

Note that R_α is not an f-divergence. However, $R_\alpha^{\alpha-1} - 1$ is an f-divergence for $f : x \mapsto x^\alpha - 1$, which allows it to indirectly benefit from f-divergence properties. We recall some properties.

Lemma 2 ([3,46]). *For two distributions $\mathcal{P}, \mathcal{Q}$ and two families of distributions $(\mathcal{P}_i)_i, (\mathcal{Q}_i)_i$, the Rényi divergence verifies these properties:*

- **Monotonicity.** $\alpha \geq 1 \mapsto R_\alpha(\mathcal{P}; \mathcal{Q})$ *is a continuous non-decreasing function.*
- **Data processing inequality.** *For any (randomized) function f, one has $R_\alpha(f(\mathcal{P}); f(\mathcal{Q})) \leq R_\alpha(\mathcal{P}; \mathcal{Q})$.*
- **Multiplicativity.** $R_\alpha(\prod_i \mathcal{P}_i; \prod_i \mathcal{Q}_i) = \prod_i R_\alpha(\mathcal{P}_i; \mathcal{Q}_i)$.
- **Probability preservation.** *For any event $E \subseteq \operatorname{Supp}(\mathcal{Q})$ and $\alpha \in (1, +\infty)$,*

$$
\mathcal{Q}(E) \geq \mathcal{P}(E)^{\frac{\alpha}{\alpha-1}} / R_\alpha(\mathcal{P}; \mathcal{Q}), \tag{1}
$$
$$
\mathcal{Q}(E) \geq \mathcal{P}(E) / R_\infty(\mathcal{P}; \mathcal{Q}). \tag{2}
$$

The following lemma bounds the Rényi divergence from the relative error Δ_{RE}.

Lemma 3 ([39]). *Let $\mathcal{P}, \mathcal{Q}$ be two distributions of same support such that $\Delta_{\mathrm{RE}}(\mathcal{P}; \mathcal{Q}) \leq \delta$. Then, for $a \in (1, +\infty)$:*

$$
R_a(\mathcal{P}; \mathcal{Q}) \leq \left(1 + \frac{a(a-1)\delta^2}{2(1-\delta)^{a+1}} \right)^{\frac{1}{a-1}} \underset{\delta \to 0}{\sim} 1 + \frac{a\delta^2}{2}
$$

We give a second lemma; it is already used implicitly in [39], but we make it formal here as it is repeatedly used in our security arguments. In particular, given Lemma 4 initial conditions, no more than $1 + \log_2 3 \leq 3$ bits of security are lost when switching from $\mathcal{I}$ to $\mathcal{P}$. The proof is in the full version of the paper.

Lemma 4. *Let $\mathcal{A}$ be an adversary performing Q queries to a distribution $\mathcal{I}$ and solving a search problem $\mathcal{S}^{\mathcal{I}}$ with probability at most $2^{-\lambda}$, where $\lambda > 1$. If one replaces $\mathcal{I}$ with a distribution $\mathcal{P}$ such that $R_\lambda(\mathcal{P}; \mathcal{I}) \leq 1 + 1/Q$, then the probability that $\mathcal{A}$ solves $\mathcal{S}^{\mathcal{P}}$ is no more than $2^{-(\lambda-1)} \cdot e$.*

Rényi divergences have entropy measure counterparts, called Rényi entropies or α-entropies. These have countless cryptographic applications [42].

Definition 3 (Rényi entropy). *Let $\alpha \in [1, +\infty]$ and X be a discrete distribution. The α-entropy (or Rényi entropy) of X is:*

$$H_\alpha(X) = \begin{cases} -\sum_x \mathbb{P}[X = x] \log_2 \mathbb{P}[X = x] & \text{if } a = 1 \\ \dfrac{1}{1-\alpha} \log_2 \left(\sum_x \mathbb{P}[X = x]^\alpha \right) & \text{if } 1 < a < \infty \\ -\max_x \log_2 \mathbb{P}[X = x] & \text{if } a = \infty \end{cases}$$

H_1 *is also called Shannon's entropy, H_2 the collision entropy and H_∞ the min-entropy. If we note U the uniform distribution over any superset of $\mathrm{Supp}\,(X)$, then all the Rényi entropies of U are equal: $H_\alpha(U) = \log_2 |\mathrm{Supp}\,(X)|$ for any $\alpha \in [1, +\infty]$. Note that Rényi divergences and entropies are closely related:*

$$\log_2 R_\alpha(X; U) = H_\alpha(U) - H_\alpha(X).$$

3 Theoretical Results

In this section, we present our theoretical results. We introduce a new cryptographic divergence; this parametric divergence seems deeply connected to several existing divergences, and possesses an unusual amplification property.

3.1 A Parametric Divergence with Peculiar Properties

We now introduce a new divergence, which we note RE_α (for *relative error*) as it can be seen as a trade-off between the statistical distance Δ_{SD} and the relative error Δ_{RE}. This trade-off is parametrized by a scalar $\alpha \in [1, \infty]$, and allows RE_α to be defined in situations where Δ_{RE} is not, all the while sharing with Δ_{RE} and Δ_{SD} a new desirable cryptographic properties.

Definition 4 (RE_α divergence). *Let $\mathcal{P}, \mathcal{Q}$ be two distributions over a countable space X such that $\mathrm{Supp}\,\mathcal{P} \subset \mathrm{Supp}\,\mathcal{Q}$. One defines the RE_α-divergence as:*

$$\mathrm{RE}_\alpha(\mathcal{P}; \mathcal{Q}) := \begin{cases} \left(\sum_{x \in \mathrm{Supp}\,\mathcal{Q}} \mathcal{Q}(x) \left| \frac{\mathcal{P}(x)}{\mathcal{Q}(x)} - 1 \right|^\alpha \right)^{\frac{1}{\alpha}} & \text{if } \alpha \geq 1 \\ \Delta_{\mathrm{RE}}(\mathcal{P}; \mathcal{Q}) = \max_{x \in \mathrm{Supp}\,\mathcal{Q}} \left| \frac{\mathcal{P}(x)}{\mathcal{Q}(x)} - 1 \right| & \text{if } \alpha = \infty \end{cases}$$

The RE_α divergence generalizes several known metrics. RE_1 is twice the statistical distance Δ_{SD}. In addition, RE_∞ is exactly the relative error Δ_{RE}. Finally, $\mathrm{RE}_\alpha^\alpha = \chi^\alpha$ is an f-divergence for $f(x) = |x - 1|^\alpha$. The χ^α divergence was first studied by Vajda [45], and χ^2 (sometimes called Pearson Chi-square divergence) has recently been used in a cryptographic context [13].

Proposition 1 provides a few properties of RE_α. Items 1. and 2. describe the behavior of RE_α when α varies, and underline our point that RE_α is a continuous trade-off between Δ_{SD} and Δ_{RE}. Items 3. and 4. show (with a tightness loss) that RE_α and the Rényi divergence R_α are equivalent. Finally, Items 5. to 8. give cryptographically useful inequalities.

Proposition 1. *Let $\mathcal{P}, \mathcal{Q}$ be two distributions over a countable space X, such that $\operatorname{Supp} \mathcal{P} \subset \operatorname{Supp} \mathcal{Q}$. The following properties hold:*

1. **Monotonicity.** $\alpha \geq 1 \mapsto \operatorname{RE}_\alpha(\mathcal{P}; \mathcal{Q})$ *is a continuous non-decreasing function.*

2. **Upper bound from Δ_{SD} and Δ_{RE}.** *It holds that:*

$$\operatorname{RE}_\alpha(\mathcal{P}; \mathcal{Q}) \leq \Delta_{\mathrm{SD}}^{1/\alpha}(\mathcal{P}; \mathcal{Q}) \cdot \Delta_{\mathrm{RE}}^{1-1/\alpha}(\mathcal{P}; \mathcal{Q}).$$

3. **Upper bound on Rényi divergence.** *It holds that:*

$$R_\alpha(\mathcal{P}; \mathcal{Q}) \leq (1 + \operatorname{RE}_\alpha(\mathcal{P}; \mathcal{Q}))^{\frac{\alpha}{\alpha-1}}. \tag{3}$$

4. **Lower bound on Rényi divergence.** *If α is an even integer, then:*

$$\operatorname{RE}_\alpha(\mathcal{P}; \mathcal{Q}) \leq 2^{1-1/\alpha} \left(R_\alpha(\mathcal{P}; \mathcal{Q})^{\alpha-1} - 1\right)^{1/\alpha}. \tag{4}$$

5. **Multiplicative probability preservation.** *For any event $E \subset X$:*

$$\mathcal{P}(E) \leq \mathcal{Q}(E)^{\frac{a-1}{a}}(1 + \operatorname{RE}_\alpha(\mathcal{P}; \mathcal{Q})).$$

6. **Additive probability preservation.** *Let $f : X \to \mathbb{R}$ be a function and $p, q > 1$ be such that $1/p + 1/q = 1$. It holds that:*

$$|\mathbb{E}[f(\mathcal{P})] - \mathbb{E}[f(\mathcal{Q})]| \leq \operatorname{RE}_p(\mathcal{P}; \mathcal{Q}) \cdot \mathbb{E}[|f(\mathcal{Q})|^q]^{1/q}.$$

In particular, for any event E:

$$|\mathcal{P}(E) - \mathcal{Q}(E)| \leq \operatorname{RE}_\alpha(\mathcal{P}; \mathcal{Q}) \cdot \mathcal{Q}(E)^{1-1/\alpha}.$$

7. **Weak triangle inequality.** *For distributions $\mathcal{P}, \mathcal{R}, \mathcal{Q}$ such that $\operatorname{Supp} \mathcal{P} \subset \operatorname{Supp} \mathcal{R} \subset \operatorname{Supp} \mathcal{Q}$:*

$$\Delta_{\mathrm{RE}}(\mathcal{P}, \mathcal{Q}) \leq \Delta_{\mathrm{RE}}(\mathcal{P}, \mathcal{R}) + \Delta_{\mathrm{RE}}(\mathcal{R}, \mathcal{Q}) + \Delta_{\mathrm{RE}}(\mathcal{P}, \mathcal{R}) \cdot \Delta_{\mathrm{RE}}(\mathcal{R}, \mathcal{Q})$$

8. **Data processing inequality.** *For any randomized function g, it holds that:*

$$\operatorname{RE}_\alpha(g(\mathcal{P}), g(\mathcal{Q})) \leq \operatorname{RE}_\alpha(\mathcal{P}, \mathcal{Q}).$$

Most of the properties in Proposition 1 are proven in a rather straightforward manner by using either convexity, Minkowski's inequality or generic properties of f-divergences. This is no coincidence as the RE_α divergence is directly connected to an f-divergence, and can also be interpreted as an L_α norm. The detailed proofs are given in the full version of the paper.

Interestingly, the RE_α divergence does not have a native multiplicative property but the security analysis scales with the number of queries if we combine it with the Rényi divergence. However, the RE_α divergence benefits from native properties that the Rényi divergence does not have, such as an additive probability preservation property. This indicates that these divergences are complementary to some extent: depending on the situation, one may be preferable to the other.

One last property allows the RE_α divergence to stand out. It was known for the statistical distance but seems not to be known for other divergences. We call it *proxy amplification* and it will be discussed in Sect. 5, but for now we move on to applications of the results of this section to prime number generators.

4   Security Proofs for Prime Number Generators

We now improve the security proofs for two known prime number generators: PRIMEINC [8] and Fouque-Tibouchi generator [17]. What we mean by security is that the output distribution of the algorithm should be as close as possible from the random one. For the first one, we show a bound on the Rényi divergence between the output distribution of the algorithm and the random distribution. For the second, we improve the results shown in [17] and show a bound on the RE_α divergence between the output distribution and the random one. We then show how those proofs show security against known attacks towards prime number generators.

Algorithm 1. PRIMEINC(x, s)

Require: Parameters x, s

Ensure: a prime number between $x/2$ and x

1: Sample odd p uniformly in $[\![x/2; x]\!]$

2: **for** $i = 1$ to s **do**
3:   **if** p is prime **then**
4:     **return** p
5:   **else**
6:     $p \leftarrow p + 2$
7:   **end if**
8: **end for**
9: **return** "failure"

Algorithm 2. Fouque and Tibouchi's prime number generator

Require: $x, \epsilon, q \propto x^{1-\epsilon}$

Ensure: A prime number $p \in [\![2; x]\!]$

1: Sample $a \xleftarrow{\$} (\mathbb{Z}/q\mathbb{Z})^*$
2: **repeat**
3:   Sample $t \xleftarrow{\$} \left\{0, ..., \left\lfloor \frac{x-a}{q} \right\rfloor\right\}$
4: **until** $p = a + tq$ is prime
5: **return** p

4.1   Provable Security of the Prime Number Generator PRIMEINC

This section and Sect. 4.2 study prime number generators. The motivation for studying them is given in Sect. 1.1. We first describe the simplest variant of PRIMEINC in Algorithm 1.[5]

Previous Analyses. Let $\mathcal{P}$ denote the output of PRIMEINC, and $\mathcal{U}$ the uniform distribution over primes in $[\![x/2; x]\!]$. It was shown in [8] (resp. [17]) that under the prime r-tuple conjecture:

$$\frac{H_1(\mathcal{P})}{H_1(\mathcal{U})} \underset{x \to \infty}{\sim} 1 \tag{5}$$

$$\Delta_{\mathrm{SD}}(\mathcal{P}; \mathcal{U}) \geq 0.86 + o(1) \tag{6}$$

On one hand, (5) seems to offer some security guarantees. However, Skórski [42, Corollary 4] showed that even when Shannon's entropy $H_1(\mathcal{P})$ is close to its

---

[5] Security-efficiency trade-offs have been presented in [8], and OpenSSL implements a variant of PRIMEINC.

trivial upper bound $\log_2 |\mathrm{Supp}\,(\mathcal{P})|$, the collision entropy $H_2(\mathcal{P})$ might still be low. Hence, (5) does not even preclude simple attacks such as common factors attacks [24,28] on RSA. On the other hand, (6) is clearly a negative result.

New Analysis. We now provide an improved security analysis. We first bound the Rényi divergence between the output of PRIMEINC and the uniform distribution. We then show that in common usecases, PRIMEINC may be safely used without compromising security. We first recall the prime r-tuple conjecture, which is instrumental in the proofs of [8,17] and in ours.

Conjecture 1 (Hardy-Littlewood's prime r-tuple conjecture [23]). Let $d = (d_1, ..., d_r)$ be a r-tuple of integers. Denote by $\pi_d(x)$ the number of integers $n \leq x$ such that for all $i, n + d_i$ is a prime number. It holds that:

$$\pi_d(x) \sim_{x \to \infty} S_d \cdot \frac{x}{\log(x)^r},$$

where $S_d = \prod_{p \text{ prime}} \left(\frac{p}{p-1}\right)^r \frac{p - \nu_d(p)}{p-1}$, and $\nu_d(p)$ is the number of distinct residue classes modulo p of the tuple d.

The following statement holds under the prime r-tuple conjecture.

Theorem 1 (Theorem 1, [19]). *Let x, k be integers. Then the number of integers n such that there are exactly k primes in $[\![n, n + \lambda \log x]\!]$ is $\simeq x \frac{e^{-\lambda} \lambda^k}{k!}$ when $x \to \infty$.*

In particular, if $d(n)$ denotes the distance of n to the next larger prime, then the probability that $d(n) > \lambda \log x$ is $e^{-\lambda}$.

Theorem 2 is the main result of this section and implies that this algorithm is asymptotically secure by computing the Rényi divergence between its output distribution and the uniform distribution over a superset of its support. The proof of Theorem 2 is in the full version of this paper.

Theorem 2 (Security of PRIMEINC). *Let $\mathcal{P}$ be the output distribution of PRIMEINC with $s = c \log x$ and $c > 0$, and $\mathcal{U}$ be the uniform distribution over the prime numbers between $x/2$ and x. Under the prime r-tuple conjecture:*

$$R_\infty(\mathcal{P}; \mathcal{U}) \leq 2c(1 + o_{c,x}(1)). \tag{7}$$

Equivalently, for all $\alpha \geq 2$,

$$H_\alpha(\mathcal{P}) \geq H_\alpha(\mathcal{U}) - \log(2c) + o_{c,x}(1). \tag{8}$$

Practical Implications I. Theorem 2 implies that for a constant number of calls to a prime number generator, a scheme secure with a uniform generator (ideal case) remains secure when using PRIMEINC instead (real case). One application is key generation for RSA signatures [41]. In the single-target setting, there are two calls to the prime number generator.[6] Combining (2) with (7), any adversary breaking the real cryptosystem with probability ϵ will break the ideal cryptosystem with probability at least $\epsilon/(2c + 1 + o_{c,x}(1))^2$; therefore at most $\approx 2 \cdot \log_2(1 + 2c)$ bits of security are lost.

Practical Implications II. Even for a large number of queries, Theorem 2 provide security guarantees against some specific attacks. For example, taking $\alpha = 2$ in (8) gives a lower bound of $n - \log(2c) + o_{c,x}(1)$ on the collision entropy of PRIMEINC. As long as $n \geq \lambda + \log(2c) + o_{c,x}(1)$ (which is always the case in practice), this is more than enough to argue resistance against common factors attacks [24,28].

4.2 Provable Security of the Fouque-Tibouchi Generator

We now study a prime number generator proposed by Fouque and Tibouchi in [16,17]. Fouque and Tibouchi actually propose several algorithms, which provide trade-offs between simplicity and the number-theoretic conjectures they base their security on: the Friedlander-Granville-Montgomery conjecture, the generalized Riemann hypothesis or full unconditionality.

We only study the simplest variant of Fouque and Tibouchi's algorithms, and leave other variants for future work. The idea of this variant is to sample a random number, and then resample only its most significant bits until a prime number is found. It is described in Algorithm 2.

Previous Analysis. In [17], it is shown under Conjecture 2 that:[7]

$$\Delta_{\mathrm{SD}}(\mathcal{P};\mathcal{U}) \ll \frac{\log x}{x^{\epsilon/4}}. \tag{9}$$

In addition, the average entropy consumption of Algorithm 2 is:

$$(\epsilon + o(1)) \cdot \frac{\varphi(q)}{q} \cdot \frac{(\log x)^2}{\log 2}. \tag{10}$$

The statistical distance requires $\Delta_{\mathrm{SD}}(\mathcal{P};\mathcal{U}) \leq 2^{-\lambda}$ in order to provide λ bits of security. As noted by [17], taking q to be a primordial (a product of small distinct primes) allows to reduce entropy consumption by a factor $O(\log \log q)$.

The Friedlander-Granville-Montgomery conjecture studies the quantity:

$$\pi(x, q, a) := \mathrm{Card}\,\{p \leq x \text{ prime} \mid p \equiv a \bmod q\}.$$

The prime number theorem establishes that $\pi(x, q, a) \underset{x \to \infty}{\sim} \frac{x}{\varphi(q)\log(x)}$ when a, q are fixed. The Friedlander-Granville-Montgomery conjecture gives a bound on the error given by this estimate.

---

[6] This is true without loss of generality; even if more primes are generated and rejected if they fail some requirements (e.g. being safe primes), the adversary only has access to the product of exactly two outputs of the generator (p and q).

[7] As stated in the preliminaries, this section will use Vinogradov's notation, which is common in number theory: $(f \ll_s g) \Leftrightarrow (f =_s O(g))$.

Conjecture 2 [Friedlander-Granville-Montgomery [18]] For $q < x, (a, q) = 1$ and all $\epsilon > 0$, one has:

$$\left| \pi(x, q, a) - \frac{\pi(x)}{\varphi(q)} \right| \ll_\epsilon \left(\frac{x}{q} \right)^{1/2} x^{\epsilon/4}.$$

Since $q \sim x^{1-\epsilon}$, it holds that $\left(\frac{x}{q} \right)^{1/2} x^{\epsilon/4} \sim x^{3\epsilon/4}$, which is negligible compared to the ratio $\pi(x)/\varphi(q) \gg x^\epsilon / \log(x)$. Thus this conjecture implies:

$$\pi(x, q, a) = \frac{\pi(x)}{\varphi(q)}(1 + o_x(1)) = \frac{x}{\varphi(q) \cdot \log x}(1 + o_x(1)).$$

Theorem 3 is the main result of this section. It bounds the relative error and the RE_α divergence between the output distribution of the Fouque-Tibouchi generator and the uniform distribution over a superset of its support. Our result is a generalization of Fouque-Tibouchi's result as we show that the relative error of any order decreases with the same exponential rate $\epsilon/4$. Again, the proof of Theorem 3 is in the full version of the paper.

Theorem 3 (Security of the Fouque-Tibouchi generator). *Denote by $\mathcal{P}$ the output distribution of Algorithm 2 and by $\mathcal{U}$ the uniform distribution over $[\![2; x]\!]$. Under the Friedlander-Granville-Montgomery conjecture:*

$$\Delta_{\mathrm{RE}}(\mathcal{P}; \mathcal{U}_{|\mathrm{Supp}\,\mathcal{P}}) \ll \frac{\log x}{x^{\epsilon/4}} \quad and \quad \mathbb{P}[\mathrm{Supp}\,\mathcal{P}^c] \leq \frac{\log(x)^2}{x}. \tag{11}$$

$$\forall \alpha \in (1, \infty), \mathrm{RE}_\alpha(\mathcal{P}; \mathcal{U}) \ll_\alpha \frac{\log x}{x^{\epsilon/4}} + \left(\frac{\log x}{x^2} \right)^{1/\alpha}. \tag{12}$$

We now make explicit the implications of Theorem 3. Since the Fouque-Tibouchi generator is more provable security-oriented than PRIMEINC, it is unsurprising that Theorem 3 is intrinsically stronger than Theorem 2 and that we can assert security for more usecases than with PRIMEINC. Compared to [16,17], our analysis divides the entropy requirement by an order of magnitude.

Practical Implications I. We study the *generic* security of RSA signature schemes in a multi-target setting. As an concrete example, consider a company producing a hardware security module (HSM); this HSM targets a bit-security $\lambda = 128$. At most 2^{31} copies of it are produced, hence at most 2^{32} queries to the prime number generator are made. For RSA signatures, NIST and ENISA recommend RSA-3072. If HSMs generate RSA private keys with Algorithm 2, this translates to $x = 2^{1536}$.

A statistical distance argument requires – via (9) – that $\frac{\log x}{x^{\epsilon/4}} \leq 2^{-\lambda}$, which here is satisfied for $\epsilon \geq \frac{4\lambda \log \log x}{\log x} \approx 0.36$. Using a Rényi-based argument instead, we combine Lemmas 3 and 4 with (11); this gives the milder requirement $\lambda Q \frac{(\log x)^2}{2x^{\epsilon/2}} \leq 1$, which is satisfied for $\epsilon \geq \frac{2\log(\lambda Q)\log \log x}{\log x} \approx 0.076$. Since entropy consumption is essentially linear in ϵ, our new analysis provides a gain of a factor roughly 5. In practice, we take a primordial $q = \prod_{\{p \leq 1049, p \text{ prime}\}} p$ as suggested by [17]. As per (10), this gives an entropy consumption of less than 20 000 uniform bits for generating two prime numbers.

Practical Implications II. We now study signature schemes based on the strong RSA assumption: this includes but is not limited to derivatives of Cramer-Shoup signatures [11]. As in the previous example, we consider 128 bits of security, hence RSA-3072. Some of these schemes only require collision resistance of the prime number generator, in which case it is sufficient to use PRIMEINC since Theorem 2 showed that its collision entropy is high.

Other schemes only specify that the output of the generator should be statistically close to the uniform distribution over primes in an interval, in which case it is more prudent to use Fouque and Tibouchi's generator. Suppose that a user is queried at most 2^{64} signatures. As before, an statistical distance analysis gives $\epsilon \gtrsim 0.36$, whereas our Rényi-based analysis gives $\epsilon \gtrsim 0.12$. The entropy consumption is divided by 3.

5   Proxy-Amplification and Application to Circuit-Private FHE

In this section, we come back to the RE_α divergence. We showed some standard properties in Sect. 3 and now we focus on a quite unique property that we call *proxy amplification*. In our opinion, this property justifies the definition of our new divergence as other divergences do not enjoy a similar property – to the best of our knowledge. We then apply this property to circuit-privacy on fully-homomorphic encryption in the fashion of [15].

5.1   Proxy Amplification

Proxy amplification is a unique property of the RE_α divergence. It generalizes an amplification property of the statistical distance [15, Lemma 2.3]. A major twist is that our property allows the RE_α divergence to "borrow" the amplification of the statistical distance: RE_α will be made increasingly small even if it is > 1, as long as $\Delta_{\mathrm{SD}} < 1$. For this reason, we call it proxy amplification. Proposition 2 states this property, and its proof is given in the full version of the paper.

Proposition 2 (Proxy amplification). *Let X be a finite space, $f : X \to X$ be a randomized function and $\alpha \in [1; +\infty]$. Suppose that for all $x \in X, \mathrm{Supp}\, f(x) = X$ and that there exists $\delta > 0$ such that:*

$$\forall a, b \in X, \quad \mathrm{RE}_\alpha(f(a); f(b)) \leq \delta.$$

Then, for all integer $k \geq 1$:

$$\mathrm{RE}_\alpha(f^k(a); f^k(b)) \leq 2 \cdot \delta \cdot \Delta_{\mathrm{SD}}(f(a); f(b))^{k-1}$$
$$\leq \delta^k / 2^{k-2}.$$

This property was already known in the particular case of the statistical distance Δ_{SD} [15, Lemma 2.3]. This generalization is useful when the relative error is too big or infinite, which is for example the case for shifted Gaussian distributions. Indeed, denote by $D_{\mathbb{Z},\sigma,c}$ the Gaussian distribution of center x and standard deviation σ over $\mathbb{Z}$. Then, in the case of the relative error:

$$\forall x \neq y, \Delta_{RE}(D_{\mathbb{Z},\sigma,x}; D_{\mathbb{Z},\sigma,y}) = \infty.$$

On the other hand, $RE_\alpha(D_{\mathbb{Z},\sigma,x}, D_{\mathbb{Z},\sigma,y}) = e^{\Theta_{x,y,\sigma}(\alpha)}$. Therefore, RE_α lies in a sweet spot between the statistical distance Δ_{SD} and the relative error Δ_{RE}. On one hand, Δ_{SD} enjoys an amplification property, but not a multiplicative probability preservation. On the other hand, Δ_{RE} enjoys both, but may not be finite. Finally, RE_α enjoys all three properties at once. Obviously in the case of Gaussian distribution, a tailcut would be fine for security proofs but this shows that from a theoretical point of view there are pathological cases with the relative error.

5.2   Circuit-Private FHE: Setting the Washing Machine in Economy Mode

We recall that the motivation for circuit privacy in FHE schemes is given in Sect. 1.1. In the following section, we show how to get improved circuit privacy guarantees using a new analysis.

The Ducas-Stehlé Strategy. Circuit privacy is guaranteed if the output distribution of the ciphertext c' does not depend on the circuit f. We briefly describe the *"washing machine"* strategy introduced by Ducas and Stehlé [15] to achieve it, and refer to [15] for a complete exposition. Ducas and Stehlé realize circuit privacy by applying a randomized function Wash = Rerand ∘ Refresh that scrambles the ciphertext c'. Here, Refresh is the bootstrapping operation, which reduces the ciphertext noise down to some level. On the other hand, Rerand injects entropy in the ciphertext, see (13). [15] shows that applying Wash many times makes the output distribution increasingly independent of the original ciphertext, and compares this to a washing machine which repeats a cycle several times to "clean up" the ciphertext.

New Security Analysis. The security analysis in [15] leverages an amplification property of the statistical distance. It guarantees λ bits of security if Wash is applied $O(\lambda)$ times. However, bootstrapping (Refresh) is extremely expensive, and it is desirable to perform it as rarely as possible. In this section, we provide a new security analysis based on the amplification property of the RE_α divergence (Proposition 2). It allows us to claim that Wash needs only to be applied $O(\log_2 Q)$ times, where Q is the number of (homomorphically encrypted) queries to f and the constants in $O(\cdot)$ are equivalent. Since one can expect $\log_2 Q$ to be much smaller than λ, this entails much lighter requirements on the number of cycles, hence a more practical protocol.

For brevity we only revisit [15, Section 4.1], but we expect our improvements to be applicable to other examples in [15], as well as newer schemes such as [25]. Suppose one wants to encrypt one bit $\mu \in \{0,1\}$ under a private key $s \in \mathbb{Z}_q^n$ with modulus q and error rate less than η. The set of LWE ciphertexts decrypting to μ is:

$$\text{LWE}_s^q(\mu, \eta) = \left\{ \left(\mathbf{a}, \langle \mathbf{a}, \mathbf{s} \rangle + \mu \cdot \left\lfloor \frac{q}{2} \right\rfloor + e \right) \in \mathbb{Z}_q^{n+1} \;\middle|\; \mathbf{a} \in \mathbb{Z}_q^n, |e| < \eta q \right\}.$$

Correct decryption is ensured provided that $\eta < 1/4$. We now describe the Rerand function. Assume that the public key contains $\ell = O(n \log q)$ encryptions of 0:

$$\forall i \leq \ell, r_i = (\mathbf{a}_i, \langle \mathbf{a}_i, \mathbf{s} \rangle + e_i) \in \text{LWE}_s^q(\eta, 0).$$

For $c \in \text{LWE}_s^q(\eta, \mu)$, define:

$$\text{Rerand}(pk, c) = c + \sum_i \epsilon_i r_i + (\mathbf{0}, err), \tag{13}$$

where the ϵ_i's are sampled uniformly in $\{0, \pm 1\}$ and $err \in \mathbb{Z}_q$ is sampled from the discrete Gaussian $D_{\mathbb{Z}, \sigma, 0} =: D_\sigma$. We note that in [15], err is instead sampled uniformly over $[\![-B, B]\!]$ with a B suitable for correctness of decryption. In our case, the relative error precludes the use of this distribution as the support of $\text{Rerand}(pk, c)$ should not depend on c. Therefore, every ciphertext should have a non-zero probability of appearance. We will set parameters that ensure that a bad ciphertext almost never (i.e with exponentially low probability) appears. To do so, we use Proposition 3.

Proposition 3. *For all $k \in \mathbb{N}$, it holds that $\mathbb{P}[|t| > k\sigma; t \hookleftarrow D_\sigma] \leq 2e^{-\frac{k^2}{2}}$.*

Next, Theorem 4 is the main result of this section and provides parameters that guarantee that Ducas and Stehlé's protocol is circuit-private. We bound the relative error between the output distributions of Rerand applied on two different ciphertexts. The theorem transfers directly to the function Wash = Rerand $\circ$ Refresh, as Refresh is deterministic and therefore has no impact on our analysis. This will subsequently allow to apply our amplification theorem on Wash, followed by a Rényi divergence argument.

Theorem 4. *Given parameters η, n, q, s, ℓ. Let Q be the number of queries and k be the number of calls to the washing machine. If*

$$k > \frac{\frac{\log Q}{2}}{\log \left(\frac{1/\eta}{4(\ell+1)} \right) - \log(8\lambda)}, \tag{14}$$

then there exists a standard deviation $\sigma > 0$ such that:

1. *The probability of Rerand outputting a bad ciphertext is $< 2^{-\lambda}$.*
2. *In the event that Rerand always output a good ciphertext, one has*

$$\forall c_1, c_2 \in \text{LWE}_s^q(\eta, \mu), \quad \Delta_{\text{RE}}(\text{Rerand}(pk, c_1); \text{Rerand}(pk, c_2)) \leq Q^{-1/2k}.$$

This gives an upper bound M on σ. For security, we require that the relative error $\Delta_{\mathrm{RE}}(\mathsf{Rerand}(pk, c); \mathsf{Rerand}(pk, c')$ for two ciphertextst c, c' is lower than $Q^{-1/2k}$ in order to use the amplification property[8] and Lemma 4. This will give a lower bound m on σ. To find a suitable σ, one only needs $m \leq M$ and this gives the lower bound on k given in (14). Note that the analysis of [15] leads to
$$k > \frac{\lambda}{\log\left(\frac{1/\eta}{4(\ell+1)}\right)}.$$

Remark 1. Security is immediate via using Proposition 2 with taking X to be the space $\mathsf{LWE}_{\mathbf{s}}^q(\mu, \eta) = \{(\mathbf{a}, \langle \mathbf{a}, \mathbf{s}\rangle + \mu \cdot \lfloor\frac{q}{2}\rfloor + e \in \mathbf{Z}_q^{n+1} \mid |e| < \eta q\}$, and for the random function f to be Wash (conditioned on the correctness of decryption). More precisely, we use the relative error by tailcutting the event where Wash outputs a bad ciphertext.

Practical Implications. Consider a cloud service proposing homomorphic evaluation of a proprietary function f over encrypted data. An adversarial user $\mathcal{A}$ tries to learn f or replicate it to some extent.

To apply a Rényi-based argument, we need to formalize the problem that $\mathcal{A}$ tackles as a search problem. This is the most delicate part of our analysis and really depends on the application: in the special case where the function f solves a search problem, then one may simply say that the problem $\mathcal{A}$ tries to solve is to find a function f' which solves the same problem on a non-negligible fraction of the inputs. All usecases may not be formalized by a search problem, but we believe that most practical ones can.

If the conditions of Theorem 4 hold, then k applications of Wash will provide a relative error $\Delta_{\mathrm{RE}} \leq 1/\sqrt{Q}$. We now apply the proof blueprint $(a) \Rightarrow (b) \Rightarrow (c)$ outlined in Section 1.1. Combining Theorem 4 with Lemma 3 and applying (1) with $\alpha = \Theta(\lambda)$, one can claim that $O(\log \lambda)$ bits of security are lost.[9]

Applied on the washing machine technique of Ducas and Stehlé, our new analysis allows to reduce the number of cycles by $\frac{2\lambda}{\log Q}$ for the same asymptotic bit security. For $\lambda = 256$ and $Q = 2^{64}$, this is an order of magnitude. Given that bootstrapping often is a computational bottleneck, this can potentially make the whole protocol faster by an order of magnitude.

Acknowledgements. The authors are indebted to Takahiro Matsuda and Shuichi Katsumata for their insightful discussions and for pointing out a flaw in an earlier version of the paper. Thomas Prest is supported by the Innovate UK Research Grant 104423 (PQ Cybersecurity).

---

[8] One would find it odd that we are not using the *proxy amplification* property here but the computations we made showed that it wouldn't give here a significantly better result than the *amplification property* for this application, so we chose not to complexify the computations done in the proof.

[9] Alternatively, one can replace Q by λQ in Theorem 4 and use Lemma 4; this results in a loss of $O(1)$ bits of security and has a negligible effect on the parameters.

References

1. Agrawal, R., Chen, Y.-H., Horel, T., Vadhan, S.: Unifying computational entropies via Kullback–Leibler divergence. In: Boldyreva, A., Micciancio, D. (eds.) CRYPTO 2019. LNCS, vol. 11693, pp. 831–858. Springer, Cham (2019). https://doi.org/10.1007/978-3-030-26951-7_28
2. Ali, S.M., Silvey, S.D.: A general class of coefficients of divergence of one distribution from another. J. Roy. Stat. Soc. Ser. B (Methodol.) **28**(1), 131–142 (1966)
3. Bai, S., Langlois, A., Lepoint, T., Stehlé, D., Steinfeld, R.: Improved security proofs in lattice-based cryptography: using the Rényi divergence rather than the statistical distance. In: Iwata, T., Cheon, J.H. (eds.) ASIACRYPT 2015. LNCS, vol. 9452, pp. 3–24. Springer, Heidelberg (2015). https://doi.org/10.1007/978-3-662-48797-6_1
4. Bai, S., Lepoint, T., Roux-Langlois, A., Sakzad, A., Stehlé, D., Steinfeld, R.: Improved security proofs in lattice-based cryptography: using the Rényi divergence rather than the statistical distance. J. Cryptol. **31**(2), 610–640 (2018)
5. Bernstein, D.J., et al.: Factoring RSA keys from certified smart cards: coppersmith in the wild. In: Sako, K., Sarkar, P. (eds.) ASIACRYPT 2013. LNCS, vol. 8270, pp. 341–360. Springer, Heidelberg (2013). https://doi.org/10.1007/978-3-642-42045-0_18
6. Bogdanov, A., Guo, S., Masny, D., Richelson, S., Rosen, A.: On the hardness of learning with rounding over small modulus. In: Kushilevitz, E., Malkin, T. (eds.) TCC 2016. LNCS, vol. 9562, pp. 209–224. Springer, Heidelberg (2016). https://doi.org/10.1007/978-3-662-49096-9_9
7. Bourse, F., Del Pino, R., Minelli, M., Wee, H.: FHE circuit privacy almost for free. In: Robshaw, M., Katz, J. (eds.) CRYPTO 2016. LNCS, vol. 9815, pp. 62–89. Springer, Heidelberg (2016). https://doi.org/10.1007/978-3-662-53008-5_3
8. Brandt, J., Damgård, I.: On generation of probable primes by incremental search. In: Brickell, E.F. (ed.) CRYPTO 1992. LNCS, vol. 740, pp. 358–370. Springer, Heidelberg (1993). https://doi.org/10.1007/3-540-48071-4_26
9. Coppersmith, D.: Finding a small root of a bivariate integer equation; factoring with high bits known. In: Maurer [31], pp. 178–189
10. Coppersmith, D.: Finding a small root of a univariate modular equation. In: Maurer [31], pp. 155–165
11. Cramer, R., Shoup, V.: Signature schemes based on the strong RSA assumption. In: Motiwalla, J., Tsudik, G. (eds.) ACM CCS 99, pp. 46–51. ACM Press, November 1999
12. Csiszár, I.: Eine informationstheoretische ungleichung und ihre anwendung auf den beweis der ergodizitat von markoffschen ketten. Magyar. Tud. Akad. Mat. Kutató Int. Közl. **8**, 85–108 (1963)
13. Dai, W., Hoang, V.T., Tessaro, S.: Information-theoretic indistinguishability via the chi-squared method. In: Katz, J., Shacham, H. (eds.) CRYPTO 2017. LNCS, vol. 10403, pp. 497–523. Springer, Cham (2017). https://doi.org/10.1007/978-3-319-63697-9_17
14. Ducas, L., Lyubashevsky, V., Prest, T.: Efficient identity-based encryption over NTRU lattices. In: Sarkar, P., Iwata, T. (eds.) ASIACRYPT 2014. LNCS, vol. 8874, pp. 22–41. Springer, Heidelberg (2014). https://doi.org/10.1007/978-3-662-45608-8_2
15. Ducas, L., Stehlé, D.: Sanitization of FHE ciphertexts. In: Fischlin, M., Coron, J.-S. (eds.) EUROCRYPT 2016. LNCS, vol. 9665, pp. 294–310. Springer, Heidelberg (2016). https://doi.org/10.1007/978-3-662-49890-3_12

16. Fouque, P.-A., Tibouchi, M.: Close to uniform prime number generation with fewer random bits. In: Esparza, J., Fraigniaud, P., Husfeldt, T., Koutsoupias, E. (eds.) ICALP 2014. LNCS, vol. 8572, pp. 991–1002. Springer, Heidelberg (2014). https://doi.org/10.1007/978-3-662-43948-7_82

17. Fouque, P.-A., Tibouchi, M.: Close to uniform prime number generation with fewer random bits. IEEE Trans. Inf. Theor. **65**(2), 1307–1317 (2019)

18. Friedlander, J., Granville, A.: Limitations to the equi-distribution of primes I. Ann. Math. **129**(2), 363–382 (1989)

19. Gallagher, P.X.: On the distribution of primes in short intervals. Mathematika **23**(1), 4–9 (1976)

20. Gentry, C.: Fully homomorphic encryption using ideal lattices. In: Mitzenmacher, M. (ed.) 41st ACM STOC, pp. 169–178. ACM Press, May/June 2009

21. Gerchinovitz, S., Ménard, P., Stoltz, G.: Fano's inequality for random variables (2017). https://arxiv.org/abs/1702.05985

22. Gierlichs, B., Batina, L., Tuyls, P., Preneel, B.: Mutual information analysis. In: Oswald, E., Rohatgi, P. (eds.) CHES 2008. LNCS, vol. 5154, pp. 426–442. Springer, Heidelberg (2008). https://doi.org/10.1007/978-3-540-85053-3_27

23. Hardy, G.H., Littlewood, J.E.: Some problems of 'partitio numerorum'; iii: On the expression of a number as a sum of primes. Acta Math. **44**, 1–70 (1923)

24. Heninger, N., Durumeric, Z., Wustrow, E., Alex Halderman, J.: Mining your Ps and Qs: detection of widespread weak keys in network devices. In: Kohno, T. (ed.) USENIX Security 2012, pp. 205–220. USENIX Association, August 2012

25. Joux, A.: Fully homomorphic encryption modulo Fermat numbers. Cryptology ePrint Archive, Report 2019/187 (2019). https://eprint.iacr.org/2019/187

26. Langlois, A., Stehlé, D., Steinfeld, R.: GGHLite: more efficient multilinear maps from ideal lattices. In: Nguyen, P.Q., Oswald, E. (eds.) EUROCRYPT 2014. LNCS, vol. 8441, pp. 239–256. Springer, Heidelberg (2014). https://doi.org/10.1007/978-3-642-55220-5_14

27. Lenstra, A.K., Hughes, J.P., Augier, M., Bos, J.W., Kleinjung, T., Wachter, C.: Public keys. In: Safavi-Naini, R., Canetti, R. (eds.) CRYPTO 2012. LNCS, vol. 7417, pp. 626–642. Springer, Heidelberg (2012). https://doi.org/10.1007/978-3-642-32009-5_37

28. Lenstra, A.K., Hughes, J.P., Augier, M., Bos, J.W., Kleinjung, T., Wachter, C.: Ron was wrong, whit is right. Cryptology ePrint Archive, Report 2012/064 (2012). http://eprint.iacr.org/2012/064

29. Ling, S., Phan, D.H., Stehlé, D., Steinfeld, R.: Hardness of k-LWE and applications in traitor tracing. In: Garay, J.A., Gennaro, R. (eds.) CRYPTO 2014. LNCS, vol. 8616, pp. 315–334. Springer, Heidelberg (2014). https://doi.org/10.1007/978-3-662-44371-2_18

30. Matsuda, T., Takahashi, K., Murakami, T., Hanaoka, G.: Improved security evaluation techniques for imperfect randomness from arbitrary distributions. In: Lin, D., Sako, K. (eds.) PKC 2019. LNCS, vol. 11442, pp. 549–580. Springer, Cham (2019). https://doi.org/10.1007/978-3-030-17253-4_19

31. Maurer, U.M. (ed.): EUROCRYPT '96. LNCS, vol. 1070. Springer, Heidelberg (1996)

32. Micciancio, D., Walter, M.: Gaussian sampling over the integers: efficient, generic, constant-time. In: Katz, J., Shacham, H. (eds.) CRYPTO 2017. LNCS, vol. 10402, pp. 455–485. Springer, Cham (2017). https://doi.org/10.1007/978-3-319-63715-0_16

33. Micciancio, D., Walter, M.: On the bit security of cryptographic primitives. In: Nielsen, J.B., Rijmen, V. (eds.) EUROCRYPT 2018. LNCS, vol. 10820, pp. 3–28. Springer, Cham (2018). https://doi.org/10.1007/978-3-319-78381-9_1

34. Mihailescu, P.: Fast generation of provable primes using search in arithmetic progressions. In: Desmedt, Y.G. (ed.) CRYPTO 1994. LNCS, vol. 839, pp. 282–293. Springer, Heidelberg (1994). https://doi.org/10.1007/3-540-48658-5_27

35. Mironov, I.: Renyi differential privacy. In: Proceedings of 30th IEEE Computer Security Foundations Symposium (2017). http://arxiv.org/abs/1702.07476

36. Morimoto, T.: Markov processes and the h-theorem. J. Phys. Soc. Japan **18**(3), 328–331 (1963)

37. Nemec, M., Sýs, M., Svenda, P., Klinec, D., Matyas, V.: The return of coppersmith's attack: practical factorization of widely used RSA moduli. In: Thuraisingham, B.M., Evans, D., Malkin, T., Xu, D. (eds.) ACM CCS 2017, pp. 1631–1648. ACM Press, October/November 2017

38. Pöppelmann, T., Ducas, L., Güneysu, T.: Enhanced lattice-based signatures on reconfigurable hardware. In: Batina, L., Robshaw, M. (eds.) CHES 2014. LNCS, vol. 8731, pp. 353–370. Springer, Heidelberg (2014). https://doi.org/10.1007/978-3-662-44709-3_20

39. Prest, T.: Sharper bounds in lattice-based cryptography using the Rényi divergence. In: Takagi, T., Peyrin, T. (eds.) ASIACRYPT 2017. LNCS, vol. 10624, pp. 347–374. Springer, Cham (2017). https://doi.org/10.1007/978-3-319-70694-8_13

40. Prest, T., Goudarzi, D., Martinelli, A., Passelègue, A.: Unifying leakage models on a Rényi day. In: Boldyreva, A., Micciancio, D. (eds.) CRYPTO 2019. LNCS, vol. 11692, pp. 683–712. Springer, Cham (2019). https://doi.org/10.1007/978-3-030-26948-7_24

41. Rivest, R.L., Shamir, A., Adleman, L.M.: A method for obtaining digital signatures and public-key cryptosystems. Commun. Assoc. Comput. Mach. **21**(2), 120–126 (1978)

42. Skórski, M.: Shannon entropy versus Renyi entropy from a cryptographic viewpoint. In: Groth, J. (ed.) IMACC 2015. LNCS, vol. 9496, pp. 257–274. Springer, Cham (2015). https://doi.org/10.1007/978-3-319-27239-9_16

43. Steinberger, J.: Improved security bounds for key-alternating ciphers via hellinger distance. Cryptology ePrint Archive, Report 2012/481 (2012). http://eprint.iacr.org/2012/481

44. Takashima, K., Takayasu, A.: Tighter security for efficient lattice cryptography via the Rényi divergence of optimized orders. In: Au, M.-H., Miyaji, A. (eds.) ProvSec 2015. LNCS, vol. 9451, pp. 412–431. Springer, Cham (2015). https://doi.org/10.1007/978-3-319-26059-4_23

45. Vajda, I.: $\chi\alpha$-divergence and generalized fisher information. In: Transactions of the Sixth Prague Conference on Information Theory, Statistical Decision Functions and Random Processes, p. 223. Academia (1973)

46. van Erven, T., Harremoës, P.: Rényi divergence and Kullback-Leibler divergence. IEEE Trans. Inf. Theor. **60**(7), 3797–3820 (2014)

Impossibility of Strong KDM Security with Auxiliary Input

Cody Freitag[1]([⊠]), Ilan Komargodski[2], and Rafael Pass[1]

[1] Cornell Tech, New York City, NY, USA
{cfreitag,rafael}@cs.cornell.edu
[2] NTT Research, Palo Alto, CA, USA
ilan.komargodski@ntt-research.com

Abstract. We show that a strong notion of KDM security cannot be obtained by any encryption scheme in the auxiliary input setting, assuming Learning With Errors (LWE) and one-way permutations. The notion of security we deal with guarantees that for any (possibly inefficient) function f, it is computationally hard to distinguish between an encryption of $\mathbf{0}$ and an encryption of $f(\mathsf{pk}, z)$, where pk is the public key and z is the auxiliary input. Furthermore, we show that this holds even when restricted to bounded-length auxiliary input where z is much shorter than pk under the additional assumption that (non-leveled) fully homomorphic encryption exists.

1 Introduction

An encryption scheme is said to be key-dependent message (KDM) secure if it is secure even against adversaries who have access to encryptions of messages that depend on the secret key. This notion captures settings where there might be correlations between the secret key and the encrypted messages. Since its introduction by Black et al. [3], this notion has been extensively studied and many different definitions have been proposed and used.

We address a strong notion of KDM security with auxiliary input and show that no encryption scheme can satisfy it under widely believed cryptographic assumptions (Learning With Errors [16] and one-way permutations). At a high level, our notion of security, called *strong KDM security with auxiliary input*, requires that, for a distribution D used to (maliciously) sample public keys together with some auxiliary input, if

$$\{(z, \mathsf{pk}^*, \mathsf{Enc}_{\mathsf{pk}^*}(0))\}_{\lambda \in \mathbb{N}} \approx_c \{(z, \mathsf{pk}^*, \mathsf{Enc}_{\mathsf{pk}^*}(1))\}_{\lambda \in \mathbb{N}}$$

for $(z, \mathsf{pk}^*) \leftarrow D(1^\lambda)$, then for every (not necessarily efficient) function f such that $f(\mathsf{pk}^*, z) \in \{0,1\}^\lambda$,

$$\{(z, \mathsf{pk}^*, \mathsf{Enc}_{\mathsf{pk}^*}(0^\lambda))\}_{\lambda \in \mathbb{N}} \approx_c \{(z, \mathsf{pk}^*, \mathsf{Enc}_{\mathsf{pk}^*}(f(\mathsf{pk}^*, z)))\}_{\lambda \in \mathbb{N}}.$$

Our main result is that the above notion of security cannot exist under Learning with Errors (LWE) and one-way permutations. More generally, our result can

© Springer Nature Switzerland AG 2020
C. Galdi and V. Kolesnikov (Eds.): SCN 2020, LNCS 12238, pp. 512–524, 2020.
https://doi.org/10.1007/978-3-030-57990-6_25

be instantiated with any implementation of a *compute-and-compare* obfuscation (introduced and constructed by Goyal, Koppula, and Waters [12] and by Wichs and Zirdelis [17]) for a specific high pseudo-entropy distribution. We use the construction of [12,17] of such an obfuscator from LWE and use one-way permutations to create the aforementioned distribution.

Theorem 1 (Informal). *Assuming LWE and one-way permutations, no semantically secure encryption scheme satisfies strong KDM security with auxiliary input.*

Furthermore, we show that even if the auxiliary input z might be short, even sublinear in the size of pk, we can use *succinct* compute-and-compare obfuscation to break the assumption. Such an obfuscator is constructed in [17] from (non-leveled) fully homomorphic encryption, which exists under LWE plus an additional circular security assumption.

Theorem 2 (Informal). *Assuming LWE, (non-leveled) FHE, and one-way permutations, there is no semantically secure encryption scheme that satisfies strong KDM security with bounded auxiliary input.*

Remark 1. In a recent work, Deshpande and Kalai [7] use this notion of strong KDM security with auxiliary input to construct a 2-message witness hiding protocol. In a preliminary version [7], they define the notion without auxiliary input, but their proof of witness hiding implicitly relies on strong KDM security with respect to auxiliary input. We have communicated a preliminary version of this note to the authors of [7], and they have acknowledged the issue with their definition. In a follow-up [8], they show that considering short auxiliary input suffices for their result. However, as we show in this work, even strong KDM security with short auxiliary input is impossible, assuming standard cryptographic assumptions.

1.1   Overview of Techniques

We give a brief overview of our main techniques. Full details are given in Sect. 4. For any semantically secure encryption scheme, our goal is to construct a distribution D that outputs a (possibly malicious) public key pk* and auxiliary input z such that for some (inefficient) function f, z makes it possible to distinguish encryptions of 0^λ and $f(\text{pk}^*, z)$ but not encryptions of 0 and 1.

We start by considering the case where the auxiliary input may be of arbitrary length. We makes use of a specific pseudorandom generator G that on input a seed s outputs two parts y_1 and y_2. We require that y_1 is information theoretically determined by y_2, but y_1 is computationally indistinguishable from random given y_2. The latter property is standard for any PRG, whereas the former property can be satisfied assuming one-way permutations. The distribution D honestly samples keys (pk, sk) for an encryption scheme and will output the honestly generated public key pk. It additionally outputs auxiliary input z that depends on sk in the following way. D samples a seed s and computes $(y_1, y_2) = G(s)$.

It then computes an obfuscated circuit $\widetilde{\mathsf{CC}}$ that outputs 1 on encryptions of y_1, and outputs 0 otherwise. We emphasize that $\widetilde{\mathsf{CC}}$ depends on sk as it needs to hardcode the decryption circuit. The auxiliary input z is simply $(y_2, \widetilde{\mathsf{CC}})$. The function f on input $(\mathsf{pk}, (y_2, \widetilde{\mathsf{CC}}))$ inefficiently computes the value of y_1 that is the unique value corresponding to y_2 based on G. Then, an encryption of $f(\mathsf{pk}, (y_2, \widetilde{\mathsf{CC}}))$ is simply an encryption of y_1, which when fed as input to $\widetilde{\mathsf{CC}}$ always outputs 1. On the other hand, if $\widetilde{\mathsf{CC}}$ is obfuscated using compute-and-compare obfuscation [17] (known to exist based on LWE), we can show that encryptions of 0 and 1 are indistinguishable, even given $z = (y_2, \widetilde{\mathsf{CC}})$.

For the case of bounded auxiliary input, it suffices to make that attack work when $z = (y_2, \widetilde{\mathsf{CC}})$ is much shorter than λ. To do so, we rely on *succinct* compute-and-compare obfuscation (known to exist based on LWE and (non-leveled) FHE) for $\widetilde{\mathsf{CC}}$. We additionally *maliciously* generate the keys $(\mathsf{pk}^*, \mathsf{sk}^*)$ for the encryption scheme using randomness computed from a PRG on input a small seed. This means that sk^*—and hence $\widetilde{\mathsf{CC}}$—has a short representation. In particular, we can make y_2 and $\widetilde{\mathsf{CC}}$ in the above argument have size bounded by λ^δ for any constant $\delta \in (0, 1)$.

1.2   Related Work

In the special case where the size of the auxiliary input is unbounded (c.f. Theorem 1), an impossibility for strong KDM security follows assuming indistinguishability obfuscation for polynomial size circuits by combining the results of Canetti, Kalai, Varia, and Wichs [6] and of Brzuska and Mittelbach [4]. Our result not only relies only on LWE (rather than indistinguishability obfuscation), but we also rule out encryption schemes where the size of the auxiliary input is bounded (and in particular it is much shorter than the public-key) by additionally assuming non-leveled FHE (see Theorem 2). Such a result was not previously known even assuming indistinguishability obfuscation for all polynomial size circuits. Thus, our result is the first to show that Deshpande and Kalai's [8] encryption scheme (with bounded auxiliary input) cannot exist.

Our construction is very related to the one of Brzuska and Mittelbach [4] but the proofs are different since we use different building blocks. Following [4], Bellare, Stepanovs, and Tessaro [2] show the impossibility of key-message leakage-resilient (KM-LR) symmetric encryption assuming indistinguishability obfuscation. KM-LR requires semantic security to hold as long as the key is computationally unpredictable given the auxiliary input, which may depend on both the key and the encrypted message. While the settings are different, we believe our techniques could be adapted to rule out KM-LR security as well. We leave the details for future work.

Canetti, Chen, Reyzin, and Rothblum [5] define and give candidate encryption schemes for a similar notion of strong KDM security for symmetric key encryption schemes, but their notion does not consider auxiliary input. As such, it is not ruled out by our impossibility.

2 Preliminaries

A function μ is negligible if for every polynomial p and all sufficiently large $\lambda \in \mathbb{N}$, $\mu(\lambda) \leq 1/p(\lambda)$. A probabilistic, polynomial time (PPT) algorithm $\mathcal{A}$ is a Turing machine with access to an infinite random tape that on input x halts in time $p(|x|)$ for some polynomial p. A non-uniform PPT algorithm $\mathcal{A} = \{\mathcal{A}_\lambda\}_{\lambda \in \mathbb{N}}$ also receives polynomial-size non-uniform advice $z = z(\lambda) \in \{0,1\}^{\mathsf{poly}(\lambda)}$. We can equivalently consider each $\mathcal{A}_\lambda$ as a circuit of polynomial size. For a probabilistic algorithm $\mathcal{A}$, we write $\mathcal{A}(x;r)$ to denote running $\mathcal{A}$ on input x with a fixed random tape r, and when r is not provided, we assume that it is generated from a uniform distribution. Without loss of generality, we assume that for a non-uniform PPT algorithm $\mathcal{A}_\lambda$ receives 1^λ as its first input for all $\lambda \in \mathbb{N}$.

2.1 Computational Indistinguishability and Pseudo-Entropy

An ensemble is a sequence $X = \{X_\lambda\}_{\lambda \in \mathbb{N}}$ where for each $\lambda \in \mathbb{N}$, X_λ is a probability distribution over $\{0,1\}^*$. Let X be a probability distribution and $\mathcal{A}$ be an algorithm, then we write $\mathcal{A}(X)$ to denote the probability distribution formed by first drawing $x \leftarrow X$ and outputting $\mathcal{A}(x)$. We define the computational indistinguishability of two ensembles as follows.

Definition 1 (Computational Indistinguishability). *Let* $X = \{X_\lambda\}_{\lambda \in \mathbb{N}}$ *and* $Y = \{Y_\lambda\}_{\lambda \in \mathbb{N}}$ *be ensembles. We say that* X *and* Y *are* computationally indistinguishable, *written* $X \approx_c Y$, *if for every non-uniform PPT algorithm* $\mathcal{A} = \{\mathcal{A}_\lambda\}_{\lambda \in \mathbb{N}}$ *there exists a negligible function* μ *such that for every* $\lambda \in \mathbb{N}$,

$$| \Pr[\mathcal{A}_\lambda(1^\lambda, X_\lambda) = 1] - \Pr[\mathcal{A}_\lambda(1^\lambda, Y_\lambda) = 1] | \leq \mu(\lambda).$$

We also define what it means for an ensemble X to have "pseudo-entropy" conditioned on Y. Informally, we say that X has high pseudo-entropy conditioned on Y if there exists an ensemble X' that is computationally indistinguishable from X such that X' has high min-entropy conditioned on Y. The conditional min-entropy of two random variables X and Y, denoted $H_\infty(X \mid Y)$, is defined as follows,

$$H_\infty(X \mid Y) = -\log\left(\mathbb{E}_{y \leftarrow Y}\left[\max_x \Pr[X = x \mid Y = y] \right] \right).$$

Definition 2 (Conditional (HILL) Pseudo-Entropy) [13,14]. *Let* $X = \{X_\lambda\}_{\lambda \in \mathbb{N}}$ *and* $Y = \{Y_\lambda\}_{\lambda \in \mathbb{N}}$ *be (possibly dependent) ensembles. We say that* X *has* $\ell(\lambda)$*-pseudo-entropy conditioned on* Y, *denoted by* $H_{\mathsf{HILL}}(X \mid Y) \geq \ell(\lambda)$, *if there exists some* $X' = \{X'_\lambda\}_{\lambda \in \mathbb{N}}$ *jointly distributed with* Y *such that* $(X, Y) \approx_c (X', Y)$ *and for all* $\lambda \in \mathbb{N}$, $H_\infty(X'_\lambda \mid Y_\lambda) \geq \ell(\lambda)$.

Furthermore, when it is clear from context, we may say that a random variable X_λ has $\ell(\lambda)$-pseudo-entropy conditioned on Y_λ (which holds only for sufficiently large $\lambda \in \mathbb{N}$) when the associated ensembles X and Y satisfy $H_{\mathsf{HILL}}(X \mid Y) \geq \ell(\lambda)$.

2.2   One-Way Functions and Pseudo-Random Generators

A one-way function is a function that can be computed easily but is hard to invert for a random input, defined formally as follows.

Definition 3. *A polynomial-time computable function* $f\colon \{0,1\}^* \to \{0,1\}^*$ *is a one-way function if for every non-uniform PPT algorithm* $\mathcal{A} = \{\mathcal{A}_\lambda\}_{\lambda \in \mathbb{N}}$, *there exists a negligible function* μ *such that for every* $\lambda \in \mathbb{N}$,

$$\Pr[x \leftarrow \{0,1\}^\lambda; y \leftarrow f(x) : f(\mathcal{A}_\lambda(1^\lambda, y)) = y] \leq \mu(\lambda).$$

Given a one-way function f, a hard-core predicate h for f is a function that outputs a single bit $h(x)$ that is hard to predict given only $f(x)$.

Definition 4. *A predicate* $h\colon \{0,1\}^\lambda \to \{0,1\}$ *is a hard-core predicate for* f *if* h *is polynomial-time computable, and for every non-uniform PPT algorithm* $\mathcal{A} = \{\mathcal{A}_\lambda\}_{\lambda \in \mathbb{N}}$, *there exists a negligible function* μ *such that for every* $\lambda \in \mathbb{N}$,

$$\Pr[x \leftarrow \{0,1\}^\lambda : \mathcal{A}_\lambda(1^\lambda, f(x)) = h(x)] \leq 1/2 + \mu(\lambda).$$

Goldreich and Levin [10] construct a hard-core predicate from every one-way function.

A pseudo-random generator (PRG) is an efficiently computable function that is expanding and whose output is computationally indistinguishable from uniform random bits. It is well known that the existence of one-way functions imply the existence of pseudo-random generators [13].

Definition 5 (Pseudo-Random Generator (PRG)). *Let* $m\colon \mathbb{N} \to \mathbb{N}$ *be a function such that* $m(\lambda) > \lambda$ *for all* $\lambda \in \mathbb{N}$. *An efficiently computable function* $G\colon \{0,1\}^* \to \{0,1\}^*$ *is a* pseudo-random generator for length m *if*

$$\{x \leftarrow U_\lambda : G(x)\}_{\lambda \in \mathbb{N}} \approx_c \{U_{m(\lambda)}\}_{\lambda \in \mathbb{N}}.$$

2.3   Semantically Secure Encryption

A public-key encryption scheme consists of key generation, encryption, and decryption algorithms. At a high level, semantic security guarantees that anything that can be learned (by a non-uniform PPT algorithm) about a plaintext given an encryption of the plaintext can be learned without the encryption. Goldwasser and Micali [11] first introduced this security notion and showed that it is equivalent to an indistinguishability-based notion, which guarantees that the encryptions of any pair of messages are computationally indistinguishable. We use the indistinguishability-based notion, defined formally as follows.

Definition 6. *A semantically secure public-key encryption scheme* $\mathcal{E} = ($Gen, Enc, Dec$)$ *satisfies the following:*

- **Correctness:** *For every message* $m \in \{0,1\}^*$ *and* $\lambda \in \mathbb{N}$,

$$\Pr[(\mathsf{sk}, \mathsf{pk}) \leftarrow \mathsf{Gen}(1^\lambda) : \mathsf{Dec}_{\mathsf{sk}}(\mathsf{Enc}_{\mathsf{pk}}(m)) = m] = 1.$$

- **Semantic security:** *For ever pair of messages* $m, m' \in \{0,1\}^*$ *such that* $|m| = |m'|$,

$$\{(\mathsf{pk}, \mathsf{Enc}_{\mathsf{pk}}(m))\}_{\lambda \in \mathbb{N}} \approx_c \{(\mathsf{pk}, \mathsf{Enc}_{\mathsf{pk}}(m'))\}_{\lambda \in \mathbb{N}}$$

for $(\mathsf{sk}, \mathsf{pk}) \leftarrow \mathsf{Gen}(1^\lambda)$.

2.4 Compute-and-Compare Obfuscation

Compute-and-compare obfuscation (also known as lockable obfuscation) was first defined and constructed concurrently by [12,17]. A compute-and-compare program $\mathsf{CC}[f, u]$ has hard coded a function f and a target value u. $\mathsf{CC}[f, u](x)$ outputs 1 if $f(x) = u$ and 0 otherwise. A compute-and-compare obfuscator $\mathcal{O}$ is an efficient algorithm that takes as input a compute-and-compare program $\mathsf{CC}[f, u]$ and outputs an obfuscated circuit $\widetilde{\mathsf{CC}}$ that satisfies distributional indistinguishability for specified class of distributions $\mathcal{D}$. We define this formally as follows.

Definition 7 (Compute-and-Compare Obfuscation). *A compute-and-compare obfuscator* $\mathcal{O}$ *for a class of distributions* $\mathcal{D}$ *is a PPT algorithm that satisfies:*

1. *Correctness: there exists a negligible function* ν *such that for all* $\lambda \in \mathbb{N}$, *circuits* $f \colon \{0,1\}^n \to \{0,1\}^\lambda$, $x \in \{0,1\}^n$, $u \in \{0,1\}^\lambda$,

$$\Pr[\widetilde{\mathsf{CC}} \leftarrow \mathcal{O}(1^\lambda, \mathsf{CC}[f, u]) : \widetilde{\mathsf{CC}}(x) = \mathsf{CC}[f, u](x)] \geq 1 - \nu(\lambda);$$

2. *Simulation: there exists a simulator* Sim *such that for every distribution* $D \in \mathcal{D}$ *where* $(z, f, u) \leftarrow D(1^\lambda)$, *it holds that*

$$\{(z, \mathcal{O}(1^\lambda, \mathsf{CC}[f, u]))\}_{\lambda \in \mathbb{N}} \approx_c \{(z, \mathsf{Sim}(1^\lambda, 1^\ell))\}_{\lambda \in \mathbb{N}}$$

for $(z, f, u) \leftarrow D(1^\lambda)$, *where* f *is an* ℓ*-size circuit for* $\ell \in \mathsf{poly}(\lambda)$.

Wichs and Zirdelis [17] construct compute-and-compare obfuscation for polynomial-time samplable distributions D where $(z, f, u) \leftarrow D(1^\lambda)$ such that D is in the class of $\alpha(\cdot)$-pseudo-entropy distributions $\mathcal{D}_{\alpha\text{-pe}}$, where $H_{\mathsf{HILL}}(u \mid z, f) \geq \alpha(\lambda)$. They show how to construct compute-and-compare obfuscation for $\mathcal{D}_{\lambda^\epsilon\text{-pe}}$ for any $\epsilon > 0$ under LWE.

Let f be a circuit of size t with depth d. We say that a compute-and-compare obfuscator $\mathcal{O}$ is *succinct* if $|\mathcal{O}(1^\lambda, \mathsf{CC}[f, u])| \in \mathsf{poly}(\lambda, |f|, |u|, \log t)$ and is *weakly succinct* if $|\mathcal{O}(1^\lambda, \mathsf{CC}[f, u])| \in \mathsf{poly}(\lambda, |f|, |u|, \log t, d)$. We may also consider compute-and-compare obfuscation for Turing machines where $t(n)$ is the bound on the running time for inputs of length n. In [17], they show how to use (non-leveled) FHE for Turing machines (which exists under LWE plus additional circular security assumptions [9]) to achieve succinct compute-and-compare obfuscation. Relying on only leveled FHE (known from LWE), they also give a *weakly succinct* obfuscator.

Finally, we note that compute-and-compare obfuscation implies one-way functions [1,15] and hence pseudo-random generators [13].

3   KDM Security

We consider a definition of KDM security where a distribution D (maliciously) samples auxiliary input in addition to a public key for *any* semantically secure encryption scheme.

Definition 8 (Strong KDM Security with Auxiliary Input). *A semantically secure public-key encryption scheme* (Gen, Enc, Dec) *is said to be* strong KDM *secure with auxiliary input if for every efficiently computable (by a non-uniform PPT algorithm) distribution D used to (maliciously) sample public keys and auxiliary input it holds that if*

$$\{(z, \mathsf{pk}^*, \mathsf{Enc}_{\mathsf{pk}^*}(0))\}_{\lambda \in \mathbb{N}} \approx_c \{(z, \mathsf{pk}^*, \mathsf{Enc}_{\mathsf{pk}^*}(1))\}_{\lambda \in \mathbb{N}}$$

for $(z, \mathsf{pk}^*) \leftarrow D(1^\lambda)$, then for every (not necessarily efficient) function f such that $f(\mathsf{pk}^*, z) \in \{0,1\}^\lambda$,

$$\{(z, \mathsf{pk}^*, \mathsf{Enc}_{\mathsf{pk}^*}(0^\lambda))\}_{\lambda \in \mathbb{N}} \approx_c \{(z, \mathsf{pk}^*, \mathsf{Enc}_{\mathsf{pk}^*}(f(\mathsf{pk}^*, z)))\}_{\lambda \in \mathbb{N}}.$$

We lastly consider a more general definition where the auxiliary input z is restricted to be bounded by some arbitrary function α of the relevant parameters. Specifically, we say that a semantically secure public-key encryption scheme (Gen, Enc, Dec) is said to be *strong KDM secure with $\alpha(\cdot)$-bounded auxiliary input* if the above definition holds when D is restricted to outputting auxiliary input z such that $|z| \leq \alpha(\lambda)$. We recover the case of no auxiliary input when $\alpha = 0$ and Definition 8 when $\alpha = \infty$, i.e., unbounded auxiliary input.

4   Breaking KDM Security with Auxiliary Input

We show that strong KDM security with auxiliary input can be generically broken for any semantically secure encryption scheme assuming the existence of compute-and-compare obfuscation for a class of λ-pseudo-entropy distributions $\mathcal{D}_{\lambda\text{-pe}}$. Specifically, for any semantically secure encryption scheme, we construct a distribution D outputting a public key pk^* and auxiliary input z such that for some function f, z makes it possible to distinguish encryptions of 0^λ and $f(\mathsf{pk}^*, z)$ but not encryptions of 0 and 1. We note that, for longer messages, it is enough to consider bit-by-bit encryption in our attack.

Theorem 3 (Restatement of Theorem 1). *Assuming any semantically secure public-key encryption scheme, any compute-and-compare obfuscation scheme for λ-pseudo-entropy distributions, and one-way permutations, no semantically secure encryption scheme satisfies strong KDM security with auxiliary input.*

In the above statement, the encryption scheme and compute-and-compare obfuscation scheme are known to exist assuming LWE [17], which gives Theorem 1.

Proof. Let $\mathcal{E} = (\mathsf{Gen}, \mathsf{Enc}, \mathsf{Dec})$ be any semantically secure encryption scheme and $\mathcal{O}$ be a compute-and-compare obfuscator for λ-pseudo-entropy distributions of [17] (which exists based on LWE). Let $G\colon \{0,1\}^\lambda \to \{0,1\}^\lambda \times \{0,1\}^\lambda$ be a PRG that satisfies the following two properties:

1. *Uniqueness:* There exists a (possibly inefficient) function g such that

$$\Pr[s \leftarrow \{0,1\}^\lambda; (y_1, y_2) = G(s) : g(y_2) = y_1] = 1.$$

2. *Indistinguishability:* The following two ensembles are computationally indistinguishable:

$$\{(y_1, y_2)\}_{\lambda \in \mathbb{N}} \approx_c \{r \leftarrow \{0,1\}^\lambda : (r, y_2)\}_{\lambda \in \mathbb{N}},$$

where $(y_1, y_2) \leftarrow G(s)$ for $s \leftarrow \{0,1\}^\lambda$.

Note that the first property is specific for our application, while the second property follows from pseudorandomness.

Given such a PRG G, it immediately follows that y_1 has λ-pseudo-entropy conditioned on y_2 where $(y_1, y_2) = G(s)$ for $s \leftarrow \{0,1\}^\lambda$. Specifically, $H_{\mathsf{HILL}}(y_1 \mid y_2) \geq \lambda$ since by assumption y_1 is indistinguishable from U_λ given y_2 and $H_\infty(U_\lambda \mid y_2) = \lambda$.

We note that the standard construction of a PRG from any one-way permutation and hardcore predicate satisfies this notion. Specifically, let P be a one-way permutation with hard-core bit h, and let $P^{(i)}$ be the composition of P i times. We define

$$G(x) = (h(x) \,\|\, h(P(x)) \,\|\, \ldots \,\|\, h(P^{(\lambda-1)}(x)), P^{(\lambda)}(x)) = (y_1, y_2).$$

Uniqueness follows since P is a permutation and hence $P^{(\lambda)}$ has a unique preimage that can be used to compute y_1. Using a standard hybrid argument, indistinguishability follows by the security of the hard-core predicate h and since $P^{(i)}$ is a one-way permutation for all $i \in \mathbb{N}$.

Using the above ingredients, we consider the following distribution D.

$D(1^\lambda)$:

1. Sample $s \leftarrow \{0,1\}^\lambda$, $(y_1, y_2) = G(s)$, and $(\mathsf{pk}, \mathsf{sk}) \leftarrow \mathsf{Gen}(1^\lambda)$.
2. Compute $\widetilde{\mathsf{CC}} \leftarrow \mathcal{O}(1^\lambda, \mathsf{CC}[\mathsf{Dec}_{\mathsf{sk}}, y_1])$.
3. Let $z = (y_2, \widetilde{\mathsf{CC}})$.
4. Output (z, pk).

We show that the definition of strong KDM security with auxiliary input is broken for $\mathcal{E}$ with respect to the distribution D for function $f(\mathsf{pk}, z) = g(y_2) = y_1$, where g is the (possibly inefficient) function that exists by the uniqueness property of G. Namely, for $(z, \mathsf{pk}^*) \leftarrow D(1^\lambda)$, we show

$$\{(z, \mathsf{pk}^*, \mathsf{Enc}_{\mathsf{pk}^*}(0^\lambda))\}_{\lambda \in \mathbb{N}} \not\approx_c \{(z, \mathsf{pk}^*, \mathsf{Enc}_{\mathsf{pk}^*}(f(\mathsf{pk}^*, z)))\}_{\lambda \in \mathbb{N}}, \qquad \text{(A)}$$

but

$$\{(z, \mathsf{pk}^*, \mathsf{Enc}_{\mathsf{pk}^*}(0))\}_{\lambda \in \mathbb{N}} \approx_c \{(z, \mathsf{pk}^*, \mathsf{Enc}_{\mathsf{pk}^*}(1))\}_{\lambda \in \mathbb{N}}. \tag{B}$$

It remains to prove that (A) and (B) hold.

Proof of (A). We construct a non-uniform PPT algorithm $\mathcal{A} = \{\mathcal{A}_\lambda\}_{\lambda \in \mathbb{N}}$ such that there exists a negligible function μ that for all $\lambda \in \mathbb{N}$

$$|\Pr[\mathcal{A}_\lambda(z, \mathsf{pk}^*, \mathsf{Enc}_{\mathsf{pk}^*}(0^\lambda)) = 1] - \Pr[\mathcal{A}_\lambda(z, \mathsf{pk}^*, \mathsf{Enc}_{\mathsf{pk}^*}(f(\mathsf{pk}^*, z)))]| \geq 1 - \mu(\lambda), \tag{1}$$

for $(z, \mathsf{pk}^*) \leftarrow D(1^\lambda)$. Each $\mathcal{A}_\lambda$ is defined as follows.

$\mathcal{A}_\lambda(1^\lambda, z, \mathsf{pk}^*, \mathsf{ct})$:

1. Parse z as $(y_2, \widetilde{\mathsf{CC}})$.
2. Output $\widetilde{\mathsf{CC}}(\mathsf{ct})$.

We first bound $\Pr[\mathcal{A}_\lambda(1^\lambda, z, \mathsf{pk}^*, \mathsf{ct}) = 1]$ for $\mathsf{ct} = \mathsf{Enc}_{\mathsf{pk}^*}(f(\mathsf{pk}^*, z))$. By definition, $\mathsf{CC}[\mathsf{Dec}_{\mathsf{sk}}, y_1](\mathsf{ct})$ outputs 1 if and only if $\mathsf{Dec}_{\mathsf{sk}}(\mathsf{ct}) = y_1$. By the correctness guarantee of compute-and-compare obfuscation, there is a negligible function ν_1 such that $\widetilde{\mathsf{CC}}(\mathsf{ct}) = 1$ when $\mathsf{Dec}_{\mathsf{sk}}(\mathsf{ct}) = y_1$ with probability at least $1 - \nu_1(\lambda)$. Thus,

$$\Pr[\mathcal{A}_\lambda(z, \mathsf{pk}^*, \mathsf{Enc}_{\mathsf{pk}^*}(f(\mathsf{pk}^*, z))) = 1] \geq 1 - \nu_1(\lambda).$$

Next we bound $\Pr[\mathcal{A}_\lambda(1^\lambda, z, \mathsf{pk}^*, \mathsf{ct}) = 1]$ for $\mathsf{ct} = \mathsf{Enc}_{\mathsf{pk}^*}(0^\lambda)$. Let BAD be the event that $y_1 = 0^\lambda$. By the security of the PRG G, it must be the case that $\Pr[\mathsf{BAD}] \leq \nu_2(\lambda)$ for some negligible function ν_2. Suppose otherwise that $\Pr[\mathsf{BAD}] > 1/q(\lambda)$ for some polynomial q. Then we can construct a non-uniform PPT algorithm that distinguishes $G(U_\lambda)$ from $U_{2\lambda}$ with noticeable probability by checking if the first λ bits are all 0, which would happen with $2^{-\lambda}$ probability for $U_{2\lambda}$ and at least $1/q(\lambda)$ probability for $G(U_\lambda)$ by assumption.

Given BAD doesn't occur, $\mathsf{Dec}_{\mathsf{sk}}(\mathsf{ct}) \neq u$ by correctness of the underlying encryption scheme $\mathcal{E}$. Then by the correctness guarantee of compute-and-compare obfuscation, $\Pr[\mathcal{A}_\lambda(1^\lambda, z, \mathsf{pk}^*, \mathsf{ct}) = 1 \mid \neg\mathsf{BAD}] \leq \nu_1(\lambda)$. It follows then that for infinitely many $\lambda \in \mathbb{N}$,

$$\Pr[\mathcal{A}_\lambda(1^\lambda, z, \mathsf{pk}^*, \mathsf{Enc}_{\mathsf{pk}^*}(0^\lambda)) = 1] \leq \Pr[\mathcal{A}_\lambda(1^\lambda, z, \mathsf{pk}^*, \mathsf{Enc}_{\mathsf{pk}^*}(0^\lambda)) = 1 \mid \neg\mathsf{BAD}]$$
$$+ \Pr[\mathsf{BAD}]$$
$$\leq \nu_1(\lambda) + \nu_2(\lambda).$$

Finally, we note that Eq. 1 holds for negligible $\mu = 2\nu_1 + \nu_2$, which completes the proof of (A).

Before proving (B), we define a hybrid distribution D_{Sim} that replaces $\widetilde{\mathsf{CC}}$ with the simulated circuit Sim, which is now independent of y_1.

$D_{\mathsf{Sim}}(1^\lambda)$:

1. Sample $s \leftarrow \{0, 1\}^\lambda$, $(y_1, y_2) = G(s)$, and $(\mathsf{pk}, \mathsf{sk}) \leftarrow \mathsf{Gen}(1^\lambda)$.

2. Compute $\widetilde{\mathsf{CC}} \leftarrow \mathsf{Sim}(1^\lambda, 1^\ell)$ where ℓ is the size of the circuit computing $\mathsf{Dec_{sk}}$.
3. Let $z = (y_2, \widetilde{\mathsf{CC}})$.
4. Output (z, pk).

Fix any message m and then consider sampling $z = ((y_2, \mathcal{O}(1^\lambda, \mathsf{CC}[\mathsf{Dec_{sk}}, y_1])), \mathsf{pk}) \leftarrow D(1^\lambda)$. Since m, sk, and pk are independent of y_1 and y_1 has λ-pseudo-entropy given y_2, it follows that y_1 still has λ-pseudo-entropy given $(y_2, \mathsf{Dec_{sk}}, \mathsf{pk}, \mathsf{Enc_{pk}}(m))$. This allows us to indistinguishably replace D with D_{Sim} as long as ct is an encryption of a message m that is independent of y_1. Specifically, by the simulation guarantee of compute-and-compare obfuscation, the following equation holds for m independent of y_1,

$$\{(z, \mathsf{pk}^*) \leftarrow D(1^\lambda) : (z, \mathsf{pk}^*, \mathsf{Enc_{pk^*}}(m))\}_{\lambda \in \mathbb{N}} \approx_c \qquad (2)$$
$$\{(z, \mathsf{pk}^*) \leftarrow D_{\mathsf{Sim}}(1^\lambda) : (z, \mathsf{pk}^*, \mathsf{Enc_{pk^*}}(m))\}_{\lambda \in \mathbb{N}}$$

We are now ready to prove (B).
Proof of (B). We construct a sequence of computationally indistinguishable hybrid ensembles H_0, H_1, H_2, H_3.

– H_0: This ensemble is the left-hand side of (B).

$$H_0 = \{(z, \mathsf{pk}^*) \leftarrow D(1^\lambda) : (z, \mathsf{pk}^*, \mathsf{Enc_{pk^*}}(0))\}_{\lambda \in \mathbb{N}}$$

– H_1: This ensemble is H_0 except D is replaced with D_{Sim}.

$$H_1 = \{(z, \mathsf{pk}^*) \leftarrow D_{\mathsf{Sim}}(1^\lambda) : (z, \mathsf{pk}^*, \mathsf{Enc_{pk^*}}(0))\}_{\lambda \in \mathbb{N}}$$

– H_2: This ensemble is H_1 except $\mathsf{Enc_{pk^*}}(0)$ is replaced with $\mathsf{Enc_{pk^*}}(1)$.

$$H_2 = \{(z, \mathsf{pk}^*) \leftarrow D_{\mathsf{Sim}}(1^\lambda) : (z, \mathsf{pk}^*, \mathsf{Enc_{pk^*}}(1))\}_{\lambda \in \mathbb{N}}$$

– H_3: This ensemble is the right-hand side of (B).

$$H_3 = \{(z, \mathsf{pk}^*) \leftarrow D(1^\lambda) : (z, \mathsf{pk}^*, \mathsf{Enc_{pk^*}}(1))\}_{\lambda \in \mathbb{N}}$$

$H_0 \approx_c H_1$ and $H_2 \approx_c H_3$: These follow from Eq. 2.
$H_1 \approx_c H_2$: Suppose by way of contradiction that H_1 and H_2 are not computationally indistinguishable. Namely, there exists a non-uniform PPT algorithm $\mathcal{A} = \{\mathcal{A}_\lambda\}_{\lambda \in \mathbb{N}}$ and a polynomial p such that for infinitely many $\lambda \in \mathbb{N}$,

$$|\Pr[\mathcal{A}_\lambda(1^\lambda, z, \mathsf{pk}^*, \mathsf{Enc_{pk^*}}(0)) = 1] - \Pr[\mathcal{A}_\lambda(1^\lambda, z, \mathsf{pk}^*, \mathsf{Enc_{pk^*}}(1)) = 1]| > 1/p(\lambda),$$

for $(z, \mathsf{pk}^*) \leftarrow D_{\mathsf{Sim}}(1^\lambda)$. We use $\mathcal{A}$ to construct a non-uniform PPT algorithm $\mathcal{B} = \{\mathcal{B}_\lambda\}_{\lambda \in \mathbb{N}}$ that breaks the semantic security of $\mathcal{E}$. For $\lambda \in \mathbb{N}$, $\mathcal{B}_\lambda$ has g, Sim, and $\ell(\lambda)$ hard coded where $\ell \in \mathsf{poly}(\lambda)$ is the size of the circuit computing $\mathsf{Dec_{sk}}$. We define $\mathcal{B}_\lambda$ as follows.

$\mathcal{B}_\lambda(1^\lambda, \mathsf{pk}, \mathsf{ct})$:

1. Sample $s \leftarrow \{0,1\}^\lambda$ and compute $(y_1, y_2) = G(s)$.
2. Compute $\widetilde{\mathsf{CC}} \leftarrow \mathsf{Sim}(1^\lambda, 1^\ell)$.
3. Output $\mathcal{A}_\lambda(1^\lambda, (y_2, \widetilde{\mathsf{CC}}), \mathsf{pk}, \mathsf{ct})$.

Because $\mathcal{B}_\lambda$ computes $(y_2, \widetilde{\mathsf{CC}})$ identically to D_{Sim}, $\mathcal{B}_\lambda$ outputs 1 with the same probability as $\mathcal{A}_\lambda$. Thus, for infinitely many $\lambda \in \mathbb{N}$,

$$|\Pr[\mathcal{B}_\lambda(1^\lambda, \mathsf{pk}, \mathsf{Enc}_{\mathsf{pk}}(0)) = 1] - \Pr[\mathcal{B}_\lambda(1^\lambda, \mathsf{pk}, \mathsf{Enc}_{\mathsf{pk}}(1)) = 1] > 1/p(\lambda),$$

contradicting the semantic security of $\mathcal{E}$.
This completes the proof of (B) and hence Theorem 3.

4.1   Dealing with Bounded Auxiliary Input

We show how to deal with auxiliary input sublinear in the size of pk, which we assume to be equal to λ. We rely on the following two new ideas to deal with bounded auxiliary input:

1. We replace the compute-and-compare obfuscation with a succinct one (which requires the stronger assumption of (non-leveled) FHE).
2. We use a PRG to generate the randomness needed for key generation, which allows us to use a compressed version of the secret key sk in the obfuscation.

We note that for encryption schemes $\mathcal{E}$ where decryption can be computed by a low depth circuit, *weakly succinct* compute-and-compare obfuscation suffices, which is known from leveled FHE and can be based on LWE alone.

Theorem 4 (Restatement of Theorem 2). *Assuming any semantically secure public-key encryption scheme, any succinct compute-and-compare obfuscation scheme for λ-pseudo-entropy distributions, and one-way permutations, no semantically secure encryption scheme satisfies strong KDM security with λ^δ-bounded auxiliary input for any $\delta > 0$.*

In the above statement, the encryption scheme and succinct compute-and-compare obfuscation scheme are known to exist assuming LWE and (non-leveled) FHE [16,17], which gives Theorem 2.

Proof. For a constant $\epsilon \in (0, 1)$ (to be chosen later), we instantiate the attack of Theorem 3 with the following modifications:

1. We use a standard PRG G with seed r to maliciously choose the keys for the encryption scheme, which allows us to compute $\mathsf{Dec}_{\mathsf{sk}}$ with a function Dec_r^* such that $|\mathsf{Dec}_r^*| \leq \lambda^\epsilon$.
2. We use a PRG $G': \{0,1\}^{\lambda^\epsilon} \rightarrow \{0,1\}^{\lambda^\epsilon} \times \{0,1\}^{\lambda^\epsilon}$, i.e., the seed s is sampled from $\{0,1\}^{\lambda^\epsilon}$, satisfying uniqueness and indistinguishability as in Theorem 3. Since ϵ is constant, G' satisfies polynomial security in λ.

3. We use λ^ϵ as the security parameter for a *succinct* compute-and-compare obfuscation for λ^ϵ-pseudo-entropy distributions, i.e., $\widetilde{CC} = \mathcal{O}(1^{\lambda^\epsilon}, CC[Dec_r^*, y_1])$. Such a succinct obfuscator exists using (non-leveled) FHE by [17]. Also, since ϵ is constant, $\mathcal{O}$ satisfies polynomial security in λ.

Let $\mathcal{E} = (Gen, Enc, Dec)$ be any semantically secure encryption scheme such that Gen uses $k(\lambda)$ bits of randomness, and let G be a secure PRG for length $k^{1/\epsilon}(\lambda) \in poly(\lambda)$. Consider the following distribution D.

$D(1^\lambda)$:

1. Sample $s \leftarrow \{0,1\}^{\lambda^\epsilon}$, $(y_1, y_2) = G'(s)$, $r \leftarrow \{0,1\}^{\lambda^\epsilon}$, and $(pk^*, sk^*) \leftarrow Gen(1^\lambda; G(r))$.
2. Construct Dec_r^* to be the function that, on input ct, first computes $(pk^*, sk^*) \leftarrow Gen(1^\lambda; G(r))$ and outputs $Dec_{sk^*}(ct)$.
3. Compute $\widetilde{CC} \leftarrow \mathcal{O}(1^{\lambda^\epsilon}, CC[Dec_r^*, y_1])$.
4. Let $z = (y_2, \widetilde{CC})$.
5. Output (z, pk^*).

We note that we can represent Dec_r^* with $O(1) + \lambda^\epsilon$ bits as a constant size Turing machine that runs in polynomial-time with r hard-coded. Since the compute-and-compare obfuscator is succinct, this implies that $|z| \leq (\lambda^\epsilon)^c$ for some constant c. We choose $\epsilon \leq \delta/c$ such that $|z| \leq \lambda^\delta$.

To finish the proof of the theorem, it remains to argue that correctness and semantic security of the encryption scheme still hold when maliciously using a PRG to generate the keys as in D. Correctness holds since $\mathcal{E}$ satisfies perfect correctness, i.e., correctness holds no matter what randomness is used by Gen. Semantic security holds by the PRG security of G and semantic security of the underlying encryption scheme. Specifically, if we could distinguish encryptions of m and m' when the randomness for Gen is generated by G, we could either distinguish $G(U_{\lambda^\epsilon})$ from $U_{k(\lambda)}$ or distinguish encryptions of m and m' for $\mathcal{E}$. The rest of the proof is identical to that of Theorem 3.

Acknowledgements. This work was supported in part by NSF Award SATC-1704788, NSF Award RI-1703846, AFOSR Award FA9550-18-1-0267, and by NSF Award DGE-1650441. This research is based upon work supported in part by the Office of the Director of National Intelligence (ODNI), Intelligence Advanced Research Projects Activity (IARPA), via 2019-19-020700006. The views and conclusions contained herein are those of the authors and should not be interpreted as necessarily representing the official policies, either expressed or implied, of ODNI, IARPA, or the U.S. Government. The U.S. Government is authorized to reproduce and distribute reprints for governmental purposes notwithstanding any copyright annotation therein.

References

1. Barak, B., et al.: On the (im)possibility of obfuscating programs. J. ACM **59**(2), 6:1–6:48 (2012)

2. Bellare, M., Stepanovs, I., Tessaro, S.: Contention in cryptoland: obfuscation, leakage and UCE. In: Kushilevitz, E., Malkin, T. (eds.) TCC 2016. LNCS, vol. 9563, pp. 542–564. Springer, Heidelberg (2016). https://doi.org/10.1007/978-3-662-49099-0_20

3. Black, J., Rogaway, P., Shrimpton, T.: Encryption-scheme security in the presence of key-dependent messages. In: Nyberg, K., Heys, H. (eds.) SAC 2002. LNCS, vol. 2595, pp. 62–75. Springer, Heidelberg (2003). https://doi.org/10.1007/3-540-36492-7_6

4. Brzuska, C., Mittelbach, A.: Indistinguishability obfuscation versus multi-bit point obfuscation with auxiliary input. In: Sarkar, P., Iwata, T. (eds.) ASIACRYPT 2014. LNCS, vol. 8874, pp. 142–161. Springer, Heidelberg (2014). https://doi.org/10.1007/978-3-662-45608-8_8

5. Canetti, R., Chen, Y., Reyzin, L., Rothblum, R.D.: Fiat-Shamir and correlation intractability from strong KDM-secure encryption. In: Nielsen, J.B., Rijmen, V. (eds.) EUROCRYPT 2018. LNCS, vol. 10820, pp. 91–122. Springer, Cham (2018). https://doi.org/10.1007/978-3-319-78381-9_4

6. Canetti, R., Tauman Kalai, Y., Varia, M., Wichs, D.: On symmetric encryption and point obfuscation. In: Micciancio, D. (ed.) TCC 2010. LNCS, vol. 5978, pp. 52–71. Springer, Heidelberg (2010). https://doi.org/10.1007/978-3-642-11799-2_4

7. Deshpande, A., Kalai, Y.: Proofs of ignorance and applications to 2-message witness hiding. IACR Cryptology ePrint Archive 2018/896 (2018). version dated: 25-Sept- 2018

8. Deshpande, A., Kalai, Y.: Proofs of ignorance and applications to 2-message witness hiding. IACR Cryptology ePrint Archive 2018/896 (2018). version dated: 02-Mar-2019

9. Gentry, C., Sahai, A., Waters, B.: Homomorphic encryption from learning with errors: conceptually-simpler, asymptotically-faster, attribute-based. In: Canetti, R., Garay, J.A. (eds.) CRYPTO 2013. LNCS, vol. 8042, pp. 75–92. Springer, Heidelberg (2013). https://doi.org/10.1007/978-3-642-40041-4_5

10. Goldreich, O., Levin, L.A.: A hard-core predicate for all one-way functions. In: STOC, pp. 25–32. ACM (1989)

11. Goldwasser, S., Micali, S.: Probabilistic encryption. J. Comput. Syst. Sci. 28(2), 270–299 (1984)

12. Goyal, R., Koppula, V., Waters, B.: Lockable obfuscation. In: 58th IEEE Annual Symposium on Foundations of Computer Science (FOCS), pp. 612–621 (2017)

13. Håstad, J., Impagliazzo, R., Levin, L.A., Luby, M.: A pseudorandom generator from any one-way function. SIAM J. Comput. 28(4), 1364–1396 (1999)

14. Hsiao, C.-Y., Lu, C.-J., Reyzin, L.: Conditional computational entropy, or toward separating pseudoentropy from compressibility. In: Naor, M. (ed.) EUROCRYPT 2007. LNCS, vol. 4515, pp. 169–186. Springer, Heidelberg (2007). https://doi.org/10.1007/978-3-540-72540-4_10

15. Komargodski, I., Moran, T., Naor, M., Pass, R., Rosen, A., Yogev, E.: One-way functions and (im)perfect obfuscation. In: 55th IEEE Annual Symposium on Foundations of Computer Science (FOCS), pp. 374–383 (2014)

16. Regev, O.: On lattices, learning with errors, random linear codes, and cryptography. In: STOC, pp. 84–93. ACM (2005)

17. Wichs, D., Zirdelis, G.: Obfuscating compute-and-compare programs under LWE. In: 58th IEEE Annual Symposium on Foundations of Computer Science (FOCS), pp. 600–611 (2017)

Multi-Client Inner-Product Functional Encryption in the Random-Oracle Model

Michel Abdalla[1,2](✉) (iD), Florian Bourse[1,2](✉), Hugo Marival[1,2](✉),
David Pointcheval[1,2](✉) (iD), Azam Soleimanian[1,2](✉),
and Hendrik Waldner[3](✉) (iD)

[1] DIENS, École normale supérieure, CNRS, PSL University, Paris, France
{michel.abdalla,florian.bourse,hugo.marival,david.pointcheval,
azam.soleimanian}@ens.fr
[2] INRIA, Paris, France
[3] University of Edinburgh, Edinburgh, UK
hendrik.waldner@ed.ac.uk

Abstract. Multi-client functional encryption (MCFE) is an extension of functional encryption (FE) in which the decryption procedure involves ciphertexts from multiple parties. It is particularly useful in the context of data outsourcing and cloud computing where the data may come from different sources and where some data centers or servers may need to perform different types of computation on this data. In order to protect the privacy of the encrypted data, the server, in possession of a functional decryption key, should only be able to compute the final result in the clear, but no other information regarding the encrypted data. In this paper, we consider MCFE schemes supporting encryption labels, which allow the encryptor to limit the amount of possible mix-and-match that can take place during the decryption. This is achieved by only allowing the decryption of ciphertexts that were generated with respect to the same label. This flexible form of FE was already investigated by Chotard et al. at Asiacrypt 2018 and Abdalla et al. at Asiacrypt 2019. The former provided a general construction based on different standard assumptions, but its ciphertext size grows quadratically with the number of clients. The latter gave a MCFE based on Decisional Diffie-Hellman (DDH) assumption which requires a small inner-product space. In this work, we overcome the deficiency of these works by presenting three constructions with linear-sized ciphertexts based on the Matrix-DDH (MDDH), Decisional Composite Residuosity (DCR) and Learning with Errors (LWE) assumption in the random-oracle model. We also implement our constructions to evaluate their concrete efficiency.

Keywords: Functional encryption · Multi-client · Inner-product functionality · Random oracle

1 Introduction

Functional encryption (FE) [9,22] is an encryption scheme that goes beyond all-or-nothing decryption, allowing users in possession of a secret functional decryp-

© Springer Nature Switzerland AG 2020
C. Galdi and V. Kolesnikov (Eds.): SCN 2020, LNCS 12238, pp. 525–545, 2020.
https://doi.org/10.1007/978-3-030-57990-6_26

tion key to learn a specific function of the encrypted message, and nothing else. More formally, in an FE scheme for a class of functions F, a ciphertext encrypting a message x can be used in conjunction with a functional decryption key dk_f, derived for a function f from F, in order to compute $f(x)$ while no more information about x is leaked. Due to its generality, FE encompasses many existing notions, such as identity-based encryption [8,13,27] and attribute-based encryption [19,23,25]. Now, general purpose FE is seen as a holy grail for modern cryptography. Several works have made progress towards this goal [10,15,26], but no constructions are known from standard assumptions. Since general-purpose FE still remains far from reality, different lines of work focused on building FE for specialized classes of functions, such as predicate encryption or inner-product FE.

Inner-product FE (IPFE) is a special case of FE [2] in which the encrypted messages are vectors x, and the functional decryption keys dk_y, are associated with vectors y of the same dimension, and the decryption yields the inner-product between those two vectors (i.e., $\langle x, y \rangle$). It was first considered in [2] as the first efficient encryption scheme going beyond all-or-nothing decryption. The class of functions defined is simple enough to allow practical instantiations, as it is only linear, but still allows for many applications. In particular, it allows for any bounded depth computation by properly increasing the size of the inputs [6,7].

Multi-client FE (MCFE), introduced in [18] , is a natural extension of FE where data comes from different sources/clients that may not trust each other and can be independently and adaptively corrupted by the adversary. The special case of Multi-input FE (MIFE) [4,5] corresponds to the setting where the clients are honest but curious, and each coordinate of a vector can be encrypted separately before being combined during the decryption procedure. The main challenge to overcome when designing MCFE is that the different parts of the ciphertext have to be crafted without sharing any randomness, as opposed to what happens in all the existing constructions for single-input IPFE (or simply IPFE).

MCFE with labels, introduced in [18] and recast in the context of the inner-product functionality by [11], allows for more control over the data during the encryption. In an MCFE scheme with labels, ciphertexts strictly depend on labels. When combining ciphertexts during the decryption procedure, data associated with different labels cannot be mixed to give a valid decryption or useful information. Thus, the data from different sources can only be combined if they have the same label. The construction suggested in [11] for the inner-product functionality is based on the Decisional Diffie-Hellman (DDH) assumption, and one of its drawbacks is that the decryption algorithm needs to compute the discrete logarithm of a group element, which means it can only support a small range of values for the inner-products, thus limiting its possible applications. Abdalla et al. [1] proposed a general compiler from single-input FE to MCFE. In their scheme, each client i encrypts its message x_i as the vector $(0||\ldots||0||x_i||0||\ldots||0) + t_{i,\ell}$ where $t_{i,\ell}$ is generated by a PRF with shared keys such that $\sum_{i=1}^{n} t_{i,\ell} = 0$, with n the number of clients. From there, by applying a layer of single-input IPFE they get a labeled MCFE scheme. This explains why the size of the ciphertext in their scheme is quadratic w.r.t the number of the slots/clients. Note that their scheme also needs a master secret key of size $O(n^2)$ which is the number of keys $k_{i,j}$ shared between clients i and j.

1.1   Challenges and Contributions

This paper aims at constructing efficient labeled MCFE schemes based on different assumptions. Our contributions can be summarized as follows:

Efficient Decryption and Shorter Ciphertext. We present two constructions: one based on the Decisional Composite Residuosity (DCR) assumption and the other one based on the Learning with Errors (LWE) assumption. These constructions can cope with the drawbacks in the constructions of [11] and [1], i.e. the size of the ciphertext is smaller (w.r.t the number of clients) and, compared to [11], they do not require a discrete-logarithm computation in the decryption algorithm. The security proof of our constructions based on DCR and LWE can be more challenging than the proof of MCFE schemes based on DDH. This difficulty comes from the fact that MCFE is in the symmetric key setting and the hybrid argument for many challenges can be complicated. More precisely, one needs to show that in the current hybrid game, given the information regarding the master secret key that is leaked through all other queries (encryption, functional keys, and random-oracle (RO) queries) the master secret key still has enough entropy to hide the chosen bit in the challenge ciphertext. This is easier to prove in DDH-based MCFE schemes since the master secret key is uniformly distributed over $\mathbb{Z}_q$ and the ciphertexts are defined in a group with the same order. This common modulus not only helps to interpret the leaked information more straightforwardly, but also to prove that the chosen bit can be perfectly hidden. However, for our DCR-based MCFE, this is not the case, and one needs to check how the leaked information can change the lattice to which the master secret key belongs (since the master secret key is distributed over the lattice $\mathbb{Z}^n$) and how it can affect the challenge which is a value modulo N. By relying on a theorem from lattice-based cryptography, setting the parameters similarly to the single-input IPFE of [6], and also by a proper simulation of random-oracle queries one can guarantee that the information leaked through the encryption queries is still tolerable, and that the security proof works. Slightly in detail, the proper simulation of random-oracle queries let us unify the leakage from all other ciphertexts. This unified information is the same as the leaked information from the public-key in [6]. Then, we can use the same strategy of [6] to show that the challenge ciphertext hides the chosen bit statistically w.r.t a selective-security notion. But the good point is that all other steps which are based on the computational-assumption DCR are adaptively secure. Thus, we only need to lift the security from selective to adaptive in our statistical argument, which is possible by a proper choice of parameters. All left to discuss is the simulation of the RO queries such that it can unify and properly interpret the leakage from all other ciphertexts. Here, we use the random self-reducibility of the DCR assumption which lets us build polynomially many random samples of DCR from one given sample. RO queries can the be replaced by these random samples. The common point about all these samples is that they are indistinguishable from elements in the class of N residues in $\mathbb{Z}_{N^2}$ and so they all have the same structure $z_\ell^N \mod N^2$. Having this N common among all the RO queries is what we needed as a tool to unify the leakage from ciphertexts. More precisely, the leakage from all other ciphertexts can be interpreted independently of ℓ as $s \mod \lambda$ (where s is the secret-key, $\mathcal{H}(\ell)^s$ appears in the ciphertexts, and λ is such that $z_\ell^{N\lambda} = 1 \mod N^2$).

For our LWE-based MCFE scheme (which can bee seen as the main contribution), it is more challenging since the information that is leaked through the encryption queries cannot be simulated during the security proof, due to the noise terms introduced by the LWE assumption. We overcome this challenge using noise flooding techniques, and by avoiding the inefficiency drawback by rounding the ciphertext down to a smaller space. This way, the noise vanishes during this rounding operation. The remaining leakage concerns as part of the master secret key that is uniformly random, and can easily be simulated. More precisely, in our LWE-based construction, ciphertexts include a multiplication term $\mathbf{Z}_i \cdot \mathcal{H}(\ell)$ where $\mathbf{Z}_i = (s_i, t_i)$ comes from the master key and $\mathcal{H}(\ell)$ is a hash function modeled as a RO. This has to be a RO on $\mathbb{Z}_q$ leading us to replace it with LWE samples (which give randomness over $\mathbb{Z}_q$) i.e., $\mathcal{H}(\ell) = (a_\ell, \mathbf{S}a_\ell + e_\ell)$. The term $t_i \cdot e_\ell$ is what can dramatically leak information about $\mathbf{Z}_i$. In the proof of Agrawal et al. [6] for IPFE, the term $\mathbf{S}a$ can be placed in the ciphertext directly since the client knows the secret $\mathbf{S}$. But for our labeled MCFE this is not the case and the term e_ℓ has to be there which leads to the leakage $t_i \cdot e_\ell$. Thus, we map the ciphertext from $\mathbb{Z}_q$ to a small space $\mathbb{Z}_{q_0}$ such that the term $t_i \cdot e_\ell$ is small enough to be neglected after this change. The term $t_i \cdot \mathbf{S}a_\ell$ would be hidden through the term $s_i \cdot a_\ell$ where s_i is uniform[1]. These two strategies give us the guarantee that no information about t_i is leaked through encryption queries. We then show that given the other sources of information that the adversary may access (functional keys and corruption queries), the master secret key t_i still has enough entropy to be used in a left-over hash lemma argument and statistically hides the message-challenge w.r.t a selective-security notion. Then similar to our discussion for DCR-based MCFE, one can simply lift the security to the adaptive case by a proper choice of parameters.

Now we discuss the simulation of the RO queries in the LWE-based construction. A curious reader may already have noticed that unlike the DCR-based MCFE scheme where we use the random self-reducibility of the DCR assumption, we may not be able to do the same here. Fortunately, the definition of the LWE problem already provides polynomially many samples for the same secret $\mathbf{S}$ as $(a_\ell, \mathbf{S}a_\ell + e_\ell)$ where $\mathbf{S}$ is a vector. We simply extend it to the case where $\mathbf{S}$ is a matrix. Note that the requirement for a matrix-secret instead of vector-secret comes from the security proof, since having $\mathbf{S}$ as a matrix gives t_i as a

---

[1] Note that we have $\mathbf{Z}_i \cdot \mathcal{H}(\ell) = s_i \cdot a_\ell + t_i \cdot (\mathbf{S}a_\ell + e_\ell)$.

vector (note that in the ciphertext we have $\mathbf{Z}_i \cdot \mathcal{H}(\ell) = \mathbf{s}_i \cdot \mathbf{a}_\ell + \mathbf{t}_i \cdot (\mathbf{S}\mathbf{a}_\ell + \mathbf{e}_\ell)$
where $\mathbf{Z}_i = (\mathbf{s}_i, \mathbf{t}_i)$ is the secret-key). Then having $\mathbf{t}_i$ as a vector provides enough
entropy in the term $(x^1 - x^0) \cdot (\mathbf{t}_1, \ldots, \mathbf{t}_n)^T$ which will be used in a left-over-
hash-lemma argument to conclude that the challenge ciphertext is statistically
independent of the chosen bit.

Various Assumptions. Following the constructions proposed by Chotard et
al. [11], we present a generalization of their scheme, relying on the Matrix-DDH
(MDDH) assumption[2]. Our Labeled MCFE scheme based on DCR assumption is
the first labeled MCFE scheme with linear ciphertext size based on this assumption. Our labeled MCFE scheme based on LWE is the most efficient MCFE
scheme based on this assumption compared to [1,21], albeit in the ROM.

Implementation. We have also implemented our constructions showing that
for applications with large message spaces our DCR-based MCFE scheme is
quite reliable while for small message space our LWE-based MCFE scheme is
more efficient. This gives enough flexibility to choose the scheme that better fits
the application. Apart from the size of the message space, other parameters are
chosen so that the schemes can support different applications.

1.2   Related Work

Here, we mainly discuss the three mentioned works [1,11,21] which are directly
relevant to our contributions. The main security notions used in these papers are
one-security and pos$^+$-security. In one-security, the adversary can ask for many
labels but for each label it can ask only one complete ciphertext. In pos$^+$-security,
the adversary can ask for many ciphertexts per label[3].

In [11], instead of proving pos$^+$-security, the authors first prove one-security
for their construction and then apply a compiler similar to [4,5] to lift the security
to pos$^+$. As in [4,5], this compiler is actually a single-input IPFE layer. We
also use this technique in this paper. The security in [11] relies on the DDH
assumption in the ROM. The ciphertext in their scheme has the form $\mathsf{ct}_{i,\ell} = g^{x_i} \cdot \mathcal{H}(\ell)^{s_i}$. The main challenge in the proof is to bound the leakage from the
ciphertexts (as we are in the symmetric key setting with many ciphertexts to be
handled directly). The idea is to change the RO queries in an indistinguishable
way such that all the encryption queries, except for the challenge query, have
the same form (i.e., $\mathcal{H}(\ell) = g^{u_\ell}$ where $u_\ell = r_\ell \cdot a$, $a = (1 \ a)^T$, $r_\ell, a \xleftarrow{R} \mathbb{Z}_p$)
leading to the same leakage $s_i \cdot a$ from all other encryption queries. This leakage,
along with the leakage from the functional secret keys and corrupted individual
encryption keys, would change the distribution of the master secret key such
that the multiplication $s_i \cdot u_{\ell^*}$ (where $u_{\ell^*} = u_1 a + u_2 a^\perp$, $u_1 \xleftarrow{R} \mathbb{Z}_p$, $u_2 \xleftarrow{R} \mathbb{Z}_p^*$)
perfectly hides the chosen bit in the challenge. More precisely, the secret key

---

[2] Which is a generalization of the DDH assumption including many other assumptions
such as k-LIN and 2-SCasc [14], as special cases.

[3] Note that these security notions are respectively called *without repetition* and *with
repetition* in [11,12] . Here we are following the terminologies of [1].

is computed as $s_i + a^\perp \gamma(x_i^1 - x_i^0)$ where $\gamma = -1/u_{\ell^*} \cdot a^T$ and $s_i \xleftarrow{R} \mathbb{Z}_p^2$. The ciphertext is of linear size while one needs to compute a discrete-logarithm during the decryption.

In [1], as we mentioned at the beginning of this section, each client builds a value $t_{i,\ell}$ such that $\sum t_{i,\ell} = 0$. For the security proof, they simply change the values of $t_{i,\ell}$ among the slots such that each $t_{i,\ell}$ is replaced with a random value except one of them associated with an honest slot, called i^*, which takes care of the relation $\sum t_{i,\ell} = 0$. Then, one-security would be reduced to the PRF property[4]. Despite relying on standard assumptions, their scheme needs $O(n^2)$ secret keys and the ciphertext-size is $O(n^2)$.

In [21], similarly to [11], each ciphertext $\mathsf{ct}_{i,\ell} = \mathbf{G}_0^T \cdot x_i + \mathbf{A}(\ell)^T \cdot s_i + \mathsf{noise}$ has a product term $\mathbf{A}^T(\ell) \cdot s_i$ which hides the chosen bit in the challenge. Unlike our constructions, the matrix $\mathbf{A}(\ell)$ is built from some public matrices and the label ℓ, rather than a RO, using an idea from [20] to derive $\mathbf{A}(\ell)$ from some public matrices using the Gentry-Sahai-Waters (GSW) fully homomorphic encryption scheme [16] (which is a source of inefficiency for the resulting MCFE scheme). That is, $\mathbf{A}(\ell)$ is the product of GSW ciphertexts dictated by a special hash applied to ℓ. The security proof relies on the fact that, with noticeable probability, $\mathbf{A}(\ell)$ is a GSW encryption of 1. From there, it can be indistinguishably changed to the GSW-encryption of 0 in all other encryption queries, except for the challenge. Finally, an argument similar to [11] (through the lossy form of matrix $\mathbf{A}$) is used to conclude the proof. Another point is that in [21], they use noise flooding to prevent the noise terms from leaking information on the master secret key, while we are using the rounding-map leading to smaller ciphertexts.

Figure 1 compares our LWE-based MCFE scheme with the schemes of [1] and [21]. We have considered the instantiation of [1] based on the LWE-based IPFE scheme of [6]. In this table, κ and n_0 are security parameters where n_0 is the size of the secret. In our scheme, $m_0 > \Omega(\log q)$ for selective security and $m_0 > \Omega(\log q + 4n \cdot \log P)$ for the adaptive case where n is the number of slots and P defines the bound of the message-space. And we also have $q_0 = \mathsf{poly}(n_0)$ and B is a constant as the bound of the error-space. And σ stands for the standard-deviation used in the generation of msk. So, as one can conclude from this table, for the client i, the size of its secret-key sk_i and also the size of public-parameters pp in [1], depend on the number of clients n, while in [21] and in our scheme they are constant (w.r.t n). Still one can argue that for the scheme of [21], the size of sk_i and pp is much larger comparing with our scheme. Note that the security parameter for their scheme is κ and for our scheme is n_0 which means that our scheme has linear-size of sk_i and pp w.r.t to the security parameter. While in [21] they are polynomials respectively of degree 5 and 13 (w.r.t the security parameter). In [1], the size of public-parameters also depends on n_0 which is the security-parameter for the underlying LWE scheme [6]. In our scheme the only public-parameter is the hash function (modeled as a random oracle) and it is a vector of size $n_0 + m_0$. While [6] has some matrices as the public parameters

---

[4] In their construction, they apply the compiler, for going from one to pos^+, which gives pos^+ directly.

Scheme	$|\mathsf{sk}_i|$	$|\mathsf{pp}|$	$|\mathsf{ct}|$	q	σ (msk)	model
[1] [6]	$O(n\kappa)$	$O(n_0(n_0+n)\log q)$	$n^2\log q$	$\mathrm{poly}(n_0)$	$\mathrm{poly}(n_0)$	SM
[21]	$O(\kappa^5)$	$O(\kappa^{13})$	$O(n\kappa^7\log q)$	2^{κ^2}	$O(2^{\kappa^2})$	SM
our scheme	n_0+m_0	n_0+m_0	$n\log q_0$	$\Omega(n_0{}^{\omega(1)}q_0 B)$	$\omega(1)$	ROM

Fig. 1. Comparison for LWE-based MCFE schemes

leading to a size of degree 2 polynomial for $|\mathsf{pp}|$ (w.r.t the security parameter), while in our scheme it is linear. About size of the ciphertext ct, in [1], it has square-size w.r.t the number of clients and in [21] has 7-degree-size w.r.t the security parameter. While in our scheme it is linear w.r.t to n and logarithmic w.r.t the security parameter.

Putting everything together, this table shows that having constant or linear size of sk_i, pp or ct w.r.t n can be challenging and leads to a polynomial-size of large degree w.r.t other parameters. We avoid this inefficiency by relying on the random oracle.

2   Preliminaries

Notation. We use $[n]$ to denote the set $\{1,\ldots,n\}$. We write $\boldsymbol{x}$ for vectors and x_i for the i-th element. In this paper, κ stands for the security parameter. The function $\mathrm{poly}(\cdot)$ shows an arbitrary polynomial function. The computational indistinguishability of two distributions G_0 and G_1, is denoted by $\mathsf{G}_0 \cong \mathsf{G}_1$. The function $\mathrm{negl}(\cdot)$ denotes the negligible function. In this paper all the algorithms are Probabilistic Polynomial Time (p.p.t.) with respect to the length of the input. For security parameter κ and additional parameters n, we denote the winning probability of an adversary $\mathcal{A}$ in a game or experiment G as $\mathsf{Win}_{\mathcal{A}}^{\mathsf{G}}(\kappa, n)$. The probability is taken over the random coins of G and $\mathcal{A}$. We define the distinguishing advantage between games G_0 and G_1 of an adversary $\mathcal{A}$ in the following way: $\mathsf{Adv}_{\mathcal{A}}^{\mathsf{G}}(\kappa, n) = \left|\mathsf{Win}_{\mathcal{A}}^{\mathsf{G}_0}(\kappa, n) - \mathsf{Win}_{\mathcal{A}}^{\mathsf{G}_1}(\kappa, n)\right|$.

2.1   Multi-Client Functional Encryption

A labeled MCFE scheme is formally defined as follows, which is an adaptation of the MIFE definition [17] with labels.

Definition 1 (Multi-Client Functional Encryption). *Let $\mathcal{F} = \{\mathcal{F}_\rho\}_\rho$ be a family (indexed by ρ) of sets $\mathcal{F}_\rho$ of functions $f\colon \mathcal{X}_{\rho,1} \times \cdots \times \mathcal{X}_{\rho,n_\rho} \to \mathcal{Y}_\rho{}^5$. Let $\mathsf{Labels} = \{0,1\}^*$ or $\{\bot\}$ be a set of labels. A multi-client functional encryption scheme (MCFE) for the function family $\mathcal{F}$ and the label set Labels is a tuple of five algorithms $\mathsf{MCFE} = (\mathsf{Setup}, \mathsf{KeyGen}, \mathsf{KeyDer}, \mathsf{Enc}, \mathsf{Dec})$:*

---

[5] All the functions inside the same set $\mathcal{F}_\rho$ have the same domain and the same range.

Setup($1^\kappa, 1^n$): *Takes as input a security parameter κ and the number of parties n, and generates public parameters* pp. *The public parameters implicitly define an index ρ corresponding to a set $\mathcal{F}_\rho$ of n-ary functions (i.e., $n = n_\rho$).*

KeyGen(pp): *Takes as input the public parameters* pp *and outputs n secret keys $\{sk_i\}_{i \in [n]}$ and a master secret key* msk.

KeyDer(pp, msk, f): *Takes as input the public parameters* pp, *the master secret key* msk *and a function $f \in \mathcal{F}_\rho$, and outputs a functional decryption key* sk_f.

Enc(pp, sk_i, x_i, ℓ): *Takes as input the public parameters* pp, *a secret key* sk_i, *a message $x_i \in \mathcal{X}_{\rho,i}$ to encrypt, a label $\ell \in$* Labels, *and outputs ciphertext* $ct_{i,\ell}$.

Dec(pp, $sk_f, ct_{1,\ell}, \ldots, ct_{n,\ell}$): *Takes as input the public parameters* pp, *a functional key sk_f and n ciphertexts under the same label ℓ and outputs a value $y \in \mathcal{Y}_\rho$.*

A *scheme* MCFE *is correct, if for all $\kappa, n \in \mathbb{N}$,* pp $\leftarrow$ Setup($1^\kappa, 1^n$)*, $f \in \mathcal{F}_\rho$, $\ell \in$ Labels, $x_i \in \mathcal{X}_{\rho,i}$, when $(\{sk_i\}_{i \in [n]},$ msk$) \leftarrow$ KeyGen(pp) and $sk_f \leftarrow$ KeyDer(pp, msk, f), we have*

$$\Pr\left[\text{Dec}(\text{pp}, sk_f, \text{Enc}(\text{pp}, sk_1, x_1, \ell), \ldots, \text{Enc}(\text{pp}, sk_n, x_n, \ell)) = f(x_1, \ldots, x_n)\right] = 1.$$

Please note that each slot i in a MCFE scheme has a different secret key sk_i, which can be individually corrupted. In addition, one also needs to consider corruptions to handle possible collusions between different parties. In the following, we formally define the security notion of a MCFE scheme.

Definition 2 (Security of MCFE). *Let* MCFE *be an MCFE scheme and* Labels *a label set. For $\beta \in \{0, 1\}$, we define the experiment IND_β^{MCFE} in Fig. 2, where the oracles are defined as:*

Corruption oracle QCor(i): *Outputs the encryption key sk_i of slot i. We denote by $\mathcal{CS}$ the set of corrupted slots at the end of the experiment.*

Left-Right oracle QLeftRight(i, x_i^0, x_i^1, ℓ): *Outputs $ct_{i,\ell} =$ Enc(pp, sk_i, x_i^β, ℓ) on a query (i, x_i^0, x_i^1, ℓ). We denote by $Q_{i,\ell}$ the number of queries of the form* QLeftRight($i, \cdot, \cdot, \ell$).

Encryption oracle QEnc(i, x_i, ℓ): *Outputs $ct_{i,\ell} =$ Enc(sk_i, x_i, ℓ) on a query (i, x_i, ℓ).*

Key derivation oracle QKeyD(f): *Outputs $dk_f =$ KeyGen(msk, f).*

and where Condition (*) *holds if all the following conditions hold:*

- *If $i \in \mathcal{CS}$ (i.e., slot i is corrupted): for any query* QLeftRight(i, x_i^0, x_i^1, ℓ), *$x_i^0 = x_i^1$.*
- *For any label $\ell \in$ Labels, for any family of queries $\{$QLeftRight(i, x_i^0, x_i^1, ℓ) or QEnc(i, x_i, ℓ)$\}_{i \in [n] \setminus \mathcal{CS}}$, for any family of inputs $\{x_i \in \mathcal{X}\}_{i \in \mathcal{CS}}$, for any query* QKeyD($f$)*, we define $x_i^0 = x_i^1 = x_i$ for any slot $i \in \mathcal{CS}$ and any slot queried to* QEnc(i, x_i, ℓ)*, we require that: $f(\boldsymbol{x}^0) = f(\boldsymbol{x}^1)$ where $\boldsymbol{x}^b = (x_1^b, \ldots, x_n^b)$ for $b \in \{0, 1\}$.*
  We insist that, if one index $i \notin \mathcal{CS}$ is not queried for the label ℓ, there is no restriction.

$$\mathbf{IND}_\beta^{\mathsf{MCFE}}(\kappa, n, \mathcal{A})$$

$\mathsf{pp} \leftarrow \mathsf{Setup}(1^\kappa, 1^n)$

$(\{\mathsf{sk}_i\}_{i \in [n]}, \mathsf{msk}) \leftarrow \mathsf{KeyGen}(\mathsf{pp})$

$\alpha \leftarrow \mathcal{A}^{\mathsf{QCor}(\cdot), \mathsf{QLeftRight}(\cdot, \cdot, \cdot, \cdot), \mathsf{QEnc}(\cdot, \cdot, \cdot, \cdot), \mathsf{QKeyD}(\cdot)}(\mathsf{pp})$

Output: α if Condition (*) is satisfied,

or a uniform bit otherwise

Fig. 2. Security games for MCFE

The weaker versions of the security are defined as xx-yy-zz-$IND_\beta^{\mathsf{MCFE}}$ *(*xx, yy, zz *may be empty when we do not have the corresponding restriction), where,*

- *When* xx = sta*: the adversary should output the set $\mathcal{CS}$ at the beginning of the game, and it does not have access to the oracle* QCor *after that.*
- *When* yy = one*: for any slot $i \in [n]$ and $\ell \in$ Labels, $Q_{i,\ell} \in \{0,1\}$, and if $Q_{i,\ell} = 1$, then for any slot $j \in [n] \setminus \mathcal{CS}$, $Q_{j,\ell} = 1$. In other words, for any label, either the adversary makes no left-right query or makes exactly one left-right query for each $i \in [n] \setminus \mathcal{CS}$.*
- *When* yy = pos$^+$*: for any slot $i \in [n]$ and $\ell \in$ Labels, if $Q_{i,\ell} > 0$, then for any slot $j \in [n] \setminus \mathcal{CS}$, $Q_{j,\ell} > 0$. In other words, for any label, either the adversary makes no left-right encryption query or makes at least one left-right encryption query for each slot $i \in [n] \setminus \mathcal{CS}$.*
- *When* zz = sel*: the adversary should output the challenges at the beginning of the game, and it does not have access to the oracle* QLeftRight *after that. This case is referred as the selective security.*

We define the advantage of an adversary $\mathcal{A}$ in the following way:

$$\mathsf{Adv}_{\mathsf{MCFE}, \mathcal{A}}^{\text{xx-yy-zz-IND}}(\kappa, n) = \big| \Pr[\text{xx-yy-zz-IND}_0^{\mathsf{MCFE}}(\kappa, n, \mathcal{A}) = 1]$$

$$- \Pr[\text{xx-yy-zz-IND}_1^{\mathsf{MCFE}}(\kappa, n, \mathcal{A}) = 1] \big|.$$

A multi-client functional encryption scheme MCFE *is* xx-yy-zz-*IND secure, if for any p.p.t. adversary $\mathcal{A}$, there exists a negligible function* negl *such that:* $\mathsf{Adv}_{\mathsf{MCFE}, \mathcal{A}}^{\text{xx-yy-zz-}IND}(\kappa, n) \leq \text{negl}(\kappa)$.

We omit n when it is clear from the context. We also often omit $\mathcal{A}$ from the parameter of experiments or games when it is clear from context.

Definition 3 (1-label Security). *Let* MCFE *be an MCFE scheme, $\mathcal{F} = \{\mathcal{F}_\rho\}_\rho$ a function family indexed by ρ and* Labels *a label set. For* xx, yy, zz *defined as Definition 2, and $\beta \in \{0,1\}$, we define the experiment* xx-yy-zz-1-label$_\beta^{\mathsf{MCFE}}$ *exactly as in Fig. 2, where the oracles are defined as for Definition 2, except:*

Left-Right oracle QLeftRight(i, x_i^0, x_i^1, ℓ): *Outputs* $\mathsf{ct}_{i,\ell} = \mathsf{Enc}(\mathsf{pp}, \mathsf{sk}_i, x_i^\beta, \ell)$ *on a query (i, x_i^0, x_i^1, ℓ). This oracle can be queried at most on one label. Further queries with distinct labels will be ignored.*

Encryption oracle $\mathsf{QEnc}(i, x_i, \ell)$ *Outputs* $\mathsf{ct}_{i,\ell} = \mathsf{Enc}(\mathsf{pp}, \mathsf{sk}_i, x_i, \ell)$. *If this oracle is queried on the same label that is queried to* $\mathsf{QLeftRight}$, *the game ends and returns 0.*

Condition (*) *is defined as for Definition 2. We define the advantage of an* $\mathcal{A}$ *as follows:*

$$\mathsf{Adv}_{\mathsf{MCFE},\mathcal{A}}^{\text{xx-yy-zz-}IND\text{-}1\text{-}label}(\kappa, n) = \big| \Pr[\text{xx-yy-zz-IND-1-label}_0^{\mathsf{MCFE}}(\kappa, n, \mathcal{A}) = 1]$$
$$- \Pr[\text{xx-yy-zz-IND-1-label}_1^{\mathsf{MCFE}}(\kappa, n, \mathcal{A}) = 1] \big|.$$

Lemma 1 (From one to many labels [1]**).** *Let* MCFE *be a scheme that is* xx-yy-zz-*IND-1-label secure. Then it is also secure against p.p.t. adversaries that query* $\mathsf{QLeftRight}$ *on many distinct labels (*xx-yy-zz-*IND security). Namely, for any p.p.t. adversary* $\mathcal{A}$, *there exists a p.p.t. adversary* $\mathcal{B}$ *such that:*

$$\mathsf{Adv}_{\mathsf{MCFE},\mathcal{A}}^{\text{xx-yy-zz-IND}}(\kappa, n) \leq q_{\mathsf{Enc}} \cdot \mathsf{Adv}_{\mathsf{MCFE},\mathcal{B}}^{\text{xx-yy-zz-IND-1-label}}(\kappa, n),$$

By q_{Enc} *we denote the number of distinct labels queried by* $\mathcal{A}$ *to* $\mathsf{QLeftRight}$.

2.2 Inner-Product Functionality

We describe the functionalities supported by the constructions in this paper, by considering the index ρ of $\mathcal{F}$ in more detail.

The index of the family is defined as $\rho = (\mathcal{R}, n, m, X, Y)$ where $\mathcal{R}$ is either $\mathbb{Z}$ or $\mathbb{Z}_L$ for some integer L, and n, m, X, Y are positive integers. If X, Y are omitted, then $X = Y = L$ is used (i.e., no constraint). This defines $\mathcal{F}_\rho = \{f_{\boldsymbol{y}_1,\ldots,\boldsymbol{y}_n} : (\mathcal{R}^m)^n \to \mathcal{R}\}$ where $f_{\boldsymbol{y}_1,\ldots,\boldsymbol{y}_n}(\boldsymbol{x}_1,\ldots,\boldsymbol{x}_n) = \sum_{i=1}^{n}\langle \boldsymbol{x}_i, \boldsymbol{y}_i \rangle = \langle \boldsymbol{x}, \boldsymbol{y} \rangle$, the vectors satisfy the following bounds: $\|\boldsymbol{x}_i\|_\infty < X, \|\boldsymbol{y}_i\|_\infty < Y$ for $i \in [n]$, and $\boldsymbol{x} \in \mathcal{R}^{mn}$ and $\boldsymbol{y} \in \mathcal{R}^{mn}$ are the vectors corresponding to the concatenation of the n vectors $\boldsymbol{x}_1, \ldots, \boldsymbol{x}_n$ and $\boldsymbol{y}_1, \ldots, \boldsymbol{y}_n$ respectively.

We note that since this work focuses on labeled MCFE schemes for the IP functionality, the setup algorithm of all our constructions implicitly takes this functionality as an input.

3   Constructions

In this section, we present our MCFE constructions for the inner-product functionality based on the MDDH, DCR and LWR assumptions. Intuitively, we extend the single-input IPFE techniques to their counterpart MCFE schemes by considering each slot as an independent client such that the clients can share the required randomness through the random oracle. While the IPFE constructions are based on a combination of the randomness and the public-key, we replace it with a combination of the random oracle and the master key in our MCFE schemes. The use of random oracles for generating randomness also explains why we ended up with one-IND security (which can be easily extended to pos$^+$-security via an existing compiler [12]). In Sect. 3.5 we present a general proof sketch covering the main proof idea of all three constructions, we refer to the full version [3].

Setup($1^\kappa, n$) :	KeyDer($pp, msk, y \in \mathbb{Z}_p^{mn}$) :
$\mathcal{G} := (\mathbb{G}, p, g) \leftarrow \mathsf{GGen}(1^\kappa)$	For $y = (y_1, \ldots, y_n)$, with $y_i \in \mathbb{Z}_p^m$
Select $\mathcal{H} : \mathsf{Labels} \to \mathbb{G}^{k+1}$	$sk_y := \sum_{i \in [n]} \mathbf{S}_i^\top y_i$
Return $pp := (\mathcal{G}, \mathcal{H})$.	
KeyGen(pp) :	Return sk_y
$\mathbf{S}_i \leftarrow \mathbb{Z}_p^{m \times (k+1)}$, $sk_i = \mathbf{S}_i, msk = \{\mathbf{S}_i\}_{i \in [n]}$	Dec($pp, sk_y, \{ct_{i,\ell}\}_{i \in [n]}, y, \ell$) :
Return $(\{sk_i\}_{i \in [n]}, msk)$	$[u_\ell] = \mathcal{H}(\ell) \in \mathbb{G}^{k+1}$
Enc($pp, sk_i, x_i \in \mathbb{Z}_p^m, \ell$) :	$C := \sum_{i \in [n]} [c_{i,\ell}] \cdot y_i - [u_\ell^\top] \cdot sk_y$
$c_{i,\ell} := \mathbf{S}_i \cdot u_\ell + x_i$ where $[u_\ell] := \mathcal{H}(\ell) \in \mathbb{G}^{k+1}$	
Return $ct_{i,\ell} := [c_{i,\ell}] \in \mathbb{Z}_p^m$	Return $\log(C)$

Fig. 3. MCFE based on the MDDH assumption.

3.1 MCFE Based on the MDDH Assumption

In this section, we present a MCFE scheme supporting labels, based on the MDDH assumption. One can see this construction as an extension of the single-input IPFE scheme where the term h_i^r is replaced with $\mathcal{H}(\ell)^{\mathbf{S}_i}$ (the value h_i is the public-key of IPFE scheme) and the value $\mathcal{H}(\ell)$ generates the required randomness. The MDDH assumption was initially introduced in [14]. We recap it here:

Definition 4 (Matrix Distribution [14]). Let $\ell, k \in \mathbb{N}$ with $\ell > k$. We call $\mathcal{D}_{\ell,k}$ a matrix distribution if it outputs (in polynomial time and with overwhelming probability) matrices in $\mathbb{Z}_p^{\ell \times k}$ of full rank k. We define $\mathcal{D}_k = \mathcal{D}_{k+1,k}$.

Definition 5 ($\mathcal{D}_{\ell,k}$-Matrix Diffie-Hellman Assumption [14]). Let $\mathcal{D}_{\ell,k}$ be a matrix distribution. We define the advantage of an adversary $\mathcal{A}$ for the $\mathcal{D}_{\ell,k}$-Matrix Diffie-Hellman Assumption in the following way:

$$\mathsf{Adv}_{\mathcal{D}_{\ell,k}, \mathcal{A}}^{\mathsf{MDDH}}(\kappa) := |\Pr[\mathcal{A}(1^\kappa, \mathcal{G}, [\mathbf{A}], [\mathbf{A}w]) = 1] - \Pr[\mathcal{A}(1^\kappa, \mathcal{G}, [\mathbf{A}], [u]) = 1]|,$$

where $\mathcal{G} = (\mathbb{G}, g, p) \leftarrow \mathsf{GGen}(1^\kappa), \mathbf{A} \leftarrow \mathcal{D}_{\ell,k}, w \leftarrow \mathbb{Z}_p^k, u \leftarrow \mathbb{Z}_p^\ell$. We say that the $\mathcal{D}_{\ell,k}$-Matrix Diffie-Hellman Assumption ($\mathcal{D}_{\ell,k}$-MDDH) holds in group $\mathbb{G}$, if for all p.p.t. adversaries $\mathcal{A}$, there exists a negligible function negl such that: $\mathsf{Adv}_{\mathcal{D}_{\ell,k}, \mathcal{A}}^{\mathsf{MDDH}}(\kappa) \leq \mathsf{negl}(\kappa)$.

Our MDDH-based MCFE construction is given in Fig. 3.

Theorem 1. Assume that the $\mathcal{D}_k$-MDDH assumption holds, then the MCFE scheme described in Fig. 3 is one-IND-secure in the random oracle model.

3.2 MCFE Based on the DCR Assumption

In this section we present a MCFE scheme based on the DCR assumption in the random oracle model. As we mentioned, the main benefit of this construction is that one can retrieve the final result without computing the discrete-logarithm. The following notations are used in this section. $\mathcal{D}_{\mathbb{Z}^k,\sigma}$ stands for the Gaussian distribution over $\mathbb{Z}^k$ with the standard deviation σ and the mean 0 (this notation is also used in the next section). $\mathbb{Z}_N$ is the additive group of integers modulo N and $\mathbb{Z}_N^*$ denotes the multiplicative group of integers modulo N. That is, including all $a \in \mathbb{Z}_N$ such that $\gcd(a, N) = 1$ where $\gcd(b, c)$ is the greatest common divisor of b and c. Let $N = pq$ be a safe modulus, meaning that p and q are large safe primes in the form of $p = 2p' + 1$ and $q = 2q' + 1$, where $p', q' > 2^\kappa$. In this paper $\mathsf{SP}(\kappa)$ is the algorithm producing safe-primes p, q as above. It is believed that for a given N as above it is hard to find p, q.

The single-input functional encryption scheme based on the Paillier cryptosystem has been proposed by Agrawal et al. [6]. In their construction, the encryption algorithm includes two main parts: $\mathsf{ct}_0 = g^r$ where $r \xleftarrow{R} \{1, \ldots, [\frac{N}{4}]\}$ and $\mathsf{ct}_i = (1+N)^{x_i} \cdot h_i^r$ for $i = 1, \ldots, n$ where $h_i = g^{s_i}$ is the public key. The term $h_i^r = g^{rs_i}$ can be replaced with $\mathcal{H}(\ell)^{s_i}$ which removes the need for sharing a random r among the clients, since the random oracle $\mathcal{H}(\cdot)$ is publicly known. This explains the intuition for our MCFE scheme represented in Fig. 4. Regarding the security proof, the indistinguishable changes in RO-queries lead to an indistinguishable change in the (sub)lattice the master secret key belongs to (Note that the master secret key is chosen from lattice $\mathbb{Z}^n$ by a Gaussian distribution $\mathcal{D}_\sigma$). From there, a theorem from lattice-based cryptography and similar parameter setting to the single-input IPFE [6] guarantees that the new distribution of the master secret key (along side the proper change in the RO-query associated with the challenge) is sufficient for the security proof.

Definition 6 (Decisional Composite Residuosity (DCR) Assumption). *Let $N = pq$ for two safe-primes p and q. We define the advantage of an adversary $\mathcal{A}$ for the DCR assumption in the following way:*

$$\mathsf{Adv}_{N,\mathcal{A}}^{\mathrm{DCR}}(\kappa) := |\Pr[\mathcal{A}(1^\kappa, z^N \bmod N^2) = 1] - \Pr[\mathcal{A}(1^\kappa, z) = 1]|, \quad \text{where } z \leftarrow \mathbb{Z}_{N^2}^*.$$

We say that the DCR Assumption holds, if for all p.p.t. adversaries $\mathcal{A}$, there exists a negligible function negl *such that:* $\mathsf{Adv}_{N,\mathcal{A}}^{\mathrm{DCR}}(\kappa) \leq \mathrm{negl}(\kappa)$.

Theorem 2. *Assume that the DCR assumption holds, then the MCFE scheme described in Fig. 4 is one-IND-secure in the random-oracle model.*

3.3   MCFE Based on LWE Assumption

In this section, the notation $\lfloor a \rfloor$ denotes the largest integer smaller than a.

Learning With Errors. The problem of Learning with Errors (LWE) was introduced in a seminal work of Regev [24]. The idea of the LWE problem is to provide a system of linear equations such that each equation is associated with an error term. Regev showed that in this case the number of equations does not really matter and it is hard to find any information about the secret. This problem is formally defined as follows.

Setup$(1^\kappa, n)$:	Enc$(\mathsf{pp}, \mathsf{sk}_i, x_i, i, \ell)$:
Run SP(κ) to get (p, q) and	To encrypt a message $\boldsymbol{x} \in \mathbb{Z}^n$ with $|x_i| \leq X$:
Compute $N = pq$.	Compute: $\mathsf{ct}_i = (1 + N)^{x_i}.\mathcal{H}(\ell)^{s_i} \mod N^2$.
Let $\mathcal{H}$: Labels $\rightarrow \mathbb{Z}_{N^2}^*$ be a full-domain	Return $\mathsf{ct} = \{\mathsf{ct}_i\}_i$
hash function.	KeyDer$(\mathsf{pp}, \mathsf{msk}, \boldsymbol{y})$:
Set $X < \sqrt{N/2n}$	For vector $\boldsymbol{y} \in \mathbb{Z}^n$ with $|y_i| \leq Y < \sqrt{N/2n}$:
Return $\mathsf{pp} = (N, \mathcal{H}, X)$	Compute $\mathsf{sk}_{\boldsymbol{y}} = \Sigma_i y_i \cdot s_i$
KeyGen(pp) :	Return $\mathsf{sk}_{\boldsymbol{y}}$
Sample $\boldsymbol{s} \leftarrow \mathcal{D}_{\mathbb{Z}^n, \sigma}$ where	Dec$(\mathsf{pp}, \boldsymbol{y}, \mathsf{sk}, \{\mathsf{ct}_{i,\ell}\}_{i \in [n]}, l)$:
$\sigma > \sqrt{\kappa} \cdot N^{5/2}$ for the selective security	Compute $C = \prod_i \mathsf{ct}_{i,\ell}^{y_i} \cdot \mathcal{H}(\ell)^{-\mathsf{sk}}$
$\sigma > \sqrt{\kappa + 2n \cdot \log(2X)} \cdot N^{5/2}$ for the	
adaptive security.	Return $\dfrac{C - 1 \mod N^2}{N}$
Return $\mathsf{msk} = \boldsymbol{s}$ and $\mathsf{sk}_i = s_i$.	

Fig. 4. MCFE based on the DCR assumption

Definition 7 (Decisional LWE assumption). *Let q, α be functions of parameter n_0. The Learning with Error ($\mathsf{LWE}_{q,\alpha}$) problem is to distinguish two following distributions given access to polynomially many samples for a fixed vector $\boldsymbol{s} \xleftarrow{R} \mathbb{Z}_q^{n_0}$,*

$$\mathcal{D} = \{(\boldsymbol{a}, \langle \boldsymbol{a}, \boldsymbol{s} \rangle + e) \; : \; \boldsymbol{a} \xleftarrow{R} \mathbb{Z}_q^{n_0}, e \xleftarrow{R} \mathcal{D}_{\mathbb{Z}, \alpha q}\}, \; \mathcal{D}' = \{(\boldsymbol{a}, u) \; : \; \boldsymbol{a} \xleftarrow{R} \mathbb{Z}_q^{n_0}, u \xleftarrow{R} \mathbb{Z}_q\}$$

Concretely, for any adversary $\mathcal{A}$ there exists a negligible function negl such that:

$$\mathsf{Adv}_{\mathcal{A}}^{LWE}(n_0) = |\Pr[\mathcal{A}^{\mathcal{D}(\boldsymbol{s}, \cdot)}(\alpha, q, n_0) = 1] - \Pr[\mathcal{A}^{\mathcal{D}'(\cdot)}(\alpha, q, n_0) = 1]| \leq \mathsf{negl}(n_0)$$

where the oracles $\mathcal{D}(\boldsymbol{s}, \cdot)$ and $\mathcal{D}'(\cdot)$ output samples respectively from $\mathcal{D}$ (with a fixed secret $\boldsymbol{s}$) and $\mathcal{D}'$.

3.4   Our MCFE Construction Based on LWE

In this section we propose a MCFE construction based on the LWE problem as an extension of single-input FE presented by Agrawal et al. [6]. Although the intuition for our construction is similar to the previous constructions, we highlight here the differences that are the use of a rounding-map, and the part of the secret key that is uniform. In [6] the mheLWE assumption is used to simulate all the queries in a correct way, as the inputs of the assumption are enough for this purpose. After applying this assumption (on one ciphertext) a product between parts of the master secret key and a uniformly random vector appears in the ciphertext. If the first factor of this multiplication has enough min-entropy, conditioned on the information available to the adversary, applying the leftover hash lemma guarantees that this product seems uniform, which concludes the proof. Now all is left to prove is that the part of the master secret key that is involved has enough min-entropy conditioned on what the adversary can see. Since in [6], we are in the public-key setting, all the information (regarding the master secret key) that the adversary can extract from honestly generated ciphertexts is the same as what it can extract from the public-key. Thus, the leakage of all the honestly generated ciphertexts can be precisely quantified, and simulated using only the information contained in the public parameters. In this work, we need to change to the symmetric-key setting (as is the case in MCFE), so it is not as straightforward how to quantify the leakage from all the ciphertext queries, and the information required to simulate the ciphertexts during the proof cannot be hidden in the public parameters. And in fact, in our case this leakage is really noticeable, especially since the ciphertexts are generated by different parties and each ciphertexts can leak information about different parts of the master secret key. Leveraging the use of a random oracle, we argue that the leakage coming from all the ciphertext queries can be deduced from the leakage of some secret matrix, together with some noise term, under the LWE assumption. The leakage about the secret matrix is completely hidden by the uniform secret key s_i, whereas the rounding-map completely removes the noise term $t_i \cdot e_\ell$ when the parameters are carefully selected.

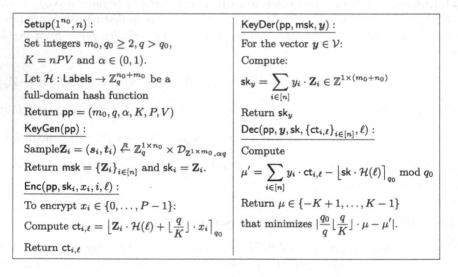

Fig. 5. MCFE based on the LWE assumption.

In our construction we are using a rounding-map which is formally defined as follows.

Definition 8 (Rounding-map from $\mathbb{Z}_q$ to $\mathbb{Z}_{q_0}$). *For $q \geq q_0 \geq 2$, a rounding map $\lfloor . \rceil_{q_0} : \mathbb{Z}_q \longrightarrow \mathbb{Z}_{q_0}$ is defined as $\lfloor x \rceil_{q_0} = \lfloor (q_0/q) \cdot \bar{x} \rceil$ where $\bar{x} = x \mod q$*

and $\lceil \cdot \rceil$ is a classical rounding function over integers[6]. This notation can be extended component-wise to vectors and matrices over $\mathbb{Z}_q$.

Our MCFE scheme based on the LWE assumption is given in Fig. 5. The setting of the parameters is discussed separately in the full version [3].

Theorem 3. *The presented MCFE scheme in Fig. 5, is an one-IND-secure MCFE scheme under the LWE assumption and in the random-oracle model.*

3.5   Security Analysis

Proof (Overview). To prove the security of our constructions under the different assumptions, we consider the case where $\mathcal{A}$ only queries QLeftRight on one label ℓ^*, and never queries QEnc on ℓ^*. In more detail, we show that: $\mathsf{Adv}_{\mathsf{MCFE},\mathcal{A}'}^{\mathsf{one\text{-}1\text{-}label}}(\kappa, n) \leq \mathsf{negl}(\kappa)$, where $\mathsf{Adv}_{\mathsf{MCFE},\mathcal{A}}^{\mathsf{one\text{-}1\text{-}label}}(\kappa, n)$ is defined as described in Definition 3. Then we use Lemma 1 to obtain the theorem.

For the proof of the 1-label security we proceed via a hybrid argument, using the games described in Fig. 6. The game G_0 corresponds to one-1-label$_0^{\mathsf{MCFE}}(\kappa, n, \mathcal{A})$ and the game G_7 to one-1-label$_1^{\mathsf{MCFE}}(\kappa, n, \mathcal{A})$. This yields: $\mathsf{Adv}_{\mathsf{MCFE},\mathcal{A}}^{\mathsf{one\text{-}1\text{-}label}}(\kappa, n) = |\mathsf{Win}_{\mathcal{A}}^{\mathsf{G}_0}(\kappa, n) - \mathsf{Win}_{\mathcal{A}}^{\mathsf{G}_7}(\kappa, n)|$.

Intuitively, we change the random-oracle queries for $\ell \neq \ell^*$ and $\ell = \ell^*$ in a somehow orthogonal way. Meaning that, the proper change for $\ell \neq \ell^*$, changes the distribution of the master key (indistinguishable in the adversary's view) such that the multiplication of this master secret key and the new value for RO-query associated with ℓ^* can perfectly (for MDDH scheme) or statistically (for DCR and LWE schemes) hide the message in the challenge.

Game G_1: In game G_1, we replace the hash function $\mathcal{H}$, that is evaluated in every random-oracle query ℓ, with a random function RF. The random function has different outputs corresponding to the different schemes: The random function outputs an element $z \leftarrow \mathbb{Z}_p^{k+1}$ in the case of the MDDH scheme, an element $z \leftarrow \mathbb{Z}_{N^2}^*$ in the case of the DCR scheme and a couple $(\boldsymbol{a}, \boldsymbol{u})$ with $\boldsymbol{a} \leftarrow \mathbb{Z}_q^{n_0}$ and $\boldsymbol{u} \leftarrow \mathbb{Z}_q^{m_0}$ in the case of the LWE scheme. This results in a perfect transition from G_0 to G_1. This results in: $|\mathsf{Win}_{\mathcal{A}}^{\mathsf{G}_0}(\kappa, n) - \mathsf{Win}_{\mathcal{A}}^{\mathsf{G}_1}(\kappa, n)| = 0$.

Game G_2: In game G_2, we answer the random-oracle queries for the label $\ell \neq \ell^*$ with an element that is indistinguishable from a random element, by relying on the corresponding computational assumption. We describe the random-oracle outputs under the label ℓ in more detail:

MDDH: we output a vector z such that z is contained in the span of $\mathbf{A}$, i.e.
$z = \mathbf{A}\boldsymbol{y}$ with a random vector $\boldsymbol{y} \leftarrow \mathbb{Z}_p^k$.

DCR: we output an element $z^N \bmod N^2$, with a random element $z \leftarrow \mathbb{Z}_{N^2}^*$.

---

[6] I.e., $\lceil a \rceil$ is $\lfloor a \rfloor$ if $a \leq \lfloor a \rfloor + 1/2$ and it is $(\lfloor a \rfloor + 1)$ if $a > \lfloor a \rfloor + 1/2$.

LWE: we output a tuple $(a, \mathbf{S} \cdot a + e)$, with $\mathbf{S} \xleftarrow{R} \mathbb{Z}^{m_0 \times n_0}$, $a \xleftarrow{R} \mathbb{Z}_q^{n_0}$, $e \xleftarrow{R} \mathcal{D}_{\mathbb{Z}^{m_0}, \alpha q}$. (we note that before proceeding to the next game for LWE scheme we need some extra games where we remove $t_i \cdot e$ and $t_i \cdot \mathbf{S}$ from all ciphertexts queries through the property of the rounding-map and the uniform distribution of s_i).

This results in: $|\mathsf{Win}_{\mathcal{A}}^{\mathsf{G}_1}(\kappa, n) - \mathsf{Win}_{\mathcal{A}}^{\mathsf{G}_2}(\kappa, n)| \leq \mathsf{negl}(\kappa)$. where $\mathsf{negl}(\kappa)$ depends on the advantage of the attacker to the underlying assumption.

Here we note that the current modifications also change the distribution of the master secret key in the adversary's view (in an indistinguishable way).

MDDH the master secret key for MDDH scheme is distributed as $\mathbf{S} + \gamma(x_1^{\ell^*} - x_0^{\ell^*}) \cdot (a^\perp)^T$ for some $\gamma \in \mathbb{Z}_q$.

DCR the master secret key for DCR scheme is distributed as $s + \lambda(x_1^{\ell^*} - x_0^{\ell^*}) \cdot \mu$ for some $\mu \in \mathbb{Z}^n$. Where $\lambda = 2p'q'$ is the order of elements z^N mod N^2.

LWE the master secret key t for LWE scheme is distributed as $t + (x_1^{\ell^*} - x_0^{\ell^*}) \cdot \mu$ for some $\mu \in \mathbb{Z}^n$ (here for the sake of simplicity, many details are missing).

Game G_3: In game G_3, we answer random-oracle queries for the label ℓ^* as follows:

MDDH: we rely on the fact that $\mathbf{A}$ has rank k and find a vector $a^\perp \leftarrow \mathbb{Z}_p^{k+1}$ such that $(a^\perp)^\top \mathbf{A} = \mathbf{0}$ (this means $(\mathbf{A}, a^\perp)$ is a base for $\mathbb{Z}^{k+1}$). Then we set $\mathsf{RF}(\ell^*) = \mathbf{A} \cdot \mathsf{RF}'(\ell^*) + a^\perp \cdot \mathsf{RF}''(\ell^*)$ such that $\mathsf{RF}''(\ell) \neq 0$ (which is satisfies except with negligible probability negl), for random functions RF' and RF''.

DCR: we rely on an isomorphism ε from $\mathbb{Z}_N \times \mathbb{Z}_N^*$ to $\mathbb{Z}_{N^2}^*$ to write the random element $\mathsf{RF}(\ell^*) = z \bmod N^2$ in its corresponding representation $\varepsilon^{-1}(z) = (1 + N)^a \cdot b^N \bmod N^2$ for $a, b \in \mathbb{Z}_N^*$ (which is satisfied expect with negligible probability negl).

LWE: we set $\mathsf{RF}(\ell^*) = \mathbf{S} \cdot a + e + \mathsf{RF}'(\ell^*)$ where RF' is a random function (again here there is an extra game which remove the term $t_i \cdot e$ from the ciphertext-challenge).

This results in: $|\mathsf{Win}_{\mathcal{A}}^{\mathsf{G}_2}(\kappa, n) - \mathsf{Win}_{\mathcal{A}}^{\mathsf{G}_3}(\kappa, n)| \leq \mathsf{negl}(\kappa)$.

Game G_4: In game G_4, we change the answers for left-or-right oracle queries under ℓ^* from encryptions of x_i^0 to encryptions of x_i^1. for the MDDH we manage to show this change is perfectly-indistinguishable, while for the DCR and LWE schemes it needs a statistical argument to justify the transition from game G_3 to game G_4. It follows that: $|\mathsf{Win}_{\mathcal{A}}^{\mathsf{G}_3}(\kappa, n) - \mathsf{Win}_{\mathcal{A}}^{\mathsf{G}_4}(\kappa, n)| = f(\kappa)$. where for MDDH, $f(\kappa) = 0$ and for DCR and LWE schemes $f(\kappa) = 2^{-\kappa}$. In fact, we prove that a multiplication (which has already appeared in the ciphertext-challenge) of the master secret key (in its new representation) and the new values $\mathsf{RF}(\ell^*)$ can perfectly (for MDDH) or statistically (for DCR and LWE) hide the message in the challenge.

Games $\mathsf{G}_5, \ldots, \mathsf{G}_8$ One can define these games as the backward-counterparts of games G_3 to G_0 while hidden bit associated with the challenge is $b = 1$.

Putting everything together, we obtain the theorem.   □

Game	ct_{i,ℓ^*}	u_ℓ	justification/remark
G_0	$\mathsf{Enc}(pp, sk_i, x_i^0, \ell^*)$	$\mathcal{H}(\ell)$	
G_1	$\mathsf{Enc}(pp, sk_i, x_i^0, \ell^*)$	$\boxed{RF(\ell)}$	Replace the hash function with a random function
G_2	$\mathsf{Enc}(pp, sk_i, x_i^0, \ell^*)$	$RF(\ell), \ell = \ell^*$ $\boxed{z,\ \ell \neq \ell^*}$	Simulate the hash function for $\ell \neq \ell^*$ using z which is indistinguishable from a random element if the underlying hardness assumption (MDDH, DCR, LWE) holds
G_3	$\mathsf{Enc}(pp, sk_i, x_i^0, \ell^*)$	$\boxed{\overline{RF}(\ell)}, \ell = \ell^*$ $z,\ \ell \neq \ell^*$	Simulate the hash function for $\ell = \ell^*$ using a different representation of $RF(\ell^*)$ corresponding to the underlying assumption
G_4	$\mathsf{Enc}(pp, sk_i, \boxed{x_i^1}, \ell^*)$	$\overline{RF}(\ell), \ell = \ell^*$ $z',\ \ell \neq \ell^*$	Change from left to right encryption

Fig. 6. Overview of the games to prove the security of the MCFE schemes.

4   Implementation

To show the efficiency of our schemes, we provide three implementations of schemes described in Figs. 3 to 5. In this table the encryption time is considered per slot. Before describing the choices made during implementation, we show the timings for these implementations in Fig. 7.

Operation	mpk Generation	msk Generation	sk_y Derivation	Encryption	Decryption
DDH	0.038843 s	0.028417 s	negligible	0.000439 s	m μs
DCR	0.201445 s	1.576873 s	negligible	0.280378 s	0.313167 s
LWE	n/a	0.017957 s	0.048872 s	0.001207 s	0.000989 s

Fig. 7. Timings of the concrete implementations, encrypting vectors of dimension 100. The code was run on a laptop running an Intel(R) Core(TM) i7-8750H CPU @ 2.20GHz. m is the discrete-logarithm value to be retrieved (the inner-product value).

Before heading into details relative to each implementation, let us review the choices common to the three implementations.

Instantiating the Random Oracle. We chose to replace the random oracle by the SHA-256 hash function, thus we were able to take advantage of the OpenSSL library, that provides efficient and well spread implementation of SHA-256. As the size of the random oracle were different to the output size of SHA-256, we used it multiple times, changing the input each time by incrementing a counter that was concatenated with the label.

Choice of the Message Space. We tested our code with vectors of dimension 100, computing the sum of the first 100 squares. We wanted to keep the message space as small as $2^{20} = 1048576$, in order for the LWE ciphertexts to be held by 32 bits integers. The message space was kept the same for the DCR implementation for fair comparison. It is worth noting that the DCR implementation could have encrypted vectors with coordinates up to 4000 bits large without being any slower, since the complexity only depends on the dimensions of the vectors, and the only bound on the message space is that it has to stay smaller than the RSA number N. On the other hand, the DDH implementation is limited by the computation of a discrete logarithm regardless of the parameter choice, and the LWE implementation can hardly increase the message space without having to pump the parameters. Indeed, the modulus is tied only to the message space and not so to security as in the case of DCR, so we don't have this spare space in the message space. We wanted to keep the ciphertexts small enough so that we can rely on fast hardware optimizations of arithmetic operations, using bigger message spaces would require to use large number libraries, which is doable.

Parameter	Message space	Ciphertext size	Secret key size
DDH	bounded by computation	512 bits	512 bits
DCR	4096 bits	9192 bits	55152 bits
LWE	20 bits	32 bits	704000 bits

Fig. 8. Capacity of the implementations and memory cost.

Discussion. The timings are very reasonable, and can be brought down quite a lot for any given application. We tried to push the parameters so that our implementations can be trusted as proofs of concept without knowing what applications will come in the future, but for given specific requirements in terms of security and efficiency, there is a lot of room for improvement. We also tried to give a flexible implementation that can be used to estimate the timings for different parameters easily. This also leaves room for optimization once the parameters are chosen for a particular application. If we are to compare the different schemes, it looks like the scheme based on LWE is much more efficient than the scheme based on DCR. One has to be careful when making such comparisons. Indeed, the DCR scheme supports very big messages, because the modulus N has to be set very large for security reasons. In comparison, the efficiency of the LWE scheme would degrade with the size of the messages to encrypt, so for applications with large messages, the DCR implementation might actually become much faster.

A summary of our results can be found in Fig. 8. Details of implementation for each of the mentioned schemes are separately discussed in the full version [3].

Acknowledgments. This work was supported in part by the European Union's Horizon 2020 Research and Innovation Programme FENTEC (Grant Agreement no.

780108), by the European Union's Seventh Framework Programme (FP7/2007–2013 Grant Agreement no. 339563 – CryptoCloud), and by the French FUI project ANBLIC.

References

1. Abdalla, M., Benhamouda, F., Gay, R.: From single-input to multi-client inner-product functional encryption. In: Galbraith, S.D., Moriai, S. (eds.) ASIACRYPT 2019. LNCS, vol. 11923, pp. 552–582. Springer, Cham (2019). https://doi.org/10.1007/978-3-030-34618-8_19

2. Abdalla, M., Bourse, F., De Caro, A., Pointcheval, D.: Simple functional encryption schemes for inner products. In: Katz, J. (ed.) PKC 2015. LNCS, vol. 9020, pp. 733–751. Springer, Heidelberg (2015). https://doi.org/10.1007/978-3-662-46447-2_33

3. Abdalla, M., Bourse, F., Marival, H., Pointcheval, D., Soleimanian, A., Waldner, H.: Multi-client inner-product functional encryption in the random-oracle model. Cryptology ePrint Archive, Report 2020/788 (2020). https://eprint.iacr.org/2020/788

4. Abdalla, M., Catalano, D., Fiore, D., Gay, R., Ursu, B.: Multi-input functional encryption for inner products: function-hiding realizations and constructions without pairings. In: Shacham, H., Boldyreva, A. (eds.) CRYPTO 2018. LNCS, vol. 10991, pp. 597–627. Springer, Cham (2018). https://doi.org/10.1007/978-3-319-96884-1_20

5. Abdalla, M., Gay, R., Raykova, M., Wee, H.: Multi-input inner-product functional encryption from pairings. In: Coron, J.-S., Nielsen, J.B. (eds.) EUROCRYPT 2017. LNCS, vol. 10210, pp. 601–626. Springer, Cham (2017). https://doi.org/10.1007/978-3-319-56620-7_21

6. Agrawal, S., Libert, B., Stehlé, D.: Fully secure functional encryption for inner products, from standard assumptions. In: Robshaw, M., Katz, J. (eds.) CRYPTO 2016. LNCS, vol. 9816, pp. 333–362. Springer, Heidelberg (2016). https://doi.org/10.1007/978-3-662-53015-3_12

7. Agrawal, S., Rosen, A.: Functional encryption for bounded collusions, revisited. In: Kalai, Y., Reyzin, L. (eds.) TCC 2017. LNCS, vol. 10677, pp. 173–205. Springer, Cham (2017). https://doi.org/10.1007/978-3-319-70500-2_7

8. Boneh, D., Franklin, M.: Identity-based encryption from the weil pairing. In: Kilian, J. (ed.) CRYPTO 2001. LNCS, vol. 2139, pp. 213–229. Springer, Heidelberg (2001). https://doi.org/10.1007/3-540-44647-8_13

9. Boneh, D., Sahai, A., Waters, B.: Functional encryption: definitions and challenges. In: Ishai, Y. (ed.) TCC 2011. LNCS, vol. 6597, pp. 253–273. Springer, Heidelberg (2011). https://doi.org/10.1007/978-3-642-19571-6_16

10. Boyle, E., Chung, K.-M., Pass, R.: On extractability obfuscation. In: Lindell, Y. (ed.) TCC 2014. LNCS, vol. 8349, pp. 52–73. Springer, Heidelberg (2014). https://doi.org/10.1007/978-3-642-54242-8_3

11. Chotard, J., Dufour Sans, E., Gay, R., Phan, D.H., Pointcheval, D.: Decentralized multi-client functional encryption for inner product. In: Peyrin, T., Galbraith, S. (eds.) ASIACRYPT 2018. LNCS, vol. 11273, pp. 703–732. Springer, Cham (2018). https://doi.org/10.1007/978-3-030-03329-3_24

12. Chotard, J., Dufour Sans, E., Gay, R., Phan, D.H., Pointcheval, D.: Multi-client functional encryption with repetition for inner product. Cryptology ePrint Archive, Report 2018/1021 (2018). https://eprint.iacr.org/2018/1021

13. Cocks, C.: An identity based encryption scheme based on quadratic residues. In: Honary, B. (ed.) Cryptography and Coding 2001. LNCS, vol. 2260, pp. 360–363. Springer, Heidelberg (2001). https://doi.org/10.1007/3-540-45325-3_32

14. Escala, A., Herold, G., Kiltz, E., Ràfols, C., Villar, J.: An algebraic framework for Diffie-Hellman assumptions. In: Canetti, R., Garay, J.A. (eds.) CRYPTO 2013. LNCS, vol. 8043, pp. 129–147. Springer, Heidelberg (2013). https://doi.org/10.1007/978-3-642-40084-1_8

15. Garg, S., Gentry, C., Halevi, S., Raykova, M., Sahai, A., Waters, B.: Candidate indistinguishability obfuscation and functional encryption for all circuits. In: 54th FOCS, pp. 40–49. IEEE Computer Society Press (2013). https://doi.org/10.1109/FOCS.2013.13

16. Gentry, C., Sahai, A., Waters, B.: Homomorphic encryption from learning with errors: conceptually-simpler, asymptotically-faster, attribute-based. In: Canetti, R., Garay, J.A. (eds.) CRYPTO 2013. LNCS, vol. 8042, pp. 75–92. Springer, Heidelberg (2013). https://doi.org/10.1007/978-3-642-40041-4_5

17. Goldwasser, S., et al.: Multi-input functional encryption. In: Nguyen, P.Q., Oswald, E. (eds.) EUROCRYPT 2014. LNCS, vol. 8441, pp. 578–602. Springer, Heidelberg (2014). https://doi.org/10.1007/978-3-642-55220-5_32

18. Gordon, S.D., Katz, J., Liu, F.H., Shi, E., Zhou, H.S.: Multi-input functional encryption. Cryptology ePrint Archive, Report 2013/774 (2013). http://eprint.iacr.org/2013/774

19. Goyal, V., Pandey, O., Sahai, A., Waters, B.: Attribute-based encryption for fine-grained access control of encrypted data. In: Juels, A., Wright, R.N., De Capitani di Vimercati, S. (eds.) ACM CCS 2006, pp. 89–98. ACM Press (2006). https://doi.org/10.1145/1180405.1180418, available as Cryptology ePrint Archive Report 2006/309

20. Libert, B., Stehlé, D., Titiu, R.: Adaptively secure distributed PRFs from LWE. In: Beimel, A., Dziembowski, S. (eds.) TCC 2018. LNCS, vol. 11240, pp. 391–421. Springer, Cham (2018). https://doi.org/10.1007/978-3-030-03810-6_15

21. Libert, B., Ţiţiu, R.: Multi-client functional encryption for linear functions in the standard model from LWE. In: Galbraith, S.D., Moriai, S. (eds.) ASIACRYPT 2019. LNCS, vol. 11923, pp. 520–551. Springer, Cham (2019). https://doi.org/10.1007/978-3-030-34618-8_18

22. O'Neill, A.: Definitional issues in functional encryption. Cryptology ePrint Archive, Report 2010/556 (2010). http://eprint.iacr.org/2010/556

23. Ostrovsky, R., Sahai, A., Waters, B.: Attribute-based encryption with non-monotonic access structures. In: Ning, P., De Capitani di Vimercati, S., Syverson, P.F. (eds.) ACM CCS 2007, pp. 195–203. ACM Press (2007). https://doi.org/10.1145/1315245.1315270

24. Regev, O.: On lattices, learning with errors, random linear codes, and cryptography. In: Gabow, H.N., Fagin, R. (eds.) 37th ACM STOC, pp. 84–93. ACM Press (2005). https://doi.org/10.1145/1060590.1060603

25. Waters, B.: Ciphertext-policy attribute-based encryption: an expressive, efficient, and provably secure realization. In: Catalano, D., Fazio, N., Gennaro, R., Nicolosi, A. (eds.) PKC 2011. LNCS, vol. 6571, pp. 53–70. Springer, Heidelberg (2011). https://doi.org/10.1007/978-3-642-19379-8_4

26. Waters, B.: A punctured programming approach to adaptively secure functional encryption. In: Gennaro, R., Robshaw, M. (eds.) CRYPTO 2015. LNCS, vol. 9216, pp. 678–697. Springer, Heidelberg (2015). https://doi.org/10.1007/978-3-662-48000-7_33
27. Waters, B.: Efficient identity-based encryption without random oracles. In: Cramer, R. (ed.) EUROCRYPT 2005. LNCS, vol. 3494, pp. 114–127. Springer, Heidelberg (2005). https://doi.org/10.1007/11426639_7

On the Query Complexity of Constructing PRFs from Non-adaptive PRFs

Pratik Soni[1(✉)] and Stefano Tessaro[2]

[1] University of California, Santa Barbara, USA
pratik_soni@cs.ucsb.edu
[2] Paul G. Allen School of Computer Science & Engineering,
University of Washington, Seattle, USA
tessaro@cs.washington.edu

Abstract. This paper studies constructions of pseudorandom functions (PRFs) from *non-adaptive* PRFs (naPRFs), i.e., PRFs which are secure only against distinguishers issuing all of their queries at once.

Berman and Haitner (Journal of Cryptology, '15) gave a *one-call* construction which, however, is not hardness preserving – to obtain a secure PRF (against polynomial-time distinguishers), they need to rely on a naPRF secure against *superpolynomial-time* distinguishers; in contrast, all known hardness-preserving constructions require $\omega(1)$ calls. This leaves open the question of whether a stronger superpolynomial-time assumption is necessary for one-call (or constant-call) approaches. Here, we show that a large class of one-call constructions (which in particular includes the one of Berman and Haitner) cannot be proved to be a secure PRF under a black-box reduction to the (polynomial-time) naPRF security of the underlying function.

Our result complements existing impossibility results (Myers, EURO-CRYPT '04; Pietrzak, CRYPTO '05) ruling out natural specific approaches, such as parallel and sequential composition. Furthermore, we show that our techniques extend to rule out a natural class of constructions making *parallel* but arbitrary number of calls which in particular includes parallel composition and the two-call, cuckoo-hashing based construction of Berman et al. (Journal of Cryptology, '19).

Keywords: Pseudorandom functions · Black-box separations · Foundations

1 Introduction

We study the problem of building a *pseudorandom function* (PRF) which resists *adaptive attackers* from a *non-adaptive* PRF (naPRF), i.e., a PRF which is only secure against adversaries choosing their inputs non-adaptively at once. This problem has attracted substantial amounts of interest (see [4,5,8,14,15,17–19] for examples) – indeed, a naPRF may initially be *easier* to devise than a full-

© Springer Nature Switzerland AG 2020
C. Galdi and V. Kolesnikov (Eds.): SCN 2020, LNCS 12238, pp. 546–565, 2020.
https://doi.org/10.1007/978-3-030-57990-6_27

fledged PRF.[1] However, to date, the complexity of the best possible transformation remains unknown,[2] and natural approaches such as sequential and parallel composition have been proved to fail.

The main contribution of this paper is a proof that highly-efficient black-box naPRF-to-PRF transformations are unlikely to exist: We rule out a large class of *one-call* constructions with respect to *hardness-preserving* black-box security proofs. Here, hardness preserving means that the transformation preserves security against PPT adversaries. As we argue below, understanding one-call constructions is a challenging first step towards understanding the overall problem. This in particular shows that previous work by Berman and Haitner (BH) [4], giving a one-call construction relying on complexity leveraging in the security proof, is best possible. Also, it is consistent with the fact that all hardness-preserving transformations make $\omega(1)$ calls.

We also extend our result to a class of *multi*-call parallel constructions, and prove that these, too, do not transform a naPRF into a PRF. This result can be seen as a generalization of Myers [17] black-box separation for the parallel composition. We elaborate on this below, but first give some more context. An overview of our results is given in Table 1.

FROM NON-ADAPTIVE TO ADAPTIVE SECURITY. The problem of building PRFs from naPRFs is well-understood in the information-theoretic case, i.e., attackers are only bounded in query complexity (but not in their running time). Here, simple constructions are sufficient (e.g., sequential and parallel composition). This was first proved by Vaudenay [22], and also follows as the application of general composition theorems [14,15].

However, negative results have shown that such simple approaches fail in the computational regime, both with respect to black-box reductions [17], as well as without any proof restriction, but assuming DDH holds [18]. Later, it was also shown [19] that public-key assumptions are necessary for counter-examples. This already suggests that the computational setting is harder, but note that these results only cover specific constructions. Here, we aim for more general impossibility, and this presents several additional challenges – in fact, already for *one-call* constructions, which are the main focus of this work.

FROM NAPRFS TO PRFS: PRIOR WORKS. The most efficient known transformations can be cast in terms of the same two steps: (1) we use a naPRF H (say, in the following, with n-bit seeds, inputs, and outputs) to build a PRF with a "small" domain, i.e., the strings of length $\ell = \omega(\log \lambda)$; (2) the domain of the resulting PRF is extended without extra calls by using (almost) universal hashing – this is often referred to as "Levin's trick", and is also reminiscent of universal-hashing based MACs [21,24].[3]

---

[1] See [1] for a concrete example.

[2] Note that as naPRFs imply one-way functions and PRGs, and thus in turn also PRFs, such transformations are always possible.

[3] We stress that this approach inherently relies on an asymptotic view targeting PPT security, which we take in this paper – if we are interested in concrete security, the best we can hope for is $2^{\ell/2}$ security, and thus we may need even more calls to the underlying naPRF.

There are two ways to accomplish step (1):

- CASCADING. A first, folkore approach (which is hardness-preserving) is via a variant of the cascade construction [3]. For a fixed polynomial $p = p(\lambda)$, we first fix distinct n-bit strings $z_1, \ldots, z_p$. Now, let $\ell = d \log p$ for some $d = \omega(1)$, and think of an ℓ-bit input x as a vector $x = (x_1, \ldots, x_d) \in [p]^d$. Then, the output with seed k is y_d, where

$$y_0 = k, \quad y_i = H(y_{i-1}, z_{x_i}) \text{ for all } i = 1, \ldots, d.$$

  This is a secure PRF as long as H is a secure PRF on the domain $\{z_1, \ldots, z_p\}$, and since p is a fixed polynomial, it is enough that H is a naPRF for p-query distinguishers that query all of $z_1, \ldots z_p$ at once.
- THE BH APPROACH. The core idea of the BH construction can be cast as the fact that every sufficiently secure naPRF secure against $(t = O(2^\ell))$-time distinguishers, where $\ell = \omega(\log \lambda)$, is *already an adaptively secure PRF* for polynomial-time distinguishers, as long as we only query a (fixed) subset of the domain of size 2^ℓ. (This follows by a straightforward reduction which queries all of these points beforehand.) I.e., we can then obtain an adaptively secure PRF with ℓ-bit domain as $F(k, x) = H(k, x \| 0^{n-\ell})$. Note that it is necessary to fix a super-polynomial t a-priori, since the construction depends on t and we want security for all polynomial-time distinguishers.

MAIN RESULT. This still leaves open the question whether the BH construction is secure only assuming H to be secure against PPT adversaries. Here, we consider the general class of constructions of the form

$$F((s, k), x) = y, \quad \text{where} \quad w = C(s, x), \quad z = H(k, w), \quad y = G(s, x, z),$$

where C is an arbitrary (seeded) pre-processing function from n bits to n bits.[4] In particular, the BH construction takes this form. We show that there exists no (fully) black-box reduction to show PRF security assuming H is a naPRF.

This class in fact includes *all* possible constructions which do not manipulate the seed k of the underlying naPRF. As our main result, we show an oracle with respect to which (1) naPRFs exist, but (2) the above construction is insecure, provided C satisfies a mild combinatorial property *and* the output length of G is lower bounded by a small constant. This implies the impossibility of providing a fully-BB reduction of security for such a construction to the (polynomial-time) security of H as a naPRF.

The combinatorial condition is that for some constant $c = O(1)$, the function C satisfies a notion we refer to as c-universal, which means that for any choice of c distinct n-bit strings $x_1, \ldots, x_c$, and a random seed s, the values $C(s, x_1), \ldots, C(s, x_c)$ are unlikely to be all equal. While this condition appears

---

[4] The choice of an n-bit input for C is arbitrary here, because for any domain length $\ell = \omega(\log n)$, we can modify C to make the domain n bits, either by appending $0^{\ell-n}$ to the input if $\ell > n$, or by using universal hashing as described above if $\ell < n$.

inherent using traditional security proofs (which often requires the input to H to be "fresh"), it is not clear how to prove it is necessary for any post-processing function G.

However, we can drop this condition for some special cases. For example, when G simply outputs (part of) z, then we see that if C is not 2-universal, then we can break PRF security of the construction directly, provided the output length is $\omega(\log \lambda)$. There are cases where however our result does not completely rule out construction – it is possible that C is not 2-universal and we can achieve security nonetheless when the naPRF has a single-bit output.

MULTI-CALL CONSTRUCTIONS. We also extend the techniques to prove our main result on one-call constructions to a restricted class of *parallel* κ-call constructions that output, on input x,

$$y = \mathsf{G}(s_{\kappa+1}, x) \oplus \bigoplus_{i \in [\kappa]} \mathsf{H}(k_i, \mathsf{C}(s_i, x))$$

where C is a c-universal pre-processing function, whereas G can be arbitrary. This family includes e.g. the Cuckoo-Hashing based construction from [5]. This result can be seen as a generalization of the work of Myers [17], which studies the special case without any pre-processing.

IMPOSSIBILITY FOR GENERAL REDUCTIONS. One may wonder whether the results claimed in this paper can be extended to rule out general reductions, e.g., from DDH, following the paradigm of Pietrzak [18]. This is unlikely to be true. In particular, Pietrzak [18] separation holds even if DDH is exponentially hard – however, under such strong hardness, one can simply use the BH construction.

A PERSPECTIVE. We believe the question of assessing how efficiently we can obtain a PRF from a non-adaptive object like a naPRF to be among the most fascinating ones in classical cryptography (although perhaps somewhat overlooked). Constructions are easy in retrospect, and, like in many other instances, seemingly very hard to improve, yet proving that they are indeed best possible appears to be out of reach.

This in particular justifies the perhaps limited-looking scope of our results – we hope to provide evidence that ruling out even a subclass of one-call constructions is a challenging problem *and* substantial progress. It would be of course desirable to provide impossibility for *all* constant-query constructions – a statement we conjecture to be true. However, we believe this to remain a challenging open question. Our work can be seen as one among a large body of results that provide lower bounds on the efficiency of black-box constructions, e.g. [2,6,9,10,12,16,23].

2   Preliminaries

For $n, m \in \mathbb{N}$, $\mathsf{Funcs}(n, m)$ denotes the set of all functions $\{0,1\}^n \to \{0,1\}^m$. By $[n]$ we denote the set $\{1, \ldots, n\}$. By $d \xleftarrow{\$} D$ we denote the process of sampling a random element from some finite set D and assigning it to d. For $l \in \mathbb{N}$,

Table 1. We rule out fully black-box constructions of PRF F from n bits to m bits of the form described in first and second column from a naPRF H from n bits to r bits, whenever the conditions in the third column are true for some constant $c \geq 2$. C is a (keyed) function family from n bits to n bits and g is a function from $2n + r$ bits to m bits. For first row, G is a function family from $n + r$ bits to m bits and G is a family from n bits to r bits for second row.

Construction	Evaluation $y = F((s, k), x)$	Rule out for any $c = O(1)$
$F^H[C, G]$ (Sect. 3)	$y = G(s, x, z)$ where $w = C(s, x); z = H(k, w)$	C is c-universal, any r any $m \geq \log(8ce)$
$F^H[\kappa, C, G]$ (Sect. 5)	$y = G(s_{\kappa+1}, x) \oplus \bigoplus_{i=1}^{\kappa} H(k_i, C(s_i, x))$	C is c-universal any κ, r, G
$F^H[C, g]$ (full version)	$y = g(x, w, z)$ where $w = C(s, x); z = H(k, w)$	any C, g, r and any $m \geq (n + r)/c + \omega(\log n)$
$F^H[C]$ (full version)	$y = H(k, C(s, x))[1, \ldots, m]$	any C any $m, r = \omega(\log n)$

$(d_1, \ldots, d_l) \xleftarrow{\$} (D)^l$ and $(d_1, \ldots, d_l) \xleftarrow{\$} (D)^{[l]}$ denote the process of sampling l elements from D where each d_i is sampled independently and uniformly from D with and without replacement, respectively. For $l, p \in \mathbb{N}$ and $f \in \mathsf{Funcs}(n, m)$, $X = (x_1, \ldots, x_l)$ denotes an ordered tuple where $x_1, \ldots, x_l \in \{0, 1\}^n$ and $X[i]$ denotes the i-th element in the tuple. $f(X)$ denotes the ordered tuple $(f(x_1), \ldots, f(x_l))$. For $X = (x_1, \ldots, x_l)$ and $Y = (y_1, \ldots, y_p)$, by $X \| Y$ we denote $(x_1, \ldots, x_l, y_1, \ldots, y_p)$. We use capital letters to denote both tuples and sets, our usage will be clear from the context. A function $\alpha : \mathbb{N} \to \mathbb{R}_{\geq 0}$ is negligible if for every $c \in \mathbb{N}$, there exists n_0 such that $\alpha(n) \leq n^{-c}$ for all $n \geq n_0$.

FUNCTION FAMILIES. For polynomially bounded functions $m, \sigma : \mathbb{N} \to \mathbb{N}$, a *function family* $F = (F.Kg, F.Eval)$ from n bits to m bits with σ-bit keys/seeds consists of two polynomial-time algorithms – the *key (or seed) generation algorithm* F.Kg and the *evaluation algorithm* F.Eval. In particular, F.Kg is a randomized algorithm that on input the security parameter 1^n returns a key k sampled uniformly from $\{0, 1\}^{\sigma(n)}$. F.Eval is a deterministic algorithm that takes three inputs: 1^n, key $k \in \{0, 1\}^{\sigma(n)}$ and query $x \in \{0, 1\}^n$ and returns an $m(n)$-bit string $y = F.Eval(1^n, k, x)$. We generally write $F(1^n, k, \cdot) = F.Eval(1^n, k, \cdot)$ and even drop the first input (i.e., 1^n) of both Kg and Eval for ease of notation. By $f \xleftarrow{\$} F$ we denote the process of sampling $k \xleftarrow{\$} F.Kg$ and assigning $f = F(k, \cdot)$.

ORACLE FUNCTION FAMILIES. In this work, we consider function families F where F.Kg and F.Eval can make queries to another function family modeled as an oracle O. We refer to such families as oracle function families and denote it by $F^{(\cdot)}$ and by F^O when the underlying oracle is O. By $F^{(\cdot)}[C]$ we denote function family F having access to the entire description of the function family C.

UNIVERSAL FUNCTION FAMILIES. Below we define a generalization of the well-known notion of almost α-universal hash function family.

Definition 1. *For polynomially bounded functions m, σ, let C be a function family from n bits to m bits with σ-bit seeds, α be some function from $\mathbb{N}$ to $\mathbb{R}_{\geq 0}$, and $c \in \mathbb{N}$. We say that C is (α, c)-universal family if for all $n \in \mathbb{N}$, every $X \in (\{0,1\}^n)^{[c]}$,*

$$\Pr_{s \xleftarrow{\$} C.\mathsf{Kg}(1^n)} [C(s, X[1]) = C(s, X[2]) = \ldots = C(s, X[c])] \leq \alpha(n).$$

We retrieve the standard notion of almost α-universal hash function family when $c = 2$. Whenever α is a negligible function, we refer to C as a c-universal function family. We emphasize that the reader should not confuse our notion of c-universality with the notion of c-wise independent hashing.

2.1 (Non-) Adaptive Pseudo-Random Functions Relative to Oracles

In this work, we consider pseudo-randomness of function families relative to an oracle which we define next.

Definition 2. *Let m be a polynomially bounded function over $\mathbb{N}$ and O be some oracle. Let $F^{(\cdot)}$ be an oracle function family from n bits to m bits. For probabilistic polynomial-time (PPT) distinguisher A, let*

$$\mathsf{Adv}_{A,F,O}^{rel-prf}(n) = \left| \Pr_{f \xleftarrow{\$} F} [A^{f^O, O}(1^n) = 1] - \Pr_{g \xleftarrow{\$} \mathsf{Funcs}(n, m(n))} [A^{g, O}(1^n) = 1] \right|,$$

where probability is also taken over the random coins of A.

We say that $F^{(\cdot)}$ is a pseudo-random function (PRF) relative to oracle O if for all PPT distinguishers A $\mathsf{Adv}_{A,F,O}^{rel-prf}(1^n)$ is negligible in n. $F^{(\cdot)}$ is a non-adaptive PRF (naPRF) relative to O if the above is true for all PPT distinguishers that only make non-adaptive queries to the challenge oracle f/g.

In naPRF definition, we require that A only make non-adaptive queries to the challenge oracle f/g and can query O adaptively. In the absence of the oracle O we recover the standard notions of PRFs and naPRFs. Although as stated the oracle O is deterministic, in this work we will consider randomized oracles O and the above probabilities is taken also over the random choices made by O.

2.2 Black-Box Separations

The study of black-box separations for cryptographic primitives was initiated by the seminal paper of Impagliazzo and Rudich [13] which provided a framework (later formalized by [20]) to provide such results. They observed that fully black-box constructions relativize w.r.t. any oracle and hence to rule out fully black-box constructions it suffices to show the existence of an oracle relative to which there exists a naPRF H but $F^H[C, G]$ is not a PRF. Furthermore, Gertner, Malkin and Reingold [11] observed that the oracle can depend on the construction F.

Theorem 1 ([11]). *An oracle function family* $F^{(\cdot)}$ *is not a fully BB construction of a PRF from naPRF if there exists an oracle* O *and an oracle function family* $H^{(\cdot)}$ *such that* H^O *is a naPRF relative to* O *but* F^H *is not a PRF relative to* O.

When restricting to uniform adversaries (which is the focus of this work) it is sufficient to exhibit a oracle that makes random choices (or a distribution of oracles) and show that Theorem 1 holds except with negligible probability. This is the approach adopted in all previous works on black-box separations. We formally state this as the following Proposition.

Proposition 1. *An oracle function family* $F^{(\cdot)}$ *is not a fully BB construction of a PRF from naPRF if there exists a randomized oracle* O *and an oracle function family* $H^{(\cdot)}$ *such that* H^O *is a naPRF relative to* O *but* F^H *is not a PRF.*

Theorem 1 for the uniform setting follows from Proposition 1 by relying on the Borel-Cantelli Lemma and on the countability of the family of uniform Turing machines. All results in this work will be of the flavor of Proposition 1. Establishing Proposition 1 w.r.t. non-uniform adversaries may not be sufficient to lift BB separations to the non-uniform model due to the uncountability of non-uniform Turing Machines. We leave it to future work to lift our results to the non-uniform setting, following ideas from [7,10].

3   Main Result

In Sect. 3.1 we formally describe the class of one-call constructions to which our separation result applies. Then in Sect. 3.2 we state our main result and provide its proof's overview in Sect. 3.3.

3.1   General 1-call Construction

Let σ, r, m be any polynomially bounded functions. Let C be a function family from n bits to n bits with σ-bit seeds, let H be a function family on n bits to r bits with n-bit seeds and let G be a function family from $n + r$ bits to m bits with σ-bit seeds. Consider the family $F^H[C, G]$ (depicted in Fig. 1a) from n bits to m bits with $\sigma + n$-bit seeds such that for every $n \in \mathbb{N}$, $F.Kg(1^n)$ outputs (s, k) where s and k are randomly chosen $\sigma(n)$-bit seeds for both C and G, and n-bit key for H respectively. The evaluation of F on $x \in \{0, 1\}^n$ proceeds as follows,

$$y = F^H((s, k), x) = G(s, x, z) \text{ where } z = H(k, C(s, x)) . \tag{1}$$

Remark 1. Note that the function families C and G in Eq. 1 share the same seed s. This, in fact, is a generalization of the case when C and G have independent seeds s_1 and s_2 respectively – for every such C and G we can construct families C' and G' which share the same seed $s = (s_1, s_2)$,

$$C'(s = (s_1, s_2), \cdot) = C(s_1, \cdot) \; ; \; G'(s = (s_1, s_2), \cdot, \cdot) = G(s_2, \cdot, \cdot) .$$

Furthermore, as G and C share the same seed s, G can compute $w = C(s, x)$ from its inputs (s, x, z) and hence w.l.o.g. we do not feed w as an input to G.

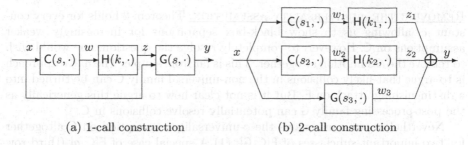

(a) 1-call construction   (b) 2-call construction

Fig. 1. (a) General 1-call construction $F^H[C, G]$ where C (resp., G) is a family from n bits (resp., $n + r$ bits) to n bits (resp., m bits) with σ-bit keys and H is a function family from n bits to r bits with n-bit keys. Figure shows the evaluation of F on input x and key (s, k) where s is the key for both C and G and k is key for H. (b) Two-call construction $F^H[C, G]$ where C (resp., G) is a family from n bits (resp., n bits) to n bits (resp., m bits) with σ-bit keys and H is a function family from n bits to m bits with n-bit keys. Figure shows the evaluation of F on input x and key (s, k) where $s = (s_1, s_2, s_3)$ and $k = (k_1, k_2)$ is key for H.

Remark 2. The choice of the input length of C is arbitrary as any C mapping $l = \omega(\log n)$-bit strings to n-bit strings can be converted into C' which maps n-bit strings to n-bit strings by padding 0^{l-n} to the input whenever $l \geq n$ and pre-processing the input via a universal hash family from n bits to l bits whenever $l < n$. Furthermore, the resulting family C' is c-universal hash family whenever C is c-universal for any $c \geq 2$.

The construction in Eq. 1 covers all one-call constructions which do not modify the key of the naPRF. In particular, it also covers the Berman-Haitner [4] construction – one recovers the BH construction from $F[C, G]$ by letting C be a universal hash family and letting $G(s, (x, z)) = z$.

3.2 Main Theorem

Below we state our main theorem which provides an oracle relative to which a naPRF H exists but the construction $F^H[C, G]$ is not a PRF as long as C is universal function family. This in turn implies that F cannot be a fully black-box construction of a PRF from a naPRF.

Theorem 2 (Main Theorem). *Let $c = O(1)$ and r, σ, m be any polynomially bounded functions such that $m \geq \log(8ce)$. Let C be a c-universal family from n bits to n bits. Then, for every $F^{(\cdot)}[C, G]$ (as in Eq. 1) from n bits to m bits there exists a randomized oracle (O, R) such that,*[5]

1. *There exists an oracle function family $H^{(\cdot)}$ from n bits to r bits with n-bit keys that is a naPRF relative to (O, R).*
2. *$F^H[C, G]$ is not a PRF relative to (O, R).*

---
[5] For simplicity we present our oracle as a pair (O, R).

REMOVING THE c-UNIVERSALITY ASSUMPTION. Theorem 2 holds for every constant c, allowing us to show black-box separations for increasingly weaker assumptions on C. However, to completely resolve the question, one would wish to remove the assumption altogether. This is far from simple: The naive approach is to argue that likely collisions in the non-universal family C can be turned into a distinguishing attack on F. But it is not clear how to argue this generically as the post-processing family G can potentially resolve collisions in C.

Nevertheless, we can remove the c-universality assumption on C altogether for two important subclasses of F[C, G]: (1) A special case of F[C, g] (third row in Table 1), where G consists of a single function g (i.e., independent of any seed material) and (2) A special case of F[C] (forth row in Table 1) where G is a family that on input (s, x, z) just outputs z. At a very high level, note that for the construction F[C], collisions in C lead to collisions in F, however such collisions occur for a random function only with negligible probability when the output length satisfies $m = \omega(\log n)$. Therefore, an adversary that knows collisions in C can trivially break the PRF security of F. For the construction F[C, g] one needs to go a step further and analyze the entropy of the output $(F(x_1), \ldots, F(x_c))$ for inputs x_i's for which collisions under C are likely. We can show a distinguishing attack whenever $m = \Omega(n)$. We defer the formal proofs to the full version.

Overall, we believe removing c-universality from Theorem 2 for all one-call constructions is closely related to the long-standing open problem in symmetric-key cryptography of proving security beyond the birthday barrier for the composition of a non-universal hash family and a short-output PRF. The challenge is that collisions in the hash function may still be less likely than actual output collisions when the range is small. We believe removing the c-universality assumption is unlikely to happen without making progress on this open question, and we believe that the answer depends on a more fine-grained understanding of the combinatorics of C.

3.3   Proof Overview Of Theorem 2

We prove Theorem 2 in two parts: First, in Proposition 2 we provide an oracle for constructions F[C, G] that satisfies a structural property – "unbiasedness" (define next) and provide an oracle for "biased" constructions in Proposition 3. $(1 - \delta)$-UNBIASED $F^{(\cdot)}[C, G]$. Before we formally define the structural property of "$(1 - \delta)$-unbiasedness" of F it would be helpful to consider the following definition.

Definition 3. *For the function family G, for some $n \in \mathbb{N}$, let $x \in \{0, 1\}^n$, $s \in \{0, 1\}^{\sigma(n)}$ and $y \in \{0, 1\}^{m(n)}$, we say that y is $1/2$-bad w.r.t. (s, x) if $\Pr_z[y = G(s, x, z)] > 1/2$ otherwise y is $1/2$-good w.r.t. (s, x).*

If for some pair (s, x) there exists a $1/2$-bad y then the output of F (on input x and seed s) will be biased towards y even if H is a truly random function family. We call F as unbiased if at least $(1 - \delta)$ fraction of the outputs y's will be $1/2$-good for some $\delta < 1$.

Definition 4 ($(1 - \delta)$-unbiased). *For any functions r, m, σ, let C be a family from n bits to n bits and G be a family from $n + r$ bits to m bits. Then for $\delta \leq 1$ we say that $\mathsf{F}^{(\cdot)}[\mathsf{C}, \mathsf{G}]$ is $(1 - \delta)$-unbiased if for all polynomials $l = \omega(\sigma)/\delta$ there exists some negligible function $\nu(\cdot)$ such that*

$$\Pr_{X,s,f} \left[|\{i : Y[i] \text{ is } 1/2\text{-bad } w.r.t. (s, X[i])\}| \geq \delta \cdot l \right] \leq \nu(n),$$

for every $n \in \mathbb{N}$ where $Y[i] = \mathsf{F}^f(s, X[i])$, $s \xleftarrow{\$} \{0,1\}^{\sigma(n)}$, $f \xleftarrow{\$} \mathrm{Funcs}(n, r(n))$ and $X \xleftarrow{\$} (\{0,1\}^n)^{[l(n)]}$. Otherwise, we call $\mathsf{F}^{(\cdot)}[\mathsf{C}, \mathsf{G}]$ as δ-biased.

We state Proposition 2 (proof in Sect. 4) which handles unbiased F's.

Proposition 2. *Let $c = O(1)$ and r, m, σ be any polynomially bounded functions. Let C be a c-universal family from n bits to n bits with σ-bit seeds and G be a family from $n + r$ bits to m bits with σ-bit seeds such that $\mathsf{F}^{(\cdot)}[\mathsf{C}, \mathsf{G}]$ is $\left(1 - \frac{1}{4c}\right)$-unbiased. Then, there exists a randomized oracle (O, R) such that there exists an oracle function family $\mathsf{H}^{(\cdot)}$ from n bits to r bits with n-bit keys that is a naPRF relative to (O, R) but $\mathsf{F}^{\mathsf{H}}[\mathsf{C}, \mathsf{G}]$ is not a PRF relative to (O, R).*

Next, Proposition 3 considers a biased F, the proof is in the full version.

Proposition 3. *Let $c = O(1)$ and let r, σ, m be polynomially bounded functions such that $m \geq \log(2ce)$. For every $\mathsf{F}^{(\cdot)}[\mathsf{C}, \mathsf{G}]$ from n bits to m bits, if $\mathsf{F}^{(\cdot)}[\mathsf{C}, \mathsf{G}]$ is $1/c$-biased then there exists a randomized oracle (O, R) such that there exists an oracle function family $\mathsf{H}^{(\cdot)}$ from n bits to r bits with n-bit keys that is a naPRF relative to (O, R) but $\mathsf{F}^{\mathsf{H}}[\mathsf{C}, \mathsf{G}]$ is not a PRF relative to (O, R).*

Remark 3. Note that Proposition 2 rules out F for any output length m (even $m = 1$). However, we can only prove Proposition 3 when $m \geq \log(2ce)$ for some constant c. For this reason Theorem 2 requires $m \geq \log(2ce)$. It is an important open question to extend our results for smaller m's.

Proof of Theorem 2. Given Propositions 2 and 3, Theorem 2 follows immediately by analyzing the following two cases: (1) If $\mathsf{F}^{(\cdot)}[\mathsf{C}, \mathsf{G}]$ is $\frac{1}{4c}$-biased then Theorem 2 follows from Proposition 3 with parameter $4c$ (instead of c), and (2) If $\mathsf{F}^{(\cdot)}[\mathsf{C}, \mathsf{G}]$ is $\left(1 - \frac{1}{4c}\right)$-unbiased then Theorem 2 follows from Proposition 2.   □

4   Proof of Proposition 2

First, in Sect. 4.1 we establish some preliminary notation necessary to describe our oracles (O, R) and the naPRF family H (which are defined in Sect. 4.2). Then, in Sect. 4.3 we argue the insecurity of F relative to (O, R) and in Sect. 4.4 we argue that H is a naPRF relative to (O, R).

4.1   Preliminary Notation for Defining (O, R)

First, we observe an important property of c-universal function families called (β, δ)-sparseness.

Definition 5 (*s is β-sparse*). *Let* C *be a family from n bits to n bits with σ-bit seeds. For $n \in \mathbb{N}$, $\beta \leq 1$, we say that $s \in \{0,1\}^{\sigma(n)}$ is β-sparse if* $\Pr_x[C(s,x) = w] \leq \beta$ *for every $w \in \{0,1\}^n$.*

Definition 6 (C *is (β, δ)-sparse*). *Let* C *be a function family from n bits to n bits. For functions β and δ we say that* C *is (β, δ)-sparse if* $\Pr[s \text{ not } \beta(n)\text{-sparse }] \leq \delta(n)$ *for all $n \in \mathbb{N}$ over the random choice of $s \xleftarrow{\$} $ C.Kg.*

Lemma 1. *For any $c = O(1)$, any (α, c)-universal function family* C *from n bits to n bits is also (β, δ)-sparse for $\beta = \max(\alpha^{1/2c}, \frac{2c}{2^n})$, $\delta = 2^{c-1}\sqrt{\alpha}$. Furthermore, β and δ are both negligible for $c = O(1)$ and negligible α.*

For the rest of this section let us fix some (α, c)-universal function family C from n bits to n bits with σ-bit seeds, some $n + r$ bit to m bit function family G with σ-bit seeds such that F = F[C, G] is a $(1 - 1/4c)$-unbiased function family (as in the statement of Proposition 2). Furthermore, for (α, c) let β, δ be functions (as defined by Lemma 1) such that C is (β, δ)-sparse. For C and F we define two sets of "good" seeds namely Good_C and Good_F necessary to describe (O, R).

THE SET $\text{Good}_C(\beta, X)$. For some tuple $X \in (\{0,1\}^n)^l$, the set $\text{Good}_C(\beta, X)$ is a set of β-sparse seeds for which there are no c-way collisions among $C(s, X[i])$'s. To match the usage of Good_C later in the proof, we define $\text{Good}_C(\beta, X)$ for $X = X_1 \| X_2$ where each X_i's are l-length tuples.

Definition 7. *For $n, l \in \mathbb{N}, \beta \leq 1$, $X = X_1 \| X_2 \in (\{0,1\}^n)^{[2l]}$ where $X_i \in (\{0,1\}^n)^{[l]}$, let $\text{Good}_C(\beta, X)$ denote the set of all $s \in \{0,1\}^\sigma$ such that s is β-sparse and there are no c-way collisions in $C(s, X)$ – for every $I \subseteq [2l]$ of size c there exists $i, j \in I$ such that $C(s, X[i]) \neq C(s, X[j])$ where we are viewing $C(s, X)$ as a set instead of the tuples.*

THE SET $\text{Good}_F(\beta, X, Y)$. Here we extend the definition of "good" seeds relative to the outputs Y. Recall that F is $(1 - 1/4c)$-unbiased and so for some sufficiently large l we expect at most $1/4c$ fraction of the $Y[i]$'s to be $1/2$-bad. Good_F is the set of seeds that are in Good_C for which $1/4c$ fraction of the $Y[i]$'s are $1/2$-bad.

Definition 8. *For X as in Definition 7 and $Y \in (\{0,1\}^n)^{2l}$, let $\text{Good}_F(\beta, X, Y)$ denote the set of seeds $s \in \{0,1\}^\sigma$ such that $s \in \text{Good}_C(\beta, X)$ and $|\{i : Y[i] \text{ is } 1/2\text{-bad w.r.t. } (s, X[i])\}| \leq 2l/4c = l/2c$.*[6]

---

[6] Note that we have $2l/4c$ because our X, Y are tuples of $2l$ length tuples.

Oracle $R_1(1^n)$:

if $T_1^n = \bot$ then $T_1^n \xleftarrow{\$} (\{0,1\}^n)^{[l(n)]}$
return T_1^n

Oracle $R_2(1^n, X, Y)$:
if $\neg\mathsf{isValid}(1^n, l, X, Y)$ then return 1
if $X \neq T_1^n$ then return $\bot$

if $T_2^n[Y] = \bot$ then $T_2^n[Y] \xleftarrow{\$} (\{0,1\}^n \setminus T_1^n)^{[l(n)]}$
return $T_2^n[Y]$

Oracle $R_3(1^n, X = X_1 \| X_2, Y = Y_1 \| Y_2)$:
if $\neg\mathsf{isValid}(1^n, 2l, X, Y)$ then return $\bot$
if $X_1 \neq T_1^n \vee X_2 \neq T_2^n[Y_1]$ then return $\bot$
if $\exists (s, k) \in \mathsf{Good}_F(\beta, \hat{X}, Y) \times \{0,1\}^n$:

   $\quad F^{H^O}[C, G]((s, k), X) = Y$ then return 1
return $\bot$

Proc. $\mathsf{isValid}(1^n, t, X, Y)$
if $X \notin (\{0,1\}^n)^{[t]}$ then return 0
if $Y \notin (\{0,1\}^m)^t$ then return 0
return 1

Adversary $A^{(O,R),f}(1^n)$:
$X_1 \leftarrow R_1(1^n)$
$Y_1 \leftarrow f(X_1)$
$X_2 \leftarrow R_2(1^n, X_1, Y_1)$
$Y_2 \leftarrow f(X_2)$
if $R_3(1^n, X_1 \| X_2, Y_1 \| Y_2) = 1$ then
   return 1
return 0

Fig. 2. Description of oracle R and adaptive adversary A that breaks the security of F relative to (O, R).

4.2   Oracles (O, R) and H^O

Recall that we are designing (O, R) for constructions $F^{(\cdot)}[C, G]$ where C is (α, c)-universal and also (β, δ)-sparse (as observed in Lemma 1), and $F^{(\cdot)}[C, G]$ is $(1 - 1/4c)$-unbiased for some $c = O(1)$ and negligible α. Let us, furthermore, fix some sufficiently large $l = \omega(\sigma + n)$. Next, we describe our oracles (O, R) which will depend on the families C, G, F and parameters β, c, l.

ORACLE O AND H^O. Oracle O embeds an information theoretically secure PRF. That is, for every $n \in \mathbb{N}$ and every $k \in \{0,1\}^n$, $O(1^n, k, \cdot)$ is implemented by a function from $\mathsf{Funcs}(n, r)$ which is sampled uniformly and independently at random with replacement. Relative to such an oracle there exists a naPRF H^O from n bits to r bits with n-bit keys. $H.\mathsf{Kg}(1^n)$ returns a randomly chosen key $k \in \{0,1\}^n$ and $H^O(k, x) = O(k, x)$ for every key $k \in \{0,1\}^n$ and input x.

ORACLE R. We decompose R into three oracles (R_1, R_2, R_3) as described in Fig. 2.

Oracle R_1: Oracle R_1 for every $n \in \mathbb{N}$ samples an $l(n)$ length tuple T_1^n of n-bit strings *without* replacement. It accepts as input the security parameter 1^n and outputs the corresponding T_1^n.

Oracle R_2: Oracle R_2 works identically to the oracle R_1 except that it takes as inputs the security parameter 1^n, and tuples $X \in (\{0,1\}^n)^{[l(n)]}$ and $Y \in (\{0,1\}^n)^{l(n)}$ and returns a random $l(n)$-length tuple of n-bit strings $(T_2^n[Y]$ in Fig. 2) iff $X = T_1^n$. The tuple $T_2^n[Y]$ is sampled without replacement from $\{0,1\}^n \setminus T_1^n$. We should think of R_1 as providing the first challenge tuple $X_1 = T_1^n$ and R_2 as providing the second, "adaptive" challenge tuple $X_2 = T_2^n[Y_1]$ after receiving the response Y_1 for the first challenge X_1.

Oracle R_3: R_1 and R_2 are just fancy random string generators and provide no way to break the security of F as both these oracles are in fact independent of F. The responsibility of ensuring that one can break F is on R_3. More precisely, R_3 accepts as queries a tuple $(X = X_1 \| X_2, Y = Y_1 \| Y_2)$ outputs 1 iff it finds some key (s, k) for F which maps X to Y where $k \in \{0, 1\}^n$ and $s \in \mathsf{Good}_\mathsf{F}(\beta, X, Y)$ and it is also required that $X_1 = R_1(1^n) = T_1^n$ and $X_2 = R_2(1^n, X_1, Y_1) = T_2^n[Y_1]$.

This completes the description of R. Note that R depends on the entire description of oracle O in addition to the function families C and G and the parameters l, β. For notational convenience, we will drop the superscript n from T_i^n and the input 1^n from all oracles. Next, in Sect. 4.3 we establish the insecurity of F as a PRF and in Sect. 4.4 the security of H as a naPRF relative to (O, R) which put together will conclude the proof of Proposition 2.

4.3 F Is Not a PRF Relative to (O, R)

Relative to the oracle (O, R) there exists a trivial uniform adversary $A^{(\mathsf{O},\mathsf{R}),f}$ which uses adaptive access to the challenge oracle f to compute $Y_i = f(X_i)$ for X_1, X_2 provided by R. In Lemma 2 we show that A indeed breaks the PRF security of F. The detail the proof in the full version.

Lemma 2 (F is insecure relative to (O, R)). *For A described in Fig. 2 there exists a non-negligible function ϵ such that,* $\mathsf{Adv}^{\mathsf{rel-prf}}_{A,\mathsf{F},(\mathsf{O},\mathsf{R})}(n) \geq \epsilon(n)$.

4.4 H Is a NaPRF Relative to (O, R)

In this section, we establish the non-adaptive security of H relative to (O, R) by reducing it to the non-adaptive security of H relative to *only* O. That is, for every A relative to (O, R) making only non-adaptive queries to its challenge oracle f but adaptive queries to O and R, we construct an adversary B relative to *only* O that also only makes non-adaptive queries to its challenge oracle f and is just as successful as A in the non-adaptive security game of H. The adversary $B^{\mathsf{O},f}$ internally runs $A^{(\mathsf{O},\mathsf{R}),f}$ and answers all of its queries to O and f by forwarding to its own oracles. For the queries to R, B attempts to simulate the oracle R internally for A. Recall that R is decomposed into three oracles (R_1, R_2, R_3) where R_1 and R_2 just output random l-length tuples of n-bit strings and hence are easy to simulate. The challenge is to simulate the oracle R_3, which depends on the entire description of O, with only oracle access to O. Nevertheless, we show that B can still simulate R_3 queries correctly. We emphasize that the non-adaptive query restriction on A is only w.r.t. querying f. It can query (O, R) adaptively.

Lemma 3 (H is a naPRF relative to (O, R)). *For any non-adaptive adversary A that makes at most $q \leq 2^{n/2}$ to its oracles we have for every $n \in \mathbb{N}$,* $\mathsf{Adv}^{\mathsf{rel-naprf}}_{A,\mathsf{H},(\mathsf{O},\mathsf{R})}(n) \leq 2q \cdot \epsilon + \frac{2q}{2^n}$ *where*

$$\epsilon = \frac{(q+1)2^\sigma}{2^t} + \frac{2^{\sigma+n}}{2^{t(c+1)}} + \frac{6q}{2^n} + q\, 2^\sigma \binom{l}{l/2} (2\beta q)^{l/2} \; ; \; t = \frac{l}{2c(c-1)} \,.$$

Game G_0, G_1:
foreach $k \in \{0,1\}^n$ **do**
  $\pi_k \xleftarrow{\$} \mathsf{Funcs}(n, m)$
$k^* \xleftarrow{\$} \{0,1\}^n$
$b \xleftarrow{\$} A^{(O,R),f}$
return b

Oracle $R_3(X = X_1 \| X_2, Y = Y_1 \| Y_2)$: //Game G_0
if $\neg \mathsf{isValid}(2l, X, Y)$ **then return** $\bot$
if $X_1 \neq T_1 \vee X_2 \neq T_2[Y_1]$ **then return** $\bot$
if $\exists (s, k) \in \mathsf{Good}_F(\beta, X, Y) \times \{0,1\}^n$:
  $F^H[C, G]((s, k), X) = Y$ **then return** 1
return $\bot$

Oracle $R_3(X = X_1 \| X_2, Y = Y_1 \| Y_2)$: //Game G_1
if $\neg \mathsf{isValid}(2l, X, Y)$ **then return** $\bot$
if $X_1 \neq T_1 \vee X_2 \neq T_2[Y_1]$ **then return** $\bot$
if $\exists (s, k) \in \mathsf{Good}_F(\beta, X, Y) \times Q$:
  $F^H[C, G]((s, k), X) = Y$ **then return** 1
return $\bot$

Oracle $R_1()$:
if $T_1 = \bot$ **then** $T_1 \xleftarrow{\$} (\{0,1\}^n)^{[l]}$
return T_1

Oracle $R_2(X, Y)$:
if $\neg \mathsf{isValid}(1^n, l, X, Y)$ **then return** 1
if $X \neq T_1$ **then return** $\bot$
if $T_2[Y] = \bot$ **then**
  $T_2[Y] \xleftarrow{\$} (\{0,1\}^n \setminus T_1)^{[l(n)]}$
return $T_2[Y]$

Oracle $O(k, x)$:
$Q \leftarrow Q \cup \{k\}$
return $\pi_k(x)$

Oracle $f(x)$:
$y \leftarrow \pi_{k^*}(x)$
return y

Fig. 3. Games G_0 and G_1 used in the proof of naPRF security of H relative to (O, R). The only difference is the implementation of the R_3 oracle – in G_0 the R_3 oracle while answering its queries considers all $k \in \{0,1\}^n$ while in G_1 it only considers $k \in Q$. The isValid procedure (omitted here) is as described in Fig. 2.

Note that since $l = \omega(\sigma + n)$ and β is negligible, the advantage of A for any polynomial q is negligible. This, with Lemma 2 concludes Proposition 2's proof.

Remark 4. Although for concreteness we state A's advantage for $q \leq 2^{n/2}$, note that for the advantage to be negligible we require $q < 1/2\beta$. Therefore, we can only prove non-adaptive security of H (in an asymptotic sense) only when $q < 1/2\beta$. We note that an adversary A making $q \geq 1/\beta$ queries can, indeed, break the non-adaptive security of H. This is because, the range of function $C(s, \cdot)$ for any β-sparse s has at least $\frac{1}{\beta}$ elements and hence an A can just query the challenge oracle f on the entire range of $C(s, \cdot)$ and force R_3 to return 1 when $f \xleftarrow{\$} H$. This is how we avoid the 1-call non-security preserving proof of Berman and Haitner [4]. More precisely, they establish PRF security of their construction assuming the naPRF is secure against $q = \beta^{-1}$-queries for some negligible β.

Proof of Lemma 3. Fix some computationally unbounded adversary A making q queries and also some $n \in \mathbb{N}$. Let us assume w.l.o.g. that A makes q distinct queries to its oracles and is deterministic. We will proceed via a sequence of games and then appropriately describe the adversary B relative to O.

Game G_0 is identical to the real-world of the non-adaptive game for H except that G_0 maintains a set Q of all keys k for which A had issued an O-query on (k, x) for some x. The code for G_0 is shown in Fig. 3. This is just a syntactic change, therefore $\Pr[G_0] = \Pr_{O,R,f \xleftarrow{\$} F} [A^{(O,R),f} = 1]$.

Recall that any R_3 query $(X = X_1 \| X_2, Y = Y_1 \| Y_2)$ in G_0 returns 1 iff it finds a key (s, k) for F such that $F((s, k), X) = Y$ where $k \in \{0, 1\}^n$ and $s \in \mathsf{Good}_F(\beta, X, Y)$. Such an R_3 seems too generous in providing help to A. This is because it also considers k's for which A has not made an $(k, \cdot)$ query to O, or equivalently $k \notin Q$, to determine its answer. Since for each k, O_k (implemented by the function π_k in Fig. 3) behaves as a random function independent of other k''s it is unlikely that A has any information about O_k for any $k \notin Q$. Hence A's queries to R_3 should only depend on $k \in Q$. Carrying this intuition we move to the game G_1 where R_3 only considers $k \in Q$ as opposed to $k \in \{0, 1\}^n$.

Games G_0 and G_1 are Close: To give an intuition of why G_0 and G_1 are close, let us assume that A only makes one R_3 query and furthermore is its last query. It is easy to see that the games remain identical until the R_3 query. Let the query be on some $(X = X_1 \| X_2, Y = Y_1 \| Y_2)$. Furthermore, let us assume that $X_1 = R_1(1^n)$ and $X_2 = R_2(X_1, Y_1)$ as otherwise R_3 outputs $\bot$ in both G_0 and G_1, hence identical responses. Now, the output of the R_3 query in G_0 differs from that in G_1 if there exists some $k \notin Q$ and some $s \in \mathsf{Good}_F(\beta, X, Y)$ such that $F((s, k), X) = Y$. Fix one such $k \notin Q$ and some $s \in \mathsf{Good}_F(\beta, X, Y)$. The probability that R_3 in G_1 errs by ignoring this (s, k) can be upper bounded by the probability that over the choice of O_k (a random function) that for each $i \in [l]$, we have $Y_1[i] = F^{O_k}(s, X_1[i])$. Let $W_1[i] = C(s, X_1[i])$ for all $i \in [l]$. Since, $s \in \mathsf{Good}_F(\beta, X, Y)$ (Definition 8) we know that there exists at least $l/(c-1)$ distinct $W_1[i]$'s as $|C(s, X_1)| > l/(c-1)$. Furthermore, we know that for $Y = Y_1 \| Y_2$ at most $l/2c$ of the $Y[i]$'s are 1/2-bad w.r.t. $(s, X[i])$. Therefore, we can safely conclude that there exists a subset $I_s \subseteq [l]$ of size at least $l/(c-1) - l/2c$ such that for every $i \neq j \in I_s$, we have

1. $W_1[i] \neq W_1[j]$, where recall that $W_1 = C(s, X_1)$
2. $Y_1[i]$ is 1/2-good w.r.t. $(s, X_1[i])$.[7]

Furthermore, none of the $W_1[i]$ have been queried before and hence $Z_1[i] = O(k, W_1[i])$ are random independent strings. Therefore, the probability that

$$\Pr_{O_k}[\forall i \in I_s : F^{O_k}(s, X_1[i]) = Y_1[i]] \leq \Pr_{O_k}[\forall i \in I_s : G(s, X_1[i], Z_1[i]) = Y_1[i]] \leq \frac{1}{2^t},$$

where $t = |I_s| \geq \frac{(c+1) \cdot l}{2c(c-1)} = \Omega(l)$ as $c = O(1)$. Taking the union bound over all σ-bit s's and n-bit k's we can show that the probability that G_1 errs on the first R_3 query is negligible. In other words, G_1 can safely ignore $k \notin Q$ and this is because if for some X and Y and some s if A has not already determined that $F((s, k), X) = Y$ then the probability that it is indeed the case is small. We will use this fact a number of times in the proof. Let us make this formal.

Definition 9. *We say that a set $Q \subseteq \{0, 1\}^n \times \{0, 1\}^m$ is a (n, m)-query-set if for every w there exists at most one y such that $(w, y) \in Q$. Furthermore, let $\mathsf{Query}(Q)$ define the set of queries, that is, $\mathsf{Query}(Q) = \{w : \exists y \ s.t. (w, y) \in Q\}$.*

---
[7] Recall that y is 1/2-good w.r.t. (s, x) if $\Pr_z[G(s, x, z) = y] \leq 1/2$.

Lemma 4. *For $n, l, t \in \mathbb{N}$, consider $X \in (\{0,1\}^n)^{[l]}$, $Y \in (\{0,1\}^m)^l$ and let $Q \subseteq \{0,1\}^n \times \{0,1\}^m$ be an (n, m)-query set. Let s be such that there exists $I_s \subseteq [l]$ of size t such that $\forall i \neq j \in I_s$ the following holds: (1) $\mathsf{C}(s, X[i]) \neq \mathsf{C}(s, X[j])$, (2) $\mathsf{C}(s, X[i]) \notin \mathsf{Query}(Q)$, and (3) $Y[i]$ are $1/2$-good w.r.t. $(s, X[i])$. Then,*

$$\Pr_{g \overset{\$}{\leftarrow} \mathsf{Funcs}(n,m)|Q} [\mathsf{F}^g(s, X) = Y] \leq 2^{-t} ,$$

where $g \overset{\$}{\leftarrow} \mathsf{Funcs}(n, m)|Q$ is the process of sampling a function uniformly at random from $\mathsf{Funcs}(n, m)$ such that for every $(w, y) \in Q$ we have $g(w) = y$.

But is bounding the above probability for $k \notin Q$ enough to show that G_0 and G_1 *close?* Recall that A has access to the oracle f which internally calls O_{k^*} (where k^* is the random key sampled by the games to implement f. That is, $f = \mathsf{O}_{k^*}$). It could very well be that $k^* \notin Q$ but that hardly ensures that A has made no queries to O on $(k^*, \cdot)$. In fact if A manages to find some s such that $\mathsf{F}^f(s, X) = Y$ then R_3 queries answered in G_1 are necessarily incorrect. For this to happen, A needs to find some s such that $\mathsf{F}^f(s, X_1) = Y_1$ and $\mathsf{F}^f(s, X_2) = Y_2$. This is where the iterative nature of R_1, R_2 is supremely crucial which ensures that A learns X_2 after committing to Y_1 (i.e., after querying R_2 on (X_1, Y_1)). Since A only makes non-adaptive queries to f it is either in one of the following cases: (1) Issues all f queries after committing to Y_1 or (2) Issues all f queries before learning X_2. In (1) A succeeds only if the challenge oracle f agrees with Y_1 on all of X_1 (for some $s \in \mathsf{Good}_{\mathsf{C}}(\beta, X)$) which is unlikely by a discussion we made in the context of handling $k \notin Q$ and in (2) A succeeds only if $\mathsf{C}(s, X_2)$ falls inside the set of f queries it had issued. Fortunately, such an event is also unlikely for s that is β-sparse and randomly sampled X_2. In both cases, for every $s \in \mathsf{Good}_{\mathsf{C}}(\beta, X)$ the conditions of Lemma 4 are satisfied for some $t = \Theta(l)$. We defer the formal proof to indistinguishability of G_0 and G_1 to the full version.

Lemma 5. *For $t = l/(2c(c-1))$,*

$$|\Pr[\mathsf{G}_0] - \Pr[\mathsf{G}_1]| < q \cdot \left(\frac{(q+1)2^{\sigma}}{2^t} + \frac{2^{\sigma+n}}{2^{t(c+1)}} + \frac{6q}{2^n} + q\, 2^{\sigma} \binom{l}{l/2} (2\beta q)^{l/2} \right) .$$

Next, we consider a similar transition from the game H_0 (identical to the random world of the naPRF security game of H) to a game H_1 where R_3 queries are answered only by considering $k \in Q$ as done in G_1. By a similar analysis,

Lemma 6. *For $t = l/(2c(c-1))$,*

$$|\Pr[\mathsf{H}_0] - \Pr[\mathsf{H}_1]| < q \cdot \left(\frac{(q+1)2^{\sigma}}{2^t} + \frac{2^{\sigma+n}}{2^{t(c+1)}} + \frac{6q}{2^n} + q\, 2^{\sigma} \binom{l}{l/2} (2\beta q)^{l/2} \right) .$$

Now, we are set to describe our adversary B relative to O. Note that in both G_1 and H_1 the R_3 queries only depend on $k \in Q$. Consider the following adversary B which is relative to O and has non-adaptive access to the challenge oracle f. It internally runs A and answers its queries to O and f by forwarding them to its own oracles. It internally simulates R_1 and R_2 and to simulate R_3 we allow B to learn the entire description of O_k whenever the first query to O_k is made by A. Such a B can then perfectly simulate the game G_1 (resp., H_1) for A. Therefore, we have argued that,

$$\Pr[G_1] = \Pr_{O, k^* \xleftarrow{\$} \{0,1\}^n} [B^{O, f = H^O_{k^*}} = 1] \; ; \Pr[H_1] = \Pr_{O, f \xleftarrow{\$} \mathsf{Funcs}(n,m)} [B^{O, f} = 1] \; . \quad (2)$$

The final step is to invoke the security of H relative to O. For this, we consider an extended version of the security game of H relative to O where for every (k, x) query to O instead of just getting $O(k, x)$ the adversary B gets the entire description of O_k – we refer to such queries as "advanced" queries. Note that B makes exactly q "advanced" queries and also only makes non-adaptive queries to f. Then, we claim the following whose proof follows from standard techniques,

$$\left| \Pr_{O, k^* \xleftarrow{\$} \{0,1\}^n} [B^{O, f = H^O_{k^*}} = 1] - \Pr_{O, f \xleftarrow{\$} \mathsf{Funcs}(n,r)} [B^{O, f} = 1] \right| \leq \frac{2q}{2^n} \; . \quad (3)$$

Combining Lemmas 5, 6 with Eq. 2, 3 concludes the proof of Lemma 3. We defer the proofs of Lemmas 5 and 6 to the full version.

□

5   On Ruling Out Multiple-Call Constructions

In this section, we lift our techniques from Sect. 3 to a specific 2-call construction (and its generalization to arbitrary calls). This result is a generalization of [17] which only rules our arbitrary parallel composition of naPRFs as a PRF.

5.1   Cuckoo-Hashing Construction

Let σ, m be polynomially bounded functions, C (resp., G) be a function family from n bits to n bits (resp., m bits) with σ-bit seeds, and let H be a function family on n bits to m bits with n-bit seeds. Consider the family $F^H[C, G]$ ((Fig. 1b) from n bits to m bits with $(3\sigma + 2n)$-bit seeds such that for every $n \in \mathbb{N}$, $F.\mathsf{Kg}(1^n)$ outputs (s, k) where $s \xleftarrow{\$} (\{0,1\}^{\sigma(n)})^3$ and $k \xleftarrow{\$} (\{0,1\}^n)^2$. The evaluation of F on $x \in \{0,1\}^n$ with $s = (s_1, s_2, s_3)$ and $k = (k_1, k_2)$ is,

$$y = F^H((s, k), x) = H(k_1, C(s_1, x)) \oplus H(k_2, C(s_2, x)) \oplus G(s_3, x) \; . \quad (4)$$

We note that the construction in Eq. 4 covers the cuckoo-hashing based naPRF to PRF construction [5] – one recovers their construction by letting C and G be hash function family with sufficient independence. Informally, they showed that for every polynomial time computable function t, if C and G are $O(\log t(n))$-wise independent and H is a naPRF secure for adversaries making at most t queries, then F is a PRF for adversaries making at most $t/4$ queries.[8]

Below we state our result which provides an oracle relative to which there exists an naPRF H such that F (in Eq. 4) is not a PRF as long as C is a 2-universal hash function family. This in turn implies that F cannot be a fully black-box construction of a PRF from a naPRF.

Theorem 3. *Let σ, m be polynomially bounded functions, C be a 2-universal family from n bits to n bits and G be a function family from n bits to m bits. Then, for $\mathsf{F}^{(\cdot)}[\mathsf{C}, \mathsf{G}]$ (Eq. 4) from n bits to m bits there exists a randomized oracle (O, R) and an oracle function family $\mathsf{H}^{(\cdot)}$ from n bits to m bits with n-bit keys such that $\mathsf{H}^{(\cdot)}$ is a naPRF relative to (O, R) but $\mathsf{F}^{\mathsf{H}}[\mathsf{C}, \mathsf{G}]$ is not a PRF.*

First, we emphasize that our result rules out any output length m (even $m = 1$). Secondly, the proof of security from [5] requires C to be a $O(\log n)$-wise independent, the later implies our notion of 2-universality. However, we here rule out F as a construction of a PRF which, at first, seems to be contradictory to [5]. Here, we emphasize that our focus is on fully-black-box constructions (which are meant to work for any secure naPRF H) whereas the construction [5] depends on the purported security of the underlying naPRF H and hence is not fully-black-box. Thirdly, we note that Theorem 3 readily extends to the case when C is assumed to only be c-universal for some constant $c > 2$.

Finally, the construction in Sect. 5.1 is a specific case of the following $\kappa(n)$-call function family $\mathsf{F}_\kappa^{(\cdot)}[\mathsf{C}, \mathsf{G}]$ which takes as seed $(\boldsymbol{s}, \boldsymbol{k})$ where $\boldsymbol{s} \in (\{0,1\}^\sigma)^{[\kappa+1]}$ and $\boldsymbol{k} \in (\{0,1\}^n)^{[\kappa]}$ and on input $x \in \{0,1\}^n$ evaluates to $y \in \{0,1\}^m$ where

$$ y = \mathsf{F}_\kappa^{\mathsf{H}}((\boldsymbol{s}, \boldsymbol{k}), x) = \mathsf{G}(s_{\kappa+1}, x) \oplus \bigoplus_{i \in [\kappa(n)]} \mathsf{H}(k_i, \mathsf{C}(s_i, x)) . $$

We note that Theorem 3 also extends to rule out $\mathsf{F}_\kappa^{(\cdot)}$ for every polynomially bounded, polynomial-time computable function κ.

Theorem 4. *Let σ, m, κ be polynomially bounded functions and $c \geq 2$. Let C be a c-universal family from n bits to n bits with σ-bit seeds, and G be any function family from n bits to m bits with σ-bit seeds. Then, for $\mathsf{F}^{(\cdot)}[\mathsf{C}, \mathsf{G}]$ (as in Eq. 5.1) from n bits to m bits there exists a randomized oracle (O, R) and an oracle function family $\mathsf{H}^{(\cdot)}$ from n bits to m bits with n-bit keys such that $\mathsf{H}^{(\cdot)}$ is a naPRF relative to (O, R) but $\mathsf{F}^{\mathsf{H}}[\mathsf{C}, \mathsf{G}]$ is not a PRF relative to (O, R).*

ON PROOFS OF THEOREM 3 AND THEOREM 4. The proof of Theorem 3 closely follows that of Theorem 2. At a high level the main challenge in proving Theorem 3 is to show that O remains a secure naPRF relative to (O, R). Recall that a non-adaptive adversary A can break naPRF challenge oracle f relative (O, R) if it can predict the output of F on challenges $X = X_1 \| X_2$ issued by R under

---

[8] They require the range of C to be restricted to the first $4t(n)$ elements of $\{0,1\}^n$.

some (s, k) where either (a) $k = (\cdot, f)$ or (b) $k = (f, \cdot)$. Because of non-adaptive access to f and iterative nature of R, A is forced to make all its queries to f either after committing to Y_1 (potential outputs for X_1) or before learning X_2. Irrespective of which is the case, A (to trigger case (a)) needs to hope that for sufficiently large set $I \subseteq [\|X\|]$: $\forall i \in I$ where $X[i]$ is a fresh query to f we have

$$f(\mathsf{C}(s_1, X[i])) = \mathsf{G}(s_3, X[i]) \oplus \mathsf{H}(k, \mathsf{C}(s_2, X[i])) \oplus Y[i] .$$

Restricting R to only consider "good" seeds s_1 ensures that enough of $\mathsf{C}(s_1, X[i])$'s are distinct and since f is randomly sampled for fresh queries, this happens with exponentially small probability. Case (b) is symmetrical. The general case of κ-calls is a syntactic generalization of Theorem 3, defer proofs to the full version.

Acknowledgements. This work was partially supported by NSF grants CNS-1553758 (CAREER), CNS-1719146 and by a Sloan Research Fellowship. The first author was additionally supported by NSF grants CNS-1528178, CNS-1929901, CNS-1936825 (CAREER), the Defense Advanced Research Projects Agency (DARPA) and Army Research Office (ARO) under Contract No. W911NF-15-C-0236, and a subcontract No. 2017-002 through Galois. The views and conclusions contained in this document are those of the authors and should not be interpreted as the official policies, either expressed or implied, of the Defense Advanced Research Projects Agency or the US Government.

References

1. Applebaum, B., Raykov, P.: Fast pseudorandom functions based on expander graphs. In: Hirt, M., Smith, A. (eds.) TCC 2016-B, Part I. LNCS, vol. 9985, pp. 27–56. Springer, Heidelberg (2016). https://doi.org/10.1007/978-3-662-53641-4_2
2. Barak, B., Mahmoody-Ghidary, M.: Lower bounds on signatures from symmetric primitives. In: 48th FOCS, pp. 680–688. IEEE Computer Society Press, October 2007
3. Bellare, M., Canetti, R., Krawczyk, H.: Pseudorandom functions revisited: the cascade construction and its concrete security. In: 37th FOCS, pp. 514–523. IEEE Computer Society Press, October 1996
4. Berman, I., Haitner, I.: From non-adaptive to adaptive pseudorandom functions. J. Cryptol. **28**(2), 297–311 (2013). https://doi.org/10.1007/s00145-013-9169-2
5. Berman, I., Haitner, I., Komargodski, I., Naor, M.: Hardness-preserving reductions via cuckoo hashing. J. Cryptol. **32**(2), 361–392 (2019). https://doi.org/10.1007/s00145-018-9293-0
6. Bronson, J., Juma, A., Papakonstantinou, P.A.: Limits on the stretch of non-adaptive constructions of pseudo-random generators. In: Ishai, Y. (ed.) TCC 2011. LNCS, vol. 6597, pp. 504–521. Springer, Heidelberg (2011). https://doi.org/10.1007/978-3-642-19571-6_30
7. Buldas, A., Laur, S., Niitsoo, M.: Oracle separation in the non-uniform model. In: Pieprzyk, J., Zhang, F. (eds.) ProvSec 2009. LNCS, vol. 5848, pp. 230–244. Springer, Heidelberg (2009). https://doi.org/10.1007/978-3-642-04642-1_19

8. Cho, C., Lee, C.-K., Ostrovsky, R.: Equivalence of uniform key agreement and composition insecurity. In: Rabin, T. (ed.) CRYPTO 2010. LNCS, vol. 6223, pp. 447–464. Springer, Heidelberg (2010). https://doi.org/10.1007/978-3-642-14623-7_24

9. Gennaro, R., Gertner, Y., Katz, J.: Lower bounds on the efficiency of encryption and digital signature schemes. In: 35th ACM STOC, pp. 417–425. ACM Press, June 2003

10. Gennaro, R., Trevisan, L.: Lower bounds on the efficiency of generic cryptographic constructions. In: 41st FOCS, pp. 305–313. IEEE Computer Society Press, November 2000

11. Gertner, Y., Malkin, T., Reingold, O.: On the impossibility of basing trapdoor functions on trapdoor predicates. In: 42nd FOCS, pp. 126–135. IEEE Computer Society Press, October 2001

12. Holenstein, T., Sinha, M.: Constructing a pseudorandom generator requires an almost linear number of calls. In: 53rd FOCS, pp. 698–707. IEEE Computer Society Press, October 2012

13. Impagliazzo, R., Rudich, S.: Limits on the provable consequences of one-way permutations. In: Goldwasser, S. (ed.) CRYPTO 1988. LNCS, vol. 403, pp. 8–26. Springer, New York (1990). https://doi.org/10.1007/0-387-34799-2_2

14. Maurer, U., Pietrzak, K.: Composition of random systems: when two weak make one strong. In: Naor, M. (ed.) TCC 2004. LNCS, vol. 2951, pp. 410–427. Springer, Heidelberg (2004). https://doi.org/10.1007/978-3-540-24638-1_23

15. Maurer, U., Pietrzak, K., Renner, R.: Indistinguishability amplification. In: Menezes, A. (ed.) CRYPTO 2007. LNCS, vol. 4622, pp. 130–149. Springer, Heidelberg (2007). https://doi.org/10.1007/978-3-540-74143-5_8

16. Miles, E., Viola, E.: On the complexity of non-adaptively increasing the stretch of pseudorandom generators. In: Ishai, Y. (ed.) TCC 2011. LNCS, vol. 6597, pp. 522–539. Springer, Heidelberg (2011). https://doi.org/10.1007/978-3-642-19571-6_31

17. Myers, S.: Black-box composition does not imply adaptive security. In: Cachin, C., Camenisch, J.L. (eds.) EUROCRYPT 2004. LNCS, vol. 3027, pp. 189–206. Springer, Heidelberg (2004). https://doi.org/10.1007/978-3-540-24676-3_12

18. Pietrzak, K.: Composition does not imply adaptive security. In: Shoup, V. (ed.) CRYPTO 2005. LNCS, vol. 3621, pp. 55–65. Springer, Heidelberg (2005). https://doi.org/10.1007/11535218_4

19. Pietrzak, K.: Composition implies adaptive security in minicrypt. In: Vaudenay, S. (ed.) EUROCRYPT 2006. LNCS, vol. 4004, pp. 328–338. Springer, Heidelberg (2006). https://doi.org/10.1007/11761679_20

20. Reingold, O., Trevisan, L., Vadhan, S.: Notions of reducibility between cryptographic primitives. In: Naor, M. (ed.) TCC 2004. LNCS, vol. 2951, pp. 1–20. Springer, Heidelberg (2004). https://doi.org/10.1007/978-3-540-24638-1_1

21. Stinson, D.R.: Universal hashing and authentication codes. In: Feigenbaum, J. (ed.) CRYPTO 1991. LNCS, vol. 576, pp. 74–85. Springer, Heidelberg (1992). https://doi.org/10.1007/3-540-46766-1_5

22. Vaudenay, S.: Decorrelation: a theory for block cipher security. J. Cryptol. 16(4), 249–286 (2003)

23. Viola, E.: On constructing parallel pseudorandom generators from one-way functions. Cryptology ePrint Archive, Report 2005/159 (2005). http://eprint.iacr.org/2005/159

24. Wegman, M.N., Carter, L.: New hash functions and their use in authentication and set equality. J. Comput. Syst. Sci. 22, 265–279 (1981)

Secret Sharing Lower Bound: Either Reconstruction is Hard or Shares are Long

Kasper Green Larsen and Mark Simkin[✉]

Aarhus University, Aarhus, Denmark
{larsen,simkin}@cs.au.dk

Abstract. A secret sharing scheme allows a dealer to distribute shares of a secret among a set of n parties $P = \{p_1, \ldots, p_n\}$ such that any authorized subset of parties can reconstruct the secret, yet any unauthorized subset learns nothing about it. The family $\mathcal{A} \subseteq 2^P$ of all authorized subsets is called the access structure. Classic results show that if $\mathcal{A}$ contains precisely all subsets of cardinality at least t, then there exists a secret sharing scheme where the length of the shares is proportional to $\lg n$ bits plus the length of the secret. However, for general access structures, the best known upper bounds have shares of length exponential in n, whereas the strongest lower bound shows that the shares must have length at least $n/\lg n$. Beimel conjectured that the exponential upper bound is tight, but proving it has so far resisted all attempts. In this paper we make progress towards proving the conjecture by showing that there exists an access structure $\mathcal{A}$, such that any secret sharing scheme for $\mathcal{A}$ must have either exponential share length, or the function used for reconstructing the secret by authorized parties must have an exponentially long description. As an example corollary, we conclude that if one insists that authorized parties can reconstruct the secret via a constant fan-in boolean circuit of size polynomial in the share length, then there exists an access structure that requires a share length that is exponential in n.

1 Introduction

A secret sharing scheme allows a dealer to distribute shares of a secret among a set of parties $P = \{p_1, \ldots, p_n\}$ such that any authorized subset $A \subseteq P$ can reconstruct the secret, yet any unauthorized subset learns nothing about it. The family $\mathcal{A} \subseteq 2^{\{p_1,\ldots,p_n\}}$ of all authorized subsets is called the access structure. Secret

K. G. Larsen—Supported by a Villum Young Investigator grant and an AUFF starting grant.

M. Simkin—Supported by the European Research Council (ERC) under the European Unions's Horizon 2020 research and innovation programme under grant agreement No 669255 (MPCPRO), grant agreement No 803096 (SPEC), Danish Independent Research Council under Grant-ID DFF-6108-00169 (FoCC), and the Concordium Blockhain Research Center.

© Springer Nature Switzerland AG 2020
C. Galdi and V. Kolesnikov (Eds.): SCN 2020, LNCS 12238, pp. 566–578, 2020.
https://doi.org/10.1007/978-3-030-57990-6_28

sharing was introduced independently by Shamir [35] and Blakley [11], who presented constructions for threshold access structures that contains all subsets with a cardinality larger than some threshold t. The first construction for general (monotone) access structures was presented by Ito, Saito, and Nishizeki [21].

The main measure of efficiency for secret sharing schemes is the share size. For threshold access structures it is known that Shamir's secret sharing, which has a share size of $\Theta(\lg n)$, is optimal up to additive constants [13]. This stands in stark contrast to the smallest share sizes we can achieve for general monotone access structures. The construction of Ito, Saito, and Nishizeki has a share size of $\mathcal{O}(2^n/\sqrt{n})$ and 29 years later the best known upper bound on the share size, due to Applebaum et al. [3] is still $2^{0.892n}$. A widely believed conjecture suggests that these upper bounds are, up to constants, the best ones one can hope for. More concretely, Beimel conjectured:

Conjecture 1 ([5,6]). There exists an $\epsilon > 0$ such that for every integer n there exists an access structure with n parties for which every secret sharing scheme distributes shares of length exponential in the number of parties, that is, $2^{\epsilon n}$.

Proving this conjecture is a major open problem in the research area of secret sharing schemes. Karnin, Greene, and Hellman [23] initiated a line of works [12, 14, 17, 18] that proved different lower bounds on the share size using tools from information theory. The best of those lower bounds is due to Csirmaz [17, 18], who uses Shannon information inequalities to prove that there exists an explicit access structure that requires shares of size $\Omega(n/\lg n)$. Csirmaz himself and subsequent works [9, 30] indicate that it is unlikely that one can prove a super-polynomial lower bound on the share size using such information inequalities.

A different line of works focuses on linear secret sharing schemes, where the shared secret is a linear combination of the shares. Many of the existing schemes, e.g. [35], are linear and applications like multiparty computation [10, 16, 34] crucially rely on this property. Karchmer and Wigderson [22] introduce monotone span programs and show that these are closely related to linear secret sharing schemes. Through the lens of monotone span programs, a series of works obtained increasingly stronger lower bounds. Karchmer and Wigderson prove the first super-linear lower bound on the share size. Babai, Gál, and Wigderson [4] prove the first super-polynomial lower bound. Finally, Pitassi and Robere [33] prove an exponential lower bound, however, the gap between the constants in the exponent of the lower and upper bound remain far apart.

Several works consider different flavors of the original secret sharing notion. Beimel and Franklin [7] consider a relaxed security notion of weak privacy, which only requires that any unauthorized subset can not exclude any secret value with certainty. The unauthorized subset can, however, conclude that some secret is more probable than another one. The authors show that this notion is strictly weaker than the original notion of secret sharing by constructing schemes with share sizes that are impossible for secret sharing schemes with perfect privacy. Among other results, the authors construct a weakly-private secret sharing scheme for the threshold access structures, where the share size is independent of n. The authors conclude that any sensible lower bound proof has to make use of the privacy requirement of secret sharing schemes. Applebaum et al. [1,2] consider the efficiency of secret sharing schemes for large secrets. The authors show that, for a certain class of access structures, one can construct secret sharing schemes, where the share size does not grow with an increasing number n of parties. Their approach requires the secrets to be exponentially large in n.

A different line of works, which is closely related to secret sharing, deals with the conditional disclosure of secrets (CDS) problem [20]. In this setting, n parties have a common secret s, some common randomness r and separate inputs x_i. The goal of the parties is to each send a single message to a referee, who should learn the secret s iff the inputs x_i satisfy some publicly known predicate F, i.e. if $F(x_1, \ldots, x_n) = 1$. Beimel et al. [8] show that any predicate F can be realized with communication complexity $\mathcal{O}(2^{n/2})$ and subsequently Liu, Vaikuntanathan and Wee [29] improve this upper bound to $2^{\widetilde{\mathcal{O}}(\sqrt{n})}$. Gay, Kerenidis, and Wee [19] prove a lower bound for CDS schemes, which, very roughly speaking, shows that the communication complexity of any CDS is at least as large as the one-way communication complexity of the underlying predicate F. The techniques in this work are similar to some of the techniques in their work and our lower bound proof can be seen as a non-trivial generalization of their initial proof strategy to the case of secret sharing schemes. In contrast to their linear lower bound, our lower bound here is exponential.

Apart from being an interesting primitive on its own, CDS is also the main building block underlying the secret sharing scheme of Liu and Vaikuntanathan [28] described above. All of the CDS schemes mentioned above run in time exponential in n for certain predicates F.

Despite all progress that was made towards understanding the complexity of secret sharing, a lower bound on the share size of secret sharing schemes for general access structures remained out of reach.

1.1   Our Contribution

In this work we make some progress towards proving Beimel's conjecture. Informally, we show that either the total share size or the computational effort for reconstructing the secret has to be exponential in n. A bit more formally, let us consider a secret sharing scheme Σ for some access structure $\mathcal{A}$ that takes a 1-bit secret as input and outputs n shares, which are at most k bits long in total. Let $\mathcal{F}$ be some family of reconstruction functions. We require that for any authorized subset of parties $A \subseteq \mathcal{A}$, there exists at least one function in $\mathcal{F}$ that these parties can use to reconstruct the correct secret with probability at least $3/4$. For any $A \notin \mathcal{A}$, we require that all functions in $\mathcal{F}$ reconstruct the correct secret with probability at most $1/4$. These correctness and privacy requirements are very weak. Neither do we require perfect correctness, nor do we require privacy against an unauthorized set of parties that may use some function outside of $\mathcal{F}$ to reconstruct the secret. Proving a lower bound for such a secret sharing scheme makes our result only stronger, since any lower bound we can prove here also applies to any secret sharing scheme with better correctness and privacy guarantees. In this work we prove:

Theorem 1 (Informal). *For any secret sharing scheme Σ for general access structures, with domain of secrets $\{0,1\}$ and total share length k, then there exists an access structure $\mathcal{A}$ such that*

$$\lg(|\mathcal{F}|) \cdot k = \Omega(2^n/\sqrt{n}).$$

Our result does not prove Beimel's conjecture, but it tells us that any secret sharing scheme for 1-bit secrets for general access structures, which has a reconstruction function whose description is sub-exponentially large in n, must have a share size that is exponential in n. In particular, this holds even if the secret sharing itself runs in time exponential in n.

To get a better feeling of what $\mathcal{F}$ is, one can, for example, imagine it to be the set of all functions from $\{0,1\}^k \rightarrow \{0,1\}$ that are computable by a constant fan-in boolean circuit of some size $t(k) \geq k$. Any one circuit can compute exactly one function, there are a constant amount of different gates types, and for any gate with constant fan-in, there are $t(k)^{O(1)}$ choices for the input wires. It follows that there are at most $t(k)^{O(t(k))}$ different reconstruction functions in $\mathcal{F}$. Now, if for example $t(k) \leq k^c$ for a constant $c \geq 1$ (decoding by a circuit of size polynomial in the secret share length), then our theorem says that there exists an access structure $\mathcal{A}$ for which the share length k must be exponential in n. On the other hand, if k is for example polynomial in n, then our theorem tells us that there exists some access structure $\mathcal{A}$ which requires an exponentially large reconstruction circuit.

We prove Theorem 1 via a counting argument, meaning that we do not explicitly provide an access structure $\mathcal{A}$ that is affected by the lower bound. The high-level idea of our proof is as follows. Assume that there exists some secret sharing scheme $\Sigma_{\mathcal{A}}$ for every access structure $\mathcal{A}$ with the desired correctness and privacy properties and a total share size of $k^{\mathcal{A}} \leq k$. In the first step, we construct a family D that contains all access structures $\mathcal{A}$ of a certain type and we show that the size of this family is $2^{\Omega(2^n/\sqrt{n})}$. By the pigeon-hole principle, we know that the description of any $\mathcal{A} \in \mathcal{D}$ is at least $\lg|\mathcal{D}| = \Omega(2^n/\sqrt{n})$ bits long. On the other hand, we show that for any $\mathcal{A} \in \mathcal{D}$ one can use $\Sigma_{\mathcal{A}}$ to construct a $\mathcal{O}(\lg|\mathcal{F}| \cdot k)$-bit long *lossless* encoding from which $\mathcal{A}$ can be uniquely recovered. Combining the two observations directly yields the theorem stated above. The main challenge in realizing this proof idea lies in the construction of an appropriate encoding (and decoding) algorithm with the desired efficiency. Our encoding algorithm proceeds in two steps. First, we exploit the correctness and privacy properties of our secret sharing scheme to construct a randomized lossless encoding algorithm that works well for 99% of the sets A in any given $\mathcal{A}$ and encodes them into $\mathcal{O}(\lg|\mathcal{F}| \cdot k)$ bits. A careful analysis reveals that we can simply write out the remaining 1% of $A \in \mathcal{A}$ as part of the encoding and still obtain a lower bound on $\lg|\mathcal{F}| \cdot k$.

Proving lower bounds via such encoding arguments has been done quite extensively in the area of data structure lower bounds, see e.g. [15,24,25,31,32,36] and was also used recently to prove optimality of the Johnson-Lindenstrauss lemma in dimensionality reduction [26] and to prove optimality of ORAMs without balls-in-bins assumptions [27].

Remark. At first sight it may seem that the reconstruction function must take the access structure as input to be able to reconstruct. If this was the case, then our lower bound would be meaningless, since we can construct exponentially large access structures. This, however, is *not* the case. Consider the following trivial secret sharing scheme for some bitstring x among parties $p_1, \ldots, p_n$ for any access structure $\mathcal{A}$. For each authorized set $A = \{p_{i_1}, \ldots, p_{i_m}\} \in \mathcal{A}$, we pick uniformly random $s_{i_1}, \ldots, s_{i_m}$ such that $x = s_{i_1} \oplus \cdots \oplus s_{i_m}$ and give (A, s_{i_j}) to p_{i_j}. If a set A wants to reconstruct a secret, they check whether they have a share corresponding to A and xor their corresponding shares together if this is the case. If they do not have a share corresponding to A, they conclude that they are not an authorized set. Note that reconstruction function *only* takes the shares as input and not the access structure itself.

2   Formal Model and Result

In this section, we formally define secret sharing schemes and the precise conditions under which our lower bounds holds. Except for the security requirements, we define a secret sharing scheme precisely as in [6].

Definition 1. *Let $\{p_1, \ldots, p_n\}$ be a set of parties. A collection $\mathcal{A} \subseteq 2^{\{p_1, \ldots, p_n\}}$ is monotone if $B \in \mathcal{A}$ and $B \subseteq C$ imply $C \in \mathcal{A}$. An* access structure *is a monotone collection $\mathcal{A} \subseteq 2^{\{p_1, \ldots, p_n\}}$ of non-empty subsets of $\{p_1, \ldots, p_n\}$. Sets in $\mathcal{A}$ are called* authorized*, and sets not in $\mathcal{A}$ are called* unauthorized*.*

Definition 2. *Let $\{p_1, \ldots, p_n\}$ be a set of parties. A distribution scheme $\Sigma = (\Pi, \mu)$ with domain of secrets $\{0, 1\}$ is a pair, where μ is a probability distribution on some finite set R called the set of random strings and Π is a mapping from $\{0, 1\} \times R$ to a set of n-tuples $\{0, 1\}^{k_1} \times \cdots \times \{0, 1\}^{k_n}$, where $\{0, 1\}^{k_j}$ is called the* domain of shares *of p_j. A dealer distributes a secret $b \in \{0, 1\}$ according to Σ by first sampling a random string $r \in R$ according to μ, computing a vector of shares $\Pi(b, r) = (s_1, \ldots, s_n)$ and privately communicating each share s_j to party p_j. For a set $A \subseteq \{p_1, \ldots, p_n\}$, we denote $\Pi(b, r)_A$ as the restriction of $\Pi(b, r)$ to its A-entries.*

When designing secret sharing schemes, one would typically consider larger domains of secrets than just a single bit as in Definition 2. In this paper we are proving a lower bound, so focusing on the simplest possible setting of a secret consisting of a single bit only makes our lower bound stronger and the proof simpler. The lower bound we prove in this paper holds for secret sharing schemes that are computationally more efficient when authorized parties reconstruct the secret than when unauthorized parties attempt to. We define this formally in the following:

Definition 3. *Let $\{p_1, \ldots, p_n\}$ be a set of parties, let $\mathcal{A} \subseteq 2^{\{p_1, \ldots, p_n\}}$ be an access structure and $\Sigma = (\Pi, \mu)$ a distribution scheme with domain of secrets $\{0, 1\}$ and domain of shares $\{0, 1\}^{k_1} \times \cdots \times \{0, 1\}^{k_n}$. Let $\mathcal{F}$ be a family of functions from $\cup_{i=1}^{\infty} (\{0, 1\}^i \to \{0, 1\})$ and let $\mathcal{U}$ be the uniform distribution on $\{0, 1\}$. We say that $(\mathcal{F}, \mathcal{A}, \Sigma)$ is an* efficient secret sharing scheme *if it satisfies the following two conditions:*

For any $A \in \mathcal{A}$, there exists a function $f_A \in \left(\mathcal{F} \cap \left(\{0, 1\}^{\sum_{j \in A} k_j} \to \{0, 1\} \right) \right)$ such that

$$\left| \Pr_{b \sim \mathcal{U}, r \sim \mu} [f_A(\Pi(b, r)_A) = b] - \Pr_{b \sim \mathcal{U}, r \sim \mu} [f_A(\Pi(b, r)_A) \neq b] \right| \geq 3/4.$$

For any $A \notin \mathcal{A}$, it holds for all functions $f \in \left(\mathcal{F} \cap \left(\{0, 1\}^{\sum_{j \in A} k_j} \to \{0, 1\} \right) \right)$ that

$$\left| \Pr_{b \sim \mathcal{U}, r \sim \mu} [f(\Pi(b, r)_A) = b] - \Pr_{b \sim \mathcal{U}, r \sim \mu} [f(\Pi(b, r)_A) \neq b] \right| \leq 1/4.$$

For intuition on Definition 3, consider as an example instantiating $\mathcal{F}$ to be the set that contains for each i, the set of all functions from $\{0, 1\}^i \to \{0, 1\}$ that are computable by a constant fan-in boolean circuit of size $t(i) \leq i^c$ for a constant $c > 1$, i.e. $\mathcal{F}$ contains functions computable by polynomially sized circuits. With this choice of $\mathcal{F}$, consider an access structure $\mathcal{A}$. A distribution scheme Σ gives an efficient secret sharing scheme $(\mathcal{F}, \mathcal{A}, \Sigma)$ precisely if any authorized set of parties $A \in \mathcal{A}$ can recover the secret using *some* constant fan-in boolean circuit with size polynomial in the share length, whereas no unauthorized set of parties can recover the secret using *any* constant fan-in boolean circuit with size polynomial in the share length. We can thus think of $\mathcal{F}$ as defining the computational resources with which authorized parties can recover the secret, but unauthorized parties cannot. For ease of notation, define $\mathcal{F}_{\leq k}$ as

$$\mathcal{F}_{\leq k} := \mathcal{F} \cap \left(\cup_{i=1}^{k} (\{0, 1\}^i \to \{0, 1\}) \right)$$

and define

$$\mathcal{F}_{=k} := \mathcal{F} \cap \left(\{0, 1\}^k \to \{0, 1\} \right).$$

in the remainder of the paper.

Discussion 1. When designing secret sharing schemes, one would typically insist that authorized parties can reconstruct the secret with probability $1 - \text{negl}(n)$. Similarly, one would insist that unauthorized parties cannot reconstruct the secret except with probability $\text{negl}(n)$. Since we are proving a lower bound, using the constants 3/4 and 1/4 in Definition 3 only makes our results stronger.

Discussion 2. One could consider allowing randomization in the algorithms used for reconstructing the secret, both for the authorized and unauthorized parties. That is, a natural extension of Definition 3 would say that *there exists a distribution γ_A over functions in*

$$\left(\mathcal{F} \cap \left(\{0,1\}^{\Sigma_{j \in A} k_j} \to \{0,1\}\right)\right)$$

such that $\mathrm{Pr}_{b \sim \mathcal{U}, r \sim \mu, f_A \sim \gamma_A}[\cdots$. We remark that the definition would be equivalent to Definition 3 since one can always fix the randomness in f_A to achieve the same guarantees (equivalent to one direction of Yao's minimax principle).

Discussion 3. Our definition may seem superficially similar to the definition of weakly-private secret sharing schemes by Beimel and Franklin [7]. Their definition states that any unauthorized set cannot exclude any potential secret with probability 1. It does, however, allow the adversary to guess the secret correctly with a probability that is arbitrarily close to 1. In contrast to their definition, ours is strictly stronger, since it requires a sharp upper bound on the probability that an unqualified set of parties guesses the correct secret.

We are ready to present our main theorem in its full generality:

Theorem 2. *Let $\mathcal{F}$ be a family of functions from $\cup_{i=1}^{\infty} \left(\{0,1\}^i \to \{0,1\}\right)$ and let $\{p_1, \ldots, p_n\}$ be a set of parties. There exists an access structure $\mathcal{A} \subseteq 2^{\{p_1, \ldots, p_n\}}$ such that any efficient secret sharing scheme $(\mathcal{F}, \mathcal{A}, \Sigma)$ with domain of secrets $\{0,1\}$ and domain of shares $\{0,1\}^{k_1} \times \cdots \times \{0,1\}^{k_n}$ with $k = \sum_j k_j$, satisfies*

$$\lg(|\mathcal{F}_{\leq k}|) \cdot k = \Omega(2^n / \sqrt{n}).$$

To appreciate Theorem 2, consider instantiating $\mathcal{F}$ to be the set that contains for each i, the set of all functions from $\{0,1\}^i \to \{0,1\}$ that are computable by a constant fan-in boolean circuit of size $t(i)$ (with $t(i) \geq i$). A simple counting argument shows that $|\mathcal{F}_{\leq k}| \leq t(k)^{O(t(k))}$ (A circuit computes only one function and there are $t(k)^{O(1)}$ choices for the input wires to each gate, there are $O(1)$ choices for the function computed by each gate, and there are $t(k)$ gates). Theorem 2 thus gives us that there must exist an access structure $\mathcal{A}$ such that any efficient secret sharing scheme $(\mathcal{F}, \mathcal{A}, \Sigma)$ with domain of shares $\{0,1\}^{k_1} \times \cdots \{0,1\}^{k_n}$ with $k = \sum_j k_j$ must satisfy $t(k) \lg(t(k))k = \Omega(2^n / n^{1/2})$. If we plug in polynomially sized constant fan-in boolean circuits, i.e. $t(i) \leq i^c$ for a constant $c \geq 1$, this gives us that $k^{c+2} = \Omega(2^n / n^{1/2}) \Rightarrow k = 2^{\Omega(n)}$, i.e. any secret sharing scheme for $\mathcal{A}$ must have shares with exponential length if decoding can be done by constant fan-in boolean circuits with size polynomial in the share length. Moreover, the lower bound holds *even if* we *only require* that unauthorized parties cannot reconstruct the secret using a polynomially sized constant fan-in boolean circuit (polynomial in the length of the shares). Notice that since this is a lower bound, it only makes the result stronger than if we e.g. required that a computationally unbounded set of parties cannot reconstruct the secret. We can also deduce from Theorem 2 that the size of the decoding circuit must be exponential in n, regardless of the share length.

Another interesting instantiation of Theorem 2 is to let $\mathcal{F}$ consist of all functions computable by a Turing machine with at most 10^6 states and alphabet $\{0,1\}$ (or some other constant number of states). Then $|\mathcal{F} \cap (\{0,1\}^i \to \{0,1\})| = O(1)$ and the lower bound says that there exists an access structure $\mathcal{A}$ for which any efficient secret sharing scheme $(\mathcal{F}, \mathcal{A}, \Sigma)$ must satisfy $k^2 = \Omega(2^n/\sqrt{n}) \Rightarrow k = 2^{\Omega(n)}$, i.e. shares must have exponential length if the secret can be reconstructed by authorized parties using a Turing machine with at most 10^6 states and binary alphabet. The lower bound holds as long as we require that unauthorized parties cannot recover the secret using a Turing machine with at most 10^6 states and alphabet $\{0,1\}$.

An even more exotic instantiation of Theorem 2 follows by letting $\mathcal{F}$ contain, for every i, the set of functions from $\{0,1\}^i \to \{0,1\}$ that are computable by a C-program with up to t ASCII characters. A counting argument shows that $|\mathcal{F}_{\leq k}| \leq k 2^{O(t)}$ (there are $2^{O(t)}$ sequences of t ASCII characters, and any program computes at most one function from $\{0,1\}^i \to \{0,1\}$) and we conclude that it must be the case that there exists an access structure $\mathcal{A}$ such that any efficient secret sharing $(\mathcal{F}, \mathcal{A}, \Sigma)$ must have $(t + \lg k) \cdot k = \Omega(2^n/\sqrt{n})$. This means that either the length of the C-program has to grow exponentially with the number of parties n, or the length of the shares has to grow exponentially with n. Thus if we insist on short shares, then the C-programs for reconstructing the secret have to be extremely non-uniform, and if we insist on reconstructing secrets using C-programs of any constant length t independent of n, then the shares must have exponential length. This lower bound holds as long as we require that unauthorized parties cannot recover the secret via a C-program of length t or less.

Finally, if one insist that authorized parties can *efficiently* reconstruct the secret via a C-program of length at most t ASCII characters, then the previous lower bound is strengthened. That is, we can now let $\mathcal{F}$ contain, for every i, the set of functions from $\{0,1\}^i \to \{0,1\}$ that are computable by a C-program with up to t ASCII characters that terminates in at most h steps. If we insist that authorized parties can reconstruct the secret by running such a C-program, then the lower bound $(t + \lg k) \cdot k = \Omega(2^n/\sqrt{n})$ holds even if we only require that unauthorized parties cannot reconstruct the secret via a C-program of length t and running time at most h steps.

3   Lower Bound Proof

To prove Theorem 2, let $\{p_1, \ldots, p_n\}$ be a set of parties and let $\mathcal{F}$ be a family of functions from $\cup_{i=1}^{\infty} (\{0,1\}^i \to \{0,1\})$. Assume that there is a parameter k such that it holds for all access structures $\mathcal{A} \subseteq 2^{\{p_1, \ldots, p_n\}}$, that there exists an efficient secret sharing scheme $(\mathcal{F}, \mathcal{A}, (\Pi_{\mathcal{A}}, \mu_{\mathcal{A}}))$ with domain of secrets $\{0,1\}$ and domain of shares $\{0,1\}^{k_1^{\mathcal{A}}} \times \cdots \times \{0,1\}^{k_n^{\mathcal{A}}}$ with $\sum_j k_j^{\mathcal{A}} = k^{\mathcal{A}} \leq k$.

We will prove a lower bound on $\lg(|\mathcal{F}_{\leq k}|) \cdot k$ via a counting argument. The high level intuition is that two distinct access structures $\mathcal{A}_1$ and $\mathcal{A}_2$ must be different either in terms of the shares they use, or in terms of the procedures used for reconstructing the secrets. Since there are overwhelmingly many distinct access structures, this gives a lower bound on either the share length (a lower bound on k), or on the descriptional size of the procedures used for reconstructing secrets (a lower bound on $\lg(|\mathcal{F}_{\leq k}|)$).

More formally, let $\mathcal{D}$ be the family containing all access structures $\mathcal{A} \subseteq 2^{\{p_1,\ldots,p_n\}}$ such that $\mathcal{A}$ contains no sets A of cardinality less than $\lfloor n/2 \rfloor$ and $\mathcal{A}$ contains all sets A of cardinality more than $\lfloor n/2 \rfloor$. We claim that $|\mathcal{D}| = 2^{\binom{n}{\lfloor n/2 \rfloor}} = 2^{\Omega(2^n/\sqrt{n})}$. To see this, observe that $\mathcal{A}$ is monotone for any choice of subsets with cardinality $\lfloor n/2 \rfloor$ that we might include in it. Since there are $\binom{n}{\lfloor n/2 \rfloor}$ subsets of cardinality $\lfloor n/2 \rfloor$, we conclude that there are $2^{\binom{n}{\lfloor n/2 \rfloor}}$ ways of choosing which subsets to include in $\mathcal{A}$.

We will show that we can encode any $\mathcal{A} \in \mathcal{D}$ into

$$\lambda = O(\lg(|\mathcal{F}_{\leq k}|) \cdot k) + 0.1 \cdot \binom{n}{\lfloor n/2 \rfloor}$$

bits and still uniquely recover $\mathcal{A}$ from the encoding alone. The encoding procedure thus defines an injective mapping from $\mathcal{D}$ to $\{0,1\}^\lambda$. By the pigeon-hole principle, this implies that

$$\lambda \geq \lg |\mathcal{D}| \Rightarrow$$
$$O(\lg(|\mathcal{F}_{\leq k}|) \cdot k) \geq 0.9 \cdot \binom{n}{\lfloor n/2 \rfloor} \Rightarrow$$
$$\lg(|\mathcal{F}_{\leq k}|) \cdot k = \Omega(2^n/\sqrt{n}).$$

We are now ready to describe our encoding and decoding procedures.

Encoding. Let $\mathcal{A} \in \mathcal{D}$. Our procedure for uniquely encoding $\mathcal{A}$ is as follows:

1. For $i = 1,\ldots,T$ for a parameter T to be fixed, consider sampling $b_i \sim \mathcal{U}$ as a uniform random bit, and sample $r_i \sim \mu_{\mathcal{A}}$. Let $A \subseteq \{p_1,\ldots,p_n\}$ be an arbitrary set of cardinality $\lfloor n/2 \rfloor$ and define $k_A^{\mathcal{A}} = \sum_{j \in A} k_j^{\mathcal{A}}$. By Definition 3, it holds that:
   - If $A \in \mathcal{A}$, then there exists a function $f_A \in \mathcal{F}_{=k_A^{\mathcal{A}}}$ such that

   $$\left| \Pr_{b_i,r_i} [f_A(\Pi_{\mathcal{A}}(b_i, r_i)_A) = b_i] - \Pr_{b_i,r_i} [f_A(\Pi_{\mathcal{A}}(b_i, r_i)_A) \neq b_i] \right| \geq 3/4.$$

   - If $A \notin \mathcal{A}$, then for all functions $f \in \mathcal{F}_{=k_A^{\mathcal{A}}}$, it holds that

   $$\left| \Pr_{b_i,r_i} [f(\Pi_{\mathcal{A}}(b_i, r_i)_A) = b_i] - \Pr_{b_i,r_i} [f(\Pi_{\mathcal{A}}(b_i, r_i)_A) \neq b_i] \right| \leq 1/4.$$

We use this observation as follows: We set $T = c \lg |\mathcal{F}_{\leq k}|$ for a sufficiently large constant $c > 1$. If $A \notin \mathcal{A}$, then since $|\mathcal{F}_{=k_A^{\mathcal{A}}}| \leq |\mathcal{F}_{\leq k}|$, we can use a

Chernoff bound and a union bound over all $f \in \mathcal{F}_{=k_A^A}$ to conclude that with probability at least 99/100, it holds simultaneously for all $f \in \mathcal{F}_{=k_A^A}$ that

$$||\{i : f(\Pi_A(b_i, r_i)_A) = b_i\}| - |\{i : f(\Pi_A(b_i, r_i)_A) \neq b_i\}|| < T/3.$$

At the same time, if $A \in \mathcal{A}$ and we have $T = c \lg |\mathcal{F}_{\leq k}|$, then with overwhelming probability, we will have that there exists at least one function $f \in \mathcal{F}_{=k_A^A}$ such that

$$||\{i : f(\Pi_A(b_i, r_i)_A) = b_i\}| - |\{i : f(\Pi_A(b_i, r_i)_A) \neq b_i\}|| > T/3.$$

Thus intuitively, the variables $b_1, \ldots, b_T$ and $r_1, \ldots, r_T$ reveal whether A is in $\mathcal{A}$ or not, i.e. they carry information about A. We exploit this as follows: Let χ_A be the random variable taking the value 1 if the test

$$\exists f \in \mathcal{F}_{=k_A^A} :$$
$$||\{i : f(\Pi_A(b_i, r_i)_A) = b_i\}| - |\{i : f(\Pi_A(b_i, r_i)_A) \neq b_i\}|| > T/3?$$

correctly predicts whether $A \in \mathcal{A}$. Then $\Pr[\chi_A = 1] \geq 99/100$. Let $\mathcal{S}$ be the family of all subsets of $\{p_1, \ldots, p_n\}$ that have cardinality $\lfloor n/2 \rfloor$. It follows by linearity of expectation that $\mathbb{E}[\sum_{A \in \mathcal{S}} \chi_A] \geq 99|\mathcal{S}|/100$. This means that there must exist a choice values $\hat{b}_1, \ldots, \hat{b}_T$ and $\hat{r}_1, \ldots, \hat{r}_T$ such that the test $\exists f \in \mathcal{F}_{=k_A^A} : ||\{i : f(\Pi_A(\hat{b}_i, \hat{r}_i)_A) = \hat{b}_i\}| - |\{i : f(\Pi_A(\hat{b}_i, \hat{r}_i)_A) \neq \hat{b}_i\}|| > T/3?$ correctly predicts whether $A \in \mathcal{A}$ for at least $99|\mathcal{S}|/100$ sets $A \in \mathcal{S}$. Fix such values.

2. Write down $\lg k$ bits specifying k^A, followed by k bits specifying $k_1^A, \ldots, k_n^A$ (this can be done by writing a length k bit string, where positions $\sum_{i=1}^j k_i^A$ are set to 1 for all $j = 1, \ldots, n$). Then write down the bits $\hat{b}_1, \cdots, \hat{b}_T$ and $\Pi_A(\hat{b}_1, \hat{r}_1)), \cdots, \Pi_A(\hat{b}_T, \hat{r}_T))$ for a total of at most $\lg k + k + T(1 + k)$ bits.

3. Let $\bar{\mathcal{S}}$ be the subset of sets from $\mathcal{S}$ where the prediction is incorrect. Encode $\bar{\mathcal{S}}$ as a subset of $\mathcal{S}$ using $\lg \binom{n}{\lfloor n/2 \rfloor} \leq n$ bits to specify $|\bar{\mathcal{S}}|$ and $\lg \binom{|\mathcal{S}|}{|\bar{\mathcal{S}}|} \leq |\bar{\mathcal{S}}| \lg(e|\mathcal{S}|/|\bar{\mathcal{S}}|) \leq (|\mathcal{S}|/100) \lg(100e) < 0.1 \cdot \binom{n}{\lfloor n/2 \rfloor}$ bits to specify the subset.

Next we argue how to recover $\mathcal{A}$ from the above encoding:

Decoding.

1. Read the first $\lg k + k$ bits to recover k^A and $k_1^A, \ldots, k_n^A$. Then use the following $T(k+1)$ bits to recover $\hat{b}_1, \ldots, \hat{b}_T$ and $\Pi_A(\hat{b}_1, \hat{r}_1), \ldots, \Pi_A(\hat{b}_T, \hat{r}_T)$.

2. For each $A \in \mathcal{S}$, iterate over all $f \in \mathcal{F}_{=k_A^A}$ and compute the value

$$\Delta_f := \left| |\{i : f(\Pi_A(\hat{b}_i, \hat{r}_i)_A) = \hat{b}_i\}| - |\{i : f(\Pi_A(\hat{b}_i, \hat{r}_i)_A) \neq \hat{b}_i\}| \right|.$$

Observe that the decoder can extract $\Pi_A(\hat{b}_i, \hat{r}_i)_A$ from $\Pi_A(\hat{b}_i, \hat{r}_i)$ since the decoder knows $k_1^A, \ldots, k_n^A$. Thus the decoder can indeed compute Δ_f. If there is at least one f with $\Delta_f \geq T/3$, we initially predict that $A \in \mathcal{A}$ and otherwise, we predict that $A \notin \mathcal{A}$. These predictions are correct, except for $A \in \bar{\mathcal{S}}$.

3. Finally we read the last part of the encoding to determine which sets $\mathcal{A}$ that were predicted incorrectly in step 2. Together with the correct predictions from step 2., this recovers $\mathcal{A}$.

Analysis. Finally we derive the lower bound. We have just argued that we can give a unique encoding of each $\mathcal{A} \in \mathcal{D}$, hence the length of the encoding must be at least $\lg |\mathcal{D}| = \binom{n}{\lfloor n/2 \rfloor}$ bits. But the above encoding uses at most:

$$\lg k + k + T(1 + k) + n + 0.1 \cdot \binom{n}{\lfloor n/2 \rfloor}$$

bits. Thus we must have

$$\lg k + k + T(1 + k) + n + 0.1 \cdot \binom{n}{\lfloor n/2 \rfloor} \geq \binom{n}{\lfloor n/2 \rfloor} \Rightarrow$$

$$Tk = \Omega\left(\binom{n}{\lfloor n/2 \rfloor}\right) = \Omega(2^n/\sqrt{n}).$$

But $T = c \lg |\mathcal{F}_{\leq k}|$ and we conclude:

$$\lg |\mathcal{F}_{\leq k}| \cdot k = \Omega(2^n/\sqrt{n}).$$

References

1. Applebaum, B., Arkis, B.: On the power of amortization in secret sharing: d-uniform secret sharing and CDS with constant information rate. In: Beimel, A., Dziembowski, S. (eds.) TCC 2018. LNCS, vol. 11239, pp. 317–344. Springer, Cham (2018). https://doi.org/10.1007/978-3-030-03807-6_12
2. Applebaum, B., Arkis, B., Raykov, P., Vasudevan, P.N.: Conditional disclosure of secrets: amplification, closure, amortization, lower-bounds, and separations. In: Katz, J., Shacham, H. (eds.) CRYPTO 2017. LNCS, vol. 10401, pp. 727–757. Springer, Cham (2017). https://doi.org/10.1007/978-3-319-63688-7_24
3. Applebaum, B., Beimel, A., Farràs, O., Nir, O., Peter, N.: Secret-sharing schemes for general and uniform access structures. In: Ishai, Y., Rijmen, V. (eds.) EUROCRYPT 2019. LNCS, vol. 11478, pp. 441–471. Springer, Cham (2019). https://doi.org/10.1007/978-3-030-17659-4_15
4. Babai, L., Gál, A., Wigderson, A.: Superpolynomial lower bounds for monotone span programs. Combinatorica **19**(3), 301–319 (1999)
5. Beimel, A.: Secure schemes for secret sharing and key distribution. Technion-Israel Institute of technology, Faculty of computer science (1996)
6. Beimel, A.: Secret-sharing schemes: a survey. In: Chee, Y.M., et al. (eds.) IWCC 2011. LNCS, vol. 6639, pp. 11–46. Springer, Heidelberg (2011). https://doi.org/10.1007/978-3-642-20901-7_2
7. Beimel, A., Franklin, M.: Weakly-private secret sharing schemes. In: Vadhan, S.P. (ed.) TCC 2007. LNCS, vol. 4392, pp. 253–272. Springer, Heidelberg (2007). https://doi.org/10.1007/978-3-540-70936-7_14
8. Beimel, A., Ishai, Y., Kumaresan, R., Kushilevitz, E.: On the cryptographic complexity of the worst functions. In: Lindell, Y. (ed.) TCC 2014. LNCS, vol. 8349, pp. 317–342. Springer, Heidelberg (2014). https://doi.org/10.1007/978-3-642-54242-8_14

9. Beimel, A., Orlov, I.: Secret sharing and non-Shannon information inequalities. In: Reingold, O. (ed.) TCC 2009. LNCS, vol. 5444, pp. 539–557. Springer, Heidelberg (2009). https://doi.org/10.1007/978-3-642-00457-5_32

10. Ben-Or, M., Goldwasser, S., Wigderson, A.: Completeness theorems for non-cryptographic fault-tolerant distributed computation (extended abstract). In: 20th Annual ACM Symposium on Theory of Computing, Chicago, IL, USA, 2–4 May 1988, pp. 1–10. ACM Press (1988)

11. Blakley, G.R.: Safeguarding cryptographic keys, pp. 313–317. AFIPS Press (1979)

12. Blundo, C., De Santis, A., Gargano, L., Vaccaro, U.: On the information rate of secret sharing schemes. In: Brickell, E.F. (ed.) CRYPTO 1992. LNCS, vol. 740, pp. 148–167. Springer, Heidelberg (1993). https://doi.org/10.1007/3-540-48071-4_11

13. Bogdanov, A., Guo, S., Komargodski, I.: Threshold secret sharing requires a linear size alphabet. In: Hirt, M., Smith, A. (eds.) TCC 2016. LNCS, vol. 9986, pp. 471–484. Springer, Heidelberg (2016). https://doi.org/10.1007/978-3-662-53644-5_18

14. Capocelli, R.M., De Santis, A., Gargano, L., Vaccaro, U.: On the size of shares for secret sharing schemes. In: Feigenbaum, J. (ed.) CRYPTO 1991. LNCS, vol. 576, pp. 101–113. Springer, Heidelberg (1992). https://doi.org/10.1007/3-540-46766-1_7

15. Chakraborty, D., Kamma, L., Larsen, K.G.: Tight cell probe bounds for succinct Boolean matrix-vector multiplication. In: Proceedings of the 50th Annual ACM SIGACT Symposium on Theory of Computing, STOC 2018, Los Angeles, CA, USA, 25–29 June 2018, pp. 1297–1306 (2018)

16. Chaum, D., Crépeau, C., Damgård, I.: Multiparty unconditionally secure protocols (extended abstract). In: 20th Annual ACM Symposium on Theory of Computing, Chicago, IL, USA, 2–4 May 1988, pp. 11–19. ACM Press (1988)

17. Csirmaz, L.: The size of a share must be large. In: De Santis, A. (ed.) EUROCRYPT 1994. LNCS, vol. 950, pp. 13–22. Springer, Heidelberg (1995). https://doi.org/10.1007/BFb0053420

18. Csirmaz, L.: The dealer's random bits in perfect secret sharing schemes. Studia Scientiarum Mathematicarum Hungarica 32(3), 429–438 (1996)

19. Gay, R., Kerenidis, I., Wee, H.: Communication complexity of conditional disclosure of secrets and attribute-based encryption. In: Gennaro, R., Robshaw, M. (eds.) CRYPTO 2015. LNCS, vol. 9216, pp. 485–502. Springer, Heidelberg (2015). https://doi.org/10.1007/978-3-662-48000-7_24

20. Gertner, Y., Ishai, Y., Kushilevitz, E., Malkin, T.: Protecting data privacy in private information retrieval schemes. In: 30th Annual ACM Symposium on Theory of Computing, Dallas, TX, USA, 23–26 May 1998, pp. 151–160. ACM Press (1988)

21. Ito, M., Saito, A., Nishizeki, T.: Secret sharing scheme realizing general access structure. Electron. Commun. Jpn. (Part III Fundam. Electron. Sci.) 72(9), 56–64 (1989)

22. Karchmer, M., Wigderson, A.: On span programs. In: Proceedings of the Eighth Annual Structure in Complexity Theory Conference 1993, pp. 102–111. IEEE (1993)

23. Karnin, E., Greene, J., Hellman, M.: On secret sharing systems. IEEE Trans. Inf. Theory 29(1), 35–41 (1983)

24. Larsen, K.G.: The cell probe complexity of dynamic range counting. In: Proceedings of the 44th Symposium on Theory of Computing Conference, STOC 2012, New York, NY, USA, 19–22 May 2012, pp. 85–94 (2012)

25. Larsen, K.G.: Higher cell probe lower bounds for evaluating polynomials. In: 53rd Annual IEEE Symposium on Foundations of Computer Science, FOCS 2012, New Brunswick, NJ, USA, 20–23 October 2012, pp. 293–301 (2012)

26. Larsen, K.G., Nelson, J.: Optimality of the Johnson-Lindenstrauss lemma. In: 58th IEEE Annual Symposium on Foundations of Computer Science, FOCS 2017, Berkeley, CA, USA, 15–17 October 2017, pp. 633–638 (2017)
27. Larsen, K.G., Nielsen, J.B.: Yes, there is an oblivious RAM lower bound!. In: Shacham, H., Boldyreva, A. (eds.) CRYPTO 2018. LNCS, vol. 10992, pp. 523–542. Springer, Cham (2018). https://doi.org/10.1007/978-3-319-96881-0_18
28. Liu, T., Vaikuntanathan, V.: Breaking the circuit-size barrier in secret sharing. In: Diakonikolas, I., Kempe, D., Henzinger, M. (eds.) 50th Annual ACM Symposium on Theory of Computing, Los Angeles, CA, USA, 25–29 June 2018, pp. 699–708. ACM Press (2018)
29. Liu, T., Vaikuntanathan, V., Wee, H.: Conditional disclosure of secrets via non-linear reconstruction. In: Katz, J., Shacham, H. (eds.) CRYPTO 2017. LNCS, vol. 10401, pp. 758–790. Springer, Cham (2017). https://doi.org/10.1007/978-3-319-63688-7_25
30. Martín, S., Padró, C., Yang, A.: Secret sharing, rank inequalities and information inequalities. In: Canetti, R., Garay, J.A. (eds.) CRYPTO 2013. LNCS, vol. 8043, pp. 277–288. Springer, Heidelberg (2013). https://doi.org/10.1007/978-3-642-40084-1_16
31. Pătrașcu, M., Demaine, E.D.: Logarithmic lower bounds in the cell-probe model. SIAM J. Comput. **35**(4), 932–963 (2006)
32. Pătrașcu, M., Viola, E.: Cell-probe lower bounds for succinct partial sums. In: Proceedings of the 21st ACM/SIAM Symposium on Discrete Algorithms (SODA), pp. 117–122 (2010)
33. Pitassi, T., Robere, R.: Lifting Nullstellensatz to monotone span programs over any field. In: Diakonikolas, I., Kempe, D., Henzinger, M. (eds.) 50th Annual ACM Symposium on Theory of Computing, Los Angeles, CA, USA, 25–29 June 2018, pp. 1207–1219. ACM Press (2018)
34. Rabin, T., Ben-Or, M.: Verifiable secret sharing and multiparty protocols with honest majority (extended abstract). In: 21st Annual ACM Symposium on Theory of Computing, Seattle, WA, USA, 15–17 May 1989, pp. 73–85. ACM Press (1989)
35. Shamir, A.: How to share a secret. Commun. ACM **22**(11), 612–613 (1979)
36. Verbin, E., Zhang, Q.: The limits of buffering: a tight lower bound for dynamic membership in the external memory model. SIAM J. Comput. **42**(1), 212–229 (2013)

Separating Symmetric and Asymmetric Password-Authenticated Key Exchange

Julia Hesse(✉) (iD)

IBM Research, Zurich, Switzerland
jhs@zurich.ibm.com

Abstract. Password-Authenticated Key Exchange (PAKE) is a method to establish cryptographic keys between two users sharing a low-entropy password. In its asymmetric version, one of the users acts as a server and only stores some function of the password, e.g., a hash. Upon server compromise, the adversary learns $H(\mathsf{pw})$. Depending on the strength of the password, the attacker now has to invest more or less work to reconstruct pw from $H(\mathsf{pw})$. Intuitively, asymmetric PAKE seems more challenging than symmetric PAKE since the latter is not supposed to protect the password upon compromise. In this paper, we provide three contributions:

- **Separating symmetric and asymmetric PAKE.** We prove that a strong assumption like a programmable random oracle is necessary to achieve security of asymmetric PAKE in the Universal Composability (UC) framework. For symmetric PAKE, programmability is not required. Our results also rule out the existence of UC-secure asymmetric PAKE in the CRS model.
- **Revising the security definition.** We identify and close some gaps in the UC security definition of 2-party asymmetric PAKE given by Gentry, MacKenzie and Ramzan (Crypto 2006). For this, we specify a natural corruption model for server compromise attacks. We further remove an undesirable weakness that lets parties wrongly believe in security of compromised session keys. We demonstrate usefulness by proving that the Ω-method proposed by Gentry et al. satisfies our new security notion for asymmetric PAKE. To our knowledge, this is the first formal security proof of the Ω-method in the literature.
- **Composable multi-party asymmetric PAKE.** We showcase how our revisited security notion for 2-party asymmetric PAKE can be used to obtain asymmetric PAKE protocols in the multi-user setting and discuss important aspects for implementing such a protocol.

Keywords: Asymmetric password-authenticated key exchange · Universal Composability

---

J. Hesse—This work has received funding from the European Union's Horizon 2020 research and innovation programme under grant agreement No. 786725 – OLYMPUS.

© Springer Nature Switzerland AG 2020
C. Galdi and V. Kolesnikov (Eds.): SCN 2020, LNCS 12238, pp. 579–599, 2020.
https://doi.org/10.1007/978-3-030-57990-6_29

1   Introduction

Establishing secure communication channels in untrusted environments is an important measure to ensure privacy, authenticity or integrity on the internet. An important cryptographic building block for securing channels are key exchange protocols. The exchanged keys can be used to, e.g., encrypt messages using a symmetric cipher, or to authenticate users. *Password-authenticated key exchange* (PAKE), introduced by Bellovin and Merrit [2], is a method to establish cryptographic keys between two users sharing a *password*. A PAKE manages to "convert" this possibly low-entropy password into a random-looking key with high entropy, which is the same for both users if and only if they both used the same password. What makes these schemes interesting for practice is that they tie authentication solely to passwords, while other methods such as password-over-TLS involve more authentication material such as a certificate. The probably most prominent implementation of PAKE is the TLS-SRP ciphersuite (specified in RFCs 2945 and 5054), which is used by GnuTLS, OpenSSL and Apache.

In most applications, users of a PAKE actually take quite different roles. Namely, some may act as servers, maintaining sessions with various clients, and storing passwords of clients in a file. For better security, it seems reasonable to not write the password to the file system in the clear, but store, e.g., a hash of the password. A PAKE protocol that lets users take the roles of a client or a server is called *asymmetric* PAKE (aPAKE) (sometimes also *augmented* or *verifier-based* in the literature). To emphasize that we talk about a PAKE protocol without different roles, we write *symmetric* PAKE.

Security of PAKE. Since a password is potentially of low entropy, an attacker can always engage in a PAKE execution with another user by just trying a password, resulting in key agreement with non-negligible probability. Such an attack is called an *on-line dictionary attack* since the attacker only has one password guess per run of the protocol. A security requirement for symmetric PAKE is that an on-line dictionary attack is the "worst the adversary can do". Especially, the attacker should not be able to mount *off-line* dictionary attacks on the password, e.g., by deriving information about the password by just looking at the transcript. For an asymmetric PAKE, we can require more: if an attacker gets his hands on a password file, in which case the server is called *compromised*, the attacker should not learn the password directly. At least, some computation such as hashing password guesses is required.

Is Asymmetric PAKE Harder than Symmetric PAKE? Intuitively, asymmetric PAKE seems more challenging than symmetric PAKE, since asymmetric PAKE protocols provide a guarantee on top: they are supposed to protect passwords whenever the storage of a server is leaked to the adversary. This claim has evidence in the literature: there are symmetric PAKE schemes that are BPR-secure (BPR is the most widely used game-based notion for PAKE, introduced by

Table 1. Comparison of static security of different PAKE and aPAKE schemes, where "strong" denotes schemes that prevent precomputation of password files (e.g., via precomputing hash tables). RO means random oracle and GGM means generic group model.

Reference	Type	Sec. notion	Model
[1]	Symmetric	BPR	Non-prog. RO
E.g., [17, 18]	Symmetric	BPR	Standard
[3]	Asymmetric	BPR	Non-prog. RO
[20]	Asymmetric	BPR	GGM
E.g., [9, 18]	Symmetric	UC	Standard
[12]	Asymmetric	UC	Progr. RO
[16]	Asymmetric	UC	Limited progr. RO
[13]	Asymmetric	UC	Progr. RO
[15]	Asymmetric	UC, strong	Progr. RO
[4]	Asymmetric	UC, strong	Non-prog. RO & GGM

Bellare et al. [1]) in the standard model, while current aPAKE schemes satisfying the asymmetric variant of BPR security are only proven in an idealized model such as the non-programmable random oracle (NPRO) or the generic group model (GGM). The situation is similar when considering PAKE/aPAKE in the Universal Composability (UC) framework of Canetti [6]. UC-secure PAKE protocols exist in the non-programmable random oracle model and even in the standard model, while proofs of current aPAKE schemes additionally rely on some form of programmability of the random oracle (RO) or the GGM. See Table 1 for a comparison.

To our knowledge, in none of the aforementioned models there exist any formal proof of asymmetric PAKE being harder to achieve than symmetric PAKE. A close look at Table 1 reveals that the "gap" in the assumption is bigger in case of UC security. Can we make this gap as small as for BPR secure schemes? For sure we would like to answer this question in the affirmative, since for asymmetric PAKE, UC-security has two notable advantages over BPR security: it comes with a composability guarantee, and it considers adversarially-chosen passwords.

Our Contributions. In this paper, we rule out the existence of UC-secure aPAKE protocols from assumptions that are enough to obtain (even adaptively) UC-secure symmetric PAKE. Namely, we show that aPAKE is impossible to achieve w.r.t a non-programmable random oracle (NPRO). To our knowledge, this is the first formal evidence that universally composable asymmetric PAKE is harder to achieve than symmetric PAKE. Interestingly, our impossibility result directly extends to a setting where parties, additionally to the NPRO, have access to a common reference string (CRS). Although such a CRS offers a limited form of programmability, we can show that this is not enough to obtain UC-secure asymmetric PAKE.

In preparation of this formal result, and as a separate contribution, we revisit the ideal functionality $\mathcal{F}_{\text{apwKE}}$ for asymmetric PAKE of Gentry, MacKenzie and Ramzan [12]. Our changes summarize as follows:

- We show that $\mathcal{F}_{\text{apwKE}}$ is not realizable due to an incorrect modeling of server compromise attacks. We fix this by formally viewing server compromise as partial corruption of the server. This was already proposed but not enforced by Gentry et al. [12].
- We show that $\mathcal{F}_{\text{apwKE}}$ allows attacks on *explicit authentication*. In a PAKE protocol with explicit authentication, parties are informed whether the other party held the same password and thus computed the same session key. However, $\mathcal{F}_{\text{apwKE}}$ allows the adversary to make parties believe in the security of adversarially chosen session keys. This is clearly devastating for applications such as secure channels. In our revisited functionality $\mathcal{F}_{\text{aPAKE}}$ we exclude such attacks by introducing a proper modeling of explicit authentication.

We argue plausibility of our revisited functionality $\mathcal{F}_{\text{aPAKE}}$ by showing that it is realized by an asymmetric PAKE protocol called the Ω-method, introduced by Gentry et al. [12]. To our knowledge, this is the first proof of security of the Ω-method in the literature. Not surprisingly, the original publication of the Ω-method did not include a proof but only a claim of security, which is invalidated with our findings of their functionality being impossible to realize. Finally, we showcase how our 2-party functionality $\mathcal{F}_{\text{aPAKE}}$ can be used to obtain multi-user asymmetric PAKE protocols. We highlight a specific artifact of UC-security that has to be considered when implementing such a scheme. Let us now explain our results in more detail.

Separating Symmetric and Asymmetric PAKE. As already mentioned, asymmetric PAKE protocols are supposed to provide some protection of the password in case of a server compromise. Essentially, in case of a security breach where account data of users are leaked to the adversary, we want that the adversary does not obtain all user passwords in the clear. Formally, this attack is modeled via a partial leakage of the internal state of the server who already stored the user's account data. The adversary is however not allowed to *control* the behaviour of the compromised server, which distinguishes compromising a server from corrupting a server. Nevertheless, a server compromise allows the attacker to mount an *adaptive* attack.

In simulation-based security notions such as ones stated in the UC model, adaptive attacks often impose a problem. Such problems are often referred to as "commitment problem": they require the simulator to explain how, e.g., a transcript that he committed to in the beginning of the protocol matches certain secrets of honest participants that are revealed only later. The first mentioning of such a commitment problem is the work of Nielsen [19], who showed that an NPRO is not enough to obtain non-committing encryption. One contribution of the paper is to formalize NPROs. In a nutshell, an NPRO is modeled as an external oracle that informs the adversary about all queries, but chooses values truly at random, especially not letting the adversary in any way influence the outputs of the oracle.

Inspired by the work of Nielsen, we obtain the following result: UC-secure asymmetric PAKE is impossible to achieve in the NPRO model. The intuition is as follows: due to the adaptive nature of the server compromise attack, the simulator needs to commit to a password file without knowing the password that the file contains. The attacker can now test whether some password is contained in the simulated file. Since accessing the external oracle is sufficient to compute this test, the simulator merely learns the tested password but cannot influence the outcome of the test.

While the result itself is not very surprising, we stress that the techniques to prove it are actually completely different from the techniques used by Nielsen [19]. For non-committing encryption, their strategy is to let the simulator commit to "too many" ciphertexts such that there simply does not exist a secret key of reasonable size to explain all these ciphertexts later. However, in asymmetric PAKE there exists only one password file at the server. And indeed, there is a bit more hope for a simulator of asymmetric PAKE to actually find a good password file if he only guesses the password correctly. Our formal argument thus heavily relies on the fact that, in the UC model, the simulator does not have an arbitrary amount of runtime to simulate the password file. We formally prove that, with high probability, he will exhaust before finding a good file.

We further investigate how our proof technique extends to more setup assumptions. We find that our impossibility result directly extends to the NPRO model where parties can access an ideal common reference string (CRS). While the CRS can be "programmed" in the simulation, it does not resolve the simulator's commitment issue: neither does usage of the CRS provide the simulator with any information about the server's password prior to simulating the file, nor does determining the CRS let the simulator influence the aforementioned test. We can thus rule out the existence of UC-secure asymmetric PAKE protocols plain CRS as well as the NPRO+CRS model.

Opposed to our findings for asymmetric PAKE, UC-secure *symmetric* PAKE can be constructed even in the standard model (see Table 1). While already the NPRO model suffers from the uninstantiability results of Canetti et al. [8], requiring programmability of a RO is crucially strengthening the model. In a security proof w.r.t an NPRO, the reduction does not need to determine any output values and thus could use, e.g., a hash function like SHA-3 to answer RO queries. This is not possible for a reduction that makes use of the programmability property of the RO. Thus, our results indicate that, while going from symmetric to asymmetric PAKE in the UC model, we are forced to move further away from realistic setup assumptions.

Modeling Server Compromise. Towards separating symmetric and asymmetric PAKE, we first carefully revisit the ideal functionality $\mathcal{F}_{\mathsf{apwKE}}$ (see Fig. 1) for asymmetric PAKE of Gentry et al. [12], which adopts the ideal functionality for symmetric PAKE [9] to the asymmetric case. For the reader not familiar with

$\mathcal{F}_{\mathsf{apwKE}}$, we provide the functionality and a thorough introduction to it in the full version [14]. For providing an overview of our contributions, we first focus on how server compromise attacks are modeled by $\mathcal{F}_{\mathsf{apwKE}}$. After learning about a server compromise attack, $\mathcal{F}_{\mathsf{apwKE}}$ enables the adversary to (a) make off-line password guesses against the file and (b) impersonate the server using the file. $\mathcal{F}_{\mathsf{apwKE}}$ only allows the adversary to compromise and make password guesses upon getting instructions from the distinguisher $\mathcal{Z}$.

We show that it is necessary to revisit $\mathcal{F}_{\mathsf{apwKE}}$ by proving that restricting the adversary to only submit off-line password guesses upon instructions from $\mathcal{Z}$ results in $\mathcal{F}_{\mathsf{apwKE}}$ being impossible to realize. By this, we invalidate the claimed security of the Ω-method [12]. We also observe that putting restrictions such as "only ask query x if $\mathcal{Z}$ tells you" on the adversary is not conform with the UC framework and invalidates important properties of the framework such as simulation with respect to the dummy adversary.

Towards a better modeling, and towards resolving the now-open question which security guarantees the Ω-method fulfils, we revisit $\mathcal{F}_{\mathsf{apwKE}}$ and propose our own ideal functionality $\mathcal{F}_{\mathsf{aPAKE}}$. The changes are as follows: we lift the aforementioned restriction on the adversary regarding off-line password guesses and argue why the resulting security notion captures what we expect from an asymmetric PAKE. We further propose a UC-conform modeling of server compromise attacks as "partial" corruption queries which, in the real execution of the protocol, partly leak the internal state of an honest party to the adversary (i.e., the password file). Our new functionality $\mathcal{F}_{\mathsf{aPAKE}}$ differs in another aspect from $\mathcal{F}_{\mathsf{apwKE}}$, which we will now explain in more detail.

Modeling Explicit Authentication. A protocol is said to have *explicit authentication* if the parties can learn whether the key agreement was successful or not, in which case they might opt for, e.g., reporting failure. $\mathcal{F}_{\mathsf{apwKE}}$ features a TESTABORT interface which allows the adversary to obtain information about the authentication status and also to decide whether parties should abort if their computed session keys do not match. The idea behind modeling explicit authentication via an interface that the adversary may or may not decide to use is to keep $\mathcal{F}_{\mathsf{apwKE}}$ flexible: both protocols with or without explicit authentication can be proven to realize it. However, we show that this results in $\mathcal{F}_{\mathsf{apwKE}}$ providing very weak security guarantees regarding explicit authentication. One property that a protocol with authentication should have is that parties reliably abort if they detect authentication failure. However, $\mathcal{F}_{\mathsf{apwKE}}$ does not enforce this property since the adversary can simply decide *not* to use the TESTABORT interface. We propose a stronger version of $\mathcal{F}_{\mathsf{aPAKE}}$ that enforces explicit authentication *within the functionality*.

To demonstrate usefulness of our revisited functionality $\mathcal{F}_{\mathsf{aPAKE}}$, we show that the Ω-method UC-realizes it. To our knowledge, this is the first full proof of security for the Ω-method.

From 2-Party aPAKE to Multi-party aPAKE. $\mathcal{F}_{\mathsf{apwKE}}$ as well as our $\mathcal{F}_{\mathsf{aPAKE}}$ are *two-party* functionalities running with one client and one server. But realistic scenarios for PAKE comprise thousands of users and hundreds of servers all using the same protocol to establish secure communication channels or to authenticate clients. This however is usually not a problem: the UC framework comes with a composition theorem, which allows to instantiate an arbitrary number of instances of the two-party functionality with its realization. Each client would invoke an instance of $\mathcal{F}_{\mathsf{aPAKE}}$, and a server can participates in arbitrarily many of them. To avoid that all instances use their "own" setup, which would require a server to use, e.g., a different hash function for each client, all functionalities could share their setups. This can be achieved by transforming the setup, e.g., a RO $\mathcal{F}_{\mathsf{RO}}$ to a multi-party functionality $\hat{\mathcal{F}}_{\mathsf{RO}}$ that acts as a wrapper for multiple copies of $\mathcal{F}_{\mathsf{RO}}$. This approach is widely used and called UC with joint state (JUC) [10]. We showcase this transformation to the multi-user setting for the Ω-method. Interestingly, a client in the multi-user Ω-method is now required to remember which is "her" copy of the RO. We demonstrate that this does not hinder practicality of the scheme since we can identify a party's RO by information that this party, in any implementation, has to remember anyway (e.g., the server's URL and her own username). Due to space constraints, details are exclusive to the full version [14].

Related Work. Canetti et al. [9] show impossibility of $\mathcal{F}_{\mathsf{apwKE}}$ in the plain model. Gentry et al. [12] show how to transform a UC-secure PAKE into a UC-secure asymmetric PAKE (the opposite direction is trivial). However, as we will show while proving security of their resulting aPAKE, their transformation seem to require a strong assumption such as a programmable RO. Thus, this does not contradict our separation result.

Since its publication, (the unrealizable) $\mathcal{F}_{\mathsf{apwKE}}$ has been used to argue security of asymmetric PAKE schemes, most notably the OPAQUE protocol [15], which was recently selected as recommended asymmetric PAKE protocol by the Crypto Forum Research Group (CFRG). The CFRG is an Internet Research Task Force providing recommendations for IETF. To our knowledge, the proof of security of OPAQUE can be modified to realize our revisited functionality $\mathcal{F}_{\mathsf{aPAKE}}$. Finally, in a concurrently published work, Shoup [21] also identifies some of the modeling issues in $\mathcal{F}_{\mathsf{apwKE}}$ pointed out in our work, but takes a different approach in fixing them. While their approach requires restricting the UC environment, ours requires restriction of the simulator.

2   The aPAKE Security Model, Revisited

The notion of universally composable asymmetric PAKE was introduced in 2006 by Gentry, MacKenzie and Ramzan [12]. Their two-party functionality $\mathcal{F}_{\mathsf{apwKE}}$ augments the functionality for (symmetric) PAKE by Canetti et al. [9] by adding an interface for server compromise attacks. The presentation is slightly more involved due to the different roles that the two participating users can take in the asymmetric version of PAKE: while the client can initiate multiple key exchange sessions by providing a fresh password each time, the server has to

The functionality $\mathcal{F}_{\mathsf{apwKE}}$ is parameterized with a security parameter λ. It interacts with an adversary $\mathcal{S}$, a client $\mathcal{P}_C$ and a server $\mathcal{P}_S$ via the following queries:

Password Registration

- On (STOREPWDFILE, sid, $\mathcal{P}_C$, pw) from $\mathcal{P}_S$, if this is the first STOREPWDFILE message, record (FILE, $\mathcal{P}_C$, $\mathcal{P}_S$, pw) and mark it uncompromised.

Stealing Password Data

- On (STEALPWDFILE, sid) from $\mathcal{S}$, if there is no record (FILE, $\mathcal{P}_C$, $\mathcal{P}_S$, pw), return "no password file" to $\mathcal{S}$. Otherwise, if the record is marked uncompromised, mark it compromised and
  - ▷ If there is a record (OFFLINE, pw), send pw to $\mathcal{S}$.
  - ▷ Else, return "password file stolen" to $\mathcal{S}$.
- On (OFFLINETESTPWD, sid, pw') from $\mathcal{S}$, do:
  - ▷ If there is a record (FILE, $\mathcal{P}_C$, $\mathcal{P}_S$, pw) marked compromised, do: if pw = pw', return "correct guess" to $\mathcal{S}$; else, return "wrong guess".
  - ▷ Else, record (OFFLINE, pw').

Password Authentication

- On (USRSESSION, sid, ssid, $\mathcal{P}_S$, pw') from $\mathcal{P}_C$, send (USRSESSION, sid, ssid, $\mathcal{P}_C$, $\mathcal{P}_S$) to $\mathcal{S}$. Also, if this is the first USRSESSION message for ssid, record (ssid, $\mathcal{P}_C$, $\mathcal{P}_S$, pw') and mark it fresh.
- On (SRVSESSION, sid, ssid) from $\mathcal{P}_S$, ignore the query if there is no record (FILE, $\mathcal{P}_C$, $\mathcal{P}_S$, pw). Else send (SRVSESSION, sid, ssid, $\mathcal{P}_C$, $\mathcal{P}_S$) to $\mathcal{S}$ and, if this is the first SRVSESSION message for ssid, record (ssid, $\mathcal{P}_S$, $\mathcal{P}_C$, pw) and mark it fresh.

Active Session Attacks

- On (TESTPWD, sid, ssid, $\mathcal{P}$, pw') from $\mathcal{S}$, if there is a record (ssid, $\mathcal{P}$, $\mathcal{P}'$, pw) marked fresh, do: if pw' = pw, mark it compromised and return "correct guess" to $\mathcal{S}$; else, mark it interrupted and return "wrong guess" to $\mathcal{S}$.
- On (IMPERSONATE, sid, ssid) from $\mathcal{S}$, if there is a record (ssid, $\mathcal{P}_C$, $\mathcal{P}_S$, pw') marked fresh, do: if there is a record (FILE, $\mathcal{P}_C$, $\mathcal{P}_S$, pw) marked compromised and pw' = pw, mark (ssid, $\mathcal{P}_C$, $\mathcal{P}_S$, pw') compromised and return "correct guess" to $\mathcal{S}$; else, mark it interrupted and return "wrong guess" to $\mathcal{S}$.

Key Generation and Authentication

- On (NEWKEY, sid, ssid, $\mathcal{P}$, K) from $\mathcal{S}$ where $|K| = \lambda$, if there is a record (ssid, $\mathcal{P}$, $\mathcal{P}'$, pw) not marked completed, do:
  - ▷ If the record is marked compromised, or either $\mathcal{P}$ or $\mathcal{P}'$ is corrupted, send (sid, ssid, K) to $\mathcal{P}$.
  - ▷ Else, if the record is marked fresh, (sid, ssid, K') was sent to $\mathcal{P}'$, and at that time there was a record (ssid, $\mathcal{P}'$, $\mathcal{P}$, pw') marked fresh, send (sid, ssid, K') to $\mathcal{P}$.
  - ▷ Else, pick $K'' \xleftarrow{\$} \{0,1\}^\lambda$ and send (sid, ssid, K'') to $\mathcal{P}$.
  Finally, mark (ssid, $\mathcal{P}$, $\mathcal{P}'$, pw) completed.
- On (TESTABORT, sid, ssid, $\mathcal{P}$) from $\mathcal{S}$, if there is a record (ssid, $\mathcal{P}$, $\mathcal{P}'$, pw) not marked completed, do:
  - ▷ If it is marked fresh and record (ssid, $\mathcal{P}'$, $\mathcal{P}$, pw) exists, send "success" to $\mathcal{S}$.
  - ▷ Else, send "fail" to $\mathcal{S}$ and (ABORT, sid, ssid) to $\mathcal{P}$, and mark (ssid, $\mathcal{P}$, $\mathcal{P}'$, pw) completed.

Fig. 1. Ideal functionality $\mathcal{F}_{\mathsf{apwKE}}$ for asymmetric PAKE from [12], but phrased as in [15] with slight notational changes to avoid confusion between the adversary ($\mathcal{S}$) and server ($\mathcal{P}_S$). Framed queries can only be asked upon getting instructions from $\mathcal{Z}$.

register a password file once which is then used in every key exchange session with the client. We recall $\mathcal{F}_{\mathsf{apwKE}}$ in Fig. 1 and refer the reader not familiar with it to the full version [14] for a thorough introduction to the functionality. To model a server compromise attack, $\mathcal{F}_{\mathsf{apwKE}}$ provides three interfaces STEALPWDFILE, OFFLINETESTPWD and IMPERSONATE, which we now describe.

- STEALPWDFILE initiates a server compromise attack. The output is a bit, depending on whether the server already registered a password file or not, and the query can only be made by the simulator if $\mathcal{Z}$ gives the instruction for it.
- OFFLINETESTPWD enables an off-line dictionary attack: the adversary can test whether some password is contained in the password file. The answer is a bit, depending on whether the guess was correct or not. The attack is called "off-line" since it can be mounted by the adversary without interacting with the client. Like STEALPWDFILE, this attack can only be mounted by the simulator if $\mathcal{Z}$ instructs him to do so. The adversary gets confirmation on a correct guess only after a STEALPWDFILE query happened.
- IMPERSONATE can be used by the adversary *after* STEALPWDFILE was issued by $\mathcal{Z}$. This interface enables the adversary to engage in a key exchange session with the client, using the stolen password file as authenticating data.

Definitional Issues with STEALPWDFILE *and* OFFLINETESTPWD *Interfaces of* $\mathcal{F}_{\mathsf{apwKE}}$. Let us make two observations about these interfaces. Firstly, the restriction of letting the adversary ask specific queries only upon receiving them from $\mathcal{Z}$ constitutes a change of the UC framework (Gentry et al. [12] propose to change the control function of the UC framework to enforce it). This needs to be done carefully to not invalidate important properties of the framework such as the composition theorem and emulation w.r.t the dummy adversary. Without further restrictions, at least the latter does not hold anymore. To provide an example, consider an environment $\mathcal{Z}$ that asks an "encoded" STEALPWD-FILE query, e.g., (ask-STEALPWDFILE-query, sid) and sends it to the adversary. A real-world adversary $\mathcal{A}$ can easily decode this query and perform the desired attack, while the simulator in the ideal world cannot accomplish the corruption at $\mathcal{F}_{\mathsf{aPAKE}}$ due to the wrong message format. This way, $\mathcal{Z}$ can keep the simulator from using his interfaces, leaving him with no leverage to presume his simulation. Clearly, such an "intelligent" real-world adversary is worse than a dummy adversary, who would just relay the message without any effect. To get a meaningful definition that inherits all properties of the UC framework, such environments would have to be excluded.

Our second observation concerns the real execution of the protocol, where $\mathcal{A}$ obtains STEALPWDFILE and OFFLINETESTPWD queries from $\mathcal{Z}$. Gentry et al. [12] assume that $\mathcal{A}$ now *mounts a server-compromise attack* and does not behave as the dummy adversary, as usually assumed in the UC framework (see [7], Section 4.3.1). Let us explain why this underspecification is problematic. In the UC framework, the real-world adversary $\mathcal{A}$ only has influence on the communication channel and corrupted parties, and none of this helps him to steal a password file from the server. For analyzing UC security of a protocol with respect to $\mathcal{F}_{\mathsf{apwKE}}$, it is however crucial to formally specify the outputs of $\mathcal{A}$ upon these queries, since $\mathcal{A}$'s output has to be simulated by $\mathcal{S}$.

2.1   Fix No. 1: Defining the Corruption Model

To address the aforementioned issues, we first define server compromise to be *party corruption*. This possibility was already pointed out by Gentry et al. [12]. Modeling server compromise via corruption offers the following advantages:

- It captures the intuition that compromising the server, like Byzantine party corruption, constitutes an attack that the environment $\mathcal{Z}$ can mount to distinguish real and ideal execution.
- It takes care of definitional issues by using the special properties of corruption queries in UC, e.g., that they can only be asked by $\mathcal{S}$ and $\mathcal{A}$ if $\mathcal{Z}$ instructs them to do so. As a consequence, there is no need to adjust the control function or to put restrictions on the environment, nor to consider adversaries other than the dummy adversary.
- It lets us flexibly define the effect of server compromise in the real world w.r.t internal state of the server. For example, one can choose whether upon compromising the server the adversary merely learns that a password file exists or even leak the whole file to him. We note that this leads to a UC-conform modeling since arbitrary corruption models can be integrated into the UC framework (see [7], Section 7.1).

Formally, besides Byzantine party corruption that is usually modeled via a query $(\mathrm{CORRUPT}, \mathcal{P}, \mathsf{sid})$ from $\mathcal{Z}$ to $\mathcal{A}$, we allow $\mathcal{Z}$ to issue an additional corruption query $(\mathrm{STEALPWDFILE}, \mathsf{sid})$. To formalize what happens upon this query in the ideal world, we adopt the conventions for corruption queries from the UC framework [7] (see Section 7.1) and let dummy parties in the ideal world ignore corruption messages. Instead, these queries are handeled by the ideal functionality, who receives them directly from $\mathcal{S}$.

Server Compromise

Real World: Let $f : \{0,1\}^* \to \{0,1\}^*$ be an efficiently computable function. We denote the internal state of $\mathcal{P}_S$ with state, consisting of all messages received by and sent to the server, its random coins and current program's state. Upon receiving a message $(\mathrm{STEALPWDFILE}, \mathsf{sid})$ from $\mathcal{Z}$, $\mathcal{A}$ delivers the message to $\mathcal{P}_S$, who immediately sends $f(\mathsf{state})$ to $\mathcal{A}$. This definition of corruption resembles what Canetti [7] describes as *physical "side channel" attacks* since it results in leaking a function of the internal state of a party. A natural choice is $f(\mathsf{state}) = $ file, with file being the variable in the server's code storing the password file, which we will use in this work.

Ideal World: Upon (STEALPWDFILE, sid) from $\mathcal{Z}$, $\mathcal{S}$ sends this message to $\mathcal{F}_{\text{apwKE}}$. $\mathcal{F}_{\text{apwKE}}$ marks $\mathcal{P}_S$ as compromised. If there are records (FILE, $\mathcal{P}_C$, $\mathcal{P}_S$, pw) ("server $\mathcal{P}_S$ used pw to generate password file") and (OFFLINE, pw) ("$\mathcal{S}$ guessed that file contains pw"), $\mathcal{F}_{\text{apwKE}}$ sends pw to $\mathcal{S}$.

Let us emphasize that, while we now model STEALPWDFILE queries formally as corruption queries, this does not mean that the adversary gets to control the behavior of the server afterwards. The reader should keep in mind that there are different variants of corruption, some more severe and some less. As common in the UC model, we refer to a party having received a Byzantine corruption message as *corrupted* (acknowledging that Byzantine party corruption is the "default" type of corruption used in the literature). Also, we refer to a server having received a STEALPWDFILE corruption query as *compromised*. In line with the aPAKE literature [12,15], we only consider static Byzantine corruption (meaning that Byzantine corruption messages are ignored after the first party obtained input from $\mathcal{Z}$). Contrarily, STEALPWDFILE corruption messages can be asked by $\mathcal{Z}$ at any time. This makes server compromise an *adaptive* attack. Obviously, static server compromise is not very interesting since it results in leakage of an empty file.

2.2 Fix No. 2: Bounding Offline Attacks

We now turn our attention to the OFFLINETESTPWD interface. If the server is compromised, which we formalized via the corruption query STEALPWDFILE, the adversary can query OFFLINETESTPWD to figure out the password within the password file. Such an attack on the password file is called "off-line" to emphasize that there is no further interaction with the client required.

Clearly, a meaningful aPAKE security notion should offer means to tell a protocol with file = pw apart from a protocol with, e.g., file = $H(pw)$ for some hash function H. The latter requires the adversary to compute hashes of passwords until it guesses the correct password, while the former directly leaks the password to the adversary without any computational effort. If we want to distinguish between these protocols, we need to make the number of OFFLINETEST-PWD queries, which in this example represent computations of the function $H()$, explicit to $\mathcal{Z}$.

To this end, Gentry et al. [12] define $\mathcal{F}_{\text{apwKE}}$ such that $\mathcal{A}$ is allowed to query OFFLINETESTPWD only by relaying queries of $\mathcal{Z}$. Clearly, this gives $\mathcal{Z}$ a way to bound the number of OFFLINETESTPWD guesses and does not allow to prove a protocol with file = pw secure. However, $\mathcal{F}_{\text{apwKE}}$ with OFFLINETESTPWD instructed by $\mathcal{Z}$ is inherently impossible to realize for natural asymmetric PAKE protocols even under strong assumptions such as a programmable random oracle. In a nutshell, the reason is that requiring $\mathcal{Z}$'s permission to issue OFFLINETEST-PWD queries keeps the simulator from using this interface and prevents successful simulation of any aPAKE protocol. We formally prove this impossibility result in the full version [14].

To circumvent the impossibility result, we change the model by letting OFFLINETESTPWD constitute an interface provided to the adversary by $\mathcal{F}_{\text{apwKE}}$

without requiring instructions from $\mathcal{Z}$. Consequently, OFFLINETESTPWD queries by $\mathcal{Z}$ do not have any effect nor produce any output in the real world. Of course, we now need means to bound the simulator's usage of this interface. Fortunately, the UC framework provides a technical tool for this, as we will detail now.

Bounding the Simulator's Computation. Unlimited access to the interface OFFLINETESTPWD lets $\mathcal{S}$ find out the server's password eventually, within polynomial time if we assume passwords to be human memorable. Knowing the password, simulation of the server becomes trivial and even protocols that we would consider insecure can be simulated (e.g., a protocol with file = pw).

One possible countermeasure is to require the simulator have runtime similar to the real-world adversary. Letting $\mathcal{S}$ only issue OFFLINETESTPWD when being instructed by $\mathcal{Z}$ enforces this, and was probably the reason for Gentry et al. [12] to use this limitation in the first place. However, as we show in the full version [14], Theorem D.1, this restriction on $\mathcal{S}$ is too heavy. Instead, we propose to lift this restriction, as formalized above, and instead require that the simulator's runtime is linked to the runtime of the real-world adversary. In the UC model, all entities are *locally T-bounded* interactive Turing machines (see full version [14]). Intuitively, each input bit can be seen as a ticket. Each ticket can be used to either send $T(1)$ input bits to another machine, or it can be consumed as $T(1)$ computation steps. Since input to the simulator comes from the environment, $\mathcal{Z}$ can decide how many OFFLINETESTPWD queries $\mathcal{S}$ is allowed to make. (This argument requires that $\mathcal{S}$ cannot use the ideal functionality to augment its input bits. However, all PAKE functionalities give only answers that are shorter than the corresponding queries. Thus, $\mathcal{S}$ can obtain additional "input tickets" only from $\mathcal{Z}$ and each query to the ideal functionality results in losing tickets.) Finally, let $T : \mathbb{N} \rightarrow \mathbb{N}$ denote the bound of the real-world adversary. We can now link the number of OFFLINETESTPWD guesses of the simulator to the number of guesses computed by the real-world adversary by requiring that for every locally T-bounded real-world adversary there exists a locally T-bounded simulator.

We are now ready to state our revisited functionality $\mathcal{F}_{\mathsf{aPAKE}}$ in Fig. 2. All differences to $\mathcal{F}_{\mathsf{apwKE}}$ were already explained above, except for changes regarding the TESTABORT interface concerning explicit authentication which we describe in Sect. 4.1. The reasons for postponing are two-fold: the changes can be best explained when investigating security of the Ω-method, and the interface is not relevant for our separation result in the upcoming section. To summarize, the differences between using $\mathcal{F}_{\mathsf{apwKE}}$ or our revisited $\mathcal{F}_{\mathsf{aPAKE}}$ are as follows:

- STEALPWDFILE is now a corruption query (change does not show in $\mathcal{F}_{\mathsf{aPAKE}}$ but in the assumed corruption model).
- OFFLINETESTPWD can be asked without getting instructions from $\mathcal{Z}$, but a simulator interacting with $\mathcal{F}_{\mathsf{aPAKE}}$ can only access OFFLINETESTPWD as long as its runtime remains locally T-bounded.
- The TESTABORT interface is removed and NEWKEY is adjusted to analyze *either* protocols with *or* without explicit authentication.

3 The Separation Result

After revisiting the UC security notion for aPAKE and closing some of its definitional gaps in the previous section, we will now turn to our main result. Namely, we give the first formal evidence that UC secure asymmetric PAKE is indeed harder to achieve than symmetric PAKE.

The functionality $\mathcal{F}_{\mathsf{aPAKE}}$ is parameterized with a security parameter λ. It interacts with an adversary $\mathcal{S}$ and a client and a server $\mathcal{P} \in \{\mathcal{P}_C, \mathcal{P}_S\}$ via the following queries:

Stealing Password Data

- On (STEALPWDFILE, sid) from $\mathcal{S}$, if there is no record (FILE, $\mathcal{P}_C, \mathcal{P}_S, \mathsf{pw}$), return "no password file" to $\mathcal{S}$. Otherwise, mark $\mathcal{P}_S$ as compromised and
  ▷ If there is a record (OFFLINE, pw), send pw to $\mathcal{S}$.
  ▷ Else, return "password file stolen" to $\mathcal{S}$.
- On (OFFLINETESTPWD, sid, pw') from $\mathcal{S}$, do:
  ▷ If there is a record (FILE, $\mathcal{P}_C, \mathcal{P}_S, \mathsf{pw}$) and $\mathcal{P}_S$ is compromised, do: if pw = pw', return "correct guess" to $\mathcal{S}$; else, return "wrong guess".
  ▷ Else, record (OFFLINE, pw').

Password Registration, Password Authentication & Active Session Attacks (as in Figure 1)

Key Generation and Authentication

- On (NEWKEY, sid, ssid, $\mathcal{P}$, K) from $\mathcal{S}$ where $|\mathsf{K}| = \lambda$, if there is a record (ssid, $\mathcal{P}, \mathcal{P}', \mathsf{pw}$) not completed, do:
  ▷ If the record is compromised, or $\mathcal{P}$ or $\mathcal{P}'$ is corrupted, or K = ⊥, send (sid, ssid, K) to $\mathcal{P}$.
  ▷ If the record is fresh, (sid, ssid, K') was sent to $\mathcal{P}'$, and at that time there was a record (ssid, $\mathcal{P}', \mathcal{P}, \mathsf{pw}$) marked fresh, send (sid, ssid, K') to $\mathcal{P}$.
  ▷ Else if the record is interrupted or if it is fresh and there is a record (sid, $\mathcal{P}', \mathcal{P}, \mathsf{pw}'$) with pw ≠ pw', then send (sid, ssid, ⊥) to $\mathcal{P}$ and $\mathcal{S}$.
  ▷ Else, pick $\mathsf{K}'' \overset{\$}{\leftarrow} \{0,1\}^\lambda$ and send (sid, ssid, K'') to $\mathcal{P}$.
  Finally, mark (ssid, $\mathcal{P}, \mathcal{P}', \mathsf{pw}$) as completed.

Fig. 2. Our revisited $\mathcal{F}_{\mathsf{aPAKE}}$ for asymmetric PAKE, with explicit authentication (see Sect. 4.1). Framed queries can only be asked upon getting instructions from $\mathcal{Z}$. Gray boxes indicate queries that required instructions from $\mathcal{Z}$ according to Gentry et al. [12], but not in our $\mathcal{F}_{\mathsf{aPAKE}}$.

The Non-programmable Random Oracle Model. In his seminal paper, Nielsen [19] formalizes the non-programmable random oracle model (NPRO) as a variant of the UC framework where all entities (including $\mathcal{Z}$) are granted direct access to an oracle $\mathcal{O}$. This oracle answers fresh values with fresh randomness, and maintains state to consistently answer queries that were asked before. We recall the formalism of Nielsen to integrate such a random oracle in the UC framework.

In the NPRO model, all interactive Touring machines (ITM) that exist in the UC framework are equipped with additional oracle tapes, namely an oracle query tape and an oracle input tape. To denote an ITM $\mathcal{Z}$ communicating with oracle $\mathcal{O}$ via these tapes, we write $\mathcal{Z}^{\mathcal{O}}$. $\mathcal{Z}$ can write on his oracle query tape, while the oracle input tape is read-only. As soon as $\mathcal{Z}$ enters a special oracle query state, the content of the oracle query tape is sent to $\mathcal{O}$. The output of $\mathcal{O}$ is then written on the oracle input tape of $\mathcal{Z}$. A random oracle can be implemented by letting $\mathcal{O}$ denote an ITM defining a uniformly random function $\mathcal{H} : \{0,1\}^* \rightarrow \{0,1\}^{\lambda}$. We now say that a protocol π *UC-realizes a functionality $\mathcal{F}$ in the NPRO model* if $\forall \mathcal{A}^{\mathcal{O}} \exists \mathcal{S}^{\mathcal{O}}$ s.t. $\forall \mathcal{Z}^{\mathcal{O}} : View_{\pi^{\mathcal{O}}, \mathcal{A}^{\mathcal{O}}}(\mathcal{Z}^{\mathcal{O}}) \overset{c}{\approx} View_{\mathcal{F}^{\mathcal{O}}, \mathcal{S}^{\mathcal{O}}}(\mathcal{Z}^{\mathcal{O}})$.

Verifiable Password Files. To state our separation result, we need to formally capture what it means for an aPAKE protocol formulated in the UC framework to have a *verifiable password file*. In a nutshell, the definition captures whether for a password file file leaked by a compromised server, the environment $\mathcal{Z}$ is provided with all necessary information and interfaces at hybrid functionalities to determine whether any given pw is contained in file. We do not specify how $\mathcal{Z}$ determines this, e.g., whether $\mathcal{Z}$ tries to recompute file from pw or whether $\mathcal{Z}$ runs the aPAKE protocol internally on inputs pw and file. For example, hashing the password results in a verifiable file $H(pw)$ if $\mathcal{Z}$ posesses the description of $H()$ or can access a functionality computing $H()$.

Definition 1 (Verifiable Password File). *Let π be an asymmetric PAKE protocol in an $\mathcal{F}$-hybrid model, where $\mathcal{F}$ is an arbitrary set of ideal functionalities. We say that π has a* verifiable password file file *if, for a given* pw*, $\mathcal{Z}$ can efficiently determine whether* file *was created upon input* pw*, by only interacting with the ideal functionalities $\mathcal{F}$ (via $\mathcal{A}$).*

We emphasize that only adversarial interfaces at hybrid functionalities may help $\mathcal{Z}$ in verifying correctness of the password file, and no further inputs to other ITMs are required. This will become crucial in proving our impossibility result. Let us emphasize that Definition 1 does not actually restrict the class of asymmetric PAKE protocols. In fact, the only asymmetric PAKE protocol formulated in the UC framework that does not have a verifiable password file that we are aware of is the ideal protocol $\mathcal{F}_{\mathsf{aPAKE}}$ itself. This protocol has a trivial password file ("no password file"/"password file stolen" are possible outputs upon server compromise), requires no hybrid functionalities and thus the password file is not verifiable. And indeed, the following Theorem would not hold w.r.t the ideal protocol $\mathcal{F}_{\mathsf{aPAKE}}$, due to the well-known fact that every UC functionality realizes itself. Let us stress though that all practical aPAKE protocols proposed in the literature do have verifiable password files, simply because a password at the client side and a file at the server side need to be enough to complete the key exchange. Definition 1 should thus be viewed as a necessary formalism to prove our separation result and not as a restriction of it.

With the NPRO model and the property of verifiable password files we now have all tools to prove our separation result in the following theorem.

Theorem 1. *The functionality $\mathcal{F}_{\mathsf{aPAKE}}$ as depicted in Fig. 2 is not realizable in the NPRO model by any protocol with verifiable password file. More detailed, for every such protocol π there exists a polynomial T, a locally T-bounded attacker $\mathcal{A}$ and an environment $\mathcal{Z}$ restricted to static Byzantine corruptions and adaptive server compromise, such that there is no locally T-bounded simulator $\mathcal{S}$ such that π UC-realizes $\mathcal{F}_{\mathsf{aPAKE}}$ in the NPRO model.*

Proof. Let π be a protocol with verifiable password file that UC-realizes $\mathcal{F}_{\mathsf{aPAKE}}$ in the NPRO model. Consider the following environment $\mathcal{Z}$ running either with an adversary or the simulator.

- $\mathcal{Z}^{\mathcal{O}}$ starts the protocol with $(\textsc{StorePwdFile}, \mathsf{sid}, \mathcal{P}_C, \mathsf{pw})$ as input to $\mathcal{P}_S$, where $\mathsf{pw} \xleftarrow{\$} \{0,1\}^{\lceil\sqrt{2\lambda}\rceil}$. All parties remain uncorrupted.
- $\mathcal{Z}^{\mathcal{O}}$ sends $(\textsc{StealPwdFile}, \mathsf{sid})$ to the adversary to compromise the server. $\mathcal{Z}$ obtains file as answer from the adversary.
- $\mathcal{Z}^{\mathcal{O}}$ verifies $(\mathsf{pw}, \mathsf{file})$.
- $\mathcal{Z}^{\mathcal{O}}$ outputs 0 if verification succeeds, else it outputs 1.

Note that step 3 can be performed by $\mathcal{Z}^{\mathcal{O}}$ without any interaction with $\mathcal{A}$, simply since it has the same oracle access as $\mathcal{A}^{\mathcal{O}}$. To verify the file, $\mathcal{Z}$ runs π internally, using pw as input to the client and file for the server. It outputs 0 if both client and server compute the same session key. Due to the file verifiability of π, $\mathcal{Z}^{\mathcal{O}}$ always outputs 0 in the real execution. It remains to compute the probability that $\mathcal{S}^{\mathcal{O}}$ outputs file$_{\mathcal{S}}$ such that $\mathcal{Z}^{\mathcal{O}}$ outputs 0 in the ideal execution. Since $\mathcal{Z}^{\mathcal{O}}$ issues only $\textsc{StorePwdFile}$ and $\textsc{StealPwdFile}$ queries (which both do not produce any output in this case), no $(\textsc{Offline}, \dots)$ or $(\mathsf{ssid}, \dots)$ records are ever created within $\mathcal{F}_{\mathsf{aPAKE}}$. Due to the absence of these records, the only interface of $\mathcal{F}_{\mathsf{aPAKE}}$ provided to $\mathcal{S}^{\mathcal{O}}$ that produces any pw-depending output is $\textsc{OfflineTestPwd}$. This interface provides $\mathcal{S}^{\mathcal{O}}$ with a bit, depending on whether the submitted password was equal to pw or not.

The real-world adversary $\mathcal{A}$ considered above only needs to read its inputs ($\textsc{StealPwdFile}$ and file) and forward them. Thus, $\mathcal{A}$ is locally T-bounded with $T(n) := n$. Since $\mathcal{S}^{\mathcal{O}}$ is required to be locally T-bounded as well, it has runtime $n = n_I - n_e$, n_I is the number of bits written to $\mathcal{S}^{\mathcal{O}}$'s input tapes and n_e the number of bits $\mathcal{S}^{\mathcal{O}}$ writes to other input tapes. Since $\mathcal{S}^{\mathcal{O}}$ cannot have a negative runtime, the maximum number of password bits that he can submit to $\textsc{OfflineTestPwd}$ is n_I. In the above attack, n_I consists of the minimal input 1^λ, $(\textsc{StealPwdFile}, \mathsf{sid})$ from $\mathcal{Z}^{\mathcal{O}}$ as well as a bit as answer to each $\textsc{StealPwdFile}$ and $\textsc{OfflineTestPwd}$ query that $\mathcal{S}^{\mathcal{O}}$ issues. We now upper bound the number of total password guesses that $\mathcal{S}^{\mathcal{O}}$ can submit. We simplify the analysis by ignoring names and session IDs in queries, and by assuming that $(\textsc{StealPwdFile}, \mathsf{sid})$ has the same bitsize as $\mathcal{S}^{\mathcal{O}}$'s answer file$_{\mathcal{S}}$. Additionally, we let $\mathcal{S}^{\mathcal{O}}$ know k, i.e., the length of the password of the server. The simplifications yield $n_I = \lambda + m$, where m is the number of $\textsc{OfflineTestPwd}$ queries of $\mathcal{S}^{\mathcal{O}}$. Since $|\mathsf{pw}| \geq 1$, we have $m < \lambda$, and thus the maximum number of k-bit long passwords that $\mathcal{S}^{\mathcal{O}}$ can write in queries is $2\lambda/k$. Setting $k = log_2(\lambda) + 2$, and using the fact that $\mathcal{Z}^{\mathcal{O}}$ draws pw at random, the probability that $\mathcal{S}^{\mathcal{O}}$ obtains

1 from OFFLINETESTPWD is at most $1/2$. It follows that $\Pr[\mathcal{Z} \to 1|$ ideal $] = \Pr[\mathcal{A}^{\mathcal{O}}(\text{pw}) = \text{file}_{\mathcal{S}}] \leq 1/2 + 1/2^{k-1}$, contradicting the UC-security of π, which concludes the proof.

Theorem 1 indicates that some form of programmability is required to realize $\mathcal{F}_{\text{aPAKE}}$. However, our proof technique differs significantly from other NPRO impossibility results such as the one from Nielsen [19] for non-committing encryption. Essentially, in non-committing encryption, simulation of *arbitrarily many* ciphertexts are necessary, while for asymmetric PAKE as specified by $\mathcal{F}_{\text{aPAKE}}$ *just one* password file needs to be simulated. An interesting question is thus whether a setup assumption such as a common reference string (CRS), which offers a limited form of programmability, is enough to realize $\mathcal{F}_{\text{aPAKE}}$. Unfortunately, we answer this question negatively by extending the impossibility result of Theorem 1 to a setting where a common reference string (CRS) is used as additional setup assumption.

Theorem 2. *Theorem 1 holds also in a setting where all entities are additionally granted access to an ideal common reference string (CRS).*

Proof (Sketch.). The argumentation is the same as before, but additionally showing that the CRS does not help the simulator since he *does not know* which password to program the CRS for.

We modify the proof of Theorem 1 as follows: as a new first step, $\mathcal{Z}$ asks for the CRS value. Since this completely "consumes" the CRS functionality, meaning that no further interaction with $\mathcal{A}$ is necessary to verify the file, $\mathcal{Z}$'s verification result in the real world is again always 0. The analysis of the probability of file depending on pw in the ideal world remains the same as for Theorem 1 since $\mathcal{Z}$ does not provide $\mathcal{S}$ with any information about pw when querying the CRS.

Remark 1. **Extending Theorem 1 to variants of random oracles.** Since in the above attack the oracle $\mathcal{O}$ is not queried before $\mathcal{S}^{\mathcal{O}}$ provides his output, any flavor of observability can be added without invalidating Theorem 1. That is, even observing random oracle queries from parties and the environment does not help the simulator to prevent the described attack. Contrarily, our result does not apply with respect to an oracle offering limited programability such as random or weak programmability [11]. In a nutshell, these oracles give the adversary the freedom to assign images that are chosen by the oracle to inputs of his choice. This is enough to circumvent our impossibility result since the simulator is now able to solve its commitment issue, while it does not rely on choosing the images itself (e.g., taking a DDH challenge as image). This claim is supported by Jutla and Roy [16]. We leave it as an open question to broaden or invalidate our result for more notions of random oracles, especially different flavors of *global* random oracles [5].

Since UC-secure symmetric PAKE can be obtained without relying on any idealized assumptions (see Table 1), our findings in this section demonstrate that UC-secure asymmetric PAKE is indeed harder to achieve than symmetric PAKE.

4 UC-Security of the Ω-Method

Gentry et al. [12] propose a generic method for obtaining an asymmetric PAKE protocol from a symmetric PAKE protocol called the Ω-method. In this section, we analyze the UC-security of the Ω-method. Let us first recall the protocol in Fig. 3 and describe its phases.

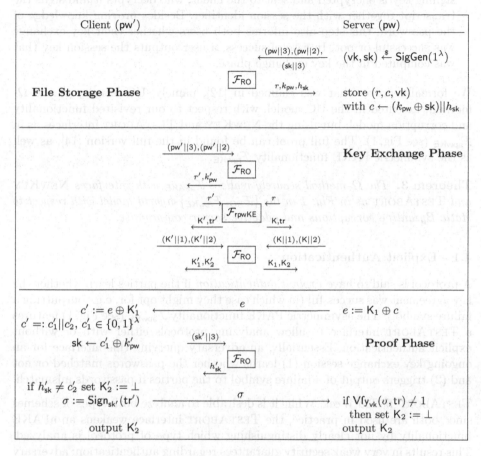

Fig. 3. The Ω-method [12]. We assume $\mathcal{F}_{\mathsf{rpwKE}}$ outputs transcripts together with keys. To merge instantiations of $\mathcal{F}_{\mathsf{RO}}$, we implicitly assume that $\mathcal{F}_{\mathsf{RO}}$ outputs random values of length 2λ for inputs ending with 1, and of length λ for inputs ending with 2 or 3.

- **File Storage Phase:** The server stores a hash of a password together with a signing key pair. This file is then used for all further sessions with a specific client.
- **Key Exchange Phase:** Client and server run a symmetric PAKE protocol using password hashes as input. To obtain more than one session key, this phase can be repeated.

- **Proof Phase:** For each key exchange phase, the client has to prove that he actually knows the password. This phase is necessary since otherwise a server compromise would enable the attacker to impersonate a client using only the hash of the password. This is clearly undesirable and reflected in the functionality that, upon server compromise, only allows to impersonate the server. Using the (hash of the) password as an encryption key, the stored signing key is encrypted and sent to the client, who decrypts it and signs the transcript together with the session identifier. Besides proving knowledge of the password, this step also informs both users whether their key exchange was successful or not. In case of success, a user outputs the session key that was computed in the key exchange phase.

We formally prove what was claimed in [12], namely, UC-security of the Ω-method, executed in the UC model, with respect to our revisited functionality and corruption model, but using the NEWKEY and TESTABORT interfaces as in $\mathcal{F}_{\mathsf{apwKE}}$ (see Fig. 1). The full proof can be found in the full version [14], as well as the symmetric PAKE functionality $\mathcal{F}_{\mathsf{rpwKE}}$.

Theorem 3. *The Ω-method securely realizes $\mathcal{F}_{\mathsf{aPAKE}}$ with interfaces NEWKEY and TESTABORT as in Fig. 1 in the $\{\mathcal{F}_{RO}, \mathcal{F}_{\mathsf{rpwKE}}\}$-hybrid model with respect to static Byzantine corruptions and adaptive server compromise.*

4.1 Explicit Authentication

A protocol is said to have *explicit authentication* if the parties learn whether the key agreement was successful (in which case they might opt for, e.g., outputting a failure symbol). The asymmetric PAKE functionality $\mathcal{F}_{\mathsf{apwKE}}$ (see Fig. 1) features a TESTABORT interface to allow analyzing protocols either with or without explicit authentication. Essentially, an adversary querying this interface for an ongoing key exchange session (1) learns whether the passwords matched or not and (2) triggers output of a failure symbol to the parties if passwords mismatch.

TESTABORT *is Too Weak.* While it is desirable to analyze both types of schemes since both are used in practice, the TESTABORT interface weakens an aPAKE functionality by not clearly distinguishing which type of protocol is analyzed. This results in very weak security guarantees regarding authentication: adversary can force a party in a protocol with explicit authentication to output whatever key it computed by *not* making use of the TESTABORT interface. This is particularly troubling since, intuitively, a protocol featuring explicit authentication should reliably inform participants whether the key exchange was successful or not. On top of that, no security guarantee about session keys is granted whatsoever in a session under attack. This means parties would even faithfully use adversarially determined keys to, e.g., encrypt their secrets.

We disclose this weakness of $\mathcal{F}_{aPAKE}$ with TESTABORT by demonstrating with Theorem 3 that the Ω-method is securely realizing $\mathcal{F}_{aPAKE}$ with TESTABORT *even if the signature scheme is insecure.* The purpose of the signature is to convince the server that the client holds the correct password. If an attacker manages to inject a forgery as last message, it can convince the server to output a session key in the real execution *even if the client holds a different password, or only the file and no password at all.* However, this can be easily simulated in the ideal world by letting the simulator *not* issue a TESTABORT query for the server (as he would do for a protocol not featuring explicit authentication). Using this simulation strategy in the proof, we do not have to rely on forgeries being unlikely.

Let us emphasize. Inspired by the above simulation strategies, we make the following claim: a modified Ω-method where the client sends a text message "accept"/"do not accept" to the server also realizes $\mathcal{F}_{aPAKE}$ with TESTABORT in the $(\mathcal{F}_{RO}, \mathcal{F}_{rpwKE})$-hybrid model. Of course, we do not recommend to use this modified version of the protocol, nor to use it with a flawed signature scheme. This is just a thought experiment to demonstrate the severe weaknesses introduced by the TESTABORT interface.

We correct this weakness of $\mathcal{F}_{apwKE}$ by equipping $\mathcal{F}_{aPAKE}$ with a NEWKEY interface enforcing explicit authentication, following informal recommendations of Canetti et al. [9]. We let the functionality send a special failure symbol $\perp$ to parties with mismatching passwords or in case of a failed online attack. The adversary gets informed about such failure. While $\mathcal{F}_{aPAKE}$ would be stronger without this leakage, the Ω-method requires it. Namely, in a session where none of the parties is corrupted but the server is compromised, the verification key used by the server is leaked to the adversary via the password file. The adversary can thus learn whether key exchange succeeded by checking validity of the signature sent by the client.

An adversary can always mount a DoS attack by, e.g., injecting messages of wrong format to make the receiving party output failure. We incorporate this attack into $\mathcal{F}_{aPAKE}$ by letting the adversary propose failure in his NEWKEY response. $\mathcal{F}_{aPAKE}$ enforcing explicit authentication is depicted in Fig. 2[1]. We are now ready to state a stronger version of Theorem 3, which captures security of the Ω-method more precisely. The proof can be found in the full version [14].

Theorem 4. *If the signature scheme is EUF-CMA secure, the Ω-method securely realizes $\mathcal{F}_{aPAKE}$ in the $\{\mathcal{F}_{RO}, \mathcal{F}_{rpwKE}\}$-hybrid model with respect to static Byzantine corruptions and adaptive server compromise.*

Acknowledgements. The author would like to thank Jiayu Xu, Dennis Hofheinz, David Pointcheval and Victor Shoup for helpful discussions. Discussion with Victor on how to resolve issues with session identifiers for the multi-user setting were particularly instructing.

---

[1] A protocol without explicit authentication can be proven to securely realize $\mathcal{F}_{aPAKE}$ with the NEWKEY interface of the symmetric PAKE functionality $\mathcal{F}_{rpwKE}$.

References

1. Bellare, M., Pointcheval, D., Rogaway, P.: Authenticated key exchange secure against dictionary attacks. In: Preneel, B. (ed.) EUROCRYPT 2000. LNCS, vol. 1807, pp. 139–155. Springer, Heidelberg (2000). https://doi.org/10.1007/3-540-45539-6_11
2. Bellovin, S.M., Merritt, M.: Encrypted key exchange: password-based protocols secure against dictionary attacks. In: 1992 IEEE Symposium on Security and Privacy, pp. 72–84. IEEE Computer Society Press, May 1992
3. Benhamouda, F., Pointcheval, D.: Verifier-based password-authenticated key exchange: new models and constructions. IACR Cryptology ePrint Archive 2013/833 (2013)
4. Bradley, T., Jarecki, S., Xu, J.: Strong asymmetric PAKE based on trapdoor CKEM. In: Boldyreva, A., Micciancio, D. (eds.) CRYPTO 2019. LNCS, vol. 11694, pp. 798–825. Springer, Cham (2019). https://doi.org/10.1007/978-3-030-26954-8_26
5. Camenisch, J., Drijvers, M., Gagliardoni, T., Lehmann, A., Neven, G.: The wonderful world of global random oracles. In: Nielsen, J.B., Rijmen, V. (eds.) EUROCRYPT 2018. LNCS, vol. 10820, pp. 280–312. Springer, Cham (2018). https://doi.org/10.1007/978-3-319-78381-9_11
6. Canetti, R.: Universally composable security: a new paradigm for cryptographic protocols. In: 42nd FOCS, pp. 136–145. IEEE Computer Society Press, October 2001
7. Canetti, R.: Universally composable security: a new paradigm for cryptographic protocols. Cryptology ePrint Archive, Report 2000/067, revised version 2020–02-11 (2020). https://eprint.iacr.org/2000/067
8. Canetti, R., Goldreich, O., Halevi, S.: The random oracle methodology, revisited (preliminary version). In: 30th ACM STOC, pp. 209–218. ACM Press, May 1998
9. Canetti, R., Halevi, S., Katz, J., Lindell, Y., MacKenzie, P.: Universally composable password-based key exchange. In: Cramer, R. (ed.) EUROCRYPT 2005. LNCS, vol. 3494, pp. 404–421. Springer, Heidelberg (2005). https://doi.org/10.1007/11426639_24
10. Canetti, R., Rabin, T.: Universal composition with joint state. In: Boneh, D. (ed.) CRYPTO 2003. LNCS, vol. 2729, pp. 265–281. Springer, Heidelberg (2003). https://doi.org/10.1007/978-3-540-45146-4_16
11. Fischlin, M., Lehmann, A., Ristenpart, T., Shrimpton, T., Stam, M., Tessaro, S.: Random oracles with(out) programmability. In: Abe, M. (ed.) ASIACRYPT 2010. LNCS, vol. 6477, pp. 303–320. Springer, Heidelberg (2010). https://doi.org/10.1007/978-3-642-17373-8_18
12. Gentry, C., MacKenzie, P., Ramzan, Z.: A method for making password-based key exchange resilient to server compromise. In: Dwork, C. (ed.) CRYPTO 2006. LNCS, vol. 4117, pp. 142–159. Springer, Heidelberg (2006). https://doi.org/10.1007/11818175_9
13. Haase, B., Labrique, B.: AuCPace: efficient verifier-based PAKE protocol tailored for the IIoT. IACR Cryptology ePrint Archive 2018/286 (2018)
14. Hesse, J.: Separating standard and asymmetric password-authenticated key exchange. IACR Cryptology ePrint Archive 2019/1064 (2019)
15. Jarecki, S., Krawczyk, H., Xu, J.: OPAQUE: an asymmetric PAKE protocol secure against pre-computation attacks. In: Nielsen, J.B., Rijmen, V. (eds.) EUROCRYPT 2018. LNCS, vol. 10822, pp. 456–486. Springer, Cham (2018). https://doi.org/10.1007/978-3-319-78372-7_15

16. Jutla, C.S., Roy, A.: Smooth NIZK arguments with applications to asymmetric UC-PAKE. IACR Cryptology ePrint Archive 2016/233 (2016)
17. Katz, J., Ostrovsky, R., Yung, M.: Efficient password-authenticated key exchange using human-memorable passwords. In: Pfitzmann, B. (ed.) EUROCRYPT 2001. LNCS, vol. 2045, pp. 475–494. Springer, Heidelberg (2001). https://doi.org/10.1007/3-540-44987-6_29
18. Katz, J., Vaikuntanathan, V.: Round-optimal password-based authenticated key exchange. In: Ishai, Y. (ed.) TCC 2011. LNCS, vol. 6597, pp. 293–310. Springer, Heidelberg (2011). https://doi.org/10.1007/978-3-642-19571-6_18
19. Nielsen, J.B.: Separating random oracle proofs from complexity theoretic proofs: the non-committing encryption case. In: Yung, M. (ed.) CRYPTO 2002. LNCS, vol. 2442, pp. 111–126. Springer, Heidelberg (2002). https://doi.org/10.1007/3-540-45708-9_8
20. Pointcheval, D., Wang, G.: VTBPEKE: verifier-based two-basis password exponential key exchange. In: Karri, R., Sinanoglu, O., Sadeghi, A.-R., Yi, X. (eds.) Proceedings of the 2017 ACM on Asia Conference on Computer and Communications Security, AsiaCCS 2017, Abu Dhabi, United Arab Emirates, 2–6 April 2017, pp. 301–312. ACM (2017)
21. Shoup, V.: Security analysis of SPAKE2+. IACR Cryptology ePrint Archive 2020/313 (2020)

The Round Complexity of Secure Computation Against Covert Adversaries

Arka Rai Choudhuri[1]($^{(\boxtimes)}$)(iD), Vipul Goyal[2], and Abhishek Jain[1]

[1] Johns Hopkins University, Baltimore, USA
{achoud,abhishek}@cs.jhu.edu
[2] Carnegie Mellon University, Pittsburgh, USA
goyal@cs.cmu.edu

Abstract. We investigate the exact round complexity of secure multiparty computation (MPC) against *covert* adversaries who may attempt to cheat, but do not wish to be caught doing so. Covert adversaries lie in between semi-honest adversaries who follow protocol specification and malicious adversaries who may deviate arbitrarily.

Recently, two round protocols for semi-honest MPC and four round protocols for malicious-secure MPC were constructed, both of which are optimal. While these results can be viewed as constituting two end points of a security spectrum, we investigate the design of protocols that potentially span the spectrum.

Our main result is an MPC protocol against covert adversaries with variable round complexity: when the detection probability is set to the lowest setting, our protocol requires two rounds and offers same security as semi-honest MPC. By increasing the detecting probability, we can increase the security guarantees, with round complexity five in the extreme case. The security of our protocol is based on standard cryptographic assumptions.

We supplement our positive result with a negative result, ruling out *strict* three round protocols with respect to black-box simulation.

Keywords: Secure computation · Covert adversary · Round complexity

1 Introduction

The ability to securely compute on private datasets of individuals has wide applications of tremendous benefits to society. Secure multiparty computation (MPC) [20,29] provides a solution to the problem of computing on private data by allowing a group of parties to jointly evaluate any function over their private inputs in such a manner that no one learns anything beyond the output of the function.

Since its introduction nearly three decades ago, MPC has been extensively studied with respect to various complexity measures. In this work, we focus on the *round complexity* of MPC. This topic has recently seen a burst of activity along the following two lines:

© Springer Nature Switzerland AG 2020
C. Galdi and V. Kolesnikov (Eds.): SCN 2020, LNCS 12238, pp. 600–620, 2020.
https://doi.org/10.1007/978-3-030-57990-6_30

- *Semi-honest adversaries*: Recently, several works have constructed *two* round MPC protocols [6,14,16,17,25] that achieve security against semi-honest adversaries who follow protocol specifications but may try to learn additional information from the protocol transcript. The round complexity of these protocols is optimal [23].
- *Malicious adversaries*: A separate sequence of works have constructed *four* round MPC protocols [1,4,22] that achieve security against malicious adversaries who may arbitrarily deviate from the protocol specification. The round complexity of these protocols is optimal w.r.t. black-box simulation and crossing this barrier via non-black-box techniques remains a significant challenge.

These two lines of work can be viewed as constituting two ends of a security spectrum: on the one hand, the two round protocols do not offer any security whatsoever against malicious behavior, and may therefore not be suitable in many settings. On the other hand, the four round protocols provide very strong security guarantees against all malicious strategies.

Our Question. The two end points suggest there might be interesting intermediate points along the spectrum that provide a trade-off between security and round complexity. In this work, we ask whether it is possible to devise protocols that span the security spectrum (as opposed to just the two end points), but do not always require the cost of four rounds. More specifically, is it possible to devise MPC protocols with a "tunable parameter" ϵ such that the security, and consequently, the round complexity of the protocol can be tuned to a desired "level" by setting ϵ appropriately?

Background: MPC Against Covert Adversaries. Towards answering this question, we look to the notion of MPC against *covert adversaries*, first studied by Aumann and Lindell [3]. Intuitively, covert adversaries may deviate arbitrarily from the protocol specification in an attempt to cheat, but do not wish to be "caught" doing so. As Aumann and Lindell argue, this notion closely resembles real-world adversaries in many commercial, political and social settings, where individuals and institutions are potentially willing to cheat to gain advantage, but do not wish to suffer the loss of reputation or potential punishment associated with being caught cheating. Such adversaries may weigh the risk of being caught against the benefits of cheating, and may act accordingly.

Aumann and Lindell model security against covert adversaries by extending the real/ideal paradigm for secure computation. Roughly, the ideal world adversary (a.k.a. simulator) is allowed to send a special cheat instruction to the trusted party. Upon receiving such an instruction, the trusted party hands all the honest parties' inputs to the adversary. Then, it tosses coins and with probability ϵ, announces to the honest parties that cheating has taken place. This refers to the case where the adversary's cheating has been *detected*. However, with probability $1 - \epsilon$, the trusted party does not announce that cheating has taken place. This refers to the case where the adversary's cheating has not been detected.[1]

Our Results. Towards answering the aforementioned question, we investigate the round complexity of MPC against covert adversaries. We provide both positive and negative results on this topic.

Positive Result. Our main result is an MPC protocol against covert adversaries with round complexity $2 + 5 \cdot q$, where q is a protocol parameter that is a function of the cheating detection parameter ϵ. When $q = 0$, our protocol requires only two rounds and provides security against semi-honest adversaries. By increasing q, we can increase the security guarantees of our protocol, all the way up to $q = 1$, when our protocol requires seven rounds. We note, however, that by appropriately parallelizing rounds, the round complexity in this case can in fact be decreased to five (see the technical sections for more details). Our protocol relies on injective one-way functions, two-round oblivious transfer and Zaps (two-message public coin witness indistinguishable proofs introduced in [13]).

As mentioned earlier, in this work, we consider the aforementioned formulation of security against covert adversaries where the adversary always learns the honest party inputs whenever it decides to cheat. An interesting open question is whether our positive result can be extended to the stronger model where the adversary only learns the honest party inputs when its cheating goes undetected.

Negative Result. We supplement our positive result with a negative result. Namely, we show that security against covert adversaries is impossible to achieve in *strict* three rounds with respect to black-box simulation. We prove this result for the zero-knowledge proofs functionality in the simultaneous-broadcast model for MPC.

1.1 Technical Overview

Negative Result. We start by briefly summarizing the main ideas underlying our negative result.

Recall that a black-box simulator works by rewinding the adversary in order to simulate its view. In a three round protocol over simultaneous-broadcast model, the simulator has three potential opportunities to rewind – one for each round. In order to rule out three round ZK against covert adversaries, we devise a covert verifier strategy that foils all rewinding strategies in every round.

As a starting point, let us consider the first round of the protocol. In this case, a rushing covert verifier can choose a fresh new first round message upon being rewound, which effectively leads to protocol restart. Next, let's consider the second round. Here, the covert verifier can choose to not be rushing, and instead compute its second round message independent of the prover's message in the second round. That is, upon being rewound, the verifier simply re-sends

---

[1] The work of [3] also provides two other formulations of security. In this work, we focus on the above formulation.

the same message again and again, thereby making the rewinding useless. Indeed, the main challenge is in ruling out successful rewinding in the third round.

One potential strategy for the covert verifier is to simply always *abort* in the third round. While such a strategy would indeed work if our goal was to rule out ZK against *malicious* verifiers, it does not quite work in the covert setting. This is because in this case, the simulator can simply request the prover's input (namely, the witness) from the trusted party and then use it to generate the view. Note that, this strategy works because protocol abort counts as cheating behavior on behalf of the verifier.[2]

To rule out such "trivial" simulation, we devise a covert verifier strategy that "cheats only if cheated with." More specifically, our covert verifier behaves honestly in the third round if it receives an accepting message from the prover; however, upon receiving a non-accepting message, it simply aborts. Clearly, this verifier never aborts in the real world. However, when the simulator runs this verifier, it may always find that the verifier aborts. Indeed, without the knowledge of the prover's witness, and no advantage of rewinding in the first two rounds, the simulator would not be able to generate an accepting third message. Moreover, querying the trusted party on the prover's input to generate the view would lead to a skewed distribution.

To establish a formal proof of impossibility, we show that the existence of a simulator can be used to break soundness of the ZK protocol. We refer the reader to Sect. 5 for more details.

Positive Result. We now summarize the main ideas underlying our positive result.

The main insight behind our protocol is to perform *random checking* to ensure that the parties are behaving honestly. Our strategy differs from prior works on MPC against covert adversaries in the following manner: while prior works *always* check for malicious behavior in a manner such that the adversary is caught with certain probability, *we only initiate the checking procedure with certain probability*. More specifically, in our protocol, the parties initiate the checking procedure with probability q. Indeed, this is what leads to the variable round complexity of our protocol.

Armed with the above insight, we implement our protocol as follows:

- In the first round, the parties execute the first round of a two-round semi-malicious MPC protocol (semi-malicious security proposed by [2] considers semi-malicious attackers that follow the protocol specification, but may adaptively choose arbitrary inputs and random tapes for computing each of its

---

[2] One may ask whether modeling protocol abort as cheating could lead to scenarios where honest parties, in the presence of network interruptions, are labeled as adversarial. We imagine that in such a scenario, one could put in place countermeasures, where, e.g., a party is allowed to prove (in zero knowledge) honest behavior in the protocol (up to the point of purported abort) to other parties in order to defend itself.

messages). In addition, the parties also commit to their inputs and random tapes, and exchange the first round message of Zaps.

- In the second round, each party tosses a coin to determine with probability q, whether or not to vote for initiating the *verification mode*. If its vote is "yes," it announces it to the other parties. Otherwise, it computes and sends the second round of semi-malicious MPC together with a Zap proving that the second round message was computed honestly.

- If the total vote count is non-zero, then the parties execute the verification phase where each party proves in zero-knowledge that it behaved honestly in the first round using the committed input and randomness. To avoid malleability concerns, we in fact use simulation-extractable zero knowledge (SE-ZK). When the verification mode ends (or if it was never executed), the parties execute the last round of the protocol. Here, the parties who did not already vote for the verification phase complete the second round of the two-round semi-malicious MPC, and additionally prove via Zap that the second round was computed honestly.

- To enable simulation, we establish an alternative "trapdoor" witness for the Zap as follows. The parties are required to commit to 0 in the first round, and prove in the verification mode that they indeed committed to 0. Now, the trapdoor mode for Zap simply amounts to proving that a party had in fact committed to 1.

At a first glance, the above protocol suggests a seemingly simple simulation strategy:

- The simulator starts by simulating the first round of the semi-malicious MPC, and commits to 1 (instead of 0).

- Next, the simulator *always* initiates the verification phase, where it uses the simulator-extractor of SE-ZK to simulate the proofs as well as extract the adversary's input and randomness.

- Finally, it simulates the second round of the semi-malicious MPC and completes the Zap using the trapdoor witness.

A closer inspection, however, reveals several problems with the above strategy. A minor issue is that the above strategy leads to a skewed distribution since the verification phase is executed with probability 1. This, however, can be easily resolved as follows: after completing extraction, the simulator rewinds to the end of the first round and then uses random coins to determine whether or not to execute the verification phase.

A more important issue is that the simulator may potentially fail in extracting adversary's input and randomness, possibly because of premature aborts by the adversary. Since aborts constitute cheating behavior, a natural recourse for the simulator in this case is to send the cheat signal to the ideal functionality. Now, upon learning the honest party inputs, the simulator rewinds to the beginning of the protocol, and re-computes the first round messages of the semi-malicious MPC using the honest party inputs. But what if now, when the verification phase is executed, the adversary no longer aborts? In this case, the distribution, once again, would be skewed.

To tackle this issue, we develop a procedure to sample the first round message in a manner such that the adversary aborts with roughly the same probability as before. We build on techniques from [18] to devise our sampling technique, with the key difference that unlike [18] which perform similar sampling with respect to a fixed prefix of the protocol, in our setting, we are sampling the very first message itself without any prefix. We refer the reader to the technical section for more details on this subject.

Now, suppose that the trusted party sends the "detect" signal to the simulator. In this case, the simulator must make sure that the verification phase is executed, and that an aborting transcript is generated. Towards this end, the simulator tries repeatedly until it is able to find such a transcript. Indeed, this is guaranteed given the aforementioned property of the re-sampled first round message. However, if the trusted party sends "non-detect" signal, the simulator may still end up with an aborting transcript. One may notice that this is not necessarily a bad thing since the simulator is able to detect cheating behavior with probability higher than what is required by the trusted party. To this end, we consider a strengthened formulation of MPC against covert adversaries where we allow the simulator to *increase* the detection probability by sending a parameter $\epsilon_{sim} > \epsilon$ to the trusted party. Upon receiving this parameter, the trusted party declares cheating to the honest parties with probability ϵ_{sim} as opposed to ϵ.

We now highlight another technical issue that arises during simulation. In an honest protocol execution, only a subset (and not necessarily *all*) of the honest parties may vote to initiate the verification phase. This means that when the simulator attempts to launch the verification phase for the first time in order to extract adversary's inputs, it must use random coins for the honest parties repeatedly until it leads to at least one honest party voting yes. In this case, the honest parties who do not vote for the verification phase must send their second round messages of semi-malicious MPC (as well as Zaps) *before* the extraction of adversary's input and randomness has been performed. A priori, it is unclear how this can be done without trivially failing the simulation.

We resolve this issue by using a new notion of *free simulation* for semi-malicious MPC. Roughly, we say that semi-malicious MPC protocol has free-simulation property if it possible to simulate the messages of all but one honest party using honest strategy (with respect to some random inputs) without the knowledge of adversary's inputs or output. Fortunately, as we discuss in the technical sections, the recent protocol of [6] based on two-round semi-malicious OT satisfies the free simulation property.

The above discussion is oversimplified and ignores several other issues that arise during simulation; we refer the reader to the technical sections for more details.

We address two natural questions that arise from our protocol

- *Can we build a protocol that has a worst case round complexity of 4?* We believe that similar ideas from our work may in fact eventually result in a protocol with a worst case complexity of four rounds. But given the complex nature of the known four round protocols [4,9,22], any attempt to transform them in to the setting of covert adversaries is unlikely to yield a clean protocol and will only detract from the main underlying ideas of our presented protocol.

- *A malicious party can always force a worst case complexity of five rounds.* Our expected number of rounds is in fact for honest parties. On the one hand an adversarial party can always force the protocol into *verification mode*, and such a strategy would force the adversarial party to provide a proof of honest behavior. On the other hand, an adversary can cheat undetected if the protocol does not go into *verification mode* thereby incentivizing a cheating adversary not to force *verification mode*.

1.2 Related Work

The round complexity of MPC has been extensively studied over the years in a variety of models. Here, we provide a short survey of this topic in the plain model, focusing on the dishonest majority setting. We refer the reader to [4] for a more comprehensive survey.

Beaver et al. [5] initiated the study of constant round MPC in the honest majority setting. Several follow-up works subsequently constructed constant round MPC against dishonest majority [21,24,26–28]. Garg et al. [15] established a lower bound of four rounds for MPC. They constructed five and six round MPC protocols using indistinguishability obfuscation and LWE, respectively, together with three-round robust non-malleable commitments.

The first four round MPC protocols were constructed independently by Ananth et al. [1] and Brakerski et al. [8] based on different sub-exponential-time hardness assumptions. [1] also constructed a five round MPC protocol based on polynomial-time hardness assumptions. Ciampi et al. constructed four-round protocols for multiparty coin-tossing [10] and two-party computation [12] from polynomial-time assumptions. Benhamouda and Lin [6] gave a general transformation from any k-round OT with alternating messages to k-round MPC, for $k > 5$. More recently, independent works of Badrinarayanan et al. [4] and Halevi et al. [22] constructed four round MPC protocols for general functionalities based on different polynomial-time assumptions. Specifically, [4] rely on DDH (or QR or N-th Residuosity), and [22] rely on Zaps, affine-homomorphic encryption schemes and injective one-way functions (which can all be instantiated from QR).

Asharov et al. [2] constructed three round semi-honest MPC protocols in the CRS model. Subsequently, two-round semi-honest MPC protocols in the CRS model were constructed by Garg et al. [14] using indistinguishability obfuscation, and by Mukherjee and Wichs [25] using LWE assumption. Recently, two-round semi-honest protocols in the plain model were constructed by Garg and Srinivasan [16,17] and Benhamouda and Lin [6] from two-round OT.

2   Definitions

Below, we provide the relevant definitions and preliminaries. Consider two distributions $\mathcal{D}_0$ and $\mathcal{D}_1$. We denote by $\mathcal{D}_0 \approx_c \mathcal{D}_1$ if $\mathcal{D}_0$ and $\mathcal{D}_1$ are computationally indistinguishable.

2.1   Zero Knowledge

Definition 1. *An interactive protocol* (P, V) *for a language L is zero knowledge if the following properties hold:*

- **Completeness.** *For every $x \in L$,*

$$\Pr\Big[\mathsf{out}_\mathsf{V}\left[\mathsf{P}(x, w) \leftrightarrow \mathsf{V}(x)\right] = 1\Big] = 1$$

- **Soundness.** *There exists a negligible function* $\mathsf{negl}(\cdot)$ *s.t.* $\forall x \notin L$ *and for all adversarial prover* P^*.

$$\Pr\Big[\mathsf{out}_\mathsf{V}\left[\mathsf{P}^*(x) \leftrightarrow \mathsf{V}(x)\right] = 1\Big] \leq \mathsf{negl}(\lambda)$$

- **Zero Knowledge.** *For every PPT adversary V^*, there exists a PPT simulator* Sim *such that the probability ensembles*

$$\Big\{\mathsf{view}_\mathsf{V}\left[\mathsf{P}(x, w) \leftrightarrow \mathsf{V}(x)\right]\Big\}_{x \in L, w \in R_L(x)} \quad and \quad \Big\{\mathsf{Sim}(x)\Big\}_{x \in L, w \in R_L(x)}$$

are computationally indistinguishable.

Remark 1. An interactive protocol is an argument system if it satisfies the completeness and soundness properties. We say an interactive proof is *input delayed* if both the statement and witness are required only for the computation of the last prover message.

2.2   Input Delayed Non-malleable Zero Knowledge

Let $\Pi_{\mathsf{nmzk}} = \langle P, V \rangle$ be a input delayed interactive argument system for an NP-language L with witness relation Rel_L. Consider a PPT Man in the Middle (MiM) adversary $\mathcal{A}$ that is simultaneously participating in one left session and one right session. Before the execution starts, both P, V and $\mathcal{A}$ receive as a common input the security parameter 1^λ, and $\mathcal{A}$ receives as auxiliary input $z \in \{0, 1\}^*$.

In the left session $\mathcal{A}$ interacts with P using identity id of his choice. In the right session, $\mathcal{A}$ interacts with V, using identity $\widetilde{\mathsf{id}}$ of his choice. In the left session, before the last round of the protocol, P gets the statement x. Also, in the right session $\mathcal{A}$, during the last round of the protocol selects the statement $\tilde{x}$ to be proved and sends it to V. Let $\mathsf{View}^\mathcal{A}(1^\lambda, z)$ denote a random variable that describes the view of $\mathcal{A}$ in the above experiment.

Definition 2 (Input Delayed NMZK). *A input delayed argument system* $\Pi_{\mathsf{nmzk}} = \langle P, V \rangle$ *for* NP-*language* L *with witness relation* Rel_L *is Non-Malleable Zero Knowledge (NMZK) if for any MiM adversary* $\mathcal{A}$ *that participates in one left session and one right session, there exists a* PPT *machine* $\mathsf{Sim}(1^\lambda, z)$ *such that*

1. *The probability ensembles* $\{\mathsf{Sim}^1(1^\lambda, z)\}_{1^\lambda \in \mathbb{N}, z \in \{0,1\}^*}$ *and* $\{\mathsf{View}^{\mathcal{A}}(1^\lambda, z)\}_{\lambda \in \mathbb{N}, z \in \{0,1\}^*}$ *are computationally indistinguishable over* 1^λ, *where* $\mathsf{Sim}^1(1^\lambda, z)$ *denotes the first output of* $\mathsf{Sim}(1^\lambda, z)$.
2. *Let* $z \in \{0,1\}^*$ *and let* $(\mathsf{View}, \tilde{w})$ *denote the output of* $\mathsf{Sim}(1^\lambda, z)$. *Let* $\tilde{x}$ *be the right-session statement appearing in* View *and let* id *and* $\tilde{\mathsf{id}}$ *be the identities of the left and right sessions appearing in* View. *If the right session is accepting and* $\mathsf{id} \neq \tilde{\mathsf{id}}$, *then* $\mathsf{Rel}_L(\tilde{x}, \tilde{w}) = 1$.

2.3   ZAP

Zap [13] are two-message public coin witness indistinguishable proofs, are defined as follows.

Definition 3. *A pair of algorithms* $\langle P, V \rangle$ *where* P *is PPT and* V *is (deterministic) polytime, is a* Zap *for an* NP *relation* Rel_L *if it satisfies:*

1. **Completeness:** *there exists a polynomial* r *such that for every* $(x, w) \in \mathsf{Rel}_L$,

$$\Pr_{P, r \xleftarrow{\$} \{0,1\}^{r(|x|)}} \left[V(x, \pi, r) = 1 : \pi \leftarrow P(x, w, r) \right] = 1$$

2. **Adaptive Soundness:** *for every malicious prover* P^* *and every* $\lambda \in \mathbb{N}$:

$$\Pr_{r \xleftarrow{\$} \{0,1\}^{r(|x|)}} \left[\begin{array}{c} \exists x \in \{0,1\}^\lambda \setminus L \\ \pi \in \{0,1\}^* \end{array} : V(x, \pi, r) = 1 \right] \leq 2^{-\lambda}$$

3. **Witness Indistinguishability:** *for any instance* $\mathcal{I} = \{(x, w_1, w_2) : w_1, w_2 \in \mathsf{Rel}_L(x)\}$ *and any first message sequence* $\mathcal{R} = \{r_{x,w_1,w_2} : (x, w_1, w_2) \in \mathcal{I}\}$:

$$\{\pi \leftarrow P(x, w_1, r_{x,w_1,w_2})\}_{(x,w_1,w_2) \in \mathcal{I}} \approx_c \{\pi \leftarrow P(x, w_2, r_{x,w_1,w_2})\}_{(x,w_1,w_2) \in \mathcal{I}}$$

2.4   Free-Simulatability

We define below the property of free-simulatability for a semi-malicious protocol. At a high level, a 2-round protocol computing f is said to satisfy the notion of *free simulatability* if there exists a simulator that can simulate the view for an adversary, consisting of second round messages for all *strict* subsets of honest parties, without querying the ideal functionality computing f. In addition, when it receives the output from the ideal functionality, it should be able to complete simulation of the view. The definition augments the definition of semi-malicious protocols introduced in [7]. Roughly speaking, semi-malicious adversaries behave like semi-honest adversaries (i.e. honest but curious, following the protocol instructions), except that they may choose arbitrary random tapes.

Definition 4. *Let f be an n-party functionality. A semi-malicious protocol computing f is said to satisfy **free simulatability** if for all semi-malicious PPT adversary $\mathcal{A}$ controlling a set of parties I in the real world, there exists a PPT simulator* Sim *controlling the same set of parties such that for every input vector $\overrightarrow{x}$, every auxiliary input z, for every strict subset $J \subset \mathcal{H}$ of honest parties, the following is satisfied*

- *free simulatability*

$$\left\{ \left(\mathsf{REAL}_1^{\mathcal{A}}(\overrightarrow{x}, z), \mathsf{REAL}_{2,J}^{\mathcal{A}}(\overrightarrow{x}, z) \right) \right\} \approx_c \left\{ (\gamma_1, \gamma_2) \,\middle|\, \begin{array}{l} (\gamma_1, \mathsf{state}_1) = \mathsf{Sim}(z) \\ (\gamma_2, \mathsf{state}_2) = \mathsf{Sim}(J, \mathsf{state}_1, z) \end{array} \right\}$$

- *full simulatability*

$$\left\{ \left(\mathsf{REAL}^{\mathcal{A}}(\overrightarrow{x}, z) \right) \right\} \approx_c \left\{ (\gamma_1, (\gamma_2, \gamma_3)) \,\middle|\, \begin{array}{l} (\gamma_1, \mathsf{state}_1) = \mathsf{Sim}(z) \\ (\gamma_2, \mathsf{state}_2) = \mathsf{Sim}(J, \mathsf{state}_1, z) \\ \gamma_3 = \mathsf{Sim}(J, y, \mathsf{state}_2, z) \end{array} \right\}$$

$\mathcal{H}$ *is the set of honest parties* $\mathcal{H} := [n] \setminus I$, $\mathsf{REAL}_1^{\mathcal{A}}(\overrightarrow{x}, z)$ *is the view of the adversary in the first round for the real execution of the protocol,* $\mathsf{REAL}_{2,J}^{\mathcal{A}}$ *is the view of the adversary $\mathcal{A}$ consisting of only messages from honest parties in the set J in the second round of the real execution of the protocol, and* $\mathsf{REAL}^{\mathcal{A}}(\overrightarrow{x}, z)$ *is the entire view of the adversary in the real execution of the protocol. Here y is the output received from the ideal functionality computing the function f on the input vector $\overrightarrow{x}^*$ where the adversarial inputs have been replaced by $\{x_i^*\}_{i \in I}$.*

Remark 2. Note that this notion extends to any L round protocol, where instead of round 2, as in the definition above, we require the properties for partial view of the L-th round of the protocol. The basic GMW [20] construction when instantiated with an appropriate semi-malicious OT (oblivious transfer) protocol gives us such an L round protocol satisfying *free simulatability*.

For the 2 round setting, consider the 2 round semi-malicious protocol construction by Benhamouda and Lin [6]. At a very high level, the protocol in [6] compiles any L-round semi-malicious protocol into a 2 round protocol by garbling each next message function of the underlying L-round protocol. These garbled circuits are sent in the second round of the protocol, where the evaluation of these garbled circuits are enabled via a semi-malicious OT protocol. Importantly, to simulate the second round of their protocol, the simulator proceeds by first simulating the underlying L-round protocol, and then using the simulated transcript to simulate the garbled circuits. If the underlying L-round protocol satisfies *free simulatability*, then a transcript absent some messages from the last round is simulated without querying an ideal functionality. For the parties whose garbled circuits need to be simulated, i.e. parties in the subset J as described above, this transcript is sufficient since in the underlying L-round protocol parties send their last message of the protocol independent of the last message from the other parties. Once the full transcript is generated on querying the ideal functionality, the remaining garbled circuits are simulated. We refer the reader to [6] for the details.

3   Model

We describe in brief the motivation behind the model described in [3]. The model is intermediary to that of semi-honest and malicious. At a high level, the model allows for the adversary to be caught sufficiently often if it attempts to "cheat" during the protocol. The model formalizes the notion of "cheating" in the manner described below.

We parameterize adversarial cheating with the parameter $\varepsilon \in (0, 1]$, called the **deterrence factor**. The parameter signifies that honest parties detect cheating with probability at least ε. The notion is also referred to as **security in the presence of covert adversaries with ε-deterrent**. The ideal functionality is modified to accept a special cheat message from the adversary. On receiving the message, the ideal functionality sends the inputs of the honest parties to the adversary, and allows the adversary to set the output of honest parties. It then tosses coins internally and announces, with probability ε, to the honest parties that cheating has been detected. It should be noted that the adversary can always choose to cheat in the ideal world, but would be detected with probability ε.

The following text is taken largely verbatim from [3] but for a few important changes. We discuss these changes subsequent to the definition. At a high level, we strengthen the definition by allowing the simulator to override the situation that the ideal functionality did not send a cheat detection message to the honest parties, by forcing a detection message to be sent. This captures the intuition our protocol results in the adversary getting caught with a higher probability than parameterized by ε.

We also note that for simplicity we only consider the setting where all parties receive the same output and the definition naturally extends to the setting of each party receiving a different output. We denote the set of adversarial parties by I.

Input: Each party obtains an input; the party P_i's input is denoted by x_i; we assume that all inputs are of the same length denoted ℓ. The adversary receives an auxiliary-input z.

Send inputs to trusted party: An honest party P_i sends its received input x_i to the trusted party. The adversarial parties, controlled by $\mathcal{A}$, may either send their received input, or send some other input of the same length ot the trusted party. This decision is made by $\mathcal{A}$ and may depend on the values x_j for $j \in I$ and the auxiliary input z. Denote the vector of inputs sent to the trusted party by $\vec{w}$.

Abort options: If an adversarial party sends $w_j = \text{abort}_j$ to the trusted part as its input, then the trusted party sends abort_j to all of the honest parties and halts. If multiple parties send abort_j, then the trusted party picks only one of them (say, the one with the smallest j).

Attempted cheat option: If an adversarial party sends $w_j = \text{cheat}_j$ to the trusted party as its input, then the trusted party sends to the adversary all of the honest parties' inputs $\{x_j\}_{j \notin I}$ (as above, if multiple cheat_j messages are sent, the trusted party ignores all but one). In addition,

1. With probability ε, the trusted party sends corrupted$_j$ to the adversary and all of the honest parties.
2. With probability $1 - \varepsilon$, the trusted party sends undetected to the adversary. Following this, the adversary can either:
    - send corrupted$_i$ to the trusted party on behalf of a party in I. Then the trusted party sends corrupted$_i$ to all of the honest parties and halts; or
    - send output y of its choice for the honest parties to the trusted party. Then the trusted party sends y to all honest parties.

    The ideal execution ends at this point.
    If no w_j equals abort$_j$ or cheat$_j$, the ideal execution continues below.

Trusted party answers adversary: The trusted party computes $y = f(\overrightarrow{w})$ and sends y to $\mathcal{A}$.

Trusted party answers honest parties: After receiving the output, the adversary either sends abort$_j$ for some $j \in I$, or continue to the trusted party. If the trusted party receives continue then it sends y to all honest parties. Otherwise, if it receives abort$_j$ for some $j \in I$, it sends abort$_j$ to all honest parties.

Outputs: An honest party always outputs the message it obtained from the trusted party. The adversarial parties output nothing. The adversary $\mathcal{A}$ outputs any arbitrary (probabilistic polynomial-time computable) function of the initial inputs $\{x_j\}_{j \in I}$, the auxiliary input z, and the messages obtained from the trusted party.

The output of the honest parties and the adversary in an execution of the above ideal model is denoted by $\mathsf{IDEALC}^{\varepsilon}_{f,\mathsf{Sim}(z),I}(\overrightarrow{x}, \lambda)$ where $\overrightarrow{x}$ is the vector of inputs, z is the auxiliary input to $\mathcal{A}$, I is the set of adversarial parties, and λ is the security parameter. $\mathsf{REAL}_{\pi,\mathcal{A}(z),I}(\overrightarrow{x}, \lambda)$ denotes the analogous outputs in a real execution of the protocol π. When we talk about the corrupted$_i$ message, it is easier to think of this as a "detect" message sent to the ideal functionality to alert the honest parties of a detected cheating.

Definition 5. *Let* $f : (\{0,1\}^*)^n \to \{0,1\}^*$ *be a function computed on* n *inputs,* π *be an* n-*party protocol, and* $\varepsilon : \mathbb{N} \to [0,1]$ *be a function. Protocol* π *is said to* **securely compute** f **in the presence of covert adversaries with** ε-**deterrent** *if for every non-uniform probabilistic polynomial time adversary* $\mathcal{A}$ *for the real model, there exists a non-uniform probabilistic polynomial-time adversary* Sim *for the ideal model such that for every* $I \subseteq [n]$:

$$\left\{\mathsf{IDEALC}^{\varepsilon}_{f,\mathsf{Sim}(z),I}(\overrightarrow{x}, \lambda)\right\}_{\overrightarrow{x}, z \in (\{0,1\}^*)^{n+1}; \ell \in \mathbb{N}} \approx_c \left\{\mathsf{REAL}_{\pi,\mathcal{A}(z),I}(\overrightarrow{x}, \lambda)\right\}_{\overrightarrow{x}, z \in (\{0,1\}^*)^{n+1}; \ell \in \mathbb{N}}$$

where every element of $\overrightarrow{x}$ *is of the same length.*

Remarks About Our Definition. We discuss the small but important changes to the definition of the ideal functionality from that in [3]:

- We work with the *explicit-cheat formulation* in [3], wherein we don't guarantee security of honest party inputs if the adversary cheats. This is opposed to the setting where the honest party inputs are secure if the adversary is caught cheating.
- In addition, we allow for the ideal world adversary to change the non-detection of cheating to a detection. Specifically, when the ideal functionality sends undetected to the ideal world adversary, it can choose to override this by subsequently sending a corrupted message to the ideal functionality which is then sent to all honest parties. We note that the adversary can only change a non-detect to detect, but not the other way round. This arguably strengthens the model allowing a cheating adversary to be detected with a higher probability.
- While we define the above model, for our proofs we find it more convenient to work with an equivalent model to the one described. In this model, the ideal world adversary can choose to send an additional parameter $\varepsilon_{\mathsf{Sim}} > \varepsilon$ in addition to the cheat message it sends to the trusted party. The trusted party now uses this new $\varepsilon_{\mathsf{Sim}}$ to determine whether or not cheating is detected by the honest parties. We still allow the ideal world adversary to override an undetected message. Equivalence between the models is easy to see since we essentially need to bias coins that detects with probability ε to one that detects with probability $\varepsilon_{\mathsf{Sim}}$ using the override option.

4   Protocol

Overview. The goal of covert secure computation is to provide the adversary enough of a deterrent to deviate from the protocol. We want to do this while also minimizing the number of communication rounds in our protocol. The basic idea is to run the protocol in two "modes". The *normal mode*, where an adversary can possibly get away by cheating; and the *extend mode* where the parties prove honest behavior via a (non-malleable) zero-knowledge protocol. The normal mode requires only two rounds of communication, while the extended mode requires five rounds. At the end of the first round of the *normal mode*, parties vote to determine whether they enter *extend mode*, where the vote of a party is determined by sampling coins with parameter q. If there is even a single party that votes to go into *extend mode*, then all players run the *extend mode* prior to executing the second round of the normal mode.

While it is possible to parallelize rounds of the non-malleable zero knowledge with the first and voting rounds of the protocol, for simplicity of exposition we ignore this point for now. We shall make a note of this at the end of our protocol.

Expected Number of Rounds. If the probability with which each party decides to vote for the *extend mode* is q, the expected number of rounds for an honest execution of the protocol with n-parties will be $2 + 5 \cdot (1 - (1 - q)^n)$.

We set the voting parameter to be $q = 2 \cdot \varepsilon$, where ε is the deterrent parameter. This gives us a total of $2 + 5 \cdot \left(1 - \frac{1}{e^{2 \cdot \varepsilon \cdot n}}\right)$ rounds in expectation.

We achieve a simpler expression if we use the union bound. By the union bound, the probability of going into extend mode is upper bounded by $2 \cdot \varepsilon \cdot n$. This gives us $2 + 5 \cdot (2n\varepsilon)$ rounds in expectation, which is close to 2 for small values of ε.

Note that an adversary can always choose to ignore q and always go into the *extend mode* thereby forcing the worst case scenario of 7 rounds in the presence of an active adversary. As alluded to, our protocol can be easily modified to be 5 rounds in the worst case (see Remark 3).

4.1 Components

We list below the components of our protocol.

- Com is a non interactive commitment which can be instantiated from injective one-way functions. We use two instances of the protocol and denote the messages by , and icom, where the former will be used as the commitment to the "trapdoor witness" for the Zap while the latter is the commitment to the inputs. Subsequently referred to as "trapdoor commitment" and "input commitment" respectively.
- NMZK = (NMZK$_1$, NMZK$_2$, NMZK$_3$, NMZK$_4$, NMZK.Ver) is a four round non-malleable zero knowledge protocol (NMZK) which can be instantiated from collision resistant hash functions [11]. The language for the NMZK protocol is described below. The corresponding simulator-extractor for the NMZK is denoted by Sim$_{nmzk}$.
- Zap = (Zap$_1$, Zap$_2$, Zap.Ver) is Zap, i.e., a two-message public-coin witness indistinguishable proof. The language for the Zap is described below.
- $\Pi = (\Pi_1, \Pi_2, \text{OUT})$ is a two round semi-malicious protocol computing the function f. OUT denotes the algorithm to compute the final output. Let Sim$_\Pi$ denote the simulator for the protocol.

  We additionally require the protocol Π to satisfy the property of **Free Simulatability**, formally defined in Appendix 2.4. The property ensures that we can simulate the second round messages of the protocol for a strict subset of the honest parties without requiring the output. Such a protocol can be instantiated from a two round semi-malicious OT protocol [6].

Notation. For notational convenience we make the use of the following conventions (i) we will ignore as input to the protocols the security parameter, which we assume is implicit; (ii) for multi-round protocols, we assume that the protocol maintains state and the previous round messages for the corresponding instances are implicit inputs; (iii) $\mathbf{T}_X[k]$ will indicate the transcript of protocol X for the first k round of the protocol, with suitable superscripts as required. For the underlying semi-malicious protocol Π, this corresponds to collecting all messages broadcast by the parties.

NP Languages. In our construction, we use proofs for the following NP languages:

1. Zap: We use Zap for language L, which is characterized by the following relation R

$$\mathsf{st} = (\mathbf{T}_\Pi[1], \mathsf{msg}_2, \mathsf{com}, \mathsf{icom})$$
$$\mathsf{w} = (\mathsf{x}, \mathsf{r}, \mathsf{r}_{\mathsf{com}}, \mathsf{r}_{\mathsf{icom}})$$

$R(\mathsf{st}, \mathsf{w}) = 1$ if *either* of the following conditions is satisfied:
   (a) **Honest:** *all* of the following conditions hold
       - icom is a commitment of Com w.r.t. to input (x, r and randomness $\mathsf{r}_{\mathsf{icom}}$).
       - msg_1 is honestly computed 1st round message of Π w.r.t. to input x and r.
       - msg_2 is honestly computed 2nd round message of Π w.r.t. to input x, transcript $\mathbf{T}_\Pi[1]$ and r.
       where $\mathbf{T}_\Pi[1]$ includes msg_1.
   (b) **Trapdoor:** com is a commitment of Com w.r.t. to input 1 and randomness $\mathsf{r}_{\mathsf{com}}$

---

2. NMZK: We use NMZK for language $\widetilde{L}$, which is characterized by the following relation $\widetilde{R}$

$$\widetilde{\mathsf{st}} = (\mathsf{msg}_1, \mathsf{icom}, \mathsf{com})$$
$$\widetilde{\mathsf{w}} = (\mathsf{x}, \mathsf{r}, \mathsf{r}_{\mathsf{icom}}, \mathsf{r}_{\mathsf{com}})$$

$\widetilde{R}(\widetilde{\mathsf{st}}, \widetilde{\mathsf{w}}) = 1$ if *all* of the following conditions hold:
   - icom is a commitment of Com w.r.t. to input (x, r and randomness $\mathsf{r}_{\mathsf{icom}}$).
   - com is a commitment of Com w.r.t. to input 0 and randomness $\mathsf{r}_{\mathsf{com}}$
   - msg_1 is honestly computed 1st round message of Π w.r.t. to input x and r.

Our protocol will crucially use the fact that if relation $\widetilde{R}$ holds, then the trapdoor witness for R cannot hold.

4.2 Protocol Description

We now describe our protocol between n parties $P_1, \cdots, P_n$. The input of party P_i is denoted by x_i. The protocol is parameterized by q which is set to be $2 \cdot \varepsilon$.

Round 1: P_i computes and broadcasts the following:
   1. First round of the following protocols
       - Semi-malicious MPC Π: $\mathsf{msg}_{1,i} \leftarrow \Pi_1(\mathsf{x}_i, \mathsf{r}_i)$ using randomness r_i.
       - Zap: for all $j \neq i$: $\mathsf{zap}_1^{j \rightarrow i} \leftarrow \mathsf{Zap}$
   2. Non-interactive commitments Com
       - $\mathsf{icom}_i \leftarrow \mathsf{Com}((\mathsf{x}_i, \mathsf{r}_i); \mathsf{r}_{\mathsf{icom},i})$ to $(\mathsf{x}_i, \mathsf{r}_i)$
       - $_{,i} \leftarrow \mathsf{Com}(0; \mathsf{r}_{\mathsf{com},i})$ to 0.

Round 2 (E.1): At the end of round 1, P_i determines whether it votes to go into *extend mode*, or directly go to *normal mode*. It does so by tossing a coin that outputs 1 with probability q. If the output is 1, set voteExtend $= 1$, broadcast extend$_i$ and go to **Extend Mode**. Else, set voteExtend $= 0$ and go to **Normal Mode** and broadcast messages of **Normal Mode** described below.

Extend Mode: If there is even a single party that votes to go into the extend, then round **E.1** counts as the first round of the extend mode. The parties prove honest behavior of the first round via a four round non-malleable zero-knowledge protocol. If during the **Extend Mode**, a party does not send the expected message, P_i aborts and sets its output as corrupted.

Round E.2 P_i does the following:
1. If parties sent **Normal Mode** messages, store them for later use.
2. Compute and broadcast the following first round messages:
   - NMZK: for all $j \neq i$, $\mathsf{nmzk}_1^{j \to i} \leftarrow \mathsf{NMZK}_1$

Round E.3 P_i computes and broadcasts the following second round messages:
1. NMZK: for all $j \neq i$, $\mathsf{nmzk}_2^{i \to j} \leftarrow \mathsf{NMZK}_2$

Round E.4 P_i computes and broadcasts the following third round messages:
1. NMZK: for all $j \neq i$, $\mathsf{nmzk}_3^{j \to i} \leftarrow \mathsf{NMZK}_3$

Round E.5 P_i computes and broadcasts the following fourth round messages:
1. NMZK: for all $j \neq i$, $\mathsf{nmzk}_4^{i \to j} \leftarrow \mathsf{NMZK}_4(\widetilde{\mathsf{st}}_i, \widetilde{\mathsf{w}}_i)$ to prove that $\widetilde{R}(\widetilde{\mathsf{st}}_i, \widetilde{\mathsf{w}}_i) = 1$, where

$$\text{Statement } \widetilde{\mathsf{st}}_i := \left(\mathsf{msg}_{1,i}, \mathsf{icom}_i, \mathsf{com}_i\right)$$

$$\text{Witness } \widetilde{\mathsf{w}}_i := \left(\mathsf{x}_i, r_i, r_{\mathsf{icom},i}, r_{\mathsf{com},i}\right)$$

Normal Mode: [a] P_i does the following:
We separate out the steps performed based on how P_i arrived at the **Normal Mode**.
   - If P_i sent extend$_i$ it performs all the operations. Since we're guaranteed that the party has already completed execution of **Extend Mode**.
   - If P_i did not send extend$_i$, we split its arrival into two cases:
     - if it comes prior to completion of **Extend Mode**, it performs all the operations other than the NMZK check.
     - if it comes after completion of **Extend Mode**, then we do only the checks for the NMZK. This is because it has already sent out its corresponding messages of **Normal Mode** when it sent out the second round message without voting to go to **Extend Mode**.
1. If voteExtend $= 1$, check the NMZK proofs. If any of the checks do not succeed, abort computation and output corrupted.
   - for all $k, j \neq i$, $\mathsf{NMZK.Ver}\left(\widetilde{\mathsf{st}}_j, \mathbf{T}_{\mathsf{nmzk}}^{j \to k}[4]\right) \stackrel{?}{=} 1$
2. Compute and broadcast second round messages of the following protocols:

- Π: $\mathsf{msg}_{2,i} \leftarrow \Pi_2\left(\mathsf{x}_i, \mathbf{T}_\Pi[1], r_i\right)$
- Zap: for all $j \neq i$, $\mathsf{zap}_2^{i \to j} \leftarrow \mathsf{Zap}_2\left(\mathsf{st}_i, \mathsf{w}_i\right)$ to prove that $R(\mathsf{st}_i, \mathsf{w}_i) = 1$, where
  Statement $\mathsf{st}_i := \left(\mathbf{T}_\Pi[1], \mathsf{msg}_{2,i}, \mathsf{com}_i, \mathsf{icom}_i\right)$

  "Honest" Witness $\mathsf{w}_i := (\mathsf{x}_i, r_i, r_{\mathsf{com},i}, \bot)$

If voteExtend $= 0$, check if $\exists \mathsf{P}_j$ that sends extend_j at the end of the first round. If so, set voteExtend $= 1$ and go to **Extend Mode**. In this case we will have to run the **Normal Mode** again.
If no party has voted to go into extend mode, then we're done.

Output Phase. P_i does the following,
1. Check the Zap proofs. If any of the checks do not succeed, abort computation and output $\bot$.
   - for all $k, j \neq i$, $\mathsf{Zap.Ver}\left(\mathsf{st}_j, \mathbf{T}_{\mathsf{zap}}^{j \to k}[2]\right) \overset{?}{=} 1$
2. Compute the output of the function $y \leftarrow \mathsf{OUT}(\mathsf{x}_i, r_i, \mathbf{T}_\Pi[2])$

---

[a] Different parties may execute parts of **Normal Mode** at different points in the protocol.

Remark 3. It is easy to observe that we can bring down the worst case round complexity to five rounds if the computations performed in E.2 and E.3 are moved to Round 1 and 2 respectively.

Theorem 1. *Assuming the existence of injective one-way functions, collision resistant hash functions, semi-malicious oblivious transfer and ZAPs, the above protocol securely computes f in the presence of covert adversaries with deterrent ε.*

To ensure that honest parties correctly identify when an adversarial party has cheated, the proof of our protocol is quite intricate, and can be found in the full version.

5   3 Round Lower Bound

In this section, we show that it is impossible to achieve security against covert adversaries in *fixed* 3 rounds via black-box simulation. We shall do this by considering the **zero knowledge (ZK) functionality in the simultaneous message model**, where both the prover and verifier send messages in each round, including the last. As in [4], zero-knowledge is only required to hold against verifiers that do not send invalid messages, *even in the last round of the protocol.*[4]

There are two main challenges in ruling out a protocol secure against covert adversaries in the simultaneous message model: (i) the setting of covert adversaries allows the simulator to send a cheat message to the ideal functionality if

---

[4] This in particular means we cannot ignore the verifier's last message to transform the protocol to a three round protocol in the alternating message model as in [15].

the verifier attempts to cheat. This allows the simulator to receive the prover's input to the functionality, the witness w, thereby allowing an easy completion of simulation; (ii) the setting of simultaneous message model allows for a simulator to potentially use the third round of the verifier to extract some form of trapdoor in order to produce a simulated transcript.

To rule out the latter simulation strategy while preventing the simulator to take the "easy way out" by sending a cheat message to the ideal functionality, we define an adversarial verifier V* with the strategy "cheat if cheated with", which roughly translates to an adversarial verifier that will abort protocol execution if the protocol messages received are "incorrect". First we see why this prevents a simulator from taking the easy way out. In the real world, V* behaves honestly while interacting with honest provers. This prevents the simulator from sending a cheat message to the trusted party to receive the prover's input since it would result in a distinguishable distribution from the real execution, where the V* does not cheat.

Next, the rough idea to rule out any simulation strategy is the following: to simulate such a covert adversarial verifier V*, the simulator needs to provide an accepting proof in the third round, else the rushing adversarial verifier V* will always abort, thereby constraining the simulator to rewinding only the first or second rounds of the protocol. Rewinding the first round is not useful to the simulator because a rushing verifier can always restart afresh with new randomness. Thus the simulator can only rewind the second round. But the verifier can choose its second round message to be independent of the simulator's second round message, as in the honest protocol. Thus, the simulator seemingly gains no advantage by rewinding the second round. At best the simulator can make its own second round depend on the adversarial verifier's second round message.

In the full version, we provide the formal description of the cheating verifier V* and show that if there exists a simulator Sim* that succeeds in simulating the view for adversarial verifier V*, then the language must be in BPP. The proof borrows ideas from [19]. We refer the reader to the full version for the details.

Acknowledgments. Vipul Goyal is supported in part by the NSF award 1916939, a gift from Ripple, a JP Morgan Faculty Fellowship, a PNC center for financial services innovation award, and a Cylab seed funding award.

Arka Rai Choudhuri and Abhishek Jain are supported in part by DARPA/ARL Safeware Grant W911NF-15-C-0213, NSF CNS-1814919, NSF CAREER 1942789, Samsung Global Research Outreach award and Johns Hopkins University Catalyst award. Arka Rai Choudhuri is also supported by NSF Grants CNS-1908181 and CNS-1414023.

References

1. Ananth, P., Choudhuri, A.R., Jain, A.: A new approach to round-optimal secure multiparty computation. In: Katz, J., Shacham, H. (eds.) CRYPTO 2017. LNCS, vol. 10401, pp. 468–499. Springer, Cham (2017). https://doi.org/10.1007/978-3-319-63688-7_16

2. Asharov, G., Jain, A., López-Alt, A., Tromer, E., Vaikuntanathan, V., Wichs, D.: Multiparty computation with low communication, computation and interaction via threshold FHE. In: Pointcheval, D., Johansson, T. (eds.) EUROCRYPT 2012. LNCS, vol. 7237, pp. 483–501. Springer, Heidelberg (2012). https://doi.org/10.1007/978-3-642-29011-4_29

3. Aumann, Y., Lindell, Y.: Security against covert adversaries: efficient protocols for realistic adversaries. In: Vadhan, S.P. (ed.) TCC 2007. LNCS, vol. 4392, pp. 137–156. Springer, Heidelberg (2007). https://doi.org/10.1007/978-3-540-70936-7_8

4. Badrinarayanan, S., Goyal, V., Jain, A., Kalai, Y.T., Khurana, D., Sahai, A.: Promise zero knowledge and its applications to round optimal MPC. In: Shacham, H., Boldyreva, A. (eds.) CRYPTO 2018. LNCS, vol. 10992, pp. 459–487. Springer, Cham (2018). https://doi.org/10.1007/978-3-319-96881-0_16

5. Beaver, D., Micali, S., Rogaway, P.: The round complexity of secure protocols (extended abstract). In: 22nd ACM STOC, pp. 503–513. ACM Press (May 1990). https://doi.org/10.1145/100216.100287

6. Benhamouda, F., Lin, H.: k-round multiparty computation from k-round oblivious transfer via garbled interactive circuits. In: Nielsen, J.B., Rijmen, V. (eds.) EURO-CRYPT 2018. LNCS, vol. 10821, pp. 500–532. Springer, Cham (2018). https://doi.org/10.1007/978-3-319-78375-8_17

7. Boyle, E., Garg, S., Jain, A., Kalai, Y.T., Sahai, A.: Secure computation against adaptive auxiliary information. In: Canetti, R., Garay, J.A. (eds.) CRYPTO 2013. LNCS, vol. 8042, pp. 316–334. Springer, Heidelberg (2013). https://doi.org/10.1007/978-3-642-40041-4_18

8. Brakerski, Z., Halevi, S., Polychroniadou, A.: Four round secure computation without setup. In: Kalai, Y., Reyzin, L. (eds.) TCC 2017. LNCS, vol. 10677, pp. 645–677. Springer, Cham (2017). https://doi.org/10.1007/978-3-319-70500-2_22

9. Choudhuri, A.R., Ciampi, M., Goyal, V., Jain, A., Ostrovsky, R.: Round optimal secure multiparty computation from minimal assumptions. Cryptology ePrint Archive, Report 2019/216 (2019). https://eprint.iacr.org/2019/216

10. Ciampi, M., Ostrovsky, R., Siniscalchi, L., Visconti, I.: Delayed-input non-malleable zero knowledge and multi-party coin tossing in four rounds. In: Kalai, Y., Reyzin, L. (eds.) TCC 2017. LNCS, vol. 10677, pp. 711–742. Springer, Cham (2017). https://doi.org/10.1007/978-3-319-70500-2_24

11. Ciampi, M., Ostrovsky, R., Siniscalchi, L., Visconti, I.: Four-round concurrent non-malleable commitments from one-way functions. In: Katz, J., Shacham, H. (eds.) CRYPTO 2017. LNCS, vol. 10402, pp. 127–157. Springer, Cham (2017). https://doi.org/10.1007/978-3-319-63715-0_5

12. Ciampi, M., Ostrovsky, R., Siniscalchi, L., Visconti, I.: Round-optimal secure two-party computation from trapdoor permutations. In: Kalai, Y., Reyzin, L. (eds.) TCC 2017. LNCS, vol. 10677, pp. 678–710. Springer, Cham (2017). https://doi.org/10.1007/978-3-319-70500-2_23

13. Dwork, C., Naor, M.: Zaps and their applications. In: 41st FOCS, pp. 283–293. IEEE Computer Society Press (November 2000). https://doi.org/10.1109/SFCS.2000.892117

14. Garg, S., Gentry, C., Halevi, S., Raykova, M.: Two-round secure MPC from indistinguishability obfuscation. In: Lindell, Y. (ed.) TCC 2014. LNCS, vol. 8349, pp. 74–94. Springer, Heidelberg (2014). https://doi.org/10.1007/978-3-642-54242-8_4

15. Garg, S., Mukherjee, P., Pandey, O., Polychroniadou, A.: The exact round complexity of secure computation. In: Fischlin, M., Coron, J.-S. (eds.) EUROCRYPT 2016. LNCS, vol. 9666, pp. 448–476. Springer, Heidelberg (2016). https://doi.org/10.1007/978-3-662-49896-5_16

16. Garg, S., Srinivasan, A.: Garbled protocols and two-round MPC from bilinear maps. In: Umans, C. (ed.) 58th FOCS, pp. 588–599. IEEE Computer Society Press (October 2017). https://doi.org/10.1109/FOCS.2017.60

17. Garg, S., Srinivasan, A.: Two-round multiparty secure computation from minimal assumptions. In: Nielsen, J.B., Rijmen, V. (eds.) EUROCRYPT 2018. LNCS, vol. 10821, pp. 468–499. Springer, Cham (2018). https://doi.org/10.1007/978-3-319-78375-8_16

18. Goldreich, O., Kahan, A.: How to construct constant-round zero-knowledge proof systems for NP. J. Cryptol. 9(3), 167–189 (1996). https://doi.org/10.1007/BF00208001

19. Goldreich, O., Krawczyk, H.: On the composition of zero-knowledge proof-systems. SIAM J. Comput. 25(1), 169–192 (1996). https://doi.org/10.1137/S0097539791220688

20. Goldreich, O., Micali, S., Wigderson, A.: How to play any mental game or a completeness theorem for protocols with honest majority. In: Aho, A. (ed.) 19th ACM STOC, pp. 218–229. ACM Press (May 1987). https://doi.org/10.1145/28395.28420

21. Goyal, V.: Constant round non-malleable protocols using one way functions. In: Fortnow, L., Vadhan, S.P. (eds.) 43rd ACM STOC, pp. 695–704. ACM Press (June 2011). https://doi.org/10.1145/1993636.1993729

22. Halevi, S., Hazay, C., Polychroniadou, A., Venkitasubramaniam, M.: Round-optimal secure multi-party computation. In: Shacham, H., Boldyreva, A. (eds.) CRYPTO 2018. LNCS, vol. 10992, pp. 488–520. Springer, Cham (2018). https://doi.org/10.1007/978-3-319-96881-0_17

23. Halevi, S., Lindell, Y., Pinkas, B.: Secure computation on the web: computing without simultaneous interaction. In: Rogaway, P. (ed.) CRYPTO 2011. LNCS, vol. 6841, pp. 132–150. Springer, Heidelberg (2011). https://doi.org/10.1007/978-3-642-22792-9_8

24. Katz, J., Ostrovsky, R., Smith, A.: Round efficiency of multi-party computation with a dishonest majority. In: Biham, E. (ed.) EUROCRYPT 2003. LNCS, vol. 2656, pp. 578–595. Springer, Heidelberg (2003). https://doi.org/10.1007/3-540-39200-9_36

25. Mukherjee, P., Wichs, D.: Two round multiparty computation via multi-key FHE. In: Fischlin, M., Coron, J.-S. (eds.) EUROCRYPT 2016. LNCS, vol. 9666, pp. 735–763. Springer, Heidelberg (2016). https://doi.org/10.1007/978-3-662-49896-5_26

26. Pass, R.: Bounded-concurrent secure multi-party computation with a dishonest majority. In: Babai, L. (ed.) 36th ACM STOC, pp. 232–241. ACM Press (June 2004). https://doi.org/10.1145/1007352.1007393

27. Pass, R., Wee, H.: Constant-round non-malleable commitments from sub-exponential one-way functions. In: Gilbert, H. (ed.) EUROCRYPT 2010. LNCS, vol. 6110, pp. 638–655. Springer, Heidelberg (2010). https://doi.org/10.1007/978-3-642-13190-5_32

28. Wee, H.: Black-box, round-efficient secure computation via non-malleability amplification. In: 51st FOCS, pp. 531–540. IEEE Computer Society Press (October 2010). https://doi.org/10.1109/FOCS.2010.87
29. Yao, A.C.C.: How to generate and exchange secrets (extended abstract). In: 27th FOCS, pp. 162–167. IEEE Computer Society Press (October 1986). https://doi.org/10.1109/SFCS.1986.25

Unprovability of Leakage-Resilient Cryptography Beyond the Information-Theoretic Limit

Rafael Pass$^{(\boxtimes)}$

Cornell Tech, New York, NY, USA
rafael@cs.cornell.edu

Abstract. In recent years, *leakage-resilient* cryptography—the design of cryptographic protocols resilient to bounded leakage of honest players' secrets—has received significant attention. A major limitation of known provably-secure constructions (based on polynomial hardness assumptions) is that they require the secrets to have sufficient *actual* (i.e., information-theoretic), as opposed to *comptutational*, min-entropy even after the leakage.

In this work, we present barriers to provably-secure constructions beyond the "information-theoretic barrier": Assume the existence of collision-resistant hash functions. Then, no $\mathcal{NP}$ search problem with (2^{n^ϵ})-bounded number of witnesses can be proven (even worst-case) hard in the presence of $O(n^\epsilon)$ bits of computationally-efficient leakage of the witness, using a black-box reduction to any $O(1)$-round assumption. In particular, this implies that $O(n^\epsilon)$-leakage resilient *injective* one-way functions, and more generally, one-way functions with at most 2^{n^ϵ} pre-images, cannot be based on any "standard" complexity assumption using a black-box reduction.

1 Introduction

Modern Cryptography relies on the principle that cryptographic schemes are proven secure based on mathematically precise assumptions; these can be *general*—such as the existence of one-way functions—or *specific*—such as the hardness of factoring products of large primes. The security proof is a *reduction* that transforms any attacker A of the scheme into a machine that breaks the

---

R. Pass—Supported in part by a JP Morgan Faculty Award, NSF Award SATC-1704788, NSF Award RI-1703846, and AFOSR Award FA9550-18-1-0267. This research is based upon work supported in part by the Office of the Director of National Intelligence (ODNI), Intelligence Advanced Research Projects Activity (IARPA), via 2019-19-020700006. The views and conclusions contained herein are those of the authors and should not be interpreted as necessarily representing the official policies, either expressed or implied, of ODNI, IARPA, or the U.S. Government. The U.S. Government is authorized to reproduce and distribute reprints for governmental purposes notwithstanding any copyright annotation therein.

© Springer Nature Switzerland AG 2020
C. Galdi and V. Kolesnikov (Eds.): SCN 2020, LNCS 12238, pp. 621–642, 2020.
https://doi.org/10.1007/978-3-030-57990-6_31

underlying assumption (e.g., inverts an alleged one-way function). This study has been extremely successful, and during the past three decades many cryptographic tasks have been put under rigorous treatment and numerous constructions realizing these tasks have been proposed under a number of well-studied complexity-theoretic hardness assumptions. In this work, we focus on *black-box* (a.k.a. *Turing*) reductions M that only use the presumed attacker A as a black-box.

Leakage-Resilient Cryptography. In recent years, *leakage-resilient* cryptography [2,12,21,27]—the design of cryptographic protocols resilient to some forms of leakage of honest players' secrets—has received significant attention. Our focus on one of the most popular and simplest way of formalizing leakage resilience— the *bounded leakage model* [2,26]—where the attacker may receive some bounded amount of leakage on the secret. For concreteness, consider a one-way function f. We say that a one-way function is $\ell(\cdot)$-*leakage resilient* [2,3,22,26] if no efficient attacker can invert $y = f(x)$ for a randomly sampled x even if it gets access to an oracle $\mathsf{leak}_x(\cdot)$ that on input a circuit C outputs $C(x)$, as long as the total amount of bits received from the oracle is bounded by $\ell(|x|)$. We emphasize that the attacker may repeatedly access the oracle and may adaptively select the leakage function based on earlier leakage. access In other words, it should be hard to find a pre-image, even if you get to see arbitrary efficiently computable but adaptively-selected "leakage" functions of a pre-image x, as long as the total *length* of the leakage is bounded by $\ell(|x|)$. Clearly, no one-way function f can be leakage resilient to $\ell(\cdot)$-leakage when $\ell(n) = n$, as this enables leaking the whole pre-image. Yet, every one-way function f is $\ell(\cdot)$-leakage resilient for $\ell(n) = O(\log n)$, as an efficient attacker can simply guess the leakage with inverse polynomial probability.

The non-trivial problem is to construct cryptographic schemes that are *polynomially* (i.e., $\ell(n) = n^\epsilon$ for some $\epsilon > 0$) or even *linearly* (i.e., $\ell(n) = O(n)$) leakage resilient. Of course, if we assume that a one-way function f is *subexponentially* (resp. exponentially) secure, then the same guessing argument suffices to conclude that f is polynomially (resp. linearly) leakage resilient. More interestingly, as shown in [3,22][1] any sufficiently compressing *second-preimage resistant* hash function (which can be constructed from any (polynomially-secure) one-way function [32]) is also linearly leakage resilient.

It is instructive to recall their argument. Recall that a second-preimage resistant hash function h is a function such that no efficient attacker can, given random $i \leftarrow \{0,1\}^{p(n)}, x \leftarrow \{0,1\}^n$, find an $x' \neq x$ such that $h(i,x) = h(i,x')$. Given a second-preimage resistant hash function h, consider the function $f(i,x) = i, h(i,x)$; we aim to show that f is a leakage resilient one-way function. Towards this, assume for contradiction that there exists an efficient attacker A that, on input $i, y = h(i,x)$ and bounded leakage on x, manages to find a pre-image (i, x'). We can use this attacker to break the second-preimage resistance property of h

---

[1] As far as we know, this was first observed by Ramarathan Venkatesan in 2005 (in personal communication).

as follows: Given i, x, we run $A(i, h(i, x))$ and *simulate* the answers to A's leakage queries by computing the leakage function on x until A outputs an inverse (i, x'). Now, if the number of pre-images to $y = h(i, x)$ is sufficiently large— which is guaranteed by the compressing property of h—a bounded number of bits of leakage does not suffice to even information-theoretically determine x and thus with high probability, $x' \neq x$ and A must have found a "second" (different) preimage, thus breaking the second-preimage resistance property of h.

Leakage Resilience Beyond the Information-Theoretic Barrier? Note that a central part of the above argument (as well as arguments to analyze other cryptographic primitives in the presence of leakage, based on the polynomial security of standard assumption), is that even after the leakage queries, there is still sufficient min-entropy in the original secret (i.e., the input x). In essence, the original input/secret x is *information-theoretically* unpredictable given the output of the function and the leakage. A natural question is whether leakage resilience for secrets that are only *computationally* hidden can be based on standard (polynomial) hardness assumptions. For instance:

Can we base polynomial leakage resilience of an injective one-way function on "standard" complexity assumptions?

Note that for an injective one-way function f, the output of the function, $y = f(x)$, fully determines the secret x and thus there is no actual entropy in x (even before leakage). More generally, is it possible to just slightly beat the "information-theoretic barrier"? We say that a function has $B(\cdot)$-*bounded number of preimages* if for every $x \in \{0,1\}^n$, there exists at most $B(n)$ values $x' \in \{0,1\}^n$ such that $f(x') = f(x)$. For a function f with $B(n)$-bounded number of preimages, $(\log B(\cdot))$ bits of leakage is required to information-theoretically determine the input, so:

Can we base $O(\log B(\cdot))$-leakage resilience of a one-way function with $B(\cdot)$-bounded number of preimages on "standard" complexity assumptions?

Towards Barriers for Leakage Resilience. An elegant work by Wichs from 2013 [34] presents some initial barriers to affirmatively answering question 1. He shows that *certain restricted types of* black-box reductions cannot be used to base polynomially leakage-resilient injective one-way functions on *any* assumption that can be modelled as a security game between a challenger $\mathcal{C}$ and a polynomial-time attacker (such as all standard cryptographic assumptions). The restriction imposed by his result is that the black-box reduction does not get to access the code of the leakage queries issues by the attacker, and can simply "run" the code as a black-box.

The idea behind his result is simple: Consider a black-box reduction M that, given any attacker A that breaks polynomial leakage resilience of some injective one-way function f, breaks some assumption $\mathcal{C}$. Consider an (unbounded) attacker A that given an image y, issues a *random oracle* leakage query H, and next upon getting a response z, inverts f on y to get a pre-image x and returns x if and only if $H(x) = z$, and $\perp$ otherwise. The point is that this attacker A is essentially never useful to the reduction:

- If M does not query the random oracle on the actual (and unique by the injective property of f) pre-image x, then with overwhelming probability, the answer z to the leakage query will not satisfy the condition that $H(x) = z$ (we here rely on the fact that H is a random oracle) and thus A will answer $\perp$;
- and if M queries H on x, it already knows the pre-image itself, and thus can perfectly emulate the answer of A. So M never needs to use A and can break $\mathcal{C}$ on its own!

Let us point out, however, that the restriction to only allowing M to access the leakage query as a black-box (which is what enables the ideal attacker A to issue random oracle leakage queries) is quite severe: it prevents us from distinguishing between computationally unbounded leakage (which clearly is unrealistic) and *computationally restricted* classes of leakage, which more realistically model "real-life" leakage. In fact, as demonstrated in a beautiful work by Barak et al. [6] (see also [25]), in the closely related context of *key-dependent message (KDM) security*, there are non-trivial black-box reductions that (inherently) treat leakage queries in a non black-box way to establish feasibility results for a-priori bounded polynomial-sized leakage. Thus, in light of the above issue, even just question 1 remains largely open.

1.1 Our Results

In this work, assuming the existence of collision-resistant hash functions, we present strong barriers to providing an affirmative answer to question 2 (and thus also question 1) from any "standard" complexity assumption w.r.t. *any* black-box (i.e., Turing) reduction. Our impossibility rules out not just leakage-resilient one-way functions but even (worst-case) leakage-resilient hardness of $\mathcal{NP}$-*search problems* with subexponentially bounded number of witnesses. More precisely, we say that an $\mathcal{NP}$-relation R_L for a language L is (ℓ, s)-*leakage resilient* if there does not exists an efficient attacker A such that for *every* $x \in L$, $y \in R_L(x)$, A given x and $\ell(|x|)$ bits of leakage on y that is computable by $s(|x|)$ size circuits, recovers a witness $y' \in R_L(x)$ with probability 1. We remark that leakage-resilience of search problems was first considered by Aggarwal and Maurer [1], where they relate the leakage-resilience limit ℓ of a search problem to various other computational task related to the search problem; most notably, to the success probability of the best PPT algorithm for solving the problem (without leakage). We note that their results do not present any limitations on leakage-resilience for search problems but rather emphasize the importance of studying leakage-resilience of search problems.

Our main result presents a barrier to leakage-resilience of $\mathcal{NP}$-search problems beyond the information-theoretic limit with respect to polynomial-size computable leakage.

Theorem 1 (Informally Stated). *Assume the existence of collision-resistant hash functions and let R_L be an $\mathcal{NP}$-relation where statements of length n have at most 2^{n^ϵ} witnesses. Then there exists some polynomial s such that if there exists a black-box reduction M for basing $(O(n^\epsilon \cdot r(n)), s(n))$-leakage resilience of R_L on some $r(n)$-round assumption $\mathcal{C}$, then $\mathcal{C}$ can be broken in polynomial-time.*

By an $r(\cdot)$-round assumption $\mathcal{C}$, we refer to a security game between a challenger $\mathcal{C}$ and a polynomial-time attacker $\mathcal{A}$ that proceed in $r(n)$ rounds (given security parameter n), and the goal of the attacker is to make the challenger output 1. We note that all "standard" complexity assumptions used in Cryptography (e.g., hardness of factoring, discrete logarithms, lattice-problems etc) can be modeled as 2-round assumptions. $r(\cdot)$-round assumptions for $r(n) > 2$ capture an even larger class of assumption (e.g., the assumption that an $r(n)$-round protocol hides some secret).

We emphasize that every leakage-resilient one-way function f with (2^{n^ϵ})-bounded number of preimages directly yields an leakage-resilient $\mathcal{NP}$-relation with (2^{n^ϵ})-bounded number of witnesses and as such Theorem 1 shows barriers to basing (weak forms of) leakage-resilient one-wayness of any function with 2^{n^ϵ}-bounded number of pre-images on "standard" complexity assumptions using a black-box reduction.

We also highlight that we do not impose any restrictions on the black-box reduction. In particular, we allow the reduction to access the code of the leakage circuit. As a consequence, (in contrast to [34]), our impossibility only applies to assumptions with an *a-priori bounded*, $r(n)$, number of rounds. This is *inherent*, as otherwise the assumption that an efficiently computable function f is an $(\ell(\cdot), s(\cdot))$-leakage resilient one-way function can itself be modeled as an $\ell(\cdot)$-round assumption. (We remark, however, that our impossibility result relies on the existence of collision-resistant hash functions, whereas Wichs' result is unconditional.)

On Non-Black-Box Reductions. We emphasize that in our leakage model, the attacker gets "interactive" leakage on the secret x—i.e., it gets to repeatedly and *adaptively* select the leakage functions as a result of answers to earlier queries. A more restricted notion of leakage resilience provides the attacker with just a single *non-adaptive* leakage query. In general, the two leakage models are equivalent (see e.g., [1]) as we can view the whole leakage-selection process by the attacker as a single leakage query; this transformation, however, uses the attacker in a non-black-box way. This observation shows that *non-black-box* reductions can be used to overcome our barrier in its most general form: the assumption that a particular function f is (ℓ, s)-leakage resilient can be based on a 2-round assumption where the attacker first submits an "attack circuit" (of unbounded polynomial size) and the challenger checks whether the circuit indeed breaks (ℓ, s)-leakage resilience of f. This "non-black-box feasibility" is not specific to the particular tasks we consider—rather, it shows that any (multi-round) falsifiable assumption (i.e., assumption where the challenger runs in polynomial time) can be based on a 2-round falsifiable assumption using a non-black-box reduction. Given this "trivial" non-black-box reduction, the best way to interpret our results is as a barrier to basing leakage-resilience on "adversary-independent" assumptions where the communication complexity of the security game is some fixed polynomial (independent of the attacker). This restriction on the assumption (which indeed is satisfied by all "standard" complexity assumption) prevents relying on the trivial non-black-box reduction (which requires communicating the code of the attacker).

1.2 Impossibility vs Unprovability

We briefly mention a related work by Ilan Komargodski [24] that shows *impossibility* of leakage-resilient one-way functions in the presence of "one-way leakage". More precisely, Komargodksi considers a model where the attacker can receive leakage of *unbounded* length, but the leakage function is restricted to be *one way* (so that the input cannot be trivially leaked). He shows, using various obfuscation-type assumptions, that for every one-way function f, there exists some one-way leakage function h such that given $h(x)$ alone, x is (computationally) hard to recover, yet given both $f(x)$ and $h(x)$, x can be recovered. His result motivates why restricting to *bounded-length* leakage is crucial.

We note that the key difference between our results and his is that he considers a notion of leakage that makes leakage resilience impossible. In contrast (as we restrict the leakage to being short), the notion of leakage-resilience we consider is weak and it is generally believed that the primitives we consider exists. Indeed, as mentioned above, any *subexponentially-secure* one-way permutation is polynomially leakage resilient. Rather, our results are *unprovability* results: we show that leakage-resilient primitives, beyond the information-theoretic barrier, cannot be based on standard (bounded-round) assumptions using *polynomial-time* black-box reductions.

1.3 Proof Overview

Assume there exists a security reduction M such that M^A breaks the assumption $\mathcal{C}$ whenever A breaks leakage resilience of some witness relation R_L with 2^{n^ϵ} bounded number of witnesses. We want to use M to directly break $\mathcal{C}$ *without the help of* A. So, following the meta-reduction paradigm of [7], the goal will be to efficiently emulate A for M—that is, we will construct a meta-reduction that uses the underlying reduction M to break $\mathcal{C}$.

Ruling Out "Simple" Reductions. To explain the ideas, let us first assume that M only invokes a *single instance* of A and *does not rewind* A—this is clearly oversimplifying a lot, but we shall see later on how to overcome these restrictions. These types of reductions are sometimes referred to as "simple" reductions. Additionally, let us (for now) restrict our attention to assumptions $\mathcal{C}$ that only have two rounds (i.e., the challenger sends a single message, and the attacker provides his response).

Consider a particular unbounded attacker A that on input a statement x picks a 2-universal hash function $h : \{0,1\}^* \rightarrow \{0,1\}^{3n^\epsilon}$ and issues h as a leakage query—we highlight that h is not a random oracle but rather a concrete hash function sampled from a 2-universal family of functions. Looking forward, the idea for this leakage query is to ensure that, conditioned on this leakage, the witness is uniquely defined (with high probability).

After receiving back an answer z (supposedly $z = h(y)$ where $y \in R_L(x)$), A next "requests" to hear *a succint interactive argument of knowledge* [23] of the statement that "there exists some y' such that $h(y') = z$ and $y' \in R_L(x)$". Such argument systems exist based on the existence of collision-resistant hash functions [23] and relying on the PCP theorem [4,14]. Additionally, the prover in such an argument can be deterministic. As such, and due to the *succinct* nature of the argument—in particular, due to the fact that the prover's messages are "short"— the prover's next-messages function can be viewed as bounded polynomial-time computable leakage query to the witness. Finally, if A gets convinced by the argument of knowledge (that it requests through its leakage queries), it recovers (in exponential time) a witness $y'' \in R_L(x)$ such that $h(y'') = z$, and returns it.

We remark that the idea of using a succint arguments of knowledge to present impossibility results for leakage resilience originated in [29] and was subsequently used in [30]; this idea goes back to even earlier work in a related context [20]. While we use this idea here for a very similar purpose, we note that these earlier works used them to rule out leakage resilience to significantly more complex primitives (secure computations [17,35] and black-box zero-knowledge proofs [16,18]). As such, we will have to work a bit harder to present an impossibility result for just leakage-resilience of a search problem.

We would now like to argue that M can simulate the answer to queries to *this particular A* on its own (and thus break $\mathcal{C}$ in polynomial time). The point is that for A to "say anything useful" (i.e., to provide a witness y'), M first needs to provide a convincing argument of knowledge of the statement "there exists some y' such that $H(y') = z$ and $y' \in R_L(x)$" to A, and from this argument *of knowledge*—and since M is only invoking a single instance of A and does not rewind A—a witness y'' such that $y' \in R_L(x)$" and $H(y'') = z$ can be extracted in (expected) polynomial time. M can thus simulate A's response by sending y'' to itself. Note that we here also need to rely on the fact that $\mathcal{C}$ only has 2 rounds, so that when we extract a witness from A, this can be done without having to rewind $\mathcal{C}$.

It remains, however, to argue that y'' is distributed in the same way as the witness y' that A would have returned. This follows from the fact that, with overwhelming probability over the choice of h, by the 2-universal property of h, there exists a *unique* y' such that $h(y') = z$ and $y' \in R_L(x)$—we here rely on the fact that the leakage is "beyond the information-theoretic limit" so that the output of h can uniquely determine y'.

Dealing with General (i.e., Rewinding) Reductions. The above proof sketch, however, relies on the fact that M does not rewind A; if M can *rewind A* and reset A, and start many *concurrent* sessions with A, then it is no longer clear how to extract a witness from the proof it is providing. In particular, if the proof is not "resettably-sound" [5], then a rewinding reduction may convince A of even false statements!

Additionally, as mentioned, it also relies on C only having 2 rounds, or else, we may rewind C when extracting the witness. Luckily, both of these problems have arisen in earlier black-box separations for interactive proofs. Consider some assumption C with $r(n)$ communication rounds. In [31], a technique was developed for extracting witnesses from reductions that arbitrarily rewind its oracle—even if they start many interleaved, concurrent, interactions with the oracle—as long as the reduction needs to provide sufficiently many *sequential* interactive arguments of knowledge of a certain "special-sound" [10] type. More precisely, $O(r(n) \cdot n^\epsilon)$ sequential proofs of this special-sound type need to be provided to ensure an appropriate level of "resettable-soundness", while avoiding rewindings communication with C. We here show how to adopt the above proof idea to fit into the framework of [31], which we need to generalize as it only considers languages with *unique witnesses*. More precisely, we proceed in two steps:

- We show how to modify Kilian's protocol to satisfy an appropriate special-soundness property needed for the meta reduction in [31]—doing this, however, requires making the communication complexity of the protocol greater than n, and thus the protocol no longer seems useful! The point is that, even if the communication complexity is large, the prover of the protocol is *laconic*—in other words, the length of the prover messages is still small and thus we can still view the prover messages as "short" leakage.
- Rather than reproving the result from [31], we rely on the meta-reduction from [31] in a black-box way, and instead present a meta-reduction that turns our attacker into an attacker for a primitive (namely sequentially witness hiding public-coin arguments for unique-witness relations) that is covered by the impossibility of [31]. In more details, we present a meta-reduction showing that any reduction for leakage-resilience can be turned into a different reduction that satisfies the "unique witness" requirement needed for the result in [31] to kick in. We can then apply the meta-reduction of [31] on top of our meta-reduction. As far as we know, this techniques of "nested" meta-reductions (or composition of meta-reductions) is new and we hope that is may be useful elsewhere.

2   General Preliminaries

In this section we recall some standard definitions and preliminaries.

2.1   Notation

Integer, Strings and Vectors. We denote by N the set of natural numbers: 0, 1, 2, ... Unless otherwise specified, a natural number is presented in its binary expansion (with no *leading* 0s) whenever given as an input to an algorithm. If $n \in N$, we denote by 1^n the unary expansion of n (i.e., the concatenation of n 1's). Given a string x, we let $x|_i$ denote the i'th bit of x. We denote by $\boldsymbol{x}$ a finite sequence of elements $x_1, x_2, \ldots x_n$, and we let $|\boldsymbol{x}|$ denote the number of elements in the sequence.

Algorithms. We employ the following notation for algorithms.

Probabilistic algorithms. By a probabilistic algorithm we mean a Turing machine that receives an auxiliary random tape as input. If M is a probabilistic algorithm, then for any input x, the notation "$M_r(x)$" denotes the output of the M on input x when receiving r as random tape. We let the notation "$M(x)$" denote the probability distribution over the outputs of M on input x where each bit of the random tape r is selected at random and independently, and then outputting $M_r(x)$.

Interactive Algorithms. We assume familiarity with the basic notions of an *Interactive Turing Machine* [18] (ITM for brevity) and a *protocol*. (Briefly, a protocol is pair of ITMs computing in turns. In each turn, called a round, only one ITM is active. A round ends with the active machine either halting—in which case the protocol halts—or by sending a message m to the other machine, which becomes active with m as a special input. By an interactive algorithm we mean a (probabilistic) interactive Turing Machine.

Given a pair of interactive algorithms (A, B), we let $\langle A(a), B(b) \rangle (x)$ denote the probability distribution over the outputs of $B(b)$ after interacting with $A(a)$ on the common input x.

Oracle algorithms. An oracle algorithm is a machine that gets oracle access to another machine. We will restrict our attention to oracle algorithms that get access to *deterministic* interactive algorithms. Given a probabilistic oracle algorithm M, and a *deterministic* interactive algorithm A, we let $M^A(1^n)$ denote the probability distribution over the outputs of the algorithm M on input 1^n, when given oracle access to a function that on input a *partial transcript* $T = (q_1, r_1, .., q_l)$ outputs the next message r_i sent by A on input 1^n and receiving the messages $(q_1, .., q_l)$ if $r_1, \ldots r_{k-1}$ are the correct next-messages of A on all the earlier prefixes of T and $\perp$ otherwise. Note that this is well defined since we only consider deterministic oracles A.

Negligible and Overwhelming Functions. The term "negligible" is used for denoting functions that are asymptotically smaller than the inverse of any fixed polynomial. More precisely, a function $\nu(\cdot)$ from non-negative integers to reals is called *negligible* if for every constant $c > 0$ and all sufficiently large n, it holds that $\nu(n) < n^{-c}$. A function $\mu(\cdot)$ is *overwhelming* if there exists some negligible function $\nu(\cdot)$ such that $\mu(n) \geq 1 - \nu(n)$ for all n.

2.2 Witness Relations

We recall the definition of a witness relation for an $\mathcal{NP}$ language [15].

Definition 1 (Witness relation). *A witness relation for a language $L \in \mathcal{NP}$ is a binary relation R_L that is polynomially bounded, polynomial time recognizable and characterizes L by $L = \{x : \exists w \; s.t. \; (x, w) \in R_L\}$.*

We say that w is a witness for the membership $x \in L$ if $(x, w) \in R_L$. We will also let $R_L(x)$ denote the set of witnesses for the membership $x \in L$, i.e., $R_L(x) = \{w : (x, w) \in L\}$. If for each $x \in L$, there exists a single $w \in R_L(x)$, we say that R_L is a *unique witness relation*. If for each $x \in L$, there exists at most $k(\cdot)$ different witnesses $w \in R_L(x)$, we say that R_L is a $k(\cdot)$-witness relation. If there exists some constant ϵ such that R_L is a 2^{n^ϵ}-witness relation, we refer to R_L as a *witness relation with subexponentially bounded number of witnesses*.

2.3   Interactive Proofs and Arguments

We recall the standard definitions of interactive proofs and arguments.

Definition 2 (Interactive Proofs and Arguments [8,18]). *A pair of probabilistic interactive algorithms (P, V) is called an* interactive proof system *for a language L with witness relation R_L if V is polynomial-time and the following two conditions hold.*

- Completeness: *For every $x \in L$, and every $y \in R_L(x)$,*

$$\Pr\Big[\langle P(y), V\rangle(x) = 1\Big] = 1$$

- Soundness: *For every interactive algorithm P^*, there exists a negligible function ν such that for every $x \notin L$, every $z \in \{0,1\}^*$,*

$$\Pr\Big[(\langle P^*(z), V\rangle(x) = 0\Big] \geq 1 - \nu(|x|)$$

In case that the soundness condition holds only with respect to a provers P^* whose running-time is polynomially bounded in the common input, the pair (P, V) is called an interactive argument system. *If P is probabilistic polynomial-time, (P, V) is an* efficient prover *interactive proof/argument system.*

2.4   Intractability Assumptions and Black-Box Reductions

Our definition of intractability assumptions and black-box reductions closely follows [31] (the text below is taken almost verbatim from there). Following Naor [28] (see also [11,19,33]), we model an intractability assumption as an interactive game between a probabilistic machine $\mathcal{C}$—called the challenger—and an attacker A. Both parties get as input 1^n where n is the security parameter. For any $t(n) \in [0, 1]$ and any "adversary" A, if $\Pr[\langle A, \mathcal{C}\rangle(1^n) = 1] \geq t(n) + p(n)$, then we say that A *breaks* $\mathcal{C}$ *with advantage* $p(n)$ over the "threshold" $t(n)$. When this happens, we might also say that A *breaks* $(\mathcal{C}, t)$ *with advantage* $p(n)$. Any pair $(\mathcal{C}, t)$ intuitively corresponds to the following assumption:

For every polynomial-time adversary A, there exists a negligible function $\nu(\cdot)$ such that for every $n \in \mathbb{N}$, A breaks C with advantage at most $\nu(n)$ over the threshold $t(n)$.

We refer to (C, t) as an $r(\cdot)$-round assumption if C on input 1^n communicates with the attacker A in at most $r(n)$ communication rounds.

Black-Box Reductions. We consider probabilistic polynomial-time Turing reductions—i.e., *black-box reductions*. A black-box reduction refers to a probabilistic polynomial-time oracle algorithm. Roughly speaking, a black-box reduction for basing the security of a primitive P on the hardness of an assumption (C, t), is a probabilistic polynomial-time oracle machine M such that whenever the oracle O "breaks" P with respect to the security parameter n, then M^O "breaks" (C, t) with respect to a polynomially related security parameter n' such that n' can be efficiently computed given n. We restrict ourselves to the case where $n' = n$, since without loss of generality we can always redefine the challenger C so that it acts as if its input was actually n' (since n' can be efficiently computed given n). To formalize this notion, we thus restrict ourselves to oracle machines M that on input 1^n always query the oracle on inputs of the form $(1^n, \cdot)$.

Definition 3. *We say that M is a* fixed-parameter black-box reduction *if M is an oracle machine such that $M(1^n)$ only queries its oracle with inputs of the form $(1^n, x)$, where $x \in \{0, 1\}^*$.*

A more liberal notion of a black-box reduction allows the reduction M to (on input 1^n) query its oracle on multiple security parameters (that are all polynomially related to n). In our eyes, such a liberal notion is less justified from a practical point of view (and as far as we are aware, cryptographic reductions typically do not rely on such liberal reductions); nevertheless, our proofs directly applies also for such a notion of black-box reductions.

3   Preliminaries from [31]

We recall some notions and results from [31] which will be useful to us. (Some of the text is taken almost verbatim from there.)

Special Soundness. We start by recalling a strong notion of a *proof of knowledge* [13,18] that will be instrumental to us. Recall that a three-round public-coin interactive proof is said to be *special-sound* [10], if a valid witness to the statement x can be efficiently computed from any two accepting proof-transcripts of x which have the same first message but different second messages. [31] considers a relaxation of this notion—referred to as *computational special-soundness*—where (a) the number of communication rounds is any constant (instead of just three), (b) the extractor may need a polynomial number of accepting transcripts (instead of just two), and (c) extraction need only succeed if the transcripts are generated by communicating with a computationally-bounded prover.

Definition 4 (Computational Special-Soundness). *Let* (P, V) *be a k-round (where* k *is a constant) public-coin interactive argument for the language* $L \in \mathcal{NP}$ *with witness relation* R_L. (P, V) *is said to be* computationally special-sound *if there exists a constant* $i < k$, *some polynomial* $m(\cdot)$, *and a polynomial-time extractor machine* X, *such that for every polynomial-time deterministic machine* P^*, *and every polynomial* $p(\cdot)$, *there exists a negligible function* $\mu(\cdot)$ *such that the following holds for every* $x \in L$ *and every auxiliary input* z *for* P^*. *Let* $\boldsymbol{T} = (T_1, T_2, \ldots T_{p(|x|)})$ *denote transcripts in* $p(|x|)$ *random executions between* $P^*(x, z)$ *and* $V(x)$ *where* V *uses the same randomness for the first* $k - i - 1$ *messages (thus, the first* $k - i - 1$ *messages are the same in all transcripts). Then, the probability (over the randomness used to generate* $\boldsymbol{T}$) *that:*

1. $\boldsymbol{T}$ *contains a set of* $m(|x|)$ *accepting transcripts with different round* $k - i$ *messages; and*
2. $X(\boldsymbol{T})$ *does not output a witness* $w \in R_L(x)$

is smaller than $\mu(|x|)$. *We say that a computationally special-sound protocol has a* large challenge space *if the length of the verifier challenge is* $\omega(\log n)$ *on common inputs of length* n.

In this work, we introduce a relaxation of computational special soundness where above extraction property only needs to hold on instances x that have a unique witness (i.e., only for $x \in L$ such that there exits a single $y \in R_L(x)$); we refer to such a notion as *unique-witness computational special-soundness*.

Witness Hiding. A desirable property of interactive proofs is that they "hide" the witness used by the prover. We will consider a very weak notion of *worst-case* sequential witness hiding: roughly speaking, a protocol is said to be *worst-case sequential witness hiding* if no polynomial time attacker can *always* recover the witness for any statement x that it hears $\ell(|x|)$ sequential proofs of.

Definition 5 (Worst-Case Witness Hiding). *Let* (P, V) *be an argument for the language* L *with witness relation* R_L. *We say that (a potentially unbounded)* A *breaks worst-case* $\ell(\cdot)$-*sequential witness hiding of* (P, V) *with respect to* R_L *if for every* $n \in \mathbb{N}$, $x \in L \cap \{0, 1\}^n$, *and* $w \in R_L(x)$, A *wins in the following experiment with probability 1: Let* $A(x)$ *sequentially communicate with* $P(x, w)$ $\ell(n)$ *times;* A *is said to win if it outputs a witness* w' *such that* $w' \in R_L(x)$. (P, V) *is called* worst-case $\ell(\cdot)$-*sequentially witness hiding w.r.t* R_L *if no polynomial time algorithm* A *breaks worst-case* $\ell(\cdot)$-*sequential witness hiding of* (P, V) *w.r.t* R_L.

Definition 6 (Black-Box Reductions for Worst-Case Sequential Witness Hiding). *We say that* M *is a* black-box reduction for basing worst-case $\ell(\cdot)$-*sequential witness hiding of* (P, V) *w.r.t* R_L *on the hardness of* $(\mathcal{C}, t)$ *if* M *is a probabilistic polynomial-time oracle machine, such that for every deterministic machine* A *that breaks worst-case* $\ell(\cdot)$-*sequential witness hiding of* (P, V) *with respect to* R_L, *there exists a polynomial* $p(\cdot)$ *such that for infinitely many* $n \in \mathbb{N}$, S^A *breaks the assumption* $(\mathcal{C}, t)$ *with advantage* $\frac{1}{p(n)}$ *on input* 1^n.

The Result of [31] We now state (a simplified form) of the main result of [31].

Theorem 2 (Main Result of [31]**).** *Let* (P, V) *be a computationally-special-sound argument with large challenge space for the language* L *with a unique witness relation* R_L, *and let* $(\mathcal{C}, t)$ *be an* $r(\cdot)$-*round assumption where* $r(\cdot)$ *is a polynomial. Let* $\ell(n) = r(n)n^\epsilon$ *for some constant* $\epsilon > 0$. *If there exists a fixed-parameter black-box reduction* M *for basing worst-case* $\ell(\cdot)$-*sequential witness hiding of* (P, V) *w.r.t* R_L *on the hardness of* $(\mathcal{C}, t)$, *then there exists a polynomial* $p(\cdot)$ *and an efficient algorithm* B *such that* $B(1^n)$ *breaks* $(\mathcal{C}, t)$ *with advantage* $\frac{1}{p(n)}$ *on input* 1^n *for infinitely many* $n \in N$.

For convenience of the reader (and because we will need to slightly generalize this result), let us provide a very high-level overview of the proof of this theorem. Assume there exists a security reduction M such that M^A breaks the assumption $\mathcal{C}$ whenever A breaks worst-case sequential witness hiding of a (computationally) special-sound argument (P, V) for a language with unique witnesses. We want to use M to directly break $\mathcal{C}$ without the help of A—that is, we will construct a "meta-reduction" [7] B that uses the underlying reduction M to break $\mathcal{C}$.

Towards this, we consider a particular computationally unbounded oracle A that after hearing an appropriate number of proofs using (P, V) (acting as a verifier) simply outputs a witness to the statement proved. The meta-reduction B next needs to *efficiently* emulate A for M and thereby can efficiently break $\mathcal{C}$ (without the help of A). To enable such an emulation of A, the idea is to "extract" out the witness that A would have provide to M *from* M *itself* by "rewinding" M—since (P, V) is computationally special-sound, M, intuitively, must know a witness for all statements x that it proves to A. There are several obstacles in formalizing this approach. The main one is that the reduction M is not a "stand-alone" prover—it might *rewind and reset* the oracle A—so it is no longer clear that it needs to "know" a witness for x in order to convince A of x. It is here that the proof of [31] relies on the fact that there are *multiple* proofs being provided by S; this gives the meta-reduction more opportunities to rewind M, which enables extraction even if M "nests" its queries to A in an arbitrary way. Let us point out that the unique witness requirement is needed to guarantee that the witness extracted out by the meta-reduction is identically the same as the witness used by the unbounded attacker A.

We remark that the proof in [31] directly also extends to languages *without unique witnesses* as long as the reduction rarely "hits" instances that do not have unique witnesses; additionally, we only require the special soundness condition to hold whenever the statement proved has a unique witness. (As can be seen in the high-level description above, this this suffices to ensure that the witnesses extracted by the meta-reduction is identically the same as the witness used by the unbounded attacker A *with overwhelming probability*.)

Theorem 3 (Slight Generalization of [31]**).** *Let* (P, V) *be a unique-witness computationally-special-sound argument with large challenge space for the language* L *with witness relation* R_L, *and let* $(\mathcal{C}, t)$ *be an* $r(\cdot)$-*round assumption where* $r(\cdot)$ *is a polynomial. Let* $\ell(n) = r(n)n^\epsilon$ *for some constant* $\epsilon > 0$. *Let*

M be a fixed-parameter black-box reduction for basing worst-case $\ell(\cdot)$-sequential witness hiding of (P, V) w.r.t R_L on the hardness of (C, t). Assume further that with overwhelming probability, $M(1^n)$ only queries its oracle on statements x that have a unique witness $w \in R_L(x)$. Then, there exists a polynomial $p(\cdot)$ and an efficient algorithm B such that $B(1^n)$ breaks (C, t) with advantage $\frac{1}{p(n)}$ on input 1^n for infinitely many $n \in N$.

4 Leakage-Resilient Witness Relations and the Main Theorem

To define leakage-resilient witness relations, we consider an attacker A that receives as input a statement x and may adaptively ask for leakage of a witness y; A succeeds if it recovers any witness to x, while having seen less than $\ell(|x|)$ bits of leakage of y. More formally, let $\mathsf{leak}_y(\cdot)$ be a function that on input a circuit C outputs $C(y)$.

Definition 7 (Leakage-Resilient Relations). Let R_L be a witness relation for the language L. We say that (a potentially unbounded) A breaks $(\ell(\cdot), s(\cdot))$-leakage resilience of R_L if for every $n \in \mathbb{N}, x \in L \cap \{0,1\}^n, y \in R_L(x)$, with probability 1, it holds that (a) $A_y^{\mathsf{leak}}(1^n, x) \in R_L(x)$ and (b) A received at most $\ell(|x|)$ bits from its oracle and (c) A only queries its oracle with circuits of size at most $s(|x|)$, where the probability is over the randomness of A. R_L is said to be a $(\ell(\cdot), s(\cdot))$-leakage resilient if there does not exists an efficient attacker A that breaks $(\ell(\cdot), s(\cdot)$-leakage resilience of R_L.

Let us make some remarks about this notion of leakage resilience:

- $(0, s)$-leakage resilience of an $\mathcal{NP}$-relation is equivalent to stating that the $\mathcal{NP}$ search problem associated with it is hard for probabilistic polynomial time; thus, $(0, s)$-leakage resilient witness relations exists assuming $\mathcal{NP} \not\subseteq \mathcal{BPP}$. $(O(\log n), s)$-leakage resilience of a witness relation is equivalent to $(0, s)$-leakage resilience since we can simply enumerate all possible answers to the leakage queries.
- By enumerating the answers to all leakage queries, (n^ϵ, s)-leakage resilience of a witness relation R_L can be based on the assumption that the $\mathcal{NP}$ search problem associated with it cannot be solved in time poly(2^{n^ϵ}).

Our main result will present barriers to basing leakage-resilient relations on polynomial-time hardness assumption. Towards this, we turn to defining what it means to base leakage resilience of R_L on some assumption using a black-box reduction.

Definition 8 (Black-Box Reductions for Leakage-Resilient Relations). We say that M is a black-box reduction for basing $(\ell(\cdot), s(\cdot))$-leakage resilience on the hardness of (C, t) if M is a probabilistic polynomial-time oracle machine, such that for every deterministic machine A that breaks $(\ell(\cdot), s(\cdot))$-leakage resilience of R_L, there exists a polynomial $p(\cdot)$ such that for infinitely many $n \in \mathbb{N}$, S^A breaks the assumption (C, t) with advantage $\frac{1}{p(n)}$ on input 1^n.

The Main Theorem. We are now ready to state our main theorem.

Theorem 4. *Assume the existence of families of collision-resistant hash functions. Let R_L be a (2^{n^ϵ})-witness relation for some constant $\epsilon > 0$, let $(\mathcal{C}, t)$ be a $r(\cdot)$-round assumption where $r(\cdot)$ is a polynomial.. Then there exists some polynomial s and some constant $c \geq 1$ such that for $\ell(n) = c \cdot r(n) \cdot n^\epsilon$, if there exists a fixed-parameter black-box reduction M for basing $(\ell(\cdot), s(\cdot))$-leakage resilience of R_L on the hardness of $(\mathcal{C}, t)$, then there exists a polynomial $p(\cdot)$ and an efficient algorithm B such that $B(1^n)$ breaks $(\mathcal{C}, t)$ with advantage $\frac{1}{p(n)}$ on input 1^n for infinitely many $n \in N$.*

5   Proof of the Main Theorem

Towards proving Theorem 4, we first present a $O(1)$-round unique-witness computationally special-sound argument for $\mathcal{NP}$ with a small prover communication complexity (i.e., with a laconic prover) and with a deterministic, efficient, prover strategy.

Next, as a warm up (and stepping-stone) to the complete proof of Theorem 4, we focus on leakage resilience of *unique witness relations* and observe that any leakage resilient *unique witness relations* with a black-box security proof together with our laconic prover argument, yields a $O(1)$-round computationally special-sound worst-case $O(n^\epsilon)$-sequentially witness hiding argument for a unique witness language: we can simply view the prover messages (which are deterministic and efficiently computable) as leakage—which is small as the length of the prover messages, as well as the number of sequential repetitions, are small—and as such leakage resilience of the relation implies worst-case witness hiding. The special case of Theorem 4 for unique witness relations can next be concluded by appealing to Theorem 2 (which rules out black-box reductions for basing worst-case $O(n^\epsilon)$-sequential witness hiding for unique witness languages on bounded-round assumptions) . In fact, if we rely on the (more general) Theorem 3, we can conclude an even stronger version that applies to any (potentially non-unique) witness relations, as long as we restrict to reductions that (with overwhelming probability) only query its oracle on instances with unique witnesses.

To conclude the full proof of Theorem 4, we next show that for any witness relation R_L with subexponentially bounded number of witnesses, there exists a different witness relation $R_{L'}$ such that any reduction for basing leakage resilience of R_L on some assumption $(\mathcal{C}, t)$ can be turned into a reduction $\tilde{M}$ for basing leakage resilience of $R_{L'}$ on $(\mathcal{C}, t)$ such that, with overwhelming probability, $\tilde{M}$ only queries its oracle on instances that have a unique witness (and as such, by the result above, is ruled out).

This is done by letting $R_{L'}$ be the set of pairs $((x, h, z), y)$ such that $y \in R_L(x)$ and $h(y) = z$ and having $\tilde{M}$ internally emulating M but for every interaction with the oracle that M initiates on input an instance x, $\tilde{M}$ first samples a 2-universal hash function h and internally issues h as a leakage query to M. Upon receiving an answer z (which is supposed to be $h(y)$ such that $y \in R_L(x)$), $\tilde{M}$ next queries the outside oracle on the instance (x, h, z) and subsequentially forwards all communication between M and the leakage oracle. By the 2-universal property of the hash function (and a union bound), it follows that if the output of the hash function is sufficiently long, then with overwhelming probability, there exists a unique pre-image for every image z and thus $\tilde{M}$ only queries its oracle on instances with unique witnesses. The point is that if the number of witnesses of x is bounded by 2^{n^ϵ}, it suffices to make the length of the output of the hash function $3n^\epsilon$ to ensure uniqueness (while at the same time ensuring that the length of the leakage is small).

5.1 A Laconic-Prover Computationally Special-Sound Argument for $\mathcal{NP}$

We here present a *laconic-prover* (namely with prover communication-complexity $O(n^\epsilon)$ for any ϵ) unique-witness computationally special-sound argument for every language in $\mathcal{NP}$ with a deterministic prover, based on the existence of collision-resistant hash functions. This construction will rely on Kilian's [23] succinct argument for $\mathcal{NP}$, which in turn relies on the PCP theorem [4,14].

Theorem 5. *Assume the existence of families of collision-resistant hash functions. Then, for every $\epsilon > 0$ and every language L with witness relation R_L, there exists a constant c and an efficient-prover unique-witness computationally special-sound interactive argument $\Pi = (P, V)$ for L, R_L with large challenge space, where (a) the prover is deterministic, and (b) the prover communication complexity is bounded by $c \cdot n^\epsilon$.*

Proof. Recall that by the result of Kilian [23], assuming the existence of families of collision-resistant hash function, for every $\epsilon > 0$ and every language L with witness relation R_L, there exists an efficient-prover 4-round interactive argument for L, R_L where the prover strategy is deterministic, and the prover communication complexity is $O(n^\epsilon)$. The protocol (P, V) proceeds as follows on common input a statement $x \in L$, and a witness $y \in R_L(x)$ as private input to P. Let $p(n)$ be a polynomial upper-bound on the length of witnesses for statements of length n.

- V picks a uniformly random string $r \leftarrow \{0, 1\}^{p(|x|)}$ and sends it to P.
- P returns $b = \sum_{i=1}^{p(|x|)} y_i r_i \mod 2$.
- P and V next invokes Kilian's (4-round) interactive argument, letting P prove that $b = \sum_{i=1}^{p(|x|)} y_i r_i \mod 2$ and $y \in R_L(x)$.

It follows directly by Gaussian elimination and the soundness of the efficient argument that (P, V) is a unique-witness computationally special-sound interactive argument. (Note that extraction using Gaussian elimination is only guaranteed to work when the witness is unique or else the malicious prover may potentially mix and match witnesses.) By definition, P is deterministic and for each $\epsilon > 0$, we can ensure that the communication complexity of P is bounded by $c \cdot n^\epsilon$ for some sufficiently large constant c. Additionally, by the efficient prover property of Kilian's argument, P can also be implemented in polynomial time.

5.2 Unprovability of Leakage-Resilient Unique-Witness Relations

As a stepping stone (and warm-up), we start by showing barriers to showing that *unique* witness relations are $(O(n^\epsilon), poly)$-leakage resilient, for any constant $\epsilon > 0$. In fact, we directly show black-box unprovability of $(O(n^\epsilon), poly)$-leakage resilience of (potentially non-unique) witness relations using any reduction that with overwhelming probability only queries its oracle on instances with unique witnesses.

Lemma 1. *Assume the existence of families of collision-resistant hash functions. Let R_L be a witness relation, let $(\mathcal{C}, t)$ be an $r(\cdot)$-round assumption where $r(\cdot)$ is a polynomial, and let $\epsilon > 0$. Then, there exists some polynomial $s(\cdot)$ such that for $\ell(n) = c \cdot r(n) \cdot n^\epsilon$, if (1) there exists a fixed-parameter black-box reduction M for basing (ℓ, s)-leakage resilience of R_L on the hardness of $(\mathcal{C}, t)$ and (2) with overwhelming probability, M only queries its oracle on instances with unique witnesses, then there exists a polynomial $p(\cdot)$ and an efficient algorithm B such that $B(1^n)$ breaks $(\mathcal{C}, t)$ with advantage $\frac{1}{p(n)}$ on input 1^n for infinitely many $n \in N$.*

Proof. Consider $R_L, \epsilon, r(\cdot)$ and $(\mathcal{C}, t)$ as in the statement of the lemma and assume the existence of families of collision-resistant hash functions. Pick a constant ϵ' such that $0 < \epsilon' < \epsilon$. By Theorem 5, there exists some polynomial $s(\cdot)$ and a unique-witness computationally special-sound argument (P, V) for R_L with communication complexity $c \cdot n^{\epsilon'}$ and with a deterministic prover with computational complexity $s(n)$. Let $m(n) = r(n)n^{\epsilon-\epsilon'}$ and let $\ell(n) = c \cdot r(n)n^\epsilon$ and consider some fixed-parameter black-box reduction M for basing (ℓ, s)-leakage resilience of R_L on the hardness of $(\mathcal{C}, t)$, such that with overwhelming probability M only queries its oracle on instances with unique witnesses.

We will show how to construct a reduction $\tilde{M}$ for basing worst-case $m(n)$-sequential witness hiding of the protocol (P, V) w.r.t. L, R_L on $(\mathcal{C}, t)$ such that with overwhelming probability $\tilde{M}$ only queries its oracle on instances with unique witnesses. By Theorem 3, this implies that there exists a polynomial $p(\cdot)$ and an efficient algorithm B such that $B(1^n)$ breaks $(\mathcal{C}, t)$ with advantage $\frac{1}{p(n)}$ on input 1^n for infinitely many $n \in N$, and thus concludes the proof of the lemma.

Let $\mathsf{code}_P(x, q_1, \ldots, q_k)$ denote the circuit $C(\cdot)$ that on input y computes P's $(k+1)$'st message given the input (x, y) and receiving messages $q_1, \ldots, q_k$. $\tilde{M}(1^n)$ internally emulates $M(1^n)$ and proceeds as follows:

- Whenever M wants to send an oracle query $(x, p_1, q_1, \ldots, p_k)$, $\tilde{M}'$ externally forwards it to its oracle. Upon receiving back a response q_{k+1}, if $k = 2m(n)$ (i.e., the response is the last message from the oracle for this interaction, that is a witness), or if $q_{k+1} = \bot$, $\tilde{M}$ simply returns q_{k+1} to M. Otherwise, it returns $\mathsf{code}_P(q_1, \ldots, q_{k+1})$ to M.

- All messages that M wants to send to $\mathcal{C}$ are forwarded externally without modification, and messages that $\tilde{M}$ receives from $\mathcal{C}$ are directly forwarded to M.

Consider some attacker A that breaks worst-case $m(n)$-sequential witness hiding of (P, V) with probability 1. Let $\tilde{A}$ be a "wrapped" version of A that post-processes responses from A in exactly the same way as $\tilde{M}$ does. It directly follows from the definition of $\tilde{A}$ and the fact that (P, V) has prover communication complexity $c \cdot n^{\epsilon'}$ and computation complexity $s(n)$ that $\tilde{A}$ breaks leakage resilience of R_L with probability 1 using

$$ c \cdot n^{\epsilon'} \cdot m(n) = c \cdot n^{\epsilon'} \cdot r(n) \cdot n^{\epsilon - \epsilon'} = c \cdot r(n) \cdot n^{\epsilon} = \ell(n) $$

bits of leakage. Thus, $\tilde{A}$ breaks (ℓ, s)-leakage resilience of R_L with probability 1, and consequently, $M^{\tilde{A}}$ breaks $(\mathcal{C}, t)$ with advantage $\frac{1}{p(n)}$ on input 1^n for infinitely many $n \in N$ for some polynomial $p(\cdot)$. It follows that the same holds with respect to $\tilde{M}^A = M^{\tilde{A}}$, and thus $\tilde{M}$ is a black-box reduction for basing worst-case witness hiding of (P, V) w.r.t. R_L on $(\mathcal{C}, t)$. Additionally, since with overwhelming probability, M only queries its oracle on instances x that have unique witnesses, the same holds for $\tilde{M}$.

5.3   Unprovability of Leakage-Resilient Bounded-Witness Relations

We proceed to prove Theorem 4 in its full generality. Recall that we will do this by arguing that it is essentially without loss of generality to consider reductions that with overwhelming probability only query its oracle on instances with unique witnesses. To do this, we will rely on 2-universal hash functions.

Definition 9 (2-Universal Hash Functions [9]). *A family of hash functions* $\mathcal{H} = \{h : S \to T\}$ *is* 2-universal *if for every* $x_1 \neq x_2 \in S$, *it holds that*

$$ \Pr[h(x_1) = h(x_2)] \leq \frac{1}{|T|} $$

where the probability is over $h \leftarrow \mathcal{H}$.

Recall that for every prime p and every $N \in \mathbb{N}$, $\mathcal{H} = \{h_{a,b}(x) = (ax + b \mod p) \mod N\}_{a,b \in \mathbb{Z}_p}$ is a family of 2-universal hash functions [9]. Thus for every $m \geq n \in \mathbb{N}$, by picking a prime p between 2^n and 2^{n+1}, letting $N = 2^n$, and using truncation, we have that exists a family of 2-universal hash functions over $\mathcal{H} = \{h_i = \{0,1\}^m \to \{0,1\}^n\}$ where each h_i can be computed using a polynomial-size circuit. Furthermore, by Chebychev's theorem on the concentration of primes, we can also efficiently sample such functions in expected polynomial time, or in strict polynomial-time with overwhelming probability.

  The following simple lemma shows how we can use a 2-universal hash function to turn a subexponentially-bounded witness relation into an "almost" unique witness relation. Given a witness relation R_L, let $R_{L'}$ be the set of pairs $((x, h, z), y)$ such that $y \in R_L(x)$ and $h(y) = z$.

Lemma 2. *Let R_L be a $2^{n^{\epsilon}}$-witness relation; let $p(n)$ be a polynomial upper-bound on the length of a witness for statements of length n, $T_n = \{0,1\}^{3n^{\epsilon}}$ and $\mathcal{H}_n = \{h : \{0,1\}^{p(n)} \rightarrow T_n\}$ be a family of 2-universal hash functions. Then, for every n, every $x \in \{0,1\}^n$, with probability $1 - 2^{-n^{\epsilon}}$ over $h \leftarrow \mathcal{H}_n$, it holds that for every $z \in T_n$, there exists at most one y such that $((x,h,z),y) \in R_{L'}$.*

Proof. Consider some $x \in \{0,1\}^n$. By definition, there exists at most $2^{n^{\epsilon}}$ witnesses y such that $(x,y) \in R_L$; let S_x be the set of these witnesses. By the 2-universal property of the hash function, for every two $y_1 \neq y_2 \in S_x$,

$$\Pr\left[h(y_1) = h(y_2)\right] \leq \frac{1}{|T_n|} = \frac{1}{2^{3n^{\epsilon}}}$$

where the probability is over the choice of h. By a union bound over $y_1, y_2 \in S_x$, it follows that the probability (over h) that there exists $y_1 \neq y_2 \in S$ such that $h(y_1) = h(y_2)$ is bounded by

$$\frac{2^{2n^{\epsilon}}}{2^{3n^{\epsilon}}} = 2^{-n^{\epsilon}}.$$

We now use this lemma to show how to turn any reduction for basing leakage resilience of a witness relation with subexponentially bounded number of witnesses on some assumption $(\mathcal{C}, t)$ into a reduction $\tilde{M}$ for basing leakage resilience of $R_{L'}$ on $(\mathcal{C}, t)$ such that, with overwhelming probability, $\tilde{M}$ only queries its oracle on instances that have a unique witness.

Lemma 3. *Let $\epsilon > 0$, let $s(\cdot), r(\cdot)$ be polynomials, let R_L be a $(2^{n^{\epsilon}})$-witness relation, let $(\mathcal{C}, t)$ be an $r(\cdot)$-round assumption and let $\ell(n) \geq n^{\epsilon}$ be a polynomial. There exist some polynomial $s'(\cdot)$ such that, if there exists a fixed-parameter black-box reduction M for basing $(4\ell(\cdot), s'(\cdot)+s(\cdot))$-leakage resilience of R_L on the hardness of $(\mathcal{C}, t)$, then there exists a witness relation $R_{L'}$ and a fixed-parameter black-box reduction $\tilde{M}$ for basing $(\ell(\cdot), s(\cdot))$-leakage resilience of $R_{L'}$ on the hardness of $(\mathcal{C}, t)$. Furthermore, with overwhelming probability $\tilde{M}$ only queries its oracle on instances with unique witnesses.*

Proof. Consider $R_L, (\mathcal{C}, t), M, r(\cdot), \ell, s, \epsilon$ be as in statement of the lemma. Let $s'(n)$ be a polynomial bounding the circuit size of every $h \in \mathcal{H}_n$. Consider the relation $R_{L'}$ defined above, and consider a black-box reduction $\tilde{M}$ that internally emulates M but for every interaction with the oracle that M initiates on input an (new) instance x, $\tilde{M}$ first samples a $h \leftarrow \mathcal{H}_n$ and returns h as a "leakage query" to M. Recall that sampling $h \leftarrow \mathcal{H}_n$ requires sampling a random poly(n)-bit prime, which can be done with overwhelming probability in strict polynomial time. If the sampling fails, M simply lets h be a dummy circuit that outputs 0. Upon receiving an answer z, $\tilde{M}$ next queries the outside oracle on the instance (x, h, z) and subsequently forwards messages back and forth between the oracle and M for that interaction.

Consider some attacker A that breaks (ℓ, s)-leakage resilience of $R_{L'}$ with probability 1. Let $g(n)$ be a polynomial that bounds the amount of randomness used to sample h (as done by $\tilde{M}$). Given some function $f : \{0,1\}^n \rightarrow \{0,1\}^{g(n)}$

(later we will instantiate f with a truly random function), let $\tilde{A}_f$ be a "wrapped" version of A that on input x picks a hash function $h \in \mathcal{H}_n$ using randomness $f(x)$ (in the same way as $\tilde{M}$ does), and next responds with h; upon receiving z as a response, it feeds the statement (x, h, z) to A and subsequently simply forwards all external messages back and forth to A. Note that since A breaks (ℓ, s)-leakage resilience of $R_{L'}$ with probability 1, $\tilde{A}$ breaks $(\ell(n) + 3n^\epsilon \leq 4\ell(n), s'(n) + s(n))$-leakage resilience of R_L with probability 1. Thus, for *every* function f, $M^{\tilde{A}_f}$ breaks $(\mathcal{C}, t)$ with advantage $\frac{1}{p(n)}$ on input 1^n for infinitely many $n \in N$ for some polynomial $p(\cdot)$; it follows that the same holds with respect to $\tilde{M}^A = M^{\tilde{A}_{RO}}$ where RO is a randomly chosen function over $\{0,1\}^n \to \{0,1\}^{g(n)}$. Additionally, note that by Lemma 2, we have that if the sampling of h succeeds, $\tilde{M}^A$ only queries A on instances x that have unique witnesses, except with probability 2^{-n^ϵ}. Finally, recall that the sampling of h succeeds with overwhelming probability, thus by a union bound we have that with overwhelming probability, $\tilde{M}$ only queries A on instances with unique witnesses.

Concluding the Proof of Theorem 4. Let R_L be a (2^{n^ϵ})-witness relation for some constant $\epsilon > 0$ and let $(\mathcal{C}, t)$ be a $r(\cdot)$-round assumption where $r(\cdot)$ is a polynomial. Let c, s be, respectively, the constant and polynomial guaranteed to exist due to Lemma 1, and let $\ell(n) = c \cdot r(n) \cdot n^\epsilon$. By Lemma 3, there exists some polynomial s' such that the existence of a fixed-parameter black-box reduction M for basing $(4\ell, s + s')$-leakage resilience of R_L on the hardness of $(\mathcal{C}, t)$ implies the existence of some witness relation $R_{L'}$ and a fixed-parameter black-box reduction $\tilde{M}$ for basing (ℓ, s)-leakage resilience of R_L on the hardness of $(\mathcal{C}, t)$, such that with overwhelming probability M only queries its oracle on instances with unique witnesses. By Lemma 1, this implies the existence of a polynomial $p(\cdot)$ and an efficient algorithm B such that $B(1^n)$ breaks $(\mathcal{C}, t)$ with advantage $\frac{1}{p(n)}$ on input 1^n for infinitely many $n \in N$.

Acknowledgments. We are very grateful to the SCN anonymous reviewers for their helpful comments.

References

1. Aggarwal, D., Maurer, U.: The leakage-resilience limit of a computational problem is equal to its unpredictability entropy. In: Lee, D.H., Wang, X. (eds.) ASIACRYPT 2011. LNCS, vol. 7073, pp. 686–701. Springer, Heidelberg (2011). https://doi.org/10.1007/978-3-642-25385-0_37
2. Akavia, A., Goldwasser, S., Vaikuntanathan, V.: Simultaneous hardcore bits and cryptography against memory attacks. In: Reingold, O. (ed.) TCC 2009. LNCS, vol. 5444, pp. 474–495. Springer, Heidelberg (2009). https://doi.org/10.1007/978-3-642-00457-5_28
3. Alwen, J., Dodis, Y., Wichs, D.: Survey: leakage resilience and the bounded retrieval model. In: Kurosawa, K. (ed.) ICITS 2009. LNCS, vol. 5973, pp. 1–18. Springer, Heidelberg (2010). https://doi.org/10.1007/978-3-642-14496-7_1

4. Babai, L., Fortnow, L., Levin, L.A., Szegedy, M.: Checking computations in poly-logarithmic time. In: Proceedings of the 23rd Annual ACM Symposium on Theory of Computing, New Orleans, Louisiana, USA, May 5–8, 1991, pp. 21–31. ACM (1991)
5. Barak, B., Goldreich, O., Goldwasser, S., Lindell, Y.: Resettably-sound zero-knowledge and its applications. In: FOCS 2002, pp. 116–125 (2001)
6. Barak, B., Haitner, I., Hofheinz, D., Ishai, Y.: Bounded key-dependent message security. In: Gilbert, H. (ed.) EUROCRYPT 2010. LNCS, vol. 6110, pp. 423–444. Springer, Heidelberg (2010). https://doi.org/10.1007/978-3-642-13190-5_22
7. Boneh, D., Venkatesan, R.: Breaking RSA may not be equivalent to factoring. In: Nyberg, K. (ed.) EUROCRYPT 1998. LNCS, vol. 1403, pp. 59–71. Springer, Heidelberg (1998). https://doi.org/10.1007/BFb0054117
8. Brassard, G., Chaum, D., Crépeau, C.: Minimum disclosure proofs of knowledge. J. Comput. Syst. Sci. **37**(2), 156–189 (1988)
9. Carter, L., Wegman, M.N.: Universal classes of hash functions. J. Comput. Syst. Sci. **18**(2), 143–154 (1979)
10. Cramer, R., Damgård, I., Schoenmakers, B.: Proofs of partial knowledge and simplified design of witness hiding protocols. In: Desmedt, Y.G. (ed.) CRYPTO 1994. LNCS, vol. 839, pp. 174–187. Springer, Heidelberg (1994). https://doi.org/10.1007/3-540-48658-5_19
11. Dodis, Y., Oliveira, R., Pietrzak, K.: On the generic insecurity of the full domain hash. In: Shoup, V. (ed.) CRYPTO 2005. LNCS, vol. 3621, pp. 449–466. Springer, Heidelberg (2005). https://doi.org/10.1007/11535218_27
12. Dziembowski, S., Pietrzak, K.: Leakage-resilient cryptography. In: 49th Annual IEEE Symposium on Foundations of Computer Science, FOCS 2008, Philadelphia, PA, USA, October 25–28, 2008, pp. 293–302 (2008)
13. Feige, U., Fiat, A., Shamir, A.: Zero knowledge proofs of identity. In: STOC, pp. 210–217 (1987)
14. Feige, U., Goldwasser, S., Lovász, L., Safra, S., Szegedy, M.: Interactive proofs and the hardness of approximating cliques. J. ACM **43**(2), 268–292 (1996)
15. Goldreich, O.: Foundations of Cryptography – Basic Tools. Cambridge University Press (2001)
16. Goldreich, O., Krawczyk, H.: On the composition of zero-knowledge proof systems. SIAM J. Comput. **25**(1), 169–192 (1996)
17. Goldreich, O., Micali, S., Wigderson, A.: How to play any mental game. In: STOC 1987: Proceedings of the Nineteenth Annual ACM Symposium on Theory of Computing, pp. 218–229. ACM, New York (1987)
18. Goldwasser, S., Micali, S., Rackoff, C.: The knowledge complexity of interactive proof systems. SIAM J. Comput. **18**(1), 186–208 (1989)
19. Haitner, I., Holenstein, T.: On the (im)possibility of key dependent encryption. In: Reingold, O. (ed.) TCC 2009. LNCS, vol. 5444, pp. 202–219. Springer, Heidelberg (2009). https://doi.org/10.1007/978-3-642-00457-5_13
20. Halevi, S., Myers, S., Rackoff, C.: On seed-incompressible functions. In: Canetti, R. (ed.) TCC 2008. LNCS, vol. 4948, pp. 19–36. Springer, Heidelberg (2008). https://doi.org/10.1007/978-3-540-78524-8_2
21. Ishai, Y., Sahai, A., Wagner, D.: Private circuits: securing hardware against probing attacks. In: Boneh, D. (ed.) CRYPTO 2003. LNCS, vol. 2729, pp. 463–481. Springer, Heidelberg (2003). https://doi.org/10.1007/978-3-540-45146-4_27
22. Katz, J., Vaikuntanathan, V.: Signature schemes with bounded leakage resilience. In: Matsui, M. (ed.) ASIACRYPT 2009. LNCS, vol. 5912, pp. 703–720. Springer, Heidelberg (2009). https://doi.org/10.1007/978-3-642-10366-7_41

23. Kilian, J.: A note on efficient zero-knowledge proofs and arguments (extended abstract). In: STOC 2002, pp. 723–732 (1992)
24. Komargodski, I.: Leakage resilient one-way functions: the auxiliary-input setting. Theor. Comput. Sci. **746**, 6–18 (2018)
25. Marcedone, A., Pass, R., Shelat, A.: Bounded KDM security from iO and OWF. In: Zikas, V., De Prisco, R. (eds.) SCN 2016. LNCS, vol. 9841, pp. 571–586. Springer, Cham (2016). https://doi.org/10.1007/978-3-319-44618-9_30
26. Maurer, U.M.: Factoring with an oracle. In: Rueppel, R.A. (ed.) EUROCRYPT 1992. LNCS, vol. 658, pp. 429–436. Springer, Heidelberg (1993). https://doi.org/10.1007/3-540-47555-9_35
27. Micali, S., Reyzin, L.: Physically observable cryptography. In: Naor, M. (ed.) TCC 2004. LNCS, vol. 2951, pp. 278–296. Springer, Heidelberg (2004). https://doi.org/10.1007/978-3-540-24638-1_16
28. Naor, M.: On cryptographic assumptions and challenges. In: Boneh, D. (ed.) CRYPTO 2003. LNCS, vol. 2729, pp. 96–109. Springer, Heidelberg (2003). https://doi.org/10.1007/978-3-540-45146-4_6
29. Nielsen, J.B., Venturi, D., Zottarel, A.: On the connection between leakage tolerance and adaptive security. IACR Cryptology ePrint Archive, 2014:517 (2014)
30. Ostrovsky, R., Persiano, G., Visconti, I.: Impossibility of black-box simulation against leakage attacks. In: Gennaro, R., Robshaw, M. (eds.) CRYPTO 2015. LNCS, vol. 9216, pp. 130–149. Springer, Heidelberg (2015). https://doi.org/10.1007/978-3-662-48000-7_7
31. Pass, R.: Limits of provable security from standard assumptions. In: STOC, pp. 109–118 (2011)
32. Rompel, J.: One-way functions are necessary and sufficient for secure signatures. In: STOC 1990, pp. 387–394 (1990)
33. Rothblum, G.N., Vadhan, S.P.: Are PCPS inherent in efficient arguments? Comput. Complex. **19**(2), 265–304 (2010)
34. Wichs, D.: Barriers in cryptography with weak, correlated and leaky sources. In: Innovations in Theoretical Computer Science, ITCS 2013, Berkeley, CA, USA, January 9–12, 2013, pp. 111–126 (2013)
35. Yao, A.C.-C.: How to generate and exchange secrets. In: Proceedings of the 27th Annual Symposium on Foundations of Computer Science (FOCS), pp. 162–167. IEEE Computer Society (1986)

Zero-Knowledge

Key-and-Argument-Updatable QA-NIZKs

Helger Lipmaa[1,2]([✉]) [iD]

[1] Simula UiB, Bergen, Norway
helger.lipmaa@gmail.com
[2] University of Tartu, Tartu, Estonia

Abstract. There are several new efficient approaches to decreasing trust in the CRS creators for NIZK proofs in the CRS model. Recently, Groth *et al.* (CRYPTO 2018) defined the notion of NIZK with updatable CRS (*updatable NIZK*) and described an updatable SNARK. We consider the same problem in the case of QA-NIZKs. We also define an important new property: we require that after updating the CRS, one should be able to update a previously generated argument to a new argument that is valid with the new CRS. We propose a general definitional framework for *key-and-argument-updatable QA-NIZKs*. After that, we describe a key-and-argument-updatable version of the most efficient known QA-NIZK for linear subspaces by Kiltz and Wee. Importantly, for obtaining soundness, it suffices to update a universal public key that just consists of a matrix drawn from a KerMDH-hard distribution and thus can be shared by *any pairing-based application that relies on the same hardness assumption*. After specializing the universal public key to the concrete language parameter, one can use the proposed key-and-argument updating algorithms to continue updating to strengthen the soundness guarantee.

Keywords: BPK model · CRS model · QA-NIZK · Subversion security · Updatable public key · Updatable argument

1 Introduction

SNARKs. Zero-knowledge succinct non-interactive arguments of knowledge (zk-SNARKs [15,19,24,25,27,35,36,43]) have become widely researched and deployed, in particular because of their applicability in verifiable computation and anonymous cryptocurrencies. However, due to a well-known impossibility result [20], the soundness of SNARKs can only be based on non-falsifiable assumptions [42]. Moreover, a new security concern has arisen recently.

Most of the existing pairing-based zk-SNARKs are defined in the common reference string (CRS) model assuming the existence of a trusted third party TTP that samples a CRS from the correct distribution and does not leak any trapdoors. The existence of such a TTP is often a too strong assumption. Recently, several efficient approaches have been proposed to decrease trust in the CRS creation, like the use of multi-party CRS generation [2,7,9,10] and the notion of subversion-resistant zero-knowledge (Sub-ZK) SNARKs [3,6,17]. A Sub-ZK

© Springer Nature Switzerland AG 2020
C. Galdi and V. Kolesnikov (Eds.): SCN 2020, LNCS 12238, pp. 645–669, 2020.
https://doi.org/10.1007/978-3-030-57990-6_32

SNARK guarantees to the prover P the zero-knowledge property even if the CRS was maliciously created, as long as P checks that a public algorithm V_{crs} accepts the CRS. Existing Sub-ZK SNARKs use a non-falsifiable assumption to extract from a V_{crs}-accepted CRS its trapdoor td. Then, one simulates CRS by using td. Since one cannot at the same time achieve subversion-soundness and Sub-ZK [6], Sub-ZK SNARKs only achieve the usual (knowledge-)soundness property.

Groth *et al.* [26] defined CRS updating and showed how to implement it in the case of SNARKs. The main idea behind it is that given a CRS based on some trapdoor td, one can update the CRS to a new CRS crs' based on some trapdoor td'. Updating can be repeated many times, obtaining a sequence

$$crs_0 \to crs_1 \to crs_2 \to \ldots \to crs_n$$

of CRSs, updated by some parties $\mathcal{P}_1, \ldots, \mathcal{P}_n$. The SNARK will be sound (and the CRS will be correctly distributed) if at least one of the CRS updaters was honest; this allows one to get soundness (if at least one updater was honest) and zero-knowledge (without any assumption on the updaters). At some moment, the prover will create an argument. The verifier only accepts when she trusts some updater *at the moment of argument creation*. Groth *et al.* [26] constructed an updatable SNARK with a quadratically-long universal CRS (valid for all circuits of the given size) and linearly-long specialized CRS (constructed from the universal CRS when a circuit is fixed and actually used to create an argument). The subject of updatable SNARKs has become very popular, with many new schemes proposed within two years [5,12,14,18,39].

As a drawback, since the argument itself is not updatable, the CRS updates after an argument has been created cannot be taken to account; in particular, it means that the verifier has to signal to the prover that she is ready to trust the argument created at some moment (since the CRS at that moment has been updated by a verifier-trusted party).

QA-NIZKs. Starting from the seminal work of Jutla and Roy [28], QA-NIZKs has been a (quite different) alternative research direction as compared to SNARKs with quite different applications and quite different underlying techniques. Intuitively, in QA-NIZKs, the prover and the verifier have access to an honestly generated language parameter lpar, and then prove a statement with respect to a lpar-dependent language $\mathcal{L}_{lpar}$. Like SNARKs, QA-NIZKs offer succinct arguments and super-efficient verification. On the positive side, contemporary QA-NIZKs are based on very standard assumptions like MDDH [16] (e.g., DDH) and KerMDH [41] (e.g., CDH). On the negative side, efficient and succinct QA-NIZKs are known only for a much smaller class of languages like the language of linear subspaces [1,28–30,32,33] and some related languages, including the language of quadratic relations [22] and shuffles [23]. [13] proposed a non-succinct QA-NIZK for SSP; non-succinctness is expected due to known impossibility results [20]. QA-NIZKs have applications in the construction of efficient cryptographic primitives (like KDM-CCA2-secure encryption,

IND-CCA2-secure IBE, and UC-secure commitments and linearly homomorphic structure-preserving signatures) based on standard assumptions.

Abdolmaleki et al. [4] recently studied subversion-resistant QA-NIZKs. They showed that Sub-ZK in the CRS model is equal to the known notion of no-auxiliary-string non-black-box zero knowledge in the significantly weaker Bare Public Key (BPK) model. Like [4], we will thus use the notions of "Sub-ZK" and "no-auxiliary-string non-black-box zero knowledge" interchangeably, but we will usually explicitly mention the trust model (CRS, BPK, plain). Due to known impossibility results, this provides a simple proof that one has to use no-auxiliary-string non-black-box NIZK to construct argument systems for non-trivial languages in the BPK model. Abdolmaleki et al. [4] also proposed an efficient V_{crs} algorithm for the most efficient known QA-NIZK Π'_{as} for linear subspaces by Kiltz and Wee [30] and proved that the resulting construction achieves Sub-ZK in the BPK model. In fact, they went one step further: they considered the case when the language parameter lpar itself is subverted and showed how to achieve soundness and Sub-ZK even in this case. More precisely, they defined separate Sub-ZK (black-box Sub-ZK, given an honestly generated lpar) and persistent Sub-ZK (non-black-box Sub-ZK, given a subverted lpar) properties, and showed that these two properties are in fact incomparable.[1]

The proof methods of [4] are quite non-trivial. In particular, [4] proved the Sub-ZK property under a new tautological KW-KE knowledge assumption, and then showed that KW-KE is secure in the subversion generic bilinear group model of [3,6] (named GBGM with hashing in [6]). Especially the latter proof is quite complicated. Moreover, they proved so-called Sub-PAR soundness (soundness in the case lpar is subverted, but the CRS is untrusted) under natural but little-studied, non-falsifiable, interactive non-adaptive assumptions [21,34].

As in the case of SNARKs, it is natural to ask if efficient QA-NIZKs like Π'_{as} can be updated. No published research has been done on this topic.

Our Contributions. We define updatable QA-NIZK by roughly following the definitional guidelines of [26] for updatable SNARKs. However, we make two significant changes to the model itself. The second change (the ability to update also the argument) is especially important, allowing for new applications. No succinct argument-updatable NIZKs, either SNARKs or QA-NIZKs, were known before. Crucially, for updating Π'_{as}, it is sufficient to update a single public key $\text{PK} = [\bar{A}]_2$, where $[A]_2$ is a KerMDH-hard matrix, and $[\bar{A}]_2$ denotes its upmost square submatrix. This means that one can share the same updatable universal public key PK between any applications where the security of one party relies on the (bare) public key, created by another party.

Firstly, since QA-NIZK security definitions differ from SNARKs (with lpar having an important and distinct role), we redefine updatable versions of com-

---

[1] To show incomparability, [4] constructed a contrived persistent Sub-ZK argument where the simulator first uses a knowledge assumption on the language parameter to extract witness, and then uses this witness as input to the honest prover. Such an argument is obviously not black-box Sub-ZK.

pleteness, soundness, and (persistent) zero-knowledge. We add to them the natural requirement of hiding (an updated key and a fresh key are indistinguishable). We will follow the framework of [4] by relying on Sub-ZK QA-NIZK in the BPK model. According to [4], the prover and the verifier of a QA-NIZK argument share a (possibly malformed) generated language parameter lpar together with a (possibly malformed) verifier's public key PK. We add the key-updating and update-verification algorithms with the corresponding security requirements: key-update completeness, key-update hiding, strong key-update hiding, key-update soundness, and key-update (persistent) Sub-ZK.

Secondly, and more importantly, we add to the QA-NIZK the ability to update the argument. That is, given a PK and an argument π constructed while using PK, one can then update PK (to a new key PK') and π to a new valid argument π' (corresponding to PK'). There are two different ways to update the argument. First, the honest argument updater must know the witness (but no secret information about the key update). Second, the argument-update simulator must know some secret key-update trapdoor (but he does not have to know the witness). We require that these two different ways of updating are indistinguishable; thus, updating does not leak information about the witness.

Argument-updating has various non-obvious implications. The key-updater can, knowing the key-update trapdoor, simulate the argument-update; this means that we will not get soundness unless at least one of the argument-creators or argument-updaters does not collaborate with the corresponding key-creator or key-updater. (See Sect. 4.) One can obtain different trust models by handling the updating process differently. For example, the honest argument-updater can have additional anonymity since it is not revealed which of the argument-updaters knows the witness. On the other hand, if there exists at least one update such that the corresponding key-updater and argument-updater do not trust each other, we are guaranteed that one of the argument-updater actually "knows" the witness and thus the statement is true.

We will give rigorous security definitions for *key-and-argument-updatable* QA-NIZKs, requiring them to satisfy argument-update completeness, argument-update hiding, strong argument-update hiding, argument-update soundness, and argument-update (persistent) Sub-ZK. We use the terminology of convolution semigroups while arguing about the hiding properties; since this terminology is very natural, we argue that one should use it more widely in the context of updatable cryptographic protocols. We prove that argument-update soundness and argument-update (persistent) Sub-ZK follow from simpler security requirements and thus do not have to be proven anew in the case of each new QA-NIZK.

We implement the provided security definitions, by proposing an updatable version $\Pi_{\mathsf{bpk}}^{\mathsf{upd}}$ of the Kiltz-Wee QA-NIZK Π'_{as} for linear subspace [30]. Our construction uses crucially the fact that all operations (like the public key generation and proving) in Π'_{as} consist of only linear operations. Hence, the new update-related algorithms are relatively simple but still non-trivial. For example, we update some elements of the public key additively and some elements multiplicatively.[2] This is a major difference to (known to us) SNARKs, where one only does multiplicative updating. Interestingly, we update the argument π by adding to it an (honestly created or simulated) argument when using the appropriately defined "difference" $\widehat{\text{PK}}$ of the new and the old public key as a one-time public key. This is why we can update arguments without the knowledge of either the witness or the trapdoor of either PK or PK'; instead, it suffices to use the trapdoor corresponding to the concrete update.

We prove that $\Pi_{\mathsf{bpk}}^{\mathsf{upd}}$ satisfies all defined security properties, and in particular, that (like the non-updatable Sub-ZK QA-NIZK of [4]) it is Sub-PAR sound either under the KerMDH^{dl} assumption [4,41] or the SKerMDH^{dl} assumption [4,22] (depending on the values of the system parameters) and argument-update persistent Sub-ZK under the KW-KE assumption of [4]. If the language parameter is trusted, then as in [4], a falsifiable assumption (either KerMDH or SKerMDH) suffices for soundness. As in [4], one can even obtain Sub-PAR knowledge-soundness.

The hiding properties rely on certain, well-defined, properties of the distributions of the secret key K and $\bar{A}$: namely, these distributions are assumed to be (essentially) stable [31]. We hope that this observation motivates study of other stable distributions for cryptographic purposes. In particular, stable distributions seem to be natural in the setting of various updatable primitives.

Updatable Universal Public Key. The goal of updatability [26] is to protect soundness in the case PK may be subverted since Sub-ZK can be obtained by running the public algorithm V_{pk} [3]. In Π'_{as}, soundness is guaranteed by one of the elements of PK (namely, $[\bar{A}]_2$, see Fig. 2) coming from a KerMDH-hard distribution, and another element $[C]_2$ being correctly computed from $[\bar{A}]_2$. Since the latter can be verified by the public-key verification algorithm, it suffices only to update $[\bar{A}]_2$. Then, $[\bar{A}]_2$ will be a "universal public key" [26] for all possible language parameters in all applications that rely on the concrete (i.e., using the same distribution) KerMDH *assumption*.

The possibility to rely just on $[\bar{A}]_2$ is a major difference with known updatable SNARKs where the universal key is quite complex, and each universal key of length $\Theta(n)$ can only be used for circuits of size $\leq n$.

Importantly, one is not restricted to QA-NIZK: *any* application that relies on KerMDH and where it suffices to know $[\bar{A}]_2$ (instead of $[A]_2$) can use the same matrix $[\bar{A}]_2$. A standard example is the 1-Lin [8,16] distribution $\mathcal{L}_1 = \{A = \binom{a}{1} : a \leftarrow_{\$} \mathbb{Z}_p\}$. We emphasize that the possibility to rely just on $[\bar{A}]_2$ is a major difference with updatable SNARKs [26,39] where the universal key is quite complex and each universal key of length $\Omega(n)$ can only be used for circuits of size $\leq n$. See Sect. 7.

Some of the proofs are given in the full version [37].

---

[2] Groth *et al.* [26] proved that in the case of multiplicative updating, each element of PK must be a monomial in secret trapdoors. Since we update various elements of PK either multiplicatively or additively, it is unclear whether this impossibility result holds. We leave this as an interesting open question.

2 Preliminaries

We denote the empty string by ϵ. Let PPT denote probabilistic polynomial-time and let $\lambda \in \mathbb{N}$ be the security parameter. All adversaries will be stateful. For an algorithm $\mathcal{A}$, let range($\mathcal{A}$) be the range of $\mathcal{A}$, i.e., the set of valid outputs of $\mathcal{A}$, let $\mathsf{RND}_\lambda(\mathcal{A})$ denote the random tape of $\mathcal{A}$ (for fixed λ), and let $r \leftarrow_\$ \mathsf{RND}_\lambda(\mathcal{A})$ denote the uniformly random choice of the randomizer r from $\mathsf{RND}_\lambda(\mathcal{A})$. By $y \leftarrow \mathcal{A}(\mathsf{x}; r)$ we denote the fact that $\mathcal{A}$, given an input x and a randomizer r, outputs y. When we use this notation, then r represents the full random tape of $\mathcal{A}$. We denote by $\mathsf{negl}(\lambda)$ an arbitrary negligible function, and by $\mathsf{poly}(\lambda)$ an arbitrary polynomial function. We write $a \approx_\lambda b$ if $|a - b| = \mathsf{negl}(\lambda)$.

Probability Theory. Let μ and ν be probability measures on $(\mathbb{Z}, 2^{\mathbb{Z}})$. The *convolution* [31, Def. 14.46] $\mu * \nu$ is defined as the probability measure on $(\mathbb{Z}, 2^{\mathbb{Z}})$ such that $(\mu * \nu)(\{n\}) = \sum_{m=-\infty}^{\infty} \mu(\{m\})\nu(\{n - m\})$. We define the nth *convolution power* recursively by $\mu^{*1} = \mu$ and $\mu^{*(n+1)} = \mu^{*n} * \mu$. Let $I \subset [0, \infty)$ be a semigroup. A family $\nu = (\nu_t : t \in I)$ of probability distributions on $\mathbb{R}^d$ is called a *convolution semigroup* [31, Def. 14.46] if $\nu_{s+t} = \nu_s * \nu_t$ holds for all $s, t \in I$. Let $X_1, X_2, \ldots$ be i.i.d random variables with distribution μ. The distribution μ is called *stable* [31, Def. 16.20] with index $\alpha \in (0, 2]$ if $X_1 + \ldots + X_n = n^{1/\alpha} X_n$ for all $n \in \mathbb{N}$.

Bilinear Pairings. A bilinear group generator $\mathsf{Pgen}(1^\lambda)$ returns $(p, \mathbb{G}_1, \mathbb{G}_2, \mathbb{G}_T, \hat{e})$, where $\mathbb{G}_1, \mathbb{G}_2, \mathbb{G}_T$ are three additive cyclic groups of prime order p, and $\hat{e} : \mathbb{G}_1 \times \mathbb{G}_2 \to \mathbb{G}_T$ is a non-degenerate efficiently computable bilinear pairing. We require the bilinear pairing to be Type-3, i.e., we assume that there is no efficient isomorphism between $\mathbb{G}_1$ and $\mathbb{G}_2$. We use the bracket notation of [16], e.g., we write $[a]_\iota$ to denote ag_ι where $a \in \mathbb{Z}_p$ and g_ι is a fixed generator of $\mathbb{G}_\iota$. We denote $\hat{e}([a]_1, [b]_2)$ as $[a]_1 \cdot [b]_2$. We use the bracket notation freely together with matrix notation, e.g., $\boldsymbol{AB} = \boldsymbol{C}$ iff $[\boldsymbol{A}]_1 \cdot [\boldsymbol{B}]_2 = [\boldsymbol{C}]_T$.

Matrix Diffie-Hellman Assumptions. Kernel Matrix Diffie-Hellman Assumption (KerMDH) is a well-known assumption family formally introduced in [41] and say, used in [30] to show the soundness of their QA-NIZK argument system for linear subspaces. The KerMDH assumption states that for a matrix $\boldsymbol{A}$ from some well-defined distribution, it is difficult to find a representation of a vector that belongs to the kernel of $\boldsymbol{A}^\top$ provided that the matrix is given in exponents only, i.e., as $[\boldsymbol{A}]_\iota$.

For fixed p, denote by $\mathcal{D}_{\ell k}$ a probability distribution over matrices in $\mathbb{Z}_p^{\ell \times k}$, where $\ell > k$. We assume that $\mathcal{D}_{\ell k}$ outputs matrices $\boldsymbol{A}$ where the upper $k \times k$ submatrix $\bar{\boldsymbol{A}}$ is always invertible. Let $\bar{\mathcal{D}}_{\ell k}$ that outputs $\bar{\boldsymbol{A}}$, where $\boldsymbol{A}$ is sampled from $\mathcal{D}_{\ell k}$. When $\ell = k+1$, we denote $\mathcal{D}_k = \mathcal{D}_{\ell k}$. In the full version [37], we define five commonly used distributions. There, we also define assumptions, needed by the constructions in [4,30], and thus, also by the current paper.

Bare Public Key (BPK) Model. In the BPK model [11,40], parties have access to a public file F, a polynomial-size collection of records (id, PK_{id}), where id is a string identifying a party (e.g., a verifier), and PK_{id} is her (alleged) public key. In a typical zero-knowledge protocol in the BPK model, a key-owning party $\mathcal{P}_{id}$ works in two stages. In stage one (the *key-generation stage*), on input a security parameter 1^λ and randomizer r, $\mathcal{P}_{id}$ outputs a public key PK_{id} and stores the corresponding secret key SK_{id}. We assume the *no-auxiliary-string BPK* model where from this it follows that $\mathcal{P}_{id}$ actually created PK_{id}. After that, F will include (id, PK_{id}). In stage two, each party has access to F, while $\mathcal{P}_{id}$ has possible access to SK_{id} (however, the latter will be not required by us). It is commonly assumed that only the verifier of a NIZK argument system in the BPK model has a public key [40].

No-Auxiliary-String Non-Black-Box (Sub-ZK) QA-NIZK in the BPK Model. The original QA-NIZK security definitions, [28], were given in the CRS model. The following description of QA-NIZKs in the BPK model is taken from [4], and we refer to [4] for additional discussion. Since black-box and even auxiliary-input non-black-box NIZK in the BPK model is impossible for non-trivial languages, we will give an explicit definition of no-auxiliary-string non-black-box NIZK. As explained in [4], no-auxiliary-string non-black-box zero knowledge in the BPK model is the same as Sub-ZK [6] in the CRS model.

As in [6], we assume that the system parameters p are generated deterministically from λ; in particular, the choice of p could not be subverted. A QA-NIZK argument system enables one to prove membership in a language defined by a relation $\mathbf{R}_{\mathsf{lpar}} = \{(\mathsf{x}, \mathsf{w})\}$, which in turn is completely determined by a parameter lpar sampled (in the honest case) from a distribution $\mathcal{D}_{\mathsf{p}}$. We will assume implicitly that lpar contains p and thus not include p as an argument to algorithms that also input lpar; recall that we assumed that p cannot be subverted. A distribution $\mathcal{D}_{\mathsf{p}}$ on $\mathcal{L}_{\mathsf{lpar}}$ is *witness-sampleable* [28] if there exists a PPT algorithm $\mathcal{D}'_{\mathsf{p}}$ that samples $(\mathsf{lpar}, \mathsf{td}_{\mathsf{lpar}}) \in \mathbf{R}_{\mathsf{p}}$ such that lpar is distributed according to $\mathcal{D}_{\mathsf{p}}$.

The zero-knowledge simulator is usually required to be a single (non-black-box) PPT algorithm that works for the whole collection of relations $\mathbf{R}_{\mathsf{p}} = \{\mathbf{R}_{\mathsf{lpar}}\}_{\mathsf{lpar}\in\mathrm{im}(\mathcal{D}_{\mathsf{p}})}$; i.e., one requires *uniform simulation* (see [28] for a discussion). Following [3], we accompany the universal simulator with an adversary-dependent extractor. We assume Sim also works in the case when one cannot efficiently establish whether $\mathsf{lpar} \in \mathrm{im}(\mathcal{D}_{\mathsf{p}})$. Sim is not allowed to create new lpar or PK but receive them as an input.

A tuple of PPT algorithms $\Pi = (\mathsf{Pgen}, \mathsf{K}_{\mathsf{bpk}}, \mathsf{V}_{\mathsf{par}}, \mathsf{V}_{\mathsf{pk}}, \mathsf{P}, \mathsf{V}, \mathsf{Sim})$ is a *no-auxiliary-string non-black-box zero knowledge (Sub-ZK) QA-NIZK argument system* in the BPK model for a set of witness-relations $\mathbf{R}_{\mathsf{p}} = \{\mathbf{R}_{\mathsf{lpar}}\}_{\mathsf{lpar}\in\mathrm{Supp}(\mathcal{D}_{\mathsf{p}})}$, if the following Items i, ii, iv and v hold. Π is a *Sub-ZK QA-NIZK argument of knowledge*, if additionally Item iii holds. Here, Pgen is the parameter generation algorithm, $\mathsf{K}_{\mathsf{bpk}}$ is the public key generation algorithm, $\mathsf{V}_{\mathsf{par}}$ is the lpar-verification algorithm, V_{pk} is the public-key verification algorithm, P is the prover, V is the verifier, and Sim is the simulator. We abbreviate quasi-adaptive to QA (Fig. 1).

$\mathrm{Exp}^{zk}_{Z,\mathcal{A}}(\mathsf{lpar})$	$O_0(\mathsf{x},\mathsf{w})$:
$r \leftarrow_\$ \mathsf{RND}_\lambda(Z);$	**if** $(\mathsf{x},\mathsf{w}) \notin \mathbf{R}_{\mathsf{lpar}}$ **then return** $\bot;$
$(\mathrm{PK}, \mathrm{aux}_Z) \leftarrow Z(\mathsf{lpar}; r);$	**else return** $\pi \leftarrow \mathsf{P}(\mathsf{lpar}, \mathrm{PK}; \mathsf{x}, \mathsf{w}); \mathbf{fi}$
$\mathrm{SK} \leftarrow \mathsf{Ext}_Z(\mathsf{lpar}; r);$	
$b \leftarrow_\$ \{0,1\};$	$O_1(\mathsf{x},\mathsf{w})$:
$b' \leftarrow \mathcal{A}^{O_b(\cdot,\cdot)}(\mathsf{lpar}; \mathrm{PK}, \mathrm{aux}_Z);$	
return $\mathsf{V}_{\mathsf{pk}}(\mathsf{lpar}; \mathrm{PK}) = 1 \wedge b' = b;$	**if** $(\mathsf{x},\mathsf{w}) \notin \mathbf{R}_{\mathsf{lpar}}$ **then return** $\bot;$
	else return $\pi_{\mathsf{Sim}} \leftarrow \mathsf{Sim}(\mathsf{lpar}, \mathrm{PK}, \mathrm{SK}; \mathsf{x}); \mathbf{fi}$

Fig. 1. Experiment $\mathrm{Exp}^{zk}_{Z,\mathcal{A}}(\mathsf{lpar})$

(i) **Perfect Completeness:** for any λ, PPT $\mathcal{A}$, given $\mathsf{p} \leftarrow \mathsf{Pgen}(1^\lambda)$, $\mathsf{lpar} \leftarrow_\$ \mathcal{D}_\mathsf{p}$, $(\mathrm{PK}, \mathrm{SK}) \leftarrow \mathsf{K}_{\mathsf{bpk}}(\mathsf{lpar})$, $(\mathsf{x},\mathsf{w}) \leftarrow \mathcal{A}(\mathrm{PK})$, $\pi \leftarrow \mathsf{P}(\mathsf{lpar}, \mathrm{PK}, \mathsf{x}, \mathsf{w})$, it holds that $\mathsf{V}_{\mathsf{par}}(\mathsf{lpar}) = 1$ and $\mathsf{V}_{\mathsf{pk}}(\mathsf{lpar}, \mathrm{PK}) = 1$ and $((\mathsf{x},\mathsf{w}) \notin \mathbf{R}_{\mathsf{lpar}} \vee \mathsf{V}(\mathsf{lpar}, \mathrm{PK}, \mathsf{x}, \pi) = 1)$.

(ii) **Computational QA Sub-PAR Soundness:** $\forall$ PPT $\mathcal{A}$, given $\mathsf{p} \leftarrow \mathsf{Pgen}(1^\lambda)$, $\mathsf{lpar} \leftarrow \mathcal{A}(\mathsf{p})$, $(\mathrm{PK}, \mathrm{SK}) \leftarrow \mathsf{K}_{\mathsf{bpk}}(\mathsf{lpar})$, and $(\mathsf{x},\pi) \leftarrow \mathcal{A}(\mathrm{PK})$, the following holds with negligible probability: $\mathsf{V}_{\mathsf{par}}(\mathsf{lpar}) = 1 \wedge \mathsf{V}(\mathsf{lpar}, \mathrm{PK}, \mathsf{x}, \pi) = 1 \wedge \neg(\exists \mathsf{w} : \mathbf{R}_{\mathsf{lpar}}(\mathsf{x}, \mathsf{w}) = 1)).$

(iii) **Computational QA Sub-PAR Knowledge-Soundness:** for any PPT $\mathcal{A}$, there exist a PPT extractor $\mathsf{Ext}_\mathcal{A}$, s.t. given $\mathsf{p} \leftarrow \mathsf{Pgen}(1^\lambda)$, $r \leftarrow_\$ \mathsf{RND}_\lambda(\mathcal{A})$, $\mathsf{lpar} \leftarrow \mathcal{A}(\mathsf{p}; r)$, $(\mathrm{PK}, \mathrm{SK}) \leftarrow \mathsf{K}_{\mathsf{bpk}}(\mathsf{lpar})$, $(\mathsf{x}, \pi) \leftarrow \mathcal{A}(\mathrm{PK}; r)$, $\mathsf{w} \leftarrow \mathsf{Ext}_\mathcal{A}(\mathsf{p}, \mathrm{PK}; r)$, the following holds with a negligible probability: $\mathsf{V}_{\mathsf{par}}(\mathsf{lpar}) = 1 \wedge \mathsf{V}(\mathsf{lpar}, \mathrm{PK}, \mathsf{x}, \pi) = 1 \wedge \mathbf{R}_{\mathsf{lpar}}(\mathsf{x}, \mathsf{w}) = 0.$

(iv) **Statistical Zero Knowledge:** for any unbounded $\mathcal{A}$, $|\varepsilon_0^{zk} - \varepsilon_1^{zk}| \approx_\lambda 0$, where ε_b^{zk} is the probability that given $\mathsf{p} \leftarrow \mathsf{Pgen}(1^\lambda)$, $\mathsf{lpar} \leftarrow \mathcal{D}_\mathsf{p}$, $(\mathrm{PK}, \mathrm{SK}) \leftarrow \mathsf{K}_{\mathsf{bpk}}(\mathsf{lpar})$, it holds that $\mathcal{A}^{O_b(\cdot,\cdot)}(\mathsf{lpar}, \mathrm{PK}) = 1$. The oracle $O_0(\mathsf{x},\mathsf{w})$ returns $\bot$ (reject) if $(\mathsf{x},\mathsf{w}) \notin \mathbf{R}_{\mathsf{lpar}}$, and otherwise it returns $\mathsf{P}(\mathsf{lpar}, \mathrm{PK}, \mathsf{x}, \mathsf{w})$. Similarly, $O_1(\mathsf{x},\mathsf{w})$ returns $\bot$ (reject) if $(\mathsf{x},\mathsf{w}) \notin \mathbf{R}_{\mathsf{lpar}}$, and otherwise it returns $\mathsf{Sim}(\mathsf{lpar}, \mathrm{PK}, \mathrm{SK}, \mathsf{x})$.

(v) **Statistical Persistent Zero Knowledge:** for any PPT subverter Z, there exists a PPT extractor Ext_Z, s.t. for any computationally unbounded adversary $\mathcal{A}$, $|\varepsilon_0^{zk} - \varepsilon_b^{zk}| \approx_\lambda 0$, where ε_b^{zk} is the probability that given $\mathsf{p} \leftarrow \mathsf{Pgen}(1^\lambda)$, $r \leftarrow_\$ \mathsf{RND}_\lambda(Z)$, $(\mathsf{lpar}, \mathrm{PK}, \mathsf{aux}) \leftarrow Z(\mathsf{p}; r)$, $\mathrm{SK} \leftarrow \mathsf{Ext}_Z(\mathsf{p}; r)$, the following holds with a negligible probability: $\mathsf{V}_{\mathsf{par}}(\mathsf{lpar}) = 1 \wedge \mathsf{V}_{\mathsf{pk}}(\mathsf{lpar}, \mathrm{PK}) = 1 \wedge \mathcal{A}^{O_b(\cdot,\cdot)}(\mathsf{lpar}, \mathrm{PK}, \mathsf{aux}) = 1$. The oracle $O_0(\mathsf{x},\mathsf{w})$ returns $\bot$ (reject) if $(\mathsf{x},\mathsf{w}) \notin \mathbf{R}_{\mathsf{lpar}}$, and otherwise it returns $\mathsf{P}(\mathsf{lpar}, \mathrm{PK}, \mathsf{x}, \mathsf{w})$. Similarly, $O_1(\mathsf{x},\mathsf{w})$ returns $\bot$ (reject) if $(\mathsf{x},\mathsf{w}) \notin \mathbf{R}_{\mathsf{lpar}}$, and otherwise it returns $\mathsf{Sim}(\mathsf{lpar}, \mathrm{PK}, \mathrm{SK}, \mathsf{x})$.

Π is *statistically no-auxiliary-string*[3] *non-black-box zero knowledge (Sub-ZK)* if it is both statistically zero-knowledge and statistically persistent zero-knowledge.

---

[3] Auxiliary-string non-black-box ZK means that definitions hold even if any aux $\in \{0,1\}^{\mathsf{poly}(\lambda)}$ is given as an additional input to $\mathcal{A}$ and Z_{PK} (and Ext_Z).

---

isinvertible($[\bar{A}]_2, \text{PK}_{\text{Vpk}}$) // $\bar{A} = (a_{ij})$

Check $\text{PK}_{\text{Vpk}} = [a_{11}^*, a_{12}^*]_1 \in \mathbb{G}_1^{1\times2} \wedge [a_{11}^*]_1 \cdot [1]_2 = [1]_1 \cdot [a_{11}]_2 \wedge$
$[a_{12}^*]_1 \cdot [1]_2 = [1]_1 \cdot [a_{12}]_2 \wedge [a_{11}^*]_1 \cdot [a_{22}]_2 - [a_{12}^*]_1 \cdot [a_{21}]_2 \neq [0]_T;$

$\mathsf{K}_{\text{bpk}}(\text{lpar} := [M]_1 \in \mathbb{G}_1^{n\times m})$: $A \leftarrow_\$ \mathcal{D}_k$; $K \leftarrow_\$ \mathbb{Z}_p^{n\times k}$; $[C]_2 \leftarrow [K\bar{A}]_2 \in \mathbb{G}_2^{n\times k}$;
$\quad [P]_1 \leftarrow [M]_1^\top K \in \mathbb{G}_1^{m\times k}$; if $\mathcal{D}_k$ is efficiently verifiable then $\text{PK}_{\text{Vpk}} \leftarrow \epsilon$;
$\quad$ elseif $\mathcal{D}_k = \mathcal{U}_2$ then $\text{PK}_{\text{Vpk}} \leftarrow [a_{11}, a_{12}]_1$; fi ; $\text{PK}_{\text{snd}} \leftarrow [\bar{A}, C]_2$; $\text{PK}_{\text{zk}} \leftarrow [P]_1$;
$\quad \text{PK} \leftarrow (\text{PK}_{\text{snd}}, \text{PK}_{\text{zk}}, \text{PK}_{\text{Vpk}})$; $\text{SK} \leftarrow K$; return (PK, SK);
$\mathsf{P}([M]_1, \text{PK}, [y]_1, w)$: return $[\pi]_1 \leftarrow [P]_1^\top w \in \mathbb{G}_1^k$;
$\mathsf{Sim}([M]_1, \text{PK}, \text{SK}, [y]_1)$: // SK is extracted by using a knowledge assumption;
$\quad$ return $[\pi]_1 \leftarrow K^\top [y]_1 \in \mathbb{G}_1^k$;
$\mathsf{V}([M]_1, \text{PK}, [y]_1, [\pi]_1)$: check that $[y]_1^\top [C]_2 = [\pi]_1^\top [\bar{A}]_2$; // $\in \mathbb{G}_T^{1\times k}$
$\mathsf{V}_{\text{pk}}([M]_1, \text{PK})$: Return 1 only if the following checks all succeed:
$\quad \text{PK} = (\text{PK}_{\text{snd}}, \text{PK}_{\text{zk}}, \text{PK}_{\text{Vpk}}) \wedge \text{PK}_{\text{snd}} = [\bar{A}, C]_2 \wedge \text{PK}_{\text{zk}} = [P]_1$;
$\quad [P]_1 \in \mathbb{G}_1^{m\times k} \wedge [\bar{A}]_2 \in \mathbb{G}_2^{k\times k} \wedge [C]_2 \in \mathbb{G}_2^{n\times k}$;
$(*) \quad [M]_1^\top [C]_2 = [P]_1 [\bar{A}]_2$;
$\quad$ if $\mathcal{D}_k$ is efficiently verifiable then $\mathsf{MATV}([\bar{A}]_2)$;
$\quad$ else check isinvertible($[\bar{A}]_2, \text{PK}_{\text{Vpk}}$); fi

---

Fig. 2. Sub-ZK QA-NIZK Π_{bpk} for $[y]_1 = [M]_1 w$ in the BPK model, where either (1) $\mathcal{D}_k$ is efficiently verifiable or (2) $\mathcal{D}_k = \mathcal{U}_2$.

Kiltz-Wee QA-NIZK in the BPK Model. Kiltz and Wee [30] described a very efficient QA-NIZK Π'_{as} for linear subspaces. Abdolmaleki *et al.* [4] modified Π'_{as} and proved that the resulting QA-NIZK Π_{bpk} is Sub-ZK in the BPK model, assuming a novel KW-KE knowledge assumption. In addition, [4] proved that the KW-KE assumption holds under a hash-knowledge assumption (HAK, [38]). The soundness of Π'_{as} holds in the BPK model under a suitable KerMDH assumption for any $k \geq 1$; one obtain optimal efficiency when $k = 1$.

The distribution $\mathcal{D}_k$ is *efficiently verifiable*, if there exists an algorithm $\mathsf{MATV}([\bar{A}]_2)$ that outputs 1 if $\bar{A}$ is invertible (recall that we assume that the matrix distribution is robust) and well-formed with respect to $\mathcal{D}_k$ and otherwise outputs 0. We refer to [4] for the construction of MATV for common distributions. Figure 2 describes the Sub-ZK QA-NIZK Π_{bpk} from [4]. Here, as observed in [4], the correctness of $[P]_1$ is needed to guarantee zero knowledge and $[\bar{A}, C]_2$ is needed to guarantee soundness [4]. Apart from restating Π'_{as} by using the terminology of the BPK model, Π_{bpk} differs from Π'_{as} only by having an additional entry PK_{Vpk} in the PK and by including the V_{pk} algorithm. For the sake of completeness, we will next state the main security results of [4]. See [4] for the definition of the KW-KE assumption.

Proposition 1 (Security of Π_{bpk} [4]). *Let Π_{bpk} be the QA-NIZK argument system for linear subspaces from Fig. 2. The following statements hold in the BPK model. Assume that $\mathcal{D}_p$ is such that V_{par} is efficient. (i) Π_{bpk} is perfectly complete and perfectly zero-knowledge. (ii) If $(\mathcal{D}_p, k, \mathcal{D}_k)$-KW-KE$_{\mathbb{G}_1}$ holds relative to Pgen then Π_{bpk} is statistically persistent zero-knowledge. (iii)*

Assume $\mathcal{D}_k$ is efficiently verifiable (resp., $\mathcal{D}_k = \mathcal{U}_2$). If $\mathcal{D}_k$-KerMDH^{dl} (resp., $\mathcal{D}_k$-SKerMDH^{dl}) holds relative to Pgen then Π_{bpk} is computationally quasi-adaptively Sub-PAR sound.

3   Key-and-Argument-Updatable QA-NIZK: Definitions

Following [4], we will consider QA-NIZK in the BPK model and thus with a public-key updating (and not CRS-updating like in [26]) algorithm. Also, we allow updating of a previously created argument to one that corresponds to the new public key PK, obtaining what we will call a *key-and-argument-updatable* QA-NIZK. As in [26], the updatable PK and the corresponding secret key will be "shared" by more than one party. Thus, executing multiple updates of PK by independent parties means that the updated version of PK is not "created" solely by a single verifier. To achieve soundness, it suffices that V (or an entity trusted by her) was one of the parties involved in the creation or updating of PK. It even suffices if, up to the currently last available updated argument, at least one key-updater does not collaborate with the corresponding proof-updater.

This moves us out from designated-verifier arguments, typical for the BPK model, to (somewhat-)transferable arguments. The CRS model corresponds to the case where PK belongs to a universally trusted third party (TTP); updating the public key of the TTP by another party decreases trust requirements in the TTP. E.g., the PK can originally belong to the TTP, and then updated by two interested verifiers.

New Algorithms. An (argument-)updatable Sub-ZK QA-NIZK has the following additional PPT algorithms on top of (Pgen, K$_{bpk}$, V$_{pk}$, P, V, Sim):

K$_{upd}$(lpar, PK): a randomized *key updater* algorithm that, given an old PK, generates a new updated public key PK$'$, and returns (PK$'$, $\widehat{sk}$) where $\widehat{sk}$ is a trapdoor corresponding to the PK-update.

V$_{Kupd}$(lpar, PK, PK$'$): a deterministic *key-update verifier* algorithm that, given PK and PK$'$, verifies that PK$'$ is a correct update of PK.

P$_{upd}$(lpar, PK, PK$'$; x, w, π): a possibly randomized *argument-updater* algorithm that, given $(x, w) \in \mathbf{R}_{lpar}$, an argument π (made by using the old public key PK), and the updated public key PK$'$, outputs an argument π' that corresponds to the updated public key PK$'$. P$_{upd}$ must be executable without the knowledge of either SK, SK$'$ (the secret key corresponding to PK$'$), or any trapdoor $\widehat{sk}$ about the update. Hence, P$_{upd}$ can be used to update either a prover-generated or a simulated argument, but only honestly, i.e., when the prover knows the witness.

Sim$_{upd}$(lpar, $\widehat{sk}$; x, π): a (randomized) *argument-update simulator* algorithm that, given an argument π (made with an old public key PK) and a PK-update trapdoor $\widehat{sk}$ (corresponding to the update from π to π'), outputs an argument π' with an updated public key PK$'$. Sim$_{upd}$ is executed without the knowledge of either w, SK, or SK$'$ (the secret keys corresponding to PK and PK$'$, respectively). Thus, $\mathsf{Sim}_{\mathsf{upd}}$ can be used to update either a prover-generated or a simulated argument, but only when knowing the trapdoor $\widehat{\mathsf{SK}}$ of the key-update. $\mathsf{Sim}_{\mathsf{upd}}$ can have more inputs (like PK); in our constructions, we do not need them.

$\mathsf{V}_{\mathsf{Pupd}}(\mathsf{lpar}, \mathrm{PK}, \mathrm{PK}'; \mathrm{x}, \pi, \pi')$: a deterministic *argument-update verifier* algorithm that verifies that π' is a correct (updated either by $\mathsf{P}_{\mathsf{upd}}$ or $\mathsf{Sim}_{\mathsf{upd}}$ on correct inputs) update of π when PK was updated to PK'.

We require that there exists an efficient algorithm Comb that, on input $(\mathsf{lpar}; \mathrm{SK}, \widehat{\mathrm{SK}})$ (where SK is the secret key corresponding to PK and $\widehat{\mathrm{SK}}$ is the trapdoor of the update PK $\Rightarrow$ PK'), returns SK' (the secret key corresponding to PK').

New Security Requirements. We introduce several new security requirements that accompany the new algorithms. They include requirements that guarantee that the standard definitions of completeness, (computational) soundness, and (statistical) zero-knowledge also hold after the key or the key-and-argument updates. We complete them with the various hiding requirements that guarantee that an updated key (and argument) are indistinguishable from the freshly generated key (and argument), assuming that either the pre-update key (and argument) were honestly created or the update was honest. While hiding is a natural security objective by itself, we will see that it allows us to get general reductions between soundness (and key/argument-update soundness) and Sub-ZK (and key/argument-update Sub-ZK).

We will consider two versions of argument-update soundness. Argument-update soundness (I) holds when PK was created honestly, but the updater is malicious, and argument-update soundness (II) holds when PK was created maliciously, but the updater is honest. Argument-update soundness (I) (resp., (II)) is defined in the case when PK and π were created honestly (resp., updated honestly) since it is impossible to get both subversion-soundness (which corresponds to the case both the PK creator and the updater are malicious) and zero-knowledge [6]. We want to guarantee soundness even in the case when only one of the key and argument updaters was honest, but various verification algorithms accept the updates of other updaters.

In the case of key-update Sub-ZK, we are interested in the case when only the public key has been updated, but the update could have been done maliciously. Since the argument is not updated, we require that an argument and simulated argument, given with the updated key (where both the old key and the key-update verify), are indistinguishable.

Similarly, in the case of argument-update Sub-ZK, the key update does not depend on the witness and may be done maliciously (possibly not by P). However, the argument is updated by P who uses the witness but does not have to know the key-update trapdoor $\widehat{\mathrm{SK}}$. This motivates the use of $\mathsf{K}_{\mathsf{upd}}$ and $\mathsf{Sim}_{\mathsf{upd}}$ in the update process in $\mathsf{Exp}_{Z,\mathcal{A}}^{\mathsf{au-pzk}}(\mathsf{lpar})$. Thus, key-update Sub-ZK and argument-update Sub-ZK are different notions and have to be handled separately.

We give all security notions for a single update; this results in simple reductions between these notions, and simple security proofs of the QA-NIZK. All notions can be composed over several updates, and the composed properties can then be proved by using standard hybrid arguments. We will omit further discussion, see [26] for more information. We divide the considerable number of definitions into completeness, hiding, soundness, and zero-knowledge sections.

Completeness

Key-update completeness: $\forall \lambda$, $p \leftarrow \mathsf{Pgen}(1^\lambda)$, $\forall \mathsf{lpar} \in \mathcal{D}_p$, $(\mathrm{PK}, \mathrm{SK}) \leftarrow \mathsf{K}_{\mathsf{bpk}}(\mathsf{lpar})$, $(\mathrm{PK}', \widehat{\mathrm{SK}}) \leftarrow \mathsf{K}_{\mathsf{upd}}(\mathsf{lpar}, \mathrm{PK})$: $\mathsf{V}_{\mathsf{Kupd}}(\mathsf{lpar}, \mathrm{PK}, \mathrm{PK}') = 1$. Moreover, if $\mathsf{V}_{\mathsf{Kupd}}(\mathsf{lpar}, \mathrm{PK}, \mathrm{PK}') = 1$ then $\mathsf{V}_{\mathsf{pk}}(\mathsf{lpar}; \mathrm{PK}) = 1$ iff $\mathsf{V}_{\mathsf{pk}}(\mathsf{lpar}; \mathrm{PK}') = 1$.

Argument-update completeness: $\forall \lambda$, $p \leftarrow \mathsf{Pgen}(1^\lambda)$, $\forall \mathsf{lpar} \in \mathcal{D}_p$, $(\mathrm{PK}, \mathrm{SK}) \leftarrow \mathsf{K}_{\mathsf{bpk}}(\mathsf{lpar})$, $\forall (\mathsf{x}, \mathsf{w}) \in \mathbf{R}_{\mathsf{lpar}}$, $\pi \leftarrow \mathsf{P}(\mathsf{lpar}, \mathrm{PK}; \mathsf{x}, \mathsf{w})$, $(\mathrm{PK}', \widehat{\mathrm{SK}}) \leftarrow \mathsf{K}_{\mathsf{upd}}(\mathsf{lpar}, \mathrm{PK})$, $\pi' \leftarrow \mathsf{P}_{\mathsf{upd}}(\mathsf{lpar}, \mathrm{PK}, \mathrm{PK}'; \mathsf{x}, \mathsf{w}, \pi)$: $\mathsf{V}_{\mathsf{Pupd}}(\mathsf{lpar}, \mathrm{PK}, \mathrm{PK}'; \mathsf{x}, \pi, \pi') = 1$. Moreover, if $\mathsf{V}_{\mathsf{Kupd}}(\mathsf{lpar}, \mathrm{PK}, \mathrm{PK}') = 1$ and $\mathsf{V}_{\mathsf{Pupd}}(\mathsf{lpar}, \mathrm{PK}, \mathrm{PK}'; \mathsf{x}, \pi, \pi') = 1$ then $\mathsf{V}(\mathsf{lpar}, \mathrm{PK}; \mathsf{x}, \pi) = 1$ iff $\mathsf{V}(\mathsf{lpar}, \mathrm{PK}'; \mathsf{x}, \pi') = 1$.

Simulator-update completeness: $\forall \lambda$, $p \leftarrow \mathsf{Pgen}(1^\lambda)$, $\forall \mathsf{lpar} \in \mathcal{D}_p$, $(\mathrm{PK}, \mathrm{SK}) \leftarrow \mathsf{K}_{\mathsf{bpk}}(\mathsf{lpar})$, $\forall (\mathsf{x}, \mathsf{w}) \in \mathbf{R}_{\mathsf{lpar}}$, $\pi_{\mathsf{Sim}} \leftarrow \mathsf{Sim}(\mathsf{lpar}, \mathrm{PK}, \mathrm{SK}; \mathsf{x})$, $(\mathrm{PK}', \widehat{\mathrm{SK}}) \leftarrow \mathsf{K}_{\mathsf{upd}}(\mathsf{lpar}, \mathrm{PK})$, $\pi' \leftarrow \mathsf{Sim}_{\mathsf{upd}}(\mathsf{lpar}, \widehat{\mathrm{SK}}; \mathsf{x}, \pi)$: $\mathsf{V}_{\mathsf{Pupd}}(\mathsf{lpar}, \mathrm{PK}, \mathrm{PK}'; \mathsf{x}, \pi, \pi') = 1$. Moreover, if $\mathsf{V}_{\mathsf{Kupd}}(\mathsf{lpar}, \mathrm{PK}, \mathrm{PK}') = 1$ and $\mathsf{V}_{\mathsf{Pupd}}(\mathsf{lpar}, \mathrm{PK}, \mathrm{PK}'; \mathsf{x}, \pi, \pi') = 1$ then $\mathsf{V}(\mathsf{lpar}, \mathrm{PK}; \mathsf{x}, \pi) = 1$ iff $\mathsf{V}(\mathsf{lpar}, \mathrm{PK}'; \mathsf{x}, \pi') = 1$.

Hiding

Key-update hiding: $\forall \lambda$, $p \leftarrow \mathsf{Pgen}(1^\lambda)$, $\forall \mathsf{lpar} \in \mathcal{D}_p$: if $(\mathrm{PK}, \mathrm{SK}) \leftarrow \mathsf{K}_{\mathsf{bpk}}(\mathsf{lpar})$ and $(\mathrm{PK}', \widehat{\mathrm{SK}}) \leftarrow \mathsf{K}_{\mathsf{upd}}(\mathsf{lpar}, \mathrm{PK})$, then $\mathrm{PK}' \approx_\lambda \mathsf{K}_{\mathsf{bpk}}(\mathsf{lpar})$.

Strong key-update hiding: $\forall \lambda$, $p \leftarrow \mathsf{Pgen}(1^\lambda)$, $\forall \mathsf{lpar} \in \mathcal{D}_p$, $\forall (\mathrm{PK}, \mathrm{PK}')$: $\mathrm{PK}' \approx_\lambda \mathsf{K}_{\mathsf{bpk}}(\mathsf{lpar})$ holds if either

1. the old public key was honestly generated and the key-update verifies: $(\mathrm{PK}, \mathrm{SK}) \leftarrow \mathsf{K}_{\mathsf{bpk}}(\mathsf{lpar})$ and $\mathsf{V}_{\mathsf{Kupd}}(\mathsf{lpar}, \mathrm{PK}, \mathrm{PK}') = 1$, or
2. the old public key verifies and the key-update was honest: $\mathsf{V}_{\mathsf{pk}}(\mathsf{lpar}, \mathrm{PK}) = 1$ and $(\mathrm{PK}', \widehat{\mathrm{SK}}) \leftarrow \mathsf{K}_{\mathsf{upd}}(\mathsf{lpar}, \mathrm{PK})$.

Argument-update hiding: $\forall \lambda$, $p \leftarrow \mathsf{Pgen}(1^\lambda)$, $\forall \mathsf{lpar} \in \mathcal{D}_p$, $(\mathrm{PK}, \mathrm{SK}) \leftarrow \mathsf{K}_{\mathsf{bpk}}(\mathsf{lpar})$, $(\mathrm{PK}', \widehat{\mathrm{SK}}) \leftarrow \mathsf{K}_{\mathsf{upd}}(\mathsf{lpar}, \mathrm{PK})$, $\pi \leftarrow \mathsf{P}(\mathsf{lpar}, \mathrm{PK}; \mathsf{x}, \mathsf{w})$, $\pi_{\mathsf{Sim}} \leftarrow \mathsf{Sim}(\mathsf{lpar}, \mathrm{PK}, \mathrm{SK}; \mathsf{x})$, $\pi' \leftarrow \mathsf{P}_{\mathsf{upd}}(\mathsf{lpar}, \mathrm{PK}, \mathrm{PK}'; \mathsf{x}, \mathsf{w}, \pi)$, $\pi'_{\mathsf{Sim}} \leftarrow \mathsf{Sim}_{\mathsf{upd}}(\mathsf{lpar}, \widehat{\mathrm{SK}}; \mathsf{x}, \pi)$: $\pi' \approx_\lambda \mathsf{P}(\mathsf{lpar}, \mathrm{PK}'; \mathsf{x}, \mathsf{w})$ and $\pi'_{\mathsf{Sim}} \approx_\lambda \mathsf{Sim}(\mathsf{lpar}, \mathrm{PK}', \mathrm{SK}'; \mathsf{x})$.

Strong argument-update hiding: $\forall \lambda$, $p \leftarrow \mathsf{Pgen}(1^\lambda)$, $\forall \mathsf{lpar} \in \mathcal{D}_p$, $\forall (\mathsf{x}, \mathsf{w}) \in \mathbf{R}_{\mathsf{lpar}}$, $\forall (\mathrm{PK}, \mathrm{PK}'; \mathsf{x}, \pi, \pi')$: $\mathrm{PK}' \approx_\lambda \mathsf{K}_{\mathsf{bpk}}(\mathsf{lpar})$, $\pi' \approx_\lambda \mathsf{P}(\mathsf{lpar}, \mathrm{PK}'; \mathsf{x}, \mathsf{w})$, and $\pi'_{\mathsf{Sim}} \approx_\lambda \mathsf{Sim}(\mathsf{lpar}, \mathrm{PK}', \mathrm{SK}'; \mathsf{x})$ hold if either

(i) the old public key and argument were honestly generated and the updates verify: $(\mathrm{PK}, \mathrm{SK}) \leftarrow \mathsf{K}_{\mathsf{bpk}}(\mathsf{lpar})$, $\pi \leftarrow \mathsf{P}(\mathsf{lpar}, \mathrm{PK}; \mathsf{x}, \mathsf{w})$, $\pi_{\mathsf{Sim}} \leftarrow \mathsf{Sim}(\mathsf{lpar}, \mathrm{PK}, \mathrm{SK}; \mathsf{x})$, $\mathsf{V}_{\mathsf{Kupd}}(\mathsf{lpar}, \mathrm{PK}, \mathrm{PK}') = 1$, $\mathsf{V}_{\mathsf{Pupd}}(\mathsf{lpar}, \mathrm{PK}, \mathrm{PK}'; \mathsf{x}, \pi, \pi') = 1$, and $\mathsf{V}_{\mathsf{Pupd}}(\mathsf{lpar}, \mathrm{PK}, \mathrm{PK}'; \mathsf{x}, \pi_{\mathsf{Sim}}, \pi'_{\mathsf{Sim}}) = 1$, or

(ii) the old public key and argument verify and the updates were honestly generated: $V_{pk}(\mathsf{lpar}, \mathrm{PK}) = 1$, $V(\mathsf{lpar}, \mathrm{PK}; x, \pi) = 1$, $V(\mathsf{lpar}, \mathrm{PK}; x, \pi_{Sim}) = 1$, $(\mathrm{PK}', \widehat{\mathrm{SK}}) \leftarrow \mathsf{K}_{upd}(\mathsf{lpar}, \mathrm{PK})$, $\pi' \leftarrow \mathsf{P}_{upd}(\mathsf{lpar}, \mathrm{PK}, \mathrm{PK}'; x, w, \pi)$, and $\pi'_{Sim} \leftarrow \mathsf{Sim}_{upd}(\mathsf{lpar}, \widehat{\mathrm{SK}}; x, \pi_{Sim})$.

Soundness. Here, we abbreviate quasi-adaptive to QA.

(Computational QA) Sub-PAR key-update soundness (I): for any PPT $\mathcal{A}$, $\mathrm{Adv}^{sndku1}_{\mathcal{A},\Pi}(\lambda) \approx_{\lambda} 0$, where $\mathrm{Adv}^{sndku1}_{\mathcal{A},\Pi}(\lambda)$ is the probability that given $p \leftarrow \mathsf{Pgen}(1^{\lambda})$, $\mathsf{lpar} \leftarrow_{\$} \mathcal{A}(p)$; $(\mathrm{PK}, \mathrm{SK}) \leftarrow \mathsf{K}_{bpk}(\mathsf{lpar})$, $(\mathrm{PK}', x, \pi') \leftarrow \mathcal{A}(\mathrm{PK})$, the following holds: $V_{par}(\mathsf{lpar}) = 1 \wedge V_{K_{upd}}(\mathsf{lpar}, \mathrm{PK}, \mathrm{PK}') = 1 \wedge V(\mathsf{lpar}, \mathrm{PK}'; x, \pi') = 1 \wedge \neg(\exists w : \mathbf{R}_{\mathsf{lpar}}(x, w) = 1)$.

(Computational QA) Sub-PAR key-update soundness (II): for any PPT $\mathcal{A}$, $\mathrm{Adv}^{sndku2}_{\mathcal{A},\Pi}(\lambda) \approx_{\lambda} 0$, where $\mathrm{Adv}^{sndku2}_{\mathcal{A},\Pi}(\lambda)$ is the probability that given $p \leftarrow \mathsf{Pgen}(1^{\lambda})$, $(\mathsf{lpar}, \mathrm{PK}) \leftarrow_{\$} \mathcal{A}(p)$, $(\mathrm{PK}', \widehat{\mathrm{SK}}) \leftarrow \mathsf{K}_{upd}(\mathsf{lpar}, \mathrm{PK})$, $\pi' \leftarrow \mathcal{A}(\mathrm{PK}')$, the following holds: $V_{par}(\mathsf{lpar}) = 1 \wedge V_{pk}(\mathsf{lpar}, \mathrm{PK}) = 1 \wedge V(\mathsf{lpar}, \mathrm{PK}'; x, \pi') = 1 \wedge \neg(\exists w : \mathbf{R}_{\mathsf{lpar}}(x, w) = 1)$.

(Computational QA) Sub-PAR key-update soundness: iff both Sub-PAR key-update soundness (I) and (II) hold.

(Computational QA) argument-update soundness (I): for any PPT $\mathcal{A}$, $\mathrm{Adv}^{sndpu1}_{\mathcal{A},\Pi}(\lambda) \approx_{\lambda} 0$, where $\mathrm{Adv}^{sndpu1}_{\mathcal{A},\Pi}(\lambda)$ is the probability that given $p \leftarrow \mathsf{Pgen}(1^{\lambda})$; $\mathsf{lpar} \leftarrow_{\$} \mathcal{A}(p)$; $(\mathrm{PK}, \mathrm{SK}) \leftarrow \mathsf{K}_{bpk}(\mathsf{lpar})$, $(\mathrm{PK}', x, \pi, \pi') \leftarrow \mathcal{A}(\mathrm{PK})$, the following holds: $V_{par}(\mathsf{lpar}) = 1 \wedge V_{K_{upd}}(\mathsf{lpar}, \mathrm{PK}, \mathrm{PK}') = 1 \wedge V_{P_{upd}}(\mathsf{lpar}, \mathrm{PK}, \mathrm{PK}'; x, \pi, \pi') = 1 \wedge V(\mathsf{lpar}, \mathrm{PK}; x, \pi) = 1 \wedge \neg(\exists w : \mathbf{R}_{\mathsf{lpar}}(x, w) = 1)$.

(Computational QA) Sub-PAR argument-update soundness (II): for any PPT $\mathcal{A}$, $\mathrm{Adv}^{sndpu2}_{\mathcal{A},\Pi}(\lambda) \approx_{\lambda} 0$, where $\mathrm{Adv}^{sndpu2}_{\mathcal{A},\Pi}(\lambda)$ is the probability that given $p \leftarrow \mathsf{Pgen}(1^{\lambda})$, $(\mathsf{lpar}, \mathrm{PK}, \pi) \leftarrow_{\$} \mathcal{A}(p)$, $(\mathrm{PK}', \widehat{\mathrm{SK}}) \leftarrow \mathsf{K}_{upd}(\mathsf{lpar}, \mathrm{PK})$, $\pi' \leftarrow \mathsf{P}_{upd}(\mathsf{lpar}, \mathrm{PK}, \mathrm{PK}'; x, w, \pi)$, the following holds: $V_{par}(\mathsf{lpar}) = 1 \wedge V_{pk}(\mathsf{lpar}, \mathrm{PK}) = 1 \wedge V(\mathsf{lpar}, \mathrm{PK}; x, \pi) = 1 \wedge \neg(\exists w : \mathbf{R}_{\mathsf{lpar}}(x, w))$.

(Computational QA) Sub-PAR argument-update soundness: iff both Sub-PAR argument-update soundness (I) and Sub-PAR argument-update soundness (II) hold.

Zero-Knowledge. Here, all experiments are described in Fig. 3.

(Statistical) key-update ZK: for any computationally unbounded $\mathcal{A}$, $|\mathrm{Exp}^{ku-zk}_{Z,\mathcal{A}}(\mathsf{lpar}) - 1/2| \approx_{\lambda} 0$.

(Statistical) argument-update ZK: for any computationally unbounded $\mathcal{A}$, $|\mathrm{Exp}^{au-zk}_{Z,\mathcal{A}}(\mathsf{lpar}) - 1/2| \approx_{\lambda} 0$.

(Statistical) key-update persistent Sub-ZK: for any PPT subverter Z there exists a PPT Ext_Z, such that for any computationally unbounded $\mathcal{A}$, $|\mathrm{Exp}^{ku-pzk}_{Z,\mathcal{A}}(\mathsf{lpar}) - 1/2| \approx_{\lambda} 0$.

(Statistical) argument-update persistent Sub-ZK: for any PPT subverter Z there exists a PPT Ext_Z, such that for any computationally unbounded $\mathcal{A}$, $|\mathrm{Exp}^{au-pzk}_{Z,\mathcal{A}}(\mathsf{lpar}) - 1/2| \approx_{\lambda} 0$.

$$\begin{array}{ll}
\underline{\mathsf{Exp}_{\mathcal{A}}^{\mathsf{ku-zk}}(\mathsf{lpar})} & \underline{\mathsf{Exp}_{Z,\mathcal{A}}^{\mathsf{ku-pzk}}(\mathsf{lpar})} \\
\end{array}$$

$\mathsf{Exp}_{\mathcal{A}}^{\mathsf{ku-zk}}(\mathsf{lpar})$	$\mathsf{Exp}_{Z,\mathcal{A}}^{\mathsf{ku-pzk}}(\mathsf{lpar})$
$\mathsf{p} \leftarrow \mathsf{Pgen}(1^{\lambda}); \mathsf{lpar} \leftarrow \mathcal{D}_{\mathsf{p}};$	$\mathsf{p} \leftarrow \mathsf{Pgen}(1^{\lambda}); r \leftarrow_{\$} \mathsf{RND}_{\lambda}(Z);$
$(\mathrm{PK}, \mathrm{SK}) \leftarrow \mathsf{K}_{\mathsf{bpk}}(\mathsf{lpar});$	$(\mathsf{lpar}, \mathrm{PK}, \mathrm{PK}', \mathsf{aux}_Z) \leftarrow Z(\mathsf{p}; r);$
$(\mathrm{PK}', \widehat{\mathrm{SK}}) \leftarrow \mathsf{K}_{\mathsf{upd}}(\mathsf{lpar}, \mathrm{PK});$	$(\mathrm{SK}, \widehat{\mathrm{SK}}) \leftarrow \mathsf{Ext}_Z(\mathsf{p}; r);$
$\mathrm{SK}' \leftarrow \mathsf{Comb}(\mathsf{lpar}; \mathrm{SK}, \widehat{\mathrm{SK}});$	$\mathrm{SK}' \leftarrow \mathsf{Comb}(\mathsf{lpar}; \mathrm{SK}, \widehat{\mathrm{SK}});$
$b \leftarrow_{\$} \{0,1\};$	$b \leftarrow_{\$} \{0,1\};$
$b' \leftarrow \mathcal{A}^{O_b^k(\cdot,\cdot)}(\mathsf{lpar}; \mathrm{PK}, \mathrm{PK}');$	$b' \leftarrow \mathcal{A}^{O_b^k(\cdot,\cdot)}(\mathsf{lpar}; \mathrm{PK}, \mathrm{PK}', \mathsf{aux}_Z);$
$\mathbf{return}\ \mathsf{V}_{\mathsf{Kupd}}(\mathsf{lpar}, \mathrm{PK}, \mathrm{PK}') = 1 \wedge$	$\mathbf{return}\ \mathsf{V}_{\mathsf{par}}(\mathsf{lpar}) = 1 \wedge \mathsf{V}_{\mathsf{pk}}(\mathsf{lpar}; \mathrm{PK}) = 1 \wedge$
$\quad b' = b;$	$\quad \mathsf{V}_{\mathsf{Kupd}}(\mathsf{lpar}, \mathrm{PK}, \mathrm{PK}') = 1 \wedge b' = b;$
$\underline{O_0^k(\mathsf{x}, \mathsf{w}):}$	$\underline{O_1^k(\mathsf{x}, \mathsf{w}):}$
$\mathbf{if}\ (\mathsf{x}, \mathsf{w}) \notin \mathbf{R}_{\mathsf{lpar}}\ \mathbf{then\ return}\ \bot;$	$\mathbf{if}\ (\mathsf{x}, \mathsf{w}) \notin \mathbf{R}_{\mathsf{lpar}}\ \mathbf{then\ return}\ \bot;$
$\mathbf{else}\ \pi' \leftarrow \mathsf{P}(\mathsf{lpar}, \mathrm{PK}'; \mathsf{x}, \mathsf{w});$	$\mathbf{else}\ \pi'_{\mathsf{Sim}} \leftarrow \mathsf{Sim}(\mathsf{lpar}, \mathrm{PK}', \mathrm{SK}'; \mathsf{x});$
$\quad \mathbf{return}\ \pi'; \mathbf{fi}$	$\quad \mathbf{return}\ \pi'_{\mathsf{Sim}}; \mathbf{fi}$
$\underline{O_0^a(\mathsf{x}, \mathsf{w}):}$	$\underline{O_1^a(\mathsf{x}, \mathsf{w}):}$
$\mathbf{if}\ (\mathsf{x}, \mathsf{w}) \notin \mathbf{R}_{\mathsf{lpar}}\ \mathbf{then\ return}\ \bot;$	$\mathbf{if}\ (\mathsf{x}, \mathsf{w}) \notin \mathbf{R}_{\mathsf{lpar}}\ \mathbf{then\ return}\ \bot;$
$\mathbf{else}\ \pi \leftarrow \mathsf{P}(\mathsf{lpar}, \mathrm{PK}; \mathsf{x}, \mathsf{w});$	$\mathbf{else}\ \pi_{\mathsf{Sim}} \leftarrow \mathsf{Sim}(\mathsf{lpar}, \mathrm{PK}, \mathrm{SK}; \mathsf{x});$
$\quad \pi' \leftarrow \mathsf{P}_{\mathsf{upd}}(\mathsf{lpar}, \mathrm{PK}, \mathrm{PK}'; \mathsf{x}, \mathsf{w}, \pi);$	$\quad \pi'_{\mathsf{Sim}} \leftarrow \mathsf{Sim}_{\mathsf{upd}}(\mathsf{lpar}, \widehat{\mathrm{SK}}; \mathsf{x}, \pi_{\mathsf{Sim}});$
$\quad \mathbf{return}\ (\pi, \pi'); \mathbf{fi}$	$\quad \mathbf{return}\ (\pi_{\mathsf{Sim}}, \pi'_{\mathsf{Sim}}); \mathbf{fi}$

Fig. 3. Zero-knowledge experiments. Experiments $\mathsf{Exp}_{Z,\mathcal{A}}^{\mathsf{ku-zk}}(\mathsf{lpar})$ and $\mathsf{Exp}_{Z,\mathcal{A}}^{\mathsf{ku-pzk}}(\mathsf{lpar})$ are described first. Experiments $\mathsf{Exp}_{Z,\mathcal{A}}^{\mathsf{au-zk}}(\mathsf{lpar})$ and $\mathsf{Exp}_{Z,\mathcal{A}}^{\mathsf{au-pzk}}(\mathsf{lpar})$ are like $\mathsf{Exp}_{Z,\mathcal{A}}^{\mathsf{ku-zk}}(\mathsf{lpar})$ and $\mathsf{Exp}_{Z,\mathcal{A}}^{\mathsf{ku-pzk}}(\mathsf{lpar})$, except the adversary has access to oracle O_b^a instead of O_b^k.

Table 1. Relations between security requirements due to Lemmas 1 to 2, 3, 4

Requirement	Follows from
Sub-PAR key-update soundness	Key-update complete, Sub-PAR sound, strong key-update hiding
Sub-PAR argument-update soundness	Argument-update complete, Sub-PAR sound, strong key-update hiding, strong argument-update hiding
(Persistent) key-update Sub-ZK	Key-update complete, (persistent) Sub-ZK
(Persistent) argument-update Sub-ZK	Key-update complete, (persistent) Sub-ZK

Argument-updatable variants of ZK are stronger than key-updatable variants. Our constructions satisfy the stronger definitions, but for the sake of completeness, it is interesting to consider also the weaker notions.

We will now show that the key-update soundness, argument-update soundness, key-update Sub-ZK, and argument-update Sub-ZK properties follow from simpler security requirements. Hence, in the case of a concrete updatable QA-NIZK, it will suffice to prove computational soundness, Sub-ZK, (key-update and argument-update) completeness and strong (key-update and argument-update) hiding. Dependency between security properties is summarized in Table 1.

Lemma 1. *Assume Π is a Sub-PAR sound and strongly key-update hiding non-interactive argument system. (i) Π is Sub-PAR key-update sound (I). (ii) If Π is additionally key-update complete, then Π is Sub-PAR key-update sound (II).*

Proof. **(i)** By strong key-update hiding, PK$'$ comes from the correct distribution. Thus, by Sub-PAR soundness, it is computationally hard to come up with an acceptable argument π' unless x belongs to the language.

(ii) From key-update completeness it follows that in the definition of Sub-PAR key-update soundness (II), we can replace the condition $V_{pk}(\text{lpar}, \text{PK}) = 1$ with the condition $V_{pk}(\text{lpar}, \text{PK}') = 1$. Because of the strong key-update hiding, PK$'$ is indistinguishable from an honestly generated PK$'$. From Sub-PAR soundness, we now obtain Sub-PAR key-update soundness (II). □

Lemma 2. *Assume Π is a Sub-PAR sound non-interactive argument system. (i) Π is Sub-PAR argument-update sound (I). (ii) If Π is also argument-update complete, strongly key-update hiding, and strongly argument-update hiding, then Π is Sub-PAR argument-update sound (II).*

Proof. **(i)** Let $\mathcal{A}$ be an adversary against Sub-PAR argument-update soundness (I). We construct the following adversary B against Sub-PAR soundness. If $\mathcal{A}$ returns lpar, B returns the same lpar. After the generation of PK, B(PK) obtains $(\text{PK}'; x, \pi, \pi') \leftarrow \mathcal{A}(\text{PK})$ and returns (x, π). Clearly, if $\mathcal{A}$ is successful then V accepts π with honestly chosen PK but $x \notin \mathcal{L}_{\text{lpar}}$. Thus, B is successful.

(ii) From argument-update completeness, it follows that in the definition of Sub-PAR argument-update soundness (II), we can replace the condition $V(\text{lpar}, \text{PK}; x, \pi) = 1$ with the condition $V(\text{lpar}, \text{PK}'; x, \pi') = 1$. Because of the strong key-update hiding, PK$'$ is indistinguishable from an honestly generated PK$'$. Because of the strong argument-update hiding, π' is indistinguishable from an honestly generated argument given PK$'$. From Sub-PAR soundness, we get Sub-PAR argument-update soundness. □

Lemma 3. *Assume Π is a key-update complete non-interactive argument system. (i) if Π is zero-knowledge then Π is key-update zero-knowledge. (ii) if Π is persistent Sub-ZK then Π is persistent key-update Sub-ZK.*

Proof. **(i)** Consider a creation of (PK, π) (that returns SK) followed by a update of (PK, π) to (PK', π') (that returns $\widehat{\text{SK}}$). Due to key-update completeness, $V_{pk}(\text{lpar}; \text{PK}') = 1$. Then, by the zero-knowledge property, for SK$' \leftarrow$ Comb(lpar; SK, $\widehat{\text{SK}}$), Sim(lpar, PK$'$, SK$'$; x) $\approx_\lambda$ P(lpar, PK$'$; x, w).

(ii) Consider a possibly malicious creation of (PK, π) followed by a possibly malicious update of (PK, π) to (PK', π'), such that all verifications accept. Due to key-update completeness, we have $V_{pk}(\text{lpar}; \text{PK}') = 1$. Then, by the Sub-ZK property, there exist an extractor Ext_Z that extracts (SK, $\widehat{\text{SK}}$), such that for SK$' \leftarrow$ Comb(lpar; SK, $\widehat{\text{SK}}$), Sim(lpar, PK$'$, SK$'$; x) $\approx_\lambda$ P(lpar, PK$'$; x, w). □

Lemma 4. *Assume that* $\widehat{\text{SK}}$ *is efficiently computable from* SK *and* SK'. *Assume* Π *is a key-update complete and simulator-update complete non-interactive argument system. (i) If* Π *is zero-knowledge then* Π *is persistent argument-update zero-knowledge. (ii) If* Π *is persistent Sub-ZK then* Π *is persistent argument-update Sub-ZK.*

Proof (Sketch.). **(i)** Consider an honest creation of (PK, π) (that also returns SK) followed by an honest update of (PK, π) to (PK', π') (that also returns $\widehat{\text{SK}}$). By zero-knowledge, $\pi \leftarrow \text{P}(\text{lpar}, \text{PK}; x, w)$ and $\pi_{\text{Sim}} \leftarrow \text{Sim}(\text{lpar}, \text{PK}, \text{SK}; x)$ are indistinguishable. By the key-update completeness, $\text{V}_{\text{pk}}(\text{lpar}; \text{PK}') = 1$ and thus, by zero-knowledge, for $\text{SK}' \leftarrow \text{Comb}(\text{SK}, \widehat{\text{SK}})$, π' and $\pi''_{\text{Sim}} \leftarrow \text{Sim}(\text{lpar}, \text{PK}', \text{SK}'; x)$ are indistinguishable. By the simulator-update completeness, $\pi''_{\text{Sim}} \approx_\lambda \pi'_{\text{Sim}}$, where $\pi'_{\text{Sim}} \leftarrow \text{Sim}_{\text{upd}}(\text{lpar}, \widehat{\text{SK}}; x, \pi_{\text{Sim}})$. Thus, the joint distributions (π, π') and $(\pi_{\text{Sim}}, \pi'_{\text{Sim}})$ are indistinguishable.

(ii) Consider a possibly malicious creation of (PK, π) followed by a possibly malicious update of (PK, π) to (PK', π'), such that all verifications accept. By persistent Sub-ZK, there exists an extractor Ext_{Z_1} that extracts SK, such that $\pi \leftarrow \text{P}(\text{lpar}, \text{PK}; x, w)$ and $\pi_{\text{Sim}} \leftarrow \text{Sim}(\text{lpar}, \text{PK}, \text{SK}; x)$ are indistinguishable. By the key-update completeness, $\text{V}_{\text{pk}}(\text{lpar}; \text{PK}') = 1$ and thus, by persistent Sub-ZK, there exists an extractor Ext_{Z_2} that extracts SK' such that π' and $\pi''_{\text{Sim}} \leftarrow \text{Sim}(\text{lpar}, \text{PK}', \text{SK}'; x)$ are indistinguishable. By the simulator-update completeness, $\pi''_{\text{Sim}} \approx_\lambda \pi'_{\text{Sim}}$, where $\pi'_{\text{Sim}} \leftarrow \text{Sim}_{\text{upd}}(\text{lpar}, \widehat{\text{SK}}; x, \pi_{\text{Sim}})$. Thus, the joint distributions (π, π') and $(\pi_{\text{Sim}}, \pi'_{\text{Sim}})$ are indistinguishable. $\square$

Handling Multiple Updates. All security notions given above are for a single update, but they can be generalized for many updates, by using standard hybrid arguments. We will omit further details and point to [26] for more discussion.

4   Updatable Kiltz-Wee QA-NIZK

Since the public key of Π'_{as} consists of (bracketed) matrices, one may hope to construct a quite simple updating process where all PK elements are updated additively. In such a case, an updater would create a "difference" public key $\widehat{\text{PK}}$ (by choosing the trapdoor privately) and update PK by adding $\widehat{\text{PK}}$ componentwise to it, $\text{PK}' \leftarrow \text{PK} + \widehat{\text{PK}}$. However, this simple idea does not work since in the case of additive updating (see Fig. 4 for notation), when we define $\bar{A}' \leftarrow \bar{A} + \hat{A}$, we need to compute

$$[C']_2 = [K'\bar{A}']_2 = [(K + \widehat{K})(\bar{A} + \hat{A})]_2 = [C]_2 + [K]_2\hat{A} + \widehat{K}([\bar{A}]_2 + [\hat{A}]_2) \ .$$

An arbitrary party cannot compute the last formula since $[K]_2$ is not public. To overcome this issue, we have chosen to update the square matrix $\bar{A}$ multiplicatively, that is, $\bar{A}' \leftarrow \bar{A}\hat{A}$. On the other hand, we cannot update $[K]_2$ multiplicatively since $[K]_2$ is (usually) not a square matrix. Thus, we use different updating strategies for different elements of PK, updating some of them

---

$\mathsf{K}_{\mathsf{bpk}}$, P, Sim, V, V_{pk}: exactly as in Fig. 2.

$\mathsf{K}_{\mathsf{upd}}([M]_1, \mathrm{PK})$: // Updates $\mathrm{PK} = ([P]_1, [\bar{A}, C]_2)$ to $\mathrm{PK}' = ([P']_1, [\bar{A}', C']_2)$
    $\widehat{A} \leftarrow_{\$} \bar{\mathcal{D}}_k; [\bar{A}']_2 \leftarrow [\bar{A}]_2 \widehat{A}; \widehat{K} \leftarrow_{\$} \mathbb{Z}_p^{n \times k};$
    $[\widehat{C}]_2 \leftarrow \widehat{K}[\bar{A}']_2; [C']_2 \leftarrow ([C]_2 \widehat{A} + [\widehat{C}]_2)/\beta;$
    $[\widehat{P}]_1 \leftarrow [M]_1^\top \widehat{K}; [P']_1 \leftarrow ([P]_1 + [\widehat{P}]_1)/\beta;$ // Implicitly, $K' = (K + \widehat{K})/\beta$
    $\mathrm{PK}_{\mathsf{upd}} \leftarrow ([\widehat{A}]_1, [\widehat{A}, \widehat{C}]_2); \mathrm{PK}' \leftarrow ([P']_1, [\bar{A}', C']_2, \mathrm{PK}_{\mathsf{upd}}); \widehat{\mathrm{SK}} \leftarrow \widehat{K};$
    return $(\mathrm{PK}', \widehat{\mathrm{SK}});$

$\mathsf{V}_{\mathsf{K}_{\mathsf{upd}}}([M]_1, \mathrm{PK}, \mathrm{PK}')$: $[\widehat{P}]_1 \leftarrow [\beta P' - P]_1; \widehat{\mathrm{PK}} \leftarrow ([\widehat{P}]_1, [\bar{A}', \widehat{C}]_2);$
    if isinvertible$([\bar{A}]_1, \mathrm{PK}_{\mathsf{V}_{\mathsf{pk}}}) \wedge$ isinvertible$([\widehat{A}]_1, \mathrm{PK}_{\mathsf{V}_{\mathsf{pk}}}) \wedge [\bar{A}']_1 \cdot [1]_2 = [\bar{A}]_1 \cdot [\widehat{A}]_2$
    $\wedge [\widehat{A}]_1 \cdot [1]_2 = [1]_1 \cdot [\widehat{A}]_2 \wedge$
    $[1]_1 \cdot [C']_2 = ([C]_2 \cdot [\widehat{A}]_1 + [1]_1 \cdot [\widehat{C}]_2)/\beta \wedge \mathsf{V}_{\mathsf{pk}}([M]_1, \widehat{\mathrm{PK}}) = 1$
    then return 1 else return 0 fi

$\mathsf{P}_{\mathsf{upd}}([M]_1, \mathrm{PK}; [y]_1, [\mathsf{w}]_1, [\pi]_1)$: $[\widehat{\pi}]_1 \leftarrow [\widehat{P}]_1^\top \mathsf{w};$ return $[\pi']_1 \leftarrow ([\pi]_1 + [\widehat{\pi}]_1)/\beta;$

$\mathsf{Sim}_{\mathsf{upd}}([M]_1, \widehat{\mathrm{SK}}; [y]_1, [\pi]_1)$: $[\widehat{\pi}_{\mathsf{Sim}}]_1 \leftarrow \widehat{K}^\top [y]_1;$ return $[\pi']_1 \leftarrow ([\pi]_1 + [\widehat{\pi}_{\mathsf{Sim}}]_1)/\beta;$

$\mathsf{V}_{\mathsf{P}_{\mathsf{upd}}}([M]_1, \mathrm{PK}, \mathrm{PK}'; [y]_1, [\pi]_1, [\pi']_1)$:
    $[\widehat{P}]_1 \leftarrow [\beta P' - P]_1; \widehat{\mathrm{PK}} \leftarrow ([\widehat{P}]_1, [\bar{A}', \widehat{C}]_2); [\widehat{\pi}]_1 \leftarrow [\beta \pi' - \pi]_1;$
    if $\mathsf{V}([M]_1, \widehat{\mathrm{PK}}; [y]_1; [\widehat{\pi}]_1) = 1$ then return 1 else return 0 fi

---

Fig. 4. Variant $\Pi_{\mathsf{bpk}}^{\mathsf{upd}}$ of Kiltz-Wee QA-NIZK for $[y]_1 = [M]_1 \mathsf{w}$ in the Sub-ZK model. Here, $k \in \{1, 2\}$, and $\alpha, \beta \geq 1$.

additively, and some of them multiplicatively. This differs significantly from the known updating procedures for SNARKs like [26] (and all subsequent works that we are aware of), where all PK elements are updated multiplicatively. Finally, to allow for a larger variety of distributions $\mathcal{D}_K$ of K, we introduce a scaling factor β. That is, we update K to $K' = (K + \widehat{K})/\beta$. (For example, with $\beta = 2$, strong key-update and argument-updating hold even when $\mathcal{D}_K = \mathcal{L}_k$.) We recommend to usually take $\beta = 2$, but other choices of β may be appropriate. We leave it as an interesting open question to similarly generalize the updating of $\bar{A}$. We depict an updatable version of Π'_{as} in Fig. 4.

Note that (i) $\mathsf{P}_{\mathsf{upd}}$ updates a QA-NIZK argument $[\pi]_1$ by adding to it a honest argument $[\widehat{\pi}]_1$ under the "difference" public key $\widehat{\mathrm{PK}}$, given the witness w. Thus, $\mathsf{P}_{\mathsf{upd}}$ can be run by a party who knows w. (ii) $\mathsf{Sim}_{\mathsf{upd}}$ updates the existing QA-NIZK argument $[\pi]_1$ by adding to it a simulation $[\widehat{\pi}_{\mathsf{Sim}}]_1$ of the argument given $\widehat{\mathrm{SK}} = \widehat{K}$ (that is known to the key-updater) as the trapdoor. Thus, $\mathsf{Sim}_{\mathsf{upd}}$ can be run by the key-updater. Thus, to be sure that at least one update was made by a party who knows the witness, one should make sure that at least one key-updater will not collude with the argument-updater of the same round.

5 Security of $\Pi_{\mathsf{bpk}}^{\mathsf{upd}}$

Lemma 5. $\Pi_{\mathsf{bpk}}^{\mathsf{upd}}$ *is (i) key-update complete, (ii) argument-update complete, and (iii) simulator-update complete.*

Proof. (**i: Key-update completeness**) We need to show that for $(\mathrm{PK}', \widehat{\mathrm{SK}}) \leftarrow \mathsf{K}_{\mathsf{upd}}(\mathsf{lpar}, \mathrm{PK})$, $\mathsf{V}_{\mathsf{Kupd}}(\mathsf{lpar}, \mathrm{PK}, \mathrm{PK}') = 1$.

Really, PK' is defined by $\bar{A}' = \bar{A}\widehat{A}$, $C' = (C\widehat{A} + \widehat{K}\bar{A}')/\beta$, and $P' = (P + M^\top \widehat{K})/\beta$. Thus, the first two verification equations in $\mathsf{V}_{\mathsf{Kupd}}$ hold by the definition of $\bar{A}$ and $\widehat{A}$ (they are invertible), and the next three ones hold trivially. Let $\widetilde{\mathrm{PK}} \leftarrow ([P]_1, [\bar{A}, C]_2)$ and $\widetilde{\mathrm{PK}}' \leftarrow ([P']_1, [\bar{A}', C']_2)$. We get $\mathsf{V}_{\mathsf{pk}}([M]_1, \widetilde{\mathrm{PK}}') = 1$ from

$$M^\top C' - P'\bar{A}' = M^\top(C\widehat{A} + \widehat{K}\bar{A}')/\beta - (P + M^\top\widehat{K})/\beta \cdot \bar{A}\widehat{A}$$
$$= \left(\left(M^\top C - P\bar{A}\right)\widehat{A} + M^\top\widehat{K}\left(\bar{A}' - \bar{A}\widehat{A}\right)\right)/\beta = 0$$

since $\mathsf{V}_{\mathsf{pk}}([M]_1, \widetilde{\mathrm{PK}}) = 1$ (and thus $M^\top C = P\bar{A}$) and $\bar{A}' = \bar{A}\widehat{A}$.
On the other hand, if $\mathsf{V}_{\mathsf{Kupd}}([M]_1; \mathrm{PK}, \mathrm{PK}') = 1$ then

$$0 = M^\top\widehat{C} - \widehat{P}\bar{A}' = M^\top(\beta C' - C\widehat{A}) - (\beta P' - P)\bar{A}'$$
$$= \beta(M^\top C' - P'\bar{A}') - (M^\top C - P\bar{A})\widehat{A}$$

and thus, since $\widehat{A}$ is invertible, $\mathsf{V}_{\mathsf{pk}}([M]_1; \mathrm{PK}') = 1$ iff $\mathsf{V}_{\mathsf{pk}}([M]_1; \mathrm{PK}) = 1$.

(**ii: Argument-update completeness**) Clearly, $y^\top\widehat{C} - \widehat{\pi}^\top\bar{A}' = y^\top\widehat{K}\bar{A}' - (\widehat{P}^\top w)^\top\bar{A}' = (w^\top M^\top\widehat{K} - w^\top M^\top\widehat{K})\bar{A}' = 0$ and thus $\mathsf{V}([M]_1, \widetilde{\mathrm{PK}}; [y]_1; [\widehat{\pi}]_1) = 1$. On the other hand, $y^\top\widehat{C} - \widehat{\pi}^\top\bar{A}' = y^\top(\beta C' - C\widehat{A}) - (\beta\pi' - \pi)^\top\bar{A}\widehat{A} = \beta\left(y^\top C' - \pi'^\top\bar{A}'\right) - (y^\top C - \pi^\top\bar{A})\widehat{A}$ and thus if $\mathsf{V}_{\mathsf{Pupd}}$ accepts then, since $\widehat{A}$ is invertible, $\mathsf{V}([M]_1, \mathrm{PK}'; [y]_1, [\pi']_1) = 1$ iff $\mathsf{V}([M]_1, \mathrm{PK}; [y]_1, [\pi]_1) = 1$.

(**iii: Simulator-update completeness**) Clearly, $y^\top\widehat{C} - \widehat{\pi}^\top\bar{A}' = (y^\top\widehat{K} - (\widehat{K}^\top y)^\top) = 0$ and thus $\mathsf{V}([M]_1, \widetilde{\mathrm{PK}}; [y]_1; [\widehat{\pi}]_1) = 1$. The proof that if $\mathsf{V}_{\mathsf{Pupd}}$ accepts then $\mathsf{V}([M]_1, \mathrm{PK}'; [y]_1, [\pi']_1) = 1$ iff $\mathsf{V}([M]_1, \mathrm{PK}; [y]_1, [\pi]_1) = 1$ is the same as in the case (ii). $\square$

Lemma 6 (Key-update hiding and argument-update hiding). *Assume that $K, \widehat{K} \sim \mathcal{D}_K$ and $\bar{A}, \widehat{A} \sim \mathcal{D}_{\bar{A}}$, where $\mathcal{D}_K$ and $\mathcal{D}_{\bar{A}}$ satisfy the following conditions: for i.i.d random variables X_1 and X_2,*

- *if $X_i \sim \mathcal{D}_K$ for both i then $X_1 + X_2 \sim \beta\mathcal{D}_K$. (Thus, $\mathcal{D}_K^{*2} = \beta\mathcal{D}_K$, where $\mathcal{D}^{*s}$ is the sth convolution power of $\mathcal{D}$. That is, $\mathcal{D}_K$ is a stable distribution with index $1/\log_2 \beta$.)*
- *if $X_i \sim \mathcal{D}_{\bar{A}}$ for both i then $X_1 \cdot X_2 \sim \mathcal{D}_{\bar{A}}$.*

Then, $\Pi_{\mathsf{bpk}}^{\mathsf{upd}}$ is (i) key-update hiding and (ii) (assuming perfect simulation) argument-update hiding.

Proof. (i) Since PK is honestly created, $C = K\bar{A}$ and thus $C' = (C\widehat{A} + \widehat{K}\bar{A}')/\beta = (K\bar{A}\widehat{A} + \widehat{K}\bar{A}')/\beta = (K + \widehat{K})/\beta \cdot \bar{A}' = K'\bar{A}'$. Similarly, $P = M^\top K$ and $P' = (P + M^\top \widehat{K})/\beta = M^\top(K + \widehat{K})/\beta = M^\top K'$. Due to the assumption on $\mathcal{D}_{\bar{A}}$ and $\mathcal{D}_K$, PK and PK$'$ come from the same distribution.

(ii) We already know PK and PK$'$ come from the same distribution. Assume that $[y]_1 = [M]_1 \mathsf{w}$. Due to the perfect simulation, $\pi = \mathsf{Sim}([M]_1, \mathrm{PK}; [y]_1, [\pi]_1) = K^\top y$. Thus, $\pi' = (K^\top y + \widehat{K}^\top y)/\beta = K'^\top y = \mathsf{Sim}([M]_1, \mathrm{PK}'; [y]_1, [\pi']_1) = \mathsf{P}([M]_1, \mathrm{PK}', [y]_1, \mathsf{w})$. □

Remark 1. In Lemma 6, we need a convolution semigroup consisting of a single element. It is possible to generalize to the case of a general convolution semigroup (i.e., allowing $\widehat{K}$ to come from a different distribution than K).

Theorem 1 (Strong key-update hiding and strong argument-update hiding). *Assume that $K, \widehat{K} \sim \mathcal{D}_K$ and $\bar{A}, \widehat{A} \sim \mathcal{D}_{\bar{A}}$, where $\mathcal{D}_K$ and $\mathcal{D}_{\bar{A}}$ satisfy the following conditions: for i.i.d random variables X_1 and X_2,*

- *if $X_i \sim \mathcal{D}_K$ for at least one i then $X_1 + X_2 \sim \beta\mathcal{D}_K$. (Thus, the convolution of $\mathcal{D}_K$ with any other distribution — over the support of $\mathcal{D}_K$ — is $\beta\mathcal{D}_K$, or $\mathcal{D}_K$ is belongs to a generalized ideal of a convolution semigroup.)*
- *if $X_i \sim \mathcal{D}_{\bar{A}}$ for at least one i then $X_1 \cdot X_2 \sim \mathcal{D}_{\bar{A}}$. (Thus, the log of $\mathcal{D}_{\bar{A}}$ belongs to an ideal of a convolution semigroup.)*

Then, $\Pi_{\mathsf{bpk}}^{\mathsf{upd}}$ is (i) strong key-update hiding and (ii) (assuming perfect simulation) strong argument-update hiding.

Proof. We will prove (i) and (ii) together in two different cases: (1) when PK (and the argument) was honestly created, and (2) when PK$'$ (and the argument) was honestly updated.

(1: PK / π were honestly created and the updates verify) Since PK is honestly created, $C = K\bar{A}$ and $P = M^\top K$. Since $\mathsf{V}_{\mathsf{Kupd}}$ accepts, we have $\bar{A}' = \bar{A}\widehat{A}$ (thus, by the assumption on $\mathcal{D}_{\bar{A}}$, $\bar{A}'$ comes from the correct distribution), $C' - (C\widehat{A} + \widehat{C})/\beta$, and $M^\top \widehat{C} = \widehat{P}\bar{A}'$ where $\widehat{P} = \beta P' - P$. Thus, $C' = (C\widehat{A} + \widehat{C})/\beta = (K\bar{A}\widehat{A} + \widehat{C})/\beta = (K\bar{A}' + \widehat{C})/\beta$. Define implicitly $K' := C'\bar{A}'^{-1} = (K\bar{A}' + \widehat{C})/\beta \cdot \bar{A}'^{-1} = (K + \widehat{C}\bar{A}'^{-1})/\beta$ (note that $\bar{A}'$ is invertible). Thus, obviously, $C' = K'\bar{A}'$. On the other hand, $M^\top K' = M^\top(K + \widehat{C}\bar{A}'^{-1})/\beta = (P + M^\top \widehat{C}\bar{A}'^{-1})/\beta = (P + \widehat{P}\bar{A}'\bar{A}'^{-1})/\beta = (P + \widehat{P})/\beta = P'$ and thus $P' = M^\top K'$. To show that PK and PK$'$ come from the same distribution, we now only need to show that $K' = (K + \widehat{C}\bar{A}'^{-1})/\beta$ comes from the same distribution as K. This holds assuming that $\mathcal{D}_K$ is a generalized ideal of a convolution semigroup.

Consider the argument $[\pi']_1$. We have, in addition to equations above, that

- since $[\pi]_1$ is honestly created: $\pi = P^\top \mathsf{w}$.
- since $[\pi']_1$ verifies: $y^\top \widehat{C} = \widehat{\pi}\bar{A}$.

Due to completeness, $\boldsymbol{y}^\top \boldsymbol{C} = \boldsymbol{\pi}^\top \bar{\boldsymbol{A}}$. Thus,

$$\beta(\boldsymbol{y}^\top \boldsymbol{C}' - \boldsymbol{\pi}' \bar{\boldsymbol{A}}') = \boldsymbol{y}^\top(\boldsymbol{C}\widehat{\boldsymbol{A}} + \widehat{\boldsymbol{C}}) - (\boldsymbol{\pi} + \widehat{\boldsymbol{\pi}})\bar{\boldsymbol{A}}'$$
$$= \underbrace{(\boldsymbol{y}^\top \boldsymbol{C} - \boldsymbol{\pi}\bar{\boldsymbol{A}})}_{=0}\widehat{\boldsymbol{A}} + \underbrace{(\boldsymbol{y}^\top \widehat{\boldsymbol{C}} - \widehat{\boldsymbol{\pi}}\bar{\boldsymbol{A}}')}_{=0}$$

and thus $\boldsymbol{C}'$ verifies. But then clearly, $\boldsymbol{\pi}' = \boldsymbol{y}^\top \boldsymbol{C}' \bar{\boldsymbol{A}}'^{-1}$ is the unique correct argument for $\boldsymbol{y} \in \mathrm{ColSpace}(\boldsymbol{M})$ when using the public key PK′.

(2: PK **verifies and the update was honestly done**) We have the following equations:

- since PK verifies: $\boldsymbol{M}^\top \boldsymbol{C} = \boldsymbol{P}\bar{\boldsymbol{A}}$,
- since PK′ was honestly updated: for correctly distributed $\widehat{\boldsymbol{A}}$ and $\widehat{\boldsymbol{K}}$, $\bar{\boldsymbol{A}}' = \bar{\boldsymbol{A}}\widehat{\boldsymbol{A}}$, $\widehat{\boldsymbol{C}} = \widehat{\boldsymbol{K}}\bar{\boldsymbol{A}}'$, $\boldsymbol{C}' = (\boldsymbol{C}\widehat{\boldsymbol{A}} + \widehat{\boldsymbol{C}})/\beta$, $\widehat{\boldsymbol{P}} = \boldsymbol{M}^\top \widehat{\boldsymbol{K}}$, $\boldsymbol{P}' = (\boldsymbol{P} + \widehat{\boldsymbol{P}})/\beta$.

Due to the assumption on $\mathcal{D}_{\bar{A}}$, $\bar{\boldsymbol{A}}'$ comes from the correct distribution. Define implicitly $\boldsymbol{P} := \boldsymbol{M}^\top \boldsymbol{C}\bar{\boldsymbol{A}}^{-1}$ (note that $\bar{\boldsymbol{A}}$ is invertible) and $\boldsymbol{K} := \boldsymbol{C}\bar{\boldsymbol{A}}^{-1}$. Then, $\boldsymbol{K}' = (\boldsymbol{K} + \widehat{\boldsymbol{K}})/\beta = (\boldsymbol{K} + \widehat{\boldsymbol{C}}\bar{\boldsymbol{A}}'^{-1})/\beta = (\boldsymbol{C}\widehat{\boldsymbol{A}} + \widehat{\boldsymbol{C}})/\beta \cdot \bar{\boldsymbol{A}}'^{-1} = \boldsymbol{C}'\bar{\boldsymbol{A}}'^{-1}$. Next, $\boldsymbol{K}' = (\boldsymbol{K} + \widehat{\boldsymbol{K}})/\beta$ has the same distribution as $\widehat{\boldsymbol{K}}$ by the assumption on $\mathcal{D}_K$. Because both $\boldsymbol{K}'$ and $\bar{\boldsymbol{A}}'$ have correct distributions, also $\boldsymbol{C}' = \boldsymbol{K}'\bar{\boldsymbol{A}}'$ has correct distribution.

Next, obviously $\boldsymbol{P}' = \boldsymbol{M}^\top(\boldsymbol{C}\bar{\boldsymbol{A}}^{-1} + \widehat{\boldsymbol{K}})/\beta = \boldsymbol{M}^\top(\boldsymbol{K} + \beta\boldsymbol{K}' - \boldsymbol{K})/\beta = \boldsymbol{M}^\top\boldsymbol{K}'$ has the correct distribution. This proves strong key-updating.

In the case of strong argument-updating, additionally, the following holds:

- the original argument verifies: $\boldsymbol{y}^\top \boldsymbol{C} = \boldsymbol{\pi}^\top \bar{\boldsymbol{A}}$,
- $[\boldsymbol{\pi}]_1$ was updated honestly: $\boldsymbol{\pi}' = (\boldsymbol{\pi} + \widehat{\boldsymbol{K}}^\top \boldsymbol{y})/\beta$ for honestly distributed $\widehat{\boldsymbol{K}} \sim \mathcal{D}_K$.

From this, we get that $\boldsymbol{\pi} = (\boldsymbol{y}^\top \boldsymbol{C}\bar{\boldsymbol{A}}^{-1})^\top = (\boldsymbol{y}^\top \boldsymbol{K})^\top = \boldsymbol{K}^\top \boldsymbol{y}$. Thus, $\boldsymbol{\pi}' = (\boldsymbol{\pi} + \widehat{\boldsymbol{K}}^\top \boldsymbol{y})/\beta = (\boldsymbol{K}^\top \boldsymbol{y} + \widehat{\boldsymbol{K}}^\top \boldsymbol{y})/\beta = (\boldsymbol{K} + \widehat{\boldsymbol{K}})^\top/\beta \cdot \boldsymbol{y} = \boldsymbol{K}'^\top \boldsymbol{y}$ which is equal to the simulated argument of $\boldsymbol{y} = \boldsymbol{M}\mathbf{w}$ (when using the public key PK′) and by perfect simulation, thus also to the real argument (when using PK′). □

Example 1 (Of the required distributions). $\mathcal{D}_K$ is the uniform distribution over $k \times k$ matrices over $\mathbb{Z}_p$ and $\mathcal{D}_{\bar{A}}$ is the uniform distribution over $k \times k$ invertible matrices over $\mathbb{Z}_p$ where as the sanity check, one checks that both matrices $[\bar{\boldsymbol{A}}]_1$ and $[\widehat{\boldsymbol{A}}]_1$ are invertible.[4] As mentioned before, in the actual instantiation of Π'_{as} (at least in the most efficient case $k = 1$) both $\mathcal{D}_K$ and $\mathcal{D}_{\bar{A}}$ are equal to the uniform distribution over $\mathbb{Z}_p$ and thus satisfy the required properties. □

Theorem 2. *Let $\mathcal{D}_k$ be efficiently verifiable (resp., $\mathcal{D}_k = \mathcal{U}_2$). If the $\mathcal{D}_k$-KerMDH^{dl} (resp., $\mathcal{D}_k$-SKerMDH^{dl}) assumption holds relative to Pgen then $\Pi_{\mathrm{bpk}}^{\mathrm{upd}}$ is (i) computationally quasi-adaptively Sub-PAR argument-update sound (I), and (ii) assuming that the preconditions of Theorem 1 are fulfilled, also computationally quasi-adaptively Sub-PAR argument-update sound (II) in the BPK model.*

---

[4] Intuitively, we require the family ν of probability distributions to be an ideal of a convolution semigroup: $\nu_s * \mu = \nu_t$, for some t, for any element μ of the semigroup.

Proof. **(i: Sub-PAR argument-update soundness (I))** follows from Proposition 1 (Π_{bpk} is computationally quasi-adaptively Sub-PAR sound under the $\mathsf{KerMDH}^{\mathsf{dl}}$ / $\mathsf{SKerMDH}^{\mathsf{dl}}$ assumption) and Lemma 2 (any Sub-PAR sound argument system is also Sub-PAR argument-update sound (I)).

(ii: Sub-PAR argument-update soundness (II)) follows from Proposition 1 (Π_{bpk} is computationally quasi-adaptively Sub-PAR sound under the $\mathsf{KerMDH}^{\mathsf{dl}}$ / $\mathsf{SKerMDH}^{\mathsf{dl}}$ assumption), Lemma 2 (any Sub-PAR sound, argument-update complete, strongly-key-update hiding, and strongly argument-update hiding argument system is also Sub-PAR argument-update sound (II)), Lemma 5 ($\Pi_{\mathsf{bpk}}^{\mathsf{upd}}$ is argument-update complete), and Theorem 1 ($\Pi_{\mathsf{bpk}}^{\mathsf{upd}}$ is strongly key-update hiding and strongly argument-update hiding). $\square$

We emphasize that Sub-PAR argument-update soundness (II) follows only when the update has been done by a honest prover (who knows the witness and does not know the key-update secret key $\widehat{\mathsf{sk}}$).

Interestingly, next, we rely on KW-KE that is a tautological knowledge assumption for Π_{bpk}, but not for $\Pi_{\mathsf{bpk}}^{\mathsf{upd}}$. This gives more credence to KW-KE as an assumption that is of independent interest.

Lemma 7. *Let $\Pi_{\mathsf{bpk}}^{\mathsf{upd}}$ be the updatable QA-NIZK argument system for linear subspaces from Fig. 4. Assume that $\mathcal{D}_p$ is such that $\mathsf{V}_{\mathsf{par}}$ is efficient. (i) Π_{bpk} is key-update statistical zero-knowledge in the BPK model. (ii) If the $(\mathcal{D}_p, k, \mathcal{D}_k)$-$\mathsf{KW\text{-}KE}_{\mathbb{G}_1}$ assumption holds relative to Pgen then Π_{bpk} is key-update statistical persistent Sub-ZK in the BPK model.*

Lemma 8. *Let $\Pi_{\mathsf{bpk}}^{\mathsf{upd}}$ be the updatable QA-NIZK argument system for linear subspaces from Fig. 4. Assume that $\mathcal{D}_p$ is such that $\mathsf{V}_{\mathsf{par}}$ is efficient. (i) Π_{bpk} is argument-update statistical zero-knowledge in the BPK model. (ii) If the $(\mathcal{D}_p, k, \mathcal{D}_k)$-$\mathsf{KW\text{-}KE}_{\mathbb{G}_1}$ assumption holds relative to Pgen then Π_{bpk} is argument-update statistical persistent Sub-ZK in the BPK model.*

6 Discussion

Why updating M might be difficult. In certain applications, one might also be interested in updating M (e.g., if $[M]_1$ is a public key of some trusted third party). Assume $[M]_1$ is updated to $[M']_1 = [M]_1 + [\widehat{M}]_1$, then $[\beta P']_1 - [P]_1 = [\beta M'^\top K']_1 - [M^\top K_{i-1}]_1 = [\beta M'^\top (K_{i-1} + \widehat{K})/\beta]_1 - [M^\top K_{i-1}]_1 = [\widehat{M}^\top K_{i-1}]_1 + [M'^\top]_1 \widehat{K}$ that can be computed assuming the updater knows either (1) both $\widehat{M}$ and $[K_{i-1}]_1$ or (2) K_{i-1}, or if all previous parties help him to compute $[\widehat{M}^\top K_{i-1}]_1$. Since neither possibility seems realistic (note that even $[K_{i-1}]_1$ is not public), one cannot probably update the language parameter.

7 Updatable Universal Public Key

Consider updatability in a more generic setting of pairing-based protocols, where the language parameter may not exist at all. The goal of updatability is to protect soundness in the case PK may be subverted, since Sub-ZK can be obtained by running the public algorithm V_{pk} [3]. In Π'_{as}, soundness is guaranteed by one of the elements of PK (namely, $[\bar{A}]_2$, see Fig. 2) coming from a KerMDH-hard distribution[5], and another element $[C]_2$ being correctly computed from $[\bar{A}]_2$. Since the latter can be verified by V_{pk}, to obtain soundness it suffices to update $[\bar{A}]_2$. (The procedure of this is the same as creating $[\bar{A}']_2$ by K_{upd} in Fig. 4, and verifying this update consists of the first four verification equations in V_{Kupd}.) Then, $[\bar{A}]_2$ will be a "universal public key" [26] for all possible language parameters in all applications that trust the concrete KerMDH *assumption*.

Importantly, one is here not restricted to Π'_{as} or even QA-NIZK: *any* application that relies on KerMDH-hardness of $\mathcal{D}_{\bar{A}}$, where it suffices to know $[\bar{A}]_2$ (instead of $[A]_2$), and where $\mathcal{D}_{\bar{A}}$ satisfies the conditions of Theorem 1, can use the same matrix $[\bar{A}]_2$. A standard example is the 1-Lin distribution $\mathcal{L}_1 = \{A = \binom{a}{1} : a \leftarrow_\$ \mathbb{Z}_p\}$. After potentially many updates of $[\bar{A}]_2$, one can create the whole public key PK corresponding to a concrete language parameter. Thereafter, one can continue updating $[\bar{A}]_2$ together with all known public keys and arguments that use (the same version of) $[\bar{A}]_2$ for soundness. Such one-phase updating can be formalized like in [26], adding to it QA-NIZK and argument-update specifics, and is out of the scope of the current paper.

We emphasize that the possibility to rely just on $[\bar{A}]_2$ is a major difference with updatable SNARKs [26] where the universal key is quite complex and each universal key of length $\Theta(n)$ can only be used for circuits of size $\leq n$.

History Further Work. The first version of this paper was written a few days after [26] was posted on eprint; and then eprinted as [37]. The current version mainly differs by taking in the account the newer version of [4]. We leave the definition and study of updatable Sub-PAR *knowledge-sound* QA-NIZKs as an open question. We also leave the study of other applications that can make use of the described universal public key updating method to the further work. We conjecture that many other such applications will be found shortly.

Acknowledgment. We would like to thank Dario Fiore and Markulf Kohlweiss for useful comments. The authors were partially supported by the Estonian Research Council grant (PRG49).

References

1. Abdalla, M., Benhamouda, F., Pointcheval, D.: Disjunctions for hash proof systems: new constructions and applications. In: Oswald, E., Fischlin, M. (eds.) EUROCRYPT 2015. LNCS, vol. 9057, pp. 69–100. Springer, Heidelberg (2015). https://doi.org/10.1007/978-3-662-46803-6_3

---

[5] Technically, A comes from a KerMDH-hard distribution, not $\bar{A}$. However, in the case of some distributions (like DLIN-related distributions), A has an extra constant column compared to $\bar{A}$. The knowledge of $[A]_2$ and $[\bar{A}]_2$ is equivalent in such a case.

2. Abdolmaleki, B., Baghery, K., Lipmaa, H., Siim, J., Zając, M.: UC-secure CRS generation for SNARKs. In: Buchmann, J., Nitaj, A., Rachidi, T. (eds.) AFRICACRYPT 2019. LNCS, vol. 11627, pp. 99–117. Springer, Cham (2019). https://doi.org/10.1007/978-3-030-23696-0_6

3. Abdolmaleki, B., Baghery, K., Lipmaa, H., Zając, M.: A subversion-resistant SNARK. In: Takagi, T., Peyrin, T. (eds.) ASIACRYPT 2017. LNCS, vol. 10626, pp. 3–33. Springer, Cham (2017). https://doi.org/10.1007/978-3-319-70700-6_1

4. Abdolmaleki, B., Lipmaa, H., Siim, J., Zając, M.: On QA-NIZK in the BPK model. In: Kiayias, A., Kohlweiss, M., Wallden, P., Zikas, V. (eds.) PKC 2020. LNCS, vol. 12110, pp. 590–620. Springer, Cham (2020). https://doi.org/10.1007/978-3-030-45374-9_20

5. Abdolmaleki, B., Ramacher, S., Slamanig, D.: Lift-and-shift: obtaining simulation extractable subversion and updatable SNARKs generically. Technical report 2020/062, IACR (2020)

6. Bellare, M., Fuchsbauer, G., Scafuro, A.: NIZKs with an untrusted CRS: security in the face of parameter subversion. In: Cheon, J.H., Takagi, T. (eds.) ASIACRYPT 2016. LNCS, vol. 10032, pp. 777–804. Springer, Heidelberg (2016). https://doi.org/10.1007/978-3-662-53890-6_26

7. Ben-Sasson, E., Chiesa, A., Green, M., Tromer, E., Virza, M.: Secure sampling of public parameters for succinct zero knowledge proofs. In: 2015 IEEE Symposium on Security and Privacy, pp. 287–304 (2015)

8. Boneh, D., Boyen, X., Shacham, H.: Short group signatures. In: Franklin, M. (ed.) CRYPTO 2004. LNCS, vol. 3152, pp. 41–55. Springer, Heidelberg (2004). https://doi.org/10.1007/978-3-540-28628-8_3

9. Bowe, S., Gabizon, A., Green, M.D.: A multi-party protocol for constructing the public parameters of the pinocchio zk-SNARK. Cryptology ePrint Archive, Report 2017/602 (2017). http://eprint.iacr.org/2017/602

10. Bowe, S., Gabizon, A., Miers, I.: Scalable multi-party computation for zk-SNARK parameters in the random beacon model. Cryptology ePrint Archive, Report 2017/1050 (2017). http://eprint.iacr.org/2017/1050

11. Canetti, R., Goldreich, O., Goldwasser, S., Micali, S.: Resettable zero-knowledge (extended abstract). In: 32nd ACM STOC, pp. 235–244 (2000)

12. Chiesa, A., Hu, Y., Maller, M., Mishra, P., Vesely, N., Ward, N.: Marlin: preprocessing zkSNARKs with universal and updatable SRS. In: Canteaut, A., Ishai, Y. (eds.) EUROCRYPT 2020. LNCS, vol. 12105, pp. 738–768. Springer, Cham (2020). https://doi.org/10.1007/978-3-030-45721-1_26

13. Daza, V., González, A., Pindado, Z., Ràfols, C., Silva, J.: Shorter quadratic QA-NIZK proofs. In: Lin, D., Sako, K. (eds.) PKC 2019. LNCS, vol. 11442, pp. 314–343. Springer, Cham (2019). https://doi.org/10.1007/978-3-030-17253-4_11

14. Daza, V., Ràfols, C., Zacharakis, A.: Updateable inner product argument with logarithmic verifier and applications. In: Kiayias, A., Kohlweiss, M., Wallden, P., Zikas, V. (eds.) PKC 2020. LNCS, vol. 12110, pp. 527–557. Springer, Cham (2020). https://doi.org/10.1007/978-3-030-45374-9_18

15. Di Crescenzo, G., Lipmaa, H.: Succinct NP proofs from an extractability assumption. In: Beckmann, A., Dimitracopoulos, C., Löwe, B. (eds.) CiE 2008. LNCS, vol. 5028, pp. 175–185. Springer, Heidelberg (2008). https://doi.org/10.1007/978-3-540-69407-6_21

16. Escala, A., Herold, G., Kiltz, E., Ràfols, C., Villar, J.: An algebraic framework for Diffie-Hellman assumptions. In: Canetti, R., Garay, J.A. (eds.) CRYPTO 2013. LNCS, vol. 8043, pp. 129–147. Springer, Heidelberg (2013). https://doi.org/10.1007/978-3-642-40084-1_8

17. Fuchsbauer, G.: Subversion-zero-knowledge SNARKs. In: Abdalla, M., Dahab, R. (eds.) PKC 2018. LNCS, vol. 10769, pp. 315–347. Springer, Cham (2018). https://doi.org/10.1007/978-3-319-76578-5_11

18. Gabizon, A., Williamson, Z.J., Ciobotaru, O.: PLONK: permutations over Lagrange-bases for oecumenical noninteractive arguments of knowledge. Cryptology ePrint Archive, Report 2019/953 (2019). https://eprint.iacr.org/2019/953

19. Gennaro, R., Gentry, C., Parno, B., Raykova, M.: Quadratic span programs and succinct NIZKs without PCPs. In: Johansson, T., Nguyen, P.Q. (eds.) EUROCRYPT 2013. LNCS, vol. 7881, pp. 626–645. Springer, Heidelberg (2013). https://doi.org/10.1007/978-3-642-38348-9_37

20. Gentry, C., Wichs, D.: Separating succinct non-interactive arguments from all falsifiable assumptions. In: 43rd ACM STOC, pp. 99–108 (2011)

21. Gjøsteen, K.: A new security proof for Damgård's ElGamal. In: Pointcheval, D. (ed.) CT-RSA 2006. LNCS, vol. 3860, pp. 150–158. Springer, Heidelberg (2006). https://doi.org/10.1007/11605805_10

22. González, A., Hevia, A., Ràfols, C.: QA-NIZK arguments in asymmetric groups: new tools and new constructions. In: Iwata, T., Cheon, J.H. (eds.) ASIACRYPT 2015. LNCS, vol. 9452, pp. 605–629. Springer, Heidelberg (2015). https://doi.org/10.1007/978-3-662-48797-6_25

23. González, A., Ráfols, C.: New techniques for non-interactive shuffle and range arguments. In: Manulis, M., Sadeghi, A.-R., Schneider, S. (eds.) ACNS 2016. LNCS, vol. 9696, pp. 427–444. Springer, Cham (2016). https://doi.org/10.1007/978-3-319-39555-5_23

24. Groth, J.: Short pairing-based non-interactive zero-knowledge arguments. In: Abe, M. (ed.) ASIACRYPT 2010. LNCS, vol. 6477, pp. 321–340. Springer, Heidelberg (2010). https://doi.org/10.1007/978-3-642-17373-8_19

25. Groth, J.: On the size of pairing-based non-interactive arguments. In: Fischlin, M., Coron, J.-S. (eds.) EUROCRYPT 2016. LNCS, vol. 9666, pp. 305–326. Springer, Heidelberg (2016). https://doi.org/10.1007/978-3-662-49896-5_11

26. Groth, J., Kohlweiss, M., Maller, M., Meiklejohn, S., Miers, I.: Updatable and universal common reference strings with applications to zk-SNARKs. In: Shacham, H., Boldyreva, A. (eds.) CRYPTO 2018. LNCS, vol. 10993, pp. 698–728. Springer, Cham (2018). https://doi.org/10.1007/978-3-319-96878-0_24

27. Groth, J., Maller, M.: Snarky signatures: minimal signatures of knowledge from simulation-extractable SNARKs. In: Katz, J., Shacham, H. (eds.) CRYPTO 2017. LNCS, vol. 10402, pp. 581–612. Springer, Cham (2017). https://doi.org/10.1007/978-3-319-63715-0_20

28. Jutla, C.S., Roy, A.: Shorter quasi-adaptive NIZK proofs for linear subspaces. In: Sako, K., Sarkar, P. (eds.) ASIACRYPT 2013. LNCS, vol. 8269, pp. 1–20. Springer, Heidelberg (2013). https://doi.org/10.1007/978-3-642-42033-7_1

29. Jutla, C.S., Roy, A.: Switching lemma for bilinear tests and constant-size NIZK proofs for linear subspaces. In: Garay, J.A., Gennaro, R. (eds.) CRYPTO 2014. LNCS, vol. 8617, pp. 295–312. Springer, Heidelberg (2014). https://doi.org/10.1007/978-3-662-44381-1_17

30. Kiltz, E., Wee, H.: Quasi-adaptive NIZK for linear subspaces revisited. In: Oswald, E., Fischlin, M. (eds.) EUROCRYPT 2015. LNCS, vol. 9057, pp. 101–128. Springer, Heidelberg (2015). https://doi.org/10.1007/978-3-662-46803-6_4

31. Klenke, A.: Probability Theory: A Comprehensive Course. Universitext, 1st edn. Springer, London (2008)

32. Libert, B., Peters, T., Joye, M., Yung, M.: Non-malleability from malleability: simulation-sound quasi-adaptive NIZK proofs and CCA2-secure encryption from homomorphic signatures. In: Nguyen, P.Q., Oswald, E. (eds.) EUROCRYPT 2014. LNCS, vol. 8441, pp. 514–532. Springer, Heidelberg (2014). https://doi.org/10.1007/978-3-642-55220-5_29

33. Libert, B., Peters, T., Joye, M., Yung, M.: Compactly hiding linear spans. In: Iwata, T., Cheon, J.H. (eds.) ASIACRYPT 2015. LNCS, vol. 9452, pp. 681–707. Springer, Heidelberg (2015). https://doi.org/10.1007/978-3-662-48797-6_28

34. Lipmaa, H.: On the CCA1-security of Elgamal and Damgård's Elgamal. In: Lai, X., Yung, M., Lin, D. (eds.) Inscrypt 2010. LNCS, vol. 6584, pp. 18–35. Springer, Heidelberg (2011). https://doi.org/10.1007/978-3-642-21518-6_2

35. Lipmaa, H.: Progression-free sets and sublinear pairing-based non-interactive zero-knowledge arguments. In: Cramer, R. (ed.) TCC 2012. LNCS, vol. 7194, pp. 169–189. Springer, Heidelberg (2012). https://doi.org/10.1007/978-3-642-28914-9_10

36. Lipmaa, H.: Succinct non-interactive zero knowledge arguments from span programs and linear error-correcting codes. In: Sako, K., Sarkar, P. (eds.) ASIACRYPT 2013. LNCS, vol. 8269, pp. 41–60. Springer, Heidelberg (2013). https://doi.org/10.1007/978-3-642-42033-7_3

37. Lipmaa, H.: Key-and-Argument-Updatable QA-NIZKs. Technical report 2019/333, IACR (2019). https://eprint.iacr.org/2019/333

38. Lipmaa, H.: Simulation-extractable ZK-SNARKs revisited. Technical report 2019/612, IACR (2019). https://eprint.iacr.org/2019/612. Accessed 8 Feb 2020

39. Maller, M., Bowe, S., Kohlweiss, M., Meiklejohn, S.: Sonic: zero-knowledge SNARKs from linear-size universal and updatable structured reference strings. In: ACM CCS 2019, pp. 2111–2128 (2019)

40. Micali, S., Reyzin, L.: Soundness in the Public-Key Model. In: Kilian, J. (ed.) CRYPTO 2001. LNCS, vol. 2139, pp. 542–565. Springer, Heidelberg (2001). https://doi.org/10.1007/3-540-44647-8_32

41. Morillo, P., Ràfols, C., Villar, J.L.: The kernel matrix Diffie-Hellman assumption. In: Cheon, J.H., Takagi, T. (eds.) ASIACRYPT 2016. LNCS, vol. 10031, pp. 729–758. Springer, Heidelberg (2016). https://doi.org/10.1007/978-3-662-53887-6_27

42. Naor, M.: On cryptographic assumptions and challenges. In: Boneh, D. (ed.) CRYPTO 2003. LNCS, vol. 2729, pp. 96–109. Springer, Heidelberg (2003). https://doi.org/10.1007/978-3-540-45146-4_6

43. Parno, B., Howell, J., Gentry, C., Raykova, M.: Pinocchio: nearly practical verifiable computation. In: 2013 IEEE Symposium on Security and Privacy, pp. 238–252 (2013)

On Adaptive Security of Delayed-Input Sigma Protocols and Fiat-Shamir NIZKs

Michele Ciampi[1]([✉])[iD], Roberto Parisella[2], and Daniele Venturi[3][iD]

[1] The University of Edinburgh, Edinburgh, UK
mciampi@ed.ac.uk
[2] Simula UiB, Bergen, Norway
roberto@simula.no
[3] Sapienza University of Rome, Rome, Italy
venturi@di.uniroma1.it

Abstract. We study *adaptive security* of delayed-input Sigma protocols and non-interactive zero-knowledge (NIZK) proof systems in the common reference string (CRS) model. Our contributions are threefold:

- We exhibit a generic compiler taking any delayed-input Sigma protocol and returning a delayed-input Sigma protocol satisfying *adaptive-input* special honest-verifier zero knowledge (SHVZK). In case the initial Sigma protocol also satisfies *adaptive-input* special soundness, our compiler preserves this property.
- We revisit the recent paradigm by Canetti et al. (STOC 2019) for obtaining NIZK proof systems in the CRS model via the Fiat-Shamir transform applied to so-called *trapdoor* Sigma protocols, in the context of adaptive security. In particular, assuming correlation-intractable hash functions for all sparse relations, we prove that Fiat-Shamir NIZKs satisfy either:
  - (i) Adaptive soundness (and non-adaptive zero knowledge), so long as the challenge is obtained by hashing both the prover's first round and the instance being proven;
  - (ii) Adaptive zero knowledge (and non-adaptive soundness), so long as the challenge is obtained by hashing only the prover's first round, and further assuming that the initial trapdoor Sigma protocol satisfies adaptive-input SHVZK.
- We exhibit a generic compiler taking any Sigma protocol and returning a *trapdoor* Sigma protocol. Unfortunately, this transform does not preserve the delayed-input property of the initial Sigma protocol (if any). To complement this result, we also give yet another compiler taking any delayed-input trapdoor Sigma protocol and returning a delayed-input trapdoor Sigma protocol with adaptive-input SHVZK.

An attractive feature of our first two compilers is that they allow obtaining *efficient* delayed-input Sigma protocols with adaptive security, and *efficient* Fiat-Shamir NIZKs with adaptive soundness (and non-adaptive zero knowledge) in the CRS model. Prior to our work, the latter was only possible using generic NP reductions.

M. Ciampi—Supported by H2020 project PRIVILEDGE #780477.

© Springer Nature Switzerland AG 2020
C. Galdi and V. Kolesnikov (Eds.): SCN 2020, LNCS 12238, pp. 670–690, 2020.
https://doi.org/10.1007/978-3-030-57990-6_33

Keywords: Sigma protocols · Non-interactive zero knowledge · Adaptive security

1 Introduction

Sigma protocols are a special class of three-round public-coin interactive proofs between a prover $\mathcal{P}$ and a verifier $\mathcal{V}$, where $\mathcal{P}$'s goal is to convince $\mathcal{V}$ that a common statement x belongs to a given NP language L. The prover knows a witness w (corresponding to x) as auxiliary input, and starts the interaction by sending a first message a (possibly depending on both x, w); the verifier then sends a uniformly random ℓ-bit challenge c, to which the prover replies with a last message z. Finally, the verifier decides whether $x \in L$ based on x and the transcript (a, c, z). Despite *completeness* (*i.e.*, the honest prover always convinces the honest verifier about true statements), Sigma protocols satisfy two additional properties known as *special soundness* (SS) and *special honest-verifier zero knowledge* (SHVZK). The former is a strong form of *soundness* (*i.e.*, no malicious prover can convince the verifier about the veracity of *false* statements $x \notin L$), which in fact implies that Sigma protocols are proofs of knowledge [6,35]; the latter requires the existence of an efficient simulator $\mathcal{S}$ that, given any *true* statement $x \in L$ and any possible challenge c, is able to simulate an *honest* transcript (a, c, z) between the prover and the verifier, which in particular implies that honest transcripts do not reveal anything about the witness to the eyes of an honest-but-curious verifier. While Sigma protocols exist for all of NP (as Blum's protocol [11] for Hamiltonian Graphs is a Sigma protocol), the latter comes at the price of expensive NP reductions. Luckily, Sigma protocols also exist for many concrete languages based on number theory and lattices (such as Quadratic Residuosity [35], Discrete Log [47,50], Factoring [33], and Learning with Errors [2,45,51]), and these protocols are very efficient, thus opening the way to a plethora of cryptographic applications, *e.g.* to constructing different kinds of commitment schemes [18,24,26,28,39,44] and trapdoor hash functions [7], and for obtaining non-interactive zero-knowledge (NIZK) proofs and digital signatures via the celebrated Fiat-Shamir transform [8,32,49]. In this paper we study *adaptive security* for both Sigma protocols and Fiat-Shamir NIZKs.

Delayed-Input Sigma Protocols. The classical Sigma protocol by Feige, Lapidot and Shamir [31,43] for Graph Hamiltonicity (henceforth denoted by FLS) has the special property that the prover can compute the first round of the proof without knowing the graph, so long as it knows the number of vertices ahead of time. In particular, the graph and the corresponding Hamiltonian cycle are only needed to compute the prover's last round. More generally, a Sigma protocol is called *delayed-input* if the prover's first round can be computed given only $n = |x|$ (and without knowing x, w). For such Sigma protocols, the standard definitions of SS and SHVZK may not be sufficient as they do not take into account attackers choosing the statement x adaptively based on a partial transcript (a, c). This limitation may have a negative impact[1] on the applications of delayed-input Sigma protocols, particularly in settings where adaptive security is required. While, the FLS protocol already satisfies both *adaptive-input* SS and *adaptive-input* SHVZK,[2] the latter is only of theoretical interest. Partially motivated by this shortcoming, Ciampi et al. [23] proposed a general transformation for turning any delayed-input Sigma protocol into one satisfying *adaptive-input* SS. This leaves the following open problem. **Q1:** *"Do there exist efficient delayed-input Sigma protocols with adaptive security (i.e., satisfying both adaptive-input SS and adaptive-input SHVZK)?"*

Fiat-Shamir NIZKs. The Fiat-Shamir transform [32] allows to turn a Sigma protocol into a non-interactive proof system by means of a hash functions h with ℓ-bit output. The idea is for the prover to compute a and z as prescribed by the Sigma protocol, where the challenge c is set to $c := h(a\|x)$. One can show that this yields a secure NIZK starting from any Sigma protocol, so long as the hash function h is modelled as a random oracle [8,30]. Whether security of the Fiat-Shamir transform can be proven without resorting to random oracles has been a question subject of intensive study. Here, the goal is to instantiate the random oracle with a set of efficiently computable hash functions $\mathcal{H} = \{h_k\}$, where the hash key k is made available to all parties in the form of a common reference string (CRS). Unfortunately, several negative results are known in this respect [4, 10,29,34], which, however, only exclude the possibility of instantiating the Fiat-Shamir transform starting with *any* Sigma protocol or via black-box reductions to falsifiable assumptions. Indeed, a recent line of research[3] established the above negative results can be circumvented:

- Assuming the initial interactive protocol is a *trapdoor* Sigma protocols [14]. Informally, a trapdoor Sigma protocol is a special Sigma protocol in the CRS model satisfying the following two properties:(i) If the statement x is false, then for every first message a, there is a unique challenge c for which there is an accepting third message z that results in an accepting transcript (a, c, z); (ii) There is a trapdoor associated with the CRS that allows us to efficiently compute this "bad challenge" c from the first message a and the statement x being proven.
- Assuming that $\mathcal{H}$ is a family of correlation-intractable (CI) hash functions [17]. Informally, a family $\mathcal{H}$ satisfies CI w.r.t. some relation R if no efficient attacker given the hash key k can produce an input x such

---

[1] We discuss practical applications where adaptive security is of concern in Sect. 1.3.

[2] Intuitively, adaptive-input SS guarantees extraction even for transcripts (a, c, z) and (a, c', z') for different (possibly adaptively chosen) statements. Similarly, adaptive-input SHVZK requires the simulator to fake the prover's first message given only $n = |x|$.

[3] This research extends previous results showing that CI is sufficient for proving *soundness* of the Fiat-Shamir transform [5,29,38].

that $(x, h_k(x)) \in R$. CI hash functions w.r.t. broad-enough[4] relations have recently been constructed from a variety of assumptions including program obfuscation [15, 41, 46], strong one-way functions [40], key-dependent message secure encryption [16], circularly-secure fully-homomorphic encryption [14], LWE [48], and LPN along with DDH/QR/DCR/LWE [13].

A natural question is whether Fiat-Shamir NIZKs obtained via CI hash functions are adaptively secure, *i.e.* whether the non-interactive proof resulting from applying the Fiat-Shamir transform to a trapdoor Sigma protocol satisfies both *adaptive* soundness and *adaptive* zero-knowledge in the CRS model.[5] Canetti et al. [14] proved that a slight variant of the FLS protocol directly achieves adaptive security, however, in order to be used in applications, the latter requires expensive NP reductions, and thus results in very inefficient NIZKs. They also provide an efficient instantiation using the classical Sigma protocol for Quadratic Residuosity [35], and more in general starting with any *instance-dependent* trapdoor Sigma protocol (in which the trapdoor is allowed to depend on the statement being proven). Unfortunately, instance-dependent trapdoor Sigma protocols are not sufficient to prove adaptive security of Fiat-Shamir NIZKs, thus leaving the following intriguing open question. **Q2:** *"Do there exist efficient trapdoor Sigma protocols allowing to obtain Fiat-Shamir NIZKs with <u>adaptive</u> security (i.e., satisfying both adaptive soundness and adaptive zero knowledge in the CRS model)?"*

1.1 Our Contributions

In this work, we make progress towards answering the above two open questions in the affirmative. Our first contribution is a general compiler taking any delayed-input Sigma protocol and outputting another delayed-input Sigma protocol (for the same language) with adaptive-input SHVZK. Furthermore, assuming the initial Sigma protocol already satisfies adaptive-input SS, so does the Sigma protocol produced by our compiler. Hence, using the transformation by Ciampi et al. [23], we obtain a general compiler which allows to turn any delayed-input Sigma protocol into one with adaptive security, which is a positive answer to **Q1**. Next, we revisit the framework for obtaining adaptively-secure NIZKs via the Fiat-Shamir transform using CI hash functions. In particular, we show the following two results:

- In case the challenge c is obtained by hashing both the prover's first round a and the statement x (*i.e.,* $c = h_k(a\|x)$), trapdoor Sigma protocols are

---

[4] In particular, sufficient for proving security of Fiat-Shamir NIZKs without random oracles.

[5] The former means that no malicious prover, given the CRS, can produce a false statement along with an accepting non-interactive proof. The latter means that no malicious verifier, given the CRS, can produce a true statement, along with the corresponding witness, for which a non-interactive proof cannot be simulated in polynomial time given the statement alone.

sufficient for proving *adaptive soundness* and *non-adaptive zero knowledge* of Fiat-Shamir NIZKs in the CRS model.

- In case the challenge c is obtained by hashing only the prover's first round a (*i.e.*, $c = h_k(a)$), trapdoor Sigma protocols satisfying soundness (which in turn follows by SS) and *adaptive-input* SHVZK are sufficient for proving *non-adaptive soundness* and *adaptive zero knowledge* of Fiat-Shamir NIZKs in the CRS model.

The fact that hashing both the prover's first message and the statement is essential for obtaining adaptive soundness was already known for the random oracle model [9]. In this vein, our paper confirms this to be sufficient in the plain model as well. Our second contribution is a compiler taking any Sigma protocol and outputting a *trapdoor* Sigma protocol (for the same language). Unfortunately, this compiler does not preserve the delayed-input property of the initial Sigma protocol (if any), and thus, by our result from above, only implies Fiat-Shamir NIZKs with adaptive soundness (but not adaptive zero knowledge). This result can still be interpreted as a partial (positive) answer to **Q2**, as it allows to obtain *efficient* Fiat-Shamir NIZKs with *adaptive soundness* (and non-adaptive zero knowledge) in the CRS model for any language admitting a Sigma protocol. Previously to our work, the latter was possible only using expensive NP reductions. Finally, we also show that any delayed-input trapdoor Sigma protocol can be turned into a delayed-input trapdoor Sigma protocol with adaptive-input SHVZK, which (again by our generalization of [14]) would be sufficient for obtaining Fiat-Shamir NIZKs with adaptive zero knowledge (and non-adaptive soundness) in the CRS model. Unfortunately, the only example we know of a delayed-input trapdoor Sigma protocol is FLS (for which [14] directly proved adaptive security of the corresponding Fiat-Shamir NIZK), and thus we view this more as a conceptual contribution providing a possible path towards obtaining efficient Fiat-Shamir NIZKs with adaptive zero knowledge in the future.

1.2   Technical Overview

Adaptive-Input SHVZK. Our first compiler exploits so-called instance-dependent trapdoor commitment (IDTC) schemes. Intuitively, this primitive is parameterized by an NP language L and allows a sender to create a commitment com (with opening dec) to a message m using a statement x as a label. The main idea is that: (i) In case $x \notin L$ is a *false* statement, the commitment satisfies the standard *binding* property. (ii) In case $x \in L$ is a *true* statement, the commitment satisfies the standard *hiding* property and additionally, given a valid witness w for x, one can generate a fake commitment com that is distributed like an honest commitment but that can later be opened to any message (the so-called *trapdoorness* property). It is well known that IDTCs for any language L can be constructed in a black-box way given any Sigma protocol for L [24,26,27,44].

We now explain how to compile any delayed-input Sigma protocol Σ for a language L into a delayed-input Sigma protocol Σ'' for L that satisfies adaptive-input SHVZK. The transformation relies on an IDTC Π for the language L_{DH}

of Diffie-Hellman (DH) tuples, and on a Sigma protocol Σ' for the complement language $\overline{L}_{DH}$ of non-DH tuples.[6]

- The prover, given only $x \in L$, starts by sampling a random non-DH tuple $T \in \overline{L}_{DH}$, along with the corresponding witness, and then computes a commitment com (with decommitment dec) to the first round a of Σ using T as label. Next, it computes the first round a' of Σ' and forwards (com, a', T) to the verifier.
- The verifier sends a random ℓ-bit challenge c to the prover.
- Upon receiving a valid witness w for x, the prover computes the third round z and z' of both Σ and Σ', and forwards them to the verifier along with the opening (a, dec) of commitment com.

The proof of (adaptive-input) SS of Σ'' follows readily from the (adaptive-input) SS of Σ and the binding property of Π. Hence, we here focus on the proof of adaptive-input SHVZK. The simulator proceeds as follows:

- Upon receiving challenge $c \in \{0, 1\}^{\ell}$, the simulator first samples a random DH tuple $T \in L_{DH}$ and generates a fake commitment com using T and its corresponding witness. Next, it runs the SHVZK simulator of Σ' upon input T and c obtaining (a', z') and returns a simulated first round $a'' = (\text{com}, a', T)$.
- Upon receiving statement $x \in L$, the simulator runs the SHVZK simulator of Σ upon input x and c obtaining (a, z). Hence, it opens the commitment com to a obtaining decommitment dec, and returns a simulated third round $z'' = (z, z', (a, \text{dec}))$.

In the proof, we first move to a mental experiment with a modified simulator that generates (a, z) using the real prover of Σ; this is possible thanks to the SHVZK property of Σ. Next, we replace $T \in L_{DH}$ with $T \in \overline{L}_{DH}$ and (com, dec) with an honestly computed commitment to a. The DDH assumption and the trapdoorness property of Π imply that no efficient distinguisher can notice such a change. Finally, we use the SHVZK property of Σ' to compute (a', z') as the real prover of Σ' would do, which yields exactly the same distribution of proofs as generated by our compiler, and thus concludes the proof. Note that, besides running Σ, our transformation requires to run an IDTC in parallel with Σ' (to prove that a tuple is DH). The cost of running the IDTC corresponds to running a Sigma protocol for DH tuples. The cost of running a Sigma protocol that proves that a tuple is DH is of 2 exponentiations for the prover and 4 exponentiations for the verifier. Therefore, our compiler adds an overhead of 4 exponentiations for the prover and 8 exponentiations for the verifier.

Adaptive Security of Fiat-Shamir NIZKs. We start by recalling the notion of trapdoor Sigma protocols in more details. Intuitively, a trapdoor Sigma protocol is a special kind of three-round public-coin proof system in the CRS model[7]

---

[6] We refer the reader to the full version for a description of Σ'.

[7] The latter means that, at setup, a CRS ω is generated and distributed to both the prover and the verifier.

with the guarantee that, for every valid CRS ω, every false statement $x \notin L$, and every first round a, there is *at most one* challenge $c := f(\omega, a, x)$ such that, for some z, the transcript (a, c, z) is accepting w.r.t. (ω, x). The function f is called the *bad-challenge function*. Moreover, it is possible to generate an honest-looking CRS ω along with a trapdoor τ which allows to efficiently compute the bad challenge c given the first round a and the statement x.

Let Σ be a trapdoor Sigma protocol for language L, and Π be the non-interactive proof derived from Σ via the Fiat-Shamir transform using a CI hash family $\mathcal{H}$ for all "efficiently searchable" sparse relations. The proof of adaptive security of Π follows closely the approached used in [14], with a few crucial differences. In particular:

- To show adaptive soundness, one first argues that any prover which, given an honestly-computed CRS (ω, k), is able to produce a statement $x \notin L$ and a non-interactive proof $\pi = (a, z)$ such that (a, c, z) is accepting w.r.t. (ω, x) for $c = h_k(a||x)$ with non-negligible probability, must do so even in case the CRS ω of Σ is generated along with the trapdoor τ. The latter, however, contradicts the CI property of the hash family $\mathcal{H}$ w.r.t. the (efficiently searchable) relation $R_{\omega,\tau} := \{(a||x, c) : x \notin L \land c = f(\tau, \omega, a, x)\}$, which is easily seen to be sparse thanks to the soundness property of Σ. The key observation that allows to prove adaptive security here is the fact that the hash function takes also x as input, which allows the reduction to CI to go through without knowing x in advance.

- The simulator for adaptive zero knowledge picks a random challenge c and then obtains a invoking the adaptive-input SHVZK simulator of Σ. Hence, it samples a fresh CRS ω and a random hash key k from the conditional distribution $h_k(a) = c$, yielding a simulated CRS (ω, k). Finally, upon receiving $x \in L$ from the adversary, it obtains z from the adaptive-input SHVZK simulator and outputs a simulated proof $\pi = (a, z)$. We note that for this to work it is essential that the challenge c is obtained by hashing only the prover's first message a, as otherwise the simulator would not be able to sample k uniformly from the conditional distribution $c = h_k(a||x)$ without being given x in advance.

From Sigma protocols to Trapdoor Sigma Protocols. Let us now explain our compiler for turning any Sigma protocol Σ into a *trapdoor* Sigma protocol Σ'. The CRS ω' of Σ' consists of the CRS ω of Σ (if any), along with the public key pk of a (committing) public-key encryption (PKE) scheme. For simplicity, let us assume that the challenge space of Σ is $\{0, 1\}$; it is immediate to extend the challenge space arbitrarily using parallel repetition. The prover of Σ' simply obtains a by running the prover of Σ. Hence, it computes both answers z_0 and z_1 corresponding to the two possible challenges $c = 0$ and $c = 1$, and it encrypts z_0 and z_1 under pk obtaining two ciphertexts e_0, e_1. The prover's first message consists of $a' = (a, e_0, e_1)$. Finally, upon receiving a challenge c, the prover's last message z' consists of the response z_c along with the random coins r_c used to obtain e_c. The verifier accepts if and only if (a, c, z_c) is a valid transcript w.r.t. (ω, x), and additionally (z_c, r_c) is consistent with e_c. It is not hard to show that the above transformation preserves both SS and SHVZK of the underlying protocol Σ, so long as the PKE scheme is semantically secure. To prove that Σ' is a trapdoor Sigma protocol it remains to show how to efficiently compute the bad-challenge function. The main idea here is to let the secret key sk corresponding to pk be the trapdoor τ. This way, given a' and x, we can decrypt e_0, e_1 obtaining[8] the responses z_0, z_1. Note that in case both transcripts $(a, 0, z_0)$ and $(a, 1, z_1)$ are accepting w.r.t. (ω, x), the SS property of Σ implies that $x \in L$. On the other hand, if $x \notin L$, there exists at most one challenge c such that (a, c, z_c) is accepting, and we can determine c efficiently by simply running the verifier algorithm upon input both transcripts $(a, 0, z_0)$ and $(a, _1, z_1)$. Note that, besides running Σ, our transformation requires to encrypt two values using a public-key encryption scheme. Moreover, if we want a trapdoor Sigma protocol with challenge space $\{0, 1\}^\ell$ for some $\ell \in \mathbb{N}$, and consequently better soundness, we need to repeat our protocol in parallel ℓ times. If the cost of running Σ is C_P for the prover and C_V for the verifier, and the cost of computing an encryption is C_E, then the cost of running our protocol for the prover is $(C_P + 2C_E)\ell$ and for the verifier is $(C_V + C_E)\ell$.

Adding Adaptive-Input SHVZK. Note that Σ' as defined above is inherently not delayed-input, even assuming Σ is delayed-input. This is because the prover needs the witness in order to compute the two possible responses z_0, z_1 already in the first round. Our last compiler overcomes this problem by extending our very first transform (for obtaining delayed-input Sigma protocols with adaptive-input SHVZK) to *trapdoor* Sigma protocols. The main idea is to work in the CRS model and replace the IDTC with an *extractable* IDTC (a new notion that we introduce). Intuitively, the difference between IDTCs and extractable IDTCs is that the latter are defined in the CRS model, and the CRS can be generated together with a trapdoor in such a way that, given a commitment of the extractable IDTC scheme with respect to a false instance, it is possible to extract the committed value (which is unique) using the trapdoor. Moreover, the commitment procedure now outputs a message com and an instance T such that the verifier can check if the first two components of T are consistent with the CRS. As we show, the latter allows to preserve the trapdoorness property of Σ when applying the transformation described before, while at the same time boosting SHVZK to adaptive-input SHVZK. Finally, we give a simple construction of an extractable IDTC Π for the language L_{DH} of DH tuples. This construction is based on the observation that the classical Sigma protocol for DH tuples has a special extractor which, on input the first round $a = (g^r, h^{r'})$ and γ such that $h = g^\gamma$, outputs the only possible challenge c that would make the transcript (a, c, z) accepting w.r.t. a non-DH tuple (for some z). Given a Sigma protocol Σ for L_{DH}, we then show how to obtain an extractable IDTC. The main idea is to set the CRS to $(g, h = g^\gamma)$ and the trapdoor to $\tau = \gamma$. Each commitment com is then equipped with a value $T = (g^\alpha, h^\beta)$ with $\alpha \neq \beta$. Note that in this case

---

[8] Due to the committing property of the PKE scheme.

(ω, T) corresponds to a non-DH tuple, hence the extractor can be run on com, which corresponds to the first round of Σ.

1.3 Applications

Our results directly allow to achieve adaptive security of delayed-input Sigma protocols and Fiat-Shamir NIZKs. Since applications of the latter are well known, below we elaborate on the impact of our results on applications of the former. The delayed-input property directly improves the round complexity of any cryptographic protocol consisting of the following two steps: (1) an NP-statement x and a witness w is defined via an interactive process; and (2) one of the parties involved in the protocol provides a proof that x is a true statement. Indeed, using a delayed-input Sigma protocol that allows proving the validity of x, it is possible to parallelize the above two steps, thus decreasing the round complexity of the overall process. Furthermore, the delayed-input property of FLS has proven to be particularly powerful for providing round-efficient constructions from general assumptions, such as: 4-round (optimal) secure 2PC where only one player gets the output (5 rounds when both players get the output) [42], 4-round 2PC in the simultaneous message exchange model where both parties get the output [22], 4-round MPC for any functionality [1,3,12,19], 3-round non-malleable commitments [20,36] and 4-round non-malleable commitments [21,37]. In many cryptographic applications, one party needs to prove an OR statement of the form *"either x is true or I know a trapdoor"*, where neither x nor the trapdoor might be known at the beginning of the protocol. Our adaptive-input SHVZK Sigma protocols can be used to prove exactly this kind of statements, as we can combine adaptive-input (and non-adaptive-input) SHVZK Sigma protocols using the well-known OR composition technique of [25], which yields an adaptive witness-indistinguishable (WI) Sigma protocol (*i.e.*, a Sigma protocol that retains the WI property even when the statement is adaptively chosen after the first round). The notion of adaptive WI was formalized in [23], where the authors proposed a general compiler to obtain this property. The advantage of our approach is that we obtain a more efficient compiler. Indeed, the compiler of [23] requires to compute at least one additional commitment for each statement that composes the OR theorem.

2   Preliminaries

We assume familiarity with the notions of negligible functions, computational indistinguishability, and public-key encryption. We refer to the full version for additional standard definitions. We start the section by introducing our notation. For a string x, we denote its length by $|x|$; if S is a set, $|S|$ represents the number of elements in S. When x is chosen randomly in S, we write $x \leftarrow_{\$} S$. When $\mathcal{A}$ is a randomized algorithm, we write $y \leftarrow_{\$} \mathcal{A}(x)$ to denote a run of $\mathcal{A}$ on input x (and implicit random coins r) and output y; the value y is a random variable, and $\mathcal{A}(x; r)$ denotes a run of $\mathcal{A}$ on input x and randomness r. An algorithm

$\mathcal{A}$ is *probabilistic polynomial-time* (PPT) if $\mathcal{A}$ is randomized and for any input $x, r \in \{0,1\}^*$ the computation of $\mathcal{A}(x;r)$ terminates in a polynomial number of steps (in the size of the input). A *polynomial-time* relation R is a relation for which membership of (x,w) w.r.t. R can be decided in time polynomial in $|x|$. If $(x,w) \in R$ then we say that w is a *witness* for *instance* x. A polynomial-time relation R is naturally associated with the NP language L_R defined as $L_R = \{x : \exists w \text{ s.t. } (x,w) \in R\}$. (When R is clear from the context, we simply write L.) Similarly, an NP language is naturally associated with a polynomial-time relation. We denote by $\hat{L}_R$ the language such that $L_R \subseteq \hat{L}_R$ and membership in $\hat{L}_R$ may be tested in polynomial time.

Sigma Protocols. Let L be an NP language, with corresponding relation R. A Sigma protocol $\Sigma = (\mathcal{P}, \mathcal{V})$ for R is a 3-round public-coin protocol. In particular, an execution of Σ proceeds as follows:

- The prover $\mathcal{P}$ computes the first message using as input the instance to be proved $x \in L$ with the corresponding witness w, and outputs the first message a with an auxiliary information st; we denote this action with $(a, st) \leftarrow_\$ \mathcal{P}(x, w)$.
- The verifier $\mathcal{V}$, upon receiving a, sends a random string $c \leftarrow_\$ \{0,1\}^\ell$ with $\ell \in \mathbb{N}$.
- The prover $\mathcal{P}$, upon input c and st, computes and sends z to $\mathcal{V}$; we denote this action with $z \leftarrow_\$ \mathcal{P}(st, c)$.
- The verifier $\mathcal{V}$, upon input (x, a, c, z), outputs 1 to accept and 0 to reject; we denote this action with $\mathcal{V}(x, a, c, z) = d$ where $d \in \{0,1\}$ denotes whether $\mathcal{V}$ accepts or not.

Definition 1 (Sigma protocol [25]). *A 3-move protocol Σ with challenge length $\ell \in \mathbb{N}$ is a Sigma protocol for a relation R if it enjoys the following properties:*

- ***Completeness.*** *If $(x,w) \in R$, then all honest 3-move transcripts for (x,w) are accepting.*
- ***Special soundness.*** *There exists an efficient algorithm $\mathcal{K}$ that, on input two accepting transcripts (a, c, z) and (a, c', z') for x with $c' \neq c$ (we refer to such two accepting transcripts as a* collision) *outputs a witness w such that $(x, w) \in R$.*
- ***Special honest-verifier zero knowledge (SHVZK).*** *There exists a PPT simulator algorithm $\mathcal{S}$ that takes as input security parameter 1^λ, $x \in L$ and $c \in \{0,1\}^\ell$, and outputs an accepting transcript for x where c is the challenge (we denote this action with $(a, z) \leftarrow_\$ \mathcal{S}(x, c)$). Moreover, for all ℓ-bit strings c, the distribution of the output of the simulator on input (x, c) is computationally indistinguishable from the distribution of the 3-move honest transcript obtained when $\mathcal{V}$ sends c as challenge and $\mathcal{P}$ runs on common input x and any private input w such that $(x, w) \in R$.*

The DDH Assumption. We give a high level overview on the DDH assumption and its variants. We refer the reader to the full version for a more formal and complete treatment. Let $\mathcal{G}$ be a cyclic group with generator g, and let A, B and X be elements of $\mathcal{G}$. We say that (g, A, B, X) is a *Diffie-Hellman tuple* (a *DH tuple*, in short) if $A = g^\alpha, B = g^\beta$ for some integers $0 \leq \alpha, \beta \leq |\mathcal{G}| - 1$, and $X = g^{\alpha\beta}$. If this is not the case, (g, A, B, X) is called a *non-DH tuple*.

The *Decisional Diffie-Hellman* (DDH) assumption posits the hardness of distinguishing a randomly selected DH tuple from a randomly selected non-DH tuple. Consider now the polynomial-time relation $R_{1nDH} := \{((g, A, B, X), \alpha) : A = g^\alpha \text{ and } X = g \cdot B^\alpha\}$. A *1-non-DH tuple* is a tuple $T = (g, A, B, X)$ such that $A = g^\alpha$, $B = g^\beta$ and $X = g \cdot B^\alpha = g^{\alpha \cdot \beta + 1}$. Under the DDH assumption random 1-non-DH tuples are indistinguishable from random non-DH tuple. As showed in [23], a Sigma protocol Σ_{1nDH} for the relation R_{1nDH} can be constructed based on the Sigma protocol Σ_{DH} of [25] to prove that a given tuple is DH. The compiler of [23] is almost as efficient as Σ_{DH} and works as follows. On input tuples (g, A, B, X), the prover and the verifier construct tuples (g, A, B, Y) by setting $Y = X/g$. Then, they simply run Sigma protocol Σ_{DH} upon input the theorem (g, A, B, Y).

2.1   Instance-Dependent Trapdoor Commitment

An *instance-dependent trapdoor commitment* scheme for polynomial-time relation R with message space M is a quadruple of PPT algorithms (Com, Dec, Fake$_1$, Fake$_2$) specified as follows:

- Com is the randomized *commitment* algorithm that takes as input an instance $x \in \hat{L}$ and a message $m \in M$, and outputs *commitment* com and *decommitment* dec;
- Dec is the *verification* algorithm that takes as input $x \in \hat{L}$, com, dec and $m \in M$, and decides whether m is the decommitment of com;
- Fake$_1$ takes as input $(x, w) \in R$ and outputs *commitment* com, and *equivocation information* rand;
- Fake$_2$ takes as input $(x, w) \in R$, message $m \in M$, and (com, rand), and outputs dec;

Definition 2 (Instance-dependent trapdoor commitment scheme). *Let R be a polynomial-time relation. We call $\Pi = (\text{Com}, \text{Dec}, \text{Fake}_1, \text{Fake}_2)$ an instance-dependent trapdoor commitment scheme (an IDTC, in short) for R if it enjoys the following properties:*

- *Correctness. For all $x \in \hat{L}$, and all $m \in M$, it holds that*

$$\mathbb{P}\left[\text{Dec}(x, \text{com}, \text{dec}, m) = 1 : (\text{com}, \text{dec}) \leftarrow_\$ \text{Com}(x, m)\right] = 1.$$

- *Binding. For all $x \notin L$, and for every commitment com, there exists at most one message $m \in M$ for which there is a valid decommitment dec (i.e. $\text{Dec}(x, \text{com}, \text{dec}, m) = 1$).*

- **Hiding.** *For every $x \in L$, and every $m_0, m_1 \in M$, the two ensembles* $\{\text{com} : (\text{com}, \text{dec}) \leftarrow_\$ \text{Com}(1^\lambda, x, m_0)\}_{\lambda \in \mathbb{N}}$ *and* $\{\text{com} : (\text{com}, \text{dec}) \leftarrow_\$ \text{Com}(1^\lambda, x, m_1)\}_{\lambda \in \mathbb{N}}$ *are identically distributed.*
- **Trapdoorness.** *For all $(x, w) \in R$ and $m \in M$ the following two distributions coincide:*

$$\{(\text{com}, \text{dec}) : (\text{com}, \text{rand}) \leftarrow_\$ \text{Fake}_1(x, w); \text{dec} \leftarrow_\$ \text{Fake}_2(x, w, m, \text{com}, \text{rand})\}$$
$$\{(\text{com}, \text{dec}) : (\text{com}, \text{dec}) \leftarrow \text{Com}(x, m)\}.$$

An IDTC can be easily constructed from any Sigma protocol as shown in [23, 26, 28, 39].

2.2 Correlation-Intractable Hash Families

Definition 3 (Hash family). *For a pair of efficiently computable functions $(n(\cdot), m(\cdot))$, a hash family with input length n and output length m is a collection $\mathcal{H} = \{h_k : \{0,1\}^{n(\lambda)} \to \{0,1\}^{m(\lambda)}\}_{\lambda \in \mathbb{N}, k \in \{0,1\}^{s(\lambda)}}$ of keyed hash functions, along with a pair of PPT algorithms specified as follows: (i) $\mathcal{H}.\text{Gen}(1^\lambda)$ outputs a hash key $k \in \{0,1\}^{s(\lambda)}$; (ii) $\mathcal{H}.\text{Hash}(k, x)$ computes the function $h_k(x)$.*

Definition 4 (Correlation intractability). *For a given relation ensemble $R := \{R_\lambda \subseteq \{0,1\}^{n(\lambda)} \times \{0,1\}^{m(\lambda)}\}$, a hash family $\mathcal{H} = \{h_k : \{0,1\}^{n(\lambda)} \to \{0,1\}^{m(\lambda)}\}_{\lambda \in \mathbb{N}, k \in \{0,1\}^{s(\lambda)}}$ is said to be R-correlation intractable with security (σ, δ) if for every σ-size attacker $\mathcal{A} := \{\mathcal{A}_\lambda\}$:*
$$\mathbb{P}\left[(x, h_k(x)) \in R_\lambda : k \leftarrow_\$ \mathcal{H}.\text{Gen}(1^\lambda); x \leftarrow_\$ \mathcal{A}(k)\right] = O(\delta(\lambda)).$$
We say that $\mathcal{H}$ is R-correlation intractable if it is R-correlation intractable with security $(\lambda^c, \lambda^{-c})$ for all constants $c > 1$.

Correlation intractability is a useful and versatile property of random oracles that we would like to guarantee in the standard model. However, even a random oracle is only R-correlation intractable for so-called *sparse* relations.

Definition 5 (Sparsity). *For any relation ensemble $R := \{R_\lambda \subseteq \{0,1\}^{n(\lambda)} \times \{0,1\}^{m(\lambda)}\}_\lambda$, we say that R is $\rho(\cdot)$-sparse if for all $\lambda \in \mathbb{N}$ and for any $x \in \{0,1\}^{n(\lambda)}$ it holds that $(x, y) \in R_\lambda$ with probability at most $\rho(\lambda)$ over the choice of $y \leftarrow_\$ \{0,1\}^{m(\lambda)}$. When ρ is a negligible function, we say that R is sparse.*

Efficiently Searchable Relations. In this work, we will need hash families achieving correlation intractability for relations R with a unique output $y = f(x)$ associated to each input x, and such that $y = f(x)$ is an efficiently computable function of x.

Definition 6 (Unique output relation). *We say that a relation R is a unique output relation if for every input x, there exists at most one output y such that $(x, y) \in R$.*

Definition 7 (Efficiently searchable relation). *We say that a (necessarily unique-output) relation ensemble R is searchable in (non-uniform) time t if there exists a function $f = f_R : \{0,1\}^* \to \{0,1\}^*$ computable in (non-uniform) time t such that for any input x, if $(x,y) \in R$ then $y = f(x)$; that is, $f(x)$ is the unique y such that $(x,y) \in R$, provided that such a y exists. We say that R is efficiently searchable if it is searchable in time $poly(n)$.*

Programmability. The following property turns out to be very useful in order to prove the zero-knowledge property of non-interactive proofs derived using correlation-intractable hash families.

Definition 8 (1-universality). *We say that a hash family $\mathcal{H}$ is 1-universal if for any $\lambda \in \mathbb{N}$, input $x \in \{0,1\}^{n(\lambda)}$, and output $y \in \{0,1\}^{m(\lambda)}$, we have $\mathbb{P}\left[h_k(x) = y : k \leftarrow_{\$} \mathcal{H}.\mathsf{Gen}(1^\lambda)\right] = 2^{-m(\lambda)}$.*

We say that a hash family $\mathcal{H}$ is programmable if it is 1-universal, and if there exists an efficient sampling algorithm $\mathsf{Sample}(1^\lambda, x, y)$ that samples from the conditional distribution $k \leftarrow_{\$} \mathcal{H}.\mathsf{Gen}(1^\lambda)|h_k(x) = y$.

2.3   Non-interactive Argument Systems

Definition 9 (NIZK argument systems). *A non-interactive zero-knowledge argument system (NIZK) for an NP-language L consists of three PPT machines $\Pi := (\mathsf{Gen}, \mathcal{P}, \mathcal{V})$, that have the following properties:*

- **Completeness.** *For all $\lambda \in \mathbb{N}$, and all $(x,w) \in R$, it holds that:*
  $\mathbb{P}\left[\mathcal{V}(\omega, x, \mathcal{P}(\omega, x, w)) = 1 : \omega \leftarrow_{\$} \mathsf{Gen}(1^\lambda, 1^{|x|})\right] = 1$.
- **Soundness.** *For all PPT provers $\mathcal{P}^*$, there exists a negligible function $\nu : \mathbb{N} \to [0,1]$, such that for all $\lambda \in \mathbb{N}$ and for all $x \notin L$:*
  $\mathbb{P}\left[\mathcal{V}(\omega, x, \pi) = 1 : \omega \leftarrow_{\$} \mathsf{Gen}(1^\lambda, 1^{|x|}); \pi \leftarrow_{\$} \mathcal{P}^*(\omega)\right] \leq \nu(\lambda)$.
- **Zero knowledge.** *There exists a PPT simulator $\mathcal{S}$ such that for every $(x,w) \in R$, the distribution ensembles $\{(\omega, \pi) : \omega \leftarrow_{\$} \mathsf{Gen}(1^\lambda, 1^{|x|}); \pi \leftarrow_{\$} \mathcal{P}(\omega, x, w)\}_{\lambda \in \mathbb{N}}$ and $\{\mathcal{S}(1^\lambda, x)\}_{\lambda \in \mathbb{N}}$ are computationally indistinguishable.*

A NIZK argument system can also satisfy various stronger properties. We list them below.

- **Adaptive zero knowledge.** *For all PPT verifiers $\mathcal{V}^*$ there exists a PPT simulator $\mathcal{S} := (\mathcal{S}_0, \mathcal{S}_1)$ such that the following distribution ensembles are computationally indistinguishable:*
  $\{(\omega, \pi) : \omega \leftarrow_{\$} \mathsf{Gen}(1^\lambda, 1^{|x|}); (x,w) \leftarrow_{\$} \mathcal{V}^*(\omega); \pi \leftarrow_{\$} \mathcal{P}(\omega, x, w); (x,w) \in R\}_{\lambda \in \mathbb{N}}$
  $\{(\omega, \pi) : (\omega, \tau) \leftarrow_{\$} \mathcal{S}_0(1^\lambda, 1^{|x|}); (x,w) \leftarrow_{\$} \mathcal{V}^*(\omega); \pi \leftarrow_{\$} \mathcal{S}_1(\omega, \tau, x); (x,w) \in R\}_{\lambda \in \mathbb{N}}$
- **Adaptive soundness.** *For all PPT prover $\mathcal{P}^*$, there exists a negligible function $\nu : \mathbb{N} \to [0,1]$, such that for all $\lambda \in \mathbb{N}$:*
  $\mathbb{P}\left[\mathcal{V}(\omega, x, \pi) = 1 : \omega \leftarrow_{\$} \mathsf{Gen}(1^\lambda, 1^{|x|}); (x, \pi) \leftarrow_{\$} \mathcal{P}^*(\omega); x \notin L\right] \leq \nu(\lambda)$.

3 A Compiler for Adaptive-Input HVZK

Definition 10 (Delayed-input protocols [23]). *A delayed-input three-move protocol for polynomial-time relation R is a three-move protocol $(\mathcal{P}, \mathcal{V})$ in which the first message of $\mathcal{P}$ can be computed on input the length n of the common theorem in unary notation.*[9]

Definition 11 (Adaptive-input special soundness). *A delayed-input 3-round protocol $\Sigma = (\mathcal{P}, \mathcal{V})$ for relation R enjoys adaptive-input special soundness if there exists a polynomial-time algorithm $\mathcal{K}$ such that, for any $x_1, x_2 \in L$, and for any pair of accepting transcripts (a, c_1, z_1) for input x_1 and (a, c_2, z_2) for input x_2 with $c_1 \neq c_2$, outputs witnesses w_1 and w_2 such that $(x_1, w_1) \in R$ and $(x_2, w_2) \in R$.*

Definition 12 (Adaptive-input SHVZK). *A delayed-input 3-round protocol $\Sigma = (\mathcal{P}, \mathcal{V})$ for relation R satisfies adaptive-input special honest-verifier zero-knowledge (adaptive-input SHVZK) if there exists a PPT simulator algorithm $\mathcal{S} = (\mathcal{S}_0, \mathcal{S}_1)$ such that for all PPT adversaries $\mathcal{A}$ and for all challenges $c \in \{0,1\}^{\ell}$ there is a negligible function $\nu : \mathbb{N} \to [0,1]$ for which $\left| \mathbb{P}\left[b' = b\right] - \frac{1}{2} \right| \leq \nu(\lambda)$ in the following game:*

1. *The challenger sends (a, c) to $\mathcal{A}$, where the value a is either computed using $(a, st) \leftarrow_{\$} \mathcal{P}(1^{\lambda}, 1^{n})$ (in case $b = 0$) or $(a, st) \leftarrow_{\$} \mathcal{S}_0(1^{\lambda}, 1^{n}, c)$ (in case $b = 1$).*
2. *The adversary $\mathcal{A}$ sends a pair (x, w) to the challenger, where $|x| = n$. Hence, if $(x, w) \in R$, the challenger sends z to $\mathcal{A}$, where the value z is either computed using $z \leftarrow_{\$} \mathcal{P}(x, w, st, c)$ (in case $b = 0$) or $z \leftarrow_{\$} \mathcal{S}_1(x, st)$ (in case $b = 1$); Else, the challenger sends $z = \bot$ to $\mathcal{A}$.*
3. *The adversary $\mathcal{A}$ outputs a bit b'.*

The Transformation. It turns out that the celebrated Sigma protocol by Lapidot and Shamir [43] is already delayed-input, and moreover it satisfies both adaptive-input special soundness[10] and adaptive-input SHVZK. While this protocol works for any NP relation, it is very inefficient as it requires generic NP reductions. Hence, it is a natural question whether there are efficient Sigma protocols that are delayed-input and satisfy both adaptive-input special soundness and SHVZK. A partial answer to this question was given in [23], which shows how to transform a large class of delayed-input Sigma protocols into ones with adaptive-input special soundness. In this section, we give yet another transform that allows to turn *any* delayed-input Sigma protocol into one satisfying adaptive-input SHVZK. Moreover, assuming the initial Sigma protocol already satisfies adaptive-input special soundness, our transformation preserves this property. Let Σ be a delayed-input Sigma protocol for a polynomial-time

---

[9] For simplicity, in what follows, we sometimes drop input 1^{n} when describing the prover of a delayed-input Sigma protocol.

[10] Strictly speaking, [43] only achieves a weaker flavor of adaptive-input special soundness that allows to extract the witness for only one of the two theorems.

relation R. We construct a Sigma protocol Σ'' for R based on the following additional building blocks: (i) An IDTC $\Pi = (\text{Com}, \text{Dec}, \text{Fake}_1, \text{Fake}_2)$ for the relation R_{DH} (see Sect. 2); and (ii) A Sigma protocol $\Sigma' = (\mathcal{P}', \mathcal{V}')$ for the relation R_{1nDH} (see Sect. 2). Intuitively, the prover starts by computing the first round a of the Sigma protocol Σ. Hence, it commits to message a using the IDTC with a random 1-non-DH tuple $T \in L_{1nDH}$ as instance (*i.e.*, $A = g^\alpha$, $B = g^\beta$ and $C = g \cdot B^\alpha = g^{\alpha \cdot \beta + 1}$ for random $\alpha, \beta \in \mathbb{Z}_q$)), obtaining a commitment com and decommitment dec. Next, the prover computes the first round a' of the Sigma protocol Σ' for showing that T is indeed a 1-non-DH tuple, and sends (com, a', T) to the verifier, which replies with a random challenge $c \in \{0, 1\}^\ell$. Finally, the prover completes the transcripts of both Σ and Σ' using c as challenge, obtaining values z, z' that are forwarded to the verifier together with the decommitment information (dec, a) corresponding to commitment com. In the full version we formally prove that the above construction yields to a delayed-input Sigma protocol for R satisfying both adaptive-input special soundness and adaptive-input SHVZK.

4 Adaptive Security of the Fiat-Shamir Transform

Trapdoor Sigma Protocols. Informally, a trapdoor Sigma protocol is a special Sigma protocol in the CRS model satisfying the following two properties: (i) If the statement x is false, then for every first message a, there is a unique challenge c for which there is an accepting third message z that results in an accepting transcript (a, c, z); (ii) There is a trapdoor associated with the CRS that allows us to efficiently compute this "bad challenge" c from the first message a and the statement x being proven. We now slightly revisit the definition of trapdoor Sigma protocols from [14], and show that the Fiat-Shamir transform applied to a trapdoor Sigma protocol (where the hash function takes as input both the statement and the first round of the prover) yields a NIZK with *adaptive soundness*. The only difference between the definition in [14] and ours is that we require the honestly generated CRS to be identically distributed to the CRS generated together with the trapdoor.[11] We also show that, assuming the trapdoor Sigma protocol admits an adaptive-input SHVZK simulator, then the NIZK resulting from the FS transform (where the hash function now takes as input only the first round of the prover) satisfies *adaptive zero knowledge*.

Definition 13 (CRSigma protocols). *We say that a three-round public-coin SHVZK proof system $\Sigma = (\text{Gen}, \mathcal{P}, \mathcal{V})$[12] in the CRS model is a CRSigma protocol if for every valid CRS ω, every instance $x \notin L$, and every first round a, there is at most one challenge $c := f(\omega, x, a)$ such that (ω, x, a, c, z) is an accepting*

---

[11] This modification is related to the fact that we want to prove adaptive soundness (more on this later).

[12] In this case the SHVZK simulator computes also the CRS.

transcript for some z. We informally call f the "bad-challenge function" associated to Σ, and note that f may not be efficiently computable.[13]

Definition 14 (Trapdoor Sigma protocol). *We say that a CRSigma protocol $\Sigma = (\mathsf{Gen}, \mathcal{P}, \mathcal{V})$ with bad-challenge function f is a trapdoor Sigma protocol if there are PPT algorithms* $\mathsf{TrapGen}$, $\mathsf{BadChallenge}$ *with the following syntax:*

- $\mathsf{TrapGen}$ *takes as input the unary representation of the security parameter and outputs a common reference string ω with a trapdoor τ.*
- $\mathsf{BadChallenge}$ *takes as input a trapdoor τ, common reference string ω, an instance x and the first message a and outputs a challenge c.*

We additionally require the following properties.

- **CRS indistinguishability.** *An honestly generated common reference string ω is identically distributed to a common reference string output by* $\mathsf{TrapGen}(1^\lambda)$.
- **Correctness.** *For every instance $x \notin L$ and for all $(\omega, \tau) \leftarrow_\$ \mathsf{TrapGen}(1^\lambda)$ we have that* $\mathsf{BadChallenge}(\tau, \omega, x, a) = f(\omega, x, a)$.

The Fiat-Shamir Transform. Let $\mathcal{H}$ be a hash family and $\Sigma = (\mathsf{Gen}, \mathcal{P}, \mathcal{V})$ be a (delayed-input) CRSigma protocol for some relation R. Consider the following non-interactive argument systems $\Pi' = (\mathsf{Gen}', \mathcal{P}', \mathcal{V}')$ and $\Pi'' = (\mathsf{Gen}', \mathcal{P}'', \mathcal{V}')$ for R:

- The common reference string $\omega' := (\omega, k)$ consists of the common reference string of Σ (*i.e.,* $\omega \leftarrow_\$ \mathsf{Gen}(1^\lambda)$) along with a hash key $k \leftarrow_\$ \mathcal{H}.\mathsf{Gen}(1^\lambda)$.
- Upon input $(x, w) \in R$, the prover $\mathcal{P}'$ (resp. $\mathcal{P}''$) computes $(a, st) \leftarrow_\$ \mathcal{P}(1^\lambda, \omega, x, w)$ (resp. $(a, st) \leftarrow_\$ \mathcal{P}(1^\lambda, \omega)$), $c := h_k(a||x)$ (resp. $c := h_k(a)$) and $z \leftarrow_\$ \mathcal{P}(st, c)$ (resp. $z \leftarrow_\$ \mathcal{P}(st, x, w, c)$), and outputs[14] (a, c, z).
- The verifier $\mathcal{V}'$ (resp. $\mathcal{V}''$) accepts the transcript (a, c, z) w.r.t. CRS $\omega' = (\omega, k)$ and statement x if $\mathcal{V}(\omega, x, a, c, z) = 1$ and $h_k(a||x) = c$ (resp. $h_k(a) = c$).

Theorem 1. *Suppose that $\mathcal{H}$ is a hash family that is correlation intractable for all sub-exponentially sparse relations that are searchable in time t, and that $\mathcal{H}$ enjoys programmability. Moreover, assume that $\Sigma = (\mathsf{Gen}, \mathcal{P}, \mathcal{V}, \mathsf{TrapGen}, \mathsf{BadChallenge})$ is a trapdoor Sigma protocol with SHVZK and challenge (second message) space $\{0, 1\}^{\lambda^\epsilon}$ for some $\epsilon > 0$, such that $\mathsf{BadChallenge}(\tau, \omega, x, a)$ is computable in time t. Then, the non-interactive argument system Π' described above satisfies zero-knowledge and adaptive soundness in the CRS model.*

Theorem 2. *Suppose that $\mathcal{H}$ is a hash family that is correlation intractable for all sub-exponentially sparse relations that are searchable in time t, and that $\mathcal{H}$ enjoys programmability. Moreover, assume that $\Sigma = (\mathsf{Gen}, \mathcal{P}, \mathcal{V}, \mathsf{TrapGen},$*

---

[13] We observe that this notion implies that a trapdoor Sigma protocol is sound with soundness error $2^{-|c|}$.

[14] Equivalently, the prover can just output (a, z) as c can be re-computed by the verifier.

BadChallenge) *is a trapdoor Sigma protocol with* adaptive-input $SHVZK^{15}$ *and challenge space* $\{0,1\}^{\lambda^{\epsilon}}$ *for some* $\epsilon > 0$, *such that* BadChallenge(τ, ω, x, a) *is computable in time* t. *Then, the non-interactive argument system* Π'' *described above satisfies soundness and* adaptive zero knowledge *in the CRS model.*

We refer to the full version for the proofs of the Theorems 1 and 2

From CRSigma Protocols to Trapdoor Sigma Protocols. In [14], the authors show that a modified version of the protocol for Hamiltonian graphs [31,43] is a trapdoor Sigma protocol. This allows to obtain a trapdoor Sigma protocol for any NP relation R by just making an NP reduction. In this section we show that *any* CRSigma protocol can be turned into a trapdoor Sigma protocol without making use of expensive NP reductions. Let $\Sigma = (\mathsf{Gen}, \mathcal{P}, \mathcal{V})$ be a CRSigma protocol for a polynomial-time relation R. Without loss of generality, we assume that the challenge space of Σ is $\{0,1\}$. We construct a trapdoor Sigma protocol $\Sigma' := (\mathsf{Gen}', \mathcal{P}', \mathcal{V}')$ for R based on Σ and on a public-key encryption (PKE) scheme $(\mathsf{KGen}, \mathsf{Enc}, \mathsf{Dec})$ with perfect correctness. The PKE scheme is essentially used as a commitment, similarly to what is done in [14]. At a high level our transform works as follows. The CRS consists of a public key for the PKE scheme and of a CRS for Σ. To compute a proof, the prover generates the first message of Σ and the replies to the challenge 0 and 1 that we denote respectively with z_0 and z_1. Then, the prover encrypts z_0 and z_1 and sends these encrypted values together with the first round of Σ to the verifier. The verifier sends a random bit c, and the prover replies with z_c and the randomness used to compute the encryption of z_c. Finally, the verifier accepts if the randomness and the value z_c are consistent with the commitment received in the first round and if the transcript for Σ is accepting. We note that given the secret key of the encryption scheme it is possible to extract the bad challenge (if any). And this is the intuitive reason why our protocol is a trapdoor Sigma protocol. We refer to the full version for the formal description of the protocol and the proof. We remark that it is always possible to extend the challenge space of the above protocol to $\{0,1\}^{\kappa}$ for any $\kappa \in \mathbb{N}$ without compromising its completeness, by just repeating it in parallel κ times. Then, using Theorem 1, we obtain an *adaptively-sound* NIZK.

Adding Adaptive-Input SHVZK. To transform a delayed-input trapdoor Sigma protocol $\Sigma = (\mathsf{Gen}, \mathcal{P}, \mathcal{V})$ into one with adaptive-input SHVZK Σ'' we follow the same approach proposed in Sect. 3. The prover computes the first round of Σ and commits to it using an IDTC that enjoys a special form of extractability. We refer the reader to the full version for the formal definition of extractable IDTCs, its concrete instantiation based on the DDH assumption, and for the formal description of Σ'' with its security analysis.

---

[15] As in the definition of adaptive-input SHVZK, the simulator is defined by two algorithms $(\mathcal{S}_0, \mathcal{S}_1)$. The difference is that $\mathcal{S}_0$ outputs the CRS in addition.

References

1. Ananth, P., Choudhuri, A.R., Jain, A.: A new approach to round-optimal secure multiparty computation. In: Katz, J., Shacham, H. (eds.) CRYPTO 2017. LNCS, vol. 10401, pp. 468–499. Springer, Cham (2017). https://doi.org/10.1007/978-3-319-63688-7_16
2. Asharov, G., Jain, A., López-Alt, A., Tromer, E., Vaikuntanathan, V., Wichs, D.: Multiparty computation with low communication, computation and interaction via threshold FHE. In: Pointcheval, D., Johansson, T. (eds.) EUROCRYPT 2012. LNCS, vol. 7237, pp. 483–501. Springer, Heidelberg (2012). https://doi.org/10.1007/978-3-642-29011-4_29
3. Badrinarayanan, S., Goyal, V., Jain, A., Kalai, Y.T., Khurana, D., Sahai, A.: Promise zero knowledge and its applications to round optimal MPC. In: Shacham, H., Boldyreva, A. (eds.) CRYPTO 2018. LNCS, vol. 10992, pp. 459–487. Springer, Cham (2018). https://doi.org/10.1007/978-3-319-96881-0_16
4. Barak, B.: How to go beyond the black-box simulation barrier. In: 42nd FOCS, pp. 106–115. IEEE Computer Society Press (October 2001). https://doi.org/10.1109/SFCS.2001.959885
5. Barak, B., Lindell, Y., Vadhan, S.P.: Lower bounds for non-black-box zero knowledge. In: 44th FOCS, pp. 384–393. IEEE Computer Society Press (October 2003). https://doi.org/10.1109/SFCS.2003.1238212
6. Bellare, M., Goldreich, O.: On defining proofs of knowledge. In: Brickell, E.F. (ed.) CRYPTO 1992. LNCS, vol. 740, pp. 390–420. Springer, Heidelberg (1993). https://doi.org/10.1007/3-540-48071-4_28
7. Bellare, M., Ristov, T.: A characterization of chameleon hash functions and new, efficient designs. J. Cryptol. 27(4), 799–823 (2013). https://doi.org/10.1007/s00145-013-9155-8
8. Bellare, M., Rogaway, P.: Random oracles are practical: a paradigm for designing efficient protocols. In: Denning, D.E., Pyle, R., Ganesan, R., Sandhu, R.S., Ashby, V. (eds.) ACM CCS 93, pp. 62–73. ACM Press (November 1993). https://doi.org/10.1145/168588.168596
9. Bernhard, D., Pereira, O., Warinschi, B.: How not to prove yourself: pitfalls of the Fiat-Shamir heuristic and applications to Helios. In: Wang, X., Sako, K. (eds.) ASIACRYPT 2012. LNCS, vol. 7658, pp. 626–643. Springer, Heidelberg (2012). https://doi.org/10.1007/978-3-642-34961-4_38
10. Bitansky, N., et al.: Why "Fiat-Shamir for proofs" lacks a proof. In: Sahai, A. (ed.) TCC 2013. LNCS, vol. 7785, pp. 182–201. Springer, Heidelberg (2013). https://doi.org/10.1007/978-3-642-36594-2_11
11. Blum, M.: How to prove a theorem so no one else can claim it. In: Proceedings of the International Congress of Mathematicians, pp. 444–451 (1986)
12. Brakerski, Z., Halevi, S., Polychroniadou, A.: Four round secure computation without setup. In: Kalai, Y., Reyzin, L. (eds.) TCC 2017. LNCS, vol. 10677, pp. 645–677. Springer, Cham (2017). https://doi.org/10.1007/978-3-319-70500-2_22
13. Brakerski, Z., Koppula, V., Mour, T.: NIZK from LPN and trapdoor hash via correlation intractability for approximable relations. IACR Cryptol. ePrint Arch. 2020, 258 (2020). https://eprint.iacr.org/2020/258
14. Canetti, R., et al.: Fiat-Shamir: from practice to theory. In: Charikar, M., Cohen, E. (eds.) 51st ACM STOC, pp. 1082–1090. ACM Press (June 2019). https://doi.org/10.1145/3313276.3316380

15. Canetti, R., Chen, Y., Reyzin, L.: On the correlation intractability of obfuscated pseudorandom functions. In: Kushilevitz, E., Malkin, T. (eds.) TCC 2016. LNCS, vol. 9562, pp. 389–415. Springer, Heidelberg (2016). https://doi.org/10.1007/978-3-662-49096-9_17

16. Canetti, R., Chen, Y., Reyzin, L., Rothblum, R.D.: Fiat-Shamir and correlation intractability from strong KDM-secure encryption. In: Nielsen, J.B., Rijmen, V. (eds.) EUROCRYPT 2018. LNCS, vol. 10820, pp. 91–122. Springer, Cham (2018). https://doi.org/10.1007/978-3-319-78381-9_4

17. Canetti, R., Goldreich, O., Halevi, S.: The random oracle methodology, revisited (preliminary version). In: 30th ACM STOC, pp. 209–218. ACM Press (May 1998). https://doi.org/10.1145/276698.276741

18. Catalano, D., Visconti, I.: Hybrid trapdoor commitments and their applications. In: Caires, L., Italiano, G.F., Monteiro, L., Palamidessi, C., Yung, M. (eds.) ICALP 2005. LNCS, vol. 3580, pp. 298–310. Springer, Heidelberg (2005). https://doi.org/10.1007/11523468_25

19. Choudhuri, A.R., Ciampi, M., Goyal, V., Jain, A., Ostrovsky, R.: Round optimal secure multiparty computation from minimal assumptions. Cryptology ePrint Archive, Report 2019/216 (2019). https://eprint.iacr.org/2019/216

20. Ciampi, M., Ostrovsky, R., Siniscalchi, L., Visconti, I.: Concurrent non-malleable commitments (and more) in 3 rounds. In: Robshaw, M., Katz, J. (eds.) CRYPTO 2016. LNCS, vol. 9816, pp. 270–299. Springer, Heidelberg (2016). https://doi.org/10.1007/978-3-662-53015-3_10

21. Ciampi, M., Ostrovsky, R., Siniscalchi, L., Visconti, I.: Four-round concurrent non-malleable commitments from one-way functions. In: Katz, J., Shacham, H. (eds.) CRYPTO 2017. LNCS, vol. 10402, pp. 127–157. Springer, Cham (2017). https://doi.org/10.1007/978-3-319-63715-0_5

22. Ciampi, M., Ostrovsky, R., Siniscalchi, L., Visconti, I.: Round-optimal secure two-party computation from trapdoor permutations. In: Kalai, Y., Reyzin, L. (eds.) TCC 2017. LNCS, vol. 10677, pp. 678–710. Springer, Cham (2017). https://doi.org/10.1007/978-3-319-70500-2_23

23. Ciampi, M., Persiano, G., Scafuro, A., Siniscalchi, L., Visconti, I.: Online/offline OR composition of sigma protocols. In: Fischlin, M., Coron, J.-S. (eds.) EUROCRYPT 2016. LNCS, vol. 9666, pp. 63–92. Springer, Heidelberg (2016). https://doi.org/10.1007/978-3-662-49896-5_3

24. Ciampi, M., Persiano, G., Siniscalchi, L., Visconti, I.: A transform for NIZK almost as efficient and general as the Fiat-Shamir transform without programmable random oracles. In: Kushilevitz, E., Malkin, T. (eds.) TCC 2016. LNCS, vol. 9563, pp. 83–111. Springer, Heidelberg (2016). https://doi.org/10.1007/978-3-662-49099-0_4

25. Cramer, R., Damgård, I., Schoenmakers, B.: Proofs of partial knowledge and simplified design of witness hiding protocols. In: Desmedt, Y.G. (ed.) CRYPTO 1994. LNCS, vol. 839, pp. 174–187. Springer, Heidelberg (1994). https://doi.org/10.1007/3-540-48658-5_19

26. Damgård, I.: On Σ-protocol (2010). http://www.cs.au.dk/~ivan/Sigma.pdf

27. Damgård, I., Groth, J.: Non-interactive and reusable non-malleable commitment schemes. In: 35th ACM STOC, pp. 426–437. ACM Press (June 2003). https://doi.org/10.1145/780542.780605

28. Damgård, I., Nielsen, J.B.: Perfect hiding and perfect binding universally composable commitment schemes with constant expansion factor. In: Yung, M. (ed.) CRYPTO 2002. LNCS, vol. 2442, pp. 581–596. Springer, Heidelberg (2002). https://doi.org/10.1007/3-540-45708-9_37

29. Dwork, C., Naor, M., Reingold, O., Stockmeyer, L.J.: Magic functions. In: 40th FOCS, pp. 523–534. IEEE Computer Society Press (October 1999). https://doi.org/10.1109/SFFCS.1999.814626

30. Faust, S., Kohlweiss, M., Marson, G.A., Venturi, D.: On the non-malleability of the Fiat-Shamir transform. In: Galbraith, S., Nandi, M. (eds.) INDOCRYPT 2012. LNCS, vol. 7668, pp. 60–79. Springer, Heidelberg (2012). https://doi.org/10.1007/978-3-642-34931-7_5

31. Feige, U., Lapidot, D., Shamir, A.: Multiple non-interactive zero knowledge proofs based on a single random string (extended abstract). In: 31st FOCS, pp. 308–317. IEEE Computer Society Press (October 1990). https://doi.org/10.1109/FSCS.1990.89549

32. Fiat, A., Shamir, A.: How to prove yourself: practical solutions to identification and signature problems. In: Odlyzko, A.M. (ed.) CRYPTO 1986. LNCS, vol. 263, pp. 186–194. Springer, Heidelberg (1987). https://doi.org/10.1007/3-540-47721-7_12

33. Fischlin, M., Fischlin, R.: The representation problem based on factoring. In: Preneel, B. (ed.) CT-RSA 2002. LNCS, vol. 2271, pp. 96–113. Springer, Heidelberg (2002). https://doi.org/10.1007/3-540-45760-7_8

34. Goldwasser, S., Kalai, Y.T.: On the (in)security of the Fiat-Shamir paradigm. In: 44th FOCS, pp. 102–115. IEEE Computer Society Press (October 2003). https://doi.org/10.1109/SFCS.2003.1238185

35. Goldwasser, S., Micali, S., Rackoff, C.: The knowledge complexity of interactive proof-systems (extended abstract). In: 17th ACM STOC, pp. 291–304. ACM Press (May 1985). https://doi.org/10.1145/22145.22178

36. Goyal, V., Richelson, S.: Non-malleable commitments using Goldreich-Levin list decoding. In: Zuckerman, D. (ed.) 60th FOCS, pp. 686–699. IEEE Computer Society Press (November 2019). https://doi.org/10.1109/FOCS.2019.00047

37. Goyal, V., Richelson, S., Rosen, A., Vald, M.: An algebraic approach to non-malleability. In: 55th FOCS, pp. 41–50. IEEE Computer Society Press (October 2014). https://doi.org/10.1109/FOCS.2014.13

38. Halevi, S., Myers, S., Rackoff, C.: On seed-incompressible functions. In: Canetti, R. (ed.) TCC 2008. LNCS, vol. 4948, pp. 19–36. Springer, Heidelberg (2008). https://doi.org/10.1007/978-3-540-78524-8_2

39. Hazay, C., Lindell, Y.: Efficient Secure Two-Party Protocols. ISC. Springer, Heidelberg (2010). https://doi.org/10.1007/978-3-642-14303-8

40. Holmgren, J., Lombardi, A.: Cryptographic hashing from strong one-way functions (or: one-way product functions and their applications). In: Thorup, M. (ed.) 59th FOCS, pp. 850–858. IEEE Computer Society Press (October 2018). https://doi.org/10.1109/FOCS.2018.00085

41. Kalai, Y.T., Rothblum, G.N., Rothblum, R.D.: From obfuscation to the security of Fiat-Shamir for proofs. In: Katz, J., Shacham, H. (eds.) CRYPTO 2017. LNCS, vol. 10402, pp. 224–251. Springer, Cham (2017). https://doi.org/10.1007/978-3-319-63715-0_8

42. Katz, J., Ostrovsky, R.: Round-optimal secure two-party computation. In: Franklin, M. (ed.) CRYPTO 2004. LNCS, vol. 3152, pp. 335–354. Springer, Heidelberg (2004). https://doi.org/10.1007/978-3-540-28628-8_21

43. Lapidot, D., Shamir, A.: Publicly verifiable non-interactive zero-knowledge proofs. In: Menezes, A.J., Vanstone, S.A. (eds.) CRYPTO 1990. LNCS, vol. 537, pp. 353–365. Springer, Heidelberg (1991). https://doi.org/10.1007/3-540-38424-3_26

44. Lindell, Y.: An efficient transform from sigma protocols to NIZK with a CRS and non-programmable random oracle. In: Dodis, Y., Nielsen, J.B. (eds.) TCC 2015. LNCS, vol. 9014, pp. 93–109. Springer, Heidelberg (2015). https://doi.org/10.1007/978-3-662-46494-6_5

45. Lyubashevsky, V.: Fiat-Shamir with aborts: applications to lattice and factoring-based signatures. In: Matsui, M. (ed.) ASIACRYPT 2009. LNCS, vol. 5912, pp. 598–616. Springer, Heidelberg (2009). https://doi.org/10.1007/978-3-642-10366-7_35

46. Mittelbach, A., Venturi, D.: Fiat–Shamir for highly sound protocols is instantiable. In: Zikas, V., De Prisco, R. (eds.) SCN 2016. LNCS, vol. 9841, pp. 198–215. Springer, Cham (2016). https://doi.org/10.1007/978-3-319-44618-9_11

47. Okamoto, T.: Provably secure and practical identification schemes and corresponding signature schemes. In: Brickell, E.F. (ed.) CRYPTO 1992. LNCS, vol. 740, pp. 31–53. Springer, Heidelberg (1993). https://doi.org/10.1007/3-540-48071-4_3

48. Peikert, C., Shiehian, S.: Noninteractive zero knowledge for NP from (plain) learning with errors. In: Boldyreva, A., Micciancio, D. (eds.) CRYPTO 2019. LNCS, vol. 11692, pp. 89–114. Springer, Cham (2019). https://doi.org/10.1007/978-3-030-26948-7_4

49. Pointcheval, D., Stern, J.: Security proofs for signature schemes. In: Maurer, U. (ed.) EUROCRYPT 1996. LNCS, vol. 1070, pp. 387–398. Springer, Heidelberg (1996). https://doi.org/10.1007/3-540-68339-9_33

50. Schnorr, C.P.: Efficient identification and signatures for smart cards. In: Brassard, G. (ed.) CRYPTO 1989. LNCS, vol. 435, pp. 239–252. Springer, New York (1990). https://doi.org/10.1007/0-387-34805-0_22

51. Stern, J.: A new identification scheme based on syndrome decoding. In: Stinson, D.R. (ed.) CRYPTO 1993. LNCS, vol. 773, pp. 13–21. Springer, Heidelberg (1994). https://doi.org/10.1007/3-540-48329-2_2

Author Index

Printed in the United States
By Bookmasters

Printed in the United States
By Bookmasters